WORD BIBLICAL COMMENTARY

WORD BIBLICAL COMMENTARY

Volume 35B

Luke 9:21–18:34

JOHN NOLLAND

NELSON REFERENCE & ELECTRONIC
A Division of Thomas Nelson Publishers
Since 1798

Word Biblical Commentary
Luke 9:21–18:34

Library of Congress Cataloging-in-Publication Data
Main entry under title:

Word biblical commentary.

Includes bibliographies.
1. Bible—Commentaries—Collected works.
BS491.2.W67 220.7'7 81–71768
ISBN-10: 0849902541 (v. 35B) AACR2
ISBN-13: 9780849902543
Printed in Colombia

The author's own translation of the Scripture text appears in italic type under the heading *Translation.*

09 10 11 12 QWB 09 08 07 06

To my mother
and in memory of my father

Editor's Note

For the convenience of the reader, page numbers for volumes one and two of this commentary on Luke (35A and 35B) are included in the Contents. Page numbers for the volume in hand are printed in boldface type, while those for the other volume are in lightface.

In addition, all of the front matter from Vol. 35A but the Introduction has been repeated in Vol. 35B so that the reader may have abbreviations, bibliography, and other pertinent information readily at hand.

Contents

Editorial Preface

The launching of the *Word Biblical Commentary* brings to fulfillment an enterprise of several years' planning. The publishers and the members of the editorial board met in 1977 to explore the possibility of a new commentary on the books of the Bible that would incorporate several distinctive features. Prospective readers of these volumes are entitled to know what such features were intended to be; whether the aims of the commentary have been fully achieved time alone will tell.

First, we have tried to cast a wide net to include as contributors a number of scholars from around the world who not only share our aims, but are in the main engaged in the ministry of teaching in university, college, and seminary. They represent a rich diversity of denominational allegiance. The broad stance of our contributors can rightly be called evangelical, and this term is to be understood in its positive, historic sense of a commitment to Scripture as divine revelation, and to the truth and power of the Christian gospel.

Then, the commentaries in our series are all commissioned and written for the purpose of inclusion in the *Word Biblical Commentary*. Unlike several of our distinguished counterparts in the field of commentary writing, there are no translated works, originally written in a non-English language. Also, our commentators were asked to prepare their own rendering of the original biblical text and to use those languages as the basis of their own comments and exegesis. What may be claimed as distinctive with this series is that it is based on the biblical languages, yet it seeks to make the technical and scholarly approach to the theological understanding of Scripture understandable by—and useful to—the fledgling student, the working minister, and colleagues in the guild of professional scholars and teachers as well.

Finally, a word must be said about the format of the series. The layout, in clearly defined sections, has been consciously devised to assist readers at different levels. Those wishing to learn about the textual witnesses on which the translation is offered are invited to consult the section headed *Notes*. If the readers' concern is with the state of modern scholarship on any given portion of Scripture, they should turn to the sections on *Bibliography* and *Form/Structure/Setting*. For a clear exposition of the passage's meaning and its relevance to the ongoing biblical revelation, the *Comment* and concluding *Explanation* are designed expressly to meet that need. There is therefore something for everyone who may pick up and use these volumes.

If these aims come anywhere near realization, the intention of the editors will have been met, and the labor of our team of contributors rewarded.

General Editors: *David A. Hubbard*
Glenn W. Barker†
Old Testament: *John D. W. Watts*
New Testament: *Ralph P. Martin*

Author's Preface

In 1966 W. C. van Unnik wrote an article under the title "Luke-Acts, A Storm Center in Contemporary Scholarship" (In *Studies in Luke-Acts,* ed. L. E. Keck and J. L. Martyn). It is probably fair to say that the intensity of the storm has since considerably abated, but there has continued to be an immense devotion of scholarly labor dedicated to the elucidation of the Lukan writings. And as some issues in dispute have clarified with the emergence of a good degree of scholarly consensus, other issues have come forward to take their place as matters in hot dispute.

A commentary such as the present one is partly a digest of the present state of this ongoing debate. In this guise it seeks to synthesize the insights that are scattered through the specialist literature and to evaluate in connection with the development of a coherent understanding of the whole Lukan enterprise the competing suggestions that have been offered in the literature for the understanding of individual items. It has, however, also been my intention to offer a fresh reading of each passage of the Gospel. In this guise the perusal of the literature has been a kind of apprenticeship or an initiation, entitling me to move on beyond the place where the accumulated discussion has taken us. Here my ambition has been to improve the answers that have been given to the issues thrown up by the particular features of the individual passages and at points to add my own questions to the scholarly agenda.

I have focused my engagement with the scholarly literature on the journal literature and the specialist monographs rather than upon the existing commentaries, largely because of the greater possibility there for exploring the detailed reasoning that stands behind the particular judgments which have been made. That said, I have learned much from the commentators. Schürmann and Fitzmyer have been constant companions. Marshall and Grundmann have also been of special use, as in different ways have the earlier works of Schlatter, Godet, and Loisy. Other commentators have periodically left their mark upon the present work. D. M. Goulder's recent work (*Luke: A New Paradigm* [2 vols., JSNTSup 20; Sheffield: JSOT, 1989]) did not appear before the manuscript left my hands in January 1989. I have tried to keep an eye constantly upon Luke's second volume, and the scholarship devoted to its elucidation, but here I have necessarily been much more selective.

While I have attempted to take something like comprehensive responsibility for all the issues involved in attempting to provide a modern reading of the ancient Lukan text, inevitably my own sense of the relative importance of things, as well as of my own areas of greater strength, will be reflected in the allocation of space (and of effort). The central paradigm for my work has been provided by seeing the Gospel text as an exercise in communication, deliberately undertaken by the Gospel writer with at least some focused sense of the actual or potential needs of his audience. I use "communication" here in a broad sense to encompass all the ways in which the Gospel may be intended to have an impact upon the reader.

To give one example that goes beyond what we might call the theological message of the book, there is a considerable sense of literature about Luke's work. Some of that will be due to Luke's instincts as artist and in that sense will be an expression of his own person as artist; some of that will be due to the fact that Luke stands heir (from the Old Testament, but also from his Christian context) to a narrative method of doing theology, along with which comes an investment in the artistry of story-telling; but for part of the explanation of this literary phenomenon we need to look in a totally nonliterary direction. Luke's ambition was not to make a name for himself in the literary world of the day (his work probably does not come up to the level). His efforts were directed towards being taken with a certain kind of seriousness in this attempt that he has made to commend and elucidate the Christian faith: Luke seeks to write at a level that would commend itself to the cultural level of his readers and implicitly make certain claims about how they as readers should orient themselves to his work. That is, Luke uses literary means to nonliterary ends. With an eye upon each of these roles for literary technique, I have sought to pay particular attention to the literary strategies of Luke at both the micro-level and the macro-level.

While the main paradigm for inquiry has been provided by a concern for the nexus of communication, the commentary also pays considerable attention to issues concerning the ultimate origin of the materials that Luke has used. Luke seems to have a concern to present his material as capable of standing up to "secular" scrutiny. He is the Gospel writer who is most clearly aware of a distance between his own reporting and the events that it is his concern to report (Luke 1:1–4), and he is the one Gospel writer who seems to work with a fairly clear conceptual distinction between the place for religious testimony and the role of "historical" evidence in commending the Christian faith. His own approach, therefore, invites our attention to the questions of origin.

The commentary may be accessed at various levels. Most readers will find the *Explanation* for each passage the best point of entry. Here the major results of the detailed work of the earlier sections are outlined in nontechnical language. Also important for keeping in view the overall thrust of the Lukan text are the brief summaries which begin each major section of the commentary, and which at the next level down constitute the opening paragraphs for both the *Form/Structure/Setting* and the *Comment* for each passage.

Libraries are finally what make humanistic scholarship possible, and I am deeply grateful for the library resources that have been made available to me at Regent College, Vancouver; the University of British Columbia; Tyndale House Cambridge; the University of Cambridge; and Trinity College Bristol. I am particularly grateful for the inter-library loan services which have given me access to a great many items not held by the particular libraries where I have worked from time to time. I wish to pay a particular tribute to the series of teaching assistants who in the early years of this project gathered library resources for me and to Su Brown, assistant librarian at Trinity College Bristol, who was of such assistance in the final stages of readying the manuscript for the press.

I owe a debt of gratitude to Regent College, for the year of sabbatical leave in which a considerable part of the manuscript was written.

Finally I pay tribute to my wife Lisa and son David who have borne with my having this project on my mind for many a year, and particularly to my wife who "journeyed [with me to] a foreign land" far "away from [her] country and [her] kindred and [her] father's house" in order that I might be able to stay in the kind of employment that would allow me to continue with this work.

October 1989 JOHN NOLLAND
Trinity College, Bristol

Abbreviations

A. General Abbreviations

A	Codex Alexandrinus	id.	*idem,* the same
ad	comment on	i.e.	*id est,* that is
Akkad.	Akkadian	impf.	imperfect
א	Codex Sinaiticus	infra	below
Ap. Lit.	Apocalyptic Literature	in loc.	*in loco,* in the place cited
Apoc.	Apocrypha	Jos.	Josephus
Aq.	Aquila's Greek Translation of the OT	lat	Latin
		lit.	literally
Arab.	Arabic	loc. cit.	the place cited
Aram.	Aramaic	LXX	Septuagint
B	Codex Vaticanus	M	Mishna
C	Codex Ephraemi Syri	masc.	masculine
c.	*circa,* about	mg.	margin
cent.	century	MS(S)	manuscript(s)
cf.	*confer,* compare	MT	Masoretic text (of the Old Testament)
chap(s).	chapter(s)		
cod., codd.	codex, codices	n.	note
contra	in contrast to	n.d.	no date
CUP	Cambridge University Press	Nestle	Nestle (ed.), *Novum Testamentum Graece* [26], rev. by K. and B. Aland
D	Codex Bezae		
DSS	Dead Sea Scrolls		
ed.	edited by, editor(s)	no.	number
e.g.	*exempli gratia,* for example	n.s.	new series
et al.	*et alii,* and others	NT	New Testament
ET	English translation	obs.	obsolete
EV	English Versions of the Bible	o.s.	old series
		OT	Old Testament
f., ff.	following (verse or verses, pages, etc.)	p., pp.	page, pages
		pace	with due respect to, but differing from
fem.	feminine		
frag.	fragments	//, par(s).	parallel(s)
FS	Festschrift, volume written in honor of	par.	paragraph
		passim	elsewhere
ft.	foot, feet	pl.	plural
gen.	genitive	Pseudep.	Pseudepigrapha
Gr.	Greek	Q	Quelle ("Sayings" source for the Gospels)
hap. leg.	*hapax legomenon,* sole occurrence		
		q.v.	*quod vide,* which see
Heb.	Hebrew	rev.	revised, reviser, revision
Hitt.	Hittite	Rom.	Roman
ibid.	*ibidem,* in the same place	RVmg	Revised Version margin

Sam.	Samaritan recension	UBSGT	The United Bible Societies Greek Text
sc.	*scilicet,* that is to say	Ugar.	Ugaritic
Sem.	Semitic	UP	University Press
sing.	singular	u.s.	*ut supra,* as above
Sumer.	Sumerian	v, vv	verse, verses
s.v.	*sub verbo,* under the word	viz.	*videlicet,* namely
sy	Syriac	vg	Vulgate
Symm.	Symmachus	v.l.	*varia lectio,* alternative reading
Tg.	Targum		
Theod.	Theodotion		
TR	Textus Receptus	vol.	volume
tr.	translator, translated by	x	times (2x = two times, etc.)

For abbreviations of Greek MSS used in *Notes,* see Nestle[26].

B. Abbreviations for Translations and Paraphrases

AmT	Smith and Goodspeed, *The Complete Bible, An American Translation*	Moffatt	J. Moffatt, *A New Translation of the Bible* (NT 1913)
		NAB	The New American Bible
AB	Anchor Bible	NEB	The New English Bible
ASV	American Standard Version, American Revised Version (1901)	NIV	The New International Version (1978)
		NJB	New Jerusalem Bible (1985)
AV	Authorized Version = KJV	Phillips	J. B. Phillips, *The New Testament in Modern English*
GNB	Good News Bible = Today's English Version	RSV	Revised Standard Version (NT 1946, OT 1952, Apoc. 1957)
JB	Jerusalem Bible		
JPS	Jewish Publication Society, *The Holy Scriptures*	RV	Revised Version, 1881–85
KJV	King James Version (1611) = AV	Wey	R. F. Weymouth, *The New Testament in Modern Speech*
Knox	R. A. Knox, *The Holy Bible: A Translation from the Latin Vulgate in the Light of the Hebrew and Greek Original*	Wms	C. B. Williams, *The New Testament: A Translation in the Language of the People*

C. Abbreviations of Commonly Used Periodicals, Reference Works, and Serials

AARSR	American Academy of Religion Studies in Religion	ACNT	Augsburg Commentary on the New Testament
		AcOr	*Acta orientalia*
AAS	*Acta apostolicae sedis*	ACW	Ancient Christian Writers
AASOR	Annual of the American Schools of Oriental Research	*ADAJ*	*Annual of the Department of Antiquities of Jordan*
		AER	*American Ecclesiastical Review*
AB	Anchor Bible	*AfJT*	*African Journal of Theology*
ABR	*Australian Biblical Review*	AFLN-WG	Arbeitsgemeinschaft für Forschung des Landes
AbrN	*Abr-Nahrain*		

	Nordrhein-Westfalen, Geistgewissenschaften
AfO	*Archiv für Orientforschung*
AGJU	Arbeiten zur Geschichte des antiken Judentums und des Urchristentums
AGSU	Arbeiten zur Geschichte des Spätjudentums und Urchristentums
AH	F. Resenthal, *An Aramaic Handbook*
AHR	*American Historical Review*
AHW	W. von Soden, *Akkadisches Handwörterbuch*
AION	*Annali dell'istituto orientali di Napoli*
AJA	*American Journal of Archaeology*
AJAS	*American Journal of Arabic Studies*
AJBA	*Australian Journal of Biblical Archaeology*
AJBI	*Annual of the Japanese Biblical Institute*
AJP	*American Journal of Philology*
AJSL	*American Journal of Semitic Languages and Literature*
AJT	*American Journal of Theology*
ALBO	Analecta lovaniensia biblica et orientalia
ALGHJ	Arbeiten zur Literatur und Geschichte des hellenistischen Judentums
ALUOS	Annual of Leeds University Oriental Society
AmCl	*Ami du clergé*
AnBib	Analecta biblica
AnBoll	Analecta Bollandiana
ANEP	J. B. Pritchard (ed.), *Ancient Near East in Pictures*
ANESTP	J. B. Pritchard (ed.), *Ancient Near East Supplementary Texts and Pictures*
ANET	J. B. Pritchard (ed.), *Ancient Near Eastern Texts*
ANF	The Ante-Nicene Fathers
Ang	*Anglicum*
AnnPhil	*Annales de Philosophie* (Beirut)
AnnThéol	*L'Année théologique*
AnOr	Analecta orientalia
ANQ	*Andover Newton Quarterly*
ANRW	*Aufstieg und Niedergang der römischen Welt,* ed. H. Temporini and W. Haase, Berlin
ANT	Arbeiten zur Neutestamentlichen Textforschung
ANTJ	Arbeiten zum Neuen Testament und zum Judentum
Anton	*Antonianum*
AOAT	Alter orient und Altes Testament
AOS	American Oriental Series
AP	J. Marouzeau (ed.), *L'année philologique*
APOT	R. H. Charles (ed.), *Apocrypha and Pseudepigrapha of the Old Testament*
ArchLing	*Archivum linguisticum*
ARG	*Archiv für Reformationsgeschichte*
ARM	Archives royales de Mari
ArOr	*Archiv orientální*
ARSHLL	Acta Reg. Societatis Humaniorum Litterarum Lundensis
ARW	*Archiv für Religionswissenschaft*
ASB	*Austin Seminary Bulletin*
AshTB	*Ashland Theological Bulletin*
AshTJ	*Ashland Theological Journal*
ASNU	Acta seminarii neotestamentici upsaliensis
ASS	*Acta sanctae sedis*
AsSeign	*Assemblées du Seigneur*
ASSR	*Archives des sciences sociales des religions*
ASTI	*Annual of the Swedish Theological Institute*
ATAbh	Alttestamentliche Abhandlungen
ATANT	Abhandlungen zur Theologie des Alten und Neuen Testaments
ATD	Das Alte Testament Deutsch

ATDan	Acta Theologica Danica
ATJ	*African Theological Journal*
ATR	*Anglican Theological Review*
AuCoeurAfr	*Au Coeur de l'Afrique: Revue interdiocésaine* (Burundi)
AUSS	*Andrews University Seminary Studies*
AzNTT	Arbeiten zur neutestamentlichen Textforschung
BA	*Biblical Archaeologist*
BAC	Biblioteca de autores cristianos
BAGD	W. Bauer, *A Greek-English Lexicon of the New Testament and Other Early Christian Literature,* ET, ed. W. F. Arndt and F. W. Gingrich; 2d ed. rev. F. W. Gingrich and F. W. Danker (University of Chicago, 1979)
BAH	Bibliothèque archéologique et historique
BangTF	*Bangalore Theological Forum*
BAR	*Biblical Archaeology Review*
BASOR	*Bulletin of the American Schools of Oriental Research*
BASP	*Bulletin of the American Society of Papyrologists*
BBB	Bonner biblische Beiträge
BBudé	*Bulletin de l'Association G. Budé* (Rome)
BCSR	*Bulletin of the Council on the Study of Religion*
BDB	F. Brown, S. R. Driver, and C. A. Briggs, *Hebrew and English Lexicon of the Old Testament* (Oxford: Clarendon, 1907)
BDF	F. Blass, A. Debrunner, and R. W. Funk, *A Greek Grammar of the New Testament* (University of Chicago/University of Cambridge, 1961)
BDR	F. Blass, A. Debrunner, and F. Rehkopf, *Grammatik des neutestamentlichen Griechisch*
BeO	*Bibbia e oriente*
BenM	*Benediktinische Monatschrift*
BerlinTZ	*Berliner Theologische Zeitschrift* (Berlin)
BET	Beiträge zur biblischen Exegese und Theologie
BETL	Bibliotheca ephemeridum theologicarum lovaniensium
BEvT	Beiträge zur evangelischen Theologie
BFCT	Beiträge zur Förderung christlicher Theologie
BGBE	Beiträge zur Geschichte der biblischen Exegese
BHH	*Biblisch-Historisches Handwörterbuch*
BHK	R. Kittel, *Biblia hebraica*
BHS	*Biblia hebraica stuttgartensia*
BHT	Beiträge zur historischen Theologie
Bib	*Biblica*
BibB	Biblische Beiträge
BibLeb	*Bibel und Leben*
BibLit	*Bibel und Liturgie*
BiblScRel	*Biblioteca di Scienze Religiose*
BibNot	*Biblische Notizen*
BibOr	Biblica et orientalia
BibS(F)	Biblische Studien (Freiburg, 1895–)
BibS(N)	Biblische Studien (Neukirchen, 1951–)
BIES	*Bulletin of the Israel Exploration Society (= Yediot)*
BIFAO	*Bulletin de l'institut français d'archéologie orientale*
BILL	Bibliothèque des cahiers de l'Institut de Linguistique de Louvain
BiTod	*The Bible Today*
BJRL	*Bulletin of the John Rylands University Library of Manchester*
BJS	Brown Judaic Studies
BK	*Bibel und Kirche*
BKAT	Biblischer Kommentar: Altes Testament

BL	*Book List*
BLE	*Bulletin de littérature ecclésiastique*
BLit	*Bibel und Liturgie*
BLS	Bible and Literature Series
BLT	*Brethren of Life and Thought*
BNTC	Black's New Testament Commentaries
BO	*Bibliotheca orientalis*
BPAA	Bibliotheca Pontificii Athenaei Antoniani
BR	*Biblical Research*
BRev	*Bible Review*
BS	Biblische Studien
BSac	*Bibliotheca Sacra*
BSO(A) S	*Bulletin of the School of Oriental (and African) Studies*
BSR	Bibliothèque de sciences religieuses
BT	*The Bible Translator*
BTB	*Biblical Theology Bulletin*
BTS	*Bible et Terre Saint*
BU	Biblische Untersuchungen
BulBR	*Bulletin for Biblical Research*
BulCPE	*Bulletin du Centre Protestant d'Études* (Geneva)
BulCRIMGU	*Bulletin of the Christian Research Institute Meiji Gakuin University* (Tokyo)
BulSSul	*Bulletin de Saint Sulpice* (Paris)
BVC	*Bible et vie chrétienne*
BW	*Biblical World*
BWANT	Beiträge zur Wissenschaft vom Alten und Neuen Testament
BZ	*Biblische Zeitschrift*
BZAW	Beihefte zur *ZAW*
BZET	Beihefte zur Evangelische Theologie
BZNW	Beihefte zur *ZNW*
BZRGG	Beihefte zur *ZRGG*
CAD	*The Assyrian Dictionary of the Oriental Institute of the University of Chicago*
CAH	*Cambridge Ancient History*
CAT	Commentaire de l'Ancien Testament
CB	*Cultura biblica*
CBFV	Cahiers biblique de Foi et Vie
CBG	*Collationes Brugenses et Gandavenses*
CBQ	*Catholic Biblical Quarterly*
CBQMS	CBQ Monograph Series
CBVE	*Comenius Blätter für Volkserziehung*
CCath	Corpus Catholicorum
CCER	*Cahiers du cercle Ernest Renan*
CChr	Corpus Christianorum
CGTC	Cambridge Greek Testament Commentary
CGTSC	Cambridge Greek Testament for Schools and Colleges
CH	*Church History*
ChicStud	*Chicago Studies*
CHR	*Catholic Historical Review*
ChrTod	*Christianity Today*
CHSP	*Centre for Hermeneutical Study in Hellenistic and Modern Culture Protocol of the Colloquy*
CIG	*Corpus inscriptionum graecarum*
CII	*Corpus inscriptionum iudaicarum*
CIL	*Corpus inscriptionum latinarum*
CIS	*Corpus inscriptionum semiticarum*
CJT	*Canadian Journal of Theology*
ClerMon	*Clergy Monthly*
ClerRev	*Clergy Review*
CLit	*Christianity and Literature*
ClQ	*The Classical Quarterly*
ClW	*Classical Weekly*
CM	*Cahiers marials*
CnS	*Cristianesimo nella Storia*
CNT	Commentaire du Nouveau Testament
CollMech	*Collectanea Mechliniensia*
CollTheol	*Collectanea Theologica*
ComLit	*Communautes et liturgies*
Communio	*Communio: International Catholic Review* (Notre Dame)

ConB	Coniectanea biblica
Concil	*Concilium*
ConcJ	*Concordia Journal*
CongQ	*The Congregational Quarterly*
ConNT	*Coniectanea neotestamentica*
CQ	*Church Quarterly*
CQR	*Church Quarterly Review*
CRAIBL	*Comptes rendus de l'Académie des inscriptions et belles-lettres*
CrisTR	*Criswell Theological Review*
CrQ	*Crozier Quarterly*
CSCO	Corpus scriptorum christianorum orientalium
CSEL	Corpus scriptorum ecclesiasticorum latinorum
CTA	A. Herdner, *Corpus des tablettes en cunéiformes alphabétiques*
CTJ	*Calvin Theological Journal*
CTM	Calwer Theologische Monographien
CTMonth	*Concordia Theological Monthly*
CTQ	*Concordia Theological Quarterly*
CurTM	*Currents in Theology and Mission*
CuW	*Christentum und Wissenschaft*
CV	*Communio viatorum*
CW	*Die christliche Welt*
DACL	*Dictionnaire d'archéologie chrétienne et de liturgie*
DBSup	*Dictionnaire de la Bible, Supplément*
Diak	*Diakonia*
DISO	C.-F. Jean and J. Hoftijzer, *Dictionnaire des inscriptions sémitiques de l'ouest*
DJD	Discoveries in the Judean Desert
DL	*Doctrine and Life*
DOTT	D. W. Thomas (ed.), *Documents from Old Testament Times*
DR	*Downside Review*
DS	Denzinger-Schönmetzer, *Enchiridion symbolorum*
DT	*Deutsche Theologie*
DTC	*Dictionnaire de théologie catholique*
DTT	*Dansk teologisk tidsskrift*
DunRev	*Dunwoodie Review*
EBib	Etudes bibliques
EBT	*Encyclopedia of Biblical Theology*
EcR	*Ecclesiastical Review*
ED	*Euntes Docete* (Rome)
EE	*Estudios Eclesiásticos*
EglT	*Église et théologie*
EHAT	Exegetisches Handbuch zum Alten Testament
EKKNT	Evangelisch-katholischer Kommentar zum Neuen Testament
EKL	*Evangelisches Kirchenlexikon*
EL	*Ephemerides Liturgicae*
Emman	*Emmanuel*
EnchBib	*Enchiridion biblicum*
EncJud	*Encyclopedia judaica* (1971)
EphMar	*Ephemerides mariologique* (Madrid)
EpR	*Epworth Review*
ER	*Ecumenical Review*
ErJb	*Eranos Jahrbuch*
EstBib	*Estudios biblicos*
EstTeol	*Estudios teologicos* (Guatemala)
ETL	*Ephemerides theologicae lovanienses*
ETR	*Etudes théologiques et religieuses*
ETS	Erfurter Theologische Studien
EuA	*Erbe und Auftrag*
EV	*Esprit et Vie*
EvErz	*Das evangelische Erzieher*
EvJ	*Evangelical Journal*
EvK	Evangelische Kommentar
EvQ	*Evangelical Quarterly*
EvT	*Evangelische Theologie*
EW	*Exegetisches Wörterbuch zum Neuen Testament (EWNT)*, ed. H. Balz and G. Schneider, 3 vols.

	(Stuttgart: Kohlhammer, 1980–83)
ExAuditu	*Ex Auditu: An International Journal of Theological Interpretation of Scripture*
Exp	*Expositor*
ExpTim	*The Expository Times*
FB	Forschung zur Bibel
FBBS	Facet Books, Biblical Series
FC	Fathers of the Church
FilolNT	*Filologia Neotestamentaria* (Córdoba, Spain)
FM	*Faith and Mission*
FoiTemps	*La Foi et le temps* (Tournai)
FriedIsr	*Friede über Israel: Zeitschrift für Kirche und Judentum* (Nürnberg)
FRLANT	Forschungen zur Religion und Literatur des Alten und Neuen Testaments
FTS	Frankfurter Theologische Studien
FV	*Foi et Vie*
FZPT	*Freiburg Zeitschrift für Philosophie und Theologie*
GAG	W. von Soden, *Grundriss der akkadischen Grammatik*
GBZKA	*Grazer Beiträge: Zeitschrift für die klassischen Altertumwissenschaft*
GCS	Griechische christliche Schriftsteller
GJ	*Grace Journal*
GKB	Gesenius-Kautzsch-Bergsträsser, *Hebräische Grammatik*
GKC	*Gesenius' Hebrew Grammar*, ed. E. Kautzsch, tr. A. E. Cowley
GNT	Grundrisse zum Neuen Testament
GOTR	*Greek Orthodox Theological Review*
GR	*Greece and Rome*
GRBS	*Greek, Roman, and Byzantine Studies*
Greg	*Gregorianum*
GTA	Göttinger Theologische Arbeiten
GThT	*Geformelet Theologisch Tijdschrift*
GTJ	*Grace Theological Journal*
GuL	*Geist und Leben*
HALAT	W. Baumgartner et al., *Hebräisches und aramäisches Lexikon zum Alten Testament*
HAT	Handbuch zum Alten Testament
HB	*Homiletica en Biblica*
HBT	*Horizons of Biblical Theology*
HD	*Heiliger Dienst* (Salzburg)
HDR	Harvard Dissertations in Religion
HerKor	*Herder Korrespondenz*
HeyJ	*Heythrop Journal*
HibJ	*Hibbert Journal*
HKAT	Handkommentar zum Alten Testament
HKNT	Handkommentar zum Neuen Testament
HL	*Das heilige Land*
HNT	Handbuch zum Neuen Testament
HNTC	Harper's NT Commentaries
HR	*History of Religions*
HSM	Harvard Semitic Monographs
HTKNT	Herders theologischer Kommentar zum Neuen Testament
HTR	*Harvard Theological Review*
HTS	Harvard Theological Studies
HTS	*Hervormde Teologiese Studies* (Pretoria)
HUCA	*Hebrew Union College Annual*
HUTH	Hermeneutische Untersuchungen zur Theologie
IB	*Interpreter's Bible*
IBD	*Illustrated Bible Dictionary*, ed. J. D. Douglas and N. Hillyer
IBS	*Irish Biblical Studies*

ICC International Critical Commentary
IDB G. A. Buttrick (ed.), *Interpreter's Dictionary of the Bible*
IDBSup Supplementary volume to *IDB*
IEJ *Israel Exploration Journal*
IER *Irish Ecclesiastical Record*
IES *Indian Ecclesiastical Studies*
IKZ *Internationale Kirchliche Zeitschrift*
IKZCom *Internationale Katholische Zeitschrift "Communion"* (Rodenkirchen)
ILS H. Dessau (ed.), *Inscriptiones Latinae Selectae* (Berlin, 1892)
Int *Interpretation*
ISBE *International Standard Bible Encyclopedia*, ed. G. W. Bromiley
ITQ *Irish Theological Quarterly*
ITS *Indian Theological Studies*

JA *Journal asiatique*
JAAR *Journal of the American Academy of Religion*
JAC *Jahrbuch für Antike und Christentum*
JAMA *Journal of the American Medical Association*
JANESCU *Journal of the Ancient Near Eastern Society of Columbia University*
JAOS *Journal of the American Oriental Society*
JAS *Journal of Asian Studies*
JBC R. E. Brown et al. (eds.), *The Jerome Biblical Commentary*
JBL *Journal of Biblical Literature*
JBR *Journal of Bible and Religion*
JBT *Jahrbuch für biblische Theologie* (Neukirchen)
JCS *Journal of Cuneiform Studies*
JDS Judean Desert Studies
JEA *Journal of Egyptian Archaeology*
JEH *Journal of Ecclesiastical History*
JerPersp *Jerusalem Perspectives*
JES *Journal of Ecumenical Studies*
JETS *Journal of the Evangelical Theological Society*
JHS *Journal of Hellenic Studies*
JIBS *Journal of Indian and Buddhist Studies*
JIPh *Journal of Indian Philosophy*
JJS *Journal of Jewish Studies*
JLH *Jahrbuch für Liturgie und Hymnologie*
JLitTheol *Journal of Literature and Theology*
JMES *Journal of Middle Eastern Studies*
JMS *Journal of Mithraic Studies*
JNES *Journal of Near Eastern Studies*
JPOS *Journal of the Palestine Oriental Society*
JQ *Jewish Quarterly* (London)
JQR *Jewish Quarterly Review*
JQRMS Jewish Quarterly Review Monograph Series
JR *Journal of Religion*
JRAS *Journal of the Royal Asiatic Society*
JRE *Journal of Religious Ethics*
JRelS *Journal of Religious Studies*
JRH *Journal of Religious History*
JRomH *Journal of Roman History*
JRT *Journal of Religious Thought*
JSJ *Journal for the Study of Judaism*
JSNT *Journal for the Study of the New Testament*
JSNTSup JSNT Supplement Series
JSOT *Journal for the Study of the Old Testament*
JSOTSup JSOT Supplement Series
JSS *Journal of Semitic Studies*
JSSR *Journal for the Scientific Study of Religion*
JTC *Journal for Theology and the Church*
JTS *Journal of Theological Studies*
JTSA *Journal of Theology for South Africa*
Jud *Judaica*

KAI H. Donner and W. Röllig, *Kanaanäische und aramäische Inschriften*

KAT	E. Sellin (ed.), *Kommentar zum Alten Testament*
KatBl	*Katechetische Blätter*
KB	L. Koehler and W. Baumgartner, *Lexicon in Veteris Testamenti libros*
KD	*Kerygma und Dogma*
KEK	Kritisch-exegetischer Kommentar über das Neue Testament
KeTh	*Kerken en Theologie*
KF	*Der Kirchenfreund*
KlT	Kleine Texte
KM	*Katholischen Missionen*
KRS	*Kirchenblatt für die reformierte Schweiz*
KTR	*King's Theological Review* (London)
KuBANT	Kommentare und Beiträge zum Alten und Neuen Testament
LCC	Library of Christian Classics
LCL	Loeb Classical Library
LD	Lectio divina
LebSeel	*Lebendige Seelsorge*
Leš	*Lešonénu*
LexTQ	*Lexington Theological Quarterly*
LingBib	*Linguistica Biblica*
LitMönch	*Liturgie et Mönchtum*
LitTheol	*Literature and Theology* (Oxford)
LLAVT	E. Vogt, *Lexicon linguae aramaicae Veteris Testamenti*
LM	*Lutherische Monatshefte*
LouvStud	*Louvain Studies*
LPGL	G. W. H. Lampe, *Patristic Greek Lexicon*
LQ	*Lutheran Quarterly*
LR	*Lutherische Rundschau*
LS	*Louvain Studies*
LSJ	Liddell-Scott-Jones, *Greek-English Lexicon*
LTK	*Lexikon für Theologie und Kirche*
LTP	*Laval théologique et philosophique*
LTSB	*Lutheran Theological Seminary Bulletin*
LUÅ	Lunds universitets årsskrift
LumVie	*Lumière et Vie*
LumVieSup	*Supplement to LumVie*
LVit	*Lumen Vitae*
LW	*Lutheran World*
ManQ	*The Manking Quarterly*
MarStud	*Marian Studies*
MC	*Modern Churchman*
McCQ	*McCormick Quarterly*
MDOG	Mitteilungen der deutschen Orient-Gesellschaft
MelT	*Melita Theologica*
MeyerK	H. A. W. Meyer, *Kritisch-exegetischer Kommentar über das Neue Testament*
MGWJ	*Monatschrift für Geschichte und Wissenschaft des Judentums*
MilltownStud	*Milltown Studies* (Dublin)
MM	J. H. Moulton and G. Milligan, *The Vocabulary of the Greek Testament* (London: Hodder, 1930)
MNTC	Moffatt NT Commentary
MonPast	*Monatschrift für Pastoraltheologie*
MPAIBL	*Mémoires présentés a l'Académie des inscriptions et belles-lettres*
MPG	*Patrologia Graeca*, ed. J. P. Migne, 1844 ff.
MScRel	*Mélanges de science religieuse*
MTS	Marburger theologische Studien
MTZ	*Münchener theologische Zeitschrift*
MUSJ	*Mélanges de l'université Saint-Joseph*
MVAG	Mitteilungen der vorder-asiatisch-ägyptischen Gesellschaft
NAG	*Nachrichten von der Akademie der Wissenschaften in Göttingen*
NB	*New Blackfriars*
NCB	New Century Bible (new ed.)
NCCHS	R. C. Fuller et al. (eds.), *New Catholic Commentary on Holy Scripture*

NCE M. R. P. McGuire et al. (eds.), *New Catholic Encyclopedia*
NClB New Clarendon Bible
NedTTs *Nederlands theologisch tijdschrift*
Neot *Neotestamentica*
NESTR *Near East School of Theology Review*
NewDocs *New Documents Illustrating Early Christianity, A Review of Greek Inscriptions, etc.,* ed. G. H. R. Horsley, North Ryde, NSW, Australia
NFT New Frontiers in Theology
NGS New Gospel Studies
NHS Nag Hammadi Studies
NICNT New International Commentary on the New Testament
NieuTS *Nieuwe theologische studiën*
NiewTT *Niew theologisch tijdschrift*
NIGTC New International Greek Testament Commentary
NJDT *Neue Jahrbücher für deutsche Theologie*
NKZ *Neue kirchliche Zeitschrift*
NorTT *Norsk Teologisk Tijdsskrift*
NovT *Novum Testamentum*
NovTSup Supplement to *NovT*
NovVet *Nova et vetera*
NPNF Nicene and Post-Nicene Fathers
NRF *Nouvelle revue française*
NRT *La nouvelle revue théologique*
NSK *Neues Sächsisches Kirchenblatt*
NTA *New Testament Abstracts*
NTAbh Neutestamentliche Abhandlungen
NTD Das Neue Testament Deutsch
NTF Neutestamentliche Forschungen
NTL New Testament Library
NTR *New Theology Review*
NTS *New Testament Studies*
NTSR The New Testament for Spiritual Reading
NTTS New Testament Tools and Studies
Numen *Numen: International Review for the History of Religions*
NZM *Neue Zeitschrift für Missionswissenschaft*
NZSTR *Neue Zeitschrift für systematische Theologie und Religionsphilosophie*

OAK *Österreichisches Archiv für Kirchenrecht*
OberrheinPast *Oberrheinisches Pastoralblatt*
OBO Orbis biblicus et orientalis
ÖBS Österreichische Biblische Studien
OCD *Oxford Classical Dictionary*
OCP *Orientalia christiana periodica*
OGI W. Dittenberger (ed.), *Orientis graeci inscriptiones selectae* (Leipzig: Hirzel, 1903–5)
OIP Oriental Institute Publications
OLP Orientalia lovaniensia periodica
OLZ *Orientalische Literaturzeitung*
OPTAT *Occasional Papers in Translation and Textlinguistics* (Dallas)
Or *Orientalia* (Rome)
OrAnt *Oriens antiquus*
OrChr *Oriens christianus*
OrSyr *L'orient syrien*
ÖTKNT Ökumenischer Taschenbuch-Kommentar zum NT
OTM Oxford Theological Monographs
OTS Oudtestamentische Studiën

PAAJR *Proceedings of the American Academy of Jewish Research*
Parlit *Paroisse et liturgie*
PastB *Pastoralblätter*
PC Proclamation Commentaries
PCB M. Black and H. H. Rowley (eds.), *Peake's Commentary on the Bible*

PEFQS	*Palestine Exploration Fund, Quarterly Statement*
PenHom	*La Pensée et les hommes*
PEQ	*Palestine Exploration Quarterly*
PerTeo	*Perspectiva Teologica*
PFay	Fayûm Papyri
PG	*Patrologia graeca,* ed. J. P. Migne
PGM	K. Preisendanz (ed.), *Papyri graecae magicae*
PhEW	*Philosophy East and West*
PhRev	*Philosophical Review*
PJ	*Palästina-Jahrbuch*
PLL	*Papers on Language and Literature*
PM	*Protestantische Monatshefte*
PNTC	Pelican New Testament Commentaries
PO	Patrologia orientalis
POxy	Oxyrhynchus Papyri
ProcCTSA	*Proceedings of the Catholic Theological Society of America*
ProcGLBS	*Proceedings Eastern Great Lakes Bible Society*
ProcIBA	*Proceedings of the Irish Biblical Association*
PRS	*Perspectives in Religious Studies*
PRU	*Le Palais royal d'Ugarit*
PSTJ	*Perkins (School of Theology) Journal*
PTMS	Pittsburgh Theological Monograph Series
PTR	*Princeton Theological Review*
PVTG	Pseudepigrapha Veteris Testamenti graece
PW	Pauly-Wissowa, *Real-Encyklopädie der klassischen Altertumswissenschaft*
PWSup	Supplement to PW
QD	Quaestiones Disputatae
QDAP	*Quarterly of the Department of Antiquities in Palestine*
QLP	*Questions liturgiques et paroissiales* (Louvain)
QRev	*Quarterly Review* (Nashville)
RA	*Revue d'assyriologie et d'archéologie orientale*
RAC	*Reallexikon für Antike und Christentum*
RArch	*Revue archéologique*
RB	*Revue biblique*
RBén	*Revue Bénedictine*
RCB	*Revista de cultura biblica*
RDC	*Revue de droit canonique*
RE	*Realencyklopädie für protestantische Theologie und Kirche*
REA	*Revue des Études Augustiniennes*
REAnc	*Revue des études anciennes* (Bordeaux)
RecAcLég	*Recueil de l'Académie de Législation* (Toulouse)
RechBib	Recherches bibliques
REg	*Revue d'égyptologie*
REG	*Revue des études grecques*
REJ	*Revue des études juives*
RelArts	Religion and the Arts
RELiège	*Revue Ecclésiastique de Liège*
RelLif	*Religion in Life*
RelS	*Religious Studies*
RelSoc	*Religion and Society*
RelSRev	*Religious Studies Review*
RES	*Répertoire d'épigraphie sémitique*
RestQ	*Restoration Quarterly*
RevAfTh	*Revue Africaine de Théologie* (Kinshasa-Limette, Zaire)
RevApol	*Revue Apologétique*
RevArch	*Revue archéologique*
RevDioc Namur	*Revue diocésaine de Namur*
RevDTournai	*Revue diocésaine de Tournai*
RevExp	*Review and Expositor*
RevistB	*Revista biblica*
RevQ	*Revue de Qumrân*
RevRef	*Revue Réformée*
RevRel	*Review for Religious*
RevScRel	*Revue des sciences religieuses*
RevSém	*Revue sémitique*
RevSR	*Revue des sciences religieuses* (Strasbourg)
RevThom	*Revue thomiste*

RevUB — *Revue de l'Université de Bruxelles*
RGG — *Religion in Geschichte und Gegenwart*
RHD — *Revue de l'histoire de droit*
RHE — *Revue d'histoire ecclésiastique*
RHPR — *Revue d'histoire et de philosophie religieuses*
RHR — *Revue de l'histoire des religions*
RHS — *Revue d'histoire de la spiritualité*
RICP — *Revue de l'Institut Catholique de Paris*
RIL — *Religion and Intellectual Life*
RivB — *Rivista biblica*
RM — *Rheinisches Museum für Philologie*
RNT — Regensburger Neues Testament
RR — *Review of Religion*
RSB — *Religious Studies Bulletin*
RSLR — *Rivista di Storiae Letteratura Religiosa* (Turin)
RSO — *Rivista degli studi orientali*
RSPT — *Revue des sciences philosophiques et théologiques*
RSR — *Recherches de science religieuse*
RST — Regensburger Studien zur Theologie
RTL — *Revue théologique de Louvain*
RTP — *Revue de théologie et de philosophie*
RTQR — *Revue de théologie et des questions religieuses* (Montaublon)
RTR — *Reformed Theological Review*
RUO — *Revue de l'université Ottawa*
RUV — *La Revue de l'Université Laval*

SaatHof — *Saat auf Hoffnung*
SacPag — *Sacra Pagina*
SAH — *Sitzungberichte der Heidelberger Akademie der Wissenschaften (phil.-hist. Klasse)*
Sal — *Salmanticensis*
SANT — Studien zum Alten und Neuen Testament
SAQ — Sammlung ausgewählter kirchen- und dogmengeschichtlicher Quellenschriften
SAWB — *Sitzungsberichte der (königlich preussischen) Akademie der Wissenschaften zu Berlin (phil.-hist. Klasse)*
SB — Sources bibliques
SBB — Stuttgarter biblische Monographien
SBFLA — *Studii biblici franciscani liber annuus*
SBJ — *La sainte bible de Jérusalem*
SBLASP — Society of Biblical Literature Abstracts and Seminar Papers
SBLDS — SBL Dissertation Series
SBLMasS — SBL Masoretic Studies
SBLMS — SBL Monograph Series
SBLSBS — SBL Sources for Biblical Study
SBLSCS — SBL Septuagint and Cognate Studies
SBLTT — SBL Texts and Translations
SBM — Stuttgarter biblische Monographien
SBS — Stuttgarter Bibelstudien
SBT — Studies in Biblical Theology
SC — Sources chrétiennes
ScEccl — *Sciences ecclésiastiques*
ScEs — *Science et esprit*
SCR — *Studies in Comparative Religion*
Scr — *Scripture*
ScrB — *Scripture Bulletin*
SD — Studies and Documents
SE — *Studia Evangelica* 1, 2, 3, 4, 5, 6 (= TU 73 [1959], 87 [1964], 88 [1964], 102 [1968], 103 [1968], 112 [1973]
SEÅ — *Svensk exegetisk årsbok*
Sef — *Sefarad*
SeinSend — *Sein und Sendung*
Sem — *Semitica*

SémiotBib *Sémiotique et Bible*
SHAW Sitzungsberichte heidelbergen Akademie der Wissenschaften
SHT Studies in Historical Theology
SHVL Skrifter Utgivna Av Kungl. Humanistika Vetenskapssamfundet i Lund
SIDJC *Service international de documentation judéo-chrétienne*
SJLA Studies in Judaism in Late Antiquity
SJT *Scottish Journal of Theology*
SLJT *St Luke's Journal of Theology*
SMSR *Studi e materiali di storia delle religioni*
SNT Studien zum Neuen Testament
SNTA Studiorum Novi Testamenti Auxilia
SNTSMS Society for New Testament Studies Monograph Series
SNTU *Studien zum Neuen Testament und seiner Umwelt*
SO *Symbolae osloenses*
SOTSMS Society for Old Testament Study Monograph Series
SPap *Studia papyrologica*
SPAW Sitzungsberichte der preussischen Akademie der Wissenschaften
SPB Studia postbiblica
SR *Studies in Religion/Sciences Religieuses*
SSS Semitic Study Series
ST *Studia theologica*
STÅ *Svensk teologisk årsskrift*
StBibT *Studia biblica et theologica*
STDJ Studies on the Texts of the Desert of Judah
STK *Svensk teologisk kvartalskrift*
StMon *Studia Monastica*
StMor *Studia Moralia*
Str-B H. Strack and P. Billerbeck, *Kommentar zum Neuen Testament*, 4 vols. (Munich: Beck'sche, 1926–28)
StudBib *Studia biblica*
StudClas *Studii clasice* (Bukarest)
StudMiss *Studia Missionalia*
StudNeot Studia neotestamentica
StudPat *Studia Patristica*
STZ *Schweizerische theologische Zeitschrift*
SUNT Studien zur Umwelt des Neuen Testaments
SVTP Studia in Veteris Testamenti pseudepigrapha
SWJT *Southwestern Journal of Theology*
SymBU Symbolae biblicae upsalienses

TantY *Tantur Yearbook*
TAPA *Transactions of the American Philological Association*
TB *Theologische Beiträge*
TBC Torch Bible Commentaries
TBl *Theologische Blätter*
TBü Theologische Bücherei
TC Theological Collection (SPCK)
TD *Theology Digest*
TDNT G. Kittel and G. Friedrich (eds.), *Theological Dictionary of the New Testament*, 10 vols., ET (Grand Rapids: Eerdmans, 1964–76)
TE *Theologica Evangelica*
TextsS Texts and Studies
TF *Theologische Forschung*
TGeg *Theologie der Gegenwart*
TGl *Theologie und Glaube*
Th *Theology*
ThA *Theologische Arbeiten*
ThBer *Theologische Berichte*
THKNT Theologischer Handkommentar zum Neuen Testament
ThViat *Theologia Viatorum*
TJ *Trinity Journal*

TJT *Toronto Journal of Theology*
TK *Texte und Kontexte* (Stuttgart)
TLZ *Theologische Literaturzeitung*
TNTC Tyndale New Testament Commentaries
TP *Theologie und Philosophie (ThPh)*
TPQ *Theologisch-Praktische Quartalschrift*
TQ *Theologische Quartalschrift*
TRev *Theologische Revue*
TrinSemRev *Trinity Seminary Review* (Columbus, OH)
TRRHD *Tijdschrift voor Rechtsgeschiednis: Revue d'histoire de droit*
TRu *Theologische Rundschau*
TS *Theological Studies*
TSAJ Texte und Studien zum Antiken Judentum
TSFB *Theological Students Fellowship Bulletin*
TSK *Theologische Studien und Kritiken*
TT *Teologisk Tidsskrift*
TTKi *Tidsskrift for Teologi og Kirke*
TToday *Theology Today*
TTS Trier theologische Studien
TTZ *Trierer theologische Zeitschrift*
TU Texte und Untersuchungen
TVers *Theologische Versuche* (Berlin)
TWAT G. J. Botterweck and H. Ringgren (eds.), *Theologisches Wörterbuch zum Alten Testament*
TWNT G. Kittel and G. Friedrich (eds.), *Theologisches Wörterbuch zum Neuen Testament*
TynB *Tyndale Bulletin*
TZ *Theologische Zeitschrift*

UBSGNT United Bible Societies Greek New Testament
UCL Universitas Catholica Lovaniensis
UF *Ugaritische Forschungen*
UFHM University of Florida Humanities Monograph
UnaSanc *Una Sancta* (Freising)
UNT Untersuchungen zum Neuen Testament
US *Una Sancta*
USQR *Union Seminary Quarterly Review*
USR *Union Seminary Review* (Richmond, VA)
UT C. H. Gordon, *Ugaritic Textbook*
UUÅ Uppsala universitetsårsskrift
UUC *Unitarian Universalist Christian*

VC *Vigilae christianae*
VCaro *Verbum caro*
VChr *Vigiliae Christianae*
VD *Verbum domini*
VetC *Vetera Christianorum*
VF *Verkündigung und Forschung*
VKGNT K. Aland (ed.), *Vollständige Konkordanz zum griechischen Neuen Testament*
VoxEv *Vox Evangelica* (London)
VS Verbum salutis
VSpir *Vie spirituelle*
VT *Vetus Testamentum*
VTSup Vetus Testamentum, Supplements

WA M. Luther, Kritische Gesamtausgabe (="Weimar" edition)
WBC Word Biblical Commentary
WC Westminster Commentary
WD *Wort und Dienst*
WDB *Westminster Dictionary of the Bible*
WF Wege der Forschung
WHAB *Westminster Historical Atlas of the Bible*
WMANT Wissenschaftliche Monographien zum Alten und Neuen Testament
WO *Die Welt des Orients*
WortWahr *Wort und Wahrheit*

WTJ	*Westminster Theological Journal*
WUNT	Wissenschaftliche Untersuchungen zum Neuen Testament
WW	*Word and World*
WZKM	*Wiener Zeitschrift für die Kunde des Morgenlandes*
WZKSO	*Wiener Zeitschrift für die Kunde Süd- und Ostasiens*
ZA	*Zeitschrift für Assyriologie*
ZAW	*Zeitschrift für die alttestamentliche Wissenschaft*
ZDMG	*Zeitschrift der deutschen morgenländischen Gesellschaft*
ZDPV	*Zeitschrift des deutschen Palästina-Vereins*
ZdZ	*Die Zeichen der Zeit*
ZEE	*Zeitschrift für evangelische Ethik*
ZHT	*Zeitschrift für historische Theologie*
ZKG	*Zeitschrift für Kirchengeschichte*
ZKNT	*Zahn's Kommentar zum NT*
ZKT	*Zeitschrift für katholische Theologie*
ZMR	*Zeitschrift für Missionskunde und Religionswissenschaft*
ZNW	*Zeitschrift für die neutestamentliche Wissenschaft*
ZPE	*Zeitschrift für Papyrologie und Epigraphik*
ZRGG	*Zeitschrift für Religions- und Geistesgeschichte*
ZSSR	*Zeitschrift der Savigny Stiftung für Rechtsgeschichte, romantische Abteilung*
ZST	*Zeitschrift für systematische Theologie*
ZTK	*Zeitschrift für Theologie und Kirche*
ZWT	*Zeitschrift für wissenschaftliche Theologie*

D. Abbreviations for Books of the Bible, the Apocrypha, and the Pseudepigrapha

OLD TESTAMENT

Gen	2 Chr	Dan
Exod	Ezra	Hos
Lev	Neh	Joel
Num	Esth	Amos
Deut	Job	Obad
Josh	Ps(Pss)	Jonah
Judg	Prov	Mic
Ruth	Eccl	Nah
1 Sam	Cant	Hab
2 Sam	Isa	Zeph
1 Kgs	Jer	Hag
2 Kgs	Lam	Zech
1 Chr	Ezek	Mal

NEW TESTAMENT

Matt	1 Tim
Mark	2 Tim
Luke	Titus
John	Philem
Acts	Heb
Rom	Jas
1 Cor	1 Peter
2 Cor	2 Peter
Gal	1 John
Eph	2 John
Phil	3 John
Col	Jude
1 Thess	Rev
2 Thess	

APOCRYPHA

1 Esd	1 Esdras
2 Esd	2 Esdras
Tob	Tobit
Jdt	Judith
Add Esth	Additions to Esther
Wis	Wisdom of Solomon
Sir	Ecclesiasticus (Wisdom of Jesus the son of Sirach)
Bar	Baruch
Ep Jer	Epistle of Jeremy

S Th Ch	Song of the Three Children (or Young Men)	Pr Man	Prayer of Manasseh
Sus	Susanna	1 Macc	1 Maccabees
Bel	Bel and the Dragon	2 Macc	2 Maccabees

E. Abbreviations of the Names of Pseudepigraphical and Early Patristic Books

Adam and Eve	Life of Adam and Eve	*Barn.*	Barnabas
Apoc. Abr.	Apocalypse of Abraham (1st to 2nd cent. A.D.)	*1–2 Clem.*	1–2 Clement
		Did.	Didache
2–3 Apoc. Bar.	Syriac, Greek Apocalypse of Baruch	*Diogn.*	Diognetus
		Herm. *Man.*	Hermas, Mandates
Apoc. Mos.	Apocalypse of Moses	*Sim.*	Similitudes
As. Mos.	(See *T. Mos.*)	*Vis.*	Visions
1–2–3 Enoch	Ethiopic, Slavonic, Hebrew Enoch	Ign. *Eph.*	Ignatius, Letter to the Ephesians
Ep. Arist.	Epistle of Aristeas	*Magn.*	Ignatius, Letter to the Magnesians
Ep. Diognetus	Epistle to Diognetus		
Jub.	Jubilees	*Phil.*	Ignatius, Letter to the Philadelphians
Mart. Isa.	Martyrdom of Isaiah		
Odes Sol.	Odes of Solomon	*Pol.*	Ignatius, Letter to Polycarp
Pss. Sol.	Psalms of Solomon		
Sib. Or.	Sibylline Oracles	*Rom.*	Ignatius, Letter to the Romans
T. 12 Patr.	Testaments of the Twelve Patriarchs	*Smyrn.*	Ignatius, Letter to the Smyrnaeans
T. Abr.	Testament of Abraham		
T. Judah	Testament of Judah	*Trall.*	Ignatius, Letter to the Trallians
T. Levi	Testament of Levi, etc.		
Apoc. Pet.	Apocalypse of Peter	*Mart. Pol.*	Martyrdom of Polycarp
Gos. Eb.	Gospel of the Ebionites	Pol. *Phil.*	Polycarp to the Philippians
Gos. Eg.	Gospel of the Egyptians		
Gos. Heb.	Gospel of the Hebrews	*Adv. Haer.*	Irenaeus, Against All Heresies
Gos. Naass.	Gospel of the Naassenes		
Gos. Pet.	Gospel of Peter	*De Praesc. Haer.*	Tertullian, On the Proscribing of Heretics
Gos. Thom.	Gospel of Thomas		
Prot. Jas.	Protevangelium of James		

F. Abbreviations of Names of Dead Sea Scrolls and Related Texts

CD	Cairo (Genizah text of the) Damascus (Document)
Ḥev	Naḥal Ḥever texts
Mas	Masada texts
Mird	Khirbet Mird texts
Mur	Wadi Murabbaʿat texts
P	Pesher (commentary)
Q	Qumran
1Q, 2Q 3Q, etc.	Numbered caves of Qumran, yielding written material; followed by abbreviation of biblical or apocryphal book
QL	Qumran literature
1QapGen	*Genesis Apocryphon* of Qumran Cave 1
1QH	*Hôdāyôt (Thanksgiving Hymns)* from Qumran Cave 1

1QIsa^{a,b}	First or second copy of Isaiah from Qumran Cave 1
1QpHab	*Pesher on Habakkuk* from Qumran Cave 1
1QM	*Milḥāmāh* (War Scroll)
1QS	*Serek hayyaḥad (Rule of the Community, Manual of Discipline)*
1QSa	Appendix A *(Rule of the Congregation)* to 1QS
1QSb	Appendix B *(Blessings)* to 1QS
3Q*15*	Copper Scroll from Qumran Cave 3
4QFlor	*Florilegium* (or *Eschatological Midrashim)* from Qumran Cave 4
4QMess ar	Aramaic "Messianic" text from Qumran Cave 4
4QPrNab	Prayer of Nabonidus from Qumran Cave 4
4QTestim	*Testimonia* text from Qumran Cave 4
4QTLevi	*Testament of Levi* from Qumran Cave 4
4QPhyl	Phylacteries from Qumran Cave 4
11QMelch	*Melchizedek* text from Qumran Cave 11
11QtgJob	*Targum of Job* from Qumran Cave 11

G. Abbreviaations of Targumic Material

Tg. Onq.	*Targum Onqelos*
Tg. Neb.	*Targum of the Prophets*
Tg. Ket.	*Targum of the Writings*
Frg. Tg.	*Fragmentary Targum*
Sam. Tg.	*Samaritan Targum*
Tg. Isa.	*Targum of Isaiah*
Pal. Tgs.	*Palestinian Targums*
Tg. Neof.	*Targum Neofiti I*
Tg. Ps.-J.	*Targum Pseudo-Jonathan*
Tg. Yer. I	*Targum Yerušalmi I**
Tg. Yer. II	*Targum Yerušalmi II**
Yem. Tg.	*Yemenite Targum*
Tg. Esth I, II	*First or Second Targum of Esther*

*optional title

H. Abbreviations of Other Rabbinic Works

ʾAbot	*ʾAbot de Rabbi Nathan*
ʾAg. Ber.	*ʾAggadat Berešit*
Bab.	*Babylonian*
Bar.	*Baraita*
Der. Er. Rab.	*Derek Ereṣ Rabba*
Der. Er. Zuṭ.	*Derek Ereṣ Zuṭa*
Gem.	*Gemara*
Kalla	*Kalla*
Mek.	*Mekilta*
Midr.	*Midraš;* cited with usual abbreviation for biblical book; but *Midr. Qoh.* = *Midraš Qohelet*
Pal.	*Palestinian*
Pesiq. R.	*Pesiqta Rabbati*
Pesiq. Rab Kah.	*Pesiqta de Rab Kahana*
Pirqe R. El.	*Pirqe Rabbi Eliezer*
Rab.	*Rabbah* (following abbreviation for biblical book: *Gen. Rab.* [with periods] = *Genesis Rabbah*)
Sem.	*Semaḥot*
Sipra	*Sipra*
Sipre	*Sipre*
Sop.	*Soperim*
S. ʿOlam Rab.	*Seder ʿOlam Rabbah*
Talm.	*Talmud*
Yal.	*Yalquṭ*

I. Abbreviations of Orders and Tractates in Mishnaic and Related Literature

(Italicized m., t., b., or y. used before name to distinguish among tractates in Mishnah, Tosepta, Babylonian Talmud, and Jerusalem Talmud.)

ʾAbot	*ʾAbot*	*Nazir*	*Nazir*
ʿArak.	*ʿArakin*	*Ned.*	*Nedarim*
ʿAbod. Zar.	*ʿAboda Zara*	*Neg.*	*Negaʿim*
B. Bat.	*Baba Batra*	*Nez.*	*Neziqin*
Bek.	*Bekorot*	*Nid.*	*Niddah*
Ber.	*Berakot*	*Ohol.*	*Oholot*
Beṣa	*Beṣa (= Yom Tob)*	*ʿOr.*	*ʿOrla*
Bik.	*Bikkurim*	*Para*	*Para*
B. Meṣ.	*Baba Meṣiʿa*	*Peʾa*	*Peʾa*
B. Qam.	*Baba Qamma*	*Pesaḥ.*	*Pesaḥim*
Dem.	*Demai*	*Qinnim*	*Qinnim*
ʿEd.	*ʿEduyyot*	*Qidd.*	*Qiddušin*
ʿErub.	*ʿErubin*	*Qod.*	*Qodašin*
Giṭ.	*Giṭṭin*	*Roš. Haš.*	*Roš Haššana*
Ḥag.	*Ḥagiga*	*Sanh.*	*Sanhedrin*
Ḥal.	*Ḥalla*	*Šabb.*	*Šabbat*
Hor.	*Horayot*	*Šeb.*	*Šebiʿit*
Ḥul.	*Ḥullin*	*Šebu.*	*Šebuʿot*
Kelim	*Kelim*	*Šeqal.*	*Šeqalim*
Ker.	*Keritot*	*Soṭa*	*Soṭa*
Ketub.	*Ketubot*	*Sukk.*	*Sukka*
Kil.	*Kilʾayim*	*Taʿan.*	*Taʿanit*
Maʿaś.	*Maʿaśerot*	*Tamid*	*Tamid*
Mak.	*Makkot*	*Tem.*	*Temura*
Makš.	*Makširin (=Mašqin)*	*Ter.*	*Terumot*
Meg.	*Megilla*	*Ṭohar.*	*Ṭoharot*
Meʿil.	*Meʿila*	*T. Yom*	*Tebul Yom*
Menaḥ.	*Menaḥot*	*ʿUq.*	*ʿUqṣin*
Mid.	*Middot*	*Yad.*	*Yadayim*
Miqw.	*Miqwaʾot*	*Yebam.*	*Yebamot*
Moʿed	*Moʿed*	*Yoma*	*Yoma (= Kippurim)*
Moʿed Qat.	*Moʿed Qatan*	*Zabim*	*Zabim*
Maʿaś. Š.	*Maʿaśer Šeni*	*Zebaḥ.*	*Zebaḥim*
Našim	*Našim*	*Zer.*	*Zeraʿim*

J. Abbreviations of Nag Hammadi Tractates

Acts Pet. 12 Apost.	*Acts of Peter and the Twelve Apostles*	*1 Apoc. Jas.*	*First Apocalypse of James*
		2 Apoc. Jas.	*Second Apocalypse of James*
Allogenes	*Allogenes*	*Apoc. Paul*	*Apocalypse of Paul*
Ap. Jas.	*Apocryphon of James*	*Apoc. Pet.*	*Apocalypse of Peter*
Ap. John	*Apocryphon of John*	*Asclepius*	*Asclepius 21–29*
Apoc. Adam	*Apocalypse of Adam*	*Auth. Teach.*	*Authoritative Teaching*

Dial. Sav.	*Dialogue of the Savior*
Disc. 8–9	*Discourse on the Eighth and Ninth*
Ep. Pet. Phil.	*Letter of Peter to Philip*
Eugnostos	*Eugnostos the Blessed*
Exeg. Soul	*Exegesis on the Soul*
Gos. Eg.	*Gospel of the Egyptians*
Gos. Phil.	*Gospel of Philip*
Gos. Thom.	*Gospel of Thomas*
Gos. Truth	*Gospel of Truth*
Great Pow.	*Concept of our Great Power*
Hyp. Arch.	*Hypostasis of the Archons*
Hypsiph.	*Hypsiphrone*
Interp. Know.	*Interpretation of Knowledge*
Marsanes	*Marsanes*
Melch.	*Melchizedek*
Norea	*Thought of Norea*
On Bap. A	*On Baptism A*
On Bap. B	*On Baptism B*
On Bap. C	*On Baptism C*
On Euch. A	*On the Eucharist A*
On Euch. B	*On the Eucharist B*
Orig. World	*On the Origin of the World*
Paraph. Shem	*Paraphrase of Shem*
Pr. Paul	*Prayer of the Apostle Paul*
Pr. Thanks.	*Prayer of Thanksgiving*
Prot. Jas.	*Protevangelium of James*
Sent. Sextus	*Sentences of Sextus*
Soph. Jes. Chr.	*Sophia of Jesus Christ*
Steles Seth	*Three Steles of Seth*
Teach. Silv.	*Teachings of Silvanus*
Testim. Truth	*Testimony of Truth*
Thom. Cont.	*Book of Thomas the Contender*
Thund.	*Thunder, Perfect Mind*
Treat. Res.	*Treatise on Resurrection*
Treat. Seth	*Second Treatise of the Great Seth*
Tri. Trac.	*Tripartite Tractate*
Trim. Prot.	*Trimorphic Protennoia*
Val. Exp.	*A Valentinian Exposition*
Zost.	*Zostrianos*

Note: The textual notes and numbers used to indicate individual manuscripts are those found in the apparatus criticus of *Novum Testamentum Graece*, ed. E. Nestle and K. Aland et al. (Stuttgart: Deutsche Bibelgesellschaft, 1979[26]). This edition of the Greek New Testament is the basis for the *Translation* sections.

Commentary Bibliography

Barclay, W. *The Gospel of Luke.* Daily Study Bible Series. 2nd ed. Philadelphia: Westminster, 1956. **Barrel, E. V.,** and **Barrell, K. G.** *St. Luke's Gospel: An Introductory Study.* London: Murray, 1982. **Bossuyt, P.,** and **Radermakers, J.** *Jésus, parole de la Grâce selon saint Luc 1: Texte. 2 Lecture continue.* Brussels: Institut d'Études Théologique, 1981. **Bovon, F.** *Das Evangelism nach Lukas.* 1, 1–9, 50. EKKNT 3/1. Neukirchen/Einsiedeln: Neukirchener/Benziger, 1989. **Bratcher, R. G.** *A Translator's Guide to the Gospel of Luke.* Helps for Translators. London/New York/Stuttgart: UBS, 1982. **Busse, U., et. al.** *Jesus zwischen Arm und Reich: Lukas-Evangelium.* Bibelauslegung für die Praxis 18. Stuttgart: Katholisches Bibelwerk, 1980. **Caird, G. B.** *The Gospel of St. Luke.* London: Penguin, 1963. **Craddock, F. B.** *Luke.* Louisville: John Knox, 1990. **Creed, J. M.** *The Gospel according to St. Luke.* London: Macmillan, 1942. **Danker, F. W.** *Jesus and the New Age according to St. Luke.* St. Louis: Clayton, 1972. ———. *Luke.* Proclamation Commentaries, 2nd ed. Philadelphia: Fortress, 1987. **D'Arc, J., Sr.** *Évangile selon Luc: Présentation du texte grec, traduction et notes.* Nouvelle collection de textes et documents . . . G. Budé. Paris: Les Belles Lettres/Desclée de Brouwer, 1986. **Dean, R. J.** *Luke.* Layman's Bible Book Commentary 17. Nashville, TN: Broadman, 1983. **Delebecque, É.** *Évangile de Luc: Texte traduit et annoté.* Études anciennes de l'Association G. Budé. Paris: Les Belles Lettres, 1976. **Dieterlé, C., et al.** *Manuel du traducteur pour l'évangile de Luc.* Stuttgart/Paris: Alliance biblique universelle, 1977. **Drury, J.** *Luke.* J. B. Phillips Commentaries, Fontana Books. London: Collins, 1973. **Easton, B. S.** *The Gospel according to St. Luke: A Critical and Exegetical Commentary.* New York: Scribner, 1926. **Ellis, E. E.** *The Gospel of Luke.* 2nd ed. London: Oliphants, 1974. **Ernst, J.** *Das Evangelium nach Lukas, übersetzt und erklärt.* RNT. Regensburg: Pustet, 1977. **Evans, C. A.** *Luke.* Peabody, MA: Hendrickson Publishers, 1990. **Evans, C. F.** *Saint Luke.* London/Philadelphia: SCM/Trinity, 1990. **Fitzmyer, J. A.** *The Gospel according to Luke.* AB 28, 28A. 2 vols. Garden City, NY: Doubleday, 1981–85. **Geldenhuys, N.** *Commentary on the Gospel of Luke: The English Text with Introduction, Exposition, and Notes.* NICNT. Grand Rapids: Eerdmans, 1951. **Gilmour, S. M.** "The Gospel according to St. Luke." *Interpreter's Bible.* Nashville: Abingdon, 1952. 8:1–434. **Godet, F.** *A Commentary on the Gospel of St. Luke.* Tr. E. W. Shelders. 2 vols. Edinburgh: T. & T. Clark, repr. 1976 (1887, 1889). **Gooding, D.** *According to Luke: A New Exposition of the Third Gospel.* Grand Rapids/Leicester, UK: Eerdmans/Inter-Varsity, 1987. **Goulder, M. D.** *Luke: A New Paradigm.* JSNTSup 20. 2 vols. Sheffield: Sheffield Academic, 1989. **Grundmann, W.** *Das Evangelium nach Lukas.* THKNT 3. 2nd ed. East Berlin: Evangelische Verlaganstalt, 1961. **Harrington, W. J.** *The Gospel according to St. Luke: A Commentary.* Westminster, MD/Toronto: Newman, 1967. **Hauck, F.** *Das Evangelium des Lukas.* Leipzig: Deichertsche Verlagsbuchhandlung, 1934. **Hendriksen, W.** *Exposition of the Gospel according to Luke.* New Testament Commentaries. Grand Rapids, MI: Baker, 1978. **Hobbs, H.** *An Exposition of the Gospel of Luke.* Grand Rapids: Baker, 1966. **Johnson, L. T.** *The Gospel of Luke.* Sacra Pagina 3. Collegeville, MN: Liturgical, 1991. **Karris, R. J.** *Invitation to Luke: A Commentary on the Gospel of Luke with Complete Text from the Jerusalem Bible.* New York: Doubleday, 1977. **Kealy, S. P.** *The Gospel of Luke.* Denville, NJ: Dimension Books, 1979. **Kilgallen, J. J.** *A Brief Commentary on the Gospel of Luke.* New York/Mahwah, NJ: Paulist, 1988. **Klostermann, E.** *Das Lukasevangelium.* HNT 5. Tübingen: Mohr (Siebeck), 1975 = 1929. **Kodell, J.** *The Gospel according to Luke.* Collegeville Bible Commentary 3. Collegeville, MN: Liturgical Press, 1983. **Kremer, J.** *Lukasevangelium: Die Neue Echter Bible, Kommentar zum Neuen Testament mit der Einheitsübersetzung 3.* Würzburg: Echter, 1988. **Lachs, S. T.** *A Rabbinic Commentary on the New Testament: The Gospels of Matthew, Mark, and Luke.* Hoboken, NJ: Ktav, 1987. **Lagrange, M.-J.** *Évangile selon Saint Luc.* 2nd ed. Paris: Gabalda, 1921. **Larson, B.** *Luke.*

Communicator's Commentary 3. Waco, TX: Word Books, 1983. **LaVerdiere, E.** *Luke.* Wilmington, DE: Glazier, 1980. **Leaney, A. R. C.** *A Commentary on the Gospel according to St. Luke.* BNTC. London: A. & C. Black, 1958. **Lenski, R. C. H.** *The Interpretation of St. Mark's and St. Luke's Gospel.* Columbus, OH: Lutheran Book Concern, 1934. **Liefeld, W.** "Luke." In *The Expositor's Bible Commentary,* ed. F. Gaebelein et al. 8:797–1059. **Linden, P. van.** *The Gospel of Luke and Acts.* Message of Biblical Spirituality 10. Wilmington, DE: Glazier, 1986. **Loisy, A.** *L'évangile selon Luc.* Paris: E. Nourry, 1924. **Luce, H. K.** *The Gospel according to St. Luke.* CGTSC. Cambridge: University Press, 1949. **Manson, W.** *The Gospel of Luke.* London: Hodder & Stoughton, 1930. **Marshall, I. H.** *The Gospel of Luke: A Commentary on the Greek Text.* NIGTC. Exeter: Paternoster, 1978. **McBride, D.** *The Gospel of Luke: A Reflective Commentary.* Dublin/Northfort, NY: Dominican Publications/Castello, 1982. **Mentz, H.** *Das Lukas-Evangelium neu erzählt.* Göttingen: Vandenhoeck, 1987. **Meynet, R.** *L'évangile selon saint Luc: Analyse rhétorique. I. Planches; II. Commentaire.* Paris: Cerf, 1988. **Miller, D. G.** *The Gospel according to Luke.* Richmond: John Knox, 1959. **Morris, L.** *The Gospel according to St. Luke: An Introduction and Commentary.* TNTC. London: Inter-Varsity, 1974. ———. *The Gospel according to St. Luke: An Introduction and Commentary.* TNTC. 2nd ed. London: Inter-Varsity, 1988. **Müller, P.-G.** *Lukas-Evangelium.* Stuttgarter kleiner Kommentar, Neues Testament 3. Stuttgart: Katholisches Bibelwerk, 1984. **Obach, R. E.,** and **Kirk, A.** *A Commentary on the Gospel of Luke.* New York/Mahwah, NJ: Paulist, 1986. **Osty, E.** *La Sainte Bible traduite en français sous la direction de l'École Biblique de Jérusalem. L'évangile selon Saint Luc. Traduction, introduction et notes.* Paris: Cerf, 1961. **Plummer, A.** *A Critical and Exegetical Commentary on the Gospel according to S. Luke.* ICC. 5th ed. New York: Scribner, 1922. **Ragg, L.** *St. Luke.* WC. London: Methuen, 1922. **Rengstorf, K. H.** *Das Evangelium nach Lukas.* NTD 3. 9th ed. Göttingen: Vandenhoeck & Ruprecht, 1962. **Rice, E.** *Commentary on the Gospel according to Luke.* Philadelphia: Union, 1900. **Rienecker, F.** *Das Evangelium des Lukas.* Wuppertaler Studienbibel. 4th ed. Wuppertal: Brockhaus, 1972. **Sabourin, L.** *L'évangile de Luc: Introduction et commentaire.* Rome: Gregorian University, 1985. **Schlatter, A. von.** *Das Evangelium des Lukas aus seinen Quellen erklärt.* Stuttgart: Calwer, 1931. **Schmid, J.** *Das Evangelium nach Lukas.* RNT 3. 4th ed. Regensburg: Pustet, 1960. **Schmithals, W.** *Das Evangelium nach Lukas.* Zürcher Bibelkommentar NT 3.1. Zürich: Theologischer Verlag, 1980. **Schneider, G.** *Das Evangelium nach Lukas.* 2 vols. Gütersloh: Mohn, 1977. **Schürmann, H.** *Das Lukasevangelium: Erster Teil: Kommentar zu Kap. 1, 1–9, 50.* HTKNT 3/1. Freiburg/Basel/Vienna: Herder, 1969. **Schweizer, E.** *The Good News according to Luke.* Tr. D. E. Green. London: SPCK, 1984. **Stöger, A.** *The Gospel according to St. Luke.* The New Testament for Spiritual Reading 3. Tr. B. Fahy. London: Sheed, 1977. **Stoll, R.** *The Gospel according to St. Luke.* New York: Pustet, 1931. **Summers, R.** *Jesus the Universal Savior: Commentary on Luke.* Waco, TX: Word, 1972. **Talbert, C. H.** *Reading Luke: A Literary and Theological Commentary on the Third Gospel.* New York: Crossroad, 1982. **Thompson, G. H. P.** *The Gospel according to Luke in the Revised Standard Version.* The New Clarendon Bible. New York/Oxford: Oxford University Press, 1972. **Tiede, D. L.** *Luke.* Augsburg Commentary on the New Testament. Minneapolis, MN: Augsburg, 1988. **Tinsley, E. J.** *The Cambridge Bible Commentary in the New English Bible: The Gospel according to Luke.* New York/London: Cambridge University, 1965. **Title, E.** *The Gospel according to Luke.* New York: Harper and Bros., 1951. **Tresmontant, C.** *Évangile de Luc: Traduction et notes.* Paris: O.E.I.L., 1987. **Wellhausen, J.** *Das Evangelium Lucae, übersetzt und erklärt.* Berlin: Georg Reimer, 1904. **Wiefel, W.** *Das Evangelium nach Lukas.* THKNT 3. Berlin: Evangelische, 1988. **Zahn, T. von.** *Das Evangelium des Lukas ausgelegt.* 4th ed. Leipzig: Deichert, 1930.

General Bibliography

Aalen, S. "St. Luke's Gospel and the Last Chapters of I Enoch." *NTS* 1 (1966) 1–13. **Aarde, A. G. van.** "'The most high God does live in houses, but not houses built by men . . .': The relativity of the metaphor 'temple' in Luke-Acts." *Neot* 25 (1991) 51–64. **Abraham, M. V.** "Good News to the Poor in Luke's Gospel." *Biblebhashyam* 14 (1988) 65–77. **Achtemeier, P. J.** "Towards the Isolation of Pre-Markan Miracle Catenae." *JBL* 89 (1970) 265–91. ———. "The Lukan Perspective on the Miracles of Jesus: A Preliminary Sketch." *JBL* 94 (1975) 547–62. ———. "Carlston's Parables: A Review Article." *ANQ* 16 (1976) 227–31. **Ades, J. I.** "Literary Aspects of Luke." *PLL* 15 (1979) 193–99. **Allison, D. C.** "Was There a 'Lukan Community'?" *IBS* 10 (1988) 62–70. **Arai, S.** "Individual- und Gemeindeethik bei Lukas." *AJBI* 9 (1983) 88–127. **Argyle, A. W.** "'Hypocrites' and the Aramaic Theory." *ExpTim* 75 (1963–64) 113–14. ———. "Evidence for the View That St. Luke Used St. Matthew's Gospel." *JBL* 83 (1964) 390–96. ———. "The Greek of Luke and Acts." *NTS* 20 (1974) 441–45. **Asante, E.** "The Theological Jerusalem of Luke-Acts." *ATJ* 15 (1986) 172–82. **Asting, R.** *Die Verkündigung des Wortes im Urchristentum, dargestellt an den Begriffen "Worte Gottes," "Evangelium" und "Zeugnis."* Stuttgart: Kohlhammer, 1939. **Aune, D. E.** "The Significance of the Delay of the Parousia for Early Christianity." In *Current Issues in Biblical and Patristic Interpretation,* ed. G. F. Hawthorne. Grand Rapids: Eerdmans, 1975. 87–109. ———. "The Gospels, Biography or Theology?" *BRev* 6 (1990) 14–21, 37. **Aurelio, T.** *Disclosures in den Gleichnissen Jesu.* RST. Frankfurt am M./Berne/Las Vegas: Lang, 1977. **Baasland, E.** "Zum Beispiel der Beispielerzählungen: Zur Formenlehre der Gleichnisse und zum Methodik der Gleichnisauslegung." *NovT* 28 (1986) 193–219. **Bachmann, M.** *Jerusalem und der Tempel: Die geographisch-theologischen Elemente in der lukanischen Sicht des jüdischen Kulzentrums.* BWANT 6/9. Stuttgart: Kohlhammer, 1980. **Baer, H. von.** *Der heilige Geist in den Lukasschriften.* BWANT 3/3. Stuttgart: Kohlhammer, 1926. **Bailey, J. A.** *The Tradition Common to the Gospels of Luke and John.* NovTSup 7. Leiden: Brill, 1963. **Bailey, K. E.** *Poet and Peasant: A Literary-Cultural Approach to the Parables in Luke.* Grand Rapids: Eerdmans, 1976. ———. *Through Peasant Eyes: More Lukan Parables, Their Culture and Style.* Grand Rapids: Eerdmans, 1980. **Baird, J. A.** "A Pragmatic Approach to Parable Exegesis: Some New Evidence on Mark 4:11, 33–34." *JBL* 76 (1957) 201–7. **Baker, J.** "Luke, the Critical Evangelist." *ExpTim* 68 (1957) 123–25. **Balch, D. L.** "Comments on the Genre and a Political Theme of Luke-Acts: A Preliminary Comparison of Two Hellenistic Historians." In *SBL 1989 Seminar Papers,* ed. D. J. Lull. 343–61. ———. "The Genre of Luke-Acts: Individual Biography, Adventure Novel, or Political History?" *SWJT* 33 (1990) 5–19. **Baltzer, K.** "The Meaning of the Temple in the Lukan Writings." *HTR* 58 (1965) 263–77. **Bammel, E.** "The Baptist in Early Christian Tradition." *NTS* 18 (1971–72) 95–128. ——— and **Moule, C. F. D.**, eds. *Jesus and the Politics of His Day.* Cambridge: University Press, 1984. **Barr, D. L.** "Speaking in Parables: A Survey of Recent Research." *TSFB* 6 (1983) 8–10. ——— and **Wentling, J. L.** "The Conventions of Classical Biography and the Genre of Luke-Acts: A Preliminary Study." In *Luke-Acts: New Perspectives,* ed. C. H. Talbert. 63–88. **Barraclough, R.** "A Reassessment of Luke's Political Perspective." *RTR* 38 (1979) 10–18. **Barrett, C. K.** *The Holy Spirit and the Gospel Tradition.* London: SPCK, 1947. ———. *Luke the Historian in Recent Study.* FBBS 24. 2nd ed. Philadelphia: Fortress, 1970. ———. *The Gospel according to St. John: An Introduction with Commentary and Notes on the Greek Text.* 2nd ed. London: SPCK, 1978. **Bartsch, H.-W.** *Wachet aber zu jeder Zeit!* Hamburg/Bergstedt: Reich, 1963. ———. "Das Thomas-Evangelium und die synoptischen Evangelien." *NTS* 6 (1959–60) 249–61. ———. "Die stehenden Bilder in den Gleichnissen als Beispiel für eine existentiale Interpretation des Bildes." In *Kerygma und Mythos,* vol. 6. 2, ed. H. W. Bartsch.

TF 31. Hamburg/Bergstedt: Reich, 1964. 103–17. ———. "Early Christian Eschatology in the Synoptic Gospels (A Contribution to Form-Critical Research)." *NTS* 11 (1965) 387–97. **Bauer, J. B.** "Evangelium und Geschichtlichkeit: Vom heutigen Stand der Erforschung des Neuen Testaments." In *Evangelienforschung: Ausgewählte Aufsätze deutscher Exegeten*, ed. J. B. Bauer. Graz: Verlag Styria, 1968. 9–32. ———. "Gleichnisse Jesu und Gleichnisse der Rabbinen." *TPQ* 119 (1971) 297–307. **Bauernfeind, O.** *Die Worte der Dämonen im Markusevangelium.* BWANT 3/8. Stuttgart: Kohlhammer, 1927. **Baumbach, G.** *Das Verständnis des Bösen in den synoptischen Evangelien.* East Berlin: Evangelische Verlagsanstalt, 1963. ———. "Gott und die Welt in der Theologie des Lukas." *BLit* 45 (1972) 241–55. **Bayer, H. F.** *Jesus' Predictions of Vindication and Resurrection: The Provenance, Meaning, and Correlation of the Synoptic Predictions.* WUNT 2/20. Tübingen: Mohr (Siebeck), 1986. **Beardslee, W. A.** "Parable Interpretation and the World Disclosed by the Parable." *PRS* 3 (1976) 123–39. ———. "Parable, Proverb, and Koan." *Semeia* 12 (1978) 151–77. **Beare, F. W.** *The Gospel according to Matthew.* Oxford: Blackwell, 1981. **Beasley-Murray, G. R.** *Baptism in the New Testament.* Exeter: Paternoster, 1972=1962. **Beck, B. E.** "The Common Authorship of Luke and Acts." *NTS* 23 (1977) 346–52. **Becker, J.** *Johannes der Täufer und Jesus von Nazareth.* BS 63. Neukirchen-Vluyn: Neukirchener, 1972. **Behm, J. M.** *Die Handauflegung im Urchristentum: Nach Verwendung, Herkunft und Bedeutung in religionsgeschichtlichen Zusammenhang untersucht.* Darmstadt: Wissenschaftliche Buchgesellschaft, 1968. **Beilner, W.** *Christus und die Pharisäer: Exegetische Untersuchung über Grund und Verlauf der Auseinandersetzungen.* Vienna: Herder, 1959. **Benoit, P., et al.** *Aux sources de la tradition chrétienne.* FS M. Goguel. Bibliothèque théologique. Neuchâtel/Paris: Delachaux et Niestlé, 1950. ——— and **Boismard, M.-E.** *Synopse des Quatre Évangiles en français: Tome 2, Commentaire.* Paris: Cerf, 1972. **Berchmans, J.** "Some Aspects of Lukan Christology." *Biblebhashyam* 2 (1976) 5–22. **Berger, K.** *Die Auferstehung des Propheten und die Erhöhung des Menschensohnes: Traditionsgeschichtliche Untersuchungen zur Geschickes Jesu in frühchristlichen Texten.* SUNT 13. Göttingen: Vandenhoeck & Ruprecht, 1976. ———. "Zum traditionsgeschichtlichen Hintergrund christologischer Hoheitstitel." *NTS* 17 (1970–71) 391–425. ———. "Materialen zu Form- und Überlieferungsgeschichte neutestamentlicher Gleichnisse." *NovT* 15 (1973) 1–37. **Bergquist, J. A.** "'Good News to the Poor'—Why Does This Lukan Motif Appear to Run Dry in the Book of Acts?" *BangTF* 18 (1986) 1–16. **Bernadicou, P. J.** "The Lukan Theology of Joy." *ScEs* 25 (1973) 75–98. **Berry, D. L.** "Revisioning Christology: The Logic of Messianic Ascription." *ATR* 70 (1988) 129–40. **Betz, O.** "The Kerygma of Luke." *Int* 22 (1968) 131–46. **Beyer, K.** *Semitische Syntax im Neuen Testament.* Vol. 1. SUNT 1. 2nd ed. Göttingen: Vandenhoeck & Ruprecht, 1968. **Black, M.** *An Aramaic Approach to the Gospels and Acts.* Oxford: Clarendon, 1946. ———. "The Parables as Allegory." *BJRL* 42 (1960) 273–87. **Blackman, E. C.** "New Methods of Parable Interpretation." *CJT* 15 (1969) 3–13. **Blass, F.** *Philology of the Gospels.* London: Macmillan, 1898. **Blomberg, C. L.** "New Horizons in Parable Research." *TJ* 3 (1982) 3–17. ———. "The Law in Luke-Acts." *JSNT* 22 (1984) 53–80. ———. "When Is a Parallel Really a Parallel? A Test Case in the Lukan Parables." *WTJ* 46 (1984) 78–103. **Böcher, O.** *Dämonenfurcht und Dämonenabwehr: Ein Beitrag zur Vorgeschichte der christlichen Taufe.* BWANT 90. Stuttgart: Kohlhammer, 1970. ——— and **Haacker, K.**, eds. *Verborum Veritas.* FS G. Stählin. Wuppertal: Theologischer Verlag R. Brockhaus, 1970. **Bock, D. L.** *Proclamation from Prophecy and Pattern: Lucan Old Testament Christology.* JSNTSup 12. Sheffield: JSOT, 1987. ———. "The Use of the Old Testament in Luke-Acts." In *SBL 1990 Seminar Papers*, ed. D. J. Lull. Atlanta, GA: Scholars, 1990. 494–511. **Bonnard, P.-E.** "Le psaume 72: Ses relectures, ses traces dans l'oeuvre de Luc?" *RSR* 69 (1981) 259–78. **Borg, M. J.** *Conflict, Holiness, and Politics in the Teaching of Jesus.* Studies in the Bible and Early Christianity 5. New York/Toronto: Edwin Mellen, 1984. **Borgen, P.** "From Paul to Luke: Observations towards Clarification of the Theology of Luke-Acts." *CBQ* 31 (1969) 168–82. **Boring, M. E.** *Sayings of the Risen Jesus: Christian Prophecy in the Synoptic Tradition.* Cambridge: University Press, 1982. **Boucher, M.** *The Mysterious Parable: A Literary Study.* CBQMS 6. Washington: Catholic Biblical Association of America, 1977. **Bouttier, M.**

"L'humanité de Jésus selon Saint Luc." *RSR* 69 (1981) 33–44. **Bouwman, G.** *Das dritte Evangelium: Einübung in die formgeschichtliche Methode.* Tr. H. Zulauf. Düsseldorf: Patmos, 1968. **Bovon, F.** *Luc le théologien: Vingt-cinq ans de recherches (1950–1975).* Le Monde de la Bible. Neuchâtel/Paris: Delachaux et Niestlé, 1978. ———. "Le salut dans les écrits de Luc: Essai." *RTP* 23 (1973) 296–307. ———. "L'importance des médiations dans le projet théologique de Luc." *NTS* 21 (1974) 23–39. ———. "Orientations actuelles des études lucaniennes." *RTP* 26 (1976) 161–90. ———. "Effet de réel et flou prophétique dans l'oeuvre de Luc." In *À cause de l'Évangile,* ed. R. Refoulé. 349–60. ———. "La figure de Moïse dans l'oeuvre de Luc." In *Lafigure de Moïse: Ecriture et relectures.* Geneva: Publications de la Faculté de Théologie de l'Université de Genève, 1978. 47–65. ———. "Le Dieu de Luc." *RSR* 69 (1981) 279–300. ———. "Luc: portrait et projet." *LVit* 30 (1981) 9–18. ———. "Du côté de chez Luc." *RTP* 115 (1983) 175–89. ———. "Israel, die Kirche und die Völker im lukanischen Doppelwerk." *TLZ* 108 (1983) 403–14. **Boys, M. C.** "The Parabolic Ways of Teaching." *BTB* 13 (1983) 82–89. **Braumann, G.** "Das Mittel der Zeit: Erwägungen zur Theologie des Lukasevangeliums." *ZNW* 54 (1963) 117–45. ———, ed. *Das Lukas-Evangelium: Die redaktions- und kompositionsgeschichtliche Forschung.* WF 280. Darmstadt: Wissenschaftliche Buchgesellschaft, 1974. **Braun, H.** *Qumran und das Neue Testament.* Vol. 1. Tübingen: Mohr (Siebeck), 1966. **Brawley, R. L.** *Centering on God: Method and Message in Luke-Acts.* Literary Currents in Biblical Interpretation. Louisville, KY: Westminster/John Knox, 1990. ———. *Luke-Acts and the Jews: Conflict, Apology, and Conciliation.* SBLMS 33. Atlanta: Scholars, 1987. **Breech, E.** "Kingdom of God and the Parables of Jesus." *Semeia* 12 (1978) 15–41. **Breech, J.** *The Silence of Jesus: The Authentic Voice of the Historical Man.* Philadelphia: Fortress, 1983. **Brown, F. B.**, and **Malbon, E. S.** "Parables as a *Via Negativa*: A Critical Review of the Work of John Dominic Crossan." *JR* 64 (1984) 530–38. **Brown, R. E.** *The Gospel according to John.* AB 29, 29A. 2 vols. Garden City, NY: Doubleday, 1966–70. ———. "Parable and Allegory Reconsidered." *NovT* 5 (1962) 36–45. **Brown, S.** *Apostasy and Perseverance in the Theology of Luke.* AnBib 36. Rome: Pontifical Biblical Institute, 1969. ———. "Precis of Eckhard Plümacher, *Lukas als hellenistischer Schriftsteller.*" In *Society of Biblical Literature. Seminar Papers, 1974,* ed. G. MacRae. 2 vols. Cambridge, MA: Society of Biblical Literature, 1974. 103–13. ———. "'Water Baptism' and 'Spirit Baptism' in Luke-Acts." *ATR* 59 (1977) 135–51. **Brox, N.** *Zeuge und Märtyrer: Untersuchungen zur frühchristlichen Zeugnis-Terminologie.* SANT 5. Munich: Kösel-Verlag, 1961. **Bruce, F. F.** *The Acts of the Apostles.* Grand Rapids: Eerdmans, 1951. ———. *The Book of the Acts.* NICNT. Rev. ed. Grand Rapids: Eerdmans, 1988. **Bruners, W.** "Lukas-Literat und Theologe: Neue Literatur zum lukanischen Doppelwerk." *BK* 35 (1980) 110–12, 141–51. **Büchele, A.** *Der Tod Jesu im Lukasevangelium.* Theologische Studien 26. Frankfurt am Main: Joseph Knecht, 1978. **Bultmann, R.** *Theology of the New Testament.* Tr. K. Grobel. 2 vols. London: SCM, 1952–55. ———. *The History of the Synoptic Tradition.* Tr. J. Marsh. 2nd ed. Oxford: Blackwell, 1972. **Bundy, W. E.** *Jesus and the First Three Gospels: An Introduction for the Synoptic Tradition.* Cambridge, MA: Harvard University, 1955. **Burridge, R. A.** *What are the Gospels? A Comparison with Graeco-Roman Biography.* SNTSMS 70. Cambridge: University Press, 1992. **Busse, U.** *Die Wunder des Propheten Jesus: Die Rezeption, Komposition und Interpretation der Wundertradition im Evangelium des Lukas.* FB 24. Stuttgart: Katholisches Bibelwerk, 1977. ———. *Das Nazareth-Manifest: Eine Einführung in das lukanische Jesusbild nach Lk 4: 16–30.* SBS 91. Stuttgart: Katholisches Bibelwerk, 1978. **Bussman, C.**, and **Radl, W.**, eds. *Der Treue Gottes trauen: Beiträge zum Werk des Lukas.* FS G. Schneider. Freiburg/Basel/Vienna: Herder, 1991. **Buzy, D.** *Les Paraboles: Traduites et commentées.* VS 6. Paris: Beauchesne, 1932. **Cadbury, H. J.** *The Style and Literary Method of Luke.* HTS 6. 2 vols. Cambridge, MA: Harvard University, 1919–20. ———. "The Tradition." In *Beginnings,* ed. F. J. Foakes-Jackson and K. Lake. 2:209–64. ———. *The Making of Luke-Acts.* New York: Macmillan, 1927. ———. "Four Features of Lucan Style." In *Studies in Luke-Acts,* ed. L. E. Keck and J. L. Martyn. ———. "Lexical Notes on Luke-Acts: II. Recent Arguments for Medical Language." *JBL* 45 (1926) 190–209. ———.

"Lexical Notes on Luke-Acts: V. Luke and the Horse-Doctors." *JBL* 52 (1933) 55–65. ————. "Soluble Difficulties in the Parables." In *New Testament Sidelights.* FS A. C. Purdy, ed. H. K. McArthur. Hartford: Hartford Seminary Foundation, 1960. 118–23. ————. "Acts and Eschatology." In *The Background of the New Testament and Its Eschatology,* ed. D. Daube and W. D. Davies. Cambridge: University Press, 1964. 300–321. **Cadoux, A. T.** *The Parables of Jesus: Their Art and Use.* London: Clarke, 1930. **Caird, G. B.** "Eschatology and Politics: Some Misconceptions." In *Biblical Studies.* FS W. Barclay, ed. J. R. McKay. Philadelphia: Westminster, 1976. 72–86. ————. *The Language and Imagery of the Bible.* Duckworth Studies in Theology. London: Duckworth, 1980. **Cambe, M.** "La *ΧΑΡΙΣ* chez Saint Luc: Remarques sur quelques textes, notamment le *κεχαριτωμένη.*" *RB* 70 (1963) 193–207. ————. "Bulletin de Nouveau Testament: Études lucaniennes." *ETR* 56 (1981) 159–67. **Carlston, C.** *The Parables of the Triple Tradition.* Philadelphia: Fortress, 1975. ————. "Changing Fashions in Interpreting the Parables." *ANQ* 14 (1974) 227–33. ————. "Proverbs, Maxims, and the Historical Jesus." *JBL* 99 (1980) 87–105. ————. "Parable and Allegory Revisited: An Interpretive Review." *CBQ* 43 (1981) 228–42. **Carroll, J. T.** "Luke's Portrayal of the Pharisees." *CBQ* 50 (1988) 604–21. ————. *Response to the End of History: Eschatology and Situation in Luke-Acts.* SBLDS 92. Atlanta, GA: Scholars, 1988. **Cartlidge, D.,** and **Dungan, D.** *Documents for the Study of the Gospels.* Philadelphia: Fortress, 1980. **Casetti, P., et al.,** eds. *Mélange Dominique Barthélemy.* FS. D. Barthélemy. OBO 38. Fribourg/Göttingen: Editions universitaires/Vandenhoeck & Ruprecht, 1981. **Cassidy, R. J.** *Society and Politics in the Acts of the Apostles.* Maryknoll, NY: Orbis, 1987. ———— and **Scharper, P. J.,** eds. *Political Issues in Luke-Acts.* Maryknoll, NY: Orbis, 1983. **Cave, C. H.** "The Parables and the Scriptures." *NTS* 11 (1964–65) 374–87. **Chance, J. B.** *Jerusalem, the Temple and the New Age in Luke-Acts.* Macon, GA: Mercer University, 1988. **Charlesworth, J. H.** *Jesus within Judaism: New Light from Exciting Archaelogical Discoveries.* Anchor Bible Reference Library. New York: Doubleday, 1988. ————, ed. *The Old Testament Pseudepigrapha.* 2 vols. London: Darton, Longman & Todd, 1983–85. **Chevallier, M.-A.** *L'Esprit et le Messie dans le bas-judaïsme et le Nouveau Testament.* Études d'histoire et de philosophie religieuse 49. Paris: Presses Universitaires de France, 1958. ————. "Luc et l'Esprit saint." *RSR* 56 (1982) 1–16. ————. "Apparentements entre Luc et Jean en matière de pneumatologie." In *À cause de l'Évangile,* ed. R. Refoulé. 377–408. **Chilton, B. D.** *God in Strength: Jesus' Announcement of the Kingdom.* SNTU B, 1. Freistadt: Plöchl, 1979. **Christ, F.** *Jesus Sophia: Die Sophia-Christologie bei den Synoptikern.* ATANT 57. Zürich: Zwingli, 1970. **Clines, D. J. A., et al.,** eds. *The Bible in Three Dimensions: Essays in Celebration of Forty Years of Biblical Studies at Sheffield.* JSOTSup 87. Sheffield: Sheffield Academic, 1990. **Collison, J. G. F.** "Eschatology in the Gospel of Luke." In *New Synoptic Studies,* ed. W. R. Farmer. Macon, GA: Mercer University, 1983. 363–71. **Conzelmann, H.** *The Theology of St. Luke.* Tr. G. Buswell. New York: Harper & Brothers, 1960. ————. *An Outline of the Theology of the New Testament.* NTL. Tr. J. Bowden. London: SCM, 1969. ————. *Die Apostelgeschichte.* Tübingen: Mohr, 1972. **Cook, C.** "The Sense of Audience in Luke: A Literary Examination." *NB* 72 (1991) 19–30. **Cook, D. E.** "A Gospel Portrait of the Pharisees." *RevExp* 84 (1987) 221–33. **Cope, L., et al.** "Narrative Outline of the Composition of Luke according to the Two Gospel Hypothesis." In *SBL 1992 Seminar Papers,* ed. E. H. Lovering, Jr. 98–120. **Cosgrove, C. H.** "The Divine *Δεῖ* in Luke-Acts: Investigations into the Lukan Understanding of God's Providence." *NovT* 26 (1984) 168–90. **Cranfield, C. E. B.** *The Gospel according to Saint Mark.* CGTC. Cambridge: University Press, 1959. **Crehan, J. H.** "The Purpose of Luke in Acts." *SE* 2 [= TU 87] (1964) 354–68. **Cribbs, F. L.** "A Study of the Contacts that Exist between St. Luke and St. John." In *SBL Seminar Papers 1973,* ed. G. MacRae. Cambridge, MA: Society of Biblical Literature, 1973. 2:1–93. **Crossan, J. D.** *In Parables: The Challenge of the Historical Jesus.* New York: Harper & Row, 1973. ————. *Raid on the Articulate: Comic Eschatology in Borges and Jesus.* New York: Harper & Row, 1976. ————. *Finding Is the First Act: Trove Folktales and Jesus' Treasure Parables.* Philadelphia: Fortress, 1979. ————. *Cliffs of Fall: Paradox and Polyvalence in the Parables of Jesus.* New York: Seabury, 1980. ————. *In Fragments: The Aphorisms of Jesus.*

San Francisco: Harper and Row, 1983. ————. *The Historical Jesus: The Life of a Mediterranean Jewish Peasant.* San Francisco: HarperSanFrancisco, 1991. ————. "Parable as Religious and Poetic Experience." *JR* 53 (1973) 330–58. ————. "The Servant Parables of Jesus." *Semeia* 1 (1974) 17–62. ————. "Parable and Example in the Teaching of Jesus." *Semeia* 1 (1974) 63–104. ————. "Structuralist Analysis and the Parables of Jesus." *Semeia* 1 (1974) 192–221. ————. "Paradox Gives Rise to Metaphor: Paul Ricoeur's Hermeneutics and the Parables of Jesus." *BR* 24–25 (1979–80) 20–37. **Crump, D. M.** "Jesus the Intercessor: Prayer and Christology in Luke-Acts." Ph.D. diss., University of Aberdeen, 1988. **Cullmann, O.** *The Christology of the New Testament.* Tr. S. C. Guthrie and C. A. M. Hall. 2nd ed. London: SCM, 1963. **Culpepper, R. A.** "Paul's Mission to the Gentile World: Acts 13–19." *RevExp* 71 (1974) 487–97. **Dahl, N. A.** "The Purpose of Luke-Acts." In *Jesus in the Memory of the Early Church: Essays.* Minneapolis: Augsburg, 1976. 87–98. **Dalman, G.** *Orte und Wege Jesu.* BFCT 2/1. 3rd ed. Gütersloh: Bertelsmann, 1924. **D'Angelo, M. R.** "Images of Jesus and the Christian Call in the Gospels of Luke and John." *Spirituality Today* 37 (1985) 196–212. **Danker, F. W.** "Imaged through Beneficence." In *Reimaging,* ed. D. D. Sylva. 57–67, 184–86. ————. "Theological Presuppositions of St. Luke." *CurTM* 4 (1977) 98–103. **Darr, J. A.** "Discerning the Lukan Voice: The Narrator as Character in Luke-Acts." In *SBL 1992 Seminar Papers,* ed. E. H. Lovering, Jr. 255–65. **Daube, D.** *The New Testament and Rabbinic Judaism.* London: Athlone, 1956. ————. "Shame Culture in Luke." In *Paul and Paulinism.* FS C. K. Barrett, ed. M. Hooker and S. G. Wilson. London: SPCK, 1982. 355–72. **Dauer, A.** *Beobachtungen zur literarischen Arbeitstechnik des Lukas.* Athenäums Monografien, Theologie. BBB 79. Frankfurt. Hain, 1990. **Davies, W. D.** *The Setting of the Sermon on the Mount.* Cambridge: University Press, 1964. ———— and **Allison, D. C.** *A Critical and Exegetical Commentary on the Gospel according to Saint Matthew: Vol. 1. Introduction and Commentary on Matthew I-VII.* ICC. Edinburgh: Clark, 1988. **Dawsey, J. M.** *The Lukan Voice: Confusion and Irony in the Gospel of Luke.* Macon, GA: Mercer University, 1986. ————. "What's in a Name? Characterization in Luke." *BTB* 16 (1986) 143–47. ————. "The Temple-Theme in Luke." *MelT* 38 (1987) 26–32. ————. "The Unexpected Christ: The Lucan Image." *ExpTim* 98 (1987) 296–300. ————. "The Literary Unity of Luke-Acts: Questions of Style—a Task for Literary Critics." *NTS* 35 (1989) 48–66. **Degenhardt, H.-J.** *Lukas, Evangelist der Armen: Besitz und Besitzverzicht in den lukanischen Schriften. Eine traditions- und redaktionsgeschichtliche Untersuchung.* Stuttgart: Katholisches Bibelwerk, 1965. **Dehandschutter, B.** "The Gospel of Thomas and the Synoptics: The Status Quaestionis." *SE* 7 [= TU 126] (1982) 157–60. **Delebecque, É.** *Etudes grecques sur l'évangile de Luc.* Paris: Société d'édition "Les Belles Lettres," 1976. ————. "L'Hellénisme de la 'relative complexe' dans le Nouveau Testament et principalement chez Luc." *Bib* 62 (1981) 229–38. **Delobel, J.,** ed. *Logia: Les paroles de Jésus—The Sayings of Jesus.* FS J. Coppens. BETL 59. Leuven: Peeters/University Press, 1982. **Delorme, J.,** and **Duplacy, J.,** eds. *La parole de grâce: Études lucaniennes.* FS A. George. Paris: Recherches de Science Religieuse, 1981. **Demel, S.** "Jesu Umgang mit Frauen nach dem Lukasevangelium." *BibNot* 57 (1991) 41–95. **Derrett, J. D. M.** *Law in the New Testament.* London: Darton, Longman, and Todd, 1970. ————. *New Resolutions of Old Conundrums: A Fresh Insight into Luke's Gospel.* Shipton-on-Stour: Drinkwater, 1986. **Descamps, A.,** and **Halleux, A. de,** eds. *Mélange bibliques.* FS B. Rigaux. Gembloux: Duculot, 1970. **Diamond, G.** "Reflections upon Recent Developments in the Study of Parables in Luke." *ABR* 29 (1981) 1–9. **Dibelius, M.** *Die urchristliche Überlieferung von Johannes dem Täufer.* FRLANT 15. Göttingen: Vandenhoeck & Ruprecht, 1911. ————. *From Tradition to Gospel.* Tr. B. L. Woolf. London: Ivor Nicholson & Watson, 1934. ————. *Studies in the Acts of the Apostles,* ed. H. Greeven. Tr. M. Ling. London: SCM, 1956. **Dietrich, W.** *Das Petrusbild der lukanischen Schriften.* BWANT 94. Stuttgart: Kohlhammer, 1972. **Dihle, A.** "Die Evangelien und die biographische Tradition der Antike." *ZTK* 80 (1983) 33–49. **Dillon, R. J.** *From Eye-witnesses to Ministers of the Word.* Rome: Biblical Institute Press, 1978. **Dodd, C. H.** *The Parables of the Kingdom.* 3rd ed. New York: Scribner's, 1961. **Dömer, M.** *Das Heil Gottes: Studien zur Theologie des lukanischen Doppelwerkes.* BBB 51. Cologne/Bonn: Peter Hanstein,

1978. **Domeris, W. R.** "The Holy One of God as a Title of Jesus." *Neot* 19 (1985) 9–17. **Donahue, J. R.** *The Gospel in Parable: Metaphor, Narrative, and Theology in the Synoptic Gospels.* Minneapolis, MN: Fortress, 1990. **Downing, F. G.** "Law and Custom: Luke-Acts and Late Hellenism." In *Law and Religion,* ed. B. Lindars. 148–58, 187–91. ————. "Common Ground with Paganism in Luke and Josephus." *NTS* 28 (1982) 546–59. ————. "Freedom from the Law in Luke-Acts." *JSNT* 26 (1986) 49–52. ————. "A bas les aristos: The Relevance of Higher Literature for the Understanding of the Earliest Christian Writing." *NovT* 30 (1988) 212–30. **Drazin, I.** *Targum Onkelos to Deuteronomy: An English Translation of the Text with Analysis and Commentary*. New York: Ktav, 1982. **Drury, J.** *Tradition and Design in Luke's Gospel: A Study in Early Christian Historiography.* London: Darton, Longman & Todd, 1976. ————. *The Parables in the Gospels: History and Allegory.* New York: Crossroad, 1985. ————. "The Sower, the Vineyard, and the Place of Allegory in the Interpretation of Mark's Parables." *JTS,* n.s., 24 (1973) 367–79. **D'Sa, T.** "The Salvation of the Rich in the Gospel of Luke." *Vidyajyoti* 52 (1988) 170–80. **Dschulnigg, P.** "Positionen des Gleichnisverständnisses im 20. Jahrhundert: Kurze Darstellung von fünf wichtigen Positionen der Gleichnistheorie (Jülicher, Jeremias, Weder, Arens, Harnisch)." *TZ* 45 (1989) 335-51. **Dubois, J.-D.** "La figure d'Elie dans la perspective lucanienne." *RHPR* 53 (1973) 155–76. **Dumais, M.** "Ministères, charismes et esprit dans l'oeuvre de Luc." *EglT* 9 (1978) 413–53. ————. "L'évangélisation des pauvres dans l'oeuvre de Luc." *ScEs* 36 (1984) 297–321. **Dungan, D. L.** "Jesus and Violence." In *Jesus, the Gospels, and the Church.* FS W. R. Farmer, ed. E. P. Sanders. Macon, GA: Mercer, 1987. 135–62. **Dunn, J. D. G.** *Baptism in the Holy Spirit.* London: SCM, 1970. ————. *Jesus and the Spirit: A Study of the Religious and Charismatic Experience of Jesus and the First Christians as Reflected in the New Testament.* London: SCM, 1975. ————. "Pharisees, Sinners and Jesus." In *The Social World of Formative Christianity and Judaism,* ed. J. Neusner et al. 264–89. **Dupont, J.** *Les actes des Apôtres.* Paris: Cerf, 1953. ————. *Les béatitudes.* 3 vols. Louvain: Nauwelaerts, 1958, 1969, 1973. ————. *Le discours de Milet: Testament pastoral de saint Paul (Actes 20, 18–36).* LD 32. Paris: Cerf, 1962. ————. "Die individuelle Eschatologie im Lukasevangelium und in der Apostelgeschichte." In *Orientierung an Jesus.* FS J. Schmid, ed. P. Hoffmann et al. 37–47. ————. *Pourquoi les paraboles? La méthode parabolique de Jésus.* Lire la Bible. Paris: Cerf, 1977. ————. *Études sur les évangiles synoptiques.* BETL 70. 2 vols. Leuven: University Press/Peeters, 1985. ————. "Le salut des Gentiles et la signification théologique du Livre des Actes." *NTS* 6 (1959–60) 132–55. ————. "Le chapître des paraboles." *NRT* 89 (1967) 800–820. ————. "L'après mort dans l'oeuvre de Luc." *RTL* 3 (1972) 3–21. ————. "The Poor and Poverty in the Gospel and Acts." In *Gospel Poverty: Essays in Biblical Theology*. Chicago: Franciscan Herald, 1977. 25–52. ————. "La prière et son efficacité dans l'évangile de Luc." *RSR* 69 (1981) 45–56. **Easton, B. S.** "The Purpose of Acts." In *Early Christianity: "The Purpose of Acts" and Other Papers,* ed. F. C. Grant. London: Seabury, 1955. 33–118. **Ebertz, M. N.** *Das Charisma des Gekreuzigten: Zur Soziologie der Jesusbewegung.* WUNT 1/45. Tübingen: Mohr (Siebeck), 1987. **Edwards, D. R.** "Acts of the Apostles and the Graeco-Roman World: Narrative Communication in Social Contexts." In *SBL 1989 Seminar Papers,* ed. D. J. Lull. 362-77. **Edwards, O. C., Jr.** *Luke's Story of Jesus.* Philadelphia: Fortress, 1981. **Ehrhardt, A.** "The Construction and Purpose of the Acts of the Apostles." *ST* 12 (1958) 45–79. **Ehrhardt, E.** *The Framework of the New Testament Stories.* Manchester: University Press, 1964. **Eichholz, G.** *Einführung in die Gleichnisse.* Neukirchen-Vluyn: Neukirchener, 1963. ————. *Gleichnisse der Evangelien: Form, Überlieferung, Auslegung.* 3rd ed. Neukirchen-Vluyn: Neukirchener, 1979. **Elliott, J. H.** "Temple versus Household in Luke-Acts: A Contrast in Social Institutions." *HTS* 47 (1991) 88–120. ————. "Household and Meals vs. Temple Purity: Replication Patterns in Luke-Acts." *BTB* 21 (1991) 102–8. **Ellis E. E.** "The Making of Narratives in the Synoptic Gospels." In *Jesus and the Oral Gospel Tradition,* ed. H. Wansbrough. 301–24. ————. *Eschatology in Luke.* Philadelphia: Fortress, 1972. ————. "Present and Future Eschatology in Luke." *NTS* 12 (1965–66) 27–41. ————. "'Those of the Circumcision' and the Early Christian Mission." *SE* 4 [= TU 102] (1968) 390–99. **Eltester, W.** "Israel im lukanischen Werk und die Nazarethperikope."

In *Jesus in Nazareth,* ed. W. Eltester. 76–147. ———, ed. *Neutestamentliche Studien.* FS R. Bultmann. BZNW 21. Berlin: Töpelmann, 1954.———, ed. *Jesus in Nazareth.* Berlin: de Gruyter, 1972. **Enslin, M. S.** "Luke, the Literary Physician." In *Studies in New Testament and Early Christian Literature.* FS A. P. Wikgren, ed. D. E. Aune. NovTSup 33. Leiden: Brill, 1972. 135–43. **Ernst, J.** *Herr der Geschichte: Perspektiven der lukanischen Eschatologie.* SBS 88. Stuttgart: Katholisches Bibelwerk, 1978. ———. *Lukas: Ein theologisches Portrait.* Düsseldorf: Patmos, 1985. ———. "Das Evangelium nach Lukas—kein soziales Evangelium." *TGl* 67 (1977) 415–21. **Esler, P. F.** *Community and Gospel in Luke-Acts: The Social and Political Motivations of Lucan Theology.* SNTSMS 57. Cambridge/New York: Cambridge University Press, 1987. **Evans, C. A.** "Is Luke's View of the Jewish Rejection of Jesus Anti-Semitic?" In *Reimaging,* ed. D. D. Sylva. 29–56, 174–83. ———. "Luke's Use of the Elijah/Elisha Narratives and the Ethic of Election." *JBL* 106 (1987) 75–83. **Farmer, W. R.** *The Synoptic Problem: A Critical Analysis.* Macon, GA: Mercer University, 1976. ———. "Luke's Use of Matthew: A Christological Inquiry." *PSTJ* 40 (1987) 39–50. **Feldkämper, L.** *Der betende Jesus als Heilsmittler nach Lukas.* Veröffentlichung des Missionspriesterseminars 29. St. Augustin bei Bonn: Steyler, 1978. **Fiebig, P.** "Jesu Gleichnisse im Lichte der rabbinischen Gleichnisse." *ZNW* 13 (1912) 192–211. **Fiedler, P.** *Jesus und die Sünder.* BET 3. Frankfurt am M./Bern: Lang, 1976. **Fiedler, W.** *Antiker Wetterzauber.* Würzburger Studien zur Altertumswissenschaft 1. Stuttgart: Kohlhammer, 1931. **Finegan, J.** *The Archaeology of the New Testament: The Mediterranean World of the Early Christian Apostles.* Boulder, CO: Westview, 1981. **Fisher, N. F.** *The Parables of Jesus: Glimpses of God's Reign.* New York: Crossroad/Continuum, 1990. **Fitzmyer, J. A.** *Luke the Theologian: Aspects of His Teaching.* New York/Mahwah, NJ: Paulist, 1989. ———. "The Priority of Mark and the 'Q' Source in Luke." In *Jesus and Man's Hope,* ed. D. G. Miller. Perspective Books. 2 vols. Pittsburgh: Pittsburgh Theological Seminary, 1970. 1:131–70. ———. *Essays on the Semitic Background of he New Testament.* Missoula, MT: Scholars, 1974. ———. "Jesus in the Early Church through the Eyes of Luke-Acts." *ScrB* 17 (1987) 26–35. ———. "The Use of the Old Testament in Luke-Acts." In *SBL 1992 Seminar Papers,* ed. E. H. Lovering, Jr. 524–38. ——— **et al.** *À cause de l'Évangile: Études sur les Synoptiques et les Actes.* FS J. Dupont. LD 123. Paris: Cerf, 1985. **Flanagan, N. M.** "The What and How of Salvation in Luke-Acts." In *Sin, Salvation and the Spirit,* ed. D. Durkin. Collegeville: Liturgical, 1979. 203–13. ———. "The Position of Women in the Writings of St. Luke." *Marianum* 40 (1978) 288–304. **Flender, H.** *St. Luke: Theologian of Redemptive History.* Tr. R. H. and I. Fuller. London: SPCK, 1967. **Foakes-Jackson, F. J.,** and **Lake, K.,** eds. *The Beginnings of Christianity.* Part 1, *The Acts of the Apostles.* 5 vols. London: Macmillan, 1920–33. **Focant, C.** "La chute de Jérusalem et la datation des évangiles." *RTL* 19 (1988) 17-37. **Ford, J. M.** *My Enemy Is My Guest: Jesus and Violence in Luke.* Maryknoll, NY: Orbis, 1984. **France, R. T.** *Jesus and the Old Testament: His Application of Old Testament Passages to Himself and His Mission.* London: Tyndale, 1971. **Francis, F. O.** "Eschatology and History in Luke-Acts." *JAAR* 37 (1969) 49–63. **Frankemölle, H.** "Hat Jesus sich selbst verkündet? Christologische Implicationen in den vormarkinischen Parabeln." *BibLeb* 13 (1972) 184–207. ———. "Kommunikatives Handeln in Gleichnissen Jesu. Historichkritische und pragmatische Exegese. Eine kritische Sichtung." *NTS* 28 (1982) 61–90. **Franklin, E.** *Christ the Lord: A Study in the Purpose and Theology of Luke-Acts.* Philadelphia: Westminster, 1975. **Freire, C. E.** "Jesús profeta, libertador del hombre: Vision lucana de su ministerio terrestre." *EE* 51 (1976) 463–95. **Freyne, S.** *The Twelve: Disciples and Apostles. An Introduction to the Theology of the First Three Gospels.* London: Sheed and Ward, 1968. ———. *Galilee, Jesus and the Gospels: Literary Approaches and Historical Investigations.* Dublin: Gill and Macmillan, 1988. **Fridrichsen, A.** *Le problème du miracle dans le Christianisme primitif.* Strasbourg/Paris: Istra. 1925. ———. "Jesu Kampf gegen die unreinen Geister." In *Der Wunderbegriff im Neuen Testament,* ed. A. Suhl. WF 295. Darmstadt: Wissenschaftliche Buchgesellschaft, 1980. 248–65. **Friedrichsen, T. A.** "The Matthew-Luke Agreements against Mark: A Survey of Recent Studies: 1974–89." In *L'Évangile de Luc* (1989), ed. F. Neirynck. 335–91. **Frye, R. M.** "The Jesus of the Gospels: Approaches through Narrative Structure."

In *From Faith to Faith.* FS D. G. Miller, ed. D. Y. Hadidian. PTMS 31. Pittsburgh: Pickwick, 1979. 75–89. **Fuchs, A.** *Sprachliche Untersuchungen zum Matthäeus und Lukas: Ein Beitrag zur Quellenkritik.* AnBib 49. Rome: Pontifical Institute, 1971. **Fuchs, E.** "Bemerkungen zur Gleichnisauslegung." In *Zur Frage nach dem historischen Jesus: Gesammelte Aufsätze II.* 2nd ed. Tübingen: Mohr, 1960. 136–42. ———. "Die Analogie." In *Die neutestamentliche Gleichnisforschung,* ed. W. Harnisch. 1–19. **Fuller, R. H.** *Interpreting the Miracles.* Philadelphia: Westminster, 1963. **Funk, R. W.** "The Narrative Parables: The Birth of a Language Tradition." In *God's Christ and His People,* ed. J. Jervell and W. A. Meeks. Oslo: Universitetsforlaget, 1977. 42–50. ———. *Parables and Presence: Forms of the New Testament Tradition.* Philadelphia: Fortress, 1982. ———. "Critical Note." *Semeia* 1 (1974) 182–91. ———. "Structure in the Narrative Parables of Jesus." *Semeia* 2 (1974) 51–73. ———. "Parable, Paradox, Power: The Prodigal Samaritan." *JAAR* 48 (1981) 83–97. ———. "From Parable to Gospel: Domesticating the Tradition." *Forum* 1 (1985) 3–24. ———. "Unraveling the Jesus Tradition." *Forum* 5.2 (1989) 31–62. **Fusco, V.** "Tendences récentes dans l'interpretation des paraboles." In *Les paraboles évangéliques: Perspectives nouvelles. XIIe congrès de l'ACEF,* ed. J. Delorme. LD 135. Paris: Cerf, 1989. 19–60 **Gaechter, P.** *Maria im Erdleben: Neutestamentliche Mariestudien.* 3rd ed. Innsbruck: Tyrolia, 1955. **Gager, J. G.** *Kingdom and Community: The Social World of Early Christianity.* Engelwood Cliffs: Prentice-Hall, 1975. ———. *The Origins of Anti-Semitism: Attitudes towards Judaism in Pagan and Christian Antiquity.* New York/Oxford: Oxford University Press, 1985. **Garrett, S. R.** *The Demise of the Devil: Magic and the Demonic in Luke's Writings.* Minneapolis, MN: Fortress, 1989. **Gärtner, B. E.** "The Person of Jesus and the Kingdom of God." *TToday* 27 (1970) 32–43. **Gasque, W. W.** *A History of the Criticism of the Acts of the Apostles.* Grand Rapids: Eerdmans, 1975. **Gaston, L.** *No Stone on Another: Studies in the Significance of the Fall of Jerusalem in the Synoptic Gospels.* NovTSup 22. Leiden: Brill, 1970. **Gault, J. A.** "The Discourse Function of *Kai Egeneto* in Luke and Acts." *OPTAT* 4 (1990) 388-99. **Gaventa, B. R.** "The Eschatology of Luke-Acts Revisited." *Encounter* 43 (1982) 27–42. **Geiger, R.** "Gesprächspartner Jesu im Lukasevangelium." In *Biblische Randbemerkungen.* FS R. Schnackenburg, ed. H. Merklein and J. Lange. Würzburg: Echter, 1974. 150–56. **George, A.** "Miracles dans le monde hellenistique." In *Les miracles de Jésus,* ed. X. Léon-Dufour. 95–108. ———. "Le miracle dans l'oeuvre de Luc." In *Les miracles de Jésus,* ed. X. Léon-Dufour. 249–68. ———. *Études sur l'oeuvre de Luc.* SB. Paris: Gabalda, 1978. ———. "La royauté de Jésus selon l'évangile de Luc." *ScEccl* 14 (1962) 57–69. ———. "Jésus Fils de Dieu dans l'évangile selon Saint Luc." *RB* 72 (1965) 185–209. ———. "Tradition et rédaction chez Luc: La construction du troisième évangile." *ETL* 43 (1967) 100–129. ———. "Israël dans l'oeuvre de Luc." *RB* 75 (1968) 481–525. ———. "L'emploi chez Luc du vocabulaire de salut." *NTS* 23 (1977) 308–20. ———. "L'Esprit-Saint dans l'oeuvre de Luc." *RB* 85 (1978) 500–542. **Gerhardsson, B.** "The Narrative Meshalim in the Synoptic Gospels." *NTS* 34 (1988) 339–63. ———. "If We Do Not Cut the Parables out of Their Frames." *NTS* 37 (1991) 321–35. **Gewalt, D.** "Das 'Petrusbild' der lukanischen Schriften als Problem einer ganzheitlichen Exegese." *LingBib* 34 (1975) 1–22. **Gibbs, J. M.** "Mark 1.1–15, Matthew 1.1–4.16, Luke 1.1–4.30, John 1.1–51: The Gospel Prologues and Their Function." *SE* 6 [= TU 112] (1973) 154–88. **Giblin, C. H.** *The Destruction of Jerusalem according to Luke's Gospel: A Historical-Typological Moral.* AnBib 107. Rome: Biblical Institute, 1985. ———. "Discerning Gospel Genre." *Thought* 47 (1972) 225–52. **Giet, S.** "Un procédé littéraire d'exposition: l'anticipation chronologique." *REA* 2 (1956) 243–53. **Gilbert, A.** "Où fut écrit l'évangile de Luc?" *ScEs* 39 (1987) 211–28. **Giles, K.** "Salvation in Lukan Theology (1)." *RTR* 42 (1983) 10–16. ———. "The Church in the Gospel of Luke." *SJT* 34 (1981) 121–46. ———. "Is Luke an Exponent of 'Early Protestantism'?: Church Order in the Lukan Writings (Part I)." *EvQ* 54 (1982) 193–205. **Gillman, J.** *Possessions and the Life of Faith: A Reading of Luke-Acts.* Zacchaeus Studies: New Testament. Collegeville, MN: Liturgical, 1991. **Gils, F.** *Jésus prophète d'après les évangiles synoptiques.* Orientalia et Biblica Lovaniensia 2. Louvain: Université de Louvain, 1957. **Glen, J. S.** *The Parables of Conflict in Luke.* Philadelphia:

Westminster, 1962. **Glöckner, R.** *Die Verkündigung des Heils beim Evangelisten Lukas.* Walberger Studien der Albertus-Magnus-Akademie. Theologische Reihe 9. Mainz: Grünewald, n.d. (1976). **Glombitza, O.** "Die Titel διδάσκαλος und ἐπιστάτης für Jesus bei Lukas." *ZNW* 49 (1958) 275–78. **Glover, W. W.** "The Kingdom of God' in Luke." *BT* 29 (1978) 231–37. **Gnilka, J.** *Das Matthäusevangelium.* HTKNT. 2 vols. Freiburg/Basel/Vienna: Herder, 1986-88. ———. *Die Verstockung Israels: Isaias 6, 9–10 in der Theologie der Synoptiker.* SANT 3. Munich: Kösel, 1961. **Goudoever, J. van.** "The Place of Israel in Luke's Gospel." *NovT* 8 (1966) 111–23. **Goulder, M. D.** *Midrash and Lection in Matthew.* London: SPCK, 1974. 452–71. ———. *The Evangelists' Calendar.* London: SCM, 1978. ———. "Characteristics of the Parables in the Several Gospels." *JTS,* n.s., 19 (1968) 51–69. ———. "On Putting Q to the Test." *NTS* 24 (1978) 218–34. ———. "Did Luke Know Any of the Pauline Letters?" *PRS* 13 (1986) 97–112. **Gowler, D. B.** *Host, Guest, Enemy and Friend: Portraits of the Pharisees in Luke and Acts.* Emory Studies in Early Christianity 2. New York/Bern: Lang, 1991. ———. "Characterization in Luke: A Socio-Narratological Approach." *BTB* 19 (1989) 54–62. **Grässer, E.** *Das Problem der Parusieverzögerung in den synoptischen Evangelien.* BZNW 22. 2nd ed. Berlin: Töpelmann, 1960. **Grassi, J. A.** *God Makes Me Laugh: A New Approach to Luke.* Wilmington: Glazier, 1986. **Green, J. B.** "'The Message of Salvation' in Luke-Acts." *ExAud* 5 (1989) 21–34. **Grelot, P.** "Miracles de Jésus et la démonologie juive." In *Les miracles de Jésus,* ed. X. Léon-Dufour. 59–72. **Grundmann, W.** *Das Evangelium nach Markus.* THKNT 2. 2nd ed. East Berlin: Evangelische Verlaganstalt, 1959. ———. "Weisheit im Horizont des Reiches Gottes: Eine Studie zur Verkündigung Jesu nach der Spruchüberlieferung Q." In *Die Kirche des Anfangs.* FS H. Schürmann, ed. R. Schnackenburg, J. Ernst, and J. Wanke. Freiburg/Basel/Vienna: Herder, 1978. 175–200. **Guillet, J.** "Bulletin d'exégèse lucanienne." *RSR* 69 (1981) 425–42. **Gundry, R. H.** *Matthew: A Commentary on His Literary and Theological Art.* Grand Rapids: Eerdmans, 1982. **Güttgemanns, E.** "Narrative Analyse synoptischer Texte." In *Die neutestamentliche Gleichnisforschung,* ed. W. Harnisch. 179–223. **Haaker, K.** "Verwendung und Vermeidung des Apostelbegriffs im lukanischen Werk." *NovT* 30 (1988) 9–38. **Hadidan, D. Y.,** ed. *Signs and Parables.* PTMS 23. Pittsburgh: Pickwick, 1978. **Haenchen, E.** *Der Weg Jesu: Eine Erklärung des Markus-Evangeliums und der kanonischen Parallelen.* Berlin: Töpelmann, 1966. ———. *Die Bibel und wir: Gesammelte Aufsätze.* 2 vols. Tübingen: Mohr (Siebeck), 1968. ———. *The Acts of the Apostles: A Commentary.* Tr. B. Noble and G. Shinn. Oxford: Blackwell, 1971. ———. "Historie und Verkündigung bei Markus und Lukas." In *Das Lukas-Evangelium,* ed. G. Braumann. 287–316. ———. "Petrus-Probleme." *NTS* 7 (1960–61) 187–97. **Hahn, F.** *The Titles of Jesus in Christology: Their History in Early Christianity.* Tr. H. Knight and G. Ogg. London: Lutterworth, 1969. **Hamm, D.** "Sight to the Blind: Vision as Metaphor in Luke." *Bib* 67 (1986) 457–77. **Hammer, R. A.** "Elijah and Jesus: A Quest for Identity." *Judaism* 19 (1970) 207–18. **Hanford, W. R.** "Deutero-Isaiah and Luke-Acts: Straightforward Universalism?" *CQR* 168 (1967) 141–52. **Harnack, A. von.** *Luke the Physician: The Author of the Third Gospel and the Acts of the Apostles.* New Testament Studies 1. Tr. J. R. Wilkinson. New York: Putnam, 1907. ———. *The Acts of the Apostles.* New Testament Studies 3. Tr. J. R. Wilkinson. London/New York: Williams & Norgate/G. P. Putnam's Sons, 1909. ———. "'Ich bin gekommen': Die ausdrücklichen Selbstzeugnisse Jesu über den Zweck seiner Sendung und seines Kommens." *ZTK* 22 (1912) 1–30. **Harnisch, W.** *Die Gleichniserzählungen Jesu: Eine hermeneutische Einführung.* Unitaschenbücher 1343. Göttingen: Vandenhoeck & Ruprecht, 1985. ———. "Die Ironie als Stilsmittel in Gleichnisse Jesu." *EvT* 32 (1972) 421–36. ———. "Die sprachkraft der Analogie: Zur These vom 'argumentativen Character' der Gleichnisse Jesu." *ST* 28 (1974) 1–20. ———. "Die Metaphor als heuristisches Prinzip: Neuerscheinungen zur Hermeneutik der Gleichnisreden Jesu." *VF* 24 (1979) 53–89. ———, ed. *Die neutestamentliche Gleichnisforschung im Horizont von Hermeneutik und Literaturwissenschaft.* WF 575. Darmstadt: Wissenschaftliche Buchgesellschaft, 1982. ———, ed. *Gleichnisse Jesu: Positionen der Auslegung von Adolf Jülicher bis zur Formgeschichte.* WF 366. Darmstadt: Wissenschaftliche Buchgesellschaft, 1982. **Hartman, L.** *Testimonium Linguae:*

Participial Constructions in the Synoptic Gospels: A Linguistic Examination of Luke 21, 13. ConNT 19. Lund: Gleerup, 1963. **Harvey, A. E.** *Jesus and the Constraints of History.* Philadelphia: Westminster, 1982. **Hasler, V.** *Amen.* Zürich/Stuttgart: Gotthelf-Verlag, 1969. **Hastings, A.** *Prophet and Witness in Jerusalem.* Baltimore: Helicon, 1958. **Haubeck, W.,** and **Bachmann, M.,** eds. *Wort in der Zeit: Neutestamentliche Studien.* FS K. H. Rengstorf. Leiden: Brill, 1980. **Hauerwas, S.** "The Politics of Charity." *Int* 31 (1977) 251–62. **Hawkins, J. C.** *Horae Synopticae: Contributions to the Study of the Synoptic Problem.* 2nd ed. Oxford: Clarendon, 1909. **Heard, W.** "Luke's Attitude toward the Rich and the Poor." *TJ* 9 (1988) 47–80. **Heinemann, J.** "The Triennial Lectionary Cycle." *JJS* 19 (1968) 41–48. **Heininger, B.** *Metaphorik, Erzählstruktur und szenisch-dramatische Gestaltung in den Sondergutgleichnissen bei Lukas.* NTAbh n.f. 24. Münster: Aschendorff, 1991. **Hemer, C. J.** *The Book of Acts in the Setting of Hellenistic History,* ed. C. H. Gempf. WUNT 49. Tübingen: Mohr-Siebeck, 1989. **Hengel, M.** *The Charismatic Leader and His Followers.* Tr. J. C. G. Greig. New York: Crossroad, 1981. **Hennecke, E.** *New Testament Apocrypha.* Ed. W. Schneemelcher. Tr. R. McL. Wilson. 2 vols. London: Lutterworth, 1963–65. **Heutger, N.** "Münzen im Lukasevangelium." *BZ* 27 (1983) 97–101. **Hiers, R. H.** *The Kingdom of God in the Synoptic Tradition.* UFHM 33. Gainesville: University of Florida, 1970. ———. "The Problem of the Delay of the Parousia in Luke-Acts." *NTS* 20 (1974) 145–55. **Higgins, A. J. B.** *Jesus and the Son of Man.* London/Philadelphia: Lutterworth/Fortress, 1964. ———. "Non-Gnostic Sayings in the Gospel of Thomas." *NovT* 4 (1960) 292–306. **Hill, E.** "Messianic Fulfilment in St. Luke." *SE* 1 [= TU 73] (1959) 190–98. **Hinnebusch, P.** "Jesus, the New Elijah, in Saint Luke." *BiTod* 31 (1967) 2175–82; 32 (1967) 2237–44. **Hirsch, E.** *Die Auferstehungsgeschichten und der christliche Glaube.* Tübingen: Mohr (Siebeck), 1940. **Hobart, W. K.** *The Medical Language of St. Luke: A Proof from Internal Evidence that "The Gospel according to St. Luke" and "The Acts of the Apostles" Were Written by the Same Person, and that the Writer Was a Medical Man.* Grand Rapids: Baker, 1954 = 1882. **Hoehner, H. W.** *Herod Antipas.* SNTSMS 17. Cambridge: University Press, 1972. **Hoffmann, J. C.** "Story as Mythoparabolic Medium: Reflections on Crossan's Interpretation of the Parables of Jesus." *USQR* 37 (1983) 323–33. **Hoffmann, P.** *Studien zur Theologie der Logienquelle.* Münster: Aschendorff, 1972. ——— **et al.,** eds. *Orientierung an Jesus: Zur Theologie der Synoptiker.* FS J. Schmid. Freiburg/Basel/Vienna: Herder, 1973. **Hollenbach, P. H.** "From Parable to Gospel: A Response Using the Social Sciences." *Forum* 2.3 (1986) 67–75. **Holtz, T.** *Untersuchungen über die alttestamentlichen Zitate bei Lukas.* TU 104. Berlin: Akademie, 1968. **Holtzmann, H. J.** *Die Synoptiker.* HKNT. 3rd ed. Tübingen: Mohr, 1901. **Hooker, M. D.** *The Son of Man in Mark: A Study of the Background of the Term "Son of Man" and Its Use in St. Mark's Gospel.* Montreal: McGill University, 1967. **Horn, F. W.** *Glaube und Handeln in der Theologie des Lukas.* GTA 26. Göttingen: Vandenhoeck & Ruprecht, 1983. **Horsley, R. A.** *Sociology and the Jesus Movement.* New York: Crossroad, 1989. **Houlden, J. L.** "The Purpose of Luke." *JSNT* 21 (1984) 53–65. **House, P.** "Suffering and the Purpose of Acts." *JETS* 33 (1990) 317–30. **Hubbard, B. J.** "Commissioning Stories in Luke-Acts: A Study of Their Antecedents, Form, and Content." *Semeia* 8 (1977) 103–26. ———. "Luke, Josephus, and Rome: A Comparative Approach to the Lukan *Sitz im Leben.*" In *1978 SBL Seminar Papers,* ed. P. J. Achtemeier. Missoula: Scholars, 1978. 1:59–68. **Huffman, N. A.** "Atypical Features in the Parables of Jesus." *JBL* 97 (1978) 207–20. **Hull, J. M.** *Hellenistic Magic and the Synoptic Tradition.* SBT 2/28. London: SCM, 1974. **Hultgren, A. J.** "Interpreting the Gospel of Luke." *Int* 30 (1976) 353–65. **Hunkin, J. W.** "'Pleonastic' *ἄρχομαι* in the New Testament." *JTS,* o.s., 25 (1924) 390–402. **Hunter, A. M.** *The Parables for Today.* London: SCM, 1983. ———. "Interpreting the Parables." *Int* 14 (1960) 70–84; 167–85; 315–54. **Jackson, D.** "Luke and Paul: A Theology of One Spirit from Two Perspectives." *JETS* 32 (1989) 335–43. **Jellicoe, S.** "St. Luke and the Letter of Aristeas." *JBL* 80 (1961) 149–55. **Jeremias, J.** *Jesus' Promise to the Nations.* SBT 24. Tr. S. H. Hooke. London: SCM, 1958. ———. *Jerusalem in the Time of Jesus.* Philadelphia: Fortress, 1969. ———. *New Testament Theology.* Vol. 1. London: SCM, 1971. ———. *The Parables of Jesus.* Tr. S. H. Hooke et al. 3rd ed. London: SCM, 1972. ———. *Die Sprache des Lukasevangeliums: Redaktion* *und Tradition im Nicht-Markusstoff des dritten Evangeliums.* KEK, Sonderband. Göttingen: Vandenhoeck & Ruprecht, 1980. ———. "Pericopen-Umstellungen bei Lukas?" *NTS* 4 (1958) 115–19. **Jervell, J.** *Imago Dei.* FRLANT 58. Göttingen: Vandenhoeck & Ruprecht, 1960. ———. *Luke and the People of God.* Minneapolis: Augsburg, 1972. ———. *The Unknown Paul: Essays on Luke-Acts and Early Christian History.* Minneapolis: Augsburg, 1984. ———. "Die Mitte der Schrift: Zum lukanischen Verständnis des Alten Testaments." In *Die Mitte des Neuen Testaments,* ed. U. Luz and H. Weder. 79–96. ———. "God's Faithfulness to the Faithless People: Trends in Interpretation of Luke-Acts." *WW* 12 (1992) 29–36. ———. "Retrospect and Prospect in Luke-Acts Interpretation." In *SBL 1991 Seminar Papers,* ed. E. H. Lovering, Jr. 283–404. ———. "The Church of Jews and Godfearers." In *Luke-Acts and the Jewish People,* ed. J. B. Tyson. 11–20, 138–40. **Johnson, L. T.** *The Literary Function of Possessions in Luke-Acts.* SBLDS 39. Missoula, MT: Scholars, 1977. ———. *Luke-Acts: A Story of Prophet and People.* Chicago: Franciscan Herald, 1981. **Johnston, R. M.** "The Study of Rabbinic Parables: Some Preliminary Observations." In *Society of Biblical Literature. 1976 Seminar Paper.* Missoula, MT: Scholars, 1976. 337–57. **Jones, C. P. M.** "The Epistle to the Hebrews and the Lukan Writings." In *Studies in the Gospels.* FS R. H. Lightfoot, ed. D. E. Nineham. Oxford: Blackwell, 1955. 113–43. **Jones, D. L.** "Luke's Unique Interest in Historical Chronology." In *1989 SBL Seminar Papers,* ed. D. J. Lull. 378–87. **Jones, G. V.** *The Art and Truth of the Parables.* London: SPCK, 1964. **Jonge, M. de,** ed. *The Testaments of the Twelve Patriarchs: A Critical Edition of the Greek Text.* Leiden: Brill, 1978. ——— and **Woude, A. S. van der.** "11 Q Melchizedek and the New Testament." *NTS* 12 (1965–66) 301–26. **Jörns, K. P.** "Die Gleichnisverkündigung Jesu: Reden von Gott als Wort Gottes." In *Der Ruf Jesu und die Antwort der Gemeinde.* FS J. Jeremias, ed. E. Lohse. Göttingen: Vandenhoeck & Ruprecht, 1970. 157–77. **Judge, E. A.** "The Social Identity of the First Christians." *JRomH* 11 (1980) 201–17. **Juel, D.** *Luke-Acts: The Promise of History.* Atlanta: John Knox, 1983. **Jülicher, A.** *Die Gleichnisreden Jesu.* 2 vols. 2nd ed. Tübingen: Mohr, 1910. **Jüngel, E.** *Paulus und Jesus: Eine Untersuchung zur Präzisierung der Frage nach dem Ursprung der Christologie.* HUTh 2. 4th ed. Tübingen: Mohr, 1972. 71–215. **Kaestli, J.-D.** *L'Eschatologie dans l'oeuvre de Luc.* Geneva: Labor et Fides, 1969. **Kahlefeld, H.** *Gleichnisse als Lehrstücke im Evangelium.* 2 vols. 2nd ed. Frankfurt: Knecht, 1964–65. **Kähler, M.** *The So-Called Historical Jesus and the Historic Biblical Christ.* Tr. C. E. Braaten. Fortress: Philadelphia, 1964. **Kampling, R.** "Jesus von Nazaret—Lehrer und Exorzist." *BZ* 30 (1986) 237–48. **Karris, R. J.** *Invitation to Luke.* Garden City: Doubleday Image, 1977. ———. *What Are They Saying about Luke and Acts? A Theology of the Faithful God.* New York: Paulist, 1979. ———. *Luke: Artist and Theologian.* New York: Paulist, 1985. ———. "Poor and Rich: The Lukan *Sitz im Leben.*" In *Perspectives on Luke-Acts,* ed. C. H. Talbert. 112–25. ———. "Windows and Mirrors: Literary Criticism and Luke's *Sitz im Leben.*" In *1979 SBL Seminar Papers,* ed. P. J. Achtemeier. Missoula: Scholars, 1979. 1:47–58. ———. "The Lukan *Sitz im Leben:* Methodology and Prospects." In *Society of Biblical Literature. 1976 Seminar Papers.* Missoula, MT: Scholars, 1976. 219–33. ———. "Missionary Communities: A New Paradigm for the Study of Luke-Acts." *CBQ* 41 (1979) 80–97. **Käsemann, E.** *Essays on New Testament Themes.* SBT 41. London: SCM, 1964. **Keathley, N. H.** "The Temple in Luke and Acts: Implications for the Synoptic Problem and Proto-Luke." In *With Steadfast Purpose: Essays on Acts.* FS H. J. Flanders, Jr., ed. N. H. Keathley. Waco, TX: Baylor University, 1990. 77–105. **Keck, L. E.,** and **Martyn, J. L.,** eds. *Studies in Luke-Acts.* FS P. Schubert. Philadelphia: Fortress, 1980 = 1966. **Kee, H. C.** *Christian Origins in Sociological Perspective.* London: SCM, 1980. ———. *Miracle in the Early Christian World: A Study in Sociohistorical Method.* New Haven: Yale University, 1983. **Kellner, W.** *Der Traum vom Menschensohn: Die politisch-theologische Botschaft Jesu.* Munich: Kösel, 1985. **Kelly, J. F.** "The Patristic Biography of Luke." *BiTod* 74 (1974) 113–19. **Kelly, J. G.** "Lucan Christology and the Jewish-Christian Dialogue." *JES* 21 (1984) 688–708. **Kenny, A.** *A Stylometric Study of the New Testament.* Oxford/New York: University Press/Clarendon, 1986. **Kertelge, K.** *Die Wunder Jesu im Markusevangelium: Eine redaktionsgeschichtliche Untersuchung.* SANT 33. Munich: Kösel, 1970. ———. "Die Wunder Jesu in der neueren

Exegese." *TBl* 5 (1976) 71–105. **Kilgallen, J. J.** "The Function of Stephen's Speech (Acts 7,2–53)." *Bib* 70 (1989) 173–93. ———. "Social Development and the Lukan Writings." *StudMiss* 39 (1990) 21–47. **Kilpatrick, G. D.** "The Gentiles and the Strata of Luke." In *Verborum Veritas,* ed. O. Böcher. 83–88. **King, N. Q.** "The 'Universalism of the Third Gospel." *SE* 1 [= TU 73] (1959) 199–205. **Kingsbury, J. D.** *Jesus Christ in Matthew, Mark, and Luke.* Philadelphia: Fortress, 1981. ———. *Conflict in Luke: Jesus, Authorities, Disciples.* Minneapolis, MN: Fortress, 1990. ———. "Ernst Fuchs' Existentialist Interpretation of the Parables." *LQ* 22 (1970) 380–95. ———. "Major Trends in Parable Interpretation." *CTM* 42 (1971) 579–96. ———. "The Parables of Jesus in Current Research." *Dialog* 11 (1972) 101–7. **Kirchschläger, W.** *Jesu exorzistisches Wirken aus der Sicht des Lukas: Ein Beitrag zur lukanischen Redaktion.* OBS 3. Klosterneuburg: Österreichisches Katholisches Bibelwerk, 1981. **Kissinger, W. S.** *The Parables of Jesus: A History of Interpretation and Bibliography.* Metuchen, NJ: Scarecrow and ATLA, 1979. **Kistemaker, S. J.** *The Parables of Jesus.* Grand Rapids: Baker, 1980. **Klauck, H.-J.** *Allegorie und Allegorese in synoptischen Gleichnistexten.* Münster: Aschendorff, 1978. ———. "Neue Beiträge zur Gleichnisforschung." *BibLeb* 13 (1972) 214–30. ———. "Die Armut der Jünger in der Sicht des Lukas." *Claretianum* 26 (1986) 5–47. ———. "Die heilige Stadt: Jerusalem bei Philo und Lukas." *Kairos* 28 (1986) 129–51. **Klein A. F. J.** "Joden en heidenen in Lukas-Handelingen." *KeTh* 13 (1962) 16–24. **Klein, H.** "Zur Frage nach dem Abfassungsort der Lukasschriften." *EvT* 32 (1972) 467–77. **Klinghardt, M.** *Gesetz und Volk Gottes: Das lukanische Verständnis des Gesetzes nach Herkunft, Funktion und seinem Ort in der Geschichte des Urchristentums.* WUNT 2/32. Tübingen: Mohr, 1988. **Klostermann, E.** *Das Markusevangelium.* HNT 3. Tübingen: Mohr, 1926. **Knox, W. L.** *The Sources of the Synoptic Gospels.* Vol. 2, *St. Luke and St. Matthew.* Ed. H. Chadwick. Cambridge: University Press, 1957. **Koch, R.** "Die Wertung des Besitzes im Lukasevangelium." *Bib* 38 (1957) 151–69. **Kodell, J.** "Luke's Use of *laos,* 'People,' Especially in the Jerusalem Narrative (Lk 19,28–24,53)." *CBQ* 31 (1969) 327–43. ———. "The Theology of Luke in Recent Study." *BTB* 1 (1971) 115–44. **Koenig, J.** "Occasions of Grace in Paul, Luke, and First Century Judaism." *ATR* 64 (1982) 562–76. **Koester, H.** *Ancient Christian Gospels: Their History and Development.* Philadelphia, PA: Trinity, 1991. ———. "From the Kerygma-Gospel to Written Gospels." *NTS* 35 (1989) 361–81. **Koet, B. J.** *Five Studies of Scripture in Luke-Acts.* SNTA 14. Leuven: University Press, 1989. **Kopas, J.** "Jesus and Women: Luke's Gospel." *TToday* 43 (1986) 192–202. **Kraybill, D. B.** "Possessions in Luke-Acts: A Sociological Perspective." *PRS* 10 (1983) 215–39. **Kremer, J.**, ed. *Les Actes des Apôtres: Traditions, rédaction, théologie.* BETL 48. Gembloux: Duculot, 1979. **Kühschelm, R.** *Jüngerverfolgung und Geschick Jesu: Eine exegetisch-bibeltheologische Untersuchung der synoptischen Verfolgungsankündigungen Mk 13, 9–13 par und Mt 23, 29–36 par.* OBS 5. Klosterneuburg: Österreichisches Katholisches Bibelwerk, 1983. **Kümmel, W. G.** "Noch einmal: Das Gleichnis von der selbstwachsenden Saat: Bemerkungen zur neuesten Diskussion um die Auslegung der Gleichnisse Jesu." In *Orientierung an Jesus.* FS J. Schmid, ed. P. Hoffmann et al. 220–37. ———. *Promise and Fulfilment: The Eschatological Message of Jesus.* SBT 1/23. Tr. D. M. Barton. Naperville/London: Allenson/SCM, 1957. ———. *Introduction to the New Testament.* Tr. H. C. Kee. 2nd ed. London: SCM, 1975. ———. "Futurische und präsentische Eschatologie im ältesten Christentum." *NTS* 5 (1958–59) 113–26. ———. "Current Theological Accusations against Luke." *ANQ* 16 (1975) 131–45. **Kurz, W. S.** "Narrative Approaches to Luke-Acts." *Bib* 68 (1987) 195–220. ———. "Narrative Models for Imitation in Luke-Acts." In *Greeks, Romans and Christians.* FS A. J. Malherbe, ed. D. L. Balch et al. Minneapolis, MN: Fortress, 1990. 171–89. **Lacan, M.-F.** "Conversion et Royaume dans les Évangiles synoptiques." *LumVie* 9 (1960) 25–47. **Ladd, G. E.** "The Life-Setting of the Parables of the Kingdom." *JBR* 31 (1963) 193–99. **Lambrecht, J.** "Les parables dans les synoptiques." *NRT* 102 (1980) 672–91. **Lampe, G. W. H.** "The Holy Spirit in the Writings of St. Luke." In *Studies in the Gospels.* FS R. H. Lightfoot, ed. D. E. Nineham. Oxford: Blackwell, 1955. 159–200. ———. "The Lukan Portrait of Christ." *NTS* 2 (1956) 160–75. **Lane, W. L.** *The Gospel according to Mark.* NICNT. Grand Rapids: Eerdmans, 1974.

——— and **Robertson, M. J., III,** eds. *The Gospels Today: A Guide to Some Recent Developments.* Philadelphia: Skilton House, 1990. **Lategan, B. C.** "Tradition and Interpretation—Two Methodological Remarks." *Neot* 7 (1973) 95–103. **Laufen, R.** *Die Doppelüberlieferungen der Logienquelle und des Markusevangeliums.* BBB 54. Königstein/Bonn: Hanstein, 1980. **LaVerdiere, E.** "The Gospel of Luke." *BiTod* 18 (1980) 226–35. ——— and **Thompson, W. G.** "New Testament Communities in Transition: A Study of Matthew and Luke." *TS* 37 (1976) 567–97. **Légasse, S.** *Jésus et l'enfant: "Enfant," "petits" et "simple" dans la tradition synoptique.* Paris: Gabalda, 1969. **Legrand, L.** "Christ's Miracles as 'Social Work.'" *IES* 1 (1962) 43–64. ———. "The Parables of Jesus Viewed from the Dekkan Plateau." *ITS* 23 (1986) 154–70. **Lemcio, E. E.** *The Past of Jesus in the Gospels.* SNTSMS 68. Cambridge: University Press, 1991. **Léon-Dufour, X.** *Études d'évangile.* Parole de Dieu. Paris: Seuil, 1965. ———, ed. *Les miracles de Jésus selon le Nouveau Testament.* Paris: Seuil, 1977. **Levy, J.** *Neuhebräisches und chaldäisches Wörterbuch über die Talmudim und Midraschim.* 4 vols. Leipzig: Brockhaus, 1876–89. **Lightfoot, R. H.** *Locality and Doctrine in the Gospels.* London: Hodder & Stoughton, 1938. **Lindars, B.** "Elijah, Elisha, and the Gospel Miracles." In *Miracles: Cambridge Studies in Their Philosophy and History,* ed. C. F. D. Moule. London: Mowbray, 1965. 63–79. ———. *Jesus Son of Man: A Fresh Examination of the Son of Man Sayings in the Gospels in the Light of Recent Research.* London: SPCK, 1983. ———, ed. *Law and Religion: Essays on the Place of the Law in Israel and Early Christianity.* Cambridge: J. Clarke and Co., 1988. **Lindeboom, G. A.** "Luke the Evangelist and the Ancient Greek Writers on Medicine." *Janus: Revue internationale de l'histoire des sciences, de la médicine, de la pharmacie et de la technique* 52 (1965) 143–48. **Lindemann, A.** "Erwägungen zum Problem einer 'Theologie der synoptischen Evangelien.'" *ZNW* 77 (1986) 1–33. **Lindeskog, G.** "Johannes der Täufer: Einige Randbemerkungen zum heutigen Stand der Forschung." *ASTI* 12 (1983) 55–83. **Lindsey, R. L.** "A Modified Two-Document Theory of the Synoptic Dependence and Interdependence." *NovT* 6 (1963) 239–63. **Linnemann, E.** *Jesus of the Parables: Introduction and Exposition.* New York: Harper and Row, 1966. ———. *Parables of Jesus.* Tr. J. Sturdy. New York: Harper & Row, 1966. **Linton, O.** "Coordinated Sayings and Parables in the Synoptic Gospels: Analysis versus Theories." *NTS* 26 (1980) 139–63. **Little, J. C.** "Parable Research in the Twentieth Century." *ExpTim* 87 (1975–76) 356–60; 88 (1976–77) 40–44, 71–75. **Lohfink, G.** *Die Sammlung Israels: Eine Untersuchung zur lukanischen Ekklesiologie.* SANT 34. Munich: Kösel, 1975. **Lohmeyer, E.** *Das Evangelium des Markus.* KEK. Göttingen: Vandenhoeck & Ruprecht, 1953. **Lohse, E.** "Missionarisches Handeln Jesu nach dem Evangelium des Lukas." *TZ* 10 (1954) 1–13. ———. "Lukas als Theologe der Heilsgeschichte." *EvT* 14 (1954) 256–75. ——— **et al.,** eds. *Der Ruf Jesu und die Antwort der Gemeinde: Exegetische Untersuchungen.* FS J. Jeremias. Göttingen: Vandenhoeck & Ruprecht, 1970. **Loisy, A.** *Les évangiles synoptiques.* Vol. 1. Cliffonds: Chez l'auteur, 1907. **Loos, H. van der.** *The Miracles of Jesus.* NovTSup 9. Leiden: Brill, 1965. **Lovering, E. H., Jr.,** ed. *Society of Biblical Literature 1991 Seminar Papers.* Atlanta: Scholars, 1991. ———, ed. *Society of Biblical Literature 1992 Seminar Papers.* Atlanta: Scholars, 1992. **Lövestam, E.** *Son and Saviour: A Study of Acts 13,32–37. With an Appendix: 'Son of God' in the Synoptic Gospels.* ConNT 18. Tr. M. J. Petry. Lund: Gleerup, 1961. **Luck, U.** "Kerygma, Tradition, und Geschichte Jesu bei Lukas." *ZTK* 57 (1960) 51–66. **Lührmann, D.** *Die Redaktion der Logienquelle.* WMANT 33. Neukirchen: Neukirchener, 1969. ———. "The Gospel of Mark and the Sayings Collection Q." *JBL* 108 (1989) 51–71. **Lull, D. J.,** ed. *1989 SBL Seminar Papers.* Atlanta, GA: Scholars, 1989. **Luomanen, P.,** ed. *Luke-Acts Scandinavian Perspectives.* Publications of the Finnish Exegetical Society 54. Helsinki/Göttingen: Finnish Exegetical Society/Vandenhoeck & Ruprecht, 1991. **Luz, U.,** and **Weder, H.,** eds. *Die Mitte des Neuen Testaments: Einheit und Vielfalt neutestamentlicher Theologie.* FS E. Schweizer. Göttingen: Vandenhoeck & Ruprecht, 1983. **Mack, B. L.** *Rhetoric and the New Testament.* Minneapolis: Fortress, 1990. ——— and **Robbins, V. K.** *Patterns of Persuasion in the Gospels.* Sonoma, CA: Polebridge, 1989. **MacRae, G. W.** "The Gospel of Thomas—*Logia Iesou?*" *CBQ* 22 (1960) 56–71. **Maddox, R.** *The Purpose of Luke-Acts.* Edinburgh: Clark, 1982. **Magass, W.**

"Die magistralen Schlusssignale der Gleichnisse Jesu." *LingBib* 36 (1976) 1–20. **Mainville, O.** *L'esprit dans l'oeuvre de Luc.* Héritage et Projet 45. Montreal: Fides, 1991. ————. "Jésus et l'Esprit dans l'oeuvre de Luc: Éclairage à partir d'Ac 2, 33." *ScEs* 42 (1990) 193–208. **Malina, B. J.** *The New Testament World: Insights from Cultural Anthropology.* Atlanta: Knox, 1981. ————. "Interpreting the Bible with Anthropology: The Case of the Rich and the Poor." *Listening* 21 (1986) 148–59. ————. "Wealth and Poverty in the New Testament and Its World." *Int* 41 (1987) 354–67. **Maloney, F. J.** "Reading Eucharistic Texts in Luke." *ProcIBA* 14 (1991) 25–45. **Maly, E. H.** "Women and the Gospel of Luke." *BiTod* 10 (1980) 99–104. **Mánek, J.** "Das Aposteldekret im Kontext der Lukastheologie." *CV* 15 (1972) 151–60. **Mangatt, G.** "The Gospel of Salvation." *Biblebhashyam* 2 (1976) 60–80. **Manson, T. W.** *The Sayings of Jesus.* London: SCM, 1949. ————. *The Teaching of Jesus: Studies in Its Form and Context.* Cambridge: University Press, 1959 = 1935. **Manson, W.** *Jesus the Messiah: The Synoptic Tradition of the Revelation of God in Christ, with Special Reference to Form-Criticism.* London: Hodder & Stoughton, 1943. **Marin, L.** "Pour une théorie du texte parabolique." In *Le récit évangélique,* ed. C. Chabrol and C. Marin. BSR. Paris: Aubrier Montagne/Delachaux et Niestlé/Cerf/Brouwer, 1974. 165–92. **Marshall, I. H.** *Eschatology and the Parables.* London: Tyndale, 1963. ————. *Luke: Historian and Theologian.* Exeter: Paternoster, 1970. ————. *The Acts of the Apostles.* Leicester: Inter-Varsity Press, 1980. ————. *Luke: Historian and Theologian.* 3rd ed. Exeter Paternoster, 1988. ————. *Luke: Historian and Theologian.* Enl. ed. Grand Rapids: Zondervan, 1989. ————. "The Present State of Lukan Studies." *Themelios* 14 (1988–89) 52–57. ————, ed. *New Testament Interpretation: Essays on Principles and Methods.* Exeter: Paternoster, 1977. **Martin, R. A.** *Syntactical Evidence of Semitic Sources in Greek Documents.* SBLSCS 3. Missoula, MT: Scholars, 1974. ————. *Syntax Criticism of the Synoptic Gospels.* Studies in the Bible and Early Christianity 10. Lewiston, NY/Queenston, Ont.: Mellen, 1987. **Martin, R. P.** "Salvation and Discipleship in Luke's Gospel." *Int* 30 (1976) 366–80. **Marx, W. G.** "Luke, the Physician, Re-examined." *ExpTim* 91 (1980) 168–72. **Marxsen, W.** *Der "Frühkatholizismus" im Neuen Testament.* BibS(N) 21. Neukirchen: Neukirchener, 1958. **März, C.-P.** *Das Wort Gottes bei Lukas: Die lukanische Worttheologie als Frage an die neuere Lukasforschung.* ETS 11. Leipzig: St. Benno, 1974. **Masson, C.** *Vers les sources d'eau vive: Études d'exégèse et de théologie du Nouveau Testament.* Publication de la Faculté de théologie, Université de Lausanne 2. Lausanne: Libraire Payot, 1961. **Matera, F. J.** "Responsibility for the Death of Jesus according to the Acts of the Apostles." *JSNT* 39 (1990) 77–93. **Matthey, J.** "Puissance et pauvreté: Notes sur la mission de l'Eglise à partir de la théologie de Luc." *BulCPE* 30 (1978) 47–54. **Mattill, A. J., Jr.** "The Purpose of Acts: Schneckenburger Reconsidered." In *Apostolic History and the Gospel: Biblical and Historical Essays.* FS F. F. Bruce, ed. W. W. Gasque and R. P. Martin. Exeter/Grand Rapids: Paternoster/Eerdmans, 1970. 108–22. ————. *Luke and the Last Things: A Perspective for the Understanding of Lukan Thought.* Dillsboro, NC: Western North Carolina, 1979. ————. "*Naherwartung, Fernerwartung,* and the Purpose of Luke-Acts: Weymouth Reconsidered." *CBQ* 34 (1972) 276–93. ————. "The Jesus-Paul Parallels and the Purpose of Luke-Acts: H. H. Evans Reconsidered." *NovT* 17 (1975) 15–46. **McArthur, K. H.,** and **Johnston, R. M.** *They Also Taught in Parables: Rabbinic Parables from the First Centuries of the Christian Era.* Grand Rapids: Zondervan, 1990. **McBride, D.** *Emmaus: The Gracious Visit of God according to Luke.* Dublin: Dominican Publications, 1991. **McDowell, E. A.** "The Gospel of Luke." *SWJT* 10 (1967–68) 7–24. **McEachern, V. E.** "Dual Witness and Sabbath Motif in Luke." *CJT* 12 (1966) 267–80. **McLaren, J. S.** *Power and Politics in Palestine: The Jews and the Governing of Their Land 100 B.C.–A.D. 70.* JSNTSup 63. Sheffield: JSOT, 1991. **McLoughlin, S.** "Les accords mineurs Mt-Lc contre Mc et le problème synoptique: Vers la théorie des deux sources." *ETL* 43 (1967) 17–40. **McPolin, J.** "Holy Spirit in Luke and John." *ITQ* 45 (1978) 117–31. **Melbourne, B. L.** *Slow to Understand: The Disciples in Synoptic Perspective.* Lanham, MD/New York/London: UP of America, 1988. **Mellon, C.** "La parabole, manière de parler, manière d'entendre." In *Le récit évangélique,* ed. C. Chabrol and L. Marin. Paris: Aubrier-Montaigne/Delachaux et Niestlé/Cerf/Brouwer, 1974. 147–61. **Menoud, P.-H.** *Jésus-Christ* *et la foi: Recherches néotestamentaires.* Bibliothèque théologique. Neuchâtel/Paris: Delachaux et Niestlé, 1975. ———. *Jesus Christ and the Faith.* PTMS 18. Tr. E. M. Paul. Pittsburg: Pickwick, 1978. ———. "Jésus et ses témoins: Remarques sur l'unité de l'oeuvre de Luc." *EglT* 23 (1960) 7–20. **Menzies, R. P.** *The Development of Early Christian Pneumatology with Special Reference to Luke-Acts.* JSNTSup 54. Sheffield: Sheffield Academic, 1991. **Merk, O.** "Das Reich Gottes in den lukanischen Schriften." In *Jesus und Paulus.* FS W. G. Kümmel, ed. E. E. Ellis and E. Grässer. Göttingen: Vandenhoeck & Ruprecht, 1975. 201–20. **Metzger, B. M.** *A Textual Commentary on the Greek New Testament: A Companion Volume to the United Bible Societies' Greek New Testament. 3rd ed.* United Bible Societies, 1971. **Meyer, A.** *Jesu Muttersprache: Das galiläische Aramäisch in seiner Bedeutung für die Erklärung der Reden Jesu und der Evangelien überhaupt.* Freiburg i. B./Leipzig: Mohr (Siebeck), 1896. **Meyer, B. F.** *The Aims of Jesus.* London: SCM, 1979. ———. *Critical Realism and the New Testament.* Princeton Theological Monograph Series 17. Allison Park, PA: Pickwick Publications, 1989. ———. "How Jesus Charged Language with Meaning: A Study of Rhetoric." *SR* 19 (1990) 273–85. **Meyer, E.** *Ursprung und Anfänge des Christentums.* 3 vols. Darmstadt: Wissenschaftliche Buchgesellschaft, 1962 = 1921–23. **Meynet, R.** *Quelle est donc cette parole? Lecture "rhétorique" de l'évangile de Luc (1–9, 22–24).* LD 99. 2 vols. Paris: Cerf, 1979. ———. *Avey-vous lu saint Luc? Guide pour la rencontre.* Lire la Bible 88. Paris: Cerf, 1990. ———. "Crie de joie, stérile!" *Christus* 33 (1986) 481–89. **Michaelis, W.** *Die Gleichnisse Jesu: Eine Einführung.* 2nd ed. Hamburg: Furche, 1956. ———. "Das unbetonte *καὶ αὐτός* bei Lukas." *ST* 4 (1950) 86–93. **Michalczyk, J. J.** "The Experience of Prayer in Luke/Acts." *RevRel* 34 (1975) 789–801. **Michiels, R.** "La conception lucanienne de la conversion." *ETL* 41 (1965) 42–78. **Miller, M. H.** "The Character of Miracles in Luke-Acts." Th.D. diss., Graduate Theological Union, Berkeley, 1971. **Miller, R. J.** "Elijah, John and Jesus in the Gospel of Luke." *NTS* 34 (1988) 611-22. **Mills, M. E.** *Human Agents of Cosmic Power in Hellenistic Judaism and the Synoptic Tradition.* JSNTSup 41. Sheffield: JSOT, 1990. **Minear, P. S.** *To Heal and to Reveal: The Prophetic Vocation according to Luke.* Crossroad Books. New York: Seabury, 1976. ———. "Dear Theo." *Int* 27 (1973) 131–50. ———. "Jesus' Audiences, according to Luke." *NovT* 16 (1974) 81–109. **Miyoshi, M.** *Der Anfang des Reiseberichts Lk 9, 51–10, 24: Eine redaktionsgeschichtliche Untersuchung.* AnBib 60. Rome: Biblical Institute, 1974. **Moessner, D. P.** "'The Christ Must Suffer': New Light on the Jesus—Peter, Stephen, Paul Parallels in Luke-Acts." *NovT* 28 (1986) 220–56. ———. "The 'Leaven of the Pharisees' and 'This Generation': Israel's Rejection of Jesus according to Luke." *JSNT* 34 (1988) 21–46 . ———. "Paul in Acts: Preacher of Eschatological Repentance to Israel." *NTS* 34 (1988) 96–104. **Moffatt, J.** *An Introduction to the Literature of the New Testament.* International Theological Library. 3rd ed. Edinburgh: T. & T. Clark, 1918. **Monloubou, L.** *La prière selon Saint Luc: Recherche d'une structure.* LD 89. Paris: Cerf, 1976. **Moore, S. D.** "Luke's Economy of Knowledge." In *1989 SBL Seminar Papers,* ed. D. J. Lull. Atlanta, GA: Scholars, 1989, 38–56. ———. *Literary Criticism and the Gospels: The Theoretical Challenge.* New Haven, CT/London: Yale UP, 1989. ———. "The Gospel of the Look." *Semeia* 54 (1991) 159–96. **Morgenthaler, R.** *Die lukanische Geschichtsschreibung als Zeugnis: Gestalt und Gehalt der Kunst des Lukas.* ATANT 14–15. 2 vols. Zürich: Zwingli, 1949. ———. *Statistik des neutestamentlichen Wortschatzes.* Zürich/Frankfurt am Main: Gothelf, 1958. **Morris, L.** *The New Testament and the Jewish Lectionaries.* London: Tyndale, 1964. ———. *The Cross in the New Testament.* Grand Rapids: Eerdmans, 1965. ———. "Luke and Early Catholicism." *JTSA* 40 (1982) 4–16. **Morton, A. Q.,** and **MacGregor, H. C.** *The Structure of Luke and Acts.* New York/Evanston, IL: Harper & Row, 1965. **Moscato, M.** "Current Theories regarding the Audience of Luke-Acts." *CurTM* 3 (1976) 355–61. **Most, W.** "Did St. Luke Imitate the Septuagint?" *JSNT* 15 (1982) 30–41. **Moule, C. F. D.** "The Intention of the Evangelists." In *New Testament Essays.* FS T. W. Manson, ed. A. J. B. Higgins. Manchester University, 1959. 165–79. ———. *An Idiom Book of New Testament Greek.* 2nd ed. Cambridge: University Press, 1963. **Moulton, J. H.,** and **Milligan, G.** *The Vocabulary of the Greek Testament, Illustrated from the Papyri and Other Non-literary Sources.* London: Hodder & Stoughton, 1930. **Moxnes, H.** *The Economy of the*

Kingdom: Social Conflict and Economic Relations in Luke's Gospel. Philadelphia: Fortress, 1988. ———. "Meals and the New Community in Luke." *SEÅ* 51–52 (1986–87) 158–67. **Muhlack, G.** *Die Parallelen von Lukas-Evangelium und Apostelgeschichte.* Theologie und Wirklichkeit 8. Bern/Frankfurt/Las Vegas: Lang, 1979. **Mulder, H.** "Theophilus de 'godvrezende.'" In *Arcana revelata.* FS F. W. Grosheide, ed. N. J. Hommes et al. Kampen: Kok, 1951. 77–88. **Müller, P.-G.** "Conzelmann und die Folgen: Zwanzig Jahre redaktionsgeschichtliche Forschung am Lukas-Evangelium." *BK* 28 (1974) 138–42. **Mussner, F.** "Wege zum Selbstbewusstsein Jesu: Ein Versuch." *BZ* 12 (1968) 161–72. **Navone, J.** *Themes of St. Luke.* Rome: Gregorian University, 1971. ———. "Three Aspects of Lucan Theology of History." *BTB* 3 (1973) 115–32. **Neale, D. A.** *"None but the Sinners": Religious Categories in the Gospel of Luke.* JSNTSup 58. Sheffield: Sheffield Academic, 1991. **Nebe, G.** *Prophetische Züge im Bilde Jesu bei Lukas.* BWANT 127. Stuttgart/Berlin/Cologne: Kohlhammer, 1989. **Neirynck, F.** "La matière marcienne dans l'évangile de Luc." In *Problèmes.* FS L. Cerfaux, ed. F. Neirynck, 157–201. ———. "Recent Developments in the Study of Q." In *Logia.* FS J. Coppens, ed. J. Delobel. 29–75. ———. *Evangelica. Gospel Studies. Collected Essays.* Ed. F. van Segbroeck. BETL 60. Leuven: University Press, 1982. ———. "The Argument from Order and St. Luke's Transpositions." *ETL* 49 (1973) 784–815. ———, ed. *L'évangile de Luc: Problèmes littéraires et théologiques.* FS L. Cerfaux. BETL 32. Gembloux: Duculot, 1973. ———, ed. *L'évangile de Luc—The Gospel of Luke. Revised and Enlarged Edition of L'Évangile de Luc: Probleme littéraires et théologique.* BETL 32. 2nd ed. Leuven: University Press/Peeters, 1989. ———, ed. *The Minor Agreements of Matthew and Luke against Mark: With a Cumulative List.* In collaboration with T. Hanson and F. van Segbroeck. BETL 37. Leuven: University Press, 1974. **Nelson, P. K.** "Leadership and Discipleship: A Study of Luke 22:24–30." Ph.D. diss., Trinity College, Bristol, 1991. **Nestle, E.** *Philologica Sacra: Bemerkungen über die Urgestalt der Evangelien und Apostelgeschichte.* Berlin: von Reuther und Reichard, 1896. **Neusner, J., et al.,** eds. *The Social World of Formative Christianity and Judaism.* FS H. C. Kee. Philadelphia: Fortress, 1988. **Nevius, R. C.** "*Kyrios* and *Iēsous* in St. Luke." *ATR* 48 (1966) 75–77. **Neyrey, J. H.,** ed. *The Social World of Luke-Acts: Models for Interpretation.* Peabody, MA: Hendrickson, 1991. **Nickelsburg, G. W. E.** "Riches, the Rich, and God's Judgment in I Enoch 92–105 and the Gospel according to Luke." *NTS* 25 (1978–79) 324–44. **Nielsen, H. K.** *Heilung und Verkündigung: Das Verständnis der Heilung und ihres Verhältnisses zur Verkündigung bei Jesus und in der ältesten Kirche.* ATDan 22. Tr. D. Harbsmeier. Leiden/New York: Brill, 1987. **Nodet, E.** "Jésus et Jean-Baptiste selon Josèphe." *RB* 92 (1985) 497–524. **Nolland, J. L.** "Luke's Readers: A Study of Luke 4.22–8; Acts 13.46; 18.6; 28.28 and Luke 21.5–36." Ph.D. diss., Cambridge, 1977. ———. "Luke's Use of *χάρις*." *NTS* 32 (1986) 614–20. **Norden, E.** *Agnostos Theos: Untersuchungen zur Formgeschichte religiöser Rede.* Stuttgart: Teubner, 1956 = 1923. **Nuttall, G. F.** *The Moment of Recognition: Luke as Story-Teller.* London: Athlone, 1978. **Nützel, J. M.** *Jesus als Offenbarer Gottes nach den lukanischen Schriften.* FB 39. Würzburg: Echter, 1980. **O'Brien, P. T.** "Prayer in Luke-Acts." *TynB* 24 (1973) 111–27. **Oesterley, W. O. E.** *The Gospel Parables in the Light of Their Jewish Background.* New York: Macmillan, 1936. **Ó Fearghail, F.** "Israel in Luke-Acts." *ProcIBA* 11 (1988) 23–43. **Ommeren, N. M. van.** "Was Luke an Accurate Historian?" *BSac* 148 (1991) 57–71. **O'Neill, J. C.** *The Theology of Acts in Its Historical Setting.* 2nd ed. London: SPCK, 1970. ———. "The Six Amen Sayings in Luke." *JTS,* n.s., 10 (1959) 1–9. ———. "The Silence of Jesus." *NTS* 15 (1968-69) 153–67. **Orchard, J. B.** "Some Reflections on the Relationship of Luke to Matthew." In *Jesus, the Gospels, and the Church.* FS W. R. Farmer, ed. E. P. Sanders. Macon, GA: Mercer, 1987. 33–46. **O'Rourke, J. J.** "The Construction with a Verb of Saying as an Indication of Sources in Luke." *NTS* 21 (1975) 421–23. **Osborne, G. R.** "Luke: Theologian of Social Concern." *TJ* 7 (1978) 135–48. **O'Toole, R. F.** *The Unity of Luke's Theology: An Analysis of Luke-Acts.* Wilmington, DE: Glazier, 1984. ———. "Why Did Luke Write Acts (Lk-Acts)?" *BTB* 7 (1977) 66–76. ———. "Parallels between Jesus and His Disciples in Luke-Acts: A Further Study." *BZ* 27 (1983) 195–212. ———. "Luke's Message in Luke 9:1–50." *CBQ* 49 (1987) 74–98. ———. "The Parallels between Jesus and Moses." *BTB* 20 (1990) 22–29.

———. "Poverty and Wealth in Luke-Acts." *ChicStud* 30 (1991) 29–41. **Ott, W.** *Gebet und Heil: Die Bedeutung der Gebetsparänese in der lukanischen Theologie.* ANT 12. Munich: Kösel, 1965. **Parsons, M. C.** "'Allegorizing Allegory': Narrative Analysis and Parable Interpretation." *PRS* 15 (1988) 147–64. **Patte, D.**, ed. *Semiology and Parables: Exploration of the Possibilities Offered by Structuralism for Exegesis.* PTMS 9. Pittsburgh: Pickwick, 1976. **Payne, P. B.** "Metaphor as a Model for Interpretation of the Parables of Jesus with Special Reference to the Parable of the Sower." Ph.D. diss., Cambridge, 1975. **Percy, E.** *Die Botschaft Jesu: Eine traditionskritische und exegetische Untersuchung.* LUÅ 1, 49, 5. Lund: Gleerup, 1953. **Perkins, P.** *Hearing the Parables of Jesus.* New York: Paulist, 1981. **Pernot, H.** *Études sur la langue des évangiles.* Collection de l'Institut Néo-hellénique de l'Université de Paris 6. Paris: Societé d'Édition "Les belles lettres," 1927. **Perrin, N.** *Rediscovering the Teaching of Jesus.* NTL. London: SCM, 1967. ———. *Jesus and the Language of the Kingdom.* Philadelphia: Fortress, 1976. ———. "The Modern Interpretation of the Parables of Jesus and the Problem of Hermeneutics." *Int* 25 (1971) 131–48. ———. "Historical Criticism, Literary Criticism, and Hermeneutics: The Interpretation of the Parables of Jesus and the Gospel of Mark Today." *JR* 52 (1972) 361–75. **Pervo, R. I.** "Must Luke and Acts Belong to the Same Genre?" In *1989 SBL Seminar Papers,* ed. D. J. Lull. 309-16. **Pesch, R.** *Das Markusevangelium.* 2 vols. Freiburg: Herder, 1976–77. ———. *Die Apostelgeschichte.* 2 vols. Neukirchen-Vluyn: Neukirchener, 1986. **Petersen, N. R.** *Literary Criticism for New Testament Critics.* Philadelphia: Fortress, 1978. ———. "On the Notion of Genre in Via's 'Parable and Example Story: A Literary-Structuralist Approach.'" *Semeia* 1 (1974) 134–81. **Petzke, G.** *Das Sondergut des Evangeliums nach Lukas.* Zürcher Werkkommentare zur Bibel. Zurich: Theologischer, 1990. **Pilgrim, W. E.** *Good News to the Poor: Wealth and Poverty in Luke-Acts.* Minneapolis: Augsburg, 1981. ———. "Luke-Acts as a Theology of Creation." *WW* 12 (1992) 51–58. **Piper, R. A.** *Wisdom in the Q-Tradition.* SNTSMS 61. Cambridge: University Press, 1989. **Pittner, B.** *Studien zum lukanischen Sondergut: Sprachliche, theologische und form-kritische Untersuchungen zu Sonderguttexten in Lk 5–19.* ETS 18. Leipzig: St. Beno, 1991. **Plooy, G. P. V. du.** "The Use of the Optative in Luke-Acts: Grammatical Classification and Implications for Translation." *Scriptura* 19 (1986) 25–43. ———. "The Author in Luke-Acts." *Scriptura* 32 (1990) 28-35. **Plümacher, E.** *Lukas als hellenistischer Schriftsteller: Studien zur Apostelgeschichte.* SUNT 9. Göttingen: Vandenhoeck & Ruprecht, 1972. **Plymale, S. F.** "Luke's Theology of Prayer." In *1990 SBL Seminar Papers,* ed. D. J. Lull. Atlanta, GA: Scholars, 1990. 529-51. ———. *The Prayer Texts of Luke-Acts.* American University Studies. 7/118. New York/San Francisco/Bern: Lang, 1991. **Pokorný, P.** "Strategies of Social Formation in the Gospel of Luke." In *Gospel Origins and Christian Beginnings.* FS J. M. Robinson, ed. J. E. Goehring et al. Forum Fascicles. Sonoma, CA: Polebridge, 1990. 106–18. **Portefaix, L.** *Sisters Rejoice: Paul's Letter to the Philippians and Luke-Acts as Seen by First Century Philippian Women.* ConBNT 20. Stockholm: Amlqvist & Wiksell, 1988. **Potterie, I. de la.** "Le titre κύριος appliqué à Jésus dans l'évangile de Luc." In *Mélanges bibliques.* FS B. Rigaux, ed. A. Descamps and A. de Halleux. Gembloux: Duculot, 1970. 117–46. ———. "Les deux noms de Jérusalem dans l'évangile de Luc." *RSR* 69 (1981) 57–70. **Powell, M. A.** *What Are They Saying about Luke?* New York/Mahwah, NJ: Paulist, 1989. ———. "Are the Sands Still Shifting? An Update on Lukan Scholarship." *TrinSemRev* 11 (1989) 15–22. ———. "The Religious Leaders in Luke: A Literary-Critical Study." *JBL* 109 (1990) 93–110. ———. "Salvation in Luke-Acts." *WW* 12 (1992) 5–10. **Praeder, M.** "Jesus-Paul, Peter-Paul, and Jesus-Peter Parallelisms in Luke-Acts: A History of Reader Response." *SBLASP* 23 (1984) 23–39. **Prior, M.** "Revisiting Luke." *ScrB* 10 (1979) 2–11. **Radl, W.** *Das Lukas-Evangelium.* Erträge der Forschung 261. Darmstadt: Wissenschaftliche Buchgesellschaft, 1988. ———. *Paulus und Jesus im lukanischen Doppelwerk.* Bern/Frankfurt: Lang, 1975. **Ramsay, W. M.** *The Bearing of Recent Discovery on the Trustworthiness of the New Testament.* 2nd ed. London: Hodder & Stoughton, 1915. ———. *"Luke the Physician" and Other Studies in the History of Religion.* Grand Rapids: Baker, 1956 = 1908. **Ravens, D. A. S.** "St. Luke and Atonement." *ExpTim* 97 (1986) 291–94. ———. "Luke 9:7–62 and the Prophetic Role of Jesus." *NTS* 36 (1990)

119–29. **Reese, T.** "The Political Theology of Luke-Acts." *BTB* 22 (1972) 62–65. **Refoulé, F.,** ed. *À cause de l'Évangile: Études sur les Synoptiques et les Actes.* FS J. Dupont. LD 123. Paris: Cerf, 1985. **Rehkopf, F.** *Die lukanische Sonderquelle: Ihr Umfang und Sprachgebrauch.* WUNT 5. Tübingen: Mohr (Siebeck), 1959. **Reicke, B.** *The Gospel of Luke.* Richmond: John Knox, 1964. **Reid, B. E.** "The Centerpiece of Salvation History." *BiTod* 29 (1991) 20–24. **Reiling, J.** "The Use and Translation of *kai egeneto,* 'And It Happened,' in the New Testament." *BT* 16 (1965) 153–63. **Reitzel, F. X.** "St. Luke's Use of the Temple Imagery." *RevRel* 38 (1979) 520–39. **Rese, M.** *Alttestamentliche Motive in der Christologie des Lukas.* Gütersloh: Mohn, 1969. ———. "Das Lukas-Evangelium: Eine Forschungsbericht." *ANRW* II/25. 3 (1985) 2259–328. ———. "Neurere Lukas-Arbeiten: Bemerkungen zur gegenwärtigen Forschungslage." *TLZ* 106 (1981) 225–37. **Richard, E.** "Jesus' Passion and Death in Acts." In *Reimaging,* ed. D. D. Sylva. 153–69, 204–10. ———. "The Divine Purpose: The Jews and the Gentile Mission." *SBLASP* 17 (1978) 267–82. ———. "Luke—Writer, Theologian, Historian: Research and Orientation of the 1970's." *BTB* 13 (1983) 3–15. ———, ed. *New Views on Luke and Acts.* Collegeville, MN: Liturgical, 1990. **Richards, K. H.,** ed. *Society of Biblical Literature. 1982 Seminar Papers.* Chico, CA: Scholars, 1982. **Riches, J.** "Parables and the Search for a New Community." In *The Social World of Formative Christianity and Judaism,* ed. J. Neusner et al. 235–63. ———. *The World of Jesus: First-Century Judaism in Crisis.* Understanding Jesus Today. Cambridge: University Press, 1990. **Ricoeur, P.** "Biblical Hermeneutics." *Semeia* 4 (1975) 29–148. **Riddle, D. W.** "The Occasion of Luke-Acts." *JR* 10 (1930) 545–62. **Riesenfeld, H.** *The Gospel Tradition and Its Beginnings.* London: Mowbray, 1957. **Riesner, R.** *Jesus als Lehrer: Eine Untersuchung zum Ursprung der Evangelien-Überlieferung.* WUNT 2/7, 2nd ed. Tübingen: Mohr (Siebeck), 1984. **Rigaux, B.** *Témoignage de l'évangile de Luc.* Pour une histoire de Jésus 4. Bruges/Paris: Brouwer, 1970. **Ringgren, H.** "Luke's Use of the Old Testament." *HTR* 79 (1986) 227–35. **Robbins, V. K.** "Writing as a Rhetorical Act in Plutarch and the Gospels." In *Persuasive Artistry: Studies in New Testament Rhetoric.* FS G. A. Kennedy, ed. D. F. Watson. JSNTSup 50. Sheffield: JSOT, 1991. 142–68. **Robertson, A. T.** *A Grammar of the Greek New Testament in the Light of Historical Research.* 3rd ed. New York: Hodder & Stoughton, 1919. **Robinson, D. W. B.** "The Use of *Parabolē* in the Synoptic Gospels." *EvQ* 21 (1944) 93–108. **Robinson, J. A. T.** *Twelve New Testament Studies.* SBT 34. London: SCM, 1962. ———. *Redating the New Testament.* Philadelphia: Fortress, 1976. ———. "Elijah, John, and Jesus: An Essay in Detection." *NTS* 4 (1957–58) 263–81. **Robinson, J. M.** *The Problem of History in Mark.* SBT 1/21. London: SCM, 1957. ———. "Jesus' Parables as God Happening." In *Jesus and the Historian.* FS E. C. Colwell, ed. F. T. Trotter. Philadelphia: Fortress, 1968. 134–50. **Robinson, W. C., Jr.** *Der Weg des Herrn: Studien zur Geschichte und Eschatologie im Lukas-Evangelium.* TF 36. Hamburg/Bergstedt: Herbert Reich, 1964. **Rohde, J.** *Rediscovering the Teaching of the Evangelists.* NTL. Tr. D. M. Barton. London: SCM, 1968. **Rolland, P.** "L'arrière-fond sémiotique des évangiles synoptiques." *ETL* 60 (1984) 358–62. ———. "L'organisation du Livre des Actes et de l'ensemble de l'oeuvre de Luc." *Bib* 65 (1984) 81–86. **Roloff, J.** *Apostolat—Verkündigung—Kirche: Ursprung, Inhalt und Funktion des kirchlichen Apostelamptes nach Paulus, Lukas und den Pastoralbriefen.* Gütersloh: Mohn, 1985. ———. *Das Kerygma und der irdische Jesus: Historische Motive in den Jesus-Erzählungen der Evangelien.* Göttingen: Vandenhoeck & Ruprecht, 1970. **Rosenblatt, M.-E.** "Landless and Homeless." *BiTod* 29 (1991) 346–50. **Runnalls, D. R.** "The King as Temple Builder: A Messianic Typology." In *Spirit within Structure.* FS G. Johnston, ed. E. J. Furcha. Allison Park, PA: Pickwick, 1983. 15–38. **Russell, H. G.** "Which Was Written First, Luke or Acts?" *HTR* 48 (1955) 167–74. **Russell, W.** "The Anointing with the Holy Spirit in Luke-Acts." *TJ* 7 (1986) 47–63. **Sahlin, H.** *Der Messias und das Gottesvolk: Studien zur protolukanischen Theologie.* ASNU 12. Uppsala: Almqvist & Wiksells, 1945. ———. *Studien zum dritten Kapitel des Lukasevangeliums.* UUÅ 2. Uppsala/Leipzig: Lundeqvistska/Harrassowitz, 1949. **Saldarini, A. J.** "Interpretation of Luke-Acts and Implications for Jewish-Christian Dialogue." *WW* 12 (1992) 37–42. **Sanders, E. P.** "Jesus and the Kingdom: The Restoration of Israel and the New People of God." In *Jesus, the Gospels, and the Church.* FS

W. R. Farmer, ed. E. P. Sanders. Macon, GA: Mercer, 1987. 225-39. ———. *Jesus and Judaism.* Philadelphia: Fortress, 1985. ———. *Judaism: Practice and Belief 63 B.C.E.–66 C.E.* London/Philadelphia: SCM/Trinity, 1992. ——— and **Davies, M.** *Studying the Synoptic Gospels.* London/Philadelphia: SCM/Trinity Press International, 1989. **Sanders, J. A.** "Isaiah in Luke." *Int* 36 (1982) 144–55. **Sanders, J. T.** "The Prophetic Use of Scripture in Luke-Acts." In *Early Jewish and Christian Exegesis.* FS W. H. Brownlee, ed. C. A. Evans and W. F. Stinespring. Atlanta, GA: Scholars, 1987. 191–98. ———. "The Salvation of the Jews in Luke-Acts." In *Luke-Acts: New Perspectives,* ed. C. H. Talbert. 104–28. ———. *The Jews in Luke-Acts.* Philadelphia: Fortress, 1987. ———. "Who Is a Jew and Who Is a Gentile in the Book of Acts?" *NTS* 37 (1991) 434–55. **Sato, M.** *Q und Prophetie.* WUNT 2/29. Tübingen: Mohr-Siebeck, 1988. **Saxer, V.** "Le 'Juste Crucifié' de Platon à Théodoret." *RSLR* 19 (1983) 189–215. **Schaberg, J.** "Daniel 7, 12, and the New Testament Passion-Resurrection Predictions." *NTS* 31 (1985) 208–22. **Schelkle, K. H.** *Die Passion Jesu in der Verkündigung das Neuen Testaments: Ein Beitrag zur Formgeschichte und zur Theologie des Neuen Testaments.* Heidelberg: F. H. Kerle, 1949. ———. "Der Zweck der Gleichnisreden." In *Neues Testament und Kirche.* FS R. Schnackenburg, ed. J. Gnilka. Freiburg: Herder, 1974. 71–75. **Schenk, W.** *Evangelium-Evangelien-Evangeliologie: Ein "hermeneutisches" Manifest.* Theologische Existenz heute 216. Munich: Kaiser, 1983. **Schenke, L.** *Die Wundererzählungen des Markusevangeliums.* SBB. Stuttgart: Katholisches Bibelwerk, n.d. [1974]. **Schlatter, A. von.** *Die Evangelien nach Markus und Lukas.* Stuttgart: Calwer, 1947. ———. *Der Evangelist Matthäus.* 6th ed. Stuttgart: Calwer, 1963 = 1929. **Schlosser, J.** *La règne de Dieu dans les dits de Jésus.* Paris: Gabalda, 1981. **Schmauch, W.** "In der Wüste." In *In Memoriam Ernst Lohmeyer,* ed. W. Schmauch. Stuttgart: Evangelischen Verlagswerk, 1951. 202–23. ———. *Orte der Offenbarung und der Offenbarungsort im Neuen Testament.* Göttingen: Vandenhoeck & Ruprecht, 1956. **Schmid, J.** *Das Evangelium nach Markus.* RNT 2. Regensburg: Pustet, 1963. **Schmidt, D. D.** "Syntactical Style in the 'We' Sections of Acts: How Lukan Is It?" In *1989 SBL Seminar Papers,* ed. D. J. Lull. 300–308. **Schmidt, K. L.** *Die Rahmen der Geschichte Jesu: Literarkritische Untersuchungen zur ältesten Jesusüberlieferung.* Berlin: Trowitzsch & Sohn, 1919. **Schmidt, T. E.** *Hostility to Wealth in the Synoptic Gospels.* JSNTSup 15. Sheffield: JSOT, 1987. **Schmithals, W.** "Lukas—Evangelist der Armen." *ThViat* 12 (1975–76) 153–67. ———. "Die Berichte des Apostelgeschichte über die Bekehrung des Paulus und die 'Tendenz' des Lukas." *ThViat* 14 (1977–78) 145–65. **Schnackenburg, R.** "Die lukanische Eschatologie im Lichte von Aussagen der Apostelgeschichte." In *Glaube und Eschatologie,* ed. E. Grässer and O. Merk. Tübingen: Mohr, 1985. 249–65. ——— **et al.,** eds. *Die Kirche des Anfangs.* FS H. Schürmann. Leipzig: St. Benno, 1977. **Schneider, G.** *Parusiegleichnisse im Lukasevangelium.* Stuttgart: Katholisches Bibelwerk, 1975. ———. *Die Apostelgeschichte.* HTKNT. 2 vols. Freiburg: Herder, 1980–82. ———. *Lukas, Theologe der Heilsgeschichte: Aufsätze zum lukanischen Doppelwerk.* BBB 59. Bonn: Hanstein, 1985. ———. "Der Zweck des lukanischen Doppelwerks." *BZ* 21 (1977) 45–66. ———. "Schrift und Tradition in der theologischen Neuinterpretation der lukanischen Schriften." *BK* 34 (1979) 112–15. ———. "Jesu überraschende Antworten: Beobachtungen zu den Apophthegmen des dritten Evangeliums." *NTS* 29 (1983) 321–36. ———. "Neuere Literatur zum dritten Evangelium (1987–1989)." *TRev* 86 (1990) 353–60. **Schnider, F.** *Jesus der Prophet.* OBO 2. Fribourg/Göttingen: Universitätsverlag/Vandenhoeck & Ruprecht, 1973. **Schottroff, L.,** and **Stegemann, W.** *Jesus von Nazareth: Hoffnung der Armen.* Stuttgart: Kohlhammer, 1978. **Schrage, W.,** ed. *Studien zum Text und zur Ethik des Neuen Testaments.* FS H. Greeven. Berlin/New York: de Gruyter, 1986. **Schramm, T.** *Der Markus-Stoff bei Lukas: Eine literarkritische und redaktionsgeschichtliche Untersuchung.* SNTSMS 14. Cambridge: University Press, 1971. **Schreckenburg, H.** "Flavius Josephus und die lukanischen Schriften." In *Wort in der Zeit: Neutestamentliche Studien.* FS K. H. Rengstorf, ed. W. Haubeck and M. Backmann. Leiden: Brill, 1980. 179–209. **Schroeder, E. H.** "Luke's Gospel through a Systematician's Lens." *CurTM* 3 (1976) 337–46. **Schroeder, H.-H.** "Haben Jesu Worte über Armut und Reichtum Folgen für das soziale Verhalten?" In *Studien zum Text,* ed. W. Schrage. 397–409. **Schulz, S.**

Die Stunde der Botschaft: Einführung in die Theologie der vier Evangelisten. 2nd ed. Hamburg Zürich: Furche/Zwingli, 1970. ———. *Q: Die Spruchquelle der Evangelisten.* Zürich: Theologischer Verlag, 1972. ———. "Gottes Vorsehung bei Lukas." *ZNW* 54 (1963) 104–16. **Schürer, E.** *The History of the Jewish People in the Age of Jesus Christ (175 B.C.–A.D. 135),* rev. ed. G. Vermes et al. 4 vols. Edinburgh: Clark, 1973, 1979, 1986, 1987. **Schürmann, H.** *Quellenkritische Untersuchung des lukanischen Abendmahlsberichtes Lk 22,7–38.* NTAbh 19/5, 20/4–5. 3 vols. Münster in W.: Aschendorff, 1953–57. ———. *Traditionsgeschichtliche Untersuchungen zu den synoptischen Evangelien.* Düsseldorf: Patmos, 1968. ———. *Ursprung und Gestalt: Erörterungen und Besinnungen zum Neuen Testament.* Kommentare und Beiträge zum Alten und Neuen Testament. Düsseldorf: Patmos, 1970. ———. *Gottes Reich—Jesus Geschick: Jesus ureiniger Tod im Licht seiner Basileia-Verkündigung (Teildruck).* Die Botschaft Gottes 2/34. Leipzig: St. Benno-Verlag, 1985. ———. "Sprachliche Reminiszenzen an abgeänderte oder ausgelassene Bestandteile der Spruchsammlung im Lukas- und Matthäusevangelium." *NTS* 6 (1960) 193–210. ———. "Das Thomasevangelium und das lukanische Sondergut." *BZ* 7 (1963) 236–60. **Schütz, F.** *Der leidende Christus: Die angefochtene Gemeinde und das Christuskerygma der lukanischen Schriften.* BWANT 9. Stuttgart: Kohlhammer, 1969. **Schwarz, G.** *Jesus und Judas: Aramaische Untersuchungen zur Jesus-Judas-Überlieferung der Evangelien und der Apostelgeschichte.* BWANT 123. Stuttgart/Berlin/Cologne/Mainz: Kohlhammer, 1988. **Schweizer, E.** *Church Order in the New Testament.* SBT 32. London: SCM, 1961. ———. *Luke: A Challenge to Present Theology.* Atlanta: John Knox, 1982. ———. "Zur lukanischen Christologie." In *Verifikation.* FS G. Ebeling, ed. E. Jungel, J. Wallmann, and W. Werbeck. Tübingen: Mohr, 1982. 43–65. ———. "Zur Frage der Quellenbenutzung durch Lukas." In *Neues Testament und Christologie im Werden: Aufsätze.* Göttingen: Vandenhoeck & Ruprecht, 1982. 33–85. ———. "Plädoyer der Verteidigung in Sachen: Moderne Theologie versus Lukas." *TLZ* 105 (1980) 241–52. **Scott, B. B.** *Jesus, Symbol-Maker for the Kingdom.* Philadelphia: Fortress, 1981. ———. "Parables of Growth Revisited: Notes on the Current State of Parable Research." *BTB* 11 (1981) 3–9. ———. "Essaying the Rock: The Authenticity of the Jesus Parable Tradition." *Forum* 2.1 (1986) 3–53. **Scott, J. A.** *Luke: Greek Physician and Historian.* Evanston: Northwestern University, 1930. **Scroggs, R.** "The Sociological Interpretation of the New Testament: The Present State of Research." *NTS* 26 (1980) 164–79. **Seccombe, D. P.** *Possessions and the Poor in Luke-Acts.* SNTU B/6. Linz, 1982. ———. "Luke and Isaiah." *NTS* 27 (1981) 252–59. **Segbroeck, F. van.** *The Gospel of Luke: A Cumulative Bibliography 1973–88.* BETL 88. Leuven: Leuven UP/Peeters, 1989. **Seifrid, M. A.** "Messiah and Mission in Acts: A Brief Response to J. B. Tyson." *JSNT* 36 (1989) 47–50. **Sellin, G.** "Allegorie und 'Gleichnis': Zur Formenlehre der synoptischen Gleichnisse." *ZTK* 75 (1978) 281–335. **Sheeley, S. M.** *Narrative Asides in Luke-Acts.* JSNTSup 72. Sheffield: JSOT, 1992. ———. "Narrative Asides and Narrative Authority in Luke-Acts." *BTB* 18 (1988) 102–7. **Shelton, J. B.** *Mighty in Word and Deed: The Role of the Holy Spirit in Luke-Acts.* Peabody, MA: Hendrickson, 1991. **Sheridan, M.** "Disciples and Discipleship in Matthew and Luke." *BTB* 3 (1973) 235–55. **Shuler, P. L.** *A Genre for the Gospels.* Philadelphia: Fortress, 1982. **Sider, J. W.** "The Meaning of *Parabole* in the Usage of the Synoptic Evangelists." *Bib* 62 (1981) 453–70. ———. "Nurturing Our Nurse: Literary Scholars and Biblical Exegesis." *CLit* 32 (1982) 15–21. ———. "Rediscovering the Parables: The Logic of the Jeremias Tradition." *JBL* 102 (1983) 61–83. ———. "Proportional Analogy in the Gospel Parables." *NTS* 31 (1985) 1–23. **Siegert, F.** "Lukas—ein Historiker, d.h. ein Rhetor? Freundschaftliche Entgegnung auf Erhardt Güttgemanns." *LingBib* 55 (1984) 57–60. **Simson, P.** "The Drama of the City of God: Jerusalem in St. Luke's Gospel." *Scr* 15 (1963) 65–80. **Siotis, M. A.** "Luke the Evangelist as St. Paul's Collaborator." In *Neues Testament und Geschichte: Historisches Geschehen und Deutung im Neuen Testament.* FS O. Cullmann, ed. H. Baltensweiler and B. Reicke. Zürich/Tübingen: Theologischer Verlag/Mohr (Siebeck), 1972. 105–11. **Siverns, L. E.** "A Definition of Parable." *NESTR* 9 (1988) 60–75. **Sloan, R. B.** *The Favorable Year of the Lord: A Study of Jubilary Theology in the Gospel of Luke.* Fort Worth, TX: Schola, 1977. **Smalley, S. S.** "Spirit, Kingdom, and Prayer in Luke-Acts." *NovT* 15 (1973)

59–71. **Smith, B. T. B.** *The Parables of the Synoptic Gospels.* Cambridge: SPCK, 1937. **Smith, D. E.** "The Eschatology of Acts and Contemporary Exegesis." *CTM* 29 (1958) 881–901. ———. "Table Fellowship as a Literary Motif in the Gospel of Luke." *JBL* 106 (1987) 613–38. **Smith, R. H.** "History and Eschatology in Luke-Acts." *CTM* 29 (1958) 881–901. **Snape, H. C.** "The Composition of the Lukan Writings: A Re-assessment." *HTR* 53 (1960) 27–46. **Snodgrass, K. R.** "Streams of Tradition Emerging from Isaiah 40:1–5 and Their Adaption in the New Testament." *JSNT* 8 (1980) 24–45. **Sparks, H. F. D.** "The Semitisms of St. Luke's Gospel." *JTS,* o.s., 44 (1943) 129–38. ———. "St. Luke's Transpositions." *NTS* 3 (1957) 219–23. **Spicq, C.** *Agapè dans le Nouveau Testament: Analyse des textes.* Vol. 1. EBib. Paris: Gabalda, 1958. **Stalder, K.** "Der heilige Geist in der lukanischen Ekklesiologie." *US* 30 (1975) 287–93. **Standaert, B.** "L'art de composer dans l'oeuvre de Luc." In *À cause de l'Évangile,* ed. F. Refoulé. 323–48. **Stegemann, W.** *Zwischen Synagoge und Obrigkeit: Zur historischen Situation der lukanischen Christen.* FRLANT 152. Göttingen: Vandenhoeck & Ruprecht, 1991. **Stein, R. H.** *An Introduction to the Parables of Jesus.* Philadelphia: Westminster, 1981. ———. "The Matthew-Luke Agreements against Mark: Insight from John." *CBQ* 54 (1992) 482–502. **Stendahl, K.** *The School of St. Matthew, and Its Use of the Old Testament.* Philadelphia: Fortress, 1968. **Stenning, J. F.,** ed. *The Targum of Isaiah.* Oxford: Clarendon, 1949. **Sterling, G. E.** "Luke-Acts and Apologetic Historiography." In *1989 SBL Seminar Papers,* ed. D. J. Lull. 326–42. **Stewart, R. A.** "The Parable Form in the Old Testament and the Rabbinic Literature." *EvQ* 36 (1964) 133–47. **Steyn, G. J.** "Intertextual Similarities between Septuagint Pretexts and Luke's Gospel." *Neot* 24 (1990) 229–46. **Stöger, A.** "Armut und Ehelosigkeit: Besitz und Ehe der Jünger nach dem Lukasevangelium." *GuL* 40 (1967) 43–59. ———. "Die Theologie des Lukasevangeliums." *BLit* 46 (1973) 227–36. **Stonehouse, N. B.** *The Witness of Luke to Christ.* London: Tyndale, 1951. **Strauss, D. F.** *The Life of Jesus Critically Examined.* Ed. P. C. Hodgson. Tr. G. Elliot. SCM Press Lives of Jesus. London: SCM, 1973. **Strobel, A.** "Lukas der Antiochener (Bemerkungen zu Act 11, 28D)." *ZNW* 49 (1958) 131–34. **Stronstad, R.** *The Charismatic Theology of St. Luke.* Peabody, MA: Hendrickson, 1984. **Stuhlmacher, P.** *Das paulinische Evangelium.* Vol. 1, *Vorgeschichte.* FRLANT 95. Göttingen: Vandenhoeck & Ruprecht, 1968. ———. "Warum musste Jesus sterben?" *TB* 16 (1985) 273–85. ———, ed. *Das Evangelium und die Evangelien: Vorträger vom Tübinger Symposium 1982.* WUNT 28. Tübingen: Mohr (Siebeck), 1983. ———, ed. *The Gospel and the Gospels.* Grand Rapids: Eerdmans, 1991. **Suggs, M. J.** *Wisdom, Christology, and Law in Matthew's Gospel.* Cambridge, MA: Harvard University, 1970. **Sundwall, J.** *Die Zusammensetzung des Markusevangeliums.* Acta Academiae Aboensis. Humaniore 9/2. Abo: Tilgmanns, 1934. **Sutcliffe, E. F.** "A Note on the Date of St. Luke's Gospel." *Scr* 3 (1948) 45–46. **Swaeles, R.** "Jesus nouvel Élie dans S. Luc." *AsSeign* 69 (1964) 41–66. ———. "L'évangile du salut: Saint Luc." *ComLit* 1 (1977) 45–70. **Sylva, D. D.** "*Ierousalēm* and *Hierosoluma* in Luke-Acts." *ZNW* 74 (1983) 207–21. ———. "Death and Life at the Center of the World." In *Reimaging,* ed. D. D. Sylva. 153–169, 211–17. ———, ed. *Reimaging the Death of the Lukan Jesus.* Athenäums Monografien. BBS 73. Frankfurt am M.: Anton Hain, 1990. **Taeger, J.-W.** *Der Mensch und sein Heil: Studien zum Bild des Menschen und zur Sicht der Bekehrung bei Lukas.* SNT 14. Gütersloh: Mohn, 1982. ———. "Paulus und Lukas über den Menschen." *ZNW* 71 (1980) 96–108. **Talbert, C. H.** *Luke and the Gnostics: An Examination of the Lukan Purpose.* Nashville: Abingdon, 1966. ———. *The Certainty of the Gospel: The Perspective of Luke-Acts.* Deland, FL: Stetson University, 1981. ———. "The Redaction Critical Quest for Luke the Theologian." In *Jesus and Man's Hope: Proceedings of the Pittsburgh Festival on the Gospels,* ed. D. G. Miller. 2 vols. Pittsburgh: Pittsburgh Theological Seminary, 1970. 1:171–222. ———. *Literary Patterns, Theological Themes, and the Genre of Luke-Acts.* SBLMS 20. Missoula, MT: Scholars, 1974. ———. *What Is a Gospel? The Genre of the Canonical Gospels.* Philadelphia: Fortress, 1977. ———. "The Lukan Presentation of Jesus' Ministry in Galilee: Luke 4:31–9:50." *RevExp* 64 (1967) 485–97. ———. "An Anti-Gnostic Tendency in Lukan Christology." *NTS* 14 (1967–68) 259–71. ———. "Shifting Sands: The Recent Study of the Gospel of Luke." *Int* 30 (1976) 381–95. ———, ed. *Perspectives on Luke-Acts.* Perspectives in Religious Studies 5. Danville, VA/Edinburgh: Association of Baptist Professors of Religion/T. & T. Clark, 1978. ———, ed. *Luke-Acts: New Perspectives from the Society of Biblical Literature Seminar.* New York: Crossroad, 1984. **Tannehill, R. C.** "A Study in the Theology of Luke-Acts." *ATR* 43 (1961) 195–203. ———. *The Sword of His Mouth.* Philadelphia/ Missoula, MT: Fortress/Scholars, 1975. ———. *The Narrative Unity of Luke-Acts: A Literary Interpretation.* Vol. 1, *The Gospel according to Luke.* Foundations and Facets. Philadelphia: Fortress, 1986. ———. "Israel in Luke-Acts: A Tragic Story." *JBL* 104 (1985) 69–85. ———. "What Kind of King? What Kind of Kingdom? A Study of Luke." *WW* 12 (1992) 17–22. **Taylor, V.** *Behind the Third Gospel.* Oxford: Clarendon, 1926. ———. *The Gospel according to St. Mark.* 2nd ed. London/New York: Macmillan/St. Martin's 1966. ———. "Rehkopf's List of Words and Phrases Illustrative of Pre-Lukan Speech Usage." *JTS,* n.s., 15 (1964) 59–62. **Tenney, M. C.** "Historical Verities in the Gospel of Luke." *BSac* 135 (1978) 126–38. **TeSelle, S. M.** *Speaking in Parables.* Philadelphia: Fortress, 1975. ———. "Parable, Metaphor and Theology." *JAAR* 42 (1974) 630–45. **Theissen, G.** *The First Followers of Jesus: A Sociological Analysis of the Earliest Christianity.* Tr. J. Bowden. London: SCM, 1978. ———. *The Miracle Stories of the Early Christian Tradition.* Tr. F. McDonagh. Edinburgh: T. & T. Clark, 1983. ———. *Localkolorit und Zeitgeschichte in den Evangelien: Ein Beitrage zur Geschichte der synoptischen Tradition.* Novum Testamentum et Orbis Antiquus 8. Fribourg: Universitätsverlag, 1989. ———. *The Gospels in Context: Social and Political History in the Synoptic Tradition.* Tr. L. Maloney. Minneapolis, MN: Fortress, 1991. ———. "Jesusbewegung als charismatische Wertrevolution." *NTS* 35 (1989) 343–60. **Theobald, M.** "Die Anfänge der Kirche: Zur Struktur von Lk 5.1–6.19." *NTS* 30 (1984) 91–108. **Thériault, J.-Y.** "Les dimensions sociales, économiques et politiques dans l'oeuvre de Luc." *ScEs* 26 (1974) 205–31. **Thiselton, A. C.** "On Models and Metaphors: A Critical Dialogue with Robert Morgan." In *The Bible in Three Dimensions,* ed. D. J. A. Clines et al. 337–56. ———. "The Parables as Language-Event: Some Comments on Fuchs's Hermeneutics in the Light of Linguistic Philosophy." *SJT* 23 (1970) 437–68. **Thrall, M. E.** *Greek Particles in the New Testament: Linguistic and Exegetical Studies.* NTTS 3. Leiden: Brill, 1962. **Tiede, D. L.** "'Glory to Thy People, Israel': Luke-Acts and the Jews." In *The Social World of Formative Christianity and Judaism,* ed. J. Neusner et al. 327–41. ———. *Prophecy and History in Luke-Acts.* Philadelphia: Fortress, 1980. **Tinsley, E. J.** "Parable, Allegory, and Mysticism." In *Vindications: Essays in the Historical Basis of Christianity,* ed. A. Hanson. London: SCM, 1966. 153–92. ———. "Parable and Allegory: Some Literary Criteria for the Interpretation of the Parables of Christ." *CQ* 3 (1970) 32–39. ———. "Parables and the Self-Awareness of Jesus." *CQ* 4 (1971) 18–27. **Tödt, H. E.** *The Son of Man in the Synoptic Tradition.* NTL. Tr. D. M. Barton. London: SCM, 1965. **Tolbert, M.** "Leading Ideas of the Gospel of Luke." *RevExp* 64 (1967) 441–51. **Tolbert, M. A.** *Perspectives on the Parables: An Approach to Multiple Interpretations.* Philadelphia: Fortress, 1979. **Tooley, W.** "The Shepherd and Sheep Image in the Teaching of Jesus." *NovT* 7 (1964) 15–25. **Torrey, C. C.** "The Translations Made from the Original Aramaic Gospels." In *Studies in the History of Religions.* FS C. H. Toy, ed. D. G. Lyon and G. F. Moore. New York: Macmillan, 1912. 269–317. ———. *Our Translated Gospels: Some of the Evidence.* New York: Harper, 1936. **Trocmé, É.** *Le "Livre des Actes" et l'histoire.* Études d'histoire et de philosophie religieuses 45. Paris: Presses Universitaires de France, 1957. ———. "The Jews as Seen by Paul and Luke." In *"To See Ourselves as Others See Us": Christians, Jews, and "Others" in Late Antiquity,* ed. J. Neusner and E. S. Frerichs. Chico, CA: Scholars, 1985. 145–61. **Tuckett, C. M.** "The Argument from Order and the Synoptic Problem." *TZ* 36 (1980) 338–54. ———. "Q, the Law and Judaism." In *Law and Religion,* ed. B. Lindars. 90–101, 176–80. ———, ed. *Synoptic Studies: The Ampleforth Conferences of 1982 and 1983.* JSOTSup 7. Sheffield: JSOT, 1984. **Turner, M.** "Spirit Endowment in Luke/ Acts: Some Linguistic Considerations." *VoxEv* 12 (1981) 45–63. ———. "The Significance of Receiving the Spirit in Luke-Acts: A Survey of Modern Scholarship." *TJ* 2 (1981) 131–58. ———. "The Spirit and the Power of Jesus' Miracles in the Lucan Conception." *NovT* 33 (1991) 124–52. ———. "The Spirit of Prophecy and the Power of Authoritative

Preaching in Luke-Acts: A Question of Origins." *NTS* 38 (1992) 66–88. **Turner, N.** *Grammatical Insights into the New Testament.* Edinburgh: T. & T. Clark, 1965. ———. "The Minor Verbal Agreements of Mt. and Lk. against Mk." *SE* 1 [= TU 73] (1959) 223–34. **Tyson, J. B.** *The Death of Jesus in Luke-Acts.* Columbia: University of South Carolina, 1986. ———. *Luke-Acts and the Jewish People: Eight Critical Perspectives.* Minneapolis: Augsburg, 1988. ———. *Images of Judaism in Luke-Acts.* Columbia, SC: University of South Carolina, 1992. ———. "The Opposition to Jesus in the Gospel of Luke." *PRS* 5 (1978) 144–50. ———. "The Jewish Public in Luke-Acts." *NTS* 30 (1984) 574–83. ———. "The Gentile Mission and the Authority of Scripture in Acts." *NTS* 33 (1987) 619–31. ———. "Scripture, Torah, and Sabbath in Luke-Acts." In *Jesus, the Gospels, and the Church.* FS W. R. Farmer, ed. E. P. Sanders. Macon, GA: Mercer, 1987. 89–104. ———. "Source Criticism of the Gospel of Luke." In *Perspectives on Luke-Acts,* ed. C. H. Talbert. 24–39. ———. "Torah and Prophets in Luke-Acts: Temporary or Permanent?" In *SBL 1992 Seminar Papers,* ed. E. H. Lovering, Jr. 539–48. **Unnik, W. C. van.** "Luke's Second Book and the Rules of Hellenistic Historiography." In *Les Actes des Apôtres,* ed. J. Kremer. 37–60. ———. "The 'Book of Acts' the Confirmation of the Gospel." *NovT* 4 (1960–61) 26–59. ———. "Jesus the Christ." *NTS* 8 (1961–62) 101–16. **Untergassmair, F. G.** *Kreuzweg und Kreuzigung Jesu: Ein Beitrag zur lukanischen Redaktionsgeschichte und zur Frage nach der lukanischen "Kreuzestheologie."* Paderborner theologische Studien 10. Paderborn: Schöningh, 1980. **Vaage, L. E.** "Q1 and the Historical Jesus: Some Peculiar Sayings (7:33–34; 9:57–58, 59–60; 14:26–27)." *Forum* 5.2 (1989) 160–76. **Vermes, G.** *Scripture and Tradition in Judaism: Haggadic Studies.* SPB 4. Leiden: Brill, 1961. **Vesco, J.-L.** *Jérusalem et son prophète: Une lecture de l'Évangile selon saint Luc.* Paris: Cerf, 1988. **Via, D. O., Jr.** *The Parables: Their Literary and Existential Dimension.* Philadelphia: Fortress, 1967. ———. "Parable and Example Story: A Literary-Structuralist Approach." *Semeia* 1 (1974) 105–33. ———. "A Response to Crossan, Funk, and Petersen." *Semeia* 1 (1974) 222–35. **Via, E. J.** "Women in the Gospel of Luke." In *Women in the World's Religions: Past and Present,* ed. U. King. New York: Paragon, 1987. 38–55. ———. "Women, the Discipleship of Service and the Early Christian Ritual Meal in the Gospel of Luke." *SLJT* 29 (1985) 37–60. **Vielhauer, P.** "Zum 'Paulinismus' der Apostelgeschichte." *EvT* 10 (1950–51) 1–15. **Vincent, J. J.** "The Parables of Jesus as Self-Revelation." *SE* 1 [= TU 73] (1959) 79–99. **Vögtle, A.** "Exegetische Erwägungen über das Wissen und Selbstbewusstsein Jesu." In *Gott in Welt.* FS K. Rahner, ed. J. B. Metz et al. Freiburg/Basel/Vienna: Herder, 1964. 608–67. **Völkel, M.** "Der Anfang Jesu in Galiläa: Bemerkungen zum Gebrauch und zur Funktion Galiläas in den lukanischen Schriften." *ZNW* 64 (1973) 222–32. ———. "Zur Deutung des 'Reiches Gottes' bei Lukas." *ZNW* 65 (1974) 57–70. **Voss, G.** *Die Christologie der lukanischen Schriften in Grundzügen.* StudNeot 2. Paris/Bruges: Brouwer, 1965. **Votaw, C. W.** "The Gospels and Contemporary Biography." *AJT* 19 (1915) 45–73, 217–49. **Vriezen, T. C.** "Leert Lukas de verwerping van Israël?" *KeTh* 13 (1962) 25–31. **Waal, C. van der.** "The Temple in the Gospel according to Luke." *Neot* 7 (1973) 49–59. **Wagner, G.,** ed. *An Exegetical Bibliography of the New Testament:* Vol. 2, *Luke and Acts.* Macon, GA: Mercer University, 1985. **Wainwright, A. W.** "Luke and the Restoration of the Kingdom to Israel." *ExpTim* 89 (1977) 76–79. **Walaskay, P. W.** *"And so we came to Rome": The Political Perspective of St. Luke.* SNTSMS 49. Cambridge: University Press, 1983. ———. "The Trial and Death of Jesus in the Gospel of Luke." *JBL* 94 (1975) 81–93. **Walker, W. O.** "'Nazareth': A Clue to Synoptic Relations." In *Jesus, the Gospels, and the Church.* FS W. R. Farmer, ed. E. P. Sanders. Macon, GA: Mercer, 1987. 105–18. **Wallis, E. E.** "Aristotelian Echoes in Luke's Discourse Structure." *OPTAT* 2 (1988) 81–88. **Wanke, J.** *Beobachtungen zum Eucharistieverständnis des Lukas auf Grund der lukanischen Mahlberichte.* ETS 8. Leipzig: St. Benno, 1973. **Wansbrough, H.,** ed. *Jesus and the Oral Gospel Tradition.* Sheffield: Sheffield Academic Press, 1991. ———. "Poverty in the Gospel Tradition." *ProcIBA* 6 (1982) 47–57. **Watson, F.** "Why Was Jesus Crucified?" *Theology* 88 (1985) 105–12. **Weatherly, J. A.** "The Jews in Luke-Acts." *TynB* 40 (1989) 107–17. **Weder, H.** *Die Gleichnisse Jesu als Metaphern.* Göttingen: Vandenhoeck & Ruprecht, 1978. **Wehnert, J.** *Die Wir-Passagen der*

Apostelgeschichte: Ein lukanisches Stilsmittel aus jüdischer Tradition. GTA 40. Göttingen: Vandenhoeck & Ruprecht, 1989. **Weinert, F. D.** "The Meaning of the Temple in Luke-Acts." *BTB* 11 (1981) 85–89. ———. "Luke, Stephen, and the Temple in Luke-Acts." *BTB* 17 (1987) 88–90. **Weiser, A.** *Die Knechtsgleichnisse der synoptischen Evangelien.* SANT 29. Munich: Kössel, 1971. **Wenham, J.** *Redating Matthew, Mark and Luke: A Fresh Assault on the Synoptic Problem.* London: Hodder and Stoughton, 1991. ———. "The Identification of Luke." *EvQ* 63 (1991) 3–44. **Wernle, P.** *Die synoptische Frage.* Freiburg i. B./Leipzig: Mohr, 1899. **Wescott, B. F.**, and **Hort, F. J. A.** *The New Testament in the Original Greek.* 2 vols. Cambridge/London: Macmillan, 1890, 1896. **Westermann, C.** *The Parables of Jesus in the Light of the Old Testament,* ed. F. W. Golka and A. H. B. Logan. Tr. F. W. Golka and A. H. B. Logan. Minneapolis, MN: Fortress, 1990. **Wettstein, J. J.** *Novum Testamentum Graecum . . . Opera et Studia.* 2 vols. Amsterdam: Officina Dommeriana, 1751–52. **Wilckens, U.** *Die Missionsreden der Apostelgeschichte: Form- und traditionsgeschichtliche Untersuchungen.* WMANT 5. 2nd ed. Neukirchen-Vluyn: Neukirchener, 1963. **Wilcox, M.** *The Semitisms of Acts.* Oxford: Clarendon, 1965. **Wilder, A.** *Early Christian Rhetoric: The Language of the Gospel.* NTL. London: SCM, 1964; rev. ed., Cambridge, MA: Harvard University, 1971. ———. *Jesus' Parables and the War of Myths: Essays in Imagination in Scripture.* Ed. J. Breech. Philadelphia: Fortress, 1982. ———. "Eschatological Images and Earthly Circumstances." *NTS* 5 (1959) 229–45. **Wilkens, W.** "Die theologische Struktur der Komposition des Lukasevangeliums." *TZ* 34 (1978) 1–13. **Williams, C. S. C.** "The Date of Luke-Acts." *ExpTim* 64 (1952–53) 283–84. **Williams, J. G.** "Neither Here nor There." *Forum* 5.2 (1989) 7–30. **Wilshire, L. E.** "Was Canonical Luke Written in the Second Century?—A Continuing Discussion." *NTS* 20 (1974) 246–53. **Wilson, R. M.** "Farrer and Streeter in the Minor Agreements of Mt. and Lk. against Mk." *SE* 1 [= TU 73] (1959) 254–57. **Wilson, S. G.** *The Gentiles and the Gentile Mission in Luke-Acts.* SNTSMS 23. Cambridge: University Press, 1973. ———. *Luke and the Pastoral Epistles.* London: SPCK, 1979. ———. *Luke and the Law.* SNTSMS 50. Cambridge: University Press, 1983. ———. "Lukan Eschatology." *NTS* 15 (1969–70) 330–47. **Wimmer, J. F.** *Fasting in the New Testament: A Study in Biblical Theology.* Theological Inquiries. New York: Paulist, 1982. **Wink, W.** *John the Baptist in the Gospel Tradition.* SNTSMS 7. Cambridge: University Press, 1968. **Wittig, S.** "A Theory of Multiple Meanings." *Semeia* 9 (1977) 75–103. **Wojcik, J.** *The Road to Emmaus: Reading Luke's Gospel.* West Lafayette, IN: Purdue University Press, 1989. **Wolfe, K. R.** "The Chiastic Structure of Luke-Acts and Some Implications for Worship." *SWJT* 22 (1980) 60–71. **Wren, M.** "Sonship in Luke: The Advantage of a Literary Approach." *SJT* 37 (1984) 301–11. **Yadin, Y.** "A Note on Melchizedek and Qumran." *IEJ* 15 (1965) 152–54. **Yarnold, E.** "The Trinitarian Implications of Luke and Acts." *HeyJ* 7 (1966) 18–32. **Yoder, J. H.** *The Politics of Jesus.* Grand Rapids: Eerdmans, 1972. **Zahn, T. von.** *Introduction to the New Testament.* Tr. J. M. Trout et al. 3 vols. Edinburgh: T. & T. Clark, 1909. **Zeilinger, F.** "Die Bewertung der irdischen Güter im lukanischen Doppelwerk und in den Pastoralbriefen." *BK* 58 (1985) 75–80. **Zeller, D.** *Kommentar zum Logienquelle.* Stuttgarter kleiner Kommentar, Neues Testament 21. Stuttgart: Katholisches Bibelwerk, 1984. **Zerwick, M.** *Biblical Greek, Illustrated by Examples.* Ed. and tr. J. Smith. Scripta Pontifici Instituti Biblici 114. Rome: Pontifical Biblical Institute, 1963. **Ziesler, J. A.** "Luke and the Pharisees." *NTS* 25 (1979) 146–57. **Zimmermann, A. F.** *Neutestamentliche Methodenlehre: Darstellung der historischkritischen Methode.* Stuttgart: Katholisches Bibelwerk, 1968. ———. *Der urchristlichen Lehrer: Studien zum Tradentkreis der διδάσκαλος im frühen Urchristentum.* Tübingen: Mohr (Siebeck), 1984. **Zingg, P.** *Das Wachsen der Kirche: Beiträge zur Frage der lukanischen Redaktion und Theologie.* OBO 3. Fribourg/Göttingen: Universitätsverlag/Vandenhoeck & Ruprecht, 1974. ———. "Die Stellung des Lukas zur Heidenmission." *NZM* 29 (1973) 200–209.

Luke 9:21–18:34

Making Ready for the Trip to Jerusalem (9:21–50)

A broad-ranging ministry throughout Palestine gives way now to a focus upon Jesus' coming fate in Jerusalem: this will be his pathway to full glory. The glorious one must suffer to achieve his proper glory and enter his proper sphere. Such a destiny maps out a pathway of discipleship along which the followers of Jesus must be prepared to give up their lives. This strange way to greatness also redefines human measures of greatness and achievement.

Tell No One, Because the Son of Man Must Suffer (9:21–22)

Bibliography

Barton, G. A. "The Use of ἐπιτιμᾶν in Mark 8, 30 and 3, 12." *JBL* 41 (1922) 233–36. **Bastin, M.** "L'annonce dela Passion et les critères de l'historicité." *RSR* 50 (1976), 289–329; 51 (1977) 187–213. **Bennett, W. J., Jr.** "'The Son of Man Must. . . .'" *NovT* 17 (1975) 113–129. **Berger, K.** *Die Auferstehung des Propheten und die Erhöhung des Menschensohnes.* 125–41, 406–22. **Büchele, A.** *Der Tod Jesu im Lukasevangelium.* 125–28. **Claudel, G.** *La confession de Pierre: Trajectoire d'une péricope évangelique.* Paris: Gabalda, 1988. 247–307. **Farmer, W. R.** "The Passion Prediction Passages and the Synoptic Problem: a Test Case." *NTS* 36 (1990) 558–70, esp. 559–60. **Feuillet, A.** "Les trois grandes prophéties de la passion et de la résurrection des évangiles synoptiques." *RevThom* 67 (1967) 533–60; 68 (1968) 41–71. **Gils, F.** *Jésus prophète.* 134–54. **Goppelt, I.** *Theology of the New Testament: Volume 1. The Ministry of Jesus in Its Theological Significance,* ed. J. Roloff. Tr. J. Alsup. Eerdmans: Grand Rapids, 1981. 187–99. **Haenchen, E.** "Die Komposition von Mk vii 27–ix 1 und Par." *NovT* 6 (1963) 81–109. **Hoffmann, P.** "Mk 8,31: zur Herkunft und markinischen Rezeption einer alten Überlieferung." In *Orientierung an Jesus: Zur Theologie der Synoptiker.* FS J. Schmid, ed. P. Hoffmann et al. Freiburg im B.: Herder, 1973. 170–204. **Howard, V.** "Did Jesus Speak about His Own Death?" *CBQ* 39 (1977) 515–27. **Jeremias, J.** *New Testament Theology.* 276–99. **Michel, O.** "Der Umbruch: Messianität = Menschensohn: Fragen zu Markus 8,31." In *Tradition und Glaube: Das frühe Christentum in seiner Umwelt.* FS K.G. Kuhn, ed. G. Jeremias et al. Göttingen: Vandenhoeck & Ruprecht, 1971. 310–16. **Neirynck, F.,** and **Friedrichsen, T. A.** "Note on Luke 9,22: A Response to M. D. Goulder." In *L'Évangile de Luc* (1989), ed. F. Neirynck. 293–98. **Oberlinner, L.** *Todeserwartung und Todesgewissheit Jesu: Zum Problem einer historischen Begründung.* SBB 10. Stuttgart: Katholisches Bibelwerk, 1980. **Patsch, H.** *Abendmahl und historischer Jesus.* Stuttgart: Calwer, 1972. 186–97. **Perry, J. M.** "The Three Days in the Synoptic Passion Predictions." *CBQ* 48 (1986) 637–54. **Pesch, R.** "Die Passion des Menschensohns: Eine Studie zu den Menschensohnsworten der vormarkinischen Passionsgeschichte." In *Jesus und der Menschensohn.* FS A. Vögtle, ed. R. Pesch and R. Schnackenburg. Freiburg/Basel/Vienna: Herder, 1975. 166–95. **Popkes, W.** *Christus traditus: Eine Untersuchung zum Begriff der Dahingabe im Neuen Testament.* ATANT 49. Zürich/

Stuttgart: Zwingli, 1967. 153–69, 216–39, 240–70, 271–73, 279–82. **Roloff, J.** "Anfänge der soteriologischen Deutung des Todes Jesu (Mk. x. 45 und Lk. xxii. 27)." *NTS* 19 (1972–73) 38–64. **Schaberg, J.** "Daniel 7, 12 and the New Testament Passion-Resurrection Predictions." *NTS* 31 (1985) 208–22. **Schenke, L.** *Studien zur Passionsgeschichte des Markus: Tradition und Redaktion in Markus 14,1–42.* FB 4. Würzburg: Echter, 1971. 244–71. **Schürmann, H.** "Wie hat Jesus seinen Tod bestanden und verstanden? Eine methodenkritische Besinnung." In *Orientierung an Jesus: Zur Theologie der Synoptiker.* FS J. Schmid, ed. P. Hoffmann et al. Freiburg im B.: Herder, 1973. 325–63. **Strecker, G.** "Die Leidens- und Auferstehungsvorausagen im Markusevangelium (Mk 8,31; 9,31; 10,32–24)." *ZTK* 64 (1967) 16–39. **Taylor, V.** "The Origin of the Markan Passion-Sayings." *NTS* 1 (1954–55) 159–67. **Walker, N.** "'After Three Days.'" *NovT* 4 (1960) 261–62.

And see at 9:18–20 and the "Son of Man" excursus that follows this unit.

Translation

[21] *With a rebuke, he commanded them to tell nobody this,* [22] *saying, "It is necessary for the Son of Man to suffer many things and to be rejected by the elders and chief priests and scribes, and to be killed, and on the third day to be raised."*

Notes

There are no significant textual variants: a few texts align elements of the Lukan text with the Markan.

Form/Structure/Setting

The section that begins here continues to v 50, after which Jesus sets his face to go to Jerusalem. It is a transition section that provides the basis in Jesus' teaching for appreciating what Luke will do in structuring his material from 9:51 onwards: from 9:51 Luke will have Jesus on an elaborate and rather artificial journey to Jerusalem; the journeying motif there will function as a constant reiteration of the teaching here of the need for the Son of Man to suffer and be rejected before he enters into his glory. Luke continues here to follow the Markan sequence of material, with some abbreviation and editing to sharpen its focus in relation to his own concerns.

The single scene, 9:18–22, has been split into two because of the way in which vv 18–20 form the climax of a whole development and thus have their major links with what precedes, while vv 21–22 start a new development and should, therefore, be read primarily in connection with what is yet to come (for more detail see at 9:18–20). Though vv 18–22 describe a single scene, already in the Markan form there are two distinct episodes reported. The disciple's hard-won recognition that Jesus is the Christ is silenced because it is not the end of the road, but only the place from which to begin.

At 9:18–20 it was argued (with Pesch [*BZ* 17 (1973) 186–88]) that we have there a narrative whose concern is to describe events and to provide information concerning factual opinions, and which therefore does not fit standard form-critical categories. If that is correct, then it is more likely that the following material (Mark 8:31–33), which in our narratives is closely connected, is more of the same (the question of the historicity of the passion predictions is discussed in some detail below). The connection between the Petrine confession and the beginning of Jesus' insistence that he must suffer and be rejected is likely to be not just editorially useful for Mark but an original feature of these traditions. At the very least Mark 8:31–33 requires a certain platform of recognition of the dignity of Jesus (in different ways, both on the part of Jesus himself and on the part of Peter) for its own internal dynamic to be successful.

Farmer (*NTS* 36 [1990] 559) draws attention to a series of minor agreements with Matt 16:21, but when his count of five agreements is reduced to the basic two (see *Comment* below), nothing more than an influence from common diction need be suspected: Luke's written source here is likely to be nothing more than his Markan source. Luke deletes the Petrine response (and with it the emphasis on the clarity of Jesus' teaching) and Jesus' counter-response (he may find it difficult for Peter to be both the one through whom Satanic trial comes and one of those who has continued with Jesus in his trials [22:28]; another possible motivation is the closer unity with vv 23–27 made possible by the deletion [cf. Marshall, 367]). Luke also re-sections the two Markan episodes so that the call to silence now belongs to the second and not, as in Mark, to the first: the call to silence about the Christ identity now has its explanation clearly in the need for the Son of Man to suffer.

We turn now to the question of historicity. Did Jesus in fact predict his own death? or are the Gospel texts that attribute such predictions to him only a reading back by the later church on the basis of the conviction that Jesus' death was indeed a necessary part of God's will for him and not merely some horrible accident? This issue has attracted a great deal of scholarly attention from both sides of the debate, and, alongside the vigorous defense of both views, a number of mediating positions have emerged.

A full review of all the issues and arguments cannot be offered here, but attention will be drawn to some of the main views and lines of argument. Much of the discussion is entwined with the discussion of the origin and meaning of the phrase "Son of Man," which so often accompanies the words attributed to Jesus that anticipate his coming passion. A consideration of this phrase has been deferred to an excursus to be found at the end of the treatment of this pericope. We will here assume that discussion. The material there, however, does not address the questions as to the historicity of different groups of Son of Man sayings, and so some attention to that matter will be included in the present discussion.

What, then are the main difficulties in the way of accepting the words of Mark 8:31 (and the other passion predictions) as straightforwardly reflecting the words of the historical Jesus? We begin with general consideration before moving to more textually based arguments.

Those who most confidently deny these words to Jesus are the scholars who most rigorously impose the criterion of dissimilarity in forming their judgments as to what we may attribute to the historical Jesus. This criterion is based on the reasonable claim that we may be most confident that we have identified the views of the historical Jesus at those points where his views are neither those of the Jewish environment nor those of the early church. An extreme application of this criterion, however, requires that we deny to Jesus anything that would link him to his environment or to the early church. None of the scholars is consistently quite so extreme, but we do frequently get the assumption that if it may be shown that the early church *could* have formed a view along some other track and subsequently attributed it to Jesus, then this is in fact what must have happened (Hoffmann's study ["Herkunft und markinischen Rezeption"] provides examples of such assumptions). In my judgment it is inappropriate to use the criterion of dissimilarity to produce negative judgments concerning the historicity of items of the Gospel tradition. The early church certainly knew the outcome of Jesus' life, and its views on this matter go to the heart of its faith. It could have attributed its own knowledge and views to the historical Jesus, but that must be demonstrated and not assumed.

Studies frequently evaluate the passion predictions by correlating them with an existing understanding of the stages of development of early Christian views of Jesus and of the significance of his death. This is an entirely reasonable procedure if we have "assured" results to bring to bear upon the study of an individual item of the tradition. Within certain schools of thought in NT scholarship there is considerable confidence that this is the case. But I prefer to think that the individual item has as much right to place in question the prevailing view as the prevailing view has to place in question the historicity of the individual item.

The very possibility of prophetic prediction has had a bad reception in influential scholarly circles. Bultmann made a theological virtue out of the skepticism that Wrede (*Messianic Secret*) brought to the study of the Gospel sources and influenced a generation and more of Gospel scholars. It is not more scholarly to assume the impossibility of prediction. Both accurate prediction and a reading back must be considered as possible explanations of the Gospel texts.

It is frequently assumed that a decision about the correct background for the phrase "Son of Man" must necessarily eliminate from any claim to historicity one or more of the groups of Son of Man sayings. The sayings that anticipate Jesus' death and resurrection are generally considered to be the most vulnerable in this process. The view canvassed in the following excursus, concerning the fundamental sense for Son of Man in Jesus' diction, has no difficulties with any of the main groups of Son of Man sayings: the partially anonymous mysterious figure of dignity is claimed to be present as a person of significance; he experiences difficulties, and his rejection and even execution are anticipated, indeed insisted upon as his necessary coming fate, although such does not at all befit his dignity; his future vindication is, however, assured both as speedy resurrection from the dead and as installation with God and coming in glory. Those who are most confident that "Son of Man" is a piece of diction from apocalyptic circles, referring to an expected heavenly redeemer, have most difficulty with its use in connection with the announcement of a suffering fate. The evidence for such a use is, however, extremely sparse and problematic.

The close link between the rebuke of Mark 8:30 and the Petrine confession counts strongly in favor of the historicity of the confession (against, e.g., Strecker, *ZTK* 64 [1967] 32–33; see further at 9:18–20). The immediate context for Mark 8:31 in the exchange of rebukes between Peter and Jesus counts strongly in favor of historical authenticity (cf. Jeremias, *TDNT* 5:715), since none of the proposed settings in the early church for this exchange of rebukes is at all persuasive.

The apparent absence from the Q tradition of predictions of the Son of Man's coming suffering and resurrection is considered by some to be a strong argument against the authenticity of this strand of Son of Man sayings (e.g., Hoffmann, *Theologie des Logienquelle*, 141–42, 187–88). But Q is at best a hypothetically reconstructed document that needs to be used with caution. The extent of overlap with Markan tradition is evaluated quite variously (at one extreme, Bayer, *Jesus' Predictions*, 212, even considers that Luke 9:22 may stem from Q!). Further, on any reckoning, Q is an incomplete rendering of the Jesus tradition in a range of respects, and so its gaps are no strong argument against the historicity of the missing material.

Sometimes in connection with the Q discussion, the claim is made that the predictions of the passion and resurrection and those of the Parousia/future position of glory of the Son of Man come from separate strands of tradition and cannot both be original (e.g., Bultmann, *Theology*, 1:30–31; Jeremias, *New Testament Theology*, 285–86, and others would treat them as variants of a single tradition, but the time references and the intended roles are very different). Certainly, the only straightforward bridge between the two types of sayings is to be found in Luke 17:24–25, and this is generally not thought to be an original unity. Though not using Son of Man language, the Last Supper narrative provides something of a link between the two strands by bridging from the death of Jesus to the messianic banquet. Berger's investigation of Jewish traditions concerning the resurrection of prophetic figures (*Auferstehung des Propheten*) remains at many points speculative, but it is valuable in questioning the necessary link between the resurrection of the Son of Man and the general eschatological resurrection from the dead, and in showing how traditions of vindication by resurrection and of a future role in glory (judgment) may be naturally fitted together: resurrection is both vindication and availability for a subsequent role. While problems remain, it is perhaps no more difficult to reconcile suffering and resurrection Son of Man sayings with future role of glory Son of Man sayings, than it is to bring together traditions that affirm the authority of the Son of Man on the earth with those that anticipate suffering and rejection. Jesus' teaching is frequently somewhat cryptic and apparently designed to leave the hearer with most of the task of integration.

The response of the disciples to Jesus' revelation of his suffering fate, or for the most part the lack of response, has been found difficult to square with a claim to historicity for the passion predictions. However much what Jesus proposes may have been outside the disciples' expectations, the words preserved seem to be altogether too plain to have evoked from even the most simple-minded of the disciples the sequence of instances of incomprehension that Mark reports. The picture Mark presents is seen to be psychologically improbable (see especially 9:10 after 8:31; 9:32 and vv 33–34; and 10:35–37 after vv 33–34; and more generally the Gospel portrayal of the disciples' reaction to the passion and resurrection). To the present writer, this objection presents a much more serious challenge.

We may with relative ease deal with difficulties in connection with the passion part of the predictions. The refusal of Peter and the others to countenance the suffering and death of this uniquely great figure to whom they had attached themselves is intrinsically plausible and is presented with psychological credibility in 8:32–33. The verse 10:32 suggests that, at least in the context of the final trip to Jerusalem, a measure of ominous expectation had developed. The immediate juxtaposition of the passion predictions and the glory seeking of the disciples is most likely to be a piece of Markan artistry designed, in part, to explicate the content of Peter's activity in 8:32. Mark's theology of a suffering messiah is presented in sharp relief by means of such juxtapositions. The juxtaposition may not be historically plausible, but it is theologically profound.

Not the passion predictions, but the resurrection predictions pose the real difficulty. There is some cogency in the suggestion that resurrection has no place in the thought of those who are unprepared to anticipate a death. But one might have expected all this to come into clear focus on Good Friday. Bayer (*Jesus' Predictions,* 227–28, 255) may be on the right course when he speaks of a cluster of enigmatic vindication predictions, though he can hardly be right to locate this enigma in a range of possible contexts for a literal resurrection. It may be helpful to have in mind the way in which both at Qumran and in the NT the text form of quotations from the OT is affected by the terms in which it was believed to have found contemporary fulfillment (see for example the differences of the composite quotation in Mark 1:2–3 from both MT and LXX). Can the same have occurred with Jesus' predictions? In particular, has a more general term pointing to vindication been displaced by a specific term for resurrection, in light of the resurrection experience? The difficulties for a straighforward correlation with the passion narrative of the reference to "after three days" provide some confidence that the anticipation of resurrection has not been added *post eventum* to what was originally only a passion prediction. Other indications that Jesus was confident of divine vindication count in the same direction. (An equivalent imprecision for the resurrection component would be achieved without change of wording if, as is suggested as possible below, the specific references to death are a later precision in the passion predictions.)

Syntactical difficulties and unevenness are regularly brought forward as arguments against the original integrity of the passion predictions as preserved in Mark. In 8:31, "to be rejected by the elders and the chief priests and the scribes" falls under suspicion on various grounds. This item stands out syntactically because of its disproportionate length and the precision of its development. It is also difficult to identify the logic that would locate "to be rejected" after "to suffer" and before "to be put to death" and "to rise." The rejection motif is also suspected of being drawn from the early Christian use of Ps 118(117):22, some suggesting that Mark added this item at the same time as adding the reference to Ps 118(117):22 in Mark 12:12. The three groups mentioned are those that feature in Mark's passion account (though they are not introduced in the same sequence, and they are the obvious terms for identifying the Jewish leadership). The case is not decisive, but it is not unreasonable to treat this phrase as less secure in its claim to be an original part of the passion prediction. The arguments for its deletion are, however, considerably weakened if the direction of development of the passion predictions is toward making precise the mention of the actual death of the Son of Man (see below).

The older view championed by Lohmeyer (*Markus,* 165) that Luke 17:25 preserves the original short form is well answered by Strecker (*ZTK* 64 [1967] 19–23). Particularly, we should note Strecker's point that no satisfactory setting in the early church can be proposed for the isolated transmission of Luke 17:25; and Mark 8:31 is much more securely anchored in its context than Luke 17:25 is in its context. The long form would naturally have been shortened to allow it to function in its new context.

Mark 9:31 also has its own share of problems. The verbs are present passive, future active, aorist passive participle, and finally a future middle. The move from present to future, the repetitive participle, and the moves between passive and active have each caused the original integrity of the text to be disputed. These difficulties have formed the basis for arguing that the text has developed from a short original along the lines of Mark 14:41 (and cf. Luke 9:44). There is a striking agreement of language, but the short form in Mark 14:41 is dictated by the context and is, therefore, best taken as a resume of a longer form, and most of the unevenness in 9:31 is not touched by this suggestion: in particular the repetition of reference to putting to death/being put to death does not coincide with the join between putative original and addition. A better suggestion might be to consider "and they will kill him" to be a (Markan?) expansion. The addition would be designed to lay greater stress on the fact that Jesus anticipated his own death, where the earlier form had been content to have the death initially implied in the handing over into the hands of men, and then resumed by the participle as link to the following resurrection statement. It is even possible, as has been intimated above, that a general tendency in the development of the wording of the passion predictions becomes visible here, and that even the participial reference is a development. The original form will have spoken of a delivering into the hands of men and a rising after three days. In a post-resurrection situation, when it is clear that the rising is a resurrection from death, the participle is added to clarify the logical link between the two clauses, now understood to refer to the death and resurrection of Jesus. On later reflection this form was thought not to do justice to the importance of Jesus' having predicted his coming death, and the Markan form emerges.

The third main passion prediction is not so much uneven as filled with terms that are immediately those of the Markan passion account. Only the use of μαστιγώσουσιν, "scourge," in place of the passion account's use of φραγελλώσας, "scourged," saves the account from being totally composed of terms used in the passion narrative or the earlier passion predictions. There may be some value in pointing out that there is some difference in the sequence of terms between the prediction and the passion account. It is also possible to claim that there is reflected in the terms used a tissue of scriptural allusions for both the prediction and the passion narrative. It is not so clear to me (as argued by Feuillet [*RevThom* 67 (1967) 551] and others) that this prediction focuses the scandal contemplated on the handing over to the Gentiles, while the Markan passion narrative locates the supreme scandal in the cross. Although it seems quite clear to me that Mark inherited from the tradition more than one form of the passion prediction, it is quite unlikely that the tradition preserved a memory of a particular number of separate passion predictions whose individual wordings were separatedly preserved. Mark's point is really that Jesus kept up (and perhaps even intensified) his insistence on a coming suffering fate (note the "began" in 8:31). Mark may or may not have received from the tradition a third form of the passion prediction.

The more indirect indications in the Gospel material that Jesus anticipated his fate provide stronger positive argument for the authenticity of the direct passion predictions than these do for themselves. We may point in particular to the fire and baptism imagery of Luke 12:49–50 (cf. Mark 10:38); to the sequence leading to climax in Jesus' response to the threat of Herod (Luke 13:32), especially if the sequel in v 33 is original; with slightly less confidence, to the removal of the bridegroom (Mark 2:19–20 [see discussion at Luke 5:27–39]). The saying concerning the destruction and renewal of the temple may also be relevant here (Mark 14:58; John 2:19). With all its difficulties, the Last Supper narrative also offers strong support for Jesus, at least at that late stage, having anticipated his death and having integrated it into his sense of God's purpose for him.

Schürmann ("Wie hat Jesus," and cf. *Gottes Reich*) has argued forcefully that the investigation of this problem has been too narrowly focused on the words of Jesus about himself and needs to be expanded in two directions: there needs to be attention to his actions as much as to his words; and there needs to be a recognition that the religious and ethical demands with which he challenged his disciples are also relevant to how he viewed and conducted his own life. Along these lines, Schürmann has demonstrated that we may gain increased confidence in Jesus' expectation of his own suffering and vindication by God.

We do seem to have then a good basis for maintaining that Jesus anticipated his own suffering and rejection, and subsequent restoration by God. It is with less confidence that we trace back particular wording to Jesus.

Comment

The difficult face of the gospel has been anticipated obliquely in earlier sections of the Gospel narrative (e.g., 4:16–30; 5:35), but the large shape of the story has been that of steady progress and of positive achievement, to a climax in Peter's confession. The significance of the intimations of the arrival of the kingdom of God seems to fall into place with this disclosure of the identity of Jesus as messiah. But where Peter and the others would have wished to treat their recognition of Jesus as the all-illuminating conclusion to their journey of discovery, for the Lukan Jesus this is no more than the minimal foundation upon which an understanding of the shape of his ministry and its priorities is to be built.

21–22 Where in Mark the principal verb is ἐπιτιμᾶν, "to rebuke," Luke uses the participle form to subordinate this idea. The command to silence comes to the fore, and here uses παραγγέλειν, "to command," which Luke has introduced in a similar linguistic context in 5:14. Mark's ἵνα, "that," clause becomes an infinitive construction (cf. 5:14 again). Mark's less focused "about him" becomes "this." Instead of having the break at this point, Luke runs the sentence on by linking the passion prediction here by using the participle εἰπών, "saying." Luke's changes to the passion prediction itself are slight: he groups the elders, chief priests, and scribes more closely together by having the terms share a definite article; his use of ἀπό (lit. "from") for Mark's ὑπό, "by," illustrates the developing interchangeability of these terms; he replaces Mark's "after three days" with "on the third day"; Mark's ἀναστῆναι, "to rise," becomes ἐγερθῆναι, "to be raised." (The listed changes are also made by Matthew in 16:21, except that his use of ἀπό is differently motivated [ὑπό would not fit after "suffer"]. Both have followed common Christian idiom, and have wanted to see the leadership groups as a single entity here. No implications for source analysis should be drawn from the commonality.)

With Luke's deletion of Mark 8:32–33 (Peter's rebuke of Jesus and its consequence), it is more difficult to see what to make of the language of rebuke here.

Probably the Markan force remains intact, if we may judge from the disciples' incomprehension (9:44–45; 18:31–34) and preoccupation with concerns that are antithetical to those of the one whose path of service involves suffering and rejection (9:46–48, 49–50, 51–56 [note the use of "rebuked"]; 22:24–27). The disciples' "Christ of God" is not easily squared with Jesus' vision of this destiny.

The nature of the logic that makes the passion prediction the reason for silence about Jesus' messianic identity is not immediately transparent, but it is almost certainly based on the inadequacy of Peter's bare confession to the Christology that Luke is seeking to commend. Only along an elaborate track do we get to the point in 24:26 where it becomes possible to speak easily of a view that the Christ should suffer.

For Luke the necessity of Jesus' suffering (cf. 13:33; 17:25; 24:7; Acts 17:3) is the necessity to fulfill the divine will and purpose. The influence of the language of apocalyptic is probably present here (cf. Dan 2:28 LXX). God's will and purpose are witnessed to in Scripture (18:31; 22:37; 24:25–27, 46). The necessity here is the moral necessity of obedience to God, not the inevitability of fate (though Luke can see the fulfillment of Scripture in a rather more fatalistic way [e.g., Acts 1:16]). Fitzmyer (179–80) rightly draws the link between the necessity here and Luke's sense that there is a well-mapped plan of salvation that must be unfolded through its stages.

For the interplay between "Christ" and "Son of Man" in Luke, see at 6:1–5. For the basic sense of "Son of Man" see the following excursus. For Luke there will be a deliberate switch of categories involved here, something akin to his move from Davidic messianic categories to Isaianic categories, which we have documented earlier (see e.g., 3:4–6; 4:17–19; 7:22). In Luke's narrative, "Son of Man" makes its appearance in an editorial comment as a mysterious designation of dignity and authority (5:24; see there).

It is best to give a wide reference to "to suffer many things." All that reflects the unwelcoming face of the reception given to Jesus' person, his message, and his ministry is here embraced (cf. 4:23–30; 6:11; 7:31–34, 44–46; 8:37, 53; 9:51–54, 58; 10:13–15; 13:31; 15:2; 16:14; 19:14, 27; 22:21, 45–47, 54–62; etc.). Official rejection is the culmination of the suffering of many things. Alternatively, at least for an earlier form that may have lacked the list of leadership groups, suffering and being rejected may be, as W. Michaelis (*TDNT* 5:914–15) has argued, an ancient two-membered expression referring on each side to a single reality, but with one term pointing to the divine meaning and purpose ("suffer many things") and the other term pointing to the human rejection of the Son of Man ("to be rejected"). To be rejected may involve the idea of failing to measure up to the necessary standard or test of authenticity.

Judaism had available a number of strands of tradition that could help to make sense out of the suffering of one who was close to God (see L. Rupert, *Jesus als der leidende Gerechte: Der Weg Jesu im Licht eines alt- und zwischentestamentichen Motivs* [Stuttgart: Katholisches Bibelwerk, 1972]). The suffering of the righteous is extensively recognized in Job and the Psalms (e.g., 34:19; cf. 118:22); it is the lot of the suffering servant (Isa 52:13–53:12), who has borne our griefs and carried our sorrows; it is an important motif in Wisdom of Solomon (2:10–20; 3:1–9; 5:4–5); it becomes the basis of a martyr theology in 4 Macc 17:21–22, where the death of the righteous makes atonement for the sins of the nation. Important for the Gospel tradition, and for Luke in particular, is the tradition of the rejection of the prophets by those to whom they had been sent (see at 4:24; 13:33–34). Note also *T. Moses* 3:11, which speaks of Moses suffering many things in Egypt. Probably, almost all of these play a part in NT reflection on the death of Jesus, and there is no particular reason to think that Jesus would not have access to all of them in the formation of his own sense of destiny.

Luke makes it clear that he has in mind the Sanhedrin rejection of Jesus by making a single group out of "elders and chief priests and scribes." Nonetheless, Luke does not in fact use this sequence of terms to designate the composition of the Sanhedrin. The three groups, mentioned in a different sequence, do approach Jesus in 20:1 to question him about his authority, but, as a designation of the Sanhedrin, the closest is 22:66, where the "eldership [council]" (πρεσβυτέριον) consists of the chief priests and the scribes. Elsewhere Luke makes a pair out of chief priests and elders (22:52; Acts 23:14; 25:15) and a triplet out of rulers, elders, and scribes. Fitzmyer (780–81) reports Josephus' use of the triplets: leaders, chief priests, and the council; and leaders, chief priests, and learned Pharisees. On scribes see at 5:17; on elders cf. at 7:3, but note that the elders here (those of Jerusalem) have a significance for the wider Jewish community that would not be true of the elders of 7:3. The singular of the term translated here chief priests is used of the high priest. The plural term is used of the upper echelon of the priestly order: the captain of the temple, those who headed up the priestly courses (see at 1:8), the priest who had charge of the treasury, and other high-ranking priests (see Vermes, ed., in E. Schürer, *History of the Jewish People*, 2:275–91; Schrenk, *TDNT* 3:271–72; Jeremias, *Jerusalem*, 160–81), here those who had seats on the Sanhedrin.

It is suggested in *Form/Structure/Setting* above that "to be killed" may be a later precision added in the transmission of this tradition. That is not to say that to suffer and be rejected did not from the first embrace death, only that death was not specified. To be put to death is the final outworking of total rejection.

Mark's "after three days" may be allowable in Semitic idiom as a designation of Jesus' two nights in the grave (Jeremias, *New Testament Theology*, 285: "a short time"), but Luke prefers the more precise "on the third day." The latter is sometimes claimed as the more original on the basis of Hos 6:2, but it is difficult to see how the passion narrative would allow for a move from the Lukan form to the Markan; and if the Lukan form is secondary it is hard to insist on a Hos 6:2 connection, when precision of agreement with the passion narrative is available as a motivation for the change. For a link to Hos 6:2, Luke has also moved in the wrong direction with his failure to reproduce the LXX verb ἱστάναι in his reference to the raising up of Jesus. On the three-day tradition see J. B. Bauer, "Drei Tage," *Bib* 39 (1958) 354–58; J. Dupont, "Ressuscité 'le troisième jour,'" *Bib* 40 (1959) 753–55; H. Grass, *Ostergeschehen und Osterberichte,* 2nd ed. (Göttingen: Vandenhoeck & Ruprecht, 1962) 127–35; G. M. Landes, "The 'Three Days and Three Nights' Motif in Jonah 2.1," *JBL* 86 (1967) 446–50; K. Lehmann, *Auferweckt am dritten Tag nach der Schrift,* Quastiones Disputatae 38 (Freiburg: Herder, 1968); J. Jeremias, "Die Drei-Tage-Worte der Evangelien," in *Tradition und Glaube,* FS K. G. Kuhn, ed. G. Jeremias et al. (Göttingen: Vandenhoeck & Ruprecht, 1971) 221–29; H. K. McArthur, "On the Third Day," *NTS* 18 (1972–73) 81–86; J. M. Perry, "The Three Days in the Synoptic Predictions," *CBQ* 48 (1986) 637–54.

The form of reference to the three days and the word used to speak of the resurrection are also to be found in Matthew, which may indicate (as Fitzmyer, 781) that Matthew and Luke are independently influenced by a common current confessional expression (cf. 1 Cor 15:4). A reference to resurrection from death would not have been as apparent if the original form spoke of suffering many things, being rejected and rising up after three days (a number of the psalms, some echoed in the passion narrative, reflect this move from suffering/rejection to restoration, without any thought of resurrection from death [e.g., Pss 22; 31; 41; 69]). In Luke's form with its divine passive for "to be raised" there is a clear intimation of his later contrast between the verdicts declared upon Jesus from the human side and from the divine side (Acts 2:23–24; 3:15; 10:39–40; 13:27–30).

Explanation

Luke's new section runs from 9:21 to 9:50. From the high point of Peter's confession of Jesus as the Christ of God, attention now turns in a quite somber way to Jesus' anticipation of his coming passion in Jerusalem. Peter and his companions would have liked to treat their hard-won insight as an all-illuminating conclusion to their journey of discovery. But such an attitude can only call forth Jesus' rebuke. The confession is the solid achievement of the first part of the Gospel, but as such it is no more than a basic foundation upon which one may begin to build an understanding of the goal of the ministry of Jesus. Luke will use the material of vv 21–50 to clarify for his readers what the journey to Jerusalem, which will occupy from 9:51 to 18:34, means for Jesus' ministry.

Instead of the glorious Christ language, Jesus chooses the mysterious Son of Man language, and announces suffering, rejection, and death, but then resurrection on the third day. Jesus is the Christ, but should only be announced as such by those who realize that the Christ must suffer and enter into his glory (24:26). The insistent necessity of the will of God presses upon Jesus this requirement. And that such is the case is witnessed to in the Scriptures (18:31; 24:25–27; etc.).

Jesus' suffering is not restricted to events right at the end: he was rejected in his home town (4:16–30); he was dismissed as glutton and drunkard by many (7:34); he was one who has nowhere to lay his head (9:58). Such suffering becomes official and final in his rejection by those groups that provide the highest levels of leadership for the Jews, as members of the Sanhedrin, and this rejection results naturally in the death of the one who is tried and found wanting.

We are not told here why such a path of suffering and rejection should be necessary. There were, however, several strands of Jewish tradition that could be brought to bear on an attempt to understand the suffering of one who was near to God. It was recognized that the righteous do suffer at the hands of the unrighteous, but that God would put things right. There was a strong tradition that suggested that Israel had murdered most of the prophets sent by God. There was a late tradition suggesting that the death of the righteous might atone for the sins of the nation. Finally there was the enigmatic figure of the suffering servant in Isa 52–53. Each of these has probably played some role in NT reflection on the death of Jesus. Only the last makes suffering the clear will of God, but in the circles of Jesus' day that we refer to as apocalyptic circles, the language of divine necessity is also applied to the progressive stages in the unfolding of human history as it moves to its appointed end.

By way of interpretation, we may at least say from this text that a contrast is drawn between the human verdict on Jesus and the divine. Rejection from the human side is overturned by the affirmation of resurrection from the divine side (compare Acts 2:23–24; 3:15; etc.).

Critical scholarship has seriously questioned the historicity of Jesus' prediction of his own death and resurrection. It is certainly not unlikely that the particular form in which we have these predictions has been somewhat influenced by the course of events. We may even see this in the minor changes in Luke's form compared with the form in Mark on which he depended. But while this may make us reticent about tracing a particular wording back to Jesus himself, there is a good critical basis for maintaining that Jesus anticipated his own suffering and rejection, and subsequent restoration/vindication by God.

Excursus: Son of Man

Bibliography

Bauckham, R. "The Son of Man: 'A Man in My Position' or 'Someone.'" *JSNT* 23 (1985) 23–33. **Black, M.** "Jesus and the Son of Man." *JSNT* 1 (1978) 4–18. ———. "Aramaic Barnasha and the 'Son of Man.'" *ExpTim* 95 (1984) 200–206. **Borsch, F. H.** *The Son of Man in Myth and History*. London: SCM, 1967. **Bowker, J.** "The Son of Man." *JTS* 28 (1977) 19–48. **Bruce, F. F.** "The Background to the Son of Man Sayings." In *Christ the Lord*, ed. H. H. Rowdon. Leicester: IVP, 1982. 50–70. **Caragounis, C. C.** *The Son of Man: Vision and Interpretation.* WUNT 38. Tübingen: Mohr-Siebeck, 1986. **Casey, M.** *Son of Man: The Interpretation and Influence of Daniel 7.* London: SPCK, 1979. ———. "General, Generic and Indefinite: The Use of the Term 'Son of Man' in Aramaic Sources and in the Teaching of Jesus" *JSNT* 29 (1987) 21–56. ———. "Method in Our Madness, and Madness in Their Methods: Some Approaches to the Son of Man Problem in Recent Scholarship." *JSNT* 42 (1991) 17–43. **Collins, J. J.** "The Son of Man in First-Century Judaism." *NTS* 38 (1992) 448–66. **Colpe, C.** "ὁ υἱὸς τοῦ ἀνθρώπου." *TDNT* 8:400–477. **Coppens, J.** "Où en est le problème de Jésus 'Fils de l'homme.'" *ETL* 56 (1980) 282–302. ———. "Le fils d'homme dans les traditions juives postbibliques hormis du livre des paraboles de l'Henoch éthiopiens." *ETL* 57 (1981) 58–82. **Donahue, J. R.** "Recent Studies on the Origin of 'Son of Man' in the Gospels." *CBQ* 48 (1986) 484–98. **Fitzmyer, J. A.** "The New Testament Title 'Son of Man' Philologically Considered." In *A Wandering Aramean: Collected Aramaic Essays.* SBLMS 25. Missoula, MT: Scholars Press, 1979. 143–60. ———. "Another View of the Son of Man Debate." *JSNT* 4 (1979) 58–68. **Gese, H.** "Wisdom, Son of Man and the Origins of Christology." *HBT* 3 (1981) 23–57. **Hampel, V.** *Menschensohn und historischer Jesus: Ein Rätselwort als Schlüssel zum messianischen Selbstverständnis Jesu.* Neukirchen-Vluyn: Neukirchener, 1990. **Hare, D. R. A.** *The Son of Man Tradition.* Minneapolis: Fortress, 1990. **Higgins, A. J. B.** *The Son of Man in the Teaching of Jesus.* SNTSMS 39. Cambridge: UP, 1980. **Hooker, M. D.** *The Son of Man in Mark: A Study of the Background of the Term "Son of Man" and Its Use in St Mark's Gospel.* London: SPCK, 1967. ———. "Is the Son of Man Problem Really Insoluble?" In *Text and Interpretation: Studies in the New Testament.* FS M. Black, ed. E. Best and R. McL. Wilson. Cambridge: University Press, 1979. 155–68. **Horbury, W.** "The Messianic Association of the Son of Man." *JTS* 36 (1985) 34–55. **Jeremias, J.** *New Testament*

Theology: Part One. The Proclamation of Jesus. Tr. J. Bowden. London: SCM, 1971. 257–76. **Kim, S.** *"The 'Son of Man'" as the Son of God.* WUNT 30. Tübingen: Mohr-Siebeck, 1983. **Kingsbury, J. D.** "Observations on 'the Son of Man' in the Gospel according to Luke." *CurTM* 17 (1990) 283–90. **Leivestad, R.** "Exit the Apocalyptic Son of Man." *NTS* 18 (1972) 243–67. **Lindars, B.** *Jesus Son of Man: A Fresh Examination of the Son of Man Sayings in the Gospels in the Light of Recent Research.* London: SPCK, 1983. ———. "Re-enter the Apocalyptic Son of Man." *NTS* 22 (1975–76) 52–72. ———. "The New Look on the Son of Man." *BJRL* 63 (1981) 437–62. ———. "Response to Richard Bauckham: The Idiomatic Use of Bar Enasha." *JSNT* 23 (1985) 35–41. **Manson, T. W.** "The Son of Man in Daniel, Enoch and the Gospels." *BJRL* 32 (1950) 171–93. **Marshall, I. H.** "The Synoptic Son of Man Sayings in Recent Discussion." *NTS* 12 (1965–66) 327–51. **McNeil, B.** "The Son of Man and the Messiah: A Footnote." *NTS* 26 (1980) 419–21. **Moule, C. F. D.** "Neglected Features in the Problem of 'the Son of Man.'" In *Essays in New Testament Interpretation.* Cambridge: University Press, 1982. 79–90. **Müller, M.** "The Expression 'the Son of Man' as Used by Jesus." *ST* 38 (1984) 47–64. **Müller, U. B.** *Messias und Menschensohn in jüdischen Apokalypsen und in der Offenbarung des Johannes.* SNT 6. Gütersloh: Mohn, 1972. **Perrin, N.** *A Modern Pilgrimage in New Testament Christology.* Philadelphia: Fortress, 1974. **Pesch, R.,** and **Schnackenburg, R.,** eds. *Jesus und der Menschensohn.* FS A. Vögtle. Freiburg/Basel/Vienna: Herder, 1975. **Schillebeeckx, E.** *Jesus: An Experiment in Christology.* Tr. H. Hoskins. New York: Vantage Books, 1979. 459–72. **Tödt, H. E.** *The Son of Man in the Synoptic Tradition.* Tr. D. M. Barton. Philadelphia: Westminster, 1965. **Tuckett, C.** "Recent Work on the Son of Man." *ScrB* 12 (1981) 14–18. **Vermes, G.** "The Use of בר נשא/בר נשׁ in Jewish Aramaic." Appendix E in Black, M. *An Aramaic Approach to the Gospels and Acts.* 3rd ed. Oxford: Clarendon, 1967. 310–28. ———. "'The Son of Man' Debate." *JSNT* 1 (1978) 19–32. **Vielhauer, P.** "Gottesreich und Menschensohn in der Verkündigung Jesu." In *Aufsätze zum Neuen Testament.* TBü 33. Munich: Kaiser, 1965. 55–91. **Walker, W. O.** "The Son of Man: Some Recent Developments." *CBQ* 45 (1983) 584–607.

The extensive scholarly discussion of the phrase ὁ υἱὸς τοῦ ἀνθρώπου, "the Son of Man," has not produced any solid consensus about the background of, the development to be traced in, or the sense to be given to the Gospel use of this phrase. For an overview of Luke's own use of the phrase, see at 6:1–5. The discussion here will concentrate on the pre-Lukan history of the phrase.

As a piece of unidiomatic Greek the phrase is universally recognized to be an overliteral translation of an underlying Semitic idiom. The indefinite Hebrew form בן־אדם, *ben ʾādām,* "[a] son of man," is used as God's address to Ezekiel the prophet (Ezek 2:1; etc.; cf. Dan 8:17). The same form in Pss 8:4 and 80:17 forms a poetic parallel to, in the former, the normal word for humankind (אדם, *ʾādām*) and, in the latter, the normal word for man (אישׁ, *ʾîsh*). Each of these has occasionally been claimed as the starting point for the Gospel usage, but this is quite unlikely.

A more profitable starting point is the corresponding Aramaic phrase בר אנשׁ, *bar ʾenāsh.* This is the phrase that occurs in Dan 7:13, which is clearly echoed in the present form of a number of the Gospel Son of Man sayings, and this is the phrase that has been the subject of a number of recent studies of Aramaic idiom that have a potential for illuminating the Gospel usage. (The phrase occurs with some variations of form, the important ones being the dropping of the א, *ʾe,* and/or the addition of a suffix א, *āʾ*.)

After documenting the use of our phrase to mean "a human being" and /also as an indefinite pronoun ("someone"), Vermes ("Use of בר נשא/בר נשׁ") goes on to draw attention to a series of rabbinic texts in which he claims that the phrase functions as a circumlocution for "I." He has certainly identified a use of the phrase in which the speaker intends the phrase to refer to himself, and since this appears to be what we have in the Gospel usage, such a discovery is potentially of great importance.

Jeremias (*New Testament Theology*, 261 n. 1) soon protested that Vermes had claimed too much. We do not have a true circumlocution for "I," since in none of the texts does the expression have the sense "I (and no other)." A series of other scholars have raised essentially the same objection but have recognized in Vermes' study an important foundation for further work.

Fitzmyer ("The New Testament Title," 152–53; *JSNT* 4 [1979] 58–64) has raised a quite different objection to Vermes' conclusion. Fitzmyer accepts Vermes' analysis of the idiom in the one case of Cairo Targum B to Gen 4:14, but he points to the absence of the initial א, *ʾe*, in every instance cited by Vermes in support of the use as a surrogate for "I." This contrasts with Fitzmyer's observation that in all the Aramaic evidence prior to the Second Revolt (that is before A.D. 131/2) the longer form is used. Fitzmyer warns against using what is, therefore, late evidence for identifying first-century Aramaic idiom. There is no such dating problem in the case of the use of the idiom to refer generally to "humanity (anyone)" or indefinitely to "someone" (see examples in Fitzmyer, 148).

Not everyone has been persuaded that, given the quite scant earlier Aramaic sources, we should rule out later sources for identifying likely first-century idiom. This relaxation of criteria seems more reasonable if it is not Vermes' unique idiom that is being claimed, but rather a use of one of the more widely established idioms (general or indefinite) in a context where self-reference is involved. Casey (*JSNT* 29 [1987] 22–23) has been able to support this relaxation by pointing to an eighth-century B.C. text (*Sepire* 3:14–17) in which an indefinite use of בר אנשׁ involves self-reference ("anyone of us"). Casey, Lindars (*Jesus Son of Man*), and Bauckham (*JSNT* 23 [1985] 23–33) have each developed, on the basis of this sort of use of Vermes' results, an understanding of the Aramaic idiom reflected in the Gospel usages.

Casey's argument is that the authentic Son of Man statements are those in which Jesus makes a general statement about humanity, but in a way that invites a specific application of this general truth to himself. Lindars offers a more subtle analysis, and proposes to find a way between Vermes and Casey.

Lindars identifies an idiomatic use of the generic article as the key to Vermes' Aramaic texts and to Jesus' use of the Son of Man expression. To understand Lindars we need first to attend to the presence, as was mentioned above, of the suffix א, *āʾ*, in some of the texts adduced by Vermes. Originally this functioned much as the definite article ("the") in English but gradually lost its force so that forms with and without this suffix came to be used interchangeably. Vermes and most other scholars have assumed that this interchangeability was already well advanced in the time of Jesus. Lindars thinks this is not the case, even in the later rabbinic period, at least with the particular idiomatic use of the generic article with "Son of Man," which it is his concern to establish (Fitzmyer [154], also, thinks that there was still, in the first century, more life than is normally allowed in the distinction between the forms with and without suffix). By generic article Lindars means the use of the suffix to "denot[e] a particular but unspecified member or group of members of the class" identified by the word or phrase to which the suffix is attached (as clarified in *JSNT* 23 [1985] 35–36). The particular idiom that Lindars claims to have identified is the use of this generic article in speech as an indirect means for the speaker to refer to himself. The use of the suffix indicates that the speaker has a specific person in mind, and the context encourages the hearer to identify that person with the speaker himself.

Bauckham considers that Lindars has not successfully demonstrated the existence of this distinctive idiom, and opts for a much simpler suggestion. Unlike Casey, Bauckham shares Lindars' sensitivity to the presence of the suffix as potentially affecting meaning, though, as we will see, this creates difficulties for his own position. Casey saw Jesus as achieving self-reference by making a general statement about humanity; Bauckham sees Jesus as achieving self-reference by making indefinite statements ("someone"), which he invites his hearers to recognize as pertaining to himself. Bauckham thinks that Jesus will have needed to use the form without suffix to indicate the indefiniteness. The Gospel forms are of course all definite, and this is taken by Bauckham as reflecting the translator's wish specifically to avoid Jesus' original ambiguity (33 n. 23).

Both Casey and Bauckham offer us thoroughly believable Aramaic idioms, but neither idiom is automatically to be applied to the Gospel uses. The claims of the competing idioms need to be tested by their capacity to best account for the actual texts.

My own scrutiny of the Aramaic texts used in the discussion suggests that there may indeed be an idiomatic distinction between uses of the phrase with and without the suffix (as maintained in different ways by Lindars and Bauckham, but denied by Casey). When a general truth is being expressed, the suffix seems to be uniformly present. When an indefinite statement is being made, that is, a statement about an unspecified "someone," then the suffix is uniformly absent. Only one precision needs to be added. As in other languages, the use of "someone" in a negative statement produces a statement of general validity: that is, the statement is true of "nobody"; or, said another way, the negation is true of any and every person.

Bultmann (e.g., *Theology of the New Testament*, 1:5) made popular the view that there was in the Judaism of Jesus' day an expectation of the coming of a supernatural apocalyptic Son of Man from heaven, and it is from this background that we must elucidate the Gospel usage of the phrase. This view has suffered steady erosion in more recent scholarship and has almost disappeared from English language scholarship. The view has played a more prominent role in German language scholarship, and has been more persistent there (e.g., Müller, *Messias und Menschensohn*; and the essays in Pesch and Schnackenburg, eds., *Jesus und der Menschensohn*).

There are certainly no examples of an Aramaic use of "Son of Man" as a title (e.g., Vermes, "Use of בר נשׁ/בר נשׁא," 327). The claim that it was used as a title is based on more indirect evidence. (*i*) Three similar phrases are used in *1 Enoch* (46:1–4; 48:2; 60:10; 62:5–9, 13, 14; 63:11; 69:27–29; 70:1–4; 71:14), and are applied to a figure who, having been established by God in heaven, is, in due course, revealed by God as eschatological judge and deliverer. While other parts of this composite work are represented by fragmentary texts at Qumran, this section of *1 Enoch* (The Similitudes) has survived only in late Ethiopic manuscripts. The absence from Qumran has led some to consider this section of *1 Enoch* as originating only in a later period (J. T. Milik, *The Books of Enoch* [Oxford: Clarendon, 1976], has argued that The Similitudes are actually a Christian work composed in Greek). The arguments here are not decisive, and it is certainly possible to adopt the view that The Similitudes give us a window onto ideas that would have been quite possible in Jesus' environment. The more fundamental question is that of whether this text reflects a titular use of "Son of Man." The starting point in 46:1–4 with its clear allusions to Dan 7:13 and the consistent use of the demonstrative ("this") with the Son of Man references show that the use is not titular (see the argument presented by Casey, *Son of Man*, 99–112). This is now generally recognized. What we do have is an apocalyptic form of eschatological hope that makes use of Dan 7:13 (but is certainly not based on that text); but we do not have a Son of Man title.

(*ii*) *4 Ezra* is a Jewish text generally dated around A.D. 100. It is known mostly from a Latin translation of a Greek translation, of what is probably a Hebrew original (cf. B. Metzger, *The Old Testament Pseudepigrapha*, ed. Charlesworth, 1:519–20). Chap. 13 introduces a dream figure of a man who comes up out of the sea and flies with the clouds of heaven (an obvious link with Dan 13:7, and more clearly so when set in connection with other dependences on Daniel in chaps. 11 and 12). "Son of Man" is not impossible as a Semitic original, but is hardly necessary, and may not even be likely (cf. Casey's argument [124–26] based on the change in term for man in Latin between the vision and the interpretation). Even if "Son of Man" were in the original, the translators have not seen this as a technical use, and, therefore, have not made any attempt to reproduce the idiom in translation. In original or in translation we have an image, based partly on Dan 7:13, and not a title. This image is interpreted with reference to the messiah who has been referred to earlier in the book.

(*iii*) The third main line of argument for an apocalyptic Son of Man is the claim that only such a Jewish tradition can make sense of the Son of Man references that we find in the Gospel texts (see esp. Colpe, *TDNT* 8:429, 433–37). Most of the more recent interpreters do not seem to find a compelling need to postulate such a background (but see Higgins, *The Son of Man*).

The case for a titular use of Son of Man in the period of Jesus is far from compelling. But what is quite likely is the existence of a tradition of using the Daniel text, interpreted of an individual figure, as an ingredient in eschatological reflection. Given such a setting, the questions we must ask of the Gospel texts are: How much context would be needed to make a Son of Man statement a clear or even a veiled allusion to Dan 7:13? Do we need more because the possibility of indirect self-reference is also idiomatically to hand? Or do we need less, because the text was playing an active role in contemporary eschatological reflection? We can go no further without attention to the Gospel texts themselves.

As we turn to the Gospel texts, it may be in order to register the concern that too often the reconstructed Aramaic idiom or Jewish apocalyptic background has become an infallible determinant of the authenticity of the particular Son of Man texts.

The synoptic Gospel data have traditionally been organized into three groups of texts: first, texts that refer to the time of the earthly ministry of Jesus (Mark 2:10, 28; Luke 7:34; 9:58; 11:30[?]; 12:10; 19:10; Matt 10:23[?]); second, texts that focus on the coming suffering of the Son of Man (Mark 8:31; 9:9, 12, 31; 10:33, 45; 14:21, 41: Luke 11:30[?]; 22:48; Matt 12:40); and, finally, texts that refer to a future role of glory for the Son of Man (Mark 8:38; 13:26; 14:62; Luke 12:8, 40; 17:22, 24, 26, 30, 18:8; 21:36; Matt 10:23[?]; 13:41; 19:28; 24:30, 37; 25:31). (This listing is not complete. It does not list parallels; nor does it include some of the more obvious Matthean insertions of the idiom; and there are texts that do not fit the scheme, such as Luke 6:22.)

Hooker ("Son of Man Problem," 159–60; *Son of Man*, 80) has rightly warned that this very classification and even the particular headings used to identify the categories run the danger of influencing the subsequent study of the texts. For example, all the texts that certainly belong in the second category, except for those set in the immediate context of Jesus' betrayal, actually anticipate, in themselves or in their immediate context, resurrection or glory; that is they all anticipate both suffering *and* vindication, and so have more in common with the third category than is at first evident. Similarly, Hooker has pointed out that each of the Markan texts in the third category anticipates future glory against a background of present difficulty, rejection, or persecution, and rightly uses the term "vindication" in connection with them. With more or less appropriateness the same term may be used in connection with a good number of the other texts in the third group.

Other categorizations may shed useful light upon the Son of Man sayings. We may divide among those sayings in which allusion to Dan 7:13 is clearly present, those in which it is clearly absent and in which the thought expressed does not immediately cohere with the circle of ideas in the first group, and those which, though they do not have a clear allusion to Dan 7:13, would cohere well with the texts that do have such a definite allusion. Alternatively, we may distinguish sayings that involve a vindication of the Son of Man, from those that involve his vindication or (non-vindication) of others. We could, further, distinguish between sayings that affirm the authority and dignity of the Son of Man and those that speak of his humiliation. Finally, we might want to distinguish texts in which self-reference is unambiguous from those in which this is not the case (and here we could distinguish between texts in which "Son of Man" is clearly an individual and those in which corporate reference of some kind needs to be considered as a possibility).

How well do the suggested Aramaic idioms fit the actual Son of Man sayings? Once the texts are isolated from their present context, Casey's view is effective for Luke 12:10; Mark 2:27–28; and 14:21. It is possible for Luke 22:48. For the passion predictions it is attractive, but depends heavily on a quite speculative reconstruction. His handling of Mark 8:38; Luke 7:34; and 9:58 is much less convincing. Bauckham's "someone" is most effective for Mark 2:10; Luke 7:34; 11:30; and 12:8–9. Despite his desire to include some of the texts that allude to Dan 7, the presence of such allusion seems at once to give a different role to the "Son of Man" expression. In other cases the actual idiom would seem to need to be able to carry more significance in itself, than provided for by Bauckham's approach.

Do the "Son of Man" sayings that involve a future coming or role of glory presuppose a Jewish apocalyptic titular use of "Son of Man"? In some of the texts it is certainly true that "Son of Man" is meant to evoke thoughts of an eschatological figure of glory. In most cases there is, however, an evocation of Dan 7 imagery to facilitate this. What is clear is that the "Son of Man" of Dan 7 is to be understood in a way reminiscent of the eschatological views associated with the use of the Dan 7 material in *1 Enoch* and *4 Ezra* (as discussed above). One particular point to note is the way that *4 Ezra* 13:1–4 has the same application of the Daniel imagery of a coming with the clouds of heaven to a role upon the earth as is found in the Gospel tradition (in Daniel the coming is to God; though the transition is eased by the likelihood that the imagery of Dan 7 involves the human figure coming to an earthly location where temporary thrones have been set up [7:9] in order for God to make a visit and establish the order of affairs that he has in mind). Notably absent in the Gospel texts is the emphasis in *1 Enoch* on the prior presence of the human figure in heaven, before being revealed for his earthly role. It seems fair to claim for the Gospel texts a setting in the kind of Jewish thought exemplified in these texts, but not to claim that the Gospel texts reflect a fixed set of well defined expectations, or a titular use of "Son of Man."

Is it possible to bring together some kind of indirect self-reference and allusion to Dan 7? One can certainly do this with much greater confidence in the flow of a Gospel text than when each of the component texts must be constantly under scrutiny as to its authenticity and each must be treated largely in isolation from its present Gospel context. Nonetheless, a pattern may commend itself as being more fundamental to the texts than can be attributed only to a later redactor.

I start from Bauckham's "somebody," by noting that if the "somebody" is both somebody with whom Jesus is potentially to be identified, and at the same time a "somebody" of significance, whose precise identity remains yet unspecified, then considerably more of the texts begin to fit neatly into an approach like Bauckham's. To modernize, we might think of something like "the Man of destiny." This would do justice to the way in which the "Son of Man" seems regularly to be assumed to be a figure of authority and dignity, without being identified as any specific dignitary. This would also allow for the possibility of an added precision being offered at a certain point or in certain contexts: this figure is, whatever else he may also be, the man of Dan 7. Prior to that further explication, the usage would remain somewhat mysterious, and even with the further explication we are not to understand that the contours of the phrase are exhaustively given in the Dan 7 imagery or the traditions associated with it in its contemporary usage. At times there could be real doubt as to the application to Jesus himself. If he were to be taken as referring to himself, then the claim of the idiom would be no more precise than to be a figure of importance. But all the time the idiom would be open to the precision to come with the eschatological role identified in the link to Dan 7, but not in the sense that "Son of Man" is now recognized to have been all along a cryptic reference to Dan 7:13. As is not the case with Bauckham, who needed to find an underlying form without the suffix, the usage suggested here would be better expressed with the form that uses the suffix. This is not exactly any existing Aramaic idiom.

It would be a distinct coinage remembered by the early church as a characteristic diction of Jesus, in much the way that the anticipatory amen was remembered or the use of Abba.

To Follow Me, You Must Give Away Your Life to Gain It (9:23–27)

Bibliography

Bauer, J. B. "'Wer sein Leben retten will . . .' Mk 8,35 Parr." In *Neutestamentliche Aufsätze.* FS J. Schmid, ed. J. Blinzler et al. Regensburg: Pustet, 1963. 7–10. **Beardslee, W. A.** "Saving One's Life by Losing It." *JAAR* 47 (1979) 57–72. **Bornkamm, G.** "Die Verzögerung der Parusie: Exegetische Bemerkungen zu zwei synoptischen texten." In *Memoriam E. Lohmeyer,* ed. W. Schmauch. Stuttgart: Evangelisches Verlagswerk, 1951. 116–26, esp. 116–19. ————. "Das Wort Jesus vom Bekennen." In *Geschichte und Glaube.* BEvT 48. Munich: Kaiser, 1968. 1:25–36. **Chilton, B.** *God in Strength.* 251–74. **Coppens, J.** *La relève apocalyptique du messianisme royal. III. Le Fils de l'homme néotestamentaire.* BETL 55. Leuven: Peeters/University Press, 1981. 13–16. **Dautzenberg, G.** *Sein Leben bewahren: ψυχή in den Herrenworten der Evangelien.* SANT 14. Munich: Kösel, 1966. 51–82. **Dinkler, E.** "Jesu Wort vom Kreuztragen." In *Neutestamentliche Studien.* FS R. Bultmann, ed. W. Eltester. BZNW 21. Berlin: Töpelmann, 1954. 110–29. **Doncoeur, P.** "Gagner ou perdre sa ψυχή." *RSR* 35 (1948) 113–19. **Fascher, E.** "Der unendliche Wert der Menschenseele: Zur Auslegung von Mark. 8,36." In *Forschung und Erfahrung im Dienste der Seelsorge,* ed. O. Söhngen et al. Göttingen: Vandenhoeck & Ruprecht, 1961. 46–57. **Fletcher, D. R.** "Condemned to Die: The Logion on Cross-Bearing: What Does It Mean?" *Int* 18 (1964) 156–64. **Fridrichsen, A.** "'Sich selbst verleugnen.'" *ConNT* 2 (1936) 1–8. **Fuller, R. H.** "The Clue to Jesus' Self-understanding." *SE* 3 (1964) 58–66. **George, A.** "Qui veut sauver sa vie la perdra; qui perd sa vie la sauvra." *BVC* 83 (1968) 11–24. **Glombitza, O.** "Das Kreuz: Eine neutestamentliche Studie." In *Domine dirige me in verbo tuo: Herr leite mich nach deinem Wort.* FS M. Mitzenheim, ed. E. Mauersberger et al. Berlin: Ev. Luth. Kirche in Thueringen, 1961. 60–67. **Green, M. P.** "The Meaning of Cross-Bearing." *BSac* 140 (1983) 117–33. **Griffiths, J. G.** "The Disciples's Cross." *NTS* 16 (1969–70) 358–64. **Holman, C. L.** "The Idea of an Imminent Parousia in the Synoptic Gospels." *StBibT* 3 (1973) 15–31. **Kattenbusch, F.** "Das Wort vom unersetzlichen Wert der Seele." *ZNW* 10 (1909) 329–31. **Koolmeister, R.** "Selbstverleugnung, Kreuzaufnahme und Nachfolge: eine historische Studie über Mt. xvi. 24." In *Charisteria Iohanni Kopp.* Papers of the Estonian Theological Society in Exile 7. Stockholm: ETSE, 1954. 64–94. **Kümmel, W. G.** *Promise and Fulfilment.* 25–29. ————. "Das Verhalten Jesus gegenüber und das Verhalten der Menschensohns: Markus 8,38 par und Lukas 12,3f par Mattäus 10,32f." In *Jesus und der Menschensohn.* FS A. Vögtle, ed. R. Pesch et al. Freiburg/Basel/Wien: Herder, 1975. 210–24. **Lambrecht, J.** "Q-Influence on Mark 8,34–9,1." In *Logia: Les paroles de Jésus—The Sayings of Jesus.* FS J. Coppins, ed. J. Delobel. Leuven: UP, 1982. 277–304. **McDermott, J. M.** "Luke, XII, 8–9: Stone of Scandal." *RB* 84 (1977) 523–37. **Michaelis, W.** "Zeichen, Siegel, Kreuz." *TZ* 12 (1956) 505–25. **Moore, A. L.** *The Parousia in the New Testament.* NovTSup 13. Leiden: Brill, 1966. 125–31, 175–77. **Perrin, N.** "The Composition of Mark ix 1." *NovT* 11 (1969) 67–70. **Pesch, R.** "Über die Autorität Jesu . . ." In *Die Kirche des Anfangs.* FS H. Schürmann, ed. R.

Schnackenburg et al. Leipzig: St. Benno, 1977. 25–55, esp. 26–39. **Rebell, W.** "'Sein Leben verlieren' (Mark 8.35 parr.) als Strukturmoment vor- und nachösterlichen Glaubens." *NTS* 35 (1989) 202–18. **Riesenfeld, H.** "The Meaning of the Verb ἀρνεῖσθαι." *ConNT* 11 (1947) 23–27. **Schierse, F. J.** "Historische Kritik und theologische Exegese der synoptischen Evangelien, erläutert an Mk 9,1." *Scholastik* 29 (1954) 520–36. **Schlosser, J.** *Le règne de Dieu.* 323–71. **Schneider, J.** "σταυρός." *TDNT* 7:572–80. **Schulz, A.** *Nachfolgen und Nachahmen: Studien über das Verhältnis der neutestamentlichen Jüngerschaft zur urchristlichen Vorbildethik.* SANT 6. Munich: Kösel, 1962. 82–90. **Schwarz, G.** ". . . ἀπαρνησάσθω ἑαυτόν . . .'? (Markus viii 34 Parr.)." *NovT* 17 (1975) 109–12. ———. "Der Nachfolgespruch Markus 8.34b.c Parr.: Emendation und Rückübersetzung." *NTS* 33 (1987) 255–65. **Trocmé, E.** "Marc 9, 1: prédication ou réprimand?" *SE* 2 (1964) 259–65. **Vögtle, A.** "Exegetisches Erwägungen über das Wissen und Selbstbewusstsein Jesu." In *Gott im Welt.* FS K. Rahner, ed. J. B. Metz et al. Freiburg: Herder, 1964. 1:608–67, esp. 642–47. **Wijngaards, J.** "Let Him Take up His Cross . . . ." *Vidyajyoti* 47 (1983) 106–17. **Zimmermann, H.** "Christus nachfolgen: Eine Studie zu den Nachfolge-Worten der Synoptischen Evangelien." *TGl* 53 (1963) 241–55.

See further at the "Son of Man" excursus preceding this section.

Translation

[23]*Then he said to all, "If someone wants to come after me, let him deny*[a] *himself, and let him take up his cross daily,*[b, c] *and let him follow me.* [24]*For, whoever wants to save his life will lose it; whoever loses his life for my sake, this one will save it.* [25]*For, how is a person benefited, who has gained the whole world, but who has lost or forfeited his own self?* [26]*For, whoever is ashamed of me and of my words,*[d] *of this one will the Son of Man be ashamed, when he comes in his glory, and the glory of the Father, and of the holy angels.* [27]*In fact,*[e] *I tell you truly: There are some of those who are standing here*[f] *who will certainly not taste death before they see the kingdom of God.*[g]

Notes

[a] The compound form ἀπαρνησάσθω (same sense) is quite strongly attested (P[75] B C W Ψ etc.), but this probably represents conformity to Mark or Matthew.

[b] "And let him take up his cross daily" is missing from D a l, probably due to homoeoarcton.

[c] "Daily" is absent from ℵ[1] C D etc. to conform it to the other Synoptics.

[d] "Words" is missing from D a e l sy[c] Or. This would give the sense "my [disciples]," but is certainly an accidental omission.

[e] Translating δέ as indicating here a measure of contrast, but also climax.

[f] Quite a lot of texts (A C D W Θ Ψ etc.) conform the wording here to Matthew, with no change of meaning. Luke's text involves a slightly odd use of αὐτοῦ ("here").

[g] D reads instead, "the Son of Man coming in his glory." This is based on, but not identical to, the Matthean reading.

Form/Structure/Setting

Luke connects vv 23–27 even more closely with vv 21–22 than does his Markan source. What Jesus announces for himself, is not for him alone. Despite all the horrors of the prospect, it is finally the way to life, and the values embodied must also be embraced by the would-be disciple of Jesus.

Luke uses only his Markan source, which has at this point a collection of isolated sayings of Jesus, which have been gathered by Mark, or before him, as mutually interpreting each other. In particular vv 24–27 are all offered in explanation of the primary statement to be found in v 23.

The presence of the word "cross" in v 23 (= Mark 8:34) has raised suspicions about whether this verse can be attributed to the historical Jesus. Despite the extensive skepticism that exists about the historicity of the passion predictions (see above at 9:21–22), at the end of all the discussion there is a surprising degree of consensus that the basic core of the material here should be traced back to Jesus himself. Beyond all the particular arguments, this is probably because the radical force of the verse seems to cohere so well with the distinctively radical nature of other teachings of Jesus.

Those who stand on the negative side of the argument consider that it is impossible to separate the reference to the cross from a Christian awareness of Jesus' own passion (see, e.g., E. Haenchen, *NovT* 6 [1963] 92). The same concern also motivates those who would postulate an original lacking the reference to a cross (Arvedson, *Mysterium Christi: Eine Studie zu Mt 11, 25–30* [Uppsala: Lundquist, 1937]. Vorwort, iv: "cross" is derived ultimately from "yoke" in Matt 11:29a [Schwarz, *NTS* 33 (1987) 259–60, develops Arvedson's view further by claiming that behind "cross" stands the Aramaic אגדי (*ʾgdy*), which means a yoke or bar placed across the shoulders to facilitate the balancing of heavy loads]; Dinkler, "Jesu Wort": "cross" is an interpretation in light of Jesus' passion of "sign" [σημεῖον], which referred originally to a [metaphorical] sealing of oneself with the sign of belonging to God, and which would have taken the form of the old shape of the Hebrew letter ת [*taw*, see Ezek 9:4] which was in fact cross shaped [x or +]). A similar motivation may be detected in Glombitza's attempt ("Das Kreuz") to give σταυρός the sense of one of the stakes from which a palisade is constructed. These attempts to unearth an obscured original range from the speculative to the fanciful, and we must ask whether there is not some other way of dealing with the need to separate pre- and post-resurrection perspectives here.

Apart from the word "cross" itself, there are two features of the text that bind closely the cross of Jesus and the cross of the disciple: (*i*) the Markan setting in closest proximity to the first passion prediction; (*ii*) the quasi-equivalence established between cross-carrying and following Jesus (in the rather specific sense of doing/being ready to do what he himself has done/will do). The first of these is clearly Markan or pre-Markan editing; the second, it has been suggested, is the result of development of the pericope from an original that spoke of coming after Jesus only in the sense of the idiom known to have been applied to students of Jewish rabbis (so, e.g., Laufen, *Doppelüberlieferung*, 309: הלך אחרי, *hlk ʾḥry*, "to go after" = "to be a disciple"). Laufen's view is supported by the way that the Markan form (reproduced by Luke, but contrast Matt 10:38; Luke 14:27) ends up having an awkward double reference to following Jesus, where Luke 14:27 can be understood to have "to be my disciple" as an equivalent for one of these. (Laufen argues effectively [305–8], against the more common view, which favors the negative form preserved in Luke 14:27, that the positive form reflected by Mark is likely to be original.) Does an original that said something like "He who would follow me [i.e., be my disciple] must take up his cross," and that is removed from its Markan editorial context, still reflect a post-resurrection situation?

The Jews of Jesus' day were quite familiar with crucifixion, dominantly as the Roman form of execution, but also with an awareness that crucifixion had been practiced in their own internal history (on crucifixion in Jesus' day see M. Hengel, *The Cross of the Son of God,* tr. J. Bowden [London: SCM, 1986] 93–185; for the situation in Palestine see further J. A. Fitzmyer, "Crucifixion in Ancient Palestine, Qumran Literature, and the New Testament," *CBQ* 40 [1978] 493–513). Nonetheless, there is said to be no surviving Semitic reference to carrying a cross, except in *Midr. Gen.* 22:6, where Isaac bearing the wood for the burnt offering is likened to "one who carries his stake [cross] on his shoulder," and which Dinkler takes as reflecting later Jewish response to Christian claims ("Jesu Wort," 114; Schelkle, *Passion Jesu,* 219, cites from *b. Ber.* 5c a reference to two men deemed to have been implicated in a murder: "They both go out laden with two beams," but I have not been able to confirm this reference). How heavily should the lack of Semitic parallels weigh in making a judgment about whether Jesus could have spoken of taking up one's cross? M. Hengel postulates a zealot idiom on the basis of the mortal danger from the Romans in which taking up the zealot cause in Jesus' day would have placed one (*Die Zealoten: Untersuchungen zur jüdaischen Freiheitsbewegung in der Zeit von Herodes I. bis 70 nach Christi,* AGJU 1 [Leiden/Köln: Brill, 1961] 265–66), but such a borrowing would seem to leave too much room for misunderstanding, and suggests an unlikely degree of orientation to the Roman question on the part of Jesus. But do we need this to suggest that Jesus could have coined such an idiom for "putting one's head on the block"? There is certainly plenty of Greco-Roman material about execution by crucifixion, but only quite rarely does the victim's carrying of the cross get any specific mention. Yet, there would be no difficulty in proposing the emergence of such an idiom in a Greco-Roman context. Where there are far fewer references to crucifixion in Semitic texts, it is quite likely that there will be gaps in our evidence for mapping out the linguistic possibilities, but there is no strong reason for considering that these linguistic possibilities will be much different in Jesus' language field. Jesus' demand makes an interesting antithesis to Epictetus' recommendation (in connection with whether one should provoke an opponent in a legal dispute; *Diatribes* 2.2.20): "If you want to be crucified, wait, and the cross will come," and compare also Cicero's attack on the Stoic thesis that pain is not really an evil (*de Finibus* 5.84): "Anyone who is put on a cross cannot be happy" (both cited from Hengel, *The Cross of the Son of God,* tr. J. Bowden [London: SCM, 1986] 159).

There seems to be no good reason for denying to Jesus the main core of Mark 8:34. It has the same character as other vivid and powerful, but less than precise, images by which Jesus' speech is marked. Luke may reflect the original thrust of Jesus' words when he sets his second version of this saying (14:27) alongside the call for hatred of family and even of self (v 26). As with other of Jesus' dramatic statements he would not have wanted this one to be taken in an unqualified manner. He would have wanted it to capture the attention and fire the imagination!

The saying in v 24 (= Mark 8:35) has been preserved in a number of forms in the Gospel tradition. It is also paired with versions of the saying in v 23 in Matt 10:38–39 (and cf. Luke 14:26–27 where "his own soul" in v 26 may betray the influence of a form of the 9:24 saying [as Schürmann, 544]). John 12:24–25 is also suggestive of the same combination. Luke also uses a form of the saying in 17:33.

Both Matt 10:39 (Laufen, *Doppelüberlieferung*, 322–25; Lambrecht, "Q-influence," 283–85) and Mark 8:35 (Schürmann, 545; Dautzenberg, *Sein Leben bewahren*, 60–66) have been defended as reflecting the more original form of the saying. The arguments are not decisive. In the Markan form the "he will save" is easily understood as a development making use of the Christian vocabulary of salvation, but "wishes to save" stands in the way of this explanation. The Matthean form may have resulted from the tension with the normal Christian use of salvation language observed in the second half ot the Markan form, but the more enigmatic nature of the Matthean form with its use of the language of finding and losing could be a pointer to its greater originality (but could we be dealing there with an idiom for "making it" in life?). Finding and losing form an easier antithesis than saving and losing, until we realize that the Markan form assumes a situation in which the possession of life is under threat. The loss of this context could have produced a shift to a "better" antithesis. The Johannine form relates more easily to the Matthean, but this tells us little about original forms. The sense of a critical situation that attaches to the Markan form finally inclines me to favor it as the more original.

Mark's "and the gospel's" is not found in any other form of the saying, and is likely to be a Markan development. His "for my sake" is not found in Luke 17:33, where it would not suit the context, or in the Johannine form. It may or may not have been part of the original, but it is at least an accurate gloss, pointing to the fact that we have here, not a timeless paradox of wisdom, but a challenge to respond to the situation created by the presence of the ministry of Jesus.

The historicity of this saying of Jesus is not normally questioned, but there is some measure of parallel to it in *b. Tamid* 32a; *The Sentences of the Syriac Menander*, lines 314–19 (and cf. *b. Ber.* 63b; 1Q27 1.3–4; *1 Enoch* 48:7; Epictetus 4.1.165), and this has occasionally brought suspicion on the saying (e.g., Braun, *Spätjüdisch-häretischer und früh christlicher Radikalismus*, BHT 24 [Tübingen: Mohr, 1957] 2:104 n. 5, 2:136 n. 1). There is a measure of genuine similarity, but it requires an unwarranted skepticism to turn this into dependence.

Luke continues to follow his Markan source for v 25 (= Mark 8:36), though he does not reproduce v 37, which in Mark forms a unit with it. The general form of the questions is akin to that of Jewish wisdom material (cf. esp. Eccl 1:3), but the specific link of the material is with Ps 49 (see Dautzenberg, *Sein Leben bewahren*, 69, 71–75). The link with Ps 49 is no guarantee that the sayings go back to the historical Jesus, but it does demonstrate that Bultmann (*Synoptic Tradition*, 97, 102) is wrong to separate the sayings and trace them to secular proverbs that have been made into Dominical sayings. There is no sufficient reason for denying the sayings to the historical Jesus.

V 26 continues the sequence of Markan verses (= Mark 8:37). A second form of this saying is known to Matthew (10:33) and Luke (12:9). This second form uses the language of denial rather than that of being ashamed, and it occurs in conjunction with a positive counterpart that uses the language of confession of Jesus. There is general agreement that the juxtaposition of positive and negative forms has been abbreviated to the negative half in the Markan form. Mark's "and of my words" is also regularly treated as a secondary Markan development (cf.

Mark 8:35; 10:29), as is "his Father" with its unparalleled idiom: "Father of the Son of Man," which seems quite un-Jewish. Kümmel ("Verhalten Jesus") stands against the consensus that the Markan form is secondary at every other point of difference as well, by maintaining the originality of the language of shame and the reference to the coming of the Son of Man with the holy angels. He argues persuasively that it is easier to explain, in a persecution context, a change from the less precise language of shame to the more precise language of denial, than it is to explain the opposite development (but note the explanation offered by Lambrecht ["Q-Influence," 286] that Mark is avoiding the language of denial, which has been used in another way in v 34). He cannot, however, explain the loss of reference to the coming of the Son of Man in the alternative form. Lambrecht (285–87; also Schürmann, 549–50) explains all the differences as the immediate product of Markan redaction, in terms that are generally persuasive. Note particularly the Markan interest in Jesus' future connection with glory (10:37; 13:26), the way that the mention of "his Father" prepares for the transfiguration declaration of sonship, and the way that the coming of the Son of Man echoes Mark 13:26–27. Some of the differences could equally be pre-Markan, as is often maintained.

With the exception of Matt 10:33, each of the forms of the saying either has a first person reference in the first clause, which gives way to a Son of Man reference in the second clause (Mark 8:34; Luke 9:26), or it betrays by its context that such was the original reading of its source (Matt 16:27; Luke 12:9—here the former only retains the second clause, while the latter has the me/Son of Man pattern in the positive form in 12:8, which probably gives way to a passive construction in v 9 to smooth the transition to v 10, which uses a passive construction). Because, however, there is a general tendency in the tradition to add Son of Man references (J. Jeremias, "Die älteste Schicht der Menschensohn-Logien," *ZNW* 58 [1967] 159–72), C. Colpe (*TDNT* 8:442; "Der Begriff 'Menschensohn' und die Methode der Erforschung messianischer Prototypen," *Kairos* 11 [1969] 241–63; 12 [1970] 81–122; 13 [1971] 1–17; 14 [1972] 241–57, here vol. 13, pp. 6–8) insists on an original form without Son of Man, finally settling on a form closely related to the Matt 10:33 wording (but with "before the angels"; in *TDNT* the form was developed out of Luke 12:8–9, but with "men" for Son of Man in v 8, and accepting the switch to the passive in v 9).

It seems, however, that Colpe does not reckon adequately with the oddness of a change that moves from a form in which there is personal reference to Jesus in both clauses to a Son of Man form, but introduces Son of Man in only one half of each statement (Kümmel, "Verhalten Jesus," 215, makes a similar point in connection with a discussion of Matt 19:28). Further, McDermott (*RB* 84 [1977] 531–32, 533–36) successfully identifies redactional reasons why Matthew might here have gone against his normal trend, and deleted a Son of Man reference in 10:33 (McDermott argues, further, that where Matthew produces a me/Son of Man sequence in 19:28, his basis for comfort with the juxtaposition is precisely his awareness of this juxtaposition in his source for 10:32–33). It is best, then, with most scholars, to take as original a form that moves from a personal reference to Jesus in the first clause to a Son of Man form in the second clause.

It is hotly disputed whether such a saying could go back to the historical Jesus. On the assumption that the saying assumes confession before legal authorities, it has attracted suspicion because such only became the situation for the disciples at a later date (Vielhauer, "Gottesreich," 78–80). It is, however, doubtful whether we have a straightforward court setting for either the scene in heaven or the scene on earth (see McDermott, *RB* 84 [1977] 530–31, who is interested in the scene on earth). Käsemann ("Sentences of Holy Law in the New Testament," in *New Testament Questions of Today*, NTL, tr. W. J. Montague [London: SCM, 1969] 66–81, here 77) has relegated this text to the prophetic community's activity, as one of its "sentences of Holy Law." But this category is not without difficulties (see esp. K. Berger, "Zu den sogenannten Sätzen heiligen Rechts," *NTS* 17 [1970–71] 10–40), and in any case our text has such unique features that it defies classification (McDermott, *RB* 84 [1977] 532–33).

Quite commonly the text is rescued, on the basis that Jesus makes a clear distinction between himself and the future Son of Man, as the one future Son of Man text to actually go back to the historical Jesus (following Bultmann, *Synoptic Tradition*, 128). In light of the preceding Son of Man excursus, an ambiguity of reference here is to be accepted. But of course, an ambiguity is quite different from a clear reference to another figure. The clear distinction view depends too heavily upon an apocalyptic Son of Man expectation, for which we have seen (excursus above) there is inadequate evidence. Via such an understanding of Son of Man, this view also fails to do justice to the degree of ultimacy attributed by Jesus to his own ministry (Luke 6:47; 7:23; 10:23–24; 11:20; 17:21; etc.): in no sense can he be viewed as seeing himself as only a preliminary figure, whose significance will give way to the ultimacy of the Son of Man at his appearance. The present text contains its own warning against this, in the way that the Son of Man, whoever he is, simply has the role of authenticating the ultimate significance that response to Jesus already has. Nonetheless, much of the weight of the argument for authenticity based on the distinction between Jesus and the Son of Man can still be appealed to on the view that Jesus here speaks in an ambiguous and mysterious manner. This is not how the early church will speak!

A final view to be considered is that the saying reflects a stage of development in the early church in which a distinction is being drawn between Jesus' historical ministry and his future role as the Son of Man (see P. Hoffmann, *Logienquelle*, 142–58). The background understanding of Son of Man in relation to which this view is formulated has been criticized above. This view must also push all the present Son of Man texts to a yet later date. The view and the subsequent discussion have suggested such a complexity of development and a plurality of streams of thought as to undermine the thesis involved (cf. McDermott, *RB* 84 [1977] 526–27).

We may, then, with some confidence trace back to the historical Jesus a form of the saying close to that in Matt 10:32–33, but with Son of Man in each second clause and with "before the angels," and just possibly with the language of shame rather than that of denial. Here Jesus affirms the ultimate significance of response to his ministry and opens up a place for speculation about his relationship with the man of destiny who will endorse in heaven the significance of the responses made to Jesus upon earth.

Once again in v 27, Luke reproduces his Markan source (= Mark 9:1), but with a number of significant changes, none of which, however, point to any second source. The origin of the Markan verse has been quite variously evaluated. Quite common is the view that it is a Markan creation, dependent on 8:38 and 13:26–27,

30 (J. Lambrecht, *Die Redaktion der Markus-Apokalypse: Literarische Analyse und Strukturuntersuchung*, AnBib 28 [Rome: Pontifical Biblical Institute, 1967] 202–11, affirms the link with Mark 13:30, but considers that Mark 13:30 is actually based on 9:1; Schürmann, 549–50, sees, additionally, an influence from the Dominical logion on which Matt 10:23 is based). Unique features of the verse, however, make it more likely that Mark depends here on a traditional saying (note esp. οὐ μή γεύσονται θανάτου, "they will certainly not taste death," and possibly ὧδε τῶν ἑστηκότων, "those standing here"). See the careful discussion of Chilton, *God in Strength*, 251–74 (whose conclusions, however, about the original sense of the pericope do not flow from his source analysis, and are not to be followed), who identifies καὶ ἔλεγεν αὐτοῖς, "and he said to them," ὅτι, indicating direct speech, τινες ὧδε, "certain ones here," and ἐληλυθυῖαν, "having come," as the Markan contribution, with some Markan influence on the syntax of τῶν ἑστηκότων, "of the ones standing." While these judgments are more precise than I would consider fully defensible, they do satisfactorily identify the shape of the pre-Markan logion, with two exceptions. Chilton's case for the inclusion of ἴδωσιν, "see," does not persuade: if the Markan link is with the transfiguration, then this is precisely one of those "sporadic glimpses at the true nature of Jesus" that, Chilton reports W. H. Kelber as suggesting, are referred to with this verb in Markan locution; this verb could be Markan. Chilton's case for the deletion of ἐληλυθυῖαν, "having come," is also weak, based as it is on taking the use of this verb in Mark 9:13 as referring to the transfiguration.

Detached from its present context, it is difficult to be sure of the pre-Markan sense of this verse. It seems to speak of an experience that, it is anticipated, will overtake people who are at present quite unaware, and who are not here being informed. It uses a time frame that is not immediate (contrast Luke 17:21) but is restricted to the present generation (as Mark 13:30). There is a domestically intimate note to the text, which separates it from apocalyptic texts to which it is otherwise closely related. This is a verse that could easily have been taken by the disciple band as intimating that the power of Rome would be broken in the lifetime of their contemporaries. Equally, it could be connected with a prophetic anticipation of God's judgment in history upon his people (contrast 2 Kgs 20:16–19; and cf. Luke 11:50). The verse may anticipate some powerful authentication of Jesus' ministry, but without being more precise about the nature of that authentication. There may be an implied contrast with the nature of the presence of the kingdom of God in Jesus' own ministry (cf. Mark 4:30–32).

The very difficulty of giving precision to the sense of the pre-Markan saying is a good indication that this is no early church creation.

Comment

Jesus announces a suffering fate not only for himself, but also as a necessary condition of discipleship for those who would be his followers. Vv 23–27 are to be read closely with vv 21–22; vv 24–27 provide a degree of explanation for the harsh demand of v 23.

23 Luke deletes Mark's mention of the drawing in of the crowd: he may have been sensitive to the problem of the presence of a crowd after the solitude of v 18, or his concern may be rather to draw more tightly together the passion prediction and the call to cross bearing. Luke's "all" still performs the function of the Markan crowd: it assures the reader that this is a general call for discipleship and not one that should be restricted to leaders or any group of special Christians. Mark's aorist εἶπεν, "said," becomes ἔλεγεν, "was saying": Luke is prone to adding the imperfect form of this verb. Luke softens the difficulty of Mark's form of the saying in which *following* apparently becomes a condition for *following* by using a different verb the first time. Luke reduces Mark's compound verb for "let him deny" to the simple form (more often the change is in the other direction, but both kinds of change are evident). Luke adds καθ' ἡμέραν, "daily," to indicate that the call is to an ever renewed state of affairs; it is not a call to a one-time-only decision or a response only to some unique situation.

Taking up the cross refers to the Roman custom of requiring the condemned criminal to carry to the place of execution the cross-bar to be used in the execution (cf. Plutarch, *de sera num. vind.* 9.554b: "Every criminal who is executed carries his own cross"; for further references see Schelkle, *Passion Jesu*, 218–19).

In *Form/Structure/Setting* above, a brief original form of this saying is discussed whose sense might be represented by "If you wish to be my disciple, you must put your head on the chopping block." Jesus' call was to a radical denial of self-interest and concern for one's own natural well-being. Jesus certainly anticipated that identification with himself would work itself out, on occasion, in social ostracism, persecution, and even martyrdom, and the disciple should be ready to meet this set of life-destroying responses head on. The call to "put the rope around one's neck" stands on a par with that to hate one's own family. The "let him deny himself" may be an early explanation, or it may come from the merging of two originally distinct sayings of Jesus (cf. Schulz, *Nachfolgen*, 84; despite all the psychological damage and narrowing of life that has been produced through a [mis]application of this saying, there is no good reason for positing with Schwarz, *NTS* 33 [1987] 257–59, a mistranslation of an Aramaic term, which should have been rendered "let him know [himself]").

In light of Jesus' own passion, at the very least a fresh poignancy and challenge is added to this Dominical saying, and the saying becomes clearly oriented to Jesus' own experience of rejection and death (thus the present link to the passion prediction). Now the call to be a disciple becomes a call to follow Jesus in the way of the cross. Now "to follow him" is not just a Jewish way of talking about being a disciple of a master, but a challenge to have one's whole existence determined by and patterned after a crucified messiah. Now the double reference to following gains its sense: to follow him (i.e., be his disciple) involves following him in the path to death that he chose (this is better than with Fridrichsen, *ConNT* 2 [1936] 1–8; Schulz, *Nachfolgen*, 83, to deny imperatival force to the final verb). One is now called to share in the fate of Jesus.

It is likely that in Mark we should understand that the metaphorical taking up of the cross should have led on naturally to the disciples' sharing with Jesus his fate in Jerusalem, something for which they were not yet ready. This perspective is no longer as evident in the rendering of Luke, who focuses the saying with his added "daily" as identifying a principle of Christian life, to be freshly appropriated each day. This may have the effect of weakening somewhat the degree of orientation to Jesus' own passion, but the closer connection that Luke achieves between vv 21–22 and vv 23–27 and the "daily" fact of continuing to head toward

Jerusalem, which will mark the Gospel account from 9:51 onwards, more than counterbalance the loss of precision caused by the addition. Luke has certanly not reduced the demand to an inner spiritual condition: in view is a practical denial of the claims of the inner drive to self-preservation and care for one's own interests, and a readiness for the loss of one's life.

24 Luke drops Mark's "and the gospel": this looks Markan, and is not in Luke's other form of the saying. He adds an emphatic *οὗτος*, "this one," to the final clause.

In attempting to understand Jesus' original formulation of the saying, Bauer ("Wer sein Leben retten will") suggests that we should liken it to the exhortation of a field commander who cautions his troops to recognize that the one who turns his back to run for his life is the one who gets killed in battle, while the one who stands his ground and faces the danger head on lives to tell the tale (cf. Xenophon, *Anabasis* 3.1.43). Despite obvious attractions, this view does no justice to the real loss of which Jesus speaks.

Dautzenberg (*Sein Leben bewahren,* 57) and Schürmann (543) suggest a context in which external threat to Jesus and his disciple band calls forth a challenge to be ready for martyrdom. This may indeed be correct, given the sense of threat to life that lies behind the fashioning of the antitheses. We should also, however, consider the possibility that the threat to life is not from outside, but is represented by the very challenge of Jesus' teaching itself (Beardslee [*JAAR* 47 (1979) 67] speaks helpfully of the "saying [as] extremely revealing of the interweaving of self-concern and self-transcendence which has characterized Christian existence from the beginning"). In each case the threat reaches to the very fabric of life itself and may embrace martyrdom. In each case the challenge is to be true to Jesus and to his proclamation of the kingdom of God.

ψυχή is not "the soul" as would be possible in Greek thought, but rather "life" (as in 6:9). For Luke, as for Jesus, life is not bounded by death, because there are resurrection and judgment beyond (cf. Matt 10:28). At the same time, the paradox of the verse is not to be resolved by a simple contrasting of this life and life beyond the grave (as Laufen, *Doppelüberlieferung,* 328–29). E. Schweizer (*TDNT* 9:642) catches something of the thrust with his comment "Jesus is thus telling man that he will achieve full life only when he no longer clings to it but finds it in loss or sacrifice." Grundmann (*Markus,* 228) says, "The one who trusts God, who gives life and saves through death, gains for his life freedom and eternity."

The rest of the verses of this section all link back to v 23 via a series of *γάρ,* "for," clauses. Here, wishing to save one's life is the opposite of taking up one's cross. The verse assumes a situation in which the possession of life is under threat. In the immediate literary context the threat is the call to cross-bearing. In normal circumstances it is commendable to save life (6:9), but here a choice of fundamental loyalty ("for my sake") is involved, which takes us beyond expediency. In light of v 26 to come, to seek to save one's life is likely to take the form of refusing to be identified with Jesus under the harsh glare of the spotlight of the world's scrutiny (cf. George, *BVC* 83 [1968] 16).

25 Luke retains most of Mark's vocabulary, but entirely changes the syntax: the impersonal construction *ὠφελεῖ*, "it profits/benefits," is replaced by the passive *ὠφελεῖται*, "is benefited"; participles replace Mark's infinitives in the continuation of the verse; *ἑαυτόν*, "himself," replaces *τὴν ψυχὴν αὐτοῦ*, "his life/soul" (the use of "life" has become quite complex in v 24, so the change of terms here makes it quite clear that the link is to the first and not the second reference to loss of life in v 24); to express the loss, Luke adds a second alternative verb, ἀπολέσας, "having lost" (this creates an immediate link with v 24). Luke does not reproduce Mark 8:37, the closely linked verse that follows in the Markan text. This helps to draw v 25 more immediately into the judgment/answerability framework of v 26 to come. (Matthew is almost as severe in his reformulation, but shares with Luke only the first of the listed changes [and there, Matthew uses a different tense]).

Dautzenberg (*Sein Leben bewahren*, 71–75) has shown that the original unit here, Mark 8:36–37, is to be read in connection with Ps 49 and, thus, is to be understood in terms of a critique of the pursuit of, and confidence in, riches. With the loss of v 37, the connection is no longer as clear, but this understanding fits so appropriately into Luke's interest elsewhere in the snare of riches (see at 6:20, 24) that we may assume that Luke does still have the connection in mind. The Psalm connection also encourages the setting of the loss of self into the context of death, understood in connection with God's judgment (cf. Luke 12:16–21; 16:19–31). To the one who has been secure in his riches, death is a loss of self. A totally different face of death has already surfaced in v 24.

The imagery of gain and loss is from the world of commercial transactions: the true measure of one's situation is determined when the gains and losses have been reckoned. To make the point, the entries on each side of the ledger in this case are taken to the absolute extremes. Wealth creates the illusion of security in life, but the horizon of death reveals the illusionary nature of this security.

Once again this verse is linked to the preceding by γάρ, "for." Jesus' call to "put the rope around one's own neck" becomes intelligible both as to its content and as to its good sense from the explanatory clauses in vv 24–26. Looking to one's own well-being and security in the world turns out not to be so important after all. Jesus' call to self-denial leads to life; the accumulation of the good things of this world cannot secure us against its loss.

There is no basis for finding (with Schürmann, 546–47) a distinction between ἀπολέσας, "having lost/ruined," and ζημιωθείς, "having forfeited/suffered loss," as referring, respectively, to condemnation and to suffering loss but being ultimately saved. Luke has simply added the synonym to make the link to v 24 explicit.

26 Luke changes his Markan source little: he drops Mark's "in this adulterous and sinful generation," compensating, perhaps, with his addition of an emphatic resumptive "this"; "the glory" is now the Son of Man's as well (cf. 24:26), and not just that "of the Father" (Luke has "the Father" and not Mark's "his Father"; he may be conscious of the difficulty of the idiom "Father of the Son of Man," or he may simply feel he has used Mark's "his" already in "his glory"); the angels do not now accompany the Son of Man (cf. the change from Mark 13:27), rather they, as the Father does, contribute their glory to his coming.

The warning here is against being so influenced by an environment that is hostile to Jesus and what he stands for (Luke deletes Mark's delineation of this environment in order to generalize and to allow the reader to supply for himself his own version of the environmental pressure; the language of shame ensures that we will think in terms of pressure created by others around us) that one shrinks from being identified with him or his teaching (cf. 22:54–62 for Peter as case in point, but Peter moves on from this failure). Induced by whatever crisis, such a disowning of Jesus will have its counterpart at the time of final crisis, when the Man of destiny comes in his glory. Such a figure of glory cannot identify himself with any who have failed to stand for the Jesus who goes to suffering and rejection, and who calls his followers also to place their necks in the noose. The glorious figure will be as embarrassed then by the claim to be linked as ever the erstwhile follower of Jesus could be in face of his human environment (cf. Rom 1:16; 2 Tim 1:8; 2:12).

Luke assumes an identity between Jesus and the Son of Man but preserves the ambiguity of Jesus' reference to this mysterious figure of authority and dignity (see excursus above and *Form/Structure/Setting*). A unique sense of self-importance for Jesus is reflected in the way that identification with his person and teaching is seen as eschatologically decisive. No precise future role is predicated here of the Son of Man. It is enough that as a figure of glory, indeed as the bearer of the glory of God and of the heavenly realm (the glory of the angels), he will be the figure of supreme dignity whose goodwill will be all important (cf. the importance of "glory" in Mark 10:35–37). In 21:27–28, 36, the Son of Man comes in glory as the bringer of redemption: to have made it through the crisis of the end period, to stand before the Son of man, is to have reached final deliverance. In terms of source, that the Son of Man "comes" is almost certainly to be linked back to Dan 7:13. But while Mark was probably aware of, if not responsible for, this development (see *Form/Structure/Setting* above), Luke simply followed his Markan source, and, since "comes" is a very narrow basis on which to build a link with Dan 7:13, we should probably not make any appeal to Dan 7:13 for the Lukan text at this point (there is, similarly no Dan 7:13 link for the more original form of the pericope reflected in Luke 12:8–9).

As with vv 24 and 25 this verse is linked back to v 23 with *γάρ*, "for." This final verse in the list indicates the final outcome of failing to take up one's cross and follow Jesus.

27 Luke omits Mark's linking "and he said to them," and so makes the link to the preceding closer; "amen" is the one Hebrew word that Luke at times retains (see at 4:24), but here it becomes its translation equivalent "truly"; the awkwardly placed *ὧδε*, "here," is relocated between the participle and its definite article and becomes the alternative *αὐτοῦ* (more often "there," but now "here" [as in Matt 26:36]); the whole phrase "having come in power" is deleted; other minor changes are also made.

For Mark already 8:38 and 9:1 point to the events outlined in Mark 13 (note on v 26 the linking of *δύναμις*, "power," of 9:1 and the *δόξα*, "glory," of 8:38), but with an anticipation in the transfiguration ("glory," "Father"/"Son," and "seeing" are all taken up there). Luke accepts this basic sense (note his inclusion of kingdom language in 21:31 [in connection with the language of seeing] and its link via v 28 to the Son of Man language of v 27 [note the similar Lukan linking of kingdom of God and the language of seeing in 13:28]; the language of seeing the kingdom of God may be related to the reference in 19:11 to the kingdom of God as about to appear [*ἀναφαίνεσθαι*]; Luke adds to the transfiguration account a reference to "his glory," which is also a distinctive of his rendering of v 26). The deletion of "having come in power" may be to facilitate the double reference. It is just possible that it also opens up a wider reference for "see[ing] the kingdom of God," but this is far from certain. For discussion of the kingdom of God, see at 4:43; 10:9; 11:2, 20; 17:21; 19:11.

(Not unattractive is Schürmann's view [550–51] that the reference is to the fact that some of the crowd, who at present remain outside the circle of discipleship, will respond to the early church preaching after the decisive Easter events. However, the contrast that Schürmann needs would be better supplied if there was in fact a rejecting crowd, but, when he has a crowd, Luke has a very positive crowd, and he probably does not have a crowd here at all.)

The link of v 27 to the set of linked vv 23–26 would seem to be that the time of full realization of the gains and losses flowing from the choices made in life under the challenge of Jesus is not in some remote uncertain future, but is within a single life span. Those who are not called upon to give up their lives for the sake of Jesus may even expect to live to see it. The difficulties that this creates for later generations, and perhaps even for Luke's own generation, will be discussed at chap. 21.

Explanation

What Jesus had announced for himself in vv 21–22 is not for him alone. Despite all the horrors of the prospect, the disciple too must secure his future by repeating in his own life the radical commitment that took Jesus to his death in Jerusalem.

The verses make separate but related points and were probably originally quite independent in the teaching of Jesus. Linked together they are now able mutually to interpret one another. After the passion of Jesus became a historical reality, these words of challenge would have gained fresh poignancy and challenge, and a clear focus on Jesus' own path of suffering. At various points the historicity of these verses has been challenged, but we may with some confidence trace the core of each of these sayings back to the historical Jesus.

The challenge of these verse is to all, and not to some rank of special saints or of Christian leaders. The one who would be a disciple of Jesus (as one might have become a disciple of a rabbi in Jesus' day) is called to a radical denial of self-interest and concern for his or her own natural well-being. Jesus anticipated that loyalty to himself would at times provoke a whole set of life-destroying processes (ostracism, persecution, martyrdom). The disciple needs to be ready to meet these head on; he is, as it were, to place his neck on the chopping block, or to put the rope around his own neck. (The image is from the Roman practice of having condemned criminals carry the cross-bar for their execution to the execution site.) This is rather like his talk of the need to hate one's own family (14:26). Such a radical commitment is not one that is called for only in some crisis situation, but one that needs to be renewed daily, and one that needs to undergird all that happens in our daily lives. The call is to a practical denial of our natural inner drive to self-preservation and care for our own interests. Only this is a following of Jesus to the cross.

V 24 opens up for us something of the inner logic of Jesus' call. Clinging onto life is not the way to achieve full life. Life is bounded neither by material well-being, nor by death, though it is easy to approach life as if it were bounded by both. The disciple's life is under threat from the challenge of Jesus' call to give up the security of a bounded view of that life. His life may also be quite literally under threat. It is a matter of faith to nail our colors to the mast, and to be ready for any loss for Jesus. This is the way to life. Loyalty to Jesus takes us beyond expediency and on into risk.

The imagery of v 25 is from the world of commercial transactions: we reckon up our gains and losses to determine our true situation. The background in Ps 49 shows that the focus here is on wealth as worldly security. Wealth creates the illusion of security in life, but in the face of death the illusory nature of this security becomes clear (cf. 12:16–21; 16:19–31). Death represents a total loss of the self to the one whose identity and security have been in his possessions. V 24 has already offered us a very different face for death. Where Jesus' call to self-denial leads to life, the accumulation of the good things of life cannot secure us against the loss of our lives.

If material goods can be a trap, so can the opinion of others. We all want the approval of others. In an environment that is normally hostile, incredulous, or bored in connection with Jesus, the pressure is to disown such an embarrassing connection. Peter found himself in just such a situation (22:54–62), and for a time he fell foul of its temptations. But disowning Jesus means being disowned by him, when he appears as the glorious Son of Man. Such a figure of glory cannot identify himself with those who have failed to make their stand for the Jesus who goes to suffering and rejection. Here we meet the final outcome of following or not following Jesus.

Seeing the kingdom of God points ultimately to the sequence of events delineated in chap. 23, but there may be a range of preliminary intimations of that final seeing, the first of which is about to come in the transfiguration account. The encouragement is that, for the disciple seeking to follow Jesus' in the way of the cross, the reaping of its ultimate benefits is not remote but within the scope of a human lifetime.

A Foretaste of Jesus' Future Glory (9:28–36)

Bibliography

Arvedson, T. *Das Mysterium Christi.* Uppsala/Leipzig: Lundquist/Lorentz, 1937. 126–32. **Bacon, B. W.** "The Transfiguration Story." *AJT* 6 (1902) 236–65. ———. "After Six Days." *HTR* 8 (1915) 94–121. **Badcock, F. J.** "The Transfiguration." *JTS* 22 (1920–21) 321–26. **Baltensweiler, H.** *Die Verklärung Jesu: Historisches Ereignis und synoptische Berichte.* ATANT 33. Zürich: Zwingli, 1959. **Bernadin, J. B.** "The Transfiguration." *JBL* 52 (1933) 181–89. **Best, T. F.** "The Transfiguration: A Select Bibliography. *JETS* 24 (1981) 157–61. **Blinzler, J.** *Die neutestamentlichen Berichte über die Verklärung.* NTAbh 17/4 Münster in W.: Aschendorff, 1937. **Boobyer, G. H.** *St. Mark and the Transfiguration Story.* Edinburgh: T. & T. Clarke, 1942. ———. "St. Mark and the Transfiguration." *JTS* 41 (1940) 119–20. **Bradley, W. P.** "The Transfiguration—Credential or Answer?" *CrQ* 12 (1935) 57–76. **Büchele, A.** *Der Tod Jesu im Lukasevangelium.* 139–45. **Caird, G. B.** "Expository Problems: The Transfiguration." *ExpTim* 67 (1956) 291–94. **Carlston, C. E.** "Transfiguration and Resurrection." *JBL* 80 (1961) 233–40. **Chilton, B.** "The Transfiguration: Dominical Assurance and Apostolic Vision." *NTS* 27 (1980) 115–24. **Coune, M.** "La Transfiguration dans l'exégèse des sept premiers siècles." *AsSeign* 28 (1962) 64–80. ———. "L'Évangile de la transfiguration." *Parlit*

52 (1970) 157–70. ———. "Radieuse Transfiguration, Mt 17,1–9; Mc 9,2–10; Lc 9,29–36." *AsSeign* 28 (1973) 44–84. ———. "Saint Luc et le mystère de la Transfiguration." *NRT* 108 (1986) 3–12. **Currie, S. D.** "Isaiah 63:9 and the Transfiguration in Mark." *ASB* 82 (1966) 7–34. **Dabeck, P.** "'Siehe, es erschienen Moses und Elia.' (Mt 17,3)." *Bib* 23 (1942) 175–89. **Dabrowski, E.** *La transfiguration de Jésus.* Scripta pontificii instituti biblica 85. Rome: Biblical Institute, 1939. **Davies, J. G.** "The Prefiguration of the Ascension in the Third Gospel." *JTS* 6 (1955) 229–33. **Denis, A.-M.** "Une théologie de la Rédemption: La Transfiguration chez Saint Mark." *VSpir* 41 (1959) 136–49. **Derrett, J. D. M.** "Peter and the Tabernacles (Mark 9, 5–7)." *DR* 108 (1990) 37–48. **Dietrich, W.** *Das Petrusbild der lukanischen Schriften.* 104–15. **Dignath, W.** "Die Verklärung Jesu." In *Taufe—Versuchung—Verklärung.* Gütersloh: Gütersloher/Mohn, 1966. 55–80. **Evely, L.** *The Gospels without Myth.* Tr. J. F. Bernard. New York: Doubleday, 1971. 99–114. **Feldkämper, L.** *Der betende Jesus.* 125–50. **Feuillet, A.** "Les perspectives propres à chaque évangéliste dans les récits de la transfiguration." *Bib* 39 (1958) 281–301. ———. "'L'exode' de Jésus et le déroulement du mystère rédempteur d'après S. Luc et S. Jean." *RevThom* 77 (1977) 181–206, esp. 181–92. **Fuchs, A.** "Die Verklärung des Markus-Evangeliums in der Sicht moderner Exegese." *TPQ* 125 (1977) 29–37. **Garrett, S. R.** "Exodus from Bondage: Luke 9:31 and Acts 12:1–24." *CBQ* 52 (1990) 656–80. **George, A.** "La transfiguration (Lc 9,28–36)." *BVC* 33 (1960) 21–25. **Gerber, M.** "Die Metamorphose Jesu, Mark. 9,2f. par." *TZ* 23 (1967) 385–95. **Groves, W. L.** "The Significance of the Transfiguration of Our Lord." *Theology* 11 (1925) 86–92. **Hall, S.** "Synoptic Transfigurations: Mark 9,2–10 and Partners." *KTR* 10 (1987) 41–44. **Hirsch, S.** "Taufe, Versuchung und Verklärung Jesu." *RWS* 1 (1932) 5–98. **Höller, J.** *Die Verklärung Jesu: Eine Auslegung der neutestamentlichen Berichte.* Freiburg: Herder, 1937. **Holzmeister, U.** "Einzeluntersuchungen über das Geheimnis der Verklärung Christi." *Bib* 21 (1940) 200–210. **Hooker, M. D.** "'What Doest Thou Here, Elijah?' A Look at St Mark's Account of the Transfiguration." In *The Glory of Christ in the New Testament: Studies in Christology.* FS G. B. Caird, ed. L. D. Hurst and N. T. Wright. Oxford: Clarendon, 1987, 59–70. **Johnson, S. L., Jr.** "The Transfiguration of Christ." *BSac* 124 (1967) 133–43. **Kayama, H.** "The Doxa of Moses and Jesus (2 Cor. 3: 7–18 and Luke 9: 28–32)." *BulCRIMGU* 23 (1990) 23–48. **Kee, H. C.** "The Transfiguration in Mark: Epiphany or Apocalyptic Vision?" In *Understanding the Sacred Text,* ed. J. Reumann. Valley Forge: Judson, 1972. 137–52. **Kenney, A.** "The Transfiguration and the Agony in the Garden." *CBQ* 19 (1957) 444–52. **Léon-Dufour, X.** *Études d'évangile.* 83–122. **Liefeld, W. L.** "Theological Motifs in the Transfiguration Narrative." In *New Dimensions in New Testament Study,* ed. R. N. Longenecker and M. C. Tenney. Grand Rapids: Zondervan, 1974. 162–79. **Lohmeyer, E.** "Die Verklärung Jesu nach dem Markus-Evangelium." *ZNW* 21 (1922) 185–215. **Mánek, J.** "The New Exodus in the Books of Luke." *NovT* 2 (1958) 8–23. **Masson, C.** "La transfiguration de Jésus (Marc 9,2–13)." *RTP* 3/14 (1964) 1–14. **Mauser, U. W.** *Christ in the Wilderness: The Wilderness Theme in the Second Gospel and Its Basis in the Biblical Tradition.* SBT 39. London: SCM, 1963. 110–19. **McCurley, F., Jr.** "'And after Six Days' (Mark 9:2): A Semitic Literary Device." *JBL* 93 (1974) 67–81. **McGuckin, J. A.** *The Transfiguration of Christ in Scripture and Tradition.* Studies in the Bible and Early Christianity 9. Lewiston, NY: Mellen, 1986. ———. "Jesus Transfigured: A Question of Christology." *ClerRev* 69 (1984) 271–79. **Moulton, W. J.** "The Significance of the Transfiguration." In *Biblical and Semitic Studies.* New York: Scribner's, 1901. 159–210. **Müller, H. P.** "Die Verklärung Jesu: Eine motivgeschichtliche Studie." *ZNW* 51 (1960) 56–64. **Müller, U. B.** "Die christologische Absicht des Markusevangeliums und die Verklärungsgeschichte." *ZNW* 64 (1973) 159–93. **Murphy-O'Connor, J.** "What Really Happened at the Transfiguration?" *BRev* 3 (1987) 8–21. **Neirynck, F.** "Minor Agreements Matthew-Luke in the Transfiguration Story." In *Orientierund an Jesus: Zur Theologie der Synoptiker.* FS J. Schmid, ed. P. Hoffmann et al. Freiburg: Herder, 1973. 253–66. **Niemand, C.** *Studien zu den Minor Agreements der synoptischen Verklärungsperikopen: Eine Untersuchung der literarkritischen Relevanz der gemeinsamen Abweichungen des Matthäus und Lukas von Markus 9,2–10 für die synoptische Frage.* Europäische Hochschulschriften, Reihe 23: Theologie 352. Frankfurt am M./Bern/

New York/Paris: Lang, 1989. **Nützel, J. M.** *Die Verklärungserzählung im Markusevangelium.* FB 6. Würzburg: Echter, 1973. **Pamment, M.** "Moses and Elijah in the Story of the Transfiguration." *ExpTim* 92 (1980–81) 338–39. **Pedersen, S.** "Die Proklamation Jesu als des eschatologischen Offenbarungsträgers (Mt. XVII 1–13)." *NovT* 17 (1975) 341–65. **Ramsey, A. M.** *The Glory of God and the Transfiguration of Christ.* London: Longmans, Green and Co., 1949. **Reid, B. O.** "Voices and Angels: What Were They Talking about at the Transfiguration? A Redaction-Critical Study of Luke 9:28–36." *BR* 34 (1989) 19–31. **Riesenfeld, H.** *Jésus transfiguré: L'Arrière-plan du récit évangélique de la transfiguration de Notre-Seigneur.* ASNU 16. Copenhagen: Munksgaard, 1947. **Ringe, S. H.** "Luke 9:28–36: The Beginning of an Exodus." *Semeia* 28 (1983) 83–99. **Roosen, A.** "'. . . Quand il viendra dans la gloire des saints anges' (Lk 9,26): Réflexions sur le rapport entre transfiguration et parousie dans le troisième évangile." In *La Pâque du Christ.* FS F.-X. Durrwell, ed. M. Benzerath et al. LD 112. Paris: Cerf, 1982. 147–57. **Saabe, M.** "La rédaction du récit de la transfiguration." In *La Venue du Messie: Messianisme et eschatologie.* RechBib 6. Bruges: Desclée de Brouwer, 1962. 65–100. **Schmithals, W.** "Der Markusschluss, die Verklärungsgeschichte und die Aussendung der Zwölf." *ZTK* 69 (1972) 379–411. **Stein, R. H.** "Is the Transfiguration (Mark 9:2–8) a Misplaced Resurrection-Account?" *JBL* 95 (1976) 79–96. **Thrall, M. E.** "Elijah and Moses in Mark's Account of the Transfiguration." *NTS* 16 (1970) 305–17. **Torrance, T.** "The Transfiguration of Jesus." *EvQ* 14 (1942) 214–29. **Trémel, B.** "Des recits apocalyptiques: Baptême et Transfiguration." *LumVie* 23 (1974) 70–83. **Trites, A.** "The Transfiguration in the Theology of Luke: Some Redactional Links." In *The Glory of Christ in the New Testament: Studies in Christology*. FS G. B. Caird, ed. L. D. Hurst and N. T. Wright. Oxford: Clarendon, 1987. 71–81. ———. "The Transfiguration of Jesus: The Gospel in Microcosm." *EvQ* 51 (1979) 67–79. **Voss, G.** *Die Christologie der lukanischen Schriften in Grundzügen.* 160–70. **Weeden, T. J.** *Mark—Traditions in Conflict.* Philadelphia: Fortress, 1971. 118–24. **Williams, W. H.** "The Transfiguration—A New Approach?" *SE* 6 (1973) 635–50. **Yoder, J. D.** "The Exodus of Jerusalem." *EvJ* 4 (1986) 51–69. **Ziesler, J. A.** "The Transfiguration Story and the Markan Soteriology." *ExpTim* 81 (1970) 263–68.

Translation

[28]About a week after these words, it so happened[a] that he went up the mountain to pray, taking along Peter and John and James.[b] [29]As he prayed, the form of his face became different and his clothing turned[c] a dazzling white, [30]and[d] two men talked with him, who were Moses and Elijah, [31]who, having appeared in glory, spoke about his exodus, which he was soon[e] to accomplish in Jerusalem.

[32]Peter and those with him were weighed down with sleep, but they kept awake and saw his glory and the two men who were standing with him. [33]As these[f] were about to depart[g] from them, Peter said to Jesus, "Master,[h] it is good for us to be here. Shall we make three booths, one for you and one for Moses and one for Elijah?" (not knowing what he was saying). [34]As he was still saying these things, a cloud came and enveloped them; and they were afraid as they entered the cloud. [35]Then a voice came out of the cloud saying, "This is my Son, the Chosen one; listen to him!" [36]When the voice had been, Jesus was found to be alone. They were silent and told nobody in those days anything of what they had seen.

Notes

[a] Gr. ἐγένετο; translated elsewhere as "happened/became/transpired, etc."

[b] The Markan order, "James and John," is found in P[45, 75vid] C[3] D L Ξ etc.

[c] The verb here (ἐγένετο) is shared with "the form of his face," in connection with which it is rendered "became."
[d] ἰδοὺ (lit. "behold") is here omitted in translation.
[e] Gr. ἤμελλεν.
[f] Gr. "they."
[g] Representing a present infinitive.
[h] p45 pc have διδάσκαλε, "teacher."

Form/Structure/Setting

Within the section 9:21–50, vv 28–36 provide a preliminary fulfillment of Jesus' promise in v 27, and impress upon the inner disciple band the need to hear Jesus when he outlines his own suffering path to glory and calls others to a life of bearing their crosses and coming after him. Beyond the immediate setting, the structural links for this unit are much more complex.

For the Markan account, Thrall (*NTS* 16 [1970] 310–11) has argued for a link with the resurrection morning account in 16:1–8. Saying nothing (or not knowing what to say) because of fear, seeing Jesus, (not) being here, white garments, and the central place of Peter are motifs that link the accounts (Thrall's sabbath link is not a persuasive handling of Mark's "after six days" [i.e., on the sabbath] and the difficult time expression in 16:2). Luke disturbs some of these links, but he adds two of his own: ἰδοὺ ἄνδρες δύο ("behold, two men") is now found in both accounts; and the shining of garments is expressed using the same root in both accounts (the transfiguration account uses a more intensive form of the verb). Note also the way that Luke in 24:6–8 recalls the passion prediction in a form reminiscent partly of the form this takes prior to the transfiguration and partly of the form that follows after the transfiguration (following the cure of the paralytic on the way down from the mount of transfiguration). Perhaps, for Luke, the point is that just as the transfiguration had confirmed (to little avail) Jesus' words about his journey through suffering and rejection to ultimate restoration, so now the empty tomb and these new supernatural visitors will provide further confirmation in the context of the actual fulfillment of Jesus' words (still to little avail [v 11]!).

Following Mark, but with his own touches, Luke in 9:27 points on to the eschatological events of chap. 21 (see at 9:27), and since he also agrees with Mark's linking of the transfiguration to this promise, it is not surprising that the transfiguration has its own links with chap. 21: "glory" is now connected to the transfigured Jesus (v 32) as well as to the returning Son of Man; the seeing of this glory (v 32) is echoed in the future seeing of the Son of Man; the cloud of Luke 21:27 is not Mark's plural, but the singular cloud of the transfiguration. The ultimate fulfillment of 9:27, to which the transfiguration itself points is the eschatological coming of the Son of Man in glory. The transfiguration reveals Jesus in terms of the ultimate destiny that is his beyond the anticipation of suffering and rejection that are the painful focus of this section.

Not unrelated is yet a further link, this time to the ascension (Acts 1:9–11). The phrase "behold, two men" occurs again (v 10); their garments are as white as Jesus' had become (the whiteness and the shining have been distributed between the figures at the tomb [Luke 24:4] and at the ascension, while both share a common term for garment[s]); the cloud is once again present (v 9). We should note as well the link provided in v 11 between the ascension and the coming of the Son of Man (Luke 21:27). For Luke, Jesus does not only achieve glory on his return as Son of Man. He departs from his disciples to go to enthronement at God's right hand (9:51; 19:12; 24:26; Acts 2:33–35). At the ascension Jesus is not revealed in glory but he is going to glory.

The final important link here is that with the scene of Jesus' prayer about removing the cup, and submission to his Father's will (22:39–46). Kenney (*CBQ* 19 [1957] 444–45) documents the importance of this link already from Mark. These links are not lost on Luke, and though he disturbs some of the Markan links, he forges new links of his own. We should note particularly the motif of prayer that Luke has introduced into the transfiguration narrative (9:28–29) and the problem with sleep, which again Luke has added to the transfiguration narrative (v 32; with his "having stayed awake" [*διαγρηγορήσαντες*] and with the imagery of being heavy with sleep, Luke actually anticipates the Markan rather than his own form of the Gethsemane scene). The shared mountain setting is clearer in Luke's version of the Gethsemane scene. If the verses in 22:43–44 be judged original (I do not consider them so), they provide yet further linkage. The "exodus" to be accomplished in Jerusalem is not specifically a link to the Gethsemane scene, but its presence strengthens the force of the other links.

It is not at once so obvious what Luke is making of this link with the Gethsemane scene. What Jesus prays about there has its own link to Jesus' announcement of his suffering fate, which is the context for the transfiguration. Are we to import the content of his prayer there for the unspecified praying in 9:2–3? By staying awake the disciples did see Jesus' glory, as well as Moses and Elijah; in (Mark's) Gethsemane they quite missed their opportunity. The Father's will that Jesus should suffer emerges forcefully in both contexts. In 9:31 Moses and Elijah help to prepare Jesus for his coming fate; in 22:43–44 (if original) he also receives supernatural assistance as he anticipates the suffering that awaits him. With the baptism narrative added in, this would give three specific points in Luke where the divine guidance of Jesus' life becomes visible as supernatural event.

A case has frequently been made for Luke's use of a second source here (e.g., Schramm, *Markus-Stoff*, 136–39; Dietrich, *Petrusbild*, 105–9). There are some striking agreements between the Matthean and Lukan versions, but Neirynck ("Minor Agreements Matthew-Luke in the Transfiguration Story") has demonstrated that these are not most naturally explained in terms of a second source, but in terms of redactional tendencies of the respective authors, which have incidentally produced a degree of coincidence. There is no good reason for thinking that Luke's distinctive additions and alterations reflect the use of any source beyond his main Markan source.

The Markan account does not have an easy unity, and many attempts have been made to identify an original core that manifests a greater unity, and which can be given a sense that easily takes its place within Jesus' historical ministry.

Baltensweiler (*Die Verklärung Jesu*) deletes vv 6 (the explanation of Peter's words) and 7b (the voice from heaven) and understands the event in the context of the final day of the celebration of the Feast of Tabernacles, seen in connection with the eschatological expectation of God's final tabernacling with his people forever. On the seventh and final day of the feast, in the context of messianic fervor stirred up by the feast, Jesus retreats to do battle with the temptation to political messiahship. The transfiguration is God's sign to Jesus, but it provokes Peter to believe that the eschatological fulfillment of the Feast of Tabernacles is underway, and so he wants to provide extra tabernacles for Elijah and Moses (tabernacles will have already been in place for Jesus and the three who have accompanied him). The dominant role given to the Feast of Tabernacles is less than persuasive.

Masson (*RTP* 3/14 [1964] 1–14) proposes an original that deletes vv 2c–3 (the transfiguration), 6b (the reference to the disciples' fear), and 7 (the cloud and voice from heaven), and offers an attractive reconstruction of Mark's motivation for the development of his final text. Masson takes the references to Moses as additions to the text, and suspects that probably only Peter was with Jesus in the original. The sense of Masson's original is not so self-evident as Masson seems to think, and despite his heavy-handed rewriting of the text, the transition to v 8 is far from smooth.

Müller (*ZNW* 51 [1960] 56–64) prefers to trace the account to the combination of two originals (neither of which is to be traced to the historical ministry of Jesus). One is reflected in the ascent of the mountain, the cloud and voice from heaven, and probably the descent from the mountain (vv 2ab, 7, 9). This account is built on the basis of the theophany on Mount Sinai (Exod 24; 33–34). The remainder of the account (vv 2c–6, 8) reflects a later Christology of the divine Christ (Müller's view is related to that proposed by Lohmeyer [*ZNW* 21 (1922) 185–215] but not repeated in his later commentary, which isolates v 3 as reflecting a later Hellenistic tradition from vv 4, 5, 7, and 8, which represent a Jewish Christian tradition). Saabe ("La rédaction du récit de la transfiguration," 83) notes that the radiance of the face of Moses in Exod 34:29 serves as an effective link between the two strands that Müller would seek to separate.

Nützel (*Verklärungserzählung*, 167–87, 236–52) allows as pre-Markan v 2 (without κατ' ἰδίαν μόνους ["apart by themselves"]), vv 3–4 (without reference to Moses), "[and] they were afraid" from v 6, v 7a (no voice from heaven), and v 8. The resulting text has a nice unity, but the role of the cloud is finally unconvincing in this reconstruction.

These views all reflect the difficulty created for the account by the presence both of the transfiguration and of the voice from heaven (Masson removes both). This must be reckoned as the chief obstacle in the way of accepting the original unity of the account, and several of the studies dedicate a good part of their energies to seeking to establish a peaceful co-existence between these motifs that threaten to be competing centers for the account. Gerber (*TZ* 23 [1967] 385–95) uses Jewish eschatological and mystical texts to show the natural home in a Jewish context of the Gospel transfiguration, and treats the transfiguration as a condition for meeting with the heavenly world, which is represented both by Moses and Elijah and by the cloud and voice from heaven. Pedersen (*NovT* 17 [1975] 341–65) has the same view of the place of the transfiguration and goes on to coordinate the presence with the tranfigured Jesus of Elijah and Moses (they are carriers of revelation whom Peter mistakenly puts on an equal footing with Jesus) and the designation of Jesus as Son (he is unique carrier of the eschatological revelation of God). A theological conception is reflected here according to which only God himself is able to make clear the true sense of what the disciples have seen (cf. also Trémel, *LumVie* 23 [1974] 70–83). Saabe ("La rédaction du récit de la transfiguration") coordinates the transfiguration itself and the voice from heaven. He points to a technical device of apocalyptic literature, whereby a scene that is revealed to the apocalyptist and remains somewhat opaque as to its significance is subsequently interpreted by the voice of a heavenly (angelic) figure. For Léon-Dufour (*Études d'évangile*, 83–122), the point of the account is the celestial proclamation (as with the baptism scene), and the vision that precedes only illustrates and solemnizes what the divine voice announces.

It may be observed that though the particular explanations differ, there is a common tendency to be discerned, and a more than adequate basis is to found for an original unity between the transfiguration and the voice from heaven.

The transfiguration account has often been identified as a misplaced resurrection account (for an extensive list of supporters of this view see Stein, *JBL* 95 [1976] 79 n. 2, to which we may add Coune, *AsSeign* 15 [1973] 50–51, 83). All the detailed argumentation cannot be repeated here. There are many details that can be marshalled on each side of the argument (Stein's essay gives a good indication of the range of arguments presented, as well as offering a good case for the traditional view).

By any reckoning the transfiguration account is very different from the accounts of the resurrection appearances preserved in the Gospel records (C. H. Dodd's impressive list of differences between the form of the transfiguration narrative and of the resurrection appearances is well worth noting ["The Appearances of the Risen Christ: An Essay in Form Criticism of the Gospels," in *Studies in the Gospels*, ed. D. Nineham [Oxford: Blackwell, 1967] 9–35, here, 25]). For this reason, the plausibility of the displaced resurrection view depends finally on the isolation of a tradition of resurrection appearances that is quite different from that reflected in Matthew, Luke, and John. In this postulated tradition the resurrection appearances are understood to be appearances from heaven of the glorified Christ (this is assumed for example by Carlston, *JBL* 80 [1961] 234, and Thrall, *NTS* 16 [1970] 312, in their support of the displaced resurrection appearance view).

The appearances of Jesus in Acts 7:55; 9:3–7; 22:6–11; 26:13–19; Rev 1:12–20 are appealed to, but these all come chronologically well after the resurrection period. In the Lukan frame, the experiences of Paul are not to be classed as resurrection appearances at all, and Paul himself seems to hint at some categorical distinction to be drawn between his encounter with the risen Lord and the earlier encounters "at the proper time" (1 Cor 15:8; see discussion below). Rev 1:12–20 is not a visit from heaven to John (the figure is moving among the lampstands, which are the churches), but a vision of the cosmic role and significance of Christ. Stephen sees into heaven; Jesus does not come to him. Appeal is also made to *Apoc. Pet.* 15–17 where a version of the transfiguration is used for a resurrection appearance on the Mount of Olives, which functions as a preliminary to the ascension. This is undoubtedly later than the Gospel accounts. In any case, it has in other respects the character of a pastiche and is, therefore, a dubious guide.

What remains is the possibility that Paul reflects a theological tradition in which the resurrection appearances are appearances of the Lord from heaven in his glory, and that this tradition may have known of, or produced, accounts along the lines of the transfiguration account. The direct information that Paul provides is extremely sparse (Gal 1:16; 1 Cor 9:1; 15:5–8), so the discussion must be based in part on broader features of Paul's theological understanding.

Does Paul understand Jesus to have been raised from death immediately to the presence of God? The idea that there is a distinct ascension, which separates the period of resurrection appearances from that of glory in heaven, is, in the NT, only to be found specifically in Luke/Acts (Luke 24:44–53; Acts 1:3, 6–11; etc.) and in John (20:17). Outside the Gospels and Acts (notably for Paul), resurrection appears to be the transition that bears all the weight (e.g., Rom 1:4; Phil 3:10; 1 Pet 1:3). And this could be taken to imply that Jesus' resurrection is understood to be resurrection immediately to God. Before we reach this conclusion, we do, however, need to explore the settings in which resurrection achieves this prominence. There are two main settings to be observed. The first is the eschatological significance of resurrection. With resurrection, Jesus achieves the eschatological state and opens up the same to others. This gives resurrection an important independence as a focus, which needs no completion by a complementary reference to ascension to glory. The second setting is the evidentiary role of the resurrection as the visible-in-this-world act of the power of God, which establishes for the believer the fact of salvation achieved in the death and resurrection of Jesus. Neither context encourages us to see resurrection as resurrection into the presence of God. Nowhere in the NT is resurrection understood as resurrection to God's presence, and to glory. Resurrection may bear the weight, but being raised does not itself take a person into the presence of God.

This is not to say that, for Paul, the natural sphere for Jesus' resurrected life is the Palestine in which he has lived. For Paul and other NT materials outside John, Matthew, and Luke/Acts, being raised has its natural sequel in moving on to the presence of God and, in Jesus' case, to glory at the right hand of God (Rom 8:34; 2 Cor 4:14; Eph 1:20; 2:6; 1 Pet 1:21; frequently, for the Christian, going to the presence of Christ takes the place of going to God). But in this respect, John and Luke/Acts are no different: there may be a chronological delay, but there is no thought that moving on from this world is anything other than the necessary sequel to Jesus' resurrection. The ascension is given no separate motivation or rationale. The present world is no longer the proper sphere for the one who has moved on into the resurrection life of the eschaton. A question may be asked about where the resurrected Jesus conducted his resurrected life between appearances. All the resurrection appearances are discrete happenings and leave us with no sense that the resurrected life of Jesus outside of these appearances had its own normal integrity and continuity in the present earthly sphere (this is especially the case for the Lukan and Johannine appearances). Jesus may, in the Gospel portrayal, stay for a while (but where is he between appearances?) for purposes in connection with his disciples, and certainly long enough for it to be clearly established that he is indeed risen, but there is never any doubt that from now on his place is to be elsewhere. Jesus has in the resurrection appearances already become something of a supramundane figure, who ultimately belongs elsewhere. Perhaps, for Paul, Jesus' resurrection puts him already in a sphere of "heavenly" existence (1 Cor 15:44–49), but this is not at once his glorification to the right hand of God.

Do we have any basis for determining whether Paul made any chronological distinction between the resurrection and glorification of Jesus? A conceptual distinction is not necessarily a chronological distinction. Clearly, for Paul, the period of resurrection appearances was a transitional period (1 Cor 15:1–8) in the aftermath of the resurrection itself. Resurrection appearances could not, in principle, continue forever (1 Cor 15:8: "last of all"). This fact alone creates a link between the resurrection appearances and the earthly life of Jesus. It is also clear that for all his need to claim his own experience as equivalent to that of the other apostles, Paul recognizes it to be categorically different by means of his bizarre imagery of an abortion or miscarriage (1 Cor 15:8: ἔκτρωμα). In Luke's scheme of things, Paul certainly saw the glorified Lord and had an experience categorically different from that of the the Twelve (Eleven). It would certainly be quite natural to read Paul in much the same way. But before we confidently do so, we should note that Matthew has no chronological distinction between Jesus' resurrection and God's bestowal upon him of all authority in heaven and earth (Matt 28:17–20). Jesus does not appear in Matt 28 as a figure resplendent with glory, but he does already appear as the one who has freshly received all authority from God. We cannot finally be sure whether Paul thought in terms of any chronological distinction between resurrection and exaltation to glory.

We still need, however, to do justice to the distinction Paul sensed between his own experience with Jesus and that of those before him. This may still be best accounted for by a distinction between appearances that involve a strong sense of continuity between the pre-resurrection and post-resurrection Jesus and Paul's own experience of encounter, as one who had no experience as a disciple of the Jesus of history, with the transcendent Lord of glory. Wherever Jesus is understood to be appearing from, there is still the question of the form of his appearing and what is being said by such a form. It does not help us that Paul says precisely nothing about the form of Jesus' resurrection appearance either to himself or to those before him. How happy would Paul have been with strongly visual descriptions of at least his own experiences of the resurrected one? Is "seeing" in such a context for Paul already partly metaphorical, and, as a transcendental experience, at least as much an inward as an outward experience?

For Paul, we cannot categorically rule out a view that the earlier resurrection appearances were of a glorious Jesus, but we have found nothing that counts clearly in favor of such a view. This possibility seems to be a precarious basis for mounting an argument that the transfiguration is a misplaced resurrection account.

So far as I have been able to discover, in the literature, McCurley (*JBL* 93 [1974] 79) alone seems to have noticed that there is much more to commend a view that the transfiguration account is a misplaced ascension story (but note also the view of Weeden, *Traditions in Conflict*, 118–24, that the original story viewed resurrection, ascension, and exaltation as all one process). McCurley involves himself in extensive dislocation and alteration of the text, but the likeness to ascension traditions is clear without such elaborate transformations of the text. However, finally all such views involve highly speculative alterations to the existing texts, and the likeness to the ascension is adequately accounted for by the fact that the transfiguration account and the ascension traditions share a concern to point to the (coming) instatement of Jesus in glory with the Father. The transfiguration account *could* be a misplaced ascension account, but no compelling case has been offered for denying to the transfiguration a place within the pre-resurrection ministry of Jesus.

A number of studies have despaired of any historical core to the account and have offered various proposals for understanding the account as simply a literary formation from theological motifs. Bradley (*CrQ* 12 [1935] 57–76) finds reflected here the church's first bid at answering the question: When and how did Jesus first become Son of God? For Bernadine (*JBL* 52 [1933] 181–89), the account was created to bolster Jesus' messiahship in dispute with Jewish opponents. Müller (*ZNW* 51 [1960] 56–64) sees only narratives that reflect different theological motifs and that have been fashioned to make christological affirmations. Evely (*The Gospels without Myth*, 99–114) sees the whole episode as a mythologized form for expressing a high point of intimacy with Jesus experienced by the inner circle of his disciples through being with him for an extended period and through sharing in his intense prayer life. Though there are attractive features to various of these suggestion, the very difficulties encountered in establishing the unity of the account (see above and further in *Comment*) and the elements of circumstantial detail within the account make these suggestions implausible.

It is often thought to be difficult to allow the Christology of the transfiguration account a place in the historical ministry of Jesus. The degree of difficulty depends in part on the Christology that one reads out of the account. The account itself does not demand that its christological terms have in their original setting the full post-resurrection confessional force that they easily acquire in Christian use of the account. In their present Gospel settings the account means more than it might be expected to have meant to Peter, James, and John in some original experience. By transfiguration Jesus is conditioned for his encounter with the heavenly world, while the voice from heaven affirms Jesus' unique significance in some way that has perhaps undergone Christian development to produce the present wording (note already the awareness of OT allusion reflected in the slight differences between the Synoptic forms of the words from heaven, and see discussion at 3:21–22 in connection with the baptismal voice). To find such an event in history is clearly beyond the scope of critical inquiry, but critical inquiry has not placed insuperable barriers in the way of considering that such an event may have occurred during the historical ministry of Jesus.

As an interaction with supra-mundane figures, this account shares features with the baptism account (3:21–22) and the account of Jesus' temptations (4:1–11). It also has a certain likeness to the ascension account in Acts 1:9–11. Without prejudice to its historicity, it should be identified in form-critical terms as a legend.

Luke basically follows the inherited Markan structure. The structure of the pericope is essentially provided by the sequence of actions of the episode. Luke does, however, distinguish much more sharply than Mark between the part of the narrative recounted from the perspective of the experience of Jesus (vv 28–31) and the part that is concerned with the experience of the disciples (vv 32–36). As well, the sense of logical development is much stronger in Luke's account than in Mark's: Jesus goes up the mountain to pray; Jesus' prayer leads to transfiguration; transfiguration prepares for and leads to the meeting with Moses and Elijah; the meeting occurs in order to discuss with Jesus his coming fate in Jerusalem (which has been the subject of his recent teaching and is that in relation to which the heavenly voice will soon challenge the disciples to listen to Jesus); the disciples, thus far kept out of view, apart from the initial mention of their accompanying of Jesus, are now grafted into the scene as having (barely) managed to be witnesses to the action to this point; with their re-introduction, the perspective moves from that of the experience of Jesus to that of the experience of the disciples; as the visitors prepare to leave, Peter tries to prevent the termination of the heavenly vision; he is answered not by Jesus, but by the enveloping cloud, signaling yet masking the arrival of God; the covering cloud puts on hold the scene of Jesus and his resplendent visitors, but also evokes fear in the presence of the awesome mystery of God; God, having arrived for the purpose, speaks in answer to Peter's suggestion; Jesus' suffering path to glory is not to be bypassed by any attempt to preserve the anticipation of it here vouchsafed to the three disciples. The action has now run its cycle; the episode has fulfilled its role. When the voice has spoken we return to a scene identical to that before Jesus began his prayer; Jesus is quite alone (this suggests most obviously the departure of Moses and Elijah, but secondarily it is allowed to embrace as well the departure of the cloud, and even the loss of the glory that had transfigured Jesus' appearance). Not unnaturally, the stunned disciples keep what they have experienced to themselves.

Comment

The transfiguration narrative confirms the importance of listening to Jesus, as he sets for himself and his followers a suffering fate; but it also confirms his anticipation of the glorious outcome of traveling this difficult road.

28 Luke totally reformulates Mark 9:2. Without any great departure from Mark's sense, he manages to retain of Mark's language only the names (in a different order), the reference to a mountain (but "a high mountain" has become "the mountain"), Mark's verb for "taking along" (used in a different form), and the word "days" (but now "about eight days"). As often, Luke introduces an *ἐγένετο*, "it happened," construction. He ties the account more closely with what precedes by his more specific "after these words." With his *ὡσεὶ ἡμέραι ὀκτώ* (lit. "about eight days"), Luke is probably abandoning Mark's six, which has no particular significance for him (Mark may have perceived a link with the period of preparation in Exod 24:16 before God spoke to Moses out of the cloud), and making the time frame about a week (cf. the French idiom; the idiom is not to my knowledge documented for Greek, but seems most likely here [and possibly in John 20:26]; it is too fanciful to find reference to the eighth day as the day of resurrection; see *Barn.* 15:9, "we too celebrate with gladness the eighth day when Jesus also rose from the dead . . . and ascended into heaven"). The point is the link between 9:27 and the present episode.

Luke uses the names of his three companions in the order in which he has referred to the privileged inner group in 8:51. Peter and John are paired in 22:8; Acts 3:1, 3, 4, 11; 4:13, 19; 8:14. In Gal 2:9 Peter and John come together after James (not, this time, John's brother). The pairing will reflect a historical link between the two in the early life of the church. Luke makes the account much more an experience in the life of Jesus than did the Markan version (but nonetheless this and similar texts still have a strong christological and theological focus rather than so much a psychological interest). So here already, Luke has: Jesus "went up onto the mountain to pray" instead of Mark's "he took them onto a high mountain." The phrase "onto the mountain to pray" is to be found identically in 6:12. Important events for Jesus are linked to his prayer. In light of what is to come, the trip up the mountain here may be linked to Moses' meeting with God on Mount Sinai (Exod 24; 33–34). More speculative is a link between Jesus' three companions and Moses' close associates in Exod 24:9.

29 Once again Mark's language is quite left behind. Only "became" (ἐγένετο), "his," and "white" betray his Markan source. The reference to prayer is repeated to make the link between transformation and prayer explicit. Luke takes Mark to be distinguishing between a transfiguration of Jesus himself and a transformation of the appearance of his dress. Luke represents the former in terms of an (unspecified) difference in the appearance of his face (in the longer ending of Mark [16:12], the representation of the Emmaus episode envisages Jesus as in a different form and thus unrecognizable to the disciples, but this is not Luke's approach there [24:16]). The sense we should give to the difference is only to be discerned from the parallel change to his garments (and from the resumption of v 29 in v 32 with "they saw his glory"). Much more economically than Mark, Luke has Jesus' garments becoming λευκὸς ἐξαστράπτων, "a white that flashes [like lightning]." The verb here is used in the LXX of Ezek 1:4, 7 in connection with outskirts of God's glory, as Ezekiel sees God upon his throne. It occurs also in the LXX of Dan 12:6, with reference to the splendid heavenly figure encountered by Daniel in a vision. Such a transformation of a human figure in connection with entry into the heavenly sphere is found in Jewish apocalyptic and mystical texts (*1 Enoch* 62:15; *Mart. Isa.* 9:9; *3 Enoch* 15; 48C; *2 Apoc. Bar.* 51:1–6 [here transformation in consequence of judgment day]; Gerber [*TZ* 23 (1967) 394] cites mystical texts and a late Hebrew midrash, which speaks of Moses being transformed to fit him for coming into the divine throne room with its angelic inhabitants). Not dissimilar is the effect upon Moses of speaking with God on Mount Sinai (Exod 33:29, 30, 35); but, for Luke, Jesus' own (future) glory is involved (v 32; cf. v 26). Jesus is destined to be enthroned in glory in the heavenly realm. In an anticipatory way, he here makes the trip to glory that lies beyond his suffering in Jerusalem. He goes up the mountain and in prayer finds himself to be in the sphere of the heavenly court attendants. Luke delays a mention of the disciples as witnesses to avoid any sense that it was for their sake. As with the baptismal descent, this is a private experience of Jesus.

30 Rather more of Mark survives in this verse, but with a totally restructured syntax. Luke introduces the phrase "behold, two men," which he will use to bind the transfiguration together with the resurrection-morning scene (24:4) and the ascension (Acts 1:10). He changes to "Moses and Elijah" from Mark's striking "Elijah with Moses." Again, he keeps the disciples out of the way: the two figures do not now appear to them; they appear in glory (and by implication to Jesus with whom they are to converse [v 31]). It is immediately easier to understand why we find Elijah in the heavenly sphere here (2 Kgs 2:11), than it is to see why Moses should be. Both figures, however, do meet God on Mount Sinai/Horeb (Exod 24; 1 Kgs 19); and the reference to Exodus, to come in v 31, creates a natural link to Moses. J. Jeremias (*TDNT* 4:854–55) documents a (late?) Jewish tradition that, despite Deut 34:5, considered Moses to have been taken up alive to heaven. Given the proleptic nature of the event, it may be, however, that we should think rather of the eschatological place of glory for these figures (cf. Luke 13:28).

Why should Jesus meet with these two figures? Baltensweiler (*Die Verklärung Jesu*, 69–82) points to the eschatological role of Elijah as a peaceful religious one, and not one marked by the violent zeal of the historic prophet. His presence points Jesus away from the zealot ideal of messiahship. Elijah is, however, hardly an obvious symbol for this, and, as Thrall (*NTS* 16 [1970] 307–8) notes, Elijah's anticipated gentle role is in Israel, and makes no comment on the appropriate attitude to the occupying power. Elijah is certainly understood to have an eschatological role. Does his presence here (with Moses) signal the impending arrival of the eschaton (as Coune, *AsSeign* 28 [1973] 72; *Rab. Deut.* 3:10 has Moses and Elijah both sent by God in the eschatological period)? Certainly at least for the earlier Markan form, this makes a poor fit with the identification elsewhere of this role with that of John the Baptist. Are we to find in the ministries of Moses and Elijah an antecedent to the sufferings of Jesus (e.g., Coune, *AsSeign* 28 [1973] 79)? Though not impossible, this is not at once what suggests itself from these two figures. Thrall (*NTS* 16 [1970] 308–17) has provided an elaborate argument for distinguishing between Moses and Elijah, on the one hand, and Jesus, on the other, as, respectively, figures who reached heaven by translation and a figure who reaches his glorious heavenly existence through death and resurrection. One difficulty here is that, in the most part of the Jewish tradition, Moses too died and was not translated to heaven. As we shall see below, it is not at all clear that the account is actually concerned to contrast Moses and Elijah with Jesus. The common view, offered with a number of variations, that Moses represents the law and Elijah the prophets finds difficulty with the initial Markan order, and with the need for Elijah to represent the writing prophets (Ziesler, *ExpTim* 81 [1970] 266, also notes that while Elijah is hardly a representative prophet, Moses could well be seen as a representative prophet [Deut 18:15]; in *Pesiq. R.* 4c Moses and Elijah are the two great prophets, members of the house of Levi, and men of God). More hopeful is the view of George (*BVC* 33 [1960] 22), which focuses on the roles of Moses and Elijah in forming and reforming the people of God. But, perhaps better, is the view that takes Moses and Elijah as respectively predecessor and precursor to Jesus (e.g., Ramsey, *The Glory of God*, 114; note the way in which Moses and Elijah come together in Mal 4:4–5, with one a figure of the relevant past and one a figure of the future; in Mark, the initial order may give Elijah prominence because as precursor he is more immediately to be brought into connection with Jesus). In both these last options, Moses and Elijah represent, in effect, the sweep of the unfolding of God's purposes leading on to the role of Jesus.

31 This verse is almost completely a Lukan formulation, with only the idea of the appearing itself and of the speaking with Jesus being carried over from Mark. These figures appear in glory because they appear from heaven. All the figures of the heavenly court have glory (cf. v 26). ἔξοδος, "exodus/departure," is used in Jewish Greek of death ("departure [from life]"; see Wis 3:2; 7:6), but always with contextual clarification. V 22 is not close enough to allow a simple sense of death here, but that verse cannot be ignored in the search for the meaning of "exodus" here. For a sense of what it is that Jesus is to leave behind when he departs, we can in part look to v 41. There must also be an allusion here to the exodus of the people of Israel from Egypt under Moses' leadership. It is surely, however, an excess to embrace in "exodus" the whole Mosaic saga of deliverance from Egypt through to possession of the promised land (Ringe [*Semeia* 28 (1983) 93 and n. 24] has noted how in the biblical tradition exodus language has its focus on the beginning of the process [out of Egypt] and not on its conclusion). Also, before we develop a whole typology of a new exodus forming a new people of God, we need to recognize that our text is concerned with "his exodus," rather than an exodus of which he is moving force or leader. The link between Jesus' exodus and that of others is specified in vv 23–27. In Acts 13:24 Luke uses the corresponding term εἴσοδος, "arrival," to speak of Jesus' arrival on the scene; "exodus" speaks correspondingly of his departure with task completed (note the use of πληροῦν, "to fulfill/accomplish/fill up"; in some important sense the departure is the accomplishment; here vv 21–22 are illuminating). Ringe (94) rightly draws on the journey to Jerusalem to help understand "exodus" here, but goes too far in identifying the journey to Jerusalem as the exodus: the journey rather marks Jesus' commitment to the (mode of) departure to which he has been summoned by God. Jesus' exodus is his death as departure from this world in the context of his understanding that his journey to glory at God's right hand has its beginning in an ignoble death in Jerusalem. Feuillet (*RevThom* 77 [1977] 191) helpfully correlates "exodus" here with ἀνάλημψις, "receiving up," in 9:51. Both terms designate the end of the earthly career of Jesus; where the former puts the accent on his death (but in the context of what is to follow), the latter focuses on his ascension to glory. Discussion with Elijah and Moses serves to confirm the rightness of Jesus' declared understanding of his future fate.

32 Nothing corresponds to this verse in Mark, except that Luke now allows for the disciples' degree of participation in the event, which he has earlier stripped from the Markan account. Luke has effectively divided the account into a first section, which focuses exclusively on Jesus (vv 28–31), and now a second section, which is concerned with the experience of the disciples (vv 32–36). As discussed above in *Form/Structure/Setting* (see there also for Luke's intention), Luke is here partly drawing on the Markan form of the Gethsemane scene (14:32–42; Luke uses elements that he does not reproduce in his own account of that episode). For the three there is here a preliminary fulfillment of Jesus' promise in v 27, which through human frailty they almost miss.

33 Before he rejoins Mark, Luke here establishes as time frame for Peter's offer the point at which the heavenly visitors are beginning to make their departure (cf. 24:29–29). For the remainder of the verse Luke follows Mark fairly closely, only deleting Mark's use at this point of the fear of the disciples as an explanation of Peter's befuddlement (he may find it difficult to correlate the fear with Peter's evident gladness at being present; he will use the fear motif in v 34). On ἐπιστάτα, "Master," which Luke inserts for Mark's ῥαββί (lit. "rabbi"), see at 5:5. Peter clearly counts it a privilege to be in on what he has seen (we should reject the view of Lagrange, 273, and Loisy, 27, that Peter is suggesting that his presence is good for the three dignitaries whom he can serve by constructing shelters), and he would gladly prolong the experience. Also clear is his apparent setting of the three figures on the same footing, but this may be quite innocent of christological error: he may simply be thinking of capturing forever this scene, which represents the whole drama of the history of salvation from Exodus to eschaton.

Not clear is the context of thought in relation to which we should understand the reference to σκηναί, "tents/booths/tabernacles/shelters," or the nature of Peter's failure. Any link with the OT tabernacle as the dwelling place of God seems to be totally discordant with the rude shelters that Peter might produce from the materials at hand on the mountain. There is also no clear reason for identifying the presence of God with these three figures. They participate in the glory of the heavenly court, but there is no reason to think of them as exhausting it. The attempts to link Peter's action to the Feast of Tabernacles have a little more plausibility, but they generally require far too much reading into the text, and it is difficult to see why in that context Peter would not want tabernacles for himself and the other disciples as well as for the three figures of glory. Perhaps only the glorious three are thought to be participants yet in the eschatological fulfillment of the Feast of Tabernacles (cf. Hos 12:9; Zech 14:16–20)? However that may be, Peter wants to freeze the moment. The heavenly visitors have confirmed the place of the trip to Jerusalem to die, but Peter would arrest the action at this point of anticipatory presence of the glory that is to be Jesus' beyond death. This is Peter's version of the beatific vision and he does not want it to go away! He does not fully appreciate that he is here attempting to stand in the way of the divine purpose.

34 Luke establishes a close link between Peter's words and the coming of the cloud: the sequence of action here initiated is some kind of response to Peter's words. Luke introduces here the fear motif and links it to the experience of being enveloped by the cloud, which becomes much more prominent in Luke's telling. The cloud is the sign of God's (hidden) presence (Ps 18:11; Exod 19:16; etc.) and the mode of his transportation (Isa 19:1; Pss 18:10–11; 104:3). Here the correlation of "cloud" and "voice" points uniquely to God's speaking from Mount Sinai (Exod 19:16; Deut 5:22). Where in Mark it is probably more natural to understand that only the three great figures enter the cloud (or are they there only overshadowed by it [Mark uses the dative object; Luke the accusative]?), the Lukan text more naturally implies that the whole party is enveloped (otherwise there are complex and unsignaled changes of subject and antecedents of pronouns in the latter part of the verse). The fear the disciples' experience is fear of the divine presence. The same verb ἐπισκιάζειν, "to overshadow/cover," is used of the cloud that covered the tabernacle in Exod 40:35 and made it impossible for Moses to enter. The scene evokes the terror of the Israelites at Mount Sinai (Exod 20:19–20).

35 Luke's only significant change here is the use of ἐκλελεγμένος, "chosen," in place of Mark's ἀγαπητός, "beloved." This makes explicit the connection with the use of יחיד, *yḥyd*, "chosen," in Isa 42:1, which, it was suggested at 3:22, lay behind the use of ἀγαπητός there. The adjectival form, ἐκλεκτός, "chosen [one]," is used at 23:35, but probably has a different function there. Jesus is here identified in the same terms as by the baptismal voice in 3:22 (see there), but here the voice is directed not to Jesus, but to the three disciples. The role of the voice is not particularly to take the disciples on to new christological heights. The reader is reminded of the Christology of the baptismal narrative, but the focus here is on the distinctive element, which is the call to hear Jesus.

The point is not to hear Jesus rather than Moses and Elijah: the disciples have not been party to their conversation with Jesus. The point is to hear what Jesus has been seeking to teach them. This is the response to Peter's desire to preserve inviolate the scene of glory that the three have witnessed. The glory they have seen is the glory to which Jesus is destined as chosen Son, but what they have glimpsed in this anticipatory scene comes to its fulfillment only by way of the cross. God here throws his weight behind Jesus' words in vv 22–27. In that the words "hear him" echo Deut 18:15 (cf. Acts 3:22; 7:37) a further Mosaic link is here established, but should not be pressed in terms of a Moses typology. Everything serves the end of getting Jesus listened to!

36 Luke returns to heavy reformulation here again. Nothing but the words "Jesus alone" is carried over from Mark. Luke makes use of, but totally refocuses, the Markan material on keeping silent about what they had seen. Luke tightens the link between the voice and the new scene in which Jesus is quite alone: the aloneness of Jesus is an aloneness that is divinely orchestrated and used to underline the thrust of the words spoken to the disciples. The cloud scene has been, in effect, a comment on the scene of the conversation of the three figures of splendor: it is not understood to have replaced that scene. We are presumably to understand that the cloud also disappeared, but that is not the point: having heard the voice we are now ready to return our attention to the scene that has been frozen momentarily to introduce this divine comment; but on our return we find that the scene no longer exists. Not yet literally, but figuratively, we have been dropped down to the bottom of the mountain. Just as no comment is made about the disappearance of the cloud, so there is no comment about the fading of Jesus' glory. The glory has been for the meeting with Elijah and Moses. The absence of the two companions indicates Jesus' return from the heavenly sphere (or the heavenly sphere's withdrawal from Jesus); there is no need to say that the glory has gone. The whole event has only been an anticipation; now the disciples are returned to the life of everyday realities in which Jesus calls for a taking up of one's cross.

Luke does not reproduce from Mark Jesus' call to silence. He is consistently less interested in the messianic secret. Nonetheless he reports their silence, but in a form that suggests the whole experience has been as much puzzling as illuminating. They have been overwhelmed by the experience, as well they might be. Only in the post-resurrection situation will the scriptural witness to Jesus' suffering path to glory be illuminated to them, and only with the coming of the Spirit will they be equipped to speak out (24:44–49).

Explanation

A week after the assurance of v 27, a few privileged disciples get a precious glimpse of the glory that will be Jesus' in the kingdom of God. They also hear the voice of God insisting that they must, against all their natural inclinations, listen to Jesus as he insists on suffering as the way to glory, and as he calls on them to give up their own lives to gain them, indeed to take up their own crosses and to follow him.

The transfiguration account has frequently been thought to be a misplaced resurrection account, but there is very little basis for such a suggestion. If it were to be a displaced anything, then it would be a displaced ascension account, but even this would involve a considerable reshaping of the account. While certainly now reported in the light of Easter faith, it is best to take the account at face value as relating to an experience of Jesus' earthly ministry.

In Luke's telling, the transfiguration account has links to several other parts of his narrative. There is a link to the Easter morning account: just as this transfiguration episode has, so the heavenly visitors and the empty tomb in Luke 24 will offer divine confirmation of what Jesus had been insisting upon. There is also a link to be drawn with the ascension account in Acts 1:9–11: at the ascension Jesus departs from his disciples to the glory of enthronement at God's right hand; the transfiguration anticipates just this glory. There is yet a further link with the account in Luke 21:27 of the end-time coming of the Son of Man in glory: what happens here is an anticipation of the ultimate splendor of Jesus' coming as the glorious Son of Man. There is, finally, a curious, and hard to interpret, link to the Gethsemane scene of prayer (22:39–46): though on other grounds 22:43–44 is likely not to be an original part of Luke's text, its presence would link the baptism, the transfiguration, and the praying in Gethsemane as the three specific points in Luke where the divine guidance of Jesus' life becomes visible as supernatural event.

A whole series of links can be drawn between the transfiguration account and the experience of Moses on Mount Sinai in Exod 24 and 34–35. We should see this in connection with Luke's conviction that, in what God is now doing in Jesus, he acts in line with his ways of working in the past, but transcends them in every respect. Jesus is not specifically seen as a new Moses, yet Moses is his predecessor in the unfolding of the purposes of God.

The mountain is the place of withdrawal for meeting with God. In Luke, important thresholds are crossed in the context of Jesus' prayer. Here, Jesus is confirmed in the destiny he has announced for himself, and the core group of disciples is challenged to accept his radical vision.

As he prays, Jesus is prepared for his meeting with Moses and Elijah: he takes on a form of glory suitable for being in the heavenly sphere, a form of glory, which in his own case, anticipates that which will be his by right, the other side of his death and resurrection. Jesus, as though translated into heaven itself, is found to be in the presence of the glorified figures of Moses and Elijah.

Why does Jesus meet with just these two? They are the only two figures of Scripture associated with meeting with God on Mount Sinai/Horeb (Exod 24; 1 Kgs 19). As well, Elijah would be expected to be in heaven (2 Kgs 2:11), and there was a strand of Jewish teaching that thought the same had happened with Moses. But it might only be their presence at the end, at the time of Jesus' ultimate glory, that is here in view (cf. 13:28). It is probably best to take these figures as representing the sweep of the unfolding of the purposes of God that leads on to the role of Jesus. Moses is Jesus' great predecessor because of his role in the formation of the people of God. Elijah is historically the restorer of the people of God, and for the end-time, he is the one who is to be the immediate precursor of God's final intervention in this world. The two figures come together in Mal 4:4–5 in a context that anticipates God's final intervention.

Moses and Elijah speak to Jesus about his exodus, which is to be accomplished in Jerusalem. They mean his death, but they mean this in connection with death seen as the manner in which he will take his departure from this world in order to move on to the glory of heaven (cf. v 51). Jesus' journey to glory at God's right hand has its beginnings in an ignoble death in Jerusalem. Jesus' death will be a kind of "deliverance" (cf. v 41, and in a different way vv 24–25), which can be compared to the exodus from Egypt under Moses. With the coming journey to Jerusalem, starting at 9:51 and dominating the remainder of the pre-passion account, Luke will mark Jesus' commitment to the mode of departure to which he has been summoned by God. Jesus' view of his own destiny is here confirmed by these heavenly visitors.

Thus far the account has been of Jesus' personal experience. Now Luke introduces the accompanying disciples, and from this point he will tell the story from the point of view of their experience. The three manage to see the scene of glory, but only just: they are heavy with sleep. Human frailty can so easily stand between believers and what God has for them.

The heavenly visitors look as if they are about to leave, but Peter sees represented here before him in this scene of glory the whole drama of the history of salvation from the exodus to the final glorification of the Jesus whom he has come to recognize as the Christ. He would much prefer to keep this scenario intact than return to the disturbing prospects about which Jesus has been speaking. This scene of glory accords rather better with Peter's version of the beatific vision than does Jesus' prospect of a blood-stained pathway to glory. It is just possible that Peter draws on a Jewish expectation of a special end-time fulfillment of the Jewish Feast of Tabernacles (cf. Hos 12:9; Zech 14:16–20) and sees himself as providing the necessary dwellings for these figures who have managed to reach that end-time state. Peter does not realize that he is totally in defiance here of the divine purpose, but his suggestion will have its answer in the divine voice from the cloud.

Jesus provides no answer, but immediately the cloud of the divine presence envelops them all. The awesome and fearful presence of God is both hidden and revealed by the presence of the cloud. Cloud and voice together call to mind God's speaking from Mount Sinai to Moses (Exod 19:16; Deut 5:21). There is a strong echo of the baptismal words from heaven, only (*i*) now the words address the disciples and not Jesus himself, (*ii*) "beloved" now becomes "chosen," which makes the allusion to Isa 42:1 clearer, and (*iii*) God's declaration of pleasure becomes a demand to hear Jesus (an echo of Deut 18:15). See at 3:21–22 for a discussion of Jesus as Son of God. Here, however, the main focus is on what is distinctive: the need to hear Jesus. Specifically the need is for Jesus to be heard in what he has begun to say about the way of the cross for himself and for his followers.

It is not possible—and it is not right—to freeze this moment of glory. The aftermath of the voice speaks as eloquently as had the voice itself. The moment of glory has vanished. Jesus is alone. The mountaintop experience has passed and what remains is the way of the cross as the way to permanence of glory. They have seen the glory that by right belongs to Jesus, but it belongs to him the other side of death and resurrection.

The three have been overwhelmed by their experience. They are still not in a position to understand the full significance of what they have witnessed. The experience has probably been as puzzling as it has been illuminating. Only in the post-resurrection situation will the scriptural witness to Jesus' suffering path to glory be illuminated to them, and only with the coming of the Spirit will they be equipped to speak out (24:44–49).

Jesus Heals a Possessed Boy When the Disciples Cannot (9:37–43a)

Bibliography

Aichinger, H. "Zur Traditionsgeschichte der Epileptiker-Perikope Mk 9,14–29 par Mt 17,14–21 par Lk 9,37–43a." In *Probleme der Forschung,* ed. A. Fuchs. SNTU 3. Vienna/ Munich: Herold, 1978. 114–43. **Bornkamm, G.** "*Πνεῦμα ἄλαλον*: Eine Studie zum Markusevangelium." In *Gesammelte Aufsätze: Band IV. Geschichte und Glaube: Zweiter Teil.* BEvT 53. Munich: Kaiser, 1971. 21–36. **Busse, U.** *Wunder.* 249–67. **Kertelge, K.** *Die Wunder Jesu.* 174–79. **Kirchschläger, W.** *Jesu exorzistisches Wirken aus der Sicht des Lukas.* 131–57. **Léon-Dufour, X.** "L'épisode de l'enfant épileptique." In *Études d'évangile.* 183–227. **Loos, H. van der.** *The Miracles of Jesus.* 397–405. **Reploh, K.-G.** *Markus—Lehrer der Gemeinde: Eine redaktionsgeschichtliche Studie zu den Jüngerperikopen des Markus-Evangeliums.* Stuttgart: Katholisches Bibelwerk, 1969. 211–21. **Roloff, J.** *Das Kerygma und der irdische Jesus.* 205–7. **Schenk, W.** "Tradition und Redaktion in der Epileptiker-Perikope Mk 9 14–29." *ZNW* 63 (1972) 76–94. **Schenke, L.** *Die Wundererzählungen des Markusevangeliums.* SBB. Stuttgart: Katholisches Bibelwerk, 1977. 314–49. **Vaganay, L.** "Les accords négatifs de Matthieu-Luc contre Marc: L'épisode de l'enfant épileptique (Mt. 17, 14–21; Mc. 9, 14–29; Lc. 9, 37–43a)." In *Le problème synoptique: Une hypothèse de travail.* Bibliothèque de théologie 3/1. Tournai: Desclée, 1957. 405–25. **Wilkinson, J.** "The Case of the Epileptic Boy." *ExpTim* 79 (1967) 39–42.

Translation

[37] *The next day,*[a] *it so happened*[b] *that, when they came down from the mountain, a large crowd met him;* [38] *and*[c] *a man from the crowd called out, "Teacher, I beg you to look with pity on my son, because he is my only child;* [39] *and a spirit seizes him, and suddenly he cries out, and it convulses him and produces foaming,*[d] *and even after devastating him,*[e] *it can only with difficulty be got to leave*[f] *him.* [40] *I begged your disciples to cast it out, and they were not able to."*

[41] *Jesus responded, "What an unbelieving and perverse generation! Until when must I be*[g] *with you and put up with you? Bring your son here."* [42] *While he was still coming the demon threw him down and convulsed him. Jesus rebuked the unclean spirit,* [h] *healed the child, and gave him to his father.* [43] *All were astonished at the magnificence of God.*

Notes

[a] [διά] τῆς ἡμέρας, "during the day," is read by [P[45]] D it sy[s] sa[ms], perhaps reflecting Sem. reckoning of the day from sunset to sunset.

[b] See at 9:28.

[c] ἰδού, "behold," has not been represented in translation here or at the beginning of v 39.

[d] Lit. "with foam."

[e] "Even after devastating him" represents συντρῖβον (lit. "crushing/breaking/bruising").

[f] "It can be got to leave" represents ἀποχωρεῖ (lit. "it separates [from]"). The verb has been treated as a quasi-passive following Marshall, 391.

[g] The Gr. tense is a simple future.

[h] A connecting "and" is dropped here for a better flow of the English.

Form/Structure/Setting

Luke continues to follow the Markan sequence, but first he deletes Mark 9:11–13. He may have found these verses convoluted; he may have considered that with their mention of Elijah they could create confusion after the role of Elijah in the transfiguration account, which is of a quite different kind. The link with the transfiguration account becomes closer because of the omission; and that Luke would have it so is indicated by his link in v 37 ("on the next day"; just possibly, the *μονογενής*, "only," which Luke adds to "my son" in v 38 may provide an echo of the heavenly voice in v 35 [cf. 3:21; 20:13]).

Luke also creates, with vv 42, 43, a link back to 7:11–17 (see: "he gave him to his mother" in v 15, and "They glorified God . . . God has visited his people" in v 16; Aichinger ["Epileptiker-Perikope," 143 n. 112] provides a full list of verbal agreements), which, in turn, prepares for 7:22, with its emphasis on the present as the time of fulfillment. After the future orientation of 9:27 (and vv 28–36; note the place of seeing in 7:22; 9:27, 32), is Luke concerned here to reinstate his emphasis on the presence of the kingdom of God in the ministry of Jesus? Does the presence of the majesty of God act as counterpoint to the glory of Jesus, which, as permanent possession, must await the journey through death and resurrection to the right hand of God?

Finally, Luke creates a close link between 9:37–43a and vv 43b–45. Both the proleptic glory of the transfiguration and the unparalleled power over the demonic must give way to the necessary suffering fate of the Son of Man.

There is quite a level of general agreement between Matthew and Luke in the strategy they have adopted in abbreviating the Markan version. This has suggested to some the existence of a second source here. Much of this agreement can be explained as obvious response to the difficulties of the Markan text and abbreviation of the sections where Mark is most wordy. At the level of vocabulary, there is just one striking agreement: that is the addition of *καὶ διεστραμμένη*, "and perverse," to Mark's "faithless" in v 41 (Matt 17:17). A link to Deut 32:5 is likely, but will this have independently suggested itself to Matthew and Luke? The agreement in v 40 (Matt 17:16) in the use of *ἠδυνήθησαν*, "were [not] able," is also to be noted, as is the use of the vocabulary of healing (different verbs) in v 42 (Matt 17:18). A second source is not proven, but may be suspected here.

Serious questions have been raised about the original unity of the Markan account. Among the difficulties of the narrative, the following questions about sources press to the fore. (*i*) There appears to be a doubling up of several features of the story: two dialogues with the father (vv 16–19; 21–24); two arrivals of the crowd (v 15; v 25); two presentations of the boy (vv 17–18; 21–22). (*ii*) The scribes appear at the beginning, but then play no further role in the story. (*iii*) V 19 is an odd answer to the father's dilemma. (*iv*) The father's need for faith and the failure of the disciples seem to be alternative claimants for a central place in the account: in vv 14–19, 28–29 the disciples have an important role; in vv 20–27 they fall from sight, and the action there turns on the father's readiness to believe. (*v*) Is the affliction seen at different points as epilepsy and as that of being a deaf-mute (as Bornkamm, "*Πνεῦμα ἄλαλον*," 25)?

Bultmann (*Synoptic Tradition*, 211–12) has argued for the blending of two quite separate narratives, one represented in vv 14–20, the other in vv 21–27, both having been truncated by the merging and by the addition of vv 28–29. This suggestion has been widely followed, and has produced a series of slight variations (v 20 is at times included in the second tradition; vv 28–29 are sometimes allowed as belonging to the unit vv 14–19[20]). Roloff (*Kerygma,* 144) has, however, rightly protested that there does not appear to be any adequate motivation that can be suggested for producing such an artificially unified account out of two independent originals.

Kertelge (*Wunder,* 174–79) and others have settled for one original, represented in vv 20–27, with extensive Markan or pre-Markan development (for Kertelge, the development is Markan). Kertelge is certainly correct to find Markan interests reflected in the failure of the disciples and the call for (believing) prayer, and in identifying a certain amount of Markan language. But he does not finally produce a believable process of development.

For Roloff (*Kerygma,* 141–53, 205–7), the core consists rather of the materials that concentrate on the disciples' failure, vv (14–17a?), 17b–19a, 19c–20, 25–27, with a post-Easter actualization in vv 28–29, and a further development in vv 21–24. Roloff seems to somewhat work against himself by noting that the application in vv 28–29 is in terms of elements that already find their place in the historical ministry of Jesus, and that vv 21–24 have features characteristic of Jesus' healing ministry (the call for faith) but not of the post-Easter role of healing. Also difficult is his view that vv 21–24 serve as an interpretation of the disciples' failure as a sign of the unbelief of this generation. Roloff's work is the point of departure for Reploh (*Markus—Lehrer,* 211–21), who suggests that the Markan narrative, with its evident distinction between how Jesus healed and how the disciples should do so, is formed in the context of the dwindling of the charismatic gifts of the early church.

Schenk (*ZNW* 63 [1972] 76–94) has proposed an altogether more complex separation of original and development. For him the presence of the scribes is key. Originally the account was of their failure to heal the son of a man who subsequently turns to Jesus. Almost all of vv 14–16 is development, as is Jesus' exclamation in v 19, his question in v 21, and all of vv 23–24 and vv 28–29. Going to the scribes as a group for exorcism does not convince, nor do the highly speculative excising and rewriting.

Schenke (*Wundererzählungen,* 314–49) takes as his point of departure the observation that the tensions and doublings of the story do in fact correspond to one another and harmonize with one another (Lohmeyer, *Markus,* 184–85, had earlier made the related observation that the repetitions serve the function of intensification). The problems are not in the content but, at least in some cases, in the location of the pieces. So, vv 21–22 run on easily from vv 17–18 (contra Bornkamm, the boy's problems in vv 17–18 are not those of a deaf-mute [see v 18]; rather, the demon is not a speaking demon [contrast 1:23–24; 3:11; 5:6–12]). In the double bringing of the child to Jesus (vv 17, 20), the first bringing fails with the failure of Jesus' representatives, the disciples. It is an established element of ancient miracle stories that the pupils fail to fully emulate the power of the master to perform miracles. Even v 19 and vv 23–24 are not incompatible competitors, linked as they are by the problem of unbelief. Only the twofold arrival of the crowd (vv 15, 25a) is a genuine tension. V 25a introduces a motivation for the healing that is unneeded at this point. It serves, says Schenke, to introduce here the idea that the healing is for the instruction of the disciples and not for the sake of the crowds. V 19 (apart from the last clause) is a Markan creation commenting on the failure of the disciples. Vv 23–24 are also Markan, exhibiting tensions with the context and reflecting a Markan interest in faith. The first of these insertions has disturbed the logic of the original narrative, which ran vv 14–18, 21–22, 20, 25–28 (vv 27–28 are a pre-Markan development). V 19 could only be placed after v 18, but its presence disturbs the sequence to v 21. Mark compensates for this by means of the relocation of v 20, which in turn calls for a change at the start of v 25, since v 20 is no longer there to be what Jesus saw. This gives Mark the opportunity for the insertion discussed above.

Schenke's explanation is certainly speculative, but it is by far the most coherent and satisfying of the many suggestions that have been offered. Perhaps a better alternative explanation for the change at the beginning of v 25, with its unparalleled use of ἐπισυντρέχει, "run together upon(?)," is to refer this verb to the prospect of a crush of people (cf. 3:8–9, and esp. 4:1). Schenke's arguments for vv 19 and 23–24 as insertions in their present context is more persuasive than is his case for their being Markan compositions. At least in the case of vv 23–24, we should probably preserve the possibility that we have the main content of a pronouncement story, which has been secondarily drawn into this account. With Schenke, and many others, we should probably regard "scribes" in v 14 as Markan.

The original form is that of a miracle story designed to glorify Jesus and to display his power. Luke, by abbreviating the Markan account and adding a final chorus of glorification of God, has produced an account that more clearly exhibits the miracle story form.

Luke has greatly simplified the Markan account and its complex structure. Jesus and the three came down the mountain to be met by a large crowd. A man from the crowd appeals to the compassion of Jesus, explaining that he has an only child who is repeatedly thrown into epileptic seizures by a demon, and that the disciples of Jesus have been unable to help. Jesus expresses his exasperation at the unbelief by which he is surrounded (even in the disciples). He asks for the boy to be brought, and as the child comes he suffers one of his frequent seizures. Jesus rebukes the demon, heals the child, and restores him to his father. The scene concludes with all amazed at the evident presence of the majestic power of God.

Comment

Jesus may need to go through death and resurrection to the full possession of his eschatological glory, but in his mighty works it is clear that God is present in his compassion and in his majesty.

37 Luke moves the descent statement to after his report of the silence of the three disciples. Luke heavily abbreviates, simplifies, and re-expresses, and all that survives from Mark is the genitive absolute construction, "when they came down" (with a slight change of verb), "the mountain," and the "great crowd." As in the transfiguration account, Luke begins the pericope with ἐγένετο δέ, "it [so] happened." Luke locates the account on the following day (probably reflecting a night setting for the transfiguration, which the sleepiness of the disciples suggests). As with v 28 the specified time lapse ties the adjacent accounts closely together. Without the specifying ἡμέρα, "day," τῇ ἑξῆς, "the next [day]," is found in Acts 21:1; 25:17; 27:18. From the later flow of the narrative we should probably understand the disciple group to be in the crowd.

38 Once again the formulation is mostly Luke's: only "the crowd," "teacher," and "my son" survive of Mark's formulation. ἰδοὺ ἀνήρ, "behold, a man," is also found in 5:12; 19:2; Acts 8:27; 10:30 (and cf. Luke 7:37; 8:41; 13:11; etc.). Luke's man makes a passionate and heart-rending appeal ("cried out"; "I beg you"; ἐπιβλέψαι, meaning here "look with compassion upon" [cf. 1:48]; "an only child" [μονογενής]), where Mark's gives a matter-of-fact explanation (but cf. Mark 9:22). For Luke's use of "teacher," see at 7:40. The usage here is closest to that at 8:49.

39 Luke has here his only description of the affliction (in Mark the description is resumed in v 21–22). The Lukan description is almost entirely independent of the Markan, but not such that we would think of a different condition. The common ideas are episodic seizure, convulsions, and foaming (with the idea of being thrown down added in v 42). For Luke's mention of the cries and of the extended nature of the attacks, compare from Mark's account the details of the exorcism (v 26; not used by Luke). For the emphasis on suddenness, note the attack as the boy is being brought to Jesus. The symptoms are those of epilepsy, which in this case is understood to be brought on by a demon. For the Lukan vocabulary for referring to evil spirits, see at 4:33. In this episode Luke uses "spirit" (here), "demon," and "unclean spirit" (both in v 42). μόγις, "with difficulty," and ἀφρός, "foam," are only here in the NT. καὶ ἰδού, "and behold," is a Lukanism.

40 Only slight changes to Mark's wording occur in this verse: in place of Mark's neutral "said," "I begged" repeats the same verb of entreaty used in v 38; the verb used for "they were not able" is now the one that Mark will use later in the discussion of whether Jesus is able to do anything in this case (a discussion that is deleted by Luke). With the disciples failure, Fitzmyer, 809, compares Gehazi's inability apart from Elisha in 2 Kgs 4:31. This feature of the story is discussed further in *Form/Structure/Setting* above. The mission of the Twelve in 9:1–6 had involved power and authority over all demons. While it is clear that the mission there anticipates the post-Easter role of the Twelve, it is not so clear whether the mission role was to continue in the period of the ongoing ministry of Jesus. V 41 suggests that they should have been successful, while v 49 may imply that we should understand that, as part of Jesus' band, the Twelve continued to play some part in Jesus' exorcising ministry. The failure of the disciples will be a foil for Jesus' success. Luke does not have Mark's emphasis on the failure and misunderstanding of the disciples, but this feature is still to be found in his account (cf. v 45). On Luke's use of the term "disciples," see at 5:30.

41 The Markan language is clearly visible in this verse. Luke introduces the name "Jesus" in place of Mark's ὁ δέ construction to indicate change of subject; the historic present verb becomes an aorist; "unbelieving" is glossed with "and perverse"; the rhetorical questions are combined by replacing Mark's second "until when" with "and"; Mark's φέρετε, "carry" [pl.], becomes προσάγαγε, "bring" [sing., addressed personally to the father]. The criticism would seem to be addressed to the failed disciples as representatives of the generation. The Markan text provides a broader basis for identifying the basis of criticism (see 9:14–16). The generation is already criticized in Luke 7:31, and will be further in 11:29–32, 50–51; and cf. 17:25; 21:32. Here there is an allusion to the historic failure of

Israel in Deut 32:5 (cf. v 20), now repeated in the present generation. Allusion to Isa 46:4 (as Schürmann, 570) is unlikely, because the context there is positive and here negative. There is a possible link to Moses' complaint about having to bear the people in the wilderness (Num 11:12; as Fitzmyer, 809). Clearly in mind is the exodus to come in Jerusalem (v 31), which will put an end to the present situation. Jesus appears here not as a "god," who in temporary human form is at present on the earth but who will soon return to his proper domain (as many, following Dibelius, *Tradition*, 278). Rather, he is one who, faced with the repetition of the historic failure of Israel to respond faithfully to God, anticipates his departure to glory at the right hand of God and the outpouring of the Spirit with its power to transform the human situation.

42 Luke deleted here the second conversation with the father and all the detail of the exorcism. Luke's ἔρρηξεν, "threw down," echoes Mark's use of this verb in v 18. He retains Mark's συνεσπάραξεν, "convulsed," ἐπιτίμησεν, "rebuked," and τῷ πνεύματι τῷ ἀκαθάρτῳ, "the unclean spirit." The pressure of the crowd plays no role for Luke. The non-speaking nature of the demon has been lost earlier (v 39) and disappears here too; Luke may sense a tension with the crying out of the demon (v 39). For Luke the attack occurs while the child is still coming to Jesus. He probably understands this as simply one of the sudden attacks, not specifically as a response to the sight of Jesus as is the case in Mark. As in 4:31–37 all sense of struggle disappears from the account: the rebuke of Jesus is instantly effective. Corresponding to the highly personal and heart-rending appeal of the father for his only child, Luke here speaks simply, but powerfully, of Jesus healing the child and handing him over to his father. The note of compassion comes strongly to the fore. Luke is happy to use the language of healing for exorcisms, but this does not mean that he confuses illness and exorcism (see discussion at 4:40; 6:18).

43a Nothing in Mark's account corresponds to Luke's addition here. This rounding off of the story displaces Mark 9:28–30, where the failure of the disciples is discussed privately with Jesus. Only here does Luke use either ἐκπλήσσειν, "to astonish," or μεγαλειότης, "majesty/magnificence," in connection with a healing, but other words for astonishment are used. In Jesus' mighty works, God is at work (cf. 7:16); and whatever people will finally make of it, the tangible reality of what Jesus is able to do is apparent to all.

Explanation

With his "on the next day" Luke links this exorcism account closely with the transfiguration account that precedes it: while it is true that Jesus' glory belongs to the other side of cross and resurrection, it is also true that in his works of power God is powerfully present in his compassion and his majestic splendor. While there is an important looking to the future, it is also true that the kingdom of God is present in the ministry of Jesus. Luke builds a link back to 7:11–17 (compare vv 42, 43 with 7:15, 16), an episode that leads on to 7:22, to underline this point. Luke also makes the link on to the next section (vv 43b–45) very tight: both the glory glimpsed in the transfiguration and the unparalleled power here demonstrated over the demonic must give way to the necessary suffering fate of the Son of Man.

The transfiguration is given a night setting by Luke, and it is the next day when the group descends the mountain. Upon his descent, a crowd comes to meet Jesus, which appears to have gathered around an unsuccessful attempt by Jesus' remaining disciples to exorcise a suffering boy. The father emerges from the crowd to make a heart-rending appeal to Jesus' compassion. A demon has caused the child to experience repeatedly sudden epileptic seizures, which are a great burden to his life. The man reports his earlier identical request to the disciples and their failure. The disciples do not succeed in sustaining the effective exercise of authority over all demons, which Jesus had made possible for their mission in 9:1–6. The failure of the disciples will be a foil to the success of Jesus. Jesus receives this report as just another indication of the unbelieving and perverse generation among which he finds himself. His words echo Deut 32:5. This generation fails in its response to God as had Israel in the OT story. Jesus' rhetorical question might echo Moses' words of complaint about having to bear with the difficult Israelites in the wilderness (Num 11:32). It certainly points us back to the language of exodus in v 31. In the face of this failure of even his disciples, Jesus anticipates his departure to glory at the right hand of God, and the outpouring of the Spirit with its power to transform the human situation.

Jesus asks the man to bring his son. As if to underline the man's despair, the boy experiences a seizure as he is being brought. But Jesus powerfully intervenes. He rebukes the spirit, heals the boy, and restores him to his father. In the presence of Jesus, the spirit is powerless to resist. The father experiences in full measure the compassion he had sought. The transformation in his child is a public reality evident to all. It astonishes as one might expect of the presence of the working of God. In such an exorcism the magnificent splendor of God is apparent.

The Son of Man Is to Be Delivered Up (9:43b–45)

Bibliography

Büchele, A. *Der Tod Jesu im Lukasevangelium.* 128–32. **Farmer, W. R.** "The Passion Prediction Passages and the Synoptic Problem: a Test Case." *NTS* 36 (1990) 558–70, esp. 561–63. **Perrin, N.** "The Use of (παρα)διδόναι in Connection with the Passion of Jesus in the New Testament." In *Der Ruf Jesu und die Antwort der Gemeinde.* FS J. Jeremias, ed. E. Lohse et al. Göttingen: Vandenhoeck & Ruprecht, 1970. 204–12.

And see at 9:21–22 and the "Son of Man" excursus following that pericope.

Translation

43b *While all were still*[a] *marveling at everything which he*[b] *had been doing,*[c] *he said to his disciples,* 44 *"Put these words into your ears. For I want you to know that*[d] *the Son of Man is about to be delivered up into the hands of men."*[e] 45 *They did not understand this word.*[f] *It was concealed from them, so that they could not comprehend it; and they were afraid to ask him about this word.*

Notes

[a] "Still" is added to clarify the force of the gen. absolute.

[b] Various texts make the reference to Jesus explicit here, some retaining the impf. verb (A C Θ Ψ etc.), and others changing to an aorist (W 1006 1506 etc.).

[c] Rendering an impf. here.

[d] "For I want you to know that" all renders a γάρ (lit. "for"), to make explicit the ellipse involved here (see *Comment*).

[e] Elsewhere translated "people."

[f] The Gr. text has a linking καί, "and," here.

Form/Structure/Setting

Luke continues to follow the Markan sequence. With the transition he forges in v 43b, he maximizes the contrast between the all-powerful exorcist of vv 37–43a and the soon-to-be-trapped Son of Man of vv 43b–45. A similar contrast is implicit already in the Son of Man language used in vv 21–22 to speak of Jesus' coming suffering fate (see there and the Son of Man excursus), and becomes explicit in the juxtaposition of that passion prediction and the following transfiguration scene. Where in vv 21–22 Luke had spared the disciples (or at least Peter their spokesman) their inappropriate response to Jesus' announcement of suffering (with the deletion of Mark 8:32–33), he here allows that motif to come into sharper focus than was the case in Mark, and will repeat the same forcefully in 18:34, where he will use Mark's third passion prediction.

Luke's short form here of the passion prediction is one of the claimants for being the most original form of the passion prediction. This possibility, along with the agreement between Matthew and Luke in replacing Mark's present tense "is handed over" with μέλλει παραδίδοσθαι, "is about to be handed over" (but Matthew and Luke have a different word order), has been used to argue for a second source here. This view of the most original form is argued against at 9:21–22; and μέλλειν, "to be about to be," + infinitive is a construction favored by both Matthew and Luke. There is insufficient reason to postulate a second source.

The historicity of the passion predictions is discussed at length at 9:21–22. Mark received from his tradition both a form of the passion predictions beginning with a reference to the Son of Man suffering (and being rejected) and one beginning with a reference to the Son of Man being handed over (παραδίδοσθαι). Both forms share the reference to rising after three days (on the third day). It is not clear that one needs to choose between these for a single historical original; but if we were to, then, the greater generality of the reference to suffering, the prominence given to Judas' betrayal (using the same verb) in early church tradition, and the possibility that the handing over echoes the uses of παραδίδοσθαι in the LXX of Isa 53 (vv 6 and 12; not paralleled in MT; see, however, in *Comment* below the closer fit with Dan 7:25, where the MT agrees), all point to giving preference to the former of the two patterns of wording. (It is not impossible that "rejected" in the second pattern is also a development and may be traced back to Christian reflection on Ps 118[117]:21, but Jesus was, himself, capable of such reflection.)

Comment

He who comes down from the mount of transfiguration to go on to his suffering destiny here sees beyond the impression he creates upon the crowds to the day that beckons when he will be handed over to the hostile wills of men. With solemn insistence he seeks to bring this home to disciples who are Satanically blinded by the anticipation of their share in the glory and success of the Christ.

43b Luke uses only "his disciples" from his Markan source here. He displaces Mark's quite separate setting for this pericope (privately with the disciples) with a strong link to the preceding exorcism, or better to the whole string of Jesus' mighty works ("all the things"), which seem to stand in such contrast to the coming powerlessness predicted here. The amazement of all is a statement about the sheer impressiveness of Jesus's deeds, not a statement about any particular kind of personal response from the crowds (cf. at 4:22). Luke does not think that the Markan "taught" gives the right tone to such a communication (note similarly at v 22). If it is right to see a note of rejection in the "handed over" language of v 44, then the contrast with the amazement here may be paralleled by the juxtaposition in Acts 2:22–23 of the attestation by means of mighty deeds and, nevertheless, the handing over to crucifixion and death by the hands of lawless people. The address is to disciples, but there is no suggestion of privacy or exclusion (cf. 6:20 and 7:1).

44 The opening clause here is entirely Lukan. Luke then reproduces the first clause of the Markan passion prediction with only minor changes, but does not continue with the remaining clauses of the Markan prediction with their words about death and resurrection. The absence of a resolution in resurrection allows the full force of the paradox to assert itself. εἰς τὰ ὦτα, "into the ears," is also found in 1:44 and Acts 11:22, in similar idioms (for the idiom, cf. Exod 17:14; Jer 9:20; Mal 2:2). The whole clause underlines the importance and solemnity of Jesus' coming statement (it is quite unnatural to refer the clause to the preceding praise of the crowds as Lagrange, 279; Rengstorf, 124).

The use of the γάρ, "for," is elliptical: the clause that follows both explains the solemnity of Jesus' introduction and is what he has intended to introduce. On Son of Man, see at 6:1–5 and the excursus following 9:21–22. Caragounis (*Son of Man*, 199) has pointed out that Dan 7:25 offers the closest parallel to "handed over into the hands of." There, the saints of the Most High (the equivalent to the "one like a son of man" of the vision of v 13) shall be delivered up (LXX uses the same verb, παραδιδόναι) into the hand of the final king of the kingdom represented by the fourth beast of Daniel's vision of 7:1–14. If this is the correct background for our text, then Son of Man here is already Danielic, and it is so precisely in its reference to suffering, rather than (as with other texts) in connection with vindication and glory. From Dan 7 is being drawn the view that the Man of Destiny, in his re-enactment of the decisive stages of the history of God's people, must himself undergo his own version of their humiliation. Such a re-enactment motif is strongly evidenced in the temptation narrative (4:1–13; there in connection with the testing of the wilderness period). There is no adequate basis for determining whether this Dan 7 connection for the suffering of the Son of Man should be traced back to the historical Jesus. This present text is certainly no adequate basis for assessing the whole Son of Man discussion from the point of view of the identification of the Son of Man with the saints of the Most High. In his Christology, Mark shows a sustained interest in the problem of the relationship between the "one" (Jesus) and the "many" (those who fail, yet benefit from the coming of the one); so, we may more readily attribute an importance to the Dan 7 link for this text in Mark, than is likely to be the case either in the historical ministry of Jesus, or here in Luke.

It is difficult to be sure of the correct nuance to give to *παραδίδοσθαι* (lit. "to give over") here. The core idea is simply that of transmission, but the term can carry quite a range of associations. Possible here would be betrayal (as with Judas [22:4, 6, 21, 22, 48]), being given up to a hostile group by the group to which one belongs (as 20:20; Acts 3:13; 21:11), being constrained and transmitted in legal custody (as Acts 8:3; 22:4), or the providential orchestration that, behind the scenes, allows one to gain power over another (as in Dan 7:25; Rom 8:32; cf. Luke 4:6). The divine purpose clearly attaches itself to each of the passion predictions and could be operative in this word (especially given a Dan 7:25 connection), but it is perhaps more likely that we should find expressed elements of the first two (closely related) suggestions, which may be extended slightly to include the giving up of Jesus to the will of the mob, which we find in 23:25. *ἄνθρωποι*, "people/men," has here a distinctly negative sense, almost as though the delivery is into the hands of a hostile mob (as 23:25). In 18:32 this becomes delivery to the Gentiles, and in 24:7 delivery into the hands of sinful people/men. If it is right to find a deliberate word-play with serious purpose in the juxtaposition of "Son of Man" and "men," then the handing over will need to be, after all, by God: he who should be welcomed by men is instead handed over (by God) to their destructive will.

45 Here Luke reproduces all Mark's words but offers his own extensive expansion, which underlines the importance of this saying of Jesus and introduces a supernatural dimension to the disciples' incomprehension. The disciples' failure to understand puts them, for one half of the description, on the same footing as the Jewish people of Acts 13:27 (the same verb; and cf. 3:17): since the disciples do know, at least in part, who he is, they do not positively have a part in condemning him to death. The cross and resurrection and subsequent attention to the Scriptures will sweep away such ignorance (Luke 24:25–27, 44–46). Luke sees more here than a simple intellectual failure to understand. Here and in 18:34 (and cf. 24:16) he identifies a supernatural aspect to this failure to perceive. This is normally taken to refer to the divine purpose in the blinding, but it may be better to treat the failure of insight as Satanic. This seems to fit better the broad sweep of Luke's narrative in which he treats such ignorance as a general benightedness, which is dispelled on the one hand by the resurrected Lord and on the other hand by the Spirit-empowered preaching of the early church. A role for Satan also does better justice to the degree of personal responsibility that attaches to this blindness. Schürmann (573) sees a culpable blindness lying behind the fear that leads here to a failure to ask. The personal responsibility is clear enough in 24:25. It is unlikely that in 24:45 Jesus is opening minds that are to be understood as previously shut by God. The clearest analogy for such a Satanic activity is provided by 8:12. The disciples' fear is a mark of partial understanding: whatever it is that Jesus is saying, it disturbs acutely their sense of how things should be.

Explanation

Luke establishes a sharp contrast between the all-powerful exorcist of the previous episode and the Son of Man who is soon to find himself subject to the hostile wills of men. The contrast is much the same as that which we have seen between the glorified Christ of the transfiguration and the one who must be heard when he talks of going to suffering and death, and when he defines a discipleship path which leads to the same. The Man of Destiny goes to his destiny in a way that defies human comprehension. Here Jesus underlines the importance of this path of destiny and seeks in vain to make his disciples accept his teaching.

The amazement of the crowds is still expressing itself when Jesus takes up his somber subject. The full paradox of the suffering of the Man of Destiny is more starkly present in Jesus' words here than was the case in vv 21–22, because his prediction here speaks only of being delivered up, and not of what lies beyond. That which is most difficult to accept is what it is most needful to accept. Talk of resurrection would not have posed such problems.

The language of handing over into the hands of may evoke Dan 7:25, but it is not certain that Luke makes anything of this. The connection would fit with the idea expressed elsewhere, in, for example, the temptation account (4:1–13) and the exodus of 9:31, that Jesus goes through in his own life a personal version of the decisive stages of the history of Israel.

The word translated "to be delivered up" can have quite a range of different associations. Here the thought could be of God behind the scenes orchestrating his purposes for the Son of Man, or it could operate much more at the level of the human actors and contemplate Jesus being betrayed and handed over by his own people to the occupying power, and then in turn by Pilate to the will of the mob (see 20:20; 22:4; 23:25; etc.). "Men" is normally a quite neutral expression for people in general, but here it has a distinctly negative force, almost as though Jesus is thinking in terms of being handed over to the will of a hostile mob (compare 23:25).

The Jewish people were involved in the death of Jesus because they were ignorant both of the identity of Jesus and of his destiny to suffer, witnessed to in Scripture (Acts 13:27). The disciples share one half of this ignorance, but are spared by at least a partial knowledge of Jesus' identity (9:20) from being involved in condemning Jesus. At the same time, they are more to blame for their lack of knowledge, since Jesus has gone to such pains to make his suffering fate known to them. The disciples do not know, because they do not want to know: note how they are afraid to ask him about what they have not understood. But there is also a supernatural aspect to their blindness. They are caught up in a Satanic benightedness (see 8:12; 18:34; 24:16), which will only be dispelled the other side of the cross, when the resurrected Lord is able to open their minds (24:45). In a similar way the preaching in the power of the Spirit of the early church is able to move the Jewish people on from their ignorance (see Acts 3:17–19).

Who Is the Greatest? (9:46–48)

Bibliography

Black, M. "The Marcan Parable of the Child in the Midst." *ExpTim* 59 (1947–48) 14–16. **Butler, B. C.** "M. Vaganay and the 'Community Discourse.'" *NTS* 1 (1954–55) 283–90. ————. "The Synoptic Problem Again." *DR* 73/231 (1955) 24–46. **Descampes, A.** "Du discours de Marc., ix, 33–50 aux paroles de Jésus." In *La formation des évangiles,* J. Cambier et al. RechBib 2. Bruges: Desclée de Brouwer, 1957. 152–77. **Fleddermann, H.** "The Discipleship Discourse (Mark 9:33–50)." *CBQ* 43 (1981) 57–75. **Glasson, T. F.,** and **Benger, E. L.** "The Markan Parable of the Child in the Midst." *ExpTim* 59 (1947–48) 166–67. **Kodell, J.** "Luke and the Children: The Beginning and End of the Great Interpolation (Luke 9:46–56; 18:9–23)." *CBQ* 49 (1987) 415–30. **Leaney, R.** "Jesus and the Symbol of the Child (Lc ix. 46–48)." *ExpTim* 66 (1954–55) 91–92. **Légasse, S.** *Jésus et l' enfant: 'Enfants,' 'Petits' et 'Simples' dans la tradition synoptique.* EBib. Paris: Gabalda, 1969. Esp. 17–36. **Lindeskog, G.** "Logia-Studien." *ST* 4 (1950) 129–89, esp. 171–77. **Neirynck, F.** "The Tradition of the Sayings of Jesus: Mark 9, 33–50." *Concilium* 20 (1966) 62–74. **Nolland, J.** "Luke's Readers." 315–21. **Robbins, V. K.** "Pronouncement Stories and Jesus' Blessing of the Children: A Rhetorical Approach." *Semeia* 29 (1983) 43–74. **Schnackenburg, R.** "Mk 9, 33–50." In *Synoptische Studien.* FS A. Wikenhauser, ed. J. Schmid and A. Vögtle. Munich: Zink, 1953. 184–206. **Vaganay, L.** "Le schématisme du discours communautaire." *Le problème synoptique: Une hypothèse de travail.* Bibliothèque de théologie 3/1. Tournai: Desclée, 1954. 361–404. **Wenham, D.** "A Note on Mark 9:33–42/Matt. 18:1–6/Luke 9:46–50." *JSNT* 14 (1982) 113–18.

Translation

[46]*A dispute arose among them over who might be the greatest*[a] *of them.* [47]*Being aware*[b] *of the contentious thoughts*[c] *of their hearts, Jesus took a child and placed him beside himself,* [48]*and said to them,*[d] *"Whoever receives this child as though he were me, receives me; and whoever receives me, receives the one who sent me. So,*[e] *the one who is least among you all is*[f] *a great one."*[g]

Notes

[a] Comparative for superlative.
[b] ἰδών, "seeing," is read for εἰδώς, "being aware," by A C D L W Θ Ξ Ψ etc.
[c] "Contentious thoughts" translates the same word as "dispute" in v 46.
[d] "Them" is omitted by P[45] D 2542 it sy[s, c].
[e] Translating γάρ.
[f] "Will be" in A D W Θ Ψ *f*[13] etc.
[g] "Great one" is omitted by P[45] co etc.

Form/Structure/Setting

Mark has at this point (9:33–50) a string of short items, mostly connected by catchwords, but with no thread of sense connecting the discrete items. Luke has used only vv 33–40 and has forged a single unit out of vv 33–37, where in Mark there were three, if not four, freestanding units. Vv 38–40 (with v 41) were already presented as a unit by Mark; Luke accepts this unit as exhibiting an adequate internal coherence, only dropping v 41, which seems not to be developing the same point.

Luke continues to want his readers to see a close link between this and the preceding pericopes. The disciples who need to learn the present lesson are the same disciples who, by their anticipation of their own share in the glory and success of Christ, were, in vv 43–45, Satanically blinded to what Jesus was saying.

Luke creates an enclosure around his large journey narrative (9:51–18:34), partly with the use of this episode and the echo it finds in 18:15–17. The preceding passion prediction (9:43b–45) is paralleled in 18:31–34, with which the journey narrative concludes (note the increased parallelism that Luke creates here with his addition of 18:34). Kodell (*CBQ* 49 [1987] 415–30) argues for a more elaborate pattern of parallelism, not all of which persuades (and does not perceive the role of the connections for the journey structure), but note as verbal links the *μὴ κωλύετε* ("do not forbid") common to 9:50 and 18:16, the *εἰς Ἰερουσαλήμ* ("into Jerusalem") of 9:51 and 18:31, and just possibly the use of *ἐπιτιμᾶν* ("to rebuke") in 9:55 and 18:15, and of *ἀκολουθεῖν* ("to follow") in 9:49 and 18:22, 28.

It has frequently been suggested that Luke had access to a second source here, but the basis is slight: Matt 18:4 and Luke 9:37 both have "this child," but the word order is different, and so is the immediate context; both use "this is" in their rewrite of Mark 9:35b (which both displace to later in the account). Both Matthew and Luke omit Mark's embrace of the child, but this has good independent motivation in their respective editing. There does seem, however, to be a better basis for suggesting that Matthew had access to a different version of catchword-linked sets of sayings with significant overlap with Mark 9:33–50. In particular a case can be made for a form that lacked vv 38–40 (see Wenham, *JSNT* 14 [1982] 113–18), but there is not sufficient evidence for confidence that Luke had access to this other form (the only piece of evidence that gives pause here is the presence at 10:16 in Luke's mission charge of a version of Mark 9:37b, while Matthew has at the end of his mission charge in 10:40, 42 a version of Mark 9:37b, 41, which reflects [as does 18:1–9] a form of the Markan set of linked items lacking any equivalent to Mark 9:38–40; but this only makes it likely that there was a second mission charge form, available to Matthew and Luke, which contained a version of Mark 9:37b, and which Matthew will have expanded).

There has been considerable discussion about whether the catchword linkages of the Markan text reflect an earlier oral collection (as e.g., Légasse, *Jésus et l'enfant*, 18) or whether Mark is the compiler here (as, e.g., Schnackenburg, "Mk 9, 33–50"). Schnackenburg can point to Gospel instances of editorial use of catchword linkage, but this is best taken as a continuation of a practice that had already an established place in the oral phase, rather than as a normal technique of literary composition. It is most likely that Mark worked from an existing collection here, but also quite possible that he may have added to this.

The discussion of original forms in connection with the materials of Luke 9:46–48 is convoluted and produces no certain results. Sayings about greatness are preserved in the Synoptic tradition in Mark 9:35b (par. Matt 18:4; Luke 9:48c); Mark 10:43–44 (par. Matt 20:26–27; Luke 22:26?); and Matt 23:11–12 (par. Luke 14:11; 18:14b), while there are related sayings about receiving the kingdom of God like a child in Matt 18:3; Mark 10:15; Luke 18:17; and compare finally the sayings about the first being last and the last first in Matt 20:16; Mark 10:31; Luke 13:30. Actions of Jesus involving a child (children) are reported in Mark 9:36 (par. Matt 18:2; Luke 9:47) and Mark 10:13–16 (par. Matt 19:13–15; Luke 18:15–17). More remotely related is Matt 21:14–16. Statements about receiving a child are restricted to the immediate parallels to Mark 9:37 (Matt 18:5; Luke 9:48; but note the similar statement with "you" for the child in Matt 10:40; Luke 10:16). The statement about the equivalence of receiving Jesus and the one who sent him are found not only in Mark 9:37b (par. Luke 8:48b; missing from Matt 18:5) but also in Matt 10:40; Luke 10:16.

There can be no serious doubt that Jesus commended humility and service as the way to greatness, but the present forms of these sayings exhibit various kinds of adaption to context and mutual influence, so that it is no longer possible to claim to identify original forms in original contexts. Robbins (*Semeia* 29 [1983] 43–74) has argued forcefully that Jesus' actions with children should not be relegated to the artificial framework generated for a pronouncement of Jesus as in the classical form-critical analysis of pronouncement stories; but in Mark 9:36 the independent importance of the action of Jesus is, in any case, evident from the poor fit in the present context. It is not unlikely that Jesus' setting up of a child in the midst of his chosen disciples was his cryptic answer to their questions about greatness, but of this we cannot be certain. We can, however, be sure that he did act in this way, and that in doing so he transgressed the sensibilities of his culture and in particular of his disciples, and left a lasting impression upon them. The equivalence of receiving a child and receiving Jesus clearly has some relationship to the sentiment of Matt 25:35–40 and also to that of Matt 10:42 (Mark 9:41). The present uses of the statement all envisage a post-Easter situation, but this is no basis for doubting that the saying itself goes back to the historical Jesus. In that original context any closer precision of sense can only be a matter of speculation. The equivalence of the reception given to Jesus and that given to God is pervasively present in the Jesus tradition, but once again present contexts for this saying reflect later church concerns, and obscure from us the precise force of this saying on the lips of Jesus.

Luke is not content to have, as Mark, a scattered set of items hooked together by catchwords. He forges a unified development out of his Markan materials. A dispute arises among the disciples about which of them is the greatest. Jesus senses what is on their minds and responds by placing a child beside himself. Then he claims an equivalence between receiving the child and himself (two polar opposites for the disciples). To make this polarity even more severe he goes on to assert, in turn, equivalence between receiving himself and receiving the one who sent him. On this basis, Jesus identifies as the great one among the disciples the one who swallows his pride and sets aside his dignity and is prepared to identify with the lowly and receive and care for them.

Comment

The disciples who were intoxicated with the anticipation of the glory that was to be theirs through their link to the Christ of glory were as little ready to find glory in the service of the humble as they had been to see the point in Jesus' talk of the Son of Man's betrayal.

46 Luke omits Mark's setting for this episode, making even more pointed the juxtaposition with vv 42–45, and reinforces its statement of the disciples' incapacity to understand. Luke's Jesus does not ask about the dispute, to be refused an answer. Only "who" and "greatest" survive of Mark's wording, along with a noun form of Mark's verb "dispute." The indirect reporting of the question with *τό* + subjunctive/optative is Lukan (cf. 1:62; 19:48; 22:2, 4, 23, 24; Acts 4:21; 22:30). It could be that the dispute has here become a matter of the private thoughts of each disciple (cf. v 47 where this is clearly the case), but it is probably better to stay with Mark's idea of a conversation, out of Jesus' earshot: they disputed, and while Jesus does not hear their words, he reads the content of the dispute from their hearts. The question of greatness may be linked back to the privilege of the three in being witnesses of the transfiguration: they played host (or tried to) to the figures of glory. More generally the questioning is to be linked to the sense of importance that the disciples are understood to have attached to their own special link to Jesus.

47 Luke defers his version of the statement about greatness to later in the episode (v 48c). He introduces Jesus' interest in the disciples' dispute, not via an initial questioning but in terms of his awareness of their thoughts. This is implicit in the Markan account and has some importance for Luke (4:23; 5:22; 6:8). For the Lukan wording here, cf. also 2:35; 3:15; 24:38. Luke reproduces quite closely the Markan statement about bringing the child. The significant changes are that the child is now placed beside himself, and not in the midst of the disciples, and that the Markan embrace of the child disappears (as it does in the Matthew parallel, and as it does also in the parallels to Mark 10:16 in both Matthew and Luke). The child is not now to be compared with the disciples; he is to be compared with Jesus himself. Nor is the child here received by Jesus, as some kind of example for the receiving of children in what follows. In Luke's account we cannot yet know what Jesus is seeking to achieve with this action.

48a Luke follows Mark closely here: he smooths the awkwardness of "one of these kinds of children" (there is only one) to "this child," and changes the word order and morphology slightly. Jesus and the child beside him are treated as in some sense interchangeable. How does all this answer to the dispute about greatness? A key is to recognize that greatness is here thought of as able to be measured by the company one keeps: the great have dealings with the great and handle matters of great significance. A woman or one of the servant classes deals with children. The chosen three have recently (almost) received the figures of glory of the transfiguration scene. In 15:2, Jesus will offend by not practicing the social exclusion that would express his status (and cf. 14:12–14). Just as the disciples considered Jesus too important to receive children (18:15), so they thought the same for themselves. To give attention to children would detract from their exalted status. For the low status of children in the ancient world, see A. Oepke, *TDNT* 5:639–52.

To clarify the thought here we need also to understand the sense required for the phrase *ἐπὶ τῷ ὀνόματί μου* (lit. "on/upon my name"). Possible senses would include "because he is my disciple," "for my sake," "because you are my disciple," "following my example," and "as my representative." A better thought flow for the pericope is, however, achieved if the sense is taken to be "as though he were I" (see detailed discussion in Nolland, "Luke's Readers," 315–21). The text speaks of honoring and respecting the humble child in the way one would honor and respect Jesus himself. Respect shown for the humble child turns out to be respect shown to Jesus.

Within the framework thus established, we may see that the pericope sets out to show that receiving and honoring the lowly does not mark one as inferior, but rather exalts one, because in doing so one receives Jesus and his Father: one plays host to God himself! This concept turns the pursuit of greatness on its head and shatters any thought of preserving one's self-importance. Greatness is not the possession of those who act out the part, but comes as gift to those who humbly serve the lowly.

Luke is formulating the context of the life of the church in which the Jesus member of the Jesus/child pair is no longer physically present. Jesus may not be received as was possible during his ministry. But what the child represents is always present. The high status that came to the disciples during Jesus' lifetime from their association with him is now to be found, paradoxically, in the company of the lowly.

48b Here also Luke follows the Markan text closely. His verbal changes are only to complete the parallelism between v 48a and v 48b. In its original sense "receive" may have meant something quite different from what is envisaged for the child, but in Luke's text this is not the case. The thought may usefully be compared with that of Heb 13:2. The concern is with the sense of greatness bestowed by the privilege of extending (in a hidden way) hospitality to such great ones. Christologically, the text points to the unique significance of Jesus, and behind the imagery there must be some sense expressed of fellowship with both Jesus and the one who sent him, which is established when one extends caring hospitality to the lowly.

48c Luke has delayed his equivalent to Mark 9:35b for this final climax position: the theme of greatness becomes explicit here at the end as it was at the beginning. Luke's polarities are *μέγας*, "great," and *μικρότερος* (lit. "smaller/more humble"), where Mark's had been "first," and "last of all" and "servant of all." Several suggestions have been made about the identification of the *μικρότερος*. Leaney (*ExpTim* 66 [1954–55] 91–92) takes the reference as being to Jesus himself as a junior to John the Baptist, but this hardly produces a good thought sequence. Alternatively the *μικρότερος* may be the child, who in his humble circumstances carries, for the one who welcomes him, the hidden greatness of Jesus and the one who sent him (so Schürmann, 576–77). The problem here is that *ἐν πᾶσιν ὑμῖν*, "among you all," could refer naturally to the child, if Luke had reproduced Mark's *ἐν μέσῳ αὐτῶν*, "in the midst of them," in v 47 for the phrase to refer back to. Luke instead has written *παρ' ἑαυτῷ*, "beside himself." The difficulties here would be eased if the *μικρότερος* here is not the child but simply what is symbolized by the child: the most lowly. The humblest among the disciples is great as the hidden bearer of the greatness of Jesus. But even with this modification the flow of thought is not as good as for the following view. The third possibility is that the *μικρότερος* represents that one among the disciples who is prepared to learn the lesson that Jesus is seeking to teach: the *μικρότερος* is the one who does not stand upon his dignity but is prepared to be identified with the lowly and to receive them, knowing that in so doing he, hiddenly, keeps company with the greatest of the great.

Explanation

Just as in 9:21–22, 23–27 a passion prediction had led on to a related challenge about the life of a disciple, so here a passion prediction leads on to a challenge about the nature of true greatness among the disciples of Jesus. The text does not specifically say so, but we may understand that this also fell upon deaf ears.

Those who were intimate disciples to the Christ thought of themselves as occupying the positions of great ones. For a privileged three, there had been recently the opportunity to (almost) play host to three figures of glory at the transfiguration. It helps to see more clearly the flow of the thought through this account to recognize that the measure of greatness uppermost in the disciples' minds has to do with the company one keeps and the high matters with which one is occupied. The disciples dispute over which of them is the greatest.

The disciples may have had their dispute privately, but Jesus is able to read the contentious thoughts of their hearts. This capacity is part of his distinctiveness from other men. Jesus responds at first, not verbally, but with an action: he sets a child up beside himself. The disciples are now facing a pair of figures, one of whom they value supremely and one of whom is a nobody in their eyes. In the ancient world children could eventually become something important, but had little of the intrinsic value that modern society sets, sometimes sentimentally, upon children.

Only now, with his visual aid in place, does Jesus speak. He suggests that, despite all appearances to the contrary, the two paired figures in front of them are somehow interchangeable. To receive the child "as though he were I" (literally "upon my name") is to receive me. Respect shown for the humble child turns out to be respect shown to Jesus. Keeping company with the lowly child turns out to be, in a hidden way, an extending of hospitality to Jesus himself. This is a little like Heb 13:2, "some have entertained angels unawares." Beyond the historical ministry, the possibility of honoring and receiving Jesus in the flesh is gone, but the humble people typified by the child are all around us to be received and honored. The stakes are even raised one step further: he who receives Jesus is in fact receiving the one who sent him; he is playing host to God himself.

On the basis of what Jesus is saying here, greatness is not the possession of the one who only pays attention to the great. Greatness is not for those who act out the part, but it is the gift of God to those who humbly serve the lowly. A fellowship with Jesus and with God himself is established when one extends caring hospitality to the lowly.

The one who is great in the circle of the disciples is the one who learns the lesson Jesus teaches here. His greatness comes from being the least, that is, from being prepared to identify with the most lowly. In terms of what is visible, the disciple identifies himself as one of the lowly, but hiddenly, in this activity he is keeping company with the greatest of the great.

The Exorcist Who Was Not Part of the Group (9:49–50)

Bibliography

Baltensweiler, H. "'Wer nicht gegen uns (euch) ist, is für uns (euch)!' Bemerkungen zu Mk 9,40 und Lk 9,50." *TZ* 40 (1984) 130–36. **Kirchschläger, W.** *Jesus exorzistisches Wirken aus der Sicht des Lukas.* 205–12. **Roloff, J.** *Das Kerygma und der irdische Jesus.* 185–86. **Schlosser, J.** "L'exorciste étranger (Mc, 9,38–39)." *RSR* 56 (1982) 229–39. **Wilhelms, E.** "Der fremde Exorzist: Eine Studie über Mark. 9,38ff." *ST* 3 (1949) 162–71.

Translation

[49]*John responded and said, "Master,*[a] *we saw someone casting out demons in your name, and we tried to stop*[b] *him, because he doesn't follow you*[c] *with us."* [50]*Jesus said to him, "Don't try to stop*[d] *it.*[e] *For the one who is not against you*[f] *is for you."*

Notes

[a] P45 ℵ L X etc. read "teacher" with the Markan text.

[b] "Tried to" represents the force here of the impf. The aorist is read by A C D W Θ Ψ etc.

[c] *f*1 b c q sy s,p, hmg etc. have a pl. "them," which fits better the pl. imperative to come.

[d] "Try to" represents the force of the present imperative following the previous use of the impf. of the verb.

[e] Mark had "him" at this point; Luke has no expressed object.

[f] *οὐ γὰρ ἔστιν καθ' ὑμῶν*, "for he is not against you," is added here by P45 L Ξ Ψ 33 892 etc. P45 continues *οὐδὲ ὑπὲρ ὑμῶν*, "nor for you."

Form/Structure/Setting

Vv 9:49–50 bring to a close the section 9:21–50 with its focus on preparing for the journey to Jerusalem. Right to the end the disciples exhibit little affinity with Jesus' vision of the way of the cross. The present episode makes its own assault on their self-importance. Luke uses the opening *ἀποκριθείς* (lit. "answered") to bind this pericope closely to the preceding dispute about greatness.

Luke continues here to follow the Markan sequence. He abbreviates by deleting Mark 9:39b, and he will not reproduce Mark's 9:41, which is yet another of the pieces linked by catchword rather than thematic development, but he reproduces Mark's wording here with unusual exactness, so that there can be no question of any influence from another tradition. Having finished with this pericope his selection of suitable materials from Mark's collection of catchword connected items in 9:33–50, Luke will leave his Markan source for the most part of the long journey section, which he will now begin. Luke will rejoin the Markan sequence at 18:15. Passing over the materials of Mark 10:1–12, he will pick up the Markan thread at 10:13.

The major difficulty to be faced in claiming historicity for this account is the language of casting out demons "in the name of" Jesus. While this practice is well attested for the early church, is it likely in the lifetime of Jesus himself? Josephus, *Ant.* 8.45–49, reports use of Solomon's name in this way, but he was a great hero of the past and not a living contemporary, as Jesus was. There is, however, a feature of the Gospel presentation of Jesus' exorcisms that may lie at the basis of a use of his name, even in his lifetime, as a power for exorcism. The interest in the Gospel presentation of Jesus' exorcism is in his own immediate authority over the powers of the demonic world. There is no emphasis on technique or even on prayer. All the stress falls on the compelling authority of Jesus. (For general discussion of Jesus' exorcisms, see at 4:31–37.) Despite the obvious role that this motif has in the life of the early church, there is good reason to consider that it is well grounded on historical memory. It is quite possible that even in Jesus' own lifetime a recognition of intrinsic authority connected with this man became the basis for experiments in appealing to his name in exorcism.

The strongest argument in favor of the fundamental historicity of the account is the tension between its generosity of spirit and the generally exclusivist tenor of the early church. As with other traditions that are critical of the disciples, there must, on that ground also here, be a general presumption in favor of historicity. Other arguments are proposed by Wilhelms (*ST* 3 [1949] 168–69), Pesch (*Markusevangelium*, 2:109), and Schlosser (*RSR* 56 [1982] 237–38).

General historicity does not, however, deal with the separate parts that go to make up this brief account. Each of the three parts of the Markan pericope has been suspected of being an expansion. Mark 9:38 falls foul of the general form-critical suspicion that in pronouncement stories the narrative framework is a secondary development used merely to provide a framework for the saying that is the point of the story. The specific arguments here can be formulated to favor either historicity or (Markan) development and are indecisive, but it is a little difficult to imagine v 39 circulating without any narrative setting. Schlosser argues for an original that had for v 38 not a *report* by John of an earlier attempt to stop an exorcist but rather an account of the actual attempt by the disciples to stop him (*RSR* 56 [1982] 231–33). Little is at stake since v 38 adds to v 39 only the role of John as spokesman for the disciples to Jesus and the specification that the wonder performed in Jesus' name was an exorcism.

The argument against v 39 consists mostly of skepticism about a pre-Easter use of Jesus' name as a basis for exorcism. This has been discussed above. It is in connection with v 40 that the claims for secondary development are strongest. One of the concerns has been with the context of persecution, which, it has been claimed, is the evident setting for the words of v 39–40. The move from the christological focus of v 39 to the ecclesiastical focus of v 40 has also raised suspicion. The saying in v 40 is obviously proverbial and is clearly paralleled in Cicero, *Pro Ligario* 33. While Jesus was quite capable of making use of the wisdom of a contemporary proverb, one must allow here for the possibility that the proverb is an early church development concerned to apply more generally in the life of the church the principle discerned in v 39.

The Lukan structure is quite simple. A report to Jesus is triggered by the previous episode. Jesus objects to what the disciples had done and gives a reason.

Comment

Coming as it does after the dispute about greatness, this pericope represents a further assault on the self-importance of the privileged disciples. Those around Jesus must learn to understand their position not in terms of a circle of privilege but in terms of a call to follow Jesus in the path of suffering. The work of God is not restricted to their circle.

49 Luke replaces Mark's ἔφη, "said," with ἀποκριθεὶς . . . εἶπεν, "responded and said," because he wants this episode to be seen in the light of the previous dispute about greatness: this bid by the disciples for exclusive claim upon the powers of the new age is of a piece with their earlier preoccupation with greatness. Mark's "teacher" becomes the more significant ἐπιστάτα, "master" (see at 5:5). For Mark's "was not following us" Luke has "does not follow [you] with us": this clarifies the christological focus and makes the issue one of being (permanently) part of the disciple band, and not only of whether the exorcist was traveling with the disciple band at the particular time. The role of John here bridges to his role (with James) in the opening pericope of the journey narrative (9:51–56). The success of this outsider may be contrasted with the failure of the disciple band in vv 40–41. Despite this failure, the disciples considered that the powers let loose by the presence of Jesus should be restricted to the disciple band (perhaps to the Twelve [cf. v 1]). An (unsuccessful) attempt by non-Christian exorcists to use the name of Jesus is reported in Acts 19:13–16. Sensitivity about the range of those who may dispense the power of the Spirit is reflected in Acts 8:14–24. In Acts in general there is an interplay between regularization and the sense that God is not bound by structures and standard channels. Whether we should think of this exorcist who uses the name of Jesus as "not far from the kingdom of God" (as Baltensweiler, *TZ* 40 [1984] 135) is not clear. What is clear is the recognition of the effective reality of the powers of the kingdom of God quite outside ecclesiastical structures. The exorcist does show a degree of confidence in the reality of the powers to be found in Jesus.

50 Luke changes the word order, adds "to him," which Mark had left to be supplied from context, and deletes the object ("him") after "do not try to stop him." The last change has the effect of generalizing in preparation for the general statement to come. Luke then omits the rest of Mark 9:39 before reproducing the proverb of Mark 9:40 in Mark's words, except for a change from an "us" form to a "you" form of the proverb (this change supports the Lukan focus on the disciples' concern about their own status).

The reasoning of Jesus' reply totally inverts the thinking that lies behind the disciples' stand. They would secure their own position by keeping others out of what they see as their own exclusive domain; Jesus suggests that, on the contrary, they should be grateful for the degree of recognition of their cause implied in the exorcist's activity. Modesty rather than self-importance and self-assertion should mark the Twelve as followers of Jesus. Even a minimal recognition of the reality of what is happening in the Jesus movement should be encouraged and received with gratitude; it should not be despised because of its limitations.

Because the horizon of interest here is that of the disciples and their attitudes, we should not use the proverb in relation to contemporary discussion of the place of the non-practicing Christian (as Baltenswieler [*TZ* 40 (1984) 135] points out, the exorcist was certainly not passive), or of the possibility of the anonymous Christian. The status of the exorcist is not finally of interest in the pericope.

As Schürmann (580) has noted there is a certain parallel to be drawn with Num 11:24–30.

Explanation

Vv 49–50 bring to an end the section that Luke has devoted to preparing for the journey to Jerusalem. The focus has been on Jesus' coming fate in Jerusalem and on the implications for discipleship of Jesus' pathway to glory. Here the disciples would protect the boundaries of their powers and privileges, but Jesus suggests a more modest approach in which they will be grateful for the smallest degree of recognition of their cause. The marks of the presence of the kingdom are not, in any case, to be restricted to their own circle.

Jesus' response to the dispute about greatness suggests to John that he and the other disciples may have got it wrong when they tried to stop an exorcist using the name of Jesus. So John reports the matter to Jesus for his adjudication. Despite their recent failure to successfully achieve an exorcism (vv 40–41), they would restrict to their own number the right to exorcise in Jesus' name (compare v 1). Full of self-importance, they are out to protect their privileges as the inner circle of Jesus' followers. They are affronted by this manifestation of the realities of the powers of the kingdom of God outside their own circle and sphere of influence.

Jesus, with his own generosity of spirit, in no way shares their concern. He turns their approach on its head. As those called to the way of the cross, the disciples should rather be grateful that there is any kind of recognition of their cause. They are really in no position to be acting out of self-importance to secure their own domain of influence. No matter what the shortcomings, any place where God's power is found to be at work should be joyfully recognized. Note the parallel with Num 11:24–30.

Excursus: The Journey to Jerusalem

Bibliography

Bailey, K. E. *Poet and Peasant.* 79–85. **Benoit, P.** "La section IX, 51–XVIII, 14 de saint Luc." *RB* 60 (1953) 446–48. **Bernadicou, P. J.** "Self-Fulfillment according to Luke." *BiTod* 56 (1971) 505–12. ———. "The Spirituality of Luke's Travel Narrative." *RevRel* 36 (1977) 455–66. **Blinzler, J.** "Die literarische Eigenart des sogenannten Reiseberichts im Lukasevangelium." In *Synoptische Studien.* FS A. Wikenhauser, ed. J. Schmid and A. Vögtle. Munich: Zink, 1953. 20–52. **Blomberg, C. L.** "Midrash, Chiasm, and the Outline of Luke's Central Section." In *Gospel Perspectives: Volume III. Studies in Midrash and Historiography,* ed. R. T. France and D. Wenham. Sheffield: JSOT, 1983. 217–61. **Büchele, A.** *Der Tod Jesu im Lukasevangelium.* 146–64. **Cadoux, C. J.** "The Visits of Jesus to Jerusalem." *Exp* 9/3 (1925) 175–92. **Conzelmann, H.** *The Theology of St. Luke.* 60–73. **Cook, E. J.** "Synoptic Indications of the Visits of Jesus to Jerusalem." *ExpTim* 41 (1929–30) 121–23. **Davies, J. H.** "The Purpose of the Central Section of St. Luke's Gospel." *SE* 2 (1964) 164–69. **Dawsey, J. M.** "Jesus' Pilgrimage to Jerusalem." *PRS* 14 (1987) 217–32. **Drury, J.** *Tradition and Design in Luke's Gospel.* 138–64. **Egelkraut, H. L.** *Jesus' Mission to Jerusalem: A Redaction Critical Study of the Travel Narrative in the Gospel of Luke, Lk 9:51–19:48.* Europäische Hochschulschriften 23/80. Frankfurt im M.: Peter Lang, 1976. **Enslin, M. S.** "The Samaritan Ministry and Mission." *HUCA* 51 (1980) 29–38. **Evans, C. F.** "The Central Section of St. Luke's Gospel." In *Studies in the Gospels: Essays in Memory of R. H. Lightfoot,* ed. D. E. Nineham. Oxford: Blackwell, 1955. 37–53. **Farrell, H. K.** "The Structure and Theology of Luke's Central Section." *TJ* 7 (1986) 33–54. **Filson, F. V.** "The Journey Motif in Luke-Acts." In *Apostolic History and the Gospel,* ed. W. W. Gasque and R. P. Martin. Exeter: Paternoster, 1970. 68–77. **Fransen, I.** "Cahier de Bible: La montée vers Jérusalem." *BVC* 11 (1955) 69–87. **Gasse, W.** "Zum Reisebericht des Lukas." *ZNW* 34 (1935) 293–99. **Gill, D.** "Observations on the Lukan Travel Narrative and Some Related Passages." *HTR* 63 (1970) 199–221. **Girard, L.** *L'Évangile des voyages de Jésus: Ou la section 9,51–18,14 de saint Luc.* Paris: Gabalda, 1951. **Goulder, M. D.** *The Evangelists' Calendar.* London: SPCK, 1978. 95–101.———. "The Chiastic Structure of the Lucan Journey." *SE* 2 (1964) 195–202. **Grundmann, W.** "Fragen der Komposition des lukanischen 'Reiseberichts.'" *ZNW* 50 (1959) 252–70. **Guilleband, H. E.** "The Travel in St Luke (IX:51–XVIII:14)." *BSac* 80 (1923) 237–45. **Hawkins, J. C.** "Three Limitations to St. Luke's of St. Mark's Gospel." In *Studies in the Synoptic Problem by Members of the University of Oxford,* ed. W. Sanday. Oxford: Clarendon, 1911. 27–94, esp. 29–59. **Kariamadam, P.** "Discipleship in the Lukan Journey Narrative." *Jeevadhara* 10 (1980) 111–30.———. "The Composition and Meaning of the Lukan Travel Narrative." *Biblebhashyam* 13 (1987) 179–98. **Kodell, J.** "Luke and the Children: The Beginning and End of the Great Interpolation (Luke 9:46–56; 18:9–23)." *CBQ* 49 (1987) 415–30. **Lapointe, R.** "L'Espace-temps de Lc 9, 51–19, 27." *EglT* 1 (1970) 275–90. **Lohse, E.** "Missionarisches Handeln Jesu nach dem Evangelium des Lukas." In *Die Einheit des Neuen Testaments: Exegetische Studien zur Theologie des Neuen Testaments.* Göttingen: Vandenhoek & Ruprecht, 1973. 165–77. **Marshall, I. H.** *Luke: Historian and Theologian.* 148–53. **McCown, C. C.** "The Geography of Jesus' Last Journey to Jerusalem." *JBL* 51 (1932) 107–29. ———. "The Geography of Luke's Central Section." *JBL* 57 (1938) 51–66. **Minear, P. S.** "Jesus' Audiences according to Luke." *NovT* 16 (1974) 81–109, esp. 89–103. **Miyoshi, M.** *Der Anfang des Reiseberichts Lk 9,51–10,24: Eine redaktionsgeschichtliche Untersuchung.* AnBib 60. Rome: Biblical Institute, 1974. ———. "Das jüdische Gebet Shema' und die Abfolge der Traditionsstücke im Lk 10–13." *AJBI* 7 (1981) 70–123. **Moessner, D. P.** *Lord of the Banquet: The Literary and Theological Significance of the Lukan Travel Narrative.* Minneapolis: Fortress, 1989. **Navone, J.** "Lucan Joy." *Scr* 20 (1968) 49–62. ———. "The Journey Theme in Luke-Acts." *BiTod* 58 (1972) 616–19. **Ogg, G.** "The Central Section of the Gospel according to St Luke." *NTS* 18 (1971–72) 39–53. **O'Leary, A.** "The Role of Possessions in the Journey Narrative of Luke 9:15–19:27." *MilltownStud* 28 (1991) 41–60. **Osten-Sacken, P. von der.** "Zur Christologie des lukanischen Reiseberichts." *EvT* 33 (1973) 476–96. **Reicke, B.** "Instruction and Discussion in the Travel Narrative." *SE* 1 [= TU 73] (1959) 206–16. **Resseguie, J. L.** "Interpretation of Luke's Central Section (Luke 9:51–19:44) since 1856." *StBibT* 6 (1975) 3–36. ———. "Point of View in the Central Section of Luke (9:51–19:44)." *JETS* 25 (1982) 41–47. **Robertson, J. A.** "The Passion Journey." *Exp* 8/17 (1919) 54–73, 128–43, 174–94, 322–44. **Robinson, W. C., Jr.** "The Theological Context for Interpreting Luke's Travel Narrative (9:51ff.)." *JBL* 79 (1960) 20–31. **Samain, E.** "Le récit lucanien du voyage de Jésus vers Jérusalem." *FV* 72 (1973) 3–23. **Schmidt, K. L.** *Der Rahmen der Geschichte Jesu: Literarkritische Untersuchungen zur ältesten Jesusüberlieferung.* Darmstadt: Wissenschaftliche Buchgesellschaft, 1964 = 1919. 246–73. **Schneider, J.** "Zur Analyse des lukanischen Reiseberichtes." In *Synoptische Studien.* FS A. Wikenhauser, ed. J. Schmid and A. Vögtle. Munich: Zink, 1953. 207–29. **Sellin, G.** "Komposition, Quellen und Funktion des lukanischen Reiseberichtes (Lk. ix 51–xix 28)." *NovT* 20 (1978) 100–135. **Stagg, F.** "The

Journey toward Jerusalem in Luke's Gospel: Luke 9:51–19:27." *RevExp* 64 (1967) 499–512. **Stöger, A.** "Armut und Ehelosigkeit—Besitz und Ehe der Jünger nach dem Lukasevangelium." *GuL* 40 (1967) 43–59. **Stonehouse, N. B.** *Witness of Luke.* 114–27. **Talbert, C. H.** *Literary Patterns, Theological Themes, and the Genre of Luke-Acts.* 58–65. **Trompf, G. W.** "La section médiane de l'évangile de Luc: L'organisation des documents." *RHPR* 53 (1973) 141–54. **Wenham, J. W.** "Synoptic Independence and the Origin of Luke's Travel Narrative." *NTS* 27 (1980–81) 507–15. **Wickes, D. R.** *The Sources of Luke's Perean Section.* Chicago: UCP, 1912. **Zerwick, M.** *Leben aus Gottes Wort: Erwägungen zum lukanischen Reisebericht.* Luzern: Schweizer Katholische Bibelbewegung, 1956.

The curious journey that dominates the whole central section of Luke has been the subject of extensive scholarly discussion, but with precious little agreement about major issues of the discussion.

Jesus sets his face to go to Jerusalem in 9:51, and the journey motif is reiterated in 13:22; 17:11; and 18:31; and perhaps also 9:57; 10:38; 11:53; 14:25. In 18:35 we find Jesus approaching Jericho, and so within about eighteen miles of his destination. The journey, however, makes no discernible progress by 17:11 (cf. 9:51–56; Conzelmann, *Luke,* 68–71, has argued from 17:11 that Luke thought of Samaria and Galilee as side by side [and in this way allows for the journey to have made progress], rather than one above the other, but the "between Samaria and Galilee" of v 11 is to explain the presence of a Samaritan among the group of lepers [v 16] and not to describe the progress of the journey [as, e.g., Grundmann, 336]). Furthermore, much of the material of the journey section does not easily fit into a journey setting and provides no sense that Jesus is a traveler.

Clearly Luke has from his Markan source information about a journey to Jerusalem and to death (see 8:31; 9:30; 10:1, 17, 32–33; and then consecutively from 10:46), though it is not absolutely clear until 10:32 that Jesus and the disciples are on a journey to *Jerusalem.* Already for Mark the content of this part of the Gospel is not consistently closely tied with the journeying motif. Luke chooses to make a major structural feature of his Gospel out of this journey motif. For him the journey becomes a major display case for a large part of the parables and teaching of Jesus that he has assembled. Luke appears to go to no pains to tie the particular material to the journeying motif. All that is important for him, it seems, is that this journey should provide the broad framework. Why should this be the case?

Many have examined the content of the materials in these chapters for the clue as to why these materials have been gathered into the journey section. McCown (*JBL* 57 [1938] 63–64) suggested that Luke did not want to interpolate the materials of this section into his account of the Galilean ministry because he sensed (*i*) that much of the material was of a somewhat different type, and (*ii*) that it pointed toward the approaching death of Jesus. The prominence of parables gives some mileage to the former suggestion, but the second is hardly obvious, and is most clear at points of Lukan intrusion. A number of scholars have drawn attention to the didactic and parenetic focus of the materials: here we have a manual for living out the life of discipleship in the later church. But is this more true of the travel narrative than of 6:20–49 or 8:4–15? Ultimately the whole Gospel has as its horizon of concern the post-Easter situation. Grundmann (*ZNW* 50 [1959] 252–70) relates the journey to the theme of Jesus as a wanderer on the earth, which he finds more broadly in Luke, but he does this (*i*) at the expense of relegating most of the materials of the journey section to excursuses and (*ii*) by doing less than justice to the dominant role of the goal of the journey for this particular piece of "wandering." Different studies have highlighted the importance in the journey materials of the themes of faith, obedience to the teaching of Jesus (Reicke, *SE* 1 [1959] 206–16, sees alternating blocks of instruction of disciples and discussion with opponents), love of God and neighbor, prayer, the openness to the divine revelation that comes through Jesus, the proper use of money and worldly goods, repentance, forgiveness, joy, following of Jesus as a way, the acceptance of suffering. Only the last two of these interlock at all closely with the journey theme; and these can hardly offer themselves as general descriptions of the contents of the journey narrative. Kodell (*CBQ* 49 [1987] 428) offers the rather complex "the lowliness and defenselessness of Jesus (and his true followers) as expressed in an expectancy of God's action and a willingness to follow his way of salvation, dependent on him." By casting a fairly wide net this gathers in a lot but is not finally a convincing description of the contents of the journey section.

With some justification Davies (*SE* 2 [1964] 164–69), Gill (*HTR* 63 [1970] 199–221), and Osten-Sacken (*ET* 33 [1973] 476–96) give priority to the specifically journey-related verses and/or to the pericopes immediately connected with the travel notices. Gill finds challenge to the hard road of discipleship, as following the way that Christ himself took; and he finds challenge to (gentile) mission, including its anticipation in the ministry of Jesus. The former of these is more obvious than the gentile part of the latter (which is, however, not to be completely denied), but at the end of the day the presence of all the other materials in this travel section still remains unexplained. The same difficulty arises with Osten-Sacken's view that Christology is central to the journey section, and in particular the separation and setting in sequence of the different stages of the messiah's career: most of the material of the journey section are only christological in a remote sense, if at all. Davies is only really interested in the directly travel materials; he cuts the Gordian knot by declaring that "The journey sets the tone of the teaching . . . not *vice versa*" (169 n. 1).

There does not seem, then, to be any way in which an analysis of the specific contents of the journey material can provide the key as to why these materials have been cast into the form of a journey. Sellin (*NovT* 20 [1978] 100–135) offers another approach. He accepts as his starting point this broadly recognized tension between the journey form and the wide-ranging teaching content of the section. Focusing attention on this journey as a journey to death, Sellin suggests that we should look to the Jewish testamentary literature for the clue that has been eluding us. As he goes to his death Jesus is here providing for his disciples a testament for the time of the church (134–35). This highly creative suggestion at one stroke allows for the diverse contents of the section, does justice to the church orientation of the materials, and provides a sensible reason for the journey setting. The ultimate weakness of the suggestion is finally the limited number of elements from the standard testament form that appear in the journey section. Almost none of the instruction is marked as instruction in view of Jesus' impending departure (as distinct from instruction *about* his impending departure); the material lacks the autobiographical tone of the testamentary genre; despite the large teaching content, the material is finally in narrative form, and this judgment is true even if we disregard the specifically journey aspect of the materials (the materials of Luke 22, in connection with the Last Supper do rather better at conforming to the testamentary genre). One can imagine that an account that presents itself as a report of what Jesus occupied himself with on his fateful journey to Jerusalem could be valued and related to as though it were a testament, and that such evaluation might take place under the influence of the knowledge of the testamentary genre; but Luke could have done much more to help the process along!

By casting the journey as he has, Luke has retained the focus of Mark's "passion narrative with an extended introduction" (the wording is that of Kähler, *Historic Biblical Christ,* 80 n. 11, who, however, expresses the sentiment in the plural of all of the Gospels), while introducing a huge amount of additional teaching of Jesus, most of which has no real bearing at all on the passion. Luke has expounded the purpose of the journey in his narrative, not primarily in any of the journey materials, but rather in the material of 9:21–50, the section in which he sets his reader up for the journey motif.

The journey allows the relatively brief materials of that section to be assured a dominating importance for the remainder of the Gospel account. In the journey narrative itself, the materials that sustain the journey motif, especially 9:51; 13:31–35; 18:31–34, but also other materials, reiterate and, in some cases, develop further the thrust of 9:21–50 (e.g., Resseguie, *JETS* 25 [1982] 41–47, has examined 14:1–33 as bringing into sharp relief two opposing perspectives, that of Jesus teaching renunciation, expressed as humility and giving up of possessions, and an opposing perspective of those who practice self-assertion, which takes the form of self-exaltation and the treasuring of possessions). It is the Jesus who goes to suffering and calls to suffering, and whose glory is the other side of cross and resurrection, who is the dominating figure of the journey section. All the particular thrust of the materials is to be subordinated to, and seen in the light of, this supremely important perspective.

While there is a good scholarly consensus about where to begin the journey, there is a range of opinion about where to bring this large section to a conclusion. Suggestions include 18:14, 31, 34; 19:10, 27, 28, 44, 48; 20:18. The arguments supporting the different views cannot be reproduced here. In the section 9:46–48 above, reasons are offered for finding in the materials that end in 18:34 the second half of an enclosure surrounding the journey section. In addition to those considerations, an obvious change takes place in the form of the narrative from 18:35, where consecutive sequence of events moves from being a narrative fiction used for thematic ends to being intrinsic to the materials (with certain clear exceptions) and where geographichal location becomes important in a way that it has consistently not been the case in the journey narrative (17:11 is the nearest thing to an exception). 18:34 is the end of the artificial journey structure; journeying continues, but now Luke is reporting the actual journeying from Jericho to Jerusalem which, unlike the journey narrative, involves making real geographical progress. From 18:35 on, Luke's perspective is that of preparing for the actual arrival in Jerusalem. The account of the journey itself has been driven from the materials of 9:21–50. From 18:35 the center of gravity shifts, and we are anticipating concretely events to come in Jerusalem (see especially the role of 19:11–27 in this).

An additional consideration that favors a terminus at 18:34 is the way in which themes from 9:22–50 recur in the units that, according to this understanding, begin to round off the journey narrative: the passion prediction of 18:31–34 echoes those of 9:21–22 and 9:43b–45 (as well as linking with 9:51); the call to self-denial and following of Jesus in 9:23–27 has a counterpart in 18:18–30 in the challenge to the ruler and the promise to Peter and the others who have followed; and the episode with a child in 9:46–48 is matched by the episode with infants in 18:15–17.

The internal organization of the travel narrative is yet another matter that has attracted a good measure of scholarly attention, but with no consensus. Beyond the various attempts to group materials into natural sections, there have been different attempts to find other kinds of motivation for Luke's ordering of his materials. Evans ("Central Section") has attempted to show detailed parallelism between the materials of the journey narrative and the unfolding of Deut 1–26 (excluding 14; 19; 21:1–14; 22:5–23:14). Despite some enthusiastic supporters, the view has been trenchantly criticized by, among others, Blomberg ("Central Section," 221–28): there are no real parallels in ancient literature to support such a procedure; the echoes of Deuteronomy appealed to are often not at all close; equally good parallels with Deuteronomy have been produced on quite a different basis; in many cases a parallel exists in Deuteronomy (but not in the correct sequence), which is better than the one proposed by Evans. Goulder (*Calendar*, 95–101) offers a lectionary explanation for Luke's procedure in the travel narrative. He has his own quite different set of parallels to Deuteronomy, but this time they are based on the Jewish lectionary divisions, which Goulder believed were already in use when the Third Gospel was produced. Simply at the level of fit, the parallels, as a set, fail to convince, while the assumed antiquity of the particular lectionary cycles is far from proven.

More than one attempt has been made to establish Luke's use of a chiastic structure (that is a structure in which a first set of items is paralleled in reverse order by a second set, sometimes with a central unparalleled item, which may be the stressed item) in the journey section (Morgenthaler, *Lukanische Geschichtsschreibung*, 1:156–57; Goulder, *SE* 2 [1964] 195–202; Talbert, *Patterns*, 51–52). While Morgenthaler and Goulder have not a single item of parallelism in common, Talbert builds on features of each of the earlier suggestions. Some of the alleged parallels are suggestive, but others are general or even forced, and this has led some subsequent students to look for the chiasm not in Luke's own work, but in a source that he has used in the central section of his Gospel. More recently again, Standaert ("L'art de composer," 336–45) has proposed a chiastic structure for 9:51–17:12. This structure has no common elements with any of the previous suggestions. It seems to have its basis predominantly in the need to find a chiastic structure also within each of the identified sections and is more imaginative than convincing.

Bailey (*Poet and Peasant*, 79–85) takes the journey through to 19:48 and offers a chiastic structure with a center point in 13:22–35, which incorporates nearly 90 percent of Luke's final text form. His parallels are somewhat more consistently persuasive than the earlier suggestions, though still quite uneven. Blomberg ("Central Section," 238) finds it puzzling that we should have a source that has been so dominantly used but whose structure has been so obscured by Lukan addition. This procedure, one might say, is not so different at one level from Luke's approach to Mark earlier in the Gospel, but where Luke has obscured the Markan structure he has clearly imposed upon the materials his own replacement structure; further, items in the Markan structure could be taken or left on a one-by-one basis, while items in a chiasm cannot be so treated without destroying the whole of the structure. Blomberg's point needs answering.

Blomberg builds his own approach on the recognition by various scholars that parables in the journey section can be convincingly paired. The five most obvious pairs (10:25–37 par. 18:9–14; 11:5–8 par. 18:1–8; 12:13–21 par. 16:19–31; 12:35–38 par. 16:1–13; 13:1–9 par. 15:1–32) in fact line up in chiastic order, and all belong to the travel-narrative materials distinctive to Luke. 14:7–24 offers itself as a suitable center piece. Beyond this, by Blomberg's reckoning, the only parables peculiar to this section of the Gospel are Luke 14:5; 14:28–33; and 17:7–10. Each of these begins with τίς ἐξ ὑμῶν, "which of you," and two of the three (14:5 and 14:28–33) fit neatly into the chiasm structure, while if the third is paralleled with 11:11–13 (which begins with the same τίς ἐξ ὑμῶν), it also finds a natural place in the chiasm. For the last, but only here, Blomberg moves outside the parables materials distinctive to the journey section of Luke (11:11–13 is paralleled in Matt 7:9–11), but can find support for the view that 11:11–13 formed an original unity with 11:5–8 and has not, therefore, been drawn in here by Luke from the materials he shares with Matthew. In the resulting chiasm the paralleled sections are in each case either both directed outside the disciple band in controversy, or they are both directed internally to the concerns of discipleship. One may express a slight uneasiness about Blomberg's failure to clarify the boundaries of what he will accept as parable, and one may want to delete some of the scope of certain of Blomberg's parable sections or even whole sections (14:7–24 could be divided and treated as a central pair; or we could accept only vv 15[16]–24 as part of this parable's source; or even delete this unit altogether on the basis of the parallel in Matt 22:1–10; perhaps 15:3–7 could be deleted on the basis of its parallel in Matt 18:10–14, but the detailed parallelism of 15:1–32 and 13:1–9 is against this; if 14:7–24 is deleted, we may want to exclude also the minisection 14:5 and treat 14:28–33 as the centerpiece, noting the way that its two parts form a close parallel with 15:3–7, 8–10 on the one side, and with their parallels in 13:2–3, 4–5 on the other side), while wanting to affirm that this study of Blomberg's adds up to a very strong case for the view that Luke has used a parables source as core source for the construction of his journey narrative. He has retained the parables in the original chiastic order of that source, but he has heavily expanded with other materials and seems to have made no attempt to use as his own the structure of his source (cf. on a microscale the residual indications of the earlier structure[s] of the genealogy in 3:23–28).

If this analysis is correct, it still does not provide us with a Lukan structure, but it does identify for us a series of constraints in relation to which Luke has worked in forming the journey narrative. The parables do not provide the structure, but they do set up landmarks and have the potential to become growth points in relation to which Luke has added thematically similar material. With some significant modification, the structure that Blomberg develops on this basis is here adopted. Arguments for its adoption will not be presented here. Rather, as earlier in the commentary, discussion will be provided as each of the sections is introduced. The outline (with, for the most part, my own headings in place of Blomberg's) is:

9:51–10:24	Accompanying Jesus to Jerusalem
10:25–42	Love of God and Love of Neighbor
11:1–13	Confident Prayer to the Father
11:14–54	Conflict and Contrast
12:1–13:9	Preparing for the Coming Judgment
13:10–14:35	Reversals Now and to Come
15:1–32	That Which Was Lost Is Found
16:1–31	Use and Abuse of Riches
17:1–19	Fitting Response to the Demand and Working of the Kingdom of God
17:20–18:8	Who Will Be Ready When the Son of Man Comes?
18:9–30	Entering the Kingdom Like a Child
18:31–34	Going to Jerusalem to Suffer (and Rise)

Accompanying Jesus to Jerusalem (9:51–10:24)

Now at the predetermined time in the plan of God, Jesus begins his fateful trip to Jerusalem. He goes to Jerusalem on a path of vulnerability and nonretaliation, and he calls would-be followers to face the challenge of being (with him) totally out of step with the normal values of the society of which they have hitherto been an integral part. As earlier, so on this journey he will continue his mission of outreach, and he sends the Seventy ahead of him as his representatives to engage in this same task.

Rejection in a Village of the Samaritans (9:51–56)

Bibliography

Arens, E. *The ΗΛΘΟΝ-Sayings in the Synoptic Tradition.* OBO 10. Freiburg/Göttingen: Universitätsverlag/Vandenhoeck & Ruprecht, 1976. 180–91. **Bony, P.** "Les disciples en situation d'envoyés: Une lecture de Lc 9,51–10,24." *BulSSul* 8 (1982) 130–51. **Brodie, T. L.** "The Departure for Jerusalem (Luke 9,51–56) as a Rhetorical Imitation of Elijah's Departure for the Jordan (2 Kgs 1,1–2,6)." *Bib* 70 (1989) 96–109. **Calmet, A.** "Il n'est pas digne de moi! Luc 9,51–62." *BVC* 77 (1967) 20–25. **Davies, J. G.** "The Prefigurement of the Ascension in the Third Gospel." *JTS* 6 (1955) 229–33. **Enslin, M. S.** "Luke and Matthew, Compilers or Authors?" *ANRW* 2.25.3 (1985) 2357–88, esp. 2368–74. **Evans, C. A.** "'He Set His Face': A Note on Luke 9,51." *Bib* 63 (1982) 545–48. ———. "'He Set His Face': Luke 9,51 Once More." *Bib* 68 (1987) 80–84. **Feuillet, A.** "Deux références évangéliques cachées au Serviteur martyrisé." *NRT* 106 (1984) 549–65, esp. 551–56. **Flusser, D.** "Lukas 9:51–56—ein hebräisches Fragment." In *The New Testament Age.* FS B. Reicke. Macon, GA: Mercer, 1984. 1:165–79. **Friedrich, G.** "Lk 9,51 und die Entrückungschristologie des Lukas." In *Orientierung an Jesus: Zur Theologie der Synoptiker.* FS J. Schmid, ed. P. Hoffmann et al. Freiburg: Herder, 1973. 48–77. **Heutger, N.** "Die lukanischen Samaritanererzählungen in religionspädagogischer Sicht." In *Wort in der Zeit.* FS K. H. Rengstorf, ed. W. Haubeck and M. Bachmann. Leiden: Brill, 1980. 275–87. **LaVerdiere, E.** "Calling Down Fire from Heaven." *Emman* 95 (1989) 322–29. **Radl, W.** *Paulus und Jesus.* 103–26. **Ross, J. M.** "The Rejected Words in Luke 9, 54–46." *ExpTim* 84 (1972–73) 85–88. **Starcky, J.** "Obfirmavit faciem suam ut iret Jerusalem: Sens et portée de Luc ix, 51." *RSR* 39 (1951) 197–202. **Tiede, D. L.** *Prophecy and History in Luke-Acts.* 55–63.

And see further at the excursus above: "Journey to Jerusalem."

Translation

[51]*When the days of [the period before]*[a] *his being taken up were drawing to a close, it happened that he set his face to go to Jerusalem.* [52]*He sent two messengers before his face. Having gone off, they went into a village*[b] *of the Samaritans, in order to*[c] *prepare for him.* [53]*But they would not receive him because his face was going to Jerusalem.*[d] [54]*Seeing*

this, the disciples James and John said, "Lord do you wish us to tell fire to come down from heaven and destroy them?"[e] [55]*He turned and rebuked them;*[f] [56]*and they went into a different village.*

Notes

[a] The part in square brackets is not represented in the Gr. text but is added in an attempt to render the ellipse involved in the use of *συμπληροῦσθαι* (lit. "to be fulfilled").

[b] "Town" (*πόλιν*) is read here by ℵ Γ Ψ f^{13} etc.

[c] The more usual *ὥστε* is read here by ℵ A C D L W Θ Ξ Ψ etc.

[d] This is idiomatically impossible in English but has been retained because of the role played in the account by the repetition of the word *face.*

[e] The expansion "as Moses also did" is found in A C D W Θ Ψ etc.

[f] *καὶ εἶπεν οὐκ οἴδατε ποίου πνεύματος ἐστε*, "He said, 'You do not know of what spirit you are,'" is added by D d geo; while a fuller form, which has *οἵου* for the *ποίου* and adds *ὁ γὰρ υἱὸς τοῦ ἀνθρώπου οὐκ ἦλθεν ψυχὰς ἀνθρώπων ἀπολέσαι ἀλλὰ σῶσαι*, "For the Son of Man did not come to destroy peoples' lives but to save [them]," is read by Θ $f^{1,13}$ lat sy[c,p] bo[pt] Marcion etc. There are minor variations in the readings.

Form/Structure/Setting

The journey section of the Gospel now begins as Jesus resolutely turns his face toward Jerusalem. The rejection that awaits him is prefigured in the inhospitality of the village of the Samaritans (cf. 4:16–30), while his meekness in the face of rejection in Jerusalem has its own anticipation in Jesus' response here.

The larger section is often taken to be 9:51–62: the units vv 51–56 and 57–62 both have to do with initiating disciples into the ways of Jesus. There is, however, a good case to be made for extending the section to include the mission of the Seventy (and with it the attached material to 10:24): *ἀπέστειλεν . . . πρὸ προσώπου αὐτοῦ*, "he sent . . . before his face," occurs in 9:52 and 10:1; *δέχεσθαι*, "to receive," is used with the negative in 9:53 and 10:10 in contexts that involve entering a village/town, not being received, and moving on to somewhere else (and note also the use of *εἰσέρχεσθαι*, "to enter in," in 9:52; 10:5, 8, 10); and "the kingdom of God" occurs in 9:60, 62 and 10:9, 11 (9:60 provides a further link with its call to *proclaim* the kingdom of God). If the mission is thus to be included, then the particular viewing point for the mission here will be that of initiating the disciples into an imitation of Jesus' own manner of engaging in mission. (The broader links between the mission and Jesus' own practice in the journey section will be explored at 10:1–12.)

The materials of this pericope are unparalleled elsewhere in the Gospel tradition. This makes it much more difficult to estimate the Lukan contribution. The pervasive, and partly negative, Elijah motif does not seem likely to have been a Lukan contribution. Luke is almost certainly responsible for v 51 and, with it, at least in its present form, for the explanation in v 53 of the Samaritans' behavior. He may be responsible for the reference in v 54 to "the disciples James and John" (the Elijah imagery works in a more integrated way if the messengers are the speakers here). V 56 may well be Lukan.

As in many places there is a clear affinity here with Johannine tradition (cf. John 4:4–42). There is also tension with the Matthean prohibition of mission among the Samaritans (10:5). Schmidt (*Rahmen*, 268–69) considered that the present tradition emerged as an explanation of the Matthean restriction (Goulder, 459, adopts this view but regards it as Luke's speculative reconstruction of events as he tries to make sense of Mark and Matthew). It is perhaps best to see the Elijah motif as responsible for the mission emphasis of the account and to understand an original that involved only hospitality on the pilgrim journey to Jerusalem (cf. Josephus, *Ant.* 20.118; *War* 2.232; *Life* 269). The mission emphasis of the account is in any case restrained. In form-critical terms we have here a story about Jesus.

Comment

Jesus now sets out resolutely on the journey for which he has been preparing his disciples in 9:21–50. Luke tells of some in the party going ahead to prepare his way, in the pattern of the eschatological preparatory role of Elijah, but they meet rejection, and James and John suggest a further imitation of Elijah in calling fire down from heaven. Jesus categorically rejects such a suggestion, and, in the spirit of the mission instructions to come in 10:1–12, they move on to a different village.

51 Both the first and the second half of the verse are best taken as Lukan formulations. The first half uses one of Luke's favored ἐγένετο, "it happened," idioms; and it has a notable similarity to Acts 2:1 and cf. Luke 2:6, 21. In the second half, the use of πορεύεσθαι, "to go," to Jerusalem aligns with Luke's use of this verb for the journey to Jerusalem (9:53; 13:33; and especially 17:11). Luke's τὸ πρόσωπον ἐστήρισεν + infinitive is not quite LXX idiom, but is an easy development from Ezek 21:7 (ET 21:2, but the LXX is significantly different here from the MT; and cf. 4 Kgdms 12:18), and definitely close enough to fit Luke's desire to write in "biblical Greek."

The comparison with 2:6, 21 suggests that "the days" are best taken as days of Jesus' earthly life or ministry and not as the days of death, resurrection, and ascension, as considered by many (In Acts 2:1 are we dealing with the ending of the day [at sundown], which marked the beginning of Pentecost?). When the days are finished, the time has arrived for the ἀνάλημψις (lit. "taking up"). There is an ellipse here that makes translation difficult. The verb is used to express the idea of a divine timetable for the unfolding of the salvation-history to which Luke attests (cf. Gal 4:4, but here the focus is on the end and not the beginning of Jesus' life).

ἀνάλημψις has been taken to mean "death" (esp. Friedrich, "Entrückungschristologie," 48–52) on the basis of *Pss. Sol.* 4:18, with possible support from *As. Mos.* 10:12; *Ps-Clem. Hom.* 3:47; *2 Apoc. Bar.* 46:7; and a second-century Montanist Christian inscription (the last cited by BAGD, 57). But it is disputed whether *As. Mos.* 10:12 or *2 Apoc. Bar.* 46:7 refers to death at all, while *Ps-Clem. Hom.* 3:47, and probably the Montanist inscription, do so in the context of the immortality of the soul, which is thought to be taken by God at death. This leaves only *Pss. Sol.* 4:18. The reference to death is clear, but almost certainly there is some metaphor of transference involved too. The most that can be said is that one may talk about death by using the term ἀνάλημψις, but that it is likely that some metaphor of transference is always involved in such language, whether seriously intended in some context of belief, or as a piece of pious convention, or as an imprecise reflection on the mystery of death.

The cognate verb is used in connection with the death of Moses in Philo, *Moses* 2.291. Here death is the threshold that sets Moses on the upward flight to heaven. The travel of the soul to heaven is the clear context in *T. Abr.* 15–20, as it is likely to be in another Montanist inscription (see BAGD, 56). The verb may, thus, be used in a manner quite parallel to the use explored above for the noun. But the verb is also used very clearly in connection with translation to heaven, as happened to Elijah (4 Kgdms 2:10–11; Sir 48:9; 49:14; 1 Macc 2:58; *T. Job* 39:12; Mark 16:19; Acts 1:2, 11; *Acts Pil.* A 15:1; 16:2). It is hard not to see this sort of background as pertaining also to the use of the noun in the present verse, and in particular not to see a reference to the ascension to come in Luke 24:50–51; Acts 1:9–11. At the same time it is probably right to appeal to the use of the noun in connection with death, along with the place of the passion predictions in setting the context for the present verse, and to understand the use of *ἀνάλημψις* in connection with Jesus' pathway through death to exaltation at the right hand of God. Davies (*SE* 2 [1964] 164–69) would also include the journey itself as the first stage of the *ἀνάλημψις*, but this is hardly convincing.

On the basis of OT idiom (esp. the uses with *ἐπί* in Ezekiel), some have detected hostility in the *τὸ πρόσωπον ἐστήρισεν*, "set/fix firmly the face," idiom; but this is not true for the source of the idiom suggested above (Ezek 21:7 [LXX]), nor for the words taken at face value, nor for the role of Jerusalem in the nearest context. Rather, Jesus sets out resolutely to make the trip to Jerusalem for which 9:21–50 have been a focused preparation. The specific mention of Jerusalem as the place of destiny has thus far been restricted to 9:31, but reference to the leadership group in v 22 has already implied a Jerusalem setting clearly enough.

52 Luke uses to start the journey a tradition of Jesus' seeking hospitality in a Samaritan village and being refused it. The use of *ὡς* + infinitive may be Lukan (cf. Acts 20:24). The verse strongly alludes to Mal 3:1 (not LXX): "I send my messenger to prepare the way before me." These messengers are in some sense preparing for Jesus in the way that John the Baptist, as an Elijah figure, had been called to do. By means of the allusion back, which we will find in 10:1, Luke suggests that the messengers are messengers of the presence of the kingdom as are the Seventy in 10:1–12. At the same time, the mission emphasis here is extremely subdued: the event prefigures later mission to the Samaritans (Acts 8:4–25) rather than itself truly being an instance of mission to them (in much the same way that the Pentecost crowd [of Jews and proselytes from many lands] prefigures in Luke's handling the worldwide gentile mission to come; Lohse ["Missionarisches Handeln," esp. 174–77] vastly exaggerates the indications of ministry to the Samaritans). The same connection with 10:1 will suggest that the mission there is to be seen as travel preparations for Jesus, as is the case here in 9:52–56.

The role of the Samaritan village is in the first instance to establish that Jesus is heading south for Jerusalem. The origin of the split between the Samaritans and the Jews is shrouded in mystery. Traditionally they have been taken to be the descendants of the mixed population settled in Israel after the Assyrian conquest of the Northern Kingdom (2 Kgs 17:24–41). Probably the breach of which the NT situation is the aftermath is to be dated to the late fourth century B.C., shortly before Alexander the Great. Manasseh, the brother of the high priest married the daughter of the Samaritan Sanballat and was expelled from Jerusalem. He responded by building a temple on Mount Gerizim. In 128 B.C. John Hyrcanus' destruction of the Gerizim temple created deep and lasting resentment. But it would seem that the Jewish Samaritan break was not complete until into the first century B.C. The Samaritans developed their own form of the Pentateuch (the extent of their canon), their own liturgy, and their own religious literature. The Samaritans were, however, never considered by the Jews simply as non-Jews: their affiliation to the congregation of Israel was never denied, only considered doubtful! (See J. Jeremias, *TDNT* 7:88–94; R. J. Coggins, *Samaritans and Jews: The Origins of the Samaritans Reconsidered* [Oxford: Blackwell, 1975]; J. D. Purvis, "Samaritans," In *The Interpreters Dictionary of the Bible*, supplementary vol. [Nashville: Abingdon, 1976] 776–77; W. A. Brindle, "The Origin and History of the Samaritans," *GTJ* 5 [1984] 47–75; R. Pummer, *The Samaritans* [Leiden: Brill, 1987].)

53 The Samaritans do not receive Jesus. This is just what (10:10) Jesus anticipates will happen to some of his representatives in towns they will enter. *τὸ πρόσωπον αὐτοῦ ἦν πορευόμενον εἰς* (lit. "his face was going to") sounds Semitic, but there is no true parallel to it in the LXX. Luke will have developed it out of v 51, perhaps displacing a simpler statement of the Jewish/Samaritan religious rivalry that lay at the basis of the present rejection (for the hostility that could be aroused by the traveling Jewish pilgrims, see Josephus, *Ant.* 20.118–23; *War* 2.232–33). It is hard to be sure whether Luke is to some degree excusing the Samaritans (cf. Acts 3:17), or whether the rejection and moving on should be connected closely with 10:10–12—probably the former (note Jesus' rebuke of James and John). For Luke, the restatement of Jesus' determined orientation to Jerusalem underlines the importance of this perspective for the conception of the travel narrative.

54 The suggestion of James and John is clearly based on Elijah's action in 2 Kgs 1:10, 12. The LXX wording is followed closely except that "destroy" replaces "consume." Preparing the way for the one who is heading to Jerusalem to suffer is not appropriately done with fiery judgment. A time of judgment will come (10:12, 14; 13:1–9; etc.), but it is not now. Probably the original did not distinguish between the messengers and those suggesting this further Elijah-like act. The presence of "James and John" here may be a continuation from 9:49, where John is spokesperson for an equally rejected sentiment. There may also be an element of compensation for Luke's elimination of Mark 10:35–45, where James and John are also concerned with the wielding of power. To have "the disciples" followed by names is unparalleled in the Gospel tradition. It may underline the failure here of James and John precisely as disciples. There is a certain parallel between the proposal of James and John here and that made by those with Jesus in 22:49, and a similarity in the response of Jesus.

55 The language here is reminiscent of Mark 8:33, which Luke has not used, but some such language of rebuke must always have stood at this point in the story. There is a measure of anticlimax in the account, which is compensated for in some MSS (see textual note) by means of the addition, "You do not know of what kind of spirit you are. For the Son of Man did not come to destroy peoples' lives but to save [them]." Despite the defense of the originality of this reading by Ross (*ExpTim* 84 [1972–73] 85–88), it seems best to treat it as a (quite fitting) scribal expansion. For Luke the account is dominated by the journey motif, and he does not sense any incompleteness. The journey in light of 9:21–50 is all the explanation necessary for Jesus' rebuke of James and John.

56 This verse is a Lukan formulation under the influence of (*i*) the journey motif: the journey continues; and (*ii*) the mission instructions to come in 10:10–12. There is no implication that Samaritan villages are henceforth to be avoided, nor is there any insistence that they went on (to mission) to further Samaritan villages.

Explanation

The journey to Jerusalem for which we have been prepared in 9:21–50 now commences. Jesus' resolution is writ large in this episode, and there is a prefiguring of the fate that awaits him in Jerusalem, but also of the spirit in which he will receive that final rejection.

9:51–56 is part of 9:51–10:24 as a larger section in which the focus is on initiating the disciples into the ways of Jesus. Here there is the handling of rejection. In the following verses (9:57–62) the radical nature of following Jesus is in focus. 10:1–24 will initiate the disciples into Jesus' own manner of engaging in mission. (We may note how much of the instruction there can be illustrated by Jesus' own practice in the following chapters.)

Now in the divine plan the time is fast approaching for Jesus to be taken up. The word used is sometimes a pious way of talking about death, but here, while it embraces Jesus' death in Jerusalem, its focus is clearly on his translation to glory. There is a certain analogy between this prospect for Jesus and what happened to Elijah (see 2 Kgs 2:10–11). Sensing that the time was fast coming, Jesus resolutely sets his face toward Jerusalem.

Jesus begins to head south and so toward a Samaritan village. With a play upon the words of Mal 3:1, Luke tells of messengers who go ahead to prepare for him. In a modest way they are doing what the Elijah of the end-time would do in preparation for the coming of the Lord. They are also doing what the Seventy will do in 10:1–20. In this way Luke hints at the mission to the Samaritans to come in Acts 8:4–25. Jesus is not, however, welcome in this Samaritan village.

Jewish pilgrims regularly passed through Samaria on their way to the Jerusalem feasts. Sometimes there was trouble that even led to massacre. The hostility between Jews and Samaritans at that time is well known. This village was not going to accept such a band of pilgrims destined for Jerusalem. They have no knowledge of the nature of Jesus' resolute orientation to Jerusalem. Samaritan rejection here acts as something of a foil for Jesus' positive presentation of Samaritans in 10:29–39 and 17:11–19.

James and John think that the Elijah ministry of preparation for the Lord should take on the fierce face of 2 Kgs 1:10, 12, 14. But this does not at all fit the tenor of the one who goes to Jerusalem to suffer. They earn only Jesus' rebuke. A similar interchange will come at the point of Jesus' arrest in Jerusalem (22:47–51).

Jesus is not at all daunted. His traveling band continues on its way to another village, which may or may not have been Samaritan. It makes no difference for Luke's telling. What is important is that the journeying continues.

Following Jesus without Qualification (9:57–62)

Bibliography

Bailey, K. E. *Through Peasant Eyes.* 22–32. **Blair, H. J.** "Putting One's Hand to the Plough: Luke ix. 62 in the Light of 1 Kings xix. 19–21." *ExpTim* 79 (1967–68) 342–43. **Brodie, T. L.** "Luke 9:57–62: A Systematic Adaptation of the Divine Challenge to Elijah (1 Kings 19)." In *SBL 1989 Seminar Papers,* ed. D. J. Lull. Atlanta, GA: Scholars, 1989. 237–45. **Caragounis, C. C.** *The Son of Man: Vision and Interpretation.* WUNT 68. Tübingen: Mohr-Siebeck, 1986. 175–79. **Casey, M.** "The Jackals and the Son of Man (Matt. 8.20//Luke 9.58)." *JSNT* 23 (1985) 3–22. **Cerfaux, L.** "Variantes de Lc., IX, 62." *ETL* 12 (1955) 326–28. **Coulot, C.** *Jésus et le disciple: Étude dur l'autorité messianique de Jésus.* Études bibliques n.s. 8. Paris: Gabalda, 1987. 18–40. **Derrett, J. D. M.** "Two 'Harsh' Sayings of Jesus Explained." *DR* 103 (1985) 218–25. **Ehrhardt, A. T.** "Lass die Toten die Toten begraben." *ST* 6 (1952) 128–64. **Glombitza, O.** "Die christologische Aussage des Lukas in seiner Gestaltung der drei Nachfolgeworte Lukas IX 57–62." *NovT* 13 (1971) 14–23. **Hengel, M.** *The Charismatic Leader and His Followers.* Esp. 3–15. **Hommel, H.** "Herrenworte im Lichte sokratischer Überlieferung." *ZNW* 57 (1966) 1–23. **Klemm, H. G.** "Das Wort von der Selbstbestattung der toten: Beobachtungen zur Auslegungsgeschichte von Mt. VIII. 22 par." *NTS* 16 (1969–70) 60–75. **Küven, C.** "Weisung für die Nachfolge: Eine Besinnung über Lk 9,57–62." *BibLeb* 2 (1961) 49–53. **Leser, P.** "No Man, Having Put His Hand to the Plough." In *On Language, Culture and Religion.* FS E. A. Nida, ed. M. Black and W. A. Smalley. The Hague/Paris: Mouton, 1974. 241–58. **Louw, J. P.** "Discourse Analysis and the Greek New Testament." *BT* 24 (1973) 101–18, esp . 104–8. **Luria, S.** "Zur Quelle von Mt 8,19." *ZNW* 25 (1926) 282–86. **McCane, B. R.** "'Let the Dead Bury Their Own Dead': Secondary Burial and Matt 8:21–22." *HTR* 83 (1990) 31–43. **Perles, F.** "Lass den Toten ihre Totengräber, damit er ihnen das Geleit gebe." *ZNW* 19 (1919–20) 96. ———. "Lass den Toten ihre Totengräber, damit er ihnen das Geleit gebe." *ZNW* 25 (1926) 286. **Ruegg, U.** "Luc 9, 57–62: Vivre en adultes." In *Reconnaissance à Suzanne de Dietrich.* CBFV. Paris: Foi et Vie, 1971. 126–37. **Schulz, A.** *Nachfolge und Nachahmen: Studien über das Verhältnis der neutestamentlichen Jüngerschaft zur urchristichen Vorbildethik.* SANT 6. Munich: Kössel, 1962. 105–8. **Schürmann, H.** *Gottes Reich—Jesus Geschick.* 91–96, 162–63. **Schwarz, G.** " *Ἄφες τοὺς νεκροὺς θάψαι τοὺς ἑαυτῶν νεκρούς.*" *ZNW* 72 (1981) 272–76. **Smith, M. H.** "No Place for a Son of Man." *Forum* 4.4 (1988) 84–107. **Steinhauser, M. G.** "Putting One's Hand to the Plow: The Authenticity of Q 9:61–62." *Forum* 5.1 (1989) 152–58. **Strobel, A.** "Die Nachfolge Jesu: Theologische Besinnung zu Lukas 9, 57–62." *TPQ* 98 (1950) 1–8. **Tannehill, R. C.** *The Sword of His Mouth.* 157–65. **Zimmermann, H.** *Neutestamentliche Methodenlehre: Darstellung der historischkritischen Methode.* Stuttgart: Katholisches Bibelwerk, 1967. 116–22.

And see also at the excursus: "Journey to Jerusalem."

Translation

57 *As they were going*[a] *on their*[b] *way, someone said to him, "I will follow you wherever you are heading."*[c] 58 *Jesus said to him, "Foxes have holes and the birds of the air have places to settle, but the Son of Man has nowhere to lay his head."* 59 *He said to someone else, "Follow me!" He said, "Lord,*[d] *let me first go and bury my father."* 60 *He said to him, "Leave the dead to bury their own dead; and you go and proclaim the kingdom of God."* 61 *Someone else said, "I will follow you, Lord; but first let me say good-bye to the members*

of my household." [62]*Jesus said to him, "No one who puts his hand to the plough and looks back*[e] *is fit for*[f] *the kingdom of God."*

Notes

[a] A (D) W Ψ etc. and the majority text begin the verse with an ἐγένετο ("it happened") construction.

[b] Gr. "the way."

[c] A C W Θ Ψ etc. read κύριε, "Lord," here. It could be original.

[d] "Lord" is omitted here by B D sy[s] and a few other texts, but as its presence, if original, constitutes one of several deliberate links between v 61 and the preceding, it should probably be accepted.

[e] There are a number of minor variants in this verse, the most significant of which is that of P[45] (fragmentary at this point) D it Cl, which puts the "look[ing] back" clause before the "putting [the] hand to the plough" clause.

[f] ἐν, "in," is added here by P[75] ℵ[2] 579 700 etc. εἰς τὴν βασιλείαν, "into the kingdom," is found in A C D W Θ Ψ 0181 etc.

Form/Structure/Setting

Luke has started the journey with an anticipation of the rejection that awaits Jesus in Jerusalem. Now he will stress that following the Jesus who goes the way of the cross makes radical demands upon all who would contemplate such a course.

For this section Luke draws on materials from a source that he shares with Matthew, at least for vv 57–60. Both the Matthean (8:18–22) and the Lukan forms bear the marks of the respective editor's interests and style. Luke probably does not at any point of the material preserve a form more original than the Matthean form, but neither does he show dependence on those features of the Matthean account most likely to be a product of that writer's own editing.

We have here three pronouncement stories drawn together into a set around the shared motif of the radical nature of discipleship. Each of the three pronouncements has greater need of its present narrative setting than is allowed for in standard form-critical orthodoxy. In particular the pronouncement in v 60 only makes sense as a response to something quite specific. The pronouncement of v 58 could have circulated alone. It makes best sense as a challenge about what is involved in desiring to throw in one's lot with the Son of Man, but it could have been preserved as reflecting an aspect of the self-consciousness of Jesus.

V 62 could also have circulated independently as a general challenge to recognize the consistency of commitment to which the preaching of the kingdom of God calls Jesus' hearers. Two considerations, however, make this unlikely. First, v 61 is not a colorless setting for the pronouncement to come: the permission requested is set in words that deliberately echo the words of Elisha as he is called by Elijah in 1 Kgs 19:20. Not only do we have a challenge to normal family decencies, but we have a dramatic heightening from even the exalted call to the prophetic office (cf. 10:23–24). As request and denial are seen together, the truly radical nature of Jesus' challenge is expressed. The second consideration builds on the first. Not only the request, but probably also the response, has an allusion to the call of Elisha, since Elisha is ploughing when he asks to bid farewell to his family. Request and response have been conceived together as a single unit.

The confidence with which we may trace these three scenes back into the time of the ministry of Jesus has been variously judged. The fortunes of the Son of Man saying (v 58) tend to rise or fall on the basis of the general evaluation of Son of Man sayings that refer to the present of Jesus' ministry (see excursus on Son of Man after 9:21–22, where such sayings are considered to have good claim to authenticity). Compared to the passion predictions (see at 9:21–22 for a defense of their basic historicity), there is not the same scope for considering this pronouncement to be prophecy after the event. While human rejection may be implied in the saying (see *Comment* below), the focus is on the humble lot of the Son of Man, so that it is hardly likely that the saying has been generated out of the myth of wisdom finding no home on the earth and returning to heaven (esp. *1 Enoch* 42:1–2). Bultmann has claimed proverbial origin for the saying (*Synoptic Tradition*, 28), but the statement is hardly an obvious proverb and has not been paralleled. The saying is much more at home on the lips of Jesus than as a community product (cf. Casey, *JSNT* 23 [1985] 12–13).

The call to leave the dead to bury their own dead (vv 59–60) is such a violation of all ancient versions of filial duty as to be hard to explain outside the context of Jesus' own sense of the compelling urgency of the claims of the kingdom of God. Scholarship is almost unanimous in attributing this logion to the historical Jesus (cf. Hengel, *Charismatic Leader*, 6 n. 12).

There is considerably more dispute about the third of our pronouncement stories (vv 61–62), which is reported only by Luke. The relationship here with 1 Kgs 19:19–20, especially because it is reflected in the words both of Jesus and of the one who had addressed him, is suggestive of literary activity (oral or written) rather than the simple reporting of an event. Lukan creation is frequently suspected (e.g., Glombitza, *NovT* 13 [1971] 16; Fitzmyer, 837; Goulder, 460). Luke is certainly a practitioner of the kind of allusive use of Scripture evidenced here, but he is also, and more often, an heir to it. The radical break with family involved in responding to the call of Jesus, which is reflected here, is undoubtedly historically authentic (cf. 14:26; and for the rupture of normal greeting practice provoked by the urgency of the kingdom of God, see 10:4). It is not unlikely that a remembered call scene from the ministry does underlie the present verses, perhaps incorporating the pronouncement much as we have it, and that the mention of ploughing and the call scene itself have become the basis for exploiting the similarities and differences to the call of 1 Kgs 19:19–20. The idea of saying good-bye to family may have already played a part in the scene, or it may have at this point been drawn in from the known tradition of Jesus' call to radical detachment from family, in order to make a contrast with Elijah's greater flexibility.

Luke begins by reinforcing the Journey to Jerusalem context. Then he consciously organizes the items as a triplet. In the first and third instances, those who address Jesus make the proposal to follow him; in the central episode, Jesus is the one who calls to follow. Only in the central interchange is there a specific formulation of the task that those challenged to follow are called to share in ("proclaim the kingdom of God"). In the opening item Jesus raises the difficulties that stand before the one who would follow. For the remaining two items, it is the one speaking to Jesus who raises the difficulties. In both these last cases the claims of the kingdom of God also are the basis for disallowing the concessions sought.

Comment

Luke sustains the sense of journeying as he now draws in a set of traditions that will highlight the fiercely radical nature of the call to follow Jesus, with its priorities that displace even the most solemn and sacred of filial obligations.

57 Luke provides a more decisive setting for these materials than Matthew's, in which Jesus takes leave of the crowds and crosses the lake of Galilee. Luke is still establishing for his readers the sense that the journeying to Jerusalem must not be lost sight of through all the central chapters of his Gospel account. The material of vv 21–50, in which the journeying motif is evoked makes an excellent setting for the teaching about the radical nature of Jesus' call to follow, which is to emerge here. In Matthew it is "a certain [εἷς] scribe" who addresses Jesus, but Luke has the totally neutral *τις*, "a certain person/someone." The Matthean scribe addresses Jesus as "teacher," but no mode of address is found in the Lukan form. Both these, but especially the former, are likely to be Matthean additions. Luke uses his favored *πρὸς αὐτόν*, "to him," after the verb "said." The man is proposing that he join the intimate group of Jesus' followers as they make their way to Jerusalem.

58 Apart from a "correction" of one historical present, this verse is identical with the Matthean rendering. As has been frequently noted, the Synoptists are more conservative in their rendering of Jesus' words (and of important words addressed to him) than in their handling of narrative setting. Conservation here will have been further encouraged by the rhythmical nature of the wording of Jesus' reply (to which Tannehill, *Sword of His Mouth*, 162, has drawn attention). The pathos of human homelessness has been expressed by means of a contrast with the lot of animals in Plutarch, *Life of Tib. Gracch.* 9 (928c). Homer, *Od.* 18.130–31, expresses the sentiment that the beast is more protected and persistent than the human creature. The latter has some similarity to the present text, if the sense is (with Casey, *JSNT* 23 [1985] 7–10) that, while nature provides shelters for the birds and the foxes in their (migratory) traveling, the Son of Man (or humanity in general) has no such automatic provision. The former is closer if we take the statement as in no way a general statement, but rather as a statement that is of a piece with the passion predictions: the Son of Man is ultimately a misfit in this world where the invasion of the kingdom of God is considered to be an intrusion. Either possibility could be related to the journey context, but the latter is finally more natural. The eager applicant is being told that he is offering to throw in his lot with a cause that is (quite soon) to prove to be an unpopular one.

As in each of the following encounters, there is no indication of the response of the individual. All the attention is concentrated on Jesus' powerful words (as Tannehill, *Sword of His Mouth*, 158), and it is finally the reader who is called upon to respond to the challenge.

59 It is difficult to be sure whether Matthew or Luke has made the major changes here. Probably Luke has given the initiative to Jesus by bringing forward the "follow me" from Jesus' response to the beginning point of this encounter. This makes the episode recall the summons of Levi to follow Jesus (5:27–28). Luke provides a brief introduction that uses only *ἕτερος*, "a different [person]," of Matthew's introduction (Matthew's identification of this person as a disciple is probably his own addition). The address as *κύριε*, "sir/lord," is slightly insecure in the Lukan text here. The word often carries a rather stronger sense than "sir" in Luke's usage. (For the alternative reconstruction, which sees Matthew as making the main changes, see Miyoshi, *Anfang des Reiseberichts*, 39 [his appeal to *πρῶτον*, "first," as indicating derangement in the Matthean text may be answered by suggesting that in Matthew's source the pair of pronouncement stories already had a minimal narrative setting, which indicated that Jesus was on the point of traveling].) Luke improves Matthew's coordinated infinitives by making one a participle. Despite all attempts to soften the words of Jesus to come, we must assume that the father in this case is either dead or on the point of death. The one challenged had before him a solemn filial duty, which he seeks respite from his call to perform. In Jewish tradition, the burial of a dead relative was a prime religious duty, and in the case of the death of parents, responsibility rested particularly on the son of the family (the situation is well documented in Hengel [*Charismatic Leader*, 8–10]; *b. Ber.* 31a says "He who is confronted by a dead relative is freed from reciting the Shema, from the Eighteen Benedictions, and from all the commandments stated in the Torah"; a son who contemplates the possibility of his own imminent death is troubled in Tob 6:15 that his parents "have no other son to bury them").

60 Luke once again replaces a historic present reflected in the Matthean form of this verse. He has already used the call to follow at the opening; for this loss he compensates by adding at the end "and you go and proclaim the kingdom of God" ("proclaim the kingdom of God" is frequent in Luke but with different verbs: 4:43; 8:1; 16:16; 9:2; Acts 8:12; 28:31; the verb here, *διαγγέλειν*, is found [but not with "kingdom of God"] in Acts 21:26).

The words "leave the dead to bury their own dead" could be imagined on the lips of a Cynic philosopher, with his utter disregard for his body once it is dead, but the words would not, then, have any sense that could conceivably find its way into the synoptic Gospel tradition (see Hengel, *Charismatic Leader*, 5–6, for texts). The various mistranslation theories are based solely on the desire to soften the words of Jesus, and should be rejected, as the psychologizing explanations of the man's request have been above. Jesus' words do not deny the normal claims of the pious duty to bury the dead; they simply insist that a more pressing duty is upon the one addressed. The urgent need for the man to bind himself to Jesus and to become a proclaimer of the kingdom of God takes precedence over other responsibilities in much the way that in Jewish thought the responsibility to bury a relative took precedence over one's normal obligations under the Torah (the attempt by Glombitza, *NovT* 13 [1971] 19–20, to relate the refusal of permission to bury the father to a priestly need to retain ceremonial purity involves the intrusion of a foreign idea and falls foul of Hengel's demonstration [*Charismatic Leader*, 10–11] that the NT period was seeing the relaxation, in the case of death of close family members, of the strict enforcement of such (high) priestly requirements; Hengel's own linking [11–12] of God's denial to Ezekiel of normal mourning for the death of his wife [24:15–24] is much more illuminating). The call to proclaim the kingdom of God anticipates the mission of 10:1–12, which will show how the apparent contradiction between the call to follow Jesus and the directive to go off and preach is to be resolved (the language of departure is actually borrowed from, and functions as an alternative to, the request of the man for permission to depart and bury his father). On preaching the kingdom of God, see at 4:43.

Though, as Fitzmyer (836) puts it, the view that the dead who are to do the burying are the physically dead has been "laughed off the exegetical stage," it is actually the natural reading of the text, and it may be related to the Hellenistic view that the dead belong to a different realm (the underworld) from the realm of the living, which has its own dynamic (note the Scholion on Euripides, *Andromache* 849, which is cited by Hengel [*Charismatic Leader,* 6 n. 12] and earlier drawn attention to by Ehrhardt [*ST* 6 [1952] 130]: *οἱ γὰρ νεκροὶ μέλ[λ]ουσι τοῖς νεκροῖς ὡς οἱ ζῶντες τοῖς ζῶσι,* "For the dead are an object of care to the dead as the living [are] to the living"). We may compare also the Semitic view of going down to the shades, but this is considerably less developed. This understanding of Jesus' words is only absurd if taken literally. The force of the words is finally "let other arrangements be made; you have more pressing duties." If we insist on a literal sense, we have to distinguish between the two references to the dead: let the spiritually dead bury the physically dead, but this seems less satisfactory, especially with the "their own" (*ἑαυτῶν*) in the text, which binds the two uses together.

It is not likely that Luke's readers or the early church in general had to face any major problem over funerals of church members. The text functions, rather, as what Tannehill (*Sword of His Mouth,* 163) would call a "focal instance," which because of its very extremity challenges any and every postponing of the demands of discipleship (cf. 14:15–24).

61 Vv 61–62 are not paralleled in the Synoptic tradition. The language that binds v 61 to the preceding is probably a Lukan contribution ("said," "a different [person]," "I will follow you," "Lord," "first," "allow me"). There may be further Lukan language as Miyoshi (*Anfang des Reiseberichts,* 42–43) suggests on the basis of a comparison with 14:33–35 and 17:31, but the case is not compelling.

The clash is not so violent as in the previous episode, but once more the would-be follower will propose the fulfilling of his filial responsibilities only to be denied by Jesus. The request here parallels that by Elisha to Elijah when the latter has symbolized the call of the former to the prophetic office by casting his mantel upon the other.

62 Jesus implicitly refuses the man's request. A situation is present whose demands are more pressing and urgent than were those imposed upon Elisha by his call. Marshall (412) cites as nearest parallel words from Hesiod, *Works and Days* 443: ". . . one who will attend to his work and drive a straight furrow and is past the age for gaping after his fellows, but will keep his mind on his work." The concerns of the kingdom of God require the most diligent and unremitting care. Family ties in this setting can only represent a looking back. Fittingly, Miyoshi (*Anfang des Reiseberichts,* 56) draws attention to Elisha's later refusal to leave Elijah in the context of his impending assumption to heaven (2 Kgs 2:1–15). There might be some over-exegesis involved in making, as Miyoshi does, the further connection with Luke 9:51, but the thought follows the right lines.

Explanation

Luke creates a strong bridge from the section 9:21–50 into the journey narrative for which it had been preparing. The rejection in a Samaritan village has given us an anticipation of what is to come in Jerusalem. Now these brief accounts of three men who considered following Jesus on the fateful journey to Jerusalem carry us forward from the challenging words of vv 23–27.

It is in connection with the journey to suffering in Jerusalem that the question of following Jesus is raised. The first man makes an eager and unconditional offer to follow Jesus anywhere. Do these words come too easily to him? Does he know what he is letting himself in for? One might fear that the attraction for him of joining the group of Jesus' most intimate followers might conform with what we have been seeing of the disciple band's own preoccupation with greatness and power. We will never know about the man, because his story is told for its challenge to us. We do not know how he responded to Jesus' words, but we do know what our own response is.

Jesus' words could be taken as applying a general truth pointedly to his own situation. Nature provides "housing" for the foxes and the birds, but not so for a human person. Human housing is built by human effort and is part of the fabric of human society. If you are a person in Jesus' situation, facing a journey to rejection by your society and your fellows, then this sense of the hostility of nature becomes acutely pressing.

One might better see Jesus' words as expressing a sentiment like that which stands behind the passion predictions. *Even* foxes and birds have a welcoming place to settle, but Jesus, though he is the Man of Destiny, has only the prospect of the hostile rejection that awaits him in Jerusalem. Of course in a literal sense, Jesus quite frequently found hospitality and for a time maintained a house in Capernaum. But at a deeper level, he had not found human society too welcoming, and the prospect of the cross was already casting its shadow.

The first man had made his own proposal to follow. The second is called to do so by Jesus. He is quite willing to rise to Jesus' challenge, despite the previous somber words about the Son of Man's lack of anywhere to lay his head. But the radical nature of the call is to bite yet deeper. The man's father is dead or on the point of dying. In Jewish tradition (and not only there!), as son, he was considered to have prime responsibility for providing a decent burial. In Jewish tradition this obligation was so sacred as to override any other obligations of the OT law. Jesus' words do not deny the normal claims of the pious duty to bury the dead, but, in a way that is harsh and even shocking, they insist that this man has a more pressing duty.

In his words Jesus appeals to the common sentiment that the world of the dead and of the living are, for the most part, spheres sealed off from one another. The father has moved off into the embrace of that other world. Let those who are already there take responsibility as they receive this newcomer. Of course, taken literally as an answer to the man's dilemma it is a piece of nonsense. But it is not to be taken literally. The harsh words are simply to impress upon the man that he has more pressing responsibilities, and that some other arrangements will have to do for the burial of the father. No real concern is expressed about what these other arrangements might be.

No doubt we would all rather that Jesus not have spoken in this way. And while we feel the challenge of this episode in connection with any kind of postponing of the demands of discipleship, it is very difficult for us to fit this sort of challenge into the kind of society in which most of us believe our discipleship is to be performed. The prophet Ezekiel faced a not dissimilar challenge when he was denied by God the right to mourn the death of his own wife (Ezek 24:15–24). In such words we experience the ultimate contradiction between the kingdom of God and even the best and most Christian of our humanist values.

The third encounter is in many ways a milder rerun of the second. It is a play upon the call of Elisha to be a prophet alongside Elijah and, ultimately, to replace Elijah (1 Kgs 19:19–21). That was an exalted calling, but at that time there was scope for Elisha first to take his departure from his family. This calling, because of the presence of the kingdom of God, goes beyond anything that Elisha would experience (compare Luke 10:23–24). It is more important and it is also more urgent. There is no place here for any hesitation or delay. To do anything other than to move right into the calling would be to behave like the man at the plough who is ploughing his way forward, but looking behind him, and so, loses the line of the furrow. That is not good enough for the kingdom of God! When the demand of God presses upon us, it must take priority over all that belongs to good sense, good citizenship, and good family membership.

Mission Charge for the Seventy Who Are Sent Ahead (10:1–16)

Bibliography

Black, M. "The Kingdom of God Has Come." *ExpTim* 63 (1951–52) 298–90. **Bosold, I.** *Pazifismus und prophetische Provokation: Das Grussverbot Lk 10,4b und sein historischer Kontext.* SBS 90. Stuttgart: Katholisches Bibelwerk, 1978. **Catchpole, D.** "The Mission Charge in Q." *Semeia* 55 (1991) 147–74. **Charette, B.** "A Harvest for the People? An Interpretation of Matthew 9.37f." *JSNT* 38 (1990) 29–35. **Comber, J. A.** "The Composition and Literary Characteristics of Matt 11:20–24." *CBQ* 39 (1977) 497–504. **Delebecque, É.** "Sur un hellénisme de Saint Luc." *RB* 87 (1980) 59–93. **Dillon, R. J.** "Early Christian Experience in the Gospel Sayings." *BiTod* 21 (1983) 83–88. **Edwards, R. A.** "Matthew's Use of Q in Chapter Eleven." In *Logia,* ed. J. Delobel. 257–75, esp. 263–69. **George, A.** "Paroles de Jésus sur ses miracles (Mt 11, 5. 21; 12, 27. 28 et par.)." In *Jésus aux origines de la christologie,* ed. J. Dupont. 283–301, esp. 293–96. **Harvey, A. E.** "'The Workman is Worthy of His Hire': Fortunes of a Proverb in the Early Church." *NovT* 24 (1982) 209–21. **Hoffmann, P.** "Lukas 10,5–11 in der Instruktionsrede der Logienquelle." *EKK Vorarbeiten* 3 (1971) 37–53. **Hutton, W. R.** "The Kingdom of God Has Come." *ExpTim* 64 (1952–53) 89–91. **Jacobson, A. D.** "The Literary Unity of Q: Lc 10,2–16 and Parallels as a Test Case." In *Logia,* ed. J. Delobel. 419–23. **Jellicoe, S.** "St Luke and the 'Seventy(-two).'" *NTS* 6 (1959–60) 319–21. **Jeremias, J.** "Paarweise Sendung im Neuen Testament." In *New Testament Essays: Studies in Memory of T. W. Manson,* ed. A. J. B. Higgins. Manchester: University Press, 1959. 136–43. **Klasson, W.** "'A Child of Peace' (Luke 10.6) in First Century Context." *NTS* 27 (1980–81) 488–506. **Lang, B.** "Grussverbot oder Besuchsverbot? Eine sozialgeschichtliche Deutung von Lukas 10,4b." *BZ* 26 (1982) 75–79. **Laufen, R.** *Die Doppelüberlieferung der Logionquelle und des Markusevangeliums.* 201–95, 491–542. **Lignée, H.** "La mission des soixante-douze: Lc 10, 1–12.17–20." *AsSeign* 45 (1974) 64–74. **Lührmann, D.** *Die Redaktion der Logienquelle.* 60–64. **Luz, U.** "Q 10:2–16; 11:14–23." In *SBL Seminar Papers 1985,* ed. K. H. Richards. Atlanta, GA: Scholars, 1985. 101–2. **Metzger, B. M.** "Seventy or Seventy-Two Disciples?" *NTS* 5

(1958–59) 299–306. **Mussner, F.** *Die Wunder Jesu: Eine Hinfürung.* Munich: Kösel, 1967. 24–28. **Neirynck, F.** "Paul and the Sayings of Jesus." In *L'apôtre Paul: Personnalité, style et conception du ministère,* ed. A. Vanhoye. BETL 73. Leuven: University Press/Peeters, 1986. 265–321, esp. 304–6. **Nielsen. H. K.** *Heilung und Verkündigung.* 65–71. **O'Hagan, A.** "'Greet No One on the Way' (Lk 10,4b)." *SBFLA* 16 (1965–66) 69–84. **Richards, W. L.** "Manuscript Grouping in Luke 10 by Quantitative Analysis." *JBL* 98 (1979) 379–91. **Robinson, J. M.** "The Mission and Beelzebul: Pap. Q 10:2–16; 11:14–23." In *SBL Seminar Papers 1985,* ed. K. H. Richards. Atlanta, GA: Scholars, 1985. 97–99. **Schulz, S.** *Q: Die Spruchquelle.* 360–66. ———. "'Die Gottesherrschaft ist nahe herbeigekommen' (Mt 10,7/Lk 10,9): Der kerygmatische Entwurf der Q-Gemeinde Syriens." In *Das Wort und die Wörter.* FS G. Friedrich, ed. H. Balz and S. Schulz. Stuttgart: Kohlhammer, 1973. 57–67. **Schwarz, G.** "Τῆς τροφῆς αὐτοῦ oder τῆς μισθοῦ αὐτοῦ?" *BibNot* 56 (1991) 25. **Tannehill, R. C.** *The Sword of His Mouth.* 122–28. **Thüsing, W.** "Dienstfunktion und Vollmacht kirchlicher Ämter nach dem Neuen Testament." *BibLeb* 14 (1973) 77–88, esp. 78–80. **Uro, R.** *Sheep among the Wolves: A Study on the Mission Instructions of Q.* Annales Academiae Scientiarum Fennicae. Dissertationes Humanorum Litterarum 47. Helsinki: Suomalainen Tiedeakatemia, 1987. **Venetz, H.-J.** "Bittet den Herrn der Ernte: Überlegungen zu Lk 10,2/Mt 9,37." *Diak* 11 (1980) 148–61. **Weder, H.** "Die Suche nach den Söhnen und Töchtern des Friedens: Auslegung der Botenrede der Logienquelle (Mt 10 par Lk 10)." *ZdZ* 44 (1991) 54–59.

And see also at 9:1–6 and excursus: "Journey to Jerusalem."

Translation

[1]*Afterwards the Lord appointed seventy(-two)*[a] *others*[b] *and sent them*[c] *out two by two before his face into every town and place where he was about to come.* [2]*He said to them, "The harvest is large, but the workers are few; so beg the lord of the harvest that he might send out workers into his harvest.* [3]*Go! I send you as lambs in the midst of wolves.* [4]*Do not carry a purse, a bag, or sandals, and greet no one along the way.*

[5]*"In whichever house you enter, first say 'Peace to this house.'* [6]*If there is a son of peace there, it will rest upon him; if not, it will return to you.* [7]*Remain in that*[d] *house, eating and drinking what they have. For the worker is worthy of his wages. Do not move about from house to house.*

[8]*"In whichever town you enter, and they receive you, eat what is placed before you* [9]*and heal the sick in it and say to them, 'The kingdom of God has drawn near to you.'*

[10]*"In whichever town you enter,*[e] *and they do not receive you, go out into its streets and say,* [11]*'Even the dust from your town which clings to our feet we wipe off against you. But know this: the kingdom of God has drawn near!'*[f] [12]*I tell you that it will be more tolerable for Sodom on that day than for that town.*

[13]*"Woe to you, Chorazin! Woe to you Bethsaida! because if the miracles that were performed in you had been performed in Tyre and Sidon, long ago they would have repented, sitting in sackcloth and ashes.* [14]*But it will be more tolerable in the judgment for Tyre and Sidon than for you.* [15]*And you, Capernaum! Will you be exalted to heaven?*[g] *No.*[h] *You will go down*[i] *to Hades.*

[16]*"The one who listens to you, listens to me, and the one who rejects you rejects me; and the one who rejects me, rejects the one who sent me."*

Notes

[a] *δύο*, "two," is included here by ℵ A C L W Θ Ξ Ψ etc., but not by P[75] B D 0181 etc. The loss of the *two* is easier to explain than its addition.

[b] καί, "also," is added here by ℵ A C D W Θ Ψ etc. and could be original.
[c] "Them" is not found in P[75vid] B 0181 etc.
[d] αὐτῇ (normally "itself") is taken as equivalent here to ταυτῇ.
[e] A W Θ Ψ 0181 etc. conform the verb here to that in v 8.
[f] ἐφ' ὑμᾶς, "upon you," is added here by A C W Θ Ψ etc. to conform the expression to that in v 9.
[g] ἡ ἕως τοῦ οὐρανοῦ ὑψωθεῖσα, "the one having been exalted to heaven," or similar is read here by A B[2] C W Θ Ψ etc.
[h] "No" here represents the force of the question form expecting a doubtful or negative answer (here negative).
[i] καταβιβασθήσῃ, "shall be brought down," is read here by P[45] ℵ A C L W Θ Ξ Ψ etc., but is less likely to be original because of the allusion to Isa 14:15 here (see *Comment*).

Form/Structure/Setting

If the first two pericopes of this section have focused particularly on foreshadowing Jesus' fate to come in Jerusalem (9:51–56), and on the radical commitment demanded of the follower of Jesus (9:57–62), this third block of material focuses on the continuation of Jesus' ministry of proclaiming the kingdom of God, which is extended ahead of him, as he journeys, by the disciples who go before at his direction. The present unit is the mission charge. On its links with 9:51–62, see at 9:51–56. Appended to this major unit will be the briefer units, vv 17–20, which report the success of the mission, and vv 21–24, which celebrate the revealing activity of the Father and the Son (which takes place in the proclamation of the kingdom of God) and speak about the privileged place in history of the disciples who benefit from this revelation.

It is clear that there is a great deal more in common between Matt 10:5–42 and Luke 10:1–16 than the Markan mission charge of 6:7–13. The common order in Matthew and Luke of Matt 9:37–38 (par. Luke 10:2), the main mission charge in chap. 10 (par. Luke 10:3–11), 11:20–24 (par. Luke 10:12–15), and 11:25–27 (par. Luke 10:21–22) should be noted, as should the large amount of common material not found in the Markan text (in every Lukan verse there are indications of the influence of this common source). Because both Matthew and Luke have been quite active editorially, and because the materials were from the beginning a set of isolated sayings that have been connected on the basis of common themes and catchwords, it is very difficult to ascertain the form of their additional shared source. A further complication for source reconstruction is the partial dependence on Mark 6:7–13, which in its turn shows marks of being a digest of a more extended mission charge.

The consensus view is as follows. Luke reproduces quite closely the original order and scope of the materials. The opening verse is to be regarded as redactional. No clear view emerges about whether v 4b was already to be found in the source. Luke's εἰ δὲ μή γε, "if not," is thought likely to be a Lukan abbreviation of the fuller form reflected in Matt 10:13. Hoffmann ("Lukas 10,5–11") has argued effectively that vv 10–11 are heavily marked by Lukan redaction and that the briefer form in Matt 10:14 is likely to be closer to the original. The Lukan location of v 2 is sometimes questioned.

Though the consensus view is for the most part accepted here, the following points need to be made. The opening verse should not be denied some traditional content since it is partially presupposed by Matt 10:23. Luke may well have had some traditional information that others beyond the Twelve were sent out by

Jesus, or at least an awareness that sending out was not restricted to the Twelve. He does not, however, have any tradition that suggested a differentiation between the instructions given to the respective groups (this is clear from the way in which 22:35 reflects the Luke 10 instructions and not those of 9:1–6). The originality of "Do not move from house to house" in 10: 7 is assured from the need for this to make sense of Mark 6:10b (par. Luke 9:4b). Hoffmann's argument ("Lukas 10, 5–11," 42–49) that the present prominence of the πόλις, "town/city," is entirely Luke's contribution is unpersuasive for at least two reasons. (*i*) Despite Hoffmann's attempt to provide an alternative explanation (43), the closeness between Luke 10:10a (8a) and Matt 10:11a does point to a common source. (*ii*) The awkward move from "house" to "town" in Luke 9:4–5 finds its best explanation as reflecting the longer source in which the move from "house" to "town" already plays a more developed part (note the influences of the second source on the wording of both vv 4 and 5). Even Hoffmann has to allow the presence of "town" in the second source at the end, but it makes altogether better sense for the shift from "house" to "town" to be located earlier. Hoffmann (49) may be correct that v 8b is a piece of Lukan smoothing.

More complicated source solutions are sometimes proposed (e.g., Roloff, *Apostolat*, 151 n. 53, who, following T. W. Manson, attributes Luke 10:1, 4–7, 17–20 to a third source). This allows the move from "house" to "town" to be dealt with on a source basis but is hardly to be justified when every verse of the Lukan text is reflected in the Matthean text. Goulder (464–76) accounts for the Lukan text on the basis of Luke's use of Matthew (and Mark). His suggestions are clever and sometimes plausible, but are in the end a wide-ranging imaginative exercise in what could have been, given an equally imaginative Luke. The shape of the argument seems ultimately to be that if one *can* get from Matthew to Luke, then that must have been what happened.

There is no reason to doubt that Jesus involved his disciples in his own mission, or that he provided them with directives for their part in his task. But that said, the various forms of the mission charges reflected in the NT suggest a use and adaptation of traditions in the context of the early church's own commitment to mission. Schürmann's view ("Mt 10:5b–6") that on a particular occasion a large-scale orchestrated mission to all Israel was managed by Jesus makes too much of the evidence. Though the verse expresses clearly Lukan redactional interests, 10:1 is probably not far off the mark with its sending of the disciples "into every town and place where [Jesus] himself was about to come" (cf. Matt 10:23 as noted above). A rather diffuse use of disciples, on an ad hoc basis and on different occasions, in the extension of Jesus' own ministry would best explain the sense that we are dealing here with a collection of once isolated sayings.

Though they have no real relationship to the sending out of the disciples, the materials of vv 13–15 have a strong claim to historicity (with George, "Miracles," 294–95; Mussner, *Wunder Jesu*, 24–28; Nielsen, *Heilung*, 67–69; against Lührmann, *Logienquelle*, 64; Schulz, *Spruchquelle*, 362–64) precisely because of the failure of the tradition to report any mighty works of Jesus in Chorazin or Bethsaida (Luke locates the feeding of the five thousand there [9:10], but that is hardly original, and does not, in any case, function as a mighty work of which the people of the city are aware). Chorazin is not mentioned elsewhere in the NT.

V 1 provides the setting for the mission charge and, also, in a summary way reports its content and implementation. By way of introduction, the charge begins (vv 2–3) with two general statements, one about the harvest nature of the task and the need for yet more workers, the other about the vulnerability of the messengers as they are now sent out. The charge proper begins with rules on travel (v 4). Then, there are instructions on receiving hospitality in people's homes (vv 5–7). At this point the focus widens to towns, and the general shape of the ministry to be exercised is outlined (vv 8–9). This leads on to directions for handling the situation in towns that will not receive the messengers of Jesus (vv 10–11). Jesus assures his ambassadors that those who reject them will be worse placed than Sodom in the day of judgment (v 12), and this becomes a transition to an apostrophe addressed to some of the cities that have not responded to the ministry that Jesus himself had performed in their midst (vv 13–15). The apostrophe has two sections. One has a three-membered structure and the second a two-membered structure. In the first section, two cities where Jesus had unsuccessfully ministered are linked to prepare for the traditional pairing of Tyre and Sidon that will be used in the comparison to come. Woe is first declared upon Chorazin and Bethsaida. The basis for this woe is then given, followed by a statement of the consequences for the judgment (which verbally echoes v 12). In the second section Capernaum's own expectation of destiny is explored with a question, and then contradicted with a prediction of its exact opposite. Finally, the implicit placing of the ministry of Jesus and of his messengers on an equal footing in vv 13–15 becomes explicit in the concluding statement (v 16) in which the rejection of the one sent by Jesus is equated with the rejection of Jesus and behind that with the rejection of the God who sent Jesus.

Comment

As the journey continues, Luke now marks the continuing importance of mission, as he reports the mission of the Seventy(-two) with its anticipation of the mission of the later church, which will become effective on the basis of the exaltation to glory that Jesus will achieve as the outcome of the present grim journey to Jerusalem.

1 Narrative reference to Jesus as "the Lord" is Lukan (see at 7:13). The textual evidence is finely balanced between "seventy" and "seventy-two" as the correct number for those sent out (see *Notes* above). However, as Metzger has shown (*NTS* 5 [1958–59] 303–4), the numbers seventy and seventy-two are often effectively interchangeable in Jewish traditions. In particular this is the case with the traditional number of the nations of the world, which is based ultimately on the list in Gen 10, which has seventy names in the MT but seventy-two in the LXX text. Luke is fond of anticipations and almost certainly uses the number here to anticipate later mission to all the nations of the earth. Jesus' mission is not displaced by his movement toward Jerusalem. Indeed it will only find its fullest shape the other side of his "being taken up" to glory at the right hand of God. (This is surely better in the Lukan framework than to link the number with the translators of the LXX, or with the number of members of the Jewish Sanhedrin. The seventy elders who received the Spirit to share the burden with Moses in Num 11:24–25 provide an alternative link. Here the "seventy-two" is explicable in terms of the Spirit also falling on Eldad and Medad [v 26; this link gains some support from the possible link in 9:49–50 with Num 11:26–30]. Luke is less likely, however, to use a link here that would suggest that Jesus, like Moses, had a limited capacity to cope with the situation in which God had placed him.)

Who are the Seventy(-two) different (ἑτέρους) from? The natural links pull in two different directions. The phrase "before his face," which is about to come, deliberately picks up on the phrase used of the messengers in 9:52 (and see the discussion there of the pseudo-mission role of the messengers), as does the idea that they are headed into the towns that Jesus is about to visit. On the other hand, the clear parallel with the mission of the Twelve in 9:1–5 suggests that the Seventy(-two) who are appointed are people other than the Twelve. Perhaps Luke has both in mind. The Twelve may actually be understood to be involved alongside the Seventy(-two) as a continuation of the role they already have, and by extension the same may be said for the anonymous messengers of v 52. Luke uses here (probably from his Markan source) the tradition of being sent out in pairs, which he had passed over in 9:2. In view of vv 10–11 to come, the idea of the validity of the testimony of two witnesses is probably in mind (Num 35:30; Deut 19:15). Traveling in pairs is widely reflected in the NT and becomes frequent in later Jewish tradition (see Jeremias, "Paarweise Sendung"). "Into every town and place where he was about to come" has a traditional basis, but in Luke's use it reinforces the journey motif and provides a link back to 9:52. Luke offers no explanation regarding why such a large group is needed to keep ahead of Jesus! He also does little to smooth the tension between the preparatory role that he establishes here for the Seventy(-two) and the full-fledged mission that he proceeds to outline with its decisive importance for those who fail to respond (the pattern in 9:51–56, which suggests that Jesus will not enter towns that do not receive his messengers, does, however, go some way towards resolving the tension). Because of the early church context to which these mission instructions would be related, it may not be too imaginative to think that beyond the context of the historical ministry of Jesus, Luke sees the church's mission, which is here prefigured, as a kind of preparation for the Parousia (cf. Acts 1:6–11).

2 It is not clear whether this verse was in the same position in Luke's source. Matthew's pre-mission charge position is more logical, where the following mission can then be a first answer to the prayer called for and a first response to the need identified. Since Luke is, so to speak, smuggling in the section on mission here under the guise of preparations for Jesus' journey movements, he could hardly have used this text in a separate unit. It is likely, then, that, because of its importance to his mission theme, Luke has been responsible for actually including this verse in the mission charge. The context of the trip to Jerusalem is quite lost sight of here. The words of address, though not the introduction, are almost identical to the Matthean form.

On the basis of a desire to allow the imagery to function in a unified way and as a single picture, Venetz (*Diak* 11 [1980] 148–61) has argued that we should not allegorically identify the Lord of the harvest as God, nor the harvest as an eschatological image. But this is to fail to understand the role of standard metaphors in the parables of Jesus, and such an approach produces an unsatisfactorily abstract understanding of this mini-parable. Harvest here is not exactly an image of (eschatological) judgment as in Mic 4:11–13; Isa 63:1–6; Jer 25:30–31; Joel 3:13, nor is it straightforwardly an image of the eschatological gathering of Israel as in Isa 27:12–13. It is, however, from this background (where the saving of God's people is always also involved) that it draws its force as an image for the eschatological calling of people into the kingdom of God through the dispensing of the eschatological salvation that has begun to be present in the ministry of Jesus. The harvest is the culmination of the whole history of God's dealings with Israel. The size of the harvest suggests that there has already been much achieved, in that such a crop has been brought to the point of harvest.

The imagery differs from the OT background in giving such a prominent mediating role to harvest workers. God has become the owner-manager of the property. The imagery is, as well, quite different from the sowing image of 8:4–8. The view of mission as harvest is quite distinctive from any other harvest imagery in the NT, but it is in line with elements in the Jesus tradition that identify the present of Jesus' own ministry, by means of various images, with the eschatological period (cf. Hahn, *Mission in the New Testament*, tr. F. Clarke, SBT 47 [London: SCM, 1965] 40 n. 3). The harvest imagery carries a sense of urgency: harvest will not await the pleasure of the harvesters. The possibility of avoidable waste of valuable produce and not a sense of personal stake is what, in the imagery, motivates the request to the owner for workers. The harvesters are simply laborers and have no owner's stake in the harvest. Presumably in the imagery the workers are in the employ already of the farmer, but have not been deployed as harvesters to this point. The present low number of workers and the verb here for "send out" (ἐκβάλῃ), which normally carries overtones of force, may suggest a reluctance on the part of the potential harvesters. All depends finally on the initiative of the farm owner, who must take responsibility for orchestrating the harvest. While the imagery is not found in Acts, its thrust fits well with much of Luke's recounting there.

3 Matthew uses this verse to introduce a section in the mission charge on the persecution to be expected by the missioners, but the stand-alone position that it has in Luke is probably the more original. In the Lukan sequence as it now stands, the position of the verse before v 4 (and following) emphasizes Jesus' concern that those sent not make, ahead of time or as people are encountered, self-protective responses in the face of their vulnerability in a hostile environment. The vulnerability of those sent is a mirror of Jesus' own vulnerability and is to be similarly met. Luke has "lambs" where Matthew has "sheep." This is probably a Lukan change to heighten the sense of vulnerability or perhaps to fit more exactly with the image with which he is familiar. The imagery is an obvious one and is widely paralleled. For background we need go no further than Isa 11:6 and 65:25. A sheep and wolves imagery is found in connection with Israel among the nations (see Jeremias, *TDNT* 1:340), but this not likely to be in view here. There is no way to really tell whether the ὑπάγετε, "go," at the beginning of the verse is Lukan or traditional.

4 9:4 directed the travelers to take nothing with them, and the list that followed was to be treated as suggestive rather than exhaustive. For variety Luke has a different list here, which overlaps with the earlier list only for "bag." He has already been influenced some by his second source at 9:4; here the mention of footwear comes from the second source (cf. Matt 10:9; with his use of "carry," that makes the prohibition of sandals relate to a [second] pair that is carried, Luke may be finding a way between the Markan permission of footwear [6:9] and its apparent prohibition in his second source). Matthew has the contents where Luke has "purse." The presence of "purse" in Luke 22:36 makes it more likely that the

Lukan reading is original. Here, as well, the Matthean order is different. In Matthew the restrictions are set strongly in the context of the good and valuable work that the laborer does: he has no need to bring his own provisions; he thoroughly deserves to be supported by those to whom he goes. Matthew would seem to be responsible for re-ordering the materials of Matt 10:7–8, which produce this change of context for his vv 9–10. On the role of these restrictions, see further at 9:3.

The prohibition of travel greetings is distinctive to this form of the mission charge, but probably stood in Luke's second source at this point. O'Hagan's suggestion (*SBFLA* 16 [1965–66] 69–84) that the refusal to greet is a mark of separation from the hostile environment, while it produces a plausible sense for the text, is quite insensitive to the specific Lukan context. Lang's suggestion (*BZ* 26 [1982] 75–79) serves us no better: *ἀσπάζειν* can mean to go and pay one's respects and in that sense to visit (cf. BAGD, 116), but to suggest that what is prohibited in the Lukan text is visits to friends and family is to intrude a foreign element into the text. Imagery from Gehazi's mission for Elisha (2 Kgs 4:29) is likely to be an influence here. As with the prohibitions of 9:3, this prohibition of greeting may serve as a deliberately staged prophetic sign of eschatological urgency. Motifs of haste and dedication come together (cf. 9:60) as the messengers are sent out as harvest workers.

5 Linked to what precedes, Matthew intrudes at this point in his account the saying about the laborer being worthy of his food/wages (Matt 10:10b; Luke 10:7b). The language of this verse has then been allowed to influence the following material, while the influence of the Markan account is also evident in the Matthean form. Matthew has also improved the logic by having the travelers go into a town or village before going into a house in the town, but has some minor difficulty handling the relationship between houses and towns in the further unfolding of his account. The Lukan form will be closer to the source form here than the more prudent Matthean form.

Though among wolves, the messenger is to assume that there will be an openness to his visit and his message on the part of the people of each house that he approaches. The pronouncement of the blessing of peace is in the first instance only a standard Jewish greeting, but in the setting becomes an anticipatory bestowal of the blessings of the kingdom of God (cf. Acts 10:36; and at 2:14). A generosity of approach is thereby encouraged.

6 Luke's probably Semitic "son of peace" will be more original than Matthew's text, where the language of worthiness, introduced with Matt 10:10b, is allowed to influence the thought and diction of the following verses. Since the "peace" has already come with the greeting, Luke will also be closer to the original with his "will rest upon" rather than Matthew's "let it come." Matthew, however, is probably closer to the original with his spelling out of the alternatives and the same may true of his use, for the return of the peace, of *ἐπιστρέφειν* rather than Luke's less common verb, *ἀνακάμπτειν*.

A son of peace would mean a person who is open to or ready for the salvation that is now coming into the world (cf. Simeon in 2:25 and see also v 38; Paul and his band find a "son of peace" in Lydia [Acts 16:13–15]; for other "son of" idioms in Luke see 5:34; 16:8; 20:34, 36; Acts 4:36). It is likely that the *ἐπαναπαήσεται ἐπ'*, "will rest upon," is meant to echo the use of the same idiom in the LXX of the spirit of Elijah resting upon Elisha (4 Kgdms 2:15; cf. also Num 11:25 as an alternative link): the messenger in some way reproduces himself in the recipient as he passes on to him the peace of God. One should not be grudging about bestowing the messianic peace; it will not stay where it is not appreciated but will return for reallocation. (Again the more cautious Matthew counsels a definite taking back of the peace.) The first evangelistic contact is at the same time a search for hospitality and a base of operations.

7 Matthew's corresponding material here (v 11) has been displaced under the influence of the Markan abbreviated form, and this has also influenced the Matthean wording. "Eating and drinking what they have" is not paralleled in the Matthean or Markan forms, but it is only as an abbreviation of some such longer form that the Markan (and Matthean) "stay there and go out from there" is saved from being a tautology. Similarly the Markan "go out from there" seems to be an abbreviation of something like Luke's "Do not go about from house to house." In connection with the greater originality of the present location for the sentence on the deserving laborer, see at v 4 above. Matthew's change from wages to food is partly in compensation for his loss of the eating and drinking of the present Lukan verse. While each of the sentences of the verse will have been in Luke's source, it is unlikely, because of the complexity of the sequence of thought generated, that both the second and the third belong in an original unity with the first. One or the other is a development, or the addition of a separate piece of tradition (see Harvey, *NovT* 24 [1982] 218–21, for the view that the original setting in the ministry of Jesus for the proverb about the worker deserving his wages is, if not the Lukan one, then a situation in which Jesus confronts a case of flagrant social injustice [a setting echoed in Jas 5:4]; the proverb is found at 1 Tim 5:18; and cf. 1 Cor 9:14; *Did.* 13:1).

The house where a son of peace has been found is to become a stable base of operations for the messenger. He is to be sustained there as one of the household. He is to receive this provision as God's payment to his harvest worker, and he is not to seek to better his circumstances by trying out other possible havens of hospitality. This would be both to despise God's good provision and to deny the primacy and eschatological urgency of the mission task.

8 For the originality of the first, if not the second, part of the verse see *Form/Structure/Setting* above. Note the similar structure to the opening of vv 5, 8, and 10 to come. Luke structures the account in this way, in particular, being responsible for the paralleling of vv 8 and 10. Now we have an account of the mission activity proper, which, from a base of hospitality, is to be directed to whole towns. The mention of being received bridges back to 9:53 and is part of the parallelism with v 10. In Luke's source, the juxtaposition of what to do in connection with houses was probably abruptly juxtaposed with the material on towns. Luke provides a bridge with his repetitive "eat what is put before you." The Lukan statement lacks the vital πᾶν, "everything," which would justify comparison with 1 Cor 10:27. There is no interest here in issues of kosher food. It is not clear what precise content can be given to "they receive you." Looking back to vv 5–7, it should be the finding of the initial hospitality; looking forward to vv 10–11, it should be the response of a whole town. Luke's concern here was more focused upon bridging and structuring than upon achieving precision of thought.

9 Matthew has already used his parallel material early in his mission charge (10:7–8). He has given more precision to the scope of the healing activity with his impressive "heal the sick, raise the dead, cleanse lepers, cast out demons." Matthew's "You received without pay; give without pay," which Luke does not have, is likely to have been in the common source, since it does not reflect distinctive Matthean interests. Luke may have discarded it as he reversed the standard order, reflected in Matthew, of preaching followed by healing. By placing the healing activity before the announcement of the nearness of the kingdom of God, Luke helps his paralleling of the sections vv 8–9 and 10–11. As Miyoshi (*Anfang*, 65–67) has shown, this order is repeated in the case of the three healing miracles reported in the journey section (13:10–17; 14:1–6; 17:11–19), after each of which comes teaching about the kingdom of God, which is presented in close connection with the preceding healing. This reversal of order makes it clearer that the presence of the kingdom of God is to be perceived in the healing activity itself (cf. 11:20). Luke's ἐφ' ὑμᾶς, "upon you," is not found in Matthew. It has probably been introduced by Luke under the influence of 11:20 (cf. 17:21).

In the healing activity are to be seen the effects of the arriving kingdom of God. While they bring their own immediate benefit to the afflicted, their true significance is only appreciated in connection with the kingdom of God. On the kingdom of God, see especially at 4:43; 6:20; 17:11 and 19:11. The argument over the sense here of ἤγγικεν (lit. "has drawn near") turns on whether the kingdom of God is being said to be very near (and so soon to come; or, that it is as near as Jesus is, who is on his way to these towns), or whether the kingdom of God is said to be here (it has done its drawing near and has thus arrived). The argument has mostly been conducted in terms of the meaning of Jesus' words in Aramaic, and in their setting in his own ministry (and often with reference to Mark 1:15 rather than to the present text). But both for the historical Jesus and for Luke, there can be no doubt that the time of the ministry of Jesus was a time of fulfillment and not only a time of preparation. Some of the dispute is linguistic rather than substantive, or is fueled by a desire to redress the loss of future eschatology that seemed to be part of Dodd's espousal of the kingdom of God as present (*Parables*, 28–30). Whether we are persuaded of the arguments that ἤγγικεν can mean "has arrived" (cf. Black, *ExpTim* 63 [1951–52] 289–90; Hutton, *ExpTim* 64 [1952–53] 89–91), as I am, or not, it is clear that the focus here in Luke is upon the present effects of the kingdom of God (cf. 10:23–24). For Luke the kingdom of God is a future eschatological reality that has broken in upon the world in the coming of Jesus but awaits future consummation.

10–11 Vv 10–11 provide the negative parallel to vv 8–9. Here the Matthean form, though it has been somewhat influenced by the Markan source, is nevertheless likely to be closer to the original, since Luke has created the structuring device of paralleled sections, partly by repeating material; it is likely that he is also responsible for the casting of the materials into direct speech; and it will be he who has made it clear that a public act is intended. Luke thinks largely of towns making a corporate response to the messengers and their message. On wiping off the dust, see at 9:5. The presence of the kingdom of God is not only a subjective reality, and it is not exclusively tied to the healings that signal its presence. For those who reject the message and the messengers it is still true that the kingdom of God has made its approach. The rejecting stance may, however, be reflected in Luke's failure to repeat the "upon you" of v 9: these people remain outside the experience of its blessings.

12 Matthew has a saying about Sodom (and Gomorrah) at this point (10:15), but he has another form of the saying at 11:24, which is in close connection with his version of the materials that will follow in Luke 10:13–15. This second form of the saying is closer to Luke's and thus will reflect more closely the source form. "That day" is the day of God's final judgment (Matthew expands to "the day of judgment"). The Lukan idiom is found in the OT (see Zech 12:3–4; Jer 30:8 [LXX 37:8]; cf. Isa 10:20). It is a cryptic form of the fuller expression "the day of the Lord." God's attitude toward Sodom had already been dramatically revealed in biblical history (Gen 19:24–28) and had become proverbial already in the OT (Isa 1:9–10); it continued to be vividly remembered in Jewish tradition (see Str-B, 1:574; 4.2:1188). The judgment upon Sodom in history was expected to be paralleled by its fate in the final judgment. The saying is not designed to hold out hope for Sodom but rather to suggest that the present situation created by the coming of Jesus means that what is involved in rejecting his messengers is much more serious again than had been the wickedness of Sodom. (For graded judgment, see also 12:41–48.)

13 Matthew uses the materials of vv 13–15 in 11:20–24, outside the mission charge. There it is linked to a Matthean equivalent to v 12 (Matthew's v 24), which, however, in Matthew, concludes rather than precedes the woes. Marshall (424; following Manson, *Sayings*, 76–77) suggests that Luke has reversed an earlier order that went v 12, v 16, vv 13–15. But this fails to account for an agreement between Matthew and Luke that the material of v 16 belongs to the final section of the mission charge (cf. Matt 10:40–42 and the discussion in *Form/Structure/Setting* for 9:46–48). The view that the Matthean setting is more original also has significant support (the flow from 11:20–23 into v 24 works very well, and the link with vv 25–27 is supported indirectly by Luke's location of his version of the same in 10:21–23). The presence, however, of a form of v 12 at the same point in the Matthean mission charge (10:15) as in the Lukan, and its recurrence in Matt 11:20–24 in connection with the materials that follow on in the Lukan mission charge (10:13–15), must count strongly in favor of the Lukan order. There is also a good case to be made for considerable Matthean intervention in 11:20, 23b–24 (the case is at times also argued strongly in the other direction for vv 23b–24, because of the detailed parallelism of the Matthean form; see the studies listed in Laufen, *Doppelüberlieferung*, 506 n. 195, and his own remarks on pp. 228–29; also George, "Miracles," 293–94, who, by pointing out in detail the defective nature of the Matthean parallelism, shows that Matthean priority here is less likely), which may encourage us to judge that in the location as well as the formulation we encounter Matthean formulation. V 13 is almost identical in wording to Matt 11:21. Only a different form for "happened" and a Lukan filling out with "seated" distinguish the verses.

Though I have argued that the Lukan order is that of his source, the original basis for the inclusion of the materials here will have been the catchwords ἀνεκτότερον ἔσται, "it will be more tolerable," along with the desire to illustrate (in readiness for v 16) the equivalence between responding to the ministry of those commissioned by Jesus and responding to the ministry of Jesus itself. The material appears in the form of a prophetic lamentation. These are in the OT mainly directed against the nations. In fact the mention of Tyre and Sidon specifically calls to mind the OT woes against those cities (Isa 23; Ezek 28:2–19, 20–23;

cf. Jer 47:4; Zech 9:2), and the language dealing with the pride of Capernaum echoes the oracle against the king of Babylon in Isa 14:4b–21 (esp. vv 13 and 15). Here this form is directed against Jewish towns. As with OT woes, the form of a direct address to the offending towns is no guarantee that the words were intended to address the offenders. As an oracle the words are more of a soliloquy, and this form of words was from the beginning used for its capacity to challenge others who are not so far gone as those here consigned to the severest of judgment. The original setting will not, however, have been a mission charge!

On "woe to you," see at 6:24. The location of Chorazin is not certainly known. It is probably to be identified with modern Kerazeh which is located about two and a half miles from tell Ḥum (see Fitzmyer, 853, and sources cited there). For Bethsaida, see at 9:10. Luke has not to this point used *δύναμις* (lit. "power") as a word for Jesus' miracles, but he will do so again in 19:37 and Acts 2:22; 8:13; 19:11. The usage forms a natural continuity with the Lukan understanding of the power that flowed from Jesus to achieve such wonders (see 4:14, 36; 5:17; 6:19; 8:46). While Fitzmyer (853) is correct that the account here does not restrict these miracles to Jesus, the logic of the account does, nevertheless, require the focus to be on Jesus' activity (as now paralleled by that of the Seventy). "Sackcloth" here is a cloth made from goat's hair and used as a minimal garment over the naked body in token of mourning or penitence. In the Greek world the term was used of a coarse hair cloth used for bags and sacks (as reflected in the English translation equivalent), but the penitential use of the material was also known (see Plutarch, *Superst* 7.168D). "Sackcloth" and "ashes" come together in Isa 58:5; Jonah 3:6; Esth 4:3; Dan 9:3 (the Hebrew term for "ashes" could also be translated "dust," but not the Greek, which occurs in the LXX; ashes are also a sign of mourning in the Greek world [see Euripides, *Suppl.* 827, 1160]). As a dramatic expression of lamentation, one covered oneself with sackcloth and either dusted oneself down with or sat in ashes (the latter is reflected in Luke's text). On Jesus' call to repentance, see at 5:32; 4:43; and cf. 3:3. The call to repentance is a standard prophetic challenge. The account in Jonah 3:5–9 stands as an example of an unlikely pagan city coming to repentance when challenged by a prophet's ministry.

Privilege brings responsibility to those who are beneficiaries of the ministry either of Jesus' messengers or of Jesus himself. Here the measure of the privilege is that what comes their way is so exceptional that it would have brought to repentance the most notorious of ancient sinful cities. What we have is effectively a statement about the presence of the kingdom of God in the ministry of Jesus. The text shows no awareness of the question at once posed to the concerns of a theodicy of why it is that, in the economy of God, the inhabitants of Tyre and Sidon should have been denied such an opportunity for repentance.

14 Luke does not have Matthew's emphatic new beginning "I say to you." Matthew has probably added it in the interest of presenting the materials in a form that makes of the incident, so far as this is possible, an actual encounter with the people of the cities involved. As in Matt 10:15 discussed at v 12 above, the Matthean form "the day of judgment" will be Matthew's development of "the judgment" (in v 15 of "the day") as found in the Lukan text. "Day of judgment" is a more standard formulation than "judgment" standing alone. On the role of the verse more generally, see further at v 12.

15 Apart from one definite article, Luke's wording is identical to that of Matt 11:23a, but Luke has nothing of Matthew's continuation in vv 23b–24. These verses are best taken as a Matthean development in which Matthew uses the tradition reflected in Luke 10:12, on the basis of its similarity of form to the material of Luke 10:14, as the main raw material for reformulating the materials on Capernaum in a form that parallels that used for speaking of Chorazin and Bethsaida (cf. further at v 13 above).

Luke 4:23 reflects a tradition that Jesus had worked wonders in Capernaum, and Luke reports exorcisms and healings in Capernaum in 4:31–44, and a further healing in 7:1–10. Perhaps already at 4:42 all is not well between Jesus and the residents of Capernaum, but Luke has provided no real basis for the development we find here. The pride of Capernaum is generally taken to be based on the way in which Jesus had made that city his home and base of operations (see esp. Mark 2:1; Matt 4:12). This is probably correct but plays no role in the mission charge, since such an attitude is not such a good parallel to the rejection by towns of the messengers of Jesus. For Luke, the optimistic expectations of Capernaum are only a foil for the disaster that Jesus announces for the city. While the verbal links are not exact, "exalted to heaven" is probably meant to reflect the prideful confidence of the king of Babylon in Isa 14:13: "I will ascend to heaven." The antithesis reflects the LXX of Isa 14:15, where his actual fate is said to be εἰς ᾅδην καταβήσῃ, "You will go down to Hades." Hades in the LXX represents the Sheol of the Hebrew text. Sheol was the sphere of the lingering and shadowy continuation of existence of those who had died. It is a place of deprivation and of oblivion, but not specifically of judgment. It does at times, however, carry overtones of judgment (as in Isa 14), because the proud and mighty get there by being stripped of their power and humbled in death. The Greek term Hades is properly the name of the god of the underworld as the place of the dead. It comes to mean more broadly the place of the dead, and from the Greek OT gains much of the range of meaning of the term Sheol. As a belief in resurrection became important in Judaism (cf. Dan 12:2) and with the sharpening in apocalyptic thought of the prospect of a final eschatological judgment of the dead and the living (again reflected in Dan 12:2), the understanding of Sheol and Hades was subject to corresponding refinements and adjustments. The main emphasis here is on the humiliation of the pride of Capernaum, but the note of punitive judgment probably cannot be excluded.

16 Matthew agrees in ending the mission charge with a section on the equivalence between receiving Jesus' messengers and receiving Jesus himself. Matthew has, however, expanded on the basis of Mark 9:37, 41, or more likely, on the basis of a second version of the linked sayings preserved there, but which lacked an equivalent to Mark 9:38–40 (see *Form/Structure/Setting* for 9:48–50). In its use of ἀκούειν, "to hear," and probably in the use of ἀθετεῖν, "to set at nought/reject," the verse here is Lukan (cf. the use of these verbs in 7:29–30, with their strong Lukan coloring), but it shares with Matthew the use of participial constructions. It may be more original than Matthew in its development of the negative side of the alternative possibilities, where Matthew (10:40) has the development of the positive side (under the influence of his other source here, and since he has not used at this point the material on Jesus' rejection in Galilean cities).

Because at its heart the response required has to do with receiving a message as from God, the receiving language of vv 8, 10 (and of Matt 10:40) gives way to the language of hearing/listening to (Mark 6:11 may have had some influence here, as Miyoshi [*Anfang*, 73] suggests). The antithesis between listening to and rejecting shows that ἀκούειν is to be translated here as "listen to" and not simply "hear," as is often better for Luke's usage. The core disciples have recently received their own challenge to listen to Jesus (9:35). Now the Seventy(-two) are assured that the presence and challenge of the kingdom of God are carried equally by their own endeavors as by those of Jesus himself (cf. 7:29–30). On this equivalence as it pertains particularly to the Twelve, see further *Form/Structure/Setting* at 6:12–16. On Jesus as sent by God, cf. 4:43. John stresses repeatedly the equivalence between Jesus and the one who sent him (5:23; 7:28; 12:44–45, 48; 13:20). We are to understand that the sorry fate of the towns in Galilee that have made no adequate response to the ministry of Jesus (vv 13–15) will apply just as much to those who reject the ministry of the messenger of Jesus. In this sense v 16 is a reiteration and explanation of v 12.

Explanation

Jesus' ministry of proclaiming the kingdom of God does not come to a halt when he sets his face to go to Jerusalem. Rather this activity continues to have its claim upon his energies, and it is extended ahead of his own travels by means of the sending of the Seventy(-two). From a historian's point of view, Luke has, like those before him, to some extent schematized in order to present the involvement of the disciples in the mission of Jesus. He does so because he anticipates the mission of the church to come, for which he is here providing a pattern.

The number seventy or seventy-two is used symbolically by Luke, who invites us to think of the traditional number of the nations of the world (in Gen 10 there are seventy names in the Hebrew OT and seventy-two in the Greek OT). While in fact these messengers will have spoken only to Jews (and perhaps Samaritans), the mission of Jesus is intended finally for the peoples of all the nations. The Twelve are very important for Luke as representatives of Jesus, but by depicting this further mission Luke allows us to see that the Lord can call many people into mission in his name. This we see happening in the Acts account of the life of the early church.

The Seventy mission like the Twelve have done (9:1–6), but they also are like the messengers of 9:52–53 as they go ahead of Jesus as he journeys toward Jerusalem. As he goes to Jerusalem to die, Jesus remains just as committed as ever to the preaching of the kingdom of God. The Seventy are to work in pairs as an indication of the validity of their testimony (see Num 35:30; Deut 19:15). As Luke thinks of mission in his own context, he may see the missioners here as preparing not for Jesus' arrival in that town on his way to Jerusalem but for the future coming of Jesus.

Jesus' directions for the mission start with two general statements. The first is about the harvest nature of the task and the need for extra workers. By Jesus' own example, the first response of the disciple to the needs of the situation is to be prayer. Harvest imagery is used in the OT of the final judgment (Mic 4:11–13; Isa 63:1–6; etc.) and of the final gathering of Israel (Isa 27:12–13). The present image builds on this background, but is different in its positive emphasis on calling people into the kingdom of God now and in giving such a prominent mediating role to harvest workers, where in the OT there is only the anticipation of the activity of God himself. Here is the culmination of all that God had been doing in the long history of the Jewish people: now the harvest is ready and urgently needs to be harvested. God's workers are often reluctant, and he must push them out onto the job. It all depends finally on him, but we must pray that he will get his workers out into the fields.

The second general statement that Jesus makes has to do with the hostility of the world into which the Seventy are sent. After such a statement we might have expected instructions to the Seventy about preparing to be self-sufficient as they go out as Jesus' messengers. What comes is the exact opposite. The disciples are not to make any self-protective preparations. They are to mirror Jesus' own readiness to be vulnerable.

For variety Luke has a list of prohibitions different from that found in 9:3, but to follow either list is to make the same statement. See the discussion at 9:1–6. The call not to greet along the way is an echo of the same restriction imposed on Gehazi by Elisha (2 Kgs 4:29). The worker needs to show disciplined dedication to the urgent task that is his. There may also be something here of the deliberately staged prophet sign.

Vv 5, 8, and 10 all begin in a similar way, and this marks the start of sections in the mission charge. The first section is about approaching people in their houses.

Though he knows he has been sent among wolves, in each case the messenger is to assume that there will be an openness to his visit and his message in each house he approaches. Here the greeting of peace takes on a special meaning as these messengers come with the message of the salvation of the kingdom of God. One should not be grudging about the bestowal of the messianic peace: it will not stay where it is not appreciated. But if it does stay then the messenger has, in a sense, reproduced himself, in much the way that Elijah did at the close of his own ministry as he passed on his role to Elisha (2 Kgs 2:15).

The first evangelistic contact in somebody's home is at the same time a search for hospitality and for a base for continued operations. Once received, the worker will be sustained as part of the household. He is to regard this provision of his needs as God's payment of wages to his harvest worker. His readiness to perceive God's intent will be reflected in his remaining where he is accepted and not seeking to improve his lot. He will also remain because the urgency of his task leaves no time for looking elsewhere for provision. From this base of operations the messenger is to seek to reach the whole town with his message.

The focus now moves to the whole town, but Luke partly repeats in v 8 to bridge between the two sections. Nothing less than the presence of the kingdom of God itself is to be perceived in the healing activity of the messengers. The healings bring their own immediate benefit to the afflicted but are only properly appreciated when seen in connection with the coming of the kingdom of God (compare 11:20), which has broken into the world in the ministry of Jesus and in the extension of that ministry by the Seventy.

Vv 10 and 11 provide the negative parallel to vv 8 and 9. On the symbolic act of wiping off the feet, see at 9:1–6. The kingdom of God is not only there for those who respond positively to it. Its presence is quite objective. It is, however, quite possible to miss out on what it offers, and for its presence to make those who respond negatively simply that much more liable to judgment. Luke thinks in terms of whole towns making a corporate response to the messengers.

Sodom was a notorious instance of a sinful town that had fallen under God's judgment (Gen 19:24–28). Nobody was in any doubt about how things would be for those people on that day (the day of God's final judgment). But so significant is what has happened in the coming of Jesus that to reject its messengers is to outclass Sodom in the league of sinners.

Vv 13–15 have a slightly awkward fit in the mission charge, but these verses are here because their presence underlines the equivalence between response to Jesus' own ministry and response to that of his messengers. We have here a prophetic lamentation like those spoken in the OT in connection with pagan nations. There are in fact some against Tyre and Sidon (e.g., Isa 23; Ezek 28:2–19). These function in much the same way that the OT judgment on Sodom functioned in v 12. But here it is suggested that Tyre and Sidon would have repented given the same advantages. Again the exceptional nature of what has now happened is stressed (as in vv 23–24 to come).

Capernaum had been Jesus' adopted home town (see Matt 4:12; Mark 2:1) and had received a generous share of his ministry. The town had apparently taken a certain pride in this connection with Jesus, but this had not led to a proper response to his message. The contrast between the town's own estimate of its future and that offered by Jesus is made by alluding to the pride of the king of Babylon in Isa 14:13 and the prospect of his fall in Isa 14:15.

The mission charge ends with a specific statement of the equivalence between response to Jesus' own ministry and that of his messengers. The Seventy are assured that the presence and challenge of the kingdom of God are carried equally by their own endeavors as by those of Jesus himself. V 16 is a reiteration and explanation of v 12 in the light of vv 13–15.

The Return of the Seventy(-Two) (10:17–20)

Bibliography

Boismard, M.-E. "Rapprochements littéraires entre l'évangile de Luc et l'Apocalypse." In *Synoptische Studien.* FS A. Wikenhauser, ed. J. Schmid and A. Vögtle. Munich: Zink, 1953. 53–63. **Charlier, C.** "L'action du grâces de Jésus (Luc 10, 17–24 et Matth. 11, 25–30)." *BVC* 17 (1957) 87–99. **Crump, D.** "Jesus, the Victorious Scribal-Intercessor in Luke's Gospel." *NTS* 38 (1992) 51–65. **Garrett, S. R.** *The Demise of the Devil.* 46–57. **Grelot, P.** "Étude critique de Luc 10,19." *RSR* 69 (1981) 87–100. **Hagemeyer, O.** "'Freut euch, dass eure Namen im Himmel verzeichnet sind!' (Lk 10,20)." *HD* 39 (1985) 160–63. **Hills, J. V.** "Luke 10.18—Who Saw Satan Fall?" *JSNT* 46 (1992) 25–40. **Kirchschläger, W.** *Jesu exorzistisches Wirken.* 239–42. **Kruse, H.** "'Dialektische Negation' als semitisches Idiom." *VT* 4 (1954) 385–400, esp. 389. **Lewis, F. W.** "'I Beheld Satan Fall as Lightning from Heaven' (Luke x.18)." *ExpTim* 25 (1913–14) 232–33. **Lowther Clarke, W. K.** "Studies in Texts." *Th* 7 (1923) 101–4, esp. 103–4. **Müller, U. B.** "Vision und Botschaft: Erwägungen zur prophetischen Struktur der Verkündigung Jesus." *ZTK* 74 (1977) 416–48. **Nielsen, H. K.** *Heilung und Verkündigung.* 46–51. **Paul, S. M.** "Heavenly Tablets and the Book of Life." *JANESCU* 5 (1973) 345–53. **Spitta, F.** "Der Satan als Blitz." *ZNW* 9 (1908) 160–63. **Vollenweider, S.** "'Ich sah den Satan wie einen Blitz vom Himmel fallen' (Lk 10:18)." *ZNW* 79 (1988) 187–203. **Webster, C. A.** "St. Luke x. 18." *ExpTim* 57 (1945–46) 52–53.

And see at 10:1–16 and excursus: "Journey to Jerusalem."

Translation

[17]*The seventy(-two)*[a] *returned with joy saying, "Lord, even the demons are subject to us in your name."* [18]*He said to them, "I saw Satan as he fell from heaven like a flash of lightning.*[b] [19]*I*[c] *have given*[d] *you authority to tread upon snakes and scorpions, and [authority] over all the power of the enemy; nothing will be able to harm you at all.*[e] [20]*Only, do not rejoice in this, that the spirits are subject to you, but rejoice that your names have been recorded*[f] *in heaven."*

Notes

[a] "Two" is not found in ℵ A C L W Θ Ξ Ψ etc. See discussion at 10:1.

[b] There is variation in word order in this verse, probably in connection with uncertainty about whether "from heaven" should be linked with "Satan" or with "flash of lightning."

[c] An emphatic *ἰδού*, lit. "behold," is left untranslated here, for lack of a suitable equivalent in current English.

[d] *δίδωμι*, "I give," is read by P[45] A C[3] D Θ Ψ etc. and the majority text. This probably represents a generalization, but it is just possible that it is original, and that a scribe has improved the thought sequence with the tense change to the perfect.

[e] "At all" renders the emphatic negation *οὐ μή*. This is not found in ℵ D, where there is also a corresponding change of the verb from subjunctive to future, which has a certain amount of additional textual support.

[f] *ἐγράφη*, "were written," is found in P[45 vid] A C D W Ψ etc.

Form/Structure/Setting

Luke has us imagine the travels of the Seventy(-two) between the mission charge of vv 1–16 and the return reported in vv 17–20. This unit underlines the achievement of the mission and further clarifies the relationship of mission of disciple and master, and also the relationship of both to the coming of the kingdom of God. Not power over the demons, but a secure place in the kingdom of God for those who will receive it is the ultimate issue of the ministry of Jesus. The subsequent unit in vv 21–24 links closely to the emphasis in v 20 on the attainment of a secure place in God's future, but also to the eschatological tone of vv 18–19.

On balance it seems most likely that Luke found in his second source a version of vv 17 linked to a version of v 20 (see detail in *Comment* below). He has expanded this in vv 18–19 with the use of materials that had been transmitted in the tradition as isolated sayings. With differing degrees of confidence, there is adequate ground for tracing all of the sayings back to the historical Jesus (confidence is perhaps greatest in the case of v 18 with its opacity and its striking imagery, and least in the case of v 19 where the formulation could owe something to apocalyptic circles in the early church).

The form that we now have is a literary creation and not an oral form. Luke has used the original link between vv 17 and 20 as the basis for structuring the section. The primary contrast of the pericope is between the basis for rejoicing attributed to the returning messengers in v 17 and the alternative proposed by

Jesus in v 20. The verses sandwiched within this inclusion function as comments on what is going on in the ministry that the Seventy(-two) have been exercising, and thus indirectly as comments on the nature of Jesus' own ministry.

Comment

Nothing less than the overthrow of Satan has occupied the Seventy(-two). Despite all the language of power inevitably involved in the description of this eschatological conflict, the ultimate issues of the kingdom of God are not power issues, but the sheer privilege of entry into the kingdom of God.

17 The return of the Seventy-two could easily be a secondary formulation based on 9:10a. "Returned [. . .] with joy" is found again at 24:52 and is likely to be Lukan. "The demons are subject to us" looks like it is modeled on v 20: "the spirits are subject to you" (but see at v 20 below for the suggestion that at this point the dependence may go the other way). "In your name" has been used at 9:49, which may be the basis for its use here. (For a more detailed discussion see Miyoshi, *Anfang*, 96–99; cf. Hoffmann, *Logienquelle*, 248–54.) Marshall (427) is, nonetheless, right to insist that in the source shared here by Matthew and Luke there needed to be some antecedent at this point for the materials of Luke 10:21–24 (Matt 11:25–27). Vv 17–20 do not, however, form a particularly good antecedent for vv 21–24 (though admittedly better than Matthew's alternative). The sequencing may already have been rather artificial in Luke's source and, if so, the materials of vv 17–20 (or, better, part of them) may reflect Luke's continuing source at this point. Alternatively, Luke may have displaced something here in favor of his own formulation based on isolated sayings from the tradition. See further discussion at v 20, which favors the former of these alternatives.

The mission of the Seventy(-two) is no less successful than had been that of the Twelve (9:1–6). The interchangeability of the content of the two missions is reflected again by the fact that where 10:9 has a directive to heal, but no mention of authority over demons, authority over demons is taken up in the report of the return here in v 17. By contrast, 9:1 has mention of exorcism as well as healing, but 9:6 takes up in the report of their actual activity only the healing. Mission is no narrow prerogative of the Twelve (cf. 9:49–50). The joy of the messengers reflects the eschatological nature of what they are experiencing (see at 1:14; but cf. the qualification in v 20).

On "Lord" as an address to Jesus by disciples see at 5:8; here it reflects something of their sense of the tremendous authority of Jesus in which they have experienced a sharing. On Luke's use of terms for demonology and his understanding of the place of demons, see at 4:31–37. On the submission of the demons, see further at v 20. On "in your name," see at 9:49; here for Luke, however, it is a little different in that it gives expression again to the equivalence between the ministry of the authorized messenger and the ministry of Jesus himself, which has been in view in vv 12–16. Nothing at this point reflects the journey context of the mission, nor the role of the Seventy(-two) in preparing for the visit of Jesus to the particular towns they have visited.

18 The opening εἶπεν δὲ αὐτοῖς, "he said to them," is likely to be Lukan, since he alone in the NT uses this phrase (8:25; 11:2; 22:67; cf. Miyoshi, *Anfang*, 99). The material here will have been transmitted as a detached saying, which has been considered by Luke or his source to be a useful explanatory comment on the success of the mission. This adoption into the present context involves, no doubt, some movement in the meaning, though the attempts to find an alternative precise setting and a corresponding meaning for the saying in the ministry of Jesus are inevitably speculative. Luke has thus far used the expression "the Devil." Here and for the remainder of the Gospel "Satan" will be the chosen terminology (11:18; 13:16; 22:3, 31; in Acts both terms are found). "Satan" (ὁ Σατανᾶς) is a Grecized form of the Hebrew or Aramaic term for "adversary," used, among other terms, as a name for the chief of the evil supernatural powers. The use of the aorist participle for the verb "to fall" ensures that the reference is to a final fall and not some temporary reversal, and to the fact of the fall, rather than to the movement of transition as such (cf. Zerwick, *Biblical Greek*, 269).

The present text has a clear relationship to a Jewish tradition that anticipated in the eschatological period a final conflict between God and Satan, which would result in Satan's defeat (see 1QM 15:12–16:1; 17:5–8; 11QMelch 13–14; *T. Levi* 18:12; *T. Dan.* 5:10; cf. *Sib. Or.* 3.796–807; *T. Jud.* 25:3). This tradition is reflected in various ways in the NT (Rev 12:7–10; Rev 20:1–3, 10; John 12:31; Rom 16:20). In our present text it could be either Satan's fall that is "from heaven" or the lightning that flashes "from heaven" (ἐκ τοῦ οὐρανοῦ). Either way, given Satan's residence in heaven (Job 1:6–12; 2:1–7; Zech 3:1–2), it will be from heaven that Satan is understood to have fallen (with Müller [*ZTK* 74 (1977) 418 n. 8]; against W. Michaelis, *TDNT* 6:163 n. 11; Spitta [*ZNW* 9 (1908) 160–63], beginning from the valid observation that it is natural, and no mark of failure, for a bolt of lightning to flash out of the sky, suggests that what is spoken of here is a counterattack by Satan, but he cannot finally do justice to the imagery of falling). Despite the long history of linking this verse with Isa 14:12 as applied to the fall of Satan (cf. Miyoshi, *Anfang*, 100), there is finally no adequate basis for such a connection, or for any early Jewish interpretation of the text from Isaiah as referring to the primordial fall of Satan from heaven. The closest parallel to the imagery here is provided by *T. Sol.* 20:16–17: "we [demons] . . . fall . . . like flashes of lightning to the earth."

Do we have here a graphic image, interpreting what is happening in the ministry of Jesus and/or his disciples? Or do we have a report of a visionary experience? In the latter case, is it a vision of what has already happened? of what is in the process of happening? or of what will happen in the eschatological future? Each of these possibilities has its firm supporters.

Müller (*ZTK* 74 [1977] 416–29) has offered an elaborate argument for understanding the present saying in connection with OT texts in which the prophet's vision of what has become true in heaven becomes in turn the basis for his message to his contemporaries. According to Müller, Jesus saw in a vision the fall of Satan actually being accomplished in heaven, and this was the basis for his confidence that the kingdom of God was now a present reality in heaven, ready to break through to the earthly sphere. This new development led to his split with John the Baptist.

Müller points to Amos 8:1–2; Isa 6 (understood as a judgment scene); Jer 1:13–19: Ezek 2:9–10; cf. 7:2, 6–7. Only Isa 6, and then only if it is to be seen as a judgment scene (which is not at all certain), provides any real support for Müller. In the other texts (and probably also in Isa 6) it is, rather, what God now intends that becomes visible (and is explained) in the visions, not what has in some sense already occurred; and there is really no achievement that occurs distinctly in heaven. Müller appeals also to Isa 40:9; 43:19; 52:7; 55:6. These texts (esp. 43:19 and 52:7) do lend themselves better to a beginning point of God's activity, which is not necessarily at present readily visible (though not easily able to be located in heaven), but which is the basis for a message about what is now (beginning) to work itself out on the earth. These additional texts are not, however, reports of visionary experiences.

OT prophetic vision does seem to offer us a measure of genuine similarity to our present text, but not exactly along the lines suggested by Müller. Not what is, or what has now happened in heaven, but what is to be, appears in the prophet's visionary experience (a harvest of judgment in Amos 8:1–3; a flood of boiling judgment from the North in Jer 1:13–19; the tragic developments to which the words of woe and lamentation on the scroll correspond in Ezek 2:9–10; in Isa 6 as well, the prospect of coming judgment defines the setting for the prophets role, but this is not now represented by any visionary image). In these OT texts the task of the prophet is to comment on rather than make happen what he has seen in his vision of the future, but the vision does in a more general sense define his own role. Is that not what we have here? Jesus reports a vision identifying the content of his own mission. In vision he has seen the coming triumph of the kingdom of God over the rule of Satan and has identified this triumph as his own task. He sees this as what God intends to achieve through him. This vision is becoming reality in his own ministry of exorcism, healing, and proclaiming of the kingdom of God. In the present context, the same working out of the envisioned future is seen in the extension of Jesus' ministry through his own disciples. (There is probably no special force to be found in the imperfect ἐθεώρουν [lit. "I was seeing/used to see"], since this verb is virtually never found in the aorist [BDF, 101]. If we insist on an imperfect force then it will be iterative: "I used to see [in a recurring vision]." No distinction would be evident in Aramaic tenses.) Müller's second set of texts may help us here too, with their sense that the full significance of what God is now doing may not be immediately evident from its beginnings. Jesus' exorcisms are impressive enough, but it is not automatically evident that we have in them the exercise of that authority over the demonic world that means the downfall of Satan. For a discussion on the arriving kingdom of God, see at 11:20; 16:16–18.

19 This verse will also have been transmitted as a detached saying (note the opening "behold," which suggests a fresh beginning rather than a development from v 18). There are no real signs of Lukan intervention in its wording. Mark 16:15–18 probably reflects a version of this saying. The content of the verse requires a link to some sort of commissioning of disciples by Jesus (Miyoshi, *Anfang,* 112–14 argues, but not convincingly, for a connection with the account of the choosing of the Twelve with its list of names). In the Lukan sequence, the verse explains the basis for the disciples' success as reported in v 17, and generalizes to make it clear that the authority there experienced is not restricted to that particular mission (note especially the future: "will not harm you"). For the bestowal of authority, cf. at 9:1.

It is likely that the pairing of snakes and scorpions is based upon Deut 8:15 (the only place in the OT where this pairing occurs; but cf. Sir 39:30), but this is not quite certain because there is evidence that the pairing developed into a fixed expression in Jewish tradition, perhaps coming originally from the use in Deuteronomy, but ultimately quite losing its allusive quality (see texts cited by Miyoshi, *Anfang*, 103–5, who, emphasizing the discussion of the Deuteronomy text in the early rabbinic tradition, is more confident than I can be of the allusion; note the juxtaposition in Luke 11:11–12). On the danger posed by snakes, cf. Num 21:6–9; Sir 21:2; for scorpions, cf. 1 Kgs 12:11, 14; Sir 39:30.

With slightly more confidence it may be suggested that the "treading upon" metaphor depends on Ps 91:13, where the venomous snake (פתן, *ptn*) is among the dangerous creatures trodden upon. These allusions, if such they are, link this new empowering of the disciples of Jesus with the divine protection of the people of Israel as they made their way through the wilderness and on into the promised land, and also with the promises made to the one who makes God his shelter (Ps 91:1).

The links between Luke 10:19 and Rev 9:3–4 have been drawn attention to by Boismard ("Rapprochements," 55–58; cf. Grelot, *RSR* 69 [1981] 97). The texts share the idea of the giving of authority, the mention of scorpions, and a reference to not harming. Perhaps nothing more can be made of the link than to suggest that in both cases we are dealing with imagery influenced by apocalyptic thought in which the final power conflict between the forces of good and of evil is in view.

The continuation with "and [authority] over all the powers of the enemy" (there is an asymmetry here in the construction with "authority" developed first by an infinitive phrase and then, in a parallel expression, with a prepositional phrase; Grelot [*RSR* 69 (1981) 89] maintains that re-translation into Aramaic explains this difficulty) shows that the snakes and scorpions represent more than the dangers of life. The text describes rather the orchestrated forces of the Evil One, pitted against the people of the earth, especially in the eschatological period (cf. Rev 9:1–11). Jesus equips his messengers with his own authority to enact, as he does, the triumph of the kingdom of God. "The enemy" is an unusual designation for Satan (Matt 13:19 provides the nearest NT parallel). In the NT only here and in Revelation (2:11; 7:2–3; 9:4; etc.) do we get the use of *ἀδικεῖν* (lit. "to do wrong") to mean "to harm" with no specific overtone of wrongdoing. Though the Greek vocabulary is different, Paul's experience in Acts 28:3–5 will be in Luke's mind an illustration of such protection from harm.

20 Though sometimes identified as Lukan composition (e.g., Fitzmyer, 859: "v 20 may also be of Lukan composition"), only the *πλήν* (a strong form of "but") with which the verse begins lies under suspicion of being Lukan (see the discussion in Miyoshi, *Anfang*, 107–9). There is, however, a difficulty about the form in which such a saying could have been transmitted. Different scholars have identified as the original unit vv 17, 20; vv 18, 20; and vv 19, 20. The best of these suggestions is the first (cf. Grelot, *RSR* 69 [1981] 88–89; rejoicing, the submission of the demons, and the role of the name link vv 17 and 20). This suggests that we should choose (from the options canvassed at v 17 above) in favor of heavy Lukan over-writing rather than Lukan composition. Could the original unit here have run something like, "They returned saying, 'Even the spirits are subject to us [in your name].' He said, 'Do not rejoice in this; rejoice, rather, that your names have been recorded in heaven'"? (For a negative version of this sentiment, cf. Matt 7:22–23.) Luke (or his source) will have developed the parallelism between the two parts through the insertion of vv 18, 19.

Heavenly books of life are known from ancient Sumerian and Akkadian times (see Paul, *JANESCU* 5 [1973] 345–53). In the OT see Exod 32:32–33; Pss 69:28; 87:6; Isa 4:3; and esp. Dan 12:1; and cf. Mal 3:16–17. In the NT cf. Phil 4:3; Heb 12:23; Rev 3:5; 13:8. See also *1 Enoch* 47:3; 108:3, 7; 1QM 12:2. The image is that of a register of citizens and is to be distinguished from the equally widespread image of God's record book of the deeds of the people upon earth (the images are at times merged). An assured place in the kingdom of God is the supreme benefit that emerges through the experience of God's grace in the ministry of Jesus. Note the contrast between Satan fallen from heaven and the names of the disciples now recorded in heaven.

Explanation

The Seventy(-two) have been involved in a mighty work and are excited by what they have experienced as they have in their mission explored the reality of the authority entrusted to them by Jesus. Jesus acknowledges and interprets this experience but bids them focus rather on the place secured for them in God's future for his People.

We are to glean the success of the mission from the announcement of the returning messengers. We have no broader report, but at least they have had a heady experience of the reality of supernatural and spiritual power. As they have used his name, Jesus has been demonstrably Lord over the demons.

Jesus responds by reporting to them his own vision of Satan's fall. This can be understood as simply a metaphorical description of the significance of what has been occurring in the disciples' mission, but is probably better taken as referring to an actual visionary experience, like those of some of the OT prophets (Amos 8:1–2; Jer 1:13–19; etc.). In vision the prophets saw what God intended and found their own role in relation to it. Jesus saw that God intended the downfall of Satan and that it was his task to achieve this in God's name.

In various circles of Jewish thought there was an expectation that the coming of the end-time would involve a final conflict between God and Satan, which would result in Satan's decisive defeat. Jesus shared this view and allowed it to define his own role. But not only does this define his own role; it also defines the role of the disciples who are called to share in and extend Jesus' own ministry. Through exorcism, healing, and proclaiming of the kingdom of God, Jesus' vision becomes tangible reality upon the earth.

V 19 uses the imagery of trampling down one's foes to develop the thought further. Jesus has imparted to his disciples the authority to move with impunity against all the forces of evil. In this verse there are probably allusions to Deut 8:15 and Ps 91:13. The former draws a connection between these present promises and God's protection of the Israelites in the dangers of the Exodus wanderings. The latter provides a link to the protection promised by God to the one who makes God his shelter. Similarities with Rev 9:3–4 increase our confidence that the text here is using imagery of the end-time conflict between good and evil. The reality of this divine empowering and protection is pictured in Acts (e.g., 28:3–5), but the coming fate of Jesus in Jerusalem, which is so stressed in this journey section of the Gospel and also in other elements of the Acts portrayal, should warn us against taking this language in a way that is too triumphalist and that leaves no place for the Christian call to suffering (compare the paradoxical juxtaposition in Luke 21:16–17 and v 18).

One can easily be carried away by the experience of power. In v 20 Jesus expresses to the disciples just this concern. The prime goal of his ministry has been to restore people to God—to provide for them a secure place in the kingdom of God. To put it in terms that look ahead in the Gospel, the goal of Jesus' ministry has been to see prodigals restored to their Father. The disciples are to rejoice that they have been recorded in heaven, for life in the kingdom of God (compare Dan 12:2).

Jesus Rejoices at What God Has Now Been Pleased to Reveal (10:21–24)

Bibliography

Allison, D. C. "Two Notes on a Key Text: Matthew 11:25–30." *JTS* 39 (1988) 477–85. **Arvedsen, T.** *Das Mysterium Christi: Eine Studie zu Mt 11.25–30.* Arbeiten und Mitteilungen aus dem neutestamentlichen Seminar zu Uppsala 7. Uppsala: Lundqvist, 1937. **Bacon, B. W.** "The Son as Organ of Revelation." *HTR* 9 (1916) 382–415. **Bieneck, J.** *Sohn Gottes als Christusbezeichnung der Synoptiker.* ATANT 21. Zürich: Zwingli, 1951. **Boring, M. E.** "A Proposed Reconstruction of Q 10:23–24." In *SBL Seminar Papers 1988,* ed. K. H. Richards. Atlanta, GA: Scholars, 1988. 456–71. **Cerfaux, L.** "L'Évangile de Jean et 'le logion johannique' des Synoptiques." In *Recueil Lucien Cerfaux.* Gembloux: Duculot, 1962. 3:161–74. ———. "Les sources scripturaires de Mt., XI, 25–30." *ETL* 30 (1954) 740–46; 31 (1955) 331–42. **Chapman, J.** "Dr. Harnack on Luke, X, 22: No Man Knoweth the Son." *JTS* 10 (1908–9) 552–66. **Charlier, C.** "L'Action de grâces de Jésus (Luc 10,17–24 et Matth. 11,25–30)." *BVC* 17 (1957) 87–99. **Christ, F.** *Jesus Sophia: Die Sophia-Christologie bei den Synoptikern.* AbhTANT 57. Zürich: Zwingli, 1970. 81–99. **Cullmann, O.** *The Christology of the New Testament.* 280–88. **Davies, W. D.** "'Knowledge' in the Dead Sea Scrolls and Matthew 11:25–30." *HTR* 46 (1953) 113–39. **Deutsch, C.** *Hidden Wisdom and the Easy Yoke: Wisdom, Torah and Discipleship in Matthew 11.25–30.* JSNTSup 18. Sheffield: JSOT, 1987. **Dupont, J.** "Les 'simples' (*petâyim*) dans la Bible et à Qumrân: A propos des νήπιοι de Mt 11,25; Lc. 10,21." In *Studi sull'oriente e la Bibbia.* FS G. Rinaldi. Genoa: Studio e vita, 1967. 329–36; reprinted in *Études.* 2:592–608. **Edwards, R. A.** "Matthew's Use of Q in Chapter Eleven." In *Logia,* ed. J. Delobel. 257–75, esp. 263–69. **Feldkämper, L.** *Der betende Jesus.* 151–77. **Feuillet, A.** "Jésus et la sagesse divine d'après des évangiles synoptiques." *RB* 62 (1955) 161–96. **Frankemölle, H.** *Biblische Handlungsanweisungen: Beispiele pragmatischer Exegese.* Mainz: Grünewald, 1983. 80–108. **Giblet, J.** "La prière d'action de grâce de Jésus dans son contexte lucanien (Lc 10,21–22)." In *Qu'est-ce que Dieu? Philosophie-Théologie.* FS D. Coppieters de Gibson. Publications des Facultés univ. Saint-Louis 33. Bruxelles: Fac. univ. St.-Louis, 1985. 613–35. **Grimm, W.** *Jesus und das Danielbuch: I. Jesu Einspruch gegen das Offenbarungssystem Daniels: Mt. 11,25–27; Lk. 17,20–21.* ANTJ 6. Bern/Frankfurt am M.: Lang, 1984. 1–69. ———. "Selige Augenzeugen, Luk. 10,23f: Alttestamentlicher Hintergrund und ursprünglicher Sinn." *TZ* 26 (1970) 172–83. ———. "Der Dank für die empfangene Offenbarung bei Jesus und Josephus." *BZ* 17 (1973) 249–56. **Grundmann, W.** "Matth. XI.27

und die johanneischen 'Der Vater-Der Sohn' Stellen." *NTS* 12 (1965–66) 42–49. **Hahn, F.** *The Titles of Jesus in Christology.* 307–33. **Harnack, A. von.** *The Sayings of Jesus: The Second Source of St. Matthew and St. Luke.* London/New York: William and Norgate/Putnam, 1908. 272–301. **Henaut, B. W.** "Matthew 11:27: The Thunderbolt in Corinth?" *TJT* 3 (1987) 282–300. **Hoffmann, P.** *Studien zur Theologie der Logienquelle.* 102–42. ————. "Die Offenbarung des Sohnes: Die apokalyptischen Voraussetzungen und ihre Verarbeitung im Q-Logion Mt 11,27 par Lk 10,22." *Kairos* 12 (1970) 270–88. **Hunter, A. M.** "Crux Criticorum—Matt. xi.25–30—A Re-appraisal." *NTS* 8 (1961–62) 241–49. **Iersal, B. M. F. van.** *'Der Sohn' in den synoptischen Jesusworten: Christusbezeichnung Jesu?* NovTSup 3. 2nd ed. Leiden: Brill, 1964. 146–61. **Jeremias, J.** *New Testament Theology.* 56–61. **Klijn, A. F. J.** "Matthew 11:25//Luke 10:21." In *New Testament Textual Criticism: Its Significance for Exegesis.* FS B. M. Metzger, ed. E. J. Epp and G. D. Fee. Oxford: Clarendon, 1981. 3–14. **Kloppenborg, J. S.** "Wisdom Christology in Q." *LTP* 34 (1978) 129–47. **Kopler, L.** "Die johanneische stelle bei den Synoptikern und die Gottessohnschaft Jesu Christi." *TPQ* 65 (1913) 50–68, 282–307, 561–86, 764–87; 66 (1914) 100–30, 340–71, 634–66, 825–72. **Légasse, S.** *Jésus et l'enfant.* Paris: Gabalda, 1969. 121–85. ————. "Le logion sur le Fils révélateur (Mt., IX,27 par. Lc., X,22): Essai d'analyse prérédactionnelle." In *La notion biblique de Dieu,* ed. J. Coppens. BETL 41. 2nd ed. Gembloux: Duculot, 1985. 245–74. ————. "La révelation aux *ΝΗΠΙΟΙ*." *RB* 67 (1960) 321–48. **Luck, W.** "Weisheit und Christologie in Mt 11,25–30." *WD* 13 (1975) 35–51. **Lührmann, D.** *Die Redaktion der Logienquelle.* Neukirchen/Vluyn: Neukirchener, 1968. 64–68. **Marshall, I. H.** "The Divine Sonship of Jesus." *Int* 21 (1967) 87–103. **Mertens, H.** *L'hymne de jubilation chex les Synoptiques, Matthieu xi, 25–30—Luc., x, 21–22.* Gembloux: Pontificia Universitas Gregoriana, 1957. **Nielsen, H. K.** *Heilung und Verkündigung.* 51–57. **Norden, E.** *Agnostos Theos.* Stuttgart: Teubner, 1913. 277–308. **Nützel, J. M.** *Jesus als Offenbarer Gottes nach den lukanischen Schriften.* 139–75. **Pryor, J. W.** "The Great Thanksgiving and the Fourth Gospel." *BZ* 35 (1991) 157–79. **Richardson, P.** "The Thunderbolt in Q and the Wise Man in Corinth." In *From Jesus to Paul.* FS F. W. Beare, ed. P. Richardson and J. C. Hurd. Waterloo: Laurier University, 1984. 91–111. **Rist, M.** "Is Matthew xi, 25–30 a Primitive Baptismal Hymn?" *JR* 15 (1935) 63–77. **Saabe, M.** "Can Mt 11,27 and Lk 10,22 Be Called a Johannine Logion?" In *Logia: Les paroles de Jésus—The Sayings of Jesus.* Mémorial J. Coppens, ed. J. Delobel. Leuven: University Press, 1982. 263–71. **Scaria, K. J.** "Jesus' Prayer and Christian Prayer." *Biblebhashyam* 7 (1981) 160–85. **Schmiedel, P. W.** "Die 'johanneische' Stelle bei Matthäus und Lukas und das Messiasbewusstsein Jesu." *PM* 4 (1900) 1–22. **Schulz, S.** *Q: Die Spruchquelle.* 213–28. **Schumacher, R.** *Die Selbstoffenbarung Jesus bei Mt XI, 27 (Lk X, 22).* Freibourg-en-Brisgau, 1922. **Schwarz, G.** "ὅτι ἔκρυψας ταῦτα ἀπὸ . . . συνετῶν." *BibNot* 9 (1979) 22–25. **Stöger, A.** "Die Theologie des Lukasevangeliums." *BLit* 46 (1973) 227–36. **Suggs, M. J.** *Wisdom, Christology, and Law in Matthew's Gospel.* Cambridge, MA: Harvard University, 1970. 71–97. **Weiss, J.** "Das Logion Matth. XI, 25–30." In *Georg Heinrici zu seinem 70 Geburtstag,* ed. H. Windisch. SNT 6. Leipzig: Hinrichs, 1914. 120–29. **Winter, P.** "Mt XI 27 and Lk X 22 from the First to the Fifth Century: Reflections on the Development of the Text." *NovT* 1 (1956) 112–48.

And see at excursus: "Journey to Jerusalem."

Translation

[21] *In that hour*[a] *he*[b] *rejoiced in*[c] *the Holy*[d] *Spirit and said, "I thank you Father, Lord of heaven and earth,*[e] *that you have hidden these things from the wise and understanding and revealed them to babies. Yes, Father, for such was your*[f] *good pleasure.* [22] [g]*All things have been passed on to me by my Father, and no one knows*[h] *who the Son*[i] *is, except the Father, and who the Father is, except the Son, and the one to whom the Son wishes to reveal [Him]."* [23] *Turning to the disciples privately*[j] *he said, "Fortunate are the*

eyes which see what you see. [24]For[k] I say to you that many prophets and kings wanted to see what you see and did not see [it], and to hear what you hear[l] and did not hear [it]."

Notes

[a] Lit. "in the hour itself."

[b] The reference to Jesus is made explicit in A C K L W Δ Θ Π Ψ etc.

[c] *ἐν*, "in," is omitted before the dative expression by P75 A B C W Δ Θ Ψ etc.

[d] "Holy" is missing from P45vid A W Δ Ψ etc.

[e] P45 omits "and the earth."

[f] Lit. "before you."

[g] The opening clause of v 23 (without *κατ' ἰδίαν*, "privately," in some texts with an added *αὐτοῦ*, "his") is added here by A C C2 H W Θ Ψ etc.

[h] An aorist tense is defended as original here by some earlier scholars, but is rightly not favored by any of the more recent studies. There is no textual support for the suggestion.

[i] In 1424 b the order of "Father" and "Son" is reversed here and in the following phrase.

[j] The note of privacy here is deleted by D 1424 it.

[k] Omitted by P75 syc sams boms.

[l] *μου*, "from me," is added here by P75 B 070 sa, presumably to distinguish a privileged hearing by the disciples from the wider hearing of v 16.

Form/Structure/Setting

The present verses are to be linked closely with the preceding mission of the Seventy (v 21: "in that hour"). In quite other terms, this unit spells out something of what Luke will have his reader understand by the message of the presence of the kingdom of God. Vv 21–22 celebrate the revealing activity of the Father, and that entrusted to the Son, while vv 23–24 point out the privileged place of the disciples who are the beneficiaries of this revelation.

The similar location of Matthew's equivalent of vv 21–22 (Matt 11:25–27; coming after Matthew's version of the woes on the privileged towns) indicates that both writers have been somewhat influenced by the order of the materials in their non-Markan common source. The Lukan sequence here will be the more original (see discussion at 10:1–17 and at 10:20 for a suggested reconstruction of the antecedent in Luke's source for vv 21–24).

More difficult is the question of the scope of the common source at this point, since Matt 11:28–30 is not found in Luke at all, and Luke 10:23–24 is not found in Matthew at this point, but rather at 13:16–17. Norden (*Agnostos Theos*, 281–85), taking up a correlation between Sir 51 and Matt 11:25–30 already proposed by Strauss (*ZWT* 6 [1863] 92), has been followed by a number of more recent scholars in his defense of Matt 11:25–30 as an original unit on the basis of a shared structure with Sir 51. This line of argument has become less persuasive with the addition of the Qumran evidence to the case for seeing Sir 51 as not itself an original unity (11QPsa 21:11–22:1 contains a version of Sir 51:13–19, 30 in the form of an alphabetical acrostic, which has good claim to be a more original form of this material than that found in Sir 51). As scholarship has moved away from claiming an original unity for Matt 11:25–30, it has become more common to attribute to Matthew the use of such a structure to unite disparate source materials (with perhaps some fresh Matthean composition). Since the link in Luke 10:23a looks like a Lukan formulation, it seems likely that neither Matt 11:28–30 nor Luke 10:23–24 stood at this point in the second source, but that each has introduced fresh materials here for redactional reasons.

While vv 21 and 22 stood together in Luke's source, they do not constitute an original unity but have been drawn together by the shared motif of revelation and the reference to God as "Father." There is also, perhaps, a parallel between the role in v 21 of the will of the Father and the place of the will of the Son in v 22. (Contrary to the judgment of Hoffmann [*Kairos* 12 (1970) 272], the formal links, but difference of content, between the verses would seem to exclude, rather than support, the occasionally canvassed view that v 22 was composed as an expansion of v 21.) In v 21 the Father is revealer; in v 22 the Son is the revealer, and the Father's role is transmission to the Son. V 21 is concerned with the identity of the recipients of the revelation, v 22 with the basis of revelation.

Few dispute that v 21 may be traced back to the historical Jesus (for a well-balanced discussion, see Kloppenborg [*LTP* 34 (1978) 135–39] who, however, leaves the question finally open; Légasse [*Jésus,* 147–51] argues, speculatively, for a setting in the ministry of Jesus at a point when response to his ministry is restricted to a few intimates). Even those who doubt the attribution to Jesus himself recognize the early Palestinian origin of the text.

V 22 raises altogether greater difficulties when we inquire about its place in the historical ministry of Jesus. The proposal of van Iersel (*'Der Sohn,'* 151–57) that v 22 was originally a response to Mark 6:2 has not found followers. While the Father/Son correlation is pervasive in John, it is quite rare in the Synoptic tradition, and usually taken to be a mark of later development (see Matt 28:19; Mark 13:32). On the other hand, the move away from understanding the mutual knowledge of Father and Son here in terms of Hellenistic mysticism and towards finding a Jewish setting for the ideas expressed (see Hoffmann [*Kairos* 12 (1970) 270–71]) allows for the possibility of an earlier origin for the text. There is some merit in the view that the Johannine development makes more sense if there is some such basis for it in the earliest Christian tradition, and certainly the present text is no displaced piece of Johannine tradition since the language is not at all Johannine (see Cerfaux ["L'évangile," 161–62]). Also the major part of the thought content of the verse is already implied by other features of the earliest tradition about Jesus and, in particular, by Jesus' distinctive use of "Abba." That the saying focuses ultimately on the capacity of Jesus to make the Father known, and not on Jesus himself, stands in favor of an early origin. An origin in the ministry of Jesus is the more likely if we may take the father/son statements as, on the lips of Jesus, enunciating a general principle, which is then applied to the particular case of Jesus' own relationship with God his Father (as Jeremias, *Theology,* 56–59).

There is broad agreement that vv 23–24 have a place in the historical ministry of Jesus (but see Schulz, *Q: Die Spruchquelle,* 419–21). These verses agree with other pieces of the Jesus tradition in which the present of Jesus' ministry is identified as a period of eschatological fulfillment. On the beatitude form involved here, see at 6:20–26.

Comment

Vv 21–24 complete the section that began in 9:51. This section has provided a foreshadowing of Jesus' coming fate in Jerusalem (9:51–56); it has stressed the radical commitment demanded of those who would follow the one who goes the way of the cross (9:57–62); and it has made it quite clear that Jesus' setting of his face to go to Jerusalem implies no loss of focus on the preaching of the kingdom of God but, if anything, expands the scope of Jesus' interest in mission (10:1–16, 17–20).

21 After considerable difference in this verse between the Matthean and the Lukan form for the introduction, the words of Jesus are rendered indentically in the two texts, apart from an expanded form for the verb "you have hidden" in the Lukan form (fitting in with Luke's general preference for verbs expanded with prepositional prefixes). Though Luke's "that hour" (*αὐτῇ τῇ ὥρᾳ*) and Matthew's "that time" (*ἐκείνῳ τῷ καιρῷ*) are linguistically quite different (both forms are likely to be redactional: for Matthew see 12:1; 14:1; for Luke see 2:38; and cf. 7:21; 20:19), both will reflect from the source a linkage with the antecedent. Luke's "rejoiced [*ἠγαλλιάσατο*] in the Holy Spirit" perhaps evokes the atmosphere of eschatological fulfillment that permeated the infancy Gospel (for linguistic links see 1:47, 2:27; and note in 2:38 the general similarity of sentiment, where the possibility of a link is additionally supported by the shared use of the *ομολογ* root ["(gave) thank(s)"] and the presence [though without the "in"] of the only other Lukan use of the *αὐτῇ τῇ ὥρᾳ*, "that hour," idiom found here in 10:21) and is most likely to be Lukan (as noted by Miyoshi, *Anfang*, 121, the word for "rejoiced" here and that for "thank" in the following clause are often linked in the LXX [Pss 9:2–3; 32:1–2; 66:4–5; 70:22–23; 106:21–22; Tob 13:6–8], and as *ἐξομολογεῖν* meaning "to thank" is a clear Septuagintalism, Luke may have been influenced by the LXX pattern). The Spirit plays a role in producing the rejoicing (cf. 4:1; 2:27; 1:47), not the relationship to the Spirit that is rejoiced about, as Fitzmyer (871; though he finally has it both ways).

Grimm (*BZ* 17 [1973] 249–56) is only partially successful in his attempt to identify a dependence here on a standard form for response to the revelation of apocalyptic secrets (see Dan 2:19–23; *1 Enoch* 39:9–11; and cf. *1 Enoch* 69:26; 1QH 7:26–27; etc.). The use of the same pattern in Luke 2:38 suggests that we need a broader focus than apocalyptic secrets (as does the influence of the form [recognized by Grimm] on Josephus, *Wars* 3.354, where the coming success of the Romans against the Jews is what God is said to have revealed [Grimm's form, though less widely evidenced, provides a better fit than the thanksgiving form appealed to by J. M. Robinson, "Die Hodajot-Formel in Gebet und Hymnus des Frühchristentums," *Apophoreta*, FS E. Haenchen, BZNW 30 (Berlin: Töpelmann, 1964), 194–235]). Presumably it is the presence and power of the kingdom of God that have just been revealed (in the mission of the Seventy), and to which it is fitting to respond with praise and thanksgiving. Through the Spirit, Jesus sees clearly how God's purposes are being worked out in Jesus' own ministry and all that extends that ministry.

The address of God as "Father" here may reflect an original use of the intimate term "Abba," which is found in Mark 14:36, but is less striking in its intimacy here than in that text because of the following "Lord of heaven and earth," and, therefore, cannot be said necessarily to transcend contemporary Jewish sensibilities (cf. 3 Macc 6:3, 8). At the end of the verse the second address of God as Father stands alone and is thus more intimate. The flow on into v 21, with its exclusive correlation of Father and Son, suggests that Luke and his source will have understood the address from the beginning as an expression of Jesus' distinctively intimate relationship with God.

The phrase "Lord of heaven and earth" is exactly paralleled in Tob 7:17 and 1QapGen 22:16, 21 (and cf. Gen 14:19, 22). Here it points forward to Jesus' recognition of the sovereign disposition by God of insight into the presence and working of the kingdom of God in and through Jesus' own ministry. For a somewhat similar disposition of insight into the kingdom of God, see Luke 8:10 and the discussion there. By far the closest parallel to the thought here of God's activity of hiding and revealing in connection with the wise and the little ones is found in 1 Cor 1:18–31; 2:6–13; 3:18–20 (cf. also CD 11:6–7; Prov 26:12), and suggests that we should understand the text in connection with a contrast between divine and human wisdom (cf. Isa 29:14; Job 5:13; 28:12–13, 20–22, 23, 27–28; Bar 3). It is less likely that the phrase "the wise and understanding" is based on Deut 1:13, 15, as maintained by Légasse (*Jésus*, 176–77), though the nuance of "leading citizens," which Deut 1:13, 15 would bring, is not untrue to the text here, since "wise and understanding" here has no automatically negative overtones; the overtone only becomes negative at the point where the wisdom of "the wise and understanding" will not subordinate itself to the revelation of the divine wisdom.

Who are the "babies" to whom the revelation successfully comes? Légasse (*Jésus*, 168–75) helpfully identifies three categories of Jewish metaphorical use of the term νήπιος (Hebrew: פתי, *pty*). In the LXX νήπιος never translates the dominant pejorative sense of פתי, *pty* (synonym to "mocker," "fool" etc.). The term is, however, used as the translation equivalents in contexts in which the the "babies/simple" are recipients of God's care and provision (Pss 119:30; 116:6; 19:7). Légasse probably exaggerates when he takes the reference in these texts to be to the faithful Israelite, confident of God's help in his distress or persecution; but he is right to see a link between "babies/simple" here and the place of the humble and poor as recipients of God's salvation (see at 4:16–30). Further, it is quite clear that at Qumran, as a development of this usage, a claim to piety is implied in the use of פתי, *pty*, as an identification of members of the community (see 1QpHab 12:4; 4QpIsa 2:5–6). There is also at Qumran (as well as a purely pejorative use of the term) in the hymns (1QH 2:9; frg. 15:4; 11QPs[a] 18:2, 4) and the commentaries on Nahum (4Q169 3:5) and Micah an intermediate use of the term, where it does not designate those who are committed to folly, nor the pious of the covenant commmunity, but rather the deficient, who in their deficiency may be open to being helped and enlightened. This usage, it seems to me (against Légasse) is closer to the OT Psalm usage discussed above. This usage has the best claim to illuminate our present text (as Légasse, *Jésus*, 178; see also Dupont, "Les 'simples'").

Kloppenborg (*LTP* 34 [1978] 138) has suggested that ναί, "yes," may have represented "amen" in Luke's source here (cf. esp. 11:51). There does not seem to be any adequate basis for taking ναί as an expression of agreement ("I approve," as Marshall, 434) rather than as an expression of affirmation ("it is so"). For its second occurrence the vocative "Father" is, in Greek, the nominative with the definite article, which is probably due to Semitic influence (BDF, 147[3]). The remainder of the verse is uniformly recognized to be strongly Semitic, as well, both in form and content, and is widely considered to reflect clearly the wording of an Aramaic original (for parallels see Str-B, 1:607; Schrenk, *TDNT* 2:745). While the OT takes very seriously the need for human response to God's initiatives and stresses human moral responsibility, it makes equally clear that it is finally the purposes of God that are achieved, and that these can neither be distorted or impeded by human opposition. If the wise and understanding have failed to humble themselves in the face of what God is now doing, then it is God himself who has determined not to reveal these things to them. The opponents are robbed of even the tragic dignity of being able to insist on remaining outside the purposes of God. See discussion at 3:22 on the verb that is cognate to εὐδοκία, "good pleasure," as used here, and also the discussion of the noun use at 2:14. In the immediate context the text comments on the situation of the messengers and those who have welcomed them and their message, and also on the rejection of Jesus and his messengers that has come into focus in 10:1–16.

22 Here both Matthew and Luke follow closely the wording of their source. They disagree only over Matthew's use of a compound form for the verb "knows" (opposite to v 21), his repetition of this verb, and his "knows the Father (Son)," where Luke has "knows who the Father (Son) is." The Matthean form is normally considered to have better claim to originality. Luke has reduced the repetitiveness of the original with the omission of one of the verbs and has conformed the references to knowing the Father/Son to the question form, which he has used earlier in connection with the identity of Jesus (9:9; cf. vv 18–20; 8:25).

Though formally we have here the continuation of Jesus' prayer, the content now becomes decidedly didactic. There has been considerable debate over whether the handing over of all things to Jesus should be taken as concerned with the transmission of knowledge, as the continuing development of the verse might suggest (but which the totally general "all things" counts against), or whether the transmission of full authority to Jesus is in view, for which appeal is made to Dan 7:14 and 2:37–38, but which seems less contextually appropriate. To some degree this is a false antithesis, because it imposes a greater precision upon the statement than the words are suited to bear (since no allusion to Daniel can be demonstrated). The emphasis is, rather, on the privileged status of the one who has received from God all that which it is his to dispose, not upon authorization or narrowly upon knowledge: God has treated him as Son and heir, and has handed on the inheritance; and it is the intimacy of relationship, which lies at the basis of this handing over, that is taken up in the following clauses. (John 13:3 may well be dependent on this tradition.)

The statement about the mutual knowledge of Father and Son has been carefully examined from many perspectives. The value of the classic studies by Norden and Arvedson is limited by the conviction of these scholars that the horizons of thought for understanding this verse were to be drawn from the Oriental Hellenistic religious world or from Gnosticism, rather than from the Jewish world that, methodologically, must have first claim to illuminate the Gospel tradition. This wider Hellenistic world has produced a parallel from a magic formula appealing to Hermes ("I know you, Hermes, and you know me. I am you and you are me" [P. Lond. 122.50; the text is published in K. Preisendanz, *Papyri Graecae Magicae* [Leipzig/Berlin: Teubner, 1928–30]). This sentiment inhabits a different world from our text, where the Son's knowledge leads on to a sharing of the knowledge of the Father. A further parallel, found in an extract from Akhnaton's hymn to the Sun, a much earlier Egyptian text ("No other knows you except your son, Akhnaton. You have initiated him into your plans and your power" [cited here after Bultmann, *Synoptic Tradition*, 160 n. 1]), is much closer in thought, but only because it does not immediately reflect a distinctively Hellenistic concept of the knowledge of God.

Hahn (*Titles*, 310–11) is committed to building his understanding of the mutual knowing here out of the meaning of the OT ידע, *ydʿ*, "know." For the Father to know the Son, suggests Hahn, means for him to choose and legitimate the Son, whereas, for the Son to know the Father means for him to acknowledge the Father and to live his life on the basis of fellowship with the Father. This view has rightly been criticized for the way that it destroys the parallelism involved in the mutual knowledge. The need to respect the strict parallelism of the clauses is further strengthened by the likelihood that their use is predicated upon the lack of a reciprocal pronoun in Aramaic (as Jeremias, *Theology*, 58). Hoffmann seeks to respect the parallelism, with his suggestion that to know the Son is to know the place and task that the Son has in the plan of the Father, while to know the Father is to have insight into the thus far secret plans that God has to effect salvation in the future unfolding of history (*Kairos* 12 [1970] 280). This view, however, is based upon appeal to an apocalyptic Son of Man concept for which there is no adequate basis in the text; it injects into the text a concern for the unfolding stages in the apocalyptic understanding of history that is not evident in the text; it fails to do justice to the relational language of the text; and, finally, the parallelism it achieves between the two knowledge statements involves little more than a formal equivalence between the knowledge of the Father and the Son.

Most studies assume that the wisdom tradition provides an important background here, but while the language of sonship is used by Philo of wisdom (or at least of the *λόγος*, "Word," which is elsewhere equated with wisdom), the term is *πρωτόγονος*, "first-born," and there is no thought of a father/son personal relationship (*Dreams* 215; *Confusion of Languages* 146). Also, texts in the wisdom tradition do not speak of wisdom as knowing God, or of God as knowing wisdom (exceptionally Bar 3:32, in its development of Job 28:23, and as derivative of "[God] knows all things"), or of God as handing anything over to wisdom, or of wisdom as revealing God. The appeal to a tradition of the rejection of wisdom is just as difficult to justify. Only by operating at a very general level can it be maintained that Jesus is here taking on attributes of wisdom, or that the relationship of Father and Son owes anything to that between God and wisdom.

Hoffmann (*Kairos* 12 [1970] 175) draws attention to the exclusivity of the mutual knowledge of Father and Son and is right to insist that the stress must fall on the contrast between their respective states of knowledge and the situation of all others who are, at least initially, excluded from such knowledge. The note of exclusivity is carried, however, not by an apocalyptic sense that dwellers on earth may only know earthly matters, while heavenly beings alone may know the affairs of heaven (e.g., *4 Ezra* 14:21), nor by the related view of the lofty position of wisdom (e.g., Job 28:13, 23). It is carried rather by the image of the intimacy of family relationship (as Jeremias, *Theology*, 58). (The exclusivity can be over-pressed: the exclusion is of the degree of knowledge provided by the unique intimacy of Father and Son, not of any knowledge at all.) Without the note of family intimacy of the present text (which reflects the Abba prayer usage of Jesus), the closest parallel in the OT to the present mutual knowledge would appear to be that between Moses and God in Exod 33:12–13. (The relational understanding supported here should not be understood in a mystical way, as in Hellenism; to know God is to know his ways and judgments, not to be mystically united with him.)

The above discussion does not distinguish between Matthew's "knows the Son/Father" and the Lukan form. Luke's distinctive "who the Son/Father is" is capable of being taken in various ways but is probably best taken in a sense that is very close to that of the Matthean text. As suggested above, Luke has conformed his text here to the question form he has used earlier in connection with the puzzle of the identity of Jesus (9:9; cf. vv 18–20; 8:25). In Luke's mind the first-person mode of the preceding clause carries over, and the sense may be given by "who I, the Son, am." Correspondingly we may paraphrase the reference to the Father as "who God, the Father, is." Once this adjustment is made, it is easy to see how knowing who somebody is is able to function here as equivalent to knowing and relating appropriately to the person.

The mutual knowledge of Father and Son is not the goal of the present saying, but only forms the basis for the final clause of the verse where the real intention becomes clear. If initially others are left outside the intimacy of this mutual knowing, it is only to be finally, at the Son's initiative and discretion, invited to share in a knowledge of God as Father, through Jesus' proclamation and preliminary enactment of the kingdom of God. As in v 21, the language of revelation here is probably drawn from an apocalyptic background, since it is not immediately the language that suggests itself for letting others in on an intimate father/son relationship. The will of the Son in v 22 corresponds to the will of the Father in v 21. As the verses come together, should we understand the relationship of the two activities of willing as the independent exercise of two identical wills?

We are left at the end of the text with a Son who remains unknown (we cannot with Winter [*NovT* 1 (1956) 131] save the situation by supplying "himself" after "the one to whom the Son chooses to reveal"). This phenomenon is the strongest argument for an originally non-titular use of son in this tradition. The thrust of the text is a claim to be able to reveal God on the basis of a privileged intimacy with him. In our present texts (both Matthew and Luke), Son is titular, which makes it a surprise for the reader that he is left as unknown. By drawing attention to the identity of the Son with his change to "who is the Son," Luke has, no doubt without realizing it, increased the logical difficulty here for his text.

23 The first clause is not represented in Matthew, whose parallel to vv 23–24 is found at 13:16–17. *στραφείς*, "having turned," may be Lukan (cf. 7:44; 23:28; 9:55), but *κατ' ἰδίαν*, "privately," is not likely to be so (only at 9:10 following Mark), despite Miyoshi's argument that it is used by Luke here to link the present material to 9:10 and 20 (*Anfang*, 131, 140). Matthew will be responsible for narrowing the scope of the text (". . . your eyes because they see") to fit the context to which he has attached these verses (a parallel to the Lukan form is still found in Matthew's continuing text in v 17), but Luke will be responsible for deleting a parallel reference to hearing (this fits the link that he has forged with the mission setting; the parallelism is still present in v 24 [it is easier for Luke to keep it in v 24 since that text functions both to explain and to generalize]).

The turning to the disciples signals the move from prayer to address. The private address to the disciples is not because any esoteric revelation is to be given but simply underlines yet more clearly that the beatitude to be expressed is only applicable to disciples; and it applies only to disciples, not because they have been recipients of some particular (earlier) esoteric revelation, but only because they are the ones who have, at least to some degree, been able to see the events surrounding Jesus for what they really were (contrast 11:14–23). Open-endedness is achieved for the category of the fortunate ones by the language "the eyes which see what you see." The primary contrast here is not, however, that between disciples and non-disciples, but as v 24 makes clear, that between the time period of previous generations and that of the generation privileged to witness the eschatological period associated with Jesus' own ministry (cf. *Pss. Sol.* 17:44; 18:6–7). The language of seeing is thus mainly straightforwardly literal, with just a trace of the more complex sense of "see with insight and response," which was found in 8:10. On disciples (a wider category than the Twelve), see at 5:30. The personification of eyes is paralleled in 2:30, and as Marshall (438) points out, "stresses the element of real, personal experience (cf. Job 19:27; 42:5)."

24 At the beginning of this verse, Matthew has probably added the "amen" that Luke lacks (Matthew definitely adds "amen, I say to you" at 19:23 and 24:2; Luke regularly substitutes something else when he omits an "amen," e.g., 9:27; 21:3; 11:51; 22:18). Matthew's pair "prophets and righteous ones" is paralleled in Matt 10:41; 23:29, and so is likely to be Matthean. Luke's "prophets and kings" would be a natural designation for the leading figures of much of the OT text. Luke seems to have toned down Matthew's stronger *ἐπεθύμησαν*, "longed" (only once elsewhere in Matthew [5:28] and then in the sense of sexual desire) to the colorless *ἠθέλησαν*, "wanted."

In OT times, neither those most closely linked with the purposes of God (the prophets; in *Mek.* 72a to Exod 19:11; 44a to Exod 15:2 the prophets are in a correspondingly less privileged position than those who had witnessed the Exodus events [cf. Grimm, *TZ* 26 [1970] 174–75]) nor those of greatest importance in the affairs of the day (the kings [Grimm's link here with Isa 52:13–15 is not convincing]) were privileged to experience the fulfillment of OT hopes as now the disciples of Jesus experience them (cf. 16:16; 7:19–23). Marshall notes (438; following W. Michaelis, *TDNT* 5:347) how idiosyncratic to Jesus, as compared to Jewish expectations of the age of salvation, is the placing of hearing alongside seeing as the modes for perceiving the presence of the eschatological salvation (but see the importance of the heralding function in Isa 52:7; 40:9; 41:27).

Explanation

Vv 21–24 are to be seen closely in connection with the preceding mission of the Seventy. Though the language is quite different, we learn more here about the fact that the kingdom of God is now making its presence known. Vv 21–22 celebrate the present revealing activity of the Father and that entrusted to the Son, while vv 23–34 point to the privileged place of the disciples who have received this revelation.

We have at this point reached the end of another major Lukan section (9:51–10:24). Jesus' coming fate in Jerusalem has been foreshadowed; an emphasis has been laid upon the radical commitment needed to follow the one who is heading to death in Jerusalem; and there has been a renewed insistence on the abiding and indeed expanding importance to Jesus of reaching out with the message of the kingdom of God.

Jesus' rejoicing here is not unlike the mood of celebration found in the Infancy Gospel as God begins there to fulfill his long-declared saving intentions. God is now decisively at work, and Jesus celebrates this as he receives the report of the spreading effect of his own ministry as achieved by the efforts of the Seventy.

Jesus speaks to God his Father out of his distinctively intimate relationship to him. He acknowledges that as "Lord of heaven and earth" it is his purposes that are being seen fulfilled in what is presently unfolding. And his purposes involve a collision between divine and human wisdom. Since "the wise and understanding," in their wisdom, have not been prepared to subordinate themselves to the action of divine wisdom, what God is now doing has remained opaque to them. God has, rather, made his revelation to "babies," that is to those with manifest deficiencies, but who nevertheless are open to being helped and enlightened. The people to be specially favored (see 2:14; the word there is the same as that rendered good pleasure here) are in the good purpose of God, not the most adequate in themselves but the least adequate.

While formally still part of Jesus' prayer, v 22 uses language that is quite didactic, and speaks of God in the third person. Jesus speaks here of his own privileged status as the one who has received from God all that it is his to dispose, and goes on to dwell on the unique intimacy of the relationship that underlies this role as the Father's heir. Just as in a human family there are unique strands of knowing that link (ideally) a father and the son who will be his heir and take on the family concerns, so it is with Jesus and his Father. In each case there is a distinctive insider's perspective involved, which nobody else is party to. But just as one may reveal human intimacies, so the Son chooses to share with certain others his own insider's knowledge of the Father. The early Christian boldness in taking over Jesus' own prayer practice of addressing God as Abba, Father, is a reflection of the revealing activity spoken of here. The will of the Father and the will of the Son both play a part as babies make their way into the kingdom of God.

Now Jesus turns quite explicitly to his disciples. It is the one who finds himself in the position of a disciple who knows what the "revealing" language of vv 21–22 is all about. Not that this is a closed set of people, since the same good fortune is for all who see what the disciple sees. The time for the dawning of God's salvation is now come. In OT times neither those most closely linked to the purposes of God (the prophets) nor those of greatest importance in the life of the day (the kings) had the privilege of personally experiencing the fulfillment of the hopes of Israel, as now the disciples of Jesus are able to experience them. What the greatest figures of the past could only hope for can now be experienced.

Love of God and Love of Neighbor (10:25–42)

Love of God and love of neighbor are understood by Luke to be an adequate summary of the Jewish law and a valid statement of what God requires (vv 25–28), but Luke wants us to see that Jesus pushes the scope of necessary neighborliness beyond every traditionally accepted limit (vv 29–37), and he would have us link the love of God with attachment to Jesus' own person and teaching (vv 38–42).

What Shall I Do to Inherit Eternal Life? (10:25–28)

Bibliography

Berger, K. *Die Gesetzesauslegung Jesu: Ihr historischer Hintergrund im Judentum und im Alten Testament: Teil I. Markus und Parallelen.* WMANT 40. Neukirchen-Vluyn: Neukirchener, 1972. 56–257. **Bornkamm, G.** "Das Doppelgebot der Liebe." In *Neutestamentliche Studien,* ed. W. Eltester. 85–93. **Búason, K.** "The Good Samaritan, Luke 10:25–37." In *Luke-Acts: Scandinavian Perspectives,* ed. P. Luomanen. 1–35. **Bultmann, R.** "Aimer son prochain, commandement de Dieu." *RHPR* 10 (1930) 222–41. **Burchard, C.** "Das doppelte Liebesgebot in der frühen christlichen Überlieferung." In *Der Ruf Jesu,* ed. E. Lohse et al. 39–62. **Denaux, A.,** and **Kevers, P.** "De historisch-kritische Methode." *Collationes* 26 (1980) 387–404. **Derrett, J. D. M.** "'Love Thy Neighbour as a Man Like Thyself'?" *ExpTim* 83 (1971) 55–56. **Diezinger, W.** "Zum Liebesgebot Mk xii,28–34 und Parr." *NovT* 20 (1978) 81–83. **Ernst, J.** "Die Einheit von Gottes- und Nächstenliebe in der Verkündigung Jesu." *TGl* 60 (1970) 3–14. **Fuchs, E.** "Was heisst: 'Du sollst deinen Nächsten lieben wie sich selbst'?" In *Zur Frage nach dem historischen Jesus.* Tübingen: Mohr, 1960. 3–19. **Fuller, R. H.** "Das Doppelgebot der Liebe: Ein Testfall für die Echteitskriterien der Worte Jesu." In *Jesus Christus in Historie und Theologie.* FS H. Conzelmann, ed. G. Strecker. Tübingen: Mohr, 1975. 317–29. ———. "The Double Commandment of Love: Test Case for the Criteria of Authenticity." In *Essays on the Love Commandment,* ed. L. Schottroff et al. Philadelphia: Fortress, 1978. 41–56. **Furnish, V. P.** *The Love Commandment in the New Testament.* Nashville: Abingdon, 1972. 34–45. **Hamilton, G. J.** "The First Commandment: A Theological Reflection." *NB* 69 (1988) 174–81. **Hruby, K.** "L'amour du prochain dans la pensée juive." *NRT* 41 (1969) 493–516. **Kiilunen, J.** *Der Doppelgebot der Liebe in synoptischer Sicht: Ein redaktionskritischer Versuch über Mk 12,28–34 und die Parallelen.* Annales Academiae Scientiarum Fennicae, Series B, Vol. 250. Helsinki: Suomalainen Tiedeakatemia, 1989. **Légasse, S.** "L'étendue de l'amour interhumain d'après le Nouveau Testament: limites et promesses." *RTL* 8 (1977) 137–59, 283–304. **Lohfink, N.** "Das Hauptgebot." In *Das Siegeslied am Schilfmeer: Christliche Auseinandersetzungen mit dem Alten Testament.* Frankfurt am M.: Knecht, 1965. 19–50. **Michel, O.** "Das Gebot der Nächstenliebe in der Verkündigung Jesu." In *Zur sozialen Entscheidung: Vier Vorträge,* ed. N. Koch. Tübingen: Mohr, 1947. 53–101. **Miller, J. S.** "The Neighbour." *ExpTim* 96 (1984–85) 337–39. **Nissen, A.** *Gott und der Nächste im antiken Judentum: Untersuchungen zum Doppelgebot der Liebe.* Tübingen: Mohr-Siebeck, 1974. **Phillips, G. A.** "'What Is Written? How Are You Reading?' Gospel, Intertextuality and Doing Lukewise: A Writerly Reading of Lk 10:25–37 (and 38–42)." In *SBL 1992 Seminar Papers,* ed. E. H. Lovering, Jr. 266–301. **Piper, J. S.** "Is Self-love Biblical?" *ChrTod* 21 (1977) 1150–53. **Schneider, G.** "Die Neuheit der christlichen Nächstenliebe." *TTZ* 82 (1973) 257–75. **Stegner, W. R.** "The Parable of the Good Samaritan and Leviticus 18:5." In *The Living Text.* FS E. W. Saunders, ed. D. Groh and R. Jewett. Washington: University Press of America, 1985. 27–38. **Stern, J. B.** "Jesus' Citation of Dt 6,5 and Lv 19,18 in the Light of Jewish Tradition." *CBQ* 28 (1966) 312–16. **Strecker, G.** "Gottes- und Menschenliebe in Neuen Testament." In *Tradition and Interpretation in the New Testament.* FS E. E. Ellis, ed. G. F. Hawthorne with O. Betz. Grand Rapids/Tübingen: Eerdmans/Mohr-Siebeck, 1987. 53–67. **Thomas, K. J.** "Liturgical Citations in the Synoptics." *NTS* 22 (1975–76) 205–14. **Thimmes, P. L.** "The Language of Community: Metaphors, Systems of Conviction, Ethnic, and Gender Issues in Luke 10:25–37 and 10:38–42." In *SBL 1991 Seminar Papers,* ed. E. H. Lovering, Jr. 698–713. **Venetz, H.** "Theologische Grundstrukturen in der Verkündigung Jesu? Ein Vergleich von Mk 10,17–22; Lk 10,25–37 und Mt 5,21–48." In *Mélanges Dominique Barthélemy,* ed. P. Casetti et al. 613–50. **Vouga, F.** *Jésus et la loi selon la tradition synoptique.* Le monde de la Bible. Geneva: Labor et fides, 1988. 128–33. **Wolpert. W.** "Die Liebe zum Nächsten, zum Feind und zum Sünder." *TGl* 74 (1984) 262–82. **Young, N. H.** "The Commandment to Love Your Neighbor as Yourself and the Parable of the Good Samaritan (Luke 10:25–37)." *AUSS* 21 (1983) 265–72.

And see at 10:29–37 and excursus: "Journey to Jerusalem."

Translation

[25] *Once*[a] *a certain lawyer stood up and said to test him, "Teacher, what must I do to inherit eternal life?"* [26] *He said to him, "What has been written in the Law? How do you read it?*[b] [27] *He answered, "You shall love the Lord your*[c] *God with your whole heart,*[d] *and*[e] *with your whole life,*[f] *and with your whole strength, and with your whole mind, and your neighbor as yourself."* [28] *He said to him, "You have answered correctly; do this and you shall live."*

Notes

[a] Representing καὶ ἰδού (lit. "and behold").

[b] "It" supplied for sense in translation.

[c] "Your" is not found in B H.

[d] D f^1 205 pc it support a reading for "with your whole heart," which is syntactically uniform with that found in the following parallel phrases.

[e] No "and" here in P^{45} B.

[f] A C W Θ Ψ etc. conform the reading for "with your whole life" and the following parallel phrases to the form of phrasing used in "with your whole heart."

Form/Structure/Setting

In the new section 10:25–42 we see that the challenge to love of God and of neighbor is readily available in the OT law, but that now the scope of neighbor-love is radically extended and the content of love of God is made concrete as engagement with Jesus and his teaching. The second and third units (vv 29–37, 38–42) take up in reverse order the love of God and love of neighbor, which have become the subjects of concern in the opening unit, vv 25–27. As often, Luke balances a story about men with a story about women. Both are stories that contrast a hero with a "villain" or "villains." As a pair the stories mutually qualify what one might otherwise be inclined to take from each as the proposed practical shape for love of neighbor and love of God (Martha is serving the needs of others as did the Samaritan, but is criticized; the priest and the Levite may be figures with an exclusively Godward direction to their piety [cf. Isa 58:6], who, despite the "one thing is needed" of v 42, are not above reproach). Luke has also made a pair out of 10:25–28 and 10:29–35 by using as a framework for the parable a structure parallel to that of vv 25–28. In each case we are given (*i*) a reason for the lawyer's following question; (*ii*) the lawyer's question; (*iii*) a counter question by Jesus; (*iv*) the lawyer's answer; and (*v*) Jesus' concluding challenge (cf. Horn, *Glaube und Handeln*, 109).

The source question here is extremely difficult. Only a small number of scholars claim an original unity between vv 25–28 and vv 29–37 (e.g., Manson, *Sayings*, 259–61). Most are impressed by the Lukan cast of the language used in vv 28–29, 37 to link the pericopes, by the difficult move from the concern in vv 25–28(29) with a passive definition of neighbor (the neighbor is the one to be helped) to a concern in vv (29)30–37 with an active definition of neighbor (a neighbor helps), and with finding that vv 25–28 can be well accounted for on the basis of Markan materials, with perhaps an additional second form from the tradition shared with Matthew, and significant Lukan redaction (see further below). On the other hand, to be well focused, the parable would seem to need some narrative setting (cf. Bultmann, *Synoptic Tradition*, 178), and it is difficult to see how the story could be better pointed than with the present link to the definition of the scope of neighborly love as enjoined in the law. It is perhaps best to think of a minimal original frame that already linked the parable to the idea of "neighbor" and that Luke has mostly displaced with a heavily edited version of the tradition about the greatest commandment in the Law. The move from passive to active in the definition of neighbor is no flaw but rather goes to the heart of the thrust of the parable.

Luke's Markan source is available for inspection (Mark 12:28–34), and it is likely that he has also drawn features from Mark 10:17–22 (the rich young ruler), but since the shared features of Luke 10:25–28 and Matt 34–40 are not extensive, it is hard to be sure what Luke found (beyond the shared vocabulary) in this common source. Perhaps the absence of any equivalent to Mark 12:29 is based on this influence; possibly the merging of the two commandments into a single two-pronged commandment was also there. But the inspiration for putting the double command into the mouth of the lawyer is more likely to have come from Mark 12:32–33, where (schooled first by Jesus) he *is* the one who expresses the view.

How novel in the first century was this bringing together of the two love commands? The attempt to identify fundamental principles that would encompass the whole will of God is as old as the OT itself (e.g., Mic 6:8; Pss 15 and 24; Isa 66:2b; Jer 22:3–4; Zech 8:16–17) and continued to play an active role in Jewish thought (e.g., *b. Šabb.* 31a [the golden rule as the whole torah]; *Mek.* to Exod 15:26 ["you shall hear/obey" contains the whole torah]; *b. Ber.* 63a [all the commands of the torah hang on (as in Matt 22:40) "in all your ways acknowledge him and he will lead you aright"]). Also, there is no doubt that the call for love of neighbor, which derives from Lev 19:18, had come to occupy a significant place in Jewish ethical summary well before the time of Jesus (Jub. 7:20; 36:7–8 with v 4; cf. CD 6:20–21; Sir 7:21; 34:15; *T. Ben.* 3:3–4; *Sipre* to Deut 32:29; *Sipra* to Lev 19:18). At the same time, the call to love of God, which in our texts reflects the wording of Deut 6:4–5 and which occurs again and again in the OT, was constantly kept before the ordinary Jew by the place of Deut 6:4–5 in the Shemaʾ, which was recited daily as part of Jewish prayer practice.

The evidence is not quite so straightforward concerning the bringing together of the two commandments. The Greek tradition distinguished between duty to the gods and duty to one's fellows. This distinction passed into more Hellenistic forms of Jewish thought and is represented, for example, by Philo's use of the word pairs *ὁσιότης* or *εὐσέβεια*, "piety," with *δικαιοσύνη*, "righteousness," or *φιλανθρωπία*, "kindness" (see *Spec. Leg.* 2.61–63; *Abr.* 208; *Life of Moses* 2.163; *Virtues* 54 and 76; while adopting the language, Josephus speaks against the autonomy of the sphere of human ethics which comes along with this division [if anything, in this view religion is a subdivision of virtue, but for Moses virtue is a subdivision of religion]; see *Ag. Ap.* 170). More typically in Jewish diction (using various terms) the bifurcation is between love/fear of God and keeping his commandments (e.g., Josh 22:5; Dan 9:4; Neh 1:5; 2 Sam 23:3; Deut 10:12). Klinghardt (*Gesetz*, 140–42; cf. Burchard, "Liebesgebot," 55–57; Berger, *Gesetzesauslegung*, 142–76) has argued that the formation of the double commandment to love required the influence of the Hellenistic pairing. The OT division can however, at times, express a division between, on the one hand, one's fundamental orientation to God and, on the other hand, the effect of this, as directed outward to one's fellows (see 2 Sam 23:3; Job 2:3; cf. Exod 19:21). Also, the arrangement of the Ten Commandments (Exod 20), and perhaps as well, the fact of *two* tables of stone (Exod 31:18), suggest that there no real difficulty, in a primary Jewish setting, in allocating to two distinct heads directives whose performance is strictly Godward and those which are directed to my neighbor. Certainly in the Gospel pericope my duty to my neighbor is still part of my duty to God (we are dealing with commandments of God!) and not an expression of virtue to be related only secondarily to God.

Love of God and love of neighbor are in fact brought together, though only as part of a longer list, in *T. Iss.* 5:2; *T. Dan.* 5:3; cf. *T. Iss.* 7:6(β), and there is no sufficient reason for denying the pre-Christian origins of these texts (*Did.* 1:2 also has the commandments paired, but Köster [*Synoptische Überlieferung bei den Apostolischen Vätern*, TU 65 (Berlin: Akademie, 1957) 170–72] argues effectively that only the reference to love of God as creator is part of the earlier Jewish tradition incorporated into this document). Does this pairing betray Hellenistic influence? The settings within more extensive lists of requirements show that we are not dealing in the Hellenistic manner with a fundamental bifurcation between the realm of God and the human sphere, while the related text in *T. Ben.* 3:3, which pairs "fear the Lord" and "love your neighbor," suggests that the line of derivation is more likely to be based on the OT pairings that characteristically use the language of fear of God (see above). Hellenistic influence seems to be an unnecessary suggestion.

T. Dan. 5:3 and *T. Iss.* 5:2 are clearly based on Lev 19:18; the call to love of God could be based on a text other than Deut 6:4–5, though the fact that the OT use of the precise form ואהבת, *wʾhbt*, "you [sing.] shall love," is confined on the one hand to Lev 19:18 and the related text 19:34, and on the other hand to Deut 6:5 and the related text 11:1, makes it likely, in view of Jewish exegetical practice in which such a shared form would be prized (cf. Diezinger, *NovT* 20 [1978] 81–83), that Deut 6:5 is the source text. It is likely, then, that Lev 19:18 and Deut 6:5

were brought together in Jewish tradition prior to the time of Jesus without benefit of specifically Hellenistic influence.

In the Markan text the commandments are not only brought together, but their union is also proposed as "first" and "second" in answer to a question about "which commandment is first of all." How does this procedure square with a first-century Palestinian Jewish setting? Burchard ("Liebesgebot," 51–55) insists that it does not square well at all: "Summations of the torah are called neither 'first' nor 'commandment'"(55). But this is to make altogether too much of the distinction between the present counting language and the Jewish rabbis' predilection for speaking of that which is great (גדל, *gdl*, or רב, *rb*) or weighty (חמור, *ḥmwr*, or שׁקול, *šqwl*). The rabbis happily used this language to identify what was more or less weighty and, as the texts cited three paragraphs above indicate, they were not averse to identifying a single ultimate principle (cf. also *b. Mak.* 23b–24a [par. *Tanḥ. B. Šop.* 10 to Deut 16:19 (V, 16b–17a)] [cited after Nissen (*Nächste*, 408–9, who fails, however, to allow the natural sense of the text [409–13)] where, in a sequence that runs from Moses to Amos, the number of commandments of God is successively reduced from 613 finally to one: "Seek Me and live" [Amos 5:4]). It may be that the Matthean language here is more original in its use of the word *great*, but little is at stake. Again, there is a rabbinic preference to mount the discussion in terms of principles (כלל, *kll*) rather than commandments, but this is not uniformly the case, and at times it is a biblical command that functions as such a principle (both points may be illustrated by *b. Mak.* 23b–24a). Immediately to link a second commandment with the first is unique to this Gospel tradition, but the impulse that lies behind it is not so different from that which produced the insistence in Isa 58 that the fast God chooses is for one to loose the bonds of wickedness, share one's bread with the hungry, etc.

We conclude, therefore, that the Gospel identification of the first and second commandments is thoroughly at home in a first-century Palestinian Jewish setting. It stands out not in its concern to identify the fundamental principle of the Law, nor in its interest in the love commandments, nor even in its linking of the two love commandments, but only in identifying these, rather than competing alternatives, as the fundamental principles of godliness.

Bornkamm ("Doppelgebot") may indeed be justified in suspecting Mark 12:32–34 of reflecting Christian use of the tradition in apologetics and in mission preaching, but there is no reason for denying that the core tradition here may be traced back to the ministry of the historical Jesus. The earliest transmission is likely to have been in the school debate form that is still reflected by the Markan form. Drawing on his second source, Luke makes use in v 25 of the idea of a testing of Jesus' Jewish credentials, but for the most part he develops the pericope as a challenge (esp. v 28). Luke creates an inclusio around the episode by using again at the end of v 28 ποιεῖν, "to do," and the ζω root ("life/live"), which have occurred in the opening verse (v 25). The challenge will be reiterated in v 37 at the termination of the linked parable, where the same imperative form ποιεῖν will recur.

Comment

As one who considers that he and his kind represent the true knowledge of God, the lawyer sets himself up to test the credentials of this One who claims to speak the mind of God, but Jesus answers question with question and the challenger finds that he himself is challenged.

25 The opening *καί ἰδού* (lit. "and behold") is characteristically Lukan (twenty-six times in the Gospel; here the role of its emphasis is to mark off the new section [this function is not paralleled in Luke]). Luke has all but one of the eight Gospel uses of *νομικός* for lawyer (on the role of the lawyer here see at 5:17), but Matthew probably has the same term at this point (Matt 22:34 [the term is omitted by f[1] 205 e sy[s] and could have come in from Luke]). Matthew has *πειράζων*, "testing," which Luke has strengthened with an *ἐκ* prefix and also has Luke's "teacher" (on Luke's use of "teacher" see at 7:40). So here Luke reflects the use of a second source. The question about the first commandment is displaced by the rich man's question of Mark 10:17 in exactly the language in which he will render that question in 18:18. John the Baptist in effect answers the same question in 3:10–14 (see there). "Eternal life" is an eschatological notion, first appearing in Dan 12:2 and becoming frequent in Jewish texts (cf. R. Bultmann, *TDNT* 2:855–61). Luke is not critical of the questioner's emphasis on doing. Indeed this emphasis will be reinforced in v 28 and then again in v 37.

26 Luke's *ὁ δὲ εἶπεν πρὸς αὐτόν*, "He said to him," is likely to have been influenced here by his second source (cf. Matt 22:37: *ὁ δὲ ἔφη αὐτῷ*, "He said to him") or possibly by Mark 10:18: *ὁ δὲ . . . εἶπεν αὐτοῷ*, "He said to him." For the remainder of the verse Luke has probably been inspired by Mark 10:19, where Jesus says to the questioner "You know the commandments." The man is being referred to the law in the same way as in that text. Uniquely in the NT, *ἀναγινώσκειν*, "to read," means here not the act of reading as such, but the perceiving of the sense of the text that has been read.

27 Luke repeats the *ὁ δὲ εἶπεν*, "he said," form from v 26, but now makes use as well of the Markan answering language (from 12:30), which he had displaced in v 26. His form of the double commandment differs from the Markan (*i*) in the absence of the introductory citation of Deut 6:4; (*ii*) in the lack of any counting language; (*iii*) in the use of *ἐν ὅλῃ τῇ* forms to express "with the whole" in all but the first of the list of ways in which God is to be loved; (*iv*) in the inversion of the order of the last two elements in the set; and (*v*) in having a single commandment to love with both God and neighbor as object. In (*i*) and (*iii*) there is commonality with Matthew. Distinction (*v*) seems to be a response to the problem posed by a tradition that gave an answer with two commandments to a question requiring the identification of a single commandment. This is a problem Luke had no need to address since he uses a quite different form of question. This fact and the agreements with Matthew suggest that Luke followed his second source quite closely here. The inversion of order noted in (*iv*) allows the Deut 6:5 set to stand together in their OT sequence, but also allows a chiastic arrangement for the natural pairings *καρδία*, "heart," and *διάνοια*, "mind" (cf. Luke 1:51), and *ψυχή*, "life/soul," and *ἰσχύς*, "strength" (e.g., LXX of Amos 2:14; Sir 9:2; and as variant readings in Ps 70[71]:9). Luke may be responsible for this. The Matthean text with its "heart," "soul," and "mind" set (22:37), where Deut 6:5 has "heart," "soul," and "strength" is best accounted for by assuming that this is what Matthew's and Luke's other shared source read at this point; Luke has supplemented from Mark (or from Deut 6:5). The original addition of "mind" to the list (which occurs in all forms) is probably to be related to the fact that *διάνοια*, "mind," is a variant reading for καρδία, "heart," in Deut 6:5 and elsewhere in the LXX.

Here set on the lips of the lawyer to demonstrate that Jesus stands only for what is the true and ultimate intention of the Jewish law, this is the only tradition of the synoptic Gospels that calls for the love of God (except for Luke 11:42, which is probably dependent on the present pericope; cf. also Mark 7:6; Luke 7:42, 47), but no language better sums up the passion for God, the intimacy with God, and the fidelity to God that were the hallmarks of Jesus' own life and to which he called others. "Your heart" denotes a response to God from the innermost personal center of one's being; "your life" ("soul") conjures up the role of the life force that energizes us; "your strength" introduces the element of energetic physical action; "your mind" signals the inclusion of the thinking and planning processes. The challenge is to a comprehensive engagement with God with the total capacity of all of one's faculties.

The claims of neighbor are not so grandly stated in the few words clipped from Lev 19:18 that are used to express it, but in the Lukan form this too is part of the one command to love. The call to love of one's fellows is marginally more broadly attested in the Gospel tradition with the call to love of enemy (Luke 6:27, 35 [see discussion there]) and the parable of the Good Samaritan (10:29–37). In its OT context in Lev 19:18 the "neighbor" is one's fellow Israelite, and this is extended in v 34 to cover the resident alien. However, in the mixed-living situation of Palestine in the first century, which had been created by developments that were a constant reminder to the Jews of the loss of their political autonomy, the non-Jewish populace appeared not as "innocent" resident aliens, but for the most part as an expression of the hated state of foreign domination. There are more generous sentiments in some Jewish texts (e.g., *Ep. Arist.* 228; *T. Zeb.* 5:1), but more typically the sense of group loyalty and loyalty to God found expression in firm boundaries for the reach of neighbor-love (the Qumran covenanters were to "love the sons of light . . . and hate all the sons of darkness" [1QS 1:9–10; cf. 2:24; 5:25; 1QM 1:1]; for rabbinic references see Str-B, 1:353–54). Jesus' practice and teaching supported a total abolition of boundaries to love of neighbor.

There has been some considerable debate about whether the "as yourself" reflects a need first to love oneself in order to be able to love others, or whether, rather, it proposes the replacement of self-love with love of the neighbor. While there is no active commendation of self-love, and the phrase does not mean "as much as you love yourself," the logic of the text does assume that behaving toward others as though oneself were on the receiving end will produce kindly and considerate behavior. At the same time, the text in no way suggests that kindliness and consideration of oneself is thereby displaced (cf. Eph 5:29).

28 The thought of v 28a is based on Mark 12:34, but Luke needs here a right answer and not simply a sensible answer, so the language echoes that of Luke 7:43b, where there has been a similar pattern of exchange. The remainder of the verse brings closure by taking up the language of the original question, which now has its answer. What Jesus stands for is in full agreement with the best instincts of the Judaism from which he has come: to love God and neighbor is what God requires of those who would come to him, but this is no theory to be espoused but rather a practice to be adopted.

Explanation

Luke 10:25–28 emphasizes the fact that Christian faith builds itself squarely on the best instincts of the Judaism out of which it emerged. Jesus' call is actually to practice that love of God and neighbor for which the OT law already clearly called. We now begin a new major section, 10:25–42, in which the sections that follow 10:25–28 are intended to show the full reach of the claim of neighbor-love (10:29–37) and to give concrete shape to the love of God as engagement with Jesus and his teaching (10:28–42).

The Judaism of Jesus' day has often been caricatured as anything but a religion of love, but Jewish texts often speak about the love of God, and in daily prayer Jews used Deut 6:4–5, which is the source of the wording for the challenge here to love of God. Likewise the call for love of neighbor (coming from Lev 19:18) repeatedly has a place in Jewish lists of God's ethical demands. It is even likely (early Jewish texts are hard to date) that the two commands had been brought together in Jewish tradition prior to Jesus. What is distinctive is to allow this double commandment to stand alone as identifying the fundamental principles of godliness.

To be a legal expert in Jesus' context was to be a Bible expert, and so the lawyer comes to test the credentials of this One who claims to speak the mind of God. But differing from the somewhat parallel texts in Matthew (22:34–40) and Mark (12:28–34), he asks not the theoretical question, "Which commandment is first of all?" but the pressingly practical question, "What must I do to inherit eternal life?" Eternal life here is not so much life after death as life in the end-time kingdom of God (see Dan 12:2).

Jesus turns the question back to this legal expert, who gives exactly the answer that would have been Jesus' own answer: Jesus calls only for what the Jewish law itself called for, and the best of Judaism did not need him to tell them that this was indeed the heart of God's requirements for his People.

Jesus' call for love of God has its best commentary in Jesus' own passion for God, his intimacy with God, and his fidelity to God; just as his call for love of neighbor has its best commentary in the life of this friend of tax collectors and sinners, who saw the service of others as his sacred calling.

Loving God with the heart requires a response to God from the innermost center of our beings; loving God with our life (or soul, as it is often translated) brings in the place of the vital life force that energizes us: our conscious "aliveness"; loving with the strength introduces the element of energetic physical action; loving with the mind identifies the importance, beyond the emotional, of the thinking and planning processes, which the mind contributes.

To love the neighbor as oneself does not mean to love the other as much as you love yourself, but it does mean to love the neighbor *in the way you would* love yourself. The call is to behave toward the other with the same consideration and concern that one naturally (and properly under most circumstances) shows about one's own welfare (as Eph 5:29). In the OT the mandated extent of neighbor-love is to one's fellow Israelite and to the resident alien in the land. As already seen in Luke 6:27, 35 and as the parable to follow will show further, Jesus operates on a far broader canvas.

Jesus endorsed the lawyer's answer and challenges him and us actually to practice this way that leads to eternal life.

Who Is My Neighbor? (10:29–37)

Bibliography

Aus, R. D. "Unerwartete Barmherzigkeit: Untersuchungen zur Beispielgeschichte Jesu vom barmherzigen Samariter (Lukas 10,30–37)." In *Wiehnachtsgeschichte, Barmherziger Samariter, Verloren Sohn: Studien zu ihrem jüdischen Hintergrund.* ANTZ 2. Berlin: Institut Kirche und Judentum, 1988. 59–125. **Bailey, D. M.** *Through Peasant Eyes.* 33–56. **Beauvery, R.** "La route romaine de Jérusalem à Jéricho." *RB* 64 (1957) 72–101. **Binder, H.** "Das Gleichnis vom barmherzigen Samariter." *TZ* 15 (1959) 176–94. **Biser, E.** "Wer ist mein Nächster?" *GuL* 48 (1975) 406–14. **Bishop, E. F. F.** "'Down from Jerusalem to Jericho.'" *EvQ* 2 (1963) 97–102. ———. "People on the Road to Jericho: The Good Samaritan—and the Others." *EvQ* 42 (1970) 2–6. **Boers, H.** "Traduction semantique, transculturelle de la parable du bon samaritain." *SémiotBib* 47 (1987) 18–29. **Bowman, J.** "The Parable of the Good Samaritan." *ExpTim* 59 (1947–48) 151–53, 248–49. **Braun, H.** "Der barmherzige Samariter." In *Jesus—der Mann aus Nazareth und seine Zeit. Um 12 Kapitel erweiterte Studienausgage.* Stuttgart: Kreuz, 1984. 179–89. **Cerfaux, L.** "Trois réhabilitations dans l'Evangile." In *Recueil Lucien Cerfaux.* Gembloux: Duculot, 1954. 2:51–59. **Champion, J.** "The Parable as an Ancient and a Modern Form." *JLitTheol* 3 (1989) 16–39. **Clucas, R. S.** "The neighbour questions." *TE* 17 (1984) 49–50. **Cooke, R. A.** "What Is a Person Worth? The Good Samaritan Problem Reexamined." *Listening* 23 (1988) 198–213. **Cranfield, C. E. B.** "The Good Samaritan (Luke 10:25–37)." *TToday* 11 (1954) 368–72. **Crespy, G.** "La parabole dite 'Le bon Samaritain'! Recherches structurales." *ETR* 48 (1973) 61–79. **Crossan, J. D.** "Parable and Example in the Teaching of Jesus." *NTS* 18 (1971–72) 285–307. ———, ed. "The Good Samaritan." *Semeia* 2 (1974) [whole issue]. **Daniel, C.** "Les Esséniens et l'arrière-fond historique de la parabole du Bon Samaritain." *NovT* 11 (1969) 71–104. **Daniélou, J.** "Le bon Samaritain." In *Mélanges bibliques.* FS A. Robert. Paris: Bloud et Gay, 1957. 457–65. **Derrett, J. D. M.** "Law in the New Testament: Fresh Light on the Parable of the Good Samaritan." *NTS* 11 (1964–65) 22–37. **Downey, G.** "Who Is My Neighbour? The Greek and Roman Answer." *ATR* 47 (1965) 3–15. **Dreyfus, F.** "Qui est mon prochain?" *AsSeign* 66 (1966) 32–49. **Eichholz, G.** *Gleichnisse der Evangelien.* 148–78. **Elderen, B. van.** "Another Look at the Parable of the Good Samaritan." In *Saved by Hope,* ed. J. I. Cook. Grand Rapids: Eerdmans, 1978. 109–32. **Enslin, M. S.** "Luke and the Samaritans." *HTR* 36 (1943) 277–97. ———. "The Samaritan Ministry and Mission." *HUCA* 51 (1980) 29–38. **Entrevernes Group, The.** *Signs and Parables: Semiotics and Gospel Texts.* PTMS. Tr. G. Phillips. Pittsburgh: Pickwick, 1978. 13–64. **Eulenstein, R.** "'Und wer ist mein Nächster?': Lk. 10,25–37 in der Sicht eines klassischen Philologen." *TGl* 67 (1977) 127–45. **Eynde, P. van den.** "Le bon samaritain." *BVC* 70 (1966) 22–35. **Feuillet, A.** "Le bon Samaritain (Luc 10, 25–37): Sa signification christologique et l'universalisme de Jésus." *EV* 90 (1980) 337–51, 369–82. **Funk, R. W.** *The Poetics of Biblical Narrative.* Foundations and Facets. Literary Facets. Sonoma CA: Polebridge, 1988. 183–85. ———. "'How Do You Read?' A Sermon on Luke 10:25–37." *Int* 18 (1964) 56–61. ———. "The Old Testament in Parable: A Study of Luke 10:25–37." *Encounter* 26 (1965) 251–67. ———. "The Good Samaritan as Metaphor." *Semeia* 2 (1974) 74–81. **Furness, J. M.** "Fresh Light on Luke 10:25–37." *ExpTim* 80 (1968–69) 182. **Gerhardsson, B.** "The Good Samaritan—The Good Shepherd?" *ConNT* 16 (1958) 1–31. **Gewalt, D.** "Der 'barmherzige Samariter': Zu Lukas 10,25–37." *EvT* 38 (1978) 403–17. **Gollwitzer, H.** *Das Gleichnis vom Barmherzigen Samariter.* BS 34. Neukirchen-Vluyn: Neukirchener, 1962. **Gordon, J. C.** "The Parable of the Good Samaritan (St. Luke x. 25–37): A Suggested Re-orientation." *ExpTim* 56 (1944–45) 302–4. **Gourgues, M.** "L'autre dans le récit exemplaire du Bon Samaritain (Lc 10,29–37)." In *L'altérité vivre ensemble differents,* ed. M. Gourgues and G.-D. Mailhiot. Recherches 7. Montreal: Bellarmin, 1986.

257–68. **Hermann, I.** "Wem ich der Nächste bin: Auslegung von Lk 10, 25–37." *BibLeb* 2 (1961) 17–24. **Heutger, N.** "Die lukanischen Samaritanererzählungen in religionspädagogischer Sicht." In *Wort in der Zeit.* FS K. H. Rengstorf, ed. W. Haubeck and M. Bachmann. Leiden: Brill, 1980. 275–87. **Jens, W.**, ed. *Der barmherzige Samariter.* Stuttgart: Kreuz, 1973. **Jones, P. R.** "The Love Command in Parable: Luke 10:25–37." *PRS* 6 (1978) 224–42. **Jüngel, E.** *Paulus und Jesus.* 169–73. **Kastner, K.** "Zwei Paralleltexte." *BZ* 12 (1914) 29–31. **Kieffer, R.** "Analyse sémiotique et commentaire: Quelque réflexions à propos d'études de Luc 10. 25–37." *NTS* 25 (1978–79) 454–68. **Klemm, H. G.** *Das Gleichnis vom barmherzigen Samariter: Grundzüge der Auslegung im 16./17. Jahrhundert.* BWANT 6/3 [103]. Stuttgart: Kohlhammer, 1973. **Klinghardt, M.** *Gesetz und Volk Gottes.* 136–55. **Lambrecht, J.** *Once More Astonished: The Parables of Jesus.* New York: Crossroad, 1981. 93–130. ———. "The Message of the Good Samaritan (Lk 10:25–37)." *LouvStud* 5 (1974) 121–35. **Leenhardt, F. J.** "La Parabole du Samaritain." In *Aux sources de la tradition chrétienne,* P. Benoit et al. 132–38. **Linnemann, E.** *Jesus of the Parables.* 51–58. **Mann, J.** "Jesus and the Sadducean Priests: Luke 10 25–37." *JQR* n.s. 6 (1915–16) 415–22. **Masson, W. J.** "The Parable of the Good Samaritan." *ExpTim* 48 (1936–37) 179–81. **Mattill, A. J., Jr.** "The Good Samaritan and the Purpose of Luke-Acts: Halévy Reconsidered." *Encounter* 33 (1972) 359–76. ———. "The Anonymous Victim (Luke 10,25–37): A New Look at the Story of the Good Samaritan." *UUC* 34 (1979) 38–54. **Menken, M. J. J.** "The Position of σπλαγχνίζεσθαι and σπλάγχνα in the Gospel of Luke." *NovT* 30 (1988) 107–14. **Monselewski, W.** *Der barmherzige Samariter: Eine auslegungsgeschichtliche Untersuchung zu Lukas 10,25–37.* BGBE 5. Tübingen: Mohr (Siebeck), 1967. **Mussner, F.** "Der Begriff des 'Nächsten' in der Verkündigung Jesu: Dargelegt am Gleichnis vom barmherzigen Samariter." In *Praesentia Salutis: Gesammelte Studien zu Fragen und Themen des Neuen Testamentes.* KuBANT. Düsseldorf: Patmos, 1967. 125–32. **Oakman, D. E.** "The Buying Power of Two Denarii: A Comment on Luke 10:35." *Forum* 3.4 (1987) 33–38. **Patte, D.** "An Analysis of Narrative Structure and the Good Samaritan." *Semeia* 2 (1974) 1–26. ———. "Structural Network in Narrative: The Good Samaritan." *Soundings* 58 (1975) 221–42. **Perkins, P.** *Hearing the Parables of Jesus.* New York/Ramsey, NJ: Paulist, 1982. 112–32. **Ramaroson, L.** "Comme 'le bon Samaritain,' ne chercher qu'à aimer (Lc 10,29–37)." *Bib* 56 (1975) 533–36. **Reicke, B.** "Der barmherzige Samariter." In *Verborum Veritas,* ed. O. Böcher and K. Haacker. 103–9. **Royce, J. R.** "A Philonic Use of πανδοχεῖον (Luke x 34)." *NovT* 23 (1981) 193–94. **Scheitlin, K.** "Das Gleichnis vom Mann, der unter die Räuber fiel." *KRS* 101 (1945) 322–23. **Scholz, G.** "Ästhetische Beobachtungen am Gleichnis vom reichen Mann und armen Lazarus und an drei anderen Gleichnissen (Lk 16, 19–25 [26–31]; 10, 34; 13, 9; 15, 11–32)." *LingBib* 43 (1978) 67–74. **Sellin, G.** "Lukas als Gleichniserzähler: Die Erzählung vom barmherzigen Samariter (Lk 10:25–27)." *ZNW* 65 (1974) 166–89; 66 (1975) 19–60. **Seven, F.** "Hermeneutische Erwägungen zur poetischen Realisation eines neutestamentlichen Texts ('Sprachereignis' bei E. Jüngel und E. Güttgemanns)." *LingBib* 29/30 (1973) 52–55. **Spencer, F. S.** "2 Chronicles 28:5–15 and the Parable of the Good Samaritan." *WTJ* 46 (1984) 317–49. **Spicq, C.** "The Charity of the Good Samaritan—Luke 10:25–37." In *Contemporary New Testament Studies,* ed. M. R. Ryan. Collegeville, MN: Liturgical, 1965. 218–24. **Stein, R. H.** "The Interpretation of the Parable of the Good Samaritan." In *Scripture, Tradition, and Interpretation.* FS E. F. Harrison, ed. W. W. Gasque. Grand Rapids, MI: Eerdmans, 1978. 278–95. **Suzuki, S.** "Verantwortung für den Andern: Lk 10,25–37 bei Bultmann, Barth, Bonhoeffer und K. Tagawa." *ZdZ* 30 (1976) 331–38. **Sweetland, D. M.** "The Good Samaritan and Martha and Mary." *BiTod* 21 (1983) 325–30. **Ternant, P.** "Le bon Samaritain: Lc 10,25–37." *AsSeign* 46 (1974) 66–77. **Trudinger, L. P.** "Once Again, Now 'Who Is My Neighbour?'" *EvQ* 48 (1976) 160–63. **Wickham, E. S. G.** "Studies in Texts: Luke x. 29." *Theology* 60 (1957) 417–18. **Wilkinson, F. H.** "Oded: Proto-Type of the Good Samaritan." *ExpTim* 69 (1957–58) 94. **Wink, W.** "The Parable of the Compassionate Samaritan: A Communal Exegesis Approach." *RevExp* 76 (1979) 199–217. **Young, N. H.** "Once Again, Now 'Who Is My Neighbour': A Comment." *EvQ* 49 (1977) 178–79. ———. "The Commandment to

Love Your Neighbour as Yourself and the Parable of the Good Samaritan (Luke 10:25–37)." *AUSS* 21 (1983) 265–72. **Zerwick, M.** "The Good Samaritan." *Furrow* 6 (1955) 291–95. **Zimmermann, H.** "Das Gleichnis vom barmherzigen Samariter: Lk 10,25–37." In *Die Zeit Jesu.* FS H. Schlier, ed. G. Bornkamm and K. Rahner. Freiburg im B.: Herder, 1970. 58–69.

And see at 10:25–28 and excursus: "Journey to Jerusalem."

Translation

[29] The lawyer,[a] wishing to justify[b] himself, said to Jesus, "And who is my neighbor?" [30] Jesus[c] took [him] up and said, "A certain man was going down from Jerusalem to Jericho and he fell among robbers who, having stripped him and beat [him] up,[d] went off leaving [him] half dead.[e] [31] By chance[f] a certain priest was going down that same way[g] and, seeing him, went by on the other side. [32] Similarly, a Levite as well came[h] to the place and, seeing him, went by on the other side. [33] A certain Samaritan was on a journey and came to where he was and, seeing him, he had compassion. [34] Coming to him, he bound up his wounds pouring on oil and wine; he mounted him on his own beast and led him to the inn and took care of him. [35] The next day he took out[i] and gave two denarii to the innkeeper and said, 'Take care of him, and whatever more you spend, I will repay to you when I return.' [36] Which of these three seems to you to have become a neighbor to the one who fell among robbers?" [37] He said, "The one who acted toward him with mercy." Jesus said to him, "Go[j] and do likewise!"

Notes

a The subject is not made explicit in the Gr.

b The present infinitive (instead of the aorist) is read here by A C³ W Θ Ψ *f*^1,13 and the majority text.

c An asyndeton is remedied here with a *δέ*, "and/but," by ℵ² A C² D L W Θ etc.

d Lit. "having placed blows."

e A C W Ψ etc. add *τυγχάνοντα* (lit. "happening, turning out"), presumably to insist on the reality on the man's half-dead state: "they left him for half dead as indeed he was" (BAGD, 829).

f Different expressions are used for this in part of the textual witness.

g Lit. "in that way."

h "Came" is expressed by *γενόμενος* in P⁴⁵ D etc. and by *ἐλθών* in P⁷⁵ ℵ² B L Ξ etc. (this is the more likely reading). These readings have been combined in A C W Θ Ψ etc.

i A C W Θ Ψ etc. refer this verb to the Samaritan's departure and "correct" to *ἐξελθών*, "going out."

j There is an emphatic "you" here in the text that is underlined further by the addition in P⁴⁵ of *καί*, "also."

Form/Structure/Setting

The present pericope takes up the neighbor part of the double command to love of God and neighbor of 10:25–28. More implicitly, the following pericope (vv 38–42) will take up the God part of this double commandment.

The parable here has mostly been taken as an unassailable part of the Jesus tradition, but this view has been seriously challenged by Sellin (*ZNW* 65 [1974] 166–89; 66 [1975] 19–60) and Goulder, 487–92 (and cf. his more general case in *JTS* 19 [1968] 51–69; and also the judgment of Funk, *Parables and Presence,* 28). According to Goulder, the parable is distinctly Lukan in each of the following respects: as "[an] illustration-story, [a] response-parable, [with a] sub-culture hero, [using] colorful detail, [marked by a] muddled conclusion, [terminating with a] guillotine question, [exhibiting] philo-Samaritan sympathies, [and dealing in] positive emotions." It can hardly be denied that a lot of Luke shows through in this and other of the Lukan parables (the Lukan language in 10:29–37 is well documented by Sellin *ZNW* 66 [1975] 35–37). But not all of Goulder's list is to be accepted (Luke has not muddled his conclusion [see below]; "philo-Samaritan sympathies" confuses the role played by the Samaritan in the story; positive emotion in parables is not as distinctly Lukan as Goulder would have us believe (Matt 18:13, 27; 13:44; 25:23; cf. 18:31, 33 [it may indeed be true that Luke had a special knack for detailing the actions that express positive emotions]). Illustration-story (example story would be better), response-parable, and guillotine question belong too closely together to be allowed to fill out the list independently of one another (in any case Matt 21:31 is pretty close to being a guillotine question in connection with a parable [cf. vv 28–33], which shows that the distance between example story and parable is not so far as mostly assumed; on this last point cf. Sellin *ZNW* 65 [1974] 178–79).

Sellin is rather less confident that we can establish the Lukan nature of the parable on the basis of formal and linguistic distinctives (*ZNW* 65 [1974] 188; 66 [1975] 37). The heart of his argument for Luke as the author is to be found in what he calls a motif-historical analysis designed to show that the main motifs of the narrative can only be accounted for satisfactorily on the basis of their role in the Lukan intention as this may be discerned against the background of late first-century Hellenistic Jewish thought (*ZNW* 66 [1975] 37–59). Sellin's case is in many ways impressive, and not least in the way that it points up the ultimate embarrassment of current interpretations of the parable at the point of accounting for the Samaritan identity of the hero figure. Sellin's own reconstruction suffers, however, from its own severe problems.

(*i*) To take "neighbor" as fellow member of the covenant community in vv 29, 36 either requires the same sense in v 27 and so restricts love to the covenant community (as extended in vv 29–37)—but this stands sharply in tension with 6:27—or, if the sense in v 27 is different, we are left with quite a strained transition from 10:27 to vv 29–37 (the issue is not just whether "love" is still the subject, but more importantly whether the two uses of "neighbor" must be given quite different scopes). Sellin depends finally quite heavily on the link from vv 25–28 to 29–37 and should logically be committed to the former of these options. Note also the way that the obvious reiteration of v 28 in v 37b draws into the parable pericope the perspective of vv 25–27.

(*ii*) Sellin's view requires a certain focus on the covenant status of the injured man, but while we may guess that he is Jewish, for the dynamic of the story his status in the covenant is irrelevant: he is totally generically "a certain man."

(*iii*) While Sellin recognizes the formal place of the injured man as the chief figure of the parable from whose perspective the story is told (though it is rather from the perspective of his need than from his personal perspective that the story is told), he does no justice to the subjective element introduced into the functioning of the story by this very fact. It is not behavior in conformity to covenant obligations that we are viewing, but the rescue of a half-dead man by one who "neighbored" him when other more likely candidates failed to help.

(*iv*) By leaving behind the perspective of vv 25–28 where the "neighbor" is one to be loved, Sellin gains a unity of perspective in vv 29–37a, but he has to admit a sudden change of perspective in v 37b (if we allow his assumptions he does, however, give quite a reasonable sense to this development: you too must act out practically the covenant fidelity exemplified by the formerly excluded Samaritan, or you will lose your place).

(*v*) Sellin totally fails to demonstrate the equivalence in any of the Jewish sources adduced between the question of "who is my neighbor?" and the issue of claim to membership of the covenant community. The issue is rather whether the claims of neighbor love should be allowed in the case of those who were not part of the covenant community.

(*vi*) To build the interpretation, as Sellin does, on a positive view of Samaritans as keepers of the Mosaic law (and on the priest and Levite as imaging that loveless cultic Israel that had failed the test of Jesus' coming) quite reverses the drama of the story, which depends on the arrival of unexpected help after the help that might have been expected failed to materialize (cf. Sellin's own recognition of this [*ZNW* 66 (1975) 39], which he fails to keep in view as his argument develops). The story does not actually require us to assume that in real life Samaritans would ever behave in such an exemplary manner, only that if one were to do so we should have to recognize that he had been neighbor to the one in need.

(*vii*) A Samaritan is not finally, as Sellin would have it, a convincing symbol of law-keeping without cult, despite those strands in Judaism that could positively affirm the (partial) punctilious law-keeping of Samaritans.

On the negative side then, recent attempts to identify the parable as a Lukan creation are less than compelling. On the positive side we may point to the interest that the parable shows in the perspective of the victim (see further in *Comment*). This is of a piece with that Jesus who is friend to the despised of his society and who brings good news to the poor. As well, the challenge here to the practical expression of love outside the bounds of group solidarity is in the family likeness of the radical call of Jesus to love of enemy (see at 6:27). Whatever the present parable may owe either to early church retelling or to Lukan artistry, there is every reason to think that its imaginative core goes back to the historical Jesus.

This parable has by most been allocated to the example-story category of Jülicher's classification of the parables (see Introduction excursus: "Modern Parables Research"). This allocation has, however, been challenged on two fronts. For much of the history of the church the Good Samaritan has been understood to be a Christ figure, and a range of modern studies have tried to reinstate a christological understanding of the parable in one form or another (e.g., Daniélou, Gollwitzer, Binder [Christ is the wounded man], Gerhardsson [a word play between "neighbor" and "shepherd" takes us to the Good Shepherd]). None of these views has gained scholarly acceptance. A much more attractive way of referring the parable to Jesus' own behavior is that proposed by Ternant (*AsSeign* 46 [1974] 71) and Zimmermann ("Samariter," 67), who suggest that in the original setting in the ministry of Jesus the parable was provoked by unease stirred by Jesus' own practice of compassion (cf. Luke 15). However, this too is finally to be rejected because it can do no justice to the presence of the Samaritan figure in the parable.

The other kind of attempt to avoid seeing the parable as an example story is exemplified by the work of Funk (*Parables and Presence*, 29–34) and Crossan (*In*

Parables, 57–66; and cf. Jüngel, *Paulus und Jesus*,172–73). The parable is not an example story because the kingdom of God comes to expression in it, because we have here a parable of the way that in the kingdom grace comes to those who do not expect it, and it comes from the most unexpected quarter (Funk), or because the kingdom comes as a language event in the shattering of worlds implicit in the need to put together the contradictory terms "Samaritan" and "neighbor" (Crossan [in his later work (*Raid on the Articulate*) this shattering of worlds becomes a radical iconoclasm directed at all systems of meaning]), or because the parable "shows how the near future of the kingdom of God in the present event of the love of God refers man to his present as the place for neighbor love" (Jüngel, *Paulus und Jesus*, 173). It is hard to avoid the impression that such approaches, except in the case of Crossan, impose a predetermined structuralist pattern, or the shape of an existing theological conviction, upon the text. Crossan, for his part, imports his narrow language-event understanding of the coming of the kingdom of God (why call the challenge of the parable the coming of the kingdom of God?) and turns into an abstraction the thoroughly ethical transformation implied by the parable (cf. Sellin, *ZNW* 66 [1975] 26 n. 124).

Despite the failure of these attempts to re-classify the parable, example story may still not be quite right. The story is told from the perspective of the needs of the wounded man rather than from the perspective of the Samaritan, which we might have expected for an example story (contrast 16:1–9). The story invites us to "take up a vantage point in the ditch" (I borrow the language of Funk, *Parables and Presence*, 32) in order to reflect on the question of who is my neighbor. The challenge is to allow the perspective from the ditch to still control my understanding when I come to the issue from the position of strength, where the question of neighbor will concern the breadth of my obligations (cf. Trudinger, *EvQ* 48 [1976] 161). We are to transfer a judgment made in a fictional life setting into a life setting where the roles are quite reversed (this is related to Dodd's observations [*Parables*, 20–23] about transferring judgments from the sphere of nature and everyday life into the quite different spiritual sphere). The parable has formal similarities to some of the other Lukan parables introduced with the phrase "a certain person" and in which there is a structure involving two contrasted characters (here priest and Levite count as a single role) and a central figure (cf. Sellin, *ZNW* 65 [1974] 179–85). Vv 15:11–32 and 16:19–31 offer the most instructive comparison points.

The pericope begins with an explanation for the continuation of the dialogue, after the evident terminus provided by v 28. The lawyer's new question is answered with a story (whose structure will be treated separately below), after which comes Jesus' counter-question (as in v 26). The answer to this counter-question makes Jesus' point (as it had in v 27). The pericope then concludes with a call to action, which parallels that in v 28, but now incorporates the additional insight produced by this second round of engagement. The parable itself begins with the introduction of a man on a journey, clearly the chief figure of the parable, who continues to be on stage and from whose plight, to reach slightly ahead, we are to view the action. We learn that the man is reduced, in an isolated place, to a situation of desperate need. In what seems like a lucky break, the arrival of a high-grade potential helper raises hopes, soon dashed, for the man's rescue. This scene is then replayed, slightly *sotto voce*, with a not quite so likely potential helper, who again brings no joy. Next on the scene is a classic villain figure, a Samaritan, who nonetheless has compassion on the sufferer. The story climaxes with the mention of the Samaritan's compassion. The hearer is then brought down gently from this high point of tension with a somewhat extended account of how the Samaritan tends to the injured man's immediate needs and takes responsibility for his restoration to health.

Comment

It is from the perspective of the ditch where one lies helpless and battered, and in desperate need of help, that one should reflect upon the question "who is my neighbor?" Then one will know how wide the reach of neighbor love should extend when one is in a position to be handing out favors.

29 The link with the question of neighbor probably came with the parable to Luke, but the formulation here is likely to be largely a Lukan bridge from vv 25–28. The idiom represented here by δικαιῶσαι ἑαυτὸν, "to justify himself," recurs at 16:15 (cf. 18:9, 14; 7:29) and is probably Lukan, as will be the use of πρός, "to," after a verb of speaking. The lawyer wishes to appear in a good light, despite having lost the initiative to Jesus, and having been displaced from the position of challenger to that of the one being challenged. It is finally unclear whether the self-justification is thought to involve the justifying of his earlier question ("there is still a difficulty to be cleared up"—this is the common view), or whether we should see here a preparation for making a claim to having fulfilled what the law asks of him (Bailey, *Peasant Eyes*, 39; cf. Luke 18:9–12, 21). On the question of the scope of neighbor love, see at v 27. The question assumes a restricted scope for neighbor love (cf. Sir 12:1–4: "If you do good, know to whom you do it . . . and do not help the sinner"). "Neighbor" here is discussed further in *Form/Structure/Setting* above.

30 ὑπολαμβάνειν in the sense of to take up in a conversation and so to answer is found only here in the NT but is found in the LXX (Job 2:4; 40:1; and many other times; Dan 3:28 [cf. Fitzmyer, 886]) and in secular Greek (BAGD, 845). ἄνθρωπός τις, "a certain person," occurs in the NT only in Luke's writing. It appears in the introduction of no less than seven of the Lukan parables (12:16 [gen.]; 14:16; 15:11; 16:1, 19; 19:12), as well as in two miracles stories (14:2; Acts 9:33 [acc.]). Despite the frequency, it may not be Lukan since (*i*) while ἄνθρωπός τις predominates in the Gospel, the statistics for ἀνήρ τις or τις ἀνήρ, "a certain man," are quite the converse with nine occurrences in Acts and only one in the Gospel, which may suggest that ἀνήρ τις, or τις ἀνήρ, represents Luke's free choice (cf. Jeremias, *Sprache*, 191); which finds support from (*ii*) Luke 8:27, the one Lukan text for which we have his source (Mark), where Luke adds a τις to Mark's ἄνθρωπος, and then goes to the trouble of changing the ἄνθρωπος to an ἀνήρ; and perhaps further support from (*iii*) recognizing that most of the texts using ἄνθρωπος are in pericopes that are likely to be from Luke's parables source (see excursus on the "Journey to Jerusalem," after 9:51–56). The uses of περιπίπτειν, "to fall among" (cf. Acts 27:41; elsewhere in NT only Jas 1:2), and πληγὰς ἐπιθέντες, "beat him" (elsewhere in the NT only Acts 16:23), are probably Lukan, and we begin to get in this verse already the beginning of that high concentration of composite words, which are characteristic of Luke (cf. Sellin, *ZNW* 66 [1975] 36).

It may be that the detailed touches in the development "stripped him and beat him and went off leaving him half dead" involve Lukan elaboration of something simpler ("left him half dead"?).

The Jericho of NT times is to be distinguished from ancient Jericho. Herod the Great was responsible for this town, which was about a mile and a half farther south near the mouth of the Wadi Qelt (Josephus, *War* 4.452–53; see further Fitzmyer, 886; Finegan, *Archaelogy*, 83–85). Over a distance of approximately eighteen miles there was a descent of about 3,300 feet. See Beauvery, *RB* 64 (1957) 72–101, regarding the route. The road passes through desert and rocky country (Josephus *War* 4.474), and Strabo (16.2.41) reports Pompey's dealings with robbers there. The location is suitable for robbers and for traveling priests and Levites, quite a number of whom lived in Jericho and traveled up to Jerusalem for their periodic responsibilities at the Temple (Str-B, 2:66, 180). For the dynamics of the story we need to know nothing of the man except that he has been reduced to a state of desperate need. Similarly, while the particular actions of the robbers can be given credible explanations, their only role in the narrative is to render the man entirely needy (what was stolen from the man apart from his clothing attracts no comment; it does not contribute to the man's immediately pressing need): the man is naked, beaten up, abandoned, and left half dead. The situation of need is presented as a matter of life and death, not because the resulting conclusion is only to be considered valid in the situation of extremity, but because an extreme case allows matters to emerge with clarity that might otherwise be obscured by extraneous considerations (cf. the way in which the horizon of death functions in 12:13–21; 16:19–31; and esp. 6:9 [see *Comment* there]). The *οἳ καί* (lit. "who also") may be rendered "who went so far as to," but need have no special force at all (cf. Haenchen, *Acts*, 140 n. 8, for such unstressed uses of *καί* following a relative pronoun).

31 Only the concentration of compound words offers itself here as a possible mark of Lukan intervention. By good fortune the priest comes along; the injured man is saved, or so for a moment it seems. But this prime representative of the religion that, in the person of the lawyer, has just agreed upon the fundamental place of love hardens his heart and passes by on the other side. We are not to understand that this priest is plagued by doubts about the scope of neighbor love (the naked man may not even be Jewish!); we understand simply that he failed the wounded man in his need. Much discussion has occurred about whether the priest would have considered himself justified in law to keep his distance from the (probably dead) man (see Lev 21:1–3; Num 5:2; 19:2–13; Ezek 44:25–27). But this is a misplaced interest. A half-dead man will soon become a dead man if timely help does not come along! The story's focus is on the priest's failure to help rather than on the reason that he failed to help. (In any case, the burial of a dead man without relatives able to take responsibility for the funeral appears to be a duty that in Jewish tradition takes precedence, even for a priest, over purity laws [*m. Naz.* 6:5; 7:1; Mann, *JQR* n.s. 6 (1915–16) 415–42]; the priest's failure to help is more likely to be motivated by fear of the robbers, though it is just possible that there may be a hint of a distinction between formal religious practice and covenant obligation to one's neighbor.) We are not to tar every priest with this brush (priestly worship is very positively represented in the Infancy Gospel); his priesthood should have made this man a good candidate for coming to the aid of the needy man, but in this case such an expectation was not borne out in practice. In the story the role of the priest is to raise hopes and then to dash them. The needy man's situation has now measurably worsened. Nobody else might come on the scene soon enough. Luke creates a set of chain linkages between his characters by using shared verbs in connection with adjacent characters as they appear on the scene (the man who falls among robbers and the priest were both "going down"; the priest and the Levite both "passed by on the other side"; the Levite and the Samaritan both "came" [using aorist forms of *ἔρχεσθαι κατά*]). Priest, Levite, and Samaritan will all "see" (*ἰδών*) the wounded man.

32 The action now repeats itself with minor variation in terms of a passing Levite. (In this verse *κατὰ τὸν τόπον*, "to the place," may be a Lukan touch [cf. Acts 27:2, 29 and Luke's many uses of *κατά* + accusative phrases in connection with locations].) The doubling heightens the effect, but the hearer is less surprised the second time round. This slight lessening in the intensity of the drama is reflected by the sequence "priest" then "Levite," since the Levites were second-ranking figures to the priest in Jewish religious life, from whom one might expect a little bit less (non-Aaronic descendants of Levi, they were entrusted with secondary roles in the life and worship of the Jerusalem temple). We may attribute to the same cause the failure of this figure to be introduced with *τις*, "a certain," as were the traveler, the priest, and the Samaritan. At this point the story is open to a number of possible developments. (Is it after all an anti-clerical story, and now an ordinary Israelite will come along and save the day? Will God intervene with angelic help and shame the religious figures? Is the story to be a tragedy in which the injured man's demise brings shame upon the covenant community?)

33 Only the use of *κατά* (here: "to") could suggest Lukan intervention (see at v 32). The arrival of a Samaritan will be an unexpected development in the story (marked in the Greek by putting "Samaritan" first). While there is no lack of verisimilitude in having a Samaritan travel here, this is not his native terrain. His arrival does not at once signal tragedy averted, since a Jewish audience will not expect much from him (from the audience's point of view this will be a Jewish affair into which this Samaritan man has stumbled). On Samaritans, see at 9:52. The traditional enmity between Samaritans and Jews is well captured in *m. Šeb.* 8:10: "He that eats the bread of the Samaritans is like one that eats the flesh of swine." When we come to *ἐσπλαγχνίσθη*, "he had compassion," we reach the fulcrum upon which the story turns. The word is reserved until the final position in the clause to build suspense and to allow maximum impact (Menkel [*NovT* 30 (1988) 111] produces word statistics that identify this as the central word in various ways [count of words, verbs, indicative verbs], but since such counting would need to be attributed to Luke, I would be happier with the method if it would work as well on a significant number of other Lukan pericopes).

Compassion is that which causes us so to identify with another's situation such that we are prepared to act for his or her benefit (cf. 7:13; 15:20). The content of the term is not significantly different from that of "love" in v 27, when applied to the neighbor, but the Samaritan is not being presented specifically as one who loves his neighbor and thus keeps the law (by means of the *ὁμοίως*, "likewise," he becomes so implicitly and secondarily in v 37b, in a Lukan development designed to tie the two pericopes [vv 25–28, 29–37] closer together, and to apply to the lawyer the challenge of the parable in the light of v 28). In the parable itself the

Samaritan's compassion functions on something of the same level as the giving of good gifts to one's children in 11:11–13. From the perspective created by the story (the victim's perspective) it is a self-evidently good act, but it is not there to prove anything about the Samaritan. This phenomenon stands behind the frequently noted secularity of the story (note esp. Braun, "Samariter"). If this is an example story, it is commending an example that seems to be not at all conditioned by the Godward dimension. But as we saw above in *Form/Structure/Setting*, what is being commended is the victim's perspective, not the example of the Samaritan. What he does is commendable, but from the perspective of the desperate victim it is self-evident that the law's demand for love of neighbor should bridge to any needy human being; that its practice should not be restricted to a closed community, even if that closed community is the community of the divine covenant. This is the exchange of perspective proposed in 6:31, but now developed in terms of the situation of one who is in desperate need. From a victim's perspective, if his situation is desperate enough, even a despised Samaritan is a welcome neighbor. (The parable is of course not designed to address the kind of Jewish fanaticism that would prefer death to being assisted by a Samaritan. To that degree it assumes a certain shared set of fundamental human instinctual values. Funk [*Parables and Presence*, 33] is wrong to stress the wounded man's inability to resist being helped by a Samaritan; he does not realize that the audience of the parable is, while perhaps embarrassed, finally glad of the Samaritan's rescue of the needy man.) A link with Hos 6:6 is often appealed to, a text that in Matt 9:13; 12:7 is used to commend mercy to those in need. The link is not unattractive (Bailey [*Peasant Eyes*, 49] finds no less than twelve links between Hos 6:1–10 and the parable), but it depends finally for its cogency on a reading of the parable (Samaritan as example and fulfiller of the law where the cult-oriented priest and Levite fail to fulfill the ethical demands of their own law) that has been rejected here on other grounds.

34 As in v 30 the detailed development in this verse is likely to owe something to Luke (for ἐπιβιβάσας, "put [him] on," cf. the only other NT uses in 19:35; Acts 23:24; for κτῆνος, "mount," cf. the only other NT use with this sense in Acts 23:24; for ἤγαγεν, "led," note the thirty-nine uses of this verb in Luke-Acts [Matthew four uses; Mark three]). Though the agreement is not close, it is just possible that the description has been influenced by 2 Chr 28:15 (there is little to commend the conjecture that the parable has been spun out of the account in 2 Chr 28:1–15). The Samaritan renders first aid with what he has with him (for the use of wine [antiseptic qualities?] and oil [it softens wounds in Isa 1:6] in ancient medicine, cf. Philostatus, *Hist. Plant.* 9.11.1; *m. Šabb.* 19:2); he gives up his own mount (the Greek could also support an image of the two men sharing the mount, but this is a less likely Lukan use of ἄγειν, "to lead/bring" [cf. J. A. Fitzmyer, "The Use of *Agein* and *Pherein* in the Synoptic Gospels," in *Festschrift to Honor F. Wilbur Gingrich*, ed. E. H. Barth and R. E. Cocroft (Leiden: Brill, 1972, 147–60)]) in order to bring the man back into human community from the place where he had been deserted and left to die; he puts them both up at an inn and takes care of the man until the next day. The Samaritan does what is immediately needed.

35 We may be justified in finding Lukan language again in this verse (ἐπί + accusative in time expressions is distinctly Lukan [elsewhere only Heb 11:30, apart from the distinctive idiom ἐφ' ὅσον (χρόνον)] and the exact phrase ἐπὶ τὴν αὔριον, "on the next day," occurs in Acts 4:5; ἐπανέρχεσθαι, "to return," is elsewhere in the NT only in Luke 19:15; there continues to be a noted concentration of compound words, for which Luke shows a fondness). The literature is prone to use exaggerated language of the trouble to which the Samaritan went, or of the relationship established between the Samaritan and the rescued man. The Samaritan took responsibility for the needs of the situation, but he went about his business the next day, leaving the continued care of the injured man in the hands of the innkeeper. We know nothing of a personal relationship. The two denarii would have provided for very basic board and lodging for about two weeks (N. Heutger, "Münzen im Lukasevangelium," *BZ* 27 [1983] 98). Having been robbed, the injured man would not have had with him the wherewithal to pay his own way. The rate of recovery from serious injury is an uncertain business, so the Samaritan pledged himself to meet any shortfall in the advance payment made for the injured man's care. The support continued so long as the pressing need continued. We are probably to understand that the Samaritan's business brought him regularly past this point and that he was known to the innkeeper.

36 The argument for Lukan intervention here depends upon seeing as tortuous the syntax of this verse as it now stands. The syntax is complex, but I see no basis for pronouncing the sentence composite. The lawyer wanted an in-principle answer to the scope of neighbor responsibility. Instead he is invited by the story to look at the neighbor question from the point of view of the potential recipient of neighbor-love in a situation of extremity, for whom the answer to the question can be a matter of life and death. The question of v 36 underlines this thrust of the parable. The strategy of the parable and the wording of the question assume a reciprocity in the term "neighbor" (cf. Jeremias, *Parables*, 205): if a neighbor is one to whom I will be ready to extend help, a neighbor is also one who is ready to extend help to me. One who is my neighbor must be present with me, but he is no neighbor if he is there only for himself and not for me as well. It is probably justified to press the perfect tense form γεγονέναι, "to have become," and to say that the Samaritan became a neighbor in his compassionate actions. No restrictive sense for "neighbor" is finally adequate to the realities of the human situation when viewed from the situation of a person in desperate need.

37 The final clause of the verse looks most Lukan with its repetition of elements of v 28 (for "do likewise," cf. 3:11; 6:31) and the use of πορεύου, "go," which occurs twelve times in Luke-Acts (once in Matthew; three times in John). The answer to Jesus' question is not oblique in order to avoid speaking about the hated Samaritan. Rather the wording underlines the point of the parable: looking at it from the point of view of the desperately needy, it is the practice of mercy that makes a passerby into a neighbor. Not only the language, as already noted, but also the complexity introduced into the logic of the pericope by the final clause suggests that, at least in its present form, it is a Lukan contribution. (Comparison with formally similar accounts such as 2 Sam 12:1–7a; Matt 21:28–31; Luke 7:41–43; *b. ʿAbod. Zar.* 54b–55a suggests, however, that some final statement by Jesus is a necessary part of the form [cf. Sellin, *ZNW* 66 (1975) 31]. We can only guess as to an earlier form here.) In the Lukan form the lawyer is being asked to carry away with him the approach to the question of neighbor that emerges from the parable (look at things from the perspective of the victim), and to love his neighbor, as now newly understood, with the kind of concrete expression of compassion that has just been exemplified by the Samaritan. The Samaritan has become a neighbor through his compassionate action, but integral to this concrete action has been his own seeing of the situation from the victim's point of view (cf. Eicholz, *Gleichnisse*, 170–71). The account ends with the emphasis on *doing* that runs as a thread from v 25 to v 28 to the present verse.

Explanation

This parable episode takes up the neighbor half of the command to love of God and neighbor of vv 25–28. Vv 38–42 will take up, more indirectly, the God half. The lawyer asks, "Who is my neighbor?" Jesus suggests that we should answer that question from a vantage point of isolation and desperate need, and then make use of the same answer when we come at the question from a position of strength, when it is within our gift to be handing out favors, rather than receiving them.

Recent questioning of whether the parable really goes back to the historical Jesus has highlighted the degree to which Luke took a hand in producing the detailed form of the parable as we now have it. But there is still every reason for thinking that the historical Jesus is the creative source of the parable.

For much of the history of the church the parable has been understood by taking the Samaritan to be Jesus, and this view has found fresh support in some modern scholarship. The idea has also been canvassed that the wounded man represents Jesus. The more usual modern view is that the parable is an example story in which the Samaritan shows us a compassion unrestricted by national, racial, or religious barriers. This is certainly better than the more allegorical approaches, but in the end is not quite correct. We need to keep in mind that the story is told from the perspective of the wounded man, and not from the perspective of the Samaritan. This is true in the story itself, and in the attached dialogue at the end, it is the wounded man who ends up with a neighbor, not the Samaritan. The story is a challenge to take up the victim's perspective.

Despite having lost the initiative to Jesus in vv 25–28, the lawyer thinks he can still emerge from the encounter looking good if he moves the question, on to "Who is my neighbor?" (It is not clear whether the fresh turn is to justify the earlier question, which has been disposed of so unceremoniously, or whether he is angling toward being able to announce his fulfillment of the double command.)

Jesus responds to the man's fresh initiative with a story. A man was on a lonely and rugged journey when he had the misfortune to be encountered by a robber band who takes all he has and leaves him half dead. Exposed, in a remote place, and seriously injured, the expectation must be that he will die. The extremity of the man's situation will provide sharp relief for the hearer's consideration of what is at stake as the story continues to unfold.

Despite all our fears, by a stroke of good fortune our man turns out not to be the only traveler that day. A priest comes along who surely will come to the aid of this victim. Our hopes are, however, immediately dashed: he passes by on the other side. We do not know why no help has been offered, but we do know that our man's situation looks bleaker than ever. The desperateness of his plight is underlined further when a second traveler, a Levite (not quite such a good candidate for help), repeats the pattern of the priest.

What possible developments can we as listeners expect in the story? We started out with high expectations of the cultic figures, but if now an ordinary Jew should come along and help, then we will find that we have been drawn into a piece of anti-clerical propaganda. Or will the story end tragically with shame falling upon the whole Jewish community for its lovelessness? Or will God be hero, and intervene, perhaps through an angel?

The development we get is not the development we expect (one would not find many Samaritans in this area). It is also not a hopeful development. What can one expect from these wretched people? But though we have no positive listener expectations, the arrival of the Samaritan does signal tragedy averted. The Samaritan so identifies with the situation of the needy man that he feels impelled to come to his aid. As Jewish listeners we may in principle have felt that we would not be prepared to accept any charity from a hated Samaritan. But here the extremity of the situation strips away much that is finally extraneous, and we are glad that help has finally come, even if from a Samaritan. Perhaps rather to our own surprise, we find that in extremis a Samaritan will do very well for a neighbor!

The Samaritan administered first aid, led the man on his own mount back to civilization, took care of him overnight at an inn, and then took financial responsibility for seeing to the man's full recuperation from his ordeal. Having seen to the man's pressing need, the Samaritan went on about his business. He would come back later and pay any bills.

Luke's lawyer can see clearly that in showing mercy to the needy man, the Samaritan has become a neighbor to the injured man. Despite the huge distance that separated the Samaritan from the covenant community of God's people, from a desperate victim's perspective he could be neighbor. The lawyer is challenged to take up precisely this "victim's perspective" as he is called to love his neighbor as himself.

The One Necessary Thing (10:38–42)

Bibliography

Augsten, M. "Lukanische Miszelle." *NTS* 14 (1967–68) 581–83. **Baker, A.** "One Thing Necessary." *CBQ* 27 (1965) 127–37. **Beydon, F.** "A temps nouveau, nouvelles questions: Luc 10:38–42." *FV* 88 (1989) 25–32. **Bonnardière, A.-M. de la.** "Marthe et Marie, figures de l'église d'après S. Augustin." *VSpir* 86 (1952) 404–27. **Brutscheck, J.** *Die Maria-Marta-Erzählung: Eine redaktionskritische Untersuchung zu Lk 10, 38–42.* BBB 64. Frankfurt am M./ Bonn: P. Hanstein, 1986. ———. "Lukanischen Anliegen in der Maria-Marta-Erzählung: Zu Lk10,38–42." *GuL* 62 (1989) 84–96. **Castel, F.** "Luc 10/38–42." *ETR* 55 (1980) 560–65. **Coakley, J. T.** "The Anointing at Bethany and the Priority of John." *JBL* 107 (1988) 241–56. **Csányi, D. A.** "Optima pars. Die Auslegung von Lk 10, 38–42 bein den Kirchenvätern der ersten vier Jahrhunderte." *StMon* 2 (1960) 5–78. **Dauer, A.** *Johannes und Lukas: Untersuchungen zu den johaneisch-lukanischen Parallelperikopen Joh 4,46–54/Lk 7,1–10—Joh 12,1–8/Lk 7,36–50; 10,38–42—Joh 20,19–29/Lk 24,36–49.* Forschung zur Bibel 50. Würzburg: Echter, 1984. **Davidson, J. A.** "Things to Be Understood and Things to Be Done." *ExpTim* 94 (1982–83) 306–7. **Demel, S.** "Jesu Umgang mit Frauen nach dem

Lukasevangelium." *BibNot* 57 (1991) 52–95, esp. 73–78. **Dreher, A.** "Jesus bei Marta und Maria (Lukas 10,38–42)." *EuA* 57 (1981) 277–79. **Dupont, J.** "De quoi est-il besoin (Lc x.42)?" In *Text and Interpretation.* FS M. Black, ed. E. Best and R. McL. Wilson. Cambridge: University Press, 1979. 115–20. **Eckhart, M.** "Martha and Mary: Second Discourse." *Parabola* 5 (1980) 69–73. **Erb, P. C.** "The Contemplative Life as the *Unum Necessarium:* In Defense of a Traditional Reading of Luke 10:42." *Mystics Quarterly* 11 (1985) 161–64. **Fee, G. D.** "'One Thing Is Needful?' Luke 10:42." In *New Testament Textual Criticism: Its Significance for Exegesis.* FS B. M. Metzger, ed. E. J. Epp and G. D. Fee. Oxford: Clarendon, 1981. 61–75. **George, A.** "L'Accueil du Seigneur: Lc 10,38–42." *AsSeign* n.s. 47 (1970) 75–85. **Gillieson, T.** "A Plea for Proportion: St. Luke x. 38–42." *ExpTim* 59 (1947–48) 111–12. **Henze, C. M.** "Zum Festevangelium von Mariä Himmelfahrt (Lc 10,42)." *TPQ* 94 (1941) 240–43. **Jeffrey, F.** "Martha and Mary." *ExpTim* 29 (1917) 184–88. **Kemmer, A.** "Maria und Martha: Zur Deutungsgeschichte von Lk 10,38ff. im alten Mönchtum." *EuA* 40 (1964) 355–67. **Kilgallen, J. J.** "A Suggestion regarding *gar* in Luke 10, 42." *Bib* 73 (1992) 255–58. **Knockaert, A.** "Structural Analysis of the Biblical Text." *LVit* 33 (1978) 471–81. **Lacan, M.-F.** "Une présence dont je puis jouir." *LumVie* 39 (1990) 63–80. **Laland, E.** "Die Martha-Maria-Perikope Lukas 10,38–42: Ihre Kerygmatische Aktualität für das Leben der Urkirche." *ST* 13 (1959) 70–85. ———. "Marthe et Marie: Quel message l'église primitive lisait-elle dans ce récit? Luc 10,38–42." *BVC* 76 (1967) 29–43. **LaVerdiere, E.** "The One Thing Required." *Emman* 89 (1983) 398–403. **Lotz, J. B.** "Martha und Maria." *GuL* 32 (1959) 161–65. **Louw, J.** "Quel est le sens des paroles de Notre-Seigneur disant que Marie a choisi la meilleure part (Lc. 10,39–42)?" *AmCl* 52 (1936) 171–72. **Magass, W.** "Maria und Martha—Kirche und Haus: Thesen zu einer institutionellen Konkurrenz (Lk 10,38–42). *LingBib* 27–28 (1973) 2–5. **Nicolas, J.-H.** "La meilleure part: Marthe et Marie." *VSpir* 75 (1946) 226–38. **Nolle, L.** "Bethany." *Scr* 4 (1949–51) 262–64. **O'Rahilly, A.** "The Two Sisters." *Scr* 4 (1949–51) 68–76. **Phelps, A. St.** "The Martha Heresy." *RevExp* 27 (1930) 176–82. **Rinaldi, G.** "Marta: Exegese zu Lk 10,38–42." *BeO* 5 (1963) 123–26. **Roosen, A.** "Das einzig Notwendige: Erwägungen zu Lk 10,38–42." *StMor* 17 (1979) 9–39. **Schlier, H.** "Das eine, was not ist." *Ut omnes unum* 22 (1959) 3–7. **Schmithals, W.** *Das Eine, das not tut: Ein Biblischer Vortag zu Lk 10,38–42.* Erbauliche Reden 5. Neukirchen: Neukirchener, 1977. **Schüssler Fiorenza, E.** "A Feminist Critical Interpretation for Liberation: Martha and Mary: Luke 10:38–42." *RIL* 3 (1986) 21–36. ———. "Theological Criteria and Historical Reconstruction: Martha and Mary: Luke 10:38–42." *CHSP* 53 (1987) 1–12 (with responses 13–63). **Stevenson, M.** "Martha and Mary." *ExpTim* 28 (1916–17) 478. **Sudbrack, J.** "'Nur eines ist notwendig' (Lk 10,42)." *GuL* 37 (1964) 161–64. **Sweetland, D. M.** "The Good Samaritan and Martha and Mary." *BiTod* 21 (1983) 325–30. **Venetz, H.-J.** "Die Suche nach dem 'einen Notwendigen' Beobachtungen und Verdächtigungen rund um die Marta-Maria-Perikope Lk 10,38–42)." *Orientierung* 54 (1990) 185–89. **Via, E. J.** "Women, the Discipleship of Service, and the Early Christian Ritual Meal in the Gospel of Luke." *SLJT* 29 (1985) 37–60. **Wall, R. W.** "Martha and Mary (Luke 10.38–42) in the Context of a Christian Deuteronomy." *JSNT* 35 (1989) 19–35.

Translation

38 As[a] they continued on their way, Jesus[b] entered a certain village, and a certain woman named Martha welcomed him into her house.[c] 39 She had a sister whose name was Mary who[d] sat down alongside, at the Lord's[e] feet, and was listening to[f] his word. 40 Martha was distracted with a great deal of domestic work.[g] She came up and said, "Lord,[h] do you not care that my sister left[i] me to do the domestic work alone? Tell her, then, to take her part along with me." 41 The Lord[j] responded[k] to her, "Martha, Martha, [l]you are worried and troubled about many things, 42 but only one thing is necessary.[l] For[m] Mary has chosen the good portion which shall not be taken from her."

Notes

[a] An opening ἐγένετο, "it happened," is provided by A C D W Θ Ψ etc. Along with it comes a καί (here: "that") between the first two clauses. This is a frequent Lukan construction and could possibly be original, but is more likely to be a scribal alteration designed to give better separation between the opening clauses.

[b] Gr. "he."

[c] "Into her house" is missing from P[45,75] B sa; P[3 vid] ℵ C L Ξ etc. lack "her"; the textual witness is divided over which word for house should occur here. The full phrase could be a scribal completion, but is probably original as part of the complex of terms that evoke the mission materials of Luke 9:1–6; 10:1–16 (see *Comment*).

[d] ἥ, "who," is read here by ℵ 1 A B C D W Θ Ψ etc., but not by P[45, 75] ℵ B[2] L Ξ etc. If it is accepted, then it should probably be linked to the following καί, which should be taken as indicating that what Mary does is in addition to what Martha has done.

[e] Ἰησοῦ, "Jesus," is read here by P[45, 75] A B C[2] W Θ Ψ etc. and may be original.

[f] An aorist tense is preferred here by P[45] L Ξ.

[g] Gr. διακονίαν, "service." The word is used to indicate preparations for a meal.

[h] Or possibly "Sir."

[i] A B C L Θ Ξ etc. read the impf. for the aorist here.

[j] "Jesus" occurs here in A B C D W Θ Ψ etc., but is less likely to be original here than is the better supported corresponding reading in v 39.

[k] Lit. "having answered, said."

[l-l] These words are missing from it sy[s] (and D has only θορυβάζῃ, "disturbed"). 38 syr[pal] arm geo bo[ms] read the text as translated but with "few things" (ὀλίγων) for "one thing" (ἑνός). Both forms are joined with ἤ, "or," in P[3] ℵ B C[2] etc. The text as translated is supported by P[45] P[75] A C W Θ Ξ Ψ etc. (For a detailed listing of the textual witnesses see Fee ["'One Thing Is Needful'?" 61–63], who argues forcefully as a textual critic for the fullest combined form as original, but finally at the expense of requiring "necessary" to function in the text in two quite different senses [in the wording of Godet, 2:45 (who himself considers this sense too subtle to be likely) "*There needs but little* [for the body], *or even but one thing* [for the soul].") The addition of "few things" is more likely to represent a softening of the text, which otherwise seemed extreme when taken as describing the necessities for a meal (note the sequence "many things," "few things," "one thing," which is produced by this expansion). The same impulse taken a step further led to the loss of "or of one thing" from this expanded form of the text. (See further in *Comment.*)

[m] Many texts (A C W Θ etc. and the majority text) read the colorless δέ, "and/but" here, no doubt as a result of difficulty with the sense sequence here.

Form/Structure/Setting

The preceding parable has focussed on the person-to-person aspect of God's requirement of love. The present episode is concerned with the vertical aspect of love of God, which shows itself in attentiveness to the word of God as brought by Jesus.

On the parallel roles of vv 29–37 and 38–42, see at 10:25. Beyond the considerations invoked there, we should note (*i*) the introduction of Martha as γυνή . . . τις, "a certain woman," after the ἄνθρωπος τις, "a certain man" of v 30; (*ii*) that the alliteration of Jerusalem and Jericho corresponds to that of Martha and Mary (Goulder, 494); (*iii*) the theme of journeying, which plays a role in each account; (*iv*) the use of κύριος, "Lord," here for Jesus after its use for God in v 27; (*v*) the further link between Jesus and God provided by the evident links between the present pericope, with its ἤκουεν τὸν λόγον αὐτοῦ, "was listening to/hearing his word," and the subunit 8:1–21, with its climax in τὸν λόγον τοῦ θεοῦ ἀκούοντες (καὶ ποιοῦντες), "[who] hear the word of God (and do [it])"; (*vi*) the possibility that Luke has in mind Mark's form of vv 25–27 (12:28–31) when he has "*one* thing is necessary," and just possibly also in the reference to hearing; (*vii*) that where vv 29–37 take up love of neighbor in the form of the question "who is my neighbor?" vv 38–42 implicitly take up love of God in the form of the question "how and where may I show love to God?"

The tradition here is distinctly Lukan and has been extensively worked over by Luke, but there is no adequate basis for treating the episode as a Lukan creation (as Goulder, 492–95 [on the other hand the links between Luke 10:38–42 and 1 Cor 7:32–35 constitute the strongest part of Goulder's case for Lukan knowledge of 1 Corinthians (pp. 132–41, here 136–37)]; see the thorough analysis of Brutscheck [*Maria-Marta-Erzählung*, esp. 65–95, 133–43] for a convincing delineation of the likely pre-Lukan content, which would include the naming of the two women, the extending of hospitality to Jesus, the "disciple" behavior of Mary, the "serving" role of Martha, and the arbitration of Jesus). The unevenness of the degree to which there is a Lukan caste to the language of the text suggests source material. The incidental similarities between the present pericope and John 11:1–44; 12:1–8 coupled with the very different interests of the texts provides an indirect support for a traditional basis to the present story (cf. George, *AsSeign* 47 [1970] 84–85; there is, however, sufficient vocabulary overlap to suspect a link at some point in the transmission of the traditions [cf. Brutscheck, *Maria-Marta-Erzählung*, 147–50]).

The original form of the materials is variously taken to be a pronouncement story (biographical apophthegm in Bultmann's diction [*Synoptic Tradition*, 33]), a story about Jesus (Taylor, *Formation of the Gospel Tradition* [London: Macmillan, 1957], 75) and a legend with historical basis (Dibelius, *From Tradition*, 119, 293). None of these is fully satisfactory: the narrative is too necessary to the final pronouncement for Bultmann's classification to convince; there is not the characterization of Mary that would be expected for Dibelius' approach; and Mary is too much the hero for Taylor's story about Jesus. R. C. Tannehill takes us a step further ("The Pronouncement Story and Its Types," *Semeia* 20 [1981] 1–14; "Varieties of Synoptic Pronouncement Stories," *Semeia* 20 [1981] 101–19) when he broadens the pronouncement story category by distinguishing different categories of pronouncement stories. He suggests that our present episode belongs to a mixed type of "objection-commendation stories," combining, as the name suggests, features of an objection story, where Jesus would answer an objection to his approach, with features of a commendation story, where Jesus confirms and praises what has been said or done by some protagonist. Brutscheck builds on Tannehill's observations to suggest that what we have here is a narrative about Jesus that is concerned to establish a norm of behavior (*Maria-Marta-Erzählung*, 158–59; cf. also Laland [*ST* 13 (1959) 71] who links the present narrative to others where a person turns to Jesus, convinced that he is in agreement with his/her approach, only to evoke from Jesus a statement that gains its significance precisely from the misunderstanding involved in the original statement [e.g., Mark 10:13–16]). Such a narrative would have a credible original setting in life in early Christian community gatherings with their shared meals or in the hospitality extended to early itinerant Christian preachers/apostles/ prophets (see 10:7; 1 Cor 9:4; 2 John 10; 3 John 7–8; *Did.* 11.3–8; 13.1–3; the more precise role, claimed by Via [*SLJT* 29 (1985) 58–59], at least for the Lukan form of the text, of regulating the relationship at the eucharistic celebration between the hearing of the word [must come first] and the meal itself [is a necessary part of the Christian ritual] involves, despite Luke's clear interest in eucharistic theology, a scarcely justifiable leap; E. Schüssler Fiorenza [*CHSP* 53 (1987) 9] is no more convincing in her claim that the account is designed to restrict women's ministry and authority, and in particular to silence women leaders of house churches).

In the history of the interpretation of the passage the two women have been variously taken to represent the active and the contemplative life, the present world and the world to come, Judaism and Christianity, justification by works and justification by faith (or Catholicism and Protestantism). All of these approaches treat the figures much too abstractly and fail to attend to the specific contours of the account (cf. E. Schüssler Fiorenza, *CHSP* 53 [1987] 4–5).

The episode portrays a stopover in a village in the context of Jesus' continuing journey to Jerusalem. He goes into a particular house where he is made welcome by the mistress of the house and listened to avidly by the younger sister of the mistress. Between them they exemplify the proper reception of the message of the kingdom of God. Martha's domestic service would seem to be an innocent development of the welcome given to the messenger of the kingdom of God, but is at once provided with negative overtones as that which causes her to be pulled this way and that. Martha's diagnosis of the problem is too much work and too few hands, but Jesus disagrees. Troubled by worries aroused by a preoccupation with the practical affairs of life (even if these concern hospitality to the messenger of the kingdom of God), Martha has been seduced away from the kind of trustful preoccupation with the kingdom of God that should be the orientation of the faithful disciple. Being taken up with God is the one thing necessary. Jesus will not send Mary to help, since in her listening posture she has chosen just that preoccupation with the message of the kingdom of God that Jesus would commend to Martha as well.

Comment

The one who loves God is taken up with his word, and this is received by listening to Jesus. Even when apparently given over to service of the kingdom of God, preoccupation with the practical affairs of life easily seduces one away from a wholehearted attention to the things of God.

38 The language of this verse is quite Lukan (Luke is the dominant NT user of the *ἐν τῷ* construction, and in these constructions he almost always, as here, supplies an express subject; he provides well over half of the NT uses of *πορεύεσθαι*, "to come/go"; the combination of noun + adjectival *τις*, "a certain," + *ὀνόματι*, "by name," + personal name is uniquely Lukan; Luke owns three of the four NT uses of *ὑποδέχεσθαι*, "to welcome/receive" [for details see Brutscheck, *Maria-Marta-Erzählung*, 66–74, who considers even more of the text to be identifiably Lukan]).

Luke refreshes here the motif of journeying to Jerusalem that is to be the constant backdrop for the whole journey section of the Gospel (see excursus after 9:21–22). At the same time the links established here by means of the conjunction of this traveling with entering (cf. 9:4; 10:5, 8) a village (cf. 9:6), being received/welcomed (cf. 10:8; [9:5; 10:10]) into a house (cf. 9:4; 10:5, 7) and hearing (cf. 10:16) cannot fail to draw attention to the motif of mission: the going out to preach the kingdom of God (as an extension of Jesus' own ministry). From these links it follows that, in the initial horizon of the story, hospitality to the preacher cannot be separated from "hospitality" to the message. As well as the link to earlier texts, it is probably right to find a link between the receiving of Jesus here and that reported in 19:1–10 (Brutscheck, *Maria-Marta-Erzählung*, 103, identifies no less than ten links [not all equally convincing]). Salvation has come to the house of Martha and Mary, as it will to that of Zacchaeus. While there is a tension between the challenge to homelessness implicit in the call to discipleship in 9:57–58 and the domestic setting to which salvation comes here, it is hardly necessary to resolve this in sociological terms by speaking of a change in the understanding of discipleship as Christianity developed from being a radical, but socially marginal, phenomenon to finding its place in the ongoing life of human society. Both forms of discipleship will have had their place from the beginning.

John 11:1; 12:1–3 locate Mary and Martha in the village of Bethany, but to mention that location here would disturb Luke's travel narrative structure (cf. 19:29). The name Martha is related to the Aramaic word for "master," but is not likely to be merely symbolic for her role as mistress of the household. Martha will be the householder, probably as a widow, but perhaps simply as the elder sister.

39 Lukan elements here include the use of *εἶναι*, "to be," with the dative; the use of the participle *καλουμένη*, "being called"; probably also the participial use of *παρακαθέζεσθαι*, "to take one's place beside"; the use of *ὁ κύριος*, "the Lord," for Jesus; the expression *τὸν λόγον αὐτοῦ*, "his word," for Jesus' teaching (see Brutscheck, *Maria-Marta-Erzählung*, 74–80).

Mary is sister to Martha also in John 11:1. One could claim a symbolic meaning for her name as well, since Mary is probably related etymologically to a Hebrew word meaning "height/summit," and as a name would connote something like "excellence" (Fitzmyer, 344). But a symbolic significance is no more likely here than for Martha. Mary takes up the position of a student with a rabbi and sets herself to listen to Jesus (see *m. ʾAbot* 1:4: "Let thy house be a meeting-house for the Sages and sit amidst the dust of their feet and drink in their words with thirst"; cf. further 2 Kgs 4:38). Luke has the same posture used similarly in 8:35 and Acts 22:3. "His word" is found also in 4:32, but more usually it is the "word of God" that Jesus is considered to speak (5:1; 8:11, 21; 11:28), and "his word" will be thought of here in just such a light. (In the present context the "hearing/listening to" evokes 10:16.) Between them Martha and Mary pattern the proper response to the messenger of the kingdom of God. They show love for God by opening themselves to the message/messenger that now comes to them from God (cf. Acts 16:13–15). Brutscheck (*Maria-Marta-Erzählung*, 105) is probably right, in light of the links to 19:1–10, to set the coming of Jesus here into the context of the motif of the visitation of God (see 7:16 for visitation recognized and 19:41–44 for visitation not recognized). Schüssler Fiorenza has totally missed the direction of the Lukan development with her stress on the restriction to silence of Mary (*CHSP* 53 [1987] 7). See at 8:1–3 for the way that Luke, compared to his sources, enhances the importance of the contribution of women disciples.

40 Luke is likely to be responsible for *περιεσπᾶτο περί*, "was distracted with"; the use of *ἐφιστάναι*, "to come up to"; in light of the other narrator's uses of the term before and after, maybe also the vocative *κύριε*, "Lord/Sir"; and more than likely the double compound verb *συναντιλάβηται*, "take part along with" (see Brutscheck, *Maria-Marta-Erzählung*, 80–87).

The starting point for our evaluation of Martha's service needs to be a recognition of the positive place that διακονία, "service/serving," and διακονεῖν, "to serve," have in Luke (see 4:39; 8:3; 22:26–27). The noun here refers broadly to attention to domestic affairs (with a particular focus on what pertains to meals) in the interests of her honored guest. Such domestic hospitality is envisaged in 10:7–8. Jesus is a meal guest also in 5:27–32; 7:36–50; 14:1–14; 24:13–35. περιεσπᾶτο, "she was distracted [lit. pulled about] with," tells us, however, that something is wrong. In Acts 6:1–6, esp. v 2, the good and necessary service of seeing to the sustenance needs of the Christian widows threatened to interrupt the even more important task of preaching the word of God. This was considered to be an intolerable development. By the time we reach the end of our narrative we will see that the multiple claims pulling upon Martha represent a threat to the single-minded devotion proper to the disciple. Martha's request is an entirely natural one, but one that ultimately fails to take account of the uniqueness of the situation and that reflects the outlook of a person who, despite the best of intentions, has become ensnared by "the worries and riches and pleasures of life" (8:14) and has lost sight of that in which her true life as a disciple consists (4:3). Knockaert (*LVit* 33 [1978] 474) suggests that there is a deliberate contrast here between Martha who *tells* Jesus what he *must* say and Mary who *listens* to what Jesus *wishes* to say.

41 In this verse only ὁ κύριος, "the Lord," is a clear piece of Lukan diction, but μεριμνᾷς, "you are anxious," may be Luke's bridge to 12:22–31 (see Brutscheck, *Maria-Marta-Erzählung*, 87–91).

The repetition of the name is gently critical. Martha is worried and preoccupied by the ordinary affairs of life (cf. 8:14; 12:22, 25, 26; 21:34 where the same μεριμν-, "worry" root is found), which have trapped her into operating with an earthbound frame of reference not worthy of a disciple called to spend his/her efforts in another direction (12:31). Laland (*ST* 13 [1959] 75) uses the language of temptation (cf. 4:4; 22:40) to describe Martha's experience. She shows nothing of that peace that should be the possession of one who has come to experience in the ministry of Jesus the immediacy of God's presence and provision.

42 Various parts of the vocabulary here *could* be Lukan. The use of ἐκλέγεσθαι, "to choose," is perhaps the most definite, but even here one can hardly be certain (see Brutscheck, *Maria-Marta-Erzählung*, 91–95).

The text is uncertain at this point with many MSS reading "a few things (or)" before "one thing" or instead of it (see details in textual note). These other readings have created a traditional focus for interpretation upon the question of what constitutes an adequate meal for Jesus: Jesus is suggesting simplicity. This makes for a difficult transition to the following clause, which despite the LXX use of μερίς, "part," for portions in a meal (Gen 43:34; 1 Sam 1:4–5; 9:23; Neh 8:10, 12; Esth 9:19, 22) can hardly be taken to mean that Mary has chosen the best dish from the meal! Conscious of this difficulty, interpreters have looked for a means of transition. That Mary has chosen to listen to the word of Jesus may be viewed metaphorically as the choice of the best meal (cf. 4:4), or it could be that *necessity* is seen from a double aspect: for a meal a few things will do; for one's salvation receiving the word of God is the necessary thing (e.g. Laland, *ST* 13 [1959] 76). Better than these suggestions one should drop any idea of a call to more simple domestic provisions and instead find expressed here the contrast between preoccupation with the practical affairs of life ("what shall we eat and what shall we drink" [12:29]) and engagement with the kingdom of God (12:31). This contrast of loyalties is expressed once more in 16:13 with ἑνός, "of one" (cf. 18:22). Allowed its own natural way, life in the world with its multiple concerns captures us and causes us to be stressed and fragmented. Attention to the word of God supplies an integrating center and makes possible a singleness of vision. This is the one necessary thing. It is typical of Jesus' laconic approach that there is no actual resolution of the practical question about the provision of food! The shock value provided by such violation of common sense is part of what etches his teaching upon the mind (cf. Brutscheck, *Die Maria-Mart-Erzählung*, 159). Presumably one must at times prepare food, but such concerns should never be allowed to compete with the hearing of the word of God. It may be the urgency lent by the eschatological presence of the kingdom of God (10:11) that mandates the undistracted attention to the messenger. The explanatory function of the final clause (γάρ, "for") is to clarify the implied negative answer to Martha's request (cf. Dupont, "De quoi?" 118). Mary's "good portion" (perhaps "best portion" [cf. BDF, 245]) may echo the language of Ps 72(73):26–28 where God is the *portion* of the psalmist, near to whom it is *good* to be (cf. also Ps 118[119]:57). "Portion" is used in connection with the imagery of one's share of an inheritance (Job 20:29; 27:13; Eccl 2:10; 3:22; Wis 2:9; Sir 14:9; Isa 17:14; Jer 13:25; etc; cf. George, *AsSeign* n.s. 47 [1970] 81). Mary's chosen portion is the same as the one necessary thing commended to Martha in 41b. Is Mary assured here of an eternal abiding possession (by contrast with 8:18; 12:19–21; as, Brutscheck, J. *Die Maria-Marta-Erzählung*, 130), or is it more simply that Mary will certainly not be asked to leave her listening position to help with domestic matters? (Almost certainly the latter.)

The episode is concerned to show that even when domestic service has been harnessed to the purposes of the kingdom of God, the danger remains that its concerns will take possession of us. Manifesting as the worries of this life, it will distract from the central necessity of hearing the word of God and choke off the effect of the word that has already been sown.

Explanation

The parable of the good Samaritan has provided a powerful comment on the person-to-person dimension of God's requirement of love. Now we are invited to attend to the vertical aspect of love of God, which comes to expression as a preoccupation with the word of God as brought by Jesus. The two accounts mutually qualify one another: the emphasis on practical activity in the Samaritan story keeps us from one-sidely exalting the "contemplative" life after the pattern of Mary; while the Martha/Mary episode warns that preoccupation with the practical affairs of life, even when apparently given over to the service of the kingdom of God, easily seduces one away from a wholehearted attention to the things of God.

The opening verse reminds us of the setting of all the material here into the context of Jesus' journey to death in Jerusalem. At the same time, Luke would have us think of the pattern of going out to preach the kingdom of God that has been provided in 9:1–6; 10:1–16. From this perspective we see that at the beginning of the episode Martha (in receiving Jesus) and Mary (in her attention to his teaching) between them exemplify the proper reception of the message of the kingdom of God. The account also has important links with the Zacchaeus account in 19:1–10: salvation has come to the house of Martha and Mary, as it will to that of Zacchaeus.

Mary's position at the feet of Jesus is probably that of a student with a rabbi, eager to learn. The word that Jesus speaks is elsewhere spoken of as the "word of God" (5:1; 8:11, 21; 11:28), and "his word" here is to be seen in light of this. Nothing less than a visitation of God is taking place (cf. 7:16; 19:41–44).

The word translated "domestic work" refers broadly to attention to domestic affairs, but with a particular focus on what pertains to meals. Martha is going to great efforts, as she sees it, in the interests of her honored guest. Such domestic hospitality is viewed positively in 10:7–8, but here Luke signals that something is wrong by his use of the word "distracted." In some respects the situation in Acts 6:1–6 is similar, where the good and necessary service of seeing to the sustenance needs of the Christian widows threatens to interrupt the even more important task of preaching the word of God.

Over-stretched in her busyness, Martha makes a very natural request for her sister's help. But at the end of the day her request quite fails to recognize the uniqueness of the situation and reflects the outlook of a person who, despite the best of intentions, has become ensnared by "the worries and riches and pleasures of life" (8:14), and has lost sight of what must predominate in one's true life as a disciple (4:4). The sharpness of Martha's language suggests that we should see a deliberate contrast between Martha as she *tells* Jesus what he *must* say and Mary who *listens* to what Jesus *wishes* to say.

In his response to Martha, Jesus uses the worry language that has already appeared in 8:14 and will recur in 12:22, 25, 26; 21:34. The ordinary affairs of life have trapped her into operating with an earthbound frame of reference. She is not experiencing the peace that should be the lot of the one who experiences in the ministry of Jesus the immediacy of God's presence and provision.

Martha is concerned with "what shall we eat and what shall we drink" (12:29) where her preoccupation should more properly be with the kingdom of God (12:31). Allowed its own natural way, life in the world with its multiple concerns captures us and causes us to be stressed and fragmented. Attention to the word of God supplies an integrating center and makes possible a singleness of vision. This is the one necessary thing.

There is a certain shock value in the way that Jesus, quite in the face of common sense, completely bypasses the practical question about the provision of food. Presumably one must at times prepare food, but such concerns should never be allowed to compete with the hearing of the word of God.

The one necessary thing is to be identified with Mary's good portion (the imagery is that of inheritance, and the language may echo Ps 73:26–28, where God is the portion of the psalmist near to whom it is good to be): whatever the practicalities, Mary will not be asked to relinquish hearing and go help with domestic matters.

Confident Prayer to the Father (11:1–13)

It is Jesus' own practice of prayer that is the starting point for the Christian practice of prayer. Jesus teaches the disciples, in the pattern prayer that he provides, to pray simply and directly to God as Father, but what they are to pray for is much the same as might be expected in Jewish prayer of their environment. They should pray in confident trust that God as their Father will delight to answer their prayer, just as a human father does the requests of his child.

Praying like Jesus (11:1–4)

Bibliography

General:

Amphoux, C.-B. "La révision marcionite du 'Notre Père' de Luc (11,2–4) et sa place dans l'histoire du texte." In *Recherches sur l'histoire de la Bible latine,* ed. R. Gryson and P.-M. Bogaert. Cahiers de la RTL 17. Louvain-la-Neuve: Publications de la Faculté de Théologie, 1987. 105–21. **Ashton, J.** "Our Father." *The Way* 18 (1978) 83–91. **Bahr, G. J.** "The Use of the Lord's Prayer in the Primitive Church." In *The Lord's Prayer and Jewish Liturgy*. New York: Seabury, 1978. 149–55. **Baker, A.** "What Sort of Bread Did Jesus Want Us to Pray For?" *NB* 54 (1973) 125–129. **Bandstra, A. J.** "The Original Form of the Lord's Prayer." *CTJ* 16 (1981) 15–37. ———. "The Lord's Prayer and Textual Criticism: A Response." *CTJ* 17 (1982) 88–97. **Barth, H.-M.** "Das Vaterunser als ökumenishes Gebet." *US* 45 (1990) 99–109, 113. **Brocke, M., et al.** *Das Vaterunser: Gemeinsames im Beten von Juden und Christen.* Veröffentlichungen der Stiftung Oratio Dominica. Freiburg/Vienna: Herder, 1974. **Brown, R. E.** *New Testament Essays.* Milwaukee, WI: Bruce, 1965. 217–53. **Brown, R. E.** "The Pater Noster as an Eschatological Prayer." In *New Testament Essays.* Milwaukee: Bruce, 1965. 217–53. ———. "The Pater Noster as an Eschatological Prayer." *TS* 22 (1961) 175–208. **Bruggen, J. van.** "The Lord's Prayer and Textual Criticism." *CTJ* 17 (1982) 78–87 (with a reply by J. A. Bandstra, 88–97). **Buchan, W. M.** "Research on the Lord's Prayer." *ExpTim* 100 (1989) 336–39. **Bussche, H. van den.** *Understanding the Lord's Prayer.* New York: Sheed and Ward, 1963. **Cameron, P. S.** "Lead us not into temptation." *ExpTim* 101 (1990) 299–301. **Carmignac, J.** *Recherches sur le "Notre Père."* Paris: Letouzey et Ané, 1969. ———. "Hebrew Translations of the Lord's Prayer: An Historical Survey." In *Biblical and Near Eastern Studies.* FS W. S. LaSor, ed. G. A. Tuttle. Grand Rapids, MI: Eerdmans, 1978. 18–79. **Collins, R. F.** "'Lord, Teach Us to Pray' (Luke 11:1): A Reflection on the Prayer of Petition." *LouvStud* 10 (1985) 354–71. **Dalman, G.** *Die Worte Jesu.* 2nd ed. Darmstadt: Wissenschaftliche Buchgesellschaft, 1965 = 1930. 283–365. **De Moor, J. C.** "The Reconstruction of the Aramaic Original of the Lord's Prayer." In *The Structural Analysis of Biblical and Canaanite Poetry,* ed. P. Van der Meer and J. C. De Moor. JSOTSup 74. Sheffield: JSOT, 1988. 397–422. **Dewailly, L.-M.** "'Donne-nous notre pain': Quel pain? Notes sur la quatrième demande du Pater." *RSPT* 64 (1980) 561–88. **Dorneich, M.,** ed. *Vaterunser Bibliographie.* Veröffentlichungen der Stiftung Oratio Dominica. 2nd ed. Freiburg: Herder, 1988. **Edmonds, P.** "The Lucan Our Father: A Summary of Luke's Teaching on Prayer?"

ExpTim 91 (1979–80) 140–43. **Elliott, J. K.** "Did the Lord's Prayer Originate with John the Baptist?" *TZ* 29 (1973) 215. **Feldkämper, L.** *Der betende Jesus.* 178–205. **Fiebig, P.** *Das Vaterunser: Ursprung, Sinn und Bedeutung des christlichen Hauptgebetes.* Gütersloh: Bertelsmann, 1927. **Fiedler, P.** *Jesus und die Sünder.* 204–11, 255–59. **Freudenberger, R.** "Zum Text der zweiten Vaterunserbitte." *NTS* 15 (1968–69) 419–32. **Gatzweiler, K.** "Jesus in Prayer: Texts of the Our Father." *LVit* 39 (1984) 141–54. **Goulder, M. D.** "The Composition of the Lord's Prayer." *JTS* 14 (1963) 32–45. **Grässer, E.** *Das Problem der Parusieverzögerung.* 95–113. **Grelot, P.** "L'arrière-plan araméen du 'Pater.'" *RB* 91 (1984) 531–56. **Harnack, A. von.** "Die ursprungliche Gestalt des Vaterunsers." *SAWB* 1 (1904) 195–208. **Heinemann, J.** "The Background of Jesus' Prayer in the Jewish Liturgical Tradition." In *The Lord's Prayer and Jewish Liturgy,* ed. J. J. Petvchowski and M. Brocke. New York: Seabury, 1978. 81–89. **Heinen, H.** "Göttliche Sitometrie: Beobachtungen zur Brotbitte des Vaterunser." *TTZ* 99 (1990) 72–79. **Jeremias, J.** "Abba." In *The Central Message of the New Testament.* London: SCM, 1965. 9–30. ————. *Abba: Studien zur neutestamentlichen Theologie und Zeitgeschichte.* Göttingen: Vandenhoeck & Ruprecht, 1966. 15–67. ————. *The Lord's Prayer.* FBBS 8. Philadelphia: Fortress, 1973. ————. *The Prayers of Jesus.* Philadelphia: Fortress, 1978. **Kistemaker, S. J.** "The Lord's Prayer in the First Century." *JETS* 21 (1978) 323–28. **Kratz, R.G.** "Die Gnade des täglichen Brots: Späte Psalmen auf dem Weg zum Vaterunser." *ZTK* 89 (1992) 1–40. **Kuhn, K.-G.** *Achtzehngebet und Vaterunser und der Reim.* WUNT 1. Tübingen: Mohr (Siebeck), 1950. **Kuss, O.** "Das Vaterunser." In *Auslegung und Verkündigung: Aufsätze zur Exegese des Neuen Testamentes.* Regensburg: Pustet, 1963. 2:277–333. **Lapide, P.** "Das Vaterunser—ein jüdische oder ein christliches Gebet?" *Renovatio* 47 (1991) 108–10. **Leaney, R.** "The Lucan Text of the Lord's Prayer (Lk xi 2–4)." *NovT* 1 (1956) 103–11. **Lewis, J. J.** "The Wilderness Controversy and Peirasmos." *Colloquium* 7 (1974) 42–44. **Lochman, J. M.** *The Lord's Prayer.* Tr. G. W. Bromiley. Grand Rapids, MI: Eerdmans, 1990. **Lohmeyer, E.** *The Lord's Prayer.* Tr. J. Bowden. London: Collins, 1965. **Magne, J.** "La réception de le variante 'Vienne ton Esprit saint sur nous et qu'il nous purifie' (Lc11,2) et l'origine des épiclèses, du baptême et du 'Notre Père.'" *EL* 102 (1988) 81–106 ————. "La variante du Pater de Lc 11,2." *LTP* 44 (1988) 369–74. **Marchel, W.** *Abba Père! La prière du Christ et des chrétiens.* AnBib 19. Rome: Biblical Institute, 1963. 191–202. **McCaughey, D.** "Matthew 6:13a: The Sixth Petition in the Lord's Prayer." *ABR* 33 (1985) 31–40. **Miller, R. J.** "The Lord's Prayer and Other Items from the Sermon on the Mount." *Forum* 5.2 (1989) 177–86. **Moule, C. F. D.** "An Unsolved Problem in the Temptation Clause in the Lord's Prayer." *RTR* 33 (1974) 65–75. **Ott, W.** *Gebet und Heil: Die Bedeutung der Gegetsparänese in der lukanischen Theologie.* SANT 12. Munich: Kösel, 1965. 112–23. **Petuchowski, J. J.**, and **Brocke, M.** *The Lord's Prayer and Jewish Liturgy.* New York: Seabury, 1978. **Popkes, W.** "Die letzte Bitte des Vater-Unser: Formgeschichtliche Beobachtungen zum Gebet Jesu." *ZNW* 81 (1990) 1–20. **Porter, S. E.** "Matthew 6:13 and Luke 11:4: 'Lead us not into temptation.'" *ExpTim* 101 (1989–90) 359–62. **Riet, S. Van.** "Seigneur, apprends-nous à prier! (Luc 11, 1)." *BVC* 22 (1958) 73–77. **Schlosser, J.** *Le règne de Dieu.* 247–322. **Schneider, G.** "Die Bitte um das Kommen des Geistes im lukanischen Vaterunser (Lk 11,2 v. 1.)." In *Studien zum Text und zur Ethik des Neuen Testaments,* ed. W. Schrage. 344–73. ————. "Das Vaterunser: Oratio dominica et judaica?" In *Weisheit Gottes—Weisheit der Welt.* FS J. Ratzinger I, ed. W. Baier et al. St.-Ottilien: Eos, 1987. 405–17. **Schroer, S.** "Konkretionen zum Vaterunser." *US* 45 (1990) 99–109, 110–13. **Schürmann, H.** *Gottes Reich—Jesu Geschick.* 100–104. ————. *Praying with Christ: The "Our Father" for Today.* New York: Herder and Herder, 1964. ————. *Das Gebet des Herrn als Schlüssel zum Verstehen Jesu.* 4th ed. Freiburg im B.: Herder, 1981. **Simon, L.** "La prière non religieuse chez Luc." *FV* 74 (1975) 8–22. **Soballa, G.** "Unterweisung der Jünger durch den Herrn: Betrachtungen über Herrenworte aus dem Lukasevangelium." *GuL* 30 (1957) 384–89. **Stritzky, M.-B. von.** *Studien zur Überlieferung und Interpretation des Vaterunsers in der frühchristlichen Literatur.* Münsterische Beiträge zur Theologie 57. Münster: Aschendorff, 1989. **Taussig, H.** "The Lord's Prayer." *Forum* 4.4 (1988) 25–41. **Templeton, D.** "The Lord's

Prayer as Eucharist in Daily Life." *IBS* 11 (1989) 133–40. **Theologische Fakultät Basel.** *Das universale Gebet: Studien zum Unservater.* FS J. Milič. Theologische Zeitschrift 48/1. Basel: Reinhardt, 1992. **Tilborg, S. van.** "A Form-Criticism of the Lord's Prayer." *NovT* 14 (1972) 94–105. **Topel, L. J.** "The Lukan Version of the Lord's Sermon." *BTB* 11 (1981) 48–53. **Vielhauer, P.** "Vaterunser-Probleme." *VF* 3 (1949–50) 219–24. **Vögtle, A.** "Der 'eschatologische' Bezug der Wir-Bitten des Vaterunser." In *Jesus und Paulus.* FS W. G. Kümmel. Göttingen: Vandenhoeck & Ruprecht, 1975. 344–62. **Willis, G. G.** "Lead Us Not into Temptation." *DR* 93 (1975) 281–88. **Wurzinger, A.** "Es komme Dein Königreich: Zum Gebetsanliegen nach Lukas." *BLit* 38 (1964–65) 89–94.

On ἐπιούσιος:

Baker, A. "What Sort of Bread did Jesus Want Us to Pray For?" *NB* 54 (1973) 125–29. **Bindemann, W.** "Das Brot für morgen gib uns heute: Socialgeschichtliche Erwägungen zu den Wir-Bitten des Vaterunsers." *BerlinTZ* 8 (1991) 199–215. **Black, M.** "The Aramaic of τὸν ἄρτον ἡμῶν τὸν ἐπιούσιον (Matt. vi.11 = Luke xi.3)." *JTS* 42 (1941) 186–89. **Bourgoin, H.** "Le pain quotidien." *CCER* 25 (1977) 1–17.———. "Ἐπιούσιος expliqué par la notion de préfixe vide." *Bib* 60 (1979) 91–96. **Braun, F.-M.** "Le pain dont nous avons besoin: Mt 6, 11; Lc 11, 3." *NRT* 100 (1978) 559–68. **Carmignac, J.** *Recherches sur le "Notre Père."* Paris: Letouzey et Ané, 1969. 118–221. **Debrunner, A.** "Ἐπιούσιος." *Glotta* 4 (1913) 249–53. **Delebecque, É.** *Études Grecques sur L'évangile de Luc.* Paris: Societé d'édition "Les belles lettres," 1976. 167–81. **Dornseiff, F.** "Ἐπιούσιος im Vaterunser." *Glotta* 35 (1956) 145–49. **Falcone, S. A.** "The Kind of Bread We Pray for in the Lord's Prayer." FS J. P. Brennan, ed. R. F. McNamara. Rochester, NY: St Bernard's Seminary, 1976. 36–59. **Foerster, W.** "ἐπιούσιος." *TDNT* 2:590–99. **Foucault, J.-A. de.** "Notre pain quotidien." *REG* 83 (1970) 56–62. **Grelot, P.** "La quatrième demande du 'Pater' et son arrière-plan sémitique." *NTS* 25 (1978–79) 299–314. **Hauck, F.** "Ἄρτος ἐπιούσιος." *ZNW* 33 (1934) 199–202. **Hemer, C.** "Ἐπιούσιος." *JSNT* 22 (1984) 81–94. **Hemmerdinger, B.** "Un élément pythagoricien dans le Pater." *ZNW* 63 (1972) 121. **Hennig, J.** "Our Daily Bread." *TS* 4 (1943) 445–54. **Hultgren, A. J.** "The Bread Petition of the Lord's Prayer." *ATRSup* 11 (1990) 41–54. **Kate, R. Ten.** "Geef ons heden ons 'dagelijks' brood." *NedTTs* 32 (1978) 125–39. **Metzger, B. M.** "How Many Times Does 'Epiousios' Occur outside the Lord's Prayer?" *ExpTim* 69 (1957–58) 52–54. **Müller, C.** "Ἐπιούσιος." In *EW* 1:79–81. **Orchard, B.** "The Meaning of τὸν ἐπιούσιον (Mt 6:11 = Lk 11:3)." *BTB* 3 (1973) 274–82. **Ramoroson, L.** "'Notre part de nourriture' (Mt 6, 11)." *ScEs* 43 (1991) 87–115. **Sabugal, S.** "Our Daily Bread: Mt 6:11; Lk 11:3." *SIDJC* 18 (1985) 12–15. **Schmid, W.** "Ἐπιούσιος." *Glotta* 6 (1915) 28–29. **Shearman, T. G.** "Our Daily Bread." *JBL* 53 (1934) 110–17. **Starcky, J.** "La quatrième demande du Pater." *HTR* 64 (1971) 401–9. **Wimmerer, R.** "Noch einmal ἐπιούσιος." *Glotta* 12 (1923) 68–82. **Yamauchi, E. M.** "The 'Daily Bread' Motif in Antiquity." *WTJ* 28 (1965–66) 145–56.

Translation

[1] *When he was praying in a particular place, it transpired that, when he stopped, a certain one of his disciples said to him, "Lord, teach us to pray, just as John taught his disciples."* [2] *He said to them, "Whenever you pray say,*

Father,[a]
May your name be sanctified,
May your kingdom come.[b, c]

[3] *Our bread for the day give us day by day,*
[4] *And forgive us our sins*

(For we ourselves practice forgiveness to
everyone who is indebted to us).

And do not lead us into [that which is a] trial."[d]

Notes

[a] A C D K P W X Δ Θ Ψ etc. conform the mode of address to that in Matt 6:9.

[b] For this petition, (162) 700 Marcion (both petitions) Gregory-Nyssa (Maximus [as 162] without the ἐφ' ἡμᾶς) read ἐλθέτω τὸ πνεῦμα σου τὸ ἅγιον ἐφ' ἡμᾶς καὶ καθαρισάτω ἡμᾶς, "May your Holy Spirit come upon us and cleanse us." The ἐφ' ἡμᾶς, "upon us," which is added to the normal reading by D it[d] may be a residue of this alternative petition. There is quite a strong scholarly tradition that favors the petition for the Spirit as original in Luke (e.g., Streeter, *The Four Gospels: A study of origins treating of manuscript tradition, sources, authorship, and date,* rev. ed [London: Macmillan, 1930] 276–77; Leaney, *NovT* 1 [1956] 103–11; Ott, *Gebet und Heil,* 112–23 [Schneider, "Kommen des Geistes," 344–73, provides a careful summary of the scholarly discussion and on p. 358 gives an extensive listing for and against]), but the majority opinion is clearly against the originality of this petition. The poor fit in the structure of the prayer, the difficulty of such a petition in a prayer for regular use, and, related to that, the uneasy fit for such a petition in Lukan pneumatology (in Luke the presence of the petition would require that the prayer be taken as only an interim prayer until Pentecost) are sufficient reasons for considering it a secondary addition. The most attractive view is that which suggests that a form of the Lord's Prayer adapted for baptism contained this petition (it may be that this form of the Lord's Prayer was produced under the influence of Lukan theology [beyond 11:13 noted below, cf. Acts 10:15; 11:8; 15:8–9], but the elements could also be pieced together on the basis of such texts as Pss 51:13; 143:10; Wis 9:17; Ezek 2:2; 3:24; 36:25–27), which has come into the Lukan text on the basis of evident links with Luke's interest in the Spirit, and specifically in connection with 11:13.

[c] (א) א[a] (א[c]) (A C D) K (P W) X (Δ Θ) Π Ψ etc. add here the following Matthean petition.

[d] (א[c]) A C D K W X Δ Θ Π Ψ add here the Matthean petition (Matt 6:13b).

Form/Structure/Setting

The theme of love of God and neighbor gives way now to that of prayer. As observers of Jesus' own practice of prayer, the disciples ask for instruction on prayer. They are rewarded with the Lord's Prayer, and with a body of teaching on prayer that focuses on the need to ask, and on the fatherly desire of God to give to his children what they need. The teaching of the section begins and ends on the note of the fatherhood of God.

Luke and Matthew (6:9–13) offer us the Lord's Prayer in rather different forms. Beyond variation in the actual wording of the sections of the prayer, there are two additional petitions in the Matthean form. What is the relationship between the two forms? In the detailed discussion below, it is argued that the differences belong in part to the existence prior to the present Gospel texts of more than one form of the Lord's Prayer, but also in part to the editorial activity of Luke himself. With the majority of the scholarly community, I conclude that the Matthean wording is generally the more original (as a minority opinion I argue that this is also true of the form of address to God, where the more Jewish Matthean form has been Christianized, but already prior to Luke), but that the additional Matthean petitions represent (probably pre-Matthean) developments, partly to spell out the logic of existing petitions and partly to develop them in the light of motifs from the known words of

Jesus (the clause about forgiveness of others may be a product of the same process). Some small part of the variation could be the result of different translation of a Semitic original, but nowhere is this certain, since the detailed changes make good Lukan sense. The degree of exact agreement in the Greek, especially with the shared use of the difficult term ἐπιούσιος (tr. above as "for the day") counts in favor of a single translation into Greek as ultimately behind the two forms of the prayer.

It is often maintained that the Lukan form cannot owe anything to the intervention of Luke himself, because as a text in liturgical use it will not have been possible for Luke to tamper with its wording. This judgment, however, cuts right across the complex mix of conservative preservation of wording along with adaptation and freedom of rendering that we actually observe in early Christian practice. We need here only to be reminded that the whole discussion of liturgical fragment in the NT epistles is almost uniformly based on the assumption that when incorporated into the epistles these fragments were edited in various ways. As well, the four canonical forms of Jesus' words at the Last Supper suggest quite a fluid liturgical use, probably combined with a certain amount of intervention on the part of the Evangelists themselves.

There has been little scholarly doubt about tracing the Lord's Prayer to the historical Jesus, but there has been a certain amount of recent questioning. In line with his general approach, Goulder (*JTS* 14 [1963] 32–45; and more recently, *Luke*, 496–98) has argued that the prayer was spun out of essentially the Markan record of Jesus' teaching by precept and example about prayer; Grässer (*Parousieverzögerung*, 95–113) has argued that the prayer, as we presently have it, developed at a time when the delay of the Parousia was no longer a problem; and Tilborg (*NovT* 14 [1972] 94–105) has attempted to give a form-critical analysis along the lines of Goulder's approach, but suggesting that the opening pair of petitions has been borrowed from the Jewish Qaddish prayer. None of this is compelling, but because of the thoroughly Jewish nature of the prayer (as shown below), it is quite difficult to demonstrate a necessary link to the historical Jesus. In its simplicity and directness it probably does go beyond what we would expect in the Jewish tradition of popular private prayer (see Heinemann, "Background," 81–89), but such a judgment is vulnerable to the limited scope of our sources for the period and inevitably has an element of subjectivity about it. There is of course no reason why the historical Jesus cannot have taught a thoroughly Jewish prayer. To do so would be a statement in its own right. Though an original form in Aramaic seems intrinsically more likely than a Hebrew original, the linguistic arguments that have been made on both sides of the debate remain indecisive.

The Lukan prayer consists of an address, paired petitions concerning the present honoring of God's name and the future coming of his kingdom, paired petitions concerning the sustenance needs of each day and the need for God's forgiveness (the latter supported by a statement about forgiveness on the human level), and a final petition to be spared the testing that could crush the human frailty of our devotion to God.

The prayer is provided with a setting that links it both to Jesus' own prayer practice and to the prayer practice of the disciples of John, which they had learned from their master.

Comment

A scene of Jesus at prayer becomes the starting point for a section on prayer. The disciples want to pray as Jesus prays. Jesus teaches them to speak simply and directly to God as Father. Their concern should be with the present honoring of God's name in the world and with the the coming of his kingdom; they are to pray each day for the needs of the present day (the future they should leave to God), but also for God's forgiveness of their failings (as they themselves extend the same release to their fellows who are indebted to them); in recognition of their own frailty they should pray to be spared from such trials as might crush them.

1 Except for ἐν τόπῳ τινί, "in a certain place," the first ten words are identical to the Lukan introduction in 9:18, while "certain place" is itself almost certainly a piece of Lukan diction (he has a disproportionate fondness for both terms). The phrase ὡς . . . ἐπαύσατο, "when he stopped," is found at 5:4. The εἶπεν πρός, "said to," idiom, the use of τις, "a certain," with "disciples" (cf. 7:19 contrasted with Matt 11:2), and the address of Jesus as κύριε, "Lord/Master/Sir," may also be marks of Lukan style. We cannot be certain whether the comparison with John is traditional, or whether Luke is simply reiterating the parallelism between John and Jesus, which structures the Infancy Gospel and is important in chap. 7.

It is likely that, different from its role on other occasions (see at 9:18), the motif of Jesus at prayer is introduced here to suggest that the disciples desire to pray as Jesus himself prays. On the address of Jesus as "Lord," see at 5:8. While more than "Sir," the use here need not carry the full force of that at 5:8. Only here in the Gospels do disciples request teaching from Jesus (Marshall, 456). A distinct group of disciples of the Baptist has been mentioned in 5:33; 7:18 (par. Matt 11:2; cf. Acts 19:1–6). While it is intrinsically likely, we do not know from elsewhere about John giving instruction about prayer, though perhaps as much is implied in 5:33. The disciples seek a prayer that will express the distinctive piety that Jesus' own life has expressed and into which he has drawn the disciple band.

2 ὅταν προσεύχησθε, "whenever you pray," appears in identical form in Matt 6:5, a little before Matthew's version of the Lord's Prayer, but this is probably fortuitous. Matthew actually introduces the prayer with οὕτως οὖν προσεύχεσθε ὑμεῖς, "you are, then, to pray in this way." As suggested in *Form/Structure/Setting* above, it is unlikely that Luke and Matthew drew on a common literary source for the Lord's Prayer or its setting. For Luke's simple address as "Father," Matthew has "Our Father in heaven." The discussion is finally balanced over which form of address has greater claim to originality, particularly as each form suits its present Gospel setting. (God is Father in heaven in Matt 5:16, 45, [48]; 6:1, [14, 26, 32]; 7:11, 21; 10:32, 33; 12:50; 16:17; 18:10, 14, 19, [35]; with the exception of 11:25–27 and 24:36 an accompanying personal pronoun is uniformly to be found in the forty-five references to God as Father in Matthew; beyond the Lord's Prayer, only in 11:25, 26 is God addressed as "Father," and only in the latter verse does this address stand alone as in Luke's form of the prayer. By contrast Luke never has God as Father in heaven [closest is 11:13, where it is probably the giving that is from heaven, not the Father who is from heaven (cf. Acts 2:33)]; God is addressed as "Father" in Luke 10:21[2x]; 11:2; 22:42; 23:34[?], 46; and in all but one of these texts this address stands alone.) Contrary to most scholarly opinion, we should probably favor the longer form here (or at least a longer form) as more original, on the basis that the Jewishness of the longer form fits better with the evident Jewishness of the remainder of the prayer (Heinemann, "Background," 87, notes Jewish use of the Matthean "Our Father who art in heaven"; Marchel, *Prière*, 199, cites from *Tg. Yer.* to Deut 32:6 הלא הוא אבוכון דבשמיא, *hălo hûʾ ʾăbûkôn dĕbišĕmayyāʾ*, "Is he not your Father in heaven?"). The Lukan form will represent a Christianization (but not by Luke himself) of the mode of address, to reflect the early church's adoption, on the basis of the eschatological bestowal of sonship through the Spirit (Gal 4:6; Rom 8:15), of Jesus' own intimate mode of address to God (Abba: Mark 14:36; cf. Luke 10:21). To encourage such a level of intimacy with God was no doubt the intention of the historical Jesus, but a direct expression of that intention in the mode of address of the earliest form of this prayer seems less likely.

Luke's language seems to imply that this is a set of words to be used as an actual prayer form (the Matthean language is more general). If we are to take the words literally, this prayer should be prayed on every occasion of prayer. Though the date or origin for particular elements of later Jewish liturgy is problematical, there can be little doubt that fixed forms of Jewish prayer were in existence in Jesus' day. While notable for its brevity, simplicity, and directness, the prayer of Jesus is entirely at home with this developing Jewish prayer tradition (see comparisons below for particular elements of the prayer).

Fitzmyer (902–3) has well summarized the background in the OT and the Apocrypha for speaking of God as Father.

> The people of Israel are [God's] children, his firstborn, and their king is his son (Deut 14:1; Hos 11:1–3; 2 Sam 7:14). The title [Father] is used of God explicitly when he is considered as creator (Deut 32:6; Mal 2:10), as lord of his chosen people (Jer 3:19; 31:9; Isa 63:16; Tob 13:4), as one sinned against by Israel (Jer 3:4–5; Mal 1:6), and as the one from whom mercy and forgiveness come (Ps 103:13; Isa 64:7–8 [64:8–9E]). . . . David is to address his as "my Father" (Ps 89:27).

On a broader canvas, God (Zeus) is Father in the sense of paternal lord in a wide range of religious traditions (cf. Lohmeyer, *Lord's Prayer*, 38–39), and when in Jewish tradition the fatherhood of God comes to be related to the individual pious Israelite (Sir 23:1, 4: "O Lord, Father and Master/God of my life"), it bears this general sense.

Despite dissenting voices, Jeremias' judgment stands that Jesus' own reference to God as "my Father" or "Abba" (which the Lukan text reflects) is without parallel in ancient Palestinian Judaism (see Jeremias, *Prayer*, 16–29; Fitzmyer, "Abba and Jesus' Relation to God," in *À cause de l'évangile*, 15–38; the non-Palestinian 3 Macc 6:8 [a text written in Greek] comes closest with its vocative "Father"; in the OT closest are the messianic "my Father" in Ps 89:26 and the collective "my Father" of Jer 3:4, 19). But see now also 4Q372 1:16 where God is addressed as "my Father and my God" (see E. Schuller, "The Psalm of 4Q372 1 within the Context of Second Temple Prayer," *CBQ* 54 [1992] 68, for a translation of the text).

The first petition of the prayer ("May your name be sanctified") is reported identically by Matthew and Luke. The passive verb leaves it initially open whether God or human respondents to God are the hidden subject of the verb. If it is to be the former, then the petition answers to such declarations as Ezek 36:23, where God says "I will sanctify my great name," and thus is looking to a decisive action of

God and has an eschatological tenor. This fits well with the eschatological thrust of the following petition.

The alternative is to understand the petition as a prayer that the peoples of the world (or God's People Israel) might duly honor God in action and in praise. This alternative could also have an underlying eschatological thrust (cf. Grelot, *RB* 91 [1984] 543, who thinks in terms of a manifestation of God's holiness, which elicits in turn a liturgical declaration of God's holiness) as may be seen from Isa 29:23 where, in the context of the restoration of Israel, it is anticipated that "they [the Israelites] will sanctify my [God's] name." But an eschatological thrust would on this understanding have fitted better if the kingdom petition had been placed ahead of the sanctification petition (there would then be a clear reference to an action of God to which sanctification of his name can then be the appropriate response).

A non-eschatological understanding is also possible for the petition taken as concerned with human response to God. This finds parallels in early Jewish prayer. The ancient Jewish Qaddish prayer runs, "Magnified and sanctified be God's great name in the world he has created according to his will. May he establish his kingdom during your lifetime . . ." (cited here according to B. Martin, *Prayer in Judaism* [New York: Basic Books, 1968] 147, the prayer occurs in a number of forms all of which, however, share the reference to the sanctification of God's great name [cf. Grelot, *RB* 91 (1984) 544]; see additional texts in Dalman, *Worte Jesu*, 304–6, where it may be noted that "praised" and "exalted" often stand in parallel with "sanctified"). We should note in the Qaddish prayer the juxtaposition of the sanctification of the name of God and the appeal for the coming of the kingdom.

Despite the powerful advocacy of Carmignac (*Recherches*, 81–85), it does not seem likely that we should find a deliberate double reference in the petition both to God's act of sanctification and to the human response that sanctifies his name. It does, however, remain difficult to choose between the alternatives. If the reference is to an act of God, then the opening petitions form a couplet with a force something like "reveal your glory and begin your eschatological rule." If the reference is to proper human response, then the couplet begins with a focus on how it is fitting now already to honor the name of God, and then moves on to the anticipation of the future plus of the coming of the eschatological kingdom. It is finally to the credit of the second possibility both that it provides a closer fit with Jewish prayer practice and that its wider scope leads on more naturally to the petitions of the rest of the prayer, with their focus on the living out of our lives in the present.

The second petition of the prayer is also identically reported by Matthew and Luke ("May your kingdom come"). As cited above, the Qaddish prayer offers a close Jewish parallel for a pairing of the opening petitions. Reference to the "coming" of the kingdom is not paralleled in ancient Jewish texts (in Jesus' words, cf. 22:18), but the coming of the LORD is well represented in the OT (1 Chr 16:33; Pss 96:13; 98:9; Isa 26:21; Mic 1:3), as is the coming of the Day of the LORD (Isa 13:6; Joel 2:1; Zech 14:1; Mal 4:5). Our petition here seems to reformulate in kingdom language the OT anticipation of the coming of God in judgment and salvation. The OT also looks forward to a time when God would in some greater sense become king (Isa 24:23; 33:22; 52:7; Zeph 3:15; Zech 14:9). Luke will for his part detail something of what he sees to be involved in this coming in chap. 21 (cf. 17:24–37), but he is also of the opinion that this future kingdom of God has its earlier intimations (cf. at 9:27).

3 Luke has no equivalent to Matthew's next clause, which is best taken as an expansion of the petition for the coming of the kingdom of God (then God's will *will* be done on earth as it is currently in heaven; the expansion may well owe a debt to the Gethsemane prayer [Matt 26:42; cf. Luke 22:42]). Then we find in both versions the petition about "daily bread," which has identical wording in both except that the verb is a present imperative in Luke and an aorist imperative in Matthew. This is compatible with a second difference, which is that Matthew has "today," *σήμερον*, where Luke has "day by day," *τὸ καθ' ἡμέραν*. Since this last phrase is Lukan, the alterations may be Luke's own (see 19:47 and cf. 9:23; 16:19; 22:53; Acts 2:46,47; 3:2; 17:11).

Given the regularity of the use of an opening imperative in the other petitions, it is notable that the object has here displaced the verb from this position. This may be a chiastic impulse in the interests of the pairing of this and the following petition (note also the linking *καί*, "and" [but the final petition is also introduced in this way], and the *ἡμῶν*, "our," . . . *ἡμῖν*, "[to] us," . . . *ἡμῖν*, "[to] us," . . . *ἡμῶν*, "our," sequence that links the petitions).

The bread petition has been taken in many different ways, depending mostly on the various senses given to *ἐπιούσιος* (translated above "for the day"). No other use of this term has been definitely located in Greek usage earlier than the Patristic discussion of the Gospel usage (A. H. Sayce recorded an instance of the term in what he took to be a fifth-century A.D. papyrus [W. M. Flinders Petrie, *Hawara, Biahmu and Arsinoe* (London: Leidenhall Press, 1889) 33–35], but since the papyrus in question is not available for confirmation and Sayce was prone to copying errors, more recent scholarship is reluctant to use this evidence; Origen considered that the term had been coined by the Evangelists [*Treatise on Prayer,* 27.7, but Hemer [*JSNT* 22 (1984) 89–90] notes a later use of the cognate noun [*ἐπιούσια*; with the sense "succession"] that seems to be quite independent of the Gospels and thus counts against Origen's judgment).

Three main derivations for the Gospel term have been proposed. (*i*) The term could be derived from the noun *οὐσία*. There is some debate about whether the *ι* from the prefixed *ἐπί* would not have elided if this were the derivation. It clearly would have in classical Greek, but for a later Hellinistic derivation we cannot rule out the retention of the *ι*. With various senses both for *ἐπί* and for *οὐσία* this derivation allows *ἐπιούσιος* to mean "supersubstantial" (i.e., surpassing all that belongs to the substantial world; this sense depends on a philosophical sense for *οὐσία* for which there is no evidence this early), "for subsistence" (Fitzmyer, 905, is persuaded by this sense), "above and beyond wealth/property" (this hardly fits the context of the Lord's Prayer), or "essential" (this reflects the view of Bourgoin [*Bib* 60 (1979) 91–96] that the *ἐπί* is otiose and makes no contribution to the meaning of the term; Bourgoin leaves the more precise sense of "essential" open [p. 95: "concerning the essence"], but it is difficult to identify a sense that does not stand in tension with the attached "our").

(*ii*) The derivation could be from the feminine participle of *εἶναι*, "to be." In this case the feminine gender betrays an understood *ἡμέρα*, "day," and the sense is "for this [present] day." Proposed by Debrunner (*Glotta* 4 [1913] 249–53), the view has found more recent support from Starcky (*HTR* 64 [1971] 401–9) and Grelot (*NTS* 25 [1978–79] 299–314), who argue respectively on the basis of an underlying Hebrew and Aramaic original. The accusation of tautology and the demand for an explanation as to why one of the many common words for "daily" should not have been used for this sense are only decisive if we fail to put the stress here on the present day *in contrast to* all succeeding days (cf. Matt 6:34). The appeal that Starcky and Grelot make to the idiom of Exod 16:4 is quite attractive ("[portion] of a day in its day"; cf. also Lev 23:37; 1 Kgs 8:59; Jer 52:34; Exod 5:19; Dan 1:5).

(*iii*) Finally, ἐπιούσιος could come from the participle of the verb ἰέναι, "to come, draw near." As in (*ii*) above it is usual to understand an implied ἡμέρα, "day." Here the reference could either be to bread for tomorrow (supported by Jerome's report that the Gospel according to the Hebrews uses the word "tomorrow" here [*Comm. in Matt.* 6.11]), or to bread for the day that is just beginning (see Hemer, *JSNT* 22 [1984] 81–94, for a particularly good discussion of the way in which the term could have emerged with these senses). When taken as referring to literal food and a literal tomorrow, the former view can be criticized on the basis of Matt 6:34. A non-literal reference is maintained by R. Brown ("Pater Noster," 242) on the basis of a link with the wilderness manna of Exod 16 (Brown notes that Moses told the people that the bread would come "on the *morrow*," but this is strained; along the same lines the request for tomorrow's bread today has been taken [in the light of the provision on the sabbath eve of two days' supply of bread] as a request for the provision of the sabbath manna, taken as an image of salvation, but this suggestion is more ingenious than persuasive). A link with the manna is possible (but see below) but hardly demonstrated, and in any case such a link could just as well be on the basis of seeing the provision of the wilderness manna as a paradigm of God as provider, as on the basis of anticipating the eschatological reiteration of the provision of manna. Vögtle ("Wir-Bitten," 350–51) is right to see the "our" as creating difficulties for an eschatological understanding of the bread (for "our bread" as our basic sustenance needs, cf. Lam 5:9; Ezek 4:15; 5:16; 12:19; Ps 102:4; Sir 12:5; Hos 2:7; Isa 4:1). Indeed it creates problems even for a non-eschatologically understood connection with the wilderness manna. It is more difficult to defend the "bread for today" form of this third view from the accusation of tautology than to defend the somewhat similar view in (*ii*) above. This third derivation is sometimes understood without the implied ἡμέρα, "day." The sense of coming, drawing near is then at times applied directly to the bread (as Orchard, *BTB* 3 [1973] 274–82). It is very difficult to see how this could be justified etymologically. Alternatively the sense of coming, drawing near could be applied to an understood reference to the kingdom of God, age to come, or similar. Matthew's "today" and even more Luke's "day by day" stand in the way of taking this as a variant of the petition for the coming of the kingdom. We would have to find here a reference to a flow back into the present of the eschatological benefits of the still outstanding future. This may well make for a good general fit with the eschatology of the historical Jesus, but its specific imagery has no close parallel in the historical Jesus material, and the crucial part of it must be supplied to the text rather than read out of it.

Other derivations have been proposed that have less to commend them than the main views listed here. Some studies try to bypass the problems of the Greek term, and to resolve the meaning in terms of a putative Hebrew or Aramaic original, but this is an uncontrollable speculative exercise when divorced from the meaning of the Greek term which is, after all, what we have. There is, finally, not a large difference of meaning between "bread for subsistence" from (*i*) above (cf. 1 Tim 6:8; Prov 30:8), "bread for the present day" from (*ii*) above (cf. Matt 6:34), and "bread for the dawning day" from (*iii*) above.

The discussion thus far favors understanding the petition as focusing on the mundane sustenance needs common to all. The various eschatological views have been addressed above and found wanting, as have the views that build on a use of the imagery of the manna. A form of this latter approach yet to be noted is that which links the manna to the eucharistic bread. The manna link is already a weakness here, and there is finally nothing to encourage a eucharistic link (the reference in Acts 2:46 may indeed be to a daily celebration of the eucharist under the designation "the breaking of bread," but for Luke the eucharist has to do with knowing the Lord, rather than with spiritual nourishment [see discussion at 9:12–17; 22:14–20; 24:13–35]). A prayer for our mundane sustenance needs is what would be most at home in the Jewish context (cf. Prov 30:8: "feed me with the food that is needful for me"; *Midr. Tanḥuma Deut.* 26:15–16: "I will not depart from here until you [God] satisfy the needs of this day" [cited after Dalman, *Worte Jesu*, 329]).

4 This next petition shows more variation between Matthew and Luke, but the differences are mostly in the supporting clause and not the petition itself. In the petition Luke has *τὰς ἁμαρτίας*, "sins," for Matthew's *τὰ ὀφειλήματα*, "debts." The change is likely to be Luke's, since he retains in the following clause a form cognate to Matthew's term here. Fitzmyer (906) is surely right to explain the motivation for the Lukan form by noting that Matthew's term is not attested in classical or Hellenistic Greek in a religious sense (this will still be the case if we are dealing with translation variants from the Aramaic as maintained by Grelot [*RB* 91 (1984) 546–47]). Luke links the following clause with *καὶ γάρ*, "for, also," where Matthew has *ὡς καί*, "as also." This could be a translation variant from Aramaic כדי, *kĕdî* (Grelot [*RB* 91 (1984) 547]), but is as well explained as a clarification of the ambiguity of Matthew's text, which could be read as an attempt to strike a bargain with God (as Brown ["Pater Noster," 247–48]). The emphasis on the subject is provided in Matthew by an explicit subject (*ἡμεῖς*, "we") and in Luke by *αὐτοί* used as an emphasizing adjective ("ourselves"). The change is probably Luke's since his Gospel has most of the NT occurrences of *καὶ αὐτοί*. Also likely to be Lukan is the present tense for the verb (so: "practice forgiveness"), where Matthew has the perfect; this fits with the "day by day" of Luke, where Matthew has "today." Since Luke seems to have been the one who has intervened in this sentence, the singular participle, with its qualifying "everyone" in place of Mathew's plural noun for the object, is best attributed to Luke's pen as well.

The chiastic pairing of this petition with the previous one has already been noted. This makes it likely that the "day by day" should be carried over from v 3 (in light of the present tense in the following clause, we need not take too seriously the fact that the imperative is aorist; so far as I have been able to ascertain, the present imperative of this verb, with the sense "to forgive," was not in use in this period). The forgiveness of sins contemplated here does not seem to have the eschatological thrust that we find elsewhere in the Lukan use of this idea (see at 5:24; 24:47). It reflects rather an awareness of the ongoing need for forgiveness that characterized Jewish religious sensibilities. The sixth blessing of the *Shemoneh ʿEsreh* petitions to God: "Forgive us, for we have sinned, blot out our mistakes before you, for great is your loving-kindness" (cited according to Kuhn [*Achtzehngebet*, 44]; cf. Ps 25:18; and esp. Sir 28:2 which instructs: "Forgive your neighbor's injustice; then when you pray, your own sins will be forgiven"; see further the texts cited in Dalman, *Worte Jesu*, 335–38).

The daily flow of forgiveness from God would be impeded if there were not a corresponding practice of forgiveness at the human level. The Lukan change to παντί, "everyone," with the singular adds emphasis but does not change the meaning of the Matthean form. Though he has changed from the noun form to the participial form, Luke retains here the use of the imagery of debt in connection with sin, which he has excluded from the previous clause. Though the previous clause guarantees that sin in a moral sense will be involved here, it is not impossible that Luke thinks more widely of release from other forms of indebtedness as well (cf. at 6:38). The linking here of God's forgiveness with forgiveness of others is well attested elsewhere in the Jesus tradition (esp. Luke 6:37; Mark 11:25; Matt 6:14–15; 18:23–35), but nonetheless its quite singular position in the Lord's Prayer does raise the question of whether it represents an expansion, in light of the known teaching of Jesus (as Vögtle, "Wir-Bitten," 345–46; R. Brown, "Pater Noster," 246 n. 108, seeks to make a virtue out this singularity as pointing to its necessity for the petition), along the lines of the Matthean expansions and the Lukan contraction evident from a comparison of the extant forms (see discussion at vv 2, 3 and at the end of the discussion of the present verse).

Luke's final petition is Matthew's penultimate, and is presented in identical wording. Once again this prayer has Jewish analogues (cf. *b. Ber.* 60b). The questions here are, "Does God test (tempt)?" "Is the trial in view the period of crisis that ushers in the eschaton?" "Is there any sense in asking to be spared the trials that are either an inevitable part of life (on one understanding of πειρασμός [tr. above as "that which is a trial"]) or a preordained aspect of the arrival of the end (on another understanding)?"

There is finally no linguistic justification for avoiding attribution to God of the trial in view. A Semitic original may have been ambiguous, but it has been taken in the Greek language tradition represented by our Gospel writers in a quite unambiguous way. In the Exodus setting and beyond, God is often said to put his People to the test (Exod 16:4; 20:20; Deut 8:2, 16; 13:4; 33:8; Judg 2:22).

Moule (*RTR* 33 [1974] 66–67) is rightly critical of those who move from Rev 3:10 to an understanding of πειρασμός as "a recognizable technical term for the ultimate crisis of apocalyptic expectation" (67). There is no evidence at all for such a usage. Trial may indeed occur in that eschatological setting (as Rev 3:10), but this will be indicated by the context and not merely by the presence of this term. Here, in line with the understanding of the prayer that has been emerging above, we might expect the scope of the petition to be comprehensive, and not to be specifically focused on the eschatological crisis. This view is encouraged by the lack of the definite article before πειρασμός.

To address the third question posed above, we need first to ask the question, "What kind of trial is in view here?" Trial as temptation is clearly to be excluded (cf. Jas 1:13–14); that is what the Devil is responsible for (Luke 4:2). But trial as that which establishes the true state of affairs is not quite appropriate either (the term does not in any case carry the law-court imagery that "trial" may carry in English). Trial here is rather that which puts pressure on one, that which is trying. In this sense one is not constantly under trial, but periodically in life the pressure mounts (cf. 8:13). Jesus comes under a severe form of this kind of pressure in

Gethsemane (cf. 22:28 for the use of πειρασμός in connection with Jesus' experience [here in the plural and in connection with earlier experiences in the ministry of Jesus]) as he contemplates his own coming suffering, and he suggests that his disciples pray that they might be spared the same. They want to be identified with Jesus in what he is doing, but at this point they cannot handle the pressure that Jesus' own impending fate imposes upon him (22:39–45; important here is the clause that Luke's version does not contain: "The spirit is willing, but the flesh is weak" [Mark 14:38; Matt 26:41]). There does of course remain something in the sense proposed here of a being tried out by this pressure situation. And if one does not stand up under the pressure, then the outcome is apostasy (as in 8:13). The primary image here is, then, one of standing up under pressure that threatens to overwhelm; the image is not one of validation (though the sense is not identical, the same sense of pressure is evident in the use of πειρασμός in 1 Cor 10:13; note esp. the use of the verb ὑπενεγκεῖν, "bear up under"). We can now answer our third question. Yes, it does make sense to ask to be spared trial, since the kind of trying pressure in view, while it may be an inevitable aspect of life and may also play its part in the ushering in of the eschaton, is considered here as episodic. It is not inevitable for the individual; and it is not seen in connection with the clarification of the real state of affairs (i.e., validation).

Once again, the additional petition at the end of the Matthean prayer is best taken as an expansion, but here we have simply a positive counterpart to the negatively expressed petition, and there is this time no clear link with a particular motif from the words of Jesus. The form of the prayer in *Did.* 8.2 has as well a form of the doxology of later liturgical use ("for yours is the power and the glory for ever").

Explanation

Jesus' own practice of prayer is the starting point for the Christian practice of prayer. So here, the disciples want to pray as Jesus prays and he teaches them a simple prayer in which they can address themselves confidently and directly to God as Father.

The disciples have the opportunity of observing Jesus at prayer. As they observe they are moved to seek instruction from him, and, when he finishes, they ask for his direction. They see their own relationship to him as parallel to that between John and his disciples, and John had taught his disciples a way of praying. So they now seek the same from Jesus. Such a prayer will be a way of expressing solidarity with Jesus as master. Jesus responds by giving them a pattern prayer to be used as (part of) their regular prayer.

It is notable that the prayer that Jesus gives is not particularly "Christian." It is rather a beautifully simple expression of Jewish prayer, distinguished only by its directness of expression, and in the Lukan form and setting, by the familiar address to God as Father and in its confidence in God's desire to answer the prayers of his children, as a loving human father desires to respond to the requests of his children.

The first petition is for the sanctification of God's name. It would be possible for this petition to have in mind the way that God at the end-time will reveal his glory and in this way God will sanctify his great name (see Ezek 36:23). Or it could have in mind the human response to this end-time act of God, when on seeing what God has done, people will sanctify God's name (see Isa 29:23 in its context). But more likely in the present setting, the petition has in mind that it is fitting in life now to honor God's name; the petition expresses a longing for an extensive and an intensive increase in the level of honor shown to God in our present life in the world. This understanding better fits what follows in the prayer, and also fits in with Jewish prayer practice of the day.

The second petition is unambiguously for the future coming of the kingdom of God. The wording reformulates in the kingdom language so popular with Jesus (but also present in Jewish prayers) the OT anticipation of the coming of the LORD (Ps 96:13; Mic 1:3; etc.) or of the day of the LORD (Isa 13:10; Mal 4:5; etc.). This language expressed the OT expectation of the coming of God in judgment and salvation. While the OT does not speak of the kingdom of God, it does look forward to a time when God would in some greater sense become king (Isa 24:23; Zeph 3:15; Zech 14:9; etc.). Luke will for his part detail something of what he sees to be involved in this coming in chap. 21 (and see as well 17:24–37), but he is also of the opinion that this future kingdom of God has its earlier intimations (see *Comment* at 9:27).

Luke does not have Matthew's next petition, which is probably an expansion from the original prayer. Instead the prayer moves straight to the petition for bread (which by word order and repetition of words is to be closely linked to the following petition for forgiveness). The word translated here as "for the day" has caused interpreters great difficulty. This word has not been found in other Greek of the period, which makes its meaning difficult to discover. Suggestions range from "daily," to "spiritual" (actually "supersubstantial"), to "coming," to "for subsistence," to "essential," to "for the coming day," to "for the coming period" (that is, the period of the kingdom of God), etc.

We cannot be quite sure what the word means, but those senses that link the bread firmly to our basic daily subsistence needs have most to commend them. Often the need is felt to spiritualize this petition (to relate it to the eucharist, to feeding on the Word of God, to spiritual manna, after John 6, etc.), but this is not called for by the context and misses the biblical affirmation of God's care for our bodily life in this world (compare Prov 30:8). Here we have bracketed together the concern for our material life in this petition with a concern for our moral/spiritual life in the following petition. The petition is in line with the confidence in God's one-day-at-a-time provision encouraged in Matt 6:25–34.

If we have a daily need for bread, we also have a daily need for the forgiveness of God. Elsewhere the forgiveness that Jesus extends is an experiencing ahead of time of the end-time release from the guilt and burden of our sin, but here it is our daily need for forgiveness as we are going on in life. Matthew has "debts" at this point, but someone operating in normal Greek might not understand that this is a metaphorical way of speaking about moral and religious failure, and so Luke has substituted here the normal Greek word for sins. Jewish prayer practice closely parallels this petition.

The next clause of the prayer rather disturbs its structure. It was clearly thought important to mark the necessary correlation between the receiving of forgiveness from above and extending of forgiveness to others. Sir 28:2 already makes this connection, and we find it in Jesus' teaching, both directly (Luke 6:37; Mark 11:25; Matt 6:14–15) and in parable (Matt 18:23–35). The daily flow of forgiveness from God will be impeded if there is not a corresponding practice of forgiveness at the human level. In this clause Luke does use the imagery of debt. Though the previous clause guarantees that sin in a moral sense will be involved here, it is quite likely that Luke would have us think more widely of release from other forms of indebtedness as well (see *Comment* at 6:38).

The final petition is that about being tested. Luke uses a word that can mean temptation, but it will not have that sense here, where God is the implied subject. Nor are we to think of the kind of testing that demonstrates what is actually the true state of affairs (we could not ask God not to unmask our deceits). We should probably also exclude the idea that the difficulties of the crisis period of the end-time are in view here. The context of thought that best explains the petition here is that of human frailty, the frailty that Jesus points to in Mark 14:38 in the words "The spirit is willing but the flesh is weak" (there he recommends, in words similar to the petition of the Lord's Prayer, prayer that we might not be buffeted by trial). We are to think here of what might buffet us and create a pressure upon our loyalty to God that in our frailty we might not be able to withstand (compare 8:13). As already hinted, a good example might be the kind of pressure that faced Jesus in Gethsemane as he contemplated his own imminent suffering.

Matthew has one additional petition, which seems to be the re-expression of the previous petition in a positive form. Once again this is likely to be an expansion of the original prayer. Neither Matthew nor Luke has the doxology that often concludes the liturgical use of the Lord's Prayer. While it is found in a few Greek texts of the NT, it is not found in any early texts and is certainly a liturgical development.

Help from a Friend (11:5–8)

Bibliography

Bailey, K. E. *Poet and Peasant.* 119–33. **Berger, K.** "Materialen zu Form und Überlieferungsgeschichte neutestamentlicher Gleichnisse." *NovT* 15 (1973) 1–37, esp. 33–36. **Bornkamm, G.** "'Bittet, suchet, klopfert an': Predigt über Luk. 11: 5–13." *EvT* 13 (1953) 1–5. **Buzy, D.** "L'ami importun (Lc. 11, 5–10)." *RevApol* 51 (1930) 303–20. **Catchpole, D. R.** "Q and 'The Friend at Midnight' (Luke xi. 5–8/9)." *JTS* 34 (1983) 407–24. ———. "Q, Prayer, and the Kingdom: A Rejoinder." *JTS* 40 (1989) 377–88. **Daube, D.** Neglected Nuances of Exposition in Luke-Acts." *ANRW* 2/25.3 (1984) 2329–56, esp. 2332–34. **Derrett, J. D. M.** "The Friend at Midnight: Asian Ideas in the Gospel of St. Luke." In *Donum Gentilicum.* FS D. Daube, ed. E. Bammel et al. Oxford: Clarendon, 1978. 78–87. **Fridrichsen, A.** "Exegetische zum Neuen Testament." *SO* 13 (1934) 38–46, esp. 40–43. **Haaker, K.** "Eine Auslegung von Lukas 11,5–8." *TBL* 17 (1986) 1–6. **Heininger, B.** *Sondergutgleichnisse.* 98–107. **Huffard, E. W.** "The Parable of the Friend at Midnight: God's Honor or Man's Persistence?" *RestQ* 21 (1978) 154–60. **Jeremias, J.** *Parables.* 157–60. **Johnson, A. F.** "Assurance for Man: The Fallacy of Translating Anaideia by 'Persistence' in Luke 11:5–8." *JETS* 22 (1979) 123–31. **Jülicher, A.** *Gleichnisreden.* 2:268–76. **Levison, N.** "Importunity? (Lc. 11, 8)." *Exp* 9/3 (1925) 456–60. **Magass, W., Güttgemanns, E.,** and **Bastian, H.** "Matrial zur Parabel 'Vom bittenden Freund' (Lk. 11, 5–8)." *LingBib* 2 (1970) 3–13. **Martin, A. D.** "The Parable concerning Hospitality." *ExpTim* 37 (1925–26) 414. **Ott, W.** *Gebet und Heil.* 23–31,

99–102. **Rickards, R. R.** "The Translation of Luke 11.5–13." *BT* 28 (1977) 239–43. **Tucket, C. M.** "Q, Prayer and the Kingdom." *JTS* 40 (1989) 367–76.

Translation

[5]*He said to them, "Which of you will have a friend, and you*[a] *will go to him at midnight and say to him, 'Friend, lend me three loaves,* [6]*since a friend of mine has come*[b] *to me from a journey and I do not have anything to lay before him,'* [7]*and he from inside will respond,*[c] *'Do not bother me; the door has already been bolted, and my children are with me in bed; I cannot get up and give you [anything]'?* [8]*I say to you, even if he will not get up and give him [anything] because he is his friend, because of the prospect of him being shamed,*[d] *he will get up and give him as much as he needs."*

Notes

[a] Here, and through v 7, third person forms are rendered as second person when their reference is to the one "of you" who has such a friend. It is unclear whether the same would be appropriate for v 8.

[b] Aorist tense.

[c] Lit. "having answered he will say."

[d] "The prospect of him being shamed" is lit. "his shamelessness."

Form/Structure/Setting

The divisions of this section are only convenience divisions. Vv 9–10 to follow simply spell out in direct teaching the encouragement to appeal confidently to God, which is the burden of the present parable. Linguistically, vv 9–10 have their links with vv 11–13, and are therefore treated with those verses in the next unit. In thought, however, vv 9–10 have the addressees in the petitioner role as in vv 5–8, whereas in vv 11–13a the addressees (in a fresh parabolic strategy) become the recipients of petitions. At the end God (as Father) becomes explicitly the one who receives petition, and with the mention of God as Father we are taken back again to the opening of the Lord's Prayer, on which vv 5–13 are comment.

Ott (*Gebet und Heil*, 23–29) is one of many who have noted the parallels between 11:5–8 and 18:2–5 (disputed by Haacker, *TBl* 17 [1986] 5 n. 11). In the excursus "Journey to Jerusalem," these two parables were seen to have been paired in a chiastically organized set of parables, which was one of Luke's sources for this part of his Gospel (for recent discussion of whether vv 5–8 are reproduced by Luke in their Q setting see Catchpole, *JTS* 34 [1983] 407–24; *JTS* 40 [1989] 377–88; Tucket, *JTS* 40 [1989] 367–76). This structure is not, however, retained as Luke's own, and in any case one should be wary of controlling the sense of the one parable from the other: that they are artistically paired does not at all demand that they make the same point.

Only Luke preserves this parable. Some of its language may be Lukan (μεσονύκτιον, "midnight": Luke-Acts has three of the four NT occurrences; φίλος, "friend," is dominantly Lukan in the NT; παραγινέσθαι, "arrive," is mostly Lukan as are παρέκειν [here "cause"], ἀνιστῆναι, "rise," and γέ, "at least/certainly"). But this is hardly a case for Lukan composition since the first two are specific needs of such a story, the fourth comes in a fixed idiom found also in Matthew and

Mark, and the others are indecisive and at most point to Lukan rewording. The awkward underlying Semitic syntax that holds together vv 5–7 (see at v 5 below) is hardly likely to have been penned by Luke. There is, finally, no adequate reason for denying to the historical Jesus this parabolic expression of confidence in God as one who answers prayer.

There is some question about whether v 8 formed an original unity with vv 5–7. The answer here will be influenced by the understanding proposed for the component parts. As understood below, vv 5–7 could well have stood alone, and have been later supplemented by v 8; but since the thrust of v 8 is only to reinforce what is already the natural sense of vv 5–7, there is equally no good reason for denying an original unity.

In terms of the traditional classification of the parables of Jesus (parable, similitude, and example story [see Nolland, *Luke,* 1:xliii]), this story belongs to the similitudes because it deals with a [potentially] recurring situation. It has probably been transmitted at some point without any interpretive setting but is now provided with a hortatory setting by means of vv 9–10.

In a long and complex sentence, the parable invites the listener to contemplate the possibility of a friend who would turn one away, if one came with a midnight request for food for an unexpected visitor. Assuming a negative answer to this hypothetical situation, Jesus, in v 8, reinforces this judgment by dealing with even the limiting case where the bonds of friendship might fail: even here the prospect of shame if he does not act will move the friend to action.

Comment

Just as our friends, despite inconvenience to themselves, come through for us when we appeal to them in our times of need (even though their motives might at times be mixed), so God will answer our prayer. As our Father he cannot be less dependable than our human friends.

5 καὶ εἶπεν πρὸς αὐτούς, "and he said to them," with its use of πρός after a verb of saying will be a Lukan linkage. The τίς ἐξ ὑμῶν, "which of you," is found (with slight variations) also in 11:11; 14:28; 15:4; 17:7, in each case in connection with brief parables. Since elsewhere in Luke this idiom occurs only at 12:25; 14:5 (and there in contexts that are almost parabolic), the parable will have come to Luke with this introduction (H. Greeven, "'Wer unter euch . . . ,'" *WD* 3 [1952] 86–101 [here p. 100] argues that this is part of the distinctive diction of Jesus). A subject in this form means that when this potential "you" turns up in the ongoing syntax of the story, he/she will do so in the third person (since τίς, "which," is third person). This makes at once for an ambiguity as to who goes to whom. Does our addressee go as the one with an unexpected guest, or get visited by the one with an unexpected guest? The former fits better the prayer focus of the setting and allows a clearer movement from the situation examined to that to which it points (with, e.g., Marshall, 464, who notes as well the oddness, on the alternative view, of the emphatic κἀκεῖνος, lit. "and that one,"; and against, e.g., Fitzmyer, 909; Fitzmyer could, however, appeal to v 11).

It is important to realize that the question is not finished until the end of v 7. The question asks whether such a response as that outlined in that verse is thinkable. There is an implied conditional clause ("if he goes . . .") in which the "then" clause, in Semitic manner, is introduced paratactically by κἀκεῖνος (so: "and he . . ." rather than "then he . . ."). The change of mood to subjunctive with εἴπῃ, "will say," may reflect the underlying conditional clause, but can be otherwise explained.

The motif of friendship, introduced here with two uses of the word "friend," recurs in v 6 and v 8 and makes itself felt also in v 7 (see there). The central place of this notion seems to be curiously out of sight in the studies devoted to this parable (Derrett, "Friend at Midnight," 80, is a rare exception, but does not consistently follow his insight). We cannot be sure what size of loaf would be intended, but it is likely that, in line with ancient Eastern patterns of hospitality, we should think in terms of a very generous, even excessively generous provision for the guest's needs (cf. Gen 18; see discussion in Bailey, *Poet and Peasant*, 121–22).

6 Though ancient patterns of obligations in respect to hospitality form the background setting for the action here, the bonds of friendship provide the primary dynamic, both for the actions and for the listener expectations (so the identification, now, of a second bond of friendship).

We are certainly to understand that the request is based upon need and not convenience, whether this is to be seen in terms of baking patterns in households, or it is to be related to the hours of commercial availability of bread. We should probably not think in terms of a house entirely bare of food: seasonally produced items would be kept in store for the rest of the yearly cycle. The householder does, however, lack the central food item of the meal: the bread, which would be enhanced by means of the prepared dish or dishes.

7 The question begun in v 5 is focused on whether the response contemplated here in v 7 is believable from a friend. This "friend" fails to greet his caller as "friend"; he objects to being caused trouble; and he refuses help on the grounds that the obstacles to action are too great to overcome (the door would need to be unlocked and this could be quite a business, and, if nothing else, noisy; the children in the one-room dwelling would certainly be disturbed from their sleep). The difficulties are real, but in a context of Eastern hospitality would be seen as quite tiny by comparison to the claims of hospitality. The answer to the question is surely that no imaginable friend would behave like this (a neighbor might, but certainly should not [Prov 3:28]).

8 After the beginning here with λέγω ὑμῖν, "I say to you," the one needing help should be, but is not, represented by second person pronouns (he is one of those addressed by Jesus [see at v 5]; the grammar has by this point lost sight of this identification, or else the sequence is continued as though the "I say to you" was only an aside and no integral part of the syntax). This verse is best taken as reinforcing the negative answer implied after the question of vv 5–7. It does this by taking care of the (extremely unlikely) limit case in which the positive bonds of friendship would not be motivation enough to produce the desired help. Even here the scenario of v 7 will not be played out. The thrust is: "You are quite right to think that no friend of yours would behave in such an unhelpful way. Even if your friend is not sufficiently motivated by the bonds of friendship that unite you to him, he will be shamed into rising and giving the help, by realizing what a shameless person he would show himself to be, if he did not produce the needed help for his friend." This understanding is, however, not easily reached.

Is Jesus answering his own question (as Marshall, 465)? This rather defeats the purpose of the parabolic method of persuasion. As in 15:7, 10 the story creates its own answer, which is in turn commented on or developed by Jesus (only in 18:8 does Jesus answer his own question, but there the question is rhetorical and not formed as a parable).

Should we translate the construction *εἰ καί . . . γέ* as "although . . . at least" (the point is then: friendship may prove unreliable, but the fear of shame will strengthen its hand) or as "even if . . . certainly" (the point is then: friendship is reliable, but even in the limit cases where it might fail the fear of shame will come to its aid)? Both possibilities are grammatically viable (but the odd position of *ἀναστάς*, "having risen" [noted by Marshall, 465], may be to link the *καί*, "even," closely with the negative *οὐ*, and if this is so, would favor the second option). The difference is only one of emphasis, but the second does better justice to the self-answering form of the parabolic question (the first seems to suggest an initially equivocating answer to the question of vv 5–7, which only becomes definite with the addition of v 8). (After the subjunctive uses of *εἴπῃ*, "[will] say," in the conditional clause here we get a return to the future verbs with which the story began in v 5, but this throws no particular light on the meaning.)

The greatest difficulty of the verse is posed by *ἀναίδεια*, which has been understood in a number of different ways. Most often it has been taken to mean "persistence." This sense, however, injects an element into the story for which we search in vain (the person has only *asked* his friend, nothing more), and more importantly it gives to the term a sense that cannot be demonstrated until many centuries later (only in the LXX of Jer 8:5 might it have a [somewhat different] chronological meaning [here "enduring/perpetual"]; see Johnson, *JETS* [1979] 123–31, who depends in part on Bailey, *Poet and Peasant*, 125–128).

The regular meaning of *ἀναίδεια* is "shamelessness/impudence," seen as a thoroughly negative quality. Some studies accept this sense here and apply it to the "shameful" disturbance of the man's neighbor (e.g., Jülicher, *Gleichnisreden*, 2:273) But besides injecting a very odd note into the story, this sense leaves the clauses of v 8 incommensurable (The man is rudely disturbed already in the first clause [he must get up]. How can this be introduced as an extra element in the second clause?).

Another way involves softening the harshness of the negative thrust of the word. Berger (*NovT* 15 [1973] 34) points to the uses in Herm. *Sim.* 3.3.2; 3.7.5, in the context of the seeking of revelation, of the cognate adjective and the verb, where the quality involved is something more like brashness, or a boldness that refuses to be shamed into not seeking its goal, than a quite negative shamelessness (there is a certain playfulness about the use of this language in Hermas; the term remains quite negative, but the negative thrust is not intended with full seriousness). This softened down sense does considerably better in Luke 11, but still leaves the clauses in v 8 incommensurable (as above; Derrett, "Friend at Midnight," 84 and n. 1, offers a list of texts to support an early neutral sense for the adjective, of "boldly" or "unselfconsciously," but the texts offer no definite support for his contention; without offering any linguistic base, Haaker, *TBl* 17 [1986] 4–5, assumes [appealing to the thought of Rom 1:16] a similar sense: "a not being ashamed of what one is doing").

Yet another possible move is to maintain, on the basis of the double meaning of the underlying *αἰδώς*, that the term *ἀναίδεια* (formed by adding a negative prefix) is here to be understood quite positively. *αἰδώς* means both a sense of shame (and therefore a sense of honor or self-respect) *and* actual shame or scandal. With the negative prefix added, the sense is elsewhere built upon the first of these two senses, but etymologically it could also be built upon the second. Bailey (*Poet and Peasant*, 132) suggests that such a sense might have resulted from an over-literal translation of an Aramaic original (while the main line of Bailey's argument is clear, the detail seems to have become confused in connection with the distinguishing of "shame" [negative] and "sense of shame" [positive]). *ἀναίδεια*, thus, becomes the "avoidance of shame." In Bailey's view, it is the person receiving the request who acts to avoid shame (we could also apply such a sense to the seeker: "because of the seekers's [need to] avoid shame"). This solution (in either form) is tantamount to saying that there has been a mistranslation into Greek. While the sense and flow of the narrative that emerges are without problem, the difficulty comes here once we ask what sense it would be possible for Luke to make of the narrative (and to offer to his readers) in a Greek text? Did he simply miss the oddness of the statement in Greek?

There is probably a better way to reach a quite similar sense. In a brief note, Fridrichsen (*SO* 13 [1934] 40–43) suggested that we should read the phrase here as a cryptic reference to the shamelessness of the person receiving the request *which would be brought to light if he refused the request for help* (Jeremias, *Parables*, 158, follows Fridrichsen, but is finally of two minds; Ott, *Gebet und Heil*, 29, recognizes the linguistic appropriateness of this view, but goes on to argue for a different approach). The householder would be seen to be without any proper sense of shame if he failed to come to his friend's need at this time. This proposal has been thought to be vulnerable because of the *αὐτοῦ*, "his" (Bailey, *Poet and Peasant*, 130; Fitzmyer, 912), but in the cryptic expression the *αὐτοῦ* stands precisely for the "[which would be] revealed by him" or "[which would be] attributed to him" of the spelled out sense. Because "shamelessness" and "friend" belong to different categories of thought, there is no difficulty in having the "his" attached to each refer to the different actors of our story.

Explanation

The role of this parable is to encourage the praying of the Lord's Prayer with confidence that God will, as we lay our needs before him, respond positively to our requests. Friends come through for us despite inconvenience to themselves, and sometimes despite mixed motives for their goodness. How much more can we be confident that God will come through for us.

Jesus invites his hearers to exercise their imaginations about their friends. Do any of his hearers have a friend who would refuse help if he went to him at midnight, embarrassed at his own inability to provide food for the hospitality needs of a friend who had unexpectedly arrived from a journey? In every culture the bonds of friendship involve the readiness to be put out for one's friends (who can be expected to return the favor). And in ancient (and indeed modern) Eastern cultures the responsibility of showing hospitality was seen as of extreme importance (see Gen 18:1–8; Heb 13:2). Set against these weighty matters the problems of getting up and unlocking the door and thus disturbing the children's sleep seem quite trivial. There can be little doubt that none of his hearers would have come up with a friend who fitted the image of v 7.

Just to be sure, however, Jesus handles the limit case in v 8. What of a friend for whom friendship does not mean enough positively to make him happy to get up and come to the rescue? Even such a "friend" will, nonetheless, get up and do the necessaries, because there is the prospect of the shame to be owned if one were to let down a friend in such a situation. One's name would be mud, not only with one's friend, but also with the wider community: here is the man who treated his friend like this, and caused him great embarrassment with his guest! The initial judgment is strengthened yet further: no friend, however poor a friend, would fail to come to one's rescue in such a situation.

(V 8 is actually the difficult verse of the section, and many different views as to its meaning are discussed in *Comment* above. In particular, what is translated above as "the prospect of being shamed" has been understood in quite different ways because the usual sense of the word does not seem to fit, until one realizes that the point here is being expressed in a very compact way that needs to be fleshed out.)

This is one of those "how much more . . ." kinds of arguments. Vv 11–13 below will offer a related parable where this "how much more" becomes explicit. Taking our lead from there we may say, "If in human friendship with all its flaws we confidently expect our friends to come through for us in our hour of need, how much more can we confidently ask God for his help."

Asking as a Son of the Father (11:9–13)

Bibliography

Bailey, K. E. *Poet and Peasant.* 134–41. **Brox, N.** "Suchen und finden: Zur Nachgeschichte von Mt 7,7b/Lk 11,9b." In *Orientierung an Jesus,* ed. P. Hoffmann et al. 17–36. **Delebecque, É.** "Sur un hellénisme de Saint Luc." *RB* 87 (1980) 590–93. **Dupont, J.** "La prière et son efficacité dans l'évangile de Luc." *RSR* 69 (1981) 45–56, esp. 50–54. **Goldsmith, D.** "'Ask, and It Will Be Given . . .': Toward Writing the History of a Logion." *NTS* 35 (1989) 254–65. **Hjerl-Hansen, B.** "La rapprochement posson-serpent dans la prédication de Jésus (Mt. VII, 10 et Luc. XI, 11)." *RB* 55 (1948) 195–98. **Kraeling, C. H.** "Seek and You Will Find." In *Early Christian Origins.* FS H. R. Willoughby, ed. A. Wikgren. Chicago: Quadrangle Books, 1961. 24–34. **Ott, W.** *Gebet und Heil.* 100–112. **Pegg, H.** "'A Scorpion for an Egg.'" *ExpTim* 38 (1926–27) 268–69. **Piper, R.** "Matthew 7,7–11 par. Luke 11,9–13: Evidence of Design and Argument in the Collection of Jesus' Sayings." In *Logia,* ed. J. Delobel. 411–18.

And see at 11:5–8.

Translation

[9] *"So*[a] *to you I say, 'Ask and it will be given to you; seek and you will find; knock and [the door] will be opened*[b] *for you.* [10]*For everyone who asks receives, and the one who seeks finds, and to the one who knocks [the door] will be opened.*[c] [11] *To which of you,*[d] *as the father, will the son make request*[e, f] *for a fish, and*[g] *instead of a fish you*[h] *will give him a snake: or indeed*[i] [12]*he will ask for an egg;*[j] *you will give him a scorpion?* [13]*If you*

then who are evil know to give good gifts to your children, how much more will the Father[k] *give [the] Holy Spirit*[l] *from heaven*[m] *to those who ask him?'"*

Notes

[a] καί (lit., "and").

[b] The first aorist passive form is preferred here by D E F G H W etc.

[c] It is difficult to be sure whether the future here (supported by P[45] ℵ C L R Θ Ψ etc.), which gives a better logic to the clause, or the present verb (supported by P[75] B D), which conforms this verb to the tense of the other verbs of the parallel clauses, has better claim to originality. In any case the present tenses are all futuristic.

[d] ℵ L (1245) etc., either influenced by the nominative form of the opening τίς, "which?" in the Matthean version, or to continue the pattern of vv 5–8 , in which the the hearers are to identify with the one needing to make request (a pattern that will return in v 13b), read τίς for τίνα (giving the sense, "Which of you as a son will make request to [his] father . . . ?"). The wording of v 13a makes it clear that this cannot be original.

[e] "Make request" is the same Gr. as "ask" in vv 9–10. The different translation handles better the syntactical complexity here.

[f] The first Matthean pair ("bread"/"stone") is added in here by ℵ C (D) L R W Θ Ψ etc. This is occasionally claimed as original.

[g] μή (lit."not") is read here for καί, "and," by ℵ A C D K L W X Δ Θ Π etc. This reproduces the broken syntax of the Matthean text (see *Comment*). (The same μή is inserted into the "scorpion" clause in v 12 by ℵ A C (D) W Θ Ψ etc.)

[h] Here and in the corresponding place in v 12, third person forms are rendered as second person to clarify the thought (as in vv 5–7 above).

[i] (ἐ)άν, "if," is added here by P[45] (C D) W Θ Ψ etc. This produces an easier transition into the following clause.

[j] ἄρτον, "bread," here in P[45] will be an influence from Matthew.

[k] P[45] has here ὑμῶν ὁ οὐράνιος, "our heavenly [Father]," which is probably a variant of the Matthean text.

[l] Various texts manifest here some kind of conflation with the Matthean reading (ἀγαθά, "good [things]").

[m] The reading of P[75] ℵ L Ψ etc. is accepted here, which has no definite article before the "from heaven."

Form/Structure/Setting

There are properly here two small units, vv 9–10 and vv 11–13. With vv 5–8 (and to a lesser degree vv 1–4), these provide a set of units that are to be read closely together. Vv 9–10 form the centerpiece (one should venture with God, for he will come through for you), which is prepared for by vv 5–8 (in our need he is yet more reliable than a friend) and expanded upon in vv 10–13 (as our Father, he will respond to our requests with more appropriateness and generosity than we do to the requests of our children). See also at 10:5–8.

The material here Luke shares with Matthew. It is not impossible that Matthew has disturbed a link with the Lord's Prayer in the shared source (as e.g., Schürmann, *Gottes Reich*, 100–101) by inserting additional materials between, and thus subordinating the structure of the source to his own structuring. Against this is to be set the differences in the form of the Lord's Prayer reflected in the respective sources (see at 11:1–4 above) and the likelihood that vv 11–13, at least in terms of their position, have been drawn, *not* from the source shared with Matthew (where no doubt it was also to be found), but from a parables source to which Luke had access (see discussion in the excursus, "Journey to Jerusalem").

For the most part there is close agreement between the Matthean and the Lukan wording, but less so in vv 11–13. It is likely that Luke bears the main responsibility for the significant reformulation of v 11, apparently for reasons of syntax and to clarify the thematic development of the material. In the same verse, however, he probably retains the more original form with his "egg"/"scorpion" pair, which has in Matthew been displaced by a "bread"/"stone" pair. By contrast in v 13, Matthew's "good things" will be more original than Luke's "Holy Spirit." (See *Comment* for details.)

There is nothing in the materials to alert us to a distinctive post-Easter perspective (except for the place given to the gift of the Holy Spirit, and that is a Lukan modification); and the extravagant trust in the goodness and generosity of God, along with the appeal to the Father/son relationship with God, fits well the concerns of the historical Jesus.

Vv 9–10 have the form of a prophetic admonition, reinforced by a prophetic promise, though the form of v 10 may owe something to a wisdom influence. Vv 11–13 should be classified as a similitude, in which, as was not the case in the somewhat similarly constructed vv 5–8, the comparison (here between human and divine fatherhood) is made explicit (in v 13).

Vv 9–10 are structured in terms of a repeated threefold pattern in which the challenge of v 9 is grounded in the universal promise of v 10. In vv 11–12 a father's care for his son is explored by means of a question, which sets up in parallel two equivalent and equally impossible parental responses. The (assumed) negative answer to this question then becomes the basis for a "how much more" statement, which compares flawed human response to a child's request to that of the Father God who will not withhold (even) the gift of the Spirit.

Comment

The implicit comparison in vv 5–8 of God with a friend to whom we might go at a moment of crisis has prepared for the challenge here to venturing with God in confidence that he will come through for us. As human fathers, with all their limitations, we honor and respond to our children's requests. How much more can God be expected to do the same, even to the point of giving us his own Spirit.

9 Luke provides as a link here the words *κἀγὼ ὑμῖν λέγω*, "and I to you say" (cf. 16:9; 6:27; 7:14; 23:43), to establish a thematic unity with what precedes. The remainder of this (and the following verse except for one verb tense where the textual tradition is divided) is found identically in Matt 7:7(–8). The call to venture is given along with the assurance that such venturing will have success. Three images of venturing are provided: asking for something that another may be able to provide; seeking for what has been lost, or whose location is initially unknown for some other reason; and knocking on a door to gain admission to a building. Taken alone, this challenge could be a general call to venture and risk in life, with confidence that existence offers plenitude (as Wilder's [*Semeia* 2 (1974) 137, 141, etc.] understanding of the Parable of the Sower [8:4–8]). For the historical Jesus, however, this could only exist in a strong context of venturing with and for God, and in any case, in the Lukan context, the venture is clearly that of coming expectantly to God in prayer, to the one who, yet more reliably than any friend (vv 5–8), will meet our needs as we come to him with them. (We probably should not look for different aspects of prayer in the different images [as, e.g., Marshall, 467].) The force of the present imperatives here is not to encourage persistence in prayer (as it might have been if v 8 had, as is often thought, been about persistence), but rather to suggest that such appeal to God will work again and again.

10 Here, in support of the challenge of v 9, each of the clauses of that verse is taken up in what looks rather like a set of wisdom maxims (as Piper ["Design and Argument," 413]; cf. in English, "Every effort has its reward," "Persistence has its reward," or in a negative form, "Nothing ventured, nothing gained"). If this world of wisdom is the correct starting point, then the kind of support that v 10 gives to v 9 is what might be expressed in the form "Doesn't the proverb say . . . ?" A specific challenge to particular people is supported by a universal maxim of folk wisdom.

While, however, the wisdom form is striking (but is this finally a believable proverb?), the close identity of content between v 9 and v 10 is finally best respected by taking v 10, in close connection with v 9, as the prophetic promise that undergirds the prophetic admonition of v 9. V 9 is first and foremost challenge, and the focus is on the call to ask. V 10 is first and foremost promise, and the emphasis is on the universality of the success in asking. The emphasis is, then, "You should *ask* (and it will be given to you). For *everyone* who asks *receives.*" As with v 9, there is no emphasis here on pertinacity (against Jeremias, *Parables,* 159–69).

11 There is significant difference here between Luke's formulation and that of Matthew, but it is more likely that most of this is Lukan than that it reflects distinctive language from his second source here (see *Form/Structure/Setting* above). Matthew's linking ἤ, "or," is gone from the start of the verse. Luke recasts to unite Matthew's first two clauses into a single clause and in the process smoothes both the grammar (in the second clause of Matt 7:9 the man who has a son turns up [in the Semitic but not the Greek manner] both as relative pronoun "whom" and as possessive "his") and the transitions of the unit (now the son's asking and the father's responding form the action of the successive principal clauses following the pattern of v 9 [cf. v 10]; now the father role becomes explicit, preparing for the mention of "the Father" in v 13). The argument is finely balanced between taking Luke's pairs, "fish"/"snake," followed by "egg"/"scorpion," as original ("snake" and "scorpion" make a good pair as not only not food, but also poisonous [Vara's conjecture (*Sal* 30 [1983] 225–29) that for "scorpion" we should read "animal dung," κόπριον, destroys this commonality; Kraeling's attempt ("Seek," 29–32) to support the Matthean pairing with the suggestion that a "pet" snake is in view, does not persuade]), and giving priority to Matthew's pairs, "bread"/ "stone" followed by "fish"/"snake" (Luke may have been influenced by his pairing elsewhere of "snake" and "scorpion" [10:19–20 (in the same order)]). The Lukan form probably has best claim to originality, with the Matthean being influenced by the Temptation narrative (Matt 4:3; Luke 4:3). Bailey (*Poet and Peasant,* 135–37; cf. C. L. Mitton, "Threefoldness in the Teaching Jesus," *ExpTim* 75 [1964] 228–30) gives a good account of a putative original with all three pairs, set within a poetic structure of threes, and ordered in ascending order of seriousness [useless, to unclean, to poisonous]. His case, however, is speculative and finally fails through its inability to account for the shorter forms of both of our present Gospel texts (Bailey, 136, considers the triple form to be original in Luke, or at least in Q [with T. W. Manson, *Sayings,* 81]). Matthew's third clause, which involves the breaking off of the syntax of the previous clauses and starting again, is replaced in Luke with a coordinated clause ("and . . . he will hand him").

Ott (*Gebet und Heil*, 101) and Dupont (*RSR* 69 [1981] 53–54) are right to note that Luke has somewhat separated v 11 from vv 9–10 (this could, however, reflect the influence of Luke's second source, which would have had no equivalent to vv 9–10). As well as making clear that v 11 looks beyond to v 13 rather than back to vv 9–10, this allows vv 9–10 to be equally related to vv 5–8 (with which it shares the perspective of having the hearers identified with the one who is asking) and to vv 11–13 (to which it has its natural vocabulary links). The admonition to prayer in vv 9–10 is prepared for by vv 5–8 and then supported by vv 11–13.

It is doubtful whether any link between "fish" and "snake," beyond the most general of visual similarity, is needed. If necessary one can point to the occasional landing by Galilean fishermen of a sea-snake instead of a fish (Hjerl-Hansen, *RB* 55 [1948] 195–98; Bailey, *Poet and Peasant*, 137, suggests an eel, but why this should be represented in Greek as ὄφις is not discussed).

12 Luke's second pairing is "egg" and "scorpion." For this second pair Luke is slightly briefer, and does not again highlight the substitution as he did in v 11 with "in place of a fish." The scorpion's similarity to an egg is limited, but is based no doubt on the way that these insects roll themselves into balls. An assumed negative answer to the question posed in vv 11–12 becomes the basis for the continuation in vv 12–13.

13 Luke's text here stays rather closer to Matthew's in its construction (Matthew's simple ὄντες ["being"] becomes (without change of meaning) the more elaborate ὑπάρχοντες that Luke favors; the "our" disappears from "the Father," as does Matthew's "in the heavens" (as in his version of the Lord's Prayer) probably to match 11:2 (this last is "compensated" for with the linguistically similar "from heaven," which is, however, to be linked to the following verb, "give"). The most important change is that from Matthew's "good things" to "Holy Spirit."

"Being evil" is not here any particular criticism of the hearers (against Bailey, *Poet and Peasant*, 140–41, who argues for a critical Pharisaic audience, largely from this phrase); rather there is "an implied appeal to experience" (Fitzmyer, 915) where the limitations of any and every earthly father are apparent. In this "how much more" argument, the contrast is with God who is good (cf. Mark 10:18). The mention of the Father takes us full circle back to the beginning of the Lord's Prayer in v 2. On the basis of Acts 2:33 it seems best to speak here of the Holy Spirit given from heaven. There can be little doubt that Matthew's "good things" is more original (cf. the "good gifts" which Luke still retains for the parental gifts). The reason for Luke's alteration is more disputed. Dupont (*RSR* 69 [1981] 52; and cf. Ott, *Gebet und Heil*, 107–8) argues that the change is to move the focus of prayer (at least of prayer which God will answer) away from the material, but this (despite Luke's real concern about the temptations and dangers of material possessions) hardly fits the prominent place given at the start of the section to the Lord's Prayer and its petition for "bread for the day." And in any case, such a change alone would be insufficient to cancel the broader scope intrinsic to the powerful image that controls the unit, of the father meeting the needs with which his children come to him. Bailey (*Poet and Peasant*, 137 n. 81) suggests that the change is for the sake of a smooth transition to the Beelzebub discussion (vv 14–23), but there Luke lacks the crucial reference to the Holy Spirit, which is present in the Matthean parallel, 12:28 [see at v 20]). It will be best to see that, since from a post-Pentecost early church perspective, the greatest gift that God can bestow is the Spirit, Luke wants it to be seen that God's parental bounty applies not just to everyday needs (already well represented in the text in Lord's Prayer) but even reaches so far as to this his greatest possible gift (this is not, as H.-T. Wrege [*Die Überlieferung der Bergpredigt,* WUNT 9 (Tübingen: Mohr-Siebeck, 1968) 108] to have Luke introduce here an idea of the giving of the Holy Spirit to the disciples prior to Easter; the possibility must also be kept open that Luke reflects here his second source).

Explanation

Vv 9 and 10 form the centerpiece of a development of thought that runs from v 5 through to v 13. The fact that in our need we will find God yet more reliable than any friend (vv 5–8) prepares for the challenge to venture with God, with its accompanying promise of his action in answer to our requests (vv 9–10). Challenge and promise are additionally buttressed by a comparison between the Fatherhood of God and human fatherhood: as our Father, God will respond to our requests with more appropriateness and generosity than we do to the requests of our children; he will not even withhold his Holy Spirit from those who make request to him.

Our text provides us with three images of venturing with God. These are (*i*) asking for something that another may be able to provide one with; (*ii*) seeking for what has been lost, or whose location is initially unknown for some other reason; and (*iii*) knocking on a door to gain admission to a building. The text assures us that what is ventured will be achieved. This may seem extravagant in terms of our experience, and there are other biblical texts that would circumscribe the boldness of this statement. Nonetheless this extravagant sense of the accessibility of God and of his ability and willingness to respond to us as we come to him fit well with the radical simplicity of the faith of Jesus, and Luke would have us encounter this in all its starkness.

The universally stated principles of vv 9–10 are further supported in a brief parable (like the kind in vv 5–8) in which the Fatherhood of God is explored as certainly being more dependable than flawed human fatherhood. Both fish and snakes are smooth and "slithery," but no human father is going to offer his son a venomous snake when his son asks for a fish. Similarly no curled up scorpion is going to be offered in place of an egg. As earthly fathers we provide what will properly nurture our children in their needs. So it is with God, but how much more! We hand out good things to our children; God will not even withhold his Holy Spirit from us. (Not of course that the Holy Spirit is supposed to substitute for all our other needs—to the starving person that would be altogether too close to the behavior that not even a flawed human father would be involved in. It is rather that the gift of the Holy Spirit as God's highest gift should give us every assurance that he will not withhold from us anything that we need.)

In the practical outworking of this teaching its application will need to be balanced by other biblical teaching, but here as a basic principle the logic of the Fatherhood of God is presented to us in stark simplicity.

Conflict and Contrast (11:14–54)

In this new section Jesus is involved in increasing conflict, on the one hand with those who are not ready to recognize the presence of God in his ministry, and on the other hand with the Pharisees and scribes who feel the sting of his personal criticism. Provoked by his words they seek in turn to provoke, and try to entrap him.

Casting out Demons by the Finger of God (11:14–23)

Bibliography

Aalen, S. " 'Reign' and 'House' in the Kingdom of God in the Gospels." *NTS* 8 (1962) 215–40, esp. 229–31. **Barnett, P. W.** "The Jewish Sign-Prophets—A.D. 40–70: Their Intentions and Origin." *NTS* 27 (1980–81) 679–97. **Beauvery, R.** "Jésus et Béelzéboul (Lc 11,14–28)." *AsSeign* 30 (1963) 26–36. **Berkey, R. F.** " *Ἐγγίζειν, φθάνειν*, and Realized Eschatology." *JBL* 82 (1963) 177–87. **Böcher, O.** *Das Neue Testament und die dämonischen Mächte.* SBS 58. Stuttgart: Katholisches Bibelwerk, 1972. 9–12. **Bryant, H. E.** "Note on Luke xi. 17." *ExpTim* 50 (1938–39) 525–26. **Busse, U.** *Wunder.* 275–89. **Campbell, J. Y.** "The Kingdom of God Has Come." *ExpTim* 48 (1936–37) 91–94. **Cangh, J. M. van.** " 'Par l'Esprit de Dieu—par le doigt de Dieu': Mt 12,28 par. Lc 11,20." In *Logia: Les paroles de Jésus,* ed. J. Delobel. 337–42. **Chilton, B.** "A Comparative Study of Synoptic Development: The Dispute between Cain and Abel in the Palestinian Targums and the Beelzebul Controversy in the Gospels." *JBL* 101 (1982) 553–62. **Clark, K. W.** " 'Realized Eschatology.' " *JBL* 59 (1940) 367–83. **Couroyer, B.** "Le 'doigt de Dieu' (Exode, VIII, 15)." *RB* 63 (1956) 481–95. **Craig, K. M.** and **Kristjansson, M. A.** "Women Reading as Men/Women Reading as Women: A Structural Analysis for the Historical Project." *Semeia* 51 (1990) 119–36. **Dodd, C. H.** "Changes of Scenery in Luke." *ExpTim* 33 (1921–22) 40–41. ———. "The Kingdom of God Has Come." *ExpTim* 48 (1936–37) 138–42. **Downing, F. G.** "Towards the Rehabilitation of Q." *NTS* 11 (1965) 169–81, esp. 170–76. **Dunn, J. D. G.** "Matthew 12:28/Luke 11:20—A Word of Jesus." In *Eschatology and the New Testament.* FS G. R. Beasley-Murray, ed. W. H. Gloer. Peabody, MA: Hendrickson, 1988. 29–49. **Easton, B. S.** "The Beelzebul Sections." *JBL* 32 (1913) 57–73. **Fiedler, P.** *Jesus und die Sünder.* 211–25. **Fuchs, A.** *Die Entwicklung der Beelzebulkontroverse bei den Synoptikern: Traditionsgeschichtliche und redaktionsgeschichtliche Untersuchung von Mk 3,22–27 und Parallelen, verbunden mit der Rückfrage nach Jesus.* SNTU B/5. Linz, 1980. **Garrett, S. R.** *The Demise of the Devil.* 43–46. **Gaston, L.** "Beelzebul." *TZ* 18 (1962) 247–55. **George, A.** "Notes sur quelques traits lucaniens de l'expression 'Par le doigt de Dieu' (Luc XI,20)." *ScEccl* 18 (1966) 461–66; reprinted in *Études sur l'oeuvre de Luc.* 127–32. **Grässer, E.** "Zum Verständnis des Gottesherrshaft." *ZNW* 65 (1974) 3–26. **Green, H. B.** "Matthew 12:22–50 and Parallels: An Alternative to Matthaean Conflation." In *Synoptic Studies: The Ampleforth Conferences of 1982 and 1983.* JSNTSup 7. Sheffield: JSOT, 1984. 157–76. **Hammerton-Kelly, R. G.** "A Note on Matthew XII. 28 par. Luke XI. 20." *NTS* 11 (1964–65) 167–69. **Hermann, I.** " '. . . dann ist das Gottesreich zu euch gekommen': Eine Homilie zu Luk 11,14–20." *BibLeb* 1 (1960) 198–204. **Käsemann, E.** "Lukas 11,14–

28." In *Exegetische Versuche und Besinnungen.* Göttingen: Vandenhoeck & Ruprecht, 1960, 1964. 1:242–48. **Kirchschläger, W.** *Jesu exorzistisches Wirken.* 229–36. **Klauck, H.-J.** *Allegorie und Allegorese.* 178–84. **Kloppenborg, J. S.** "A Synopsis for Q." In *SBL Seminar Papers,* ed. K. H. Richards. Atlanta: Scholars, 1985. 127–32. ————. "Q 11:14–26: Work Sheets for Reconstruction." In *SBL Seminar Papers,* ed. K. H. Richards. Atlanta, GA: Scholars, 1985. 127–32. **Kruse, H.** "Das Reich Satans." *Bib* 58 (1977) 29–61. **Kümmel, W. G.** *Promise and Fulfilment.* 24, 105–9. **Laufen, R.** *Die Doppelüberlieferung.* 126–49. **Légasse, S.** "L' 'homme fort' de Luc xi 21–22." *NovT* 5 (1962) 5–9. **Linton, O.** "The Demand for a Sign from Heaven (Mk 8, 11–12 and Parallels)." *ST* 19 (1965) 112–29. **Lorenzmeier, T.** "Zum Logion Mt 12,28; Lk 11,20." In *Neues Testament und christliche Existence.* FS H. Braun, ed. H. D. Betz and L. Schottroff. Tübingen: Mohr-Siebeck, 1973. 289–304. **Lührmann, D.** *Logienquelle.* 32–43. **Luz, U.** "Q 10:2–16; 11:14–23." In *SBL Seminar Papers 1985,* ed. K. H. Richards. Atlanta: Scholars, 1985. 101–2. **MacLauren, E. C. B.** "Beelzeboul." *NovT* 20 (1978) 156–60. **Mearns, C.** "Realized Eschatology in Q? A Consideration of the Sayings of Luke 7.22, 11.20 and 16.16." *SJT* 40 (1987) 189–210. **Meynet, R.** "Qui donc est 'le plus fort'? Analyse rhétorique de Mc 3, 22–30; Mt 12, 22–37; Luc 11, 14–26." *RB* 90 (1983) 334–50. **Neirynck, F.** "Mt 12,25a/Lc 11,17a et la rédaction des évangiles." *ETL* 62 (1986) 122–33. **Nielson, H. K.** *Heilung.* 28–45. **Oakman, D. E.** "Rulers' Houses, Thieves, and Usurpers: The Beelzebul Pericope." *Forum* 4.3 (1988) 109–23. **Perrin, N.** *Rediscovering the Teaching of Jesus.* 63–67, 77. **Robbins, V. K.** "Rhetorical Composition and the Beelzebul Controversy." In *Patterns of Persuasion in the Gospels,* ed. B. L. Mack and V. K. Robbins. Sonoma, CA: Polebridge, 1989. **Robinson, J. M.** "The Mission and Beelzebul: Pap. Q 10:2–16; 11:14–23." In *SBL Seminar Papers,* ed. K. H. Richards. Atlanta: Scholars, 1985. 97–99. **Rolland, P.** "'Jésus connaissait leurs pensées'" *ETL* 62 (1986) 118–21. **Roulin, P.** "Le péché contre l'Esprit-Saint." *BVC* 29 (1959) 38–45. **Schirock, R.** "Whose Exorcists Are They? The Referents of οἱ υἱοὶ ὑμῶν at Matthew 12.27/Luke 11.19." *JSNT* 46 (1992) 41–51. **Schlosser, J.** *Le règne de Dieu.* 127–53. **Schulz, S.** *Spruchquelle.* 203–13, 476–80. **Syx, R.** "Jesus and the Unclean Spirit: The Literary Relation between Mark and Q in the Beelzebul Controversy (Mark 3:20–30 par)." *LouvStud* 17 (1992) 166–80. **Trautmann, M.** *Zeichenhafte Handlungen Jesu: Ein Beitrag zur Frage nach dem geschichtlichen Jesus.* FB 37. Würzburg: Echter, 1980. 258–77. **Wall, R. W.** " 'The Finger of God': Deuteronomy 9.10 and Luke 11.20." *NTS* 33 (1987) 144–50. **White, L. M.** "Scaling the Strongman's 'Court' (Luke 11:21)." *Forum* 3.3 (1987) 3–28. **Yates, J. E.** "Luke's Pneumatology and Lk. 11,20." *SE* [=TU 87] 2 (1964) 295–99.

Translation

[14]*He was casting out a mute*[a] *demon. It transpired that when the demon came out*[b] *the mute person spoke and the crowds were amazed.* [15]*But some*[c] *of them said, "By Beelzeboul,*[d] *the ruler of the demons, he casts out the demons!"* [16]*Others, to test him, were wanting from him a sign from heaven.* [17]*He, knowing their thoughts, said to them, "Every kingdom divided against itself is desolated, and a house [divided] against a house falls.* [18]*If Satan, as well, has been divided against himself, how will his kingdom stand? For you say that by Beelzeboul I cast out demons.* [19]*If I cast out demons*[e] *by Beelzeboul, by whom do your sons cast [them] out? Therefore, they will be your judges.* [20]*If I*[f] *by the finger of God cast out demons, then the kingdom of God has come upon you.*

[21]*"When the*[g] *powerful man, fully armed, keeps guard over his own castle, his goods are secured.* [22]*When* [h]*one who is more powerful than he*[i] *comes upon him and conquers him, he takes away the armor in which he had put his trust and distributes the booty.*

[23]*"The one who is not with me is against me; and the one who does not gather with me scatters."* [j]

Notes

[a] In A[c] C R W Θ Ψ etc. "mute" is linked to the added words "and it was" (*καὶ αὐτὸ ἦν*).

[b] *ἐκβληθέντος*, "was cast out," is read here by A C L etc.

[c] Rather oddly, P[45] further specifies these as *ὀχυροί*, "strong ones" (it also handles the verb here differently).

[d] ℵ B 579 have the spelling *Βεεζεβούλ*, "Beezeboul," which ℵ B have as well in vv 18, 19.

[e] P[45] it lack "demons."

[f] The emphatic "I" (*ἐγώ*) is present in P[75] ℵ[1] B C (D) L R etc., omitted by P[45] ℵ A W Θ Ψ etc.

[g] ℵ omits the definite article here.

[h] A definite article is included here by A C W etc.

[i] "Than he" (*αὐτοῦ*) is missing from P[45,75] D 1241.

[j] ℵ ℵ[2] C[2] L Θ Ψ etc. have added, rather oddly, a "me" (*με*) at this point.

Form/Structure/Setting

A total change of topic marks the beginning of a new main section here. Various links bind the units of this section together: vv 24–26 are linked to vv 14–23 by means of the shared interest in the fate of the demonized; vv 27–28 are linked by means of a time statement ("it happened that while he was saying these things . . ."); vv 29–32 are linked by means of the crowd language that runs as a thread from v 14 to v 27 to v 29, but more importantly by the taking up here of the demand for a sign that has surfaced in v 16 (not paralleled at this point in Matthew or Mark!); vv 33–36 are provided with no specific links, but they are clearly meant to be understood in their Lukan setting in connection with the misunderstanding and (willful) misinterpretation that Jesus is encountering in this section; vv 37–44 are linked (as were vv 27–28) with a time statement; vv 45–52 are linked by making the lawyer's remarks a response to the incident in vv 37–44; (taking a cue from Mark's use in 3:6 of a statement about a rising surge of opposition to Jesus to round off a series of linked units) Luke ends the section in vv 53–54 with his statement about growing scribal and Pharisaic opposition. The first and the last of the units of this section begin with an amazed response to some activity of Jesus.

Luke's only source here appears to have been that which he shares with Matt 12:22–30. Where Matthew has at points been influenced by the Markan partial parallel (Mark 3:22–27), Luke shows no definite sign of such influence. The materials of the section do not have any intrinsic unity and have probably been transmitted separately before being drawn together into the present unit. While v 15 depends upon the existence of Jesus' exorcisms, the present such account in v 14 is so bare as to make it likely that it has been secondarily formed as introduction here (cf. 7:21). Vv 17–18 cannot have existed without v 15 (v 16 has been intruded by Luke), nor can v 19. V 15 will not have existed without an attached response of some kind, but v 19 and v 20 are also candidates here (one alone, or two, or all three of the choices). V 20 could have been transmitted quite independently of its present setting. Vv 21–22 (or at least the simpler Matthean version) are likely to have had an independent transmission history as a brief parabolic utterance. V 23 can also have been independently transmitted. As the material now stands, we have a controversy dialogue.

The confidence with which we may trace the various materials back to the historical Jesus is variable. With greatest confidence we may trace v 20 back to Jesus (see the recent laying out of the arguments by Nielsen, *Heilung*, 32–40). The attribution of Jesus' exorcisms, by some, to Beelzeboul also has good claim to historicity, as does the brief parabolic utterance behind vv 21–22. There is more room for uncertainty in the case of vv 17–18 and v 19 where we move into a kind of logical argumentation that probably had little place in the teaching of Jesus. Yet even here the skeptical judgment of Käsemann (*Versuche*, 243–44) depends more on an over-reading of the arguments (see below) and on a theological commitment to the fundamental "ambiguity of all mere facts" (244), than it does on balanced historical judgment.

The occasion of an exorcism produces a generally amazed response from the crowds. But some identify Beelzeboul as the power behind Jesus' exorcisms, and others call for a sign from heaven to resolve all uncertainties as to the significance of Jesus' activity. A response to the latter is kept in reserve for vv 29–32. The former is addressed first by means of images of civil war and of a divided household: how could Satan countenance such an undermining of his own kingdom? This phase of the argument is then rounded off by having Jesus reiterate the accusation being addressed. The accusation is thereby ready at hand as well for the second phase of the response: Where does this view place all other Jewish exorcists? Are they to fall under the same suspicion? These arguments are designed to dismiss the accusation leveled against him. Jesus now makes his own claims in connection with his exorcisms: these exorcisms are by the "finger of God" and manifest the coming of the kingdom of God. This claim is then elaborated in a parable, in which the presence of the mighty power of God with Jesus in his exorcisms is imaged in the vanquishing of a powerful man despite all his military precautions, when one yet more powerful comes on the scene: to return to the imagery of vv 17–18, Satan is now despoiled not by civil war, but by the arrival of the one who is more than his match. Jesus' own interpretation of the situation has now been offered. The unit concludes with the challenge to join him in what he is doing, or to be reckoned as part of the opposing military forces; to share with him in the eschatological gathering of Israel, or to be considered as one with those who have been responsible for the tragic scattering of the flock of God.

Comment

To attribute Jesus' exorcisms to the power of Satan is a patently false understanding of this liberating act of Jesus. Jesus proposes, rather, that his exorcisms are to be understood in connection with the very finger of God, powerfully making its presence felt as in Egypt of old; indeed that the very kingdom of God had now come upon the people of Jesus' own generation.

14 Matthew (12:22), more than Luke, seems to have significantly modified the wording of their shared source here. For whatever reason, Matthew appears to have made a second use of the same material in 9:32–34, where the language used provides, in part, a middle term between the the wording of Luke and the version in Matt 12:22, and shows that apart from the periphrastic ἦν ἐκβάλλων, "was casting out" (cf. esp. 1:21), and the use of ἐγένετο, "it happened," Luke has followed his source closely here. The exorcism is recounted in the briefest possible compass and serves only to provide a setting for the interchange to follow. On exorcism, see at 4:31–37. On the amazed response of the crowds, see at 9:43b. Amazement marks the impressiveness of what has been experienced, but does not signal any particular personal response to Jesus (this is evident in vv 15–16 where the amazement of some leads on to an accusation of collusion with the devil, and of others to a request for a sign from heaven).

15 One cannot be sure which is more original here, Matthew with his Pharisaic accusers (Matthew does like to highlight the tension between Jesus and the Pharisees [cf. at 3:7]) or Luke with his anonymous τινὲς δὲ ἐξ αὐτῶν, "some of them" (Luke is fond of forms of τις [lit. "(a) certain"] and in the present text τινὲς δὲ ἐξ αὐτῶν anticipates the ἕτεροι δέ, "others," which introduces the second sectional response in v 16; Mark has as a third option, "scribes from Jerusalem"!). It may be that the original is an unspecified "they" (and so most naturally to be identified with the "crowds"). For the accusation, Laufen (*Doppelüberlieferung*, 127–28 [following R. Hummel]) argues effectively that the distinctive οὐκ . . . εἰ μή, "not . . . except," construction of Matthew's text is Matthean redaction (an aftereffect of the Matthean version of the popular response in v 23b), and that Luke follows the source closely here (cf. Matt 9:34).

The reality of the power present in Jesus is not in dispute, but is it demonic or divine power with which we are dealing? The former possibility has attractions for those who preferred to sidestep the challenge to their own lives posed by the ministry of Jesus, but given the expectations of Satanic deception (Deut 13:1–3; Matt 24:24; 2 Thess 2:9; Rev 13:13–14; and cf. 2 Cor 11:14), to raise such a possibility is not, on the surface of things, without its intrinsic merits. (The contention of Böcher [*Die dämonischen Mächte*, 11] that other exorcists made use of the power of Beelzeboul is without foundation.) The accusation against John the Baptist ("he has a demon" [7:33]) has a closer parallel in the Markan form here ("he has Beelzeboul" [3:22]) unless this should be read the other way ("Beelzeboul has [him]"). Elsewhere in the NT the name "Beelzeboul" is found outside the present context, and its parallels, only at Matt 10:25. The name is a transliteration into Greek of the name of an old Canaanite god, meaning "Baal, the Prince" or "Baal of the Exalted Abode." On the basis that the gods of the nations are demons (as 1 Cor 10:20–23), they become figures in the demonic power structure (on the relationship between Satan and the demons see at 4:1–13). It would seem that as with "Belial" (2 Cor 6:15; 1QS 1:18, 24; 2:5, 19), "Mastemah" (1QS 3:23; 1QM 13:4, 11; CD 16:5; *Jub.* 10:8), and "Asmodaeus" (Tob 3:8, 17), "Beelzeboul" had become in time simply an alternative name for Satan. (For fuller discussion, see Fitzmyer, 920–21; MacLauren *NovT* 20 [1978] 156–60; Gaston, *TZ* 18 [1962] 247–55.)

16 This verse has no parallel in Matthew, and it appears to have been produced by Luke on the basis of Mark 8:11 (which is followed in v 12 by a brief Markan parallel to Luke 11:29). Mark 8:11 contributes in exact wording πειράζοντες, "being tested," σημεῖον, "sign," οὐρανοῦ, "heaven," παρ' αὐτοῦ, "from him," as well as the use of the verb ζητεῖν, "to seek." The presence of v 16 gives the necessary concrete antecedent for vv 29–32 and serves in the binding together of the materials of Luke's section here (11:14–54). The request is that Jesus should arrange for God to personally step in and confirm his (Jesus') own credibility in some miraculous way (Deut 13:1–2 reflects the assumption that a prophet might be validated by means of a miraculous sign; we might think of such things as the turning back of the sun [2 Kgs 20:8–11], the collapse of the walls of Jerusalem [Josephus, *Ant.* 20.168–72; *War* 2.261–63]; in John 6:30–31, the wilderness manna is seen as just such a sign, authenticating Moses; such signs often involve prior announcement, but it is not this, as Linton contends [*ST* 19 (1965) 112–29], that constitutes their identity as signs). From the viewpoint of this group, such is the way to test the authenticity of Jesus. Luke's inclusion of this second response at just this point has a certain fine irony about it, since it is precisely because Jesus' exorcism is not such a (morally neutral or ambiguous [as with Deut 13:1–5]) "sign from heaven," but is, rather, an act manifestly against the interests of the forces of evil, that it is finally not subject to the ambiguity intrinsic to any "sign" that is simply a display of power (God's or Satan's?).

17 *αὐτὸς δέ* (expressed subject: "he") is likely to be a Lukan addition to specify the subject change after the *τινες . . . ἕτεροι*, "some . . . others," pattern used in vv 15–16. Luke's *τὰ διανοήματα* for "the thoughts" will be the source term here, not Matthew's alternative *τὰς ἐνθυμήσεις*, which he also introduces in 9:4. The form *ἐφ' ἑαυτήν* for "against himself" could be a Markan influence, but in the absence of other Markan influences on the Lukan text of this pericope, it is probably better to consider that Matthew has introduced the less common *καθ' ἑαυτῆς* form. The compound form for "divided" in Luke will be his own touch. Luke is probably responsible for the cryptic abbreviation of the statement about houses (which uses *οἶκος* for "house" rather than the *οἰκία* of Matthew and Mark).

Luke shows a specific interest in Jesus' uncanny awareness of what goes on in people's minds (see at 4:23). We are to understand that the verbal expressions of such thoughts noted in vv 15–16 were directed only to the immediate neighbors of those who spoke and could not be overheard by Jesus. (Neirynck, *ETL* 62 [1986] 122–33, makes this tension the cornerstone of his argument that v 17a may not have been in Q and, even if it was in Q, was not part of the original account here [the latter alternative seems rather more likely than the former].) Jesus points to the desolation caused by civil war, and then to something similar with respect to houses. The second image is too elliptically expressed in Luke's text to be sure of its meaning (lit. "a house upon a house falls"). Possible senses are: (*i*) "House after house collapses" (this is how the desolation of the kingdom proceeds [a variant of this would be "House collapses against house" (as Käsemann, *Versuche*, 1:243)]). (*ii*) "House falls upon (i.e., attacks) house" (this would still be subordinate to the primary civil war of the previous clause, but it makes for an awkward sequence after the desolation already achieved by the end of the previous clause). (*iii*) "A house [pitted against its own] house falls" (this assumes a certain carelessness in Luke's abbreviation [Creed, 160, suggests that we should supply an understood *διαμερισθεῖσα*, "divided," from the previous clause], but it allows for an image parallel to that of a kingdom to be applied to a household, as is the case in Matthew and Mark here). Despite its linguistic difficulties, the third option seems most likely to be correct. These pictures of internecine warfare, or at least the first of them, are taken up in v 18 and applied to the matter in hand.

18 Unlike Luke, both Matthew and Mark provide some bridging explanation before applying the imagery of v 17 to Satan (Matthew: "if Satan casts out Satan"; Mark: "if Satan has risen up against himself"). Since Matthew's wording seems to be influenced by Mark 3:23, the Lukan text, which allows the bridging to take place implicitly, is likely to be more original. Luke's own contribution will be the rounding off of this phase of the argument and the driving home of the inner contradiction of the view that Jesus is here criticizing, by having Jesus, at the end of the verse, reiterate the accusation against him (Luke may have sensed the need for this repetition after the inclusion of v 16, after which, without the present clarification, it could be the v 16 response to Jesus' exorcizing that was receiving comment; the language is a back formation from v 19a).

The proposed role of Beelzeboul would mean, Jesus suggests, that evil has now risen up against evil. Civil wars do occur, but it is hard to see how they could be deliberately countenanced by the ruler of the kingdom of darkness, for whom it could only mean the laying waste of his kingdom and the undermining of his rule. This is something rather more than just shooting oneself in the foot! The argument has considerably more cogency (see above at end of v 16) than Käsemann dismissively allows (*Versuche*, 1:243: he cannot see that the argument addresses the possibility of Satanic deception, and he makes no distinctions within the category of the miraculous).

19 Luke's addition at the end of v 18 means that the rejected possibility, which is taken up here again, has been immediately present in the previous sentence: we are not required to search back to v 15 where it is initially proposed. The wording here is virtually identical to that of Matthew. The argument builds from the shared assumptions that (*i*) exorcism is a (morally) good thing, and not just a demonstration of power; and that (*ii*) Jesus is not the only functioning exorcist in the Jewish community (see Mark 9:38; Acts 19:13–14; Josephus, *Ant.* 8.46; 1QapGen 20:29; etc.). There may be a third assumption that all Jewish exorcisms proceed from the power of God, but this is less certain (depending as it does on the assumption that God and Satan are the two alternatives to be considered in answer to the question; in the present text, the dynamic of v 20 must be counted against this third assumption). To blacken Jesus' name as an exorcist is to cast the same doubt upon all other Jewish exorcists. To make the other Jewish exorcists the eschatolgical judges of these skeptical Jews (as, e.g., Fitzmyer, 922; Marshall, 475) is to take the image altogether too literally. The point is rather, "What will other Jewish exorcists, in light of their own exorcizing activity, make of such a view?"

20 Luke and Mark have identical wording here, except that Luke has "finger of God" for Matthew's "Spirit of God." Earlier scholarship tended to consider the Lukan form as original here (Wall, *NTS* 33 [1987] 144, still identifies this as the current consensus), but all the more recent studies that have focused attention on this matter conclude that Luke is the one who has altered the text (see Rodd, *ExpTim* 72 [1960–61] 157–58; Hamerton-Kelley, *NTS* 11 [1964–65] 167–69; Yates, "Luke's Pneumatology," 295–99; George, "Par le droigt," 127–32; van Cangh, "Par l'Esprit," 337–42; Wall, *NTS* 33 [1987] 144–50). Some of the main lines of argument are: (*i*) Lukan omissions of references to the Spirit can be documented (e.g., 21:15; cf. Mark 13:11), while Matthew cannot be shown to have added them; (*ii*) Luke alone of the Synoptists uses two other quite similar anthropomorphisms, namely "the hand of God" (1:66; Acts 4:28, 30; 7:50; 11:21; 13:11) and "the arm of God" (Luke 1:31; Acts 13:17); (*iii*) "finger of God" is (rightly) normally linked to Exod 8:15 (ET v 19; this is surely better than the much less natural link to Deut 9:10 that Wall [*NTS* 33 (1987) 144–50] defends in the context of an argument for an elaborate midrashic link here with Deut 9), where the verdict of the magicians of Pharaoh on the plagues that Moses had brought upon Egypt was, "This is the finger of God"; and it is Luke who shows the most consistent concern to show that elements in Jesus' ministry are a heightened reiteration of elements from earlier phases of the history of God's dealings with his People (this is especially true in the infancy accounts, but has been documented in many places in the present work, most recently at 9:57–62); (*iv*) there may be a link between omission of a reference to the Spirit here and addition at v 13 (the sectioning is clearer *without* a reference to the Spirit between v 13 and 12:10). Hamerton-Kelly (*NTS* 11 [1964–65] 167–69), by drawing attention to the parallelism between "hand of God" (which must have an equivalent meaning to "finger of God") and "Spirit" (Hamerton-Kelly discusses Ezek 8:1–3 and 1 Chr 28:11–19), has argued that there is no substantial change of meaning from the Matthean to the Lukan text. Luke will mean that power is present with Jesus by virtue of his possession of the Spirit of God, and with the "finger of God" language he will be likening the present to the time of the dramatic activity of God on behalf of his People at the Exodus from Egypt.

Where vv 17–19 have had the negative function of undermining the interpretation of Jesus' exorcisms proposed in v 15, the present text represents Jesus' own claim. This claim is in no sense presented as the (only) logical alternative to the view criticized in vv 17–19.

Much has been made in the (earlier) scholarly discussion of the possible relationship between the ἔφθασεν (tr. above "has come") and the ἤγγικεν (lit. "has drawn near") of 10:9 (cf. Mark 1:15). In the attempt to find a common original each has been drawn in turn into the natural orbit of the meaning of the other (see discussion of ἤγγικεν at 10:9), often in connection with attempts to identify the correct underlying Aramaic verb. The term ἔφθασεν has also been asked to bear the weight of theological concerns that have far exceeded its semantic possibilities. In particular, on the basis that the verb can mean "to come before, precede" when it is followed in the accusative by what is preceded (see BAGD, 856), a sense of "to come ahead of time" is claimed, or the verb is even taken to represent "a limit case of drawing near, that still does not signify presence" (Michaelis, *Das Evangelium nach Matthäus,* 2:154 [cited according to Nielsen, *Heilung,* 42]). Whatever larger interpretive difficulties result, in the present text the verb can bear no more than its ordinary sense (when followed by ἐπί + acc.) of "to come upon." The only questions are whether it carries here the nuance "*just* come upon," and whether there is any threatening edge to the statement (i.e., "come upon" in the sense that a disaster might "come upon/overtake" one [cf. the context of Exod 8:19]).

Because "kingdom" is clearly "realm" and not "rule" or "reign" in vv 17–18, Aalen (*NTS* 8 [1962] 229–31) has claimed that the same is true here in v 20, but this is to integrate the material in an improper manner. In the first place an original unity of these materials is not at all likely (see *Form/Structure/Setting*). But as well, even in the unity created in the present text, there is no close link to be drawn between the kingdom language of vv 17–18 and that of v 20: in the former it is the logic of a divided kingdom that is being explored; in the latter the claim is made that in the activity of Jesus, God is exercising his rule. Indeed it is the notion of exercise of dominion, implicit in the different elements drawn together here (see also vv 22–22), that holds the unit together here. In v 20 this notion comes to expression in the kingdom language.

If the historical Jesus (and here the Gospel of Luke) spoke of the kingdom of God only as a reality brought into the present in connection with the ministry of Jesus and not also as a future cosmic expectation, then it might be reasonable to understand "kingdom of God" in a manner quite different from the hopes of apocalypticism. But while there have been a whole series of attempts to relegate entirely to the later church either the future or the present strand, or to interpret away the chronological intention of one or other of the strands, none of these expedients has proved satisfactory. Jesus both announced the present coming of the kingdom of God and anticipated its future apocalyptic manifestation. The interpretive task is so to formulate an understanding of the kingdom of God that we can do justice at one and the same time to a future and a present coming without ending up with two quite different kinds of "kingdom of God." As helpful a brief statement as any is that of Nielsen (*Heilung*, 44–45):

> The healings [here the exorcisms] are signs [of the presence of the kingdom of God (i.e., expressions of its reality)] in the same way that snowdrops are signs of Spring. The power and the reality which we meet in the snowdrop are the same ones, which later—even if far more powerfully—come into prominence.

Caird (*The Language and Imagery of the Bible*, 199–271) has helpfully drawn attention to the metaphorical nature of the language use involved. In particular Caird has shown how the same sort of juxtaposition of present fulfillment and future consummation functions powerfully in the OT to set present experience into the larger context of the purposes of God in history. There is inevitably an element of paradox in the claim that, while the larger world goes on much as before, nevertheless the new world order of God's eschatological rule has now arrived in and through the activity of Jesus.

The presence of the kingdom of God is linked not to the fact of exorcism standing alone (then the same claim could be as well made for the other Jewish exorcists), but also involves the role of Jesus himself (note the emphatic "I") and the implied claim that "the finger of God" is the operative power here, that is, that the presence and power of God are here in some distinctive manner (this may have to do with the manner, and not simply the fact, of the exorcisms).

21 Here and in the following verse Luke has, without changing the basic thrust, quite reformulated his source material (Matthew and Mark are quite similar to one another at this point). The possibility of a second source has been raised, but as Légasse demonstrates (*NovT* 5 [1962] 5–9), the language is so solidly Lukan that this must be considered unlikely (secondarily Légasse suggests that, because much of the Lukan language here is used elsewhere in connection with Luke's teaching on the problems of riches, a reorientation in this direction is to be seen here as well; this seems less likely). Luke has moved the image from that of a physically strong householder to that of a well-armed lord of a castle, and the primary action from that of binding up the householder to that of his defeat at the hands of a more powerful figure. He has transformed what was little more than a modestly developed comparison into a full-blown similitude. It is to this kind of creativity that those who would give Luke the major role in the production of the distinctive Lukan parables can with good reason point. The picture in this verse is of a petty ruler, well armed and concerned to maintain the security of his estate. Since in his local context he is a powerful figure, his possessions are quite secure under his vigilant eye. The tranquility of this scene is disturbed, however, by the newcomer introduced in the following verse.

22 A well-armed and powerful man may adequately secure his goods *only* until a more powerful figure comes along. Then he can be defeated and stripped of his protective armor, and his precious goods become the spoils of victory for his adversary. Only at the very end, with the distribution of the booty, does the role of retainers in this whole episode become explicit (an allusion to Isa 53:12 LXX: *τῶν ἰσχυρῶν μεριεῖ σκῦλα*, "he will divide the spoil of the strong [pl.]," is possible here, but not likely).

It is usual to see Satan figured in the strong man, and Jesus in the one who is yet stronger. Meynet (*RB* 90 [1983] 334–50) has offered a structural argument for taking the strong man as a figure for the individual (in the larger setting confronted by Jesus and Satan) and the stronger man as Satan (according to Meynet, vv 21–22 are paralleled by 24–26, and both are oriented to the centerpiece, v 23; this is part of a larger symmetrical structuring of the chapter around vv 27–28). The view involves a forced reading of v 23 ("scatters" turns in effect into "is scattered") and is, more generally, an example of the danger of allowing an attractive structure to overrule careful attention to textual particularity. Wall (*NTS* 33 [1987] 147; following Danker, 94) also sees vv 21–22, v 23, and vv 24–26 as a set of linked units, but for him the struggle is between Israel and Satan, and the set of units condemns the Jews for their false sense of security before God. This view makes good sense of vv 24–26, but it fails to do justice to the way that the conflict imagery of vv 21–22 links back to vv 15–20 rather than on to vv 24–26 where no similar conflict is in view. It may be, however, that we should apply the figure in vv 21–22 to the activity of God (in Jesus) rather than directly to the activity of Jesus (cf. Percy, *Botschaft Jesu*, 181–87). This does best justice to "the finger of God" and the "kingdom of God" of v 20. It does, however, make the link to v 23a a little more indirect. On the triumph over Satan, see further at 10:17–20.

23 Luke's text is identical here to its Matthean counterpart. Two images are juxtaposed. The first is that of taking sides in a military conflict (cf. Josh 5:13: "Are you for us or for our adversaries?"): he who does not side with Jesus, and thus with the triumph of the kingdom of God, is reckoned to be aligned with the forces of Satan. The second image is that of gathering the flock of Israel (cf. Ezek 34, esp. vv 13, 21). Jesus is engaged in the eschatological gathering of the flock of Israel. In joining him, one becomes part of that gathering process (cf. esp. 5:1–11; 9:1–6; 10:1–16). In failing to do so, one contributes yet further to the tragic scattering that has been the historical experience of Israel. As a detached saying it has been drawn into its present setting by the appropriateness of the former image; the latter fits less well in the present context, except in the more general sense that the coming of the kingdom of God must necessarily involve the gathering of the flock of Israel (cf. also the connection in 10:17–20 between the triumph over Satan and the role of the dispatched disciples).

Explanation

In this new section of 11:14–54, Jesus is involved in increasing conflict with those who are not ready to recognize the presence of God in his ministry and who refuse to contemplate the personal change that is called for by this new work of God.

An interchange between Jesus and the crowds is set in motion by an exorcism. A demon-possessed man who is mute is exorcised, and, freed of the demon who caused his problem, he breaks into speech (on exorcism, see at 4:31–37). General amazement in the crowds marks the impressiveness of such a deed. No one doubts the impressiveness of the deed, but it is still quite possible to harbor doubts about the one who has done it.

Some accuse Jesus of being empowered by none other than Beelzeboul (originally the name of a Caananite god [the name means "Baal, the prince" or "Baal of the Exalted Abode"], it came, after these gods were identified with the demons, to be used for the prince of the demons, Satan himself). Though by the end of the section we begin to get the impression that there is a certain willfulness about this view, it is not on the surface of things an impossible suggestion. Jewish thought was well aware of the possibility of Satanic deception (see Deut 13:1–3; Matt 24:24; 2 Thess 2:9; Rev 13:13–14; 2 Cor 11:14); Jesus might be no more than an agent of the Evil One's deceitful miracles.

While some accused, others wanted a test to be run. They asked for a sign from heaven. This will have its response when we come to vv 29–32. Deut 13:1–2 reflects the assumption that a prophet or a particular message that he brings (see 2 Kgs 20:8–11) might be validated by means of a miraculous sign. Again, on the surface of things the demand for a sign seems quite reasonable. But there is finally something quite ironical about such a request sitting side by side with an exorcism: a sign, as a display of power is likely to be morally neutral (or ambiguous, as is reflected in Deut 13:1–5), but an exorcism is quite manifestly an act against the interests of the forces of evil. An exorcism is not what they want, but in the end it speaks more powerfully for Jesus than could the sign they ask for!

Jesus responds not to the second suggestion, but to the first. The view involved has been expressed discreetly to neighbors in the crowd, but Jesus is aware, nevertheless, of what is being said about him. The thrust of his response is "How can the ruler of a kingdom possibly benefit by fomenting a civil war?" Divided kingdoms get desolated and divided houses collapse; how can the kingdom of Satan fare better if he is attacking his own demons? Is it, then, really reasonable to suggest that Jesus exorcises by the power of Beelzeboul?

Jesus has a second point to make. He is not the only Jewish exorcist, and the services of other exorcists are valued in the community. Are we to suspect them also of collusion with the devil? Surely to do so would be an uncalled for piece of moral inconsistency. What would they think of this kind of judgment upon Jesus?

Thus far apologetics! Now Jesus makes his own claim. The reference to the "finger of God" (from Exod 8:19) suggests that what Jesus does is akin to what Moses did when the plagues in Egypt cleared the way for deliverance of God's People from their national slavery. Here is a similar manifestation of the presence and power of God, but there is something much more. That God should establish his rule upon the earth at the end of human history was part of the hope of pious Judaism. That hope took different forms, but there was a shared expectation that God would radically reshape the whole of the fabric of human affairs as he intervened in grace and judgment. Jesus is claiming that his exorcizing activity is nothing less than an aspect of the arrival of this hoped for kingdom of God. The hope of the future has now become present.

This is certainly a paradoxical kind of statement and clearly involves the language of metaphor. As one writer has pointed out, there should be no more need for exorcisms if the kingdom of God has in fact arrived (or at least if it has fully arrived). But

Jesus definitely desires to claim that the same power and reality that will be known in all its fullness in the arrival of the kingdom of God at the end of human history has already made its presence felt and been brought to bear on the human condition in the ministry that Jesus himself is exercising. This is a huge claim and one that is difficult to analyze precisely, but it is an important part of the NT witness to Jesus.

The coming of the kingdom of God surely means the despoiling of the kingdom of Satan, and, to this, Jesus now turns in a brief parable. Here the presence of the mighty power of God with Jesus in his exorcisms is imaged in the vanquishing of a powerful man despite all his military precautions, when one yet more powerful comes on the scene. See more on the triumph over Satan at 10:17–20.

The unit ends with a final challenge from Jesus that involves two images. The first is that of taking sides in a military conflict (cf. Josh 5:13: "Are you for us or for our adversaries?"). There is no middle ground for those who will not throw in their lot with Jesus. The second image is based on Ezek 34 (esp. vv 13, 21). In the end-time of salvation, God will gather the scattered flock of Israel. The challenge is to join Jesus in this task of gathering. One who does not is thereby one who scatters Israel, as her unfaithful leaders had done.

The False Hope of a Temporary Benefit (11:24–26)

Bibliography

Fridrichsen, A. "Nachträge." *ConNT* 2 (1936) 44–45. **Jeremias, J.** *Parables.* 197–98. **Laufen, R.** *Die Doppelüberlieferung.* 126–55, 427–55. **Nyberg, H. S.** "Zum grammatischen Verständnis von Matth. 12, 44f." *ConNT* 2 (1936) 22–35; abbreviated reprint 13 (1949) 1–11. **Plummer, A.** "The Parable of the Demon's Return." *ExpTim* 3 (1891–92) 349–51.

And see at 11:14–23.

Translation

[24] *"When*[a] *the unclean spirit departs from a*[b] *person, he travels through waterless places seeking a resting place, and, if he does not find [one],* [c]*he says, 'I will return to my house from which I departed.'* [25] *When he comes he finds [it]* [d]*swept and decorated.* [26] *Then he goes and takes along other spirits more evil than himself—seven [of them]—and they go in and take up residence there. The last state of that person has become worse than the first!"*

Notes

[a] A linking δέ, "and/but," is read here by P[45,75] D W f^1 etc.
[b] There is a generic definite article here in the Gr.
[c] τότε, "then," is found here in P[75] ℵ[2] B L Θ Ψ etc.
[d] Influenced by Matthew, ℵ[2] B C L Ξ Ψ etc. add here σχολάζοντα, "unoccupied."

Form/Structure/Setting

Vv 24–26 are really a continuation of the thought development in vv 14–23 and have only been separated here for convenience (on the structuring of the section, 11:14–54, see at 11:14–23 above). Vv 24–26 provide a negative counterpart to vv 21–22.

Again, as in vv 14–23, Luke makes use here of the second source shared with Matthew. In the Matthean order, however, this unit is preceded by the unit on the desire for a sign, which Luke will take up in vv 29–32. It is more likely to be Matthew who has changed the order here, and added the final clause to 12:45 (based on v 39) in order to allow the parable to stand quite independently.

The parable is finally too enigmatic for it to be easily attributed to the developing church. It is surely a parable of Jesus concerned to lay bare the phenomenon of false hopes. We no longer know, however, what kind of use the historical Jesus would have made of such an exposure, or how closely tied the concern of the parable would have been to the actual phenomenon of demon possession.

The story is told entirely in terms of the intentions and movements of the demon. However, the underlying concern of the parable with the state of the man becomes explicit in v 26b and is allowed to surface indirectly already in v 25. At this underlying level the movement of the story is from possession to an unanticipated release that is gladly exploited, only to be turned to disaster with the return of the bondage of possession in an even more severe form.

Comment

Where the ministry of Jesus brings solid achievement, the temporary windfalls of life can only engender a false hope that may soon be dashed.

24 Luke's wording differs from Matthew's only in the absence of a δέ, "and/but," to link with the previous materials; the use of a participial construction (in place of Matthew's coordinated principal clause) for the failure to find a suitable alternative abode; the absence of Matthew's linking "then," τότε; and a change in word order that emphasizes the returning rather than the house to which the spirit returns. The participle will be Luke's, but the other differences are more likely to be attributable to Matthew.

Luke also calls demons unclean spirits in 4:36; 6:18; 8:29; 9:42 (always following a source). It is best not to read "departs" (ἐξέλθῃ) as a hidden passive (so: "is [made to] depart"; as Jeremias, *Parables*, 197, and most scholars; in favor of this suggestion, may be cited, as a partial parallel, the use of the verb in v 14). The image here forms a contrast to the conquest imagery of vv 21–22: here the spirit is on a freely chosen journey of exploration. No good parallel has been cited for the journeying in waterless places, but the imagery is probably based on the idea that the demons will move naturally in realms where conditions are antithetical to human well-being, and devoid of the blessing of God (2 Pet 2:17–20, which uses the imagery of "waterless springs" for apostate Christians, probably reflects the present parable; in Isa 44:3 water on the thirsty ground is an image for the presence and blessing of God). We are probably to understand that it is transient accommodation that the spirit fails to locate. It is not a forgone conclusion that the spirit will find no suitable place to rest on his journey, but the case we are invited to contemplate is the one in which he does not. As the spirit was free to leave, so the spirit is free to return (note the repetition here of the language of departure [not expulsion]).

25 It is likely that Matthew has added rather than Luke deleted the *σχολάζοντα*, "standing empty" (as first of three parallel participles), of the Matthean text. Otherwise the texts are identical. In Matthew, "nature abhors a vacuum" may indeed be the point, but for Luke the refurbished house is simply now a very attractive place in which to take up residence. The spirit has wandered about in the hope of doing better than his former residence. His bad fortune at having his journey of exploration cut short is now more than compensated for by the improvements made in his absence to his former dwelling.

26 The wording here is almost identical to the Matthean (Matthew adds "with itself" to "takes along"; the "seven" is located at the beginning of its phrase in Matthew and at the end of its phrase in Luke; Matthew has an additional concluding sentence ["So it will be with this evil generation as well."], which is likely to be his own attempt at application). The improved accommodations are now fit for a whole demonic community. So the returning demon provides himself with a whole set of demonic companions, each of whom outstrips the original dweller's capacity to inflict evil upon its host. The upshot of it all is that this demonized person has known a temporary improvement in his lot, which quickly gives way, however, to a situation disastrously worse than that from which he began. The temporary improvement only masks for a time that this person is totally at the mercy of the whim of the demon(s).

In light of our exploration of the detailed contours of the story itself, some of the common understandings of this parable must be rejected at once. The story has nothing to do with the threat of repossession after exorcism (so it is not a story about how the demonic world [the seven other demons], far from empowering an exorcism [as v 15], will rather be involved in helping the dispossessed demon to regain possession; nor is it about the ineffectiveness of Jewish exorcism when compared with that practiced by Jesus; nor is it about the need, after exorcism, to replace the dispossessed demon with loyalty to Jesus [v 23] or obedience to the word of God [v 28]; nor is it about the fate of the Jews who have despised the salvation brought to them by Jesus [pictured as exorcism of their demon]). The story is, rather, about the deceptiveness of apparent improvement in one's lot, so long as the "powerful man" (v 21) is still firmly in control (the main virtue of Meynet's structural study of 11:14–26 [*RB* 90 (1983) 334–50] is to recognize a parallelism between vv 21–22 and 24–26). In the present context, it is a warning against false hope, not firmly anchored in the present coming of the kingdom of God, by the finger of God, in the person and activity of Jesus himself (v 20). Probably demon possession and its remission are to be seen only as illustration of a much wider phenomenon of false hope engendered by a short-lived improvement in the circumstances of life. The ups and downs of life, and the false hopes they engender, are contrasted with the solid and lasting achievements of the ministry of Jesus himself.

Explanation

Where the ministry of Jesus brings solid achievement, the temporary windfalls of life can only engender a false hope, which may soon be dashed.

Jesus tells the story of a person who finds him or herself freed from a state of demonic possession. It is rather like having an undesirable tenant in some rental accommodation that one owns. A sitting tenant that one has not been able successfully to evict suddenly takes himself off. Lots of soap and water, paint and repairs go into making good the dilapidation caused by such a poor tenant. Soon it is a place worth living in again. But horror of horrors, back comes the bad penny and along with him seven of his cronies who, by comparison, make him seem not such a bad tenant at all. The stroke of good luck has turned into a disaster.

From the demon's side, the story is one of making a journey of exploration to hunt out a better lair. The only trouble is that it cannot find transient accommodation for the period of search. So back it goes, only to be delighted to discover the improvements made while it was away. The improved accommodations are now fit for a whole demonic community. So the returning demon fits itself out with a whole set of demonic companions, each of whom outstrips the original dweller's capacity to damage his landlord's property.

The story is one of hopes raised and then dashed. It is offered as a negative counterpart to that of vv 21–22. The coming of the kingdom of God in Jesus' ministry is permanent achievement, to be contrasted with the normal ups and downs of life and the false hopes these can engender.

Who Is Blessed? (11:27–28)

Bibliography

Black, M. "The Aramaic Liturgical Poetry of the Jews." *JTS* o.s. 50 (1949) 179–82. **Brown, R. E., et al.** *Mary in the New Testament.* Philadelphia/New York: Fortress/Paulist, 1978. 170–72. **Corbin, M.** "Garder la parole de Dieu: Essai sur Luc 11,28." In *Le déplacement de la théologie,* ed. J. Audinet et al. Le point théologique 21. Paris: Beauchesne, 1977. 109–18. **Dewailly, L.-M.** *Jésus-Christ, Parole de Dieu.* 2nd ed. Paris: Cerf, 1969. 141–45. **Jacquemin, P.-E.** "L'Accueil de la parole de Dieu LC 11,27–28." *AsSeign* 66 (1973) 10–19. **McNamara, M.** *The New Testament and the Palestinian Targum to the Pentateuch.* AnBib 27. Rome: Biblical Institute, 1966. 131–33. **Mussner, F.** "Lk 1, 48f.; 11, 27f. und die Anfänge der Marienverehrung in der Urkirche." *Catholica* 21 (1967) 287–94, esp. 291–94; reprinted *De primordiis cultus mariani: Acta congressus mariologici-mariani in Lusitania anno 1967 celebrati.* Rome: Academia mariana, 1970. 2:25–34. **Riedl, J.** "Selig, die das Wort Gottes hören und befolgen (Lc 11,28): Theologisch-biblische Adventsbesinnung." *BibLeb* 4 (1963) 252–60. **Scott, M. P.** "A Note on the Meaning and Translation of Luke 11,28." *ITQ* 41 (1974) 235–50. **Wahlberg, R. C.** "Jesus and the Uterus Image (Lc 11,27–28)." *ITQ* 41 (1974) 235–50. **Zimmermann, H.** "'Selig, die das Wort hören und es bewahren': Eine exegetische Studie zu Lk 11, 27f." *Catholica* 29 (1975) 114–19.

Translation

[27] *It happened that while he was saying these things,*[a] *a certain woman from the crowd raised [her] voice*[b] *and said to him, "Fortunate is the womb which carried you and the*

breasts which you sucked." [28]*He said, "Yes, but fortunate rather are those who hear the word of God and keep [it]."*

Notes

[a] P[75] lacks ταῦτα, "these things."
[b] "Voice" is oddly positioned in the Gr. A C W Θ Ψ etc. provide a more normal word order.

Form/Structure/Setting

This pericope is marked by the kind of contrast language that is pervasive in this section (11:14–54). After the intervening dialogue, this piece takes up the positive impression made upon the crowds in v 14 and makes a challenge akin to that of v 23.

Matthew has in the corresponding position (12:46–50) a version of Mark 3:31–35; par. Luke 8:19–21, which seems to have influenced Luke's introductory clause here (11:27a). It seems rather less likely that Matthew has displaced a version of Luke 11:27–28 with the Markan material, than that Luke, having used a Markan version at 8:19–21, displaces the corresponding material from his second source with 11:27–28. The high component of Lukan language, the evident Lukan motifs, and the traditional nature of the language of the macarism in v 27 make it quite possible that Luke has fashioned these verses himself. That said, the basic sentiment, with its focus on response to God rather than directly to Jesus himself, is thoroughly in accord with the historical Jesus.

The first macarism uttered by the women from the crowd provides the setting for Jesus' own macarism. The form is, thus, that of a pronouncement story.

Comment

Something very impressive is present in Jesus, but to be impressed is not enough. What counts is committed response to the message that Jesus brings.

27 Luke will have provided the wording of the introduction here: ἐγένετο δὲ ἐν τῷ λέγειν αὐτὸν ταῦτα, "it happened that while he was saying these things," but in substance it has a parallel in Matt 12:46a. Lukan as well will be the ἐπάρασα φωνήν idiom ("lifted up [her] voice"; cf. [17:13]; Acts 2:14; [4:24]; 14:11; 22:22). ἐκ τοῦ ὄχλου, "from the crowd," could be Lukan (cf. 12:13), to link with v 14, but need not be, as could τις γύνη, "a certain woman" (cf. 8:2; 10:38). The targums to Gen 49:25e have an almost identical wording to the beatitude here (see Black, *JTS* o.s. 50 [1949] 182; McNamara, *Palestinian Targum,* 131–33; see also *2 Apoc. Bar.* 54:10; *m. ʾAbot* 2:8; *Gen. Rab.* 98:20), which may suggest that the wording was already proverbial.

As have been many others (most recently v 14), this woman is impressed by Jesus and gives a maternally formulated expression to this. Her words fulfill 1:48 and follow in the train of 1:42 (and cf. v 45). As far as it goes, no fault is to be found with her declaration of the good fortune of Mary.

28 The use of μενοῦν (or μὲν οὖν; tr. above "yes, but . . . rather") is predominantly Lukan in the NT, so is likely to be Luke's touch here. "Hearing the word of God and keeping (φυλάσσοντες) [it]" clearly echoes the wording of 8:21

(see discussion there and cf. 6:47): "hearing the word of God and doing (ποιοῦντες) [it]." (These verbs are paired synonyms in the LXX of Deut 4:6; 28:13, 15; etc.) 8:21 was based on an original that had simply "do the will of God" (Mark 3:35), but a double form in the source is more likely here to balance the womb and the breasts of v 27. "Word of God" is, however, likely to be Lukan (on this phrase see at 5:1).

μενοῦν can introduce a contradiction, "no, rather"; an affirmation, "yes, indeed"; or a correction or modification. The third is represented in the translation above, since only this sense fits both the measure of contrast required by the wording here, as well as the earlier role of 1:42, 45, 48 (cf. Thrall, *Greek Particles*, 34–35; Moule, *Idiom Book*, 163–64). A somewhat similar sentiment is found in 10:23–24. The kind of *keeping* in view here is that involved in the keeping of the commandments (as in 18:21). In the Lukan perspective Mary is, no doubt, one of "those who hear the word of God and keep it" but, contrary to repeated claims, this fact attracts no special attention here. For the role of v 28 after v 27 we might compare that of v 23 after the claim of v 20 (and vv 21–22). Response is all important.

Explanation

Something very impressive is present in Jesus, but to be impressed is not enough. What counts is committed response to the message that Jesus brings.

"Oh to be the mother of such a great son!" This is roughly the sentiment expressed by the woman from the crowd, and as she reflects this maternal sentiment, unbeknown to herself, she fulfills in her words Mary's prediction in 1:48. Jesus has clearly made quite an impact on her, and as far as it goes her effusive expression cannot be faulted. But the point is finally not to be impressed but to be changed. So Jesus' declaration in response moves the focus away from his own stature and onto the challenge to obediently take up the message of God that Jesus himself brings.

No Sign but the "Sign" of Jonah (11:29–32)

Bibliography

Adam, A. K. M. "The Sign of Jonah: A Fish-Eye View." *Semeia* 51 (1990) 177–91. **Bacon, B. W.** "What Was the Sign of Jonah?" *BW* 20 (1902) 99–112. **Barnett, P. W.** "The Jewish Sign-Prophets—A.D. 40–70: Their Intentions and Origin." *NTS* 27 (1980–81) 679–97. **Bonsirven, J.** "Hora talmudica: A propos du logion sur le signe de Jonas." *RSR* 24 (1934) 450–55. **Bowen, C. R.** "Was John the Baptist the Sign of Jonah?" *AJT* 20 (1916) 414–21. **Bowman, J.** "Jonah and Jesus." *Abr-Nahrain* 25 (1987) 1–12. **Correns, D.** "Jona und Salomo." In *Wort in der Zeit: Neutestamentiche Studien.* FS K. H. Rengstorf, ed. W. Haubeck and M. Bachmann. Leiden: Brill, 1980. 86–94. **Edwards, R. A.** *The Sign of Jonah in the Theology of the Evangelists and Q.* SBT 2/18. Naperville, IL: Allenson, 1971. **Glombitza, O.** "Das Zeichen des Jona (Zum Verständnis von Matthäus 12.38–42)." *NTS* 8 (1962) 359–66. **Howton, J.** "The Sign of Jonah." *SJT* 15 (1962) 288–304. **Lührmann, D.** *Die Redaktion.* 34–43. **Merrill, E. H.** "The

Sign of Jonah." *JETS* 23 (1980) 23–30. **Michael, J. H.** "The Sign of John." *JTS* 21 (1919–20) 146–59. **Mora, V.** *Le signe de Jonas.* Lire la Bible 63. Paris: Cerf, 1983. **Moxon, C.** "*τὸ σημεῖον Ἰωνᾶ.*" *ExpTim* 22 (1911) 566–67. **Murray, G.** "The Sign of Jonah." *DR* 107 (1989) 224–25. **Mussner, F.** "Wege zum Selbstbewusstsein Jesu: Ein Versuch." *BZ* 12 (1968) 161–72, esp. 169–71. **Peifer, C. J.** "Jonah and Jesus: The Prophet as Sign." *BiTod* 21 (1983) 377–83. **Schmitt, G.** "Das Zeichen des Jona." *ZNW* 69 (1978) 123–29. **Schulz, S.** *Die Spruchquelle.* 250–57. **Seidelin, P.** "Das Jonaszeichen." *ST* 5 (1951) 119–31. **Standaert, B.** "Jezus en Jona." *Heiligung* 32 (1982) 21–31. **Thibaut, R.** "Le signe de Jonas." *NRT* 60 (1933) 532–36. **Tödt, H. E.** *The Son of Man in the Synoptic Tradition.* London: SCM, 1965. 52–54, 211–14. **Vögtle, A.** "Der Spruch von Jonaszeichen." In *Synoptischen Studien.* FS A. Wikenhauser, ed. J. Schmid and A. Vögtle. Munich: Zink, 1953. 230–77; reprinted *Das Evangelium.* 103–136. **Zeller, D.** "Entrückung zur Ankunft als Menschensohn (Lk 13, 34f.; 11, 29f.)." In *À cause de l'Évangile,* ed. F. Refoulé. 513–30.

Translation

29 *As the crowds were pressing closely about [him], he began to say, "This generation is an evil generation:*[a] *it seeks a sign. No sign shall be given to it, but only the 'sign' of Jonah.*[b] 30 *For*[c] *just as Jonah became a 'sign' to the Ninevites, so the Son of Man will also*[d] *be a 'sign' to this generation.* 31 *The Queen of the South will rise in the judgment*[e] *with the men*[f] *of this generation and will condemn them,*[g] *because she came from the ends of the earth to hear the wisdom of Solomon, and now, something greater than Solomon is here.* 32 *Ninevite men will rise in the judgment with this generation and condemn it, because they repented at the preaching of Jonah, and now, something greater than Jonah is here."*

Notes

[a] The second *γενεά*, "generation," is missing from C E G H W Δ etc.
[b] A C W Θ Ψ etc. have here Matthew's added *τοῦ προφήτου*, "the prophet."
[c] ℵ and a few other texts omit *γάρ*, "for."
[d] P^{45} Ψ etc. lack the *καί*, "also," here (as Matthew).
[e] *ἐν τῇ κρίσει*, "in the judgment," is missing from P^{45} D.
[f] *ἀνθρώπων*, "people," is read in the original hand of ℵ.
[g] $P^{45,75}$ 1424 etc. have *αὐτήν*, "it" (treating "generation" as the antecedent).

Form/Structure/Setting

Vv 29–32 take up the agenda set in v 16. To ask for a sign is to fail to recognize what is truly present—far more than was ever available to the queen of Sheba or to the men of Nineveh—and it is also to fail to make the response that such a presence calls for. In such a situation, the only "sign" on offer is the announcement of coming judgment.

Luke continues to use here the source that he shares with Matthew (12:38–42). Luke is likely to reflect the order of the shared source. Matthew has brought the present material back before his parallel to vv 24–26. Within the block, the source order of vv 31, 32 is the opposite to that of Matthew. In this case, it may be Luke who has reordered, since the original union of the materials in vv 31–32 with those of v(v) 29(–30) is more likely to have taken place with the reference to

Jonah at the beginning, and, as Fitzmyer (932) suggests, "Luke's change of word order would be in the interest of investing the preaching of Jonah with wisdom overtones."

There is every likelihood that vv 31–32 have a quite separate transmission history from vv 29–30. Whether vv 31 and 32 were ever separate is less certain. Matthew does not have an equivalent to v 30. Instead he has (in 12:40) the comparison between Jonah in the whale and the Son of Man in the "heart of the earth." There is just enough structural and vocabulary overlap to suggest that the one is a development from the other. Matthew's is almost certainly the development. In a post-resurrection situation, the similarity between Jonah in the whale and delivered and the death and resurrection experience of Jesus would quite naturally become the compelling point of comparison between the two figures. Luke's v 30 has been explained as a compositional link to join together v 29 and vv 31–32 (e.g., Lührmann, *Die Redaktion*, 41). This is not impossible, but since it does little more than lay out what is implicit in v 29 (see *Comment* below), it could as well be the original continuation of that verse.

Mark has a partial parallel to v 29 (8:11–12) which has had a slight influence on both the Matthean and the Lukan forms (Matthew has repeated this tradition at 16:1, 4, but in a wording that has been heavily influenced by his other source). The relationship between this source and the longer Matthew/Luke source in the tradition history has attracted much debate and a range of opinions. The Markan source has a bald denial of any prospect of a sign. Has this been expanded with the sign of Jonah reference to facilitate the addition of vv 31–32 (further helped with the creation of v 30)? This seems unlikely as there is no real basis for wanting to bring these materials together without an original sign-of-Jonah reference. Far more likely is an abbreviation in the materials used by Mark: the full tradition was in any case a denial of the sign requested.

Of the materials here, it is the basic content of Luke 11:29 that we can with the greatest confidence trace back to the historical Jesus. There is, however, a good coherence between the materials of vv 31–32 and those of 10:13–15 (see discussion of historicity there), a text that constitutes something of a middle term between 11:31–32 and 11:20. This suggests that also in vv 31–32 we are dealing with materials that may be traced to the historical Jesus.

Comment

Whereas those who hear the word of God from Jesus and obey it are the truly fortunate (vv 27–28), the evil generation that asks for a sign condemns itself in its failure to recognize in Jesus the presence of the kingdom of God. The only "sign" for it is the announcement of its coming judgment.

29 Luke has prepared for this pericope in v 16; now he provides a further link (cf. vv 14, 17) with his addition of the press of the crowds (the verb here [ἐπαθροιζομένων, lit. "gather upon"] is often translated as "increased," but "pressed upon" suits the Lukan context better [note the similar Lukan introduction in 12:1]; the simple form of the same verb occurs in 24:33). "He began to say" is also likely to be Lukan, since the separation of v 16 requires a fresh start here (12:1 has the same words). Luke needs as well to deal with the effects of this new start in the following two clauses, as he edits something like the Matthean form

(12:39; the "adulterous" there could be a Matthean intensification; a Markan influence [Mark 8:12] is probably visible in ἡ γενεὰ αὕτη, "this generation," and the simple form ζητεῖ for "seeks"). The final clause of the verse is as in Matthew, except for Matthew's "prophet," which will be his addition (absent in the Matt 16:4 parallel).

Problems with "this generation" have already surfaced in 7:31 and 9:41; its role may be traced through vv 30, 31, 32, further in the present main section in vv 50, 51, and then in 17:25 and 21:32. One can hardly be critical of the request for a sign (cf. at v 16); the difficulty must be the request in the context of Jesus' ministry before them. Such a ministry has its own inner self-authentication; a request for a sign is already a refusal to see what is going on before one's very eyes.

The request for a sign is refused, but there is an enigmatic qualification to this refusal: "except/but only (εἰ μή) the sign of Jonah." The first question here is that of whether there is a true exception ("no sign except . . .") or it is rather an alternative ("no sign, but only . . ."). The language can support either (the former sense is more frequent, but for the latter cf. 4:26, 27). A correct choice here will depend on the sense to be given to "sign" (for both the third occurrence here and that in v 30). Is the "sign of Jonah" a sign at all in the sense of the request for a sign? In turn our answer to this question may possibly be different for the source than for the finished Lukan text. Jonah as a "sign to the Ninevites" in v 30 is not a sign at all in the sense of the request for signs, but in "sign of Jonah," standing alone, there could be such a sign. In "the sign of Jonah" (τὸ σημεῖον Ἰωνᾶ) the sign is not a sign used by Jonah (neither the OT or early Jewish tradition seems to know of any such sign; *Lives of the Prophets* 10:10 speaks exceptionally of Jonah giving a τέρας, "portent/omen/wonder," but this turns out to be a portent that he prophesies will herald the destruction of Jerusalem [Schmitt, *ZNW* 69 [1978] 123–29, thinks this tradition is appealed to in our text; this is not impossible, but the link is very slender]); it could be a sign to Jonah (it is just possible that it has been taken this way in the Matthean development in 12:40), but this would work best if the sign to this generation could be an experience for them (and not for Jesus), analogous to Jonah's experience with the whale; a further possibility is "the Jonah-sign," where "Jonah" has become adjectival, but this would seem to need an established usage of "sign" language in connection with Jonah's experience, and no evidence for this is forthcoming. (Earlier in the century even John the Baptist came up for consideration as possibly being the sign of Jonah [Bacon, *BW* 20 (1902) 99–112; Moxon, *ExpTim* 22 (1911) 566–57; Michael, *JTS* 21 (1919–20) 146–59; and cf. Bowen, *AJT* 20 (1916) 414–21].) This leaves as our best choice Jonah as himself the sign (as in v 30.) So, by analogy Jesus is speaking of himself as a sign, rather than of a sign that he gives. This now gives us the confidence to conclude that "sign" is being used here, with a touch of irony, in a sense deliberately different to that in the request for signs. Our grammatical choice, then, is for an alternative rather than for an exception. And if our line of reasoning has been sound, our conclusions hold true as much for v 29 taken alone as they do when we take the verse in its Lukan setting.

Jesus is, or will be, a sign as Jonah had been a sign, but how is this, and who is Jonah a sign to? (*i*) Jonah could be a sign to the Israelites of God's compassion for Gentiles (this is the view championed by Mora, *Signe*). (*ii*) For a naive reading of Jonah, the prophet could be a sign to Ninevah precisely because the Ninevites are assumed to have access to the experience of Jonah with the whale (just as the reader is "present" for both the whale experience and for the preaching in Nineveh [this possibility is favored by Zeller, "Entrückung," 522; Seidelin, *ST* 5 (1951) 121–22]). (*iii*) The prophet is often referred to in discussions as a preacher of repentance, but he is more accurately to be seen as a preacher of judgment; the shock of the prospect of the judgment about which he spoke led to repentance, but was not particularly intended to (see Jonah 3:4, 10; 4:1). Is Jonah a sign in his preaching of judgment? The first view has a general fit with Luke's universalism, but it is really the book and not the man that might function as such a sign, and even then the language is far from being given an obvious sense. The second view has more to commend it, but it is in the end based on a muddled reading of the book of Jonah. The third view is finally the most satisfactory (cf. for example, 10:13–15), and seems to have been the reading of the text adopted by Luke and by his tradition (from v 30).

30 Luke has no equivalent to Matthew's v 40, nor has Matthew an equivalent to Luke's verse here (except that each verse speaks both of Jonah and the Son of Man; see above for the view that it is Luke who follows the shared source here).

The present verse explains the enigmatic exception of v 29. The questions here concern, as interrelated issues, the use of "Son of Man" language and the future tense for his activity. The future tense has been taken by some as simply a logical future, which would allow the Son of Man to be already a sign to the present generation. The alternative is to understand the verb as a true future. As a true future, it has been applied variously to the coming of the Son of Man in judgment at the Parousia (e.g., Vögtle, "Jonaszeichen," 252, 269); to the overcoming of death in resurrection (along the lines of Matt 12:40; Zeller ["Entrückung," 524–25] offers a variant that combines features of these first two approaches with his claim, on the basis of somewhat tortuous appeal to traditions in *Jub.* 4:23–24; *Midr. Ps.* 26.7[110b], that in view is Jesus' translation to heaven in order to have a role in the future judgment); or even simply to the remainder of Jesus' ministry as a preacher of repentance, yet to come. None of these views is fully satisfactory. The resurrection view is no more likely here than it was found to be for v 29. A background of a Jewish apocalyptic judge understanding of "Son of Man," which has been found to be wanting in the excursus on the Son of Man (see after 9:21–22), has had a controlling influence here on those views that focus on the role of the Son of Man in the future judgment. The last view listed offers no reason for seeing the remainder of Jesus' ministry as having a different role than the earlier part had. It seems best not to return to the logical future view, in connection with which there must always be the nagging suspicion that this would have been rendered by a present here rather than the future, so where do we go from here? There is one way of taking the verb as a true future and yet relating it to the ministry of Jesus as in process. The use of ἐγένετο, "became," in the Jonah clause allows for the possibility that the future verb should be related to Jesus' ministry seen as a whole, and to that degree as (partially) future. If that does not satisfy, then we could allow something of the negative tone of the context to guide us to yet another suggestion. In the discussion of v 29 we saw that Jonah was a preacher of judgment, not of repentance. Do we have a future tense here precisely because it is the response of this evil generation to Jesus' announcement of the kingdom of God that obliges him to become in turn at this point a preacher of judgment (cf. 10:13–15)? (In the Lukan text and the source that stands behind it, the narrative goes on to announce precisely at this point the future judgment of this generation.) In either case we are concerned with the present activity of Jesus, and the use of "Son of Man" here is to be seen in connection with the line of uses, beginning in 6:5 (see there), on the lips of Jesus in connection with his role as a figure of authority and dignity.

31 Except that Matthew has the Jonah material before the Solomon material here, the two texts agree closely (Luke has probably added "the men of" to the source here, with the consequent "them" for "it" [he destroys the parallel with v 32, but may have in mind the creation of a parallel to the "men" of that verse]).

The visit of the "Queen of the South" is that of the queen of Sheba (1 Kgs 10:1–29; 2 Chr 9:1–12). Sheba was a kingdom of Semitic people in southwest Arabia, not far from Teima (Fitzmyer, 936). "Ends of the earth" is hyperbolic, and reflects biblical idiom (cf. Pss 2:8; 22:28; 59:14; etc.). The use of the term *ἄνδρων*, "men," rather than *ἄνθρωπων*, "people/human beings," is a linguistic reflection of the male domination of public life in the ancient world (elsewhere Luke is actually often at pains to present women on an equal footing with men, and even here it is the queen of Sheba who has the place of honor). The language is not intended in practice to exclude women. For a discussion of the eschatological judgment anticipated here, see at 10:13–15, which is clearly a kindred statement. There, the people of Tyre and Sidon continued in their wickedness, but they did not have the present generation's privileged situation; they will be better off in the judgment. Here the queen of Sheba responded to what God had to offer (and she came a long way for it), though what was offered does not compare to what he has now offered (and is brought right to the present generation); on this basis she will be their accuser in the judgment. The family likeness with 10:13–15 is even closer for v 32. A line is probably to be drawn from "the wisdom of Solomon" here to the operation of wisdom in the ministry of Jesus (cf. at 7:35; 11:49).

32 Matthew and Luke are identical here. The Lukan order allows the whole pericope to be a comparison with Jonah (with a comparison with Solomon embedded in it for the sake of the wisdom note thereby injected). Repentance is an even more appropriate response to the ministry of Jesus than it was to the preaching of Jonah (cf. 5:32; 10:13; etc.). There may be a deliberate balance intended between the negative judgment-preaching of Jonah and the positive availability of wisdom with Solomon.

Explanation

The request for a sign (v 16) has been a response to Jesus' exorcising activity through which he manifests the presence of the kingdom of God (v 20). The request separates the evil generation from the fortunate ones who hear the word of God from Jesus and obey it (vv 27–28). The only "sign" for this evil generation is the announcement of its coming judgment.

The "evil" of "this generation" is known precisely from its request for a sign (the problems of "this generation" first surface at 7:31). Such a ministry as that of Jesus has its own inner self-authentication, and so a request for a sign is already a refusal to see what is going on before one's very eyes. The sign requested is refused. All there is for these people is a sign in a very different sense. Jonah had announced the coming judgment of Nineveh; Jesus will announce the coming judgment of this generation. Jesus' presence and ministry, though it is concerned with salvation, will be for them a sign of coming judgment.

V 30 spells out the enigmatic formulation of this in v 29. The term "Son of Man" here is used in connection with Jesus' role as a figure of authority and dignity, as in a series of texts beginning with 6:5. It is either Jesus in his ministry taken as a whole, which will be this sign of judgment, or it will be Jesus in that aspect of his ministry provoked by the negative response of "this generation" (that is in his announcement of coming judgment, as in vv 31–32).

The queen of Sheba responded to what God had to offer (and she came a long way for it), though what was offered does not compare to what he has now offered (and is right where "this evil generation" is); on this basis she will, in the judgment, be the accuser of those who now ask for a sign. The activity of wisdom in Jesus has already been identified in 7:35. A similar comparison is made in v 32 by returning to the comparison with Jonah. The people of Nineveh repented at the preaching of this prophet of judgment, with all his limitations; this evil generation asks for a sign, though, now in the ministry of Jesus, the kingdom of God has come upon them. Repentance is a much more appropriate response to the ministry of Jesus than ever it was to the preaching of Jonah (cf. 5:32; 10:13; etc.).

Making Good Use of the Lamps (11:33–36)

Bibliography

Allison, D. C., Jr. "The Eye Is the Lamp of the Body (Matthew 6.22–23 = Luke 11.34–36)." *NTS* 33 (1987) 61–83. **Benoit, P.** "L'Oeil, lampe de corps." *RB* 60 (1953) 603–5. **Betz, H. D.** "Matthew vi.22f. and Ancient Greek Theories of Vision." In *Text and Interpretation: Studies in the New Testament.* FS M. Black, ed. E. Best and R. McL. Wilson. Cambridge: University Press, 1979. 43–56. **Brandt, W.** "Der Spruch vom lumen internum." *ZNW* 14 (1913) 97–116, 177–201. **Cadbury, H. J.** "The Single Eye." *HTR* 47 (1954) 69–74. **Cadoux, C. J.** "The Evil Eye." *ExpTim* 53 (1942) 354–55. **Delebecque, É.** *Études grecques.* 85–88. **Derrett, J. D. M.** "The Light under a Bushel: The Hanukkah Lamp?" *ExpTim* 78 (1966) 18. **Dupont, J.** "La lampe sur le lampadaire dans l'évangile de saint Luc (Lc 8,16; 11,33)." In *Études.* 2:1032–48. ———. "La transmission des paroles de Jésus sur la lampe et la mesure dans Marc 4,21–25 et dans la tradition Q." In *Logia,* ed. J. Delobel. 201–36; reprinted *Études.* 1:259–94. **Edlund, C.** *Das Auge der Einfalt: Eine Untersuchung zu Matth. 6,22–23 und Luk. 11,34–35.* ASNU 19. Copenhagen/Lund: Munksgaard/Gleerup, 1952. **Garrett, S. R.** "'Lest the Light in You Be Darkness'": Luke 11:33–36 and the Question of Commitment." *JBL* 110 (1991) 93–105. **Hahn, F.** "Die Worte vom Licht: Lk 11,33–36." In *Orientierung an Jesus,* ed. P. Hoffmann et al. 107–38. **Jülicher, A.** *Die Gleichnisreden Jesu.* 2:79–88, 98–108. **Percy, J. D.** "'An Evil Eye.'" *ExpTim* 54 (1942) 26–27. **Philonenko, M.** "La parabole sur la lampe (Luc 11:33–36) et les horoscopes qoumrâniens." *ZNW* 79 (1988) 145–51. **Ryder Smith, C.** "'An Evil Eye' (Mark vii. 22)." *ExpTim* 53 (1942) 181–82. ———. "The Evil Eye." *ExpTim* 54 (1942) 26. **Schulz, S.** *Spruchquelle.* 468–70, 474–76. **Schwenke, F.** "Das Auge ist der Leibes Licht (Mt. 6,22f., Lk. 11,33–36)." *ZWT* 55 (1913) 251–60. **Sjöberg, E.** "Das Licht in dir:

Zur Deutung von Matth. 6,22f Par." *ST* 5 (1951) 98–105. **Thienemann, T.** "A Comment on Interpretation by Prof. Cadbury." *Gordon Review* 1 (1955) 10–22.

And see at 8:16–18.

Translation

[33] *"No one lights a lamp and then puts it in a crypt,*[a] *but rather on the lampstand, so that those who would come in may see the light.*[b] [34] *Your*[c] *eye is the lamp of the body. When your eye is clear, then your whole body is*[d] *illuminated; when it is diseased, then your body [is]*[e] *darkened.* [35] *Take note then, whether the 'light' which is in you is darkness.* [36] *If, then, your whole body is illuminated, without any part*[f] *darkened, then it will be an illuminated whole, as [it will be] when the lamp [is allowed to] illuminate you with [its] shining."*

Notes

[a] Most texts add here *οὐδὲ ὑπὸ τὸν μόδιον*, "or under the peck measure," but this phrase is missing from P[45,75] L Γ Ξ 0124 *f* [1] 700 etc., and probably represents an early influence from Matt 5:15.

[b] *φέγγος*, "radiance," for *φῶς*, "light," is read here by P[45] A K L W Γ Δ Ψ etc. and may be original (*φῶς* is the reading at 8:16).

[c] *σου*, "your," is missing here in א[2] L Θ Ψ *f* [1] etc. It may have come in from its use with the next occurrence of "eye."

[d] A future tense is read here by P[45] K L *f* [1] etc.

[e] A future tense is supplied here by P[45] K Θ *f* [13] etc.

[f] P[45] has *μέλος*, "limb, member."

Form/Structure/Setting

The materials here are bound together by means of a series of catchwords and repeated phrases. In the context they serve to apply the image of the lamp to what is present in the ministry of Jesus (cf. vv 20, 31, 32) and to identify as willful blindness the failure to perceive it correctly and be appropriately transformed by it.

For v 33, Luke had two sources (cf. Mark 4:21; Matt 5:15), but has been influenced here more by his own reworking of the parallel to Mark 4:21 in 8:16 than by the wording of either of them (on v 33 see further at 8:16–18). Vv 34–35 are paralleled in Matt 6:22–23. It is probably Luke who is responsible for bringing this material together with v 33, since only he effectively unifies them, with his provision of v 36. The alternative is to say that they were together, but only by reason of catchword association (the order and proximity of the Matthean uses stand slightly in favor of this alternative). V 36 is a Lukan creation (see below).

There is no good reason for denying to the historical Jesus some original form of both of these brief similitudes. The first may have been applied originally to risks taken by Jesus in continuing the exercise of a public ministry in the face of growing opposition. The second can have had no significantly different sense than it currently does.

In the Lukan text, the first similitude makes the point that the lamp is displayed to assist people in finding their way. But in the second similitude it becomes evident that the body has its own lamp, the eye: the human interior will be illuminated or not on the basis of the health or diseased state of the eye. V 35 invites the hearer to check whether any light is getting in. V 36 draws the two similitudes into one composite image: an illuminated whole results from the exterior light shining (thanks to the intermediary role of the body's well-functioning lamp, the eye) with full intensity into every part of the body.

Comment

For those who have eyes to see it, the lamp is set upon its stand and shining forth. People bear personal responsibility if they will not allow the entry of the light with its capacity to illuminate the whole of their lives.

33 For Luke's sources here see at 8:16–18. The *εἰς κρύπτην* (lit. "into a hidden place"; used of cellars, crypts, and vaults, and perhaps here of some kind of wall recess; cf. Fitzmyer, 940: "crevice") is distinctive here. It is probably nothing more than a Lukan ornamental variation of a detail of the imagery from the wording he used in 8:16 (which is largely repeated here). In 8:16 the lamp that has been lit is the one who has heard the word of God from Jesus and responded to it. The verse contains a mission challenge. Here, however, the sequence from vv 29–32 and the sequel in vv 34–36 make it clear that the light shines out from Jesus' own ministry, which is no hidden phenomenon, but is available to cast its light upon those who wish to find their way inside (the imagery is explored more fully at 8:16). This second application is more likely to reflect the original use of this mini-parable. Light imagery has been used in connection with Jesus already by Luke in 2:32 and cf. 1:78–79.

34 Luke has made a number of minor stylistic changes to his source here (see Matt 6:22), the most obvious of which are the preference for *ὅταν . . . ἐπάν*, "when . . . when," over Matthew's *ἐάν . . . ἐάν*, "if . . . if"; the addition of some transitional uses of *καί* (here, "then"); a present tense for Matthew's logical future (note the present tense of Matt 6:23, and conversely Luke's use of this future in v 36); and the trimming away of words Luke judged to be repetitive (only the loss of *ὅλον*, "whole," from the darkening of the body might affect the meaning: partial sight is a possibility in the Lukan text).

There are two layers of metaphor here: the eye is spoken of as a lamp, but is in its turn a relatively transparent metaphor for moral and spiritual readiness to see. (It is difficult to see how Dupont ["La transmission," 229] can say, "Taken together, these four verses [vv 33–36, separated off from their Lukan context] reveal no other preoccupation than that of an ethical instruction on the good example that the believer is called to give to those around him.") The lamp metaphor may be more readily appreciated in the context of ancient Greek views of sight as involving a flow of light out from the eye to mingle with the light of the object under scrutiny, and thence to return via the eye into the body of the beholder (see Plato, *Timaeus,* 45B–46A and the summary in Delebecque, *Études,* 86, of material from C. Mugler, *Dictionnaire historique de la terminologie optique des Grecs* [Paris: Klincksieck, 1964]; Betz ["Matthew vi.22f," 43–56] appeals to this Greek view, but rather grandly finds in our text a critique of the entire approach of the Greek philosophical tradition; Allison [*NTS* 33 (1987) 61–71] has documented the range of Greek views; he confirms that the dominant Greek views agree in treating the eye as a light source, but he also demonstrates that ancient Jewish sources also assume that vision operates on the basis of light originating from the eye). The concern of the image is to demonstrate the power of the privileged part over the whole: it is a comprehensive disaster to the whole that the seeing organ should fail to do its job. Moral and spiritual illumination is not self-terminating, but rather casts its light over the whole of the living out of one's life. At this point there is no clear indication of the relationship between the lamp of v 33 and that of v 34.

ἁπλοῦς (tr. above "clear") is lit. "single." The word is used in moral contexts in connection with sincerity, wholeheartedness, guilelessness, and generosity, but is found in connection with eyes meaning "clear," "sound," or "healthy" (probably originally in connection with multiple vision). On the negative side, πονηρός (tr. above "diseased") is the normal word for "evil" or "wicked," but in connection with eyes the noun form is documented to mean "disease" (see BAGD, 690) and more generally the adverb is used in the idiom πονηρῶς ἔχειν where the sense is "to be ill." In the first instance the medical sense should be allowed for both words in the present text, but it is not impossible that the terms have been chosen with one eye also on their moral sense.

35 Matthew ends this brief similitude with a conditional statement rather than the challenge we find here, but eight of the ten words are in common. From Matthew's text one could think of an unfortunate, but irreversible, state of affairs (though in the context Matthew actually does not); in Luke there is rather a challenge to do something about it, if one discovers that the interior is dark rather than light. "The light . . . in you" is the light that shines from the eyes inwards into the body. With a diseased eye, where this light should be is only darkness.

36 Matthew has no equivalent to v 36. In its present form, its function is clearly to pull together the images that have been used in v 33 and vv 34–35. Hahn ("Die Worte," 114–17) has argued that Matt 6:23b and Luke 11:36 (without from "as" to the end of the verse) form together in antithetical parallelism the original conclusion of the similitude of the eye as a lamp. Over against this must be set the following: (*i*) the parallelism is not especially close; (*ii*) the ὅλος, "whole," deleted by Luke in v 34 is likely to be connected with the possibility of partial darkening found here (and this phrase has the only vocabulary of v 36 that is not simply repeated exactly from earlier in the similitude [the μέρος τι (lit. "a certain part") found here is used by Luke again at Acts 5:2]); and (*iii*) the shared εἰ οὖν, "if then," of the parallel parts is likely to be no more than Luke's re-use of the expression he has displaced from v 35. Lukan formulation seems altogether more likely. Only the final clause of v 36 provides a slight pause, because here the imagery of 33 is taken up again, but in a form that echoes the Matthean (original) form and not the Lukan redaction of the final clause. But Luke has shown himself capable of this kind of thing elsewhere (e.g., in 8:11–15, the explanation of the parable of the sower [see there]).

V 36 welds together the similitudes of v 33 and vv 34–35 by taking the beginning point from the first and the terminus from the second (the missing reference to the eye functions hiddenly as what mediates the light from the lamp to the interior of the body). The translation offered above is only one of many possibilities, since the formulation is cryptic and some of the phrasing units uncertain. To avoid any sense of tautology here, Hahn ["Die Worte," 130–32] finds an eschatological correlate to the present shining of the light in v 34, but this is artificial, makes no proper sense of the ὡς ὅταν, "as when," and makes altogether too much of the future tense of ἔσται,"will be." Sjöberg (*ST* 5 [1951] 98) is right to find in the light image of these verses what he calls "an ethical aspect" and "a salvation aspect."

Explanation

The presence of the kingdom of God in the ministry of Jesus is like a lamp shining out for all to see. But only sound eyesight allows the light to come from the lamp and illuminate every part of life.

The first little parable makes the point that the ministry of Jesus is no hidden and obscure thing. It shines out brightly for all who would find their way by means of its brightness. Juxtaposed is a second parable, which is a challenge about moral and spiritual eyesight. Its point is rather like that of the proverb, "There is none so blind as those who will not see." The metaphorical language here can be better appreciated if we realize that in the Greco-Roman world seeing was thought to involve a flow of a kind of light out from the eye to mingle with the light of the object under scrutiny, and thence to return via the eye into the body of the beholder. The imagery is used here to demonstrate the power of the privileged part over the whole: the whole of life is affected by the functioning, or not, of the eyes. V 35 challenges the hearers to examine whether their eyes are sending light into the body.

The words translated in v 34 as "clear" and "diseased" are also used as moral terms. The first means literally "single" and is used in connection with sincerity, wholeheartedness, guilelessness, and generosity. The second is the normal word for "evil" or "wicked." It is likely that the words have been deliberately chosen by the Greek translator so that these moral senses can provide some guidance for the application of the parable.

Each parable makes its own point, but the two are welded together in v 36. Starting from the situation of inner illumination produced by well-functioning eyes, the verse traces this inward shining light back to its ultimate source in the external lamp upon its stand. The light as it shines into a person's life brings both salvation and moral transformation.

Woes against Pharisees and Lawyers (11:37–54)

Bibliography

Beilner, W. *Christus und die Pharisäer.* 200–235. **Birch, V.** "The Petitionary Blood of the Prophets (Luke xi. 49–51)." *ExpTim* 30 (1918–19) 329–30. **Booth, R. P.** *Jesus and the Purity Laws: Tradition History and Legal History in Mark 7.* JSNTSup 13. Sheffield: JSOT, 1986. **Chapman, J.** "Zacharias, Slain between the Temple and the Altar." *JTS* 13 (1911–12) 398–410. **Christ, F.** *Jesus Sophia.* 120–35. **Correns, D.** "Die Verzehntung der Raute Luk XI 42 und M Schebi IX 1." *NovT* 6 (1963) 110–12. **Derrett, J. M. D.** "You Build the Tombs of the Prophets (Lk. 11,47–51, Mt. 23,29–31)." *SE* 4 [= TU 102] (1968) 187–93. **Ellis, E. E.** "Lk xi.49–51: An Oracle of a Christian Prophet?" *ExpTim* 74 (1962–63) 157–58. **Garland, D. E.** *The Intention of Matthew 23.* NovTSup 52. Leiden: Brill, 1979. **Haenchen, E.** "Mathäus 23."

In *Gott und Mensch: Gesammelte Aufsätze*. Tübingen: Mohr (Siebeck), 1965. 1:29–54. **Jeremias, J.** *Heiligengräber in Jesu Umwelt (Mt. 23,29; Lk. 11,47): Eine Untersuchung zur Volksreligion der Zeit Jesu*. Göttingen: Vandenhoeck & Ruprecht, 1958. ———. "Drei weitere spätjüdische Heilgengräber." *ZNW* 52 (1961) 95–101. **Klein, G.** "Die Verfolgung der Apostel, Luk 11,49." In *Neues Testament und Geschichte*. FS O. Cullmann, ed. H. Baltensweiler and B. Reicke. Zürich/Tübingen: Theologischer/Mohr, 1972. 113–24. **Kosch, D.** *Die eschatologische Tora des Menschensohnes: Untersuchungen zur Rezeption der Stellung Jesu zur Tora in Q*. Novum Testamentum et Orbis Antiquus 12. Fribourg/Göttingen: Universitätsverlag/Vandenhoeck & Ruprecht, 1989. 61–212. **Kühschelm, R.** *Jüngerverfolgung und Geschick Jesu*. 249–59. **Kümmel, W. G.** "Die Wehgerufe über die Schriftgelerten und Pharisäer." In *Antijüdisches im Neuen Testament*, ed. P. W. Eckert et al. Munich: Kaiser, 1967. 135–47. **Légasse, S.** "L'oracle contre 'cette génération' (Mt 23,34–36 par Lc 11,49–51) et la polémique judéo-chrétienne dans la Source des Logia." In *Logia*, ed. J. Delobel. 237–56. ———. "Scribes et disciples de Jésus." *RB* 68 (1961) 321–45, 481–506, esp. 323–33. **Maccoby, H.** "The Washing of Cups." *JSNT* 12 (1980) 3–15. **Marshall, I. H.** "How to Solve the Synoptic Problem: Luke 11:43 and Parallels." In *The New Testament Age*. FS B. Reicke, ed. W. C. Weinrich. Macon, GA: Mercer University, 1984. 2:313–25. **Miller, R. J.** "The Rejection of the Prophets in Q." *JBL* 107 (1988) 225–40. ———. "The Inside Is (Not) the Outside: Q 11:39–41 and GThom 89." *Forum* 5.1 (1989) 92–105. **Moxnes, H.** *The Economy of the Kingdom*. 109–26. **Nagel, W.** "Neuer Wein in alten Schläuchen (Mt 9, 17)." *VC* 14 (1960) 1–8, esp. 5–6. **Neusner, J.** "'First Cleanse the Inside': The 'Halakhic' Background of a Controversy Saying." *NTS* 22 (1975–76) 486–95. **Pernot, H.** "Matthieu, XXIII,29–36; Luc, XI,47–51." *RHPR* 13 (1933) 263–67. **Pesch, W.** *Der Lohngedanke inder Lehre Jesu verglichen mit der religiösen Lohnlehre des Spätjudentums*. MTS 1/7. Munich: Zink, 1955. 40–50. **Rice, G. E.** "Some Further Examples of Anti-Judaic Bias in the Western Text of the Gospel of Luke." *AUSS* 18 (1980) 149–56, esp. 152–54. **Sand, A.** *Das Gesetz und die Propheten: Untersuchungen zur Theologie des Evangeliums nach Matthäus*. BU 11. Regensburg: Pustet, 1974. 84–95. **Schulz, S.** *Spruchquelle*. 94–114, 336–45. **Schürmann, H.** "Die Redekomposition wider 'dieses Geschlecht' und seine Führung in der Redenquelle (vgl. Mt 23,1–39 par Lk 11,37–54): Bestand—Akoluthie—Kompositionsformen." *SNTU* 11 (1986) 33–81. **Schwarz, G.** "Unkenntliche Gräber? (Lukas xi. 44)." *NTS* 23 (1976–77) 345–46. **Seitz, O. J. F.** "The Commission of Prophets and 'Apostles': A Re-examination of Matthew 23,34 with Luke 11,49." *SE* 4 [= TU 102] (1968) 236–40. **Steck, O. H.** *Israel und die gewaltsame Geschick der Propheten*. WMANT 23. Neukirchen-Vluyn: Neukirchener, 1967. 26–33, 50–53, 282–83. **Steele, E. S.** "Luke 11:37–54: A Modified Hellenistic Symposium?" *JBL* 103 (1984) 379–94. **Vincent, H.** "Le tombeau des prophètes." *RB* 10 (1901) 72–88. **Wild, R. A.** "The Encounter between Pharisaic and Christian Judaism: Some Early Gospel Evidence." *NovT* 27 (1985) 105–24.

Translation

37 *When he had [finished] speaking, a* [a]*Pharisee asked him to dine with him. He went in and sat down.* 38 *The Pharisee, as he saw [it], marvelled that he did not get washed*[b] *first, before the meal.* 39 *The Lord said to him, "Now you Pharisees clean the outside of the cup and the platter; but the inside of you is full of rapacity and evil.* 40 *Fools! Did not he who made the outside make the inside*[c] *as well?* 41 *Rather, in connection with what is inside, you should give alms, and then*[d] *everything is*[e] *clean for you.*

42[f] *"Woe to you Pharisees! You tithe mint and rue*[g] *and every edible plant, and pass by justice and the love of God.*[h] *These, rather are what it is necessary to do (but not to leave the others undone*[i]*).* 43 *Woe to you Pharisees! You love the chief seat in the synagogues and to be greeted*[j] *in the marketplaces.*[k] 44 *Woe to you! You are like unseen tombs; the people who walk*[l] *over [them] do not realize [it]."*

[45] *A certain one of the lawyers responded and said to him, "In saying these things you insult us as well."* [46] *He said, "Woe to you lawyers as well! You load people up with loads which are difficult to carry, and you yourselves will not touch the loads with one of your* [m] *fingers.* [47] *Woe to you! You build the tombs of the prophets, and your fathers killed them.* [48] *You are, then, witnesses:*[n] *you give your approval to the deeds of your fathers. For they killed them and you do the building!*[o] [49] *Indeed, for this reason, the Wisdom of God said, 'I will send prophets and apostles to them, and some of them they will kill and persecute,* [50] *so that the blood of all the prophets poured out*[p] *since the foundation of the world may be required of this generation,* [51] *from the blood of Abel to the blood of Zechariah who perished between the altar and the sanctuary.'*[q] *Yes, I say to you, 'It will be required from this generation.'* [52] *Woe to you, lawyers! You have taken away the key of knowledge; you did not enter yourselves and have hindered those who [wanted to] enter."*

[53] *When he had gone out from there,*[r] *the scribes and the Pharisees began to oppose him violently*[s] *and to speak against him,* [54] *lying in ambush*[t] [u] *to catch at something from his mouth.*[v]

Notes

[a] τις, "a certain," is added here by A C (D) W Θ Ψ etc.

[b] "Get washed" renders the passive ἐβαπτίσθη. The middle form is read by P[45] 700 (so: "washed himself") and could possibly be original.

[c] The order of "outside" and "inside" is reversed in P[75] C D 700 a c e.

[d] ἰδού (lit. "behold").

[e] The future form is read here by P[45] (D) $f^{1,13}$ 200 etc.

[f] An opening ἀλλά (lit. "but") establishing a contrast is omitted in translation.

[g] Following Matthew, ἄνηθον, "dill," is read here by P[45] etc.

[h] "Of God" is missing from B.

[i] Many texts conform here to the Matthean reading. A variant on that is the ἀφεῖναι, "to be absent(?)" of P[75] ℵ etc. The whole clause here is missing from D it[d]. Omission could be explained in terms of the exaggeration introduced by Luke into the earlier part of the verse (see below). The final verb παρεῖναι (ἀφιέναι in Matthew) favors retention.

[j] Lit. "the greetings."

[k] P[45] appears to have the singular form here.

[l] The participle here does not have the definite article in P[75] A D W etc. So: "when/if they walk."

[m] P[75] omits "your."

[n] The Matthean μαρτυρεῖτε, "you bear witness," is found here in P[75] A C D W Θ Ψ etc.

[o] A mention of tombs here, using either μνημεῖα or τάφους (as in v 47 or the Matthean equivalent) is found in A C W Θ Ψ $f^{1,13}$ etc.

[p] P[45] ℵ A C D L W Θ Ψ etc. conform Luke's perfect participle here to the Matthean present participle.

[q] Lit. "house."

[r] As an alternative for this clause, A (D) W Θ Ψ etc. have λέγοντος δὲ αὐτοῦ ταῦτα πρὸς αὐτούς, "as he was saying these things to them."

[s] δεινῶς ἐνέχειν, lit. "have it in for terribly."

[t] Omitted by ℵ Θ Ψ etc.

[u] A C (D) W Ψ etc. add ζητοῦντες, "seeking," here.

[v] ἵνα κατηγορήσωσιν αὐτοῦ, "so that they might accuse him," (cf. Mark 3:2) is added here by A C (D) W Θ Ψ etc.

Form/Structure/Setting

The conflict and contrast of the section 11:14–54 now reaches a climax and conclusion in the present unit with its fierce denunciation of the Pharisees and the scribes and of their counter-hostility to him.

The Lukan material here has an extensive parallel in Matt 23, and the form of the original shared source has been much discussed. Though not equally convincing at every point, Schürmann's recent source analysis (*SNTU* 11 [1986] 33–81) has much to commend it. He argues for a source that has the Matthean order and consists of the materials found in Matt 23:2–4, 6b–7a, 12, 13, 15, 23, 25–26, 27, 29–31, 34–36, 37–39 and with some part of Luke 11:53–54. This source itself shows signs of having been put together of three more original units made up in turn of the verses listed above to v 13, then those from v 15 to v 27, and finally those from vv 29 to the end. The first unit was directed to scribes and the second to Pharisees, while the third had a broader audience. In the first two units there is a correspondence between the first and last elements, while in the third there is a thematic unity. Luke has drawn selectively on the source and partially modified its order of presentation.

Prior to the formation of these three identified clusters, the origins of the individual items of tradition must be individually assessed, since these are not original unities. There has been considerable scholarly reluctance to trace more than a small part of the materials here back to the historical Jesus. Scholars have been reluctant to attribute the phenomenon of criticism of the scribes and the Pharisees by class to Jesus, partly on the basis that it seems to contribute to an unfortunate caricature of first-century Pharisaism. The degree of instability in the Gospel traditions as to who is being criticized of a particular fault provides a measure of support for this reticence. Conflicts experienced in the ongoing life of the early church have clearly left their mark on such traditions as these. But perhaps the real problem is that what was originally formulated as address *to* a group of people has come to be taken as providing a description *of* a group of people. A passionate prophetic consciousness will catch attention and challenge in ways that involve the exaggeration of hyperbole and the imaginative presentation of what are only partial perspectives. The point is to challenge, not to analyze. It is clear from the tradition reflected in v 44 that the criticisms leveled were considered to be consistent with a lifestyle that led to a high level of public approbation. In the ongoing conflict between emerging church and Jewish leadership, Christians made use of these materials in a polemical context, not without some justification, but nevertheless with a real danger of distortion.

A meal setting in the home of a Pharisee is provided for the accusatory speech that Jesus makes here. Its opportunity is his host's surprise that he does not wash before eating. Jesus responds with the accusation that the Pharisees' preoccupation with outward ritual cleanness makes an unhappy contrast with their inner persons, where rapacity and evil hold sway. But God, creator of inner as much as of outer is not fooled. The path of recovery (since they, not Jesus, need to change) is said to be almsgiving—that is to be the expression of the life of the inner person.

Jesus proceeds to level three woes at the Pharisees as a class: tithing minutiae while neglecting justice and the love of God; loving public honor; being like unseen graves that contaminate unawares those who come within contact. A token lawyer sees his own kind as implicated in the accusations Jesus makes. Jesus confirms this suspicion by turning and leveling three woes at the lawyers as a class: burdening in an excessive manner those whom they instructed and then providing no support to the burdened; being the "grave-diggers" in a team exercise with their ancestors who killed the prophets; failing to enter the house of wisdom themselves and depriving others of the key. The second of these woes with its strange logic is supported by a development in vv 49–51. Jesus reports that Wisdom has announced that prophets and apostles will be sent to the present generation, who will kill and persecute them. This will demonstate the true solidarity of the generations and will justify the requiring at the hands of this generation of all the blood of the prophets, spilt over the generations and building up a cumulative burden of national guilt.

The unit (and the larger Lukan section here) concludes with Jesus' departure from the dinner party, having stirred up what will be an ongoing fierce opposition from the scribes and the Pharisees.

Comment

The Pharisees and the lawyers are blind to the light, precisely because their own lives are morally and religiously compromised and, as with their forebears, they do not want to hear the challenge of the messengers of God.

37 Luke introduces the material here with *ἐν δὲ τῷ λαλῆσαι*, "when he had [finished] speaking," to provide the link in the set of units he is using for the present section (the wording is a variant of that in v 26). The rest of the verse repeats the content (but in fairly different wording) of 7:36 and is generally considered to be entirely Lukan redaction. The only possible sign of pre-Lukan tradition is the use of the historic present tense (*ἐρωτᾷ*, "asks"), which Luke so studiously avoids in the Gospel (but not in Acts; cf. Fitzmyer, 107). Luke has probably deduced the meal setting from Mark 7:1–5 (it is more than likely that he makes use of Mark 7:2, 5 in v 38 to follow), on the basis that only by (one of their number) sharing a meal could the Pharisees become aware of the disciples' (and, therefore, Jesus') ritual cleanliness habits. Luke has Jesus dining with a Pharisee again at 14:1. On Pharisees see at 5:17.

38 The meal setting now makes possible the Pharisee's observation. It would appear that hands were rinsed and not immersed for ritual purification (Booth, *Purity*, 185). In using *ἐβαπίσθη* (lit. "was baptized" [P[75] 700 read the middle form *ἐβαπτίσατο*, "baptized himself," which could be original]), either (*i*) Luke is unclear at this point as to the exact practice and slightly mistakes Mark's sense in 7:2; or (*ii*) he uses the verb in a sense that could embrace washing without immersion (see sources at 3:3); or (*iii*) he is aware of the practice of a more strict Pharisaic group involving ritual immersion (cf. Booth, *Purity*, 200) and substitutes this as he moves from Mark's reference to the disciples' practice to a reference to the practice of their master; or (*iv*) he uses a different tradition here, which reflects a stricter kind of Pharisaic practice (as Booth, *Purity*, 23–25). Whichever is correct, the amazement of the Pharisee has to do with Jesus' failure to conform to the demands of Pharisaic piety. Presumptive impurity would in the Pharisaic view be a necessary correlate to Jesus' involvement with the crowds.

39 The opening clause is Lukan (on the use of "Lord" see at 7:13). Matthew's form here (23:25) begins with "woe to you" and is addressed to "scribes and Pharisees, hypocrites" (as is Matthew's whole series of woes). In the former respect it is likely to be more original, but not in the latter (cf. Schulz, *Spruchquelle*, 95–96; Schürmann ["Redekomposition," 58–64] offers an attractive case for seeing Matt 23:2–4, 6b–7a, 12, 13 as originally addressed to scribes, vv 15, 23, 25–26, 27 as originally addressed to Pharisees, and vv 29–39 as originally addressed to neither, but whether this was still the case in the form used by Luke is placed in question by Luke's allocation to Pharisees of the material of vv 6b–7a). Matthew's *παροψίδος*, "dish," is likely to be original, rather than Luke's *πίνακος*, "platter/dish," because Matthew accepts *πίνακος* from his source in 14:8, 11. In Matthew the outside and the inside of the cup and dish are contrasted (this is probably in accord with Jewish tradition despite Maccoby's [largely justified] criticism [*JSNT* 12 (1980) 3–15] of Neusner's particular reconstruction of the state of the tradition at the time of Jesus [*NTS* 22 (1975–76) 486–95]), though clearly the referent of this language slides from literal reference (for the outside) to being a metaphor for the lives of the those criticized (for the inside). Luke avoids this slide by abandoning the metaphor and contrasting the outside of the *cup* with the inside of the *person* (with the loss of the metaphor, Matthew's "uncleanness" becomes simply "evil"). Though the principle here is clearly applicable to the question of ritual washing of the hands/body, the text does not constitute a natural response to the situation in v 38. It is Luke who has juxtaposed the traditions (various of the Lukan changes here and in the following verses reduce the significance of the cup and dish, and in this way help to unify the traditions).

40 Matthew has no parallel to this verse, and since its contrast works better from a starting point in Luke's form in v 39, this may well be a Lukan development, or perhaps it is more likely that we have here an independent fragment of tradition that Luke has fitted in here (see Nagel's speculation, on the basis of the reversed form in *Gos. Thom.* 89 and as a variant reading here, about an original double form for this tradition [*VC* 14 (1960) 5]). The reference is not to the human artisan of the cup and dish, but to God who is creator of the human agent, inside and outside (reference to the *human* outside here helps the link with v 38). The point here is that God will be (at least) as concerned for the inside as ever for the outside.

41 Despite the skepticism of Fitzmyer (947) the links here with Matt 23:26 (*τὸ ἐντός* in Matthew, *τὰ ἐνόντα* in Luke; *καθαρόν* in Matthew, the plural in Luke; and a differently expressed but similar relationship between the two clauses) are too strong for the verses not to be variants on a single tradition. Though Torrey's view ("The Translations," 312–13) that "give alms" reflects an original better translated "make righteous" (עבדו צדקא, *ʿbdw ṣaddiqāʾ*), is not unattractive (the "rapacity and evil" of v 39 is correspondingly unrighteous), the Lukan language and interests in v 41 point rather to a recasting by him of what was essentially the Matthean form (Matthew's form continues the imagery that Luke has already disturbed; Luke's form produces a generalized contrast between the inner and the outer, which is in line with the material he has used in v 40 and helps the link between vv 37–38 and vv 39–41).

"Alms" is an effective antithesis to the "rapacity" of v 39. Almsgiving is one of the classic expressions of Jewish piety and is clearly important for Luke. Its role in his thought is to be connected on the one hand with such Jewish piety (cf. esp. Acts 10:2, 4, 31; 24:17), and on the other hand with his concerns about the destructive potential of riches (see at 6:24; and cf. 12:33). *τὰ ἐνόντα* (lit. "the [things] being within") must be translated with v 39 in mind, and so is best rendered "what is inside" and linked to the clause as an accusative of respect: "in connection with what is inside . . . ," and so, "as an expression of what is inside." V 41 makes it clear that Luke's use of "inside" and "outside" does not mark a dualism of the inner and outer life of a person: the inner life expresses itself in outward actions and is to be contrasted to that which is *only* an outward display. Taken literally Luke makes an exaggerated claim for almsgiving. But the almsgiving here, while it is to be understood quite literally, is at the same time meant to evoke Luke's whole understanding of how God alone is to be the point of our reliance; it is a proper relationship to God (and the heart for others that is inextricably connected) that finds expression in this almsgiving. Could it be that the phrase πάντα καθαρά, "all things . . . clean," echoes Mark 7:19? Matthew's text gives the primacy to the inner; Luke's text gives the totality to the inner. The only point at which Luke presents Jewish Christians as no longer bound by Jewish requirements is in connection with the fellowship established between themselves and the gentile Christians (see Acts 10:9–16, 28; 11:3–12, 17; 15:9). Because of his right relationship to God (Cornelius gave alms [10:2]), about to be demonstrated beyond doubt in his response to Peter's message, Cornelius could not be contaminated by his disregard of Jewish ritual purity requirements and, therefore, in turn could not contaminate Jewish Christians who shared table fellowship with him (there is some tension in Acts between seeing Cornelius as already clean [10:29] and as being cleansed by the Spirit as he responds in faith to Peter's message [15:8–9]; the second seems to be at one and the same time a confirmation and extension of the first). Though the text is ostensibly addressed to the Pharisees, Luke thinks here primarily of the situation of gentile Christians.

42 Luke wants the first woe that he introduces here to be seen as a continuation of the point being made in vv 39–41: petty tithing is like washing the outside of cups; justice and the love of God have an equivalence in almsgiving. Jewish tithing practices were an elaboration and adaptation of the OT materials on tithing (Lev 27:30–33; Num 18:12; Deut 12:6–9; 14:22–29; 26:12–15; Neh 10:37–38; 12:44; 13:5, 12; 2 Chr 31:5–12; Mal 3:8, 10). The Lukan form is an exaggeration of the Matthean: Matthew's list of tithed items deals with items that would be used in tiny quantities, but in connection with which tithing was practiced (cf. *m. Maᶜaś.* 4:5 for dill; *m. Dem.* 2:1 for cumin; mint has not in fact been found mentioned in the sources); Luke's list is designed to be absolutely comprehensive and so includes rue, which is exempt from tithing as something that grows wild rather than being commercially grown (*m. Šeb.* 9:1), and then the exhaustive category "every edible plant" (πᾶν λάχανον). Luke is probably not expressing a different view, but only establishing his point more forcefully by poetic exaggeration. Luke also expresses differently the areas of neglect. Matthew's "the weightier matters of the law" may be his own touch, but the other differences are to be put to Luke's account (cf. Schulz, *Spruchquelle*, 100–101): Luke keeps κρίσιν from his source (with the sense, as in the source, of "right, justice" [as in Acts 8:33]), but he thinks of the scope of the concerns of 10:27 (as Fitzmyer, 948) and so introduces "love of God" in place of the other terms found in his source (ἔλεος, "mercy," πίστιν, "fidelity/faithfulness"), which were from the human ethical sphere. The final clause, if original here (see *Note* i above), is a reminder of Luke's reluctance to criticize the place of the law in the lives of Jewish Christians. Luke replaces both Matthew's uses of ἀφιέναι (here "neglect") with more colorful words (παρέρχεσθε, "pass by," παρεῖναι, "leave undone"). The imperfect ἔδει is probably the apodosis of a present condition-contrary-to-fact clause ("[if you were to do the will of God], it would be necessary to . . ."), but this is difficult to catch precisely in translation.

43 Luke has the woe format here (Lukan?), where Matthew (23:6–7) does not. A related tradition in Mark 12:38–39 applies the criticism to scribes (this would seem historically preferable), rather than to Pharisees as here (see at v 39 above). Matthew's "the place of honor at feasts" is likely to be a Markan influence, but Matthew's *φιλοῦσιν*, "they love," for Luke's *ἀγαπᾶτε*, "you love," is likely to be original here (cf. Luke 20:46). Matthew's continuation in v 7b belongs with the continuing material of vv 8–10, which Matthew has added from elsewhere and will not have been in the shared source. "Seat of honor" is literally "first seat." "Greetings" here are, of course, those to one specially honored. Synagogue and market would have been main settings for public social interaction. In connection with rabbis and for a later period, Str-B (1:382, 915–18) documents these patterns of behavior.

44 "Pharisees" is missing from this final Lukan woe against the Pharisees. This is probably to indicate that the present woe is not independent of the earlier material but rather comments upon it (but note the similar phenomenon in v 47). Luke has here changed the imagery from that of the "whitewashed tombs" of Matt 23:27–28. Outward display of righteousness has not been Luke's target; his concern has been, rather, to expose the "rapacity and wickedness," which, lurking out of sight, are the deep motivations of these Pharisees, rather than the necessary motivation of "justice and the love of God." As he rounds off his section against the Pharisees, Luke returns again to the imagery of ceremonial uncleanness used at the beginning (vv 39–41) and suggests that contact with such Pharisees is an unwitting exposure to contamination (moral under the image of ceremonial). The imagery implies that the failings of the Pharisees that are criticized do not take blatant forms but must be discovered from more subtle indicators.

45 Luke distributes the woes between the Pharisees and the lawyers (on "lawyers" = "scribes" see at 5:17, 7:30; see *Form/Structure/Setting* and at v 39 for Schürmann's view that this distribution is original, even if not Luke's exact allocation of the items). He is likely to be responsible for the narrative introduction here as well, and may be so for the exclusive reference to lawyers here and in v 52. The point of this verse would be implicit already in Luke's source if it had, at least at points, joint reference to scribes and Pharisees. The "lawyers" here are part of the Pharisaic group and own responsibility for the formulation of the details of Pharisaic observance. For them to address Jesus as "teacher" is to acknowledge him as of their own class. On "teacher," see at 7:40.

46 Again, this is not a woe in Matthew's formulation (23:4) and has probably been made so by Luke. The wording is rather different in the two versions, probably from Lukan intervention. The Matthean imagery of tying a heavy load upon the shoulders becomes simply a loading of people with difficult-to-carry burdens. The criticism here has more to do with the failure to help than with the initial burdening (though that is not likely to be entirely free of criticism). As interpreters of the law of God, the scribes were responsible to lay the burden of the law upon the people, but not a much heavier burden, and they should have been giving support and encouragement in the shouldering of the load. Instead they were inclined to despise the ordinary people who could hardly understand, let alone successfully implement, the Pharisaic casuistry. (In the Matthean setting the concern is often taken to be about the scribal failure to practice what they preach [cf. v 3] but is most naturally taken as here.)

47 It is not clear why Luke does not address the "lawyers" as such in this woe. It is true that the criticism can hardly be narrowly applied to the scribes, but in Luke's structure (see vv 45, 46, 52, 53) it must be taken as directed to the scribes. Luke offers in vv 47–48 a rather abbreviated version of what we find in Matt 23:29–32. Though it is difficult to be sure, most of the alteration is likely to be Luke's, but the double form in Matt 23:29 of "prophets" and "righteous ones" is likely be a Matthean development, and v 32 could be as well. Building tombs for, and revering the graves of, the great figures of the past was a notable feature of Jewish life (see Acts 2:29–30; Jeremias, *Heiligengräber;* id., *ZNW* 52 [1961] 95–101; [one cannot take as seriously intended the tradition drawn attention to by Derrett (*SE* 4 [= TU 102] (1968) 187–88), which maintains that "tombstones are not erected for the righteous, as their words are their memorials" (see, e.g., *Gen. Rab.* 82:10); this is no more than a "debating point"]). Luke has distilled the final clause here out of Matt 23:30–31. He will use the same juxtaposition of building and killing in reverse order in v 48. The murder of the prophets has a firm place in Jewish tradition despite being not strongly evidenced in the OT in terms of actual instances (1 Kgs 19:10, 14; Neh 9:26; Jer 2:30; 26:20–24; cf. at Luke 6:23). Luke's point remains opaque until we move into the following verse.

48 In the Matthean text, admitted kinship with the murderers of the prophets carries the thread of the argument. Here the building of the tombs bears the argument. The "partnership" of the generations is expressed at the end of the verse as "they killed . . . ; you build." In English idiom we might get Luke's point more readily if the juxtaposed activities had been killing and burying (T. W. Manson, *Sayings,* 101, catches the point with his, "They killed the prophets: you make sure they stay dead"). Monumental tombs are normally, and rightly, taken to celebrate the life of the deceased; the Lukan polemic here interprets the tomb building as rather a celebration of the death (murder) of the prophets involved: "your fathers perpetrated the murder and you celebrate it."

Of course this is not a genuine argument; it is an ironic reinterpretation of something that those involved would want interpreted quite differently. For this reason its force depends entirely on the negative attitude to the prophets of the past, which is claimed here, being evident in other ways. Only then might one be in a position to say that the tomb-building activity should rightly carry this provocative interpretation. Vv 49–51 are designed to supply this missing link.

49 Matthew (23:34) has changed "the wisdom of God said" here to "I [i.e., Jesus]," a change that he sustains by changing the subsequent verbs from third to second person forms (and probably also by changing "will send" to the present tense [no longer the report of a past announcement, and in any case the sending has already begun [10:16; etc.]). Beyond "kill and persecute" Matthew has a development dependent in part upon 10:17b and cf. also v 23. It is more difficult to be sure whether Matthew's "wise men and scribes" or Luke's "apostles" (ἀποστόλους) is the more original, since each evangelist has what is congenial to himself (Matt 13:52 for "scribe" in an equivalent sense; Luke has six uses of "apostles" to Matthew's one). Luke may have the original, but with ἀποστόλους in his source having the wider sense "emissaries," or perhaps better is an original with σοφούς ("wise men"; this fits Wisdom as spokesperson [cf. the logic of Wis 7:15]), which Luke changes with an eye upon 10:21.

"Because of this" means here "because you are like vv 47–48 have suggested you are." For Jewish personification of Wisdom, see at 7:35. At Wis 8:8, Wisdom "predicts the things to come." We are probably to understand not that some written or traditional source is being appealed to by Jesus but rather that he has personally been informed by Wisdom (the nearest analogy is perhaps the visionary experience spoken about in 10:18) of her intention (he is himself to be part of its implementation). In the Jewish traditions that have survived, Wisdom does not send envoys but comes herself to deliver her message (e.g., Prov 1:20–21). She does, however, operate in human affairs by entering into people (in particular into those who are [to be] prophets [Wis 11:1; 7:27]). From the mediating role of Wisdom in creation broadly (Prov 8:30; Wis 7:12, 21; 8:1, 4–6), it is a small step to a mediating role for Wisdom in the working out of God's dealings with his People in history. Though Luke has probably introduced "apostles" here to evoke the role of the Twelve, "prophets and apostles" functions as a comprehensive designation for messengers of God (this other half of the double role of this term would be best respected with the translation "emissaries"). The sending here is future to the prophetic activity reflected in vv 50–51. In view will be the role of John, Jesus himself, and those who will act in Jesus' name. The tomb builders of v 47–48 will in this way reveal their true colors, and thus the real meaning of their commemoration, by continuing the pattern of their forebears (cf. at v 47; 6:23; 13:34).

50–51 Matthew's change to second person above produces "upon you" in place of "upon this generation," as well as "you murdered" for "perished." It is likely that the other differences here are also to be attributed to Matthew (cf. Schulz, *Spruchquelle*, 337–38; Légasse, "L'oracle," 243–45).

As in the segment of OT history that acculminated in the Babylonian exile, the culmination of generations of accumulated wickedness is contemplated here as bringing the judgment of God. There is both personal responsibility and inherited guilt. The idiom "to seek the blood" is an OT idiom that in the LXX uses the language found here (Gen 9:5; 42:22; 2 Kgdms 4:11; Ezek 3:18; etc.). The language evokes the OT stipulation of a death penalty for murder, with its implications of the cleansing of the land from pollution (e.g., Num 35:33). "Prophets" here is used loosely (cf. the use in Gen 20:7 in connection with Abraham) of those with an intimate link with God (this is a problem for Matthew, who speaks rather of "all the righteous blood"). The present generation is to answer for all the pollution caused by the spilling of the blood of God's servants from creation onwards (cf. Rev 18:4). This comprehensiveness finds its home in apocalyptic thought (the similarity between "from foundation of the world" here and "from the beginning of creation" in Mark 13:19, along with the general similarity of thought, suggests that the link to Dan 12:1 of that verse may be via an exegetical tradition also reflected here).

The figures Abel and Zechariah represent this comprehensiveness. The former is the very first murder (the voice of whose blood is said to cry out from the ground [Gen 4:10]) and comes from the first book of the OT, while the second probably gives us the earliest indication that, as was true later, 2 Chronicles (the priest Zechariah's murder is reported in 2 Chr 24:20–22) already came last in the

Hebrew OT. "Between the altar and the sanctuary" must come from Jewish tradition; the OT simply says he was stoned in the court of the house of the Lord. Jewish tradition reflects confusion between this Zechariah and the prophet of the same name (see Str-B, 1:940–42), and this confusion has left its mark on the Matthean text in the form of "son of Berachiah" (cf. Zech 1:1). Occasional attempts are made to identify the Zechariah here as Zechariah son of Baris, who was assassinated in the temple area by zealots in the Jewish uprising prior to the destruction of Jerusalem in A.D. 70. The one thing in favor of this suggestion is the nice timing contrast with Abel thus achieved (see, e.g., Steck, *Israel*, 37–40).

Having reported Wisdom, Jesus now appropriates Wisdom's message as his own by reiterating its major thrust after an emphatic "Yes, I say to you" (also found in 7:28; 12:5). In the Lukan structure, the coming destruction of Jerusalem will be in view, but not without overtones of final judgment as well.

52 Once again here the imagery has been transformed, though without fundamental change to the point made. If Schürmann ("Die Redekomposition," 39, 48) is right to see Matt 23:2–3 as, in the source history, beginning the block that is concluded with the source form of the present verse, then it must be the Matthean form that is to be preferred (and cf. Schulz, *Spruchquelle*, 110 n. 23). Luke's imagery is that of a key that gives access to knowledge, rather than of knowledge as itself the key. The scribes are accused of blocking access to knowledge.

Matthew's reference to the kingdom of heaven has been removed and so is not available as antecedent to the entry language of the next clause. Fitzmyer (951) is likely to be right that Luke thinks rather (after v 49) of entry into the house of Wisdom (Prov 9:1). Luke has already reported the interference of the scribes in Jesus' ministry (5:21, 30; 6:7), and will continue to do so (see further at vv 53–54). The criticism is, however, more general. (Though the scribes as such are never mentioned, Luke may think as well of the attempts to block the Christian mission, which he will report in Acts.)

53–54 These verses have no parallel in Matthew and are mostly taken to be a Lukan formulation based roughly on Mark 3:6; 12:13, but the language is quite distinctive and not Lukan. This, combined with Schürmann's source analysis (*SNTU* 11 [1986] 33–81), which calls for a concluding synthesis of some kind about Pharisees and scribes, suggests that Luke may be, at least in part, following his source here (note that Luke reverts to "scribes," found in the Matthean tradition, after his use of "lawyers" in vv 45, 46, 52). It may be that the departure statement, in the source applied to the Pharisees and scribes (cf. Mark 3:6), has been applied here to Jesus, on the basis of v 37.

The particular use of ἀποστοματίζειν here has not been closely paralleled. The word normally means "to teach by word of mouth [and so teach/speak from memory]," but here "to speak/teach against" might be suggested. Other suggestions include "to provoke him to speak" (RSV), "to question closely" (Fitzmyer, 952), "to force answers from" (JB). ἐνεδρεύοντες, "lying in ambush" (cf. Acts 23:21), and θηρεῦσαι, "catch [at]," both evoke imagery of violent intent to destroy, whether in the hunt for game or in the ambush of an enemy. They are scanning his words for anything they can oppose. Just as Luke keeps alive the journey motif through periodic reminders, so he will periodically illustrate this point as his narrative continues (note esp. 14:1; 15:2; 16:14; 17:20; 19:39; 20:19–26). Luke may also have in mind the role of the scribes in developments up to and including the trial (19:47; 22:2, 66; 23:10).

Explanation

The conflict and contrast of the section 11:14–54 now reaches a climax and conclusion in the present unit with its fierce denunciation of the Pharisees and the scribes and of their counter-hostility to him. The Pharisees and the lawyers are blind to the light, precisely because their own lives are morally and religiously compromised and, as with their forebears, they do not want to hear the challenge of the messengers of God.

Jesus has already dined with a Pharisee and will do so again (7:36; 14:1). He is in some sense one of their kind. But he offends by his failure to fit in with their exaggerated version of the need for ritual purity (they had extensively broadened the OT concern for ritual purity, which was mostly focused on purity for worship in the temple).

The implied criticism of the Pharisee's amazement is answered with a counter-criticism. Jewish tradition appears to have made a distinction, for purposes of ritual purity, between the inside and outside of a vessel for food or drink. Jesus suggests that clean outsides of cups and dishes are balanced by rapacious and evil insides of persons. (In terms of ritual purity of vessels, the inside is of chief importance: inner uncleanness transfers out, but outer uncleanness does not necessarily transfer in.) This should not be taken as suggesting that these Pharisees were unusually evil, only that their preoccupation with the ritually outer has about it an aspect of what Matthew (23:25) will call "hypocrisy." God, the creator of both "insides" and "outsides," will certainly be no less concerned for the inside than for the outside. Rapacity should give way to almsgiving, which is rather dramatically said to make all things clean for one. Taken quite literally this is no doubt an exaggeration. However, Luke thinks here on the one hand of the importance of almsgiving in traditional Jewish piety, and wants to affirm that (see Acts 10:2, 4, 31; etc.), and on the other hand of the teaching he reports about the destructive potential of riches (see 6:24; 8:14; 12:33; etc.). Almsgiving, while being literally intended, becomes at the same time a symbol for single-hearted devotion to God and not to humanly achieved security in this world. It is the kind of confidence expressed in this verse, when applied to gentile Christians, that later made it possible for Jewish Christians to share table fellowship with their newfound gentile Christian brothers and sisters (see the Cornelius discussion in Acts 10, 11, 15).

Now Jesus begins a series of woes against the Pharisees. Luke has made this woe a little comic by exaggerating the form that we find in Matthew (23:23). The picture here is of Pharisees who tithe simply everything, with no regard for what were the normal practical exemptions for minor quantities of non-commercially produced edible plants. Excessive scrupulosity on this one side in matters of tiny detail is matched by a curious comparative laxity in the areas of huge significance: social justice and love of God. Of course this description, in its second half, is hardly something that would have been obvious to a bystander in the first century. Rather, Jesus is to be understood as uncovering the hidden realities of the human condition—ours as much as ever those of first-century Pharisees. The final sentence of v 42 may not be original in Luke, but if it is, it underlines Luke's reluctance to criticize the place of the OT law, and the traditions developed from it, in the lives of Jewish Christians.

The second woe is directed at a love for public honor. This is no distinctive fault in Jesus opponents, but is clearly an endemic human failing, which may be indulged in different ways and at different levels. Synagogue and marketplace were main places for public social interaction in Jesus' setting.

The third woe adds no further content to Pharisaic failings; rather it identifies them with an image that would have caused great discomfort to these experts in ceremonial cleanness. In Jewish thought a tomb conveyed ritual uncleanness, and the problem with an invisible tomb was that it conveyed uncleanness without the one passing over realizing that this had taken place and taking steps for cleansing. The imagery implies that the failings of the Pharisees do not take blatant forms but must be discovered from more subtle indicators.

Since the lawyers here were the Scripture-and-tradition experts for the Pharisees, any criticism of Pharisees was indirectly an insult to them as well. So, the lawyer makes this point to Jesus. As had the meal invitation earlier, so here the address as teacher marks Jesus as in some sense part of their kind. Instead of giving any concessions, Jesus now addresses three additional woes toward the legal experts.

As experts in the law, the scribes rightly lay the burden of the law upon the people of God. But these scribes have made this into an exaggerated burden, and they have not provided the support and encouragement that would have made things easier for the ordinary people. Instead of encouraging, they were inclined to despise the ordinary people who could hardly understand, let alone successfully implement, the complex web of legal requirements.

Building tombs for, and revering the graves of, the great figures of the past was a notable feature of Jewish life. The idea that the earlier generations had murdered the prophets has a firm place in Jewish tradition despite being not that strongly evidenced in the OT (but see Neh 9:26; etc.). Our text puts the two together as a kind of partnership of the generations in which the tombs celebrate not the prophet but the successful extermination of the prophet! It is, of course, far from obvious that this was the purpose of tomb building, and only the development in vv 49–51 will justify this kind of language.

Uniquely, Jesus reports what Wisdom has told him is her intention (but compare the visionary experience of 10:18). Wisdom is here a personified attribute of God as in Prov 9. Through her, God implements his purposes. Aware of the true nature of the present generation (and its tomb building), Wisdom plans to reveal the truth by sending a fresh batch of prophets and apostles (or emissaries). In this way she will provoke a repetition of the ancestral behavior, and thus an exposure of the true nature of its tomb building. (In view will be the role of John, Jesus himself, and those who will act in Jesus' name.)

"Prophets" is used loosely here of God's servants (compare Gen 20:7). Abel (esp. Gen 4:10) and Zechariah (2 Chr 24:20–22) probably represent the first and last murders in the OT, in the order of books then current. The culmination of generations of accumulated wickedness is blamed for bringing the judgment of God. There is both personal responsibility and inherited guilt. The land will now be cleansed of its accumulated pollution.

Having reported Wisdom, Jesus now appropriates Wisdom's message as his own by reiterating its major thrust after an emphatic, "Yes, I say to you." In the Lukan structure, the coming destruction of Jerusalem will be in view, but not without overtones of final judgment as well.

The final woe uses the imagery of the house of Wisdom (Prov 9:1). The lawyers have not used their privileged access to knowledge about God and his will in order to enter Wisdom's house, and they have blocked the access of others who may have liked to enter. We should probably think also of the interference of the scribes in the ministry of Jesus (5:21, 30; 6:7; etc.).

Having provided the guests with this after-dinner speech, Jesus leaves the party, but the situation is now permanently different. A fresh level of violent opposition has been provoked. Both of the verbs used here of Jesus' opponents evoke imagery of violent intent to destroy, whether in the hunt for game or in the ambush of an enemy. The Pharisees and scribes are now scanning Jesus' words for anything they can oppose and contradict.

Preparing for the Coming Judgment (12:1–13:9)

There is an easy transition from the conflict and contrast of the previous section to the focus here on the coming judgment (indeed the motif of conflict continues while the prospect of judgment has already had a place in 11:14–54): judgment day will reveal things as they really are; it provides the threatening edge to the challenge for change that Jesus' ministry brings.

The Need for a Clear-cut Acknowledgment of Jesus (12:1–12)

Bibliography

GENERAL:

Allison, D. C. "The hairs of your head are all numbered." *ExpTim* 101 (1990) 334–36. **Bertrand, D.** "Hypocrites selon Luc 12,1–59." *Christus* 21 (1974) 323–33. **Brown, S.** *Apostasy and Perseverance.* 45–56. **Dupont, J.** "La transmission des paroles de Jésus sur la lampe et la mesure dans Marc 4,21–25 et dans la tradition Q." In *Logia*, ed. J. Delobel. 201–36; reprinted *Études.* 1:259–94. ———. "L'Après-mort dans l'oeuvre de Luc." *RTL* 3 (1972) 3–21. **Iwand, H. J.** *Die Gegenwart des Kommenden: Eine Auslegung von Lk 12.* BibS(N) 50. Neukirchen-Vluyn: Neukirchener, 1966. **Kloppenborg, J. S.** "The Q Saying on Anxiety (Q 12:2–7)." *Forum* 5.2 (1989) 83–97. **Laufen, R.** *Die Doppelüberlieferung.* 156–73. **MacDonald, D.** "The Worth of the Assarion." *Historia* 38 (1989) 120–23. **Marshall, I. H.** "Uncomfortable Words, VI: 'Fear Him Who Can Destroy Both Soul and Body in Hell' (Mt 10:28 R.S.V.)." *ExpTim* 81 (1969–70) 276–80. **Mitton, C. L.** "Leaven." *ExpTim* 84 (1972–73) 339–43. **Moulton, H. K.** "Luke 12:5." *BT* 25 (1974) 246–47. **Negoitā, A.**, and **Daniel, C.** "L'Enigme du levain: Ad Mc. viii 15; Mt. xvi 6; et Lc. xii 1." *NovT* 9 (1967) 306–14. **Niven, W. D.** "Luke xii.4." *ExpTim* 26 (1914–15) 44–45. **Robinson, J. M.** "Worksheets for Q 12." In *SBL Seminar Papers 1987*, ed. K. H. Richards. Atlanta, GA: Scholars, 1987. 586–605. **Sweetland, D. M.** "Discipleship and Persecution: A Study of Luke 12,1–12." *Bib* 65 (1984) 61–80. **Wuellner, W.** "The Rhetorical Genre of Jesus' Sermon in Luke 12.1–13.9." In *Persuasive Artistry: Studies in New Testament Rhetoric.* FS G. A. Kennedy, ed. D. F. Watson. Sheffield: JSOT, 1991. 93–118. ———. "The Rhetorical Structure of Luke 12 in Its Wider Context." *Neot* 22 (1988) 283–310.

FOR 12:8–9:

Catchpole, D. R. "The Angelic Son of Man in Luke 12:8." *NovT* 24 (1982) 255–65. **Copestake, D. R.** "Luke 12:8 and 'silent witness.'" *ExpTim* 94 (1983) 335. **Coppens, J.** *La relève apocalyptique du messianisme royal: III. Le Fils de l'homme néotestamentaire.* BETL 55. Leuven: Peeters/University Press, 1981. 13–16. **Fleddermann, H.** "The Q Sayings on Confessing and Denying." In *SBL Seminar Papers 1987*, ed. K. H. Richards. Atlanta, GA: Scholars, 1987. 606–16. ———. "The Cross and Discipleship in Q." In *SBL Seminar Papers 1988*, ed. D. J. Lull. Atlanta, GA: Scholars, 1988. 472–82. **Hahn, F.** *The Titles of Jesus in Christology.* 28–34. **Haufe, G.** "Das Menschensohn-Problem in der gegenwärtigen wissenschaftlichen Diskussion." *EvT* 26 (1966) 130–41. **Higgins, A. J. B.** "'Menschensohn' oder 'ich' in Q: Lk 12,8–9/Mt 10,32–33?" In *Jesus und der Menschensohn.* FS A. Vögtle, ed. R. Pesch and R. Schnackenburg. Freiburg/Basel/Vienna: Herder, 1975. 117–23. **Kümmel, W. G.** "Das Verhalten Jesu gegenüber und das Verhalten des Menschensohnes. Markus 8,38 par und Lukas 12,8f par Mattäus 10,32f." In *Jesus und der Menschensohn.* FS A. Vögtle, ed. R. Pesch, R. Schnackenburg, and O. Kaiser. Freiburg: Herder, 1975. 210–24. **Lambrecht, J.** "Q-Influence on Mark 8,34–9,1." In *Logia,* ed. J. Delobel. 277–304. **Lindars, B.** "Jesus as Advocate: A Contribution to the Christological Debate." *BJRL* 62 (1980) 476–97. **McDermott, J. M.** "Luke XII, 8–9: Stone of Scandal." *RB* 84 (1977) 523–37. ———. "Luc, xii, 8–9: Pierre angulaire." *RB* 85 (1978) 381–401. **Tödt, H. E.** *The Son of Man in the Synoptic Tradition.* NTL. Philadelphia: Westminster, 1965. 55–60, 339–47.

See further at 9:23–27 and Son of Man excursus.

FOR 12:10:

Berger, K. *Die Amen Worte Jesu.* Berlin: de Gruyter, 1970. 36–41. **Boring, M. E.** "The Unforgivable Sin Logion Mark III 28–29/Matt XII 31–32/Luke XII 10: Formal Analysis and History of the Tradition." *NovT* 18 (1976) 258–79. **Casey, P. M.** "The Son of Man Problem." *ZNW* 67 (1976) 147–54. **Colpe, C.** "Der Spruch von der Lästerung des Geistes." In *Der Ruf Jesu,* ed. E. Lohse et al. 63–79. **Denney, J.** "Speaking against the Son of Man and Blaspheming the Spirit." *Exp* 7/4 (1907) 521–32. **Evans, O. E.** "The Unforgivable Sin." *ExpTim* 68 (1956–57) 240–44. **Fitzer, G.** "Die Sünde wider den Heiligen Geist." *TZ* 13 (1957) 161–82. **Fridrichsen, A.** "Le péché contre le Saint-Esprit." *RHPR* 3 (1923) 367–72. **Holst, R.** "Reexamining Mk 3:28f. and Its Parallels." *ZNW* 63 (1972) 122–24. **Lövestam, E.** *Spiritus blasphemia: Eine Studie zu Mk 3,28f par Mt 12,31f, Lk 12 12,10.* Scripta minora regiae societatis humaniorum litterarum lundensis 1966–67:1. Lund: Gleerup, 1968. **Marshall, I. H.** "Hard Sayings—VII." *Th* 67 (1964) 65–67. **O'Neill, J. C.** "The Unforgivable Sin." *JSNT* 19 (1983) 37–42. **Roulin, P.** "Le péché contre l'Esprit Saint." *BVC* 29 (1959) 38–45. **Schippers, R.** "The Son of Man in Matt. xii. 32 = Lk. xii. 10, Compared with Mk. iii. 28." *SE* 4 [= TU 102] (1968) 231–35. **Williams, J. G.** "A Note on the 'Unforgivable Sin' Logion." *NTS* 12 (1965–66) 75–77. **Wrege, T. H.** "Zur Rolle des Geisteswortes in frühchristlichen Traditionen (Lc 12,10 parr.)." In *Logia,* ed. J. Delobel. 373–77.

FOR 12:11–12:

Giblet, J. "Les promesses de l'Esprit et la mission des apôtres dans les évangiles." *Irénikon* 30 (1957) 5–43, esp. 17–19. **Kühschelm, R.** *Jüngerverfolgung und Geschick Jesu.* 226–28, 282–86. **Reicke, B.** "A Test of Synoptic Relationships: Matthew 10,17–23 and 24,9–14 with Parallels." In *New Synoptic Studies,* ed. W. R. Farmer. Macon, GA: Mercer, 1983. 209–29. **Schürmann, H.** "Zur Traditions- und Redaktionsgeschichte von Mt 10:23." *BZ* 3 (1959) 82–88.

Translation

[1]*During this period, when the myriads of the crowd*[a] *had gathered and*[b] *they were trampling one another, he began to say (to his disciples in the first instance), "Beware of the leaven of the Pharisees, which is hypocrisy.* [2]*Nothing is covered up which shall not be revealed*[c] *and hidden which shall not become known.* [3]*Therefore, as many things as are said by you*[d] *in the darkness will be heard in the light, and what is spoken by you*[e] *to the ear, [and] in the inner chambers, will be proclaimed on the rooftops.*

[4] *"I say to you, my friends, Do not fear*[f] *those who can kill the body, and after that have nothing further they can do.* [5] *I'll show you whom you should fear: fear the one who after he kills has authority to cast into Gehenna. Yes, I say to you, fear this one!* [6] *Are not five sparrows sold for two assaria? Yet*[g] *not one of them has escaped God's notice.*[h] [7] *Indeed, even the hairs of your head are all numbered. Do not fear;*[i] *you are worth more than many sparrows!*

[8] *"I say to you, everyone who acknowledges me before people, the Son of Man will also acknowledge*[j] *before the angels of God.* [9] *But the one who denies me before people will be denied before the angels of God.* [10] *Everyone who says a word against the Son of Man—it will be forgiven him; but to the one who blasphemes against the Holy Spirit it will not be forgiven.* [11] *When they bring you before synagogues and rulers and authorities, do not be worried: How or in what words*[k] *are you to make your defense? or, What are you to say?* [12] *For the Holy Spirit will teach you in that hour what it is necessary to say."*

Notes

[a] P[45] 579 etc. read λαοῦ, "People."
[b] Gr. ὥστε (lit. "with the result that").
[c] P[45] lacks the final clause.
[d] The verb is active ("you said") but is rendered passive for the sake of English idiom.
[e] as[d].
[f] P[45] 700 have the stronger term πτοηθῆτε, "be terrified."
[g] Gr. καί.
[h] Lit. "is forgotten/neglected before God."
[i] οὖν, "then," is added (from Matthew) by ℵ A D W Θ Ψ etc.
[j] Gr. has a redundant "him" here.
[k] Gr. τί, "what."

Form/Structure/Setting

The new section, 12:1–13:9, with its concern for people's readiness for the coming judgment, begins in 12:1–12 by stressing the necessity of a clear public acknowledgment of allegiance to the Son of Man.

The materials of the unit here are presented as a single continuous statement by Jesus, made in the hearing of a huge crowd, but with special reference to the disciples. Luke presents the unit in three subunits: vv 1–4; 5–7; 8–12. The terminus of the unit is made clear by the clear change of topic introduced in v 13 by a request from a person in the crowd.

Luke establishes a continuity of audience for the materials of the section by establishing an interplay between address to the disciples and to the gathered crowd (vv 1, 22, 41), and by having the same crowd present for the duration (vv 1, 13, 54; 13:1). This, together with the general thematic unity, establishes the boundaries of the section.

The underlying tradition used in 12:1 is reflected in Mark 8:15, but probably comes to Luke along a separate track. For vv 2–9, Luke follows the order of the source he shares with Matthew (10:26–33). Most of the differences are to be set to the account of Luke, but Matthew is likely to have introduced significant changes in his version of vv 3 and 8. For v 10, Luke follows the source shared with Matthew (12:32), but with a slight influence from the wording of the Markan parallel (3:29). Luke may follow the original source order here in v 10 and in the following vv 11–12 (catchword association; the continuation in vv 11–12 with materials that in Matthew [10:19–20] are found quite close to the parallel to vv 2–9; Matthew provides no information on order for v 10 since he inserts the material of the verse into the Markan setting). In vv 11–12 Luke partly follows the shared source but also partly rewrites the Markan parallel (13:11). The materials of the unit do not constitute an original unity and must be separately assessed as to historicity. On the lips of Jesus, "the leaven of the Pharisees" may mean that which was influencing the Pharisees in a damaging way, rather than the influence they had on others. The materials of vv 2–7 all fit well into the ministry of Jesus. The historicity of vv 8–9 has been seriously challenged but is defended at 9:23–27. For v 10, with the significantly different parallel tradition in Mark 3:28–30, there is first the question of the nature of the form from which these have been ultimately derived. Despite a flurry of favor for the view that the Q form is the more original, a series of recent studies takes us back to earlier views and argues persuasively for an original that owes more to the Markan form (see esp. Boring, *NovT* 18 [1976] 274–77, who points to the chiastic parallelism and the ease with which an Aramaic לבר נשא, *lĕbār nāšāʾ*, "to [the] son of man," placed at the end of its clause after the reference to forgiveness and to blasphemy, could be taken as referring either to forgiveness of sin/blasphemy *against the Son of Man* or to forgiveness of sins/blasphemies *for humanity*). The first half of the text, with its declaration of universal forgiveness, has been the more readily conceded to the historical Jesus, while the second negative half has been given various early church settings. But the paradox of the whole, along with the extremity of both halves, fits the historical Jesus rather better than the early church. For vv 11–12, the issue of historicity turns on the historical Jesus having anticipated persecution for his followers and on whether he anticipated for them a link with the Spirit beyond that conveyed by their link to himself. Though there is only a small body of Synoptic words of Jesus that mention the Spirit (cf. G. R. Beasley-Murray, "Jesus and the Spirit," in *Mélange Biblique*, FS B. Rigaux, ed. A. Descamps et al., 463–78), Luke 3:16 and OT background would make the latter likely, while the former needs to be seen in connection with Jesus' anticipation of his own rejection, which is seen as historically plausible in the discussion at 9:21–22 (see further at 6:22 where OT and Qumran background are explored). In light of the variant form in 21:14–15 without mention of the Holy Spirit, we must reckon with the possibility of an original without this reference. It is possible that the passive construction of Mark 13:11b, without the development of v 11c, takes us closest to the original.

Comment

The hypocrisy of being one thing in private and another in public cannot survive God's searching scrutiny at the time of judgment; it is he who should be feared, rather than those whose present hostility might tempt one to dissimulation. What is needed is a clear acknowledgment before others of one's allegiance to the Son of Man; in the time of crisis the Holy Spirit himself will convince the disciples of the need for this.

1 Luke has created a similar introduction in 11:29 and will be responsible for the introduction here, which is marked by Lukan language. A version of the saying about the leaven of the Pharisees is found in Mark 8:15, which Matt 16:6

preserves in the same context, but with a use of προσέχετε, "beware," as here in Luke. It is not unlikely that Matthew and Luke have independently avoided Mark's idiom βλέπειν ἀπό (lit. "to see from"), but a Q source or even a distinctive Lukan source is at times claimed. Luke will have made use of the tradition here for the sake of the link with 11:37–54. The use of "hypocrisy" is probably from the source used there (though as suggested earlier, the Matthean use of "hypocrites" in every woe is his own touch).

ἐν οἷς (lit. "in which [times]") probably has the sense "during this period" (the sense "meanwhile" produces a strained sequel from 11:53–54 unless it is linked, rather ungrammatically, to the genitive absolute [as Fitzmyer, 953, appears to]). It is probable that ἐπισυναχθεισῶν (lit. "having been gathered together") refers to the compression (cf. Fitzmyer, 953: "had gathered closely") rather than to the arrival of the crowd, but this sense for the verb remains undocumented. "The crowd" is definite here because the reader has long been familiar with the regular attendance of a crowd upon Jesus. "The myriads" prepares for the trampling upon one another to come but does not by itself indicate an increase in the size of the crowds (with the trampling, however, it may). Luke may be inspired by crush scenes from Mark, not all of which has he used directly (3:9; 4:1; 5:24). As Jesus speaks to the disciples, the packed crowd can hear as well. πρῶτον is best taken here as "primarily/in the first instance" and related to the addressing of the disciples, rather than giving it a time sense ("first"), or linking it to the following warning ("above all"). The imagery of "leaven" is of a pervading influence. The leaven was a saved piece of old dough stored in fermenting juices until mixed into the fresh batch of dough (cf. 13:21). Its use as an image of corruption may have to do with the decomposition produced by the fermentation process, which allowed to go on for too long would spoil the dough. The Pharisee is not likely to be hypocritical in quite the same manner as the disciple may be tempted to be, but the example of one kind of religious hypocrisy is considered to have the potential of fostering another.

2 The materials of vv 2–9 are repeated in the same sequence in Matthew. Here apart from one compounded verb and the supplying of an ἐστίν, "is," the forms are identical, aside from an opening clause contributed by Matthew. The Markan form of the same tradition has been used at Luke 8:17. In view is the eschatological denouement in which nothing escapes detection.

3 Here it seems likely that Matthew (10:27) has recast the material to suit his mission-charge context (against Laufen, *Die Doppelüberlieferung*, 160–63, who, nonetheless, provides the best listing of the arguments). The linking ἀνθ' ὧν ("therefore" or "because" [here the former]) is probably Lukan (in the NT only here and 1:20; 19:44; Acts 12:23). The imagery of darkness and light points on the one hand to the secrecy of hidden failure in the present and on the other hand to the widespread use of the imagery of light in connection with the (revealing) presence of God. τοῖς ταμείοις, "inner chambers," are places for hiding away in Judg 16:9; 1 Kgs 22:25. In each of the parallel clauses there is a double pairing of opposites. Now in this verse it is what one *says* that cannot escape publicity at the judgment. Read within the thematic unity of the unit, what is said is either in acknowledgment or denial of the Son of Man.

4 Luke has added the fresh beginning here, "I say to you, my friends" (a small Johannine touch [cf. John 15:13–15] or a Hellenistic flourish?). He is also likely to be responsible for the other changes involved here, which primarily hold back information in order to allow the move to climax in v 5 to have a greater rhetorical effect. The supreme challenge to the profession of faith is the threat of death. The Acts account knows of those who have paid the supreme cost in this manner.

5 Luke adds the opening clauses (cf. 6:47) as a rhetorical improvement (completed with the concluding clauses, which are also his own), in connection with his addition at the start of v 4. The other changes look Lukan as well. That God kills is the OT perspective of Deut 32:39; 1 Sam 2:6; 2 Kgs 5:7; and cf. Job 1–2. Luke thinks in terms of a dual causality. 1 Sam 2:6 has exerted some influence on Luke's formulation here. "Gehenna" is a Jewish Greek term derived from the Hebrew גֵי הִנֹּם, *gê hinnōm*, meaning "valley of [the son(s) of] Hinnom" and referring to the valley that runs north-south on the west side of Jerusalem and then east-west on the south side. It had been a place of human sacrifice (Jer 7:32; 2 Kgs 16:3; etc.). Later it was a place where potters' kilns and rubbish dumps continually burned (Jer 18:1–4; 19:2, 10–13; Neh 2:13). Since God's judgment has a long history of being seen as a fire (e.g., Deut 32:22; Isa 31:9; 66:24; Jdt 16:21; *Jub.* 9:15), it is not difficult to understand that Gehenna could become an image for the place of God's judgment. (A further development of this is the lake of fire that appears in Rev 19:20; etc.) There are no known Jewish uses of the term that definitely pre-date the Gospel uses. In Luke's thought the three horizons of judgment (in the unfolding of national history, after death, and at the time of the coming of the Son of Man) are seen in close relationship to one another, though the nature of this interrelationship is nowhere clearly specified.

6 Sparrows were a cheap food source for the poor (for texts, see O. Bauernfeind, *TDNT* 7:730). The assarion was a Roman copper coin worth about one-sixteenth of a denarius. Luke has slightly different pricing information than that found in Matthew (would he know the current going price and correct to it?), and he moves the attention from the involvement of God in their fall to the earth (in death) to the more general point of the assurance that not even a single sparrow is neglected by God. This is the beginning of a "how much more" argument completed in v 7. The Matthean form could be read as simply asserting that the timing of one's martyrdom is in the hands of God (though Matt 10:30–31 does in fact broaden the point). The Lukan form assures of the pervasive care of God, here in the context of a concern about situations in which pressures to apostasy are encountered. No strong case for originality can be made in either direction, but given Luke's other editing, he is probably responsible here (but Luke's reference to "God" rather than to "the Father" may be original). Isa 49:15 makes the same kind of point, but using an opposite strategy.

7 Only minor differences separate the Matthean and Lukan wording here. The saying is to be related to a traditional idiom (coming from the phenomenon of male balding?), which represents total deliverance in a situation of potential danger by speaking of not having a single hair fall or be lost from one's head (1 Sam 14:45; 2 Sam 14:11; 1 Kgs 1:52). This idiom is used by Luke in 21:18; Acts 27:34. In the completion of the "how much more" comparison, God's care for the sparrows is individuated to the single hairs of the human head. Since God is vitally and caringly involved, disciples do not stand alone in the situations in which their allegiance to the Son of Man is under challenge.

8–9 The opening "I say to you" is probably a Lukan sectioning device as in v 4. Otherwise Luke will represent in v 8 the source shared with Matthew here, except possibly for the use of ὅς ἄν + subjunctive, rather than Matthew's ὅστις + future, for "who will. . . ." For v 9 Luke probably offers an abbreviated form of a version standing fully in parallel with the positive counterpart of v 8. (See discussion at 9:23–27, where Luke uses the Markan form of this tradition.)

To "acknowledge" (ὁμολογήσῃ) is a positive expression of what is expressed negatively, and with the language of shame, in 9:26. The use of the verb with ἐν, "in," reflects Semitic idiom. On "Son of Man," see at 5:24 and the excursus on Son of Man. On the role of the Son of Man here, see at 9:26. While I have kept in translation the traditional rendering "Son of Man," this does obscure the play between ἀνθρώπου, "person" (here: "Man"), and ἀνθρώπων, "people." Where the setting in 9:26 was the coming of the Son of Man, here the imagery is controlled by a concern to have a counterpart in heaven for the earthly situation of acknowledging or denying Jesus. This is the first Lukan text to express an interest in a heavenly location for the Son of Man. The text does not assume an immediate identity between Jesus himself and this Son of Man ("the Man of destiny"). In a broad sense, a judgment setting may be assumed from the context, but this could be as much a judgment following death (vv 4–5) as judgment at the Parousia. Rather than the concerns being strictly judicial, the focus is on who will own a committed link with whom. The angels here constitute the heavenly royal court (as in 15:10) rather than a court specifically for judgment. Luke gives less emphasis to the negative correlate in v 9: his concern is to draw forth a clear-cut acknowledgment of Jesus. The denial of v 9 is precisely what Peter was (temporarily) guilty of in 22:57, 61. This could possibly be of importance for v 10 to follow.

10 Matthew has amalgamated his parallel to this (12:32) with a related tradition found in Mark 3:28–30. The catchword linkage in the Lukan sequence may indicate that his order is that of the source, but this remains uncertain. Compared to vv 8–9, it is now Luke who uses a future and Matthew who has the subjunctive construction, but it is Luke again who uses a participial construction in place of the second relative clause. Luke is likely to have introduced the πᾶς, "everyone," to parallel v 8. Luke has been influenced in the wording of the second half of the verse by the parallel tradition of his Markan source (Mark 3:29a; the curious idiom introduced by Luke into the first half verse, λέγειν λόγον εἰς [lit. "to say a word into"] is to parallel the use of εἰς in the Markan clause [Luke combines the two in 22:65]). Luke's source combination weakens the parallelism of the two halves and allows him to make a sharper differentiation between the forgivable and the unforgivable ("Son of Man" versus "Holy Spirit"; "says a word against" versus "blasphemes").

Lövestam (*Spiritus blasphemia*) has shown how the language of blasphemy/speaking against the Holy Spirit is a natural development from the OT and later Jewish reflection on the failure of the Israelites at the time of the Exodus from Egypt (on the Spirit, see esp. Isa 63:10 and perhaps Ps 106:32–33). What is in view is not a matter of blasphemous speech, but rather the denial or rejection of the manifest saving intervention of God on behalf of his People (the use of Holy Spirit here is akin to that of "finger of God" in 11:20 [cf. Lövestam, *Spiritus blasphemia*, 35–43). The one who hardens himself or herself against what God is doing as he acts to save places himself or herself beyond the reach of God's present disposition of eschatological forgiveness. In the move from the pre- to post-Easter perspective, there is a move from understanding this text as referring to the ministry of Jesus in the power of the Spirit to understanding it in terms of the gift of the Spirit in the life of the church. The focus on the "Son of Man" in Luke's source form, as in his development of it, results in the disappearance of the original reference in the first half of the verse (cf. Mark 3:28) to the bestowal of eschatological forgiveness.

Luke may want here to distinguish such human failure as that of Peter's in 22:57 from a persistent hardening of oneself against what God is doing/has done in the ministry of Jesus, but it is more likely that, as in 11:13, we need a post-Easter perspective to make good Lukan sense of this verse (in fact the "Son of Man" reference here is a post-Easter development [cf. Mark 3:28]). Luke could be distinguishing a pre- and post-Easter situation (cf. Acts 5:32; 3:17): rejection of Jesus in his historical ministry is forgivable, but not the rejection of the witness of the Spirit in and through the present witness of Christians; or perhaps (since the whole unit is concerned with the proper acknowledgment by the disciples of their connection with Jesus), Luke may distinguish between the situation of a Christian who has received the Holy Spirit and someone who has yet to be convinced of the truth of the Christian message (as Sweetland, *Bib* 65 [1984] 73–74): not (yet) believing is forgivable, but apostasy, where the known experience of salvation through the Spirit is repudiated, is not (thus the contrasting of the mild "says a word against" with the forceful "blasphemes").

11–12 The content of vv 11–12 is a variant of what recurs in 21:14–15 (= Mark 13:11), but that it is based on a separate source is indicated by the common elements with Matt 10:19–20, and to a lesser extent with distinctive elements in Luke's form of 21:14–15. Luke has substantially modified the wording, but it is difficult to be quite clear about source wording here because of the evident influence of Mark 13:11 on the Matthean wording (and also on the Lukan). The list "synagogues and rulers and authorities" is likely to be from the source (cf. Mark 13:9; submerged in the Markan local context used by Matthew). ἀπολογήσησθε, "make a defense," is difficult in the construction here, but the pairing of verbs thus created is likely to have its counterpart in the paired verbs ἀντιστῆναι ἢ ἀντειπεῖν, "withstand or contradict," of the form of the second half of the saying preserved in Luke 21:15 (note the pairing there, as well, of "mouth" and "wisdom"). It is likely, therefore, to be from the second source and points to the dependence of 21:15 on this second source. The idiom ἐν αὐτῇ τῇ ὥρᾳ, "in that very hour," and possibly the use of δεῖ, "it is necessary," may be Lukan touches. (For the idiom of the Holy Spirit *teaching*, Luke may be influenced by a strand of tradition shared with John [see John 14:26].) Luke appears to have entirely rewritten 12:12 along the general lines of Mark 13:11c, but with his own wording. See further at 21:14, 15.

To be brought before a synagogue as a Jewish Christian would cause one to anticipate the fate reflected in Paul's words in Acts 22:19. "Rulers" and "authorities" will be the magistrates and other authorities of the Roman administration. Luke's two verbs for the response to be made to the situation may be to allow the second to refer specifically to the acknowledgment/denial of the Son of Man envisaged in vv 8–9 (cf. Kühschelm, *Jüngerverfolgung*, 227, who thinks rather of proclamation). The worry envisaged here will be about the preservation of one's life in this situation of threat. As an attitude, it is to be linked with the "worries of life" of 8:14 (cf. 21:34) as well as with the worrying about life of 12:22, 25, 26, and finally with the concern to save one's life in 9:24. Such a concern about one's life is both wrong in itself and a denial of God's care and of his control over the situation. "What it is necessary to say" is centrally to confess one's allegiance to the Son of Man (the role suggested here for vv 11–12 is partially recognized by Wrege, "Rolle des Geisteswortes," 374). The Holy Spirit will teach the disciple, in the hour of stress, the priority of confession over self-defense. Not to follow his promptings is potentially to move into the realm of blasphemy against the Holy Spirit; but the failure of Peter in 22:54–62 reminds us that it is settled repudiation, and not a temporary lapse into temptation, that should be labeled with this harsh language.

Explanation

The new section, 12:1–13:9, is concerned with the need to be ready for the coming judgment. The verses in 12:1–12 stress the need for a clear public acknowledgment of allegiance to the Son of Man.

Jesus speaks in the first instance to the disciples, but it is of importance for Luke that the crowds can hear this instruction also. The disciples are warned to avoid being influenced by the hypocrisy that is modeled by those Pharisees of whom Jesus is critical. However carefully it is hidden away, the hypocrisy of being one thing in reality and another in public image cannot survive God's searching scrutiny at the time of judgment.

Fear of what those who see us will think leads to such insincerity. And so the thread of thought leads on to the addressing of this fear. It is God who should be feared, rather than those whose hostility in the present might tempt one to disown discipleship. The hostility of such people can do no more than take your life; God can do that, but beyond death he can consign to fearsome judgment. When life and limb seem to be at threat from a hostile environment, we should not imagine that God has abandoned us. He doesn't even abandon the sparrows that seem beneath contempt for all except the poor whose meat they are. Far from abandoning you, who are much more precious, he has a record of every hair of your head!

Not hypocrisy but a clear acknowledgment before others of one's allegiance to the Son of Man is called for. He who owns is owned: the Son of Man will do in heaven in relation to you what you are prepared to do on earth in relation to him.

The link from here into v 10 is less certain. The role of the Holy Spirit in v 10 is rather like that of "the finger of God" in 11:20, and, as there, we should have in mind the Exodus from Egypt. Involved here is the denial or rejection of the presence of God in his saving power, when this presence is plain for all who are prepared to see. In the wilderness wanderings, the Israelites were guilty of such a response. Now, in connection with what God has done through Jesus, the same possibility stands open. And the one who hardens himself or herself against what God is doing as he acts to save, places himself or herself beyond the reach of God's present gift of nothing less than that very forgiveness for which one might hope on Judgment Day.

In contrasting speaking against the Son of Man and blasphemy against the Holy Spirit (note the difference in the force of the verbs), Luke thinks either of a pre-Easter rejection of Jesus, after which there is a second and last chance beyond Pentecost, or perhaps more likely of the difference between the person who is yet an outsider to Christian things and one who has known the experience of salvation through the Spirit: not (yet) believing is forgivable, but apostasy is not.

In vv 11–12 it is anticipated that making the Christian confession may make one vulnerable to both Jewish and Roman "justice." The worrying in view here is that concerned with the preservation of one's life and well-being in such a situation of threat (cf. 8:14; 9:24; 12:22–26). This kind of concern about one's life is wrong in itself, and is a denial both of God's care and of his control over the situation. The temptation is to repudiate one's Christian stance, but the Holy Spirit himself will in such times of crisis convince the true disciple of the need for faithful confession. Not to follow his promptings is potentially to move into the realm of blasphemy against the Holy Spirit; but the failure of Peter in 22:54–62 reminds us that it is settled repudiation, and not a temporary lapse into temptation, that should be labeled with this harsh language.

The Folly of Preoccupation with Possessions (12:13–21)

Bibliography

GENERAL:

Baarda, T. "Luke 12, 13–14: Text and Transmission from Marcion to Augustine." In *Christianity, Judaism and Other Greco-Roman Cults.* FS M. Smith, ed. J. Neusner. SJLA 12. Leiden: Brill, 1975. 1:107–62. **Bailey, K. E.** *Through Peasant Eyes.* 57–73. **Daube, D.** "Inheritance in Two Lukan Pericopes." *ZSSR* 72 (1955) 326–34. **Degenhardt, H.-J.** *Lukas, Evangelist der Armen.* 68–80. **Derrett, J. D. M.** "The Rich Fool: A Parable of Jesus Concerning Inheritance." *HeyJ* 18 (1977) 131–51. **Eibach, U.** "Jesus und die Güter dieser Erde!—Oder 'Von der Pflicht eines biblischen Exegeten'! Einige Anfragen zu einer höchst bedenklichen Art, biblische Exegese zu 'verwerten.'" *TB* 6 (1975) 27–30 (reply by G. Maier, pp. 72–74). **Eichholz, G.** "Vom reichen Kornbauern (Luk. 12, 13–21)." In *Gleichnisse der Evangelien.* 179–91. **Gaide, G.** "Le riche insensé Lc 12, 13–21." *AsSeign* 49 (1971) 82–89. **Gorringe, T.** "A Zealot Option Rejected? Luke 12:13–14." *ExpTim* 98 (1987) 267–70. **Horn, F. W.** *Glaube und Handeln.* 58–66. **Joüon, P.** "Le parabole du riche insensé (Luc, 12,13–21)." *RSR* 29 (1939) 486–89. **Maier, G.** "Verteilt Jesus die Güter dieser Erde? Eine Untersuchung zu Luk. 12, 13–15." *TB* 5 (1974) 149–58. **Seccombe, D. P.** *Possessions.* 139–45, 158–59. **Tarelli, C. C.** "A Note on Luke xii. 15." *JTS* 41 (1940) 260–62. **Weisskopf, R.** "Lächeln reicht nicht." *TB* 6 (1975) 23–27.

FOR 12:16–21:

Ameling, W. "*ΦΑΓΩΜΕΝ ΚΑΙ ΠΙΩΜΕΝ*: Grieschische Parallelen zu zwei Stellen aus dem Neuen Testament." *ZPE* 60 (1985) 35–43. **Baur, W.** "Der 'Endverbraucher': Betrachtung zum Gleichnis vom reichen Kornbauern (Lk 12,16–21)." In *Das Zeugnis des Lukas: Impulse für das Lesejahr C,* ed. P.-G. Müller. Stuttgart: Katholisches Bibelwerk, 1985. 70–74. **Birdsall, J. N.** "Lk xii. 16ff. and the Gospel of Thomas." *JTS* 13 (1962) 332–36. **Carroll, J. T.** *Response* *to the End of History.* 62–64. **Dupont, J.** *Les béatitudes.* 3:113–18. ————. "Die individuelle Eschatologie im Lukasevangelium und in der Apostelgeschichte." In *Orientierung an Jesus,* ed. P. Hoffmann et al. 37–47, esp. 38–41. ————. "L'Après-mort dans l'oeuvre de Luc." *RTL* 3 (1972) 3–21, esp. 3–7. **Heininger, B.** *Sondergutgleichnisse.* 40–46, 107–21. **Jeremias, J.** *Parables.* 164–65. **Joüon, P.** "Notes philologiques sur les Évangiles—Luc 12,21." *RSR* 18 (1928) 353–54. **Linnemann, E.** *Jesus of the Parables.* 4–5, 15–16, 22, 45. **Magass, W.** "Zur Semiotik der Hausfrömmigkeit (Lk. 12, 16–21: Die Beispielerzählung vom reichen Kornbauer)." *LingBib* 4 (1971) 2–5. **Reid, J.** "The Poor Rich Fool: Luke xii. 21." *ExpTim* 13 (1901–2) 567–68. **Schwarz, G.** "ταυτη τη νυκτι την ψυχην σου απαιτουσιν απο σου?" *BibNot* 25 (1984) 36–41. **Seng, E. W.** "Der reiche Tor: Eine Untersuchung von Lk. xii 16–21 unter besonderer Berücksichtigung form- und motivgeschichtlicher Aspekte." *NovT* 20 (1978) 136–55.

Translation

[13]*Someone from the crowd said to him, "Teacher, tell my brother to divide the inheritance with me."* [14]*He said to him, "Man, who appointed me a judge or divider*[a] *over you?* [15]*Watch out and be on guard against every kind of greed, because it is not in the abundance for someone of his possessions*[b] *that his life consists."*[c] [16]*He told them a parable:*[d] *"The estate of a certain rich person produced a bountiful crop,* [17]*and he pondered inwardly, saying, 'What shall I do? For I do not have anywhere where I can gather together my crops.'* [18]*He said, 'This is what I will do: I will pull down my barns and I will build bigger ones, and I will gather together there all my grain*[e] *and my good things.* [19]*Then I will say to my soul, 'Soul, you have many good things stored up for many years: take your rest, eat, drink, be merry!'* [20]*God said to him, 'Fool, this very night you will be asked to give back your soul;*[f] *what you have prepared—whose will it be?'* [21]*So it is with the one who stores up treasure with reference to himself and does not become rich with God in view."*[g]

Notes

[a] "Or divider" is missing from D Marcion 28 and some other texts (influence of v 51? [Evans, 522]).

[b] The Gr. here is difficult: ἐν τῷ περισσεύειν τινὶ . . . ἐκ τῶν ὑπαρχόντων αὐτῷ (lit. "in the to abound to a certain one . . . out of the goods/means/possessions"). This has been simplified in Cl by reading τὰ ὑπάρχοντα and relocating it immediately after τινι.

[c] Lit. "is."

[d] A redundant "saying" has been dropped in translation.

[e] The text as read is supported by P^{75} (as corrected) (ℵ^{2}) B L *f*^{1,13} etc. ℵ D it (sy^{s,c}) read τὰ γενήματα μου, "my produce," without the following "and my good things." A W Θ Ψ etc. have the same, but with the following words as well.

[f] Lit. "they will ask [back] from you your soul."

[g] D a b omit the whole of v 21.

Form/Structure/Setting

Under the umbrella of the concern of this section (12:1–13:9) with being ready for the judgment of God, the focus now moves from the need for a clear-cut acknowledgment of Jesus to the need for a right evaluation and use of material wealth. Aspects of this new concern will be developed in following units to v 34. Luke here bridges and unifies with v 15 what would otherwise be the quite disparate materials of vv 13–14 and 16–21.

Luke introduces a distinctive piece of tradition in vv 13–14, which is in the form of a pronouncement story. It seems unlikely to have been formulated in the ongoing life of the church. V 15 forms no original unity with vv 13–14, but while it has been significantly edited by Luke, it is unlikely to be his own composition (language not notably Lukan and syntax betraying a composite origin).

The parable of vv 16–20 is preserved by Luke and by the *Gospel of Thomas.* This latter form is not at all close to the Lukan form and could represent an independent transmission, but it is impossible to be certain. Luke's form certainly does not represent his development of a form like that in *Gos. Thom.* 63, since that version would form an easier unity with Luke 12:13–14. It has been claimed that the parable is a Lukan creation (e.g., Goulder, 534–39; cf. Sellin, *ZNW* 65 [1974] 166–89, esp. 168–89 [see *Bibliography* for 10:29]), but the case for this is not strong. Though Luke may be responsible for a certain amount of the wording (Luke may even be responsible for vv 17b–19a as argued by Heininger [*Sondergutgleichnissen,* 110–13]), the parable is likely to have come to him from the parables source around which he formed the journey section of his Gospel (see in excursus: "Journey to Jerusalem") and in which this parable is paralleled by that in 16:19–31 (Sellin, 182 n. 77, claims a detailed parallel rather with 16:1–9, but the most important agreement [the role of monologue] is shared also with 18:1–8 and 18:9–14 [the shared "what shall I do? . . . I shall . . ." is significant, but the story-line parallels with 16:19–31 are finally more telling]).

Various stories with a significant degree of commonality with this parable have been identified (see Seng, *NovT* 20 [1978] 147–50, for a survey of materials in which the untimely/fitting intervention of an early death is the common thread; one of the fables from *The Thousand and One Nights* is strikingly close, but for such themes as a rich man's satisfaction in his wealth and the intervention of sudden death, no common source needs to be postulated). The Gospel parable is likely to be a conscious development from Sir 11:18–20, but it is by no means the same story. Because of its folk-wisdom content, this parable can be traced back to the historical Jesus with less confidence than most other of his parables. By the same token the historical Jesus clearly related extensively to the wisdom traditions of his People, and the content of the parable would not be out of step with his teaching (see vv 22–31 to follow; cf. Seng, *NovT* 20 [1978] 154–55). There is no adequate basis for setting the parable into the ministry of Jesus by referring it to the horizon of the eschatological crisis rather than to the horizon of death (as does Jeremias, *Parables,* 165).

Luke will be responsible for the addition here of v 21. It is based on the tradition preserved in Matt 6:19–21.

Comment

Not the pursuit of wealth but the recognition of the full authority of Jesus to mediate the claims of the will of God should be the basis upon which Jesus is approached. Life does not consist of possessions, and it is foolish, indeed incredibly myopic, to think that one's responsibilities in life have come to an end if one has been able to secure one's economic future. True wealth is only accumulated when one has God in mind in the use of one's economic means.

13 The introduction is likely to be Lukan. The mention of the crowd links this piece into the larger section. On the address as teacher, see at 7:40. Here the term does not point to the role of the professional Scripture experts in applying the law (here the law of inheritance [see Deut 21:15–17; Num 27:1–11; 36:7–9]); and v 14 is hardly to be taken as a denial of scribal status! Rather, the person making the request is seeking to turn to his own ends Jesus' status and moral authority. For the purpose of the Gospel account, the rights and wrongs of the claim remain unimportant and out of sight, though no doubt the "plaintiff" will have considered that he had a good case. It is less likely that the concern is to break up an inheritance held in common, than to gain access to a withheld inheritance. The firstborn had a double claim on the inheritance, but all sons had a proper claim upon it.

14 The address, "man," is forceful, but need not be insulting (cf. 5:20; 22:58, 60). The reply echoes in an inverted manner wording from Exod 2:14 (cf. Acts 7:27, 35). "Divider" is not a separate designation but only a particular function of a judge. While "judge" comes from Exod 2:14, "divider" appears here because of the particular request addressed to Jesus. Is Jesus rejecting a role as second Moses (as Leaney, 199)? Is he identifying a fundamental difference between his own role and that of Moses (as Maier, *TB* 5 [1974] 151–54)? Or is there an irony involved here, based on a view that the person appealing wants to make use for his own ends of a perceived status and authority in Jesus without facing the claim upon his own life implicit in that status and authority? (While it did not suit the protagonists in Exod 2:14 to have Moses intervene and intervention did suit in the Gospel episode, in neither case is there a proper recognition of the role of the intervening/called-upon-to-intervene figure.) The last of the three options identified is the most likely. The allusion suggests that the logic of the man's request should press him to discipleship and so to the values promulgated by this new "Mosaic" figure (cf. Deut 18:18–19).

15 The introductory clause and the final phrase (ἐκ τῶν ὑπαρχόντων αὐτῷ, "out of his possessions") may betray the Lukan hand (in the NT only Luke uses the dative with τὰ ὑπάρχοντα). The other language is sufficiently distinctive for it to be likely that Luke is making use of traditional material here to provide the bridge between vv 13–14 and vv 16–21. The address is probably not to be understood as narrowly to the two brothers. Greed is identified frequently in the NT as a problem to be avoided (Rom 1:29; 2 Cor 9:5; Col 3:5; Eph 4:19; 5:3; 2 Pet 2:3, 14) as it is broadly in Greco-Roman thought (see Horn, *Glaube und Handeln*, 60, for texts). Greed is the desire to have more, to get one's hands on whatever one can, to acquire without reference to one's own specific needs or the situation of others. The basis for the warning against greed is the assertion that life is not to be found in possessions. The clause here is syntactically difficult. περισσεύειν can mean "to be present in abundance" or "to be more than enough"; and so, with the following τινί, "to have in abundance" or "to have more than enough" (the former seems preferable in the present setting). Probably the text before Luke (without the final phrase [see above]) carried one or the other of these senses, but Luke was conscious of imprecision and, wishing to specify his concern with the possession of material wealth, added the final qualifying phrase. (Alternately, the clumsiness could be seen as a product of the influence of two competing idioms [cf. C. F. D. Moule, "H. W. Moule on Acts iv. 25." *ExpTim* 65 [1953–54] 220–21].) "Life" here is neither physical life nor "spiritual" life, but rather a humanly meaningful and satisfying life. There is an appeal to the wisdom of experience. But already in 9:25 we have seen something of how these different "lives" merge together and interact; therefore we should not try to separate them too sharply. Luke is quite clear that one's attitude toward material possessions has a major effect on one's openness to what God is doing in and through Jesus, as upon how one will be received before God in judgment. While the "greed" clause relates most pointedly back to the concern over inheritance, the clause about the abundance of possessions corresponds more closely with the parable to come.

16 Once again the introductory clause will be a Lukan transition to a new unit of tradition. *ἀνθρώπου τινός*, "of a certain person," could be Lukan (for the genitive construction, cf. 7:2), but may be, rather, a style feature of one or more of Luke's sources (see further at 10:30, and, on Luke's parables source, in the excursus: "Journey to Jerusalem"). V 16:19 also introduces a parable about a rich person (cf. 16:1). For the Lukan reader the mention of wealth will already produce a rather negative set of resonances (see esp. 6:24, 8:14 and the reversal language of 1:52–53), but if this story has a pre-Lukan integrity, it will be important in the first instance not to intrude this negative evaluation prematurely into the story itself (on the other hand the possibility of reversal of fortunes may come in already from folk-tale expectations). Luke does not elsewhere use *χώρα* with the sense required here ("estate/property/fields"). The story is about this rich person's response to the bounty of one particular year's crop.

17 *τί ποιήσω*, "what shall I do," could be a Lukan touch (introduced at 20:13; found also at 16:3; cf. at 3:10), but Luke modifies this same language at 18:18. The advantage of soliloquy for a storyteller is that the character is able thereby to be rendered totally transparent. The capacity of present storage arrangements is now exhausted, presumably to the degree that the bounty of the present crop exceeded this farmer's prudent expectations.

18 To the "what shall I do" of v 17 corresponds the "I shall do this" found here. The vocabulary for storage of grain in vv 17–18 is found also at 3:17. *τὰ ἀγαθά*, "good things," generalizes from the preceding "grain," but probably not beyond the range of farm produce intended in v 16 (against Fitzmyer, 973). Thus far the man is an exemplary model of forward thinking, practical wisdom, and readiness for decisive action.

19 Luke uses *κεῖσθαι* (lit. "to place") quite often, but not elsewhere with the sense "to lay/store up." "Eat, drink, and be merry" had become a traditional trio long before this parable was coined (Eccl 2:24; 3:13; 5:18; 8:15; Judg 19:4–9; Tob 7:10; cf. Isa 22:13 [= 1 Cor 15:32]; Sir 11:19; there are also non-Jewish parallels [see Fitzmyer, 973]), but the choice of *εὐφραίνειν* for "be merry" might be Lukan. The "soul" is here the "self" but with overtones of the life-force that animates the body (as in the imagery of Gen 2:7). The enjoyment of life here is not the "last meal before execution" of Isa 22:13, nor is it the modest comfort held out by the Preacher of Ecclesiastes to the toiler in the midst of the vanity of it all; but neither is it the innocent enjoyment of a Tobit. It comes closest to the self-satisfaction of Sir 11:19: "I have found rest and now I will eat of my good things" (but not with the criticism of the means of gaining the wealth found in v 18; note the shared use of the *ἀναπαυ-* ["rest"] and *φαγ-* roots, and of *ἀγαθά*, "good things"). Sir 11:20 continues "Persevere in your duty, take pleasure in doing it, and grow old at your work." (Note the confluence with Ecclesiastes here.)

20 *ταύτῃ τῇ νυκτί*, "this very night," is likely to be Lukan wording (added at 17:34; cf. Acts 27:23), as just possibly *ἄφρων*, "fool" (cf. at 11:40), and *ἀπαιτοῦσιν*, "ask for the return [of]" (cf. at 6:30), but "fool" forms such a vital role in the drama of the story that it is best seen as original, and for ἀπαιτοῦσιν it is difficult to see Luke using the impersonal third person plural in place of the passive (the same idiom, i.e., the request for the return of the soul, is found in Wis 15:8, but with the passive form of the verb). In the parable, nothing is made of how God speaks to the farmer, but we should probably understand that his plans of v 18 have already been carried out (cf. "prepared" in v 20). Wherein lies his folly? Different answers are given: the failure to recognize the fleeting nature of life (cf. Pss 39:5–8, 13; 90:12); the failure to prepare for what lies beyond death (v 21 can easily be read in this context, esp. if linked to v 5); the failure to consider God (cf. Jas 4:13–5:6); selfish preoccupation with one's own life and pleasures; etc. If Sir 11:19–20 can be something of a guide, then the problem is likely to stem from the view that one's responsibilities in life end with the securing of one's own economic future. The farmer had no business stopping at the point where his own future has been assured by the windfall of an unusually good crop. At this point his responsibilities had only just begun (is there some negative echo of Joseph's handling of the bumper crops of Egypt?). In defining this broader responsibility, one's answerability to God is not to be left out of account. The life-force, from which stems all our power to act, one has as a trust from God, and he may ask for its return at any point. The foolishness of the farmer's narrow aims is highlighted by the contrast between his many years of supply and the few hours that remain to him of life. He has considered only his own present life, but his stockpile of good things will be of no benefit to that life, for God has now asked for its return. It may be that Ps 49:13 (in its context) has had an influence on the thought here as well, and that we should discern in the exultation of v 19 a foolish confidence that in securing his economic future, the farmer has secured the future of his life itself as well—he has not reckoned with God. In the larger Lukan section, the prospect of death necessarily introduces, as well, the prospect of judgment (see v 5).

21 While not likely to be an original part of the parable, this verse is an appropriate (Lukan and based on the tradition reflected in Matt 6:19–21 [cf. Luke 12:33–34]?) application of it. The verse does not directly criticize the accumulation of wealth (though elsewhere Luke is insistent upon its dangers) but is content to emphasize the need to be rich in a Godward direction. The detail of the imagery of the verse is difficult, probably because of Lukan compression. πλουτῶν, "being/becoming rich," is the result of θησαυρίζων, "treasuring up," and so functions as a synonym for this verb in the second phrase. If we take the dative ἑαυτῷ as "with reference to himself" and εἰς θεόν as "with God in view," then an appropriate balance is achieved. In both cases the person gets rich, but in the second case he is accumulating his treasure in heaven (cf. Matt 6:19–21; Sir 29:8–17; Tob 4:9; *Pss. Sol.* 9:5). This wealth is accumulated primarily by, in obedience to God, making use of one's material wealth to meet the needs of the poor.

Explanation

The focus of answerability moves now from the need for a clear-cut acknowledgment of Jesus to the need for a right evaluation and use of material wealth. The appeal to Jesus to intervene in an inheritance dispute threatens to be a bizarre and inverted repetition of what happened when Moses intervened in Exod 2:14. The rich man, feeling that all his life's needs are fully satisfied by his recent bumper crop, finds that he is in for a rude surprise.

The rights and wrongs of the claims of the person who asks for Jesus to intervene remain unimportant and out of sight in the Gospel account, though no doubt he will have considered that he had a good case. The story emphasizes this person's attempt to turn to his own ends Jesus' status and moral authority.

Jesus declines to intervene, and says so by means of an allusion to Exod 2:14. The tone is ironical, and Jesus seems to challenge the petitioner to recognize whether he is trying to make use of a perceived status and authority in Jesus without facing the claim upon his own life implicit in that status and authority. If Jesus is some kind of "new Moses," then he needs to be heard and obeyed (Deut 18:18–19).

This challenge gives way to teaching on greed and the nature of life. Greed is the desire to have more, to get one's hands on whatever one can, to acquire without reference to one's own specific needs or the situation of others. The greedy person is confused about life, since a humanly meaningful and satisfying life has very little to do with how extensive one's possessions are. The "greed" clause relates most pointedly back to the concern over inheritance; the clause about the abundance of possessions corresponds more closely with the parable to come.

The farmer of our story was already rich before his claim to economic sufficiency is sealed by the bounty of one of those very special years when everything has gone right. His barns have no capacity to contain all the produce of this bountiful year, so with clear-sightedness and practical wisdom he upgrades his storage capability so that all his stores can be maintained most efficiently.

When the work is done, he will be in a position to relax and enjoy his good fortune. All his responsibilities in life will have now been met, and all the needs of his life will now be satisfied, or so he thinks. (The "soul" by which the farmer addresses himself is the "self" but with overtones of the life-force that animates the body.) But God bursts in upon the self-satisfaction of his life. At this point, with so much wealth at his disposal, this person should rightly have seen that his responsibilities had only begun. (There may be a [negative] echo of how Joseph dealt with the bumper crops of Egypt in the seven good years.) This farmer has not reckoned on his answerability to God for his life. The life-force, from which stems all our power to act (see Gen 2:7), one has as a trust from God, and he may ask for its return at any point. As the parable ends, the foolishness of the farmer's narrow aims is highlighted by the contrast between his many years of supply and the few hours that remain to him of life. Did he think that in securing his economic future he had secured the future of his life as well?

V 21 offers a final application of the parable. It is really a compressed expression of what we find in Matt 6:19–21 (and compare Luke 12:32–33). The farmer was right to the extent that he saw that life is about the accumulation of wealth, but what kind of wealth should we be primarily concerned with accumulating? To "become rich with God in view" refers in the present context primarily to the use in obedience to God of one's material wealth for the relief of real needs in the world. The point could be generalized to all acts of compassion.

The Generous Provider Requires Generous Disciples (12:22–34)

Bibliography

Alon, A. *The Natural History of the Land of the Bible.* Garden City, NY: Doubleday, 1978. 155–74. **Catchpole, D.** "The ravens, the lilies and the Q hypothesis: A form-critical perspective on the source-critical problem." *SNTU* 6/7 (1981–82) 77–87. **Chilton, B. D.** *God in Strength.* 231–50. **Dalman, G.** "Die Lilie der Bibel." *PJ* 21 (1925) 98–100. **Degenhardt, H.-J.** *Lukas, Evangelist der Armen.* 80–93. **Derrett, J. M. D.** "Birds of the Air and Lilies of the Field." *DR* 105 (1987) 181–92. **Dillon, R. J.** "Ravens, Lilies, and the Kingdom of God (Matthew 6:25–33/Luke 12:22–31)." *CBQ* 53 (1991) 605–27. **Dupont, J.** *Les béatitudes.* 3:122–24. **Fuchs, E.** "Die Verkündigung Jesu: Der Spruch von der Raben." In *Der historische Jesus und der kerygmatische Christus,* ed. H. Ristow and K. Matthiae. 3rd ed. Berlin: Evangelische Verlagsanstalt, 1964. 385–88. **George, A.** "L'Attente du maître qui vient: Lc 12,32–48." *AsSeign* 50 (1974) 66–76. **Ha-Reubeni, E.** "Les lis des champs." *RB* 54 (1947) 362–64. **Healey, J. F.** "Models of Behavior: Matt 6:26 (//Luke 12:24) and Prov 6:6–8." *JBL* 108 (1989) 497–98. **Hoffmann, P.** "Der Q-Text der Sprüche vom Sorgen Mt 6,25–33/Lk 12,22–31: Ein Rekonstruktionsversuch." In *Studien zum Matthäusevangelium.* FS W. Pesch, ed. L. Schenke. SBS. Stuttgart: Katholisches Bibelwerk, 1988. 127–55. **King, G. B.** "Consider the Lilies." *CrQ* 10 (1933) 28–36. **Mealand, D. L.** "'Paradisial' Elements in the Teaching of Jesus [12, 22–32]." In *Studia Biblica, II,* ed. E. A. Livingstone. JSNTSup 2. Sheffield: JSOT, 1980. 179–84. **Mees, M.** "Das Sprichtwort Mt. 6,21/Lk. 12,34 und seine auserkanonischen Parallelen." *Augustinianum* 14 (1974) 67–89. **Meyer, B. F.** "Jesus and the Remnant of Israel." *JBL* 84 (1965) 123–30. **Molitor, J.** "Zur Überzetzung von *μετεωρίζεσθε* Lk 12,29." *BZ* 10 (1966) 107–8. **Montgomery, J. A.** "Some Correspondences between the Elephantine Papyri and the Gospels." *ExpTim* 24 (1912–13) 428–29. **Nötscher, F.** "Das Reich (Gottes) und seine Gerechtigkeit (Mt 6,33 vgl. Lc 12,31)." *Bib* 31 (1950) 237–41. **Olsthoorn, M. F.** *The Jewish Background and the Synoptic Setting of Matt. 6 ,25–33 and Luke 12, 22–31.* Studium Biblicum Franciscanum, Analecta 10. Jerusalem: Franciscan Printing Press, 1975. **Pesch, R.** "'Sei getrost, kleine Herde' (Lk 12,32): Exegetische und ekklesiologische Erwägungen." In *Krise der Kirche—Chance des Glaubens: Die 'Kleine Herde' heute und morgan,"* ed. K. Färber. Frankfurt: Knecht, 1968. 85–118. ———. *Die kleine Herde: Zur Theologie der Gemeinde.* Reihe 10. Graz: Styria, 1973. **Pesch, W.** "Zur Exegese von Mt 6,19–21 und Lk 12,33–34." *Bib* 41 (1960) 356–78. ———. "Zur Formgeschichte und Exegese von Lk 12,32." *Bib* 41 (1960) 25–40. **Riesenfeld, H.** "Vom Schätzesammeln und Sorgen—Ein Thema urchristlicher Paränese: Zu Mt VI 19–34." In *Neotestamentica et patristica.* FS O. Cullmann, ed. W. C. van Unnik. NovTSup 6. Leiden: Brill, 1962. 47–58. **Schlosser, J.** *Le règne de Dieu..* 2:573–601. **Schwarz, G.** "*προσθεῖναι ἐπὶ τὴν ἡλικίαν αὐτοῦ πῆχυν ἕνα.*" *ZNW* 71 (1980) 244–47. **Seccombe, D. P.** *Possessions.* 146–59. **Souček, J. B.** "The Good Shepherd and His Flock." *ER* 9 (1957) 143–53. **Steinhauser, M. G.** "The Sayings on Anxieties: Matt 6:25–34 and Luke 12:22–32." *Forum* 6.1 (1990) 67–79. **Tannehill, R. C.** *The Sword of His Mouth.* 61–67. **Wrege, H.-T.** *Die Überlieferung der Bergpredigt.* WUNT 9. Tübingen: Mohr-Siebeck, 1968. 116–23.

Translation

[22]*He said to his*[a] *disciples, "On this basis I say to you, Do not be worried for [your]*[b] *soul*[c]*: what shall you eat? or for [your]*[d] *body: what shall you put on?* [23]*For*[e] *the soul is more than food, and the body than clothing.* [24]*Consider*[f] *the ravens! For they do not sow,*

nor do they reap; for them there is no storeroom and no barn; yet God feeds them. How much more you are worth than the birds! [25]*Which of you by worrying can add a small amount*[g] *to his span of life?* [26]*If then, you cannot [do such] a very small thing, why do you worry about the other things?*[h] [27]*Consider the lilies—how they grow. They neither work hard nor spin; but I say to you, not even Solomon in all*[i] *his glory robed himself as one of these.* [28]*If God so clothes the grass in the field, which is there today and tomorrow is thrown into the oven, how much more you, you*[j] *people of little faith!* [29]*Do not have as your constant consideration:*[k] *what shall you eat? and*[l] *what shall you drink? And do not be anxious!* [30]*For all the nations of the world have these things as their constant consideration*[m] *and your Father knows that you need these things.* [31]*But have his*[n] *kingdom as your constant consideration*[o] *and these things will be given to you in addition.* [32]*Do not be afraid, little flock, because your Father had determined in his pleasure*[p] *to give the kingdom to you.* [33]*Sell your possessions and give alms. Make for yourselves treasure-sacks which will not age, a treasure unfailing in heaven, where a thief does not draw near and a moth does not destroy.* [34]*For where your treasure is, there will your heart be as well."*

Notes

[a] "His" is not found in P[75] B 1241 c e.

[b] Probably under the influence of the Matthean text, "your" is present in P[45] Ψ *f*[13] etc.

[c] For the sake of the antithesis with "body" and for continuity with v 20, ψυχή is here rendered "soul," but the force is close to "life."

[d] Probably under the influence of the Matthean text, "your" is present in B 070 *f*[13] etc.

[e] Omitted by P[75] A E G H Q W Δ Ψ etc.

[f] P[45] adds τὰ πετεινὰ τοῦ οὐρανοῦ καί, "the birds of heaven and," conflating the Matthean and Lukan readings.

[g] "Small amount": πηχῦν (lit. "cubit").

[h] τῶν λοιπῶν, lit. "the rest."

[i] Omitted by P[45].

[j] "You" is not repeated in the Gr.

[k] "Have as your constant consideration": ζητεῖτε (lit. "seek"). "Constant" represents here the force of the present tense.

[l] P[75] A D W Θ Ψ etc. read ἤ, "or."

[m] ἐπιζητοῦσιν. Cf. *Note* k.

[n] P[45] A D[1] W Θ etc. have τοῦ θεοῦ, "of God."

[o] As *Note* k.

[p] "Has determined in his pleasure": εὐδόκησεν.

Form/Structure/Setting

The unit here is taken as vv 22–34. One could divide before or after v 32, but it seems best to see the whole as forming a for-the-disciples parallel to vv 13–21, which maps out for them a proper orientation to material goods (note especially the relationship between v 21 and vv 33–34; the scope of the relevance of vv 35–40 to follow is then deliberately ambiguous, to be resolved in vv 41–48 in terms of a relevance to both disciples and to others, but in somewhat different ways).

Luke continues with the source he shares from Matthew, picking up again where he left off after v 12. Matthew and Luke each go their own way with v 32. For vv 33–34 Luke again takes up the shared source, probably following again its ordering of the materials (but this will not reflect an original unity). An original unity for vv 22–31 can be questioned at various points. Among recent source analyses, that of Catchpole (*SNTU* 6/7 [1980–81] 77–87) seems most cogent. He suggests that v 23 is a later insertion (different thrust and use of language), which has led to the introduction of the language of body and soul into v 22. V 25 (v 26 is probably Lukan) is likewise an addition (but the flow here, at least in the Matthean form, can be made to work better than Catchpole allows), as is v 30a (introducing the "pagans" here intrudes quite a new idea). Of these insertions, v 30a (even in the earlier Matthean form) is hardly likely to go back to the historical Jesus, but the other pieces could well be authentic fragments of the tradition. The historicity of the material in v 32 is cautiously affirmed in the discussion below. V 33 is likely to be a Lukan formulation (though v 33b is one of those places from which the case for second form for the Q tradition gains its credibility; perhaps Luke has been influenced here by the wording of another form of the tradition of Matt 6:19–21), interpreting v 34 and partly inspired by the traditional material reflected in Matt 6:19.

Comment

In a measure of conscious parallelism to vv 13–22, the present unit challenges the disciples to freedom from worry about the subsistence needs of life (God cares even for ravens and grass flowers). Instead they should be concerned with the kingdom of God (they are assured that God's good pleasure is that they shall have it) and the dispersal of one's money in almsgiving, which creates a treasure with God in heaven.

22 Luke supplies the first clause, which now moves the focus onto address to the disciples (cf. vv 1, 41). Otherwise Matthew (6:25) and Luke are close. *διὰ τοῦτο*, "on this basis," is part of the tradition here (cf. Matt 6:25 [on the basis of vocabulary links and style similarities, the original antecedent is likely to have been the source behind Luke 12:11–12]) and should be read as indicating a continuity of subject matter with what precedes. This continuity is also underlined by the presence of *τῇ ψυχῇ*, "the soul/life" (cf. v 20). Further afield, note the use of *μεριμνᾶν*, "to be worried," and the question form in v 11, as well as the soul and body language in the source behind v 4 (see there). On being worried/anxious, see at 8:14; 10:41; 12:11. Here food sustains life inwardly as necessary nourishment, and clothing protects the body outwardly from the threat of the elements. There is no dualism here of soul and body. The perspective is that of basic survival, not that of comfort or luxury.

23 Again the text forms are close: Luke has a *γάρ*, "for," clause for Matthew's *οὐχί*, "is it not?" question form. The point is that life is not simply about surviving. Indeed there are things manifestly more important than surviving. The sentiment has links with that of Matt 10:28b (in Luke's source part of the larger context of the present verse) and in a different way with Luke 12:15b. "Soul" and "body" have a wider sense than in v 22. Vv 22–31 exhibit the same interaction, seen in vv 4–7, between an affirmation of God's involvement in issues of survival and the identification of more important horizons.

24 The text forms diverge further in this verse, but with no great effect upon meaning. Both evangelists seem to have introduced changes (Luke: *κατανοήσατε*, "consider" [as in v 27; 20:23]; *ταμεῖον*, "storeroom" [cf. 12:3]; *πόσῳ* (*μᾶλλον*), "how much (more)" [as v 28; cf. 11:13]; Matthew: *τὰ πετεινά*, "the birds" [see Luke 12:24 end]; *ὁ πατὴρ ὑμῶν ὁ οὐράνιος*, "your heavenly Father" [with variation in pronoun seven times in Matthew]). The issue of food is taken up here in v 24; that of clothing will be addressed in v 27. The choice of "raven" here seems to be based on Job 38:41 (cf. Ps 147:9), where, however, the point made by pointing to God's care for the ravens is quite different. The uncleanness of such birds of prey may play a role in the choice ("God feeds even the ravens"; see Lev 11:15; Deut 14:14), as may, just possibly, an ancient image of ravens as particularly careless (for texts see Fitzmyer, 978). Sowing and reaping and the use of storeroom and barn are the ways in which people do what they can to guarantee a continued supply of their basic sustenance needs. Ravens do not take such precautions, yet God feeds them all the same! And you are much more valuable than birds.

In an agricultural economy, what could be made of what seems at first blush to be advice to abandon all farming and storage of produce? For Catchpole (*SNTU* 6/7 [1981–82] 82), this advice is to be related to the expectation of an imminent eschatological crisis. For Degenhardt (*Lukas*, 80–85), this demand is restricted to the circle of Jesus' followers, and then by implication to later Christian leaders, but not ordinary Christians. But Tannehill (*The Sword of His Mouth*, 60–67) seems closer to the mark when he says (65), "This argument has force only if the birds and flowers become resonant images for a reality which transcends them." The image is meant to evoke an awareness of God's pervasive care and provision, not to give encouragement to be as careless as the ravens. What the ravens fail to do speaks to us, but does not exactly tell us what we should do. As often with Jesus' teaching (cf. at 10:38–42), while having our present patterns of action put in question, we are not ultimately told what to do about the details of life; we are being addressed at a different level.

25 Luke follows his source closely here. This general statement about the ineffectualness of worry is located, with a certain artistry, between the developments, respectively, on worry about food and about clothing; but it does not seem possible to achieve a close integration of its sense into its immediate setting. ἡλικίαν may mean "age/span of life" or "stature" (cf. at 2:52); πῆχυς means "a cubit [c. eighteen inches]," but is probably used in a temporal sense here ("a small amount"; cf. Diogenes Laertius, *Plato* 3.11; and for a similar idiom Ps 39:5). The point is probably that no amount of worrying (or indeed the farsighted activity produced by such worry) can *guarantee* even the smallest gain in longevity. But to judge from v 26 to come, Luke takes the worrying here as something quite distinct from the preoccupation with the issues of food and clothing.

26 Did Luke have difficulty with v 25 and try to help with this addition? (Matthew has a clause that introduces the material on concern about dress from which Luke has the words "why do you worry?") If worry will not extend life even to the smallest degree, then why extend worrying into other areas, like the concern for food and clothing, where it will prove just as fruitless?

27 The differences from the Matthean text are slight (Luke will be responsible for κατανοήσατε, "consider," as in v 24, and the grammatically preferable singular verbs with the neuter plural subjects; but τοῦ ἀγροῦ, "of the field," may be Matthew's touch to underline the identity of "the lilies" and "the grass" of the Matt 6:30 [Luke 12:28]). Used technically, κρίνα may have referred to the white lily, *candidum lilium*, but the term was more often used loosely of any flowers that had a lily-like appearance. Where the activities singled out in connection with the production of food were sowing, harvesting, and storage, the activities now singled out in connection with the provision of clothing are working hard (quite a general term is used) and spinning (probably we are to think of a choice between hard work to earn enough to purchase the cloth or domestic production of one's own cloth). There is no OT comment on Solomon's dress, but the riches and pomp of his court had become legendary (1 Kgs 10:4–5, 21, 23; 2 Chr 9:4, 20, 22). There is a heightening here compared to v 24, where only subsistence was in view. The argument here turns on a shared awareness that the beauties of nature exceed those of human craft and industry. (For a contrary view, see Derrett, *DR* 105 [1987] 186 and n. 29.)

28 The changes of wording here are slight and are all likely to be Lukan (a series of symmetrical balances in the Lukan form suit his sense of artistry). When wood is valuable and in short supply, then the natural field grasses (along with the wild flowers found there), as well as the chaff from the harvest, serve to eke out the fuel supply (contrary to the comment offered in WBC 35A, this is probably the imagery of 3:17 as well). The transience of the field grasses (cf. Job 8:12; Pss 37:2; 90:5–6; 102:12; 103:15; Isa 37:27; 40:6–8) points to their limited significance when compared to that of a human life. Again the vision is of God's pervasive care and provision, this time with a note of generosity. "You people of little faith" points to the pervasiveness of human anxiety about the basic provisions for life, which, given this vision of God as generous provider, can only be described as a limitation of faith. Matthew develops the idea of disciples being "people of little faith."

29 Luke is likely to be more original here with his second person forms (cf. v 22), but his "do not be anxious" with its use of the rare *μετεωρίζεσθαι* in an unusual sense will be his own contribution, disturbing the threefold listing, which would be needed to parallel v 22. The use of *ζητεῖτε*, "seek," is likely to be secondary on the same grounds (probably from v 31 [and cf. the use of a compound form of the verb in v 30]).

30 By shifting "all" from "these things" to "nations" (this analysis is confirmed by Luke's dropping of the subsequent occurrences of "all") and adding "of the world," Luke softens the "pagans" overtones of *τὰ ἔθνη*, "nations/Gentiles," in the Matthean form. Now the reference is simply to the normal human condition. Luke changes *γάρ*, "for" (but occasionally equivalent to *δέ*), into *δέ* (here: "and") to clarify and reorder the logic of the thought, but it will be Matthew who adds "heavenly" to the reference to God as Father (cf. at v 24). The reference to God as Father with its overtones of God as provider (cf. esp. 11:2–3, 13) suits better the Matthean thought links. For Luke, the emphasis is on "you need these things."

31 Luke creates an emphatic contrast here with his introduction of *πλήν*, "but" (Matthew has *δέ*). "And his righteousness" in the Matthean version will be his own addition (cf. 5:6; etc). Luke drops the "all" from "all things" as a continuation of his changes in v 30. On "his kingdom," see at 4:43 and 6:20. Both the new experience of the rule of God, being encountered in the present ministry of Jesus, and the eschatological consummation of this are in view. For the sentiment expressed here, cf. 18:29–30. The inclusion of v 31 (and cf. the "disciples" of v 22) makes the focus of the whole unit not God as provider for all of humanity (as Matt 5:45; Luke 6:35; Acts 14:17) but God as provider for those who are committed to his rule as manifested in the ministry of Jesus.

32 This verse has no parallel in Matthew, who concludes his section with "Do not be worried about tomorrow . . ." (6:34). It is likely that both evangelists have added further (traditional) material to their shared source. "Your Father" and "kingdom" provide immediate links with vv 30–31, and "do not be afraid" can be linked with the worry/anxiety language of the unit. "Do not fear" reflects the vulnerability of the flock in its littleness (cf. Amos 7:2, 5). "Flock" is a stock image for Israel/Judah (Jer 13:17; Ezek 34; Zech 10:3; etc.). "To give you the kingdom" probably alludes to Dan 7:14, 27 (cf. vv 17, 22). Taken alone, the text announces the coming of salvation, rather than the judgment of God, or (its expression in [ongoing]) oppression by the Gentiles. It is, however, regularly (and probably correctly) assumed that this language is spoken not to a general audience but to those who have responded to the ministry of Jesus and in connection with whom the prophetic promises alluded to are to come to their fulfillment. Discussion over whether the historical Jesus could have spoken like this has been dominated by the question of whether a remnant consciousness can be predicated of him. In the terms in which the question is normally put, Jesus must be distanced from groups of his day that were concerned about the gathering of the holy remnant (e.g., Qumran). But as Meyer (*JBL* 84 [1965] 123–30) has shown, Jesus' proclamation of the kingdom and of coming judgment, his links with John the Baptist (who was concerned with the salvation of a [repentant and baptized] remnant), his experience of rejection by some, and a realization that a preserved remnant of Israel can actually co-exist with a universalist salvific mission combine to make it not unlikely that Jesus did think in terms of the salvation of a remnant. The materials here have their closest Gospel parallels in Luke 22:28–29 and Mark 14:27–28.

33 Vv 33–34 are partially paralleled in Matt 6:19–21, probably continuing where Luke broke off from this shared source after v 12. "Sell your goods and give alms" looks like a Lukan formulation (cf. 11:41 and Luke's frequent use of *τὰ ὑπάρχοντα*, "possessions/means/property"), perhaps inspired by the tradition he will use in 18:22 (from where the following "treasure in heaven" may also have come). *ἀνέκλειπτον*, "unfailing," may be Luke's formulation to contrast with v 20. It is hard to be sure whether the imagery of a non-aging purse is traditional or Luke's own. The change of verbs to "draws near" and "destroys" may well be Luke's. The doubling up of terms in the Matthean form is as likely to be Matthew's addition as Luke's deletion (Matt 6:19 itself could be a Matthean product of this doubling instinct [as Schneider, 286]).

The horizon here moves quite away from the survival concerns of vv 22–31. Built on, however, are the confidence in God as provider, the affirmation that life is about more than surviving (v 23), and the concern and confidence that God will give the kingdom (vv 31–32). In contrast to the rich man's strategy (vv 16–20), disencumberment and generous dispersal to the needy are commended (the injunction here lacks the "all" of 18:22). For the importance of almsgiving in Jewish piety, cf. Tob 4:8–9; *1 Enoch* 38:2; *2 Enoch* 50:5. It is unclear whether "treasure-sacks (*βαλλάντια*) that will not age" refers to treasure containers that will not break open and lose their contents or, perhaps better, to sacks of treasure (the containers standing for the contents; the apposition favors this) that will not be subject to any form of natural deterioration (cf. Matthew's "corrosion ruins" in 6:19, 20). Taking the latter, this treasure does not deteriorate with age, nor is it vulnerable to thieves or to insect pests. For the presence of treasure in heaven, see at 12:21. The thought is of a treasure secured with God and making one rich, i.e., valued, in his eyes. While often assumed, the idea is not specifically of a treasure that goes on before us to the heaven we will reach through death.

34 Matthew and Luke agree closely, the only notable difference being the individuation that marks the Matthean text (each individual deposits his own treasure [second person singular rather than plural forms]). Secular Greek literature can match the general sentiment of this maxim (Sextus Empiricus, *Hypotyp.* 1.136; Epictetus, *Diat.* 2.22.19). The point could either be: "follow the trail of the use of money and it will lead you to the heart," or "the heart will follow the financial investment." Probably the former. The heart that is with God (in heaven) will be the heart that has the kingdom of God as its constant consideration (v 31).

Explanation

In important ways the unit here runs parallel to that in vv 13–21. It builds upon vv 13–21 and is a more hard-hitting rendering of its concerns, fashioned specifically for the disciple rather than for the general hearer. It commends freedom from worry about the basic needs of life (God is the generous provider), preoccupation with the kingdom of God (God has determined that you shall have it), and the dispersal of one's money in charitable causes (which is like banking it with God in heaven).

Food sustains life (here the soul: the spark of life) inwardly as necessary nourishment, and clothing protects the body outwardly from the threat of the elements. The disciple is not to worry about such basic survival needs. Why? More than one line of reasoning is offered. First, such preoccupying worry is inappropriate because life is not simply about surviving. Indeed there are things manifestly more important than physical survival (cf. vv 4–7; 12:15; Matt 10:28). Yet more significant, however, is that such worry is based upon a faulty vision of God. Ravens do none of the things people do to try to guarantee a continuity of supply of their basic needs for sustenance. We are not encouraged here to be as careless as the ravens but, in recognizing that people matter much more to God than ravens, to have an awareness, evoked through this image, of God's pervasive care and provision. Ordinary human patterns are challenged here, but since Jesus is certainly not recommending that farming be given up in Palestine, it is clear that we are ultimately being addressed at a different level. In a moment, a parallel point will be made by pointing to the field lilies, but first there is a more general statement about the futility of worry: it cannot (guarantee to) extend life in the slightest, so it is not a very effective strategy in life.

The beautiful flowers of the field neither work hard to have the money to buy their clothing, nor are they, as an alternative, involved in the domestic production of cloth for their own clothing. It simply comes from the generous hand of God. For all who have the eyes to recognize the unmatchable beauties of nature, there can be no doubt that even Solomon in all his legendary splendor could not match the beauty of the flowers. But these flowers are only part of the field grasses that (in part) fuel the ovens in a land where wood is valuable and scarce. Their value is nothing like that of a person. In the light of such a vision of God, our normal human worrying must be seen as a measure of the smallness of our faith.

The opening challenge is reiterated in v 29 and then freshly supported in the following verses. This preoccupation is the normal human condition ("all the nations of the world"), and God knows that it corresponds with our actual human needs. But these sustenance needs should come to us as God's gift to those who make the kingdom of God their constant consideration. In the use of the phrase "his kingdom," Luke will have in mind both the new experience of the rule of God, being encountered in the present ministry of Jesus, and the end-time completion of this.

To our need to focus our lives on the kingdom of God corresponds Jesus' assurance that God has determined in his pleasure to give it to his own People. "Flock" is a stock image for Israel (or Judah), here carried over to those who have responded to the ministry of Jesus, in connection with whom the prophetic promises alluded to are to come to their fulfillment. "To give you the kingdom" probably alludes to Dan 7: 14, 27, where the kingdom is promised in vision to the saints of God. "Do not fear," with its counterpart in "little," reflects the vulnerability of the flock in its littleness to the judgment of God or the threat of the nations. In the Lukan context, however, it may reflect the minority response to the gospel and the pressure placed upon Christians by their neighbors.

The disciples' alternative to the rich man's behavior is radical generosity to the needy. This is how to store up treasure-sacks whose contents are not vulnerable to the ravages of time; this will create a treasure trove that will not fail one, as the rich man's treasure did at his untimely death, and that will not be accessible to the thief or to insect pests. (We need to take a rather wider view of treasure here than simply money or jewels. For example, costly garments could well be implied.) How does this work? As in 11:41, such action creates a "bank account" with God. One is considered rich, that is, valued, in his eyes. The appropriateness of this course of action is supported by the maxim with which the unit ends in v 34. If one follows the trail marked out by a person's use of money, it will lead to that person's heart. The heart that is with God (in heaven) will thereby demonstrate that it has the kingdom of God as its constant consideration (v 31).

Be Ready and Alert, and on the Job for the Master (12:35–48)

Bibliography

Aarde, A. G. van. "Narrative Point of View: An Ideological Reading of Luke 12:35–48." *Neot* 22 (1988) 235–52. **Bauckham, R.** "Synoptic Parousia Parables and the Apocalypse." *NTS* 23 (1976–77) 162–76. **Betz, O.** "The Dichotomized Servant and the End of Judas Iscariot (Light on the Dark Passages: Matthew 24,51 and parallel; Acts 1,18)." *RevQ* 5 (1964–65) 43–58. **Beyer, K.** *Semitische Syntax.* 287–93. **Botha, J.** "Iser's Wandering Viewpoint: A Reception-analytical Reading of Luke 12:35–48." *Neot* 22 (1988) 253–68. **Carroll, J. T.** *Response to the End of History.* 53–60. **Clarke, A. K.,** and **Collie, N. E. W.** "A Comment on Luke xii 41–58." *JTS* 17 (1915–16) 299–301. **Combrink, H. J. B.** "Readings, Readers and Authors: An Orientation." *Neot* 22 (1988) 189–203. **Detering, P. E.** "Eschatological and Eucharistic Motifs in Luke 12:35–40." *ConcJ* 5 (1979) 85–91. **Dewey, A. J.** "A Prophetic Pronouncement: Q 12:42–46." *Forum* 5.2 (1989) 99–108. **Ellingworth, P.** "Luke 12.46—Is There an Anticlimax Here?" *BT* 31 (1980) 242–43. **Fleddermann, H.** "The Householder and the

Servant Left in Charge [12,39–40.42–46]." In *SBL Seminar Papers 1986*, ed. K. H. Richards. Atlanta, GA: Scholars, 1986. 17–26. **George, A.** "L'attente du maître qui vient: Lc 12,32–48." *AsSeign* 50 (1974) 66–76. **Gollinger, H.** "'Ihr wisst nicht, an welchem Tag eure Herr kommt': Auslegung vom Mt 24,37–51." *BibLeb* 11 (1970) 238–47. **Grässer, E.** *Parusieverzögerung.* 84–95. **Harnisch, W.** *Eschatologische Existenz.* Göttingen: Vandenhoeck & Ruprecht, 1973. 84–95. **Hartin, P. J.** "Angst in the Household: A Deconstructive Reading of the Parable of the Supervising Servant (Lk 12:41–48)." *Neot* 22 (1988) 373–90. **Jeremias, J.** *Parables.* 48–66, 90–96, 101–2. **Joüon, P.** "La parabole du portier qui doit veiller (Mt 13, 33–37) et la parabole des serviteurs qui doivent veiller (Lc 12, 35–40)." *RSR* 30 (1940) 365–68. **Kamlah, E.** "Die Parabel vom ungerechten Verwalter (Luk 16:1ff) in Rahmen der Knechtgleichnisse." In *Abraham unser Vater*, ed. O. Betz. Leiden: Brill, 1963. 276–94, esp. 282–93. **Kollmann, B.** "Lk 12,35–38—ein Gleichnis der Logienquelle." *ZNW* 81 (1990) 254–61. **Lategan, B. C.,** and **Rousseau, J.** "Reading Luke 12:35–48: An Empirical Study." *Neot* 22 (1988) 391–413. **Lövestam, E.** *Spiritual Wakefulness in the New Testament.* Lunds Universitets Arsskrift 1/55.3. Lund: Gleerup, 1963. 79–80, 92–107. **März, C.-P.** ". . . *lasst eure Lampen brennen!" Studien zur Q-Vorlage von Lk 12, 35–14, 24.* ETS 20. Leipzig: St. Benno, 1991. **Plessis, I. J. du.** "Reading Luke 12:35–48 as Part of the Travel Narrative." *Neot* 22 (1988) 217–34. ———. "Why Did Peter Ask His Question and How Did Jesus Answer Him? Or: Implicature in Luke 12:35–48." *Neot* 22 (1988) 311–24. **Prast, F.** *Presbyter und Evangelium in nachapostolischer Zeit: Die Abschiedsrede des Paulus in Milet (Apg. 20,17–38) im Rahmen der lukanischen Konzeption der Evangeliumsverkündigung.* FB 29. Stuttgart: Katholisches Bibelwerk, 1979. 233–49. **Reicke, B.** *Diakonie, Festfreude und Zelos.* Uppsala: Lundequistka, 1951. 234–40. **Rensburg, J. J. J. van.** "A Syntactical Reading of Luke 12:35–48." *Neot* 22 (1988) 415–38. **Scheffler, E. H.** "A Psychological Reading of Luke 12:35–48." *Neot* 22 (1988) 355–71. **Schneider, G.** *Parusiegleichnisse im Lukas-Evangelium.* SBS 74. Stuttgart: Katholisches Bibelwerk, 1975. 20–37. **Schnell, C. W.** "Historical Context in Parable Interpretation: A Criticism of Current Tradition-historical Interpretations of Luke 12:35–48." *Neot* 22 (1988) 269–82. **Schulz, S.** *Spruchquelle.* 268–71, 271–77. **Schürmann, H.** "Die zwei unterschiedlichen Berufungen, Dienste und Lebensweisen im Presbyterium [12,42–46]." In *In libertatem vocati estis (Gal 5,13).* FS B. Häring. Studia Moralia 15. Roma: Academia Alfonsiana, 1977. 401–20. **Sebothoma, W.** "Luke 12:35–48: A Reading by a Black South African." *Neot* 22 (1988) 325–35. **Sellew, P.** "Reconstruction of Q 12:33–59." In *SBL Seminar Papers 1987*, ed. K. H. Richards. Atlanta, GA: Scholars, 1987. 617–68. **Smit, D. J.** "Responsible Hermeneutics: A Systematic Theologian's Response to the Readings and Readers of Luke 12:35–48." *Neot* 22 (1988) 441–84. ———. "Those were the critics, what about the real readers? An analysis of 65 published sermons and sermon guidelines on Luke 12:35–48." *Neot* 23 (1989) 61–82. **Smitmans, A.** "Das Gleichnis vom Dieb." In *Wort Gottes in der Zeit.* FS K. H. Schelke, ed. M. Feld and J. Nolte. Düsseldorf: Patmos, 1973. 43–68. **Staden, P. van.** "A Sociological Reading of Luke 12:35–48." *Neot* 22 (1988) 337–53. **Strobel, A.** *Untersuchungen zum eschatologischen Verzögerungsproblem.* Leiden: Brill, 1961. 203–33. **Theissen, G.** "Lokalkoloritforschung in den Evangelien: Plädoyer für die Erneuerung einer alten Fragestellung." *EvT* 45 (1985) 481–99. **Tilborg, S. van.** "An Interpretation from the Ideology of the Text." *Neot* 22 (1988) 205–15. **Tödt, H. E.** *The Son of Man.* 88–94. **Weder, H.** *Die Gleichnisse Jesus als Metaphern.* 162–68. **Weiser, A.** *Die Knechtsgleichnisse der synoptischen Evangelien.* SANT 29. Munich: Kösel, 1971. 161–225. **Wenham, D.** *The Rediscovery of Jesus' Eschatological Discourse.* Gospel Perspectives 4. Sheffield: JSOT Press, 1984. 15–100. **Wuellner, W.** "The Rhetorical Structure of Luke 12 in Its Wider Context." *Neot* 22 (1988) 283–310.

Translation

[35] *"Let your waists be girded and your lamps burning.* [36] *Then*[a] *you will be like people who are awaiting their master (whenever he should return from the banquet),*[b] *so that*

when he comes and knocks, they will open [the door] to him immediately. [37]*Fortunate*[c] *are those slaves whom the master finds on the alert when he comes. Amen, I say to you, 'He will gird himself [suitably], make them recline at table,* [d]*and will come and serve them.'* [38]*If he comes and finds [it] so, even*[e] *in the second or the third watch, those*[f] *ones are fortunate.*

[39]*"Know this: if the householder had known at what hour the thief was coming, he* [g]*would not have allowed his house to be broken into.*[h] [40]*So you too must be ready, because the Son of Man comes in an hour [in which] you do not think [he will come]."*

[41]*Peter said, "Lord, are you telling this parable to us or to everyone?"* [42]*The Lord said,*[i] *"Who, then, whom the master*[j] *will appoint over the food-serving arrangements, to give the food ration at the proper time,* [k]*will prove to be*[k] *the faithful and wise steward?* [43]*Fortunate is that slave who when his master comes will find him doing just so!* [44]*Truly I say to you, he will appoint him over all his goods.* [45]*But if that slave says in his heart, 'My master is delayed in coming,' and he begins to beat the male and female servants, and to eat and drink and get drunk,* [46]*then*[l] *the master of that slave will come on a day when he does not expect [him] and in an hour which he does not know about, and he will cut him in two and will allocate [him] his place with the faithless.*

[47]*"That slave who knew his master's will and did not*[m] *make preparations or act in accord with his will will be beaten with many [blows].* [48]*(But the one who did not know, and acted in a manner worthy of blows, will be beaten with a few [blows].) Everyone to whom much is given, much will be required from him, and for the one to whom much is handed over, more will be asked*[n] *of him."*

Notes

[a] Gr. *καί* (lit. "and").

[b] *γάμοι* refers normally, but not always (cf. Esth 2:18; 9:22), to the celebrations of a wedding banquet.

[c] Gr. *μακάριοι*.

[d] From here to the end of the verse is not found in ℵ.

[e] The separation here of "if" and "even" is not really grammatically justified but is likely to be the intended sense (see *Comment*).

[f] *οἱ δοῦλοι*, "the slaves," is added here by A Q W Θ Ψ etc.

[g] *ἐγρηγόρησεν (ἂν) καὶ οὐκ* is added here by (ℵ[1]) (A) B L (Q) W (Θ) Ψ etc., under the influence of the Matthean version.

[h] Lit. "dug through."

[i] *αὐτῷ*, "to him," is added by ℵ A W Θ Ψ etc.

[j] The translation of *κύριος* here as master obscures the fact that the same term is used of Jesus as "Lord" in vv 41, 42.

[k-k] Lit. "is."

[l] Added for clarity.

[m] There is an accidental omission of the negative in P[45], which also lacks the reference to preparation (as does D).

[n] The third person pl. active is here used with passive force (as in v 20).

Form/Structure/Setting

The present unit is made up of a collection of smaller units united by their shared interest in the imagery of a householder and his slaves (atypically, in vv 39–40 only the householder appears, and he becomes the image of the disciple needing to maintain constant vigilance [elsewhere the slave is the image]), and by their focus on the need to be in some appropriate state of readiness for an expected "coming" whose timing is unknown (on the internal subdivision between vv 35–40 and 41–48, see at 12:22–34). Whereas the challenge to be ready for the coming judgment, which is the leitmotif of this section (12:1–13:9), has taken the shape of concrete ethical and religious demands in the units thus far, in this unit all focus is on the challenge to readiness.

For vv 39–40, 42b–46, Luke draws here on non-Markan material shared with Matthew (cf. Matt 24:42–51). It is likely that Matthew has placed this material in his eschatological discourse because of the similarity with Mark 13:35–36, but there is no particular reason for thinking that Luke is following a source order here.

Since Matthew has no equivalent to vv 35–38, these verses could be from distinctive Lukan sources (or they could be Luke's own formulation based on fragments of tradition). Weiser (*Knechtgleichnisse*, 164–66; and cf. Schneider, *Parusiegleichnisse*, 32; Kollmann, *ZNW* 81 [1990] 254–61) has shown, however, that it is quite likely that a version of this parable was present in the source shared with Matthew. On the other hand the chiastically arranged "parables source" appealed to in the excursus: "The Journey to Jerusalem" (following Blomberg, "Midrash, Chiasmus and the Outline of Luke' Central Section," in *Gospel Perspectives, Vol. 3. Studies in Midrash and Historiography*, ed. R. T. France and D. Wenham [Sheffield: JSOT, 1983] 217–61) requires the inclusion of this parable. It may be that the (substantial) displacement of the "parables source" form by the form found in the source materials shared with Matthew accounts for the phenomenon to which Blomberg draws attention (241–42) of conceptual links but almost total absence of verbal links between 12:35–38 and 16:1–13 (its chiastic pair).

The evident relationship of vv 35–38 with Mark 13:33–37 combines with the unevenesses of both to raise questions of more original forms. Bauckham (*NTS* 23 [1977] 167–69) has drawn attention to the process of "deparabolization" that has been at work here, in which the original narrative structure has been broken down by the application of the parable. While one can never be sure in detail, there is a good measure of agreement (and see esp. Weiser, *Knechtgleichnisse*, 161–74) that the present form has developed in stages from an original that is closer to Mark 13:34–36, but which is likely (*i*) to have lacked mention of the journey or (*ii*) of the role of any other servants beyond the doorkeeper and (*iii*) to have referred to the need to watch in the third person (the doorkeeper's need to watch), and (*iv*) to have used the Lukan language of the numbered watches of the night (sometimes the suggestion is made that the first watch, missing from our present text, was included in the original, but this seems quite unnecessary). There is no sufficient reason for denying such an original to the historical Jesus.

The form of vv 39–40 differs in only minor ways from Matthew's version. Though often maintained, an original unity is unlikely between the two verses (Luke has bonded the verses more closely by conforming the thief's coming in a "watch" [so Matt 24:43] to the Son of Man's coming in "an hour"). It is likely that the later Christian use of the thief metaphor (1 Thess 5:2–4; Rev 3:3; 16:15) is a development from this brief parable of Jesus. *Gos. Thom.* 21 has a rather different form of the parable. The boldness involved in the comparison here between the coming of a thief and the coming of the day of the Lord/kingdom of God is more likely to stem from Jesus than from the early church. Since the readiness called for by v 40 consists of making an appropriate response to the challenge of Jesus' ministry, the role for the Son of Man here is not unlike that in 9:26. Nonetheless, there is somewhat more likelihood here than there that we are dealing with a secondary Christian formulation. Unpredictability of timing (cf. 12:35–38; 17:26–30; 21:34) is a quite different motivation for readiness than is the expectation of an imminent coming of the kingdom of God, but the two can function in a complementary relationship. In both, the future exerts its pressure on the present.

The verses 12:41–42a are in all likelihood a Lukan formulation to be connected with Luke's interplay in this section between disciples and crowd as audience for Jesus' words and prepare for vv 47–48, which will indicate that Luke thinks in terms of graduated responsibility in the impending eschatological answerability. (In connection with vv 47–48, the parable of vv 42–46 gains a particular focus on the distinctive responsibility laid upon the designated servant by the knowledge of the master's will implicit in his charge.)

A degree of development is likely to have taken place in vv 42–46. Suspicion has been cast by various scholars on the originality of (*i*) the description in v 42 of the slave as "faithful" and "wise"; (*ii*) the beatitude of v 43 with its development in v 44, or (*iii*) the deliberation and subsequent action of v 45 with its consequences in v 46, or (*iv*) the deliberation of v 45a; (*v*) one or other of the time statements in v 46; (*vi*) the whole of the extreme and violent response of the master in v 46, or (*vii*) the final clause of v 46: the assignment of a place with the faithless (hypocrites). Of these suggestions the first and last have much to commend them. The first seems to short-circuit the logic of the parable (but see *Comment* below); the last moves right outside the story logic of the parable.

The discussion of originality has been dominated by two issues: first, the nature of the links between the parable and the early Christian experience of the delay of the Parousia and, second, the degree of realism of the imagery of the parable. The delay motif is particularly to be associated with v 45a. While this verse will have been so linked in the ongoing life of the church, Weiser (*Knechtsgleichnisse*, 188–93) has demonstrated that the verse is best seen as an original part of the parable with no intrinsic link to the Parousia delay motif. In relation to everyday realism, all the actions and responses of the parable are extreme (other than the initial assignment of the task and its possible faithful implementation), but in the first-century world they are all finally within the horizons of the possible. The whole shape of the parable involves pushing the logic of everyday affairs to the kind of extreme that will guarantee that the hearer will sense the need to move behind the story world to search for the intention of the parable. From its inception, the whole parable is somewhat allegorical, but this should not deter us from attributing it to the historical Jesus (on allegory in the parables of Jesus, see the excursus in the Introduction of WBC 35A: "Modern Parables Research").

Vv 47–48 are distinctive to Luke, and since he has prepared for them with vv 41–42a, they are likely to have been incorporated here by him. There is probably no original unity between the mini-parable of the knowledgeable and ignorant servants (vv 47–48a) and the attached double proverb (v 48bc). It is uncertain whether either or both items may be attributed to the historical Jesus. On the one hand, there is a kind of casuistry that, however necessary it may be for the practicalities of the religious life, seems to have played little part in Jesus' pronouncements. On the other hand, the thrust here could be fitted neatly into

Jesus' critical interaction with segments of the Jewish religious leadership and his bias toward the weak and the excluded.

Comment

One should be equipped and alert at all times, ready to meet the master at the moment of his arrival. Those who are alert and ready to welcome the master at whatever time he comes will find to their surprise that they will have the experience of being served servants rather than that of being serving servants! If one is to be ready when the thief comes, then one needs to be ready all the time. That is how it is with the coming of the Son of Man. The wise and faithful slave is steadily carrying out his master's wishes when his master walks in the door. He will be promoted. The servant who takes advantage of the master's delay will find himself paying the ultimate penalty for his folly. These challenges demand more of the disciples than of the crowds, because responsibility is proportionate to awareness.

35 Luke thinks in terms of a deliberate imprecision of audience for this unit until the clarification of vv 41–42a, 47–48. The typical long robe of ancient dress was worn loose when one was at leisure in private but tied in place whenever one needed to be "dressed for the occasion" or to be active in work, travel, or warfare. "Girding" can mean either this tying in place or more broadly "getting dressed." (See Exod 12:11; 1 Kgs 18:46; 20:31–32; 2 Kgs 4:29; 9:1; Job 38:3; 40:7; Prov 31:17; Isa 32:11; 1QM 15:14; 16:11; Eph 6:14; 1 Pet 1:13). Here the image is likely to be that of being dressed fittingly to honor the arrival of the master, though perhaps with a thought as well of the bustle of activity that would accompany the arrival. Lighted lamps mean no delay in lighting the master's path into the house.

36 The readiness to which the disciple is called is likened to the readiness of servants awaiting their master's return from a party. The flow from v 35 to v 36 is difficult because v 35 has been formulated with the setting of v 36 already in mind. It is for that reason best seen as a later elaboration. In the Lukan framework, the call is to readiness for the Parousia of Jesus (cf. v 40). On the lips of Jesus, the link may be with the imminent arrival of the kingdom of God and the prospect of the coming judgment (cf. Isa 40:3–5; Luke 3:7, 9; 10:14; 21:31–32).

37 The present verse seems to have been intruded into the flow of the parable in the course of its transmission and development. In its present form the first part of the verse provides, through its similarity to v 43, a unifying link between the materials. The latter part of the verse is frequently taken to be a later formulation, which is not impossible (cf. 9:14–17; 22:27, 30; 24:30; John 13:1–17), but the imagery is arresting in its own right. We should keep open the possibility that v 37 has its own separate transmission history and originally expressed Jesus' vision of God's magnanimity to those who are alert and ready for his coming (cf. Ps 23:2, 5; Ezek 34:14–16; Luke 13:29). As an expression of the relationship of master and slave, the imagery is not at all true to life; but the point may be precisely that things are quite different in the kingdom of God. There may be some background in God's honoring of his servants the prophets and even perhaps in the meal of the elders before God in Exod 24:11.

38 The intrusion of v 37 has required reformulation here from an original, which may have simply been *κἂν ἐν τῇ δευτέρᾳ κἂν ἐν τῇ τρίτῃ φυλακῇ* (*ἔλθῃ*), "even if (he comes) in the second, even in the third watch." A reference to the

Hellenistic and Jewish pattern of three watches seems more likely than to the four-watch Roman pattern (Mark 13:35 seems to reflect the Roman pattern). There is no need to think that the first watch has been dropped out because of the delay of the Parousia: from the perspective of v 38, the first watch is implicitly accounted for already in v 36. It is a mistake to think that the need to retain readiness only becomes an issue after years of unfulfilled expectation. Even if not to the same degree, human life in the ancient world was no doubt troubled by the same momentary enthusiasms that plague modern life. Even an imminent Parousia must still be awaited. The intrusion of v 37 makes the *κἄν*, "even if," no longer grammatically appropriate. The *καὶ εὕρῃ οὕτως*, "and he finds it so," is a not entirely successful attempt to put this to rights.

39 Luke will have contributed *τοῦτο*, "this" (Matthew has *ἐκεῖνο*, "that"), and *ὥρᾳ*, "hour" (Matthew has *φυλακῇ*, "watch"), but Matthew will have added *ἐγρηγόρησεν ἂν καί*, "he would have been on the alert" (under the influence of v 37?). The point of the parable seems to be that thieves do not send calling cards ahead to announce their arrival. If one is to be ready for a thief's intrusion, one needs to be ready all the time (Matthew's language of the "watch" draws into the field of imagery the possibility of "night watchmen"). In view here is a prospect of suffering loss or damage through lack of constant readiness; the parable has been linked thematically. *διορυχθῆναι*, "to be dug through," reflects the largely mud-brick construction of Palestinian homes.

40 This verse has probably only secondarily become an application of the parable (Matthew strengthens the link with his added "because of this"). The coming of the Son of Man points here to the hour of decisive accountability to God: the eschatological denouement. On Son of Man, cf. at 6:1–5; 9:26 and the excursus: "Son of Man." The unpredictability of the timing of the coming is the basis of the appeal for present readiness (cf. 12:35–38; 17:26–30; 21:34; Matt 25:1–13). In this way the future is meant to exert its pressure already on the present and to identify the present as the time of decisive significance: the present is the time in which the Son of Man could come at any moment.

41 The language here is recognizably Lukan (note especially *τὴν παραβολὴν ταύτην λέγεις* [cf. 4:23] and *λέγεις πρὸς πάντας* [cf. 9:23]), and Matthew has no corresponding verse (there is a possible influence from Mark 13:37). "This parable" must refer immediately to vv 39–40, but by implication the answer will carry the previous parable with it. The question is not about restriction of relevance to the leadership group consisting of the Twelve, but rather restriction to those who are already disciples (on disciples, see at 5:30; on relevance to disciples and to the crowds, cf. at 12:1). As vv 35–40 can hardly be said to lend themselves to such a question, the inclusion of the verse must be judged to be a rather artificial ploy to prepare for the inclusion by Luke of vv 47–48. On the place of Peter, cf. at 5:1–11 and 9:20. With *ὁ κύριος*, "the Lord," to follow in v 42, *κύριε* here probably means more than "sir" (cf. at 5:12 and 5:8, where, however, more confidence was expressed in the frequency of Luke's use of *κύριε* to mean "sir" than I now think appropriate).

42 Luke will be responsible here for the introductory "The Lord (*ὁ κύριος*) said" (on this use of "Lord" of Jesus, see at 7:13; coming before the reference in the parable to *ὁ κύριος*, "the master," this insertion leads the reader to take the master of the parable as an image of Jesus, rather than of God [who is the more likely referent in the original use of the parable]); the switch from δοῦλος, "slave," to οἰκονόμος, "steward" (he retains the former in vv 43, 45, 46; an οἰκονόμος is the central figure of 16:1–8); the move from οἰκετείας, "(the slaves in) the household," to the more classical θεραπείας, "serving, service, care, healing," which could mean here either "(those who perform the) serving roles" or "the (food-) serving arrangements" (cf. the use of the cognate θεραπεύειν [here: "to serve"] in Acts 17:25); and the substitution for τροφήν, "food," of the more technical σιτομέτριον, "ration." Given this level of intrusion, the other differences are likely to be from his pen as well.

It is difficult to be sure how this (counter) question is meant to function. Beyer (*Semitische Syntax*, 287–93; and cf. Weiser, *Knechtsgleichnisse*, 181–83) has argued with considerable force for an original form without "faithful" and "wise." In Semitic syntax (cf. Deut 20:5) this would allow the question to function as roughly equivalent to the protasis of a conditional statement, with v 43 as the apodosis (so: "if a servant is appointed . . . , then that servant is fortunate if . . ."). But neither Luke nor his source has so taken it. The phrase "the faithful and wise steward" is clearly formulated in light of the outcome of the parabolic action (Luke underlines this fact by his change from "slave" to "steward": the slave becomes a steward in v 44). We can perhaps reflect this best by, as in the translation above, intruding the relative clause into the principal clause of the question, and taking the verb there (ἐστίν, "is") with a future force (so: "Who, then, whom the master will appoint . . . will prove to be the [or if taken generically "a"] faithful and wise steward?"). Only when we reach vv 47–48 will it become clear how the present counter question is the beginning of an answer to Peter's question.

A correlation is quite rightly to be drawn between the serving role here and the call to various forms of service in the church, but any narrow focus on church leaders is to be resisted.

43 Luke makes no change here other than to move οὕτως, "thus" (here: "just so"), to the emphatic position. Vv 43–44 constitute the answer to Jesus' rhetorical question. On beatitudes, see at 6:20–26. The basis for the declaration of good fortune is given in v 44. Note the link with v 37. The coming of the master has an original connection with the coming of the kingdom of God, but in Luke's rendering the link will be with the Parousia of Jesus as Son of Man (cf. v 40).

44 Luke intrudes only to translate ἀμήν, "amen," as ἀληθῶς, "truly" (as at 9:27). The repetition here of καταστήσει (ἐπί), "will put [him] in charge (of)," from v 42 underlines the point that fidelity in a lesser appointment leads to a more significant appointment (cf. 16:10–11, 19:17, 19; etc). Now this slave becomes the master's "steward" (cf. v 42).

45 There is no woe to balance the beatitude of v 43, but vv 45–46 provide the negative counterpart to vv 43–44. As was the case in v 42, Matthew here anticipates the outcome he is about to describe by speaking of the "wicked servant." It is unclear whether Matthew has added or Luke deleted. Luke will have underlined the Parousia link by adding ἔρχεσθαι, "to come." He will also be responsible for the distinction of male and female slaves (servants). It is rather less certain whether Luke, for whom the problem with eating and drinking is focused on excess, or Matthew, who sees the problem in the company of the drunkards, is the more original.

To "say in the heart" corresponds to Semitic idiom (cf. Rev 18:7). The servant finds that he is on a longer rein than he had at first anticipated. He will surely be able to cover his tracks before the master turns up! Now is his moment of greatness and his opportunity to kick over the traces! In the original parable there is no thought of a delayed Parousia; the master's extended absence is simply a device to achieve a situation in which the servant is not subject to immediate check by his master. His true colors are given space to emerge. At the same time, the developing consciousness among early Christians of a definite period before the Parousia in which fidelity is required of the servants of the Lord cannot but have affected the reading of this parable. This servant's excesses have their parallel in other ancient stories (see texts from the Arabic, Syriac, and Armenian versions of Ahikar [Charles, *Pseudepigrapha*, 740–41, 749]; *Bet Ha-Midrash* 4.145–46 [the texts are cited by Weiser, *Knechtsgleichnisse*, 194–95]).

46 Luke differs from Matthew only in having "unfaithful" for Matthew's "hypocrites." It is more likely that Matthew is responsible for this change than Luke. The errant servant is now to be caught in the act! While the language of "day" and "hour" is used in the NT in connection with eschatological expectation (Matt 24:36; 25:13; Mark 13:32; cf. Rev 9:15), it is in the parable no code expression for eschatological expectation but only a poetic way of heightening the impact of the sudden and unexpected shattering of the illusions of the servant. This is not to say that the ultimate referent is not eschatological.

The severity of the punishment envisaged here is matched in other ancient tales (see Weiser, *Knechtsgleichnisse*, 199 [the cited texts do, however, all involve a king and not merely a master]). Though Jewish law provided slaves with some protection and amelioration of their lot, in the Roman world slaves were for the most part entirely the property of their masters to do with as they would. The various attempts to remove the severity by appeal to mistranslation of a Semitic original require either a misreading as well as a mistranslation or are based on unproven assumptions about word meanings (see discussion in Wieser, *Knechtsgleichnisse*, 199–200). The severity of response here is of a piece with the general extremity that characterizes responses in the parable.

The final clause of the master's response moves beyond anything that can be retained within the boundaries of the story. Here we have a piece of application drawn into the telling of the story. Betz (*RevQ* 5 [1964–65] 44–47) has drawn attention to the similar statement in 1QS 2:16–17: "[God] will give his allotted portion in the midst of those accursed forever." Here we are dealing with the assignment of an eschatological destiny. This final clause is likely to have been added at a time in the transmission history when Jesus' role in assigning eschatological destinies was self-evidently the thrust of the story.

47–48 Matthew (24:51) finishes the parable with a clause about weeping and gnashing of teeth, which is likely to be his own addition (cf. 8:12; 13:42, 50; 22:13; 25:30). Luke finishes with a new mini-parable and a double proverb. Luke may be using v 47 as a comment on the slave of vv 45–46 ("*that* slave" = the slave of vv 45–46), or (more likely). vv 47–48a may function as yet another in the collection of parables here ("that" as an emphatic definite article). The principle is that answerability is proportionate to awareness. Reference may be made to the OT distinction between witting and unwitting sins (Num 15:30; Deut 17:12; Ps 19:13; cf. 1QS 5:12; 7:3; CD 8:8; 10:3; etc.). We should note the assumption that failure is never entirely blameless. The answer to Peter's question is that although the parable was for all, its challenge is more pressing and the answerability greater for the disciples than for the crowds (cf. at 12:10). The message of proportionate responsibility is supported by the secular wisdom of the parallel statements of the double proverb that follows.

Explanation

The imagery of the master of a household and his slaves and a motif built out of concern to be ready and vigilant and about the master's business when he should turn up hold together here a collection of brief parables and attached sayings. Each supports the theme of this section (12:1–13:9), which is the challenge to be ready for the coming judgment.

When waiting for their master's return from a party, the servants should stay dressed in a manner that will make them fit for immediate presentation before the master, to be available for his bidding, and they should keep the lamps lit so that there will be no delay in lighting the master's pathway into the house. Then they can respond to his knock at once. How fortunate those servants will be. The master will be so impressed (and even more so if he should come really late) that, far from making use of their services, he will for the occasion become their servant and mount a celebration for them.

Since thieves do not send calling cards ahead of them, the only way to be ready for the thief's entry is to be ready all the time. So if one does not want to be surprised, one should be ready at all times for the coming of the Son of Man.

Luke uses Peter's question to draw a distinction between how the preceding parable (and therefore also the one before) applies to the disciples and how it is relevant to the crowds. Vv 47–48 finally make the answer to the question clear: relevance is to all, but with the answerability being more severe for the disciples in their privileged state of awareness.

For Luke the "master" (same Greek word as "Lord") of each of the parables is the Lord Jesus, and so he signals this with his reference to Jesus as "Lord" in v 42. Jesus' counter-question seems at first to favor a narrow reference of the earlier parable to disciples, but the full answer becomes clear only later on. What kind of servant appointed to see to food distribution will turn out to be the wise and faithful servant and gain the more responsible and permanent role of manager of the whole estate? The one who is found to be actually on the job when his master turns up will be so favored. But if a delay in his master's return is taken by him as an opportunity to live it up and have his own moment of glory, then he will be in trouble. The master will turn up unexpectedly and catch him before he has had time to cover his tracks. Since the slave is his master's property, he (the master) will not shrink from hacking the failed servant in two. Just for good measure, and going outside the world of the story, the master will also "allocate him his place with the faithless." This reference to the end-time judgment, with its sorting of people, makes it clear that Luke has reported the parable with Jesus' return and the end-time judgment clearly in mind.

In this most recent parable the servant involved has been a privileged servant entrusted with a special task (and so corresponds to a disciple of Jesus), but the challenge to readiness has a wider relevance as well: servants are always answerable, but they are the more answerable to the degree that they are more aware of the master's will. The gifts of opportunity create the demands of responsibility.

The Prospect of Fire, Baptism, and Division (12:49–53)

Bibliography

Arens, E. *The HΛΘON-Sayings in the Synoptic Tradition.* OBO 10. Freiburg/Göttingen: Universit'atsverlag/Vandenhoeck & Ruprecht, 1976. 63–90. **Black, M.** "'Not peace but a sword': Matt 10:34ff; Luke 12:51ff." In *Jesus and the Politics of His Day,* ed. E. Bammel and C. F. D. Moule. 287–94. **Bruston, C.** "Une parole de Jésus mal comprise." *RHPR* 5 (1925) 236–56. **Delling, G.** "*Βάπτισμα βαπτισθῆναι.*" *NovT* 2 (1957–58) 92–115. **Derrett, J. M. D.** "Christ's Second Baptism (Lk 12:50; Mk 10:38–40)." *ExpTim* 100 (1989) 294–95. **Feuillet, A.** "La coupe et le baptême de la passion (Mc, X, 35–40; cf. Mt, XX, 20–23; Lc, XII, 50)." *RB* 74 (1967) 356–91. **Fuller, R. H.** *Mission and Achievement of Jesus: An Examination of the Presuppositions of New Testament Theology.* SBT. London: SCM, 1954. 59–62. **George, A.** "La venue de Jésus, cause de division entre les hommes Lc 12,49–53." *AsSeign* 51 (1972) 62–71. **Graystone, G.** "'I Have Come to Cast Fire on the Earth . . . .'" *Scr* 4 (1949–51) 135–41. **Grelot, P.** "Michée 7,6 dans les évangiles et dans la littérature rabbinique." *Bib* 67 (1986) 363–77. **Grimm, W.** *Weil ich dich liebe: Die Verkündigung Jesu und Deuterojesaja.* ANTJ 1. Bern/Frankfurt: H. Lang/P. Lang, 1976. 277–85. **Kaestli, J.-D.** "Luc 12:49–59: Diverses paroles eschatologiques." *L'Eschatologie.* 19–23. **Klein, G.** "Die Prüfung der Zeit (Lukas 12,54–56)." *ZTK* 61 (1964) 373–90, esp. 374–77. **Kuss, O.** "Zur Frage einer vorpaulinischen Todestaufe." In *Auslegung und Verkündigung: Vol. 1. Aufsätze zur Exegese des Neuen Testamentes.* Regensburg: Pustet, 1963. 162–86. **Légasse, P.** "Approche de l'épisode préévangélique des fils de Zébédée." *NTS* 20 (1974) 161–77. **März, C.-P.** "'Feuer auf die Erde zu werfen, bin ich gekommen . . .': Zum Verständnis und zur Entstehung von Lk 12, 49." In *À cause de l'Évangile,* ed. F. Refoulé. 479–512. ———. "Zur Vorgeschichte von Lk 12,49–59." *SNTU* 12 (1987) 69–84. **Patterson, S. J.** "Fire and Dissention: Ipsissima Vox Jesus in Q 12:49, 51–53?" *Forum* 5.2 (1989) 121–39. **Roberts, T. A.** "Some Comments on Matthew x. 34–36 and Luke xii. 51–53." *ExpTim* 69 (1957–58) 304–6. **Schulz, S.** *Spruchquelle.* 258–60, 421–24. **Sellew, P.** "Reconstruction of Q 12:33–59." In *SBL Seminar Papers 1987,* ed. K. H. Richards. Atlanta, GA: Scholars, 1987. 617–68. **Tannehill, R. C.** *The Sword of His Mouth.* 140–47. **Vögtle, A.** "Todesankündigung und Todesverständnis Jesu." In *Der Tod Jesu: Deutungen im Neuen Testament,* ed. K. Kertelge. Freiburg: Herder, 1976. 51–113, esp. 80–88. **Ward, R. A.** "St Luke xii. 49: *καὶ τί θέλω ει ἤδη ἀνήφθη.*" *ExpTim* 63 (1951–52) 92–93.

Translation

[49] *"I came to cast fire upon*[a] *the earth, and how I wish it were already kindled!* [50] *I have a baptism with which to be baptized, and how I am taken up [with it] until it is accomplished!* [51] *Do you consider that I came to give*[b] *peace in*[c] *the earth? No, I tell you, rather division!* [52] *For from now on there will be five in one household, three divided against two and two against three;* [53] *father will be divided against son and son against father, mother against the daughter and daughter against the mother, mother-in-law against her*[d] *daughter-in-law,*[e] *and daughter-in-law*[e] *against the*[f] *mother-in-law."*

Notes

[a] *εἰς*, "into," is read by P[45] D E G H Δ etc.

[b] D e sy[c] support *ποιῆσαι*, "make," here.

[c] ἐπι τῆς γῆς, "upon the earth," is read by P[45] etc.
[d] Omitted by P[75] ℵ Δ etc.
[e] νύμφη(ν) (lit. "bride"). Here with an extended sense.
[f] αὐτῆς, "her," in ℵ[2] A W Θ Ψ etc.

Form/Structure/Setting

In this new unit (vv 49–53) of the section on preparing for the coming judgment (12:1–13:9), attention now turns to the coming judgment itself. Jesus has been commissioned to cast down upon the earth the fire of eschatological purgation, which is associated with that coming judgment. The time for the execution of that commission is not yet, but its purging flames are already anticipated in the baptism that is to be Jesus' own fate and in the heartbreak and challenge of the strife that, with the coming of Jesus, breaks apart the closest of human ties.

Matthew offers a close parallel to vv 51 and 53, but Luke's source for vv 49, 50, and 52 is more uncertain. V 49 has been considered by some to be a Lukan formulation, but this possibility has been losing favor since the text "has no linguistic features which could be used to link it specifically with Lukan redaction" (Patterson, *Forum* 5.2 [1989] 124). If the verse is pre-Lukan, then was it part of the source materials shared with Matthew, or was it taken from a distinctive Lukan source? The arguments favor the former possibility, especially because of the link with Matt 10:34 (see esp. H. Schürmann, *Tradionsgeschichtliche Untersuchungen*, 213 and n. 24), though it is best not to claim any original unity between v 49 and Matt 10:34. Moving a stage further back, März ("Feuer auf die Erde," esp. 493–501) has made an attractive case for seeing Luke 12:49 as formulated in the (late) Q editing process (based on 3:16 and establishing a thematic connection with that verse). More commonly the origin of the verse is attributed to the historical Jesus, with appeal to claimed Semitic elements in the language (noted in *Comment* below) and to the dissimilarity of the verse from standard early church formulations and interests as well as from prevailing Jewish sentiments (the verse has a distinctively lifetime-of-Jesus perspective). Both forms of argumentation have their difficulties, but they do carry sufficient weight to give one pause in accepting März's reconstruction. (Patterson [*Forum*, 5.2 (1989) 126–27, 134–37] argues for attribution to the historical Jesus on the basis of a less than persuasive claim for the greater originality of the form of the saying in *Gos. Thom.* 10.)

V 50 clearly has some relationship with Mark 10:38–39. A Lukan formulation on the basis of that text is not impossible (as März ["Feuer auf die Erde," 482–84]), but the distinctiveness of the focus here may point to a separate origin. Légasse (*NTS* 20 [1974] 164–66, 169) has proposed an original containing the τί θέλω εἰ ἤδη [lit. "what I wish if already"] of v 49, offering arguments that have convinced Vögtle ("Todesankündigung," 85–86). While the baptism language will belong to the Greek language phase of the tradition, there is every reason to allow this anticipation of disaster to the historical Jesus. It makes very little difference whether we take v 52 as a Lukan creation or a Matthean omission (probably the former). In any case the ἀπὸ τοῦ νῦν, "from now on," is likely to be Lukan (cf. 1:48; 5:10; 22:18, 69; Acts 18:6).

Comment

Jesus has been commissioned to cast the purging fire of the coming judgment upon the earth, but while he awaits God's timing for that, and as a prelude to it, he first anticipates his own baptism of disaster to come, and also the strife among people which he himself engenders, and indeed by which he is overwhelmed in the baptism he contemplates.

49 For other first person formulations of the purpose of the coming of Jesus, see 4:43; 5:32; and cf. 19:10 (on the question of the authenticity of such sayings, see discussion at 5:27–39 and at 7:34). βαλεῖν [. . .] ἐπὶ τὴν γῆν (lit. "to cast upon the earth") occurs identically in Matthew's version of v 51 (10:34). The closest parallels are Rev 8:5, 7, 8; 20:9 with their apocalyptic imagery of judgment. Jeremias (*Parables,* 122 n. 83) and others claim a Semitic idiom meaning "to kindle," not "to cast," but this reading would cause the loss of the place of God (ἀνήφθη, "kindled," could no longer be a theological passive) as the one who determines times, which seems likely to be an original feature. The use of τί to mean "how" is probably Semitic, but the presence of this idiom in later Greek makes such a judgment not entirely certain (cf. BAGD, 819; BDF, 299[4]). The θέλω εἰ (lit. "I wish if") idiom is difficult. Marshall claims it as Semitic on the basis of the LXX of Isa 9:5 and Sir 23:14. The second of these (the first text is of uncertain meaning) certainly parallels the idiom, but unfortunately we have no Hebrew text to compare, and Marshall admits the presence of a similar idiom in Herodotus 6.52; 9.44. Other plausible Greek language suggestions have also been offered for this text.

"Fire" here certainly belongs to the apocalyptic language of eschatological purgation and judgment. See discussion at 3:16. From the OT, cf. 2 Kgs 1:10; Isa 66:15–16; Ezek 38:22; 39:6; Amos 1:4, 7, 10, 14. The linked verses suggest that while the anticipated conflagration is yet withheld, its purging flames are to have their anticipation in Jesus' own coming fate and in the divisive strife to come upon his disciples. In so doing the linked verses make it clear that Jesus does not stand over against the world as fiery judge, but that he also must make his way through the end-time distress for which it is his task to set ablaze the refiner's fire. Just how Jesus is to be seen as initiating conflagration remains unclear. Apart from the present setting (which has no particular claim to be original), the text probably points to Jesus' own expectation of an imminent eschatological denouement and to his own role in this turning of the ages. But nothing more precise can be said with any confidence.

50 The striking phrase βάπτισμα βαπτισθῆναι, "to be baptized [with] a baptism," is elsewhere found only at Mark 10:38. Such constructions with a cognate accusative are found in Hebrew, Aramaic, and Greek (see Delling, *NovT* 3 [1957] 98–99). The metaphorical use of "baptism" for an experience of being overwhelmed by disaster is not found in the LXX but is present both in Hellenistic sources and in the later Greek versions of the OT (see Delling, 242–44). There is no sufficient reason for making recourse either to the baptism of John or to Christian baptism to account for the wording of the text here. While the precise imagery must belong to the Greek language phase of the tradition, the representation of the threat of disaster in terms of a flood of water is well attested in the OT (e.g., 2 Sam 22:5; Pss 69:2–3, 15; 32:6; 124:4–5). The imprecision of the referent for the imagery counts against an early church origin. In the Lukan setting there is of course no doubt that the coming passion is in view.

Luke is the main user of συνέχειν in the NT and may be responsible for it here. Only in 2 Esd 16:10 has the present absolute use been paralleled (Fitzmyer, 997). The verb should be taken here not in the sense "to be distressed" (as proposed by those who would link it with the Gethsemane prayer), but rather as "to be preoccupied/taken up [with]" (only this respects the relationship with v 49; cf. Acts 18:5). In the Lukan frame this preoccupation is reflected in 9:51 and the passion predictions. The use of τελεῖν, "to achieve/accomplish/complete," suggests that the prospect envisaged "is no mere fate or accident but a destiny to be fulfilled" (Marshall, 547). Luke uses τελεῖν in connection with the passion in 18:31; 22:37; and Acts 13:29 (and cf. Luke 13:32).

51 Luke's δοκεῖτε ὅτι . . . οὐχί, λέγω ὑμῖν, ἀλλά . . . , "do you think that . . . no! I say to you, but . . . ," is found again in 13:2–3, 4–5, while Matthew's μὴ νομίσητε ὅτι ἦλθον . . . οὐκ ἦλθον . . . ἀλλά, "do not consider that I came . . . I did not come . . . but," uses the same pattern as in Matt 5:17. So either could be redactional. Perhaps Luke has made the change with an eye on the unity of his section. The other differences from Matthew all bear the mark of Luke's pen (note the similarities between Matthew's form and v 49; Luke's διαμερισμόν, "division," anticipates the uses of the cognate verb in v 52).

The language here is deliberately paradoxical: "peace" is self-evidently the goal of Jesus' ministry and of the Jewish eschatological hope that Luke confidently presents as finding its fulfillment in connection with Jesus (1:79; 2:14; 7:50; 8:48; 10:5–6; 19:38, 42 [see discussion at 1:79; 2:14; 7:50]). But the OT prophets had insisted that "the day of the Lord" so longed for would be "darkness and not light," "destruction," "gloom," "very terrible" (Amos 5:16; Joel 1:15; 2:1–2, 11, 31; Isa 13:6; etc.); and the apocalyptic tradition anticipated a time of great distress to usher in the end (of particular note in the present context are 4 Ezra 6:24: "At that time friends shall make war on friends like enemies"; and *Jub.* 23:16: "they will strive with one another, the young with the old and the old with the young"; cf. 4 Ezra 9:2–3; *1 Enoch* 100:1–4; etc.). Luke has disturbed the original parallelism of vv 49 and 51, but the relatedness of the coming fire and the strife being presently stirred up will nonetheless still be part of his understanding. Are we to understand that Jesus himself will be overwhelmed (i.e., "baptized") by the conflict he has set in motion?

52 Matthew has no parallel to this verse. ἀπὸ τοῦ νῦν, "from now on," will be Lukan, as will the periphrastic construction ἔσονται . . . διαμεμερισμένοι, "they will be . . . divided." But it is not certain whether Luke has added or Matthew abbreviated. The double-sidedness of the conflict identified here is reflected in Luke's form in v 53, which is fuller than in Matthew. The figure "five" is likely to be based by anticipation on a counting of the figures in v 53 (identifying the mother and the mother-in-law). The division anticipated in v 51 penetrates even into the intimacy of family. "From now on" is from the time of the ministry of Jesus.

53 By contrast with Matthew, Luke carries the two-sidedness of the conflict forward here with repetition of each pairing in reversed order. Luke continues with the verb introduced in v 52, whereas Matthew has the clause built around a fresh ἦλθον, "I came," introducing διχάσαι, "to separate/turn [someone against]." Does Matthew conform to Mic 7:6, or does Luke obscure the allusion (on the place of Mic 7:6 in the Gospel tradition, see Grelot, *Bib* 67 [1986] 363–77)? Probably the Matthean language reflects here the wording of yet another item from the original collection of ἦλθον statements (but did Luke find the διαμεριζ-, "divide," root somewhere in his source?). The continuation of the quote in Matt 10:36 may, however, be Matthew's own touch. The paradoxical language continues in the tension between this affirmation and the expectation of Luke 1:17 (albeit in connection with John the Baptist).

Explanation

In this new unit (vv 49–53) of the section on preparing for the coming judgment (12:1–13:9), attention now turns to the coming judgment itself and that which must precede it.

The use of the word "fire" here comes from a tradition in the OT of using such language to point to God's intention of mounting a painful purifying of his People by purgation and destruction. More precisely the imagery seems to be of Jesus awaiting the time when God will kindle the fire with which he (Jesus) is to set (appropriate parts of) the earth ablaze. The following verses make it clear that Jesus does not stand over against the world as fiery judge, but that he also must make his way through the end-time distress for which it is his task to set ablaze the refiner's fire. Jesus awaits with eager anticipation the fulfillment of God's purposes.

A second matter, not unlinked with the first, also preoccupies Jesus' mind. He who is to spread a fire upon the earth is himself destined to be overwhelmed by disaster: he will be "immersed" in disaster. In the Lukan account, we find this preoccupation reflected in 9:51 and in the passion predictions. What Jesus anticipates here is no mere fate or accident but a destiny, which God has set for him to fulfill.

The harsh tone continues with a paradoxical denial that the "prince of peace" has come to give peace. Though it is not said so here, of course he will bring peace. The point is that end-time expectations involve properly the prospect of a time of great distress before the full realization of the hope of God's peace is possible. Jesus himself becomes the point of division that will set people against one another, in conflict and not in peace. This conflict will penetrate even into the heart of family life, with family members set firmly against one another. This passage echoes Mic 7:6, a text that had clearly influenced Jewish expectations of Jesus' day about the shape of the end period. Once again we identify the language of paradox, as we compare this to the expectation reflected in 1:17 (in connection with John the Baptist). The conflict anticipated here has been reflected already in the challenge in 12:1–12 to make a clear-cut acknowledgment of Jesus no matter what the opposition or the personal cost.

Interpreting the Present Time (12:54–56)

Bibliography

George, A. "'Interpréter ce temps' Luc 12,54–56." *BVC* 64 (1965) 18–23. **Klein, G.** "Die Prüfung der Zeit (Lukas 12,54–56)." *ZTK* 61 (1964) 373–90. **März, C.-P.** "Lk 12,54b–56 par Mt 16,2b.3 und die Akoluthie der Redequelle." *SNTU* 11 (1986) 83–96. **Tannehill, R. C.** *The Sword of His Mouth.* 128–34. **Wood, H. G.** "Interpreting This Time." *NTS* 2 (1955–56) 262–66.

Translation

[54]*He said to the crowds as well, "When you see a cloud coming up from the west, you say at once, 'A rain-storm is coming'; and so it happens.* [55]*And when [you see]*[a] *the south [wind] blowing, you say, 'It will be*[b] *very hot'; and it happens.* [56]*Hypocrites! You know [how] to interpret the appearance of the earth and the sky.*[c] *How is it that you do not*[d] *interpret this [present] time?"*

Notes

[a] P45 it supply the missing verb.
[b] P45 ℵ D L etc. have *ἔρχεται*, "it comes," in conformity with v 54.
[c] The order of "earth" and "sky" is reversed in P45,75 ℵ2 D K L N etc.
[d] Following, as the more difficult reading, P45 A W Ψ *f* 1,13 etc., rather than P75 ℵ B L Θ etc., which add *οἴδατε*, "know [how]," and have the following verb in the infinitive.

Form/Structure/Setting

The need to be prepared for the coming judgment (12:1–13:9) becomes even more pressing for those who are prepared to see that this very judgment is presaged in the ministry of Jesus (v 56: "this present time"), who is, as we have just seen (12:49), the very one appointed by God to cast the fire of judgment upon the earth and who is in his ministry making his way through the events that are the necessary preliminary to that role.

The material here is paralleled in the textually uncertain Matt 16:2b–3 (absent from ℵ B X Γ *f* 13 etc; found in C D L W Θ *f* 1 latt etc). What is clear from the complex pattern of similarities and differences between the two forms is that these verses are no scribal insertion from Luke (cf. Klein, *ZTK* 61 [1964] 386–88; März *SNTU* 11 [1986] 90–92). März (94–95) argues on redactional grounds that the verses are necessary in their Matthean context (his argument for the Q sequence [93] on the basis of verbal reminiscences linking the Matthean form to the Lukan [Q] context is less compelling). Perhaps scribal omission was facilitated by the *γεν-* beginning shared by the second word of the omitted section and the beginning of the continuation in v 4. Klein's view (388–90) that Luke 12:56 (= Matt 16:3b) was originally separate and has been independently added to in the streams of tradition represented in Matthew and Luke is intrinsically improbable and, as Tannehill has shown (*Sword of His Mouth,* 129–31), it is also artistically insensitive.

Comment

Skilled in observing the ways of nature, people regularly examine the indicators of coming weather patterns and order their lives accordingly. It is nothing less than hypocrisy when the same skills are not brought to bear on the events of Jesus' ministry, which, just as reliably, point to the coming day of answerability to God.

54–55 The opening clause will be Luke's own formulation, as he continues in this section the pattern of address to disciples and the crowds (cf. at v 1). The καί, "as well," indicates a widening of the scope of address, rather than a turning from disciples to crowds. Since Matthew and Luke have different examples of weather prediction here (Luke's are oriented primarily to wind direction; Matthew's to the timing of the phenomena interpreted [cf. Klein, *ZTK* 61 (1964) 586]), it is not possible to identify an original form with any confidence. Perhaps the Matthean form is to be preferred as fitting best with τὸ πρόσωπον τοῦ οὐρανοῦ, "the appearance of the sky," in 16:3b (= Luke 12:56). In Palestine rain clouds come from the west, carrying the moisture taken up from the Mediterranean. νότος means "south" but is used both for southerly and southwesterly wind (see BAGD, 544). Here it needs to refer to a southerly or even a southwesterly *wind*, since these are the winds that would carry the heat of the desert. Guided by such advance indicators, people are prepared for the coming weather. The things they observe prove to be reliable indicators of what is to come.

55 The Matthean form here lacks "hypocrites." Though it is an unlikely Lukan addition, Matthew will not have deleted it. The presence of this word fits best with the form of the verse without the second οἴδατε, "you know [how]" (see above *Note* d). Luke's additional "of the earth and" appears to be (his?) generalization. Matthew's "signs of the times" looks like conformity to apocalyptic language for the periodization of world history. "Interpret" is δοκιμάζειν in Luke and διακρίνειν in Matthew, with no real difference of sense. Luke points to a failure to interpret (but see above *Note* d), while Matthew points to the inability to interpret.

"This [present] time" is the time occupied by the presence and activity of Jesus (in the Lukan frame we may fairly include also the role of John the Baptist; the close tie with vv 51–53 claimed by Klein [*ZTK* 61 (1964) 577–78] is unwarranted, especially with the expansion of audience envisaged in v 54). Current events have an "appearance" (πρόσωπον), which is just as indicative of what is to come as ever the weather indicators might be. The "hypocrisy" is the pretense involved in refusing to read the indicators for what they are. The text does not specify the future toward which the indicators point, but in the context of the larger section this can only be the eschaton, with its prospect of judgment.

Explanation

The events in the ministry of Jesus should make clear to all that the flow of world history is moving rapidly toward its appointment with the judgment of God.

Jesus' audience now widens to include the crowds, for whom some of the language is more appropriate than for the disciples, who are also addressed. He points out that people are very astute in interpreting the indicators of approaching weather. If the wind is bringing clouds from the Mediterranean, then rain is anticipated and rain duly comes. If the wind is from the south, out of the hot desert, then a scorcher is expected and a scorcher surely arrives. Guided by such advance indicators, people are prepared for the coming weather.

After these two illustrations the point is made more generally: when it comes to earth and sky (the two divisions of the natural order), people bring to bear their interpretive skills to anticipate the future and so to be prepared for it. Jesus accuses the crowds of hypocrisy because they are not ready to apply the same shrewdness to the indicators contained in the unfolding of his own ministry (and perhaps also its precursor in the ministry of John). The events of "this [present] time" point just as reliably as any weather indicators to the coming day of answerability to God.

Under Accusation and on the Way to the Court of Justice! (12:57–59)

Bibliography

Caird, G. B. "Expounding the Parables: I. The Defendant (Matthew 5:25f.; Luke 12:58f.)." *ExpTim* 77 (1965–66) 36–39. **Jeremias, J.** *Parables.* 43–44, 96, 180. **Klein, G.** "Die Prüfung der Zeit (Lukas 12,54–56)." *ZTK* 61 (1964) 373–90, esp. 380–85. **Schürmann, H.** "Eschatologie und Liebesdienst in der Verkündigung Jesu." In *Ursprung und Gestalt.* 279–98.

Translation

[57] *"Why indeed do you not make the right judgment for yourselves?* [58]*For as you go with your accuser to the official,*[a] *make an effort to be released from him on the way; otherwise he will drag you off*[b] *to the judge, and the judge will hand you over to the bailiff, and the bailiff will throw you into prison.* [59]*I say to you, you will certainly not get out of there until you have paid up the last lepton!"*

Notes

[a] Gr. ἄρχων (lit. "ruler").
[b] D it sy[s,c] have κατακρίνῃ, "he will condemn [you]."

Form/Structure/Setting

This unit consists of a challenge to make that judgment of which the hypocritical withholding has been protested in v 56, along with a parable that already points to the appropriate form for this judgment: that is, that the present time is the time when one is already on the way with one's accuser, to answer to the workings of the machinery of justice. The judgment for which the section (12:1–13:9) challenges one to prepare is seen to be imminent.

Apart from the opening transitional verse (which, despite März's defense of its place in Q [*SNTU* 11 (1986) 86–87, 93], is best taken as a Lukan formulation), the materials here have a parallel in Matt 5:25–26. The wording is quite different primarily because of Luke's intervention. In Luke the material has the form of parabolically expressed admonition, and this is probably true of the Matthean use of the parable as well, where it is more often taken as (nonparabolic) ethical admonition.

Comment

Jesus' hearers are now challenged to make the interpretation of "this [present] time," which in their hypocrisy they have avoided doing thus far. There is barely time for corrective action when one is already on the way with one's accuser to meet with the machinery of justice.

57 This verse has no parallel in Matthew's rendering. Luke's fondness for δὲ καί (lit. "but . . . also/even/indeed") and the clearly redactional ἀφ' ἑαυτῶν, "for yourselves," in 21:30 suggest that the verse is a Lukan transition. κρίνετε τὸ δίκαιον (lit. "judge the right [thing]") is best seen as equivalent to the δοκιμάζειν, "interpret," of v 56. The challenge is to move beyond the "hypocrisy" of v 56.

58 The wording (but not the sense) is almost entirely different from that in Matt 5:25. Most of the changes would seem to be Luke's (the interchange of ἄρχων [lit. "ruler"] and κριτής, "judge," is Lukan [Acts 7:27, 35; 16:19–20]; ἐργασίαν, "work/effort" is Lukan [four times in Acts, once elsewhere in the NT]; the simple form σύρειν, "drag," is found three times in Acts; πράκτωρ, "bailiff," reflects Luke's careful use of terminology [Matthew has ὑπηρέτης, "servant/assistant"]).

That the "go[ing] with" is not voluntary (against Schürmann, "Eschatologie und Liebesdienst," 281) reveals itself in the "drag you off," which becomes its equivalent (the "official" and the "judge" are one and the same person [see texts in paragraph above]; it is part of the story-telling technique that neutral terms are used to describe the action while the possibility of release remains, and threatening terms take their place for the situation in which that release has not been achieved). Though not clear in the present verse, from v 59 we should probably understand that an unpaid debt is the issue at stake. Also unclear is the anticipated strategy for achieving release from the clutches of one's creditor. Matthew has "make friends" (εὐνοῶν), and possibly ἀπηλλάχθαι here means "be reconciled" (cf. Marshall, 551; the following ἀπό, "from," counts against this sense; another possible sense is "obtain a settlement" [this would be a development from the sense "to be dismissed as settled" with reference to a matter under discussion (LSJ, 177)]). In any case some sort of accommodation with the accuser is anticipated (Klein's claim that, after vv 52–53, the call is to make a full break with those who oppose the church [*ZTK* 61 (1964) 383] makes no sense at all of the parable's story line).

Jesus' hearers are invited to see themselves as people in a compromised situation and heading toward an imminent disaster. Schürmann ("Eschatologie und Liebesdienst," 282) is surely right to link the demanded behavior here with the concern for "neighbor" that permeates Jesus' teaching. The call is to put things right with those to whom one is linked at the human level. The failure to do so will lead inexorably to the judgment of God, and that soon. It is difficult to see how Fitzmyer (1001–2) can see here no more than "a piece of prudential advice" about making "compromises in life."

59 Luke stays closer to his source here. He is likely to be responsible for the loss of an opening "amen," the addition of an emphatic "even," and the scaling down of the coin from a quadrans to a lepton (= half a quadrans and 1/128 of a denarius), which in the first century was the smallest coin in use in Palestine. Debtors' prison allowed little possibility for the retrieval of one's situation.

Explanation

"This [present] time" of v 56 is now identified parabolically as a time of being on the way to the law courts, with the prospect of an extended period of confinement. Only swift action can abort now the specified steps in the judicial process.

Jesus challenges his hearers to move beyond the hypocrisy of v 56 and to interpret aright for themselves "this present time." The parable to follow builds upon or perhaps in part seeks yet again to evoke this desired response. It paints a picture of the hearers as, individually, on the road with an accuser (apparently with respect to a matter of debt) who is after legal redress against him or her. It is a situation that screams out for each urgently to bend every effort to achieve an accommodation with the accuser. "Go[ing] with" and "official" sound innocuous enough, but if no accommodation is reached, then the true colors of these neutral terms emerge in the "drag you off" and "judge," which soon take their place and define the same state of affairs. Once the legal machinery has been put in motion, then the situation is lost. It is notoriously difficult ever to get out of a debtors' prison.

The parable points to the judgment of God, which will soon overwhelm those who do not put right those things in which their neighbors may have cause against them. Dealing justly with one's neighbor is the proper response to that process leading to the judgment of God, which Jesus has set in motion.

The Need for Timely Repentance (13:1–9)

Bibliography

Bartsch, H.-W. "Die 'Verfluchung' des Feigenbaums." *ZNW* 53 (1962) 256–60. **Blinzler, J.** "Die Niedermetzelung von Galiläern durch Pilatus." *NovT* 2 (1957–58) 24–49. ———. "Die letzte Gnadenfrist: Lk 13,6–9." *BLit* 37 (1963–64) 155–69. **Cantrell, R. A.** "The Cursed Fig Tree." *BiTod* 29 (1991) 105–8. **Denney, J.** "Three Motives to Repentance, Luke XIII. 1–9." *Exp* 4/7 (1893) 232–37. **Farmer, W. R.** "Notes on a Literary and Form-Critical Analysis of Some of the Synoptic Material Peculiar to Luke." *NTS* 8 (1962) 301–16. **Heininger, B.** *Sondergutgleichnisse.* 121–31. **Jeremias, J.** *Parables.* 169–71. **Johnson, S. E.** "A Note on Luke 13:1–5." *ATR* 17 (1935) 91–95. **Kahn, J. G.** "La parabole du figuier stérile et les arbres récalcitrants de la Genèse." *NovT* 13 (1971) 38–45. **Lasserre, J.** *La tour de Siloé: Jésus et la résistance de son temps.* Lyon, 1981. **Schwarz, G.** "Lukas XIII, 1–5: Eine Emendation." *NovT* 11 (1969) 121–26. **Telford, W. R.** *The Barren Temple and the Withered Tree: A Redaction-critical Analysis of the Cursing of the Fig-Tree Pericope in Mark's Gospel and Its Relation to the Cleansing of the Temple Tradition.* JSNTSup 1. Sheffield: JSOT, 1980. 224–39. **Ternant, P.** "Le dernier délai de la conversion Lc 13." *AsSeign* 16 (1971) 59–72. **Young, F. W.** "Luke 13:1–9." *Int* 31 (1977) 59–63.

Translation

[1] *Some were present at that time who told him about the Galileans whose blood Pilate mingled with [the blood of] their sacrifices.* [2] *In response he*[a] *said*[b] *to them, "Do you think*

that these Galileans were greater sinners than all the [other] Galileans, because they suffered these things?[c] [3]*I tell you, no! But unless you repent you will all perish in a similar manner.* [4]*Or those eighteen on whom the tower fell at Siloam and killed them—do you think that they were greater debtors than all the other people living in Jerusalem?* [5]*I tell you no! But unless you repent you will all perish just as they did."*[d]

[6]*Then he spoke this parable. "A certain person had a fig tree planted in his vineyard, and he came looking for fruit on it and did not find [any].* [7]*He said to the vineyard worker, 'Look, it is three years since I began coming*[e] *looking for fruit on this fig tree and I have not been finding*[f] *[any]. Cut it out then*[g]*! Why should it even use up the soil?'* [8]*He responded,*[h] *'Sir, leave it this year as well, until I dig around it*[i] *and put on manure.* [9]*Perhaps it will bear fruit in the coming year.*[j] *If not, you may*[k] *cut it out.'"*

Notes

[a] ὁ Ἰησοῦς, "Jesus," is found in A D W Θ Ψ etc. At this point Jesus has not been identified by name since 10:37.

[b] Lit. "having answered he said."

[c] τοιαῦτα, "such things," is read by P[75] A W Ψ etc.

[d] A W Ψ and the majority text interchange the ὡσαύτως, "just as they did," with the ὁμοίως, "in a similar manner," of v 3. P[75] D Θ 070 f^{13} conform v 5 here to v 3.

[e] Gr. ἔρχομαι (lit. "am coming").

[f] Gr. εὑρίσκω (lit. "am finding").

[g] Omitted by ℵ B D W f^1 etc.

[h] Lit. "having answered he says."

[i] τὸν τόπον, "the place/space," in B 1424.

[j] In P[45 vid] A D W Θ Ψ etc., "in the coming year" is linked to the following clause.

[k] Lit. "you will."

Form/Structure/Setting

The final unit of this section on preparing for the coming judgment (12:1–13:9) is a call for repentance. By providing a balancing vertical dimension here, the need for change toward God links with the demand in v 58 to deal with one's accuser. The limited opportunity remaining for the fig tree has its analogue in the scene painted in v 58, as well, of one on the way to meet the judge.

There is no Synoptic parallel to any of Luke's materials here. Farmer (*NTS* 8 [1962] 301–16) has argued persuasively that Luke 13:1–9 and 15:1–32 are both pre-Lukan units with a shared structure (he finds six structural characteristics that these two passages share that cannot be paralleled elsewhere). These passages were constituent parts of the chiastic parables source appealed to in the excursus: "Journey to Jerusalem." This does not, however, entitle us to claim an original unity for the materials of 13:1–9. Schwarz (*NovT* 11 [1969] 121–26) has shown how a close parallelism between vv 2–3 and 4–5 emerges if we dispense with the setting provided in v 1 and absorb the words "whose blood Pilate mingled with their sacrifices" from it into Jesus' words in v 2. This suggests that 13:1 may owe its origin to the editor of the parables source, who will be equally responsible for the joining of vv 6–9 to vv 2–5. The close parallelism of vv 2–3 and 4–5 (especially with Schwarz's reconstruction) stands in favor of an original unity for these verses.

As presented in Luke, vv 1–5 constitute a pronouncement story, but more originally the material probably lacked narrative setting and is to be seen as teaching of Jesus that admonishes on the basis of contemporary experiences. Though true enough to life, the parable of vv 6–9 is to be classified as a parable proper and not a similitude, since it deals with a particular rather than a typical situation.

Apart from the present report, the events noted in vv 1–5 are quite unknown to us from ancient sources. Concern about this has been focused on the fate of the Galileans, which, because of the political dimensions of Pilate's act here, many believe should have left some trace on Josephus' account of this period (he provides more detail for the period when Pilate was prefect than for other periods). Many attempts have been made to identify the present event with some other instance of Pilate's hostility to some of his Jewish or Samaritan subjects (see Blinzler, *NovT* 2 [1957–58] 29–37; Fitzmyer, 1006–7, offers a convenient summary). None is at all satisfactory. But, as Blinzler points out (39–40), it can be demonstrated that Josephus fails to report at least one much more politically significant act of Pilate (the attempt to introduce into Jerusalem votive shields without images but carrying the emperor's name; see Philo, *Leg. Gai.* 299–305) and that he is often content with generalized summaries. Given that the report in Luke 13:1–3 fits well with what is known about the harsh and insensitive nature of Pilate's rule (but see at 23:1–5 for the view that the image of supreme cruelty and injustice that has been formed of Pilate on the basis of Jewish sources is badly overdrawn; for a brief outline of Pilate's career in Judea, see E. Schürer, *Jewish People*, ed. G. Vermes, 1:383–87), there should, therefore, be no particular embarrassment about the lack of corroborating testimony.

The motif of a barren fig tree that faces destruction is also found in Mark 11:13–14, 20–21; par. Matt 21:18–19. While Luke's failure to include this incident may be based on the degree of similarity of the parable to this episode, the common claim that the one is derived from the other has little to commend it when it is noted how little common language is to be found (cf. Fitzmyer, 1004).

Comment

The challenge in 12:1–13:9 to prepare for the coming judgment now climaxes with a call to repent before disaster strikes. The remaining opportunity for reform is strictly limited.

1 *παρῆσαν*, "were present," and *ἐν αὐτῷ τῷ καιρῷ*, "in that time," serve to clamp the present unit with the preceding and are probably to be set to Luke's account (the former with the sense "had come" could be part of the pre-Lukan form [cf. the verb pattern in 15:2], but in the Lukan text the alternative sense is to be preferred). While there is every likelihood that these Galileans were involved in activities hostile to the state, this text should not be used to support Zeitlin's contention ("Who Were the Galileans? New Light on Josephus' Activities in Galilee," *JQR* 64 [1973–74] 189–203) that Josephus uses "Galilean" in a specialist sense for a particular revolutionary group (his case seems to involve some confusion between the connotation of the term in certain contexts of Josephus and the denotation of the term). The comparison with the eighteen deaths caused by the collapse of the tower suggests that no large number of people were involved here. Sense requires that we fill out the reference to the sacrifices with "the blood of." An idiomatic use of "mingling of blood" is known in Jewish sources (see. Str-B, 2:193), which in one text is even applied to a putting to death in the temple (Philo, *De spec. leg.* 3.91). The idiom may be literal or it may be figuratively used, but in any case requires that the related spillings of blood take place in the same time period (and probably the same place). The report to Jesus is a call for him to comment on the significance of this event. The response given operates within the framework of sin and judgment, but those who brought the matter to Jesus' attention should perhaps be understood to have been looking for a political statement.

2 Comparison with 11:4 raises the possibility that Luke may have supplied *ἁμαρτωλοί*, "sinners," here in place of an original *ὀφειλέται*, "debtors" (as in v 4). The use of *παρά* (lit. "beside") for the comparative ("more than"), along with the lack of a word for "other" (as required by the sense), suggests a Semitic original (Fitzmyer, 1007, finds an Aramaic parallel for the construction in 1QapGen 20:6–7). A connection between sin and calamity has a firm background in Jewish thought (see Job 4:7; 8:4, 20; 22:5; Pss 1:4; 37:20; Exod 20:5; 1QapGen 20:16–29; John 9:2–3; Str-B, 2:193–97) and is implicitly accepted by Jesus here. Jesus will, however, dispute the possibility of determining the *degree* of sinfulness from the experience of calamity and will shift the focus away from the passing of judgment on others to the need to put one's own house in order.

3 For the general thought here, see Ps 7:12 (cf. Jer 12:17). Three horizons of God's judgment are identified within Luke's works in *Comment* at 12:5 (human history, after death, final judgment). Only the first is intended here (even more so in the parallel v 5), but this should not be pressed, since all three horizons are understood as closely interconnected: in one way or another disaster will strike all those who will not repent in the face of the new situation created by the presence and the ministry of Jesus and by his proclamation of the coming of the kingdom of God. The coming destruction of Jerusalem is not especially anticipated here (or more specifically in vv 4–5), but takes its place in connection with this kind of thinking. On repentance, see at 3:3.

4 On the sentence construction here, cf. at v 2. Siloam was the name given to the reservoir near the southeast corner of the Jerusalem walls (Josephus, *War* 5.145; cf. John 9:7, 11). A tower at this point in the wall is otherwise unknown (and so, naturally, its collapse). *ὀφειλέται*, "debtors," for "sinners" probably reflects Aramaic idiom (חיב, *ḥayyāb*, which has an idiomatic use in connection with those who have fallen into "debt" in connection with God). "People living in Jerusalem" only because that is where the tower incident occurred, but its mention here also provides a happy counter to any who would wish to set Galilee and Judea against each another.

5 This verse differs from v 3 only in the use of *ὡσαύτως*, "just as they did," rather than the *ὁμοίως*, "in a similar manner," of v 3.

6 Luke has a particular fondness for labeling parables as such and so is probably responsible for "this parable" here. For fig trees in vineyards, see Pliny, *Nat. Hist.* 17.35.200 and Theophrastus, *De caus. plant.* 3.10.6 (which advises against it); the refrain of 1 Kgs 4:25; Mic 4:4; Zech 3:10 may reflect this ancient practice. The imagery of fruitfulness for God here may go back to Jer 8:13 (cf. Isa 5:2). See also Luke 3:9. Though frequently maintained, there is really no OT use of the imagery of the fig tree for Israel (or Judah) unless we count the passing image of fruitlessness in Jer 8:13. The argument of C. Daniel ("Esséniens, zélotes et sicaires et leur mention par paronymie dans le N.T.," *Numen* 13 [1966] 88–115, esp. 99–100) that the fig tree refers to the terrorist group the *sicarii* (because of the presence of the same consonants in the Greek) has no credibility.

7 The ἀμπελουργός, "vineyard worker," rather than the owner, would have taken care of the vineyard, under the direction of his employer. We should understand that the tree had been growing quite long enough to reach fruit-bearing maturity before the first visit. For the removal of the barren tree, cf. 3:9.

8–9 The vineyard worker pleads for one last year of opportunity for the tree, during which he will provide special nurture for it (see Heininger, *Sondergutgleichnisse,* 125 n. 2, for texts on the use of manure on fig trees). If it fares no better, he too must agree that the tree is fit only for removal.

The Lukan setting encourages an individualistic reading of the parable, but in the ministry of Jesus the thrust may have been more collective. The lack of fruit in the parable corresponds to the need for repentance in vv 1–5. The parable sets a limit on the time available for the required repentance. The image is of judgment graciously held back. Is it over-interpretation to identify Jesus' ministry with the special nurture offered to the tree in its final year?

Explanation

The challenge in 12:1–13:9, to prepare for the coming judgment, now climaxes with a call to repent before disaster strikes. The fate of the Galileans whose blood Pilate mingled with that of their sacrifices, like that of those who perished in the fall of the tower of Siloam, becomes a symbol for the coming fate of all who will not repent. The fig-tree parable identifies Jesus' hearers as being in the last season of opportunity to change their ways.

Luke uses chronological unity here to reinforce thematic unity. We have no other knowledge of the events reported here, but that is not surprising given the limited historical records available for first-century Palestine. No doubt Pilate considered these Galileans guilty of some considerable political crime, and Jesus could have commented on the rights and wrongs of their cause. But instead, his comments take their point of departure from the standard Jewish association of calamity and sin (see Job 4:7; Ps 1:4; John 9:2–3; etc.). Jesus does not dispute such a connection, but he does suggest that these people were no *more* sinful than others. In the situation created by Jesus' presence and his preaching of the kingdom of God, *all* need to repent. He moves the focus away from judgment of others with his call to put one's own house in order. Those who fail to do so will themselves perish.

Luke sees the judgment of God as falling on people in the flow of human history, after death, and on the final judgment day. The wording here literally supports the first, but in the Gospel account the three are too closely intertwined to be neatly separated.

While in vv 2–3 we were dealing with the act of a cruel leader and perhaps of people who "asked for it" by their political activity, now we are probably to think of an "act of God" falling randomly on those who just happen innocently to be present. The same judgments apply.

It was apparently quite common to grow fig trees in vineyards. This one had been mature enough for the owner to have expected fruit from it for at least three years, and it had regularly disappointed the owner. The vineyard worker was ordered to cut it down, but he asks for one more year of opportunity for the tree during which he will provide it with special nurture. The parable reinforces the need for repentance and suggests that there is a strict limit to the time available for the required repentance. The image is of judgment graciously held back for a time.

Reversals Now and to Come (13:10–14:35)

In two sets of units set in sequential parallelism (13:10–35; 14:1–35), Luke explores a series of reversals and paradoxical inversions associated with the manifestation of the kingdom of God, both in connection with its present manifestation and in connection with its manifestation at the time for the consummation of all God's purposes.

Releasing on the Sabbath the One Bound by Satan (13:10–17)

Bibliography

Busse, U. *Wunder.* 289–304. **Derrett, J. D. M.** "Positive Perspectives on Two Lucan Miracles." *DR* 104 (1986) 272–87. **Dietzfelbinger, C.** "Vom Sinn der Sabbatheilungen Jesu." *EvT* 38 (1978) 281–97. **Glöckner, R.** *Neutestamentliche Wundergeschichten und das Lob der Wundertaten Gottes in den Psalmen: Studien zur sprachlichen und theologischen Verwandtschaft zwischen neutestamentichen Wundergeschichten und Psalmen.* Walberger Studien. Theologische Reihe 13. Mainz: Grünewald, 1983. 105–24. **Green, J. B.** "Jesus and a Daughter of Abraham (Luke 13:10–17): Test Case for a Lukan Perspective on the Miracles of Jesus." *CBQ* 51 (1989) 643–54. **Hamm, M. D.** "The Freeing of the Bent Woman and the Restoration of Israel: Luke 13:10–17 and Narrative Theology." *JSNT* 31 (1987) 23–44. **Kirchschläger, W.** *Jesu exorzistisches Wirken.* 242–48. **Klein, H.** *Barmherzigkeit gegenüber den Elenden und Geächteten: Studien zur Botschaft des lukanischen Sondergutes.* Biblisch-theologische Studien 10. Neukirchen-Vluyn: Neukirchener Verlag, 1987. 17–23. **Lohse, E.** "Jesu Worte über den Sabbat." In *Judentum—Urchristentum—Kirche.* FS J. Jeremias, ed. W. Eltester. BZNT 26. Berlin: Töpelmann, 1960. 79–89. **Milot, L.** "Guérison d'une femme inferme un jour de sabbat (Luc 13,10–17): L'importance d'une comparison." *SémiotBib* 39 (1985) 23–33. **O'Toole, R. F.** "Some Exegetical Reflections on Luke 13,10–17." *Bib* 73 (1992) 84–107. **Radl, W.** "Ein 'doppeltes Leiden' in Lk 13:11? Zu einer Notiz von Günther Schwarz." *BibNot* 31 (1986) 35–36. **Roloff, J.** *Das Kerygma.* 66–69. **Schüssler Fiorenza, E.** "Lk 13:10–17: interpretation for liberation and transformation." *TD* 36 (1989) 303–19. **Schwarz, G.** "*λυθηναι απο του δεσμου τουτου.*" *BibNot* 15 (1981) 47. ———. "*και ην συγκυπτουσα.*" *BibNot* 20 (1983) 58. **Steiner, A.,** and **Stotzer, H.** "Zur Freiheit befreit: Jesu heilt eine behinderte Frau am Sabbat (Lukas 13:10–17): Ein Normenwunder." In *Wunder Jesu,* ed. A. Steiner and V. Weymann. Bibelarbeit in der Gemeinde. Themen und Materialen 2. Basel: Reinhardt, 1978. 127–46. **Trautmann, M.** *Zeichenhafte Handlungen Jesu: Ein Beitrag zur Frage nach dem geschichtlichen Jesus.* FB 37. Würzburg: Echter, 1980. 278–316. **Weiser, A.** *Eine Heilung und ihr dreifacher Bericht (Matthäus 8,5–13; Lukas 7,1–10; Johannes 4,43–54).* Werkstatt Bibelauslegung. Bilder, Interpretationen, Texte. Stuttgart: Katholisches Bibelwerk, 1976. 64–69. **Wilkinson, J.** "The Case of the Bent Woman in Luke 13:10–17." *EvQ* 49 (1977) 195–205.

Translation

[10]*He was teaching in one of the synagogues on the sabbath.* [11]*There was*[a] *a woman [there] who had had a spirit of weakness for eighteen years and was bent over and not*

able to straighten up at all. [12]*Seeing her, Jesus*[b] *called out and said to her, "Woman, you are released*[c] *from your weakness."* [13]*He placed his hand upon her and at once she became erect again and began to glorify God.* [14]*Annoyed that Jesus had healed on the sabbath, the ruler of the synagogue responded and said to the crowd, "There are six days on which one must work; come and be healed on those and not on the day of the sabbath."* [15]*The Lord responded and said, "Hypocrites,*[d] *doesn't each of you release his ox or his ass from the manger on the sabbath to lead it away to give it a drink?* [16]*And shouldn't this woman who is a daughter of Abraham, whom Satan bound these*[e] *eighteen years, be released from this bondage on the day of the sabbath?"* [17]*As he said these things, all*[f] *his opponents were put to shame, while all the crowd rejoiced at all the glorious things which were being done by him.*

Notes

[a] Lit. "and behold."
[b] Missing from P[45] b i.
[c] Perfect tense in the Gr.
[d] P[45] D W *f*[1] etc. have the sing.
[e] Lit. "behold."
[f] Omitted by P[45] D it.

Form/Structure/Setting

A new major section begins here and runs through 14:35. Thematically it is marked by contrasts or reversals, but the main device that Luke uses to identify the bounds of the section is parallelism between the units of 13:10–35 and those of 14:1–35 (13:10–17 and 14:1–6 are healings on the sabbath; 13:18–19 is closely paralleled by vv 20–21, just as 14:7–11 is by vv 12–14 [the link from the kingdom of God of 13:18–19, 20–21 to the banquet of 14:1–6, 12–14 is facilitated by 14:15 with its reference to eating food in the kingdom of God]; 13:22–30 and 14:15–24 are each concerned with who will make it into the kingdom of God; 13:31–35 deals with the coming fate of Jesus in Jerusalem, while 14:25–35 deals with its analogue in the call to bear one's own cross and come after Jesus [does the unhappy condition of Jerusalem in 13:34–35 correspond to the salt that has lost its taste in 14:34–35?]). His method here is to be compared with that involved in the structuring of 5:1–6:16. (Talbert, *Literary Patterns*, 52, recognizes part of this pattern when he parallels 13:10–17 with 14:1–6 and 13:18–30 with 14:7–24; the otherwise not unattractive chiastic structuring of 12:49–13:35 by Hamm, *JSNT* 31 [1987] 30–31, is vulnerable to criticism in its use of 12:54–13:5 as a unit.)

Here again, Luke alone reports this incident. A number of difficulties have been identified in the account, which have served to place its unity and/or authenticity in question: (*i*) novelistic coloration is suspected; (*ii*) the form of the material is thought to be caught between that of a miracle story and of a controversy dialogue; (*iii*) the synagogue ruler complains to the crowd rather than to Jesus, who is his actual opponent; (*iv*) Jesus addresses "hypocrites" where only a single synagogue ruler opposes him; (*v*) the easy claim of v 15 is said not to be true of first-century Jewish practice; (*vi*) what we have here may, in any case, be only a variant of the tradition behind Matt 12:11; (*vii*) the present narrative has a "literary" unity based on the three uses of the Greek verb *λύειν*, "to release/loose," which makes the force of the comparison in the argument depend upon a recognition and acceptance of a transferred sense of this term (most of these points are noted by Roloff, *Kerygma*, 67–68, who nonetheless in conclusion treats all the main content as original, apart from vv 14b–15 [vv 10 and 17 are seen as schematic completions and v 11 is thought to be based on v 16a]).

(*i*) Novelistic coloration is finally impossible to evaluate given a single source and Luke's free rendering of his sources. (*ii*) The question of form is adequately answered by the removal of "she glorified God" from v 13, words that may be suspected of being Lukan on the basis of other uses of this language (see 5:25, 26; 7:16; 18:43; 23:47). (*iii*) The question of the ruler's address to the crowd is to the point. It appears to be concerned, by alluding to the sabbath commandment, to make a statement in principle about Jewish objection to all Jesus' (and continuing Christian?) sabbath healing activity (if Luke had not obscured the sabbath observance in 4:40, it would be tempting to attribute the present text to Lukan reflection on that text). (*iv*) Technically, Jesus does address "hypocrites," but the response is to "you and your kind." (*v*) Interpretation of first-century practice is disputed in *Comment* below. (*vi*) Shared source with Matt 12:11 cannot be disproved, but there are no literary links to support it. (*vii*) Limited literary unity is true for the use of *λύειν* in v 12 (this is probably in the Greek text a back influence from v 16). The imagery in v 16 (of a person being constrained by Satan as animals are constrained) certainly needs to commend itself to the hearer (in the way that a parable does), but the link to v 15 is not at all narrowly language dependent. V 16 would be much weakened by the lack of v 15.

Beyond these points, some form of v 10 is required to give a sabbath setting (and probably a synagogue setting as well, to account for the role of the ruler of the synagogue). V 17 is certainly schematic and probably does not belong to the earliest form of this pericope. Its elements take up chiastically the success of Jesus in the controversy of vv 14–16 (generalizing from the shaming of the synagogue ruler) and the healing of vv 11–13 (generalizing from the single healing and from the woman's glorifying of God at the end of v 13 [this last suggests that v 17 may be Lukan]).

Comment

No amount of pious protection of the sanctity of the sabbath can stand in the way of Jesus' release of this crippled woman from her longstanding bondage, the more so when it is recognized that even the most fastidious will not let their animals go one sabbath day without being given the freedom to go and get water.

10 For this verse, see at 4:31 (cf. v 33). There is an interesting correspondence between *ἐν μιᾷ τῶν . . . ἰδοὺ ἀνήρ . . . ἰδών*, "in one of the . . . behold a man . . . seeing," in 5:12 and the role of these words and phrases (with "woman" for "man") in shaping the narrative development in vv 10–12. The teaching role is not formally taken up in the unfolding of the episode, but the controversy of vv 14–17a is effectively a piece of teaching. This is the last mention in Luke of Jesus' presence in a synagogue.

11 As yet another instance of Luke's concern to balance men and women, the parallel incident in 14:1–6 will involve a man. It remains uncertain whether we should consider a "spirit of weakness" as descriptive of a demon (see "spirit of festering" in 1QapGen 20.26; cf. v 16; "spirit of divination" in Acts 16:16) or whether it is simply an idiom for having a debilitating ailment. "Satan bound" in v 16 is not a decisive indicator, since "healing all who were oppressed by the devil" in Acts 10:38 is best taken as referring to healing in general. In all other respects the language of the account suits a healing better than an exorcism (cf. Wilkinson, *EvQ* 49 [1977] 201–2). "Eighteen" may be a conventional number (18 = 2 x 9 = "a long time") as maintained by Derrett (*DR* 104 [1986] 274 and 284 n. 14; cf. O. Stein, "The numeral 18," *Poona Orientalist* 1 [1936] 1–37; 2 [1937] 164–65). This would account for its over-representation in particular parts of the OT (see Judg 3:13–14; 10:8; 20:25, 44; 2 Sam 8:13) and for this second occurrence within eight verses of Luke's text. εἰς τὸ παντελές could link with μὴ δυναμένη (so: "completely unable") or with ἀνακύψαι (so: "to straighten up fully"), probably the former since the seriousness of the complaint seems more pertinent than precision about the degree of mobility. An informed modern medical diagnosis is *spondylitis ankylopoietica*, which produces fusion of the vertebrae (Wilkinson, 196–200), but all suggestions are necessarily speculative.

12–13 Jesus takes the initiative after seeing the woman in her need. The perfect passive used suggests: "God's release has come for you." The term for release anticipates v 15. For the laying on of hands, cf. 4:40. For her response, see at 5:26.

14 On "ruler of the synagogue," see at 8:41. It fits with his role that he should be concerned about a disturbance of the order of worship. Concern about healing on the sabbath has been an issue already in 6:6–11 (see there). The directive to the crowd alludes to the sabbath command of Exod 20:9 (Deut 5:13). Since the woman did not come to Jesus, but he, in effect, to her, and since the annoyance is with Jesus' behavior and not the crowd's, the directive fits only imperfectly in the flow of the story here. "Day of the sabbath" (also in v 16) is found also in the parallel episode at 14:5.

15 From 7:13 onward (see at 7:13), Luke often introduces Jesus as "the Lord." Jesus' response here is to the annoyance of the ruler of the synagogue rather than to his directive to the crowd. The "hypocrites" are the synagogue ruler and his kind, not the crowd of v 14. Their hypocrisy in this instance is the inconsistency to be uncovered by Jesus' continuing words. The phrase here τῷ σαββάτῳ, "on the sabbath," and the pairing of ox and ass will recur in the parallel 14:1–6 (vv 3, 5). While Roloff (*Kerygma*, 67 and n. 59) can rightly point to sabbath restrictions on *how* the needs of animals might be met (water not to be *directly* given to them, certain kinds of knots not to be untied), there is not the slightest doubt that their needs were in fact regularly met (see Marshall, 558–59, for texts; see esp. *m. Erub.* 2:1–4; CD 11:5–6 for the movement of animals on the sabbath for pasture and water). "Release" here corresponds to the binding and releasing to come in v 16.

16 This woman is a "daughter of Abraham" as Zacchaeus will later be a "son of Abraham": one of God's chosen People (cf. 1:55; 3:8; 16:24; Acts 7:2; 13:26; and for the idiom Gal 3:7 ["sons"]; 4 Macc 15:28 ["daughter"]). Satan stands behind the afflictions of life. The role given him in illness here draws all the healings into the orbit of the sentiment of 11:20. The woman's restriction is compared to that of an animal that is not free to get to the drinking water that it needs. The animal is not left tethered for *one day;* the woman has been restricted in this way for *eighteen years!* Fitzmyer (1014) documents analogous figurative use of the bondage language here. This is part of the "liberty" "to the captives" promised in 4:18.

17 There is undoubtedly an allusion to the LXX of Isa 45:16, which is seen as having a fulfillment here. The clause about the opponents is clearly schematic since apart from one of them they are not even present! Luke uses "all the crowd" as well in 6:19; Acts 21:27. Cf. the response at 7:16. The marvels promised by God for the possession of the promised land are spoken of with the same term, ἐνδόξοι, in the LXX of Exod 34:10. Again there is a schematic reference to acts beyond what has been experienced on this occasion.

Explanation

The new section "Reversals Now and to Come" (13:10–14:34) is thematically held together by the contrasts and reversals that are to be found throughout, but Luke most clearly marks the section by paralleling item by item the units of 13:10–35 and those of 14:1–35. The opening unit is paralleled by another sabbath healing in 14:1–6.

The woman healed in this unit has known a long and apparently irreversible bondage to a crippling disease. As Jesus comes across her in this sabbath setting, no amount of sabbath scrupulosity will keep him from bringing "liberty" to this particular "captive" (4:18). Those who object do better by their animals!

Here Jesus encounters a sick woman as he teaches in the synagogue as he had earlier come across a demoniac in the synagogue of Capernaum (4:31–37; there could be a demon involved here as well [see *Comment* above]), but the closest parallel is with a sick man in 14:1–6. Luke is, as we have seen already seen, fond of man/woman comparisons. There is some evidence that "eighteen" may at times be used not literally but for a large number. The disease here may have involved a fusing of the vertebrae.

Once he has seen her, Jesus takes the entire initiative in the woman's restoration: he tells her that God's release has come for her and lays his hands on her (as in 4:40). Her restoration is immediate, and she gives glory to the God who stands behind her deliverance.

Healing on the sabbath has already made trouble in 6:6–11. The ruler of the synagogue alludes to the sabbath requirement of the Ten Commandments and directs the crowd to come and be healed on the working days of the week. He has no capacity to enter into the thrill of the woman's restoration.

Jesus responds to the hidden hypocrisy of his complainant (he talks here to "you and your kind," not to the crowd). He compares the woman's restriction to that of an animal that is not free to get the water that it needs, and argues that in taking up this critical attitude such people show that they have more regard for the thirst of their animals over *one* sabbath day, than for the Satan-bound condition of this woman over *eighteen years.* Satan is understood to stand behind such afflictions. From this perspective, Jesus' healings too can demonstrate that "the kingdom of God has come upon you" (Luke 11:20).

Luke rounds off the account schematically by suggesting that Jesus puts all his opponents to shame (of course most of them would not even have been present!). By echoing the language of the Greek text of Isa 45:16, he suggests that Scripture is being fulfilled. Similarly the response of the crowd strays outside the bounds of the actual episode. The use of "glorious things" may be a deliberate echo of the same term in the Greek version of Exod 34:10.

The Kingdom of God Is like Mustard Seed (13:18–19)

Bibliography

Bartsch, H.-W. "Eine bisher übersehene Zitierung der LXX in Mark. 4,30." *TZ* 15 (1959) 126–28. **Bowen, C. R.** "The Kingdom and the Mustard Seed." *AJT* 22 (1918) 562–69. **Clark, K. W.** "The Mustard Plant." *ClW* 37 (1943–44) 81–83. **Crossan, J. D.** "The Seed Parables of Jesus." *JBL* 92 (1973) 244–66, esp. 253–59. **Dahl, N. A.** "The Parables of Growth." *ST* 5 (1951) 132–66; reprinted *Jesus in the Memory of the Early Church.* Minneapolis: Augsburg, 1976. 141–66. **Didier, M.** "Les paraboles du grain de sénevé et du levain." *RevDiocNamur* 15 (1961) 385–94. **Dupont, J.** "Le couple parabolique du sénevé et du levain." In *Études.* 2:609–23. ———. "Les parables de sénevé et du levain." *NRT* 89 (1967) 897–913. **Fleddermann, H.** "The Mustard Seed and the Leaven in Q, the Synoptics, and Thomas." In *Society of Biblical Literature 1989 Seminar Papers,* ed. D. J. Lull. Atlanta, GA: Scholars, 1989. 216–36. **Funk, R. W.** "The Looking-Glass Tree Is for the Birds: Ezekiel 17,22–24; Mark 4,30–32." *Int* 27 (1973) 3–9. **Granata, G.** "Some more Information about Mustard and the Gospel." *BeO* 25 (1983) 105–6. **Haenchen, E.** *Der Weg Jesu.* 180–86. **Hertzsch, K. P.** "Jésus herméneute: Une étude de Marc 4,30–32." In *Reconnaissance à Suzanne de Dietrich.* CBFV 70. Paris: Foi et Vie, 1971. 109–16. **Hunter, A. M.** "The Interpretation of the Parables." *ExpTim* 69 (1957–58) 100–104. **Hunzinger, C.-H.** "*σίναπι.*" *TDNT* 7:287–91. **Jehle, F.** "Sehnkorn und Sauerteig in der Heiligen Schrift." *NKZ* 34 (1923) 713–19. **Jeremias, J.** *Parables.* 146–49. **Kogler, F.** *Das Doppelgleichnis vom Senfkorn und vom Sauerteig in seiner traditionsgeschichtlichen Entwicklung: Zur Reich-Gottes-Vorstellung Jesu und ihren Aktualisierung in der Urkirche.* FB 59. Würzburg: Echter, 1988. **Kuss, O.** "Zur Senfkornparabel." *TGl* 41 (1951) 40–49; reprinted *Auslegung und Verkündigung: Aufsätze zur Exegese des Neuen Testamentes.* Regensburg: Pustet, 1963. 1:78–84 ———. "Zum Sinngehalt des Doppelgleichnisses vom Senfkorn und Sauerteig." *Bib* 40 (1959) 641–53; reprinted *Auslegung und Verkündigung: Aufsätze zur Exegese des Neuen Testamentes.* Regensburg: Pustet, 1963. 1:85–97. **Laufen, R.** *Doppelüberleiferung.* 174–200, 470–90 ———. "*Βασιλεία* und *ἐκκλησία*: Eine traditions- und redaktionsgeschichtliche Untersuchung des Gleichnisses vom Senfkorn." In *Begegnung mit dem Wort.* FS H. Zimmermann, ed. J. Zmijewski and E. Nellessen. BBB 53. Bonn: Hanstein, 1980. 105–40. **Lohfink, G.** "Senfkorn und Weltenbaum (Mk 4,30–32 Parr): Zum Verhältnis von Natur und Gesellschaft bei Jesus." In "*. . . Bäume braucht man doch*"*! Das Symbol des Baumes zwischen Hoffnung und Zerstörung,* ed. H. Schweizer. Sigmaringen: Thorbecke, 1986. 109–26. **Mare, W. H.** "The Smallest Mustard Seed: Matthew 13,32." *GJ* 9 (1968) 3–11. **Matthews, A. J.** "The Mustard 'Tree.'" *ExpTim* 39 (1927–28) 32–34. **Mayr, I.** "Vom Sauerteig." *BLit* 25 (1957–58) 255–57. **McArthur, H. K.** "The Parable of the Mustard Seed." *CBQ* 33 (1971) 198–210. **Michaelis, W.** "Die Gleichnisse vom Senfkorn und vom Sauerteig." *KF* 72 (1938) 118–21, 129–36. **Mussner, F.** "1Q Hodajoth und das Gleichnis von Senfkorn (Mk 4,30–32 Par.)." *BZ* 4 (1960) 128–30. **Pollard, S.** "The Mustard Seed." *ExpTim* 24 (1912–13) 187. **Schultze, B.** "Die ekklesiologische Bedeutung des Gleichnis vom Senfkorn (Matth. 13,31–32; Mk. 4,30–32; Lk. 13,18–19)." *OCP* 27 (1961) 362–86. **Schulz, S.** *Spruchquelle.* 298–307, 307–9. **Smith, J. H.** "The Parable of the Mustard Seed." *ExpTim* 23 (1911–12) 428–30. **Sproule, J. A.** "The Problem of the Mustard Seed." *GTJ* 1 (1980) 37–42. **Szimonidesz, L.** "Eine Rekonstruction des Senfkorngleichnisses." *NieuTS* 26 (1937) 128–55. **Zimmermann, H.** *Neutestamentliche Methodenlehre: Darstellung der historischkritischen Methode.* Stuttgart: Katholisches Bibelwerk, 1967. 123–27. **Zinng, P.** *Wachsen.* 100–115.

Translation

[18]*Then he said, "What is the kingdom of God like, and to what shall I compare it?* [19]*It is like a mustard seed which a man took and threw into his garden. And it grew up and became a*[a] *tree and the birds of the sky nested in its branches."*

Notes

[a] p[45] A W Θ Ψ etc. add μέγα, "great," probably influenced by Mark 4:32.

Form/Structure/Setting

In this second unit of the section 13:10–14:35, "Reversals Now and to Come," it is the high point (vv 13b, 17) of the reversal in 13:10–17 that corresponds to the low point of the reversal contemplated in this present parable. In the parallelism that structures the section, vv 18–19 have a close parallel in vv 20–21, and together these units have a counterpart in the paralleled 14:7–11 and 12–14 (Luke helps the link by referring to the teaching of vv 8–11 as a "parable").

The present parable and its sequel appear together in Matt 13:31–33. Mark also has the present parable (4:30–32) but not its sequel. (The *Gospel of Thomas* form of the parable [20] is likely to be secondary to the synoptic Gospel forms.) Matthew has clearly been influenced by the Markan location, and his form of the parable shows some Markan influence but is closer to the Lukan form (which shows no clear Markan influence). Luke has used here the source materials he shares with Matthew. Except for uncertainty over whether "field" or "garden" stood in the source, there is broad agreement that Luke reproduces his source verbatim. It is likely that "garden" is the source form; that it came into the parable when it was united with the following parable (to allow for a "house"/"garden" pairing along with the "woman"/"man" pairing in the linkage of the parables; as Zimmermann, *Methodenlehre,* 126; Laufen, *Doppelüberlieferung,* 178); and that Matthew has adopted "field" from 13:24 (from which he has also taken his use of the verb "sow" [more likely than from Mark 4:31 because of the link with "man"]; Matthew may also have been aware of the Jewish tradition that [in connection with the OT prohibition of sowing two kinds of seeds together] excluded mustard from gardens [*m. Kil.* 3:2; *t. Kil.* 2.8]).

Is it possible to identify a more original form behind the Q and Mark forms? It is likely that the parable of the leaven has imposed its form on the Q wording at the point where the two parables were united, and that we should therefore broadly favor the Markan form. On the other hand the grammatical awkwardness and repetition involved in the inclusion of ὃς ὅταν σπαρῇ ἐπὶ τῆς γῆς μικρότερον ὂν πάντων τῶν σπερμάτων τῶν ἐπὶ τῆς γῆς, "which when it is sown upon the ground is the smallest of all the seeds upon the ground," in the Markan form (4:31) makes it unlikely that this is an original part of the parable. Its addition will have influenced in turn the wording in v 32, "becomes the greatest of all the shrubs (λαχάνων [normally "vegetables," which in Jewish terms would allow the mustard plant back into the garden]," which perhaps should be reduced to "becomes a shrub." In the introduction the reference to "parable" may well be Markan intervention, and here the double form found in Luke 13:18 is likely to be the more original. There is no adequate basis for choosing between Mark's "under the shade" and Luke's "in the branches": the point remains much the same. (For these judgments, cf. Laufen, *Doppelüberlieferung,* 176–82; contrast Dupont, *NRT* 89 [1967] 899–900; McArthur, *CBQ* 33 [1971] 205–8). There is in any case some reason to question whether the earliest form of all will have contained this final element (McArthur, *CBQ* 33 [1971] 204: "If one wanted to create a parable culminating in the OT picture [see *Comment* below] of birds nesting in the branches of a tree is it likely that he would begin with the imagery of the mustard seed?").

On the lips of Jesus the parable has natural links to 7:23 and offers a measure of elucidation to the intrinsically paradoxical language of 11:20; 17:21.

Comment

As impressive as Luke's portrayal of the ministry of Jesus is, when we compare it to the full shape of Jewish eschatological hopes for the kingdom of God, it is only as a mustard seed is to a particularly large specimen of the adult plant.

18 While there is no change of location, neither is there any expectation that we should read these paired parables with the crowd or the synagogue ruler of vv 10–17 as audience. For the double questioning introduction, cf. 7:31 (Isa 40:18 has a somewhat similar pattern). On kingdom of God, see at 4:43; 6:20; 17:21; 11:20; 19:11.

19 Mustard seed was considered proverbially small in Jewish tradition (*m. Nid.* 5:2). While the Markan text brings this fact into prominence, it is operative here as well. Theophrastus, *Hist. plant.* 7.1, 2–3 includes mustard among the *λαχάνα*, "vegetables/edible plants" (above for Mark: "shrubs"), and can use *δένδρον*, "tree," of *λαχάνα* (cf. Clark, *ClW* 37 [1943–44] 82). An unusually large mustard plant (*sinapis nigra*) could be nine feet tall (usually about four feet [Hunzinger, *TDNT* 3:288–89]). *ἄνθρωπος* is normally "person," but here "man" in contrast with the "woman" of v 21 (the domestic activity in the "garden" is also contrasted with the woman's domestic activity, which will take place in the house). "Threw" probably reflects the same careless confidence as the sower of 8:4–8 (see there). See above for possible difficulty in a Jewish setting with the garden location. As well as emphasizing the extent of the growth, the reference to "tree" is for the sake of the OT allusion, of which it is the first trace. The relevant texts are Dan 4:12, 21 (MT 4:9, 18) and Ezek 17:22–23; 31:5–6 (and cf. also Ps 104:12). The images portray a powerful king/kingdom able to provide a widely used protective canopy of stability and peace. Ezek 17:22–23 is the most likely allusion as it has the twin advantages of an appropriate context and its own development from small beginnings (sprig to noble cedar).

The ministry of Jesus is claimed here as genuinely the beginning of what culminates in the apocalyptic coming of the kingdom of God. In the Lukan scheme the element of continuity that links the beginning and the end is partly christologically understood (see, e.g., Acts 3:21; 17:31) and partly realized in the continuity between the ministry of Jesus and the life of the Church (as well as through the decisive developments: death, resurrection, and heavenly session of Jesus; coming of the Spirit; gentile mission to the ends of the earth). The Church is not, however, identified with the kingdom, and the final coming of the kingdom is clearly not a development from the present life of the Church. Whether (as often maintained) an eschatological gathering of the Gentiles is necessarily intended by the birds remains uncertain. It is likely, however, that for Luke, for whom the Gospel inclusion of the formerly excluded prepares for the later inclusion of the Gentiles, there will be a hint of gentile entry into the kingdom of God (cf. v 29; 14:21–23).

Explanation

In this second of the "Reversals Now and to Come" of this section (13:10–14:35), we are given a picture of the contrast between the beginning of the kingdom of God in the ministry of Jesus and its culmination in the full manifestation of God's kingdom at the end. Vv 13:18–19 have a close parallel in vv 20–21, and together these units have in Luke's structure a counterpart in the paralleled 14:7–11 and 12–14.

The events of Jesus' ministry have been glorious and powerful (see 13:17), but they hardly represent the full realization of the kingdom of God. What exactly do we have? It is like comparing a tiny mustard seed to the robust plant that it can produce (at times the mustard plant can be like a small tree, as much as nine feet tall). Once a man has lodged that seed in his garden, the life and destiny of the large bush to develop is already committed. Just so, in Jesus' presence and deeds the kingdom of God is certainly present (11:20), and what is happening in his presence makes certain that future full coming of the kingdom, precisely because the life of that future kingdom is already making itself manifest.

In Luke's form of the parable, there appears to be an allusion to Ezek 17:22–23. Here and elsewhere in the OT a tree with birds nesting in its branches becomes an image for a powerful king or kingdom able to provide a widely used protective canopy of stability and peace. The birds that come are the people who find shelter and protection, but Luke will want us to think particularly (at least as we look back from his second volume, Acts) of the prospect of the coming of the Gentiles into the kingdom of God (see v 29 and 14:21–23).

The Kingdom of God Is like Leaven (13:20–21)

Bibliography

Aiken, W. "A Continental Divide in Scripture Interpretation: The Parable of the Leaven." *BSac* 95 (1938) 219–30. **Allis, O. T.** "The Parable of the Leaven." *EvQ* 19 (1947) 254–73. **Funk, R. W.** "Beyond Criticism in Quest of Literacy: The Parable of the Leaven." *Int* 25 (1971) 149–70. **Mayr, I.** "Vom Sauerteig." *BLit* 25 (1957–58) 255–57. **Waller, W.** "The Parable of the Leaven: A Sectarian Teaching and the Inclusion of Women." *USQR* 35 (1979–80) 99–109.

And see at 13:18–19.

Translation

[20] *Again he said, "To what shall I compare the kingdom of God?* [21] *It is like leaven which a woman took and hid in three sata*[a] *of flour, until the whole was leavened."*

Notes

[a] Gr. σάτα. According to Josephus (*Ant.* 9.85; cf. 9.71), a σάτον is one and a half times the Latin *modius*, and so about twelve quarts.

Form/Structure/Setting

The present unit closely parallels vv 19–20, and its place in the structure is discussed there. As with vv 19–20, the present parable is paralleled in Matt 13 (here v 33; and cf. *Gos. Thom.* 96). Again Luke seems to have reproduced the source form, whereas Matthew's form has been affected by his redaction of vv 31–32 (under the influence of Mark 4:30–32). Since the mustard seed parable was considerably changed to unite it with the present parable (see above), the present form can be accepted as original (only the "three," which makes the measure so large, has been suspected of being a development).

Comment

The presence of the kingdom of God in the ministry of Jesus has a potency that belies its small-scale operation. In the end, because of this beginning, the whole world will be transformed.

20 The present verse is an abbreviation of v 18, combining elements of both of that verse's rhetorical questions. The abbreviation could be Luke's.

21 For the operation of leaven, see at 12:1. Note the close parallelism of construction with v 19. "Hid" is an odd verb here as was "threw" in v 19 (see there). This woman had "super leaven," which, she was confident, would make its way, without being mixed in, through this huge lump of dough. σάτον (pl. σάτα, *sata*) is normally taken as equivalent to the Hebrew סאה, *sĕʾāh* (via the Aramaic סאתא, *sāʾtāʾ*). The term is, however, not used for סאה in the LXX, which makes it doubtful whether we should appeal to OT texts that mention three seahs of flour or its equivalent, one ephah (Gen 18:6; Judg 6:19; 1 Sam 1:24). (On the basis of such appeal the parable has been taken as subverting, or proposing an alternative to, the whole temple cultus with its requirement that nothing leavened be offered to God [so, e.g., Funk (*Int* 25 [1971] 166) speaks of "the loss of the received world of Judaism in favor of the gain of the world of the kingdom"].)

What has come into the world in the ministry of Jesus is no flash in the pan. Its dynamic leads inexorably to the apocalyptic manifestation of the kingdom of God. See further at v 19.

Explanation

The parable of the woman and the leaven runs closely parallel to that of the man and the mustard seed (vv 19–20). What this woman has is no ordinary leaven; she has "super leaven," which, she is confident, will make its way, without being mixed in, through this huge lump of dough (the dough will make enough bread to feed around 150 people!).

The presence of the kingdom of God in the ministry of Jesus has a potency that belies its small-scale operation. In the end, because of this beginning, the whole world will be transformed; the end-time kingdom of God will come. See further at vv 18–19.

"Is It True that Those Who Are Saved Will Be Few?" (13:22–30)

Bibliography

Allison, D. C. "Who Will Come from East and West? Observations on Matt 8:11–12—Luke 13:28–29." *IBS* 11 (1989) 158–70. **Boring, M. E.** "A Proposed Reconstruction of Q 13:28–29." In *Society of Biblical Literature 1989 Seminar Papers*, ed. D. J. Lull. Atlanta, GA: Scholars, 1989. 1–23. **Chilton, B. D.** *God in Strength.* 179–202. **Denaux, A.** "Der Spruch von den zwei Wegen im Rahmen des Epilogs des Bergpredigt (Mt 7,13–14 par Lk 13,23–24): Tradition und Redaktion." In *Logia*, ed. J. Delobel. 305–35. **Derrett, J. D. M.** "The Merits of the Narrow Gate (Mt 7:13–14, Lk 13:24)." *JSNT* 15 (1982) 20–29. **Dupont, J.** "'Beaucoup viendront du levant et du couchant . . .' (Mt 8,11–12; Lc 13,28–29)." *Études.* 2:568–82. ———. "'Beaucoup viendront du levant et du couchant . . .' (Matthieu 8,11–12; Luc 13,28–29)." *ScEccl* 19 (1967) 153–67. **Giesen, H.** "Verantwortung des Christen in der Gegenwart und Heilsvollendung: Ethik und Eschatologie nach Lk 13,24 und 16,16." *TGeg* 31 (1988) 218–28. **Grässer, E.** *Parusieverzögerung.* 192–93. **Grimm, W.** "Zum Hintergrund von Mt 8, 11f/Lk 13, 28f." *BZ* 16 (1972) 255–56. **Hoffmann, P.** "*Πάντες ἐργάται ἀδικίας:* Redaktion und Tradition in Lc 13 22–30." *ZNW* 58 (1967) 188–214. **L'Épattenier, C.** "Lecture d'une séquence lucanienne: Luc 13/22 à 14/24." *ETR* 56 (1981) 282–87. **Légasse, S.** "Jésus a-t-il annoncé la conversion final d'Israël? (à propos de Marc X. 23–7)." *NTS* 10 (1964) 480–87. **Manson, T. W.** *Sayings.* 124–26. **Mees, M.** "Auserkanonische Parallelstellen zu den Gerichtsworten Mt. 7,21–23; Lk. 6,46; 13,26–28 und ihre Bedeutung für die Formung der Jesusworte." *VetC* 10 (1973) 79–102. **Mussner, F.** "Das 'Gleichnis' vom gestrengen Mahlherrn (Lk 13,22–30): Ein Beitrag zum Redaktionsverfahren und zur Theologie des Lukas." *TTZ* 65 (1956) 129–43. **Packett, E. B.** "Luke 13:25." *ExpTim* 67 (1955–56) 178. **Parrott, R.** "Entering the Narrow Door: Matt 7:13–14//Luke 13:22–24." *Forum* 5.1 (1989) 111–20. **Rosaz, M.** "Passer sur l'autre rive." *Christus* 26 (1979) 323–32. **Schlosser, J.** *Le règne de Dieu.* 2:603–69. **Schulz, S.** *Spruchquelle.* 308–12, 323–36. **Schwarz, G.** "Matthäus VII 13a: Ein Alarmruf angesichts höchster Gefahr." *NovT* 12 (1970) 229–32. **Seynaeve, J.** "La parabole de la porte étroite: L'Acceptation 'pratique' du Christ, Lc 13,22–30." *AsSeign* 52 (1974) 68–77. **Zeller, D.** "Das Logion Mt 8,11f/Lk 13,28f und das Motif der 'Völkerwallfahrt.'" *BZ* 15 (1971) 222–37; 16 (1972) 84–93.

Translation

[22]*He went on his way from town to town and village to village, teaching and journeying to Jerusalem.* [23]*Someone said to him, "Sir,*[a] *is it true that those who are saved will be few?" He said to them,* [24]*"Make every effort to gain entry*[b] *through the narrow door.*[c] *For many, I say to you, will try to gain entry and will not be able.*

[25]*"After the householder*[d] *has risen and shut the door,* [e]*you will be* [f]*standing outside and*[f] *knocking on the door saying, 'Sir,*[g] *open up for us.' He will respond to you, 'I do not know where you are from!'* [26]*Then you will say, 'We ate and drank in your presence,*

and you taught in our streets.' [27]He will say to you,[h] 'I do not know[i] where you are from! Depart from me all workers of unrighteousness!' [28]There will be weeping and grinding of teeth there, when you see Abraham and Isaac and Jacob and all the prophets in the kingdom of God, but yourselves thrown outside.

[29]"They will come from east and west, and from north and south and sit down in the kingdom of God. [30]However,[j] there are last who will be first and first who will be last."

Notes

[a] Or perhaps "Lord" (Gr. is κύριε).

[b] Lit. "to enter."

[c] A W Ψ f^1 etc. conform the reading to Matthew's πύλης, "gate."

[d] P[75] has δεσπότης, "master."

[e] καί, "and," at this point is treated as Sem. parataxis and not represented in translation.

[f-f] Missing from ℵ bo[ms].

[g] The address is repeated in A D W Θ Ψ etc. (conforming to Matt 7:22).

[h] Lit. "he will say to you, saying." ℵ 579 lat etc. lack the redundant "saying." P[75] A D L W Θ Ψ etc. have ἐρεῖ λέγω ὑμῖν, "he will say, 'I say to you.'"

[i] P[75] B L 070 etc. omit the grammatically odd ὑμᾶς, "you," that occurs at this point.

[j] Lit. "and behold."

Form/Structure/Setting

In the parallelism that structures the section 13:10–14:35, the present unit corresponds with the parable of 14:15–24 (the link has been recognized in different ways by Mussner, *TTZ* 65 [1956] 140–41; Dupont, *ScEccl* 19 [1967] 159). It is linked to the preceding parables by the kingdom of God language and by an interest in its full eschatological manifestation, but it is kept from being read too closely with them by the intervening travel notice in v 22, which also links these verses with vv 31–35 to come.

The present unit is a complex mix of Lukan formulation and the linking together of traditional elements. Vv 22 and 23, apart from the word "few," seem to be free Lukan composition. For v 24 Luke draws, most likely, on a tradition much like Matt 7:13–14, adapting it for the link to v 25 to come. In v 25, by contrast, Luke stays with the wording of his source with all its awkwardness (some earlier link may tie v 25 with Matt 25:10–12, but Luke has not taken the verses from a version of this parable). Vv 26–27 are paralleled in Matt 7:22–23. For the sake of a parallelism to link v 25 to vv 26–27, Luke has imposed an overall structure here, but for the most part he stays closer to the source wording than Matthew does. Vv 28–29 are paralleled in Matt 8:11–12. In several details Luke has kept the more original wording (notably in not having Matthew's "sons of the kingdom"), but he has totally rearranged the materials to suit his purposes. V 30 is a floating logion represented as well in Matt 19:30; 20:16; Mark 10:31.

Matt 7:13–14 shows signs of a development under the influence of the tradition of the two ways (cf. Jer 21:8; Ps 1:6; Prov 14:2; Sir 21:10; *2 Enoch* 30:15; *T. Asher* 1:3, 5; *ʾAbot* 2:12–23; and esp. 2 Esd 7:1–9; 1QS 3:20–21; *Did.* 1:1; 2:2; 5:1; *Barn.* 18:1), but the call to enter by the narrow gate may well go back to the historical Jesus. Luke 13:25 is a fragment of something larger, and questions of its historicity must be bracketed in the absence of a larger context. Vv 13:26–27 are normally denied to the historical Jesus on the basis that a direct role for Jesus in the future judgment is openly assumed here in an atypical manner. The text may be a Christian exposition of a tradition like that in 12:8–9. As a statement of the categorical rejection of the Jews, 13:28–29 have been generally considered a Christian development. But this only applies to the Matthean form. As identifying the possibility of Israelites being excluded from the eschatological gathering of Israel, the text is of a piece with what may be confidently traced to the historical Jesus. There is no reason for denying to the historical Jesus the reversal language of v 30.

Comment

Will those who are saved be few? Jesus is quite sure that there are many who are experiencing his ministry but will not be present at the final kingdom of God banquet. But whether those who are saved will be few or not depends upon the response to be made to his challenge to strain to make every effort to gain entry through the narrow door.

22 Luke will be responsible for this verse. *διαπορεύεσθαι* (lit. "to go through") is used by Luke again in connection with the journey to Jerusalem at 18:36 (of the crowd accompanying Jesus); Luke uses *κατὰ πόλεις καὶ κώμεις*, "from town to town and village to village," in the singular at 8:1 (cf. 9:6). *πορείαν ποιούμενος*, "journeying," with its use of the middle voice and periphrastic construction, is a Lukan literary touch. The *Ἱεροσόλυμα* form for Jerusalem here is actually the form less used by Luke (cf. at 2:22). The verse keeps the journey motif alive in the readers' minds (cf. 9:51, 57; 10:1, 38) and specifically prepares for vv 31–35 (it precedes vv 23–30 so that these verses can exemplify the "teaching" that Jesus engages in on the way; cf. Hoffmann, *ZNW* 58 [1967] 192). Its presence smooths the transition from the expansive vv 18–19, 20–21 to the restrictive vv 23–30.

23 This verse may also be a Lukan formulation (use of *κύριε*, "Lord/sir" [cf. at 12:41, which has, as well, a Lukan formulation of an introductory question]; use of a Septuagintal question form introduced by *εἰ*, "if" [cf. 22:49; Acts 1:6; 7:1; 19:2; 21:37; 22:25]; use of *εἶπεν πρός* for "said to"). The presence of *ὀλίγοι*, "few," in Matt 7:14 suggests, however, that at least for that word Luke is reflecting tradition. The sentiment of the question has its closest parallels in the speculative Jewish apocalyptic concerns of 2 Esd 8:1, 3; 7:47; 9:15; *2 Apoc. Bar.* 13:2; 18:1–2; 21:11; 44:15; 48:23, 45 (contrast the generosity of *m. Sanh.* 10:1, which anticipates the salvation of all Israelites, with notable exceptions, however), but the answer takes us off into the quite different area of personal ethical responsibility.

24 Despite the unevennesses of Matt 7:13–14 (see Denaux, "Zwei Wegen," 321–23), attempts to postulate a Q form closer to Luke 13:24 remain unconvincing. It is best to think that, though Matt 7:13–14 is ultimately composite, Luke uses a form close to this: he replaces "gate" with "door" in anticipation of v 25; the imagery of the way is surplus to his needs; his other materials to come operate in terms of being in or out of the kingdom, so Luke dispenses with the "wide gate," and along with it he loses the antithesis between "destruction" and "life."

ἀγωνίζεσθε, "fight/struggle/make every effort," reflects the language of struggle or contest that can be found in the Hellenistic diatribe, but also in Jewish and early Christian ethical exhortation. In 1 Tim 4:10; 6:11–12; 2 Tim 4:7–8, as here, the language is connected with an eschatological viewpoint (cf. Hoffmann, *ZNW*

58 [1967] 196). By setting 14:15–24 (with its rounding up of totally unlikely guests for the banquet of the kingdom of God) in parallel with 13:22–30, Luke establishes a dialectic between human responsibility stressed here and the priority of God's grace and initiative. As well, there is likely a balancing dialectic to be noticed between the picture here (and in the parable to follow) of people unsuccessfully trying to get in and that in the paralleled 14:15–24 of people unconcerned about access to the banquet of the kingdom of God. The "many" corresponds to the "few" of v 23, at least hinting at a positive answer to the question there (as does the imagery of the narrow door itself). The time of effort is now, but the time of entry (or failure to gain entry) is, if we may judge from v 25, in the eschatological future. The rich ruler of 18:18–23 (and cf. comments of vv 24–25) will be offered later as an attempt to enter that was doomed to failure.

25 Luke has heavily modified v 24 to fit with v 25. Here it is more likely, therefore, that he substantially reproduces the wording of his source (Semitic features of the syntax support this possibility [possible paratactic *καί* (lit. "and"); pleonastic use of *ἄρχεσθαι* (lit. "begin")]). The string of *καί*'s makes translation difficult. The evident parallelism of vv 25 and 26–27 (v 25: *ἄρξησθε . . . λέγοντες*, "you will begin . . . saying"; *καὶ . . . ἐρεῖ ὑμῖν*, "and he will say to you"; *οὐκ οἶδα ὑμᾶς πόθεν ἐστέ*, "I do not know where you are from"; vv 26–27: *ἄρξεσθε λέγειν*, "you will begin to say"; *καὶ . . . ἐρεῖ ὑμῖν*, "and . . . he will say to you"; *οὐκ οἶδα ὑμᾶς πόθεν ἐστέ*, "I do not know where you are from") suggests that either the clause following the second *καί* should have the opening clause subordinated to it (so: "[then] you will be standing outside . . .") or coordination should be kept through the verse. The elements of v 25 have an evident relationship to the conclusion of the Matthean parable 25:1–12 (here vv 10–12), which may reflect some influence earlier in the tradition, but could indicate no more than that both draw on established Jewish imagery to express exclusion. While in the Matthean parable those excluded have come too late, in Luke the door is shut by the householder (Luke's central figure comes from inside, Matthew's from outside) at the point when all his expected guests have arrived. Those outside consider themselves invited guests, but are not so considered by the householder. Luke's addition of *πόθεν ἐστέ* (lit. "from where you are") to the *οὐκ οἶδα ὑμᾶς*, "I do not know you," of Matt 25:12 (which is reminiscent of a Jewish ban formula; cf. Str-B, 1:469; 4:293), is likely to be secondary (for its grammar, cf. Zerwick, *Biblical Greek*, 207). In either case the language expresses the lack of claim that these would-be guests have upon the host (cf. 2 Tim 2:19).

26–27 Vv 26–27 are paralleled in Matt 7:22–23. Luke will have modified the framing words to form the parallelism with v 25 identified above, but it will be Matthew who has totally reformulated the content of the (useless) defense and will be responsible for the use of *ὁμολογήσω*, "I will confess/acknowledge." In the final clause of v 27, Luke follows the Greek wording of Ps 6:9 for the first half, while Matthew follows it for the second (except that it is Luke who has the "all"). For Luke, vv 26–27 elaborate on the experience of exclusion reported in v 25. While the parable form continues, it now becomes quite explicit that the householder figure is Jesus. The statement of protest fits well the impressed and appreciative crowds that are regularly with Jesus in Luke's portrayal (cf., e.g., 4:42; 7:16; 9:17; Hoffmann [*ZNW* 58 (1967) 200 and n. 41] cannot be faulted for drawing a link to the eucharistic practice of the Lukan church, but if this is intended it remains secondary). Unless their response goes further, this experience of Jesus will be of no avail on the day of answerability. The language of making the effort in v 24 finds its Lukan exposition here.

28–30 Vv 28–29 are paralleled in Matt 8:11–12. It is clear that Luke has reordered and reworded materials that he found in a form closer to that of Matthew's text (Luke reorders the clauses to use "there" to link to v 27; adds "when you see" to link the now disordered clauses; separates into two separate sayings the coming from afar and the presence of Abraham and Isaac and Jacob [a traditional trio (Deut 1:8; 1 Kgs 18:36; 2 Kgs 13:23; Acts 3:13; 7:32) to which Luke adds "and all the prophets" (cf. 11:50; 24:27; Acts 3:18,24; 10:43)]; Matthew may be responsible for "into the outer darkness" since Luke has prepared for the simpler "outside" with his use of that term in v 25; Matthew's "the sons of the kingdom" is hardly original [Zeller, *BZ* 15 (1971) 224 is equivocal at this point, but his subsequent analysis depends heavily on the presence of this phrase]; Luke's corresponding "you" is likely to be original, but could be an adaption to his context; since the OT gathering texts have four directions represented [Ps 107:3; Isa 43:5–6 (exceptionally Isa 49:12; Jer 3:18; but these do not have Matthew's directions)], Matthew is likely to have compressed [see Mussner, *TTZ* 65 (1956) 136–37; Dupont, *ScEccl* 19 (1967) 157–58; Hoffmann, *ZNW* 58 (1967) 206–10; Zeller, *BZ* 15 (1971) 223–24]). Luke 13:30 is one of those wandering logia (cf. Matt 19:30; 20:16; Mark 10:31), and Luke's source and its wording must remain uncertain (the "many" found in two of the above forms does not suit the open-endedness that Luke prefers for his unit; for the same reason he does not take up the "many" that is likely to have been in his source for v 28).

In v 28 Luke continues the story but moves beyond the imagery of his parable: the narrow door has been that of access into the eschatological kingdom of God, where these great ones of Israel's history will be found (only in v 29, where we have left the parable far behind, will we learn that Luke has in mind that the guests in the house have been gathered for a banquet); those outside are in the position of disappointed and anguished exclusion from that climax of God's purposes for his People ("thrown out" is an unfortunate violation of the parable imagery).

Vv 29–30 act as a kind of concluding summary and no longer make any pretense of operating within the story line of the parable. While Matthew applies the text to the gathering in of the Gentiles, Luke seems to stay with its original reference to the eschatological gathering of Israel (in Acts, Luke establishes an important parallelism between the Jewish [diaspora] mission and mission to the Gentiles [see Nolland, "Luke's Readers," 90–128]; instructive here is Luke's recounting of the Pentecost account, which by means of this parallelism proclaims simultaneously God's interest in both Jews and Gentiles to the ends of the earth [see discussion, Nolland, 93–102]). The prophetically anticipated gathering of the dispersed People of God from the four corners of the earth will take place, but Jesus' hearers should be warned that this great event will not take place without some surprising reversals. In the immediate context, the surprising but ominous twist is the exclusion of some of those to whom in the first instance God sent the ministry of Jesus (cf. v 26); in the wider Gospel context we need to see hints as well of the inclusion of the excluded segments of Israel (cf. 14:21–23); and in the full Lukan context we will find anticipated the inclusion of the Gentiles in the salvation purposes of God. The challenge for each is to not be among the excluded!

Explanation

In the parallelism that structures the section 13:10–14:35, the present unit corresponds with the parable of 14:15–24. The reversal here is of the expectation of those who experience the earthly ministry of Jesus and expect to be present at the banquet of the eschatological kingdom. The answer to the question posed depends in part on the seriousness with which one takes up the challenge to make every effort to gain entry through the narrow door.

The present unit contains some of the challenging teaching of Jesus as he continues to make his way to Jerusalem—a journey that Luke would keep before the minds of his readers.

The question that is put to him is the kind of speculative question that was posed at the time in Judaism, but Jesus' response moves at once from the speculative to the realm of personal ethical challenge. His imagery of a narrow door suggests that the answer to the question is likely to be yes. Certainly many will fail to gain entry. Serious effort now will result in entry when the time comes. (With the paralleled 14:15–24, we get an emphasis on God's grace and initiative, to balance the emphasis here on human responsibility—also on typical human carelessness, lest we get the wrong idea from the image of people trying and failing here).

The challenge is reinforced with a parable, whose story continues in vv 27–28 in non-parabolic language (in v 26 already a concrete identification of the householder as Jesus [that is, by reference to his teaching ministry] breaks through the parable form). Vv 29–30 provide a summary conclusion, which is no longer part of the parable narrative.

The householder will rise and close the door when all his expected guests have arrived and are inside. Those standing outside protest that there has been some mistake. They had gone to the "revival meetings" that Jesus had run; surely they belonged. The damning response looks rather at the practical outworking in their lives of what they had heard. They had not bent their efforts to entering by the narrow gate; they had worked evil and not good. The words "I do not know where you are from" express the lack of claim that these would-be guests have upon the host.

The scene thereafter outside the closed door is now painted (in non-parabolic but still metaphorical language): those outside are in the position of disappointed and anguished exclusion from that climax of God's purposes for his People; the great heroes of the past are in and they are out.

Now Jesus summarizes: the prophesied gathering of the dispersed tribes of Israel (Ps 107:3; Isa 43:5–6) will take place, as from the four winds people are gathered into the banquet of the eschatological kingdom, but there will be some surprising reversals as to who will be present and who will be missing. The challenge for each is to not be among the excluded!

Jesus' Fate in, and the Fate of, Jerusalem (13:31–35)

Bibliography

For 13:31–33:

Blinzler, J. *Herodes Antipas und Jesus Christus.* Stuttgart: Katholisches Bibelwerk, 1947. 16–20. ———. "Wie lautet Jesu Botschaft an seinen Landesherrn?" *Haec Loquere* 38 (1944) 381–83. **Büchele, A.** *Tod Jesu.* 152–57. **Bunn, L. H.** "Herod Antipas and 'that fox.'" *ExpTim* 43 (1931–32) 380–81. **Denaux, A.** "L'hypocrisie des Pharisees et le dessein de Dieu: Analyse de Lc., XIII, 31–33." In *L'Evangile de Luc,* ed. F. Neirynck. 245–85. **Derrett, J. D. M.** "The Lucan Christ and Jerusalem: τελειοῦμαι (Lk 13 32)." *ZNW* 75 (1984) 36–43. **Farley, F. A.** "A Text (Luke xiii. 33)." *ExpTim* 34 (1922–23) 429–30. **Fulford, H. W.** "'This fox.'" *ExpTim* 19 (1908) 523. **Gilbert, A. H.** "Σήμερον καὶ αὔριον, καὶ τῇ τρίτῃ (Luke 13:32)." *JBL* 35 (1916) 315–18. **Grimm, W.** "Eschatologischer Saul wider eschatologischen David: Eine Deutung von Lc. xiii 32 ff." *NovT* 15 (1973) 114–33. **Hoehner, H. W.** *Herod Antipas.* 214–24. **Jeremias, J.** "Die Drei-Tage-Worte der Evangelien." In *Tradition und Glaube: Das frühe Christentum in seiner Umwelt.* FS K. G. Kuhn, ed. G. Jeremias et al. Göttingen: Vandenheock & Ruprecht, 1971. 221–29. **Lehmann, K.** *Auferweckt am dritten Tag nach der Schrift: Früheste Bekenntnisbildung und Schriftauslegung im Lichte von 1 Kor. 15,3–5.* QD 38. Fribourg: Herder, 1968. 231–41. **Lehmann, M.** *Synoptische Quellenanalyse und die Frage nach dem historischen Jesus: Kriterien der Jesusforschung untersucht in Auseinandersetzung mit Emmanuel Hirschs Frühgeschichte des Evangeliums.* BZNW 38. Berlin: de Gruyter, 1970. 146–48. **Rese, M.** "*Einige Überlegungen zu Lukas XIII, 31–33.*" In *Jésus aux origines de la christologie,* ed. J. Dupont. BETL 40. Gemboux/Leuven: Duculot/Leuven University, 1975. 201–25. **Schnackenburg, R.** "Lk 13, 13–33: Eine Studie zur lukanischen Redaktion und Theologie." In *Der Treue Gottes trauen,* ed. C. Bussmann and W. Radl. 229–41. **Schnider, F.** *Jesus der Prophet.* Göttingen: Vandenhoeck & Ruprecht, 1974. 167–72. **Steck, O. H.** *Israel und das gewaltsame Geschick der Propheten: Untersuchungen zur Überlieferung des deuteronomistischen Geschichtsbildes im Alten Testament, Spätjudentum und Urchristentum.* WMANT 23. Neukirchen-Vluyn: Neukirchener, 1967. 40–45. **Tiede, D. L.** *Prophesy and History in Luke-Acts.* 70–78. **Tyson, J. B.** "Jesus and Herod Antipas." *JBL* 79 (1960) 239–46. **Verrall, A. W.** "Christ before Herod (Luke xxiii 1–16)." *JTS* 10 (1908–9) 321–53, esp. 352–53.

For 13:34–35:

Allison, D. C. "Matt. 23:39 = Luke 13:35b as a Conditional Prophecy." *JSNT* 18 (1983) 75–84. **Baltzer, K.** "The Meaning of the Temple in the Lukan Writings." *HTR* 58 (1965) 263–77, esp. 272–74. **Christ, F.** *Jesus Sophia.* 136–52. **Conzelmann, H.** *Theology.* 109–10, 133, 139, 199. **Grässer, E.** *Die Naherwartung Jesu.* SBS 61. Stuttgart: Katholisches Bibelwerk, 1973. 109–12. **Hoffmann, P.** *Studien zur Theologie der Logienquelle.* NTAbh n.s. 8. Münster: Aschendorff, 1972. 171–80. **Kühschelm, R.** "Verstockung als Gericht: Eine Untersuchung zu Joh 12,35–43: Lk 13,34–35; 19,41–44." *BLit* 57 (1984) 234–43. **Kümmel, W. G.** *Promise and Fulfilment.* 79–81, 100. **Kwaak, H. van der.** "Die Klage über Jerusalem." *NovT* 8 (1966) 156–70. **Miller, R. J.** "The Rejection of the Prophets in Q." *JBL* 107 (1988) 225–40. **Schulz, S.** *Spruchquelle.* 346–60. **Steck, O. H.** *Israel und das gewaltsame Geschick der Propheten: Untersuchungen zur Überlieferung des deuteronomistischen Geschichtsbildes im Alten Testament, Spätjudentum und Urchristentum.* WMANT 23. Neukirchen-Vluyn: Neukirchener, 1967. 45–58, 227–39. **Suggs, M. J.** *Wisdom, Christology and Law in Matthew's Gospel.* Cambridge, MA: Harvard University, 1970. 63–71. **Weinert, F. D.** "Luke, the Temple and Jesus' Saying about

Jerusalem's Abandoned House (Luke 13:34–35)." *CBQ* 44 (1982) 68–76. **Zeller, D.** "Entrückung zur Ankunft als Menschensohn (Lk 13, 34f.; 11, 29f.)." In *À cause de l'Évangile*, ed. F. Refoulé. 513–30.

Translation

[31]In that very hour[a] some of the Pharisees came and said to him, "Go off and get away from here, because Herod wants to kill you." [32]He said to them, "Go and say to this fox, 'Look, I cast out demons and perform healings today and tomorrow, and the third [day][b] I am finished. [33]It is indeed necessary that I continue on my way today and tomorrow and the next[c] [day], for it is not possible for a prophet to perish outside of Jerusalem.'

[34]"Jerusalem, Jerusalem, the one which kills the prophets and stones those who have been sent to her, how often I wanted to gather your children as a hen gathers her own brood under [her] wings, and you didn't want [it]. [35]Now[d] your house is abandoned.[e] And[f] I say to you, you will not see me until the time comes[g] when you will say, 'Blessed is the one who comes in the name of the Lord.'"

Notes

[a] B[1] W Θ Ψ etc. have "day."

[b] B 346 etc. have "day."

[c] ἐρχομένῃ, "coming," for ἐχομένῃ, "next," is read by P[75] ℵ D etc.

[d] Lit. "behold."

[e] ἔρημος is added here by D E G H Δ Θ Ψ etc., which may be original for Matthew, giving the sense "left desolate."

[f] The linking δέ, "and/but," is omitted by P[45] ℵ L etc., which could be original.

[g] "The time comes" (ἥξει ὅτε) is found only in D, but with a preceding ἄν in A W (Ψ f^1 1006) 1342 and the majority text. It is omitted by P[75] B L 892 etc., while P[45] ℵ (Θ) f^{13} 205 etc. have simply ἄν. The long form is accepted as the most difficult reading.

Form/Structure/Setting

Vv 31–35 constitute the final unit in the series of units (13:10–35) for which Luke will provide parallels in 14:1–35. The present unit is bound closely with the preceding by the opening time reference and the shared link back to the journey statement in 13:22. The necessity here of Jesus' coming fate in Jerusalem finds its parallel in the necessity of the cross of discipleship (coming after Jesus) in 14:25–35. In the unit, Herod's intention for Jesus' demise is contrasted with Jesus' chosen (because the will of God) path to his destiny in Jerusalem. Jesus laments the paradox of the abandoned city that stands at the heart of God's dealings with his People but has persistently rejected those sent to her by God.

Only Luke reports vv 31–33, but he unites it with vv 34–35, which may be found as well in Matt 23:37–39. An earlier consensus that Luke 13:31–33 preserved ancient tradition has been challenged by Rese ("Einige Überlegungen," 201–25) and Denaux ("L'hypocrisie," 245–85), who both argue (with considerable mutual contradiction) for Lukan creation of these verses. Their cases have not been found persuasive. The text does, however, exhibit difficulties that call for some explanation. Particularly difficult has been the attempt to account for the relationship between vv 32 and 33 (though earlier Dibelius [*Tradition*, 162–63] questioned the narrative setting: vv 31–32a). Suggestions here range from the introduction of a reference to the need to work, remain etc. to link with the first two days of v 33 (to allow for a neat parallelism between the verses), through the excision of v 32 from "behold I cast out . . ." or of "today and tomorrow" (from v 33) or even "and the third day I am finished. Indeed it is necessary for me today and tomorrow." Each produces an adequate sense (except possibly the second), but in the absence of any textual support cannot be preferred over a satisfactory sense for the existing text. Other suggestions involve identifying parts of the text as Lukan or pre-Lukan redaction, or as being originally separate items of tradition that have been secondarily linked. Vv 31–32a, 32b, 33 have variously been taken as redactional, while v 33 has also been taken to be a second tradition. Of these suggestions by far the most satisfactory is that which takes v 33 as Lukan redaction (so K. L. Schmidt, *Rahmen*, 266–67 [partially]; Steck, *Gewaltsame Geschick*, 41–46; Schnider, *Jesus*, 168–72). The verse is a Lukan reiteration of v 32 in a form that accommodates it to the journey context in which Luke has placed it and bridges to vv 34–35, which Luke is about to use.

Despite the distinctiveness of the tradition in vv 31–32, it does not lend itself to being explained as a church development and should be traced to the historical Jesus. The material has the form of a biographical pronouncement story.

For vv 34–35, Luke stays closer than Matthew to the source they share. It is likely that the evangelists are each responsible for the present respective locations of the tradition. A large part of the scholarly literature takes the view that Wisdom is the speaker in vv 34–35a (at least in the tradition behind the verses). This view has been effectively criticized by Hoffmann (*Studien*, 173–77; cf. Zeller, "Entrückung," 513–15; Miller, *JBL* 107 [1988] 235–36), who demonstrates that the horizon is that of the climactic, historical rejection of a particular figure (the Greek tenses encourage us not to correlate the repeated wish with the series of those sent), not that of the supra-historical perspective of Wisdom (who after withdrawing returns with the Son of Man when he comes in judgment [see esp. Steck, *Israel*, 50–58]). The high Christology of the verses has caused most interpreters to treat them as either a Jewish tradition (normally set on the lips of Wisdom) transferred to Jesus, or as an early Christian formulation. If Wisdom is not the speaker, then the former becomes less likely, while the latter has not really been argued with any cogency. A related question is that of whether v 35b forms an original unity with vv 34–35a. Since the unity with vv 34–35a is much clearer from a post-ascension perspective, because of the use of Ps 118(117):26 with its assumption of a particular tradition of interpretation, and because of the presence here of the distinctive notion of Jesus being removed from the scene until the eschaton, it is best to allow for the possibility of a separate origin for v 35b as a Christian development of vv 34–35a.

Comment

Herod can offer no threat to Jesus' ministry. Jesus has a God-ordained ministry laid out for him. He goes to his destiny in Jerusalem and not to his demise at the hands of Herod. But the final, ugly response of Jerusalem to Jesus is not some deterministic necessity; it is the tragedy of the spurning by Jerusalem of its redeemer. The leaders of Jerusalem turn destructively upon the only one who could offer them protection and safety in their own threatened situation.

31 *ἐν αὐτῇ τῇ ὥρᾳ,* "in that very hour," is Lukan (cf. 10:21; 12:12; 20:19; 24:33) and serves to link with the previous episode (cf. at v 22): the coming reversal in Jerusalem's fate is an instance of the point of v 30. This is the only place in the Gospel where Pharisees seem to make common cause with Jesus (on Pharisees see at 5:17). This has led (*i*) both to a questioning of the historicity of the event and to a strong affirmation of its historicity, on the basis of the principle of dissimilarity; (*ii*) to the interpretation of the report as one falsely conjured up by the (Galilean) Pharisees to encourage Jesus to get out of their hair; or as one in which they conspire with Herod to get Jesus out of the region; and (*iii*) to a highlighting of Luke's generally more positive reporting of the Pharisees than the other Gospels (and especially in Acts). The first suggestion in (*ii*) produces what is finally an artificial reading of the text. It is hard to choose between the second suggestion in (*ii*) and a genuine warning. Luke would be interested in any measure of Pharisaic recognition of Jesus, however modest (cf. Acts 6:34–39), and his presentation of Pharisees, while tending towards the monochrome in the Gospel, is not entirely so. Such a warning is not historically unbelievable, even given strong Pharisaic feelings against Jesus: whatever their differences, over against Herod, Jesus and those of Pharisaic persuasion would have an enormous amount in common. On the other hand, the renewal in 14:1 of the perspective of 11:53–54 (cf. 6:11) suggests a continuing negative perception of the Pharisees. The suggestion is that Jesus should leave Herod's jurisdiction (presumably Galilee here [Perea would be possible as well, but suits the presence of the Pharisees rather less well]; this again speaks in favor of tradition here, since in Luke's structure Jesus has been journeying away from Galilee since chap. 9). The Herod here is that of 3:1, 19–20 (see there). His hostile intent fits well the general picture of the man, but since it stands in some slight tension with Luke's interest in Herod's desire to *see* Jesus (9:9; 23:8), it is unlikely that Luke's pen will have created the motif here of murderous intent. In Jerusalem Herod no longer considers Jesus to be a political liability to him (or he prefers to have Pilate carry the public responsibility), and he can simply indulge his curiosity (23:6–12).

The coming of the Pharisees here corresponds to the coming of the crowds with Jesus in 14:25.

32 It is unclear whether the directive to go and tell Herod is rhetorical or is literally intended (cf. 7:22). If reported, the words would be quite provocative. "Fox" is best taken as an image of craftiness or slyness (see Fitzmyer, 1031, for classical and Hellenistic Greek texts; Str-B, 2:200–201 for [later] Jewish texts). Luke can rest content with the summary here of Jesus' ongoing ministry as "casting out demons and performing healings" (cf. Acts 10:38; 2:22) because he has provided in v 22 a setting that stresses the teaching side of his ministry. The idiom "today, tomorrow . . . and on the third day" has attracted considerable attention; it is clearly not literally intended. The imagery is of one period of time giving way to another at the proper point (cf. Exod 19:10–11; with just "today" and "tomorrow," cf. Luke 12:28; Sir 10:10). The point is that Jesus will disregard the threat posed by Herod's intentions and will carry on with his ministry in Galilee for as long as it was intended. What kind of completion is expressed by *τελειοῦμαι*? There is general agreement that a passive sense is required; beyond that there is quite a range of suggestions. The term is probably meant to be about as ambiguous as the translation I have offered: "I am finished." Over against the concerns of

Herod, the term suggests that Jesus will no longer be exercising his disturbing ministry; over against the proposal of the Pharisees, it suggests that he will then be out of Herod's way; and in the wider journey to Jerusalem context (which essentially disregards the implicit geography of the text), it implies all that is involved in the "being taken up" anticipated in 9:51 (see there). In connection with all three horizons, there is the sense of accomplishment as well, and not just the idea of cessation.

33 This verse is a Lukan reiteration of v 32 in a form that accommodates it to the journey context and bridges to vv 34–35. Luke's difficulty is that his journey context for this tradition has Jesus apparently doing exactly what the Pharisees suggest (admittedly he had started doing it before the threat came to light). The verse says in effect that the journeying is not meant to be so understood, but is rather an expression of the sentiment of v 32, set into the context of the need for Jesus to get to Jerusalem for the full force of v 32 to take effect.

The contrast expressed by the opening πλήν (normally "but/only/nevertheless," but here rendered "indeed" [cf. Thrall, *Greek Particles*, 20–21]) is with Herod's murderous intentions, not with the statement in v 32 (cf. the role of this term in 10:14). The divine necessity expressed in δεῖ, "it is necessary," is that which has been expressed earlier in relation both to his ministry (4:43) and to his coming suffering (9:22), and which has already been present in the passive τελειοῦμαι, "I am finished," with its implicit reference to divine activity. Luke takes up the reference to "today . . . tomorrow . . . the third day" as "today . . . tomorrow . . . the day after" (only Luke in the NT uses the middle participle of ἔχειν, "to have," in time expressions like this). Because for Luke the journey here takes Jesus all the way to the "finish" (through death to the right hand of God [cf. at 9:51]), he no longer has a sharp break between the first two days and the third. (Luke requires us to understand "go on my way" on the basis of the Journey to Jerusalem context [indeed outside this context the verse hardly makes any kind of sense]). But at the same time the journey here is not simply the traveling to Jerusalem (and thence to heaven), but also (reiterating v 32) the ministry of teaching and healing that happens along the way (so, e.g., recently 13:10–17). Since there is no tradition of the need for prophets to perish in Jerusalem (one [later?] tradition suggests that false prophets, as other capital offenders, should be tried in Jerusalem, and the executions performed there during one of the major feasts [*m. Sanh.* 11:1, 5, 6]), the final clause should be taken ironically. It combines the idea that Jerusalem is the heart and center of Israel with the tradition that the Israelites have persistently rejected the prophets God has sent to them (see at 4:24; 6:23; and cf. 13:34 to follow): "if you must reject those sent you by God, you should do it properly, by doing it at the heart of all Jewish affairs in Jerusalem" (see Fitzmyer, 1032, for traditions linking the perishing of particular prophets with Jerusalem). That Luke intends no deterministic fatalism here is indicated by the very different language of the following verse.

The necessity for Jesus to go to his fate in Jerusalem is matched by the necessity in 14:27 (developed in vv 26–33) for the one who would follow Jesus to take up his *cross* and follow him.

34 Apart from a linking γάρ, "for," used by Matthew, Luke's text and Matthew's differ only at two points: different forms for "to gather": "her own brood" (τὴν ἑαυτῆς νοσσιάν) in Luke, "her young" (τὰ νοσσία αὐτῆς) in Matthew. The double form of address may align here with a pattern of divine revelations (cf. Gen 22:11; 46:2; Exod 3:4; 1 Sam 3:10). On stoning of false prophets, see Deut 13:1–5, 10; for the stoning of a prophet in Jerusalem, see 2 Chr 24:20–22 (see further J. Blinzler, "The Jewish Punishment of Stoning in the New Testament Period," in *The Trial of Jesus*, ed. E. Bammel [Naperville, IL: Allenson, 1970] 147–61). In the parallelism here there is no distinction of identity between "prophets" and "those sent to her." The epithet here for Jerusalem forms the background for the present spurning of Jesus. For the city as a mother, cf. Isa 54; 62:1, 4. "Your children" could be narrowly the inhabitants of Jerusalem or it could be used more broadly of all Jewry (cf. Ps 147:2; Gal 4:26). The latter fits better the Lukan pattern of the ministry of Jesus, but the multiple wish to gather does not, in any case, require multiple visits to Jerusalem (cf. Fitzmyer, 1034, 1036). For the imagery of a bird's motherly protection, cf. Deut 32:11; Pss 17:8; 36:7; Ruth 2:12; *2 Apoc. Bar.* 41:3–4; 2 Esd 1:30. The imagery certainly involves the speaker in a claim to be in a position to act in the place of God (cf. 5:8–10, 24; 8:25; etc.). Over against the desire of Jesus stands the lack of desire of the children of Jerusalem. When would Jesus have been in a position to make such a statement? Our records give us no adequate basis for deciding, but just as he reached the point of declaring a woe upon Chorazin, Bethsaida, and Capernaum (10:13–15), so, perhaps in the context of the outcome of his encounters with Jewish leadership (the scribes and Pharisees of the Gospel account), there came a time when he was ready to make a more comprehensive assessment of the uptake of his ministry. Though Luke reports no events from any earlier ministry in Jerusalem, he would have us think in terms of Jesus having exercised his ministry throughout Judea (in the wider sense of Jewish Palestine [see at 4:44]).

35 Here Matthew has dropped ἥξει ὅτε, "[the time] will come when" (as has much of the textual tradition for Luke here), and added ἀπ' ἄρτι, "from now on," in line with the Jerusalem setting he has chosen for the incident. "*Your* house" is best not taken narrowly of the temple. Jer 22:1–8 provides the closest background here, where Jerusalem is in view as the location of the royal palace. The present tense ἀφίεται, "is abandoned," suggests a fate already sealed. The thought here is close to that of 11:49–51 (see there). The coming destruction of Jerusalem will be as God's judgment, in which he abandons her to her foes (see further at Luke 21). The prospect of such a judgment in history does not preclude continuing Christian outreach to the Jews of Jerusalem by the early church. No more than was the Babylonian exile should this be seen as God finally wiping his hands of the Jewish People.

"You will not see me" must be given a stronger force than Weinert's idea of a temporary respite from the challenge of Jesus' ministry (*CBQ* 44 [1982] 73). It seems best to relate it to Acts 3:17–21 and to see here a hint of Jesus' heavenly location from the end of his ministry to the Parousia. Zeller ("Entrückung," 515–17 [further bibliography, 515 n. 13]) is probably right to appeal to Jewish traditions of figures translated to heaven in preparation for a future eschatological role (beginning from 2 Kgs 2:11–12 and the OT anticipation of a future role for Elijah; cf. esp. 2 Esd 6:26). Jesus will be snatched away (through death in his case) to heaven until it is time for his eschatological role. His return will be marked by the eschatological welcome of the messiah in the words of Ps 118(117):26 (the wording is that of the LXX text). This eschatological welcome has its anticipation in the welcome given Jesus in Jerusalem by the disciples in 19:38.

To the unrealized potential of Jerusalem corresponds the failure of the salt in 14:34–35.

Explanation

Herod can offer no threat to Jesus' ministry. It must proceed to its intended end in Jerusalem. In continuity with its earlier history, Jerusalem now rejects this ultimate divine envoy who will subsequently be whisked off to heaven to await his end-time role. The necessity here of Jesus' coming fate in Jerusalem finds its parallel in the necessity of the cross of discipleship (coming after Jesus) in the paralleled unit 14:25–35.

The advice may be sincerely intended by the Pharisees, who despite having their own dispute with Jesus, would not wish him to fall into the hands of Herod Antipas—at least not yet. Or it may be a Pharisaic collaboration with Herod to frighten him out of the realm. Later, Herod no longer has a personal interest in securing Jesus' death, when he is in Jerusalem (out of Herod's territory) and in the custody of Pilate (23:6–12).

While it is unclear whether Jesus seriously intended the response to be delivered to Herod, his words are certainly provocative. "Fox" conjures up an unflattering image of low cunning. The days are of course not literal. The point is that Herod's plans will make not a jot of difference: Jesus will carry on with his ministry in Galilee for as long as it was intended. "I am finished" is deliberately ambiguous. To Herod and the Pharisees it means "finished with the ministry that has so disturbed Herod." He will be out of Herod's hair. But in the broader Lukan context of the Journey to Jerusalem, it must include all that is anticipated (including death) in the "being taken up" of 9:51.

V 33 re-expresses v 32 precisely in the journey context. Jesus' travel here is no running away from Herod. It is rather a continuation of his ministry of exorcism and healing, as in a leisurely but deliberate manner he makes his way to Jerusalem and to the real threat to his life that Herod (under the sovereign hand of God) could never be. While some prophets had perished in Jerusalem, the end of the verse is actually ironical: "if you [Israel/Judah] must reject those sent you by God, then let's have you do it properly, by doing it at the heart of all Jewish affairs in Jerusalem."

Jesus anticipates what is to come and in a kind of soliloquy addresses absent Jerusalem. As she has rejected God's earlier emissaries, now she rejects this one. It is likely that "your children" is not narrowly the inhabitants of Jerusalem but is a broader reference to Jewry sustained from its center in Jerusalem (see Ps 147:2; Gal 4:26). Acting, as it were, in the place of God (see esp. Deut 31:11), Jesus has extended to Jerusalem's children the maternal offer of protection and safety. He wished to give; they did not wish to receive.

"Your house" is Jerusalem as the heart of the old kingdom (see Jer 22:1–8). She has been abandoned to her enemies and will, as God's judgment, be destroyed in the Jewish war in A.D. 68–70. This does not in any way mean the end of God's concern for the Jews, any more than had the destruction of Jerusalem in the sixth century and the exile period in Babylon.

After rejection by Jerusalem's children, Jesus will be taken off into heaven (via death), there to await the time for his role at the end. He will not be seen again before that day when he comes to be welcomed into Jerusalem as the end-time messiah (see Acts 3:17–21). The words of welcome are taken from Ps 118:26 and are used by the crowds of disciples in an anticipatory way in 19:38.

Healing on the Sabbath the Man with Dropsy (14:1–6)

Bibliography

Bernadicou, P. J. "The Lukan Theology of Joy (Revisited)." *ScEs* 30 (1978) 57–80. **Black, M.** "The Aramaic Spoken by Christ and Luke 14.5." *JTS* n.s. 1 (1950) 60–62. **Derrett, J. D. M.** "Positive Perspectives on Two Lucan Miracles." *DR* 104 (1986) 272–87. **Dietzfelbinger, C.** "Vom Sinn der Sabbatheilungen Jesu." *EvT* 38 (1978) 281–97. **Ernst, J.** "Gastmahmgespräche: Lk 14,1–24." In *Die Kirche des Anfangs*, ed. R. Schnackenburg et al. 57–78. **Glaue, P.** "Einige Stelle die die Bedeutung des Codex D charakterisieren." *NovT* 2 (1958) 310–15, esp. 313. **Klein, H.** *Barmherzigkeit gegenüber den Elenden und Geächteten: Studien zur Botschaft des lukanischen Sondergutes.* Biblisch-theologische Studien 10. Neukirchen-Vluyn: Neukirchener, 1987. 23–29. **Lohse, E.** "Jesus Worte über den Sabbat." In *Judentum—Urchristentum—Kirche*, ed. W. Eltester. BZNW 26. Berlin: Töpelmann, 1960. 79–89. **Meeûs, X. de.** "Composition de Lc., XIV et genre symposiaque." *ETL* 37 (1961) 847–70. **Neirynck, F.** "Luke 14, 1–6: Lukan Composition and Q Saying." In *Der Treue Gottes trauen*, ed. C. Bussmann and W. Radl. 243–63. **Roloff, J.** *Das Kerygma.* 66–69. **Simson, P.** "L'Evangile (Lc 14,1–11): Le code de beinséance de l'assemblée chrétienne." *AsSeign* o.s. 70 (1975) 31–41. **Trautmann, M.** *Zeichenhafte Handlungen Jesu: Ein Beitrag zur Frage nach dem geschichlichen Jesu.* FB 37. Würzburg: Echter, 1980. 285–91.

Translation

[1] *When he went into the house of a certain one of the rulers of Pharisees to eat bread, and they were watching him, it happened that* [2] *a certain man, suffering from dropsy, was there*[a] *in front of him.* [3] *Jesus responded [to the situation] by saying to the lawyers and Pharisees, "Is it lawful on the sabbath to heal, or not?"*[b] [4] *They were silent. He took and healed him, and dismissed him.* [5] *He said*[c] *to them, "Which of you—when his ass*[d] *or his ox falls into a well, does not straight away pull it up, on the day of the sabbath?"* [6] *They were not able to give an answer back to this.*[e]

Notes

[a] Reflecting an *ἰδού* (lit. "behold") in the text.

[b] "Or not" is missing from P[45] A W Ψ etc.

[c] *ἀποκριθείς*, "having answered," is added by א א[2] A (W) Θ Ψ f^{13} etc.

[d] Read by א K L Ψ $f^{1,13}$ etc. P[45,75] (A) B W etc. have *υἱός*, "son," which is often preferred as the more difficult reading. "Son" may, however, have been introduced in the face of a more extreme Jewish view (as reflected, e.g., in CD 11:13–14). The deliberate Lukan paralleling of 13:10–17 and 14:1–6 favors "ass" as the original reading. Others appeal to translation variants involving confusion of Aramaic terms, but this seems unlikely.

[e] Pl. in Gr.

Form/Structure/Setting

The units of 14:1–35 all have paralleled units in 13:10–35 (see further at 13:10–17). Luke provides here in 14:1–5 a sabbath healing to match that in 13:10–17 and to alert his readers to the parallelism to come. A meal setting links the first four of the five units of the chapter (in the paralleled 13:10–35, only the first three units are linked into a single occasion; Luke has reasons there for wanting, instead, items four and five to be linked). In the line of the reversals that mark this section, the powerful presence of the kingdom of God reverses for this man the damage to his body evident in his dropsy.

There is no clear parallel to this report in the synoptic Gospel materials, but Matt 12:11 has a parallel to v 5 inserted into his version of Mark 3:1–6 (with an associated comment in 12:12), and there are significant similarities between Mark 3:1–6 and Luke 14:1–6. Luke 14:1–6 is frequently treated as a Lukan creation. It is certainly true that motifs were transferred from one sabbath healing to another in the transmission of the tradition. And it is also likely to be true that Luke has had a major part in forming the present account as the front piece for the second half of his section here. But Matt 12:11–12 must have come from a sabbath healing account, and the choice of dropsy is unmotivated if it is not drawn from tradition. So it is best to conclude that Luke had an additional sabbath healing account at his disposal here, even if its visibility is finally minimal in the present account. As Luke reports it, the account has the form of a controversy dialogue.

Comment

Jesus' arguments shame and silence his adversaries, as individuals who are touched by his ministry have a new experience of the sabbath as God's day of liberation for them in their needs.

1 The opening verse here is essentially a Lukan formulation. *καὶ ἐγένετο ἐν τῷ* + inf. . . . *καὶ ἰδού* (lit. "and it happened . . . and behold") is Lukan (5:12; 9:29; 24:4; and 5:17; 9:37 without the infinitive). Unusual here is the paralleling of the infinitive phrase with a finite verb construction (*καὶ ἦσαν παρατηρούμενοι*, "and [while] they were watching him"). Luke is fond of *τις*, "a certain" phrases (cf. esp. 7:36 where Jesus is invited to eat with "a certain one of the Pharisees"). "Rulers" is ambiguous, but since the "they" who are watching him finds its best antecedent in these rulers, Luke will mean leading figures among the Pharisees (taken up as "lawyers and Pharisees" in v 3). On Pharisees, see at 5:17. The sabbath setting is required for vv 2–6; the meal setting is used for vv 7–24. Though there is no straightforward use here of such a genre, there is probably some link between the meal setting and Hellenistic *symposion* practice (a banquet with formalized "table-talk") and the loose literary genre that developed out of the practice (see J. Martin, "Symposion: Die Geschichte einer literarischen Form," *Studien zur Geschichte und Kultur des Altertums* 17 [1931] 33–148; Ernst, "Gastmahlgespräche," 57–78; de Meeûs, *ETL* 37 [1961] 847–70). If there is such a connection, it is probably for the sake of contrasting typical symposium patterns with those that are worthy of, or to be practiced in relation to, the kingdom of God (we ought not, however, to think of a Hellenistic symposium *as opposed to* a Jewish meal). The language for the meal, *φαγεῖν ἄρτον*, "to eat bread," anticipates that of v 15 (in connection with the kingdom of God): in Luke's literary handling, this sabbath meal anticipates the eschatological banquet. For the practice of festive sabbath meals and sabbath-day hospitality, see Josephus, *Life* 54.279; *m. Šabb.* 4:1–2; Str-B, 1:611–15; 2:202–3. Luke has used the verb for "watching" in the sabbath healing episode in 6:6–11 (from Mark 3:2), and he has expressed the same sentiment more powerfully in 11:53–54 (the theme continues, with the same verb, but with scribes and chief priests in 20:20).

2 *καὶ ἰδοὺ ἄνθρωπος* (lit. "and behold a person/man") here balances the same phrase with *γυνή*, "woman," in 13:11; so, *ἄνθρωπος* will be "man" here. *ἄνθρωπός τις*, "a certain man," balances "a certain one of the rulers of the Pharisees" in v 1. It may, however, be a formulation from the tradition here (see at 10:30). Dropsy is a symptom, not a disease. It refers to massive retention of fluids in the body because of what are, mostly, quite serious and even life-threatening health problems. Whether the man was a guest or an intruder plays no role in the narrative.

3 Jesus responds to the situation of watching opponents and a needy person in front of him. The language is Lukan. "Lawyers and Pharisees" are paired elsewhere in Luke only at 7:30 (in reverse order; the order here may be favored by the reference to "leaders"). *ἔξεστιν τῷ σαββάτῳ*, "it is [or is it] lawful on the sabbath," is found also at 6:9. "To heal or not" puts a simple question in the place of the polemically set alternatives in 6:9.

4 Luke has not used in 6:6–11 the failure to respond found in Mark 3:4 ("they were silent"), but he does include that motif here (using a different verb). It is one thing to criticize Jesus for healing on the sabbath; it is another thing to take responsibility oneself for denying restoration to a needy person. The language of this verse is strongly Lukan (cf. Jeremias, *Sprache*, 236). Luke does not elsewhere use *ἐπιλαμβάνειν*, "take," in connection with a healing, but cf. his introduction of the verb in 9:47. Jesus somewhat similarly "dismissed" the Gerasene demoniac in 8:38 (the same verb is used in 13:12 of the release of the woman from her debilitating complaint). In the present narrative the man is no more than the instance in relation to which the matter in dispute is considered.

5 If "an ass or an ox" is the original reading here (see *Notes* above), then Luke may be responsible for the wording, to parallel 13:15 (Matt 12:11 has "one sheep," but this may itself be secondary; there is no significant common language between the two forms of the tradition, which probably suggests that the evangelists had different sources here). A more severe view than the one assumed here is evidenced at Qumran (CD 11:13–14), but that will not have been typical (cf. *m. Šabb.* 18:3). Those who will not, on the sabbath, leave their animals to the mercy of a well into which they have fallen should not begrudge the meeting of serious human need on the sabbath. Cf. discussion at 13:15; 6:5, 9.

6 Luke takes up in a new form the silence motif of v 4a. They can make no answer to the case that Jesus makes (cf. the partial parallel in 13:17; and further 20:26; Acts 11:18). The language here is again Lukan (cf. Jeremias, *Sprache*, 150).

Explanation

With this second sabbath episode we move beyond the halfway point in the section "Reversals Now and to Come." The unit 14:1–6 stands parallel to the earlier sabbath episode (13:10–17) with which the section began, just as the following units will correspond to counterparts that have been met in the same sequence in the first half of the section. The main line of the argument here is quite similar to that in the earlier sabbath episode.

The sabbath setting is for the sake of vv 1–6, but the meal setting is for the sake of the following units to v 24: these following units become "table-talk," and even table-talk that comments critically on the patterns involved in the kind of banquets in antiquity at which such table-talk took place (the patterns that are worthy of, and fitting in, the kingdom of God are quite different). The meal setting also has another role: it allows this meal to anticipate the end-time banquet of the kingdom of God (see v 15). The watching of Jesus here is a continuation of the development noted in 11:53–54.

A man appears before Jesus who has a serious fluid-retention problem, perhaps the byproduct of a heart condition. Jesus knows he is himself under critical scrutiny and responds to the situation with a simple question. His question puts his critics on the spot, because it is one thing to criticize Jesus for healing on the sabbath; it is quite another thing to take responsibility oneself for denying restoration to a needy person because of the sabbath day. In the face of their silence, Jesus deals with the man's need and dispatches him. The report is more about the dispute than about the healing.

Just as animals need water on the sabbath (13:15), they need, as well, help if they get into an awkward situation. Jesus assumes that any of his critical hearers would rescue his or her ass or ox which had fallen into a well on the sabbath, though in fact more extreme Jewish views of the day have been recorded. Nonetheless, Jesus' assumption is effective for this set of critics. The comparison leaves them looking as if they want animals treated better than people. The critics could offer no counter.

"When You Are Invited to a Banquet . . ." (14:7–11)

Bibliography

Bivin, D. "A Measure of Humility." *JerPersp* 4 (1991) 13–14. **Degenhardt, J.-H.** *Lukas, Evangelist der Armen.* 97–113. **Jeremias, J.** *Parables.* 25–26, 191–93. **Jülicher, A.** *Gleichnisreden.* 2:246–54. **Magass, W.** "Semiotik einer Tischordnung (Lk 14,7–14)." *LingBib* 25–26 (1973) 2–8. **Moxnes, H.** *The Economy of the Kingdom.* 127–37. **Navone, J.** "The Parable of the Banquet." *BiTod* 14 (1964) 923–29. **Noël, T.** "The Parable of the Wedding Guest: A Narrative-Critical Interpretation." *PRS* 16 (1989) 17–27. **Shillito, E.** "The Gospel according to St. Luke xiv. 7–33." *ExpTim* 52 (1940–41) 432–34. **Stöger, A.** "Sentences sur les repas: Lc 14,1. 7–14." *AsSeign* n.s. 53 (1970) 78–88.

Translation

[7] *When he noticed how they were seeking out the first places, Jesus told a parable to those who had been invited.*[a] [8] *"When you are invited by someone to a banquet,*[b] *do not*

recline in the first position; it may turn out that one who is more honorable than you has been invited by him. [9]*Then the one who invited both you and him will say to you, 'Make*[c] *a place for this person.' At that point you will begin with shame to take up the last place.* [10]*Rather, when you are invited, go and recline in the last place, so that when the one who has invited you comes, he will say to you, 'Friend, go up higher!' Then you will have*[d] *glory in the presence of all those who are reclining with you.* [11]*For every one who exalts himself will be humbled and the one who humbles himself will be exalted."*

Notes

[a] A redundant "saying to them" has been omitted in translation.

[b] εἰς γάμους, "to a banquet/wedding celebration," is omitted from P[75] b sa, possibly because the "wedding celebration" setting seemed out of place in the context.

[c] Lit. "give."

[d] Lit. "there will be to you."

Form/Structure/Setting

The unit 14:7–11 corresponds in the Lukan structure to 13:18–19; and as 13:18–19 is closely paralleled by vv 20–21, so here 14:7–11 is closely matched with vv 12–14. Wise advice to guests at banquets becomes a parable about life in the kingdom of God.

The present unit is known only from Luke, apart from a version of vv 8–11 placed after Matt 20:28 (which has its much altered equivalent to Luke 14:11 at the beginning) in D Φ it sy[c], which could be independent of Luke's text. V 7 will be Luke's own introduction. V 11 he has elsewhere (18:14 and cf. Matt 18:4; 23:12). It is unclear whether Luke is the "parable maker" here, turning a piece of prudential advice into a parable of the kingdom of God, or whether this has already been Jesus' strategy, and Luke merely highlights this with his introductory words in v 7.

We should note the similar structure in vv 8 and 12, which links the present unit and that in vv 12–14 ("when you are invited" [v 8]//"when you give a dinner" [v 12]; "do not recline" [v 8]//"do not invite" [v 12]; μήποτε [v 8: "it may turn out that"; and v 12: "in case"]).

Comment

As in life so in the kingdom of God, self-importance and the self-promotion that goes with it lead not to honor but to shame.

7 Luke's introduction ties the teaching to come to the meal setting he has provided in v 1 and contributes to the adversarial mood of the units in 14:1–24. "Parable" invites us to move beyond the prudential advice that is ostensibly all that Jesus offers (v 11 will serve the same end). Love of the "seat of honor" in the synagogue is identified as a Pharisaic weakness in 11:43 (and cf. 20:46), but love of honors is widespread!

8 On γάμους, "banquet/wedding celebration," see at 12:36. Jesus' words are in the first instance critical of what he sees happening in front of him. κατακλιθῇς, "recline," will be Lukan (the six occurrences in the NT are all in Luke's Gospel). For the three uses of "recline," Luke uses three different verbs. The "first position" is the place for the most honored guest. μήποτε normally expresses a negative purpose ("lest"), but here the sense is "it may turn out that."

9 The one who issued the invitations has the final say about the ranking of his guests. This is the basis for the parabolic application of the advice. There is a correlation between promoting oneself before others and promoting oneself before God. Whereas self-importance has taken the person initially to the position of highest honor, now shame causes him to bypass intermediate ranking positions for the lowest of all.

10 A series of parallels to this prudential advice has been documented (see Str-B, 1:916; 2:204). The words of advancement echo those of Prov 25:6–7 (and cf. Sir 3:17–20). "Real honor will come not from one's self-seeking choices, but from what is bestowed on one by another" (Fitzmyer, 1045). A matching humility before God is correspondingly honored.

11 In connection with Prov 25:6–7, *Lev. Rab.* 1:5 has language similar to that here ("My humiliation—that is my exaltation, and my exaltation is my humiliation."), which may favor an original presence of v 11 here. The notable difference is the passive form in the Gospel, which makes a clear place for the role of God. The one who comes to God must come humbly recognizing his own poverty before God. God will not turn him away.

Explanation

The reversal here involves the interchange of humble and exalted standing. The unit 14:7–11 corresponds in the Lukan structure to 13:18–19. It is closely linked with vv 12–14 to follow (as 13:18–19 was with 13:20–21).

Luke calls this a parable, but it is first a piece of critical advice to people whose behavior shows clearly their need of it. Self-importance shows itself all too often in the easy and often unself-conscious assumption of one's rights. But, to take up the banquet imagery, the one who issues the invitations finally has the right to rank the guests who are enjoying the generosity of the host's hospitality.

Jesus' advice is also a parable because there is a correlation between how we might behave in promoting ourselves before others and in promoting ourselves before God. The prudential advice that might save us from humiliating shame in a social situation applies also to our claim upon the kingdom of God. Our hope is in coming to God in the humility that recognizes our own poverty before him. God lifts up the head of the one who approaches with downcast eyes (cf. 18:13).

"When You Are Going to Give a Luncheon or a Dinner . . ." (14:12–14)

Bibliography

Cavallin, C. "'Bienheureux seras-tu . . . à la résurrection des justes': Le macarisme de Lc 14,14." In *À cause de l'Évangile,* ed. F. Refoulé. 531–46. **Glombitza, O.** "Das grosse Abendmahl (Luk. xiv. 12–24)." *NovT* 5 (1962) 10–16.

And see at 14:1–7; 14:7–11.

Translation

[12]He said as well, to the one who had invited him, "When you are going to give a luncheon or a dinner do not call your friends, or your brothers, or your rich neighbors, in case they in turn call you, and there is a repayment to you. [13]Rather, when you are going to give a banquet, invite the poor, the crippled, the lame, the blind. [14]Then you will be blessed,[a] because they have no way to pay you back. For[b] there will be repayment to you at the resurrection of the righteous.

Notes

[a] The same term is translated "fortunate" at 6:20 etc., but here the future reference encourages the present translation.

[b] ℵ $f^{1,13}$ 205 1424 2542 it have the simple δέ, "and/but."

Form/Structure/Setting

In the larger Lukan section, 14:12–14 corresponds to 13:20–21 (see at 13:10–17; 14:7–11). More immediately it is tied closely to vv 7–11 by the parallelism in the grammatical structures of vv 8 and 12 (for a more elaborate structural parallelism, see Cavallin ["'Bienheureux seras-tu,'" 538–39]; de Meeûs [*ETL* 37 (1961) 868]). There is a second important parallelism between vv 12–14 and vv 15–24: the call of vv 12–14 is to extend hospitality to the same group of social undesirables that, in the end, the dinner host of the parable invites to his banquet.

There is no Gospel parallel to the present unit, and it remains unclear what traditional base Luke has for it. On the one hand, the material is marked by Lukan diction and has been influenced in syntax and wording by vv 8, 16 and 21. On the other hand, the content of the teaching and the radical form it takes align closely with the historical Jesus.

Comment

God will reward the truly generous who, like himself, extend their generosity to the most unlikely of people and who have no thought of reciprocal gain for themselves.

12 The introduction here is likely to be part of the Lukan structuring. Jesus addresses in turn the guests collectively (vv 7–11), his host (here), and one particular guest who utters an expression of standard piety (vv 15–24). "Going to give . . . a dinner" is likely to have been taken from the parable to come (v 16). The distinction between ἄριστον and δεῖπνον (translated "luncheon" and "dinner") is that between the two Jewish meals of the day (or possibly for Luke the Roman equivalents): a late morning meal and a late afternoon meal, which was the main meal of the day. The mention of both provides for comprehensiveness. The guest list is a natural one: people whose company one enjoys; those to whom one is linked by blood; and those from whom one might gain advantage. In each case, reciprocity is more than likely (on the Greco-Roman reciprocity ethic, see at 6:32). There is an irony in Luke's setting in parallel as undesirable outcomes the shame of vv 8–9 and the "repayment" here of a return invitation to a banquet—this is not a normal way of looking at things!

13 The more general term δοχήν, "banquet/feast," now displaces the meal language of v 12. Apart from the inversion of the order of the last two terms, the guest list is identical to that of v 21, from where it has probably been borrowed. The link suggests that we are being directed to arrange our meal hospitality on the same basis as God does as he makes arrangements for the great eschatological banquet which he is convening (cf. Cavallin, "'Bienheureux seras-tu,'" 540). There is a close correspondence as well with the categories of people mentioned in 7:22 as having been touched by Jesus' ministry. Xenophon, *Symposion* 1.15 criticizes the reciprocity approach to meal invitations; *m. ʾAbot* 1:5 encourages domestic hospitality to the poor ("let the poor be members of your household"). The crippled, the lame, and the blind are marked for exclusion in Lev 21:17–23; 1QM 7:4; 1QSa 2:5–6; 4QD^{b}; cf. 2 Sam 5:8 (LXX).

14 The prospect of blessing is based squarely on the inability of those benefited by one's hospitality to provide any kind of return. It is precisely this that identifies the hospitality as generosity, rather than as calculated self-interest. The thought here invites comparison with Luke's frequent commendation of almsgiving (cf. discussion at 11:41), but also with the critique of the reciprocity ethic in 6:32–36, with its commendation of open-handed generosity in imitation of the generosity of God (is this text behind Luke's linking of vv 12–14 and 15–24?). Though this is the first reference in the Gospel to resurrection, life beyond this one has been regularly assumed (e.g., 9:24; 10:14; 12:5; 13:28). Except for Jesus' own resurrection, apart from the present verse and the dispute in 20:27–40 (see there for further discussion of belief in resurrection), Luke keeps the motif of resurrection for his second volume, where the post-resurrection setting provides a particular focus for this motif. The "resurrection of the just" here is the positive half of the "resurrection both of the righteous and the unrighteous" contemplated in Acts 24:15.

Explanation

Standard patterns of reciprocity and concern for those of our own standing are overturned here. The directions for hosts correspond to the directions to guests in vv 7–11, and in turn these directions to hosts are to be found to have their counterpart in the behavior of the divine host, hidden in the parable of vv 15–24.

The natural guest list is made up of people whose company one enjoys, along with relatives, and those from whom one stands to gain in some way. We are told here to rewrite that guest list for fear that it might give us precisely what it has been drawn up to provide: a reciprocal benefit from our generosity. This cannot lead to God's blessing on the day of accountability.

Such a guest list needs to be replaced by a list consisting of the people who would never be our natural guests, and who have no capacity to return the favor. Then our hospitality will express true generosity of soul and will be like God's own generosity, extended to the most unlikely of people.

Who "Shall Eat Bread in the Kingdom of God"? (14:15–24)

Bibliography

Abel, O. "De l'obligation de croire: Les objections de Bayle au commentaire augustinien du 'constrains-les d'entrer' (Luc 14/16–23)." *ETR* 61 (1986) 35–49. **Bailey, K. E.** *Through Peasant Eyes.* 88–113. **Baker, J.** "Christ's Challenge to Straight Thinking." *ExpTim* 67 (1955–56) 179–81. **Ballard, P.** "Reasons for Refusing the Great Supper." *JTS* 23 (1972) 341–50. **Beare, F.** "The Parable of the Guests at the Banquet: A Sketch of the History of Its Interpretation." In *The Joy of Study: Papers on New Testament and Related Subjects.* FS F. C. Grant, ed. S. E. Johnson. New York: Macmillan, 1951. 1–7. **Bergen, P. van.** "La parabole des invites qui se derobent." *LumVie* 49 (1960) 1–9. **Bultmann, R.** "Lukas 14, 16–24." In *Marburger Predigten.* Tübingen: Mohr-Siebeck, 1956. 126–36. **Derrett, J. D. M.** "The Parable of the Great Supper." In *Law.* 126–55. **Dominic, A. P.** "Lucan Source of Religious Life." *ITS* 23 (1986) 273–89. **Dormeyer, D.** "Literarische und theologische Analyse der Parabel Lukas 14, 15–24." *BibLeb* 15 (1974) 206–19. **Eichholz, G.** "Vom grossen Abendmahl (Luk. 14, 16–24) und von der königlichen Hochzeit (Matth. 22, 1–14)." In *Gleichnisse der Evangelien: Form, Überlieferung, Auslegung.* 3rd ed. Neukirchen-Vluyn: Neukirchener, 1979. 126–47. **Fiedler, P.** *Jesus und die Sünder.* 238–41. **Fuchs, E.** "Trace de Dieu: la parabole." *BulCPE* 25 (1973) 19–39. **Haenchen, E.** "Das Gleichnis vom grossen Mahl." In *Die Bibel und wir: Gesammelte Aufsätze, zweiter Band.* Tübingen: Mohr-Siebeck, 1968. 135–55. **Hahn, F.** "Das Gleichnis von der Einladung zum Festmahl." In *Verborum veritas.* FS G. Stählin, ed. O. Böcher and K. Haacker. Wuppertal: Brockhaus, 1970. 51–82. **Hart, J. H. A.** "Possible References to the Foundation of Tiberias in the Teaching of Our Lord." *Exp* 8/1 (1911) 74–84. **Hasler, V.** "Die königliche Hochzeit, Matth. 22, 1–14." *TZ* 18 (1962) 25–35. **Jeremias, J.** *Parables.* 63–69, 176–80. **Jülicher, A.** *Gleichnisreden.* 2:67–79, 202–14. **Kilpatrick, G. D.** "The Aorist of γαμεῖν in the New Testament." *JTS* 18 (1967) 139–40. **Kreuzer, S.** "Der Zwang des Boten: Beobachtungen zu Lk 14,23 und 1 Kor 9,16." *ZNW* 76 (1985) 123–28. **Lemcio, E. E.** "The Parables of the Great Supper and the Wedding Feast: History, Redaction and Canon." *HBT* 8 (1986) 1–26. **Linnemann, E.** *Jesus of the Parables: Introduction and Exposition.* New York: Harper and Row, 1966. 88–97, 158–68. ———. "Überlegungen zur Parabel vom grossen Abendmahl: Lc 14 15–24/Mt 22 1–14." *ZNW* 51 (1960) 246–55. **Matura, T.** "Les invités à la noce royale: Mt 22,1–14." *AsSeign* 59 (1974) 16–27. **McCaughey, J. D.** "Two Synoptic Parables in the Gospel of Thomas." *ABR* 8 (1960) 24–28. **Navone, J.** "The Parable of the Banquet." *BiTod* 1 (1964) 923–29. **Norwood, F. A.** "'Compel Them to Come In': The History of Luke 14:23." *RelLif* 23 (1953–54) 516–27. **Palmer, H.** "Just Married, Cannot Come." *NovT* 18 (1976) 241–257. **Perkins, P.** *Hearing the Parables.* 94–98. **Perrin, N.** *Rediscovering.* 110–14. **Pousset, E.** " Les invités au banquet (Luc 14,15–24)." *Christus* 32 (1985) 81–89. **Radl, W.** "Zur Struktur der eschatologischen Gleichnisse Jesu." *TTZ* 92 (1983) 122–33. **Resenhöfft, W.** "Jesu Gleichnis von den Talenten, ergänzt durch die Lukas-Fassung." *NTS* 26 (1979–80) 318–31. **Sanders, J. A.** "The Ethic of Election in Luke's Great Banquet Parable." In *Essays in Old Testament Ethics.* FS J. P. Hyatt, ed. J. L. Cranshaw and J. T. Willis. New York: Ktav, 1974. 245–71. **Schlier, H.** "The Call of God." In *The Relevance of the New Testament.* New York: Herder and Herder, 1968. 249–58. **Schottroff, L.** "Das Gleichnis vom grossen Gastmahl in der Logienquelle." *EvT* 47 (1987) 192–211. **Schulz, S.** *Spruchquelle.* 391–403. **Stöger, A.** "Armut und Ehelosigkeit—Besitz und Ehe der Jünger nach dem Lukasevangelium." *GuL* 40 (1967) 43–49. **Sutcliffe, E. F.** "'Compel Them to Come in' (Lk 14, 23)." *Scr* 5 (1952) 20–21. **Swaeles, R.** "L'Evangile (Lc 14, 16–24): La parabole des invités qui se dérobent." *AsSeign* o.s. 55 (1962) 32–50. **Trilling, W.** "Zur

Überlieferungsgeschichte des Gleichnisses vom Hochzeitsmahl Mt 22,1–14." *BZ* 4 (1960) 251–65. **Via, D. O., Jr.** "The Relationship of Form to Content in the Parables: The Wedding Feast." *Int* 25 (1971) 171–84. **Vine, V. E.** "Luke 14:15–24 and Anti-Semitism." *ExpTim* 102 (1991) 262–63. **Vögtle, A.** "Die Einladung zum grossen Gastmahl und zum königlichen Hochzeitsmahl: Ein Paradigma für den Wandel des geschichtlichen Verständnishorizonts." In *Das Evangelium und die Evangelien: Beiträge zur Evangelienforschung.* Düsseldorf: Patmos, 1971. 171–218. **Weder, H.** *Die Gleichnisse Jesu.* 177–93. **Wegenast, K.** "Freiheit ist lernbar: Lukas 14,15–24 im Unterricht." *EvErz* 40 (1988) 592–600. **Weiser, A.** *Die Knechtsgleichnisse.* 58–71. **Zimmermann, H.** *Jesus Christus: Geschichte und Verkündigung.* 2nd ed. Stuttgart: Katholisches Bibelwerk, 1975. 110–21.

Translation

[15] *When one of those reclining with [him] heard this*[a] *he said to him, "Blessed is the one who will eat bread in the kingdom of God."* [16] *He said to him, "A certain person was going to give*[b] *a large dinner*[c] *and he had invited many.* [17] *At the time for the dinner he sent his slave to say to those who had been invited, 'Come,*[d] *because things are already prepared.'* [18] *And they all began with one [accord] to refuse. The first said to him, 'I have bought a field and I have a need to go out and see it; I ask you, have me excused.'* [19] *Another one said, 'I have bought five yoke of oxen and I am going to try them out; I ask you, have me excused.'* [20] *Another one said, 'I have married a wife, and because of this, I am not able to come.'* [21] *The slave came and reported these things to his master. The the householder was angry and said to his slave, 'Go out quickly into the streets and alleys of the town and bring in here the poor, the crippled, the blind, and the lame.'* [22] *The slave said, 'Master, I have done what you ordered and still there is space.'* [23] *The master said to the*[e] *slave, 'Go out into the highways and hedgerows and compel them to come in, so that my house may be filled.* [24] *I say to you, that none of those men*[f] *who were invited shall taste of my dinner.'"*

Notes

[a] The Gr. is pl.
[b] A D L W Θ Ψ etc. have the aorist instead of the impf.
[c] A W *f* [13] etc. have *ἄριστον*, "luncheon" (cf. v 12).
[d] ℵ A D W Δ etc. have the infinitive (so: "invited to come").
[e] "His" in P[75] D 983 etc.
[f] *ἀνθρώπων*, "people," in ℵ (D) 0233 2542 e.

Form/Structure/Setting

In the Lukan structure for the section 13:10–14:35, the present unit is paralleled with 13:22–30 (cf. there). In both cases Jesus challenges the confidence of those who take it for granted that they will be present at the great eschatological banquet. In both cases there is a reversal of expectations about those who will be in and those who will miss out. The sabbath meal setting of 14:1–24 concludes with this episode: Jesus has silenced his lawyer and Pharisee antagonists over the matter of sabbath healing; he has addressed the honors seeking of the guests in general; he has directed the leader of the Pharisees, whose guest he was, about guest lists for dinners; and now he responds to a pious remark by one of the guests.

The present unit is paralleled in Matt 22:1–10, though there is considerable dispute whether Matthew and Luke received this parable in the same form. In the end we cannot be sure, but the following points can be made. (*i*) Most of the Matthean differences can be seen to accord with Matthean theological interests and redactional tendencies and so *could* be attributed to Matthean redaction. (*ii*) Despite Goulder (588–92) it is difficult to see how the Lukan form could come from anything like the Matthean form, and much easier to see how something like the Lukan form can have developed into the Matthean form (that the *Gospel of Thomas* form [64] is quite close to the Lukan form in most of its features, and [unusually] does not appear to be secondary to the Synoptic forms, adds support to this view). (*iii*) The very small amount of verbal agreement, combined with the very high level of Matthean intervention required for any assumption that Matthew began from a parable form close to Luke's, stands in favor of some pre-Matthean development. (*iv*) In the excursus "Journey to Jerusalem" it has been suggested that the present parable was part of a parables source available to Luke (however, since in the chiastic structure, this parable is in the central position, the structure would in fact survive its omission).

The setting provided by 14:15 may well be Luke's contribution. It is perhaps more likely that the original list of guests in v 21 has been transferred to v 13, than, as is normally held, that the influence has moved in the other direction. Luke's role in the list of excuses in vv 18–20 remains uncertain. Luke's replacement guest list has the best claim to originality. It seems likely that Matthew's second sending of slaves to the first list of guests reflects an adaptation of the motif of a second sending found in vv 22–23 of Luke's text. Luke's vv 22–23 may nevertheless (apart from the final clause) represent an early development of the parable. V 24 is best taken as a later development, most likely by Luke himself in connection with 13:28 in the paralleled unit.

The most significant attack on the historicity of the parable is that of Haenchen ("Gleichnis," 153–55), who points out that the historical Jesus did not turn to the poor because he was rejected by the rich and important. The starting point is rather God's love for the tax collectors and sinners. This is a decisive criticism for any chronological reading of the parable. But the chronology belongs to the story rather than to the intention of the parable: the householder's anger is real enough against those who have refused to come, but it is only a narrative device in connection with the invitation of the poor (under normal circumstances a normal householder does not invite the poor, despite the recommendation of vv 12–14). The chronological priority of those first invited may have at its base Sanders' understanding ("Ethic of Election," 259) of the sense in which they are identified as the *κεκλημένοι*, "invited/called": they are the "apparently elect" or "those who consider themselves elected."

Comment

It is not the people with the most publicly obvious claim upon an invitation to partake of the eschatological banquet who will finally be found there. Jesus is currently being snubbed by many as he calls people to come into the kingdom of God, and it is the poor, the crippled, the lame, and the blind who are finding their way into the banquet.

15 This verse is likely to be a Lukan formulation that provides a transition from the resurrection language of v 14 to the meal imagery of the kingdom of God found in vv 16–24 (Luke uses *ἀκούσας*, "having heard," similarly in 7:29; *τις*, "a certain," is common in Luke; *τῶν συνανακειμένων* [lit. "the ones reclining together"] has just been used in v 10; *μακάριος*, "blessed," is from v 14; *φάγεται ἄρτον*, "eats bread," picks up on v 1 [it is an OT idiom for eating a meal (cf. Gen 37:25; 2 Sam 9:7; 2 Kgs 4:8; Eccl 9:7; etc.)]; "kingdom of God" here underlines the kingdom-of-God perspective that has been operative since v 7 and now becomes explicit [cf. the kingdom of God motif in the paralleled units in 13:18–30]). In the perspective of the Lukan Jesus, the kingdom-of-God banquet is not so exclusively future as this pious remark should probably be taken to assume: in Jesus' own ministry, God is saying "come, for the banquet is ready" (indeed meal fellowship with Jesus is potentially an anticipatory experience of this eschatological banquet).

16 See discussion of *ἄνθρωπός τις*, "a certain man," as likely to be traditional at 10:30. "Going to give a . . . dinner" is language we have met already at v 12. In keeping with imagery of the eschatological banquet being utilized in the parable, "large" and "many" put this dinner party on a grander scale than those anticipated in v 12. Matthew's "a man, a king" (22:2) is likely to betray a development from an original "a man." His "marriage feast for his son" is a natural allegorical development (the son plays no further role in the parable, and *γάμους* is only certainly to be translated "marriage feast" [rather than "banquet" as in Luke 12:36] because of the addition in Matthew of vv 11–14 [see v 11]). No clearly fixed group is in view for the "many." We could say that they turn out to be those who, while having some historic claim to being part of the People of God, do not in fact take up the invitation that is their birthright. This would not be wrong, but it places an emphasis on historical election that goes beyond the concern of the parable.

17 The language in Matthew and that in Luke agree most closely in this verse (in common is "he sent his slave[s] . . . those who had been invited"). As in ancient custom (see Esth 5:8 cf. 6:14; *Lam. Rab.* 4:2; Philo, *Opif.* 78; Terence, *Heaut.* 169–70; Apuleius, *Met.* 3.12), invitations had been issued and accepted ahead of time, and at the appointed time when things were quite ready, the domestic slave was sent around to summon the guests on the day. In line with earlier changes, the Matthean text raises the scale of the event with its "slaves" as with mention of the animals prepared for the feast. The action corresponds to Jesus' invitation of his contemporaries into the kingdom of God (to be rejected in v 18).

18 The anticipated course of events now takes a bizarre turn. After all is arranged, every last one of them refuses to come (Luke's *ἀπὸ μιᾶς* [lit. "from one (fem.)"] may be an Aramaism, related to an idiom known in later Christian Palestinian Aramaic or Syriac [so: "at once"] or it could involve an ellipse with *φωνῆς*, "voice," *γνώμης*, "opinion," etc. understood [see Fitzmyer, 1055]; since the shared opinion is most striking in the story line development, the latter is preferable). The action of the parable is not to be related to some remote (or even near) eschatological future, but to the present of Jesus' ministry (and by extension to the present of the early church's ministry): now is the time to be taking up the invitation and coming along to the messianic banquet.

If the *Gos. Thom.* 64 version of the parable is independent of the canonical Gospels, then Luke's series of excuses will be more original than Matthew's departure scene (Matthew's violent treatment of the servants by some is certainly secondary). At the same time the rather different excuses of the *Gospel of Thomas* version show how easily changes can occur in this kind of detail (the four *Gospel of Thomas* excuses [Luke has three] include two that involve purchase and one that involves a wedding [as Luke, but the content in each case is quite different], as well as one that concerns expectation of payments from merchants). Against the claims of several, there is not likely to be a relationship between the battle exemptions of Deut 20:5–8 (cf. 24:5) and the present excuses.

Efforts have been made to make of this first excuse (and that to follow) a credible life priority, by speaking of the intended inspection as a part of the purchase procedure (cf. *b. ʿAbod. Zar.* 15a), but our text does not speak either of a possible sale or a sale in progress. As in each of the following excuses, we are dealing with a personal preoccupation rather than with a reasonable priority. The man's priorities are ultimately those warned against in 17:31.

19 The sequence "the first," "another one" (ἕτερος), "another one" is to suggest that we are being given only a sample set of the excuses offered in turn by each of the "many" (v 16). Both here and in the previous excuse we are dealing with the behavior of the quite well off in ancient society.

20 The first two cases have been reported in closely parallel form, but the third is handled rather differently: this person speaks of his inability to come rather than of the necessity of his doing (or of his intention to do) something else, and he does not ask to be excused. No doubt we are meant to understand that the marriage is recent, but this would not have been something unforeseeable at the time of the initial invitation, and in any case hardly constitutes an adequate basis for withdrawal. Luke is clearly critical of commitment to one's wife ahead of one's commitment to the kingdom of God (note his addition of "wife" to the list of those one needs to "hate" in v 26 and of those one might need to leave in 18:29). Linnemann's case (*Jesus,* 89, 93, 164 n. 16) that this verse was no original part of the parable (and that therefore those seeking to be excused were only concerned to be excused their late arrival) falls foul of the natural sense of ἔχε με παρῃτημένον, "have me excused," in vv 18 and 19. Whatever the status of the particular excuses in Luke's account, the parable has always been about people deciding that they have better things to do and that they will not come after all.

21 Matthew has nothing corresponding to the slave's return and report to his master, but his account develops the mention of anger with an account of the destruction of those on the first guest list (their behavior has been much worse in the Matthean account) and speaks of the unworthiness of those invited. The new guest list in the Matthean account is "as many as you find" (resumed in the following verse with "all whom they found, both bad and good"), and they are to be found in the "thoroughfares" (διεξόδους τῶν ὁδῶν [resumed simply as τὰς ὁδούς, "the streets," in the following verse (cf. Luke 14:23)]).

Most of the Matthean differences look secondary, but the case is less clear for "thoroughfares" and "as many as you find" ("bad and good" will be to prepare for the added vv 11–14). The decision about the former is linked to that about whether Luke's two trips for extra guests or Matthew's one should be given priority. Here the best (though not the usual) solution seems to be to assume that the editor of the Matthean form could see no point in the two trips and has conflated them, but that the presence of this motif in his source is nonetheless reflected in the second round of slaves sent to reinforce the call to come at once to the wedding banquet (22:4; this second round stresses that no effort has been spared in getting those invited to see the need to come at once, which in turn prepares for the gravity of the outcome in v 7). This suggests that for the language of location Luke is more likely to be original (however either in v 21 or 13:26 [in the section which Luke parallels with 14:15–24], Luke is likely to be responsible, for the sake of the parallelism, for the use of πλατεῖαι, "streets"; the Lukan pairing of πλατεῖαι, "streets," and ῥύμαι, "alleys," is found in Isa 15:3; Tob 13:18; for the sake of the same parallelism Luke has introduced here οἰκοδεσπότης, "householder," from 13:25 (the parable otherwise uses κύριος, "master").

I would also give Luke priority in the case of the alternative guest list: his version fits the priorities of the ministry of Jesus rather better than Matthew's "as many as you find" (which with its generality may already be preparing for vv 11–14); and it is likely that Luke has taken the list from here for use in v 13 (not the other way round as is often supposed).

There is no thought that this list of needy people will consider refusing the invitation (Matthew has them invited, but Luke simply has them brought): concerns with the affairs of life do not have the same hold upon these needy people (there is a link here with Luke's concerns in 6:24–26; 8:14; 12:15–21; etc.). The list matches pointedly those who were targeted by Jesus' ministry.

There is of course no redirection of the ministry of Jesus to correspond to the redirection of the slave's efforts here in the story.

22 This verse assumes as its basis the unreported fulfillment of the command of v 21. The second recruitment of replacement guests (which is prepared for here), while it appears to have been known by the editor of the Matthean version, may still be a secondary development. In a small Galilean town, however, there is not likely to have been the difficulty that some have suggested with either a too great delay in serving the meal or with excessive numbers to be found in a quick gathering from the public thoroughfares of the town: there could still be room; and it is not envisaged that the slave go any great distance in his search outside the town for additional guests (he is concerned only with the rural land immediately attached to the town). Most in favor of seeing vv 22–23 as secondary is the possibility that their role is to suggest an open-ended and outward-looking ministry succeeding the ministry of Jesus to the needy of Palestine. In the setting of the original ministry of Jesus these verses need, however, no more than to anticipate the open-ended and outward-looking future that Jesus' roving ministry continued to contemplate.

23 εἶπεν . . . πρός, "said . . . to," corresponds to Luke's favored diction. "Highways and hedgerows" refer probably not to separate places but to the situation outside the town where the rural roads are abutted by the hedges or fences surrounding the fields (cf. Fitzmyer, 1057). To the supposed need to go out (ἀνάγκην ἐξελθών), of the first person on the guest list to withdrew (v 18), corresponds the need to come in (ἀνάγκασον εἰσελθεῖν) that the slave is to impose on this last set of newly found potential guests. Though the list of potential guests is not repeated from v 21, we should understand that the quest is for the same strata of people. Despite regular claims to the contrary, it is at most a ministry beyond that of Jesus (but see above), and not a ministry to the Gentiles, that is made room for here (as in 13:29–30 [see there]; in the larger Lukan perspective this will include the outreach to the Gentiles). The substance of the final clause is paralleled in Matt 22:10: despite the bizarre withdrawal of the initial guests, the banquet will go ahead as planned and with a full complement of guests.

24 This verse is a foreign body in terms of the narrative development of the story (filling the house with replacement guests will make no difference to those who do not want to come anyway [the appeal to a custom of taking portions to guests unable to come (as Derrett, "The Parable of the Great Supper," 141, appealing to Neh 8:10–12) makes adequate sense of the verse itself, but offers little help for integrating it with the flow of the story]). It also addresses a plural "you" who have no place in the story. The verse is best taken as a Lukan formulation (the similarity with Matt 22:8 is too slight to serve as basis for claiming the presence of Luke 14:24 in the source form here). The "I" who speaks here will be the master of the house who speaks, however, not to his slave, but rather (to use the words of Linnemann, *Jesus*, 90) "he steps as it were on to the apron of the stage and addresses the audience." It is likely that on the basis of 13:24–28, the master for this verse is to be identified in Luke's eyes with Jesus himself (in the original parable the master is God). The thought is that of 13:29b, and Luke is underlining the parallelism in his structuring between 13:22–30 and 14:15–24.

Explanation

Both this unit and its parallel in 13:22–30 question the confidence of those who take it for granted that they will be present at the great eschatological banquet. With the ministry of Jesus, the walls between the present and the future of the banquet of the kingdom of God dissolve; and as he calls upon people to come into the kingdom of God, it is the poor, the crippled, the lame, and the blind who are making their way into the banquet while many of the more obvious people on the invitation list are preoccupied with other concerns.

The idea of blessing at the resurrection of the righteous (v 14) leads to the pious statement of v 15. Jesus does not question the sentiment, but his story does bring the matter from the future into the present, and it does place in question a corollary of the sentiment: that such a prospect would automatically be first priority for all for whom it became a possibility.

After invitations had been issued and accepted, it was the custom to send a slave to fetch the guests as near to the appointed hour as all was ready. Incredibly, in this story, every last one of the invited guests comes up with a last-minute excuse and will not come. One is preoccupied with a newly bought field that he wants to look over; one is taken up with newly acquired oxen that he wants to try out; one has recently married and would prefer to stay home with his wife; and so on it goes. These people have the kind of preoccupations with the material affairs of life that, in Luke's view, can be a most serious trap (see 17:31; 8:14; etc.), or the kind of attachment to family relationships that cripples the possibility of any costly, committed stance (see 14:26 and 18:29). These uninterested responses paralleled some of the responses that Jesus was encountering, and continued to find their parallels in the response to the ongoing preaching of the Christian gospel. The total block-response of all the initially invited guests contributes to the drama of the story, but has no clear analogue in the experience of Jesus or of the early church.

The master of the household who learns of the way in which his invitations are snubbed is naturally angry. But instead of abandoning his dinner party, he makes a bold move quickly to supply substitute guests. He arranges for the bringing in of unpretentious folk, indeed the truly disadvantaged of his society. His slave quickly rounds up all who are around in the public roads and alleys of the town. This reaching out to the poor and disabled corresponds to the ministry of Jesus himself, but of course in reality it needs no basis in some change of plan on the part of God. That is only part of the need to provide story-line motivation.

The deed is done and yet there is room (not a lot of such people are about on the roadways at the end of the day). So the net is cast wider: the slave goes out now beyond the town to the country roads among the fields, vineyards, and market gardens adjacent to the town. The house will yet be full. In the setting of the ministry of Jesus, this move anticipates the open-ended and outward looking future that Jesus' roving ministry continued to contemplate. It also makes room for a ministry beyond that of Jesus' own lifetime, a ministry that, in Luke's larger telling of the story (Acts), extends the gospel message to the Gentiles.

V 24 is only half-heartedly part of the parable. Here the banquet host addresses the audience of the drama, so to speak, and not the characters of the drama. The thought is close to that in 13:29 (end of verse), and it is likely that for v 24, where Luke has one eye on 13:24–28, the role of banquet host has become Jesus' role (not God's, as in the body of the parable) and that Luke is underlining the parallelism that he wants us to see between 13:22–30 and 14:15–24.

The Disciple's Fate, and the Possibility of Failed Discipleship (14:25–35)

Bibliography

For 14:25–33:

Blinzler, J. "Selbstprüfung als Voraussetzung der Nachfolge." *BLit* 37 (1963–64) 288–99. **Denney, J.** "The Word 'Hate' in Luke xiv, 26." *ExpTim* 21 (1909–10) 41–42. **Derrett, J. D. M.** "Nisi dominus aedificaverit domum: Towers and Wars (Lk xiv 28–32)." *NovT* 19 (1977) 241–61. **Dupont, J.** "Renoncer à tous ses biens (Luc 14,33)." *NRT* 93 (1971) 561–82. **Eichholz, G.** "Vom Bauen und vom Kriegführen (Luk. 14, 28–32)." In *Gleichnisse der Evangelien.* 3rd. ed. Neukirchen–Vluyn: Neukirchener, 1979. 192–99. **Finlayson, T. C.** "Christ Demanding Hatred: Luke xiv. 26." *Exp* 1/9 (1879) 420–30. **Fletcher, D. R.** "Condemned to Die: The Logion on Cross-Bearing: What does It Mean?" *Int* 18 (1964) 156–64. **Gough, I. F.** "A Study on Luke 14:26: Jesus Calls His Disciples to a Life of Supreme Commitment." *AshTB* 3 (1970) 23–30. **Heininger, B.** *Sondergutgleichnisse.* 132–39. **Hempel, J.** "Luk. 14,25–33, eine 'Fall-Studie.'" In *Das lebendige Wort.* FS G. Voigt, ed. H. Seidel. Berlin: Evangelische Verlagsanstalt, 1982. 255–69. **Hommel, H.** "Herrenworte im Lichte sokratischer Überlieferung." *ZNW* 57 (1966) 1–23. **Hunzinger, C. H.** "Unbekannte Gleichnisse Jesu aus dem Thomas-Evangelium." In *Judentum-Urchristentum-Kirche*, ed. W. Eltester. BZNW 26. Berlin: Töpelmann, 1960. 209–20. **Jarvis, P. G.** "Expounding the Parables: V. The Tower-builder and the King Going to War (Luke 14:25–33)." *ExpTim* 77

(1965–66) 196–98. **Jülicher, A.** *Gleichnisreden.* 2:202–14. **Laufen, R.** *Die Doppelüberlieferung.* 302–42. **Legrand, L.** "Christian Celibacy and the Cross." *Scr* 14 (1962) 1–12. **Louw, J.** "The Parables of the Tower-Builder and the King Going to War." *ExpTim* 48 (1936–37) 478. **Manson, T. W.** *The Teaching of Jesus.* 237–40. **Mechie, S.** "The Parables of the Tower-Building and the King Going to War." *ExpTim* 48 (1936–37) 235–36. **Menoud, P. H.** "Richesses injustes et biens véritables." *RTP* 31 (1943) 5–17. **Moore, T. V.** "The Tower-Builder and the King: A Suggested Exposition of Luke xiv: 25–35." *Exp* 8/7 (1914) 519–37. **Perrin, N.** *Rediscovering.* 126–28. **Piper, R. A.** *Wisdom in the Q-Tradition.* 197–202. **Schmidt, T. E.** "Burden, Barrier, Blasphemy: Wealth in Matt 6:33, Luke 14:33, and Luke 16:15." *TJ* 9 (1988) 171–89. **Schulz, S.** *Spruchquelle.* 430–33. **Seeley, D.** "Blessings and Boundaries: Interpretations of Jesus' Death in Q." *Semeia* 55 (1991) 131–46. ———. "Jesus' Death in Q." *NTS* 38 (1992) 222–34. **Seynaeve, J.** "Exigences de la condition chrétienne: Lc 14." *AsSeign* n.s. 54 (1972) 64–75. **Stein, R. H.** "Luke 14:26 and the Question of Authenticity." *Forum* 5.2 (1989) 187–92. **Thackeray, H. St. J.** "A Study in the Parable of the Two Kings." *JTS* 14 (1913) 389–99.

And see at 9:23–27.

FOR 14:34–35:

Coleman, N.-D. "Note on Mark ix 49, 50: A New Meaning for *ἅλας*." *JTS* 24 (1922–23) 387–96. **Cullmann, O.** "Das Gleichnis vom Salz: Zur frühesten Kommentierung eines Herrenworts durch die Evangelisten." In *Vorträge und Aufsätze 1925–1962,* ed. K. Froehlich. Tübingen: Mohr-Siebeck, 1966. 192–201. ———. "Que signifie le sel dans la parabole de Jésus? Les évangélistes, premiers commentateurs du logion." *RHPR* 37 (1957) 36–43. **Deatrick, E. P.** "Salt, Soil, Savior." *BA* 25 (1962) 41–48. **Gressmann, H.** "Mitteilungen 14: Salzdüngung in den Evangelien." *TLZ* 36 (1911) 156–57. **Hauck, F.** *TDNT* 1:228–29. **Jeremias, J.** *Parables.* 168–69. **Jülicher, A.** *Gleichnisreden.* 2:67–79. **Köhler, L.** "Salz, das dumm wird." *ZDPV* 59 (1936) 133. **Krämer, M.** "Ihr seid das Salz der Erde . . . Ihr seid das Licht der Welt: Die vielgestaltige Wirkkraft des Gotteswortes der Heiligen Schrift für das Leben der Kirche aufgezeigt am Beispiel Mt 5, 13–16." *MTZ* 28 (1977) 133–57. **Nauck, W.** "Salt as a Metaphor in Instructions for Discipleship." *ST* 6 (1952) 165–78. **Perles, F.** "Zwei Übersetzungsfehler im Text der Evangelien." *ZNW* 19 (1919–20) 96. ———. "La parabole du Sel sourd." *REJ* 82 (1926) 119–23. **Schulz, S.** *Spruchquelle.* 470–72. **Schwarz, G.** *Jesus und Judas.* 37–42. **Souček, J. B.** "Salz der Erde und Licht der Welt: Zur Exegese von Matth. 5, 13–16." *TZ* 19 (1963) 169–79.

Translation

[25]*Many crowds were going along with him,*[a] *and he turned and said to them,* [26]*"If someone comes to me and does not hate his own father and mother, and wife and children, and brothers and sisters, and even his own life as well, he cannot be my disciple.* [27]*Whoever does not carry his own cross and come after me cannot be my disciple.*

[28]*"For which of you, wanting*[b] *to build a tower, does not sit down and reckon up the cost—whether he has [enough] for completion,* [29]*so that [the situation will not develop where,] when he has laid the foundation* [c]*and is not able to complete,*[c] *all who see will begin to mock him* [30]*saying, 'This person began to build and was not able to complete.'* [31]*Or what king, as he goes to engage another king in battle, will not sit down first and decide*[d] *whether he is able to meet with ten thousand [troops] the one coming upon him with twenty thousand [troops].* [32]*Otherwise, while he is still far off, he will send a delegation and sue*[e] *for terms of*[f] *peace.*

[33] *"In the same way, then, every one of you who does not give up all his goods cannot be my disciple.*

[34] *"Salt, then,*[g] *is good; but if even*[h] *the salt has become insipid,*[i] *with what shall it be seasoned?* [35] *It is fit neither for the earth nor for the dung-heap; they throw it away. Let the one who has ears to hear, hear!"*

Notes

[a] P[75] lacks "with him."

[b] P[45] W Γ f^{13} etc. have ὁ θέλων (lit. "the one wishing"), while P[75] has θέλει, "he wishes." The sense fails in the first and the grammar in the second.

[c-c] Omitted by D e. The clause is slightly repetitive.

[d] Present tense in A D L R W Ψ etc.

[e] Gr. ἐρωτᾷ (lit. "he asks" [present tense]).

[f] Gr. τὰ πρός (lit. "the to[wards]"). ℵ Γ 1241 etc. drop τά, "the"; B (K) etc. have εἰς, "into"; P[75] etc. have nothing before "peace." The original idiom caused the scribes difficulty.

[g] Omitted in A D R W Θ etc.

[h] Omitted in P[75] A E R $f^{1,13}$ etc.

[i] Gr. μωρανθῇ (lit. "has become foolish").

Form/Structure/Setting

The final unit of the section 13:10–14:35 focuses on the paradoxical nature of the resources needed for discipleship: disencumberment from family and material goods and the carrying of a cross. This unit parallels 13:31–35, the reference point for "carry his own cross and come after me" (v 27). To the failure of Jerusalem in 13:34–35 corresponds the prospect of failed discipleship, imaged in the salt of 14:34–35.

Luke forms this unit around material that he shares with Matt 10:37–38 (i.e., vv 26–27). He prefaces this with his own setting (v 25), which evokes afresh the journey motif, and he supports the challenge of the materials with two brief parables (vv 28–30, 31–32), which he alone of the Synoptists has preserved. V 30 may be a Lukan expansion of the first parable (cf. Heininger, *Sondergutgleichnisse*, 133). V 33 is likely to be of Lukan coinage, based in form on vv 26–27 and in content on 12:33; 18:22. Finally Luke adds, as conclusion to the unit, material that he shares with Matt 5:13 (and partially with Mark 9:49–50), which he uses to conjure up an image of failure, set against the challenge to follow Jesus to his fate in Jerusalem. Luke completes this item with a call to hear, which he has used already at 8:8.

Luke stays closer to his source than Matthew does for v 26, but he will be responsible for some expansion of the range of family specified. For v 27 the Matthean form of the relative clause will be more original, while Luke has the source form of the final clause. A form of vv 26–27 is also preserved in *Gos. Thom.* 55 (cf. 101), which seems to be dependent on the Synoptic forms and to merge features from Matthew and Luke (or just possibly from Matthew and a source like Luke's). Vv 26–27 do not constitute an original unity. When the materials were joined, v 27 received substantial formal modification for the sake of parallelism (for an earlier form, see 9:23, and see the extended discussion of form and historicity at 9:23–27). The incautious language of v 26 does not fit comfortably into the normally strongly family-oriented patterns of Jewish thought, nor those of developing Christianity. To postulate its origin in a sect of radical Christian itinerants runs the risk of circularity, especially since there is a perfectly good fit for such language and thought in the ministry of the historical Jesus (cf. Stein, *Forum* 5.2 [1989] 187–92).

The parables of vv 28–32 are likely to have been formulated together. They probably go back to the historical Jesus, but see *Comment* below for the possibility that their original sense was quite different from the Lukan sense. The three Synoptic forms of the salt similitude show how it has been modified in transmission. Luke is interested only in the image of disaster, but the choice of salt will originally have been made also in connection with the positive usefulness of the salt as a flavoring. Was the saying originally a statement of failure, or was it more of a challenge? Was it originally directed to Israel in connection with its role in the world as God's light to the nations, or was it always a discipleship saying, as now in the Gospels?

Comment

Jesus calls the crowds who would follow him to Jerusalem to a renunciation of all ties that would hold them back from a readiness to parallel in their own lives the fate that awaits Jesus in Jerusalem and to which he now journeys. Otherwise they will be disciples in name but not in reality.

25 Luke has formulated the setting here (for the language, cf. esp. 5:15; 7:11; and note the Lukan preference for εἶπεν πρός for "said to"). Its role is to renew the journey motif after the sedentary setting of 14:1–24. This renewal is in anticipation of the the carrying of one's cross after Jesus of v 26. In tandem with that saying, it enables Luke to tie this unit to 13:31–35: are these crowds of potential disciples, who are presently coming along with him as he heads for Jerusalem, prepared to follow him to the fate he has marked out for himself in 13:31–35?

26 Matthew has a parallel to vv 26–27 in his mission charge (10:37–38), which is certainly no original setting. Luke is likely to have contributed to the present verse the pairing of "wife and children" (this pairing is found in Jdt 7:14; Luke has this in place of Matthew's "son or daughter"; cf. the addition of "wife" at 18:29), and the addition of "and even his own life" (inspired by 9:24, which we should note follows a variant of 14:27). Perhaps he is also responsible for filling out the family set with "brothers and sisters" (based on 18:29//Mark 10:29).

The language of hate is typical Semitic hyperbole (Prov 13:24; 2 Sam 19:6; cf. Gen 29:30–33 [does ויאהב את־רחל מלאה, *wayyeʾĕhab ʾet-rāhēl milēʾāh* mean "and he loved Rachel rather than Leah"?]; Mal 1:2–3; Deut 21:15–17) that has been toned down by Matthew, but it is probably not right, as is often said, that the Semitic idiom actually means "love less than" (the language of hate is intended with all seriousness in Ps 139:21–22; 1QS 1:10; 9:21). The point here is that where there is hate no "ties that bind" limit one's freedom of action (cf. 9:59, 61). There is likely to be an allusion to Deut 33:9 with its link in turn to Exod 32:27–29, where the Levites demonstrate that they are on the Lord's side by carrying out the required slaughter with a single-mindedness that disregarded their own family ties. Hommel (*ZNW* 57 [1966] 1–23) is surely right to compare the strand in the Greek philosophical tradition reaching back to Socrates that, in the name of a single-minded devotion to truth, devalued family loyalties and concern for one's own bodily life and its needs (see Epictetus, *Diss.* 3.3.3–5; Xenophon, *Memorabilia* 1.2.49–55). Against Hommel (20–21) there is no sufficient basis for claiming a common source (but it is just possible that Luke's addition of "and even his own life" is motivated in part by a desire to point up the parallel with Socrates).

Luke's added "and even his own life" makes it quite clear that neither psychological hostility nor sectarian separation is in view. This addition also prepares for the life-threatening possibilities contemplated in v 27 to follow, thus reinforcing the structural parallelism that unites vv 26 and 27 (note also the transition from "comes to" [v 26] to "comes after" [v 27]).

"Comes to me . . . cannot be my disciple" casts Jesus in the role of a teacher with a band of disciples (according to Josephus [*Ant.* 6.84; 8.354], Joshua was a disciple of Moses and Elisha of Elijah). The analogy with a rabbinic teacher and his pupils living together for the purpose of the study of Torah is only of limited validity where such radical commitment is required. Matthew has displaced the pattern of teacher and disciples in favor of an overtly christological focus ("love more than me . . . not worthy of me"; T. W. Manson's appeal [*Teaching of Jesus*, 237–40] to a misreading of an Aramaic source is quite unnecessary). On disciples in Luke, see at 5:30.

27 Matthew's text focuses the imagery on the taking up of the cross, Luke's on carrying along of the cross. Matthew may be influenced by the Markan form (Mark 8:34, used in Matt 16:24), or Luke may think in terms of the journey already begun as a metaphorical carrying of the cross to execution in Jerusalem (probably the latter). Matthew's "follow after" may be influenced by the use of "follow" in Mark 8:34, but it may be better to think of Luke's "come after" as a product of his attention to the structural unity and flow of vv 26–27 (see above). This verse receives extensive discussion at 9:23–27, where it is closely paralleled in v 23. The discipleship framework of this verse is likely to be secondary. It will have been generated at the point where vv 26 and 27 were brought together as mutually illuminating.

28–30 The parables provide support for the challenge of vv 26–27 (linked with *γάρ*, "for"): without these necessary resources, namely "hatred" for family and a cross, there is no successful implementation of discipleship. The oddness of imagining these things as resources points to the secondary nature of the Lukan linking of the materials. "Which of you" questions in parables expect a negative answer (cf. 11:5, 11; 14:5; 17:7). The tower to be built could be a watchtower for a market garden or vineyard, or something more substantial for protective purposes ("which of you" fits the former better). Sitting is the appropriate posture for planning and calculation. The imagery of prior reckoning of resources is found in the context of moral discourse in Epictetus, *Disc.* 3.15.8, and Philo, *Abr.* 21.105. The foundations serve as a public statement of the intention to complete the tower. Fear of public ridicule, rather than the prospect of failure, provides the driving force of the parable.

Hunzinger ("Unbekannte Gleichnisse," 213–16) offers an attractive case for seeing the parable (and its pair) as more originally designed to make a comparison with God (as with the other "which of you" parables in 11:5, 11; 15:4, 8; 17:7; but see 14:5), who, having made the beginning he has with Jesus' ministry, will surely bring the kingdom to its fruition (Moore's application to Jesus [*Exp* 8/7 (1914) 519–37] is much less credible): God is not building a tower that he will be embarrassed not to complete; God has not, with insufficient troops, engaged in battle with his enemy when he should have sued for terms of peace.

31–32 There is no sign that these two parables ever circulated independently of one another. This second parable does not address "which of you," but which king, since we move beyond the field of direct applicability to Jesus' hearers. The first parable moved in the sphere of personal intention; this second begins from a situation already in place: two armies are moving toward one another with mutually hostile intent (note the correspondence of *πορευόμενος* [lit. "going"] and *ἐρχομένῳ* [lit. "coming"]). For the military use of *συμβάλλειν*, "to meet, engage," cf. 1 Macc 4:34; 2 Macc 8:23; 14:17. The king must "decide whether he is able to meet" the enemy with some reasonable chance of military success. *εἰ δὲ μή γε*, "otherwise," may be a Lukan intensification (cf. 5:36–37; 10:6). Where the first parable has concluded with the outcome of a failure to take a reckoning, the present parable spells out the alternative strategy to flow from just such a reckoning. In both cases, but for opposite reasons, it is the aftermath of the aborted project that attracts attention. *τὰ πρὸς εἰρήνην* (lit. "the [things] for peace") occurs again at 19:14. It seems to be an idiom for "terms of peace" (while not documented, this seems better than the appeal to Hebrew idiom in which "to greet [an opponent]," שאל בשלום, *šāʾal bĕšālôm,* is said to mean "to pay homage," and thence "to surrender unconditionally," which, apart from a speculative textual restoration proposed by Thackeray [*JTS* 14 (1913) 394–95], is also undocumented).

33 This verse is likely to be a Lukan formulation, inspired by 12:33 and 18:22 (cf. Dupont, *NRT* 93 [1971] 568–70). Despite the use of *οὕτως*, "in the same way/similarly," which elsewhere introduces a parable application (12:21; 156:7, 10; 17:10; 21:31), the thread of thought for v 33 reaches back rather to vv 26–27. The link is clear from the parallelism created by the use of "everyone of you who," which stands in the place of the "if someone" used v 26 and of "whoever" in v 27; and from the repetion of "he cannot be my disciple" from those verses.

τὰ ὑπάρχοντα are the goods one has at one's disposal, one's "worldly wealth" (cf. 8:3; 11:21; 12:15, 33, 44; 16:1). The call is to give up all of one's earthly goods, in much the way that those initially called by Jesus did (5:11, 28; 18:28), and in the way in which the rich ruler was challenged to do (18:22). It is likely that Acts 2:44; 4:32 portray, rather than a literal disposal of all of one's assets, Luke's notion of how this commitment should manifest itself in the ongoing life of the church. The important thing in the present context is the need to be disencumbered (as in v 26) in order to have the necessary freedom to live out the reality of discipleship. In Luke's understanding, preoccupation with property and wealth has a disastrous effect on the possibility of coming to terms with the discipleship demands of Jesus (cf. 6:24; 8:14; 16:14). In the structure of Luke's thought, disencumberment from wealth is the third of the necessary resources for discipleship, to be added to "hate" for one's family and the carrying of a cross.

34–35 Luke provides with *οὖν*, "then," the link with the preceding thought. He has drawn on two forms of the salt saying (the use of *ἀρτύειν*, "to prepare/season," indicates dependence on the Markan source [Mark 9:50], as might *καλὸν τὸ ἅλας*, "salt [is] good" [but this could have been in the second source as well], while the passive form of this verb, the presence of *μωρανθῇ*, "becomes insipid," and the general agreement of v 35 with Matt 5:13b point to the role of the second source). It is more likely that Luke has added the final saying to call for the interpretation of the similitude (cf. 8:8b) than that it was an original part of the tradition that has been suppressed by Mark and Matthew.

Salt is thought of here in connection with its use as a flavoring agent (it was also used in the ancient world as a preservative, to destroy the fertility of soil, conversely to enhance the fertility of soil, and finally as a catalyst in certain kinds of ovens). μωρανθῇ is literally "be made or become foolish/mad/stupified," and there is no documented use of the term in the sense that is clearly required here. Naturally there has been considerable discussion of the problem posed by the fact that salt cannot actually lose its flavor (*b. Bek.* 8b reflects a Jewish view that this is impossible). The issue of realism is probably a false focus of concern. Salt has been chosen for the image, because if any other savory foodstuff is or becomes insipid in taste, it can be seasoned with salt, but if the salt itself were to become insipid, then there could be no possibility of retrieval. In connection with savory food, the worst possible disaster would be that salt should lose its saltiness. (If we must look for an actual possibility of salt losing its nature, then the best of the suggestions is that reported by Deatrick [*BA* 25 (1962) 42] who refers to [impure] salt stored in [damp] mountain cabins as subject to a leaching out of the sodium chloride [salt] from the bottom layer, leaving behind only the impurities, which would then be the "salt" that had lost its saltiness.)

Matthew lacks Luke's additional spheres of uselessness of this spoiled salt (it is unclear whether expansion or contraction has occurred), but once the salt is thrown out he has it "trodden under foot by people" (which may be his own expansion [cf. Matt 7:6]). While the best salt was for table use, salt also had an agricultural use as a fertilizer for some kinds of vegetables. While other foodstuffs that have deteriorated beyond human consumption can still generally be added to the manure pile, desalinated salt is not even of this much use (alternately the point may be that salt could be used as a regulating agent in connection with the rate of fermentation of the manure pile). Luke's impersonal use of the third person plural ("they throw it out") will be more original than Matthew's passive participle construction.

Luke is interested in the similitude only as an image of disastrous failure. One might suspect also that the similitude originally conveyed the idea of (unspoiled) salt as of positive benefit to foodstuff. Matthew's "you are the salt of the earth" (5:13) retains this orientation. In the Lukan flow of thought, the salt that loses its flavor is the one who tries to embark on the project of discipleship without the necessary resources of disencumberment and cross. Unthinkingly, he will have placed himself in the position of the person who could not complete his tower, or of the king who went blindly into a battle that he could not win (vv 28–32). His discipleship will be no more discipleship than insipid salt is salt, and his bid to achieve discipleship will have become an irretrievable disaster. The final challenge is to avoid such a fate by listening to the advice and warning given in this unit.

Explanation

To be a successful disciple of Jesus involves, on one hand, disentanglement from the normal restraints imposed upon us by family commitments and the ties of property and wealth, and on the other hand, the carrying of one's own cross—traveling with Jesus, so to speak, to share his coming fate in Jerusalem.

The journey motif is renewed by the setting provided by v 25. What will it mean for these crowds who are moving along with Jesus as he heads toward Jerusalem to truly become disciples of Jesus? First there is a call to hate one's family. This is the kind of Semitic exaggeration that Jesus was quite fond of, but the point will be that where there is "hate" no "ties that bind" limit one's freedom of action (see 9:59, 61). There is an allusion to the single-mindedness of the Levites celebrated in Deut 33:9 and reported in Exod 32:27–29. Jesus' statement does not encourage alienation, or tense and strained relationships, but a particular kind of loose bond with the normal constraints that human family relationships impose. Of course even this is in a certain amount of tension with the strong affirmation of the family that is normally considered to be a central Christian ethic. In just the same way there is tension between the normal Christian affirmation of life and its goodness and the call here to hate one's own life (on this see at 9:24), which has gained inclusion in this family list. To hate one's own life can easily be taken in a psychologically destructive manner not at all intended here.

In addition to being disencumbered of family ties and the commitment to maintain one's own life, one must also carry one's own cross, in the way that Jesus was at this point, metaphorically, carrying his to Jerusalem. The need to bear a cross has already been encountered at 9:23 (see there). Here it has been prepared for by the call to hate one's own life.

The parables in 14:28–32 provide support for the challenge of vv 26–27. It is all very well to want to be a disciple, but the demands of vv 26–27 identify the necessary resources, without which there could be no successful implementation of discipleship. To rush without thought into the project of discipleship is like the person who begins to build a tower without the resources needed to complete it: he looks ridiculous. Or it is to be like the king who when challenged by another king rushes out to sure defeat, without considering that with half the troops of his opponent he can anticipate only disaster: far better if he had sued for terms of peace.

Having made the point that one needs to consider whether one possesses the proper resources, the Lukan Jesus returns to the conditions of discipleship. Now giving up one's worldly wealth is added to the earlier conditions. This is reminiscent of those who first responded to Jesus' call and is what the rich ruler failed to do. Not quite so comprehensively the same challenge has come in 11:41. It is likely that Acts 2:44; 4:32, rather than a literal disposal of all of one's assets, portray Luke's notion of how this commitment should manifest itself in the ongoing life of the church. The important thing in the present context is the need to be disencumbered (as in v 26) in order to have the necessary freedom to live out the reality of discipleship. In Luke's understanding, preoccupation with property and wealth has a disastrous effect on the possibility of coming to terms with the discipleship demands of Jesus.

The little parable that ends the unit is presented as an imaging of disastrous failure. Like discipleship, salt is a good thing. If other foods lose their taste, one can always add some salt, but if salt were to lose its taste, this would be an irretrievable disaster! It could not even be put to those secondary uses of salt, as fertilizer for certain vegetables, or to regulate the rate of decay in the manure pile. It would be useless. But no more useless than the one who tries to be a disciple without coming to terms with the necessary conditions of discipleship. We are challenged to hear the message that discipleship requires comprehensive disencumberment and cross bearing.

That Which Was Lost Is Found (15:1–32)

The section 15:1–32 defends and commends preoccupation with the lost, and overflowing joy at their restoration. We all respond this way with what is our own, and this attitude corresponds to the concerns of a father's heart for his own children, each one of whom is singularly precious in his sight.

The Joy of Finding the One Lost Sheep (15:1–7)

Bibliography

GENERAL FOR 15:1–32:

Adam, A. "Gnostische Züge in der patristischen Exegese von Luk. 15." *SE* 3 [= TU 88] (1964) 299–305. **Agnew, F. H.** "The Parables of Divine Compassion." *BiTod* 27 (1989) 35–40. **Bailey, K. E.** *The Cross and the Prodigal: The 15th chapter of Luke, seen through the eyes of Middle Eastern peasants.* St Louis: Concordia, 1973. ———. *Finding the Lost: Cultural Keys to Luke 15.* Concordia Scholarship Today. St. Louis: Concordia, 1992. ———. "Psalm 23 and Luke 15: A Vision Expanded." *IBS* 12 (1990) 54–71. **Bonnard, P.** "Approche historico-critique de Luke 15." *FV* 72 (1973) 25–37. **Bovon, F.,** and **Rouiller, G.,** eds. *Exegesis: Problems of Method and Exercises in Reading (Genesis 22 and Luke 15).* PTMS 21. Tr. D. G. Miller. Pittsburgh: Pickwick, 1978. **Cantinat, J.** "Les paraboles de la miséricorde (Lc, XV, 1–32)." *NRT* 77 (1955) 246–64; English digest in *TD* 4 (1956) 120–23. **Dupont, J.** *Les béatitudes.* 2:233–49. ———. "Réjouissez-vous avec moi! Lc 15,1–32." *AsSeign* n.s. 55 (1974) 70–79. **Entrevernes Group, The.** *Signs and Parables: Semiotics and Gospel Texts.* PTMS 23. Tr. G. Phillips. Pittsburgh: Pickwick, 1978. 117–83. **Farmer, W. R.** "Notes on a Literary and Form-Critical Analysis of Some of the Synoptic Material Peculiar to Luke." *NTS* 8 (1961–62) 301–16. **Giblin, C. H.** "Structural and Theological Considerations on Luke 15." *CBQ* 24 (1962) 15–31. ———. "Why Jesus Spoke in Parables—An Answer from Luke 15." *ChicStud* 7 (1968) 213–20. **Harrington, W.** "The Setting of the Parables." *DL* 13 (1963) 165–73. **Hickling, C. J. A.** "A Tract on Jesus and the Pharisees? A Conjecture on the Redaction of Luke 15 and 16." *HeyJ* 16 (1975) 253–65. **Jeremias, J.** "Tradition und Redaktion in Lukas 15." *ZNW* 62 (1971) 172–89. **Kossen, H. B.** "Quelques remarques sur l'ordre des paraboles dans Luc XV et sur la structure de Matthieu XVIII 8–14." *NovT* 1 (1956) 75–80. **Lambrecht, J.** *Once More Astonished.* New York: Crossroads, 1981. 24–56. **Meynet, R.** "Deux paraboles parallèles: Analyse 'rhétorique' de Luc 15, 1–32." *AnnPhil* 2 (1981) 89–105. **Nützel, J. M.** *Jesus als Offenbarer Gottes nach den lukanschen Schriften.* FB 39. Würzburg: Echter, 1980. 234–55. **Perrin, N.** *Rediscovering.* 90–102. **Ramaroson, L.** "Le coeur du troisième évangile: Lc 15." *Bib* 60 (1979) 248–60. **Ramsey, G. W.** "Plots, Gaps, Repetitions, and Ambiguity in Luke 15." *PRS* 17 (1990) 33–42. **Rasco, E.** "Les paraboles de Luc XV: Une invitation à la joie de Dieu dans le Christ." In *De Jésus aux évangiles: Tradition et rédaction dans les évangiles synoptiques.* FS I. Coppens, ed. I. de la Potterie. BETL 25. Gembloux: Duculot, 1967. 2:165–83. **Soltau, W.** "Die Anordnung der Logia in Lukas 15–18." *ZNW* 10 (1909) 230–38. **Waelkens, R.** "L'Analyse structurale des paraboles: Deux essais: Luc 15,1–32 et Matthieu 13,44–46." *RTL* 8 (1977) 160–78, esp. 160–69.

FOR 15:1–7:

Bailey, K. E. *Poet and Peasant.* 142–56. **Bishop, E. F. F.** "The Parable of the Lost or Wandering Sheep: Matthew 18.10–14; Luke 15.3–7." *ATR* 44 (1962) 44–57. **Bussby, F.** "Did a Shepherd Leave Sheep upon the Mountains or in the Desert? A Note on Matthew 18.12 and Luke 15.4." *ATR* 45 (1963) 93–94. **Buzy, D.** "La brebis perdue." *RB* 39 (1930) 47–61. **Cantinat, J.** "La Brebis et la drachme perdues (Lc 15,1–10)." *AsSeign* o.s. 57 (1965) 24–38. **Derrett, J. D. M.** "Fresh Light on the Lost Sheep and the Lost Coin." *NTS* 26 (1979–80) 36–60. **Descamps, A.** *Les Justes et la Justice dans les évangiles et le christianisme primitif hormis la doctrine proprement paulinienne.* Louvain/Gembloux: Universitas Catholica Louvaniensis, 1950. 147–54. **Dupont, J.** "Les implications christologiques de la parable de la brebis perdue." In *Jésus aux origines de la christologie,* ed. J. Dupont. BETL 40. Gembloux/Leuven: Duculot/Leuven University, 1975. 331–50. ———. "La brebis perdue et la drachme perdue." *LumVie* 34 (1957) 15–23. ———. "La parabole de la brebis perdue (Matthieu 18, 12–14; Luc 15, 4–7)." *Greg* 49 (1968) 265–87. **Fiedler, P.** *Jesus und die Sünder.* 148–53, 220–28. **George, A.** "Les paraboles." *LumVie* 23 (1974) 35–48. **Greeven, H.** "'Wer unter euch . . . ?'" *WD* 3 (1952) 86–101. **Jeremias, J.** *Parables.* 38–40, 132–36. **Kamphaus, F.** "'. . . zu suchen, was verloren war': Homilie zu Lk 15,1–10." *BibLeb* 8 (1967) 201–4. **Légasse, S.** *Jésus et l'enfant.* 54–62. **Linnemann, E.** *Jesus of the Parables.* 65–73. **Monnier, J.** "Sur la grâce, à propos de la parabole de la brebis perdue." *RHPR* 16 (1936) 191–95. **Perkins, P.** *Hearing the Parables.* 29–33, 38, 47, 52. **Peterson, W. L.** "The Parable of the Lost Sheep in the Gospel of Thomas and the Synoptics." *NovT* 23 (1981) 128–47. **Schmidt, W.** "Der gute Hirt: Biblische Besinnung über Lukas 15,1–7." *EvT* 24 (1964) 173–77. **Schnider, F.** "Das Gleichnis vom verlorenen Schaf und seine Redaktoren: Ein intertextueller Vergleich." *Kairos* 19 (1977) 146–54. **Schulz, S.** *Spruchquelle.* 387–91. **Topel, J.** "On Being 'Parabled.'" *BiTod* 87 (1976) 1010–17. **Trau, J. M.** "The Lost Sheep: A Living Metaphor." *BiTod* 28 (1990) 277–83. **Trilling, W.** "Gottes Erbarmen (Lk 15,1–10)." In *Christusverkündigung in den synoptischen Evangelien: Beispiele gattungsgemässer Auslegung.* Biblische Handbibliothek 4. Munich: Kösel, 1969. 108–22. **Weder, H.** *Die Gleichnisse.* 168–77.

Translation

[1]*All*[a] *the tax collectors and the sinners used to draw near to him to listen to him;* [2]*and the Pharisees and the scribes were grumbling, saying, "This fellow receives sinners and eats with them!"*

[3]*So he told them this parable.* [4]*"Which man among you, if he were to have*[b] *a hundred sheep and lost one of them, would not leave*[c] *the ninety-nine in the wilderness and go after the lost [one] until he finds it?* [5]*And when he finds it, would he not place*[c] *it on his shoulders rejoicing,* [6]*and when he comes to his house, would he not call together his friends and his neighbors and say to them, 'Rejoice with me, for I have found my sheep which was lost'?*

[7]*"I tell you, in the same way there will be more joy in heaven over one sinner who repents than over ninety-nine righteous people who have no need of repentance."*

Notes

[a] W lat sy^{s,c,p} sa^{ms} etc. omit this hyperbolic "all."

[b] ἔχων (lit. "having").

[c] The tense is a simple present. The conditional forms of the translation are a consequence of taking the participles in v 4 conditionally.

Form/Structure/Setting

This new section is to be identified unproblematically with the extent of the chapter (the three parables are carefully linked linguistically and thematically, while the disgruntled elder son at the end of the third parable takes up the grumbling of the Pharisees and scribes of the introductory setting [vv 1–3]). The parable proper serves effectively as a justification of Jesus' behavior, while the application verse (v 7) takes us on beyond the parable with its introduction of the note of repentance, and with its development of the note of joy into a call to share in the joy of heaven over the restoration of sinners.

It is likely that the linking of the three parables of this section is pre-Lukan. In support of this are (*i*) the tension between the Lukan setting (vv 1–3), which calls for the justification of Jesus' behavior, and the note of shared joy, which suits better an ecclesiastical setting (see below at v 6); and (*ii*) the close structural parallel in 13:1–9 (and partially in 14:28–32), which plays no role in Luke's structuring of his Gospel, but which, as is argued in the excursus "Journey to Jerusalem," is best explained as a relic of the structure of a chiastically arranged parables source used by Luke. The three parables in sequence have been correlated with Jer 31:10–20 (Kossen, *NovT* 1 [1956] 75–80), but the link is not close and the degree of parallelism is likely to be fortuitous.

Luke appears to be responsible for the setting in vv 1–3, but his role in the wording of vv 4–7 seems to have been quite minimal, despite the general concurrence of the material with his own interests. There is a second form of this parable in Matt 18:12–14 that is significantly different from the Lukan, but the divergence seems to have been almost entirely pre-Lukan and is also likely to be significantly pre-Matthean.

In our pursuit of the earliest accessible form of the parable, there is no adequate basis for choosing between Matthew and Luke for the opening section, but it is likely to have had Luke's language of the shepherd *losing* rather than Matthew's of the sheep *straying*. On the other hand, Matthew's verb for "leave" and his use of "hills" may be more original than Luke's verb and "wilderness." Though the choice is difficult, Luke's assumption that the sheep will be found is likely to be more original than Matthew's text, which leaves the possibilities open. The process by which v 5 has been lost from Matthew's version is explored in *Comment* below: originally it will have been followed by a version of Matt 18:13b (without the opening "amen, I say to you that"), which will have been the concluding statement of the parable. Matthew is likely to be responsible for the application in 18:14. Luke 15:6 and 7 have both been penned at the point where this parable was joined with that of the lost coin. V 5 has been modeled on v 9, while v 7 is a reformulation of v 10 under the influence of the tradition behind Matt 18:13b. Despite the claims of Peterson (*NovT* 23 [1981] 128–47), the *Gospel of Thomas* form of the parable has no real claim to being more primitive than the synoptic Gospel forms.

The parable is one of those that narrate a typical situation, rather than a distinctive situation, and is thus to be classified as a similitude. The close relationship of the sentiment here to that of 5:31–32 stands in favor of tracing the present parable to the historical Jesus. Though Luke's setting is secondary, it involves a correct identification of the typical setting for such a parable.

Comment

It is only natural that what has been lost should become the object of inordinate attention, and when it is found, the object of particular joy. God takes special delight in the restoration of the sinner.

1 By general consent this verse is a Lukan contribution: Luke is fond of periphrastic tenses and is the major NT user of ἐγγίζειν, "to draw near"; he is also fond of hyperbolic uses of "all" [3:16; 4:15; 7:29; etc.]; the pairing of "tax collectors" and "sinners" may be borrowed from 5:30 or possibly 7:34 [see there and cf. Mark 2:15, 16]; the phenomenon of coming to hear Jesus is formulated by Luke in 5:1, 17; 6:18; etc. The presence of the tax collectors and sinners provides the provocation for the protest in v 2, which is in turn answered in terms of the three parables of the chapter. Marshall (599), pointing to the periphrastic imperfect ("were drawing near/used to draw near"), is probably right to suggest that "the general circumstances of Jesus' ministry rather than one particular incident are in mind." Luke would have followed the line of at least the first two of his parables more closely if he had had Jesus in pursuit of tax collectors (cf. 5:27–28; 19:1–10) and sinners (5:32; perhaps 7:34). It is too much to say that this drawing near to Jesus implies the repentance of vv 7 and 10, but it is certainly a move in the direction of that possibility.

2 This verse has even stronger links to 5:30 than v 1 does (in common is [δι]ἐγόγγυζον οἱ φαρισαῖοι καὶ οἱ γραμματεῖς . . . λέγοντες . . . ἁμαραρωλ[ούς] . . . [συν]εσθί[ει], "the Pharisees and the scribes grumbled . . . saying . . . eat[s] with sinners"). Only προσδέχεται, "receives" (in the LXX the verb occasionally [Mic 6:7; Zech 3:10] takes the sense "take pleasure in/have goodwill towards" that has been claimed for the present use), which is used here with a different sense from that required for all the other Lukan uses of this verb, could possibly indicate the presence here of a source (as argued by Nützel, *Jesus*, 237–39; but the base of argumentation is too narrow for any confidence). On the significance of this behavior for Jesus and the scandal it caused, see at 7:34 and 5:30–32.

3 The language here is very close to that of 18:9 and is best seen as Lukan. As in 14:7, a (Lukan) reference to a single parable actually introduces a set of three (after 5:36 there are two).

4 Matthew (18:12–14) and Luke have very little language in common between their forms of the parable, and it is doubtful whether they have drawn this parable from a shared source. It has already been suggested above that the three parables of this chapter have come to Luke as a linked set, which in turn was probably part of a distinctive parables source available to Luke. It is likely that a good deal of the language here is that of Luke's distinctive source. On the traditional nature of the τίς ἐξ ὑμῶν, "which of you," language, see at 11:5. As in 14:2, ἄνθρωπος should be translated "man" (on the basis of the parallel with the "woman" of 15:8). This is not Luke's preferred usage and is likely to be from the source (the syntactical similarity between the introductions to the parables in 14:28 and 31 and those in 15:4 and 8 is from Luke's parables source, not his own structuring of the materials). Luke has ἀπολέσας (lit. "[the shepherd] having lost") and Matthew πλανηθῇ, "[the sheep] strayed," to express the fate of the sheep that gets separated from the flock. Matthew may be responsible for the difference, since he uses Luke's verb in connection with eternal perdition in the application that he adds in 18:14, and could hardly use the same verb with such a difference of sense in the actual parable (cf. Dupont, *Greg* 49 [1968] 274–75), but Luke's verb is also found in Luke 15:6, 8, 9, 17, 24, 32, and so belongs to the redactional unity here, probably of Luke's source. Luke's καταλείπει may be secondary to Matthew's ἀφήσει for "he leaves" (cf. Luke's change in 20:31). Given the topology of Palestine, Luke's "wilderness" and Matthew's "hills/mountains" refer to the same location. Perhaps the change is Luke's (see 8:29; cf. Mark 5:5). Luke's telling assumes a successful search, while Matthew's allows also for an unsuccessful outcome. The possibilities remain quite open, since Matthew's form suits his ecclesiastical horizon (and so Matthean redaction), while Luke's fits in with the horizon of v 1 (and so Luke may have intervened), but also with the parallelism with v 8 (and so we may have pre-Lukan redaction).

While the situation envisaged can be taken quite hypothetically, the secondary nature of Luke's setting is perhaps underlined by the oddness of thinking of a Pharisee or a scribe having and shepherding his hundred sheep (at least for later Pharisees, shepherding was a proscribed trade [cf. Jeremias, *Parables*, 132]). It is tempting to appeal to the OT use of the shepherd imagery of God (Ezek 34:11–16; Ps 23:1–3), but if this plays any role here, and it probably does, it is only in the move from the story world to the world of application and needs to be kept strictly out of sight as we seek to identify the inner dynamic of the story. Both the OT imagery and the parable base themselves on the investment of care required of *anyone* to maintain sheep under ancient conditions. The "hundred" and the "ninety-nine" are an obvious way of setting up a contrast between the vast majority and a small part of the whole; it is paralleled in Jewish texts (see. *m. Pe᾽a* 4:1, 2; Str-B, 1:784–85). To own a hundred sheep would be a mark of some wealth. We should not understand that the ninety-nine are simply left to their own devices, only that the normal level of care is withdrawn from them temporarily for the sake of the needs of the lost sheep (it is perhaps best to think of the sheep being secondarily watched over by a fellow shepherd who temporarily divides his attention between these and his own sheep, but such detail is outside of the concern of the parable). The point of the parable is the disproportionate investment of effort and concern directed toward the one sheep: in the context of losing and finding, the one is *temporarily* of more importance than the ninety-nine in connection with whom there is no particular need or problem (cf. Linnemann, *Jesus*, 66). There is an evident similarity (but also a difference) here with the thought of 5:31–32, and only the defense of Jesus' concourse with sinners provides an adequate setting for the parable. At the same time, Dupont (*Greg* 49 [1968] 282) has rightly drawn attention to the parabolic assumption of ownership, which, in the attempt to understand the thrust of the parable, inevitably draws the focus onto God (cf. Ezek 34:11–16). The implication is that in some sense Jesus takes the place of God; he performs the acts of God; "the conduct of Jesus is the concrete form taken by the salvific intervention of God" (Dupont, "Implications christologiques," 349).

5 Matthew has nothing corresponding to this verse. As things now stand, its opening καὶ εὑρών (lit. "and having found") is paralleled at the opening of v 9, while the rest of the verse (and the start of v 6) is required to move the action to a setting that enables a parallel to the remainder of v 9. On the basis of this role, the verse might be judged secondary, but it is also possible that the earliest Greek form of the parable had v 5 followed by a form of Matt 18:13b without the opening "amen I say to you that" (in a mini-chiasm the participle εὑρών, "finding," takes up εὕρῃ, "he finds," then χαίρει, "he rejoices," takes up the participle χαίρων, "rejoicing"; on this reconstruction, the addition of "amen I say to you that" disturbs the flow and subsequently leads, on the one hand, to the suppression of Luke 15:5 in the Matthean form and, on the other hand, to the moving of the declaratory statement outside the parable and its reformulation as an application in the Lukan form). A frightened and disoriented sheep is most quickly brought back to the flock not on its own legs, but carried around the shoulders of the shepherd. To the preoccupation with the single lost sheep in the search corresponds the joy at its retrieval, which finds development in vv 6, 7.

6 This verse has no parallel in Matthew, but is closely paralleled in v 9 (except for the opening words, which simply bring the man into a domestic setting in order to make possible the parallelism; cf. as well 1:58), where it has a more natural home. Its formulation belongs to the point at which the two parables were brought together (συνκαλεῖ, "he calls together," may be a Lukan touch since he has all but one of the occurrences of this verb in the NT). We are probably to understand that the sheep will have been returned to the flock, and the day's work finished, before the owner of the sheep will return to his home (not that he goes straight home with the sheep on his shoulders!).

The note of (shared) joy over the restoration of that which had been lost spans from vv 5–7, to v 9, to vv 23–24, 32. It becomes problematic in the person of the elder son of vv 25–32 (see detailed discussion there). The emphasis on shared joy (συγχάρητε is translated "rejoice with," but it connotes here some concrete activity of celebration, and not just fellow-feeling) seems to be designed primarily to encourage in the church an outward-looking concern for the winning of sinners, and participation in the joy of those who are successfully involved in such outreach. In the Lukan setting, however, the main focus has been pulled onto a justification to the scribes and Pharisees of the behavior of Jesus, and then only secondarily, via the exemplary nature of Jesus, does it provide a justification of the behavior of those in the church who continue the practice initiated by Jesus (cf. esp. Nützel, *Jesus*, 248–51). Since the emphasis on shared joy fits only with difficulty into the Lukan focus, this feature will be pre-Lukan.

7 This verse is clearly a version of Matt 18:13b, or rather it is a recasting of Luke 15:10 in the light of the tradition reflected in Matt 18:13b. The formulation will have occurred at the point when the two parables were united. The emphasis on repentance here is at times attributed to Luke (Luke introduces repentance into 5:32; repentance does not specifically feature in 15:11–32), but it is difficult to see how vv 8–10 could ever have been without the reference to repentance, and so the same element will be pre-Lukan here. On repentance, see at 3:3. The place of repentance here takes us right outside the framework of the parable, which focuses exclusively on the role of the shepherd. Studies often protest that this verse obscures the fact that Jesus scandalized the Pharisees precisely by his *failure* to demand repentance in the normal way, but the parable could not in any case serve to make such a point without appeal to Luke's redactional setting (vv 1–3), and there is good reason to think that the call to repentance did play some role in the ministry of Jesus (cf. 10:13–15).

To participate on earth in the rejoicing evoked by seeing sinners repent is to image the joy of heaven. Since Luke's Greek has no word for the "more" of the translation above, the sense could be either "joy over . . . , rather than . . ." or "more joy over . . . than . . . ." I have preferred the second, since the first may suggest a negative note that is not present in the parable. The statement affirms God's particular delight in restoration (cf. Ezek 18:23; 33:11), as well as the value he sets upon the individual. The future here (ἔσται, "will be") will be a logical future and not a distinctly eschatological future. The use of δικαίος, "righteous," here is akin to that in 1:6, 17; 2:25; etc., but the present statement completes the logic of the explanation, rather than being concerned seriously to suggest that there is a category of people who, in the context of the coming of the kingdom of God, do not stand in need of repentance. Jewish tradition could also set high value on the penitent sinner (Str-B, 2:210–12), but could as well think in terms of God's joy over the downfall of the godless (*t. Sanh.* 14.10; Str-B, 2:209).

Explanation

The new section that begins here spans the chapter and consists of two small parables that are paired and an extended parable, which itself has two distinct focuses. The present parable justifies Jesus' behavior to the Pharisees and the scribes and challenges the church in aggressive outreach to, and joyful welcome of, the "sinners" who are outside.

Jesus' success at getting close to tax collectors and sinners has already been noted (5:30; 7:34); and not only in Jesus' generation has such freedom of association proved to be a cause of scandal to the pillars of society. Sharing meals was a particular offense to the Pharisees, who practiced careful ritual cleanliness.

The force of the parable comes from the challenge to each to recognize that were the loss one's own, one's behavior would be quite the same as that described in the parable. Though the man pictured has ninety-nine other sheep, it is quite natural that he should give a disproportionate share of his attention and concern to the one that is lost. *Temporarily* in the situation of loss this one is more important than all the rest put together. The man will no doubt ask someone else to keep a general eye on the sheep he leaves grazing, but he is quite prepared to deprive them for a time of their normal level of care for the sake of the sheep that has been lost.

As we seek to move from story to application, we need to attend to the assumption of ownership that undergirds the thrust of the parable. God's ownership of the flock from which the tax collectors and sinners have strayed is the starting point (see Ezek 34:11–16; Ps 23:1–3). At the same time we need to note that in the first instance it is the behavior of *Jesus* that is being defended. Clearly there is some sense in which Jesus is performing the acts of God here.

Not only in the moment of loss but also in the moment of recovery, this one sheep is inordinately important; and so we have in the parable not only the single-mindedness of the search but also the picture of joy consequent upon the success of the recovery. A happy man carries his sheep back to the flock, and at the end of the day's work, he mounts a modest celebration, so that his friends and neighbors can share in his joy. The motif of shared joy runs as a thread through the parables of chap. 15; it functions to encourage in the church a reiteration of the pattern of Jesus' preoccupations: an outward-looking concern for the winning of sinners and participation in the joy of those who are successfully involved in such outreach.

V 7 provides a specific application for the parable. God's joy at restoration is like that of the owner of the sheep, since he too is preoccupied with the one who is lost. In this verse the restoration of the sinner is understood to involve repentance (see at 3:6). The sense of "righteous" here will be like that in 1:6, 17; etc. There are those who have not strayed like the tax collectors and sinners, and so in the logic of the explanation need no repentance. We should not, however, take this to mean that in the context of the challenge of the coming of the kingdom of God there are any who have no need of repentance. The unspoken conclusion is that we too should share this joy of God in the restoration of sinners.

The Joy of Finding the Lost Coin (15:8–10)

Bibliography

Bailey, K. E. *Poet and Peasant.* 156–58. **Güttgemanns, E.** "Struktural-generative Analyse des Bildworts 'Die verlorene Drachme' (Lk 15,8–10)." *LingBib* 6 (1971) 2–17. **Heininger, B.** *Sondergutgleichnisse.* 140–46. **Sheerin, D.** "The Theotokion *Ὀ την ευλογημενην:* Its Background in Patristic Exegesis of Luke 15.8–10, and Western Parallels." *VC* 43 (1989) 166–87. **Walls, A. F.** "'In the Presence of the Angels' (Luke xv 10)." *NovT* 3 (1959) 314–16. **Weder, H.** *Gleichnisse Jesu.* 249–52.

And see at 15:1–7.

Translation

[8] *"Or which woman who has ten drachmas—*[a]*if she loses one drachma—would not light*[b] *a lamp and sweep the house and search diligently until she finds [it]?* [9] *And when she finds it, would she not call together*[b] *her friends and neighbors and say to them, 'Rejoice with me, for I have found the drachma which I lost'?*

[10] *"I tell you, in the same way there is joy before the angels of God over one sinner who repents."*

Notes

[a] D Θ *f*[13] etc. smooth the Gr. here and improve the parallelism with v 4 by reading *καὶ ἀπολέσας*, "and having lost."

[b] As in vv 4, 5 the tenses are present. They are translated as here not for any local reason but for the sake of the parallelism with the earlier verses.

Form/Structure/Setting

The present parable forms a close parallel with the preceding, only now with a relatively poor woman and her coins in the place of the relatively rich man with his sheep.

Only Luke preserves this parable. He will have it as part of a source that already joined the three parables of this chapter (part of a larger parables source). Jeremias (*ZNW* 62 [1971] 184) may be right that Luke interferes more with the wording of this parable than in the previous parable, where he has allowed to stand features of style that are not natural to him. The parable has not always been linked with vv 4–7. The junction has had more influence on vv 4–7 than on the wording of the present text, but it is likely that "one" in v 10 is a product of the junction. V 10 as such is not a product of the junction, but there is some question whether it has always been attached to the parable. The decision is difficult. In the present setting there is a clear emphasis on repentance that goes beyond the contours of the parable. But while the contrast between the ninety-nine and the one in the former parable allows that parable quite easily to stand without application, this is more difficult (though not impossible) for the woman and her coins, where there is no focus on the contrast between the lost coin and the remaining coins. It is perhaps best to suggest that the original parable application spoke of a "restored sinner" (or something similar). While in the present sequence v 10 plays an important role in orienting the reader to vv 11–32, the lack of specific language links (contrast the links between vv 4–7 and 8–10) and the stages by means of which the formulation "before the angels of God" seems to have developed (see below) suggest that v 10 predates the link with vv 11–32. It is yet another question whether the link between vv 8–10 and vv 11–31 predates the link with vv 4–7. This is possible given the somewhat parallelism of *τίς γυνή*, "which woman," and *ἄνθρωπός τις*, "a certain man." This would provide an occasion for the introduction into v 10 of the notion of repentance. The parable is to be classified as a similitude.

See further at 15:1–7.

Comment

As was the man with his sheep, so is the woman with her silver coin: again the point is that God takes special delight in the restoration of the sinner who has been lost from his People.

8 The "of you" of v 4 would not fit Luke's conversation partners of v 2. The "of them" is also missing, since there is no particular contrast here between the lost one and the remaining nine. Has Luke corrected the hanging nominative phrase in v 4, but forgotten to do so here? The drachma was an ancient silver coin whose value changed a good deal over time. In the time of Nero it was equivalent to a denarius. Though we are not told, the coins probably represent the savings that would cushion the family against days in which no income came in, or would help toward the cost of pilgrimage to Jerusalem, etc. The one coin represents a significant part of her savings. The woman's search procedure is based on (*i*) the confidence that the coin will be in the house (Derrett [*NTS* 26 (1979) 41] notes that drachmas were heavily dished and not truly circular, and that therefore they could not roll far); (*ii*) the poor natural light inside the house (probably no window and a small door); and (*iii*) the capacity of the broom to catch up the coin with the pile of dust and perhaps to reveal the presence of the coin by causing it to tinkle. The woman does not settle for what remains to her but seeks diligently to recover her coin.

9 This verse is that upon which v 6 has been based. Note that in the Greek the friends and neighbors are specified as female. The coin has become more important to her in its recovery than it had been originally as part of her nest egg. The invitation to share in the woman's joy only takes the character of a challenge to others from the wider setting.

10 *γίνεται χαρά*, "there is joy," may be a Lukan "improvement" (cf. Acts 8:8) to the *χαρὰ . . . ἔσται* used in v 7, which may reflect the source at this point. This verse stands behind Luke's formulation in v 7. The phrase *ἐνώπιον τῶν ἀγγέλων τοῦ θεοῦ*, "before the angels of God," is odd and is probably not original. In late Hebrew and in the NT, for something to be so "before God" is an indirect method of attributing the matter to God (cf. Walls, *NovT* 3 [1959] 315). A step further toward indirectness involves substituting "the angels" for God. But then the process seems to have gone into reverse here with the addition of "of God" (Walls' suggestion [*NovT* 3 (1959) 314–16: God rejoicing before or with his angels] finally falls foul of this "of God"). God is no more content than is the woman with what remains to him. There is special importance for him too in that which has been lost but is restored to him. Because of v 7, "who repents" introduces here as well a note that takes us outside the dynamic of the parable. The parable is intrinsically interested in the recovery of the sinner, not his or her repentance as such.

Explanation

The present parable forms a close parallel with the preceding, only now with a relatively poor woman and her coins in the place of the relatively rich man with his sheep. Once again the point is that God takes special delight in the restoration of the sinner who has been lost from his People.

A drachma is probably about a day's wage for a day laborer. The coins likely represent the family nest egg, there to buffer against difficult times or to meet special needs. The one coin represents a significant part of the woman's savings. With a lamp to catch the glint of the coin and a broom to make it tinkle, she searches with care for her coin. Naturally enough, the woman is not content with what remains to her but makes every effort to retrieve her lost coin.

When the coin has been found, she invites her friends and neighbors to share in her joy. The coin has become more important to her in its recovery than it had been originally as part of her nest egg. In the wider setting there is a challenge to actively identify with the joy that results from the restoration of a sinner to God.

V 10 applies the parable to God. God is no more content than is the woman with what remains to him when some of his People are lost from him in their sin. The penitent sinner is a source of great joy to God.

The Father and His Two Sons: "We Had to Make Merry" (15:11–32)

Bibliography

Aus, R. D. "Die Rückkehr des verlorenen Sohnes: Motive aus der jüdischen Josefüberlieferung in Lukas 15,11–32." In *Weihnachtsgeschichte, Barmherziger Samariter, Verlorener Sohn: Studien zu ihrem jüdischen Hintergrund.* Arbeiten zur neutestamentlichen Theologie und Zeitgeschichte 2. Berlin: Institut Kirchen und Judentum, 1988. 126–73. ———. "Luke 15:11–32 and R. Eliezer ben Hyrcanus's Rise to Fame." *JBL* 104 (1985) 443–69. **Austin, M. R.** "The Hypocritical Son." *EvQ* 57 (1985) 307–15. **Bailey, K. E.** *Poet and Peasant.* 158–206. **Betz, O.** "Die Bedeutung von Psalm 103 für das Werk Jesu." *TB* 15 (1984) 253–69, esp. 263–65. **Blinzler, J.** "Gottes grosse Freude über die Umkehr des Sünders: Lk 15:11–32." *BLit* 37 (1963–64) 21–28. **Bornhäuser, K.** *Studien zum Sondergut des Lukas.* Gütersloh: Bertelsmann, 1934. 103–37. **Brandenburg, H.** *Das Gleichnis vom verlorenen Sohn.* 2nd ed. Gladbach: Schriftenmissions-V., 1959. **Braumann, G.** "Tot-Lebendig, verloren-gefunden (Lk 15,24 und 32)." In *Wort in der Zeit: Neutestamentliche Studien.* FS K. H. Rengstorf, ed. W. Haubeck and M. Bachmann. Leiden: Brill, 1964. 156–64. **Broer, I.** "Das Gleichnis vom verlorenen Sohn und die Theologie des Lukas." *NTS* 20 (1973–74) 453–62. **Carlston, C. E.** "A Positive Criterion of Authenticity?" *BR* 7 (1962) 33–44. ———. "Reminiscence and Redaction in Luke 15:11–32." *JBL* 94 (1975) 368–90. **Cerfaux, L.** "Trois rehabilitations dans l'évangile." In *Recueil Lucien Cerfaux.* Gembloux: Duculot, 1954. 2:51–59. **Cloete, G. D.,** and **Smit, D. J.** "'Rejoicing with God . . .' (Luke 15:11–31)." *JTSA* 66 (1989) 62–73. **Compton, J. E.** "The Prodigal's Brother." *ExpTim* 42 (1930–31) 287. **Corlett, T.** "This *brother* of yours." *ExpTim* 100 (1989) 216. **Couffignal, R.** "Un Père au coeur d'or: Approches nouvelles de Luc 15,11–32." *RevThom* 1 (1991) 95–111. **Crawford, R. G.** "A Parable of the Atonement." *EvQ* 50 (1978) 2–7. **Crossan, J. D.,** ed. *Polyvalent Narration* [= *Semeia* 9] Missoula, MT: Society of Biblical Literature, 1977. **Daube, D.** "Inheritance in Two Lukan Pericopes." *ZSSR* 72 (1955) 326–34. **Dauvillier, J.** "Le partage d'ascendant et la parabole du fils prodigue." In *Actes du Congrès de Droit Canonique: Cinquantenaire, 1947.* Bibliotheque de la Faculté de Droit Canonique de Paris. Paris: Letouzey et Ané, 1950. 223–28. **Derrett, J. D. M.** "Law in the New Testament: The Parable of the Prodigal Son." *NTS* 14 (1967–68) 56–74. ———. "The Parable of the Prodigal Son: Patristic Allegories and Jewish Midrashim." *StudPat* 10 (1970) 219–24. **Dschulnigg, P.** "Gleichnis vom Kind, das zum Vater flieht (Josas 12,8)." *ZNW* 80 (1989) 269–71. **Du, J. Le.** *Le fils prodigue: ou les chances de la transgression.* Évangile 1. Saint-Brieuc: Sofec, 1974. **Dumais, M.** "Approche historico-critique d'un texte: La parabole du père et de ses deux fils (Luc 15, 11–32)." *ScEs* 33 (1981) 191–214. **Dupont, J.** *Béatitudes.* 2:237–42. ———. "L'Évangile (Lc 15,11–32): L'Enfant prodigue." *AsSeign* o.s. 29 (1966) 52–68. ———. "Le fils prodigue: Lc 15,1–3.11–32." *AsSeign* n.s. 17 (1969) 64–72. **Eichholz, G.** *Gleichnisse der Evangelien.* 200–220. **Faley, R. J.** "'There was once a man who had two sons. . . .'" *BiTod* 1 (1965) 1181–86. **Fiedler, P.** *Jesus und die Sünder.* 155–72, 337–40. **Fuchs, E.** "Das Fest der Verlorenen: Existentiale Interpretation des Gleichnisses vom verlorenen Sohn." In *Glaube und Erfahrung: Zum christologischen Problem im Neuen Testament.* Tübingen: Mohr-Siebeck, 1965. 402–15. **Funk, R. W.** *The Poetics of Biblical Narrative.* Foundations and Facets. Literary Facets. Sonoma, CA: Polebridge, 1988. Esp. 177–83. **Giblet, J.** "La parabole de l'accueil messianique (Luc 15, 11–32)." *BVC* 47 (1962) 17–28. **Gibson, G. S.** "The Sins of the Saints." *ExpTim* 96 (1984–85) 276–77. **Golenvaux, C.** "L'Enfant prodigue." *BVC* 94 (1970) 88–93. **Goppelt, L.** *Theology of the New Testament: Vol. 1. The Ministry of Jesus in Its Theological Significance,* ed. J. Roloff. Tr. J. Alsup. Grand Rapids: Eerdmans, 1981. 124, 129–38. **Gourgues, M.** "Le père prodigue (Lc 15,

11–32): De l'exégèse à l'actualisation." *NRT* 114 (1992) 3–20. **Grelot, P.** "Le père et ses deux fils: Luc, xv, 11–32: Essai d'analyse structurale." *RB* 84 (1977) 321–48. ———. "Le père et ses deux fils: Luc, XV, 11–32 (Fin): De l'analyse structurale à l'herméneutique." *RB* 84 (1977) 538–65. **Harrington, W.** "The Prodigal Son." *Furrow* 25 (1974) 432–37. **Heininger, B.** *Sondergutgleichnisse.* 146–66. **Hiroishi, N.** "Die Gleichniserzählung vom verlorenen Sohn (Lk 15,11–32): Eine form- und traditionsgeschichtliche Untersuchung der Gleichniserzählung Jesu im lukanischen Sondergut." *AJBI* 16 (1990) 71–99. **Hirsch, E.** *Frühgeschichte des Evangeliums.* Tübingen: Mohr-Siebeck, 1941. 2:220–23. **Hofius, O.** "Alttestamentliche Motive im Gleichnis vom verlorenen Sohn." *NTS* 24 (1977–78) 240–48. **Hoppe, R.** "Gleichnis und Situation: Zu den Gleichnisses vom guten Vater (Lk 15,11–32) und gütigen Hausherrn (Mt 20,1–15)." *BZ* 28 (1984) 1–21, esp. 3–13. **Jeremias, J.** *Parables.* 87, 105, 128–32. ———. "Zum Gleichnis vom verlorenen Sohn." *TZ* 5 (1949) 228–31. ———. "Tradition und Redaktion in Lukas 15." *ZNW* 62 (1971) 172–89. **Jones, G. V.** *The Art and Truth of the Parables.* London: SPCK, 1964. 167–205. **Jones, P.** "La parabole du fils prodigue: Deux méthodes d'interpretation." *RevRef* 34 (1983) 122–37. **Jülicher, A.** *Gleichnisreden.* 2:333–65. **Jüngel, E.** *Paulus und Jesus: Eine Untersuchung zur Präzisierung der Frage nach dem Ursprung der Christologie.* 2nd ed. Tübingen: Mohr-Siebeck, 1964. 160–64. **Kloepfer, R.** "Der verschwenderische Sohn: Ein ungewöhnlich fruchtbares Gleichnis." In *Die Sprache der Bilder: Gleichnis und Metaphor in Literatur und Theologie,* ed. H. Weder. Gütersloh: Mohn, 1989. 56–75. **Klötzli, E.** *Ein Mensch hatte zwei Söhne: Eine Auslegung von Lukas 15,11–32.* Zürich/Frankfurt: Gotthelf, 1966. **Kögel, J.** *Das Gleichnis vom verlorenen Sohn.* Biblische Zeit- und Streitfragen 5/9. Berlin: Runge, 1909. **Kruse, H.** "The Return of the Prodigal: Fortunes of a Parable on Its Way to the Far East." *Orientalia* 47 (1978) 163–214. **Linnemann, E.** *Jesus of the Parables.* 73–81. **Lohfink, G.** "Das Gleichnis vom Gütiger Vater." *BibLeb* 13 (1972) 138–46. ———. "Ich habe gesündigt gegen hen Himmel und gegen dich! (Lk 15,18.21)." *TQ* 155 (1975) 51–52. **Magass, W.** "Geben, Nehmen, Teilen als Tischsequenz in Lk 15,11–32." *LingBib* 37 (1976) 31–48. **Marsch, E.** *Die verlorenen Söhne: Konstitution und Redaktion in der Parabel.* FS H. Stirnimann, ed. J. Brantschen and P. Selvatico. Unterwegs zur Einheit. Fribourg: Publications universitaires, 1980. 29–45. **Niebuhr, K.-W.** "Kommunikationsebenen im Gleichnis vom verlorenen Sohn." *TLZ* 116 (1991) 481–94. **O'Rourke, J. J.** "Some Notes on Luke xv. 11–32." *NTS* 18 (1971–72) 431–33. **Osborn, R. T.** "The Father and His Two Sons: A Parable of Liberation." *Dialog* 19 (1980) 204–9. **Patte, D.** "Structural Analysis of the Parable of the Prodigal Son: Toward a Method." In *Semiology and Parables.* 71–149 (discussion 151–78). **Penning de Vries, P.** "Der nie verlorene Vater (Lk 15, 11–32)." *GuL* 44 (1971) 74–75. **Perkins, P.** *Hearing the Parables.* New York: Paulist, 1981. 53–62, 134–36. **Pesch, R.** "Zur Exegese Gottes durch Jesus von Nazaret: Eine Auslegung des Gleichnisses vom Vater und den beiden Söhnen (Lk 15,11–32)." In *Jesus: Ort der Erfahrung Gottes.* FS B. Welte, ed. B. Casper. Freiburg im Bayern: Herder, 1976. 140–89. **Pirot, J.** "Asseignements doctrinaux de la parable de 'l'Enfant prodigue.'" *AnnThéol* 8 (1947) 262–73, 299–308. **Poensgen, H.** *Die Befreiung einer verlorenen Beziehung: Eine biblisch-homiletische Untersuchung zu Lk 15:11–32 unter besonderer Berücksichtigung familientherapeutischer Erkenntnisse.* Europäische Hochschulschriften, Reihe 23: Theologie 330. Frankfurt/Bern/New York/Paris: Lang, 1989. **Pöhlmann, W.** "Die Absichtung des verlorenen Sohnes (Lk 15:12f.) und die erzählte Welt der Parabel." *ZNW* 70 (1979) 194–213. **Price, J. L.** "Luke 15:11–32." *Int* 31 (1977) 64–69. **Rau, E.** *Reden in Vollmacht: Hintergrund, Form und Anliegen der Gleichnisse Jesu.* FRLANT 149. Göttingen: Vandenhoeck & Ruprecht, 1990. **Rengstorf, K. H.** *Die Re-investitur des verlorenen Sohnes in der Gleichniserzählung Jesu: Luk. 15, 11–33.* AFLN-WG 137. Cologne/Opladen: Westdeutscher-V., 1967. **Richards, W. L.** "Another Look at the Parable of the Two Sons." *BR* 23 (1978) 5–14. **Rickards, R. R.** "Some Points to Consider in Translating the Parable of the Prodigal Son (Lk 15,11–32)." *BT* 31 (1980) 243–45. **Robbins, J.** *Prodigal Son/Elder Brother: Interpretation and Alterity in Augustine, Petrarch, Kafka, Levinas.* Religion and Postmodernism. Chicago: University Press, 1991. **Robilliard, J. A.** "La Parabole du fils aîné: Jésus et l'amour miséricordieux." *VSpir* 106 (1962) 531–44. **Rosenkranz, G.** "Das Gleichnis vom verlorenen Sohn im Lotos-Sûtra und im Lukasevangelium." *TLZ* 79 (1954) 281–82. **Rubsys, A. L.** "The Parable of the Forgiving Father." In *Readings in Biblical Morality*, ed. C. L. Salm. Englewood Cliffs, NJ: Prentice-Hall, 1967. 103–8. **Sanders, J. T.** "Tradition and Redaction in Luke xv. 11–32." *NTS* 15 (1968–69) 433–38. **Schnider, F.** *Die verlorene Söhne: Sturkturanalytische und historisch-kritische Untersuchung zu Lk 15.* OBO 17. Freiburg/Göttingen: Editions universitaires/Vandenhoeck & Ruprecht, 1977. **Schniewind, J.** "Das Gleichnis vom verlorenen Sohn." In *Die Freude der Busse: Zur Grundfrage der Bibel.* 2nd ed. Göttingen: Vandenhoeck & Ruprecht, 1960. 34–87. **Schottroff, L.** "Das Gleichnis vom verlorenen Sohn." *ZTK* 68 (1971) 27–52. **Schweizer, E.** "Zur Frage der Lukasquellen, Analyse von Luk. 15,11–32." *TZ* 4 (1948) 469–71. ————. "Antwort." *TZ* 5 (1949) 231–33. **Scobel, G.** "Das Gleichnis vom verlorenen Sohn als metakommunikativer Text: Überlegungen zur Verständnisproblematik in Lukas 15." *FZPT* 35 (1988) 21–67. **Scott, B. B.** "The Prodigal Son: A Structuralist Interpretation." In *Polyvalent Narration*, ed. J. D. Crossan. 45–73. **Smit Sibinga, J.** "Zur Kompositionstechnik des Lukas in Lk 15:11–32." In *Tradition and Re-interpretation in Jewish and Early Christian Literature.* FS J. C. H. Lebram, by J. W. Van Henten et al. Studia postbiblica 36. Leiden: Brill, 1988. 97–113. **Stickler, H. E.** "The Prodigal's Brother." *ExpTim* 42 (1930–31) 45–46. **Strunk, R.**, and **Mausshardt, M.** "Leistung des Schöpferischen (Lk 15,11–32)." In *Doppeldeutlich*, ed. Y. Spiegel. Munich: Kaiser, 1978. 59–78. **Tolbert, M. A.** "The Prodigal Son: An Essay in Literary Criticism from a Psychoanalytic Perspective." In *Polyvalent Narration*, ed. J. D. Crossan. 1–20; revised and expanded in *Perspectives on the Parables.* 93–114. **Via, D. O., Jr.** "The Prodigal Son: A Jungian Reading." In *Polyvalent Narration*, ed. J. D. Crossan. 21–43. **Vogel, H.-J.** "Der verlorene Sohn: Lukas 15,11–32." *TK* 18 (1983) 27–34. **Weder, H.** *Gleichnisse Jesu.* 252–62. **Zauner, W.** "Busse als Fest: Eine Busspredigt zu Lk 15,11–32 (der barmherzige Vater—der heimgekehrte Sohn—der daheimgebliebene Bruder)." *TPQ* 134 (1986) 280–82.

Translation

[11]*He said, "A certain man had two sons.* [12]*The younger of them said to the father, 'Father, give me the portion of the property due [to me].' He divided the estate.* [13]*After not many days the younger son gathered up everything and journeyed to a distant land and there he squandered his property by living dissolutely.*

[14]*"When he had spent everything, there was a severe famine in that land and he began to be in want.* [15]*So he went and joined himself to one of the citizens of that land, who*[a] *sent him into his fields to feed pigs.* [16]*He would have liked to fill his belly*[b] *with the carob pods which the pigs were eating and nobody gave him [anything].*

[17]*"Coming to himself, he said, 'How many hired hands of my father have an abundance of bread; and I am perishing here in a famine.* [18]*I will set off*[c] *and go to my father and I will say to him, "Father, I have sinned against heaven and before you;* [19]*I am no longer worthy to be called your son. Instate me as*[d] *one of your hired hands."'* [20]*So he set off*[e] *and came to his father.*

"While he was still far off, his father saw him and had compassion, and he ran and fell upon his neck and kissed him. [21]*The son said, 'Father, I have sinned against heaven and before you; I am no longer worthy to be called your son.'*[f] [22]*The father said to his slaves, 'Quickly,*[g] *bring out*[h] *the best robe and put it on him; and provide a ring for his hand and sandals for [his] feet;* [23]*and bring the fatted calf, make the kill, and let us eat and make merry;* [24]*because this, my son, was dead and has come back to life again;*[i] *he was lost and has been found. So they began*[j] *to make merry.*

[25]*"His elder son was in the fields and as he came along and drew near to the house he heard music and dancing.* [26]*So calling one of the servants he inquired what this might*

be. [27]*He said to him, 'Your brother has come, and your father has killed the fatted calf, because he received him safe and sound.'*[k] [28]*He was angry and refused to go in. Then his*[l] *father came out and entreated him,* [29]*but he answered his father, 'See how many years I have slaved for you and I never disobeyed a command of yours, and you never gave me a goat*[m] *so that I could make merry with my friends;* [30]*but when this son of yours came, who has consumed your estate with prostitutes, you killed the fatted calf for him!'* [31]*He said to him, 'Child, you are always with me, and all that I have is yours!* [32]*We had to make merry and rejoice, because this, your brother, was dead and has come alive,*[n] *[was]*[o] *lost and has been found.' "*

Notes

[a] Lit. "and he sent."

[b] Reading γεμίσαι τὴν κοιλίαν αὐτοῦ with A Θ Ψ etc., rather than the better attested χορτασθῆναι, "to have his hunger satisfied" (P[75] ℵ B D L etc.), which is likely to be a tasteful correction.

[c] Lit. "arise."

[d] Or "treat me like."

[e] Lit. "arose."

[f] Many of the best texts (ℵ B D 33 700 1241 etc.) have here the full form of the prepared confession of vv 18–19. As this is a natural scribal "restoration," the shorter reading of P[75] A L W Θ Ψ $f^{1,13}$ etc. is followed.

[g] Missing from A W Θ Ψ f^1 etc.

[h] P[75] 579 etc. have ἐνέγκατε, "bring."

[i] B 579 etc. read ἔζησεν, "he came to life," which is likely to be original in v 32.

[j] P[75] 1 579 etc. have ἤρξατο, "he began."

[k] Lit. "being healthy."

[l] "The father" in ℵ L W Θ Ψ etc.

[m] ἐρίφιον, "young goat," in P[75] B etc.

[n] ℵ[2] A D W Θ Ψ etc. read ἀνέζησεν, "he has come back to life again," as in v 23.

[o] The verb ἦν, "was," is found only in ℵ 346 1006 1342 etc., but is included in the majority text as well. It is present in v 23.

Form/Structure/Setting

This third parable completes the section 15:1–32. The "joy in heaven" in vv 7, 10 orients the reader to link the father's experience in the present parable with that divine joy. The linking of the three parables also raises the profile in the present parable of the motif of repentance and that of shared joy. The prodigal and the elder brother of the parable are to be linked on the one hand to the tax collectors and sinners and on the other hand to the Pharisees and scribes of vv 1–2.

See discussion at 15:1–7 for the likelihood that these parables were already linked prior to Luke. There are certain marks of Luke's stylistic intrusion into the parable, but there are also a considerable number of Semitisms of a kind that cannot be dismissed as Septuagintal imitations. There are also linguistic features that are unlikely to have originated from Luke's pen and, perhaps, indications that the parable related to the Hebrew OT and not the Greek (some of these features are noted below; for detailed discussion, see Schweizer, *TZ* 4 [1948] 469–71; id., *TZ* 5 [1949] 231–33; Jeremias, *TZ* 5 [1949] 228–31; *ZNW* 62 [1971] 172–89; Sanders, *NTS* 15 [1968–69] 433–38; O'Rourke, *NTS* 18 [1971–72] 431–33; Carlston, *JBL* 94 [1975] 368–83; Hofius, *NTS* 24 [1977–78] 246). These features are by no means restricted to the prodigal's story and count in favor of an original unity for the two halves of the story, as do certain features of the narrative itself (see *Comment*).

Individual elements in the story have by some been judged as Lukan or pre-Lukan additions. χαρῆναι, "to rejoice," in v 32 is not likely to be Lukan, but probably does represent an addition at the point when the three parables were united. Suspicion has been cast upon all or parts of vv 24 and 32, but it is best to take them as original components of the parable, though it is not impossible that the lost-and-found language has come in at the same point of union of the parables (see further below). Heininger (*Sondergutgleichnisse*, 147) has argued with some force that vv 18–19 are likely to be a Lukan development of the son's monologue. V 21 has also been accused, but in the absence of vv 18–19 it can no longer be seen as repetitive, and the story works better with it than without. In further detail, it is impossible to make fixed judgments about the degree of narrative embellishment by Luke or before him.

Attempts to identify all (esp. Schottroff, *ZTK* 68 [1971] 27–52) or even the second half (esp. Schweizer, *TZ* 4 [1948] 469–71; id., *TZ* 5 [1949] 231–33; Sanders, *NTS* 15 [1968–69] 433–38; Heininger, *Sondergutgleichnisse*, 146–53) of the parable as Lukan fail not only on the basis of the language indicators referred to above, but also because there is a real measure of tension between the parable and the theological preoccupations of Luke himself. Repentance does not play the role in the parable that it plays in Luke's theology, and the elder son is treated much too generously for Luke's own views to be coming directly to expression here.

The shape of the parable has been disputed in terms of the best title to give such a story. Does the story focus on the father, the prodigal, or the elder son? While Grelot's reading of the parable is considerably different from the reading offered here (*RB* 84 [1977] 321–48; 538–65), his threefold reading of the parable as the story of the trials (in turn) of each of the three main characters demonstrates the unsatisfactory nature of any straightforward answer to this question. The hearer/reader is required to identify emotionally in turn with each of the characters (though in the end the hearers finds themselves directly only in the elder son). The unity of the vision behind the story can be seen when we understand it to be a story designed by Jesus to put in perspective what was going on—what sinners were doing and what God was doing—as he (Jesus) consorted with sinners, and in this way to challenge the righteous to come and welcome these reclaimed brothers and to share in the celebration of their restoration.

Comment

In the ministry of Jesus, prodigals find the free and generous love of the Father. If they will but see it rightly, there is nothing here to disturb those most deeply concerned to live out the holiness of God; on the contrary they should recognize that they are regaining brothers, and they should come and join in the celebrations.

11 εἶπεν δέ, "and he said," may be a Lukan link, but ἄνθρωπός τις, "a certain man," is likely to be pre-Lukan (see at 10:30). There is a partial parallel with vv 4 and 8. The opening language of the parable prepares the hearer to expect a role in the story for each of the sons (cf. Matt 21:28).

12 The verb-subject word order here is the first of at least nine instances of this more Semitic word order in the parable. The concentration, though not the phenomenon as such, counts against Lukan formulation (see Carlston, *JBL* 94 [1975] 376). The legal use of τὸ ἐπιβάλλον μέρος, "the portion due," is documented in the papyri and inscriptions by Pöhlmann (*ZNW* 70 [1979] 204–5). The word used for "estate" (βίος) also means "life," "manner of life," "means of subsistence." The estate is what supports the life of the family. The legalities and the social consequences of such a settlement upon the younger son in the lifetime of his father have been painstakingly and repeatedly analyzed, but without the emergence of a clear consensus on some of the main points. There is no doubt that the younger son is initiating a breakdown of the solidarity of the family, but the precise details are only of limited importance for the telling of the story. The acquiescence of the father to the son's request is itself notable, but nothing is made of it in the account (since at this point in the story we do not know what the son is up to, we have little basis for assessing the father's action). The main issues of law and custom are as follows.

The disposition of part of an estate by gift during the lifetime of the donor would not normally impair claim upon the estate at the time of death (*m. B. Bat.* 8:7; Daube, *ZSSR* 72 [1955] 330), but such claim is clearly impaired in our story. There is some possibility, however, that a custom in line with Gen 25:5–6 survived in popular practice and allowed for a settlement upon younger sons, leaving the main estate intact for the eldest son (Daube, 330–33). Without throwing any light on the legal status of any remaining estate, the practice of (partial) disposition of an estate in the lifetime of its owner is reflected in Sir 33:19–23; Tob 8:21; *b. B. Meṣ.* 75b (critically in the first and last). The possibility of such a settlement in Greek and Egyptian practice provides some further support for its likelihood in a Jewish context as well (Pöhlmann, *ZNW* 70 [1979] 200 and n. 27). One would expect that such a settlement in a Jewish context would conform to the Jewish stipulation of a double share for the firstborn son (Deut 21:17). For the son to be the initiator of such a move is striking. While in principle one might excuse the action of the younger son in connection with the prospect of a coming marriage (cf. *m. B. Bat.* 8:7) or with the possibility of emigration to better his prospects in life (cf. Jeremias, *Parables*, 129), neither of these has any place in the intention of our story. That the father takes no positive view of the move is plain from his later talk of this son as "dead" and "lost" (without benefit of any knowledge of the son's subsequent lifestyle). Though the story makes only the slightest investment in this point, in requesting the settlement, the son is behaving abominably toward his father. Away from the influence of the father, the son will go from bad to worse.

Such a disposition need not involve any concurrent settlement upon the elder son, but in our case some such seems to be implied in "he divided the estate between them." Later in the story it is clear, however, that the elder son is not exercising the main control over the estate, and it might just be possible that "divided the estate" means only worked out who would ultimately get what, and implies conferral only in the case of the younger son. Rather more likely, however, is an assignment to the elder son in the manner attested in *m. B. Bat.* 8:7: this involves assignment of capital goods, but not of claim to their produce during the lifetime of the father ("from today and after my death" is the required legal wording of the assignment). In effect the father thereby retained a lifetime interest in the property. In such a situation the main responsibility for the lifetime support of the parents is clearly taken care of by the estate, but the normal Jewish responsibility for care of aging parents would still be incumbent upon each of the sons.

13 The figure of speech (litotes) involved in μετ' οὐ πολλὰς ἡμέρας ("after not many days" = "after a few days") is one favored by Luke (seventeen uses, including 21:9: Acts 1:5; 12:18; 14:28). συνάγειν, "to gather together," is used in Plutarch, *Cato Min.* 6.7 (672c) of converting an inheritance into cash, and may be so used here. εἰς χώραν μακράν, "to a distant land," is found also at 19:12. The noun cognate with ἀσώτως, "dissolutely," is associated with the dishonoring of one's father in Prov 28:7. The departure is treated as a separate stage in the development of the saga from the initial laying of claim to the inheritance. The squandering of the property in dissolute living comes as yet another step. In this way the hearer comes only gradually to appreciate the enormity of the "crime" intended by the younger son against his father.

14 Luke has a "severe famine" also in 4:25 and Acts 11:28, but there the adjectives are μέγας and μεγάλη, not the ἰσχυρά found here. Unstressed καί αὐτός, "and he," is a Lukanism (cf. Fitzmyer, 120, who does, however, allocate too many texts to this category). At the point when his money is gone and he becomes vulnerable, "nature" intervenes against this dissolute young man.

15 πορευθεὶς ἐκολλήθη (lit. "having gone he joined"; both of these verbs in the sense required here, along with the participial use, are notable in Luke) and the use of πολίτης, "citizen" (cf. the use at 19:14; Acts 21:39) may be Lukan (cf. Carlston, *JBL* 94 [1975] 370). The unsignaled change of subject (at "he sent") is likely to be Semitic (cf. O'Rourke, *NTS* 18 [1971–72] 431). The son's choice has been for freedom, but now as he takes a menial job, his pressing need reverses the direction of his choices. The nature of the work, however, takes him still a step further away from his beginning point with the father. For the Jewish repugnance for swine, see Lev 11:7; Deut 14:8; 1 Macc 1:47; *b. B. Qam.* 82b. The link with the foreigner may already be seen as compromising his Jewish loyalties (cf. Acts 10:28) and as interfering with his practice of the faith (e.g., sabbath).

16 If it is original here, the rather crude γεμίσαι τὴν κοιλίαν αὐτοῦ, "to fill his belly," is not likely to have been penned by Luke. Bailey (*Poet*, 171–73) may be right that the carob here is not the St. John's Bread (*ceratonia silqua*) with which it is usually identified (this has pods which, while not particularly nutritious, have a sweet pulp and are eaten regularly in the Middle East), but rather its wild cousin, which was much smaller and whose fruit was bitter and was not eaten except in desperation. It is not clear whether we should understand that he was supervised in such a way as to make it impossible for him to steal the pods or whether such meager fare could not successfully "fill his belly." Bailey (*Poet*, 171) cites a rabbinic saying: "Israel needs carob to be forced to repentance." The final clause could be taken in connection with the carob pods (then supervision is the issue), or it could be independent (in which case we should probably think of a lack of any public charity to indigents). His subsistence-level salary in the economic conditions induced by the famine led in reality to gradual starvation. The younger son has reached his lowest possible point before death.

17 The idiom εἰς ἑαυτὸν ἔρχεσθαι, "to come to himself," is known also in extrabiblical Greek (see BAGD, 311), as an idiom for coming to one's senses (the

Hebrew and Aramaic idioms cited by Str-B, 2:215, are not quite the same since they involve a turning). Luke quite likes rhetorical monologue, as here, and has introduced it into his text at 20:13 (cf. Mark 12:6). However, the transition to v 20 is abrupt without vv 17–19. Perhaps it is best, with Heininger (*Sondergut-gleichnisse,* 147), to take v 17 as original and vv 18–19 as Lukan expansion. The μίσθιοι, "hired hands," would not only be better off, but probably also considerably more their own persons than the younger son was in his servile status in the foreign land. While the use of ἀπολλύναι carries a different nuance here from that in vv 24 and 32 (here "perish," there "be lost"), the present use prepares for those to come. The contrast between the two situations propels the younger son to action.

18 ἀναστάς (lit. "having arisen") is somewhat pleonastic, but it does mark the beginning of the son's decisive change of direction. There is a certain parallel with the resolve of faithless Israel to return to her first husband in Hos 2:7b (cf. Hofius, *NTS* 24 [1977–78] 241). As in the former request (v 12), he plans again to address his father as "Father." For the confession of sin against God and human beings, cf. Exod 10:16. "Heaven" is here a periphrasis for "God" (cf. at v 10), while "against" (εἰς) and "before" (ἐνώπιον) are translation variants, for stylistic reasons, of a single Semitic preposition (Hebrew ל, *lĕ,* is rendered in the LXX by both of these Greek prepositions). While the basis of the son's repentance is clearly his own situation of desperate need, and a desire to improve his lot, it is wrong-headed to question his sincerity or to detect continuing pride in his bid to become an independent employee (against Bailey, *Poet,* 173–79). The presence of God on the story line is a reminder that we must let the parable have its own integrity as story and not to simply identify the father with God.

19 The son speaks truly in speaking of his unworthiness to be called son any longer. He is quite sure that he has burned his bridges with his father and no longer has any future in the family, but at the same time he seems confident that the father will accede to this suggestion from a son who comes back to the father and confesses his fault. While this would be no foregone conclusion in real life, the hearer has no reason to question the implied confidence of the repentant son.

20 The plans formulated in the soliloquy of vv 18–19 are now reported as event in v 20a and 21. The *going* of v 19 becomes a *coming* here as the perspective shifts from that of the son to that of the father. The verbal repetition draws additional attention to this part of the parable. Luke is likely to be responsible for the use of αὐτοῦ [οὐ] μακρὰν ἀπέχοντος (lit. "he [not] being far off") in 7:6 and so may be responsible for the same idiom here. The greater the distance the clearer it is that it is the father who actively initiates the restoration. The son can do no more than come within reach. For the motif of seeing the son before his actual arrival, cf. Tob 11:5–6. Though there is an inner link between the two activities, the return to the father is yet more important than the confession of sin, since this opens up the possibility of the father's welcome; what is more, the father's welcome precedes the confession, and even qualifies it. The movement of compassion here is to be compared to that in 7:13 (Jesus to the widow of Nain) and 10:33 (the Samaritan to the man who had fallen among thieves). The language of the father's action here is likely to be based upon that of the classic reconciliation scene between Jacob and Esau (Gen 33:4; cf. Hofius, *NTS* 24 [1977–78] 242–43, 245–46; Hofius points out that the LXX wording is not reflected; Carlston,

JBL 94 [1975] 371–72, claims Gen 45:14–15 LXX as background, but it is not as close; cf. also Gen 46:29; 2 Sam 14:33; Tob 11:9; 3 Mac 5:49; etc.). There is here no qualified acceptance or cautious reception of the son but rather a wholehearted acceptance and an uninhibited expression of delight in the return of the son. Once he recognizes the figure in the distance as his son, the father cares not a whit about the fitting dignity of his years and station! (cf. Bailey, *Poet*, 181–82). The son may not be worthy any more to be called son, but, without need of words, the father has made it quite clear that he has regained a son. While this is clearly not the reaction of every father, it is a credible action of a father in such a situation (we have its fraternal equivalent in Gen 33:4; parental affection is reflected upon as a potential basis for action in the OT [Ps 103:13 (Betz, *TB* 15 [1984] 264–65, considers that this text lies behind the parable, but Jer 31:20, cf. vv 17–19, has just as good a claim); Mal 3:17], in Jewish tradition [*Gen. Rab.* 49:8; *Midr. Ps.* 9:1; etc.), and in the Greek and Roman rhetorical tradition [see esp. the story from Quintilian, *Declamation* 19, cited by Schottroff, *ZTK* 68 (1971) 45]).

21 The son does not conclude that his prepared confession has now become irrelevant. It may even be fair to say that the welcome he has just experienced makes it yet more pressingly appropriate. Now, perhaps he can see more clearly than when the words of confession were formulated the depths of his own failure. In one respect, however, his words must be altered. After this initial meeting, to say, "Instate me/treat me as one of your hired hands" would be to insult his father's love. This clause disappears from the prepared piece (this is better than making v 22 an interruption). One could have a coherent story without v 21 (as Fiedler, *Jesus*, 166; followed by Hoppe, *BZ* 28 [1984] 9), but the drama of the story is more effective with v 21, and there is no adequate basis for questioning its place in the original story. For the confession, cf. 18:13 (and compare the Pharisee's prayer with the elder son's words in 15:29).

22 The developments in vv 22–24 only indicate what was already entailed in the wordless scene of v 20b. The clothing details are often interpreted in connection with Gen 41:42 (and cf. also 1 Mac 6:15). There Joseph is being instated in high office, but Esth 6:6–11 (cf. also 8:2) may be a better comparison with its concern with "the man whom [the king] delights to honor." *στολὴν τὴν πρώτην* may be "the best robe," and thus perhaps the best of the father's own wardrobe (cf. Esth 6:8), or just possibly "the former robe," and thus the clothing that marked the son's place in the family before his departure. Despite the normal assumption, "a ring" will not be the signet ring of the father (Evans, 594, realizes this): the son is being honored, but not made the plenipotentiary of his father as Joseph and Mordecai were made plenipotentiaries of the Pharaoh and king, respectively. The shoes for the feet remind us of the son's straitened circumstances—he has made the journey from the faraway land barefoot (again, though often repeated, the point will not be that he is treated as a free man and not a slave). The son undergoes in an instant a dramatic and unexpected change of circumstances and status. The development in v 23 confirms the view that v 22 has to do with honoring rather than with reinvestment with authority.

23 The phrase "the fatted calf" occurs in the same form in the LXX of Judg 6:28 (perhaps interpreting a reading of the Hebrew as referring to a one-year-old beast) and in the indefinite plural in the LXX of Jer 26:21 (which reflects accurately the MT of 46:1), but no particular link with these texts is warranted. The

MT of 1 Sam 28:24 is rather closer. For the role of such a slaughter in the honoring of guests, cf. Gen 18:7–8. This provision of the fatted calf is more significant in first-century Palestine than it might appear to us, since meat was normally eaten only on special festive occasions (normally religious). Hours of preparation are covered by this directive. The note of celebration here is paralleled by that in 12:19; but there it was a means of private self-congratulation, while here it is a matter of joy shared in celebration. In the present sequence of parables, this is the same shared joy as that of vv 6 and 9 (and cf. vv 7 and 10), and the linking of the parables gives a higher profile to the joy motif in the third parable than would be evident in a reading of the parable as a separate item.

24 The presence of this verse in the original parable is occasionally questioned (e.g., Braumann, "Tot-Lebendig," 156–64 [who argues that vv 24, 32 were added to apply the parable to a baptismal setting]; Nützel, *Offenbarer Gottes*, 248–49). The language of lost and found could have been imported into the parable at the point of union with vv 4–10, but it is partly prepared for in v 17 (see above). The language of death and coming to life could be baptismal in a Pauline context, but hardly in Luke, and is somewhat prepared for in v 16. The language here is indeed striking, and while it does not actually break the bounds of the story, it comes closer to being immediately symbolic than at other points of the parable (the father does not use the language primarily in connection with the son's experiences in the distant land—he does not know about this except by supposition, and minimally from the state in which he finds his son—but in connection with his own "bereavement" and "finding again" of his son: the language is relational). Again the story is more powerful with vv 24 and 32 than without, and there is no adequate reason for treating the verses as additions (if anything has been added, it will be the lost-and-found language). The role of the younger son comes to a close with the beginnings of the party to celebrate his homecoming. The noise of this same celebration becomes the beginning point for the drama that is now to unfold in connection with the elder son.

25 The elder son has been waiting in the wings to take a role in the parable since vv 11–12. *ἐν ἀγρῷ* (lit. "in [a] field") is probably quasi-adverbial and so best rendered "in the fields." The economic level of the family was such that the family was actively involved in supervising and perhaps sharing in the manual work of the farm. Three-way conversations are avoided in the parables, and so it has been useful to have the elder son out of the way for the reconciliation scene. The narrative technique involves allowing the elder son to discover through a series of steps what has transpired in his absence. *συμφωνία* is etymologically the coordination of sounds and is used for "music," "band/orchestra," or for a particular instrument producing more than a single note at a time (double flute and bagpipe are proposed). The last is uncalled for here. *χορῶν* here could be "singers" or "dancers" (the latter from the tendency for such dancing to be accompanied by choral singing).

26 The use of *πυνθάνεσθαι*, "to inquire," along with its optative form may indicate Lukan formulation here (cf. Carlston, *JBL* 94 [1975] 372), as may the use of the *εἷς*, "one," + gen. construction (cf. Fitzmyer, 121–22).

27 The use of *ὑγιαίνειν*, "to be in good health," may be Lukan (5:31; cf. Mark 2:17). The servant's version of developments reflects the naturalness of the father's response, and thus in effect "supports" the father over against the reaction of the elder son about to be described.

28 An explanation of the elder son's anger is delayed until the conversation with the father. Though there is some measure of similarity between this son refusing to go into the house and the alienation of the younger son, and between the coming out of the father to speak with this son and the father's running to greet the younger son, there are no linguistic pointers to suggest that our interpretation should be guided by any sense of parallelism: the elder son is angry about the action of the father, rather than alienated from the father; the father is seeking his son's entry into the joy of restoration, appropriate to the return of the younger son, not the restoration of the elder son.

29 The frequently noted failure to address his father as "father" fits in with the angry tone, but should not be over-interpreted. Similarly, the presence of *δουλεύω*, "be/do the work of a slave," is more to point up the contrast with the ways of his younger sibling than to express fully the attitude he has adopted over the years or the nature of the service he has provided to the father (cf. the use of the same verb in the heated language of Gen 31:41). It is important not to Paulinize this language (note the very positive use of the cognate *δοῦλος*, "slave" in Luke 2:29). For the obedience of a son to his father's commandments, see Prov 2:1; 3:1; Sir 3:1 (3:7 has *δουλεύειν*, "be/do the work of a slave," of service to parents); etc. Deut 26:13 specifies as part of the tithe-time recitation before God "I have not transgressed any of your commandments." This all sticks in the elder son's throat now because of the fuss that is being made over that son for whom none of this is true! The splendid reception accorded to the prodigal causes the elder son to look back over his life of service and resent the failure of the father to provide him with recognition for his services. It is not a goat as such that he wants (it is not a question of niggardliness on the part of the father), but recognition (the imagery is of a mini-version of the reception of the younger son—only a goat, not a much more prized fatted calf; only a little occasion with my friends, not the conspicuous celebration currently taking place). Luke 17:7–10 addresses in another parable precisely this demand for recognition. Here is a yet more extreme version of the complaint of Matt 20:11: "These last worked only one hour, and you have made them equal to us who have borne the burden of the day and the scorching heat." From the elder son's point of view, his father had made the prodigal not only equal but superior.

30 While "this, your son" distances the elder son from his brother, the language also echoes wording from v 24: "this, my son." *βίος* (here: "estate"; see discussion at v 12) is used as in v 12, rather than the *οὐσία*, "property," of vv 11, 13. The elder brother is not forgetting the distribution of v 12: he thinks in terms of the accumulated family wealth the father had husbanded, which was designed to be the basis of livelihood for the family from generation to generation. The younger son has broken the chain and squandered what had been (part of) his father's livelihood and should have been kept intact for his own livelihood and that of his own sons in turn. The mention of consorting with prostitutes is new information, but is surely meant to be taken as a specification of 13, and not as a slander. Prov 29:3 may be echoed. The paradox of failing to honor the honorable, while giving honor to the dishonorable is shown up by the elder brother in stark colors. This paradox was even more striking in the ancient world, where issues of honor and shame were of considerably greater importance than in modern Western societies.

31 Though not addressed by his son as "father," the father in response addresses his son affectionately as "child." The father does not question the son's description of things, but he does address the son's sense of having been shortchanged in comparison with his brother. There has been no displacement of the elder son: his place at the father's side is as secure as ever, and his claim upon the family inheritance is in no way disturbed by this new development. The father's commitments are fully intact (cf. Matt 20:13). Since the terms of division made in v 12 are now confirmed, we may feel inclined to ask about where this leaves the younger son, so far as his long-term economic future. But this part of the parable is no longer about the restoration of the younger son. His future in respect to the legal situation is not addressed, because this is the one point at which the imagery of the parable could break down.

The interpretations that are highly critical of the elder brother cannot begin to do justice to this verse. It is also very hard to imagine Luke independently penning the words of this verse.

32 χαρῆναι, "to rejoice," may echo the language of vv 6–7, 9–10, and have been added at the point when the parables were united. It would be attractive to focus on the ambiguity of the ἔδει (the Greek is literally "it was necessary to make merry and rejoice") if the imperfect tense did not specify that the father is explaining what is already transpiring, not canvassing a present necessity. οὗτος, "this," is taken up from v 31, but the father insists upon the fraternal relationship, and thus implicitly renews his appeal for the brother to join in the celebration. If it is true that the younger son has been restored to his father, it is just as true that the younger son has, within the family, been restored to his brother. The challenge to the elder son is to recognize in what has transpired just such an enrichment of the family, and thus of himself, and to enter into the joy of celebration.

Thus far we have explored only the inner life of the story. For what kind of people was such a story formulated, and how was it intended to address them? The contours of the story that have emerged above are best suited by seeing the parable as an interpretation of what was visible to Jesus' contemporaries as his friendship with tax collectors and sinners (Luke 7:34; cf. 15:1). For all who were concerned with holiness before God, including the Pharisees and scribes, this behavior was potentially troubling. Jesus invites such listeners to realize that in this situation these needy people, who have come to the end of themselves, are finding the free and generous love of the Father in heaven. In being prepared to open up to Jesus, they have come within reach of God's present initiative. God has embraced them in overwhelming compassion as one who is delighted at the return of his prodigal sons. They have indeed recognized the error of their ways, but that is not particularly the point (there is no test of genuineness; the father's acceptance precedes the confession); what matters is that they have been restored to the Father. The only proper course of action is celebration: these newly returned sons should, so to speak, be decked out in the best of the family finery, and honored and fêted. This may seem hard to those who have borne the heat and burden of the day, but it is God's way. There is nothing here to threaten God's faithful sons. Their place with God remains secure; their inheritance is undisturbed. But they should not imagine that they have a claim upon God that excludes others. Nor should they imagine that their faithful efforts place God in their debt (cf. 17:7–10), or oblige him to give them some distinctive recognition. Like the returned prodigals, no more and no less, they are the Father's dear children, objects of his parental affection. The challenge to them is to recognize and to rejoice in this rescue operation now proceeding apace. They should come on in and join the party.

In the Lukan setting the story is more generous to the Gospel Pharisees and scribes than might have been expected (cf. Carlston's important observations in this connection [*JBL* 94 (1975) 387–88] about the unsuitability of the early church as a setting for developing a story like this, which accepts as well as criticizes the elder son). Luke may read the story on the basis of the refusal of the Pharisees and scribes to come in, and of the resistance of their heirs to the coming in of that larger group of prodigals: the Gentiles. For Luke, and for the parables compiler before him, the place of repentance gains a higher profile than it intrinsically has in the story, because of vv 7 and 10.

Explanation

This large parable completes the section 15:1–32. The "joy in heaven" of the earlier parables prepares us for thinking of the parable father in close connection with God, and also causes us to come to the parable with images of discovery, repentance, and shared joy. The parable itself helps us to see that in the ministry of Jesus, sinners, who in their need draw near, are finding the free and generous love of the heavenly Father. Despite the elder son's misgivings, there is nothing here that should disturb those who are concerned with holy living; here the faithful are regaining lost brothers whom they should welcome and whose restoration they should celebrate.

In this story, each of the two sons will have his period of centrality for the development of the story line. At first we do not know quite what to make of the younger son cashing in his share of the family inheritance. From the start it is evident that he is initiating a breakdown of the solidarity of the family, and as the story develops, it becomes clear that his motivations are all bad ones. The father gives him what he wants and lets him go, but away from the father the younger son only goes from bad to worse. Turning his inheritance into cash finances a grand spree for a time, but he has no bottomless purse from which to draw, and soon the good times are over.

The arrival of a famine only hastens the process whereby the younger son's foolish choices catch up with him. The young man has chosen freedom and extravagance: the freedom he must give up for a menial job which, in place of his extravagance, can finance nothing more than slow starvation. Yet even this desperate move has taken him a step further away from home: in this employ he would no longer be free to practice his Jewish faith without compromise, and here he is caring for swine, which are so repugnant to Jewish sensibilities. In his desperation he would have been glad for pig food, but his foreman was watching too closely for him to effectively pilfer as he worked.

In the school of hard knocks, the young man came to a new appreciation of the situation he had left behind. He assumes that he has burned his bridges with his father and no longer has any future in the family, but even the day laborers at home have things much better than he does now. In his desperation he formulates a plan: he will go home and confess his fault to his father, and beg for a job as a day laborer on the family estate. He has good hopes that his father will accede to his proposal. The son is now prepared to recognize his need and his fault, and to ask for help.

The camera shifts now from the son to the father. Though it is the son who comes back, it is the father who takes the initiative in the restoration of the family relationship. The son can do no more than to come within reach; he does not even realize what is possible with the father. Once having recognized his son, the father cares not a whit about the fitting dignity of his years and station. He does not wait for words of explanation or confession. The son has no need to prove himself. He has come back and he is at once the object of his father's overwhelming compassion (cf. Ps 103:13; Jer 31:17–20). After a passionate embrace, the son makes his confession, perhaps with rather more meaning because of what he has just experienced, yet with one modification: it would be to insult the father's love to ask now to be made a servant; he has clearly been restored as son. That this is so finds its confirmation in the directives to the servants. His tattered garments are to be covered with the best robe; the feet that have made the long journey without footwear are to be outfitted; his hand that has become a laborer's hand is to be decorated with a fine dress ring. Finally his emaciated body is to be nourished with the fatted calf, which is to be killed and dressed as pièce de résistance in the banquet at which all will make merry over this happy outcome. There is nothing less to celebrate than life from death (the father's "bereavement" has been reversed), the finding again of what had been lost (just like the sheep and the coin). While it may be painted here in vivid colors, this father's reaction, although it would not be that of every father, is an understandable parental reaction.

The elder brother did not take full possession of his share of the property when the division was made. Rather, in accord with an available Jewish custom, the father transferred ownership, to take effect at the time of his own death, retaining for himself the lifetime use of the produce of the estate. So the elder son, though holding title to the estate, had continued to work on the estate under the authority of his father. Conscientiously on the job, he only discovers little by little what has transpired while he has been busy in the fields.

To the servant who fills in the elder son, the father's practice is accepted as natural. The elder brother does not, however, find it so. He is angered and refuses to go in and thus give his approval to this development. The father implores him to come in. And this releases the flood of protest. He has been a model son. He has done everything his father ever asked of him. He has "slaved" for his father's benefit. But he has never had the recognition now accorded to the prodigal. How can it be that *he* deserves such a fuss? The prodigal gets a big party while the elder son has never even been given a little party with his friends! This is Matt 20:11 over again, but with a vengeance: "These last worked only one hour, and you have made them equal to us who have borne the burden of the day and the scorching heat." To the elder brother this honor to the dishonorable and failure to honor the honorable is unintelligible.

The father is gentle but insistent. The elder son's description is more or less accurate, but his sense of having been short-changed needed correction. There has been no displacement of the elder son: his place at the father's side is as secure as ever, and his claim upon the family inheritance is in no way disturbed by this new development. But the elder son has only been doing what is right; he should not imagine that he has placed his father in his debt. At the same time there is no question of the younger son having deserved his restoration!

The father wants the elder son to see that while he (the father) has gained a son, the elder son has, if he will but accept it, gained a brother. The challenge to the elder son is to see that just such an enrichment of the family has transpired and to enter into the joy of celebration.

The story interprets Jesus' involvement with tax collectors and sinners. It invites the righteous not to stand upon their own dignity and to be preoccupied with their own claims upon God, but rather to enter into the joy of welcoming these desperately needy sinners home into the family of God. It is not difficult to see the contemporary relevance to our respectable church membership.

Use and Abuse of Riches (16:1–31)

Already on the basis of the challenge of the law, but even more now with Jesus' preaching of the good news of the kingdom of God, the call is to give up the pretense of seeking to serve both God and mammon: the ethical demands of the Gospel are every bit as stringent as those of the law, and then some!

The Dishonest Steward: "What Am I Going to Do?" (16:1–8)

Bibliography

GENERAL FOR 16:1–31:

Byrne, B. "Forceful Stewardship and Neglected Wealth: A Contemporary Reading of Luke 16." *Pacifica* 1 (1988) 1–14. **Fassl, P.** "'Und er lobte den ungerechten Verwalter' (Lk 16,8a): Komposition und Redaktion in Lk 16." In *Eschatologie: Bibeltheologische und philosophische Studien zum Verhältnis von Erlösungswelt und Wirklichkeitsbewältigung.* FS E. Neuhäusler, ed. R. Kilian et. al. St. Ottilien: EOS, 1981. 109–43. **Feuillet, A.** "Les paraboles de Luc: Chap. 16: Recherches sur la conception chrétienne du droit de propriété et sur les fondements scripturaires de la doctrine sociale de l'église." *EV* 89 (1979) 241–50, 257–71. **Hickling, C. J. A.** "A Tract on Jesus and the Pharisees? A Conjecture on the Redaction of Luke 15 and 16." *HeyJ* 16 (1975) 253–65. **Rodenbusch, E.** "Die Komposition von Lucas 16." *ZNW* 4 (1903) 243–54. **Samain, E.** "Approche littéraire de Lc 16." *FV* 72 (1973) 39–62, 62–68.

FOR 16:1–8:

Arnott, W. "The Unjust Steward in a New Light." *ExpTim* 24 (1913) 510. **Bailey, K. E.** *Poet and Peasant.* 86–118. **Barth, M.** "The Dishonest Steward and His Lord: Reflections on Luke 16:1–13." In *From Faith to Faith,* ed. D. Y. Hadidian. Pittsburgh: Pickwick, 1979. 65–73. **Baudler, G.** "Das Gleichnis vom 'betrügerischen Verwalter' (Lk 16,1–8a) als Ausdruck der 'inneren Biographie' Jesu: Beispiel einer existenz-biographischen Gleichnisinterpretation im religionspädagogischer Absicht." *TGeg* 28 (1985) 65–76. **Baverstock, A. H.** "The Parable of the Unjust Steward: An Interpretation." *Th* 35 (1937) 78–83. **Beames, F.** "The Unrighteous Steward." *ExpTim* 24 (1912–13) 150–55. **Beavis, M. A.** "Ancient Slavery as an Interpretive Context for the New Testament Servant Parables with Special Reference to the Unjust Steward (Luke 16:1–8)." *JBL* 111 (1992) 37–54. **Bigo, P.** "La richesse comme intendance, dans l'évangile: A propos de Luc 16:1–9." *NRT* 87 (1965) 267–71. **Blinzler, J.** "Kluge Ausnützung der Gegenwart zur Sicherung der Zukunft: Lk 16,1–8." *BLit* 37 (1963–64) 357–68. **Boyd, W. F.** "The Parable of the Unjust Steward (Luke xvi. 1ff)." *ExpTim* 50 (1938–39) 46. **Breech, J.** *The Silence of Jesus.* 101–13. **Bretscher, P. G.** "Brief Studies: The Parable of the Unjust Steward—A New Approach to Luke 16:1–9." *CTM* 22 (1951) 756–62. **Brown, C.** "The Unjust Steward: A New Twist?" In *Worship, Theology and Ministry in the Early Church.* FS R. P. Martin, ed. M. J. Wilkins and T. Paige. Sheffield: Academic Press,

1992. 121–45. **Caemmerer, R. R.** "Investment for Eternity: A Study of Luke 16:1–13." *CTM* 34 (1963) 69–76. **Clavier, H.** "L'Ironie dans l'enseignement de Jésus." *NovT* 1 (1956) 3–20. **Collins, R. L.** "Is the Parable of the Unjust Steward Pure Sarcasm?" *ExpTim* 22 (1910–11) 525–26. **Comiskey, J. P.** "The Unjust Steward." *BT* 52 (1971) 229–35. **Coutts, J.** "Studies in Texts: The Unjust Steward, Lk. xvi, 1–8a." *Th* 52 (1949) 54–60. **Daube, D.** "Neglected Nuances of Exposition in Luke-Acts." *ANRW* 2/25.3 (1984) 2329–57, esp. 2334–39. **Davidson, J. A.** "A 'Conjecture' about the Parable of the Unjust Steward (Luke xvi,1–9)." *ExpTim* 66 (1954–55) 31. **Degenhardt, H.-J.** *Lukas, Evangelist der Armen.* 114–120. **Delebecque, É.** "Le régisseur infidèle (16,1–13)." In *Études grecques.* 89–97. **Derrett, J. D. M.** "Fresh Light on St Luke xvi: I. The Parable of the Unjust Steward." *NTS* 7 (1960–61) 198–219; reprinted in a slightly developed form in *Law.* 48–77. ————. "'Take Thy Bond . . . and Write Fifty.' Luke 16:6: The Value of the Bond." *JTS* 23 (1972) 438–40. **Drexler, H.** "Miszellen: Zu Lukas 16,1–7." *ZNW* 58 (1967) 286–88. **Dupont, J.** *Les béatitudes.* 1:107–11, 2:118–22, 168–72. ————. "La parabole de l'intendant avisé (Luc 16,1–13)." *LumVie* 12 (1953) 13–19. ————. "L'Example de l'intendant débrouillard: Lc 16,1–13." *AsSeign* n.s. 56 (1974) 67–78. **Dutton, F. G.** "The Unjust Steward." *ExpTim* 16 (1904–05) 44. **Essig, K.-G.** "Ammerkungen zur Bildebene des Gleichnisses vom ungerechten Verwalter (Lk 16,1–9)." In *Die Auslegung Gottes durch Jesus.* FS H. Braun, ed. L. and W. Schottroff. Mainz: University of Mainz, 1983. 116–41. **Feuillet, A.** "Les riches intendants du Christ (Luc xvi, 1–13)." *RSR* 34 (1947) 30–54. ————. "La parabole du mauvais riche et du pauvre Lazare (Lc 16,19–31) anthithèse de la parabole de l'intendant astucieux (Lc 16,1–9)." *NRT* 101 (1979) 212–23. **Firth, C. B.** "The Parable of the Unrighteous Steward (Luke xvi. 1–9)." *ExpTim* 63 (1951–52) 93–95. **Firth, H.** "The Unjust Steward." *ExpTim* 15 (1903–04) 426–27. **Fitzmyer, J. A.** "The Story of the Dishonest Manager (Lk 16:1–13)." *TS* 25 (1964) 23–42. **Fletcher, D. R.** "The Riddle of the Unjust Steward: Is Irony the Key?" *JBL* 82 (1963) 15–30. **Flusser, D.** "Jesus and the Essenes." *JerPersp* 3.3 (1990) 3–5, 13; 3.4 (1990) 6–8. **Focant, C.** "Tromper le Mammon d'iniquité (Lc 16, 1–13)." In *À cause de l'Évangile,* ed. R. Refoulé, 547–69. **Fossion, A.** "Tromper, l'argent trompeur: Lecture structurale de la parabole du gérant habile, Luc 16,1–9." *FoiTemps* 13 (1983) 342–60. **Fuchs, E.** "L'Évangile et l'argent: la parabole de l'intendant intelligent." *BulCPE* 30 (1978) 3–14. **Fyot, J.-L.** "Sur la parabole de l'intendant infidèle." *Christus* 6 (1959) 500–504. **Gächter, P.** "The Parable of the Dishonest Steward after Oriental Conceptions." *CBQ* 12 (1950) 121–31. ————. "Die Parabel vom ungetreuen Verwalter (Lk 16,1–8)." *Orientierung* 27 (1963) 149–50. **Gander, G.** "Le procédé de l'économe infidèle, décrit Luc 16.5–7, est-il répréhensible ou louable?" *VCaro* 7 (1953) 128–41. **Gibson, M. D.** "On the Parable of the Unjust Steward." *ExpTim* 14 (1902–03) 334. **Grant, J.,** and **O'Neill, F. W. S.** "The Unjust Steward." *ExpTim* 16 (1904–05) 239–40. **Griffith Thomas, W. H.** "The Unjust Steward." *ExpTim* 25 (1913–14) 44. **Hampden-Cook, E.** "The Unjust Steward." *ExpTim* 16 (1904–05) 44. **Heininger, B.** *Sondergutgleichnisse.* 167–77. **Herrmann, J.** "Rechtsgeschichtliche Überlegungen zum Gleichnis vom ungerechten Verwalter (Lk. 16:1–8)." *TRRHD* 38 (1970) 389–402. **Hooley, B. A.,** and **Mason, A. J.** "Some Thoughts on the Parable of the Unjust Steward [Luke 16:1–9]." *ABR* 6 (1958) 47–59. **Horn, F. W.** *Glaube und Handeln.* 72–80. **Hüttermann, F.** "Stand das Gleichnis vom ungerechten Verwalter in Q?" *TGl* 27 (1935) 739–42. **Ireland, D. J.** "A History of Recent Interpretation of the Parable of the Unjust Steward (Luke 16:1–13)." *WTJ* 51 (1989) 293–318. **Jalland, T. G.** "A Note on Luke 16,1–9." *SE* 1 [= TU 73] (1959) 503–5. **Jeremias, J.** *Parables.* 19, 23, 42, 45–48, 181–82. **Jülicher, A.** *Die Gleichnisreden Jesu.* 2:495–514. **Jüngel, E.** *Paulus und Jesus.* 157–60. **Kamlah, E.** "Die Parabel vom ungerechten Verwalter (Luk. 16, 1ff.) im Rahmen der Knechtsgleichnisse." In *Abraham unser Vater,* ed. O. Betz et al. 276–94. **Kannengiesser, C.** "L'intendant malhonnête." *Christus* 18 (1971) 213–18. **King, A.** "The Parable of the Unjust Steward." *ExpTim* 50 (1938–39) 474–76. **Kloppenborg, J. S.** "The Dishonoured Master (Luke 16:1–8a)." *Bib* 70 (1989) 474–95. **Knox, W. L.** *The Sources of the Synoptic Gospels.* Cambridge: University Press, 1957. 2:93–96. **Kosmala, H.** "The Parable of the Unjust Steward in the Light of Qumran." *ASTI* 3 (1964)

114–21. **Krämer, M.** *Das Rätsel der Parabel vom ungerechten Verwalter, Lk 16:1–13: Auslegungsgeschichte-Umfang-Sinn: Eine Diskussion der Probleme und Lösungsvorschläge der Verwalterparabel von den Vätern bis heute.* BiblScRel 5. Zürich: PAS, 1972. **Krüger, G.** "Die geistesgeschichtlichen Grundlagen des Gleichnisses vom ungerechten Verwalter Lk 16,1–9." *BZ* 21 (1933) 170–81. **Lenwood, F.** "An Alternative Interpretation of the Parable of the Unjust Steward." *CongQ* 6 (1928) 366–73. **Lévy, J.-Ph.** "Sur trois textes bibliques concernant des actes écrits." In *Droit biblique, Interprétation rabbinique, Communaités et société.* FS M.-H. Prévost, ed. M. Humbert. Paris: PUF, 1982. 23–48. **Lindars, B.** "Jesus and the Pharisees." In *Donum gentilicium.* FS D. Daube, ed. E. Bammel et al. Oxford: Clarendon, 1978. 51–63, esp. 53–56. **Loader, W.** "Jesus and the Rogue in Luke 16:1–8a: The Parable of the Unjust Steward." *RB* 96 (1989) 518–32. **Lunt, R. G.** "Towards an Interpretation of the Parable of the Unjust Steward (Luke xvi. 1–18)." *ExpTim* 66 (1954–55) 335–37. ———. "Expounding the Parables: III. The Parable of the Unjust Steward (Luke 16:1–15)." *ExpTim* 77 (1965–66) 132–36. **Maass, F.** "Das Gleichnis vom ungerechten Haushalter, Lukas 16,1–8." *ThViat* 8 (1961–62) 173–84. **Maillot, A.** "Notules sur Luc 16, 8b–9." *ETR* 44 (1969) 127–30. **Maiworm, J.** "Die Verwalterparabel." *BK* 13 (1958) 11–18. **Mann, C. S.** "Unjust Steward or Prudent Manager?" *ExpTim* 102 (1991) 234–35. **Marshall, H. S.** "The Parable of the Untrustworthy Steward." *ExpTim* 39 (1927–28) 120–22. **Marshall, I. H.** "Luke xvi, 8—Who Commended the Unjust Steward?" *JTS* 19 (1968) 617–19. **McFayden, J. F.** "The Parable of the Unjust Steward." *ExpTim* 37 (1925–26) 535–39. **Menoud, P.-H.** "Riches injustes et biens véritables." *RTP* n.s. 31 (1943) 5–17. **Merkelbach, R.** "Über das Gleichnis vom ungerechten Haushalter (Lucas 16, 1–13)." *VC* 33 (1979) 180–81. **Miller, W. D.** "The Unjust Steward." *ExpTim* 15 (1903–04) 332–34. **Molina, J.-P.** "Luc 16/1 à 13: L'Injuste *Mamon.*" *ETR* 53 (1978) 371–76. **Moore, F. J.** "The Parable of the Unjust Steward." *ATR* 47 (1965) 103–5. **Moxnes, H.** *The Economy of the Kingdom.* 139–46. **Murray, G.** "The Unjust Steward." *ExpTim* 15 (1903–04) 307–10. **Noonan, J. T., Jr.** "The Devious Employees." *Commonweal* 104 (1977) 681–83. **Oesterley, W. O. E.** "The Parable of the 'Unjust' Steward." *Exp* 6/7 (1903) 273–83. **Pargiter, F. E.** "The Parable of the Unrighteous Steward." *ExpTim* 32 (1920–21) 136–37. **Parrott, D. M.** "The Dishonest Steward (Luke 16.1–8a) and Luke's Special Parable Collection." *NTS* 37 (1991) 499–515. **Paterson, W. P.** "The Example of the Unjust Steward." *ExpTim* 35 (1923–24) 391–95. **Paul, G.** "The Unjust Steward and the Interpretation of Luke 16:9." *Th* 61 (1958) 189–93. **Pauly, D.** *Die Bibel gehört nicht uns.* Einwürfe 6. Munich: Kaiser, 1990. **Perkins, P.** *Hearing the Parables.* 165–71. **Pickar, C. H.** "The Unjust Steward." *CBQ* 1 (1939) 250–52. **Pirot, J.** *Jésus et la richesse, Parabole de l'intendant astucieux.* Marseille: Impr. Marsaillaise, 1944. **Plessis, I. J., du.** "Philanthropy or sarcasm? Another Look at the Parable of the Dishonest Manager (Luke 16:1–13)." *Neot* 24 (1990) 1–20. **Porter, S. E.** "The Parable of the Unjust Steward (Luke 16:1–13): Irony is the Key." In *The Bible in Three Dimensions,* ed. D. J. A. Clines et al. 127–53. **Preisker, H.** "Lukas 16,1–7." *TLZ* 74 (1949) 85–92. **Riggenbach, E.** "Villicus iniquitatis: Duo filii Mt 21,28–32." In *Aus Schrift und Geschichte.* FS A. Schlatter, ed. K. Bornhäuser et al. Stuttgart: Calver, 1922. 17–34. **Rücker, A.** *Über das Gleichnis vom ungerechten Verwalter, Lc 16:1–13.* BibS(F) 17/5. Freiburg im Breisgau: Herdersche Verlagshandlung, 1912. **Samain, P.** "Le bon usage des richesses, en Luc XVI, 1–12." *RevDTournai* 2 (1947) 330–35. **Schwarz, G.** ". . . lobte den betrügerischen Verwalter?" *BZ* 18 (1974) 94–95. **Scott, B. B.** "A Master's Praise: Luke 16,1–8a." *Bib* 64 (1983) 173–88. **Scott, R. B. Y.** "The Parable of the Unjust Steward (Luke xvi. 1ff.)." *ExpTim* 49 (1937–38) 234–35. **Seccombe, D. P.** *Possessions.* 158–72. **Smith, B. T. D.** *The Parables of the Synoptic Gospels: A Critical Study.* Cambridge: University Press, 1937. 108–12. **Snoy, S.** "Le problème de la finale de la parabole de l'intendant avisé." *FV* 12 (1973) 62–68. **Steele, J.** "The Unjust Steward." *ExpTim* 39 (1927–28) 236. **Steinhauser, M. G.** "Noah in His Generation: An Allusion in Luke 16:8b, εἰς τὴν γενεὰν τὴν ἑαυτῶν.'" *ZNW* 79 (1988) 152–57. **Stoll, R.** "The Unjust Steward: A Problem in Interpretation." *EcR* 105 (1941) 16–27. **Tillmann, F.** "Zum Gleichnis vom ungerechten Verwalter: Lk 16:1–9." *BZ* 9 (1911) 171–84. **Topel, L. J.** "On the Injustice of the Unjust Steward: Lk 16:1–13." *CBQ* 37 (1975) 216–27. **Velte, D.** "Das eschatologische

Heute im Gleichnis vom ungerechten Haushalter." *MonPast* 27 (1931) 213–14. **Vögtle, A.** "Das Gleichnis vom ungetreuen Verwalter." *OberrheinPast* 53 (1952) 263–70. **Volckaert, J.** "The Parable of the Clever Steward." *ClerMon* 17 (1953) 332–41. **Wansey, J. C.** "The Parable of the Unjust Steward: An Interpretation." *ExpTim* 47 (1935–36) 39–40. **Weber, S.** "Revision gegen die Freisprechung des ungerechen Verwalters Luk. 16, 5–8." *TQ* 93 (1911) 339–63. **Weder, H.** *Die Gleichnisse Jesu.* 262–67. **Williams, F. E.** "The Parable of the Unjust Steward (Luke xvi. 1–9)." *ExpTim* 66 (1954–55) 371–72. ———. "Is Almsgiving the Point of the 'Unjust Steward'?" *JBL* 83 (1964) 293–97. **Wilson, P. S.** "The Lost Parable of the Generous Landowner and Other Tests for Imaginative Preaching." *QRev* 9 (1989) 80–99. **Wright, A.** "The Parable of the Unjust Steward." *Interpreter* 7 (1911) 279–87. **Zimmermann, H.** "Die Botschaft der Gleichnisse Jesu." *BibLeb* 2 (1961) 92–105, 171–74, 254–61, esp. 254–61.

Translation

[1] *He went on to say, to the*[a] *disciples as well, "A certain man was rich, and he used to have a steward; and this [fellow] was accused to him as squandering his goods.* [2] *He called him and said to him, 'What is this that I hear about you? Hand over the account of your stewardship, for you may no longer act as steward.'* [3] *The steward said to himself, 'What am I going to do, since my master is taking away the stewardship from me? I don't have the strength to dig; I am ashamed to beg.* [4] *I know what I shall do, so that when I am removed from the stewardship [people] will receive me into their houses.'* [5] *Calling each one of his master's debtors, he said to the first, 'How much do you owe my master?'* [6] *He said, 'A hundred baths*[b] *of olive-oil.' He said to him, '[Here,] take your contract, and quickly sit down and write "fifty."'* [7] *Then he said to another, 'And you—how much do you owe?' He said, 'A hundred cors of wheat.' He said to him, '[Here,] take your contract and write eighty.'* [8] *The master praised the dishonest steward, because he acted shrewdly."*[c] *For the sons of this age are more shrewd*[d] *among their own generation than the sons of light!*

Notes

[a] "His" in A W Θ Ψ *f* [1,13] etc.

[b] א L W Ψ 070 579 etc. have βάδους, which seems to be only a spelling variant, but D lat and a few other texts have κάδους, "jars," and D[2] and some other texts have κάβους, "cabs" (a cab is about two quarts).

[c] φρονίμως, "wisely."

[d] φρονιμώτεροι, "wiser."

Form/Structure/Setting

The section here again is coterminous with the chapter. While chap. 15 has emphasized the divine initiative and the heavenly joy at its success, with the need for repentance as only a secondary note, now the emphasis moves onto human responsibility, focused sharply on the use of, and attitude toward, wealth (both allegiance to the law of God and response to the proclamation of the kingdom of God find their proper reflection in the handling of wealth). In this chapter the divine initiative becomes a secondary note present only in the reference in v 16 to the announcing of the good news of the kingdom of God.

A series of links suggests that the sections in chap. 15 and chap. 16 are to be read in close relation to one another. There is carefully constructed continuity of scene (see 16:1, 14); both are chapters of extended narrative parables; the final parable in each set involves three main figures arranged in a somewhat similar configuration; there are some vocabulary links; Coutts, *Theol* 52 (1949) 56, M. R. Austin ("The Hypocritical Son," *EvQ* 57 [1985] 307–15), and Bailey (*Poet*, 109), among others, have emphasized the links between the final parable of chap. 15 and the opening parable of chap. 16.

While chap. 15 had been inherited by Luke, this section has very clearly been formed by him. It seems likely that the parables of vv 1–8 and 19–31 were sequential in Luke's parables source (see excursus: "Journey to Jerusalem"). Luke has bound the parables together by providing a money focus to his interpretation of the former and has enhanced unity by developing in the section the motif of the coincidence of the demand of the law and of the preaching of the kingdom of God.

There has been very little questioning of the claim of the parable to go back to the historical Jesus (but see Horn, *Glaube und Handeln*, 72–73; Goulder, 618–21). The careful qualification of the story that we find in the following verses and the extent to which their match with the parable is less than perfect stand in the way of the view of Horn and Goulder, that it is Luke who has produced the story. Smith's point is cogent (*Parables*, 109): "The fact that we do not expect such a tale to be used to enforce a religious lesson appears to be an almost unanswerable argument in favour of the authenticity of this parable." The view of Heininger (*Sondergutgleichnisse*, 167–77) that the monologue in vv 3–4 is a Lukan development fails to convince because of the unsatisfactory nature of the story that remains and the limited sense that Heininger can give to it. The case is much more complex with the material at the end of the parable. V 8a is best taken as an original part of the parable, but v 8b is almost certainly an addition, probably by Luke himself and meant to be read as a narrator's comment (see below). The subsequent verses are discussed in connection with the following unit.

The interpretation developed below has taken into account but has not been able to interact with more than a few of the many views of the parable that have been defended in the scholarly literature. A quite wide-ranging survey of modern views prepared by D. J. Ireland may usefully be consulted in *WTJ* 51 (1989) 293–318. Loader (*RB* 96 [1989] 518–32) goes beyond the categories of interpretation handled by Ireland by suggesting that Jesus himself is the rogue figure of the parable. A more extensive treatment of the history of interpretation may be found in Krämer, *Das Rätzel*.

Comment

The worldly-wise steward has shrewdly appraised the situation that confronts and threatens him and has moved quickly to situate himself to best advantage for the future. Would that those who know the truth of the Christian gospel could see things so sharply and as effectively align their actions to the situation that confronts them!

1 The introductory clause would seem to be Lukan. Where Luke would have us see the parables of chap. 15 as being directed exclusively to the Pharisees and scribes (15:2–3), now the audience is widened to include the disciples as well (that this is the right way to take the καί, "and/even/also," is confirmed by the presence of the Pharisees in 16:14). Disciples have last been specifically identified as those addressed at 12:22. The awkwardness of the opening sequence of clauses suggests that the phrase *ἄνθρωπός τις ἦν πλούσιος*, "a certain man was rich," is a Lukan touch, borrowed from v 19 to set in parallel the two parables that dominate this section. The rich man is less important for the story than the present opening might suggest. *ἄνθρωπός τις . . . εἶχεν*, "a certain man . . . had," also establishes a link with 15:11.

οἰκονόμος, "steward," can be used in a range of ways, determined principally by the nature of the *οἶκος*, "house," for which the steward takes responsibility (domestic arrangements for those living in the home, business management of the affairs of the master's estate, financial affairs of the city, etc. [here the second is clearly intended]). On *οἰκονόμος*, see W. L. Hendricks, *SWJT* 13 (1971) 25–33; O. Michel, *οἰκονόμος*, *TDNT* 5:149–50. The master here need not be, as often assumed, an absentee landlord making one of his infrequent visits to check up on his affairs: resident landlords could also entrust their affairs to stewards and would be more likely to receive such a "tip-off." The exact extent of the steward's powers remains uncertain since it could be quite varied, but here he is clearly empowered with extensive financial responsibility and freedom and is able to make contracts in his master's name (Daube, *ANRW* 2/25.3 [1984] 2335, cites an Egyptian papyrus of the second century detailing the scope of a particular steward's authorization).

διεβλήθη, "was accused," is generally used in a hostile sense, at times with the implication of falsity and slander. It is better to take the story as developing on the basis of the steward having been "found out" than as turning upon the honor of the master, which is threatened by the fact of the report whether true or false (as Kloppenborg, *Bib* 70 [1989] 488; this improperly moves the center of gravity of the story away from the steward). *διασκορπίζειν*, "squander," is used similarly in 15:13. This may be for the purpose of reinforcing the link between the sections. The story does not require us to be concerned about the nature of the steward's delinquency, but, because it follows 15:13, it is tempting to think of the steward as siphoning off funds for his own consumption from transactions made in the name of his master.

2 In the NT only Luke uses the *ἀκούειν τι περὶ τίνος*, "to hear something about someone," idiom (Horn, *Glaube und Handeln*, 72). The master's question could be either, "What is this that I hear about you?" or (less likely) "Why do I hear this about you?" No doubt the master intends the steward to be stripped at once of his authority to act: he is asked to hand in to his master the documents relating to his conduct of affairs. But since this would take at least some time, as would the dissemination to the master's debtors of the knowledge of the steward's loss of role, there is an inevitable period of vagary which allows for the plan that the steward devises.

3 *εἶπεν δὲ ἐν ἑαυτῷ* (lit. "and he said in himself") and *τί ποιήσω*, "what am I going to do?" may be Lukan diction (Jeremias, *Sprache*, 256). The time required for the process involved in ejecting the steward from office is reflected in the present tense "is taking away." In ancient society persons displaced from their class and role were often left in a quite precarious situation. This man clearly has no private savings to fall back upon (cf. the squandering of v 1). His consideration of options is clearly based on an assumption that, with his name blackened by the present exposure, another similar job would not likely come his way. Begging and manual labor were the steps immediately above slavery in the social scale (the low status of the beggar is reflected in 18:39; for distress about the work of digging, cf. Aristophanes, *Birds* 1432). The first hearers would hardly be critical of such a reflection, even though they would mostly have been from the laboring classes themselves.

4 The aorist ἔγνων (normally, "I knew"; here, "I know") views the newly acquired knowledge as an achieved state. The time required for the removal is reflected here as well in "when I am removed." The play upon the root οἰκο- in the balanced phrases "out of the stewardship" and "into their houses" derives its sense from the fact that the loss of the man's stewardship involved as well the loss of a roof over his head. The subject of δέξωνται, "they will receive," is not specified. It is equivalent to a passive construction and may be influenced in the NT by Aramaic patterns (cf. 6:38; 12:20, 48). The continuation of the story makes it clear that the steward has in mind debtors of his master. The deposed steward probably anticipates becoming a house guest successively in a number of the houses of those with whom he has done business on behalf of his master. This may not represent a lifetime solution to his needs, but it would deal with his immediately pressing problem. (The view that the reference is to a job as steward falls foul of the plural "their houses.") It will become clear that the basis for his confidence in the outcome of his plan is the reciprocity ethic that was so important in Greco-Roman culture (see at 6:32).

5 Luke may have contributed the idiom represented in ἕνα ἕκαστον, "each one" (Jeremias, *Sprache*, 256). We are to understand that there are quite a number of debtors, of whom the two described are exemplary. The most likely basis for the debts is in connection with the leasing of the land producing the crops reflected in the different debt currencies (leasing could be on the basis of a percentage of the crop, or on the basis of an agreed quantity from the yield [cf. Bailey, *Poet*, 92]). Another possibility would be that loans of the mentioned commodities are involved (as, e.g., Derrett, *Law*, 48–77). This introduces the complicating factor of interest and questions about the nature of first-century practice against the background of the biblical prohibitions in Deut 15:7–8; 23:19–20; Exod 22:25; Lev 25:36–37. There is a good likelihood that in the first century these verses were not necessarily understood as a prohibition of business loans (only Deut 23:19–20 could be broader, but even here there may be an assumption that the basis of the loan is that the receiver has fallen on hard times; the banking system in Luke 19:23 assumes a custom of loans at interest; Josephus, *Ant.* 4.266–70, applies the prohibition only to interest on loans of food or clothing to the indigent). Where lending was likely to come under suspicion there were devices available to avoid the appearance of usury (e.g., if a person already had any amount of a commodity, it was permissible to lend him that commodity [at interest, since the person was deemed not to be in hardship in connection with that particular commodity]; though clearly not developed for this purpose [cf. the Egyptian documents cited by Kloppenborg, *Bib* 70 (1989) 483 n. 34], the ancient practice of writing contracts not in terms of the borrowed amount but in terms of a higher notional amount that included the added interest could be exploited in the interest of avoiding the appearance of usury [as though a larger amount had been loaned than was the case]). Some of the intricacies of the development of rabbinic views on usury are tracked by Derrett (*Law*, 56–66). As will become clearer below, there is finally no adequate basis for drawing into the parable the complexities of the first-century loan market. As far as the dynamic of the parable is concerned, the debt could equally be land rent or business loan. We should note that the debt is specified as owing to the master. The opening of the dialogue serves more for the hearers of the parable than for the development of the story (it is they who need to learn the base-line debt levels).

6–7 A bath is a liquid measure of about nine gallons. A cor is a Semitic dry measure whose size is not certainly known, but it is probably around ten to fifteen bushels (Josephus gives radically contradictory equivalents in *Ant.* 15.9.2 and 3.15.3; the version giving the larger measure is normally accepted as approximately accurate and has the advantage in our present context of making the reduction more or less equivalent in value [cf. Caird, 188]). Both the quantity of olive oil and of wheat mentioned here are found identically in the list that specifies the extravagant release or resources authorized by Artaxerxes for Ezra (Ezra 7:22). The quantities involved are quite huge. The oil involved would represent the annual yield of a very large olive grove. Similarly the wheat debt "would represent a half-share rent for almost 200 acres, which is perhaps twenty times the size of an average family plot" (Kloppenborg, *Bib* 70 [1989] 482). The master is dealing with large-scale business associates here, not with ordinary people and ordinary economic levels. As here, *γράμματα* is regularly used in the plural to refer to a legal document (BAGD, 165). The validity of the contract is guaranteed by being written in the handwriting of the debtor, with the document kept in the possession of the creditor (or here his steward).

The steward is instructing the debtor to reduce by 50 percent the originally specified debt. At a stroke the master has lost half of what he might have expected to receive from this particular business transaction. What exactly is happening? If this is a loan with interest, then it may be important for us to realize that ancient interest rates were very high indeed. Business risks were high, and returns on successful business were correspondingly high. On commodity loans, interest of 50 percent was typical, so much so that a contract idiom emerged *μετὰ τῆς ἡμιολίας* [or *σὺν ἡμιολίᾳ*, or *ἐπι' διαφόρῳ ἡμιολίας*], "including the added half" (for references see Kloppenborg, *Bib* 70 [1989] 483 n. 34; interest on cash loans tended to be lower, since here the fluctuations in commodity prices played no role). Even, however, with very high interest rates, despite claims to the contrary, the reduction in the olive oil debt is more than could reasonably be treated as surcharge (interest? insurance? costs?) on a loan of half the specified amount (Fitzmyer, 1101, suggests parabolic exaggeration). When we come to the wheat, the problem is the same in the other direction: the reduction is only 25 percent, where the normal interest would be 50 percent. The reductions do not represent, therefore, a reduction to the original capital amount of a loan.

Is the steward, then, eliminating a practice of overcharging? His master clearly has not benefited from such extra revenue (cf. v 1)! If the steward has been pocketing the difference (up to this point we know only of malpractice toward his master), then this present act would simply be to expose his own corruption to those he has formerly cheated and only now for the first time treats squarely. There is nothing here to serve as a basis for expecting a major investment of hospitality in return.

If we are dealing not with loans but with the rental of land, then reductions of debt would be conceivable in consideration of natural disaster in the form of crop disease or a poor season (cf. *m. Bab. Meṣ.* 9.1.6). Such powers could well have been vested in the steward. No such disaster is in sight, but the steward could use just such an available mechanism to ingratiate himself with his master's business partners. From the point of view of the debtors, the steward will have used his last moments in office, by means of an act that was quite within his powers, to show generosity to them on a grand scale. In accord with the demands of Greco-Roman reciprocity ethics, they would feel honor bound to repay a good turn with generosity also of a high level. Caught in his squandering of the master's goods, the steward retrieves the situation by means of yet further squandering.

This all assumes, however, that the steward was right in his expectations, and that his actions will at least in some measure satisfactorily assure his future. Porter ("Unjust Steward," 146) has recently suggested that, though the ploys of the steward may work, he is rather to be seen as a pathetic figure who in this last set of actions has sold out completely to villainy and does not realize how fleeting the values of this world really are. The force of Porter's case depends upon the sense he defends for the following verses (an ironic sense), which will be disputed below. One could, I suppose, also consider the possibility that the steward was simply quite mistaken in his assumptions about the outcome of his action (cf. Gächter, *CBQ* 12 [1950] 123), but this does seem to be a gratuitous imposition upon the natural flow of the story.

There is the question of what the steward thought his master might do or could do in consequence of his (the steward's) action. It seems clearly to be assumed that the master cannot undo what the steward has done. From the master's point of view, in this last set of actions the steward has not acted in a manner that is any more criminal toward his master: by acting quickly he has simply managed to squander yet more of his master's goods. The obvious difference is that this time he acts for the benefit of others (in the first instance), rather than for his own benefit. If the steward had at this point sought to move additional resources in his own direction, then the master could have done something about regaining what had been stolen from him. Instead this new third-party situation keeps the transferred wealth out of his reach (presumably nothing remains of the master's earlier losses). The master's redress seems to be still limited to the dismissal of his steward. The steward has acted very cleverly indeed! He has found a way forward where there seemed to be none.

8 Which κύριος praised the steward? Is it the master who has been κύριος in vv 3, 5, or is it "the Lord" as a Lukan (or pre-Lukan) designation for Jesus? No other appended parable application set on the lips of Jesus in the Gospel tradition involves making a value judgment upon persons or actions in a parable. As Bailey (*Poet*, 103) points out, while in a parables context the absolute ὁ κύριος is used twice of Jesus (12:42 before a parable; 18:6 after a parable), more often it is used of a figure in the parable (12:37; 12:42b; 14:23). We should also note that the clear indication of a new beginning in v 9 stands in favor of a reference to the master of the parable in v 8a. The difficulties for a reference to the master are (*i*) the continuing words of v 8b, which cannot with any realism be attributed to the master, and (*ii*) the unlikelihood that a master who has just been swindled would consider his swindler praiseworthy (this difficulty has led to theories of mistranslation ["cursed" not "praised"], as well as to the suggestion that there is heavy irony in the master's praise [the former is purely speculative and provides an inadequate closure to the story; for the latter there are no adequate signals in the preceding text, and in the form that Porter proposes it ("Unjust Steward," 146–53), it leads on to an understanding of vv 9–13 that is highly unlikely]). Point (*i*) can be countered by taking v 8b as an expansion (as in the translation above, I take it to be an expansion meant to be read as an editorial explanation [cf. the discussion at 5:24]). Point (*ii*) is more serious, and yet there is something that even the one swindled can admire about this scoundrel. Even when he had been found out in his crime and his number was clearly up, this fellow in his shrewdness could find a way to swindle his master yet again right under the master's nose and in such a way that the master, even though on the spot and alerted to the steward's ways, could do nothing to restore the situation. However grudgingly given, a recognition of the cleverness of this fellow is not out of place (Heininger, *Sondergutgleichnisse*, 168, draws attention to the approval given to the rascal slave in ancient comedy). The final argument that inclines me to favor the view that v 8a is part of the parable is that the story is curiously truncated if it must end with v 7. We must assume that the master was apprised of this latest fraud, much as he had learned of the earlier misappropriation of his goods.

The qualifying τῆς ἀδικίας (lit. "of unrighteousness") has attracted considerable attention, recurring as it does in v 9 in connection with "mammon" (see main discussion there). Its presence here stands against those interpretations that see the reduction of debts in a positive light (the steward has not stopped being unrighteous). We should note, however, that the presence of vv 8b and 9 may exert a back influence on the sense to be given in the finished text to τῆς ἀδικίας, so that in connection with the later context it may be correct to paraphrase the sense here as "worldly."

There is a broad consensus that v 8b is an expansion of the original parable, either by Luke or before him (the clause cannot be set on the lips of the master; the second ὅτι, "because/for," is awkward [note Marshall's defense of this as a move from indirect to direct speech (*JTS* 19 [1968] 617–19), which Fitzmyer (1108) dismisses much too readily]; the contrast involved is difficult to attribute to the historical Jesus [cf. Kloppenborg, *Bib* 70 [1989] 476]; in the NT "sons of this age" occurs again only at 20:34, where it appears to have been introduced by Luke). I take the clause to be a Lukan editorial comment. This is how Luke makes it clear that if we are to be challenged to follow in any way the example of the steward, then there must first be a transposition into a different frame of reference.

"Sons of this age" are those for whom the ultimate frame of reference is no larger than this age. A similar phrase, "sons of the world," with a similar meaning is found in the Qumran document CD 20:34. With reference to the parable, the phrase points to the steward's shrewd, worldly self-interest. In his own frame of reference, he is an impressive achiever. "Sons of light" is also found at Qumran (e.g., 1QS 1:9; 1QM 1:3 [see list of texts in Fitzmyer, 1108]), where it normally stands in opposition to "sons of darkness." In the NT the phrase is also found at 1 Thess 5:5; Eph 5:8; John 12:36. "Sons of light" are in the Lukan setting illuminati who are, through a knowledge of God given in this eschatological period, aware of the larger shape of reality, its moral texture, and its orientation to the future judgment. Luke draws from the parable the lesson that, despite this state of awareness,

Christians seem less effective at cutting their cloth to their situation than do the worldly wise. Is this a Lukan apology for the embarrassment to the cause of the gospel that Christians can sometimes be, or is it a challenge to Christians to rise to the occasion?

What can we make of the parable without its Lukan development? The steward has shrewdly appraised the situation in which he found himself and acted in the one way that he can to save himself. The challenge is to have the shrewdness to recognize and seize the opportunity that exists in the midst of threat. We should no doubt apply this to the challenging development in events brought about by the presence and ministry of Jesus. There is that which threatens, but at the same time there is a successful way forward for those who will be wise. Taken alone, the parable can hardly say more, but despite the skepticism of Horn (*Glaube und Handeln,* 73) there is quite enough here to warrant the parable a place in the ministry of Jesus. Perhaps the parable of the hidden treasure provides the closest point of comparison (Matt 13:44).

Explanation

A new section begins here that runs to the end of the chapter and has quite close links with the preceding section: chap. 15 has emphasized divine initiative and heavenly joy, with repentance in the background; now human responsibility is stressed, especially in connection with the attitude to and the use of wealth, and the divine initiative is only briefly alluded to. A theme developed in the section is that the law of the OT and the gospel of the NT speak with a united voice about the need for a practical moral response to be lived out in the human interactions of life.

The worldly-wise steward is confronted by a situation that threatens to be his undoing. He appraises the situation with great shrewdness and acts quickly to situate himself to best advantage for the future. Do we who have at least in theory the perspective created by a knowledge of Jesus as Christ and Lord have the incisiveness of insight to see as effectively through to the heart of the matter and the incisiveness of action to follow through with what is required?

The audience has been the scribes and Pharisees, but it now widens to include the disciples. The action of the parable that Jesus now tells is precipitated by a move by unspecified persons to expose the corruption of a certain steward who has been living high at the expense of his master. The steward was in effect a business manager who had vested in him wide-ranging powers to act on behalf of his master. Integrity was vital for the role, and this man's integrity had failed.

The master confronts the steward and asks for the return of the documents relating to his conduct of affairs. His intention is to strip the steward at once of his authority to act, but there is inevitably a brief time of transition for the steward to hand over the documents. During this time, the news will gradually spread that the steward has been relieved of his duties. In the meantime, the steward has a window of opportunity.

The steward goes off to do his master's bidding for this one last time, reflecting on the prospect of the approaching collapse of his world. In ancient society persons displaced from their class and role often found themselves in quite a precarious situation. Can he do anything? No one will want him as a steward, but his pride and class make begging or manual labor out of the question (no one would dispute this in his cultural setting). A light goes on: he has hit upon a plan. His goal becomes long-term residential hospitality with those of his own class who had been his master's debtors.

The debtors are quickly summoned. The debts involved are very large, so we are not dealing with the debts of the poor or with the borrowing of seed grain, etc. by small scale farmers. These debts are large business debts, either lease arrangements on land or commercial borrowing by the merchant classes. The steward had the authority to write and even rewrite contracts in the name of his master. For example, in times of natural calamity it was customary to reduce the amount due on the lease of farmland. The debt amounts in these contracts would be written in the hand of the debtor (this would discourage falsification). The debt amount in the contract of each of the debtors is reduced by a huge amount. (While the percentage reduction is quite different, the value of the reduction would be about the same.) From the point of view of the debtors, the steward will have used his last moments in office (though they will only learn later that these are his last moments in office) to show generosity to them on a grand scale.

The ancient world ran on the basis of a reciprocity ethic: good turns given and returned. The steward's move gave him a claim upon his master's debtors that was much more secure than any contract. Public honor required that they make some appropriate return to their benefactor. The steward had secured his future!

But what of the master's reaction to this? This last set of actions had not made him any more criminal than he was already, and the reaction to his former squandering was to be dismissal. Nothing more could be done from that angle. What about recovery? If the steward had sought to lay claim to more of his master's goods for himself at this point, the master, now alerted and present, would have made all legal moves necessary for their recovery. The stroke of brilliance was the tranfer to a series of third parties. Here the wealth is out of the master's reach, but on the basis of the reciprocity ethic, it was effectively within the reach of the steward. The master can do nothing more than he had already done. However grudgingly, the master can only acknowledge the cleverness of the now dismissed steward.

The whole of the action has taken place in connection with the less than savory nature of what so often goes on in the world of business and high finance. The ethics are at a pretty low level. But what should attract our attention is that the steward has shrewdly appraised the situation in which he found himself, and acted to save himeself. The challenge is for us to have the shrewdness to recognize and seize the opportunity that exists in the midst of threat. In the immediate context, the threat and opportunity are those created by the ministry of Jesus. But beyond that the story challenges all Christians to be as successful as the worldly wise in cutting their cloth according to their situation: to act committedly in the light of what we know (in knowing God in Christ) of the larger shape of reality, its moral texture, and its orientation to the future judgment.

Serving God and Using Mammon (16:9–13)

Bibliography

Anderson, F. C. "Luke xvi. 10." *ExpTim* 59 (1947–48) 278–79. **Colella, P.** "Zu Lk 16:7 (sic 9)." *ZNW* 64 (1973) 124–26. **Compston, H. F. B.** "Friendship and Mammon." *ExpTim* 31 (1919–20) 282. **Degenhardt, H.-J.** *Lukas, Evangelist der Armen.* 120–31. **Descamps, A.** "La composition littéraire de Luc XVI 9–13." *NovT* 1 (1956) 47–53. **Dupont, J.** "Dieu ou Mammon (Mt 6, 24; Lc 16, 13)." *CnS* 5 (1984) 441–61. **Hiers, R. H.** "Friends by Unrighteous Mammon: The Eschatological Proletariat [Luke 16:9]." *JAAR* 38 (1970) 30–36. **Hof, O.** "Luthers Auslegung von Lukas 16:9." *EvT* 8 (1948–49) 151–66. **Honeyman, A. M.** "The Etymology of Mammon." *ArchLing* 4 (1952) 60–65. **Middleton, R. D.** "St. Luke xvi. 9." *Th* 29 (1934) 41. **Pautrel, R.** "'Aeterna tabernacula' [Luc, XVI,9]." *RSR* 30 (1940) 307–27. **Rüger, H. P.** "*Μαμωνᾶς*," *ZNW* 64 (1973) 127–31. **Safrai, S.,** and **Flusser, D.** "The Slave of Two Masters." *Immanuel* 6 (1976) 30–33. **Schlögl, N.** "Die Fabel vom 'ungerechten Reichtum' und the Aufforderung Jesu, sich damit Schätze für den Himmel sammeln." *BZ* 14 (1916–17) 41–43. **Schulz, S.** *Spruchquelle.* 459–61.

And see further at 16:1–8.

Translation

[9] *"I say to you, Make friends for yourself by means of the mammon of unrighteousness, so that when it fails*[a] *they may receive you into eternal dwellings.*

[10] *"The one who is faithful in the smallest thing is also faithful in something great, and the one who is unrighteous in the smallest thing is also unrighteous in something great.* [11] *If, then, you have not been faithful in [the use of] unrighteous mammon, who will entrust to you that which is of true value?* [12] *and if you have not been faithful in [the use of] what belongs to another, who will give you what is [to be] your own?*[b]

[13] *"No servant is able to give slave service to two masters. For either he will hate the one and love the other, or he will be devoted to the one and despise the other. You cannot give slave service to God and to mammon."*

Notes

[a] The ἐκλ(ε)ίπητε, "you fail = die," of ℵ W *f* [13] etc. rightly glosses the sense here.
[b] Rather curiously B L etc. read ἡμέτερον, "our own."

Form/Structure/Setting

In this second unit of the section 16:1–31, v 9 provides an application of the previous parable to the specifically fiscal realm, and this leads in turn to other teaching about the appropriate orientation to money of a disciple of Jesus. V 10 offers a secular-sounding proverb that is applied in vv 11–12 in terms of a transformed sense of what it means to have true wealth of one's own and how such is gained. V 13a offers another secular-sounding proverb that, in a similar procedure, is applied in v 13bcd in terms of the fundamental incompatability of committed service to God and to mammon.

Despite its Semitic sound, v 9 is probably best seen as a Lukan formulation designed to provide the transition to vv 10–13, and beyond that to incorporate the preceding parable into the theme of the chapter, and in particular to align it with the parable of the rich man and Lazarus. With vv 10–12 the situation is more uncertain. Luke may have been inspired by the tradition behind 19:17 to offer the development here, but there is mileage in the suggestion that vv 10–12 (along with v 13) may show the marks of Semitic word-play. V 13 is found as well in Matt 6:24. It is an artistically unified piece (see esp. Dupont, *CnS* 5 [1984] 449–56) and, with its message of radical attachment to God, easily finds a place in the message of the historical Jesus.

In both vv 10–12 and v 13 a general truth presented in proverbial address is applied to the specific area of the appropriate orientation of a disciple of Jesus toward money.

Comment

The shrewd and timely action implicitly called for in the preceding parable is applied in v 9 to the use of money: use it for the needs of the poor, and they will be there to welcome you into eternity. The unit goes on to recommend fidelity in the use of money, which, though intrinsically of very little value, one has as a trust from God. This will lead to the possession of a true wealth that can genuinely be called one's own. Finally, there is a call to a loyalty of committed service to God that precludes any loyalty to money.

9 Luke will have provided the introductory *καὶ ἐγὼ ὑμῖν λέγω*, "and I say to you" (cf. at 11:9; but note the contrary view of Jeremias, *Sprache*, 106; Fitzmyer, 1105). The echoes of the language of v 4 in the verse make it doubtful whether this verse ever existed separately from the parable. On the other hand the difference in meaning between *τῆς ἀδικίας* (lit. "of unrighteousness") in this verse (discussed in a moment) and in v 8 makes it difficult to accept this verse as an original application of the parable. There is just enough link between the thought here and the parable of the rich man and Lazarus to make it most likely that Luke is responsible for the present formulation (drawing "mammon" from the tradition he is about to use in v 13 [and cf. v 11], and thinking of the very opposite kind of reception that the rich man is to encounter at the hands of Abraham). There are, nevertheless, two causes of reservation to be recorded: (*i*) Could Luke have spontaneously produced such a Semitic-sounding idiom as *ὁ μαμωνᾶς τῆς ἀδικίας*, "the mammon of unrighteousness"? (*ii*) Is there an underlying Semitic word-play linking "mammon" here with the uses of "faithful" in vv 10–11, along with the use of "true" in v 11 (as suggested by Dupont, *CnS* 5 [1984] 447; id., *Beatitudes*, 1:109–11; this second would be as well satisfied by considering vv 10–13, without v 9, as an earlier collection)?

Horn (*Glaube und Handeln*, 76–77; with references) points out that only Hellenistic Greek parallels can be found for Luke's *ποιήσατε φίλους*, "make friends." Luke is making use of imagery drawn from the same reciprocity ethic that we saw behind the steward's actions in the parable above. But the thought expressed ultimately shatters precisely that ethic (cf. Horn, 79–80; the underlying thought is not dissimilar to that in 6:32–36).

μαμωνᾶς, "mammon," is a grecized form of Hebrew ממון, *māmôn*, or Aramaic ממונא, *māmônāʾ*. Its etymology is disputed, but may be from a root with an original sense of "that in which one puts one's trust." However, it came to be used quite neutrally of "money" (see further Fitzmyer, 1109; Rüger, *ZNW* 64 [1973] 127–31). ממון דרשע, *mmwn drš*ʿ, "mammon of wickedness," ממון דשקר, *mmwn dšqr*, "mammon of falsehood," and ממון שיקרא, *mmwn šyqr*ʾ, "mammon of deception," are all found in the later targums (Rüger, 128–29), but the sense does not fit the Lukan context. Somewhat similar phrases at Qumran (but without "mammon") refer to wealth gained by violence or evil (though just possibly in the sense that it is gained by operating in the evil world system, rather than because it is gained through specific acts of evil [see 1QS 10:19; CD 6:15; 8:5; 19:17]). In Luke there is certainly no sense that the wealth is ill-gotten or so intrinsically contaminated that one ought to have nothing to do with it (cf. v 11). Rather the wealth is part of the present world system and as such has seductive qualities that Luke is keen to warn against. The sense for *τῆς ἀδικίας* (lit. "of unrighteousness") that emerges here could have no proper place in the parable conclusion in v 8a above.

The failure of wealth comes not at the moment when we have run out of it, but rather at the moment of death. The point is that "you can't take it with you." "They receive" is repeated from v 4. The imagery is compounded out of that of the preceding parable and a modification of that of the parable to come at the end of the chapter. From the wider Lukan context it is clear that the friends to be made are the poor to whom alms should be given in line with the injunction of 12:33 (cf. 18:22), which expresses the same thought, but with different imagery. *σκηνάς*, "tents/dwellings," is a counterpart to the "houses" of v 4. Luke probably finds a certain dignity in the use of this Septuagintal term (he certainly does not mean temporary dwellings [as in 9:33]). Such "eternal dwellings" transcend the horizons of the "sons of this age" of v 8b. In the parable to come, Lazarus is to be found in the eternal dwellings (perhaps in another sense so is the rich man).

Whereas the challenge of the parable (with Luke's editorial comment in v 8b) has remained general, here in v 9 Luke brings the general challenge to focus on the use of money. This provides a transition to the assembled collection of sayings that Luke will now present about the proper attitude toward and use of money. (The ironic understanding of v 9 [most recently Porter, "Unjust Steward," 148–50] finally fails because of the verse's clear links to the Lukan teaching on wealth and its use; the same must be said of the attempts to take *ἐκ* [either by assumed mistranslation of the Aramaic, or by claiming such a sense for the Greek] as meaning "without/apart from.")

10 Vv 10–13 have no connection at all with the preceding parable (though often repeated, Dodd's description [*Parables,* 17] of the verses [with v 9] as "notes for three separate sermons on the parable as text" is quite misleading). V 9 has established use of money as the topic, and Luke uses these verses to make a series of points about this topic. V 10 has the sound of a piece of secular wisdom but could be a Lukan formulation on the basis of 19:17, or it may reflect Jesus' own appeal to wisdom sayings. Given the present context, development from the tradition in 19:17 seems quite likely (but see at v 9 above the question of Semitic word-plays in vv 10–13). Since vv 10–12 are an integrated unit, then the judgment made for v 10 is likely to apply as well to vv 11–12. It becomes clear from v 11 that contrary to normal human estimates, it is money to which Luke wants to apply the category of "the least thing." What he thinks of as "something great" is revealed in a more riddling way in the following verses.

11 *οὖν*, "then," points to the intended application of the proverbial statement of v 10. *τῷ ἀδίκῳ μαμωνᾷ* takes up the "mammon of unrighteousness of v 9," but now in more natural Greek: "unrighteous mammon." The question form keeps the point quite general, but now there is a move from observable patterns in connection with matters of reliability to observable patterns in the behavior of those who are in a position to entrust wealth to the care of others. *τὸ ἀληθινόν* (lit. "the true") is best rendered "that which is of true value." God is clearly lurking beneath the surface of these words, since only he can deal in a currency that goes quite beyond material resources.

12 The inference to be drawn from this verse is not only that God is in the business of entrusting people with a new currency that has true value. His pattern is to entrust it not simply as to a stewardship, but to give it as a personal possession to the one who has been found trustworthy. Presumably the ownership of the mammon of the world is here assumed to be God's. The riches that one has in one's own name cannot be very different from the "treasure kept in heaven" of 12:33 (cf. "your treasure" in v 34).

13 Thus far the imagery has been of money as a resource and as a trust; here the imagery is switched to that of money as a potential master. Now Luke has used a traditional piece also found at Matt 6:24 (identical wording except for the presence in Luke of *οἰκέτης*, "servant" [probably a Matthean deletion, for the purposes of generalization (cf. Dupont, *CnS* 5 [1984] 444–49), but Luke does use the word again in Acts 10:7]). Plural ownership of slaves was in fact practiced. Ancient literature reports cases of slaves with more than one owner, citing either the impossibility of satisfying their demands or, paradoxically, the space of freedom thus created (see Dupont, *CnS* 5 [1984] 441; cf. Acts 16:16–19). The point here is that the slave's service will be less than satisfactory on the one side or the other.

The bald opening proverb is supported by two chiastically arranged formulations, sharply contrasting the alternatives: hate and love, or being attached and despising. There is actually no natural necessity in the sharpness of these antitheses. They are perhaps built upon a background assumption that fully adequate service requires an exclusive kind of love and attachment to the master (cf. Exod 21:5; Greco-Roman texts recognize the importance of affection and loyalty to the master in the appointment of a slave as steward). No doubt the thought is conditioned as well by the radical nature of Jesus' call to the kingdom of God. Dupont (*CnS* 5 [1984] 454–55) makes the point that these clauses take us from the objective realm to the realm of subjective disposition, which implicitly introduces the dimension of the servant's choice in the matter. This idea of choice is then carried forward when the final clause with its formal parallelism with the opening clause identifies the point of application of the opening proverbial saying.

There is no need to look for some demonizing of wealth here (on mammon, see at v 9) or to claim the influence of any radical dualism that disparaged the material world. Josephus knows about the possibility of being "enslaved to lucre" (*τῷ κέρδει δουλεύσας*; *Ant.* 4.238), and the idea that love of money easily transforms itself into servitude is well attested in antiquity (Wettstein, *Novum Testamentum Graecum*, 1:333, documents the sentiment in Euripides, Valerius Maximus, Libanius, Plutarch, and Demophilus, to which Dupont, *CnS* 5 [1984] 442 n. 4 adds Epictetus; closest to our present text is Wettstein's quote from Demophilus:

"it is impossible for the same person to be a lover of money and a lover of god. For the . . . lover of money is of necessity unrighteous"). Without the narrow moralism of Demophilus, in our text the call for a thoroughly uncompromised service of God is set against just this kind of background.

Explanation

The challenge of the parable in 16:1–8 has remained general. Luke now applies that challenge to the realm of the handling of money: money should be dispersed with more than one eye on eternity. Continuing the topic of money, this unit also calls for a stewardship attitude toward this commodity. Money is intrinsically of quite limited value, but when handled in this way, it can lead on to its replacement by a really valuable form of currency, which will no longer simply be a trust but will be properly one's own possession. Money is an instrument but should be no master, so finally the unit sets in absolute antithesis the proper service of God and the service of mammon.

V 9 picks up imagery from the parable of the dishonest steward (see v 4) and applies it to a situation that is partly drawn from the parable to come at the end of the chapter (the rich man and Lazarus): while we have money at our disposal during our lives, we should make use of it in meeting the needs of the Lazaruses who are around us. Then, when its usefulness has come to an end at the point of our death, we will meet in the eternal beyond with those we have helped and be welcomed by their heartfelt gratitude, which will (metaphorically) provide for a roof over our heads in this other world. In this way the money, which by its nature as part of the treasures of this age has a tendency to seduce us into false values and actions, can be put to a use that transcends the limited horizons of worldliness. This is a proper response to the challenge that the ministry of Jesus represents to us.

"The least thing" to which the proverb of v 10 is to be applied is of course money. The proverb is built upon the universal practice of trying somebody out in something that doesn't matter too much before entrusting to them something in which the stakes are rather higher. Those who do not handle their material wealth as God's faithful stewards will never know what it is like to have charge of something that is really valuable. What is more, they will miss the experience of having God give them this valuable commodity not just as a trust but as their own personal possession. (This is all rather like the treasure in heaven of 12:33–34.)

So far money has been considered a resource and a trust, but in v 13 it is considered a possible master. A slave with two masters is a slave with problems. To give proper slave service to the one master requires that exactly the opposite outlook be adopted in connection with the other master. This is just how it is with God and money. We would all prefer to think that we had a measured response to the claims of wealth. But money cries out to be a lord and master, and all too often we are quite ready to comply. V 13 is a warning that such submission is inimical to the service of God.

Lovers of Money and Seekers of Honor (16:14–15)

Bibliography

Degenhardt, H.-J. *Lukas, Evangelist der Armen.* 131–33. **Hanson, R. P. C.** "A Note on Luke xvi. 14–31." *ExpTim* 55 (1943–44) 221–22. **Klinghardt, M.** *Gesetz und Volk Gottes.* 24–40. **Moxnes, H.** *The Economy of the Kingdom.* Esp. 1–9, 146–48, 151–53. **Schmidt, T. E.** "Burden, Barrier, Blasphemy: Wealth in Matt 6:33, Luke 14:33, and Luke 16:15." *TJ* 9 (1988) 171–89. **Schürmann, H.** "'Wer daher eines dieser geringsten Gebote auflöst . . .' Wo fand Matthäus da Logion Mt 5, 19?" *BZ* 4 (1960) 238–50.

Translation

[14]*The Pharisees*[a] *(being lovers of money) heard all these things and*[b] *ridiculed him.* [15]*He said to them, "You are those who justify yourselves before [other] people, but God knows your hearts. For what is exalted among human beings*[c] *is an abomination before God!"*

Notes

[a] A W Θ $f^{1,13}$ etc. add *καί* (here: "as well") here in line with that in v 1.
[b] *καί* (lit. "even [ridiculed]").
[c] Gr. *ἀνθρώποις*, which is translated earlier in the verse as "[other] people."

Form/Structure/Setting

This brief unit strengthens the link between 15:1–32 and 16:1–31 (cf. 15:1; and see at 16:1–8). It reports and interprets the negative Pharisaic response to the teaching of vv 1–8, 9–13. The unit maintains the thematic interest in wealth that unifies the section (there is something to be said for correlation by Ellis [200–201] and others of vv 14–15 with 19–26 [with vv 16–18 correlated with vv 27–31]).

There is no parallel to this material, and it is normally taken as a Lukan construction. Schürmann (*BZ* 4 [1960] 240–49) has drawn attention to the links between material in each of vv 14, 15, 16, 17, 18 and material in Matt 5 (vv 14–15: Pharisees and the language of justification shared with Matt 5:20; v 16: "the law and/or the prophets" shared with Matt 5:17 and "into" along with "the kingdom of God" shared with Matt 5:20; v 17: closely related to Matt 5:18; v 18: closely related to Matt 5:32). Though his own source conclusions remain speculative, there is sufficient weight in these correlations to suggest the influence of some shared source here. Nonetheless the material of vv 14–15, though rooted in the tradition, is best treated as substantially Lukan.

Comment

An outwardly cultivated righteousness can only disgust God when there is no corresponding righteousness of the heart that welcomes every illumination of the path of righteousness.

14 For ἤκουον δὲ . . . ταῦτα, "they heard . . . these things," as Lukan, cf. 14:15. For ἐξεμυκτήριζον, "they ridiculed him," cf. 23:35. The use of ὑπάρχοντες for "being" is also Lukan. In Luke's opinion, in the attitude toward money the cracks are likely to show in what is otherwise an outwardly impressive veneer of righteousness. This is why he thinks in terms of the Pharisees' seeking to discredit the preceding teaching. On the problem of the love of money, see at v 13. While Luke finds love of money, among other things, to be at the root of Pharisaic disquiet about Jesus and his teaching, we should not caricature the Pharisees on this basis as more inclined to be lovers of money than any other group who benefit from some existing status quo. The Pharisees are chosen only because of Luke's need to explain ongoing Pharisaic hostility to the Christian movement in his own context of concern. The same verb for "ridiculing" is found in Ps 21(22):7 (also 34[35]:16).

15 Luke has a certain fondness for the sort of righteousness language that is found here (the same verb is found in 7:29, 35; 10:29; 18:14; and cf. 18:9; 20:20). The latter part of the verse makes clear that the contrast here is between outward image and inner reality (see 11:39, where the following verses develop the link to use of wealth; cf. further 11:44). The problem is not *self*-justification (as in Paul) but a concern that stops short by only being interested in the impression created upon other people (cf. 11:43). For a similar accusation (not of Pharisees), see *As. Mos.* 7:1–10; cf. *1 Enoch* 96:4. God's prime interest in the state of the heart has a strong OT basis (cf. 1 Sam 16:7; 1 Kgs 8:39; 1 Chr 28:9; Ps 7:10; Prov 21:2; 24:12). His access to the human heart is also spoken of in Acts 1:24; 15:8. The central importance of the heart is reflected as well in Acts 8:21.

The final clause may have existed as a saying in its own right: it has the antithetic exaggeration of a Semitic proverb and fits slightly awkwardly into the syntax here. For the kind of contrast involved, cf. 1:52; 14:11. The proverbial antithesis is applicable in particular instances but is hardly a universal truth. The use of βδέλυγμα, "abomination," no doubt gains in emotive force here from the extensive Septuagintal use of this word in connection with what God finds utterly revolting.

Explanation

The role of the Pharisees here reinforces the linking of chaps. 15 and 16. Here they seek to discredit Jesus' teaching on wealth because it represents a threat to their carefully nurtured public good standing.

Pharisees and disciples together have been the audience since 16:1. A raw nerve has been touched by this teaching, Luke suggests, precisely because it has collided with a deep-seated love of money—not that the Pharisees saw themselves as loving money; not that any of us do. Disturbed by the teaching, the Pharisees sneer at the teacher.

At least for this set of disturbed Pharisees, a hidden weakness was being revealed from behind their exemplary righteousness. Clearly it is Luke's opinion that in the attitude toward money the cracks are likely to show in what is otherwise an outwardly impressive veneer of righteousness, impressive even to ourselves. The present disquiet pointed to an underlying attitude that located righteousness in public opinion and not in the wellsprings of the human heart. But God finds abominable what is built (only) upon the basis of what impresses others and does not represent the true inner state.

The Demands of the Law and the Prophets, and Those of the Gospel of the Kingdom of God (16:16–18)

Bibliography

FOR 16:16:

Bachmann, M. "Johannes der Täufer bei Lukas: Nachzügler oder Vorläufer." In *Wort in der Zeit: Neutestamentliche Studien.* FS K. H. Rengstorf, ed. W. Haubeck and M. Bachmann. Leiden: Brill, 1964. 123–55, esp. 137–50. **Barnett, P. W.** "The Jewish Eschatological Prophets." Ph. D. diss., University of London, 1977. 145–210. **Betz, O.** "Jesu heiliger Krieg." *NovT* 2 (1957) 117–37, esp . 125–28. **Braumann, G.** "Dem Himmelreich wird Gewalt angetan." *ZNW* 52 (1961) 104–9. **Cameron, P. S.** *Violence and the Kingdom: The Interpretation of Matthew 11:12.* ANTJ 5. 2nd ed. Bern/Frankfurt: Lang, 1988. **Catchpole, D. R.** "The Law and the Prophets in Q." In *Tradition and Interpretation in the New Testament.* FS E. E. Ellis, ed. G. F. Hawthorne and O. Betz. Grand Rapids, MI/Tübingen: Eerdmans/Mohr, 1987. 95–109. ———. "On Doing Violence to the Kingdom." *JTSA* 25 (1978) 50–61. **Chamblin, K.** "John the Baptist and the Kingdom of God." *TynB* 15 (1964) 10–16. **Chilton, B. D.** *God in Strength.* 203–30. **Cortés, J. B.,** and **Gatti, F. M.** "On the Meaning of Luke 16:16." *JBL* 106 (1987) 247–59. **Danker, F. W.** "Luke 16:16: An Opposition Logion." *JBL* 77 (1958) 231–43. **Dungan, D. L.** "Jesus and Violence." In *Jesus, the Gospels, and the Church.* FS W. R. Farmer, ed. E. P. Sanders. Macon, GA: Mercer, 1987. 135–62. **Giesen, H.** "Verantwortung des Christen in der Gegenwart und Heilsvollendung: Ethik und Eschatologie nach Lk 13,24 und 16,16." *TGeg* 31 (1988) 218–28. **Haudebert, P.** "Abrogation ou accomplissement de la loi mosaïque? (Luc 16, 16–18)." *Impacts (Angers)* 4 (1984) 15–26. **Hoffmann, P.** *Studien.* 50–79. **Kaestli, J.-D.** *L'Eschatologie.* 24–27. **Kosch, D.** *Die Gottesherrschaft im Zeichen des Widerspruchs: Traditions- und redaktionsgeschichtliche Untersuchung von Lk 16,16//Mt 11,12f bei Jesus, Q, und Lukas.* Europäische Hochschulschriften 23/257. Bern/Frankfurt: Lang, 1985. ———. *Die eschatologische Tora des Menschensohnes: Untersuchungen zur Rezeption der Stellung Jesu zur Tora in Q.* Novum Testamentum et Orbis Antiquus 12. Fribourg/Göttingen: Universitätsverlag/Vandenhoeck & Ruprecht, 1989. 427–44. **Kümmel, W. G.** "'Das Gesetz und die Propheten gehen bis Johannes'-Lukas 16,16 im Zusammenhang der heilgeschichtlichen Theologie der Lukasschriften." In *Verborum Veritas,* ed. O. Böcher and K. Haacker. 89–102. ———. *Promise and Fulfilment: The Eschatological Message of Jesus.* SBT 1/23. Tr. D. M. Barton. London: SCM, 1957. 121–24. **Laufen, R.** *Die Doppelüberlieferungen.* 343–60. **Mearns, C.** "Realized Eschatology in Q? A Consideration of the Sayings in Luke 7.22, 11.20 and 16.16. *SJT* 40 (1987) 189–210. **Menoud, P.-H.** "De la manière d'entrer dans le royaume." *Flambeau (Yaoundé)* 55 (1979) 271–75. ———. "Le sens du verbe *βιάζεται* dans Lc 16,16." In *Mélanges bibliques.* FS B. Rigaux, ed. A. Descamps and A. de Halleux. 207–12; ET = "The Meaning of the Verb *βιάζεται* in Luke 16. 16." In *Jesus Christ and the Faith.* 192–201. **Moore, W. E.** "*Βιάζω, Αρπάζω* and Cognates in Josephus." *NTS* 21 (1974–75) 519–43. ———. "Violence to the Kingdom: Josephus and the Syrian Churches." *ExpTim* 100 (1989) 174–77. **Perrin, N.** *Rediscovering.* 74–77. **Prast, F.** *Presbyter und Evangelium in nachapostolischer Zeit: Die Abschiedsrede des Paulus in Milet (Apg. 20,17–38) im Rahmen der lukanischen Konzeption der Evangeliumsverkündigung.* FB 29. Stuttgart: Katholisches Bibelwerk, 1979. 278–81. **Schlosser, J.** *Le règne de Dieu.* 2:509–39. **Schnackenburg, R.** *God's Rule and Kingdom.* New York: Herder and Herder, 1963. 129–32. **Schrenk, G.** "*βιάζομαι βιαστής.*" *TDNT* 1:609–14. **Thiering, B. E.** "Are the 'Violent Men' False Teachers?" *NovT* 21 (1979) 293–97. **Wink, W.** *John the Baptist in the Gospel Tradition.*

20–23, 51–57. **Witherington, B., III.** "Jesus and the Baptist—Two of a Kind?" In *SBL 1988 Seminar Papers*, ed. D. J. Lull. Atlanta: Scholars, 1988. 225–44, esp. 237–38.

FOR 16:17:

Bammel, E. "Is Luke 16,16–18 of Baptist's Provenience?" *HTR* 51 (1958) 101–6. **Banks, R. J.** *Jesus and the Law in the Synoptic Tradition.* SNTSMS 28. Cambridge: University Press, 1975. 203–26. **Daube, D.** *The New Testament and Rabbinic Judaism.* London: Athlone, 1956. 285–300. **Dewey, A. J.** "Quibbling Over Serifs: Observations on Matt 5:18/Luke 16:17." *Forum* 5.2 (1989) 109–20. **Guelich, R. A.** *The Sermon on the Mount: A Foundation for Understanding.* Waco, TX: Word, 1982. 143–49. **Haudebert, P.** "Abrogation ou accomplissement de la loi mosaïque? (Luc 16,16–30,18)." *Impacts* 4 (1984) 15–26. **Honeyman, A. M.** "Matthew V. 18 and the Validity of the Law." *NTS* 1 (1954–55) 141–42. **Klinghardt, M.** *Gesetz und Volk Gottes.* 15–23, 78–96. **Schulz, S.** *Spruchquelle.* 114–20, 261–67. **Schürmann, H.** *Gottes Reich.* 124–29. ———. "'Wer daher eines dieser geringsten Gebote auflöst . . .': Wo fand Matthäus das Logion Mt. 5,19." *BZ* 4 (1960) 238–50. **Schwarz, G.** "*ἰῶτα ἕν ἢ μία χεραία.*" *ZNW* 66 (1975) 268–69. **Schweizer, E.** "Matth. 5, 17–20: Anmerkungen zum Gesetzverständnis des Matthäus." *Neotestamentica.* Zurich: Zwingli, 1963. 393–406. ———. "Noch einmals Mt 5,17–20." In *Das Wort und die Wörter.* FS G. Friedrich. Stuttgart: Kohlhammer, 1973. 69–73.

FOR 16:18:

Baltensweiler, H. *Die Ehe im Neuen Testament: Exegetische Untersuchungen über Ehe, Ehelosigkeit und Ehescheidung.* ATANT 52. Zürich: Zwingli, 1967. **Bammel, E.** "Markus 10,11f. und das jüdische Eherecht." *ZNW* 61 (1970) 95–101. **Berrouard, M.-F.** "L'Indissolubilité du mariage dans le Nouveau Testament." *LumVie* 4 (1952) 21–40. **Bockmuehl, M. N. A.** "Matthew 5.32; 19.9 in the Light of Pre-rabbinic Halakhah." *NTS* 35 (1989) 291–95. **Bonsirven, J.** *Le divorce dans le Nouveau Testament.* Paris/Tournai: Desclée, 1948. **Catchpole, D. R.** "The Synoptic Divorce Material as a Traditio-Historical Problem." *BJRL* 57 (1974–75) 92–127. **Coiner, H. G.** "Those 'Divorce and Remarriage' Passages (Matt. 5:32; 19:9; 1 Cor 7:10–16), with Brief Reference to the Mark and Luke Passages." *CTM* 39 (1968) 367–84. **D'Angelo, M. R.** "Remarriage and the Divorce Saying Attributed to Jesus." In *Divorce and Remarriage,* ed. W. D. Roberts. Kansas City: Ward and Ward, 1990. 78–106. **Delling, G.** "Das Logion Mk x.11 (und seine Abwandlungen) im Neuen Testament." *NovT* 1 (1956) 263–74. **Derrett, J. D.** *Law.* 363–88. **Descamps, A.-L.** "Les textes évangéliques sur le mariage." *RTL* 9 (1978) 259–86; 11 (1980) 5–50; ET = "The New Testament Doctrine on Marriage." In *Contemporary Perspectives on Christian Marriage,* ed. R. Malone and J. R. Connery. Chicago: Loyola University Press, 1984. 217–73, 347–63. **Donahue, J. R.** "Divorce: New Testament Perspectives." *The Month* 242 (1981) 113–20. **Down, M. J.** "The Sayings of Jesus about Marriage and Divorce." *ExpTim* 95 (1984) 332–34. **Dupont, J.** *Mariage et divorce dans l'évangile: Matthieu 19,3–12 et parallèles.* Bruges: Abbaye de Saint-André; Desclée de Brouwer, 1959. 45–88, 124–53. **Fitzmyer, J. A.** "Divorce among First-Century Palestinian Jews." In *H. L. Ginsberg Volume.* Eretz-Israel 14. Jerusalem: Israel Exploration Society, 1978. 103–10, 193. ———. "The Matthean Divorce Texts and Some New Palestinian Evidence." *TS* 37 (1976) 197–226; reprinted in *To Advance the Gospel: New Testament Studies.* New York: Crossroads, 1981, 79–111 (cited from here). **Greeven, H.** "Ehe nach dem Neuen Testament." *NTS* 15 (1968–69) 365–88. **Guelich, R. A.** *The Sermon on the Mount: A Foundation for Understanding.* Waco, TX: Word, 1982. 199–211. **Haacker, K.** "Ehescheidung und Wiederverheiratung im Neuen Testament." *TQ* 151 (1971) 28–38. **Harrington, W.** "Jesus' Attitude toward Divorce." *ITQ* 37 (1970) 199–209. **Hoffmann, P.** "Jesus' Saying about Divorce and Its Interpretation in the New Testament Tradition."

Concil 55 (1970) 51–66. **Isaksson, A.** *Marriage and Ministry in the New Testament: A Study with Special Reference to Mt. 19,3–12 and 1. Cor. 11,3–16.* ASNU 24. Lund: Gleerup, 1965. **Jensen, J.** "Does *Porneia* Mean Fornication? A Critique of Bruce Malina." *NovT* 20 (1978) 161–84. **Kilgallen, J. J.** "To What Are the Matthean Exception-Texts (5,32 and 19,9) an Exception." *Bib* 61 (1980) 102–5. **Kretzer, A.** "Die Frage: Ehe auf Dauer und ihre mögliche Trennung nach Mt 19,3–12." In *Biblische Randbemerkungen.* FS R. Schnackenburg, ed. H. Merklein and J. Lange. Bonn: Echter, 1974. 218–30. **Laufen, R.** *Die Doppelüberlieferung.* 343–57. **Lohfink, G.** "Jesus und die Ehrescheidung: Zur Gattung und Sprachintention von Mt 5,32." In *Biblische Randbemerkungen.* FS R. Schnackenburg, ed. H. Merklein and J. Lange. Bonn: Echter, 1974. 207–17. **MacRae, G. W.** "New Testament Perspectives on Marriage and Divorce." In *Divorce and Remarriage in the Catholic Church,* ed. L. G. Wrenn. New York: Newman, 1973. 1–15. **Mahoney, A.** "A New Look at the Divorce Clause in Mt 5,32 and 19,9." *CBQ* 30 (1968) 29–38. **Malina, B.** "Does *Porneia* Mean Fornication?" *NovT* 14 (1972) 10–17. **Mueller, J. R.** "The Temple Scroll and the Gospel Divorce Texts." *RevQ* 10 (1979–81) 247–56. **Myre, A.** "Dix ans d'exégèse sur le divorce dans le Nouveau Testament." In *Le divorce: L'Eglise catholique ne devrait-elle pas modifier son attitude séculaire à l'égard de l'indissolubilité du mariage?* Montreal: Fides, 1973. 139–62. **Nembach, U.** "Ehescheidung nach alttestamentlichem und jüdi schem Recht." *TZ* 26 (1970) 161–71. **O'Rourke, J. J.** "Does the New Testament Condemn Sexual Intercourse outside Marriage?" *TS* 37 (1976) 478–97. **Pesch, R.** *Freie Treue: Die Christen und die Ehescheidung.* Freiburg im B.: Herder, 1971. 56–60. ———. "Die neutestamentliche Weisung für die Ehe." *BibLeb* 9 (1968) 208–21. **Richards, H. J.** "Christ on Divorce." *Scr* 11 (1959) 22–32. **Ruckstuhl, E.** "Hat Jesus die Unauflösigkeit der Ehe gelehrt?" In *Jesus im Horizont der Evangelien.* Stuttgarter Biblische Aufsatzbände 3. Stuttgart: Katholisches Bibelwerk, 1988. 49–68. **Sabourin, L.** "The Divorce Clauses (Mt. 5,32; 19,9)." *BTB* 2 (1972) 80–86. **Schaller, B.** "Die Sprüche über Ehescheidung und Wiederheirat in der synoptischen Überlieferung." In *Der Ruf Jesus und die Antwort der Gemeinde.* FS J. Jeremias, ed. E. Lohse. Göttingen: Vandenhoeck & Ruprecht, 1970. 226–46. **Schneider, G.** "Jesu Wort über die Ehescheidung in der Überlieferung des Neuen Testaments." *TTZ* 80 (1971) 65–87. **Schubert, K.** "Ehescheidung im Judentum zur Zeit Jesu." *TQ* 151 (1971) 23–27. **Schürmann, H.** "Neutestamentliche Marginalien zur Frage nach der Institutionalität, Unauflösbarkeit und Sakramentalität der Ehe." In *Kirche und Bibel,* ed. O. Böcher et al. Paderborn: Schöningh, 1979. 409–30. **Smith, D. T.** "The Matthean Exception Clauses in the Light of Matthew's Theology and Community." *StBibT* 17 (1989) 55–82. **Stenger, W.** "Zur Rekonstruktion eines Jesusworts anhand der synoptischen Ehescheidungslogien." *Kairos* 26 (1984) 194–205. **Stock, A.** "Matthean Divorce Texts." *BTB* 8 (1978) 24–33. **Tosato, A.** "The Law of Leviticus 18:18: A Reexamination." *CBQ* 46 (1984) 199–214. **Vawter, B.** "The Divorce Clauses in Matt. 5:32 and 19:9." *CBQ* 16 (1954) 155–67. ———. "The Biblical Theology of Divorce." *ProcCTSA* 22 (1967) 223–43. ———. "Divorce and the New Testament." *CBQ* 39 (1977) 528–42. **Wiebe, P. H.** "Jesus' Divorce Exception." *JETS* 32 (1989) 327–33. **Wijngards, J. N. M.** "Do Jesus' Words on Divorce (Lk 16:18) Admit of No Exception." *Jeevadhara* 6 (1975) 399–411. **Wrege, H.-T.** *Die Überlieferungsgeschichte der Bergpredigt.* WUNT 9. Tübingen: Mohr-Siebeck, 1968. 66–70.

Translation

[16] *"[There was only] the law and the prophets until John; since then the good news of the kingdom of God is announced,*[a] *and everyone takes vigorous steps to enter*[b] *it.* [17] *It is easier for heaven and earth to pass away than for the projecting part of one letter of the law to drop out.* [18] *Everyone who dismisses his wife and marries another commits adultery, and the one*[c] *who marries someone who has gained dismissal from a husband commits adultery."*

Notes

[a] ℵ G 788 finish the verse here.

[b] "To enter" is only implied by the Gr. text. sy[p] supplies the verb explicitly.

[c] ℵ A W Θ Ψ $f^{1,13}$ etc. have πᾶς, "everyone," clearly to complete the parallelism with the first half of the verse.

Form/Structure/Setting

The role of the unit is to identify a fundamental parallelism between the demands of "the law and the prophets" and those of the preaching of the good news of the kingdom of God. Paradoxically the bestowal of the free and generous love of the heavenly Father makes yet more rigorous demands upon those who will respond than had the law and prophets that preceded it.

The three verses of this unit have no intrinsic unity. It seems likely that, on the basis of a measure of similarity already evident, Luke has drawn the tradition behind v 16 into a source that has influenced him already in vv 14–15 and from which he extracts vv 17 and 18 (cf. the discussion at 16:14–15 of Schürmann's source observations). I will discuss in turn the likely tradition history of each of the three verses.

A form of v 16 is preserved in Matt 11:12–13, but the wording and sense are strikingly different. Both evangelists appear to have tailored the tradition to their own concerns. For the sake of the John the Baptist setting in which he uses this tradition, Matthew delays the mention of "the law and the prophets" so as to begin with a mention of John (which he must freshly formulate since the original reference goes with "the law and the prophets"). In Matthew's hands the text is part of the clarification of the relative importance of John and Jesus (cf. esp. 11:11): with the coming of the kingdom of God in the ministry of Jesus, John, for all his importance, is a superseded figure. This boundary-marking function is enhanced by the way in which the delayed mention of "the law and the prophets" allows for a renewed reference to John. ("Of heaven," "the Baptist," "until now," the linking "for," "all" [with the reversal in order of "the prophets" and "the law" in line with the prophetic identity of John in v 9], and "prophesied" [also in view of v 9] are other minor Matthean interventions.)

Luke for his part will be responsible for εὐαγγελίζεται, "announced as good news" (for the passive use of the verb, cf. Luke 7:22), in place of Matthew's βιάζεται (normally "use violence" [if middle], or "be violently treated" [if passive]; only Luke in the NT uses this verb in connection with the kingdom of God [4:43; 8:1; cf. Acts 8:12]; Catchpole's considerations ["The Law and the Prophets," 95–98] in favor of Luke's verb in the original do not outweigh this). Perhaps somewhat in compensation, Luke transfers the Matthean verb to the following clause and in this way avoids the rare cognate noun βιαστής, "violent person" (the Matthean use is earlier than any other reported instances of the word). Along with this change comes the new subject "everyone," the added "into," and the loss of the verb ἁρπάζουσιν (normally: "steal/carry off/snatch"; perhaps here: "plunder") used in the Matthean form.

This suggests that the source form ran something like: "the law and the prophets [were] until John; since then the kingdom of God βιάζεται and violent people plunder it." Though the views are legion, it is perhaps best to take βιάζεται as referring to the kingdom of God powerfully forcing its way in the world and against the opposing forces of Satan (for the absolute use of the middle, cf. Josephus, *Life*, 303; *War* 3.518; *Ant* 4.226). The imagery, then, would be that of a newly arisen conflict situation, a power struggle, in which the power of the kingdom of God, effective in the ministry of Jesus, encounters a powerful opposition from those who would snatch away the ones who are entering the kingdom, and perhaps also the kingdom worker(s). (Taking the verb and cognate noun as both producing negative statements makes the second statement somewhat redundant, and can hardly be the sense Matthew has attributed to his source; no matter what is done with the first statement, taking the second statement as positive is, with its clearly negative terms, too cryptically parabolic to be plausible.) It is not clear whether in this earlier form John should be assigned to "the law and the prophets" or whether, with Jesus, he belongs to the dynamic of the arrival of the kingdom.

The motif of the presence of the powers of the kingdom of God and the idea of a conflict situation thereby created both find a natural place in the tradition of the historical Jesus. The evidence is equivocal over whether the historical Jesus is more likely to have included John with himself, as belonging to the new situation, or not (he probably considered that he partly did and partly did not). Though the source form leaves it quite unclear in exactly what sense the law and the prophets have now been surpassed, it does seem rather less likely that the historical Jesus would have used "the law and the prophets" to point to a preceding era (it is just possible that rather than the source analysis offered above, we should identify the source form as more like Matt 11:12 [without "until now," with "of God," and perhaps without "the Baptist"], to which Matthew has linked "all the prophets and the law," partly for the sake of the context [see above], and partly in line with his evident interest in this pairing; and to which Luke has linked "the law and the prophets" under the influence of the source into which he is incorporating this tradition [see discussion at 16:14–15; the source involved would be reflected in part in Matt 5:17, 18, 20, 32]).

A form of Luke 16:17 is preserved in Matt 5:18. Though set in different contexts, in both settings the verse is designed to reassert the validity of the law, against the background of some sort of suggestion that the Jesus movement may no longer affirm its full validity. The awkwardness (in Matthew's form) of having two consecutive ἕως ἄν, "until," clauses is normally taken as implying that one is original (and so Luke has restructured to give an "it is easier . . ." form to the comparison, perhaps under the influence of the tradition that he reproduces in 18:25 [basing himself solely on the similarity with this text, Dewey (*Forum* 5.2 [1989] 109–20) has pronounced in favor of the Lukan form, but on this assumption it is hard to see how the development of the Matthean text can be explained]), and that the other is Matthean (or pre-Matthean editing). On the basis of the ἀμὴν . . . οὐ μὴ . . . ἕως, "amen . . . will certainly not . . . until," pattern that emerges (found in Mark 9:1; 13:30; 14:25; Matt 10:23), Klinghardt (*Gesetz*, 18–19) has recently argued that it is the first of the ἕως, "until," clauses that has been added later. But it is this first clause that the Lukan form reflects, and Klinghardt's view requires a complexity in the tradition history to which he gives too little attention. The usual view is to be preferred that it is the second ἕως, "until," clause that has been added. It remains less certain whether the ἀμὴν λέγω ὑμῖν, "amen, I say to you," opening was to be found in the shared source, whether Luke's use of different verbs in the paralleled phrase or Matthew's repetition of the same verb is earlier, and whether "one iota or" is Matthew's addition or Luke's omission.

The sentiment expressed here is often denied to the historical Jesus and attributed to later rigorist Jewish Christians, but the evident difficulty that modern interpreters have in giving the text a fitting sense in the later first-century context of our present Gospels can be as well accounted for by tracing the text to the historical Jesus as by tracing it to a rigorist group whose traditions were somehow incorporated into the gospel traditions of rather less rigorous Christians. There is, however, an apparent orientation to the text, rather than to the substance of Scripture here, that fits less well with the core Jesus-of-history materials (could the original have spoken only of the failure of the law, with both the Lukan and Matthean forms reflecting polemical development? or is the apparent orientation to the text only a rhetorical figure, drawn from the rhetorical repertoire of the day [as Dewey, *Forum* 5.2 (1989) 114]?).

Luke 16:18 is related to Matt 5:32; 19:9; Mark 10:11–12, and needs to be considered, as well, in relation to 1 Cor 7:10–11; Mark 10:9 (par. Matt 19:6). The source considerations represented in the literature are both extensive and highly complex, and full justice cannot be done to them here. Some of the main points will, however, be noted and some suggestions made.

Luke does not have the "exception clause" found in both the Matthean forms of this tradition. It is most often considered a Matthean addition, but against this consensus assumption has been urged the apparently Semitic form of παρεκτὸς λόγου πορνείας (lit. "apart from a word of sexual impurity"), reinforced by the likelihood that Matthean redaction would have produced the μὴ ἐπὶ πορνείᾳ (RSV: "except for unchastity") that is found in Matt 19:9. These considerations granted, it is still much easier to explain the addition of "the exception clause" than its deletion. So if it is not a Matthean addition, it is best taken as a pre-Matthean addition (and as a case where Luke and Matthew had access to different forms of their shared material).

Caught up in this source decision are both the question of how the phrase is to be linked into its clause syntactically and that of the meaning to be ascribed to the term πορνεία here. The syntax options that have been canvassed include those represented by the following paraphrases: (*i*) "setting to one side the case of fornication (which will not be here addressed)"; (*ii*) "in addition to the defilement already caused by her immorality (which has led to the action in question)"; (*iii*) "no exception made for instances of immorality"; (*iv*) "(the judgment applies in all cases) except those involving the immorality of the wife" (here there are those who restrict the exception to dismissal, as well as those who relate the exception to both dismissal and remarriage). It can be said that most of these views would not have been canvassed if there had not been felt a need to support the indissolubility of marriage. The most natural and obvious is the second form of (*iv*), and there seems to be no adequate reason for moving away from it.

What is πορνεία here? It has mostly been taken as a less precise synonym for μοιχεία ("adultery"), cognate verbs of which are used for the (other) references in the texts to the committing of adultery. An alternative view that has become quite popular is to give πορνεία here the sense that it probably has in Acts 15:20, 29; 21:25, that is to say that the sexual impurity involved is that of having contracted a marriage within degrees of kinship proscribed in the OT (see Lev

18:6–19; 20:11–21; Deut 27:20; Ezek 22:10). That *πορνεία* could carry this sense finds support in the Qumran text CD 4:20–5:10, where זנות, *zĕnût* (a term the LXX translates with *πορνεία*) is applied to marriage within such prohibited degrees of kinship.

If the exception clause is a later development, then the correct choice for its meaning is related to the question of the cultural setting of, and the role for, this exception clause. Only in a setting where Jewish sensibilities are being imposed on gentile converts who come from a background where kinship marriage rules are less strict does the second choice make good sense: we must have a situation in which conversion involves the undoing of such marriages, not simply one in which converts are directed not to enter into such marriages (as is in view in Acts 15). Such a setting is certainly not impossible (especially if the development is pre-Matthean), but does seem less likely than the alternatives that are available.

Whatever sense we give the exception clause, it would appear to involve the attempt to develop the saying of Jesus in a manner concerned with practical implementation in the life of the church. (In working toward an implementation of the ethical vision of Jesus, it is always important to recognize the distinctive style in which much of it is presented: to go to the heart of the matter, Jesus often addresses matters as though a particular principle could be implemented in total isolation from both practical considerations and other ethical principles that make their own proper demands [cf. the discussion at 6:29–30 and 10:42]; Jesus' concern is to establish a vision, much more than to give practical directives for life; this has in practice made the implementation of certain of his tenets a continuing matter of controversy and division in the life of the church.)

A rather more likely setting than the one discussed above is supplied by the mores of a strict Jewish view of adultery. In the OT period, adultery was a capital offense (Lev 20:10; Deut 22:22), which therefore left no practical possibility for a marriage to continue beyond an act of adultery! Though there are questions about the implementation of this law in the Roman period, its continuing validity is attested in the Mishnaic and Talmudic sources (cf. Schneider, *TDNT* 4:731–32; for the intertestamental period, cf. *Jub.* 30:8–9). The early rabbinic sources reflect, however, a clear desire to circumscribe as far as possible the sphere in which such a severe penalty was to be enforced. A wife whose life was to be spared was certainly to be divorced (without return of dowry). She was said to be forbidden to her husband and to have become unclean to him (see *m. Soṭa* 5:1; 3:6; 4:2; etc. cf. *Jub.* 33:9; this understanding is probably to be traced back to Num 5:11–31 coupled with Deut 24:4, and in connection with the ideas of uncleanness, cf. as well the restriction on the marriage of priests in Lev 21:7; note, however, that *m. Soṭa* 2:6 may assume the possibility of being taken back despite all this, when it disallows from the scope of a priestly investigation cases of suspected adultery behavior that precedes such a taking back [Danby's translation glosses this text so as to make it apply to what transpired after divorce and before a subsequent remarriage to the original husband, but this rather sets the text in conflict with Deut 24:4, and is for that reason not likely to be correct (on the other hand, my own reading stands in tension with the general principle with which *m. Soṭa* 2:6 concludes)]). In a context determined by such views of forbiddenness and uncleanness, it is easy to see that the implementation of Jesus' teaching would need to make allowances for the conviction that adultery caused the total destruction of a marriage. (In such a setting the exception clause may, but need not, have been developed as an exposition of Deut 24:1.)

Somewhat analogous situations existed in the wider Greco-Roman world, but there the imperative to divorce had to do not with purity and forbiddeness but with issues of public shame and honor (see Schneider, *TDNT* 4:732–33; and cf. Malina, *New Testament World*, 25–50, for the role of shame in ancient culture). And since the teaching of Jesus (and of the early church) involved at least at points a self-consciously critical engagement with societal assumptions about the maintenance of one's public honor, it seems less likely that the Matthean texts developed as an accommodation to this particular set of cultural mores.

If we return now to the texts with the assumption that the exception clauses represent a later development, we are still left with a series of texts that manifest significant differences. Can we trace the development of our present texts? What is the original that has given rise to the present texts?

Each of the texts except Matt 19:9 includes a second half that contemplates the divorce and remarriage of a woman. So it seems more likely that Matt 19:9 is an abbreviation than that each of the other texts has been developed from the shorter form reflected in Matt 19:9 (1 Cor 7:10–11 seems to reflect an awareness of the double form, in a form that has, however, also been influenced by the tradition reflected in Mark 10:9; Klinghardt, *Gesetz*, 21, is quite wrong to appeal to Herm. *Man.* 4.1.6 as a second witness to the shorter form: only the first half of the Gospel tradition is relevant to the flow of thought there, and the reversal of male and female roles is provided for in 4.1.8 [cf. v 10]).

Matt 5:32 is distinctive in not mentioning a remarriage of the man following the divorce. On the normal understanding of *ποιεῖ αὐτὴν μοιχευθῆναι* (RSV: "makes her an adulteress"), this is sufficiently accounted for by the focus on the effect upon the future of the spurned wife. An alternative view of these words will be explored below, which will involve the assumption that originally a remarriage was specified here (and is still assumed), even though the antithesis form that Matthew has crafted to parallel the other antitheses of Matt 5 has led to the omission of specific mention of the remarriage. In any case the assumption must be in favor of the earliest source having spoken of a remarriage.

The agreement of Matt 5:32 and Luke 16:16 in *πᾶς ὁ ἀπολύων τὴν γυναῖκα αὐτοῦ* (lit. "everyone, the one loosing the wife of him") and *ἀπολελυμένην* (lit. "having been loosed") suggests that these texts have been influenced by a shared source beyond that reflected in Mark 10:11–12. For the second half of the verse, the difference is only syntactical and the question of the more original form is of little interest (probably Matthew has been somewhat influenced by the syntax of his Markan source). For the first half of the verse, while many have considered Luke to be the better witness, it seems much more likely that it is the rather puzzling Matthean form that has been rendered more simple by Luke.

Does Luke conform the sense to that of his Markan source, or could it be that he rightly renders the sense of Matthew's difficult phrase? Since the vocabulary of adultery did not lend itself to an easy syntactical pattern for identifying the one who is the wronged party in an act of adultery (in the OT [both Greek and MT] this must always be worked out from the context), and since in ancient thought the wronged party in any case was always a man, there were considerable difficulties in the way of saying that adultery had been committed against (rather than with) a woman: that her marriage had been violated by her husband's sexual infidelity. Mark has μοιχᾶται ἐπ' αὐτήν (lit. "he commits adultery upon her"), which is normally taken as "he commits adultery against her [the former wife]," on the basis that a following Gk. acc. case is the otherwise attested way of expressing "adultery with," but no parallels to this usage have been reported (it is taken as "adultery with" by Turner, *BT* 7 [1956] 151–52; Schaller, "Ehescheidung," 239–45; etc.; this option does find some support from the use in connection with a woman of μοιχευθῆναι ἐπί in the sense "to commit adultery with [a man]" in *Constitutiones Apostolorum* 1.3.4 [a late fourth-century text, which, while it echoes the thought of Matt 5:28, has no literary link with the Gospel texts under discussion]). Passive forms for μουχεύειν, "to commit adultery," are not frequent. The passive was used of a woman's involvement in adultery, but would not the passive also be required if one wished to speak of a woman as having adultery committed against her? Again this usage is not documented, but its assumption here would mean that each of the Gospel forms has essentially the same meaning for the first half of the verse (the Matthean text, with its simple acc. rather than the ἐπί, is perhaps influenced by the preceding ποιεῖ, "he causes").

Our search for the most original form of this tradition needs only now to address the question of the difference between Mark and Luke/Matthew over the second half of the tradition: the Markan text has a statement that parallels the first half with the role of man and woman interchanged. Luke/Matthew consider instead the case of a man marrying a divorced woman. Here the difference is more significant than it turned out to be in the first half of the saying, but perhaps it is not as great as at first appears. Matthew and Luke agree in not equating the dismissed wife of the first half with the dismissed wife of the second half (otherwise a definite article would have been used). Could this be because the second half envisages a situation in which the initiative for the divorce has come from the woman and not from the man? Though in Jewish law only a man can divorce (so the passive verb), it was also true in Jewish law that there were situations in which a woman could manipulate a situation to guarantee the granting of a divorce. We have seen above how this would be so in terms of uncleanness and forbiddenness. See *m. Ket.* 7:1–5, 10 for other situations of required divorce, *b. Giṭ* 90b for a situation where it is "a religious duty" to divorce, and *m. Ket.* 7:6 for other actions likely to provoke divorce. *M. Soṭa* 51 is of particular interest here: a woman who has had a liaison with a paramour is said to be forbidden both to the husband *and to the paramour.* The thought is not the same as the Gospel tradition, but there is a significant degree of parallel. It will be argued below that in the first half of the saying divorce *in order to* remarry is the subject of concern. Here I am suggesting that the same is true for the second half as well. In both cases the abandoning of one spouse in favor of a replacement is in focus. My proposal involves the suggestion that in the Jewish use of the passive of ἀπολύειν in connection with divorce there is a phenomenon that runs parallel to the use of the passive of μοιχεύειν to speak of a woman committing adultery (where the active is used for a man committing adultery). If I am correct, then the extent of the innovation of the Markan text is only to take the next step, in a wider Greco-Roman cultural setting where wives had equal ability before the law to initiate divorce, and to reformulate the tradition in terms of overt female initiation, and then to carry this through in terms of a full parallelism between the first and second halves by identifying the woman of the second half as herself guilty of adultery.

That the underlying tradition may be traced to the historical Jesus has, rightly, not been seriously questioned. It is of a piece with his equation of lustful desire and adultery (Matt 5:28; this does, however, have interesting Jewish parallels in *Rab. Lev.* 23:12 [to 18:3]; *Pesiq. R.* 24[124b]; etc.) and his insistence that divorce is a human distortion of the divine intention, which should not happen (Mark 10:9). Prohibition of divorce is sometimes said to be reflected in the Qumran texts CD 4:20–5:1; 11QTemple 57:17–19, but all that is clearly present in those texts is a prohibition of polygamy (as Vawter, *CBQ* 39 [1977] 533, aptly notes, the assumption of lifelong unions in these texts, as the background against which the words against polygamy are spoken, is no more a prohibition of divorce than is Eccl 9:9). What appears to be quite revolutionary in Jesus' words here is the identification of a man's infidelity to his wife as adultery, since in Jewish thought of the period a man could be guilty of adultery in connection with the marriage of another, but there seems to be no provision for conceiving of him as guilty of adultery against his own wife. A number of recent studies have endeavored to portray Jesus' teaching (especially the second half of the saying as normally understood) as being, on the basis of Lev 21:7, an instance of the tendency in Judaism (especially in Pharisaism) to laicize, and therefore apply to all, regulations pertaining to priests (there is a similar phenomenon to be noted in connection with royal texts), but the Lev 21:7 restriction has no real connection with issues either of divorce or adultery.

Comment

In Luke's understanding here, the preaching of the good news of the kingdom of God, quite the contrary to offering easy entry into the kingdom, involves an intensification of the demands of the law. The case of divorce is used illustratively in the unit, but in the larger shape of the section the focus will be on the confirmation and intensification of the law's demands in connection with wealth.

16 "The law and the prophets" here anticipates "Moses and the prophets" in vv 29, 31 (and cf. 24:44; Acts 28:23; in connection with synagogue readings, the identical phrase is found in Acts 13:15; the idiom is reflected at Qumran [1QS 1:3; 8:15–16; CD 5:21–6:1; etc.]). It is clear that in Lukan understanding the "law and the prophets" are in no sense superseded, but rather added to in the sense of being made yet more rigorous (behind 10:25–28 lies the assumption of the continuing ethical validity of the law; to claim that Luke maintains the validity of the law and prophets only in a prophetic sense can do no justice to Luke's thought). At the same time it must be said that in Acts 15 there will be an in-principle sparing of the Gentiles of the demands of the law as belonging fundamentally to Jewishness and not to salvation, and that in Acts 10–11 there will be a recognition that in dealings between Jewish and gentile Christians God's cleansing activity overcomes the problems that the needs of ritual purity would otherwise have presented. Luke probably believed that at the inter-human level the not-distinctly-Jewish aspects of the law were substantially the same as enlightened ethical views in the Greco-Roman world of his day.

In a Lukan framework, the beginning point for the new situation can hardly exclude John, even if the full introduction of the new situation is kept for Jesus (see Luke 1–2; 3:1–6, 7–18; 7:1–50; for a careful consideration of the Lukan linguistic evidence relevant to whether μέχρι, "until," and ἀπὸ τότε, "since then," are inclusive or exclusive of John, see Bachmann, "Johannes," 141–49). The same language of announcing the good news of the kingdom of God is found in 4:43; 8:1; cf. Acts 8:12. The good news is of the arrival of the kingdom of God: that which is heralded is at the same time introduced (cf. at 4:18). Luke means essentially the same thing as the Matthean text, which thinks in terms of the kingdom of God powerfully making its way (βιάζεται). In the following clause, however, Luke has not only reformulated, but he seems to have taken the meaning in quite a different direction. The Matthean text thinks in terms of a conflict situation, the Lukan in terms of an appropriate response. Luke is probably looking back to the decisive action of the desperate man in 16:1–8, or to the radical choice implied in v 13. Everyone who would take advantage of the good news must take vigorous steps to enter the kingdom of God. (βιάζεται εἰς means "enter forcibly into," or, somewhat weakened, "try hard to enter" [Epictetus 4.7.20–21; Josephus, *War* 4.323]. Taken as a passive, it could mean "invite pressingly into" [as Menoud, "Le sens," 207–12; Cortés and Gatti, *JBL* 106 (1987) 247–59], but this would be much less contextually appropriate.) The "everyone" is of course not comprehensive; it can refer only to everyone who cares to embrace the good news of the kingdom of God.

17 Apocalyptic eschatology is not in view here as it will be in 21:33, so there is no sense in which the time frame for the validity of the law is being limited (despite the popularity of the contrary opinion, it is likely that the same is true for Matt 5:18: with the added final clause Matthew probably intends to make room for his understanding that the process of prophetic fulfillment in Christ does involve the selective abrogation of aspects of the law, while heaven and earth continue). The continuing validity of every detail of the law is here being lent the sense of permanence that adheres to the creation itself. On the permanence of the law, cf. Bar 4:1; Tob 1:6; 4 Ezra 9:37; *2 Apoc. Bar.* 77:15. κεραία is literally a horn. The term is applied to projections (probably both ornamental and those that distinguish similar letters) in the formation of letters in writing, and also to accents and breathings (see BAGD, 428). In Philo, *Flacc.* 131; Plut. *Mor.* 1100A; Dio Chrys. 31.86 the term is used, paired with "syllable," with reference to the smallest detail of a document (yet smaller than a syllable). We probably should not find reflected here the same meticulous concern for attention to detail that was later to be expressed by the rabbis in similar language (see Str-B, 1:247–49). The addition of v 17 makes it quite clear that v 16 is not to be read as implying any kind of supersession of the law, while v 18 to follow suggests that an ethical focus should be given to the sense of v 17.

18 The use in Jewish texts of ἀπολύειν in connection with divorce finds confirmation from early second-century texts from Murabbaʿat (see details in Fitzmyer, "Matthean Divorce Texts," 90–91). Whereas the subject of the related tradition in Mark 10:2–9 is divorce, the subject here is divorce and remarriage. Indeed it is very likely that the subject here is divorce for the sake of remarriage. It can only be the existence of the Matthean exception clauses that, situated as they are between the verbs that express the two actions, has stood in the way of an adequate consideration of this understanding of the text (Descamps, *RTL* 11 [1980] 16 n. 37, has noted that among the Greek Fathers the linking καί [lit. "and"] was often understood in a final sense [that is as denoting purpose: so, "dismisses . . . in order to marry"]). Perhaps also the literary (but hardly original) link in Mark (and retained in Matthew) between the discussion on divorce in 10:2–9 and that on divorce for remarriage (as I see it) in vv 10–12 has slanted the perspective from which this tradition has been examined. Surely the remarriage is to be interpreted as adultery and in no sense the divorce already (to call divorce adultery would represent a quite arbitrary equation of incommensurables). At the very least we may say that the divorce is no more than the logically necessary antecedent to the remarriage, and since the focus of the saying is upon the remarriage, it is most natural to take the sense as "divorces in order to." As explored more fully in *Form/Structure/Setting* above, it seems best to allow the concern for remarriage to be the dominant focus as well for the second half of the verse. A Jewish woman could not initiate divorce, but she could provoke it. The paramour who is waiting in the wings for his love to extricate herself from her present marriage is, in marrying his beloved, only giving a cloak of legitimacy to the adultery that he, and therefore she, are arranging to commit. We can appreciate the full challenge of these words that much more by reminding ourselves that adultery continued to be a capital offense in Jewish eyes.

The present verse is meant to be illustrative of the way in which the demands of the kingdom of God take up and confirm the imperatives of the law and the prophets (Exod 20:14; Lev 18:20; Deut 5:18; Mal 2:14–16), but go on to be yet more demanding in very specific ways.

Explanation

Until John, there were only the law and the prophets; now the ministries of John and Jesus, involved as they were with the coming of the kingdom of God, both confirm the demands of the law and make yet more radical demands upon those who wish to come to terms with what God is now doing.

For Luke, John is already part of this new thing that is coming to pass in the ministry of Jesus, even if he represents it only in a preliminary way. The God who has been the God of the law and the prophets has now acted in a fresh and new way in connection with the establishing of his own rule. Jesus and, in a preliminary way, John before him have been heralds introducing the new reality of the presence of the kingdom of God. The power and reality of the kingdom of God make their presence felt in the ministry of Jesus and his call for a response. Those who would make their way into this kingdom must act decisively and energetically to align themselves with the rule of God that is presently being established. The status quo is no longer adequate.

We should not, however, get the impression that this development places in question the continuing validity of the demands of the law. (By the time we get to Acts 10–11 and 15 it will become clear that for gentile Christians, this apparently straightforward statement can no longer be understood in a simple manner. But nothing of that emerges here. The following verse will draw the focus onto the thought that the ethical standards of the OT are retained and even made more rigorous with the announcement now of the good news of the kingdom of God.)

Though the OT contained the impassioned "I hate divorce" of Mal 2:16, from what we can determine, Jewish divorce practice of the period seems to have been fairly loose (based on Deut 24:1), though not without protest from those who, on the basis of the same text, would restrict the ground for divorce to sexual infidelity. Just as Jesus identified the lustful look as already adultery, so he identified as adultery the use of the societal provision for divorce and remarriage in order to abandon a spouse and move on to a partner seen as more desirable. Jesus took the revolutionary step of insisting that a man also can be guilty of adultery against his wife (in Jewish understanding of the period a man could only be guilty of adultery against someone else's marriage; but a woman could also be guilty of adultery against her husband). Whether it is a case of a man leaving his wife for better pastures or a case of a woman angling for a divorce from her husband to do the same (Jewish women could not legally initiate divorce), Jesus considered the resulting union to be an adulterous violation of the previous marriage. This teaching represents a particular application of his general dictum (not reported in Luke): "what God has yoked together let no human being separate" (Mark 10:9). And it is a good illustration of the way in which the standards demanded in connection with the kingdom of God build upon, but are yet more stringent than, those set in place by the OT law.

The Outcome of Life for the Rich Man and Lazarus (16:19–31)

Bibliography

Alexandre, M. "L'Interprétation de Luc 16,19–31 chez Grégoire de Nysse." In *Epektasis: Mélanges patristiques.* FS J. Daniélou, ed. J. Fontaine and C. Kannengiesser. Paris: Beauchesne, 1972. 425–41. **Barth, K.** "Miserable Lazarus (Text: Luke 16:19–31)." *USR* 46 (1934–35) 259–68. **Batiffol, P.** "Trois Notes exégetiques: Sur Luc 16, 19." *RB* 9 (1912) 541. **Bauckham, R.** "The Rich Man and Lazarus: the Parable and the Parallels." *NTS* 37 (1991) 225–46. **Bishop, E. F.** "A Yawning Chasm." *EvQ* 45 (1973) 3–5. **Bornhäuser, K.** "Zum Verständnis der Geschichte vom reichen Mann und armen Lazarus: Luke 16, 19–31." *NKZ* 39 (1928) 833–43. ———. *Studien zum Sondergut des Lukas.* Gütersloh: Bertelsmann, 1934. 138–60. **Boyd, W. P.** "Apocalyptic and Life after Death." *SE* 5 [= TU 103] (1968) 39–56, esp. 50–51. **Bruyne, D. de.** "Chasma, Lc. 16, 26." *RB* 30 (1921) 400–405. **Cadbury, H. J.** "A Proper Name for Dives: Lexical Notes on Luke-Acts VI." *JBL* 81 (1962) 399–402. ———. "The Name of Dives." *JBL* 84 (1965) 73. **Cadron, F. H.** "'Son' in the Parable of the Rich Man and Lazarus." *ExpTim* 13 (1901–02) 523. **Cantinat, J.** "Le mauvais riche et Lazare." *BVC* 48 (1962) 19–26. **Cave, C. H.** "Lazarus and the Lukan Deuteronomy." *NTS* 15 (1968–69) 319–25. **Cölle, R.** "Zur Exegese und zur homiletischen Verwertung des Gleichnisses vom reichen Mann und armen Lazarus: Luk. 16, 19–31." *TSK* 75 (1902) 652–65. **Degenhardt, H.-J.** *Lukas, Evangelist der Armen.* 133–35. **Derrett, J. D. M.** "Fresh Light on St Luke xvi: II. Dives and Lazarus and the Preceding Sayings." *NTS* 7 (1960–61) 364–80; reprinted in *Law.* 78–99. **Dunkerley, R.** "Lazarus." *NTS* 5 (1958–59) 321–27. **Dupont, J.** *Béatitudes.* 3:60–64, 111–12, 162–82. ———. "L'Après-mort dans l'oeuvre de Luc." *RTL*

3 (1972) 3–21. **Eichholz, G.** *Gleichnisse der Evangelien.* 221–28. **Eliade, M.** "Locum refrigerii. . . ." *Zalmoxis* 1 (1938) 203–8. **Evans, C. F.** "Uncomfortable Words—V. '. . . Neither Will They Be Convinced.'" *ExpTim* 81 (1969–70) 228–31. **Feuillet, A.** "La parabole du mauvais riche et du pauvre Lazare (Lc 16, 19–31) antithèse de la parabole de l'intendant astucieux (Lc 16, 1–9)." *NRT* 101 (1979) 212–23. **George, A.** "La parabole du riche et de Lazare: Lc 16,19–31." *AsSeign* n.s. 57 (1971) 80–93. **Glombitza, O.** "Der reiche Mann und der arme Lazarus: Luk. xvi 19–31, Zur Frage nach der Botschaft des Textes." *NovT* 12 (1970) 166–80. **Grensted, L. W.** "The Use of Enoch in St. Luke XVI, 19–31." *ExpTim* 26 (1914–15) 333–34. **Gressmann, H.** *Vom reichen Mann und armen Lazarus: Eine literargeschichtliche Studie.* Abhandlungen der königlichen preussischen Akademie der Wissenschaften. Philosophisch-historische Klasse 7. Berlin: Könliglische Akademie der Wissenschaften, 1918. **Grobel, K.** "'. . . Whose Name Was Neves.'" *NTS* 10 (1963–64) 373–82. **Hafer, R. A.** "Dives and Poor Lazarus in the Light of Today." *LQ* 53 (1923) 476–81. **Hanson, R. P. C.** "A Note on Luke XVI, 14–31." *ExpTim* 55 (1943–44) 221–22. **Haupt, P.** "Abraham's Bosom." *AJP* 42 (1921) 162–67. **Heininger, B.** *Sondergutgleichnisse.* 177–91. **Hintzen, J.** *Verkündigung und Wahrnehmung: Über das Verhältnis von Evangelium und der Leser am Beispiel Lk 16, 19–31 im Rahmen des lukanischen Doppelwerkes.* Athenäums Monografien, Theologie: BBB 81. Frankfurt: Hain, 1991. **Hock, R. F.** "Lazarus and Micyllus: Greco-Roman Backgrounds to Luke 16:19–31." *JBL* 106 (1987) 447–63. **Horn, F. W.** *Glaube und Handeln.* 81–85, 144–49, 181. **Huie, W. P.** "The Poverty of Abundance: From Text to Sermon on Luke 16:19–31." *Int* 22 (1968) 403–20. **Jensen, H. J. L.** "Diesseits und Jenseits des Raumes eines Textes: Textsemiotische Bemerkungen zur Erzählung 'Vom reichen Mann und armen Lazarus' (Lk 16,19–31)." *LingBib* (1980) 39–60. **Joüon, P.** "Notes philologiques sur les Evangiles: Luc 16, 30." *RSR* 18 (1928) 354. **Jülicher, A.** *Gleichnisreden.* 2:617–41. **Köhler, K.** "Zu Luk. 16, 10–12." *TSK* 94 (1922) 173–78. **Kreitzer, L.** "Luke 16:19–31 and 1 Enoch 22." *ExpTim* 103 (1992) 139–42. **Kremer, J.** "Der arme Lazarus. Lazarus, der Freund Jesu: Beobachtung zur Beziehung zwischen Lk 16,19–31 und Joh 11,1–46." In *À cause de l'Évangile.* FS J. Dupont, ed. F. Refoulé. 571–84. **Künstlinger, D.** "Im Schosse Abrahams." *OLZ* 36 (1933) 408. **Kvalbein, H.** "Jesus and the Poor: Two Texts and a Tentative Conclusion (16,19–31)." *Themelios* 12 (1986–87) 80–87. **Lefort, L. T.** "Le nom du mauvais riche (Luc 16. 19) et la tradition copte." *ZNW* 37 (1938) 65–72. **Lorenzen, T.** "A Biblical Meditation on Luke 16:19–31: From the Text toward a Sermon." *ExpTim* 87 (1974–75) 39–43. **Marchadour, A.** *Lazar: Histoire d'un récit. Récits d'une histoire.* Lectio Divina 132. Paris: Cerf, 1988. **Mieses, M.** "Im Schosse Abrahams." *OLZ* 34 (1931) 1018–21. **North, B.** *The Rich Man and Lazarus: A Practical Exposition of Luke xvi, 19–31.* London: Banner of Truth Trust, 1960. **Omanson, R.** "Lazarus and Simon." *BT* 40 (1989) 416–19. **Osei-Bonsu, J.** "The Intermediate State in Luke-Acts." *IBS* 9 (1987) 115–30. **Pax, E.** "Der reiche und der arme Lazarus: Eine Milieustudie." *SBFLA* 25 (1975) 254–68. **Pearce, K.** "The Lucan Origins of the Raising of Lazarus." *ExpTim* 96 (1984–85) 359–61. **Powell, W.** "The Parable of Dives and Lazarus (Luke XVI, 19–31)." *ExpTim* 66 (1954–55) 350–51. **Renié, J.** "Le mauvais riche (Lc., xvi, 19–31)." *AnnTh* 6 (1945) 268–75. **Rimmer, N.** "Parable of Dives and Lazarus (Luke xvi. 19–31)." *ExpTim* 66 (1954–55) 215–16. **Schnider, F.,** and **Stenger, W.** "Die offene Tür und die unüberschreitbare Kluft: Strukturanalytische Überlegungen zum Gleichnis vom reichen Mann und armen Lazarus (Lk 16, 19–31)." *NTS* 25 (1978–79) 273–83. **Scholz, G.** "Aesthetische Beobachtungen am Gleichnis vom reichen Mann und armen Lazarus und von drei anderen Gleichnissen (Lk 16,19–25[26–31]; 10,34; 13,9; 15,11–32)." *LingBib* 43 (1978) 67–74. **Schurhammer, G.** "Eine Parabel Christi in Götzentempel." *KM* 49 (1920–21) 134–38. **Seccombe, D. P.** *Possessions.* 173–81. **Standen, A. O.** "The Parable of Dives and Lazarus and Enoch 22." *ExpTim* 33 (1921–22) 523. **Tanghe, V.** "Abraham, son fils et son envoyé (Luc 16,19–31)." *RB* 91 (1984) 557–77. **Trudinger, P.** "A 'Lazarus Motif' in Primitive Christian Preaching." *ANQ* 7 (1966) 29–32. **Vogels, W.** "Having or Longing: A Semiotic Analysis of Luke 16:19–31." *EglT* 20 (1989) 27–46. **Wehrli, E. S.** "Luke 16:19–31." *Int* 31 (1977) 276–80.

Translation

[19]*"A certain man was rich,*[a] *and he was dressed in purple and fine linen and he made merry every day in a splendid manner.* [20]*A certain poor man, whose name was Lazarus, was positioned at his gate, in an ulcerated condition,* [21]*longing to have his fill from [the things]*[b] *which fell from the table of the rich man.*[c] *But instead, the dogs used to come and lick*[d] *his ulcers.* [22]*It happened that the poor man died and was carried away by the angels to the bosom of Abraham; the rich man also died and he was buried.* [23]*Being in torment in Hades,*[e] *he raised his eyes and saw*[f] *from afar Abraham and Lazarus in his bosom.* [24]*He called out, 'Father Abraham, have mercy on me and send Lazarus to dip the tip of his finger in water and cool my tongue, for I am in pain in this flame.'* [25]*Abraham said, 'Child, remember that you received your good things in your life, and Lazarus correspondingly [received] the bad; now he is consoled here, and you are in pain.* [26]*Besides all this, between us and you a great chasm has been fixed, so that those wishing to go across from here to you are not able [to do so], and people may not cross from there*[g] *to us.'* [27]*He said, 'I ask you then, father, to send him to my father's house,* [28]*for I have five brothers, that he might warn them, so that they might not come, as well, to this place of torment.'* [29]*Abraham said,*[h] *'They have Moses and the prophets; let them listen to them.'* [30]*He said, 'No, father Abraham, but if someone goes*[i] *to them from the dead they will repent.'* [31]*He said to him, 'If they do not listen to Moses and the prophets, neither will they be persuaded if someone rises*[j] *from the dead.'"*

Notes

[a] "Dives" comes from treating the Latin adjective *dives,* "rich," as a name. P[75] adds ὀνόματι Νευης, "by name, Neues," which is partly supported by the Sahidic, which gives the name "Ninevah." Yet other names emerge later in the tradition, undoubtedly under the pressure of the missing parallel to v 20. See Fitzmyer (1130) for a detailed summary.

[b] As in Matt 15:27, τῶν ψιχίων is added by ℵ A (D) W Θ Ψ etc.

[c] The failure of the man's wishes is made explicit in *f* [13] and a few other texts, with language borrowed from 15:16: καὶ οὐδεὶς ἐδίδου αὐτῷ, "and no one gave him [anything]."

[d] The verb here, ἐπιλείχειν, with its ἐπι- prefix is quite rare and has been corrected to more common cognate forms with the prefix ἀπο- (W *f* [13] etc.), περι- (157 etc.), or without prefix (D *f* [1] 205 etc.).

[e] "In Hades" is absent from ℵ lat Marcion.

[f] Present tense in Gr. (historic present).

[g] The addition of οἵ here in ℵ[2] A L W Θ Ψ *f* [1,13] etc. produces the sense "those who are there."

[h] Present tense in Gr. (historic present).

[i] P[75] has ἐγερθῇ, "is raised"; ℵ and some other texts have ἀναστῇ, "is raised/rises."

[j] P[75] has ἐγερθῇ, "is raised," here as well.

Form/Structure/Setting

Luke concludes his section 16:1–31 ("The Use and Abuse of Riches") with the present parable, which has linguistic and/or thematic links to each of the earlier units of the section. There are also links with 15:11–32, with which it has a certain parallelism in the larger Lukan structuring. This provides for a reading of the adjacent sections 15:1–32 and 16:1–31 in close relationship to one another (see further at 16:1–8).

The parable here is likely to be from Luke's parables source, in which it stood in parallel with 12:13[16]–21 (see discussion in excursus: "Journey to Jerusalem"). There is quite a bit of Lukan language in the present form of the parable (see

Comment below). More fundamentally there has been a considerable questioning of the ultimate unity of the parable. Those who dispute the unity see in vv 19–25(26) a focus on the reversal of fortunes after death of the poor and the rich, and tend to see this as a simple reversal. Then in vv (26)27–31 they see a focus on the pessimistic judgment that even a messenger from the dead will not produce repentance among the rich, and suggest that instead of simple reversal we now have a guilty pattern of life requiring repentance. We will see, however, in *Comment* below that already in vv 19–26 the rich man's social responsibility toward Lazarus is implied by the juxtaposition of the two chief characters and details of the telling: even here the problem is not wealth alone. We will also see below that v 31 is the difficult verse to make sense of in a narrative set in the pre-resurrection period, and within the horizons of the narrative world (in a different way and with different results Horn [*Glaube und Handeln*, 84] has also recognized that vv 30–31 create the difficulties of the narrative). It is likely that the difficulties of the parable are best accounted for by treating that verse (and v 30 which prepares for it) as a post-resurrection, and perhaps even Lukan, development. The remaining narrative makes a perfectly coherent unity, which from the experience of the rich man develops a challenge for those who yet live: the rich man of the parable finds out his folly only after death; those who are yet living should not expect a personal messenger from the world of the dead to warn them; what is needed is already clearly set out for them in the law and the prophets, "let them listen to them." In a post-resurrection situation the request of v 27 lent itself to comparison with the resurrection of Jesus, and the failure of this resurrection to compel Jewish repentance and acceptance of their messiah finds its echo and explanation in the development in vv 30–31.

There is also the question of the relationship of this parable to an Egyptian folktale preserved on the reverse side of a document dated to A.D. 47. For a translation of the tale, see F. L. Griffith, *Stories of the High Priests of Memphis* (Oxford: Clarendon, 1900) 42–43. Gressmann (*Vom reichen Mann*) argued that the Gospel parable had a relationship to this tale and to a series of rabbinic texts that seem in turn to have some relationship of their own to this Egyptian tale (see also the Jewish tale appealed to by Bultmann, *History*, 197, which has a message from the afterworld for a rich and godless man; and, further, the only partially successful comparison made by Hock [*JBL* 106 (1987) 455–63] between Lazarus and the poor shoemaker Micyllus, who is introduced by the Cynic Sophist Lucian of Samosata in both *Gallus* and *Cataplus*, and for whom in relation to immoral rich men there is a reversal of fates after death). The view that the parable reflects the Egyptian tale has been widely adopted, and subsequently adapted and developed in various ways. There is indeed some commonality (the suffering of a rich man and the blessing of a poor man in the world after death [inability to get to the water of a stream plays a role in the Jewish form]), but the tours of (or dream visions of) the world of the dead and/or messages from the dead that provide the central dynamic for these tales become a rejected possibility in the Gospel parable, and none of the versions of the tale has any interest in the rich man's attitude to or use of his wealth. (What I find most curious in the appeal to these traditions is the tendency to assume that it supports an original short version of the parable [vv 19–25(26)], even though only the second half of the parable introduces even the possibility of somebody still alive coming to know of the reversal in the afterworld, which is precisely the motif of most importance for the dramatic movement of these tales.) These traditions may provide a certain background for the Gospel parable, but Jeremias (*Parables*, 183) is quite wrong to make the listeners' prior knowledge of such a tale into a hermeneutical key to the understanding of the Gospel parable. Apart from the final two verses that have been added, the parable is best taken as an independent creation by the historical Jesus, which is suitably set against the background of the cultural and religious awareness of his hearers.

A quite different tradition-history question is posed by the link with John 11 created by the shared name and the motif of resurrection. The second of these links is made yet more precise by the considerations adduced at the discussion of v 31 below, where a Johannine note is identified. Since, apart from the shared name, the links belong to what we have seen to be a secondary development of the parable, and since, further, the name can hardly be a later insertion into the narrative (the name is needed at least in v 24), it seems best to conclude that the shared name is quite fortuitous. But if Luke, or this element of his tradition, already knew something of the John 11 tradition, then we can add an extra note to the description above of the development of vv 30–31, namely the awareness that another Lazarus had come back from the dead, and that the kind of people the editor of this parable had in mind had not been brought to repentance.

Of the traditional categories, this present parable comes closest to fitting into that of example story. However, it is really a cautionary tale in which we are invited to learn from the disaster experienced by the central character of the tale. Despite the frequent mentions made of him, Lazarus is a quite secondary figure in the parable.

Comment

The rich man enjoys the social status quo, which has been most kind to him, and is oblivious to the claim upon him of the needs of his beggar neighbor, Lazarus. Those who live so will discover in Hades the bitter truth of the implications of their disregard for the basic demands of the law and thc prophets. And those who live so, despite all pretense of piety, will not mend their ways even if one should be raised from the dead to bring them warning.

19 ἄνθρωπος . . . τις, "a certain man," is likely to be traditional here (see at 10:30; but contrast 16:1, where "a certain man was rich" has been introduced to create a closer formal parallelism with the present verse), but the phrase εὐφραινόμενος καθ' ἡμέραν λαμπρῶς, "make merry every day in a splendid manner," is solidly Lukan (cf. Dupont, *Béatitudes* 3:174). It is just possible that for ἐνεδιδύσκετο πορφύραν, "dressed in purple," Luke has been influenced by the language of Mark 15:17 (which he does not use in his own trial narrative; "purple" and "fine linen" [βύσσος] occur together in Prov 31:22 and in 1QapGen 20:31, in both cases referring to female garb).

Segments of the upper classes in Palestine had developed a lifestyle involving the ostentatious display of wealth, which was modeled ultimately upon upper-class practice in Rome. Quite apart from the Lukan context, the sense of extravagance is likely to prepare the reader already for a negative outcome for the rich man (Tanghe, *RB* 91 [1984] 563, speaks of the evocation, by its contrary, of the ideal of the rich benefactor). In connection with the links that bind together chaps. 15 and 16, possibly the use of εὐφραίνεσθαι, "make merry," establishes a contrast between fitting and blasphemous merrymaking (cf. 15:23, 24, 29, 32).

20 Luke is likely to be responsible for πτωχὸς δέ τις ὀνόματι . . . (lit. "a certain poor man by name . . ."). ἐβέβλητο is literally "was thrown." The term is used of people who are confined to bed through illness (cf. Matt 8:6, 14; 9:2; Rev 2:2) and is likely to suggest here Lazarus' inability to choose freely where he will be. We are probably to understand that Lazarus is positioned at the gate to beg, and that he is to all intents and purposes stuck there, living rough in the open, more or less where he begs. "The gate" that the man is near will be an outer vestibule or portal (cf. Acts 10:17; 12:13). He would not be tolerated near the actual entry door, but his location would enable him to be noticed by all who came and went from the rich man's house. The juxtaposition of Lazarus and the rich man is not quite so pointed, but may be compared with that of the travelers and the man who had fallen among thieves in 10:29–37. The perspective on this man's poverty that emerges embraces his stricken state, his isolation, and his inability to provide for himself. The naming of Lazarus in this parable is the only use of a personal name in a Gospel parable. The name is a shortened form of the Hebrew or Aramaic Eleazar (אלעזר, *ʾElʿāzār*; the equivalence of the short and longer forms may be seen from the bilingual inscription *CII* 2.1337, in which the Greek longer form stands in parallel with the short Hebrew form). The name means "God helps/has helped," and is likely to be symbolic of the divinely orchestrated ultimate outcome of the man's desperate state. Additional suggestions about the fact of a name include (*i*) noting that this specification prevents the reversal pattern of the parable from being automatically applicable to every poor person; and (*ii*) pointing out that the naming of the poor man while the rich man remains anonymous already anticipates the coming reversal by reversing the normal anonymity of poverty and the individuating significance of wealth. Further suggestions about the particular name include (*i*) finding a link between Lazarus here and Abraham's servant Eleazar in Gen 15:2 (Tanghe's elaboration of this in terms of seeing Lazarus' role in the parable as that of the envoy of Abraham [as Gen 24] does not persuade [*RB* 91 (1984) 557–77]); (*ii*) taking the etymology to indicate that Lazarus is the one in whom God's help appears (Lazarus is then ultimately a figure for Jesus himself; see Glombitza [*NovT* 12 (1970) 166–80]; this approach is overly subtle); and (*iii*) claiming a link between this Lazarus and that of John 11 on the basis of the link in both cases to resurrection (see further in *Form/Structure/Setting* above). The medical cause of the man's weeping ulcers is uncertain, but they constitute the health problem that keeps him from gainful employment.

21 ἐπιθυμῶν χορτασθῆναι, "longing to eat his fill," may be a link to 15:16 (in the discussion there I have not accepted χορτασθῆναι as the original reading, but there is a substantial link even without that reading). Food also falls from the table (using the same words) in Matt 15:27. There it is an image of modest excess (crumbs), here something rather more extravagant. The rich man could easily have sent a servant out with some of the scraps, but we are to understand that this did not happen: the man's longing continued unfulfilled. Though the common view is that the dogs here are wild street dogs, the linkage with the meal scene is best satisfied by these being the dogs of the rich man's house (dogs were used as watch dogs and hunting dogs, and were even at times kept as domestic pets). Instead of a servant coming with the fallen scraps, the dogs come from having consumed the scraps and continue their meal with the juices that ooze from the afflicted man's sores. (It would be possible to take the dogs' action as an expression of the compassion that Lazarus' fellow human beings have failed to provide, but this fits the syntax and flow less well.)

22 *ἐγένετο δέ*, "it happened," + inf. is Lukan, as is probably the link with *δὲ καί* (lit. "and/but also"). In a chiastic pattern, the story deals with the deaths of the two figures in the reverse order to their introduction into the story. The difference between the posthumous fates of Lazarus and the rich man is expressed in the contrasting verbs "carried off" and "buried." Fitzmyer (1132) is probably right that we are to understand that Lazarus was given no burial by fellow human beings, but perhaps there is more involved here. Since there is no close parallel in connection with views of the afterlife to the role of the angels here (Hermas, *Vis.* 2.2.7 is likely to reflect the present text; there is a more remote and rather later partial parallel in Diogenes Laertius, *Lives* 8.31), it may be that we should think in terms not of the normal fate of the righteous, but of a special translation to heaven, somewhat in the tradition of that of Enoch (Gen 5:24) and Elijah (2 Kgs 2:11). There was clearly a Jewish tradition that Moses also was translated to heaven, which may, in light of Deut 34:5, have involved in some forms (as here) a translation after death (cf. J. Jeremias, *TDNT* 4:854–55). We should note also the availability for a future role of Jeremiah and Isaiah, along with Elijah in *4 Ezra* 2:18. If we are proceeding along the right lines here, then we would probably need to assume the same translation for Abraham as well. Totally obscure, Lazarus is placed on a level with the supremely privileged of the OT saints. (Because Lazarus is ultimately a secondary character in the story, there is no narrative need to account for this extraordinary good fortune: we should not understand that it is the automatic outcome of his poverty and suffering upon earth.) The location at the bosom of Abraham is likely to express close intimacy (cf. John 1:18; and see Hock, *JBL* 106 [1987] 456, for the use of "bosom" in sepulchral epigrams and epitaphs), though it is just possible that a meal setting is also evoked (cf. John 13:23 and note the fitting contrast this would make with v 21). In the later rabbinic text *b. Qidd.* 72a-b to be "in Abraham's bosom," בחיקו של אברהם, *bḥyqw šl ʾbrhm*, is probably a euphemism for being dead, at least in the case of a great rabbi, and may represent a broadening yet further of the exclusive category of those who are singled out for translation to heaven (cf. Derrett, *Law*, 87).

23 *ἐπάρας τοὺς ὀφθαλμούς*, "raised his eyes," and *ὑπάρχων*, "being," could be Lukan (more likely the latter). On Hades, see at 10:15. Though representing the place of the dead quite generally, it comes increasingly to include the idea of a preliminary experience of what is to be the individual's ultimate fate at the final judgment (see 2 Esd 7:80; *1 Enoch* 22:11; cf. Jude 6–7; 1 Pet 3:19–20). It thus embraces two of the three horizons of judgment that are to be found in Luke's thought (see at 12:5). Though this has been disputed, we should probably visualize Lazarus' location as above and the rich man's as below. But more important than this is the stress on the distance involved. The presence of Abraham certifies the upper location as a place of blessedness. With no evident change of meaning, the Greek term for "bosom" occurs this time in the plural. The contrast is between torment and tranquil intimacy with great father Abraham.

24 The unstressed καὶ αὐτός, "and he," will be Lukan, and πέμψον, "send," καταψύξῃ, "cool," and ὀδυνῶμαι, "I am in great pain," all suit Luke's diction. For Abraham as father, see at 1:73; 3:8. Such an address makes it certain that the rich man is meant to be seen as Jewish, and probably subtly insinuates the basis upon which the rich man makes his request. The call for mercy is entirely appropriate (cf. 17:13; 18:38, 39), but, as will become clear, is voiced too late. Does the rich man's knowledge of Lazarus' name inject a note of deliberateness into his earlier neglect of the poor man's needs? Does his suggestion for Lazarus reflect his conviction that the lower classes exist to see to the needs of the upper classes; or is it based on an awareness that, while he is in a place of bondage, Lazarus is in a place of freedom? Notably, the rich man asks only for an amelioration of his suffering, not for release from them: does he recognize that his sufferings are deserved, or is his modest request an understated bid for release from his miserable situation? It is natural to think of thirst in this context (cf. the juxtaposition of thirst and torment in 2 Esd 8:59), but the request, if taken literally, is for only a tiny amount of water (is this a deliberate understatement?), and the water is to be used for the cooling of the overheated tongue, not the slaking of thirst (but is the one an image for the other?). For the flame here, cf. Isa 66:24; Sir 21:9–10; *1 Enoch* 10:13; 63:10; 1QH 17:13.

25 Much of the language here is probably Lukan (see Dupont, *Béatitudes*, 3:60–61). The return address "child" shows an acknowledgement of the link claimed by the rich man. The reversal that the future has brought recalls the reversals of 1:52–53 and 6:20–26 (see esp. at 1:53; 6:24). While Abraham is certainly pointing out the equity achieved by the reversal, we should not take this, either in the Lukan framework or in the original parable, as expressing the view that there will be some kind of automatic eschatological reversal of present fortunes. The fairly subtle, but nonetheless significant, delineation of aspects of the rich man's attitude to, and use of, his riches and status show already (without vv 27–31 to come) that more is involved than an evening up of the balance of good and ill. Moreover, agony in the flame in v 24 is a punitive image, more than merely a redressing of the balance. The "now" of v 25 is the opposite of the "now" of 6:20–26 as consolation switches from the present possession of the rich to the present possession of poor Lazarus. As with the chiasm in vv 19–22, the rich man is again introduced before Lazarus, but Lazarus' fate is addressed before that of the rich man.

26 Only ἐν πᾶσι τούτοις, "besides all this," in this verse looks Lukan (cf. 24:21). Surpassing any considerations of equity is the fixed determination of the will of God: the topology of Hades objectifies the will and purpose of God, which no momentary surge of human sympathy can be allowed to dislocate.

27–28 ἐρωτῶ . . . ἵνα, "I ask . . . that" (used in a petition) is the most Lukan diction in these verses. Even if his own case is hopeless, something may yet be done for those to whom the rich man is bound by the ties of family affection. The details of the family arrangements remain unclear. It seems unlikely that the rich man's home is the shared paternal home. If the five brothers are still in the paternal home, why is the father not included in the request? It is perhaps best to understand that the father is dead, but that the five brothers have decided not to divide their share of the inheritance. The rich man continues (as in v 24) to see Lazarus as the one through whom Abraham should act.

Messengers from the dead have a place in Greek literature (Plato, *Resp.* 10.614D; Lucian, *Demonax* 43), but perhaps more pertinent is the Jewish tradition of a future role for those who have at death been translated to heaven (see at v 22; cf. further the calling up of Samuel in 1 Sam 28:7–20). The plea for a personal warning (this is better than testimony to the reality of the afterlife, which is also linguistically possible), even before the talk of repentance in v 30, implies that the rich man is aware of a moral responsibility for his own fate: he could and should have acted differently.

29 "The law and the prophets" is an attested Jewish idiom (see at 16:16), but "Moses and the prophets" is likely to be a Lukan variant on this (see 24:27, 44; Acts 28:23; cf. John 1:45). The rich man asks for special treatment for his brothers. Abraham replies that they have in the law and the prophets all that they should need: these are the appointed means by which God makes his will plain to those concerned to know it. The parable suggests that there is a profound challenge to the social status quo to be found in the law and the prophets, and that there is a desperate need for the privileged to search out their stipulations and to act upon them.

30 *οὐχί . . . ἀλλ'*, "no . . . but," and possibly the use of *πορεύεσθαι*, "to go," and *μετανοεῖν*, "to repent," betray the Lukan hand. The rich man is confident that such a dramatic visitation would cause the brothers to change their ways. Abraham will be much more pessimistic.

31 *τις ἀπό* (lit. "a certain one from"), *πεισθήσονται*, "will be persuaded," and "Moses and the prophets" are the most obvious Lukan features here. Taken as a universal principle, this final statement by Abraham raises considerable difficulties, since it would seem to presuppose that the law and the prophets constitute the decisive revelation of God: nobody can get any further than they get with the law and the prophets. But Jesus' ministry itself certainly reached people who were left outside by the law and the prophets, and the post-resurrection early church saw the repentance of both Jews and Gentiles under the impact of the message of the resurrection of Jesus. If, however, we turn the direction of perception around and look here for an explanation of how certain segments of the Jewish population could have failed to repent when they heard the message of Jesus and of his followers, even in the light of the resurrection of Jesus from the dead, the sentiment expressed becomes unproblematic: the resurrection of Jesus (as indeed the earlier ministry of Jesus himself) makes no impact upon them because, despite whatever they may seem to be on the surface, they have, in their failure to attend to God's call upon them in the law, already hardened their hearts to the voice of God (cf. Acts 7:51–53; cf. further the way that Luke in the Infancy Gospel locates perceptiveness to the new thing that God is doing in the hearts of those who are righteous according to the law [e.g., 1:6; 2:25, 39], and then later in the hearts of those who have responded to the ministry of John the Baptist [7:29–39]). Here there is yet another Johannine note in the Lukan tradition. These unpersuadable people will be identified by Luke with the Pharisaic adversaries of vv 14–15, with their love of money.

Explanation

Luke's section on the use and abuse of riches (16:1–31) comes to its climax with the present parable and its judgment emphasis. Its tale of failure is to balanced by the tale of the joyous restoration of the prodigal (15:11–32), which climaxed the previous section. For those economically benefited by the status quo, here is a salutary warning against the self-serving and self-satisfied life that so easily results from such privilege.

The rich man was doing no more than living out the life of his class, influenced as it was by the patterns of conspicuous consumption developed in Imperial Rome. He could have been a rich benefactor, but instead his extravagance was focused on his own enjoyment of the good things of life. But no man is an island, and not far away was a neighbor whose experience of life was quite different. Lazarus was stuck near the outer vestibule of the entry way into the rich man's fine house. No doubt he was there to beg, but he was too weak and ill to try for a better begging perch once he had discovered how lean the pickings were here. He lived rough, went hungry, and suffered with his ulcerated body. At this point, the only sign of hope is his name, which means "God helps" and is probably intended to point to the divinely orchestrated final outcome for Lazarus.

Lazarus would have been thrilled with scraps from the rich man's table, which the rich man could have so easily arranged to have sent out to him. But the dogs got these, and then they (and not, say, a servant laden with bread) approached poor Lazarus and finished off their meal by licking his oozing wounds.

In due course, both men died. In keeping with the indignities of his life, Lazarus had no one to bury him. But once both men are firmly across the portals of death, there is a radical reversal. Lazarus' body is not left to rot. Instead, he is translated to heaven, to that place of intimacy and consolation on the bosom of no one less than Abraham himself, the father of all Israel. In Jewish tradition, a few distinguished people, beyond Enoch (Gen 5:24) and Elijah (2 Kgs 2:11), had been translated to heaven either alive, or immediately after death. Now Lazarus had joined their privileged ranks. (The story does not tell us exactly why Lazarus is so privileged since the rich man is the protagonist of the tale: not every poor person is so privileged.) By contrast, the rich man was placed in the earth with all dignity, but he found himself in torment in Hades, the place of the departed dead. In some strands of Jewish tradition, one expected to experience in Hades in a preliminary way what would be one's fate at the last judgment. The rich man was experiencing his fate! Now Lazarus enjoys freedom and peace, and the rich man is constrained and tormented.

We should probably understand the request in terms of ancient Semitic understatement: not just the cooling of his tongue with a drop of water, but enough water to slake his raging thirst; not just a momentary relief of his torment, but release from this place of suffering. The rich man quite properly sues for mercy, but he is too late. The irrevocability of the decision of God about his fate is symbolized in the great chasm that separates the two realms of the afterlife.

Entrusted with the riches of this world, the rich man had generously rewarded himself during his lifetime. He has in fact been paid in full (see 6:24) and can expect no more. Lazarus has been dreadfully short-changed in his lifetime, but now there is a redressing of the balance. Though we ought not in the parable think in terms of a simple balancing of accounts, it is nonetheless true that God is no person's debtor.

The rich man cannot but see the justice of the situation: he could and should have acted differently; but even if his own case is hopeless, something may yet be done for those to whom he is bound by the ties of family affection. Lazarus could reappear on the earth, just as it was anticipated that Elijah and Enoch and others would appear some day. Such a personal warning would save the rich man's brothers from the fate that had befallen him.

The rich man asks for special treatment for his brothers. The reply is that they have in the law and the prophets all that they should need: these are the appointed means by which God makes his will plain to those concerned to know it. The parable suggests that there is a profound challenge to the social status quo to be found in the law and the prophets, and that there is a desperate need for the privileged to search out their stipulations and to act upon them. The gospel of the kingdom of God affirms and makes yet more radical the demands of the law and the prophets.

The rich man reiterates his request, confident that such a visitor from the realm of the dead would produce the necessary repentance. But his confidence is misplaced. Just such a visitation does take place with the resurrection of Jesus. However, the kind of people the Lukan parable addresses (see vv 14–15) do not repent and embrace the one proclaimed as messiah (of course for some Jewish folk the resurrection of Jesus does produce just such a repentance [see Acts 2], but for others, and especially among the leaders, there is continuing hardness). In the unfolding of the generations, the fact of the resurrection of Jesus has met the same fate: those who, enmeshed in their riches, have closed their ears to God hear no better because this dead man came back to warn us all.

Fitting Response to the Demand and Working of the Kingdom of God (17:1–19)

The three units of this section deal with how disciples should act and how they should understand themselves in light of the demands and working of the kingdom of God. Troubled by the extreme form of Jesus' teaching on sin, the disciples are told that they have not reckoned with the limitless powers of a faith that has met in Jesus the working of the kingdom of God. They learn, further, that no matter what heights of obedient service they rise to, they will only have done their duty. And, finally, they are reminded of the true nature of faith as decisive action on the basis of the conviction that God's help is to be found with Jesus, coupled with grateful response to God for his gracious intervention for us in our need.

Dealing with Sin in the Disciple Community (17:1–6)

Bibliography

Shelton, R. M. "Luke 17:1–10." *Int* 31 (1977) 280–85.

For 17:1–2:

Dagron, A. *Aux jours du Fils de l'Homme: Essai sur le service de la parole. Luc XVII 1 à XVIII 8. Lecture Sémiotique et Propositions Théologiques.* PROFAC Série Biblique 2. Lyon: CADIR—PROFAC, 1990. **Deming, W.** "Mark 9.41–10.12, Matthew 5.27–32, and *B. Nid.* 13b: A First Century Discussion of Male Sexuality." *NTS* 36 (1990) 130–41. **Derrett, J. D. M.** "Two 'Harsh' Sayings of Christ Explained." *DR* 103 (1985) 218–29, esp. 218–21. **Kafka, G.** "Bild und Wort in den Evangelien." *MTZ* 2 (1951) 263–87, esp. 263–65. **Michel, O.** "'Diese Kleinen'—eine Jüngerbezeichnung Jesu." *TSK* 108 (1937–38) 401–15. **Moffatt, J.** "Jesus upon 'Stumbling Blocks.'" *ExpTim* 26 (1914–15) 407–9. **Schlosser, J.** "Lk 17,2 und die Logienquelle." *SNTU* 8 (1983) 70–78. **Trilling, W.** *Hausordnung Gottes: Eine Auslegung von Matthäus 18.* Düsseldorf: Patmos, 1960. 30–35, 57–60.

For 17:3–4:

Barth, G. "Auseinandersetzungen um die Kirchenzucht im Umkreis des Matthäusevangeliums." *ZNW* 69 (1978) 158–77, esp. 169–74. **Catchpole, D.** "Reproof and Reconciliation in the Q Community: A Study of the Tradition-History of Mt 18,15–17.21–22/Lk 17,3–4." *SNTU* 8 (1983) 79–90. **Lührmann, D.** *Redaktion.* 111–14. **MacGillivray, D.** "Luke xvii. 3." *ExpTim* 25 (1913–14) 333. **Schulz, S.** *Spruchquelle.* 320–22.

For 17:4–5:

Delebecque, É. *Études grecques.* 99–107. **Derrett, J. D. M.** "Moving Mountains and Uprooting Trees (Mk 11:22; Mt 17:20,21; Lk 17:6." *BibOr* 30 (1988) 231–44. **Duplacy, J.** "La foi qui déplace les montagnes." In *A la rencontre de Dieu.* FS A. Gelin, ed. M. Jourjon et al. Bibliothèque de la Faculté de Théologie de Lyon 8. Le Puy: Mappus, 1961. 273–87. **George, A.** "La foi des apôtres: Efficacité et gratuité: Lc 17,5–10." *AsSeign* n.s. 58 (1974) 68–77. **Hahn, F.** "Jesu Wort vom bergeversetzenden Glauben." *ZNW* 76 (1985) 149–69. **Lafon, G.** "Loi, promesse, grâce: Une Lecture de Luc 17,5–10." In *Esquisses pour un christianisme.* Cognitio fidei 96. Paris: Cerf, 1979. 203–9. **Lührmann, D.** *Glaube im frühen Christentum.* Gütersloh: Mohn, 1976. 17–30. **Schulz, S.** *Spruchquelle.* 465–68. **Zmijewski, J.** "Der Glaube und seine Macht: Eine traditionsgeschichtliche Untersuchung zu Mt 17,20; 21,21; Mk 11,23; Lk 17,6." In *Begegnung mit dem Wort.* FS H. Zimmermann, ed. J. Zmijewski and E. Nellessen. Bonn: Hanstein, 1980. 81–103.

Translation

[1] *He said to his disciples, "It is impossible for things which cause one to stumble not to come; but woe [to the one] through whom they come.* [2] *It is better for such a one if a millstone is placed about his neck and he [finds that he]*[a] *has been thrown into the sea, than that he causes one of these little ones to stumble.* [3] *Be on your guard! If your brother sins,*[b] *rebuke him, and if he repents, forgive him;* [4] *and if he sins against you seven times in the day and turns to you saying, 'I repent,' you must forgive him."*

[5] *The apostles said to the Lord, "Grant [additional] faith to us."* [6] *The Lord said, "If you have faith as a mustard seed, you would say to the*[c] *sycamore, 'Be uprooted and planted in the sea,' and it would have obeyed*[d] *you."*

Notes

[a] The insertion seeks to do justice to the transition from present to perfect tense.
[b] *εἰς σέ*, "against you," is added by D Ψ f^{13} ctc., probably from v 4.
[c] *ταύτῃ*, "this," is read by A B W Θ Ψ $f^{1,13}$ etc. Omitted by P^{75} ℵ D L 579 etc.
[d] The shift in time frame here reflects the move from impf. to aorist in the Gr.

Form/Structure/Setting

Luke seems to have cobbled a unit together here out of three separate blocks of tradition (vv 1–2, 3–4, 5–6). The catchword link "into/in the sea" from v 2 to v 6 helps to give a formal unity to the piece, and it is likely that he intends the blocks, so juxtaposed, to mutually qualify the meaning of onc another.

The beginning of the new larger section here is marked by a change of subject and a fresh introduction of audience (cf. 16:1). The end of the section is marked by the change of topic in 17:20, provoked initially by the questioning of the Pharisees, to that of the coming of the kingdom and of the Son of Man. The first and last units of the present section end with an emphasis on faith in God.

Luke will be responsible for the setting in v 1a, as he will be responsible for the transition in v 3a. Parallels to vv 1bc–2 are found in Mark 9:42 (to v 2 only) and Matt 18:6–7. Luke is closer to the Markan wording for v 2, but he does betray an awareness of at least one feature of the Matthean form of v 2. While he has reordered and abbreviated, his form of v 1bc is quite close to the Matthean form. Matthew probably preserves the second source form more accurately than Luke does.

Despite Catchpole's attempt (*SNTU* 8 [1983] 79–90) to show that Luke 17:3–4 is a truncated version of the Q form as preserved in Matt 18:15–16a, 17, the more common recent view that Matthew and Luke use at this point variant forms of their shared tradition would seem to have more to commend it (see, e.g., Lührmann, *Redaktion*, 111–14). However, the additional Matthean material is to be seen ultimately as an expansion of an earlier form that is better reflected by the Lukan text, and the case for Matthean redaction is not closed. Luke seems to have retained the original unity between vv 3 and 4, in which the emphasis is intended to fall heavily on v 4. Nevertheless it is likely that Luke has imposed his own vocabulary on the material.

Luke 17:5 is best treated as a setting created by Luke for the tradition of v 6 (less the opening words, which will be Luke's as well), for which there are versions in Mark 11:22–23; Matt 17:19–20; 21:21. Luke seems to reproduce the non-Markan source form best here, where Matthew has been considerably influenced by his Markan source. It is possible, however, that "amen, I say to you," which is common to all the forms except that in Luke, was part of the non-Markan as well as the Markan source. The more difficult question is that of the greater originality of the Markan source form or the non-Markan. There are three main differences: (*i*) the Markan form has a mixed second/third person construction moving from imperative to conditional form, where the other form is second person conditional; (*ii*) the non-Markan form lacks the comparison with a mustard seed (on the mustard seed imagery, see at 13:19); (*iii*) the non-Markan form has a mulberry/sycamore tree uprooted and planted in the sea, where the Markan form has a mountain lifted up and cast into the sea. For point (*i*) the presence of second person forms in each version of the saying favors the non-Markan form. The comparison in point (*ii*) does not fit well with the development about not doubting in the Markan text, which suggests that this development may have displaced it. The presence of the contrast accentuates the massive scale of the promised outcome and makes for a harder saying. It is, therefore, likely to be original. Point (*iii*) is the most difficult. A mountain cast into the sea (cf. Rev 8:8; and the rabbinic references to the rooting up of mountains assembled at Str-B, 1:759, as well as the faith to move mountains of 1 Cor 13:2) is an easier image than a tree growing in the sea. On the other hand, the strong-rootedness of the שקמה, *šiqmāh*, "sycamore," is proverbial (see Str-B, 2:234; since συκάμινος is used in the LXX to translate שקמה, that is probably how we should take the term here, though it can at times be used to differentiate the mulberry tree from the sycamore), and there is a striking power in imagery that doubles the impossibility by imagining now a tree standing firm and erect above the sea with its root system held in place by nothing more than the flowing waters. The latter seems finally preferable, despite Hahn's attractive exposition of an original with mountain in terms of participation in the powers of the new creation (*ZNW* 76 [1985] 157–58, 166–67).

All three of these traditions grouped here by Luke have the kind of extremity that gives them good claim to be traced back to the historical Jesus. Only the authenticity of vv 3–4 seems to have been seriously questioned (by Catchpole, *SNTU* 8 [1983] 79–90), and the source reconstruction upon which this judgment depends has not been found persuasive.

There is undoubtedly some source implication in the fact that the Matthean parallels to vv 1–2, 3–4, 5–6 are all to be found in the space of thirty verses in Matthew (17:20–21; 18:15–17; 18:21–22).

Comment

The teaching of Jesus here imposes a huge burden of responsibility for in no way causing others to stumble and calls for a capacity to forgive that knows no limits and gives all the benefit of the doubt to the sinner. Faced with this challenge the apostles cry out for an increase of faith, but they are told that if they would but exercise a mustard-seed-sized faith they would have all the power they should ever need.

1 The opening setting is a variant on 16:1, and will be Lukan. Probably Luke's effectively double negative form with its use of the adjective *ἀνένδεκτον*, "impossible," is secondary to Matthew's form with *ἀνάγκη*, "necessity" (which may have suggested to Luke some unwelcome notion of apocalyptic necessity in such occasions of falling into sin; Luke has no parallel to the Matthean woe to the world as it is troubled by such causes of falling). Luke is likely to be responsible as well for the abbreviated form of the woe. (Mark has no parallel to any part of this verse.) *σκάνδαλα*, "things which cause one to stumble," is probably used in line with the Septuagintal tradition, from which it gains overtones of that which causes stumbling in addition to the imagery of a snare or trap from the Greek origins of the term. We need not think that some extreme form of sin or apostasy is in view here. The present saying has the same radical quality as Matt 5:29–30. In the Lukan sequence it is the radical nature of the teaching that calls forth the response of v 5. The verse expresses on the one hand realistic expectations in a fallen world, but on the other hand a sense of undiminished human responsibility.

2 For *εἰ . . . περίκειται . . . εἰς τὴν θάλασσαν*, "if . . . is placed about . . . into the sea," Luke agrees with Mark against Matthew. On the other hand, Luke's *ἵνα* (here: "that") seems to find an echo in Matthew's use of the term in a different but syntactically similarly placed clause. Luke stands alone with *λυσιτελεῖ . . . ἤ* for "it is better . . . than," *λίθος μυλικός*, "millstone," *ἔρριπται*, "thrown," and with the location of the final clause of the verse, its positioning of *ἕνα*, "one," and its failure to identify the little ones as believers. Though Matthew has clearly modified his distinctive source here in line with his Markan source and also introduced his own variations, it seems best, except in the case of the missing reference to believers and perhaps the positioning of *ἕνα*, to attribute the Lukan distinctives to Luke's own editorial activity (but see the contrary view of Schlosser [*SNTU* 8 (1983) 70–78]), upgrading the language and making a better fusion of the two parts of the tradition (the woe saying and the millstone saying).

Who are "these little ones"? Jesus probably means the weak, the lowly, the vulnerable (see at 7:28). Though otherwise unmentioned in the context, we are to understand that they are present as those drawn to Jesus. To cause one of these little ones to stumble morally or spiritually is to get oneself into a worse predicament than would be the case if one were to have been tossed into the sea with one's head poking through the center hole of a millstone that had been firmly secured as a kind of bizarre necklace (it is possible that, as Derrett [*DR* 103 (1985) 220] suggests, the Matthean imagery is rather of being harnessed up to the millstone in the way the working ass was; the prospect of drowning is just as certain either way).

3 The opening warning will be Lukan (cf. 21:34; 12:1 for the same wording). It is unclear whether Luke wished it to be linked backwards or forwards. Perhaps it links in both directions in order more clearly to make a pair out of vv 1–2 and 3–4.

Luke may be responsible here for *μετανοήσῃ*, "repents," and *ἐπιτίμησον*, "rebuke." In view is personal wrong of one against another (this is made clearer in v 4; and cf. at 11:4), and correspondingly repentance has an everyday sense and not the repentance toward God called for by the Gospel challenge (cf. at 3:3). "Brother" will have originally meant "fellow Jew," but in Luke should probably be read as fellow Christian. To rebuke is, for Jesus, to challenge with a view to change all that is evil, inappropriate, or defective. Jewish parallels to this call to rebuke and forgive may be found in CD 9:2–8; 1QS 5:25–6:1; and *T. Gad* 6:1–7. The "surprising lack of parallel in the Christian texts for the Jewish texts' preoccupation with the spirit in which reproof is undertaken" (Catchpole, *SNTU* 8 [1983] 82) has been noted. The presence of this element in the Jewish texts has rightly been accounted for on the basis of dependence upon Lev 19:17–18. Its absence from the Gospel tradition points to the end emphasis intended here: v 3 is a bare-bones version of a view that was already to be found in Judaism (though only in *T. Gad* does forgiveness come into clear focus, and here there is always the possibility of Christian influence [but see also Sir 28:2]); v 4 contains the radical Gospel challenge.

4 *ἐπιστρέψῃ*, "turns," and *μετανοῶ*, "I repent," may be Lukan language, but the difficulty of suggesting a suitable alternative for the second makes it more likely that both here and in v 3 the use of this verb is pre-Lukan. In traditional Jewish approaches to forgiveness, the burden lies with the one seeking forgiveness to demonstrate the genuineness of his or her repentance. With Jesus, the emphasis is on the readiness of the heart to forgive, no matter what strain is put upon the capability to forgive. The number seven is of course not a literal limit. It is meant to be sufficiently high to place the burden of responsibility on the person forgiving rather than on the person repenting (the recasting in Matt 18:21–22 makes the same point by increasing the number to seventy-seven, but without Luke's "in the day"). The benefit of the doubt lies entirely with the one being forgiven (this is finally quite different from *T. Gad* 6:7, where forgiveness is enjoined even when there has been no repentance, but where the sense of forgiveness has undergone a subtle but important change so that now it comes to mean lack of personal desire for vengeance in light of God's expected avenging of the wrong).

5 "Apostles," "Lord," and the use of *προστιθεῖναι*, "add/proceed/provide/give," are all Lukan. The request is probably given to the apostles because Luke wishes to emphasize the extreme challenge of the teaching that has just been given, to even the most committed of the followers of Jesus. At the same time Luke's use of "Lord" underlines Jesus' right to direct them in this way. The continuation in v 6 suggests that we should read "grant [additional] faith to us," rather than "give us faith," which the language could equally support (Delebecque's "have faith in us" seems hardly possible [*Études grecques,* 103]). The apostles seek additional faith to rise to the challenge of the teaching that has just been directed at the disciple band and the terrible responsibility to and for others that it creates (cf. the rather different response to teaching that was considered to be excessively challenging in Matt 19:10).

6 The opening words continue to provide the Lukan setting. As a response in the present setting, the words of v 6 say in effect that what is needed is not the *increase* of faith, but the *exercise* of faith (while the second clause is an apodosis of an unreal condition, this should not be taken as denying the reality of the apostle's faith here [cf. 22:32], any more than the similar construction in John 14:28 is intended as a denial of the disciples' love for Jesus: what is involved in each case is the failure to follow through with the behavior that *should* be implied by the preceding clause). Even the smallest possible portion of faith can achieve what is humanly impossible. For a discussion of the imagery here, see *Form/Structure/Setting* above. The imagery of uprooting and planting could possibly be ultimately derived from Jer 1:10. In its Gospel context, "faith" will be related to an awareness of the present coming of the kingdom of God in connection with the ministry of Jesus. Through faith the apostles (and by implication others) participate in the powers at work in and through Jesus himself. In Luke these powers are normally seen in connection with exorcism or healing (but note the ethical overtones of the use of the doctor image at 5:31–32, the pervasiveness of scope of "the good news to the poor" of the kingdom of God, and cf. the discussion of "authority" at 4:37), but here they are linked to the establishment of the ethical reality of the kingdom of God.

Explanation

As he opens this new section (17:1–19), Luke has brought together three small blocks of tradition to form a unit about the adequacy, despite all human frailty, of even the most meager of kingdom faiths for the radical challenge of Jesus' teaching. For those who have been touched by the coming of the kingdom of God in connection with the ministry of Jesus, what is needed is not the increase of faith, but simply the active exercise of faith.

V 1 expresses on the one hand realistic expectations in a fallen world of people influencing one another to evil, but on the other hand a sense of full responsibility for such influence. The extreme seriousness of the responsibility is illustrated by comparing, unfavorably, the state of one who has caused another to stumble into sin with that of a person tossed into the sea with a millstone jammed over his head as an unwelcome necklace of death dragging him down to the depths. The situation is seen to be at its most serious when it is one of "these little one"—the weak, the lowly, and the vulnerable who have been drawn to Jesus—who has been led astray.

In the opposite direction, the challenge is to be totally ready to forgive the person one has challenged as sinning against one. If the other repents, we must forgive. And this is still the case if the cycle of sin, repentance, and forgiveness needs to be repeated with the offender seven times in the day! Clearly the responsibility has been laid by Jesus on the one offended to show wholehearted readiness to forgive, and not upon the offender to demonstrate the reality of his or her repentance.

For us who seek to be guided by the words of Jesus, it must be said that this giving of the benefit of the doubt entirely to the one being forgiven raises serious practical difficulties. In practice, as with certain other of the dicta of Jesus (see discussion at 6:27–38), other significant and valid factors are likely to qualify the straightforward application of this teaching. But Jesus' teaching does identify in sharp contours what genuine forgiveness is all about.

Reeling under the impact of these demands, the apostles petition for an increased allocation of faith. But they have not reckoned with the limitless powers of a faith that has met in Jesus the working of the kingdom of God. It is not a matter of how much faith, but of the powers of the working of the kingdom of God that this faith, however meager and however unformed it might be, unleashes us. The need is not for more faith, but for the active exercise of faith. Our faith will prove adequate to the demands confronting us because of the adequacy of God's power to effect his own kingdom and rule.

"We Are Slaves to Whom No Favor Is Owed" (17:7–10)

Bibliography

Bailey, K. E. *Through Peasant Eyes.* 114–26. **Beyer, K.** *Semitische Syntax.* 1:287–93. **Bornhauser, K.** "Das Gleichnis von den 'unützen' Knechten: Bemerkungen zu Lk. 17, 5–10." *PastB* 82 (1939–40) 455–58. **Bultmann, R.** *Marburger Predigten.* Tübingen: Mohr, 1956. 148–58. **Derrett, J. D. M.** "The Parable of the Profitable Servant (Luke xvii.7–10)." *SE* 7 [= TU 126] (1982) 165–74. **Dupont, J.** "Le maître et son serviteur (Lc 17,7–10)." *ETL* 60 (1984) 233–51. **Eichholz, G.** "Meditation über das Gleichnis von Lk. 17, 7–10." In *Kirche, Konfession, Ökumene.* FS W. Niesel, ed. K. Halaski and W. Herrenbrück. Neukirchen-Vluyn: Neukirchener, 1973. 25–33. **Heininger, B.** *Sondergutgleichnisse.* 191–97. **Holstein, H.** "Serviteurs inutiles?" *BVC* 48 (1962) 39–45. **Jeremias, J.** *Parables.* 193. **Jülicher, A.** *Gleichnisreden.* 2:11–23. **Maasewerd, T.** "Unbekanntes Evangelium." *BLit* 28 (1960–61) 291–96. **Minear, P.** "A Note on Luke 17:7–10." *JBL* 93 (1974) 82–87. **Moffatt, J.** "The Story of the Farmer and His Man." *Exp* 8/23 (1922) 1–16. **Neuhäusler, E.** *Anspruch und Antwort Gottes: Zur Lehre von den Weisungen innerhalb der synoptischen Jesusverkündigung.* Düsseldorf: Patmos, 1962. 34–36. **Pesch, W.** *Der Lohngedanke in der Lehre Jesu verglichen mit der religiösen Lohnlehre des Spätjudentums.* MTS 7. Munich: Zink, 1955. 20–22. **Prast, F.** *Presbyter und Evangelium in nachapostolischer Zeit: Die Abschiedsrede des Paulus in Milet (Apg. 20,17–38) im Rahmen der lukanischen Konzeption der Evangeliumsverkündigung.* FB 29. Stuttgart: Katholisches Bibelwerk, 1979. 249–53. **Riggenbach, E.** "Ein Beitrag zum Verständnis der Parabel vom arbeitenden Knecht Luk. 17, 7–10." *NKZ* 34 (1923) 439–43. **Schmid, J.** "Zwei unbekannte Gleichnisse Jesu." *GuL* 33 (1960) 428–33, esp. 431–33. **Sudbrack, J.** "'Armselige Knechte sind wir: Unsere Schuldigkeit war es, was wir taten': Meditation über Lk 17,7–10." *GuL* 41 (1968) 308–12. **Ward, A. M.** "Uncomfortable Words: IV. Unprofitable Servants." *ExpTim* 81 (1969–70) 200–203. **Weiser, A.** *Die Knechtsgleichnisse.* 105–20.

Translation

[7] *"Which of you is there with*[a] *a slave that ploughs or shepherds, who, when he comes from the field, will say to him, 'Come right away and sit down to eat'?* [8] *Will he not, rather, say to him, 'Prepare*[b] *what I am to eat; then gird yourself [suitably] and wait on me while I eat and drink, and after this, you may eat and drink'?* [9] *Does he express thanks to the servant because he did what was commanded?*[c] [10] *So it is with you. When you have done all that has been commanded, say, 'We are slaves* [d]*to whom no favor is owed;*[d] *we have done [only] what we ought to do.'"*

Notes

[a] Gr. "having."
[b] μοι, "for me," is added by ℵ it sy sa[ms] bo[pt].
[c] οὐ δοκῶ, "I do not think [so]," is added by A (D) W Δ Θ Π etc. It is best taken as a marginal gloss.
[d-d] Gr. ἀχρεῖοι. The word is omitted by sy[s], and some other texts show variations in word order that may reflect a secondary reinsertion of the word.

Form/Structure/Setting

This small parable is the second unit of the present section (17:1–19). In the Lukan context it sets the heavy demands of vv 1–7 into the context of the imagery of slave and master. To meet God's demands is the duty of our station, not the basis of some special standing in his eyes.

The parable is found only in Luke. It has been subject to a modest amount of Lukan rewording, but the suggestions that v 8 and/or v 10 are secondary are without sufficient basis (see below). In the Gospel of Luke it has become a disciples' parable, but the appeal to settled life and slave ownership in the introduction to the parable hardly fits the itinerant disciple band. Though the parable is often treated as polemical, there is no reason not to see its function more positively as depicting total, selfless loyalty to an ineffably supreme God, a loyalty that Jesus promoted in all his ministry.

It is likely that Luke has the parable from a parables source in which it was chiastically paired with 11:11–13 (see excursus: "Journey to Jerusalem"). Depicting as it does a typical situation, the parable is to be classified as a similitude.

Comment

The demands of vv 1–6 may be heavy, but their fulfillment creates no claim upon God. This is nothing more than the duty owed to him.

7 There are no clearly Lukan features in the language here. Since there is no obvious verb for the opening phrase, the large shape of the syntax is difficult to untangle. Beyer (*Semitische Syntax*, 1:287–93) has claimed here a variant on a Semitic syntax pattern of sequential clauses, which he has identified, but the need to appeal to a variation, along with the lack of a negative in the ὅς, "who," clause in v 7 (supplied by D e l bo), stands against his reconstruction. The best solution seems to be to supply ἔστιν to the opening phrase. On τίς ἐξ ὑμῶν, "which of you," see at 11:5. The participles ἀροτριῶντα and ποιμαίνοντα, "ploughing" and "shepherding," could refer either to the slave's activity of the particular day or to his regular role; perhaps the latter is preferable. It is precisely the behavior contemplated here that is offered as an extraordinary act in 12:37. But here the appeal is to standard patterns, and the question presupposes the answer "None of us would do that."

8 This verse is sometimes considered to be a Lukan development (e.g., Weiser, *Knechtsgleichnisse*, 109–10), but only μετὰ ταῦτα, "after this," is notably Lukan. To remove the verse turns the option considered in v 7 into a gesture of thanks (cf. v 9). The shortened parable would not as adequately express the sense that in the master/slave relationship obligation flows in one direction alone; it would quite lose the image of comprehensive performance of duty that the full parable carries; and the full sharpness of the contrast between master and servant would be lost as well by the omission.

The parable assumes a small household with a single slave as a man of all duty. The slave is not denied the opportunity or the wherewithal to see to his own needs, but this may not interfere with the full performance of his duties. On *περιζωσάμενος*, "gird yourself [suitably]," see at 12:35. Despite Minear (*JBL* 93 [1974] 82–87) and others, neither the use of *διακονεῖν*, "serve/wait upon," nor the shepherding and ploughing imagery of v 7 should be linked specifically with the use of this imagery in connection with Christian ministry.

9 *διαταχθέντα*, "things commanded," may be Lukan here and in v 10. There is no particular personal gratitude due to the slave: he has only done what it has been his clear responsibility to do; his place in the scheme of things is to obey the directives of his master.

10 Minear (*JBL* 93 [1974] 87) protests about the change in focus here from the attitude of the master to the attitude of the slave. But that is exactly what we have as well in 11:11–13. It is a natural result of the need in application for the hearer to move from the master's position (cf. v 7), where he has been imaginatively set by the parable, to that of the slave, which is the image that in real life defines his relationship to God. There is no need to postulate a later addition of this verse.

πάντα, "everything," corresponds to the comprehensiveness of the duties of v 7 and then v 8. The main difficulty of v 10 is to find a satisfactory sense for *ἀχρεῖοι* (tr. above as "to whom no favor is owed"). It normally means "useless/worthless" and is certainly so used of slaves, but in a pejorative sense of slaves who do not work well. It could have this sense here as a piece of Oriental overstatement. A weaker sense of "unworthy" is attested for the Greek translations of the OT (see BAGD, 128) and would be a better fit here. This weaker sense also provides a measure of support for the otherwise rather speculative suggestion of Kilgallen (*Bib* 63 [1982] 549–51), based on etymological considerations, that the sense here is something like "owed nothing" (my language, not his). Kilgallen's suggestion, though it remains speculative, has been adopted because of its excellent fit and partial support from the Greek translations of the OT (Fitzmyer, 1147, suggests that Homer, *Od.* 18.163; Theocritus, *Poem.* 25.72 may provide some support for Kilgallen). The sentiment expressed in *m. ʾAbot* 1:3; 2:4 is quite similar.

Explanation

This small parable makes the point that meeting the demands of the kingdom of God (including those heavy demands of vv 1–7) is the duty of our station and gives us no special claim upon God: our obligation to him is as total as ever a slave's could be to his master's commands.

The parable begins by appealing to the commonplace of practice with slaves in the world of Jesus' day. After a man has done a hard day's work in the fields, his wife may indeed feel a reciprocal obligation to have a meal ready and waiting for him on his return. But a slave, like a farm animal, is there to work. He should not be starved or mistreated, but he is doing no favor when he works: he was purchased for that end. In the small establishment envisaged in this parable, there was but one slave and his range of responsibilities would be comprehensive. When the needs of the day were all met, then he could stop and see to his own needs.

Just as no thanks are due to the slave for fulfilling his natural societal role, so it is in our relationship to God. We exist for him, not he for us. As the one who is unimaginably supreme over us, he deserves our total loyalty and unstinting obedience. There is nothing meritorious in such obedience: it is merely the fulfillment of a natural obligation.

We, to whom slavery is naturally abhorrent, need to remind ourselves that the prospect of slavery *for oneself* was just as abhorrent to free persons in the ancient world as to us. To be sure, what is different is their acceptance (for the most part) of the institution of slavery and the societal class assumptions and patterns of behavior that went along with it. In the ancient world slavery was an available image for the total commitment of loyalty, devotion, and obedience due to God, and in this parable it illustrates the fact that our obedience as such does not create claim upon God. For us it is yet more important than in biblical times that this imagery does not stand alone to form our understanding of God. Alongside the uncomfortable austerity of this image must be set the warmth and generosity contributed by other biblical images of God. Ultimately, however, this alien image can introduce us in our democratic, individualistic hedonism to the transcendent reality of the God whom we serve in response to our inmost nature and is our natural duty.

The Response of Faith to the Healing Mercy of God (17:11–19)

Bibliography

Betz, H. D. "The Cleansing of the Ten Lepers (Luke 17:11–19)." *JBL* 90 (1971) 314–28. **Blinzler, J.** "Die literarische Eigenart des sogenannten Reiseberichts im Lukasevangelium." In *Synoptischen Studien.* FS A. Wikenhauser, ed. J. Schmid and A. Vögtle. Munich: Zink, 1953. 20–52, esp. 46–52. **Bours, J.** "Vom dankbaren Samariter: Einc Meditation über Lk 17,11–19." *BibLeb* 1 (1960) 193–98. **Bruners, W.** *Die Reinigung der zehn Aussätzigen und die Heilung des Samariters Lk 17,11–19: Ein Beitrag zur lukanischen Interpretation der Reinigung von Aussätzigen.* Forschung zur Bibel 23. Stuttgart: Katholisches Bibelwerk, 1977. **Busse, U.** *Wunder.* 313–27. **Charpentier, E.** "L'Evangile (Lc 17,11–19): L'Etranger appelé au salut." *AsSeign* o.s. 67 (1965) 36–57. ———. "L'Evangile (Lc 17,11–19): L'Etranger appelé au salut." *AsSeign* n.s. 59 (1974) 68–79. **Conzelmann, H.** *Luke.* 68–73. **Enslin, M. S.** "Luke and Matthew, Compilers or Authors?" *ANRW* 2.25.3 (1985) 2357–88, esp. 2378–84. **Glöckner, R.** *Neutestamentliche Wundergeschichten und das Lob der Wundertaten Gottes in den Psalmen: Studien zur sprachlichen und theologischen Verwandtschaft zwischen neutestamentichen Wundergeschichten und Psalmen.* Walberger Studien. Theologische Reihe 13. Mainz: Grünewald, 1983. 125–60. **Glombitza, O.** "Der dankbare Samariter, Luk. xvii 11–19." *NovT* 11 (1969) 241–46. **Heutger, N.** "Die lukanischen Samaritanererzählungen in religionspädagogischer Sicht." In *Wort in der Zeit: Neutestamentliche Studien.* FS K. H. Rengstorf, ed. W. Haubeck and M. Bachmann. Leiden: Brill, 1980. 275–87. **Meltzer, H.**

"Die Gleichnisse vom dankbaren Samariter und von der wunderbaren Speisung." *PM* 25 (1921) 198–206. **Pesch, R.** *Jesu, ureigene Taten? Ein Beitrag zur Wunderfrage.* QD 52. Freiburg im B.: Herder, 1970. 114–34. **Roloff, J.** *Das Kerygma.* 157–58.

Translation

[11] *It happened, as he was making his way to Jerusalem and going along between*[a] *Samaria and Galilee,* [12] *that, on his way into a certain village, ten leprous men met him, who stood far off.* [13] *They raised their voices*[b] *and said, "Jesus, master, have mercy on us."* [14] *When Jesus saw [them], he said to them, "Go and show yourselves to the priests"; and* [c]*what happened was*[c] *that, as they set off, they were made clean.* [15] *One of them, seeing that he had been healed, returned glorifying God with a loud voice* [16] *and fell down on his face at Jesus'*[d] *feet, giving thanks to him—and this one was a Samaritan.* [17] *Jesus responded, "Were the [whole] ten not made clean? The nine, where are they?* [18] *They have not been found returning to give glory to God—only this foreigner."* [19] *He said to him, "Get up and go; your faith has saved you."*

Notes

[a] Gr. διὰ μέσον. The oddness of this usage has generated various alternatives: D has just μέσον, "in the middle of?"; *f* [1,13] 205 etc. have ἀνὰ μέσον, "among/within/through/between," and A W Θ Ψ 33 etc. διὰ μέσου, "through the midst of/between," as more common expressions.

[b] Gr. "voice."

[c-c] Gr. καὶ ἐγένετο. Often translated "[and] it happened."

[d] Gr. "his."

Form/Structure/Setting

The sense of the heavy demand of discipleship engendered by the previous two units (vv 1–6, 7–10) of this section (vv 1–19) is lightened somewhat by this concluding unit with its emphasis on the dynamic of gratitude. The role of faith at the end of the first unit recurs here at the end of the final unit.

Again Luke is the only Synoptist to have preserved this material. Bruners (*Reinigung*, esp. 297–306) has argued at length for a purely Lukan origin for this unit. This judgment has been accepted by Busse (*Wundergeschichten*, 319–22) and others, but has been effectively countered by Glöckner (*Wundergeschichten*, 128–31; and see earlier Pesch, *Ureigene Taten*, 216–23). Note particularly the uneven distribution of Lukan language features through the material, and the fact that free composition would have produced a more free-flowing text and more thorough integration into the context.

There has been, nonetheless, significant Lukan intervention, and opinion varies as to the nature and extent of this intervention. Has Luke introduced the Samaritan motif (as Roloff, *Kerygma*, 157)? This is shown in *Comment* below to be unlikely. Has he added v 19, as frequently claimed? Again, probably not. The scope of Luke's contribution to the present narrative, beyond individual language changes, is most likely to be v 11, v 12 as far as "village," and v 15–16 from "glorifying God" through to "at his feet." That is, he has provided the setting and he has reinforced and developed the equation of response to Jesus and response to God, but has not disturbed the basic structure or scope of the narrative.

What of the earlier history of the narrative? Here we should first deal with the questions of the relationship between the present narrative and, respectively, (*i*) the healing of Naaman in 2 Kgs 5:9–19 and (*ii*) the healing of the leper in Luke 5:12–14//Mark 1:40–45. For its relationship with the healing of Naaman, Bruners (*Reinigung*, esp. 103–18) represents the maximal position. For him (118) the whole narrative is an imitative narrative of a prophetic figure who surpasses his model. The other extreme is to deny any connection (as, e.g., Glöckner, *Wundergeschichten*, 131–39). It is probably reasonable to detect a modest amount of allusion to the Elisha narrative, without this providing in any way an adequate basis for the production of the narrative or providing any interpretive key to the narrative. For the relationship of this unit to the other healing of a leper, Bultmann (*History*, 33) represents the maximizing position, according to which Luke 17:11–19 is no more than an imaginary transposition of the earlier cleansing account. Most of the commonality is simply that required for any account one might formulate of the healing of leprosy in the context of the Jewish law. "He fell on [his] face" in 17:16 does seem, however, to be a deliberate borrowing (however by Luke, not earlier) from the one account to the other (see 5:12). Again, the one narrative has no capacity to account for the other (beyond the nine and the one, which is all that Bultmann really attends to; note in particular the role of the return and the equivalence between thanks to Jesus and glory to God).

The narrative defies standard form-critical classification (it comes closest to being a pronouncement story, but much of the detail of the miracle account is essential for the pronouncement). This should not, however, be allowed automatically to disqualify the narrative as ultimately historical. At the same time, the variety of the threads that are woven together here must reduce rather than increase the confidence with which we can trace the particular elements back to the historical Jesus.

Comment

Only the one who gratefully returns to the source in Jesus makes an appropriate response to the healing mercy extended by God in the ministry of Jesus.

11 Eight of the opening nine words are to be found in a similar configuration in 9:51. Most likely the whole verse is Lukan (Pesch, *Ureigene Taten*, 117–19 defends διὰ μέσον Γαλιλαίας, "through the midst of Galilee," as pre-Lukan). Luke has last mentioned the fact that Jesus is traveling in 14:25, and has last spoken of the destination in Jerusalem in 13:31–35: it is time to renew the motif, particularly since Luke's tradition here is likely to have provided a suitable linchpin in the form of a statement implying that Jesus is traveling as he meets the lepers. This is the last renewal of the motif before that of the final unit of the large journey section in 18:31–34. Though this is often done, it is best not to take these reminders as structure markers (17:11–19 links better with what precedes than with what follows).

Though no close parallel has been cited for the use of διὰ μέσον for "between," there are instances where διά + acc. is used to mean "through," rather than the expected "because of/for the sake of." This leads reasonably enough to the sense "between" for διὰ μέσον (see BDF, 222; BAGD, 181; Fitzmyer, 1153 ["through the middle (of)" is an impossible sense with the following "Samaria and Galilee" and would not normally be the natural sense with a following pair of nouns]). There is no need, with Blinzler ("Die literarische Eigenart," 49–52), to treat μέσον Σαμαρείας καί as a gloss nor, with Conzelmann (*Luke*, 68–73), to consider that Luke betrays here his confusion about the geography of Palestine. Luke has no interest in the geographical features of the journey. The location between Samaria and Galilee merely accounts for the mixed Jewish and Samaritan makeup of the group of lepers.

12 It is likely that ἀπήντησαν, "met," is the verb controlled by the opening ἐγένετο, "it happened," construction of v 11 (cf. Fitzmyer, 1154; the closest parallels to the structure are in 5:1; 19:15), and thus that it is Luke who provides the syntax to this point (and probably the vocabulary up to but not including ἀπήντησαν). The distance of the lepers reflects Lev 13:46; Num 5:2–3 (contrast Mark 1:40; cf. v 41). That they are met outside the village is to be similarly explained. "Leprous men" rather than "lepers" may be a Lukan touch.

13 The opening unstressed καὶ αὐτοί (lit. "and they") is likely to be Lukan. In Lukan idiom "lifting up the voice" has to do with needing to be heard or wanting to be emphatic, and not specifically with prayer (only so in Acts 4:24). A mixture of the first and second is best here. ἐπιστάτα, "master," may be Lukan, but it is distinctive from Luke's other uses in not being spoken by a disciple (see at 5:5). Jesus will also be addressed by a suppliant as "Jesus" (there with "Son of David") in 18:38–39//Mark 10:47–48 (and note the presence there as well of "have mercy on me"). "Have mercy on me/us" is frequent in the Psalms (see Glöckner, *Wundergeschichten*, 139–40), but nothing should be made of this for such an imprecise expression (here it could [but should not] be taken as no more than a request for alms).

14 The point of mentioning Jesus' "seeing" is that this is the basis for his identification of the problem, and thus of his directive to the lepers. While the same motif of the need to meet the Mosaic requirement for being declared clean from leprosy is present as in 5:14 (see there), the notable difference here is that the lepers are sent off with their leprosy still not dealt with. The lepers were required to act as though doing what Jesus asked would make a difference, even though there was yet no tangible evidence that it would (they had at least to believe that it was worth a try; cf. the commands to act with the expectation of healing in 5:25; 6:10; 7:14; 8:54; and cf. further 7:7–10; John 4:50). This is the closest point to the Naaman incident (2 Kgs 5:10), but even here the link is not certain. ἐν τῷ ὑπάγειν is likely to mean here, as in 8:42, "as [they] set off": they have not gone far before they are made clean from their leprosy.

15–16 δοξάζων τὸν θεόν, "glorifying God," is likely to be Lukan here as it was in 5:25 and will be in 18:43. μετὰ φωνῆς μεγάλης, "with a loud voice," is less likely to be so, since Luke clearly prefers φωνῇ μεγάλῃ for this. ἔπεσεν ἐπὶ πρόσωπον, "he fell on [his] face" (cf. 5:12), and παρὰ τοὺς πόδας αὐτοῦ, "at his feet," are both Lukan.

ἰδών, "seeing/saw," propels the action as it did in v 14. There is no real basis for giving any profound sense of spiritual awakening to this verb in itself. Glöckner (*Wundergeschichten*, 145) has, however, pointed to the parallel role of "seeing" in 5:8 (and note the narrative there has the same double role for seeing in the forwarding of the action [see 5:2]), and this may suggest that we should see the "seeing" in each case as triggering in turn a deeper perception, to be evidenced in what ensues. ὑπέστρεψεν, "returned," is the verb that Luke uses in connection with repentance, but that nuance is out of place here (2:20 is a better comparison).

While the importance of giving glory to God is pervasively evident in the psalms, one wonders (yet more so in v 18) why it should be necessary to *return to Jesus* to give glory to God. Why not, say, go to the temple or the synagogue? Or why not even complete first what Jesus had directed? (This last may only need to be answered in terms of the short distance from Jesus when the healing took place.) It is likely that an original that simply equated returning and giving thanks to Jesus with returning and giving glory to God (for a similar kind of equation see 8:39) has been elaborated by Luke in language that points to the theophanic nature of encounter with Jesus (cf. 5:8–9). The original equation is intelligible in terms of the role of Jesus in the manifestation of the kingdom of God and has an implied Christology that Luke is keen to exploit and develop. It is just possible, as well, that the return represents a second allusion to the cleansing of Naaman (see 2 Kgs 5:15), which may find development in the expression of thanks (cf. the offered present of 2 Kgs 5:15).

There is no adequate reason for excising the Samaritan from the original account (on Samaritans, see at 9:51–56). At a literary level the text without the Samaritan cries out for a comment on the one who is so different from the nine. The point is neither pro-Samaritan nor anti-Jewish, any more than 7:9 is anti-Jewish. It points (but only implicitly) to Jewish failure, but in a manner that is designed to challenge rather than condemn. (In a secondary way, and in the larger Luke-Acts context, the present text does, however, secure a foothold for the Samaritan mission, much as 7:9 does for the mission to the Gentiles.)

17–18 None of the language here is notably Lukan. For δοῦναι δόξαν τῷ θεῷ, "to give glory to God," cf. Acts 12:23. The narrator's singling out of the one in v 15 now becomes a public contrast of the one and the nine made by Jesus himself. V 18 is normally punctuated as a question, but the syntax receives better justice when translated as a statement. Jesus equates the return to give thanks to himself with a return to give glory to God (see above). The return involves a public identification with what God is now doing in Jesus. The wording attributed to Jesus here suggests that he had no greater spontaneous expectation of good from Samaritans than did his fellow Jews. ἀλλογενής, "foreigner," is not used elsewhere in the NT. It is the term used in the temple inscription that forbade the entry of foreigners into the Jerusalem temple (cf. BAGD, 39). More strictly, the Samaritans were viewed as half-foreign, Israelites of doubtful descent (see at 9:52).

19 See discussion at 7:50 for the series of Lukan terminating statements similar to this verse, and for the sense of the present verse. This is the one in the set that stands the greatest chance of being a secondary development (and it is so judged by many). But even here the role of the return and the nature of the identification of thanksgiving to Jesus and glorification of God suggest the appropriateness of a final statement that recognizes the difference, achieved through the return, between the one and the nine. Moreover, without v 19, the returning Samaritan is discussed but, curiously, not addressed. The distinctive ἀναστάς, "get up," is produced by the prostrate position Luke has introduced in v 16. Though the Samaritan is but a foreigner to the People of God, his faith has brought salvation to him (cf. Acts 15:9, 11).

Explanation

This last unit of the section (17:1–19) provides a balance to the stern picture of discipleship that has dominated the first two units. Now gratitude comes into the picture and an image of the healing mercy that God extends to those who call on Jesus for mercy.

Luke refreshes the journey motif at this point: this too must be seen in connection with the journey to suffering and glory that climaxes the ministry of Jesus. Luke offers the vague location between Samaria and Galilee to account ahead of time for the Samaritan in the group of lepers (others of the group may have been Samaritans as well, but a mixed group is required by v 18).

Because of the need for lepers to keep themselves segregated from others, the lepers meet Jesus outside a village; for the same reason they shout out to him from a distance. They know who he is, and they address his as "master," which indicates a personal recognition of his authority. They humbly ask for his help in traditionally suppliant language.

When Jesus has sized up the situation, he asks them to go off to the priests, as required by the OT for those seeking reclassification as clean from their leprosy. The lepers are required to act as though doing what Jesus asks will make a difference, though there is yet no tangible evidence that it will. They have little to lose and all comply. It is worth a try. They are no doubt delighted to discover in a very short time that the venture has worked.

The effect on one, but only one, is to make him turn right around and head back to Jesus, full of thanks to Jesus and glory to God. Luke's elaboration of the man's behavior here suggests that he wants us to see that this man in his dealings with Jesus experiences an encounter with God. Of the ten only this one makes a public identification with what God is now doing in Jesus.

The kingdom of God has been at work, but only one of the ten makes the necessary response of gratitude and faith. As Jesus has elsewhere lamented the lack of faith of his generation (9:41), so here he expresses his distress that this one man has come back alone. The shame of it is intensified because this fellow is not really a Jew. Though the language is slightly exaggerated in connection with a Samaritan, to make the point, the man is spoken of by Jesus as a "foreigner." But as much of a foreigner as he might be, this man is now sent off by Jesus as a person who has experienced the salvation that Jesus came to bring. None of the others, despite their new-found freedom from leprosy, receives this special blessing.

Who Will Be Ready When the Son of Man Comes? (*17:20–18:8*)

The focus moves now from the presence of the kingdom of God in the ministry of Jesus to the future consummation of the kingdom of God. The coming of the Son of Man could be at any moment. When the moment comes there will be no mistaking it, though it will come upon many unawares. The call is for a constant state of heightened alertness and a readiness for decisive action. The day will come bringing both deliverance and devastating destruction, and its drama will unfold with a precision that will distinguish between those in even the closest proximity to one another. Who will rise to the occasion?

When Will the Kingdom of God Come? (*17:20–21*)

Bibliography

General for 17:20–18:8:

Allen, H. J. "The Apocalyptic Discourse in S. Luke XVII." *Exp* 9/4 (1925) 59–61. **Delcor, M.** "Jour du Fils de l'Homme." *Catholisme* 6/25 (1965) 1052–54. **Feuillet, A.** "La venue du règne de Dieu et du Fils de l'Homme (d'après Luc, XVII,20 à XVIII,8." *RSR* 35 (1948) 544–65. ———. "La double venue du règne de Dieu et du Fils de l'homme en Luc xvii,20–xviii,8: Recherches sur l'eschatologie des Synoptiques." *RevThom* 81 (1981) 5–33. **Geiger, R.** *Die lukanischen Endzeitreden: Studien zur Eschatologie des Lukas-Evangeliums.* Europäische Hochschulschriften 23/16. Bern/Frankfurt am M.: H. Lang/P. Lang, 1973. 29–169. **Hudson, J. T.** "Q's Eschatology: A Study of Luke xvii. 20–37." *ExpTim* 34 (1922–23) 187–88. **McDowell, E. A.** "The Kingdom of God and the Day of the Son of Man." *RevExp* 39 (1942) 54–65. **Schnackenburg, R.** "Der eschatologische Abschnitt Lk 17,20–37." In *Mélanges bibliques.* FS B. Rigaux, ed. A. Descamps and A. de Halleux. 213–34. **Zmijewski, J.** *Die Eschatologiereden des Lukas-Evangeliums: Eine traditions- und redaktionsgeschichtliche Untersuchung zu Lk 21,5–36 und Lk 17,20–37.* BBB 40. Bonn: Hanstein, 1972. 326–540.

For 17:20–21:

Allen, P. M. S. "Luke xvii. 21: ἰδοὺ γὰρ ἡ βασιλεία τοῦ θεοῦ ἐντὸς ὑμῶν ἐστιν." *ExpTim* 49 (1937–38) 476–77; 50 (1938–39) 233–35. **Ballard, F.** "Luke xvii. 21." *ExpTim* 38 (1926–27) 331. **Beasley-Murray, G. R.** *Jesus and the Kingdom of God.* Grand Rapids, MI/Exeter: Eerdmans/Paternoster, 1986. 313–21. **Braun, H.** "Der Irrtum der Naherwartung." In *Jesus—der Mann aus Nazareth und seine Zeit: Um 12 Kapitel erweiterte Studienausgabe.* Stuttgart: Krenz, 1984. 201–13. **Bretscher, P. M.** "Luke 17:20–21 in Recent Investigations." *CTM* 22 (1951) 895–907. **Cadbury, H. J.** "The Kingdom of God and Ourselves." *Christian Century* 67 (1950) 172–73. **Carroll, J. T.** *Response to the End of History.* 76–87. **Catchpole, D. R.** "The

Law and the Prophets in Q." In *Tradition and Interpretation in the New Testament.* FS E. E. Ellis, ed. G. F. Hawthorne and O. Betz. Tübingen/Grand Rapids, MI: Mohr/Eerdmans, 1987. 95–109. **Conzelmann, H.** *Luke.* 120–25. **Dalman, G.** *The Words of Jesus.* Edinburgh: Clark, 1909. 143–47. **Dodd, C. H.** *Parables.* 62, 83, 87, 155. **Easton, B. C.** "Luke 17:20–21: An Exegetical Study." *AJT* 16 (1912) 275–83. **Glasson, T. F.** "The Gospel of Thomas, Saying 3, and Deuteronomy xxx.11–14." *ExpTim* 78 (1966–67) 151–52. **Grässer, E.** *Parusieverzögerung.* 170–72. **Griffiths, J. G.** "'Ἐντὸς ὑμῶν (Luke xvii. 21)." *ExpTim* 63 (1951–52) 30–31. **Grimm, W.** *Jesus und das Danielbuch: I. Jesu Einspruch gegen das Offenbarungssystem Daniels: Mt. 11,25–27; Lk. 17,20–21.* ANTJ 6. Bern/Frankfurt am M.: Lang, 1984. 70–90. **Hartl, D.** "Die Aktulalität des Gottesreiches nach Lk 17,20f." In *Biblische Randbemerkungen.* FS R. Schnackenburg, ed. H. Merklein and J. Lange. Würzburg: Echter, 1974. 25–30. **Hawthorne, G. F.** "The Essential Nature of the Kingdom of God." *WTJ* 25 (1962–63) 35–47. **Héring, J.** *Le royaume de Dieu et sa venue: Etudes sur l'espérance de Jésus et de l'apôtre Paul.* New ed. Neuchâtel: Delachaux et Niestlé, 1959. 42–45. **Hiers, R. H.** "Why Will They Not Say, 'Lo, Here!' or 'There!'?" *JAAR* 35 (1967) 379–84. **Jeremias, J.** "L'Attente de la fin prochaine dans les paroles de Jésus." In *L'Infallibilità,* ed. E. Castelli. Archivio di filosofia. Padua: A. Milani, 1970. 185–94. **Joüon, P.** "Notes philologiques sur les Évangiles—Luc 17:20–21." *RSR* 18 (1928) 354–55. **Kaestli, J.-D.** *L'Eschatologie.* 28–37. **Kümmel, W. G.** *Promise and Fulfilment.* 32–36, 90, 103–5, 151. **Lebourlier, J.** *"Entos hymōn:* Le sens 'au milieu de vous' est-il possible?" *Bib* 73 (1992) 259–62. **Lewis, F. W.** "Luke xvii. 21." *ExpTim* 38 (1926–27) 187–88. **Müller, D.** "Kingdom of Heaven or Kingdom of God?" *VChr* 27 (1973) 266–76. **Mussner, F.** "'Wann kommt das Reich Gottes?' Die Antwort Jesu nach Lk 17, 20b–21." *BZ* 6 (1962) 107–11. **Nicklin, T.** "With Observation." *ExpTim* 27 (1915–16) 475. **Noack, B.** *Das Gottesreich bei Lukas: Eine Studie zu Luk. 17,20–24.* SymBU 10. Lund: Gleerup, 1948. **Percy, E.** *Die Botschaft Jesu: Eine traditionskritische und exegetische Untersuchung.* Lund: Gleerup, 1953. 216–33. **Perrin, N.** *Rediscovering.* 58, 68–74, 77, 193–96. **Proctor, K. S.** "Luke 17,20.21." *BT* 33 (1982) 245. **Proost, K. F.** "Lukas 17, 21, ἐντὸς ὑμῶν." *TT* 48 (1914) 246–53. **Riesenfeld, H.** "'Ἐμβολεύειν—Ἐντός." *Nuntius* 2 (1949) 11–12. ———. "Le règne de Dieu, parmi vous ou en vous? (Luc 17, 20–21)." *RB* 98 (1991) 190–98. ———. "τηρέω, κτλ." *TDNT* 8:140–51, esp. 148–51. **Roberts, C. H.** "The Kingdom of Heaven (Lk. xvii. 21)." *HTR* 41 (1948) 1–8. **Robinson, J. M.** "The Study of the Historical Jesus after Nag Hammadi." *Semeia* 44 (1988) 45–55, esp. 53–55. **Rüstow, A.** "*ΕΝΤΟΣ ΥΜΩΝ ΕΣΤΙΝ*: Zur Deutung von Lukas 17.30–21." *ZNW* 51 (1960) 197–224. **Schrey, H. H.** "Zu Luk. 17,21." *TLZ* 74 (1949) 759. **Sledd, A.** "The Interpretation of Luke 17,21." *ExpTim* 50 (1938–39) 235–37. **Smith, A. G.** "'The Kingdom of God Is within You.'" *ExpTim* 43 (1931–32) 378–79. **Sneed, R.** "'The Kingdom of God Is within You' (Lk 17,21)." *CBQ* 24 (1962) 363–82. **Strobel, A.** "Die Passa-Erwartung als urchristliches Problem in Lc 17,20f." *ZNW* 49 (1958) 157–96. ———. "A. Merx über Lc. 20f." *ZNW* 51 (1960) 133–34. ———. "In dieser Nacht (Luk 17,34): Zu einer älteren Form der Erwartung in Luk 17,20–37." *ZTK* 58 (1961) 16–29. ———. "Zu Lk 17,20f." *BZ* 7 (1963) 111–13. **Wabnitz, A.** "Note sur Luc XVII, 21." *RTQR* 18 (1909) 234–38. ———. "Note supplémentaire sur Luc XVII, 21." *RTQR* 18 (1909) 289–94. ———. "Seconde note supplémentaire sur Luc XVII, 21." *RTQR* 18 (1909) 456–66. **Waggett, P. N.** "Studies in Texts." *Th* 8 (1924) 163–66. **Wenham, D.** *The Rediscovery of Jesus' Eschatological Discourse.* Gospel Perspectives 4. Sheffield: JSOT Press, 1984. 107–9, 135–74. **Wikgren, A.** "*ΕΝΤΟΣ*." *Nuntius* 4 (1950) 27–28.

Translation

[20]*Being asked by the Pharisees when the kingdom of God would come, Jesus replied, "The kingdom of God will not come*[a] [b]*in a way that allows for advance observation.*[b] [21]*Nor will they say, 'Look, here [it is], or there [it is].'*[c] *No,*[d] *the kingdom of God will be*[e] *[right there] in your midst."*

Notes

[a] Gr. has present tense.
[b-b] Lit. "with observation."
[c] A D (W) Ψ $f^{1,13}$ etc. have made the correspondence with v 23 more exact.
[d] Lit. "behold."
[e] Gr. has present tense.

Form/Structure/Setting

There is a fairly broad recognition that the natural section here runs from 17:20 to 18:8: each of the units deals in some way with the timing of God's future intervention in the world (using the language of the coming of the kingdom of God or of the coming of the Son of Man). The final unit 18:1–8 is bound to the large central unit (17:22–37) by the inclusion of 18:8b with its reference to the coming of the Son of Man. The preceding 17:20–21 is bound to this same central unit by the inclusion in v 21 of ἰδοὺ ὧδε ἢ ἐκεῖ ἰδού (lit. "bchold here or there behold"), which is clearly linked to v 23.

Luke alone of the Synoptists has preserved the material of vv 21–22 (there are versions in *Gos. Thom.* 3, 51, 113 and OxyP 654:9–16, which are probably dependent on the Lukan form [but note the attribution of the question to the disciples in *Gos. Thom.* 113; see further, Fitzmycr, *Semitic Background*, 374–78], as will be the version cited by Robinson [*Semeia* 44 (1988) 52] from the *Gospel of Mary*). Schnackenburg ("Eschatologische Abschnitt," 213–34) has argued for a single source that embraces 17:20–21 and 22–37, but his source reconstruction is particularly unconvincing at the point of transition from v 21a to v 23a (he considers v 21b Lukan, along with v 22 apart from "days will comc"). There is, therefore, no reason for thinking that Matthew had access to this tradition in connection with other material he shares with Luke.

While there is no particular reason for disputing the attribution of the question to Pharisees, Luke's freedom in formulating settings for his own editorial purposes means we cannot be sure that this attribution is original. The words of Jesus have the nature of a response and will, therefore, always have been the answer to a question, rather than an independent statement. There is quite a likelihood that Luke has intruded the second negative statement (v 21a) in order to connect more obviously this kingdom-of-God tradition with the Son-of-Man tradition to come in vv 22–37.

The material here has been preserved and transmitted as a pronouncement story. The content fits with what appears to be Jesus' general antipathy toward attempts to engage in apocalyptic timetabling.

Comment

Concern with right response to the present working of the kingdom of God now gives way to an interest in the future consummation of the kingdom of God. The future coming of the kingdom of God could become operative at any moment: there will be no staged warnings to be discerned even by the most astute.

20 There is nothing particularly Lukan about any of the language of this verse, but the role of the Pharisees as conversation partners with Jesus throughout the journey narrative means that we cannot rule out the Lukan hand (the use of παρατήρησις, "observation," is sometimes considered Lukan on the basis of Luke's use of the cognate verb, but this is hardly convincing). In the Lukan structuring, conversation with the Pharisees makes vv 20–21 a public statement of what is elucidated privately in vv 22–37 to the disciples. On the *coming* of the kingdom, see at 11:2, and on the kingdom of God more generally, at 4:43; 6:20; 13:19; 19:11; 21:31. The question presupposes that the kingdom of God is yet to come, and the beginning of the answer, as the language of the question is repeated, seems to accept this starting point (although, in another sense, the kingdom of God had now already come in connection with the ministry of Jesus). The response suggests that in the Lukan text the question should be given the force "how will we know when the kingdom of God will come/has come?"

A number of suggestions have been offered about the sense to be given to μετὰ περατηρήσεως, "observation/observance." Taking his cue from the identity of the questioners and arguing for a tradition parallel in Rom 14:17 (and cf. the use of the cognate verb in Gal 4:10), Sneed (*CBQ* 24 [1962] 363–82) takes the sense to be "external observance of the requirements of the law." But Sneed's parallel is not close; his view does not make for a good connection with either the preceding or following clauses; and it is difficult to see how μετά can bear the sense required. Strobel (esp. *ZNW* 49 [1958] 157–96) has argued at length that this phrase should be correlated with a (later?) Pharisaic tradition that the messiah would come on the night of observation, i.e., the night of Passover. Beyond the difficulty of dating the traditions appealed to, there is, however, nothing in the context to encourage such a precise reference. Other suggestions include a reversion into Aramaic to uncover the sense "secretly, i.e., in a manner which cannot be observed" (the question hardly suggests that the questioners thought it might come secretly) and the idea that the coming of the kingdom will have authenticating signs with it (the response then is: it doesn't need them; its coming will be obvious to all [this is a long way from the question, and makes παρατηρήσεως a word for sign(s), which it most certainly is not]). Better than any of these is the view that recognizes that the term used here is primarily used in Greek for observations made in connection with medical diagnosis, treatment, and prognosis, as well as in connection with various kinds of scientific observations (including observation of the stars; for texts see Riesenfeld, *TDNT* 8:148–49). The words here point to the process of trying to work out, by means of concrete observations, what is happening in connection with the coming of the kingdom of God, whether these observations take the form of looking for supernatural signs, projecting from the present political situation, looking at the entrails of animals, examining the configuration of the stars, or some other form. One cannot discern when the kingdom of God will come by prognostication on the basis of the observation of preliminary indications.

21 It seems most likely that Luke is responsible for the second negative clause, which he has drawn almost verbatim from v 23 (the closeness of the wording, the structural usefulness to Luke of such a link with vv 22–37, the future verb in contrast with the [futuristic?] present verbs of the preceding and following clauses, and the difficulty of correlating the clause with the question all count in favor of a Lukan origin). The Lukan sense is best seen in connection with v 23 (where the location of the Son of Man is in view). The issue here is: might it be possible to miss the kingdom of God if one does not investigate suggestions about where it might be located; or, possibly, will there be a period for preparation between receiving a message that the kingdom of God has arrived and needing to personally encounter it for oneself? (The possibility of a localized kingdom of God is best seen in connection with traditions about the central role of Jerusalem or Mount Zion in Jewish eschatological hopes.) The Lukan Jesus emphatically rejects the possibility of missing the kingdom of God because it is happening elsewhere. His reason is given in the final clause of the verse.

The statement that the kingdom of God ἐντὸς ὑμῶν ἐστιν (lit. "is within/among you") has been the subject of extensive investigation. The view with the longest pedigree is that the phrase should be translated "is within you" and that we are being told that the kingdom of God is an inner spiritual reality and not a future apocalyptic transformation of the whole cosmos. This sense makes use of what is the most common sense of ἐντός, and makes a good contrast with the preceding negations (while requiring a slightly different nuance for the second negation than that given above). However, it requires that "you" be taken impersonally, which is a little unnatural. It also represents a view of the kingdom of God not found elsewhere in the Gospel tradition (despite Feuillet's vigorous defense [*RevThom* 81 (1981) 11–15] of a wider presence of such a view). Taken in conjunction with the preceding negations, it leaves no room for a future eschatological intervention of God as anticipated in vv 22–37.

Probably the most common modern view takes ἐντός as "among/in the midst of" and sees the kingdom of God as present in the person and ministry of Jesus. This fits well with other materials that identify a present coming of the kingdom of God in connection with the ministry of Jesus (see Luke 11:20). There is some question whether ἐντός can take the sense "among/in the midst of" other than in the sense "within your circle," a sense that runs into acute problems with the Pharisaic identity of those addressed (cf. Roberts, *HTR* 41 [1948] 3–4; Feuillet, *RevThom* 81 [1981] 7–11; Riesenfeld, *RB* 98 [1991] 190–98; BAGD, 269). It is likely that this sense is possible, though not common, but here again the same difficulty arises when the preceding negations are linked: there is no room for vv 22–27.

A third suggestion is to align the phrase here with a use of ἐντός that Rüstow (*ZNW* 51 [1960] 214–16) has documented. Here ἐντός means "within one's reach/in one's hands/under the control of" (Rüstow's analysis of the sense here is to be accepted despite the attempts by Riesenfeld [*Nuntius* 2 (1949) 11–12] and Wikgren [*Nuntius* 4 (1950) 27–28] to demonstrate that in the papyri texts appealed to ἐντός is, rather, elliptical for "in/at the home of"; this proposed alternative will only work for some of the texts and is not certain for any of them). With this understanding the same difficulty arises with the link to the preceding negations.

The final view to be considered is that of Bultmann (*History*, 121–22) and others that the reference is to a future sudden arrival of the kingdom of God. This view must first accept the possibility of giving ἐντός the sense "in your midst" and then needs to treat this idiomatically as conveying the idea of the kingdom of God being "right there," as having arrived, while all the alert observers have failed to notice anything to base their prognostications upon. This assumes that ἐστιν, "is," should be taken futuristically, but, in the absence of the second negation, this is a natural reading after the obviously futurist force of the present tense ἔρχεται (lit. "comes"). This view is somewhat vulnerable to the frequently leveled criticism that the key notion of a sudden and unheralded arrival of the kingdom of God must be taken as implied, because it is certainly not explicitly present. It is, nevertheless, the view that does best justice to the content of v 21, and the one view that easily makes room for vv 22–37 and does justice as well to Luke's evident concern to link the two sections.

Explanation

Where 17:1–19 has been concerned with making a fitting response to the *present* demands and working of the kingdom of God, the new section 17:20–18:8 concerns itself with the anticipation of the *future* coming of the kingdom of God. The kingdom of God could be right here at any moment. There is no place for advance observation of telltale signs, or a warning message that it has arrived elsewhere but has not yet reached us.

What is said here to the Pharisees, and therefore publicly, will be developed more fully for the disciples in vv 22–37, and therefore possibly privately. The response Jesus makes suggests that in the Lukan text we should take the question as having the force "how will we know when the kingdom of God will come/has come?"

Jesus responds with two negative statements and a positive one. Each is very brief, and it is difficult to be sure of the sense. The most likely meaning for the first negative statement is that Jesus is wanting to deny any place to the activity of trying to work out, by means of concrete observations of any kind, what is happening in connection with the coming of the kingdom of God. This would apply to such practices as looking for supernatural signs, attempting to project from the present political situation (even on the basis of prophecy), looking, as the ancients did, at the entrails of slaughtered animals, or examining the configuration of the stars (as in astrology).

The second negative statement has a close parallel in v 23. The concern here is either with a breathing space between the arrival of the kingdom of God and the need to personally encounter its reality, or with the possibility of missing the kingdom of God by not being in the right place at the right time. That is not how things will be, says Jesus.

These negations are explained by a positive statement whose meaning is most difficult to ascertain. Perhaps best is to see the statement as insisting that when the kingdom of God is due to come it will just be there, right in our midst, with no advance warning and no localized beginning. This understanding fits best with vv 22–37 to come.

The Days of the Son of Man (17:22–37)

Bibliography

Ashby, E. "The Days of the Son of Man." *ExpTim* 67 (1955–56) 124–25. **Black, M.** "The Aramaic Dimensions in Q with Notes on Luke 17.22 and Matthew 24.26 (Luke 17.23)." *JSNT*

40 (1990) 33–41. **Borsch, F. H.** *The Son of Man in Myth and History.* London/Philadelphia: SCM/Westminster, 1967. 307–8, 343, 347–57, 380–82, 399. **Carroll, J. T.** *Response to the End of History.* 87–96. **Colpe, C.** "ὁ υἱὸς τοῦ ἀνθρώπου." *TDNT* 8:430–61. **Guenther, H. O.** "When 'Eagles' Draw Together." *Forum* 5.2 (1989) 140–50. ———. "A Fair Face Is Half the Portion: The Lot Saying in Luke 17:28–29." *Forum* 6.1 (1990) 56–66. **Higgins, A. J. B.** *Jesus and the Son of Man.* Philadelphia: Fortress, 1964. 82–91. **Jefford, C. N.** "The Dangers of Lying in Bed: Luke 17:34–35 and Parallels." *Forum* 5.1 (1989) 106–10. **Kloppenborg, J. S.** *The Formation of Q: Trajectories in Ancient Wisdom Collections.* Studies in Antiquity and Christianity. Philadelphia: Fortress, 1987. 162–65. **Kümmel, W. G.** *Promise and Fulfilment.* 29, 36–39, 43–45, 70–71, 79, 91, 154. **Laufen, R.** *Die Doppelüberlieferungen.* 302–43, 361–84. **Léon-Dufour, X.** "Luc 17,33." *RSR* 69 (1981) 101–12. **Leaney, R.** "The Days of the Son of Man (Luke xvii. 22)." *ExpTim* 67 (1955–56) 28–29. **Lührmann, D.** *Redaktion.* 71–83. ———. "Noah und Lot (Lk 17:26–29)—Ein Nachtrag." *ZNW* 63 (1972) 130–32. **Manson, T. W.** *Sayings.* 141–47. **Meyer, D.** "πολλὰ παθεῖν." *ZNW* 55 (1964) 132. **Pesch, R.** *Naherwartungen: Tradition und Redaktion in Mk 13.* Düsseldorf: Patmos, 1968. 112, 147–48. **Powell, W.** "The Days of the Son of Man." *ExpTim* 67 (1955–56) 219. **Rigaux, B.** "La petite apocalypse de Luc (XVII, 22–37)." In *Ecclesia a Spiritu Sancto edocta, Lumen gentium, 53.* FS G. Philips. BETL 27. Gembloux: Duculot, 1970. 407–38. **Schlosser, J.** "Les jours de Noé et de Lot: À propos de Luc, xvii, 26–30." *RB* 80 (1973) 13–36. **Schneider, G.** *Parusiegleichnisse.* 42–46. **Schulz, S.** *Spruchquelle.* 277–87, 444–46. **Tannehill, R. C.** *The Sword of His Mouth.* 118–22. **Tödt, H. E.** *The Son of Man in the Synoptic Tradition.* 48–52, 104–8. **Vielhauer, P.** *Aufsätze zum Neuen Testament.* Theologische Bücherei 31. Munich: Kaiser, 1965. 74–76, 108–10. **Winstanley, E. W.** "Days of the Son of Man." *ExpTim* 24 (1912–13) 533–38. **Zmijewski, J.** "Die Eschatologiereden Luk 21 und Lk 17: Überlegungen zum Verständnis und zur Einordnung der lukanischen Eschatologie." *BibLeb* 14 (1973) 30–40.

Translation

22 *He said to the disciples, "Days will come when you will long to see one of the days of the Son of Man, and you will not see it.* 23 *Then they will say to you, 'Look, there! or look, here!'*[a] *Don't head off; don't go in pursuit.*[b] 24 *For, just as the lightning, when it flashes, lights up the [earth] from [one end] of heaven to the [other end] of heaven, so will the Son of Man be*[c] *in his day.*[c] 25 *But first it is necessary for him to suffer many things and be rejected by this generation.*

26 *"Just as it was in the days of Noah, so will it also be in the days of the Son of Man:* 27 *they were eating, they were drinking, they were marrying, they were being given in marriage, until the day in which Noah went into the ark and the flood came and destroyed [them] all.* 28 *Likewise, just as it was in the days of Lot: they were eating, they were drinking, they were buying, they were selling, they were planting, they were building;* 29 *but on the day in which Lot went out of Sodom fire and sulphur rained down from heaven and destroyed [them] all.* 30 [d] *It will be like this*[d] *on the day in which the Son of Man is revealed.*

31 *"On that day the one who is on the rooftop, and his belongings in the house, must not go down to take them away [with him], and the one who is in the field, similarly, must not turn back.* 32 *Remember Lot's wife!* 33 *Whoever tries to* [e] *retain his life [as a possession] for himself*[e] *will lose it; whoever loses [it] will preserve its*[f] *life.* 34 *I tell you, on that night there will be two in one*[g] *bed: the one will be taken and the other will be left behind.* 35 *There will be two grinding [at the mill] together: The one will be taken and the other will be left behind."*[h] 37 *Then the disciples said in response, "Where, Lord?" He said to them, "Where the body is, there the vultures will be gathered together."*

Notes

[a] There is some uncertainty here about the linking word (ἤ, "or," καί, "and," or no linking word), and about the order of "here" and "there," but no difference of sense results.

[b] Only the second of these imperatives is found in P[75] B *f*[13] sa etc. This could be original, but it is difficult to find motivation for such an addition.

[c-c] This phrase is missing from P[75] B D it sa and may not be original.

[d-d] The Gr. idiom for this phrase could be κατὰ τὰ αὐτά, as ℵ[2] B D Ψ etc., or κατὰ ταῦτα, as in P[75 vid] ℵ A L W Θ etc.

[e-e] Rendering περιποιήσασθαι. In conformity with 9:24, ℵ A W Θ Ψ etc. have σῶσαι, "to save."

[f] There is a translation difficulty here that results from translating ψυχή as "life" (represented here by αὐτήν, "it"), while also needing to reflect in translation the ζωο, "life," element of the verb ζῳογονήσει.

[g] Omitted in B and a few other texts.

[h] This verse is absent from ℵ and a few other texts. A verse 36 containing the substance of Matt 24:40 but with the syntax conformed to that of Luke 17:34, 35 is found in D *f*[13] (579) 700 1006 lat sy etc.

Form/Structure/Setting

The verses 17:22–37 constitute the central unit of the section 17:20–18:8. The unit is presented as an elaboration to the disciples of what has been said to the Pharisees in 17:20–21, and warns against being caught unawares by the sudden arrival of the Son of Man.

The section has a substantial parallel in Matt 24:26–27, 37–39, 17–18 (this piece is paralleled in Mark and presented in the Markan sequence of the earlier part of the chapter), 40–41, 28. A Matthean parallel is lacking for vv 22, 25, 28–29, 33 (but Matthew has a parallel to this verse in 10:39), 34, 37a. There is probably some residue of a source in v 22 (v 23 needs an introduction for any adequate sense), but as we have it, the verse seems to be mainly Lukan. V 23 is also known in another form from the Markan tradition (13:5–6, 21–22), where it is applied to the expectation of coming of Jesus himself, or of the messiah, rather than of the Son of Man. The accents of the Markan forms and the redactional links to the present Markan settings suggest that we should give priority to the Lukan tradition. For the most likely wording of the pre-Lukan form of this, see in *Comment* below. It remains uncertain whether the tradition was originally linked to messianic or Son of Man language. This turns in part on whether an original unity between Luke 17:23 and 24 is likely. In favor of such an original unity is that Mark 13, despite its lack of an equivalent for Luke 17:24, sets this tradition into the context of the unmistakability and cosmic scale of the coming eschatological events. This makes the connection with Son of Man language the more likely. There can be little doubt that Jesus spoke of the coming of the Son of Man; it is rather less likely that he ever spoke of the coming of the messiah. Though certainty is not possible, Luke seems to have preserved more closely the original form and imagery of v 24. There are sufficient links between this expectation of the Son of Man and that formulated in 9:26 to encourage attribution to the historical Jesus.

V 25 seems to have been drawn in secondarily by Luke on the basis of 9:22 and in connection with his concerns in 17:22. Vv 26–27 would seem to have been linked to vv 23–24 in Luke's source (Matthew has Markan material in 24:29–36 and his equivalent of Luke 17:37 in v 28), though this is hardly likely to have been an original unity. Vv 28–29 closely parallel vv 26–27 in form and will not have existed apart from that material. They are not reproduced by Matthew but are best taken as part of the common source here. The Lukan form in each case is likely to reflect the source reasonably closely. Though it has been disputed whether the historical Jesus made this kind of use of Scripture, there is no good reason to deny to him the sentiment expressed here. Compared with the Jewish use of these traditions, this use is distinctive in its failure to emphasize the sinfulness of the people and somewhat, also, in its eschatological orientation (found in Jewish texts only where the allusion is very general and often open to dispute). V 31 could have been in Luke's source here, but it is rather more likely that he has drawn it in from his Markan source (see Mark 13:15). Matthew agrees only to the extent that, in putting his parallel to the Lukan material into his development of the Mark 13 materials, he draws the materials Luke has united here into the same larger unit, but his parallel in 24:17–18 is presented within a Markan sequence. V 32 is best taken as a Lukan development designed to integrate v 31 with the preceding similitudes. V 33 has a parallel in 9:24. Since Matthew also uses this tradition twice (10:39; 16:25), it is likely that Luke knows the tradition from two different sources. Nevertheless, the lack of any distinctive links between the present verse and Matthew's non-Markan use (10:39) makes it likely that Luke has actually edited his Markan form again here rather than used language from a second form. On v 33, see further at 9:23–27.

Though Matthew has no parallel for it, it is likely that in v 34 Luke returns to the common source, and only the future tenses for the outcome and possibly the use of ὁ εἷς . . . ὁ ἕτερος, "the one . . . the other," will be Lukan. However, an original unity with the materials of vv 26–29 is unlikely. A form of v 34 is preserved in *Gos. Thom.* 61. Before the statement about the women working at the mill, which is shared by the two evangelists, Matthew has two men working in a field. The original here is likely to have had all three images, which each evangelist has economized to two (see further in *Comment* below). The challenge of such imagery has no difficulty finding a place in the words of the historical Jesus (cf. the recent discussion by Jefford [*Forum* 5.1 (1989) 106–10]). V 37a is likely to be from Luke's pen, designed to allow him to use as a final climax for his unit the striking maxim that occurs in Matthew (more originally) in the earlier position after Matthew's equivalent for v 24. Since the maxim has no particular claim to original unity with v 24 and, without a context, is of quite uncertain sense, there is no firm basis for a decision about the origins of the maxim. It cannot with any confidence be traced to the historical Jesus (cf. Guenther [*Forum* 5.2 (1989) 140–50]). The imagery may be dependent on Job 39:29–30.

Comment

The longed for presence of the Son of Man will become a reality in a spectacular public coming. The associated devastation will catch many unawares. On that day it will be important to show no hesitancy: everything must be left behind, and even life itself ventured recklessly. The divide between destruction and deliverance will separate even those who live and work side by side: one will be taken off to safety; the other will be left to destruction. Those taken will be drawn to their place of safety like vultures to a body.

22 The setting will be Lukan with its εἶπεν δὲ πρός, "he said to." The phrase "days will come" comes from Luke's pen at 21:6 (but from his tradition at 5:35).

"Days of the Son of Man" is found elsewhere only in v 26 ("days of the Messiah" is found in [later?] Jewish sources [see Str-B, 2:237; 4:826–29] but has no strong claim as the basis for the present usage) and may have been formulated here in anticipation of that verse. Since he uses "one of" often, Luke may be responsible for the "one of" that introduces this phrase. It is no longer possible to be sure what remains here of an inherited setting for v 23, and what comes from Luke (Catchpole ["The Son of Man's Search for Faith (Luke xviii 8b)," *NovT* (1977) 83] points to the use of ἐπιθυμεῖν ἰδεῖν, "to long to see," in Luke's source for 10:24 [see Matt 13:17] as the source for that idiom here).

Vv 22–37 are an elaboration to the disciples of vv 20–21 (cf. the role of 12:22–34 and see at 12:41). The coming days here are not those of eschatological(?) judgment as in 21:6, but rather those of the absence of what was being experienced by the disciples in the presence of Jesus' historical ministry. This absence motif plays nothing like the role in Luke's thought that Conzelmann (*Luke*) attributed to it by making it a structuring principle of salvation history, but it does nonetheless play some limited role in Luke's conception (cf. esp. Acts 3:21; and see issues raised in this connection at Luke 9:48). The progression of Jesus through death and resurrection to the exalted position at the right hand of God is more usually treated by Luke as all gain for the disciple community (see, e.g., Acts 2:33). Luke will use v 25 to reinforce the motif of absence (it is no mistake that the resurrection goes unmentioned there). The period of unfulfilled longing here corresponds to what in 18:1–8 is the period in which vindication has not yet been experienced. Luke points to a period in which it will be necessary to hold on in anticipation for what is deeply longed for but is not yet present.

The phrase "one of the days of the Son of Man" functions to create a certain kind of interchangeability between the days of the ministry of the historical Jesus and the period of the coming of the Son of Man in glory (see discussion of Luke's use of Son of Man at 6:1–5; for the background of the term, see the excursus: "Son of Man"; and further at 17:26 on "days of the Son of Man"): in both Jesus is present and exercising the authority of the Son of Man. As the disciples look back with nostalgia, they look to the future for the fulfillment of their longings.

(Various other explanations have been proposed for the unusual "one of," including (*i*) translation as "the first," following a Septuagintal pattern; (*ii*) appeal to mistranslation of an underlying Aramaic and retranslation as "very much"; and (*iii*) taking the "one" as emphatic with the sense "even one/just one." None of these fits as well the thought development of the text.)

23 There are strong language links with v 21, where the corresponding language has probably been derived from here. A shared source is evident from Matt 24:26, where the source shared with Luke is added to another version (or two versions) of the tradition and used in connection with the coming of the Christ (see Mark 13:5–6, 21–22; Matt 24:4–5, 23–24; after v 26 Matthew continues with his parallel to Luke 17:24, 37b). The Lukan wording may be influenced as well by the form of the tradition reflected in Mark 13:21. While certainty is impossible, the most convincing account of the original form here is that offered by Laufen (*Doppelüberlieferungen*, 361–63), who argues for this text form: ἐροῦσιν ὑμῖν. ἰδοὺ ἐν τῇ ἐρημῳ ἐστίν, μὴ ἐξέλθητε. ἰδοὺ ἐν τοῖς ταμιείοις, μὴ διώξητε (lit. "They will say to you, 'Behold he is in the wilderness.' Do not go out! 'Behold, in the inner chambers.' Do not go in pursuit!").

When hope is delayed, one is tempted to grasp at any straw: here the possibility that the Son of Man might have turned up in some remote place. A coming of this kind (with its evident similarity to the way that Jesus had been present as Son of Man in his historical ministry) is being rejected as a possible path to the fulfillment of the longings of v 22.

24 While ἀστράπτουσα (lit. "flashing"; 24:4 and cf. 9:29) is likely to be Lukan, and ἡ παρουσία, "the coming," will be Matthean, it remains unclear whether in other respects Matthew or Luke is more original. The difficulty of Luke's idiom may count in its favor, especially if the feminine gender of τῆς and τῆν (two forms of "the") betrays a Semitic influence upon the Greek idiom, rather than arising from any implied Greek word (the offered suggestions in Greek [χώρας, "region," γῆς, "earth/land," μερίδος, "part"] all leave something to be desired; Semitic words for "end" are mostly feminine [cf. esp. Jer 25:33 (LXX 32:33); Deut 4:32]). That Matthew's "east" and "west" are to be set to his account in 8:11 (see discussion at 13:28–30; Luke has all four directions) also stands in favor of Luke here as more original.

The Matthean imagery has the lightning emerging from the east and shining right across to the west; the Lukan imagery appears to be of a lightning flash that lights the whole field of vision to the extremities in both directions (in this imagery there are two ends to the earth as in Jer 25:33; cf. Matt 8:11). ὑπ' οὐρανὸν (lit. "under heaven") means "on earth" (e.g., Exod 17:14; Eccl 1:13; Acts 2:5), but the imagery of being under the vault of heaven allows here for the specific inclusion of the sky. While lightning lends itself to being an image both for suddenness and for the impossibility of remaining unaware that something has happened, the development here is all in the direction of the latter; and it is this latter that makes the appropriate contrast with v 23 (despite what is at times said, lightning actually does not lend itself as well to being an image of unexpectedness, because of the association of storms and lightning).

"In his day" is absent from some texts (see *Notes*) and may not be original. It appears to involve an application to the Son of Man of the OT idiom of the "Day of the Lord" (e.g., Isa 13:6; Joel 2:1; Zech 14:1; Mal 4:5; in 4 Ezra 13:52 "in the time of his day" is used of "my [i.e., God's] son"; *1 Enoch* 61:5 has "in the day of the elect one"; for developing Christian use see 1 Cor 1:8; 5:5; 2 Cor 1:14; Phil 2:16). The light imagery here may also have a link to glory language used in connection with the coming of the Son of Man (9:26; as Zmijewski, "Eschatologiereden," 404–6).

25 Apart from πρῶτον δὲ, "but first" (redactional at 9:62), and τῆς γενεᾶς ταύτης, "this generation" (cf. at Luke 7:31), the wording is verbally an extract from 9:22 (see detailed discussion of the passion predictions at 9:21–22) and has almost certainly been introduced from there by Luke. The days looked back to in v 22 are days that will have come to an end with the passion of Jesus. Perhaps we should understand that the longing in v 22 is further fueled by the way in which the disciples are experiencing their own counterpart to Jesus' suffering (cf. 6:22).

26 Matthew's ὥσπερ γάρ, "for as," here, along with his "parousia of the Son of Man" (24:37), is likely to be coming from his v 27 (where the second phrase is already redactional). Luke's "in the days of the Son of Man" is an unnatural idiom, based on the paralleled "in the days of Noah." Luke has borrowed and modified this idiom in v 22, but is rather less likely to be responsible for it here. Here it refers to the time period in which the revealing of the Son of Man will take place (cf. v 30). Mathhew's ἦρεν, "took away," may be more original than Luke's ἀπώλεσεν, "destroyed." The nature of the comparison only becomes explicit in v 27, but there is a Jewish tradition, probably with roots already in the OT, of typological appeal to the deluge (and more extensively to the destruction of Sodom) to demonstrate the certainty of God's judgment upon sinners (see Schlosser, *RB* 80 [1973] 13–36, for a review of these traditions; also J. P. Lewis, *A Study of the Interpretation of Noah and the Flood in Jewish and Christian Literature* [Leiden: Brill, 1968]; Lührmann, *Redaktion*, 75–83).

27 Luke's simple list of imperfect verbs is more likely to be original here than Matthew's periphrastic tenses and reference to "the days before the flood" (which detracts strongly from the artistic development). The list of activities "invites the hearer to feel the familiar, comfortable rhythm of life and recognize his involvement in it" (Tannehill, *Sword*, 119). In connection with v 25, this comfortable continuation of life suggests the possibility that people seem to have been able to escape punishment after their rejection of Jesus during his earthly ministry. But it will not be so! In the midst of their complacency, judgment will fall. In the discussion of v 31 below, the question will be raised whether Luke thinks here only of final eschatological judgment, or whether, as in Luke 21, there is a close connection to be drawn between the historical destruction of Jerusalem in A.D. 70 and the final judgment. As Schlosser has shown (*RB* 80 [1973] 13–36), Jewish use of the traditions of flood and destruction of Sodom is connected with the certainty of judgment, not with the suddenness of the arrival of judgment. But here there is clearly a note of unexpectedness, and therefore, effectively, a sense of sudden reversal of expectation (while not exactly the same, this corresponds with the sense given to v 21b above). Against the background of Jewish use of this tradition, however, the point is hardly likely to be the impossibility of knowing the timing of the coming judgment, but rather the unwillingness to reckon with the prospect of such a judgment.

28 Matthew has nothing corresponding to this appeal to the destruction of Sodom in the time of Lot. Lack of any discernible Matthean motivation for deletion is regularly appealed to as a basis for treating vv 28–29 as secondary; but Matthew frequently is simply concerned to abbreviate and need have had no additional motivation here. It is more likely that Luke has reproduced his source than that, sensitive to the Jewish use together of these traditions of judgment, he has himself composed such a fine companion piece for the appeal to the judgment of the flood. Matt 24:39b is perhaps best seen as a relic of the second similitude. Luke 17:28a is to be taken as an ellipse to be completed with the words of v 26b (to judge from Matt 24:39b, the original would have had the full form, but Luke has suppressed the second half in favor of the summary he will provide in v 30). The list of activities begins identically, so as to establish continuity, but is then completed with the introduction of four fresh areas of life. Luke knows some of these as potential "distractions from what human existence should be about" (Fitzmyer, 1171), but the emphasis is upon the normal rhythms of life.

29 The ἄχρι ἧς ἡμέρας . . . καί (lit. "until which day . . . and") of v 27 is now varied to ᾗ δὲ ἡμέρᾳ (lit. "in which day") without a linking καί, "and." Note the artistic balance between Noah going in to a place of safety and Lot going out to a place of safety. "Fire and sulphur" is from Gen 19:24 (reverse order, as in Ps

11:6; 3 Macc 2:5). The imagery will have originated in connection with the experience of volcanic eruption. The sulphur should be understood to be on fire (it is possible that we should think in terms of a hendiadys and translate not "fire and sulphur" but "burning sulphur") and should evoke both the choking smell and the persistent burning.

30 This verse is likely to be a Lukan inspiration, pulling together the thrust of the two preceding similitudes. The language of *revealing* in this verse picks up on the language of *seeing* in v 22: here will be the fulfillment of the disciples' longing. Luke sees deliverance as well as judgment imaged in his two similitudes: it is only when Noah and Lot have been taken out of the firing line that the others find that they have been left to the ravages of judgment. V 31 will develop this two-sideness.

31 Luke draws the present verse from his Markan source (see 13:15), and will be responsible for "in that day," "and his belongings in the house," and "in the same way," and for the loss of "to take his garment" (a minor agreement with Matthew is the loss of "and let him not enter"). The imagery is of a person on the flat roof that served as an important extension of the living area of a typical Mediterranean dwelling (cf. Acts 10:9). The way down was not through the house but by an exterior staircase. To leave as quickly as possible would involve leaving everything in the house behind. Luke has conformed the second illustration to the first: the deletion of "to take his garment" leaves us to understand that the person working in the field is also contemplating going back to the house for his belongings (it is possible that the reduced phrase also prepares for v 32, by alluding to the looking *back* of Lot's wife). As did Noah and Lot, individuals will need to cooporate in their own immediate removal if they are not to be engulfed in the judgment to fall. In the Markan context, in which judgment is historical and localized, the verse is about fleeing from Judea to the mountains (contrast Luke 17:23–34). But since Luke sees the first-century judgment in Judea at the hands of the Romans, which culminated in the destruction of Jerusalem, as the first installment of a universal judgment (see discussion at Luke 21), he has no difficulty in drawing upon the Markan tradition here. It is impossible to say in this wider Lukan setting precisely what kind of removal Luke had in mind, but in the readiness to leave things behind he no doubt thinks in terms of the teaching he has given warning against the snare of material riches.

32 The present verse is likely to be Lukan and makes it quite clear that Luke still had his similitudes firmly in mind in introducing v 31. The allusion is to Gen 19:26 where Lot's wife, though she was part of the group to be rescued, fails to put the requisite distance between herself and the city and is finally engulfed by the judgment that falls upon the city.

33 Luke introduces at this point a tradition that parallels 9:24 (see discussion at 9:23–27). The language changes are likely to be Lukan (ζητήσῃ, "seeks," περιποιήσασθαι, "save for oneself/acquire/bring about," ζῳογονήσει, "give life to/preserve the life of," and the omission of "his life for my sake"). Luke is applying to the crisis context, when judgment is arriving, a teaching of Jesus that he has earlier applied in the broader context of a daily taking up of one's cross to follow Jesus. The Lukan change of verbs establishes a measure of parallelism with the actions contemplated in v 31: in the critical period, trying to preserve one's life as a possession is rather like trying to detour via one's house in order to preserve one's belongings. There is the same relationship established between dispossession of one's goods and of one's life in 14:25–33 (see esp. vv 26, 33). If to any degree Luke is still carrying forward the imagery of v 31 (which is quite uncertain), then he may think in terms of the desire to retreat to one's house where it is thought to be safe, rather than running the gauntlet of dangers to be encountered in departure (cf. 21:21). Whether *ζῳογονήσει* here should be taken with reference to the preservation of life or more positively with reference to the gaining of life (eternal life) remains uncertain.

34 Matthew does not have the first of these images of separation; the second follows after the equivalent to Luke's v 28a. The presence of the non-Lukan *λέγω ὑμῖν*, "I say to you" (but he is responsible for its use in 12:4), and the *ταύτῃ τῇ νυκτί* (lit. "this night" [cf. in 12:20]), which is a little puzzling in the present Lukan setting, suggest that Luke is using tradition here, and has not himself formed a new image on the basis of that to come in v 35. The night setting fits the bedroom scene, but creates some tension with the day imagery of v 30 and even with the mill-work imagery of v 35 to come. Strobel (*ZTK* 58 [1961] 16–29; accepted by Ernst, 491) has argued for a link here (as elsewhere he has argued for 17:20 [see there]) to a Jewish tradition that expected the coming of the messiah to occur during the night of the Passover evening. This seems unlikely, but it is not easy to provide a satisfactory alternative. Perhaps in the original tradition the following images (i.e., Matt 24:40 plus Luke 17:35) were introduced with a balancing *ταύτῃ τῇ ἡμέρᾳ* (lit. "in this day"), which has been displaced as a result of the way in which each evangelist has abbreviated to a simpler twofold pattern an original threefold pattern of one item paralleled with two others, which are in turn more closely paralleled to each other.

Probably a man and wife are intended, although the terms are all masculine in the Greek (not to have all the parts masculine would have required a decision to be made already about whether the husband or the wife would be taken; in the original pattern suggested above, there would have been, then, a first night-time example involving a man and a woman, then two day-time examples, one involving two men and one involving two women). Whatever ambiguity there may be in the original, in the Lukan (and Matthean setting) the imagery of Noah and Lot encourages us to understand that being taken off is the image of deliverance and being left behind is the image of abandonment to destruction.

35 Luke has replaced "at the mill" with "together" (*ἐπὶ τὸ αὐτό*; found also in Acts 1:15; 2:1, 44, 47; 4:46). When he dropped the image of the two in the field, he also dropped the original contrast between at work and at home in favor of bringing into greater prominence the shared element of having two people together. As in v 34, Luke has future tenses where Matthew, probably more originally, has (futuristic) present tenses. Though less certainly, it is likely that Matthew's *μία . . . καὶ μία* (lit. "one . . . and one") is more original than Luke's *ἡ μία . . . ἡ δὲ ἑτέρα* (lit. "the one . . . and/but the other").

37 Matthew's equivalent to v 37 comes immediately after his equivalent to v 24, and this is generally considered to be the positioning in the shared tradition. The introductory question looks like a Lukan formulation (despite the historic present) designed to assist with his relocation of the maxim to the climactic position in his unit. The small wording differences are likely to be Luke's. The disciples' question is most easily understood to be asking where the people of vv 34–35 were to be taken. Luke's climax is graphic, but obscure. Though the image is rather gruesome, in the present setting it is likely to represent the gathering to the Son of Man of those to be delivered (see 21:28; cf. v 27): they will be gathered to him like eagles/vultures to the prey upon which they will feast (there are many other suggestions about the meaning of this imagery, which I will not take the trouble to list here). For this, Luke may have been more comfortable with *σῶμα*, "body," than with the *πτῶμα*, "corpse," which is found in Matthew (though *σῶμα* is often enough used of a corpse in Hellenistic Greek and is so used by Luke [23:52, 55; 24:3, 23; Acts 9:40]). *ἀετός* is normally "eagle," but because in the Matthew parallel (24:28) the corpse represents food for the birds (cf. Job 39:30 LXX), the reference in this maxim is more likely to be to vultures.

Explanation

This large unit elucidates in further detail for the disciples what has been said in main outline to the Pharisees in vv 20–21. The text identifies a period of time in which the Son of Man, earlier present in the ministry of Jesus, will be absent from the disciples. The main thrust of the unit is to warn against being caught unawares by the sudden arrival of the Son of Man and its associated devastation.

V 22 identifies a period beyond the ministry of Jesus in which it will be necessary for disciples to persevere in anticipation of what is deeply desired (and has in a certain sense been their experience already while Jesus was with them), but is not now available. In that context Jesus warns against grasping at straws: don't listen to people if they suggest that the Son of Man has turned up in some remote place. When the Son of Man comes, this will be as unmistakable as a lightning flash that lights up the whole earth and sky. But from the perspective of the historical ministry of Jesus, there must be loss before there is gain: the present ministry must through suffering and rejection give way to the time of Jesus' absence. The longing during this intervening period may be further fueled by the disciples' experiencing of their own counterpart to Jesus' painful suffering and rejection (see 6:22).

For most people the comfortable rhythms of everyday life went on undisturbed until the very moment in which Noah entered the ark and floodwaters overwhelmed life. So it will be in the period of the coming of the Son of Man. With v 25 in mind, the comfortable continuation of the rhythms of life suggests the thought of people apparently escaping punishment after their rejection of Jesus during his earthly ministry. But it will not be so! In the midst of comfortable complacency, judgment will fall. The experience of Lot provides a second example of the same thing. The coming of the Son of Man will be accompanied by both destruction and deliverance, but here destruction is in focus. (Though note how the revealing of the Son of Man in v 30 takes up from v 22 the idea of seeing that which is desired.)

The double possibility of destruction or deliverance comes clearly into focus in vv 31–37. And it does so by emphasizing the idea of separation. Vv 31–33 point to the need to be sufficiently detached from material goods to leave at a moment's notice in order to escape to safety as the devastation begins (compare 21:21). One must even be willing to forfeit one's life in running the gauntlet of dangers to be encountered in departure. Paradoxically, it is this very willingness to venture into mortal danger that will guarantee in a much more important sense that one's life is ultimately preserved. Only the one for whom the proffered deliverance, coming with the Son of Man, is everything and all else is valueless by comparison will be able to escape in the final moment of crisis.

Vv 34–37 introduce a different kind of separation: the separation of one person from another. In all outward respects two people may be of quite the same kind: sharing the same bed, working at the same mill. But one may be taken off to deliverance while the other is left to be enveloped by the coming destruction. "Where will the favored ones be taken?" the disciples ask. The answer is obscure, but probably the image of vultures gathered to a body is to be applied to disciples gathered to the Son of Man (compare 21:27–28).

We should note the balance between the imagery of vv 31–33, with its suggestion that the disciples must be ready to make their own way to safety, and the imagery of vv 34–37, in which the removal to safety is divinely initiated. Luke is keenly aware of the two sides of the coin.

Speedy Vindication for Any Who Have Faith (18:1–8)

Bibliography

Bailey, K. E. *Through Peasant Eyes.* 127–41. **Benjamin, D. C.** "The Persistent Widow." *BiTod* 28 (1990) 213–19. **Bindemann, W.** "Die Parabel vom ungerechten Richter." *TVers* 13 (1983) 91–97. **Bornhäuser, K.** *Studien zum Sondergut des Lukas.* Gütersloh: Bertelsmann, 1934. 161–70. **Buzy, D.** "Le juge inique." *RB* 39 (1930) 378–91. **Catchpole, D. R.** "The Son of Man's Search for Faith (Luke xviii 8b)." *NovT* 19 (1977) 81–104. **Cranfield, C. E. B.** "The Parable of the Unjust Judge and the Eschatology of Luke-Acts." *SJT* 16 (1963) 297–301. **Daube, D.** "Neglected Nuances of Exposition in Luke-Acts." *ANRW* 2/25.3 (1984) 2329–57, esp. 2339–40. **Delling, G.** *Studien zum Neuen Testament und zum hellenistischen Judentum: Gesammelte Aufsätze 1950–1968,* ed. F. Hahn et al. Göttingen: Vandenhoeck & Ruprecht, 1970. 203–25. ———. "Das Gleichnis vom gottlosen Richter." *ZNW* 53 (1962) 1–25. **Derrett, J. D. M.** "Law in the New Testament: The Parable of the Unjust Judge." *NTS* 18 (1971–72) 178–91. **Deschryver, R.** "La parabole du juge malveillant (Luc 18, 1–8)." *RHPR* 48 (1968) 355–66. **Freed, E. D.** "The Parable of the Judge and the Widow (Luke 18.1–8)." *NTS* 33 (1987) 38–60. **George, A.** "La parabole du juge qui fait attendre le jugement: Lc 18,1–8." *AsSeign* n.s. 60 (1975) 68–79. **Grässer, E.** *Parusieverzögerung.* 36–38. **Harnisch, W.** "Die Ironie als Stilmittel in Gleichnissen Jesu." *EvT* 32 (1972) 421–36. **Heininger, B.** *Sondergutgleichnisse.* 198–208. **Hicks, J. M.** "The Parable of the Persistent Widow (Luke 18:1–8)." *RestQ* 33 (1991) 209–23. **Huhn, K.** *Das Gleichnis von der 'bittenden Witwe': Gebetsaufruf Jesu an die Gemeinde der Endzeit.* Hamburg: Bethel, 1946. **Jeremias, J.** *Parables.* 87, 93, 153–57. **Jülicher, A.** *Gleichnisreden.* 2:276–90. **Linnemann, E.** *Jesus of the Parables.* 119–24. **Ljungvik, H.** "Zur Erklärung einer Lukas-Stelle (Luk. xviii. 7)." *NTS* 10 (1963–64) 289–94. **Meecham, H. G.** "The Parable of the Unjust Judge." *ExpTim* 57 (1945–46) 306–7. **Ott, W.** *Gebet und Heil.* 19, 32–72. **Paulsen, H.** "Die Witwe und der Richter (Lk 18,1–8)." *TGl* 74 (1984) 13–39. **Perkins, P.** *Hearing the Parables.* 176, 194–95. **Perrin, N.** *Rediscovering.* 129–30. **Riesenfeld, H.** "Zu μακροθυμεῖν (Lk 18,7)." In *Neutestamentlische Aufsätze.* FS J. Schmid, ed. J. Blinzler et al. Regensburg: Pustet, 1963. 214–17. **Robertson, G. P.** "Luke xviii. 8." *ExpTim* 40 (1928–29) 525–26. **Robertson, J. A.** "The Parable of the Unjust Judge (Luke xviii. 1–8)." *ExpTim* 38

(1926–27) 389–92. **Sahlin, H.** *Zwei Lukas-Stellen: Lk 6:43–45; 18:7.* Symbolae biblicae uppsalienses 4. Uppsala: Wretman, 1945. 9–20. **Schneider, G.** *Parusiegleichnisse.* 71–78. **Spicq, C.** "La parabole de la veuve obstinée et du juge inerte, aux décisions impromptues (Lc. xviii, 1–8)." *RB* 68 (1961) 68–90. **Stählin, G.** "Das Bild der Witwe: Ein Beitrag zur Bildersprache der Bibel und zum Phänomenon der Personifikation in der Antike." JAC 17 (1974) 5–20. **Via, D. O.** "The Parable of the Unjust Judge: A Metaphor of the Unrealized Self." In *Semiology and Parables: Exploration of the Possibilities Offered by Structuralism for Exegesis,* ed. D. Patte. PTMS 9. Pittsburgh: Pickwick, 1976. 1–32 (responses, 33–70). **Warfield, B. B.** "The Importunate Widow and the Alleged Failure of Faith." *ExpTim* 25 (1913–14) 69–72, 136–39. **Weder, H.** *Die Gleichnisse Jesu.* 267–73. **Weiss, K.** "ὑπωπιάζω." *TDNT* 8:590–91. **Wifstrand, A.** "Lukas xviii. 7." *NTS* 11 (1964–65) 72–74. **Zimmermann, H.** "Das Gleichnis vom Richter und der Witwe (Lk 18,1–8)." In *Die Kirche des Anfangs,* ed. R. Schnackenburg et al. 79–95.

Translation

[1]*He told them a parable about the need always to pray on and not to give up.* [2]*He said, "There was a certain judge in a certain town who neither feared God nor cared about human beings.*[a] [3]*There was a widow in that city who used to come to him and say, 'Vindicate me against my antagonist.'* [4]*He didn't want to, for a time. But later on*[b] *he said to himself, 'Though I neither fear God nor care about human beings,*[a] [5]*yet, because this widow is a bother to me, I will vindicate her, so that* [c]*her coming does not utterly*[c] *shame me.'"* [6]*The Lord said,* [d]*"Hear what the unrighteous judge says!*[d] [7]*Won't God be sure to vindicate his elect who cry out to him day and night? He [will indeed show himself] long-suffering with them.* [8]*I tell you, he will vindicate them speedily; but will the Son of Man, when he comes, find faith on the earth?"*

Notes

[a] Gr. ἄνθρωπον (normally translated "person").
[b] Lit. "after these things."
[c-c] Lit. "she, coming, in the end."
[d-d] This clause is missing from ℵ.

Form/Structure/Setting

The effect of Luke's use in 17:22–37 of vv 22 and 25 is to introduce into that unit a motif that can now be taken up in terms of the vindication theme of 18:1–8. Here too, in the unit that finishes the section 17:20–18:8, we are looking forward to the coming of the Son of Man. (The prayer language common to vv 1 and 9 could support a link between 18:1–8 and 18:9–14, but the future orientation, the role of the Son of Man, and the concern with the timing of his coming, all distinguish 18:1–8 from 18:9–14 and provide links with what precedes; 18:9–14 has its strongest links with the following pericopes.)

Luke alone preserves this parable. It has been suggested earlier (see excursus: "Journey to Jerusalem") that Luke has it from a parables source in which it stood parallel to 11:5–8 (the relationship of these two parables is widely recognized [for a partial list of supporting scholars, see Ott, *Gebet und Heil,* 24, to which we may add at once Bundy, Bultmann, Fridrichsen, T. W. Manson, Jeremias, Grässer, Catchpole, Bailey; against which may be noted Spicq and Delling]). The present parable also seems to have a deliberate relationship to Sir 35:12–24 (ET 12–20). There God is judge, and he does *not* ignore the supplication of the widow; there persistent prayer is made to God, and the assurance is given that the Lord will not delay; there μακροθυμεῖν (tr. above "[show oneself] long-suffering") is also used of God (though I argue below that the sense from Sir 35:19 is not carried over to the Gospel text: rather, as the verb is redirected from the enemies of God's People to God's People themselves, the distinctive sense that it has in Sir 35:19 gives way to the more normal meaning for this verb in a context like the present).

There has been extensive discussion regarding the original scope of the parable and its development, questions upon which the parallelism with 11:5–8 and the relationship with Sir 35:12–24 have some capacity to shed light. The discussion below argues that v 1 is a Lukan contribution; that the place of v 6 in the original parable is uncertain (other than the clearly Lukan introduction: "the Lord said"); that v 8a is likely to have originally followed the main narrative of the parable and been applied not to the elect but to the widow; and that v 7 has always been linked with the parable as an application. This does not mean, however, that we should immediately see the parable through the eyes of this application without allowing the inner dynamic of the parable to emerge on its own terms. Via ("The Unjust Judge," 1–32) has offered a reading of the parable in connection with Jungian psychological insights, which elucidates the narrative as a metaphor of the unrealized self (of the judge). While Via is right to see that the parable is primarily about the unjust judge and not about the widow, what he fails to see is that the story is about the judge precisely as the one who holds in his hands the future of the widow (in much the same way that the good Samaritan story is about the Samaritan as the one who holds in his hands the future of the wounded man). This recognition makes Via's reading quite impossible and underlines the appropriateness of reading the parable in connection with the activity of God. The form of the narrative is that of a parable proper and not a similitude.

Against the overwhelming majority of scholars, Linemann (*Parables*, 121) and Freed (*NTS* 33 [1987] 38–60) have placed in question the appropriateness of tracing this parable back to the historical Jesus. At most, their observations require a recognition that Luke uses material that is congenial to him and feels free to develop it in ways that suit his purposes and interests.

Comment

Despite the unfulfilled longing of the present time, one should keep looking to God for eschatological vindication, secure in the confidence that he will fulfill his promises magnificently and he will do so soon. The individual is challenged not to be one of those whose failure places in question the finding of faith on earth when the Son of Man comes.

1 Though the language of the verse is not heavily Lukan, there is widespread agreement that Luke has provided this introduction to the parable (for ἔλεγεν δὲ παραβολὴν αὐτοῖς [lit. "and he was saying a parable to them"], cf. esp. 5:36; 6:39; 15:3; 21:29; and further 12:16; 13:6; 18:9; δεῖν [lit. "to be necessary"] is found elsewhere in the NT only at Acts 26:9; the Lukan interest in prayer is pervasive). The disciple audience of 17:22–37 continues. The audience will be broadened again in 18:9. In light of the Lukan sectioning and the Lukan hand in 17:22, as well as vv 7–8a to come, we should think here not of prayer in general but of prayer in connection with the longing of 17:22, focused on prayer for vindication. πρός τό introduces the subject matter of the parable (an accusative of reference or respect). πάντοτε προσεύχεσθαι and μὴ ἐγκακεῖν mutually qualify one another's meaning. So the former takes the sense "always to keep on praying" (not "pray without ceasing" as the similar phrase in 1 Thess 5:17), and the latter means "not to give up" in the sense of not giving up on prayer and expresses the expectation that God will respond with vindication. (ἐγκακεῖν is quite a rare verb, not found in the LXX but present in later Greek translations of the OT and in the NT also in 2 Cor 4:1, 16; Gal 6:9; Eph 3:13; 2 Thess 3:13. The verb expresses centrally the idea of coming to a point of failure, but may secondarily take on coloring from the implied cause of such a failing: despair, weariness, etc. [cf. Spicq, *RB* 68 (1961) 69–70, 88–89; Grundmann, *TDNT* 3:486; Delling, *ZNW* 53 (1962) 6 n. 23; Ott, *Gebet und Heil*, 69–70].)

2 For a similar (Lukan) introduction to a parable, which includes the redundant λέγων, "saying," see 15:3. One of the uses of τις, "a certain," could well be Lukan, given Luke's fondness for the indefinite adjective, but the former is likely to have its parallel in the interrogative τίς, "which," of Luke 11:5. There is actually a measure of tension between this emphatic (but indefinite) particularity and the quite general way in which the story functions ultimately (this is the one piece of evidence in favor of Deschryver's contention [*RHPR* 48 (1968) 361] that the appeal is to a particular known experience). In principle a judge is a figure from whom the powerless ought to expect vindication, but this particular judge looks less than promising. For the importance for a judge of the fear of God, cf. 2 Chr 19:4–6. For similar characterizations of public figures, see Josephus, *Ant.* 10.283, cf. 1.72; Dionysius of Halcarnassus, *Rom. Ant.* 10.10.7; Livy, 22.3.4. Fearing God is of particular importance to Luke (in the NT only Luke/Acts speaks of [not] fearing God as a human attribute [but cf. 1 Pet 2:17]), but this hardly makes the phrase here Lukan. Though it can take both senses, ἐντρεπόμενος, "cared about/respected," is used here with reference to how one acts toward others, rather than with reference to how one values oneself. The distinction is important when we come to v 5.

3 ἐν τῇ πόλει ἐκείνῃ, "in that city," occurs elsewhere in the NT only in Acts 8:8 and may (particularly since it is not integral to the story) be a Lukan touch. The parataxis "and she used to come" instead of "who used to come" may reflect a Semitic substructure. "She used to come to him" finds its parallel in "he will go to him" in 11:5, while the following "and say" (λέγουσα), introducing a request for aid, has its analogue in the "and say" (καὶ εἴπῃ) that introduces a request in 11:5. Particular assumptions are frequently made about the legal and personal circumstances involved here, but most of these play no real role in the dynamic of the story. (It is not even important whether she could have gone off to another judge.) Important here is only the image of the widow as needy and vulnerable. The widow's subsequent claim to special care (see Lam 1:1; Exod 22:22–24; Ps 68:5[67:6]; Jas 1:27), not least in connection with the judicial system (Isa 1:17, 23), is a tradition available for exploitation. Against the background of v 2b, the appearance of a widow seems to doom any prospect of justice in this story.

ἐκδίκησον could be a call for vengeance, but an appeal for protective or restorative justice is permitted by the language and is much more in keeping with the widow image. ἀντίδικος is in its original use applied mainly to the initiator of a legal suit, but can also be used of the defendant. Without the court imagery, the word can mean "opponent" in a quite general sense (see Schrenk, *TDNT* 1:373–75), though that is not likely in the present judicial context. In our parable the widow is clearly initiating the suit, but her opponent is nonetheless cast in the aggressor role. Freed (*NTS* 33 [1987] 45) draws attention to the conjuntion of the same verb and noun in Jer 28:36 LXX (MT 51:36; and cf. 27:34 [MT 50:34], but the conjunction is so intrinsically appropriate that we should not make too much of this.

4 Freed demonstrates (*NTS* 33 [1987] 46–47) that Luke has a certain predilection for reference to people "not wanting/wishing to." As a classical touch ἐπὶ χρόνον could be Lukan. μετὰ ταῦτα in the sense "afterwards/later on" could also be Lukan (cf. Acts 7:7; 13:20; 15:16). If εἶπεν ἐν ἑαυτῷ (lit. "he said in himself") is the Semitism that Black (*Aramaic Approach*, 302) maintains, then it is less likely that the soliloquy form here betrays Luke's hand. The εἰ καί . . . διά γε, "although . . . yet, because," pattern of vv 4–5 is found also in 11:8. The unwillingness of the judge to help has a counterpart in the hypothetical excuses of Luke 11:7. The story thus far has set us up for a failure of justice, but in this verse we are prepared for a surprising development.

5 With the plural rather than the singular, the idiom παρέχειν μοι κόπον, "to be a bother to," occurs as well in 11:7 (this correspondence is not in sequence, as the others thus far identified have been). What sense should we give to ὑπωπιάζῃ ("shame" in translation above)? Etymologically the verb means "strike under the eye"; and there are those who would keep this sense and claim it as an instance of Gospel irony or humor (see Harnisch, *EvT* 32 [1972] 432–33). However, this is hardly convincing, especially when we move beyond the inner dynamic of the story to explore its intended role on the lips of Jesus (or in the text of Luke; Harnisch [433–36] sees the parable as intended, for the sake of the threatened and lost who were Jesus' special concern, to rob the oppressors of their power by making them look ridiculous). A weakened sense for ὑπωπιάζῃ of "annoy/exhaust/wear out" is also regularly proposed. The difficulty here is that such a sense is difficult to document. It is not an unbelievable development, but preference should probably be given to an undoubted development. To be struck is wounding to pride as well as to body. So it is not surprising that the root developed a use in the direction of "shame/dishonor/defamation" (see Plutarch, *Moralia* 2.921–22; and the references collected by Derrett, *NTS* 18 [1972] 191 [it is uncertain whether one should go further and accept Derrett's account (189–91) of the underlying Semitic idiom as meaning "blackening the face" = "bring shame upon"]). How this shaming is understood to take place remains less certain, and depends in part on how εἰς τέλος (lit. "to [the] end") should be linked into the clause. The present participle ἐρχομένη, "coming," makes it likely that we should look for a gradually achieved shaming. Linked with "coming," εἰς τέλος would mean "continually"; linked with the main verb it could mean "completely," "in the end" or "to the uttermost." Perhaps the last is the most satisfactory, and we should understand that the embarrassment of her continual coming enables the widow to triumph over the unethical judge. If we are right to understand ὑπωπιάζῃ in connection with notions of shame, then we have yet another link with Luke 11:5–8, now with v 8.

6 The introductory "The Lord said" is likely to be Lukan. κριτὴς τῆς ἀδικίας (lit. "judge of unrighteousness") could be modeled after οἰκονόμον τῆς ἀδικίας (lit. "steward of unrighteousness") of 16:8, in which case it would be Lukan. This would make it likely that the whole clause was Lukan, but this remains uncertain. The present verse is a rhetorical flourish underlining the key words "I will vindicate her" from v 5. Even this wicked judge is concerned for his reputation at some level; so *even* he will vindicate *even* a widow who keeps coming to him for access to legal protection.

7 There is very little of this verse that could be claimed as Lukan, though there is considerable likelihood that there is Septuagintal influence reflected in ποιήσῃ τὴν ἐκδίκησιν (lit. "make vindication"; the use of the active rather than the middle for this idiom is a mark of the LXX), just possibly in τῶν βοώντων αὐτῷ, "the one's crying out to him" (here the lack of the Septuagintal πρός counts against such dependence), and perhaps in the word order "day and night," which is strongly preferred in the LXX (cf. Freed, *NTS* 33 [1987] 52–53). If the link between the present parable and Sir 35:12–24 (ET 12–20), discussed in *Form/Structure/Setting* above, is accepted, it is hard to deny an original unity between this verse and the parable (see esp. vv 18–19 [ET 17b–18a]).

The parable finds its application to God's action on a "how much more" basis: now we are dealing with the judgment of God, not with a wicked judge (note the contrast between the judge of the parable and the description of God as judge in Sir 35:12–18); now we have the elect ones to whom God is pledged, not an insignificant widow who is quite unknown to the judge. It is more than likely that an eschatological vindication is intended, even without the specifically eschatological setting provided by v 8b and by the larger Lukan structure.

In chap. 13 Luke does not reproduce the references of his Markan source to "the elect" (Mark 13:20, 22, 27), and this language is not found elsewhere in the synoptic Gospel tradition except in Matt 22:14. Elsewhere Luke makes use of election language only in Acts 13:48: "as many as were ordained to eternal life believed." In the OT, election language is applied originally to the privileged status of Israel (see Pss 105:6, 43; 106:5; Isa 43:20; 45:4), but then more restrictedly to the faithful from among the People (see Isa 65:9, 15, 22). Post-biblical developments arise mainly from this more restricted use, but are notable for the way in which the language gained an eschatological orientation (see esp. the repeated uses in *1 Enoch* [e.g., 1:1, 8] and the Qumran documents [e.g., CD 4:3–4; 1QpHab 10:13]). This eschatological thrust is likely to be present in Luke 18:7. We cannot be certain that the historical Jesus made use of such election language, but the thrust of the present verse depends little on its presence.

The call for persistence in prayer has already been highlighted in v 1. This note is already present in Sir 35:17b–18a (ET 17) and is an expression of steadfastly looking to God, and not elsewhere. It, of course, communicates to those of God's people who find themselves yet unvindicated, despite their prayers.

The final clause involves a shift from an emphatic negative future verb form to a simple present. It is often taken, nevertheless, as a continuation of the question. Other possibilities are to treat it as a separate question, or as a statement and not as a question (the connecting καί is variously taken as meaning "and," "yet," or "even if"). Linked with this syntactical question is that of the sense to be given to μακροθυμεῖ (tr. above "[will show himself] long-suffering"). The verb expresses some kind of holding back, but whether this is in terms of a delay on his part or in terms of his long-suffering nature remains to be decided. Catchpole's survey (*NovT* 19 [1977] 93–98) of the texts in which this root is applied to God's People (Exod 34:6; Num 14:18; Pss 86:15[85:15]; 103[102]:8; Joel 2:13; Wis 15:1; Sir 5:4) demonstrates that the latter is to be preferred in a context determined to any degree by Jewish culture (the most attractive of the suggestions built upon the former is that of Ljungvik [*NTS* 10 (1963–64) 289–94], who takes the sense as "will he hold out [on them]?" and links this with the temporary holding out of the wicked judge). God does not in any unrestrained manner pour out his wrath upon his People, though they are far from guiltless. (God's vindication of his elect may even be from a situation into which they have been placed by God as a measured reaction to their sin; but his reaction remains well under control and ultimately takes its place as part of his generous dealings with his People.) Given this sense, it is probably best to take the final clause as a resultant statement and not a question.

8 If the opening *λέγω ὑμῖν*, "I say to you," corresponds to the use of the same phrase in 11:8, then it may be that Luke has inverted the order of vv 7 and 8a (in order to facilitate the addition of v 8b). If this is so, then v 8a originally spoke about the wicked judge ("her" has necessarily become "them" in the inversion), and, in its earlier form, makes a comment similar to that found in 11:8 (Zimmermann, "Gleichnis," 79–95, supports the same view of v 8a in the context of a quite different argument). The new piece of information here is the *ἐν τάχει*, rendered "quickly/soon" or "suddenly." Luke's other uses of the phrase (Acts 12:7; 22:18; 25:4) favor the former, and only this sense provides a good fit in the context. There are in fact no certain instances of the phrase in the second sense. It is the short period of waiting that provides full poignancy to the doubts that are nevertheless about to be expressed about what the Son of Man will find when he comes.

Despite Catchpole's elaborate defense of the place of v 8b in the original (*NovT* 19 [1977] 81–104), there is a broad consensus that this is a Lukan addition, possibly on the basis of a detached saying of Jesus. While there is no difficulty unifying the thought of this saying with the preceding, it introduces as new ideas the Son of Man, his coming, the importance of faith, and doubt about the state of faith at the time of the coming of the Son of Man. These new and unprepared for ideas make it quite unlikely that this saying formed any original unity with the preceding. Since the coming of the Son of Man is undoubtedly something Jesus spoke about (see Son of Man excursus after 9:21–22 and on Luke's use of Son of Man at 6:1–5), a concern with faith is clearly embedded in the historical Jesus materials; and, since a range of critical remarks about people's readiness for future judgment appears in these materials, nothing prevents the tracing of this logion to the historical Jesus. In Luke's hands v 8b proceeds from the role of the Son of Man in 17:22–37. The faith espoused here looks to God day and night for vindication.

Explanation

The cry for vindication and deliverance here has links back to 17:22 and 25, and the role of the Son of Man here proceeds from his role in 17:22–37. How much more can God be relied upon to provide vindication than can the wicked judge of our story who, despite his wickedness, when he faces the prospect of public embarrassment can be inveighed upon by even a widow to deliver justice.

Luke announces the thrust of the coming parable as encouragement to persist in prayer to God. He does not say it in so many words, but it is clear from the context that this prayer is about the end-time resolution of the problems of the present and not simply about answered prayer in the normal sense. (On answered prayer in the more normal sense, see 11:5–13.)

The judge is described in a manner that undermines all confidence that one could look to him for justice: he answers neither to the directives of God nor to the patent needs of those around him. He is exactly how a judge should not be. When the second character is introduced as a widow, one who has absolutely no leverage at all in society, then the hearer is prepared for a total failure of justice. In whatever issues she stands under threat from her adversary, we cannot hold out much hope. However, the widow persists in her request for the protection of the law.

The judge initially lives up to the narrator's description of him. He is stony-faced to the widow in her need. But the "for a time" in v 4 signals a coming development. The private musings of the judge first of all confirm the unsavory character of this fellow, but then they go on to reveal an unexpected vulnerability. This judge is worried that the widow's persistence is going to make a laughing stock of him. The embarrassment of her repeated pleas is finally too much for him. Against all his normal patterns, he capitulates and does her bidding.

Out of even such a hopeless case as this it is possible to get some good! Listen to the judge's words: "I will vindicate her." If there is even hope in such a case, then how much better must it be when we are dealing with the God of all goodness, and when the petitioner is one of God's own elect to whom he is deeply committed. God will certainly act for those of his own people who steadily look to him for the vindication of all that they stand for as his people.

The reference to God being long-suffering remains obscure until we look at how that verb is used of God in the OT. There we find that it expresses an aspect of the generosity of God in his dealings with his People. He does not lash out at the sins of his People, but rather exercises restraint (the word involved is often translated as "slow to anger" in the OT). On a strict scale of justice, God's own People may not deserve the vindication that they crave. But, while God may well discipline his recalcitrant People, he works for their vindication in the end.

V 8 promises that this deliverance will come quickly. This is of some embarrassment for us, many centuries later. How are we to handle this problem? Part of the answer is probably to be found in the way that Luke sees as very closely related, even somehow interchangeable, the time of one's death, the time of the destruction of Jerusalem, and the time of the end-time vindication and judgment that encompasses the whole world. They can all be versions of God's ultimate vindication of his people and the imposition of his final judgment. Moreover, the promised "quickly" is ultimately a statement about the character of God, and it will come true. But it may come true in stages, through intimations already here and now, and also in ways that are not at once obvious, before ever it comes true in the fully comprehensive sense that first springs to mind.

The final sentence makes it clear that "quickly" is not "immediately" and that one needs to hang on to this "quickly." Though the vindication comes quickly, there is doubt whether individuals will maintain their faith. The faith described here continues to look to God for vindication, day and night.

Entering the Kingdom like a Child (18:9–30)

The tax collector lacks any claim upon God but calls upon his mercy and is heard. Children are free from all the barriers that adult self-importance and self-sufficiency place between an individual and the approach of the kingdom of God, so the kingdom of God is for them and for those who will become childlike. While the commandments retain their validity as the path to life, in the presence of the call of Jesus, there must also be a radical turning away from security based upon the possession of material resources. But no one will be the poorer for giving anything up for the kingdom of God.

The Pharisee and the Tax Collector at Prayer (18:9–14)

Bibliography

Bailey, K. E. *Through Peasant Eyes.* 142–56. **Böhl, F.** "Das Fasten an Montagen und Donnerstagen: Zur Geschichte einer pharisäischen Praxis (Lk 18, 12)." *BZ* 31 (1987) 247–50. **Bruce, F. F.** "'Justification by Faith' in the Non-Pauline Writings of the New Testament." *EvQ* 24 (1952) 66–68. **Bultmann, R.** *Marburger Predigten.* Tübingen: Mohr, 1956. 107–17. **Cerfaux, L.** "Trois réhabilitations dans l'Evangile." In *Recueil Lucien Cerfaux: Etudes d'exégèse et de histoire religieuse.* Gembloux: Duculot, 1954. 2:51–59, esp. 53–55. **Charpentier, E.** "Le chrétien: Un homme 'juste' ou 'justifié'? Lc 18,9–14." *AsSeign* n.s. 61 (1972) 66–78. **Cortés, J. B.** "The Greek Text of Luke 18:14a: A Contribution to the Method of Reasoned Eclecticism." *CBQ* 46 (1984) 255–73. **Downing, F. G.** "The Ambiguity of 'The Pharisee and the Toll-Collector': Luke (18:9–14) in the Greco-Roman World of Late Antiquity." *CBQ* 54 (1992) 80–99. **Dreher, B.** "Der Pharisäer: Biblisch-homiletische Besinnung zum Evangelium des 10. Sonntags nach Pfingsten (Lk 18,9–14)." *BibLeb* 8 (1967) 128–32. **Feuillet, A.** "La signification christologique de Luc 18,14 et les références des évangiles au Serviteur souffrant." *NovVet* 55 (1980) 188–229. ———. "Le pharisien et le publicain (Luc 18,9–14): La manifestation de la miséricorde divine en Jésus Serviteur souffrant." *EV* 48 (1981) 657–65. **Fiedler, P.** *Jesus und die Sünder.* 228–33. **Green, L. C.** "Justification in Luther's Preaching on Luke 18:9–14." *CTM* 42 (1972) 732–47. **Gueuret, A.** "Le pharisien et le publicain et son contexte." In *Les paraboles évangéliques: Perspectives nouvelles. XIIe congrès de l'ACEF,* ed. J. Delorme. LD 135. Paris: Cerf, 1989. 289–307. **Heimbrock, H. G.,** and **Heimler, A.** "Das Gleichnis vom Pharisäer und Zöllner (Lk 18,9–14)." In *Doppeldeutlisch,* ed. Y. Spiegel. Munich: Kaiser, 1978. 171–88. **Heininger, B.** *Sondergutgleichnisse.* 208–18. **Hengel, M.** "Die ganz andere Gerechtigkeit: Bibelarbeit über Lk. 18,9–14." *TB* 5 (1974) 1–13. **Hoerber, R. G.** "'God Be Merciful to Me a Sinner': A Note on Lk 18:13." *CTM* 33 (1962) 283–86. **Holleran, J. W.** "The Saint and the Scoundrel." *BiTod* 25 (1987) 375–79. **Jeremias, J.** *Parables.* 139–44. **Jülicher, A.** *Gleichnisreden.* 2:598–608. **Klein, H.** *Barmherzigkeit gegenüber den Elenden und Geächteten: Studien zur Botschaft des lukanischen Sondergutes.* Biblisch-theologische Studien 10. Neukirchen-Vluyn: Neukirchener, 1987. 64–68. **Kodell, J.** "Luke and the Children: The Beginning and End of the Great Interpolation (Luke 9:46–56; 18:9–23)." *CBQ* 49 (1987) 415–30. **Linnemann, E.** *Jesus of the Parables.* 58–64. **Lorenzen, T.** "The Radicality of Grace: The Pharisee and the Tax Collector (Luke 18:9–14) as a Parable of

Jesus." *FM* 3 (1986) 66–75. **Magass, W.** *Hermeneutik und Semiotik: Schrift—Predigt—Emblematik.* Forum Theologiae Linguisticae 15. Bonn, 1983. ———. "Die magistralen Schlusssignale der Gleichnisse Jesu." *LingBib* 36 (1975) 1–20. **Mahr, F.** "Der Antipharisäer: Ein Kapitel 'Bibel verfremdet' zu Lk 18,10–14." *BK* 32 (1977) 47. **Merklein, H.** "Dieser ging als Gerechter nach Hause. . . .': Das Gottesbild Jesu und die Haltung der Menschen nach Lk 18,9–14." *BK* 32 (1977) 34–42. **Mottu, H.** "The Pharisee and the Tax Collector: Sartrian Notions as Applied to the Reading of Scripture." *USQR* 29 (1973–74) 195–213. **Nützel, J. M.** *Jesus als Offenbarer Gottes nach den lukanischen Schriften.* FB 39. Würzburg: Echter, 1980. 255–63. **Perkins, P.** *Hearing the Parables.* 38–39, 171–76. **Pesch, R.** "Jesus, a Free Man." In *Jesus Christ and Human Freedom.* Concilium 3/10. New York: Herder and Herder, 1974. 56–70. **Schlosser, J.** "Le pharisien et le publicain (Lc 18,9–14)." In *Les paraboles évangéliques: Perspectives nouvelles. XIIe congrès de l'ACEF,* ed. J. Delorme. Lectio Divina 135. Paris: Cerf, 1989. 271–88. **Schmitz, S.** "Psychologische Hilfen zum Verstehen biblischer Texte? Zum Beispiel Lk 18, 9–14." *BK* 38 (1983) 112–18. **Schnider, F.** "Ausschliessen und ausgeschlossen werden: Beobachtungen zur Struktur des Gleichnisses vom Pharisäer und Zöllner Lk 18,10–14a." *BZ* 24 (1980) 42–56. **Schottroff, L.** "Die Erzählung vom Pharisäer und Zöllner als Beispiel für die theologische Kunst des Überredens." In *Neues Testament und christliche Existenz.* FS H. Braun, ed. H. D. Betz and L. Schottroff. Tübingen: Mohr-Siebeck, 1973. 439–61. **Schweizer, H.** "Wovon reden die Exegeten? Zum Verständnis der Exegese als verstehender und deskriptiver Wissenschaft." *TQ* 164 (1984) 161–85. **Völkel, M.** "Freund der Zöllner und Sünder." *ZNW* 69 (1978) 1–10. **Vogt, E.** "Hat 'šabbāt' im. A. T. den Sinn von 'Woche'?" *Bib* 40 (1959) 1008–11. **Wimmer, J. F.** *Fasting in the New Testament.* 79–84. **Young, N. H.** "'Hilaskesthai' and Related Words in the New Testament." *EvQ* 55 (1983) 169–76. **Zimmermann, H.** *Jesus Christus: Geschichte und Verkündigung.* 2nd ed. Stuttgart: Katholisches Bibelwerk, 1975. 105–10.

Translation

[9] *With this parable he addressed as well*[a] *certain people who were confident in themselves, because they were righteous, and despised*[b] *all others.*[c] [10] *"Two people went up to the temple to pray, the one a Pharisee, the other a tax collector.* [11] *The Pharisee stood and prayed thus*[d] *about himself,*[e] *'I thank you God that I am not like the rest of humankind: robbers, evildoers, adulterers; or even like this tax collector.* [12] *I fast twice a week; I tithe all that I acquire.'* [13] *The tax collector stood far off and would not even raise his eyes to heaven. Instead he beat his breast saying, 'God be merciful to me, a sinner.'* [14] *I tell you, this one, rather than*[f] *the other, went down to his house upright in the sight of God. For everyone who exalts himself will be humbled, and the one who humbles himself will be exalted."*

Notes

[a] There is considerable recasting here to allow "as well" to fit into the requirements of English syntax.

[b] P^{75} B T etc. have the nominative here, but this is only a thoughtless conformity to the case of *δίκαιοι*, "righteous," and no satisfactory sense can be given.

[c] Lit. "the rest."

[d] Lit. "these things."

[e] The word order of *ταῦτα πρὸς ἑαυτόν* (lit. "these things to himself") is uncertain. A K W X Δ Π etc. place *ταῦτα* last (and D it[d] geo[2] with *καθ'* for *πρός*). ℵ omits *πρὸς ἑαυτόν*. The word order may have a bearing on whether to read *πρὸς ἑαυτόν* with the participle or the main verb.

[f] Reading *παρ'* with ℵ B L Q T f^1 etc. Cortés (*CBQ* 46 [1984] 255–73) has defended the reading *ἢ γάρ* of A Ψ 063 0135 f^{13} and the majority text, in the sense "certainly not," or, interrogatively, giving

"or did the other do so?" He is right to point to the difficulty, on the basis of the normally accepted text, of accounting for the introduction of the ἤ (the γάρ comes easily from a misread παρ'), but a mindless copyist's γάρ could easily be corrected to ἦ γάρ, and the senses proposed by him do not work as well in the dynamic of the narrative.

Form/Structure/Setting

The opening unit of the new section (18:9–30) is not as carefully integrated into the section as are the subsequent units, but each of the units illustrates entry into the kingdom of God from a position of inferiority (the sinfulness of the tax collector, the limitations of the children, the self-impoverishment of those who have sold or left all for the sake of the kingdom or to follow Jesus). Luke's addition of v 14b with its note of self-humiliation is partly concerned to help bring the present parable into line with the other units of the section. Luke will also be responsible for the setting provided by the opening verse.

In the excursus "Journey to Jerusalem," this parable is identified as having its parallel in 10:25–37 in a distinctive Lukan parables source, which came to Luke in a chiastically arranged set of paralleled parables. The going up of the one corresponds to the going down of the other; these are the only two Gospel parables in which the characters belong to the Jewish religious establishment; each has an unlikely "hero," whose role is contrasted with that of an (or a pair of) expected hero(s); only these parables are located in fixed locations in the geography of Palestine; the mercy shown by the good Samaritan corresponds to the call for mercy of the tax collector (different Greek words); these parables are among the few so-called example-story parables (further parallels are noted by C. Blomberg, "Midrash," 240 [see in bibliography for the excursus]).

The suggestion has been defended that the parable originally lacked v 14a and was meant to be read as a kind of teaser designed to undermine the value categories that we normally use. This produces an exposition of the parable that highlights the tension between what the hearer feels inclined to affirm about the Pharisee and what he feels he must affirm about the tax collector. This approach would work much better with a question form of v 14a (a possibility that has also been proposed). Despite some deep attractions these approaches are finally to be rejected because (*i*) v 14a must be removed or reformulated on a totally speculative basis; and more importantly, as will be shown below, (*ii*) the presentation of the Pharisee and the tax collector is not finally even-handed in the manner that would be required for such a reading.

As with most of the parables, there has not been much scholarly doubt that we have here a genuine story of the historical Jesus (allowing always for a measure of retelling in the transmission), but Schottroff ("Erzählung," 448–52) has seriously questioned this on the basis that the image of the Pharisee is such a caricature that we certainly cannot attribute it to the historical Jesus. No such caricature is visible in the analysis of the story below (though it must be admitted that the Lukan framework is in danger of moving towards caricature), so there is every reason for accepting the consensus judgment here. On the lips of Jesus, this story addressed to the pious gently puts in question the exclusivity of their claim upon the favor of God and subtly suggests that this very pattern of exclusivity is a strike against them in the eyes of God. The story is of a piece with Jesus' inclusive approach and his ministry to the outcasts. The story is not exactly an example story, since both its chief figures are morally ambiguous, but it is a story about how God values things. It does not appear to require any transfer of judgment from one realm to a quite different realm (unless we say that only the working of the kingdom of God in Jesus' own ministry accounts for such an unusual act on the part of a tax collector!).

Comment

Things are not as they might seem. The confident piety of this Pharisee, with its easy dismissal of all others, is less acceptable to God than the genuine appeal for mercy on the part of the tax collector, despite his undoubted moral inadequacy and failure of loyalty to the People of God.

9 The opening *εἶπεν δὲ καὶ πρός . . . τὴν παραβολὴν ταύτην*, "he said also to . . . this parable," fits right in with other Lukan introductions (cf. at 18:1). Luke is responsible for the use of *πεποιθέναι ἐπί*, "to trust in," in 11:22 and so is likely to be responsible for it here as well. *δίκαιοι*, "righteous," is probably based on the use of its opposite, *ἄδικοι*, "unjust," in v 11. (Though the language of Ezek 33:13 is strikingly similar to that here, the thought is so different that there is little likelihood of dependence.) *ἐξουθενεῖν*, "despise," is used by Luke again in 23:11. Finally *τοὺ λοιπούς* (lit, "the rest") is based on the use in v 11.

The Lukan audience still contains the disciples of 17:22 but now is widened. Luke sees the parable as particularly addressed to those whose attitudes correspond to those of the Pharisee figure of the parable. Since Jesus has been in conversation with Pharisees in 17:20, Luke will think here centrally, but not necessarily exclusively, of certain of the Pharisees. "Because they are righteous" fits the imagery to come better than "that they are righteous," which is also a possible translation. In the parable to come, the tax collector's lack of self-confidence is quite clear. The parable is much more subtle than Luke about the opposite quality in the Pharisee. The despising of all others is a fair enough summary of the outlook of the Pharisee of the parable.

10 *προσεύξασθαι*, "to pray," may be Luke's addition (cf. 9:28; apart from Matt 14:23 only Luke uses *ἀναβαίνειν*, "go up," with a following infinitive of purpose [Fitzmyer, 1186]). The use of *ὁ εἷς . . . ὁ ἕτερος*, "the one . . . the other," may also be from Luke's pen (cf. at 17:34). For prayer in the temple at the hours of prayer, see at 1:10, but here there could be a more private use of the temple for prayer (but see Bailey, *Through Peasant Eyes*, 145), which would be possible at any time. On Pharisees, see at 5:17. On tax collectors, see at 3:12. By this stage the reader inevitably has a double image of both Pharisees and tax collectors: Pharisees are leading figures in the religious life of the nation, but Jesus is often critical of them; tax collectors are unsavory types, but Jesus befriends them. But for the narrative audience Luke does not normally provide any sense of cumulative impact of the teaching or activity of Jesus, so for this narrative audience we should presuppose a positive image for the Pharisee and a negative image for the tax collector.

11 *σταθείς*, "stood," may be Lukan, being found in this use only in Luke/Acts (Fitzmyer, 1186). The verb probably implies a standing posture, but usually it indicates arrival at an intended destination and taking up a position there for whatever is to follow (this is difficult to represent in translation, esp. if there is intended parallel in v 13 [this is uncertain because of the use of the perfect tive participle there and the aorist passive here]). πρὸς ἑαυτόν (lit. "to himself could echo an Aramaic structure representing the possessive and be linked wi σταθείς to give the sense "taking his stand" as claimed by Torrey (*Our Translat Gospels*, 79; Bailey's "stood by himself" [*Through Peasant Eyes*, 147–48] seems li guistically unlikely) but is more likely to be linked with the following verb wit the sense "concerning himself" (the literal "prayed to himself [rather than God] is ruled out by the clear address to God).

Radically different answers have been given to the question "How should th Pharisee's prayer strike us?" For Linnemann (*Parables*, 58), we have painted her the ideal of a pious man. We respond, "Yes, that is what one should be like! Thi man can appear before God with thankful joy." For Schottroff ("Erzählung," 448–52), by contrast, the Pharisee is a deliberately overdrawn caricature. He is a figure of pride and hypocrisy who promotes himself before God in a quite blatant way. I doubt whether the Pharisee is either of these extremes, but I would want to place him closer to the first than to the second. There are similar prayers in (later) Jewish sources that are meant to be seen as fully positive (see *y. Ber.* 2.7d; *b. Ber.* 28b; but see also the earlier 1QH 7:34).

This Pharisee is suitably grateful to God for his advantages. He presumably tells the truth as he describes his own life. "All other people" is likely to mean all who do not share the strict religious commitments of the Pharisees. He seems to see them all as robbers, evildoers, adulterers, or the like. Though his own behavior is exemplary, he is down on all non-Pharisees in a way that can hardly attract reader sympathy (Pharisaic dismissal of others is also reflected in John 7:49). The tax collector is not differentiated from the robbers, evildoers, and adulterers as either better or worse; in the Pharisee's eyes, he is just another example of the same kind of human degradation. This disparaging and offhand dismissal of the tax collector will also count against our sympathy by the time we have been through v 13.

12 Whether or not שׁבּת, *šabbāt* (lit. "sabbath") ever means "week" in the OT (see Vögt, *Bib* 40 [1959] 1008–11), the corresponding Greek, σαββάτου, clearly means "week" here (cf. Mark 16:9; 1 Cor 16:2). An annual fast on the Day of Atonement is prescribed in Lev 16:29–31; 23:27–32; etc., fasting is enjoined in connection with the commemoration of the days of Purim in Esth 9:31, and other annual fast days are recognized in Zech 8:19; 7:3, 5. Beyond that, fasting in individual cases occurs as an expression of mourning, penance, or supplication. For a more frequent practice of fasting, see 5:33. Twice weekly fasting is reflected in later rabbinic texts (*b. Taᶜan. 12*a; *y. Pesaḥ* 4.1; etc.) and in the late first-century *Did.* 8:1, where it is enjoined upon Christians, but with different days from the Mondays and Thursdays of the "hypocrites." Though clearly going beyond any requirement of the OT law, the practice of the Pharisee of the parable reflected the disciplined piety practice of his group, and not some individual accomplishment. The same is probably true for his tithing practice, which, while not precisely identified by his words here (for options see Str-B, 2:244–46), is clearly more comprehensive than strictly enjoined by the law (on tithing practice, see at 11:42).

Do we have cause to be critical of the attitude expressed by this Pharisee in prayer? We are sometimes told that he is a hypocrite who has an outer righteousness but no real faith in God, or that the man's problem is that he is preempting God's sovereign right to bestow salvation on whomever he pleases, or even that he is seeking to gain salvation by works and not by faith. But whatever the man's problem might be, unless we bring a prior judgment with us from outside the story, it is not as blatant a fault as any of these criticisms suggest.

What can be said on the basis of features that are actually in the story? Should we be made suspicious by the need he apparently feels to parade his virtues before God? While he thanks God for it all, is he really boasting to God? Is that his problem? Or, does the problem have to do with the way that his own self-estimate depends upon being able to identify others as moral failures—that he can only feel good about himself if he has others to condemn by contrast? Or, are we to note his complacent acceptance of the contrast between his own happy state and that of the tax collector with whom he shares the temple at prayer? Would he, like the older brother of the prodigal, prefer the status quo to continue? Would he be firmly against any rescue mission, or even any suggestion that there could be hope for such reprobates? Certainty is not possible, but somewhere among these suggestions we may find the necessary hints of a fatal flaw.

On first appearances our Pharisee presents very well, but things are not all that they seem. In ways that are at first not easy to put one's finger on, something seems not quite right. We are not warmed by the love of God when we are in the presence of this upright and apparently godly man. When we examine this man closely, the flaw lines begin to show. And what we see, perhaps, is a man whose apparent love for God is not at the same time a heart of compassion for his fellows. Righteousness for him drives him far away from others. It builds no bonds to those with whom he shares life in Palestine. Well might the Pharisee thank God for his advantages. They were real enough. But along with them comes responsibility. If grace does not lead to grace, it turns out not to have been grace at all.

The hearer of the story is unlikely to have engaged in such secondary reflection at this stage of the telling. First impressions are more like those of a Pharisee who lives out conscientiously the high calling of his Pharisaism.

13 To the use of *οὐκ ἤθελεν*, "was unwilling," compare the use at 18:4 (with discussion there). The Septuagintal *τοὺς ὀφθαλμοὺς ἐπᾶραι*, "to lift up the eyes," could be Lukan (6:20; 16:23), but probably belonged to the language of the parables source here. A near parallel to the tax collector's reticence is found in Ezra 9:6 (cf. Josephus, *Ant.* 11.143). Both the location and the posture speak of the tax collector's intense sense of unworthiness. The beating of the breast expresses remorse here as in Joel 2:12 (LXX); *Barn.* 7:5 (both without explicit mention of the breast); and *Joseph and Asenath* 10:1, 15. See also Luke 23:48. The tax collector's petition echoes the opening words of the penitential psalm, Ps 51 (though with *ἱλάσθητι*, "be merciful/gracious," for the *ἐλέησον*, "have mercy," of the Septuagint, and with the addition of *τῷ ἁμαρτωλῷ* [lit. "the sinner"]). (In Classical Greek *ἱλάσκεσθαι* means "to be appeased"; although in the LXX it may still mean "to be mollified" [Exod 32:14], it regularly has instead the sense "to forgive/have mercy.")

As a tax collector this man is intrinsically a negative figure, and the figure he cuts in our story in its own way reinforces our prejudices about the unsavory lifestyle of tax collectors. But at the same time the depth of feeling expressed by his appeal, posture, and action means that our hearts must go out to him; and the echo of the penitential psalm reminds us that the possibility of forgiveness of even the most heinous of crimes is a fundamental aspect of Jewish faith.

14a λέγω ὑμῖν, "I say to you," statements are a feature of several of the parables that Luke reproduces from his parables source (cf. 18:8a; 11:8; 13:3, 5; 15:7, 10). "Went down" corresponds to "went up" in v 10. While it would be more natural to speak of the tax collector as leaving "having been forgiven," this language would not allow for the comparison intended. Fitzmyer's "upright in the sight of God" (1188) catches well the force here of δεδικαιωμένος (lit. "having been justified"). It is the tax collector rather than the Pharisee who, in this moment of encounter with God in the temple, has found favor with him (it is important that we not read this as a story about every Pharisee and every tax collector; it is a story about a Pharisee who acts so, and about a tax collector who acts so). For the immediate thought here, cf. 2 Esd 12:7. Without the Lukan framework it would seem more natural to take παρ' ἐκεῖνον as "more than" than as "rather than," but the Lukan frame encourages a sharper contrast, and so I have translated as "rather than" (despite the "more than" required in 13:2, 4). There is no real basis for seeing this text through Pauline eyes and finding pronounced here, through the mouth of Jesus, God's eschalogical verdict in favor of sinners. We have discussed, as the story has developed, what it might be about this Pharisee and this tax collector that, contrary to initial expectations, causes God to prefer the latter to the former.

14b Luke has used an almost identical set of words already at 14:11 (see there). It is unclear whether he draws the present use from there or is dependent upon a second source, but because of the congruity with his addition of v 9, it will be Luke rather than his parables source who will be responsible for linking this tradition with the parable. Where the parable is considerably more subtle in the means that it uses to justify to the hearer the preference of tax collector over Pharisee, Luke, in danger of mere caricature, sees the Pharisee as exalting himself before God (it is indisputable that the tax collector of our story humbles himself before God). The addition of v 14b aligns the parable with the motif of reversal that has earlier been brought into prominence (see 1:45, 48, 52), and also bridges to the following unit (18:15–17), which emphasizes receiving the kingdom like a child.

Explanation

The new section runs from 18:9–30 and brings together a series of units that illustrate entry into the kingdom of God from a position of deficiency. The opening parable shows that things are not necessarily what they seem to be on the surface. There is a future for wicked tax collectors who sue God for mercy, and there is rebuff for pious Pharisees who confidently dismiss all others in their sense of exclusive claim upon the good pleasure of God.

The Lukan framework in v 9 (along with the last half of v 14) simplifies the subtlety of the parable, first by emphasizing the confidence of the Pharisee in himself on the basis of his righteousness and also his despising of others, and then by forcing a clear either/or between the two figures, rather than the "more than" that would be quite possible for the parable without this Lukan framework.

To read our parable well requires a positive starting image for Pharisee and a negative starting image for tax collector. It is the work of the parable subtly to qualify the level of our initial approval of this Pharisee, and to cause us to begin to see that there may yet be hope for those who have been written off by respectable society.

The Pharisee attributes his own upstanding life to the grace of God and expresses his gratitude. He does, however, seem to think that all non-Pharisees are utterly lost in degradation; he is completely dismissive of the tax collector who is also in the temple to pray; and finally he is cleary impressed by his own Pharisaic super-piety in the areas of fasting and tithing. His achievements are impressive, but we might wonder why he needs to distance himself (his group) so much and so critically from all others and why he chooses to mention these particular pious practices before God. By the end of the episode a sharp contrast will have emerged between this Pharisee's attitude toward the tax collector and that of God himself. And in retrospect we may feel that we are not warmed by the love of God when we are in the presence of this upright and apparently godly man: his love for God does not move him to have compassion for his fellows; his righteousness, rather, drives him away from others.

By location and posture, the tax collector signals his sense of unworthiness before God. And, as he speaks, his words echo the opening words of Ps 51, the classic penitential psalm, which is associated with the sin and repentance of David. At one level he confirms all our prejudices about how bad tax collectors are, but at the same time the depth of feeling expressed by his appeal, posture, and action means that our hearts must go out to him, and the echo of the penitential psalm reminds us that the possibility of forgiveness of even the most heinous of crimes is a fundamental aspect of Jewish faith.

Our opening view that Pharisees are good and tax collectors are bad has certainly not been overturned, but it has been seriously qualified, at least in the case of these two believable figures. The story has gently led us by the hand to the place where we are no longer shocked by the statement with which v 14 opens. Hidden flaws have been exposed in the Pharisee, and fitting remorse is attributed to the tax collector. Things are not necessarily as they at first seem, and we are by now prepared for the declaration that the tax collector, more than the Pharisee, meets with God's approval in this encounter in the temple.

Hardened tax collectors may not normally be expected to behave like this tax collector. In the story we may well not have a general possibility but an image of how Jesus himself understood what was taking place in his own contact with tax collectors. These people were indeed being rescued for God and, through the ministry of Jesus, being brought into the kingdom of God.

In line with v 9, Luke invites us to see the judgment expressed at the end of the parable in connection with a process of reversal. He sees the Pharisee as having exalted himself, and so God's approval has been denied him. Meanwhile, it is clear that the tax collector has humbled himself before God and has, therefore, gained acceptance with him.

Entering the Kingdom of God like a Child (18:15–17)

Bibliography

Aland, K. *Did the Early Church Baptize Infants?* Philadelphia: Westminster, 1963. 95–99. **Beasley-Murray, G. R.** *Baptism in the New Testament.* London: Macmillan, 1962. 320–29. **Brown, R.** "Jesus and the Child as a Model of Spirituality." *IBS* 4 (1982) 178–92. **Crossan, J. D.** "Kingdom and Children: A Study in the Aphoristic Tradition." *Semeia* 29 (1983) 75–95. **Cullmann, O.** *Baptism in the New Testament.* SBT 1. Chicago/London: Regnery/SCM, 1950. 26, 42, 76–80. **Derrett, J. D. M.** "Why Jesus Blessed the Children (Mk 10:13–16 par.)." *NovT* 25 (1983) 1–18. **Jeremias, J.** *Infant Baptism in the First Four Centuries.* London: SCM, 1960. 48–55. ———. *The Origins of Infant Baptism: A Further Study in Reply to Kurt Aland.* SHT 1. London: SCM, 1963. 54 n. 1. **Légasse, S.** *Jésus et l'enfant: "Enfants," "petits" et "simples" dans la tradition synoptique.* EBib. Paris: Gabalda, 1969. 36–43, 195–209, 326–33. **Lindars, B.** "John and the Synoptic Gospels: A Test Case." *NTS* 27 (1981) 287–94. **Michaelis, W.** "Lukas und die Anfänge der Kindertaufe." In *Apophoreta.* FS E. Haenchen, ed. W. Eltester and F. H. Kettler. BZNW 30. Berlin: Töpelmann, 1964. 187–93. **Patte, D.** "Jesus' Pronouncement about Entering the Kingdom like a Child: A Structural Exegesis." *Semeia* 29 (1983) 3–42. **Percy, E.** *Die Botschaft Jesu.* 31–37. **Ringehausen, G.** "Kie Kinder der Weisheit: Zur Auslegung von Mk 10:13–16 par." *ZNW* 77 (1986) 33–63. **Robbins, V. K.** "Pronouncement Stories and Jesus' Blessing of the Children: A Rhetorical Approach." *Semeia* 29 (1983) 43–74. **Schilling, F. A.** "What Means the Saying about Receiving the Kingdom of God as a Little Child (τὴν βασιλείαν τοῦ θεοῦ ὡς παιδίον)? Mk x. 15; Lk xviii. 17." *ExpTim* 77 (1965–66) 56–58. **Schramm, T.** *Markus-Stoff.* 141–42.

Translation

[15] *[People] were bringing even babies for him to touch. When the disciples saw this they began to rebuke*[a] *them.* [16] *But Jesus offered them welcome, saying,*[b] *"Allow the children to come to me, and don't try to stop them. For the kingdom of God belongs to such as these.* [17] *Amen, I say to you, whoever does not receive the kingdom of God like a child, shall certainly not enter it."*

Notes

[a] A W Θ Ψ etc. have the aorist of the Markan parallel.

[b] The main verb and participle forms are interchanged here by A W Θ Ψ (f^{13}) 33 etc.

Form/Structure/Setting

The childlikeness called for in this unit is to be linked with the humbling of oneself called for in the preceding 18:9–14, and with the challenge to abandon material supports for the sake of the kingdom of God, which is to come in 18:18–30. Luke has distributed the two Markan pericopes in which Jesus has dealings with children between the section that prepares for the Journey to Jerusalem narrative (9:22–50; see vv 46–48) and this last full section of the journey narrative. Along with some other markers, this allocation functions as a kind of inclusio marking off the boundaries of the journey narrative.

Luke at this point rejoins his Markan source, which he will draw upon sequentially for the remainder of this section and also for the tail-piece for the Journey Narrative in 18:31–34. Luke reproduces the Markan wording quite closely (see details below). The original unity of the Markan piece (10:13–16) is frequently questioned on the basis that v 15 obtrudes from an account that is otherwise about the guaranteed place of young children in the kingdom of God (e.g., Bultmann, *History*, 32). That the language in v 15 of receiving the kingdom of God is not used elsewhere in the Gospel tradition may support the view that it is a later insertion (Légasse, *Jésus et l'enfant*, 187–88). (The possibility that Matt 18:3 represents a more original form of this saying [e.g., Lindars, *NTS* 27 (1980–81) 287–94] may count in either direction, since, despite having being transmitted independently, the Matthean form makes an excellent link with the Markan setting.) On the other hand, if the view that children have a place in the kingdom of God itself depends in turn on a value set upon certain aspects of children's attitudes and responses, then it would be quite natural for this point to be developed and applied to adults (cf. Marshall, 682); and the idiom of receiving the kingdom may be no more than an ellipse encouraged by the previous mention of the kingdom of God. Reflection upon Ps 131:2 may stand behind Mark 10:15.

The account as we have it is in the form of a two-pronged pronouncement story. While the material here has played an important role from quite early on in the discussion of the church's practice of baptism, none of the Gospel forms should be read as directly concerned with this matter.

Comment

Jesus welcomes infants and challenges all to receive the preaching of the kingdom of God in a childlike manner.

15 Luke makes the Markan point yet more extreme by changing *παιδία*, "children," into *βρέφη*, "babies," and by adding *καί*, "even"; he brings forward "seeing," which Mark has attributed to Jesus, and applies it to the disciples; and he makes minor tense changes to follow through more consistently from the opening imperfect tense. It is best to think that parents were bringing their infants to be blessed by this high-profile religious figure (cf. the response in 11:27). *ἅπτηται* could be "hold," but "touch" is what Luke elsewhere means by this verb, and it is likely to be the physical contact with Jesus that is thought to be beneficial to the infants (cf. 6:19). It may be that the folk-religion aspect of this contributed to the annoyance of the disciples, though perhaps more likely it is their own sense of self-importance, based upon their privileged proximity to Jesus, that is offended by the approach.

16 A Markan reference to Jesus' anger is displaced by *προσεκαλέσατο αὐτά* (lit. "he called them"; Matthew also drops the reference to anger [19:14]). Rather curiously, whereas the rebuke language of v 15 was directed at the parents, Luke now uses the neuter, which must refer to the babies themselves. Perhaps he is under the influence of the "children" of his Markan source (which Luke retains in the present verse; and cf. v 17), or it may be that Luke uses *προσεκαλέσατο* in the sense "he invited" with something like the force "he offered a welcome to" (perhaps this is what is intended by Fitzmyer's "called for them" [1191, 1194], which otherwise hardly accords with the Greek syntax).

The use of λέγων (lit. "saying") suggests that the following statement (as well as checking the disciples' behavior) constitutes the welcoming invitation. It is, then, to be seen as addressed both to the parents and to the disciples. To apply μὴ κωλύετε, on the basis of Acts 8:36; 10:47, to the possible prohibition of baptism is to introduce a thought quite alien to the context here. What is the quality in children that warrants such a statement? In the ancient world setting it is not likely to be a romantic idealization of children (note the image used in 7:32 of what may be a children's squabble). Is it openness, willingness to trust, freedom from hypocrisy or pretension, conscious weakness and readiness for dependence, or some other quality? Perhaps the metaphoric force of the challenge of these words is only preserved by keeping the options open, within a general framework set by the other Gospel challenges (Jeremias, *Infant Baptism*, 49, is, however, surely wrong to link directly here a child's use of "Abba").

On the kingdom of God, see at 4:43; 6:20; 11:20; 19:11. That the kingdom of God belongs not simply to these children but to all those who are like the children in question leads to the development of v 17.

17 The wording here is identical to Mark 10:15, but Luke drops the Markan completion of the episode in 10:16. For the force of "amen, I say to you," see at 4:24. "Receive the kingdom of God" probably stands for "receive the message/messenger of the kingdom of God" (cf. 9:2, 5; 10:11). ὡς παιδίον could mean "when [he was] a child," but will mean "in the manner that a child receives." A related thought is expressed in 10:21 (see discussion there). Entry into the kingdom of God is also in question in 18:24, 25; Acts 14:22. In this verse the line between the present manifestation of the kingdom of God and its future consummation becomes very fine indeed: the first half verse is concerned with present reception; the second must embrace both the present and ultimate manifestations of the kingdom of God.

Explanation

The call to childlikeness here links well with the need for humbling oneself of 18:9–14 and prepares for the challenge to abandon material self-sufficiency in the units that follow. Luke is starting to wind up his long Journey to Jerusalem narrative, and there will be, from now on, as signals of this, a series of echoes of material from the section 9:22–50 (which prepared for the journey narrative). Here 9:46–48 is echoed.

In the manner of folk-religion worldwide, people come to see if there might be some advantage for their children from this new religious figure who has made such a stir. His touch has healed the sick; it may be good for babies as well! The disciples are offended and see their own self-importance being undermined by this kind of casual access to Jesus. They attempt to nip it in the bud, but Jesus himself intervenes. With a generosity of spirit not yet shared by his closest followers, he asks for the children to come to him. And he goes further: he declares that children, precisely through their being like children, have a place in the kingdom of God. Though Jesus will bc no romantic about children, somewhere among their openness, willingness to trust, freedom from hypocrisy or pretension, conscious weakness, and readiness for dependence Jesus finds those qualities that are essential for entry into the kingdom of God.

It is, then, no surprise that Jesus builds on this with a challenge to all who are no longer children: only those who, when the message of the kingdom of God comes to them, are prepared to emulate the qualities of childhood can hope to find entry into the kingdom of God.

"What Must I Do to Inherit Eternal Life?" (18:18–23)

Bibliography

Bailey, K. E. *Through Peasant Eyes.* 157–70. **Berger, K.** *Die Gesetzauslegung Jesu: Ihr historischer Hintergrund im Judentum und im Alten Testament: Teil I. Markus und Parallelen.* WMANT 40. Neukirchen-Vluyn: Neukirchener, 1972. 396–460. **Best, E.** "The Camel and the Needle's Eye (Mk 10:25)." *ExpTim* 82 (1970–71) 83–89. **Caspari, A.** "Der gute Meister." *CuW* 8 (1932) 218–31. **Coulot, C.** "La structuration de la péricope de l'homme riche et ses différentes lectures (Mc 10,17–31; Mt 19,16–30; Lc 18,18–30)." *RevSR* 56 (1982) 240–52. **Degenhardt, H.-J.** *Lukas, Evangelist der Armen.* 136–59. ———. "Was muss ich tun, um das ewige Leben zu gewinnen? Zu Mk 10,17–22." In *Biblische Randbemerkungen.* FS R. Schnackenburg, ed. H. Merklein and J. Lange. Würzburg: Echter, 1974. 159–68. **Dupont, J.** *Béatitudes.* 3:153–60. **Galot, J.** "Le fondement évangélique du voeu religieux de pauvreté." *Greg* 56 (1975) 441–67. **Huuhtanen, P.** "Die Perikope vom 'Reichen Jüngling' unter Berüchsichtigung der Akzentuierungen des Lukas." *SNTU* 2 (1977) 79–98. **Klijn, A. F. J.** "The Question of the Rich Young Man in a Jewish-Christian Gospel." *NovT* 8 (1966) 149–55. **Klinghardt, M.** *Gesetz und Volk Gottes.* 124–36. **Légasse, S.** *L'Appel du riche (Marc 10,17–31 et parallèles): Contribution à l'étude des fondements scripturaires de l'état religieux.* Paris: Beauchesne, 1966. 97–110, 184–214. ———. "L'appel du riche." In *La Pauvreté évangélique.* Lire la Bible 27. Paris: Cerf, 1971. 65–91. **Luck, U.** "Die Frage nach dem Guten: Zu Mt 19,16–30 und Par." In *Studien zum Text und zur Ethik des Neuen Testaments,* ed. W. Schrage. 282–97. **Minear, P. S.** "The Needle's Eye: A Study in Form Criticism." *JBL* 61 (1942) 157–69. **Murray, G.** "The Rich Young Man (18, 18–23)." *DR* 103 (1985) 144–46. **Neuhäusler, E.** "Allem Besitz entsagen." In *Anspruch und Antwort Gottes: Zur Lehre von den Weisungen innerhalb der synoptischen Jesusverkündigung.* Düsseldorf: Patmos, 1962. 170–85. **Riga, P. J.** "Poverty as Counsel and as Precept." *BiTod* 65 (1973) 1123–28. **Schmid, J.** *Matthäus und Lukas.* 129–31. **Schramm, T.** *Markus-Stoff.* 142. **Spitta, F.** "Jesu Weigerung, sich als 'gut' bezeichnen zu lassen." *ZNW* 9 (1908) 12–20. **Swezey, C. M.** "Luke 18:18–30." *Int* 37 (1983) 68–73. **Thomas, K. J.** "Liturgical Citations in the Synoptics." *NTS* 22 (1975–76) 205–14. **Tillard, J. M. R.** "Le propos de pauvreté et l'exigence évangélique." *NRT* 100 (1978) 207–32, 359–72. **Trilling, W.** *Christusverkündigung in den synoptischen Evangelien: Beispiele gattungsgemässer Auslegung.* Biblische Handbibliothek 4. Munich: Kössel, 1969. 123–45. **Wagner, W.** "In welchem Sinne hat Jesus das Prädikat *ΑΓΑΘΟΣ* von sich abgewiesen?" *ZNW* 8 (1907) 143–61. **Walter, N.** "Zur Analyse von Mc 10,17–31." *ZNW* 53 (1962) 206–18. **Ward, R. A.** "Pin-Points and Panoramas: The Preacher's Use of the Aorist." *ExpTim* 71 (1959–60) 267–70. **Weiss, J.** "'Zum reichen Jüngling' Mk 10,13–27." *ZNW* 11 (1910) 79–83. **Wenham, J. W.** "Why Do You Ask about the Good? A Study of the Relation between Text and Source Criticism." *NTS* 28 (1982) 116–25. **Zimmerli, W.** "Die Frage des Reichen nach dem ewigen Leben." *EvT* 19 (1959) 90–97.

Translation

[18]*A certain ruler asked him, "Good teacher, what must I do to inherit eternal life?"* [19]*Jesus said to him, "Why do you call me good? No one is good, except one:*[a] *God.* [20]*You know the commandments, 'You shall not commit adultery, you shall not murder, you shall not steal, you shall not bear false witness, honor your father and*[b] *mother.'"* [21]*He said, "I have kept all these since [my]*[c] *youth."* [22]*As Jesus heard [this]*[d] *he said to him, "One thing still remains for you [to do]: sell everything that you have and distribute*[e] *to the poor, and you will have treasure in heaven; and come and follow me."* [23]*When he heard*[f] *these things he became very sad. For he was exceedingly wealthy.*

Notes

[a] ℵ B B² omit "one."
[b] A separate "your" for mother is supplied in ℵ *f*¹³ etc.
[c] Conforming to the Markan text, a word for "my" is supplied by ℵ A L W Θ Ψ etc.
[d] *ταῦτα*, "these things," is found in A W Θ Ψ *f*¹³ etc.
[e] The simple *δός*, "give" (as in Mark and Matthew), is found in ℵ A D L 078 *f*¹ etc.
[f] ℵ and a few other texts have an added "all."

Form/Structure/Setting

Those who would enter the kingdom of God will humble themselves (18:9–14); they will be childlike (18:15–17); and, now, they will, in order to follow Jesus, divest themselves of all security in life that is based upon material resources. This last is to be developed further in 18:24–30. Vv 18–23, and vv 24–30 to follow, make their own contribution to the inclusio that surrounds the journey narrative (see also at 18:15–17) by calling to mind the motif of self-renunciation in order to follow Jesus (in the way of the cross), as well as the paradox of loss leading to gain, ideas that were encountered in 9:23–27 (and cf. 9:57–62).

Luke continues to follow his Markan source and sequence here. For the most part the Markan language is followed quite closely, the main change being dispensing with the Markan introduction in order to bond the present unit more closely with the previous unit. (Luke agrees with Matthew against Mark in omitting "do not defraud" from the commandments list [it is not one of the Ten Commandments]; in replacing Mark's middle verb form in v 21 with the preferred active; in using the plural form for "heaven" in v 22; and in introducing the participle *ἀκούσας* [lit. "having heard"] in v 23. None of these warrants appeal to a second source.)

The apparently double answer to the rich man's question has caused some to dispute the original unity of the pericope. Minear (*JBL* 61 [1942] 160–61) has argued that Mark 10:20–21a is a Jewish Christian addition, concerned to see that the demands of the Law not be overlooked, while Berger (*Gesetzauslegung*) has argued in a much more extended fashion (pp. 396–417 provide an elaborate analysis of the development of Mark 10:13–31) in the opposite direction, that the original unit terminated at 21a (with: "and Jesus loved him"). Berger's view is controlled by a christological understanding of the role of "good" in Mark 10:18 that works itself out in v 19 in terms of Jesus only being able to say what God has already said (i.e., the commandments). This view involves an unbelievable early

Jewish Christian understanding of Jesus, and also does not take into account the tone given to Jesus' response by its opening words: "*you* know the commandments." Minear's view is less open to immediate criticism, but is finally an unnecessary decomposition of the text, which only taken as a whole unit witnesses to the kind of radicalization of the law that we have otherwise seen grounds for attributing to Jesus (see, e.g., at 6:27; 10:29–38). The two-stage development here has some analogy in Luke 9:7–9 and 9:18–20.

The originality of Mark 10:18 has also been questioned, but its very difficulty stands strongly in favor of treating it as an original component of the pericope. As it stands, the unit should probably be classified as an unusually elaborate pronouncement story.

Comment

The demands of discipleship reach beyond, but do not detract from, the requirements of the OT law. A radical detachment from the claims of earthly wealth is required of those who would follow Jesus.

18 Luke's omission of the Markan introduction here connects the present verse's interest in what is needed for eternal life more closely to the interest of v 17 in conditions for entry into the kingdom of God. Luke makes several minor syntactical changes and, more significantly, identifies the man who approaches Jesus as τις . . . ἄρχων, "a certain ruler." The term is used in 8:41 of a ruler of the synagogue; in 12:58 (in a parable) of a magistrate; in 14:1 of a "certain one of the rulers of the Pharisees." This first unqualified use provides a transition to the use of the term in connection with the role of the Jewish (lay-)leadership in the trial and execution of Jesus (23:13, 35; 24:20; Acts 3:17; 5:26). The present unit makes its own modest contribution to Luke's view that by and large the Jewish leadership had vested interests that kept them from embracing Jesus' proclamation of the kingdom of God.

"Good" in connection with a Jewish teacher does not seem to be evidenced in Jewish sources prior to the much later *b. Taᶜan.* 24b. Since the word is already applied to the human sphere in 6:45 (and cf. Prov 12:2; 14:14; Eccl 9:2), it is difficult to see why there should be any serious objection to its use of a religious teacher. An identical question has already been put in 10:25 (see there).

19 Luke moves "Jesus" to a later point in the opening clause and brings εἶπεν, "said," forward to produce his favored opening εἶπεν δέ. Otherwise he reproduces the Markan wording. Why does Jesus bridle at being called good? Answers canvassed range from seeing the response here as an implicit claim to divinity to finding here Jesus' recognition of his own sinfulness. Others claim that Jesus has detected insincere flattery or an attempt to trade on his kindness and to seek from him a less demanding path to eternal life. Berger (*Gesetzauslegung*, 398–402) offers the distinctive suggestion that in the original context Jesus is denying the possibility of being able to offer a new and better way to eternal life than that already given by God in the commandments. Perhaps best here is to understand that Jesus is pressing the man about what has been no more than a casual use of the term "good" and challenging him to understand the relationship between his (Jesus') own activity and God as the only truly good one (cf. 11:20). The goodness of God is a persistent OT motif (1 Chr 16:34; 2 Chr 5:13; Pss 25:8; 34:8;

106:1; 118:1, 29; 136:1; Nah 1:7; etc.). Here this motif has been combined with the Jewish monotheistic emphasis upon the oneness of God (Deut 6:4; cf. Luck, "Die Frage," 291).

20 Luke reverses the order of the first two of the listed commandments and drops "you shall not defraud" from the Markan list (as does Matthew). Since "you shall not defraud" is not among the Ten Commandments, its omission by both Matthew and Luke is understandable (it is probably a variant form of the command not to covet). The difference over the order of the first listed commandments clearly reflects different traditional orderings (Mark has the OT order; for Luke's order see Deut 5:17–20 [LXX, except the A text, which has the Masoretic order]; Philo, *De decal.* 51; Rom 13:9). The command not to bear false witness appears in a reduced form that brings it formally into line with the other commands (the same has happened to the prohibition of coveting in Rom 13:9; and cf. Philo, *De decal.* 51). Though Berger (*Gesetzauslegung,* 418–19) notes helpfully the way in which the traditional use of the command concerning parents has been influenced by its distinctive capacity to function as a transition from those commands concerning the honoring of God to those concerning the social order, no convincing explanation has been offered for its final position here. Is it a later addition to the list? Does the order reflect that family honor, and not just individual uprightness, is dependent on the fulfillment of the earlier commandments listed? Is this command given last in order to end with a positive commandment rather than a negative prohibition? Perhaps the last.

Though in quite a different way from 10:25–28, Jesus' answer here has the same concern to confirm the validity and continuing life-giving significance of the OT commandments of God. The man is first called upon to practice what he already has and knows.

21 Luke introduces the response with a simple *ὁ δὲ εἶπεν*, "he said," and also drops Mark's "teacher" and the personal pronoun *μου*, "my." He changes the verb from Mark's middle form to the more usual active (as does Matthew). On the transition from childhood to full adult responsibility under the law, see at 2:42. The man declares that he has faithfully observed the law since his youth. This is reminiscent of the consistent piety of Zechariah and Elisabeth, Simeon and Anna. The positive assessment appropriate to this statement is made explicit in Mark's following statement: "Jesus . . . loved him." Though Luke (as Matthew) is less comfortable in attributing emotion to Jesus (cf. at 5:13) and has eliminated this Markan clause (as has Matthew), this should not at all be taken as indicating a more critical stance. Such faithful obedience to the law of God is fertile soil for response to what God is now doing in Jesus.

22 Luke reduces the nonverbal part of the Markan response by Jesus to *ἀκούσας*, "having heard." Mark's reference to what is "lacking" in the young ruler's life is here replaced by a reference to what "still remains [to be done]." An added *πάντα*, "all," lays stress on the call for the ruler to dispose of all. "Give to the poor" becomes the more elegant "distribute to the poor." The word for "heaven" is changed to the plural (as Matthew).

The poor are the natural recipients of almsgiving and are in some sense the special objects of Jesus' concern. Though the contrary claim is at times made, the disposal of wealth is certainly more than simply a precursor to joining the group of intimate followers of Jesus. This is clear from the reference to treasure in heaven that precedes the call to follow, and also from the discussion to come in vv 24–30. The basic Lukan sense here will be close to that of 12:33 (see there, and cf. 6:23, 35). At the same time the call to relinquish wealth is not to be separated from the call to follow Jesus (Jesus issues specific calls for individuals to follow him in 5:27; and 9:59; and more generally in 9:23; 14:27; he is followed in the manner envisaged here in 5:11, 28; 18:28). In just this context the challenge represents the "plus" required by God in this new situation of the proclamation of the kingdom of God by Jesus. The treasure here is not the eternal life sought in v 18, but disencumberment and following do represent the way to eternal life, and not merely some higher righteousness with its own special rewards (against Galot, *Greg* 56 [1975] 441–67). The total disencumberment asked of the ruler echoes that achieved (but not specifically asked for) in 5:11, 28 (Lukan addition of *πάντα*, "all" in both cases). The generalizability of this emphasis on the "all" is moderated by Luke's change in 18:28 of Mark's *πάντα*, "all," to *τὰ ἴδια*, "what is our own," and also by the exemplary pattern of the tax collector to come in 19:1–10, who gives very generously of his wealth but does not dispose of its entirety. The money aspect of the challenge needs to be set finally into the wider context of the general call to follow of 9:23 (see there).

23 Luke somewhat abbreviates, and almost totally rewords, his Markan source here. *ἀκούσας*, "having heard," propels the action here as in v 22. Luke's omission of Mark's departure statement probably leaves the ruler present to hear the development in vv 24–30. Mark's *ἔχων κτήματα πολλά*, "having much wealth," becomes *πλούσιος σφόδρα*, "exceedingly rich." The pull of the man's material wealth was more than he could resist. He was not ready for the all-embracing nature of the claim of the kingdom of God.

Explanation

The series of requirements for entering the kingdom of God continues here. The old requirements of God continue to have their validity, but in the presence of the call of Jesus there needs to be a radical turning of one's back upon any security based upon the possession of material resources.

The ruler is a representative of the lay-leadership of the Jews, in a form that shows a very positive initial interest in Jesus. Jesus' preaching of the kingdom of God evokes the question here about the closely related topic of eternal life. Jesus bridles at the man's casual use of the word "good" in "good teacher." Jesus takes up the term in order to challenge the man to make up his mind about the relationship of this good teacher's activities to the God who is the one and only true fount of goodness. (Here Jesus applies the oneness of God from Deut 6:4 to the OT teaching of God's goodness and comes up with God as the one who has an exclusive claim upon goodness.) If the ruler is prepared to see this level of goodness in the activity of Jesus, then he will realize that nothing less than the kingdom of God is present.

In answer to the man's question, Jesus first points him back to the commandments of the decalogue, which define for the People of God the ethics of social relationships. These are the requirements of God for human life and represent the way to life (Lev 18:5; Deut 30:15–16). The commandments listed here are reordered so that the positive requirement of honor to parents should complete the list of what is otherwise a series of prohibitions. This man has been a seeker after God and can reply to Jesus that from his youth he has faithfully observed all these commands. We should not question the reality of his piety; it is to be compared to that of Zechariah, Elisabeth, Simeon, and Anna, whom we met in the Infancy Gospel. Such piety was fertile soil for response to the new thing that God was now doing.

But Jesus' answer to the man does not stop there. The coming of the kingdom of God makes its own fresh demands and sets in a new and radical light the old commandments of God. There was still something else that the man needed to do in his pursuit of eternal life. He needed to divest himself of all his worldly security and then follow Jesus. In this way his treasure would be securely invested in heaven and would no longer be only an earthbound asset. Though "everything" was important in the case of this man, and was probably true also of the apostolic band (see 5:11, 28), the coming example of Zacchaeus the tax collector, along with vv 29–31 to come, shows that the underlying principle is the readiness to renounce for the sake of the kingdom of God whatever it should prove necessary to renounce. This call takes its place within the wider call of 9:23 to take up one's cross and follow Jesus.

Luke has again and again insisted upon the dangers and temptations of wealth. His point is made yet again when this eagerly religious Jewish leader, because of the way in which his own wealth has him under its sway, cannot rise to the call of Jesus. His pursuit of God is finally choked by the claims of money (see 8:15; 16:13; 6:24; etc.).

"How Hard It Is for Those Who Have Money to Enter the Kingdom of God!" *(18:24–30)*

Bibliography

Aicher, G. *Kamel und Nadelöhr: Eine kritisch-exegetische Studie über Mt 19,24 und Parallelen.* NTAbh 1/5. Münster in W.: Aschendorff, 1908. **Denk, J.** "Camelus: 1. Kamel, 2. Schiffstau." *ZNW* 5 (1904) 256–57. ———. "Suum cuique." *BZ* 3 (1905) 367. **Fürst, H.** "Verlust der Familie—Gewinn einer neuen Familie (Mk 10, 29f. Parr.)." In *Studia Historico-Ecclesiastica.* FS L. G. Spätling, ed. I. Vazquez. BPAA 19. Rome: Pontificium Athenaeum Antonianum, 1977. 17–47. **Galot, J.** "La motivation évangélique du célibat." *Greg* 53 (1972) 731–58, esp. 750–56. **Goguel, M.** "Avec des persécutions." *RHPR* 8 (1928) 264–77. **Herklotz, F.** "Miszelle zu Mt 19,24 und Parall." *BZ* 2 (1904) 176–77. **Legrand, L.** "Christian Celibacy and the Cross." *Scr* 14 (1962) 1–12. **Lehmann, R.** "Zum Gleichnis vom Kamel und Nadelöhr und Verwandtes." *TBl* 11 (1932) 336–38. **May, D. M.** "Leaving and Receiving: A Social-Scientific Exegesis of Mark 10:29–31." *PRS* 17 (1990) 141–51, 154.

And see at 18:18–23.

Translation

[24]*Seeing him, Jesus*[a] *said, "How hard it is for those who have money*[b] *to enter the kingdom of God!* [25]*For it is easier for a camel to go into the eye of a needle than for a rich*

person to go into the kingdom of God." [26]*Those who heard said, "Who, then, can be saved?"* [27]*He said, "What is impossible for human beings is possible for God."* [28]*Peter said, "Look, we have left what was ours*[c] *and followed you."* [29]*He said to them, "Amen, I say to you, that*[d] *there is no one who has left home or wife or siblings or parents or children for the sake of the kingdom of God* [30]*who will fail to receive many times as much in this age and, in the age to come, eternal life."*

Notes

[a] περίλυπον γενόμενον, "becoming very sad," is added by A (D) W Θ Ψ f^{13} etc.
[b] χρήματα could alternatively be "possessions" or "property."
[c] ℵ A W Ψ 33 etc. have instead the ἀφήκαμεν πάντα καί, "we have left all and," of the Markan text.
[d] Missing from ℵ D Δ lat.

Form/Structure/Setting

The present unit offers a loose connection of sayings presented as a reflection on the ruler's failure to follow through on Jesus' directive: for the rich, entry into the kingdom is extremely difficult, but not impossible, with God. The apostles' following of this path of renunciation has its reward now and will lead on to eternal life. On the place of this unit in the section and on its role in the inclusio surrounding the Journey to Jerusalem narrative, see at 18:18–23.

Luke continues to follow his Markan source and its sequence, but with quite a bit of editing. Luke dispenses with the disciple audience of Mark 10:23; he omits the whole of v 24 with the difficulties that come from (*i*) its close relation to v 23, but (*ii*) its movement away from the topic of the problems of the rich; he has suppressed the difficult to account for astonishment of Mark's v 26; all through this section he has reduced the materials to a simple dialogue form; in preparation for the listing of vv 29–30, he has τὰ ἴδια (lit. "the things of one's own") for Mark's πάντα, "everything," in v 28; he has reformulated the Markan list in v 29 of what is left behind, notably adding "wife" and deleting "fields"; he drops Mark's repetition of the list for the present hundredfold compensation, and replaces Mark's "hundredfold" with the less precise "manifold"; and finally, he drops Mark's concluding v 31 with its reference to the interchange of first and last.

Luke's editing shows, among other things, his awareness of the difficulties inherent in reading Mark 10:23–31 as a coherent narrative. The artificiality of the unit has led to a series of attempts to deconstruct the stages in its formation. Important suggestions about putative sources include the following: (*i*) originally the order of vv 24, 25 was reversed (giving an easier transition from the situation of the rich to a more general statement); (*ii*) v 25a was originally the completion of v 24, and thus was not applied to the rich before the addition of v 25b (a variant on this is to accept the whole of v 25 as original, apart from the reference to "a rich person," which will have displaced an original that spoke only of "a person"); (*iii*) the interest of the whole text (here 10:17–31) in the question of the disposal of wealth is a development back through the materials of a motif that was originally restricted to vv 29–31.

What can finally be said with greatest confidence is that the core of vv 23–31 is to be found in a series of discrete sayings of Jesus, comprising vv 25 (a form of v 25 lacking a reference to riches is unbelievable, unless there were a developed setting), 27, 29–30, 31. The linking materials are likely to be secondary formulations, but v 25 may well have always had v 23b attached, and v 27 is either a fragment originally transmitted in a setting now lost to us, or it has always had some original connection with v 25. Of these, v 25 is most unproblematically to be traced to the historical Jesus; vv 29–30 show signs of considerable development, but the basic sentiment is likely to attributable to the historical Jesus; v 27 has about it the uncertainty that attaches to its original setting; and v 31, though it is a floating logion of uncertain original thrust, is likely to be a saying of the historical Jesus.

In light of the development of Mark 10:23–26a, the translation of *τὰ χρήματα* in v 24 as "riches" or the like has probably been misleading. It is likely to have referred originally not only to the situation of the wealthy but to that of all who have possessions (or perhaps property). The Markan text has a staged development, starting with the warning to all who have possessions, which provokes a response of amazement. Then the level of provocation increases in a twofold way. The general statement about the difficulty of entering the kingdom of God is repeated, but now with nothing to limit this difficulty to those who have possessions. At the same time, the extent of difficulty, now specifically for the rich, is raised to the level of impossibility. Correspondingly the response escalates from amazement to exceeding astonishment. This development cries out for some kind of resolution, and this is provided by v 27.

Comment

The renunciation required for the kingdom of God makes entry extremely difficult, not to say impossible, for the rich (but with God all things are possible), but such renunciation brings great reward now and leads on to eternal life.

24 The Markan *περιβλεψάμενος*, "looking around," becomes *ἰδών*, "seeing"; the rich man becomes its object; and "his disciples" are no longer specifically the addressees (these last two changes bond the unit here more closely with vv 18–23); Luke uses a present verb in place of Mark's future for "enter" (but ℵ D Ψ 579 etc. have Mark's future verb). With the presence of Jesus, the possibility of entry into the kingdom of God now exists (cf. at v 17), but, for those with possessions, entry is extremely difficult. It remains uncertain whether "having possessions" is synonymous here with being rich, or whether v 25 supports v 24 more generally by exploring an extreme case. Probably the former. Luke has nothing corresponding to Mark 10:24 (Matthew keeps only a small phrase of this verse).

25 Luke adds a linking *γάρ*, "for"; changes the imagery slightly from *through* the eye of the needle to *into* the eye of the needle (for the sake of uniformity between the verb applied to the movement of the camel and to entry into the kingdom of God); and uses different words for "eye of a needle" (probably words he considered to be more refined). The attempt to identify some narrow city gate as "the eye of the needle" has now largely been abandoned. Jesus was quite fond of extreme images (cf. 6:41–42). A relatively early exposition of the text involved reading *κάμιλον*, "rope, ship's cable," for *κάμηλον*, "camel" (at least from Origen). No real change of meaning is involved, but there seems to be no adequate reason for displacing "camel" with the quite weakly attested "rope." There is a later rabbinic saying about an elephant passing through the eye of a needle.

The image is a provocative statement of an impossibility. On the situation of the rich, see further at 6:24; 8:14; 11:41; 12:13–21, 33–34; and chap. 16.

26 For Mark's "they were exceedingly astonished, saying to themselves," Luke has only "those who heard said" (Matthew also introduces *ἀκούσαντες* [lit. "having heard"] here). Luke's omission of Mark 10:24 leaves the question with a less satisfactory motivation, but Luke still needs the question to prepare for v 27 (this difficulty is eased a little if we take Luke's v 24 as applying to all who have possessions and not merely to the rich; alternatively we can place to one side all the earlier Gospel materials critical of the rich and attribute to the questioners a view that riches indicate the favor of God). A somewhat similar question has been posed at 13:23. The imagery of salvation now displaces that of the kingdom of God. In v 30 this will give way in turn to reference to "eternal life."

27 Again Luke simplifies the Markan introduction, this time to *ὁ δὲ εἶπεν*, "he said." He also abbreviates the saying, reducing it to a single clause. There is no great change of meaning, but the Markan "all things are possible with God" echoes a proverbial statement of Jewish faith in the omnipotence of God (see at 1:37), in a manner that is lost in the Lukan redaction, which instead focuses on the contrast between human and divine ability. The text does not make clear how human inability and divine ability come together to achieve the salvation of (some of) the rich, but presumably the process must involve the breaking of the mesmerizing effect through which riches control those who possess them.

28 Luke displaces the Markan introduction with (another) *εἶπεν δέ*, "[he] said"; he replaces the first of Mark's coordinated verbs with a participle and uses *τὰ ἴδια* (lit. "the things of one's own") for Mark's *πάντα*, "everything" (and this despite Luke's introduction of *πάντα*, "everything," in 5:11, 28; *τὰ ἴδια* prepares better for the list to come in v 29). For the continuity of the thought here we need in part to reach back to v 22: the Apostles have put into effect a version of what v 22 demanded. The present language echoes that of the departure statements in 5:11, 28. On Peter's place as spokesperson for the Twelve, see at 9:20. There is neither more nor less reason to be critical of this statement than of the rich man's in v 21 (see there).

29 *ὁ δὲ εἶπεν*, "he said," again displaces the Markan introduction, but this time Luke adds "to them." (Matthew has these changes as well, but with *Ἰησοῦς*, "Jesus," after *ὁ δέ*; both Luke and Matthew have also added a *ὅτι*, "that," before the words of promise.) From Mark's list of things left behind, Luke deletes "fields" and has bundled "father or mother" into "parents." He probably allows *ἀδελφούς* (lit. "brothers") to stand for both brothers and sisters ("siblings"), where Mark has *ἀδελφάς*, "sisters," in the list as well. At the head of the list, after "home," Luke has added "wife." For "for my sake and the gospel's" Luke has, under the influence of vv 24–25, substituted "for the sake of the kingdom of God" (Luke has disturbed the same phrase at 9:24 [see there]).

On the force given by the use of "amen" here, see at 4:24. The context makes it clear that the "leaving behinds" of this list represent deeply felt loss rather than callous disregard. The claims of the kingdom of God finally transcend even the most sacred and binding of all human loyalties. For the thought, cf. at 9:59–62 and 14:26. In terms of an expression of fundamental loyalties, there is some genuine similarity with Jewish conversion motifs (cf. esp. *Joseph and Asenath* 13.2: "I left behind all the good things of the earth and fled to you, Lord"), but this hardly amounts to a demonstration that this is how the origin of the text is to be accounted for (against Berger, *Gesetzauslegung*, 404–7, 422–25, who identifies a series of stages in the development of Mark 10:29–30, from a straightforward promise of a hundredfold compensation for converts who leave their pagan past, through the addition of the structure of the two ages and the addition of the persecution motif, to the text as we now have it).

30 Luke considerably abbreviates the Markan form here. The main changes are: Mark's conditional form with ἐὰν μή becomes a grammatically preferable relative clause beginning ὃς οὐχὶ μή; Mark's "hundredfold" becomes the less precise πολλαπλασίονα (lit. "manifold"); the repetition of the list is abandoned (presumably as part of this reduction of precision), and with this goes the reference to persecutions (Matthew does not repeat the list either).

As a statement of manifold compensation for deprivation endured, this text (with its immediate Synoptic parallels) is unique, but its sentiment correlates well with the Gospel strand that emphasizes the present manifestation of the kingdom of God.

The distinction between this age and the age to come is found again in 20:34–35 and cf. 16:8b (cf. Str-B, 4.2:815–57 for the place of this distinction in later rabbinic thought). At the end we come back to the issue of eternal life from which we began with the ruler's question in 18:18. On "eternal life," see at 10:25. Luke has used a parallel to Mark 10:31 at 13:30 and simplifies the thought here by not repeating the saying.

Explanation

Luke presents here a series of developments from the ruler's failure to follow through on Jesus' directives. The greater wealth the greater difficulty that stands in the way of finding one's way into the kingdom of God. For the rich, entry is so difficult as to be impossible without the miracle-working ability of God. But the greatness of the outcome is on a scale that corresponds with that of the difficulty: present multiple compensation and eternal life in the future.

Jesus' words interpret the rich man's failure. Money is a problem for entry into the kingdom of God, and, for those with a lot of money, trying to get into the kingdom of God is like trying to drive a camel into the eye of a sewing needle. Here is yet another of a series of bizarre and extreme images used by Jesus for their shock value.

Jesus' hearers are suitably shocked. They feel that the possibility of salvation is becoming rather restricted. This reaction leads Jesus to offer a ray of light after his hard saying. He reminds his hearers that human impossibilities are divine possibilities. So despite it all, even rich people may be saved. The text does not make clear how human inability and divine ability come together to achieve the salvation of (some of) the rich, but presumably the process must involve the breaking of the mesmerizing effect through which riches control those who possess them.

In words that echo 5:11, 28, and take up the thought of v 22, Peter speaks of how he and the others in the Apostolic band have left what they had and followed Jesus. This occasions Jesus' promise to all who have left what is precious to them for the sake of the kingdom of God. The kingdom of God can demand much more than the leaving behind of material wealth. Even the most sacred and binding of all human loyalties must give way to its claim. Compare at 9:59–62 and 14:26.

Without intending to be very precise about the form this will take, the text promises a very generous compensation in this life for all deprivation suffered for the sake of the kingdom of God: there is a present reality of being blessed in the kingdom of God. But beyond that, in the age to come there is the assurance of eternal life—the eternal life that the ruler had initially come to Jesus to inquire about.

"Everything Written about the Son of Man Will Be Carried Out" (18:31–34)

Bibliography

Büchele, A. *Der Tod Jesu im Lukasevangelium: Eine redaktionsgeschichtliche Untersuchung zu Lk 23.* FTS 26. Frankfurt/M: Knecht, 1978. 132–35. **Farmer, W. R.** "The Passion Prediction Passages and the Synoptic Problem: a Test Case." *NTS* 36 (1990) 558–70, esp. 563–66. **Haenchen, E.** *Der Weg Jesu.* 360–62. **Lambrecht, J.** "Reading and Rereading Lk 18, 31–22, 6." In *À cause de l'Évangile,* ed. R. Refoulé. 585–612. **Schmid, J.** *Matthäus und Lukas: Eine Untersuchung des Verhältnisses ihrer Evangelien.* BibS(F) 23/2–4. Freiburg im B.: Herder, 1930. 133–34. **Schneider, G.** *Verleugnung Verspottung und Verhör Jesu nach Lukas, 22,54–71: Studien zur lukanischen Darstellung der Passion.* SANT 22. Munich: Kösel, 1969. 36–39. **Varro, R.** "Annonce de la passion et guérison de l'aveugle de Jéricho selon S. Luc, 18,31–43." *AmCl* 78 (1968) 25–27. **Zimmermann, H.** *Jesus Christus: Geschichte und Verkündigung.* Stuttgart: Katholisches Bibelwerk, 1973. 263–69.

And see at 9:21–22.

Translation

[31]*Taking aside the twelve he said to them, "Look, we are going up to Jerusalem, and everything written by the prophets about the Son of Man will be carried out.* [32]*For he will be delivered up to the Gentiles and will be ridiculed and insulted and spat upon.* [33]*They will flog him and kill him, and on the third day he will rise."* [34]*They understood nothing of these things. This word was concealed from them, and they did not know what was being said.*

Notes

There are no significant textual variants.

Form/Structure/Setting

Brief though it is, the present unit is to be identified as constituting the terminal section for the long Journey to Jerusalem narrative, which began at 9:51. In a manner similar to what has been noted for the preceding several units, by echoing the motifs of 9:21–22, 43b–45 from the section that prepared for the journey narrative, this unit makes a contribution to the inclusio effect that surrounds the journey narrative (we end where we began). This unit is separated from the preceding by a change of audience and theme, and is separated in the same way from what is to follow.

Luke continues with his Markan source and sequence (Mark 10:32–34). He trims away the Markan setting and some of the content that would be repetitive after 9:22, and then he adds a reformulation of 9:45 (which, while based on Mark 9:32, was already largely Lukan). Other minor changes are also noted below.

For extensive discussion of the passion predictions, see at 9:21–22, 9:43b–45 and the Son of Man excursus.

Comment

We come now to the last of the great passion predictions. But repetition has not made the message any clearer to the Twelve, who are quite blind to the significance of what they hear. This final prediction emphasizes the fulfillment of Scripture and focuses particularly on that which will insult and demean the Son of Man, as well as on the role of the Gentiles, the foreign overlords. For the whole unit, see the more detailed discussions at 9:21–22 and 9:43b–45.

31 The language of v 31a is borrowed directly from the Markan source (*εἶπεν πρός*, "he said to," is a Lukan touch), but no use is made of the Markan setting (10:32), and from "and everything written" to the end of the verse, except for "the Son of Man," is a Lukan contribution (cf. 24:44). A new beginning is marked by the private audience here for the Twelve. See 6:12–16 on the call of the Twelve. The Jerusalem goal first comes into clear focus in 9:51 (but cf. 9:31 and the Jerusalem location already implied by the set of leadership categories in 9:22). The language of necessity of 9:22 etc. is now revealed as having a scriptural basis. "All things" points to the way in which Luke thinks not just of the passion but of a program of events leading on to the glorification of Jesus beyond resurrection (cf. 24:26; 9:31, 51). It is not possible to be sure what Scriptures Luke had specifically in mind, though Dan 7:13 is surely to be included (but note that Daniel is not among the prophets in the Masoretic divisions of the OT; Fitzmyer, 1209, is able to avoid the question of which Scripture by linking Son of Man to "carried out" rather than to "written," but the significant parallel in 24:44, with its *περὶ ἐμοῦ*, "concerning me," makes this less likely). On the background for the Gospel role for the Son of Man, see the Son of Man excursus, and on Luke's use, see at 6:1–5.

32 Luke adopts the passive construction with which the Markan text begins here, but, passing over the role of the chief priests and the scribes (for the most part this information is already to be found in 9:22, and the condemning to death of Mark 10:33 oversteps Luke's understanding of the role of the Jewish Sanhedrin in Jesus' death), moves immediately to the role of the Gentiles. The Markan verbs here are recast into the passive, and *ὑβρισθήσεται*, "insulted/abused/mistreated," is added to the list (cf. 11:45; Acts 14:5). The new notes here are (*i*) the anticipation of actions designed to insult and demean ("ridiculed" is used in Luke's passion account at 22:63; 23:11, 36; "insulted" does not occur there, but *βλασφημεῖν*, "defame/revile," is a near equivalent and is found in 22:65; 23:39; "spat upon" is used in the Markan passion account in 14:65; 15:19, but is not reproduced by Luke); and (*ii*) the role of the Gentiles, that is, the Romans (see 20:20b; 23:1–25). Handing over to the Gentiles is a rupture of Jewish national solidarity, but the question remains whether this rupture is to be accounted for in terms of the unworthiness of the one handed over or in terms of the compromised situation of those responsible for the handing over.

33 Luke reduces the first Markan verb here to a participle and replaces Mark's "after three days" with "on the third day" (representing more accurately what is to come in the passion and resurrection account). The flogging here is represented in 22:63 by a different verb. This activity also is designed to demean and degrade. The set of means of insult and of degradation (see also v 32) is likely to constitute an allusion to Isa 50:6 (which has "floggers," "shame," and "spitting"). In 9:22 Luke replaced Mark's "to rise" with "to be raised [by God]," but here he keeps the intransitive use: "he will rise" (cf. 24:7, 46; Acts 10:41; 17:3). Luke sees it both ways.

34 Mark has nothing corresponding at this point. This verse is a Lukan reformulation of 9:45 (see there for its meaning), which had a partial basis in Mark 9:32. The illumination that answers to this benightedness will come in 24:13–35.

Explanation

The extended literary section, to which Luke has given a journey shape, now comes to an end. He began the introductory section for the journey with the suffering of the Son of Man (9:21–22) and now he ends with the same. All the teaching gathered in between is to be seen in the light of Jesus' coming fate in Jerusalem.

The first new note here is that the prophets have recorded ahead of time the future that Jesus anticipates for himself as the Son of Man. We cannot be sure what texts Luke would have thought of, but Dan 7:13 would surely be in the list. Jesus also makes it clear that his destiny will involve being handed over to the foreign overlords who controlled the government of Palestine at the highest level, and under whom the Jews were a subject people. He finally stresses that he will not only die (which might be glorious) but that he will be ridiculed, insulted, and spat upon, that is, that he will be treated in a way that is designed to humiliate, demean, and degrade.

Despite the repetition and the different approaches, the blindness of the disciples (here the Twelve), first identified at 9:45, is not to be dispelled. Only beyond the resurrection, with the exposition of Scripture and the breaking of the bread, will the blindness give way to clear understanding (see 24:13–35).

For more detail on the passion predictions, see at 9:21–22 and 9:43b–45.